STRATEGY

Process, Content, Context

AN INTERNATIONAL PERSPECTIVE

D1340253

STRATEGY

Process, Content, Context

AN INTERNATIONAL PERSPECTIVE

BOB DE WIT The Open University and Maastricht School of Management, The Netherlands

RON MEYER TiasNimbas Business School, Tilburg University, The Netherlands

SOUTH-WESTERN
CENGAGE Learning™

Australia • Brazil • Japan • Korea • Mexico • Singapore • Spain • United Kingdom • United States

SOUTH-WESTERN
CENGAGE Learning™

Strategy: Process, Content, Context, 4th Edition
Bob de Wit and Ron Meyer

Publishing Director: Linden Harris

Publisher: Thomas Rennie

Development Editor: Jennifer Seth

Content Project Editor: Lucy Arthy

Head of Production & Manufacturing:
  Alissa Chappell

Production Controller: Tom Relf

Marketing Manager: Amanda Cheung

Typesetter: MPS Limited, A Macmillan
  Company

Cover design: Adam Renvoise

Text design: Design Deluxe

For product information and technology assistance,
contact **emea.info@cengage.com.**
For permission to use material from this text or product,
and for permission queries,
email **clsuk.permissions@cengage.com**

The Author has asserted the right under the Copyright, Designs and Patents Act 1988 to be identified as Author of this Work.

British Library Cataloguing-in-Publication Data
A catalogue record for this book is available from the British Library.
ISBN: 978-1-4080-1902-3

Cengage Learning EMEA
Cheriton House, North Way, Andover, Hampshire SP10 5BE.
United Kingdom

Cengage Learning products are represented in Canada by Nelson Education Ltd.

For your lifelong learning solutions, visit
www.cengage.co.uk

Purchase your next print book, e-book or e-chapter at
www.ichapters.co.uk

Printed in Croatia by Zrinski d.d.
2 3 4 5 6 7 8 9 10 – 13 12 11

BRIEF CONTENTS

CONTENTS

SECTION

STRATEGY CONTENT 233

SECTION iv

STRATEGY CONTEXT   423

8 THE INDUSTRY CONTEXT   425

9 THE ORGANIZATIONAL CONTEXT   482

SECTION V

PURPOSE

SECTION

VI

CASES

655

LIST OF EXHIBITS

ACKNOWLEDGEMENTS

BOB DE WIT:

Imagination is more important than knowledge

Albert Einstein (1879-1955) German-American physicist

With his quote, one of the most respected knowledge workers of all times had no intention to scale down the importance of knowledge. On the contrary, for Einstein knowledge was crucial. To create new knowledge that builds on what is known, however, he considered to be even more important. For him, knowledge was the basis, and the beginning, of a thought process that never ended. He imagined what could be added to the existing knowledge base, as an inspiration to discover new paths. Researchers in strategy will recognize Einstein's enthusiasm in their work.

This fourth edition brings together the knowledge of great people in the strategy field. We thank them for creating new knowledge and insights, for their inspiration and hard work, and for developing the strategy field to where it is today. Writing our book would not have been possible without the current knowledge base and the writers of many phenomenal papers. We also apologize for not including all excellent contributions in our book. As the architects of this book we read many excellent papers, but since there is a limitation to a book's size we could select only a few. We were simply not able to include all the great papers and had to make some tough and (sometimes) personal choices.

Knowledge is not only important in research, but also in teaching. Knowledge is a crucial resource for professors and students, and the basis of a good strategy course. Teaching strategy is not just explaining current knowledge, however, and learning strategy is much more than understanding concepts and theory. Our intention with the book is to stimulate classroom discussions, and to start dialogues on key strategy topics. We thank the professors who selected our book as the basis of class discussions, to help students developing their strategic mind. Many improvements we made in this fourth edition are based on the feedback of professors who have used previous editions in their classrooms. We are grateful for their valuable insights, and for sharing their experiences.

Developing the fourth edition of our book has been a tremendous effort of many people. It takes lots of time to read and pre-select the growing number of publications and cases in the strategy field, and to develop supporting materials. We greatly appreciate the contribution of our Strategy Academy team members (in alphabetical order) Claudia Cox, Hester Duursema, Jos Eeland, Fred Huibers, Geert-Jan Knegt, Desiree Kradolfer, Wolter Lemstra, Roel Meijers, Priscilla van der Leij, Bas van Gils, and Marcel van Gils. We also thank 'external colleagues' Eric de Roos and Peter Smith. But most of all we thank colleague Casper van der Veen, who fulfilled his 'dirty job' of managing the project and leading our team with great effort and competence.

Finally we would like to thank the Cengage Learning team. In particular we would like to thank Tom Rennie, who has done an incredible job in managing this substantial project. And last but not least, we would like to thank the man who got us started fifteen years ago, our first editor, David Godden.

Thank you all very much. Your efforts have been enormous. Even beyond imagination.

RON MEYER:

It could be said of me that in this book I have only made up a bunch of other men's flowers, providing of my own only the string that ties them together.

Montaigne (1533-1592) French moralist and essayist

As Montaigne, we have created a book that is a 'bouquet of other people's flowers' – we have brought together many of the leading ideas, concepts, frameworks and theories in the field of strategic management and have arranged them in a way that each complements the 'beauty' and 'fragrance' of the others. While I am proud of the job done in selecting the most attractive flowers and arranging them into a lush bouquet, I am aware that we are much indebted to the hundreds of authors whose contribution to the topic of strategy we have used to compose this book. In particular, I am very grateful to the writers whose work we have been allowed to reprint here – without their cooperation, and the permission of their publishers, we would not have been able to create the structure of the book as envisioned.

Even when it comes to the string tying the flowers together, we have received considerable support, which should not go unmentioned. During the fifteen years since the publication of the first edition, many colleagues and readers from around the world have provided valuable feedback, leading to considerable changes in the book. I have also benefited from the comments and suggestions received from my students and executive program participants, as I have had the opportunity to present these ideas at universities and companies in dozens of countries around the world. To all of these people, I would like to express my gratitude – and I would like to encourage all to keep on contributing towards the next edition.

The work on the fourth edition started in the autumn of 2008, with the creation of an internet-based collaborative case community, to get as many book-users as possible involved in suggesting case ideas, writing case material and giving feedback. I would like to thank Martijn Rademakers of the Center for Strategy & Leadership for managing this entire process, as well as being my most important co-author on the short cases and illustrations. In the end, eight people besides Martijn joined me to write all of the new short cases and illustrations (in case order): Casper van der Veen, Marc Sniukas, Peer Ederer, Roger Cook, Graham Hubbard, Judy Hubbard, Mariapia Di Palma and Paul Knott. Many of the short cases and illustrations were based on publicly available information, but we were also lucky to get the cooperation from many companies. I would explicitly like to recognize the assistance provided by following case companies: Exact Software, Sanoma, Grohe, Faber Castell, Ducati (great factory tour!), Imtech and ING Direct.

Furthermore, I would like to thank all the other strategy lecturers who joined the collaborative case community to review the new short cases and illustrations: Ljljana Erakovic, Hans Le Fever, Paul Hunter, Pierre Maniere, Hans-Erich Müller, Raymond Oriakhi, Hanno Poeschl, Gitte Schober, Peter Smith, Didier Van Caillie and Margot Wood. And last but not least, I would like to express my appreciation to my two student assistants, Daniela Dodan and Mariapia Di Palma, for helping Martijn and me to collect all of the necessary information and fact check everything written, as well to my office manager Karin Feteris, for making sure the place didn't fall apart in the meantime.

Finally, I would also like to acknowledge the efforts of the team at Cengage throughout the years, most recently by Tom Rennie and Jennifer Seth. I realize how taxing it can be to work with a perfectionist, who not only produces a manuscript, but also has a detailed opinion about the layout and even believes he knows a lot about marketing. Thank you Tom and Jen for bringing this project to fruition. And thanks to past editors, Steven Reed, Anna Faherty and Geraldine Lyons, but most of all to the man who got us started as 'flower arrangers' fifteen years ago, our first editor, David Godden, who has now retired to a life of growing real flowers in New Zealand.

AUTHOR BIOGRAPHIES:

Bob de Wit is Professor of Strategic Leadership at the Open University and the Maastricht School of Management, The Netherlands. He is also founder and director of Strategy Works, Strategy Academy and Strategy Academy Research Foundation in Rotterdam. Bob is a member of the *Journal of Change Management* Advisory Board, and a reviewer for the International Strategic Management Society Conference. Bob's mission is to combine academic rigor and practical relevance.

Bob holds a bachelor's degree in Psychology from Utrecht University, an MBA at the Interdisciplinary Institute Bedrijfskunde in Delft, and a PhD degree in Management Science from Erasmus University Rotterdam. After graduation he became a professor in strategic management at the Rotterdam School of Management, teaching strategy in MSc programs and the international MBA program. In 1996 he started working at the Maastricht School of Management, a market leader in management education in non-Western countries. Since then, Bob has been teaching in over 30 countries at all continents. He served as the Chairman of the Interest Group 'The Practice of Strategy' of the *Strategic Management Society*, and the Dutch Society for Strategic Decision Making (VSB), and has been a member of the Academic Council of the *Ecole Nationale des Ponts et Chaussées* in Paris.

Bob de Wit has (co-) authored 9 books, over 20 cases and teaching notes, and numerous articles and book chapters in the area of strategic management.

Bob passionately loves his wife Pamela and daughter Liz.

Ron Meyer is Professor of Corporate Strategy at TiasNimbas Business School, Tilburg University, The Netherlands, where he conducts research in the areas of strategy and leadership, and teaches in a variety of educational programs. He is also managing director of the Center for Strategy & Leadership, an international consulting and management development organization, dedicated to improving companies' competences in the areas of strategic thinking, leadership, entrepreneurship, business innovation and change management.

Ron studied Political Science at the University of Alberta in his native Canada and got his MBA and PhD at the Erasmus University in Rotterdam, the Netherlands. From 1987 to 1998 he was Assistant Professor of Strategic Management at the Rotterdam School of Management. For two years he was also Associate Director of RSM, in charge of managing the MBA Program. From 1998 to 2008 he retained a position as Adjunct Professor of Strategic Management at RSM, while setting up two companies together with Bob de Wit, the strategy consulting firm Strategy Works and the management development firm Strategy Academy.

In 2008 he left both firms, to set up the Center for Strategy and Leadership, together with Martijn Rademakers, to focus more strongly on the people-side of strategy, where strategizing and leading come together. In 2009 he was appointed Professor of Corporate Strategy at TiasNimbas Business School, at the University of Tilburg, where his assignment is to manage the paradox of rigor and relevance – combining strategy research with boardroom consultancy and in-company trainings.

As consultant he works with many top international companies on such topics as corporate strategy, business innovation, strategic alliances and strategies for growth. As trainer he has given seminars and training courses to hundreds of companies around the world and lectured at more than 30 universities.

Ron has a dual nationality (Canadian and Dutch), but as that wasn't international enough, he married an Austrian, who he actually met at a Strategic Management Society conference while speaking about a previous edition of this book. They live with their four "multinational" children in Rotterdam, but together their goal is to see and experience as much of the rest of the world as possible.

PREFACE

Not only is there an art in knowing a thing,
but also a certain art in teaching it.

Cicero (106-43 B.C.) Roman orator and statesman

What is a good strategy for teaching and learning about the topic of strategy? Judging by the similarity of the strategic management textbooks currently available, there seems to be a general consensus among business professors on the best approach to this task. It is not an exaggeration to say that strategic management education is dominated by a strong *industry recipe* (Spender, 1989). Almost all textbooks share the following characteristics:

- *Few differing perspectives.* Only a limited number of perspectives and theories are presented, often as accepted knowledge, from which prescriptions can easily be derived;

- *Step-by-step structure.* A step-by-step strategic planning approach is used as the books' basic structure, to decompose strategy-making into a number of simple sequential activities;

- *No primary material.* The key academic articles and books on strategy are reworked into the textbook authors' own words to create consistent and easily digestible pieces of text;

- *Domestic orientation.* Despite fancy subtitles referring to globalization, the choice of perspectives, theories, examples and cases are heavily biased towards the textbook authors' own domestic context.

It is interesting to speculate on the causes of this isomorphism in the 'strategic management education' industry. Institutionalists would probably point to the need for legitimacy, which leads textbook authors to conform to widely accepted practices and to avoid major innovations (e.g. Abrahamson, 1996; Powell and DiMaggio, 1991). Social psychologists would likely suggest that over the years shared cognitive structures have developed within the strategic management community, which makes the prevailing educational paradigm difficult to challenge (e.g. Smircich and Stubbart, 1985, Walsh, 1995). Theorists taking a new institutional economics perspective would probably interpret the uniformity of strategic management textbooks as a form of lock-in, caused by the large investments already made by publishers and business professors based on a shared educational 'standard' (e.g. Arthur, 1996; David, 1994). Whatever the reason, it is striking that the character of strategic management textbooks has not significantly changed since the founding of the field.

But what would strategy education look like if educational orthodoxy would be actively challenged and the industry rules were broken? How might strategy be taught if the current constraints were thrown aside and the teaching process was boldly reinvented? In short, what would happen if some strategic thinking were applied to the teaching of strategy?

During the last fifteen years, we have continuously asked ourselves these questions. Our conclusion is that all four of the above features of current strategic management textbooks greatly inhibit the development of independent strategic thinkers and therefore urgently need to be changed. It is for this reason that we decided to create a book our-selves, with the following characteristics:

- *Multiple strategy perspectives.* A broad range of differing, and often conflicting, per-spectives and theories, are presented, reflecting the richness of current debate among academics and practitioners in the field of strategic management;
- *Issue-based structure.* An issue-based book structure is used, with each chapter fo-cusing on a key strategic issue, which is discussed from a variety of angles, leaving readers to draw their own conclusions;
- *Original readings.* A large number of original articles and book chapters are included, to offer readers a first hand account of the ideas and theories of influential strategy thinkers;
- *International orientation.* A strong international orientation is at the core of this book, as reflected in the choice of topics, theories, readings, examples and cases.

In the following paragraphs the rationale behind the choice for these characteristics will be explained. Following this discussion, the structure of the book and the ways in which it can be employed will be further clarified.

USING MULTIPLE STRATEGY PERSPECTIVES

Education, n. That which discloses to the wise and disguises from the foolish their lack of understanding. The Devil's Dictionary

Ambrose Bierce (1842 – 1914) American columnist

What should students learn in a strategic management or business policy course? It seems an obvious question to start with, especially for professors who teach about objective set-ting. Yet, in practice, the large majority of strategic management textbooks do not make their teaching objectives explicit. These books implicitly assume that the type of teaching objectives and teaching methods needed for a strategic management course do not radically differ from any other subject – basically, strategy can be taught in the same way as ac-counting or baking cookies. Their approach is based on the following teaching objectives:

- *Knowledge.* To get the student to clearly understand and memorize all of the major "ingredients";
- *Skills.* To develop the student's ability to follow the detailed "recipes";
- *Attitude.* To instill a disciplined frame of mind, whereby the student automatically attempts to approach all issues by following established procedures.

This is an important way of teaching – it is how all of us were taught to read and write, do arithmetic and drive a car. This type of teaching can be referred to as *instructional*, because students are told what to know and do. The instructor is the authority who has all of the necessary knowledge and skills, and it is his/her role to transfer these to the stu-dents. Thus the educational emphasis is on communicating know how and ensuring that students are able to repeat what they have heard. Students are not encouraged to question the knowledge they receive – on the contrary, it is the intention of instructional teaching to get students to absorb an accepted body of knowledge and to follow established recipes. The student should *accept, absorb* and *apply.*

However, while instructing students on a subject and programming their behavior might be useful in such areas as mathematics, cooking and karate, we believe it is not a very good way of teaching strategy. In our opinion, a strategic management professor should have a different set of teaching objectives:

- *Knowledge.* To encourage the understanding of the many, often conflicting, schools of thought and to facilitate the gaining of insight into the assumptions, possibilities and limitations of each set of theories;
- *Skills.* To develop the student's ability to define strategic issues, to critically reflect on existing theories, to creatively combine or develop conceptual models where necessary and to flexibly employ theories where useful;
- *Attitude.* To instill a critical, analytical, flexible and creative mindset, which challenges organizational, industry and national paradigms and problem-solving recipes.

In other words, strategy professors should want to achieve the opposite of instructors – not to instill recipes, but rather to encourage students to dissect and challenge recipes. Strategic thinking is in its very essence questioning, challenging, unconventional and innovative. These aspects of strategic thinking cannot be transferred through instruction. A critical, analytical, flexible and creative state of mind must be developed by practicing these very qualities. Hence, a learning situation must encourage students to be critical, must challenge them to be analytical, must force them to be mentally flexible and must demand creativity and unconventional thinking. Students cannot be instructed to be strategists, but must learn the art of strategy by thinking and acting themselves – they must *discuss, deliberate* and *do.* The role of the professor is to create the circumstances for this learning. We therefore refer to this type of teaching as *facilitative.*

This teaching philosophy has led to a radical departure from traditional textbooks that focus on knowledge transfer and application skills, and that have often been written from the perspective of just one paradigm. In this book the fundamental differences of opinion within strategic management are not ignored or smoothed over. On the contrary, it is the mission of this book to expose students to the many, often conflicting, perspectives in the field of strategy. It is our experience that the challenge of comparing and reconciling rivaling strategy perspectives sharpens the mind of the 'apprentice' strategists. Throwing students into the midst of the central strategy debates, while simultaneously demanding that they apply their thinking to practical strategic problems, is the most likely way to enhance the qualities of creativity, flexibility, independence and analytical depth that students will need to become true strategic thinkers.

FOCUSING ON STRATEGY ISSUES

Some people are so good at learning the tricks of the trade that they never get to learn the trade.

Sam Levenson (1911–1980) American teacher and comedian

While it is the objective of this book to increase students' strategic thinking abilities by exposing them to a wide range of theories and perspectives, it is not the intention to confuse and disorient. Yet in a subject area like strategic management, in which there is a broad spectrum of different views, there is a realistic threat that students might go deaf listening to the cacophony of different opinions. The variety of ideas can easily become overwhelming and difficult to integrate.

For this reason, the many theories, models, approaches and perspectives have been clustered around ten central strategy issues, each of which is discussed in a separate chapter. These ten strategy issues represent the key questions with which strategists must deal in practice. Only the theorists whose ideas have a direct bearing on the issue at hand are discussed in each chapter.

The advantage of this issue-based book structure is that it is *decision-oriented* – each chapter is about a key type of strategic decision that needs to be made. Students are challenged to look at a strategic issue holistically, taking various aspects and perspectives into account, and to arrive at a proposed course of action. This type of decision-focus closely reflects what strategizing managers need to do in practice. Step-by-step books are much more *tool-oriented,* teaching students how to go through each phase of a strategic planning process and how to use each analysis framework – useful, especially for junior analysts, but unlikely to stimulate real strategic thinking and to provide insight into difficult strategic choices.

Within each chapter, the conflicting perspectives on how the strategic issue should be approached are contrasted with one another by staging a virtual 'debate'. Two opposite perspectives are presented to kick off the debate and highlight areas of disagreement, after which the students (and their professors) are invited to further debate the issue and decide on the value and limitations of each point of view. While the chapter text offers a general introduction to the nature of the strategic issue and gives an overview of the hotly debated questions, no attempt is made to present the 'right answer' or provide a 'grand unifying theory' – students must make up their own minds based on the arguments placed before them.

The advantage of this debate-based chapter structure is that it encourages the students' engagement and that it provokes critical thinking. As students need to determine the strengths and weaknesses of each strategy perspective, they also become more adept at combining different 'lenses' to gain a fuller understanding of a problem, while becoming more skilled at balancing and mixing prescriptions to find innovative solutions to these problems. Some students will feel ill at ease not being presented the 'right approach' or the 'best practice', as they are used to getting in many other books, but this is all the more reason to avoid giving them one – as strategizing managers the security of one truth won't get them far, so it is preferable to learn to deal with (and benefit from) a variety of opinions as soon as possible.

USING ORIGINAL READINGS

Education is not filling a bucket but lighting a fire.

William Butler Yeats (1865 – 1939) Irish poet and dramatist

There are no better and livelier debates than when rivals put forward their own ideas as forcefully as they can. For this reason, we have chosen to structure the strategy debates by letting influential theorists speak for themselves. Instead of translating the important ideas of key writers into our own words, each chapter contains four original readings in which the theorists state their own case. These four readings can be viewed as the discussants in the debate, while our role is that of chairmen – we set the stage for the debate and introduce the various perspectives and 'speakers', but as conscientious chairmen we avoid taking a position in the debate ourselves.

The four readings in each chapter have been selected with a number of criteria in mind. As a starting point, we were looking for the articles or books that are widely judged to be classics in the field of strategy. However, to ensure the broad representation of different perspectives, we occasionally looked beyond established classics to find a challenging minority point of view. Finally, discussants are only as good as their ability to communicate to the non-initiated, and therefore we have sometimes excluded certain classics as too technical.

To keep the size of the book within acceptable limits, most readings have had to be reduced in length, while extensive footnotes and references have had to be dropped. At all times this editing has been guided by the principle that the author's key ideas and arguments must be preserved in tact. To compensate for the loss of references in each article, a combined list of the most important references has been added to the end of each chapter.

TAKING AN INTERNATIONAL PERSPECTIVE

He who knows only his side of the case, knows little of that.

John Stuart Mill (1806-1873) English philosopher

While almost all strategic management textbooks have been mainly produced for their author's domestic market and are later exported overseas, this book has been explicitly developed with an international audience in mind. For students the international orientation of this book has a number of distinct advantages:

- *Cross-cultural differences.* Although there has been relatively little cross-cultural research in the field of strategy, results so far indicate that there are significant differences in strategy styles between companies from different countries. This calls into question the habit among strategy researchers to present universal theories, without indicating the cultural assumptions on which their ideas have been based. It is not unlikely that strategy theories have a strong cultural bias and therefore cannot be simply transferred from one national setting to another. Much of the debate going on between strategy theorists might actually be based on such divergent cultural assumptions. In this book the issue of cross-cultural differences in strategy style is raised in each chapter, to debate whether strategists need to adapt their theories, perspectives and approaches to the country in which they are operating.

- *International context.* Besides adapting to a specific country, many companies are operating in a variety of countries at the same time. In this international arena they are confronted with a distinct set of issues, ranging from global integration and coordination, to localization and transnationalization. This set of issues presented by the international context is debated in depth in chapter 10.

- *International cases and illustrations.* To explore how the various strategy perspectives can be applied to different national contexts, it is imperative to have cases and illustrations from a wide variety of countries, spread around the world. In this book the 33 cases (22 long and 11 short cases) cover more than 20 countries and most of the cases have an international orientation. The 20 main illustrations have also been drawn from around the world. It must be noted, however, that we have had a bias towards well-known firms from developed economies, as these examples are more recognizable to most audiences around the world.

CONTACT US

A stand can be made against invasion by an army; no stand can be made against invasion by an idea.

Victor Hugo (1802–1885) French poet, novelist and playwright

Books are old-fashioned, but based on a proven technology that is still the most appropriate under most circumstances. One drawback, however, is that a book is unidirectional, allowing us to send a message to you, but not capable of transmitting your comments, questions and suggestions back to us. This is unfortunate, as we are keen on communicating with our audience and enjoy hearing what works and doesn't work 'in the field'.

Therefore, we would like to encourage both students and professors to establish contact with us. You can do this by visiting our website (www.cengage.co.uk/strategy4e) to check out the extra features we have for you and to leave your comments and suggestions. But you can also contact us directly by email at b.dewit@strategy-academy.org or r.meyer@tiasnimbas.edu

REFERENCES

Abrahamson, E. (1996), Management Fashion, *Academy of Management Review*, Vol. 21, pp. 254–285.

Arthur, W.B. (1996), Increasing Returns and the New World of Business, *Harvard Business Review*, July/August, pp. 100–109.

David, P.A. (1994), Why are Institutions the 'Carriers of History'?: Path Dependence and the Evolution of Conventions, Organizations and Institutions, *Structural Change and Economic Dynamics*, pp. 205–220.

Powell, W.W., and P.J. DiMaggio (Eds.) (1991), *The New Institutionalism in Organization Analysis*, Chicago: University of Chicago Press.

Smircich, L., and C. Stubbart (1985), Strategic Management in an Enacted World, *Academy of Management Review*, Vol. 10, pp. 724–736.

Spender, J.-C. (1989), *Industry Recipes: The Nature and Sources of Managerial Judgement*, Oxford: Basil Blackwell.

Walsh, J. (1995), Managerial and Organizational Cognition: Notes from a Trip Down Memory Lane, *Organization Science*, vol. 6, pp. 280–321.

ABOUT THE WEBSITE

Visit the *Strategy: Process, Content, Context, 4e* companion website at **www.cengage.co. uk/strategy4e** to find valuable teaching and learning material including:

For Instructors:
- Instructor's Manual
- PowerPoint Slides
- ExamView Test Bank

For Students:
- Revision Questions
- Annotated Web Links

CENGAGENOW™

Designed by lecturers for lecturers, CengageNOW™ for De Wit & Meyer's Strategy mirrors the natural teaching workflow with an easy-to-use online suite of services and resources, all in one program. With this system, lecturers can easily plan their courses, manage student assignments, automatically grade, teach with dynamic technology, and assess student progress. CengageNOW™ operates seamlessly with Blackboard/WebCT, Moodle and other virtual learning environments. Ask your Cengage Learning sales representative for a demonstration of what CengageNOW™ for De Wit & Meyer's Strategy can bring to your courses (http:/edu.cengage.co.uk/contact_us.aspx).

STRATEGY

INTRODUCTION

Men like the opinions to which
they have become accustomed
from youth; this prevents them
from finding the truth, for they
cling to the opinions of habit.
Moses Maimonides (1135–1204);
Egyptian physician and philosopher

Where there is much desire to
learn, there of necessity will be
much arguing, much writing,
many opinions; for opinion in
good men is but knowledge in the
making.
John Milton (1608–1674); English poet

THE NATURE OF STRATEGY

In a book entitled *Strategy,* it seems reasonable to expect Chapter 1 to begin with a clear definition of strategy that would be employed with consistency in all subsequent chapters. An early and precise definition would help to avoid conflicting interpretations of what should be considered strategy and, by extension, what should be understood by the term 'strategic management'. However, any such sharp definition of strategy here would actually be misleading. It would suggest that there is widespread agreement among practitioners, researchers and theorists as to what strategy is. The impression would be given that the fundamental concepts in the area of strategy are generally accepted and hardly questioned. Yet, even a quick glance through current strategy literature indicates otherwise. There are strongly differing opinions on most of the key issues and the disagreements run so deep that even a common definition of the term 'strategy' is illusive.

This is bad news for those who prefer simplicity and certainty. It means that the topic of strategy cannot be explained as a set of straightforward definitions and rules to be memorized and applied. The strongly conflicting views mean that strategy cannot be summarized into broadly agreed on definitions, rules, matrices and flow diagrams that one must simply absorb and learn to use. If the fundamental differences of opinion are not swept aside, the consequence is that a book on strategy cannot be like an instruction manual that takes you through the steps of how something should be done. On the contrary, a strategy book should acknowledge the disagreements and encourage thinking about the value of each of the different points of view. That is the intention of this book.

The philosophy embraced here is that an understanding of the topic of strategy can only be gained by grappling with the diversity of insights presented by so many prominent thinkers and by coming to terms with the fact that there is no simple answer to the question of what strategy is. Readers who prefer the certainty of reading only one opinion, as opposed to the intellectual stimulation of being confronted with a wide variety, should read no further – there are plenty of alternatives available. Those who wish to proceed should lay aside their 'opinions of habit', and open their minds to the many other opinions presented, for in these pages there is 'knowledge in the making'.

IDENTIFYING THE STRATEGY ISSUES

If the only tool you have is a hammer, you treat everything like a nail.
Abraham Maslow (1908-1970); American psychologist

The approach taken in this book is in line with the moral of Maslow's remark. To avoid hammering strategy issues with only one theory, a variety of ways of viewing strategic questions will be presented. But there are two different ways of presenting a broad spectrum of theoretical lenses. This point can be made clear by extending Maslow's hammer-and-nail analogy. To become a good carpenter, who wisely uses a variety of tools depending on what is being crafted, an apprentice carpenter will need to learn about these different instruments. One way is for the apprentice to study the characteristics and functioning of all tools individually, and only then to apply each where appropriate. However, another possibility is for the apprentice to first learn about what must be crafted, getting a feel for the materials and the problems that must be solved, and only then to turn to the study of the necessary tools. The first approach to learning can be called 'tools-driven' – understanding each tool comes first, while combining them to solve real problems comes later. The second approach to learning can be termed 'problem-driven' – understanding problems comes first, while searching for the appropriate tools is based on the type of problem.

Both options can also be used for the apprentice strategist. In a tools-driven approach to learning about strategy, all major theories would first be understood separately, to be compared or combined later when using them in practice. A logical structure for a book aiming at this mode of learning would be to allot one chapter to each of the major theories or schools of thought. The advantage of such a theory-based book structure would be that each chapter would focus on giving the reader a clear and cohesive overview of one major theory within the field of strategy. For readers with an interest in grasping the essence of each theory individually, this would probably be the ideal book format. However, the principal disadvantage of a theory-by-theory summary of the field of strategy would be that the reader would not have a clear picture of how the various theories relate to one another. The apprentice strategist would be left with important questions such as: 'Where do the theories agree and where do they differ? Which strategy phenomena does each theory claim to explain and which phenomena are left unaccounted for? Can various theories be successfully combined or are they based on mutually exclusive assumptions? And which strategy is right, or at least most appropriate under particular circumstances? Not knowing the answers to these questions, how could the apprentice strategist try to apply these new theoretical tools to practice?

This book is based on the assumption that the reader wants to be able to actively solve strategic problems. Understanding the broad spectrum of theories is not an end in itself, but a means for more effective strategizing. Therefore, the problem-driven approach to learning about strategy has been adopted. In this approach, key strategy issues are first identified and then each is looked at from the perspective of the most appropriate theories. This has resulted in an issue-based book structure, in which each chapter deals with a particular set of strategy issues. In each chapter, only the theories that shed some light on the issues under discussion are brought forward and compared to one another. Of course, some theories are relevant to more than one set of issues and therefore appear in various chapters.

In total, ten sets of strategy issues have been identified that together largely cover the entire field of strategic management. These ten will be the subjects of the remaining ten chapters of this book. How the various strategy issues have been divided into these ten sets will be explained in the following paragraphs.

Strategy dimensions: Process, content and context

The most fundamental distinction made in this book is between strategy process, strategy content and strategy context (see Figure 1.1). These are the three dimensions of strategy that can be recognized in every real-life strategic problem situation. They can be generally defined as follows:

- Strategy process. The manner in which strategies come about is referred to as the strategy process. Stated in terms of a number of questions, strategy process is concerned with the *how, who* and *when* of strategy: how is, and should, strategy be made, analysed, dreamt-up, formulated, implemented, changed and controlled; who is involved; and when do the necessary activities take place?
- Strategy content. The product of a strategy process is referred to as the strategy content. Stated in terms of a question, strategy content is concerned with the *what* of strategy: what is, and should be, the strategy for the company and each of its constituent units?
- Strategy context. The set of circumstances under which both the strategy process and the strategy content are determined is referred to as the strategy context. Stated in terms of a question, strategy context is concerned with the *where* of strategy: where (that is in which firm and which environment) are the strategy process and strategy content embedded?

It cannot be emphasized enough that strategy process, content and context are not different parts of strategy, but are distinguishable dimensions. Just as it is silly to speak of the length, width and height parts of a box, one cannot speak of the three parts of strategy either. Each strategic problem situation is by its nature three dimensional, possessing process, content and context characteristics, and only the understanding of all three dimensions will give the strategist real depth of comprehension. In particular, it must be

FIGURE 1.1   Dimensions of strategy and the organizational purpose

acknowledged that the three dimensions interact (Pettigrew and Whipp, 1991; Ketchen, Thomas and McDaniel, 1996). For instance, the manner in which the strategy process is organized will have a significant impact on the resulting strategy content, while likewise, the content of the current strategy will strongly influence the way in which the strategy process will be conducted in future. If these linkages are ignored, the strategist will have a flat view instead of a three-dimensional view of strategy. A useful analytical distinction for temporarily unravelling a strategic problem situation will have turned into a permanent means for fragmenting reality.

However, it is possible to concentrate on one of the strategy dimensions if the other two are kept in mind. In fact, to have a focused discussion it is even necessary to look at one dimension at a time. The alternative is a debate in which all topics on all three dimensions would be discussed simultaneously: such a cacophony of opinions would be lively, but most likely less than fruitful. Therefore, the process–content–context distinction will cautiously be used as the main structuring principle of this book, splitting the text into three major sections.

A fourth section has been added to these three, although strictly speaking it is not about strategy. In the above list, the questions of how, who, when, what and where were mentioned, but not yet the question of why – why do organizations exist and why do their strategies move them in a certain direction? This is the issue of organizational purpose – the impetus to strategy activities. Making strategy is not an end in itself, but a means for reaching particular objectives. Organizations exist to fulfil a purpose and strategies are employed to ensure that the organizational purpose is realized. Given the importance of this topic to the understanding of strategy, purpose has been given an equal position next to process, content and context as a separate section of this book.

This four-fold structure fits closely with the situation within the academic field of strategic management. To a large extent, strategy literature is divided along these lines. Most strategy research, by its very nature, is more atomistic than holistic, focusing on just a few variables at once. Consequently, most writings on strategy, including most of the theories discussed in this book, tend to favor just one, or at most two, strategy dimensions, which is usually complex enough given the need to remain comprehensible. In particular, the divide between strategy process and strategy content has been quite pronounced, to the extent of worrying some scholars about whether the connections between the two are being sufficiently recognized (Pettigrew, 1992). Although sharing this concern, use of the process–content–context–purpose distinction here reflects the reality of the current state of debate within the field of strategic management.

Strategy process: Thinking, forming and changing

Section II of this book will deal with the strategy process. Traditionally, most textbooks have portrayed the strategy process as a basically linear progression through a number of distinct steps. Usually a split is made between the strategy analysis stage, the strategy formulation stage and the strategy implementation stage. In the analysis stage, strategists identify the opportunities and threats in the environment, as well as the strengths and weaknesses of the organization. Next, in the formulation stage, strategists determine which strategic options are available to them, evaluate each and choose one. Finally, in the implementation stage, the selected strategic option is translated into a number of concrete activities, which are then carried out. It is commonly presumed that this process is not only linear, but also largely rational – strategists identify, determine, evaluate, choose, translate and carry out based on rigorous logic and extensive knowledge of all important factors. Furthermore, the assumption is frequently made that the strategy process is comprehensive – strategy is made for the entire organization and everything can be radically changed all at once.

All of these beliefs have been challenged. For instance, many authors have criticized the strong emphasis on rationality in these traditional views of the strategy process. Some writers have even argued that the true nature of strategic thinking is more intuitive and creative than rational. In their opinion, strategizing is about perceiving strengths and weaknesses, envisioning opportunities and threats and creating the future, for which imagination and judgement are more important than analysis and logic. This constitutes quite a fundamental disagreement about the cognitive processes of the strategizing manager. These issues surrounding the nature of strategic thinking will be discussed in Chapter 2.

The division of the strategy process into a number of sequential phases has also drawn heavy criticism from authors who believe that in reality no such identifiable stages exist. They dismiss the linear analysis–formulation–implementation distinction as an un-warranted simplification, arguing that the strategy process is messier, with analysis, formulation and implementation activities going on all the time, thoroughly intertwined with one another. In their view, organizations do not first make strategic plans and then execute them as intended. Rather, strategies are usually formed incrementally, as organizations think and act in small iterative steps, letting strategies emerge as they go along. This represents quite a difference of opinion on how strategies are formed within organizations. These issues surrounding the nature of strategy formation will be discussed in Chapter 3.

The third major assumption of the traditional view, comprehensiveness, has also been challenged. Many authors have pointed out that it is unrealistic to suppose that a company can be boldly redesigned. They argue that it is terribly difficult to orchestrate an over-arching strategy for the entire organization that is a significant departure from the current course of action. It is virtually impossible to get various aspects of an organization all lined up to go through a change at the same time, certainly if a radical change is intended. In practice, different aspects of an organization will be under different pressures, on different timetables and have different abilities to change, leading to a differentiated approach to change. Moreover, the rate and direction of change will be seriously limited by the cultural, political and cognitive inheritance of the firm. Hence, it is argued, strategic change is usually more gradual and fragmented than radical and coordinated. The issues surrounding this difference of opinion on the nature of strategic change will be discussed in Chapter 4.

These three chapter topics – strategic thinking, strategy formation and strategic change – do not constitute entirely separate subjects. Let it be clear that they are not phases, stages or elements of the strategy process that can be understood in isolation. Strategic thinking, strategy formation and strategic change are different aspects of the strategy process, which are strongly linked and partially overlapping (see Figure 1.2). They have been selected because they are sets of issues on which there is significant debate within the field of strategy. As will become clear, having a particular opinion on one of these aspects will have a consequence for views held on all other aspects as well.

Strategy content: Business, corporate and network levels

Section III of this book will deal with the strategy content. Strategies come in all shapes and sizes, and almost all strategy writers, researchers and practitioners agree that each strategy is essentially unique. There is widespread disagreement, however, about the principles to which strategies should adhere. The debates are numerous, but there are three fundamental sets of issues around which most conflicts generally centre. These three topics can be clarified by distinguishing the level of strategy at which each is most relevant.

Strategies can be made for different groups of people or activities within an organ-ization. The lowest level of aggregation is one person or task, while the highest level of

FIGURE 1.2   Aspects of the strategy process

aggregation encompasses all people or activities within an organization. The most common distinction between levels of aggregation made in the strategic management literature is between the functional, business and corporate levels (see Figure 1.3). Strategy issues at the *functional level* refer to questions regarding specific functional aspects of a company (operations strategy, marketing strategy, financial strategy, etc.). Strategy at the *business level* requires the integration of functional level strategies for a distinct set of products and/or services intended for a specific group of customers. Often companies only operate in one such business, so that this is the highest level of aggregation within the firm. However, there are also many companies that are in two or more businesses. In such companies, a multi-business or *corporate level* strategy is required, which aligns the various business level strategies.

A logical extension of the functional–business–corporate distinction is to explicitly recognize the level of aggregation higher than the individual organization. Firms often cluster together into groups of two or more collaborating organizations. This level is referred to as the multi-company or *network level*. Most multi-company groups consist of only a few parties, as is the case in strategic alliances, joint ventures and value-adding partnerships. However, networks can also have dozens, even hundreds, of participants. In some circumstances, the corporation as a whole might be a member of a group, while in other situations only a part of the firm joins forces with other organizations. In all cases, when a strategy is developed for a group of firms, this is called a network level strategy.

In line with the generally accepted boundaries of the strategic management field, this book will focus on the business, corporate and network levels of strategy, although this will often demand consideration of strategy issues at the functional level as well. In Section II, on the strategy process, this level distinction will not be emphasized yet, but in Section III, on the strategy content, the different strategy issues encountered at the different levels of strategy will be explored. And at each level of strategy, the focus will be on the fundamental differences of opinion that divide strategy theorists.

Chapter 5 will deal with strategy issues at the business level. Here the fundamental debate surrounds whether firms are, and should be, primarily market-driven or resource-driven. Some authors argue that firms should be strongly externally oriented, engaged in a game of positioning vis-à-vis customers, competitors, suppliers and other parties in the environment, and should adapt the firm to the demands of the game. In other words, companies should think 'outside-in'. Yet, other authors strongly disagree, stressing the

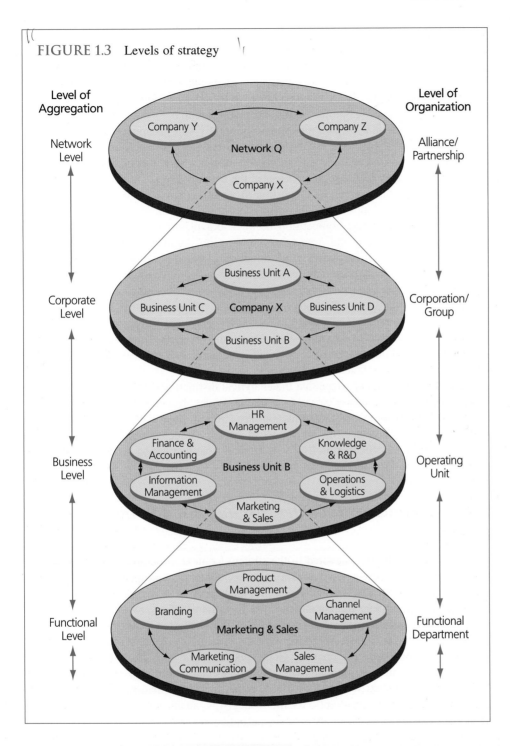

FIGURE 1.3   Levels of strategy

need for companies to exploit and expand their strengths. They recommend a more 'inside-out' view, whereby companies search for environments and positions that best fit with their resource base.

Chapter 6 is concerned with strategy issues at the corporate level. The fundamental debate in this chapter is whether corporations are, and should be, run as federations of autonomous business units or as highly integrated organizations. Some authors argue that corporate strategists should view themselves as investors, with financial stakes in a portfolio of business units. As a shrewd investor, the corporate centre should buy up cheap companies, divest underperforming business units, and put money into its business units with the highest profit potential, independent of what industry they are in. Each business unit should be judged on its merits and given a large measure of autonomy, to be optimally responsive to the specific conditions in its industry. However, other authors are at odds with this view, pointing to the enormous potential for synergy that is left untapped. They argue that corporations should be tightly knit groupings of closely related business units that share resources and align their strategies with one another. The ensuing synergies, it is forecast, will provide an important source of competitive advantage.

Chapter 7 focuses on the strategy issues at the network level. The fundamental debate in this chapter revolves around the question of whether firms should develop long-term collaborative relationships with other firms or should remain essentially independent. Some authors believe that competition between organizations is sometimes more destructive than beneficial, and argue that building up durable partnerships with other organizations can often be mutually advantageous. Participation in joint ventures, alliances and broader networks requires a higher level of inter-organizational trust and interdependence, but can pay off handsomely. It is therefore recommended to selectively engage in joint – that is, multi-company – strategy development. Other authors, however, are thoroughly skeptical about the virtues of interdependence. They prefer independence, pointing to the dangers of opportunistic partners and creeping dependence on the other. Therefore, it is recommended to avoid multi-company level strategy development and only to use alliances as a temporary measure.

Again, it must be emphasized that the analytical distinction employed here should not be interpreted as an absolute means for isolating issues. In reality, these three levels of strategy do not exist as tidy categories, but are strongly interrelated and partially overlapping. As a consequence, the three sets of strategy issues identified above are also linked to one another. In Section III it will become clear that taking a stand in one debate will affect the position that one can take in others.

Strategy context: Industry, organizational and international

Section IV in this book is devoted to the strategy context. Strategy researchers, writers and practitioners largely agree that every strategy context is unique. Moreover, they are almost unanimous that it is usually wise for managers to strive for a fit between the strategy process, strategy content and the specific circumstances prevalent in the strategy context. However, disagreement arises as soon as the discussion turns to the details of the alignments. Does the context determine what the strategizing manager must do, or can the manager actually shape the context? Some people argue or assume that the strategy context has a dynamic all its own, which strategists can hardly influence, and therefore that the strategy context sets strict confines on the freedom to manoeuvre. The context is not malleable and hence the motto for the strategist is 'adapt or die'. Others believe that strategists should not be driven by the context, but have a large measure of freedom to set their own course of action. Frequently it is argued that strategizing managers can, and should, create their own circumstances, instead of being enslaved by the circumstances they find. In short, the strategy context can be determined, instead of letting it determine.

In Section IV, the difference of opinion hinges on the power of the context to determine strategy surfaces when discussing the various aspects of the strategy context. The section has been split into three chapters, each focusing on a different aspect of the strategy context. Two distinctions have been used to arrive at the division into three chapters (see Figure 1.4). The first dichotomy employed is that between the organization

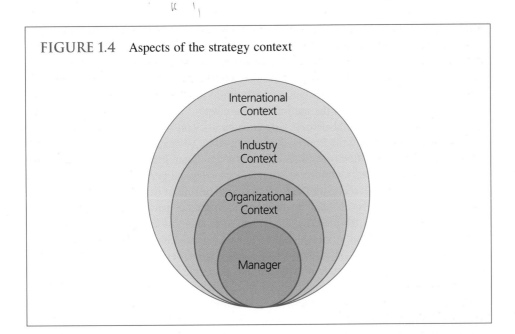

FIGURE 1.4   Aspects of the strategy context

and its industry environment. The *industry context* will be the subject of Chapter 8. In this chapter, the strategic issues revolve around the question of whether the industry circumstances set the rules to which companies must comply, or whether companies have the freedom to choose their own strategy and even change the industry conditions. The *organizational context* will be dealt with in Chapter 9. Here, the key strategic issues have to do with the question of whether the organizational circumstances largely determine the strategy process and strategy content followed, or whether the strategist has a significant amount of control over the course of action adopted.

The second dichotomy employed is that between the domestic and the international strategy context. The domestic context does not raise any additional strategic issues, but the *international context* clearly does. Strategists must deal with the question of whether adaptation to the diversity of the international context is strictly required or whether companies have considerable freedom to choose their strategy process and content irrespective of the international context. The difference of opinion between writers on the international context actually goes one step further. Some authors predict that the diversity of the international context will decline over time and that companies can encourage this process. If global convergence takes place, it is argued, adaptation to the international context will become a non-issue. Other authors, however, disagree that international diversity is declining and therefore argue that the international context will remain an issue that strategists must attempt to deal with. This debate on the future of the international context is conducted in Chapter 10.

Organizational purpose

Oddly enough, most authors write about strategy without any reference to the organizational purpose being pursued. It is generally assumed that all organizations exist for the same basic reasons, and that this purpose is self-evident. However, in reality, there is extensive disagreement about what the current purposes of organizations are, and especially about what their purpose should be. Some people argue that it is the business of business to make money. In their view, firms are owned by shareholders and therefore should pursue shareholders' interests. And it is the primary interest of shareholders to see the value of their stocks increase. On the other hand, others believe that companies exist to serve the interests of multiple stakeholders. In their opinion, having a financial stake in a firm should not give shareholders a dominant position vis-à-vis other groups that also have an interest in what the organization does. Other stakeholders usually include employees, customers, suppliers and bankers, but could also include the local community, the broader industry and even the natural environment.

This is a very fundamental debate, with broader societal implications than any of the other strategy issues. Given the important role played by business organizations in modern times, the purposes they attempt to fulfil will have a significant impact on the functioning of society. It is not surprising, therefore, to see that organizational purpose is also discussed by people other than strategy theorists and practitioners. The role of firms and the interests they should pursue are widely debated by members of political parties, environmental conservation groups, unions, the media, political action groups and the general public.

Arguably, in a book on strategy, organizational purpose should be discussed before moving on to the subject of strategy itself – as Figure 1.1 visualizes, organizational purpose is the impetus for strategy activities. In principle this is true, but the 'issue of existence' is not an easy topic with which to start a book – it would be quite a hefty appetizer with which to begin a strategy meal. Therefore, to avoid intellectual indigestion, the topic of purpose will be saved for dessert. The last text part of the book, Section V, will be devoted to the issues surrounding purpose. This section comprises only one chapter, Chapter 11 entitled 'Organizational purpose', as the discussion will be staged broadly, asking what drives organizations forward.

STRUCTURING THE STRATEGY DEBATES

For every complex problem there is a simple solution that is wrong.
George Bernard Shaw (1856–1950); Irish playwright and critic

Every real-life strategic problem is complex. Most of the strategic issues outlined earlier in this chapter will be present in every strategic problem, making the prospect of a simple solution an illusion. Yet, even if each set of strategy issues is looked at independently, it seems that strategy theorists cannot agree on the right way to approach them. On each of the topics, there is widespread disagreement, indicating that no simple solution can be expected here either.

Why is it that theorists cannot agree on how to solve strategic problems? Might it be that some theorists are right, while others are just plain wrong? In that case, it would be wise for problem-solvers to select the valid theory and discard the false ones. While this might be true in some cases, it seems unlikely that false theories would stay around long enough to keep a lively debate going. Eventually, the right (i.e. unfalsified) theory would prevail and disagreements would disappear. Yet, this does not seem to be happening in the field of strategic management.

Could it be that each theorist only emphasizes one aspect of an issue – only takes one cut of a multi-faceted reality? In that case, it would be wise for problem-solvers to combine the various theories that each look at the problem from a different angle. However, if this were true, one would expect the different theories to be largely complementary. Each theory would simply be a piece in the bigger puzzle of strategic management. Yet, this does not explain why there is so much disagreement, and even contradiction, within the field of strategy.

It could also be that strategy theorists start from divergent assumptions about the nature of each strategy issue and therefore logically arrive at a different perspective on how to solve strategic problems. In that case, it would be wise for problem-solvers to combine the various theories, in order to look at the problem from a number of different angles.

All three possibilities for explaining the existing theoretical disagreements should be kept open. However, entertaining the thought that divergent positions are rooted in fundamentally different assumptions about strategy issues is by far the most fruitful to the strategist confronted with complex problems. It is too simple to hope that one can deal with the contradictory opinions within the field of strategy by discovering which strategy theories are right and which are wrong. But it is also not particularly practical to accept all divergent theories as valid depictions of different aspects of reality – if two theories suggest a different approach to the same problem, the strategist will have to sort out this contradiction. Therefore, in this book the emphasis will be on surfacing the basic assumptions underlying the major theoretical perspectives on strategy, and to debate whether, or under which circumstances, these assumptions are appropriate.

Assumptions about strategy tensions

At the heart of every set of strategic issues, a fundamental tension between apparent opposites can be identified. For instance, in Chapter 7 on network level strategy, the issues revolve around the fundamental tension between competition and cooperation. In Chapter 8 on the industry context, the fundamental tension between the opposites of compliance and choice lies at the centre of the subject (see Figure 1.5). Each pair of opposites creates a tension, as they seem to be inconsistent, or even incompatible, with one another; it seems as if both elements cannot be fully true at the same time. If firms are competing, they are not cooperating. If firms must comply with the industry context, they have no choice. Yet, although these opposites confront strategizing managers with conflicting pressures, somehow they must be dealt with simultaneously. Strategists are caught in a bind, trying to cope with contradictory forces at the same time.

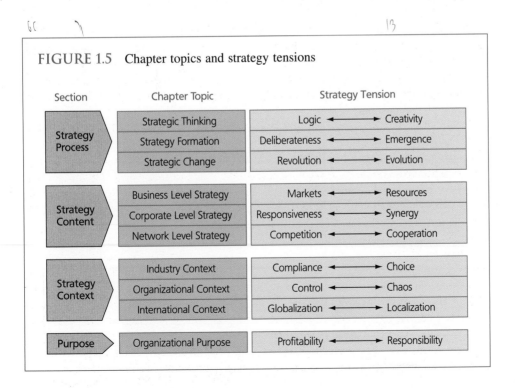

FIGURE 1.5   Chapter topics and strategy tensions

Section	Chapter Topic	Strategy Tension
Strategy Process	Strategic Thinking	Logic ←→ Creativity
	Strategy Formation	Deliberateness ←→ Emergence
	Strategic Change	Revolution ←→ Evolution
Strategy Content	Business Level Strategy	Markets ←→ Resources
	Corporate Level Strategy	Responsiveness ←→ Synergy
	Network Level Strategy	Competition ←→ Cooperation
Strategy Context	Industry Context	Compliance ←→ Choice
	Organizational Context	Control ←→ Chaos
	International Context	Globalization ←→ Localization
Purpose	Organizational Purpose	Profitability ←→ Responsibility

The challenge of strategic management is to wrestle with these tricky strategy tensions. All strategy theories make assumptions, explicitly or implicitly, about the nature of these tensions and devise ways in which to deal with them. However, every theorist's assumptions differ, giving rise to a wide variety of positions. In fact, many of the major disagreements within the field of strategic management are rooted in the different assumptions made about coping with these strategy tensions. For this reason, the theoretical debate in each chapter will be centred around the different perspectives on dealing with a particular strategy tension.

Identifying strategy perspectives

The strategy issues in each chapter can be viewed from many perspectives. On each topic there are many different theories and hundreds of books and articles. While very interesting, a comparison or debate between all of these would probably be very chaotic, unfocused and incomprehensible. Therefore, in each chapter the debate has been condensed into its most powerful form – two diametrically opposed perspectives are confronted with one another. These two poles of each debate are not always the most widely held perspectives on the particular set of strategy issues, but they do expose the major points of contention within the topic area.

In every chapter, the two strategy perspectives selected for the debate each emphasize one side of a strategy tension over the other (see Figure 1.6). For instance, in Chapter 7 the discrete organization perspective stresses competition over cooperation, while the embedded organization perspective does the opposite. In Chapter 8, the industry dynamics perspective accentuates compliance over choice, while the industry leadership perspective

FIGURE 1.6   Strategy topics, paradoxes and perspectives

Strategy Topics	Strategy Paradoxes	Strategy Perspectives
Strategic Thinking	Logic vs. Creativity	Rational Reasoning vs. Generative Reasoning
Strategy Formation	Deliberateness vs. Emergence	Strategic Planning vs. Strategic Incrementalism
Strategic Change	Revolution vs. Evolution	Discontinuous Renewal vs. Continuous Renewal
Business Level Strategy	Markets vs. Resources	Outside-in vs. Inside-out
Corporate Level Strategy	Responsiveness vs. Synergy	Portfolio Organization vs. Integrated Organization
Network Level Strategy	Competition vs. Cooperation	Discrete Organization vs. Embedded Organization
Industry Context	Compliance vs. Choice	Industry Dynamics vs. Industry Leadership
Organizational Context	Control vs. Chaos	Organizational Leadership vs. Organizational Dynamics
International Context	Globalization vs. Localization	Global Convergence vs. International Diversity
Organizational Purpose	Profitability vs. Responsibility	Shareholder Value vs. Stakeholder Values

does the opposite. In other words, the two perspectives represent the two extreme ways of dealing with a strategy tension, emphasizing one side or emphasizing the other.

In the first part of each chapter, the core strategic issue and the underlying strategy tension will be explained. Also, the two strategy perspectives will be outlined and compared. However, such a measured overview of the perspectives lacks colour, depth and vigour. Reading the summary of a debate does not do it justice – just like reading the summary of a sports match is nothing like watching a game live. Therefore, to give readers a first-hand impression of the debate, theorists representing both sides will be given an opportunity to state their own case by means of a reading. Readers will be part of a virtual debate in which the authors of four readings will participate.

The first two readings in each chapter will speak on behalf of the two-pole perspectives. The second set of two readings is intended to bring in additional issues and arguments not fully covered in the two lead contributions. All of the readings will receive a short introduction, to assist in understanding their pertinence to the debate at hand. The only thing that will not be done – and cannot be done – is to give readers the outcome of the debate. Readers will have to decide on this for themselves.

Viewing strategy tensions as strategy paradoxes

So, what should readers be getting out of each debate? With both strategy perspectives emphasizing the importance of one side of a strategy tension over the other, how should readers deal with these opposites? Of course, after hearing the arguments, it is up to readers to judge for themselves how the strategy tensions should be handled. However, there are four general ways of approaching them:

- As a puzzle. A puzzle is a challenging problem with an optimal solution. Think of a crossword puzzle as an example. Puzzles can be quite complex and extremely difficult to analyse, but there is a best way of solving them. Some of the most devious puzzles are those with seemingly contradictory premises. Strategy tensions can also be viewed as puzzles. While the pair of opposites seems to be incompatible with one another, this is only because the puzzle is not well understood yet. In reality, there is one best way of relieving the tension, but the strategist must unravel the problem first. Some writers seem to suggest that there are optimal ways of dealing with strategy tensions under all circumstances, but others argue that the optimal solution is situation dependent.

- As a dilemma. A dilemma is a vexing problem with two possible solutions, neither of which is logically the best. Think of the famous prisoner's dilemma as an example. Dilemmas confront problem-solvers with difficult either–or choices, each with its own advantages and disadvantages, but neither clearly superior to the other. The uneasy feeling this gives the decision-maker is reflected in the often-used expression 'horns of a dilemma' – neither choice is particularly comfortable. Strategy tensions can also be viewed as dilemmas. If this approach is taken, the incompatibility of the opposites is accepted, and the strategist is forced to make a choice in favour of either one or the other. For instance, the strategist must choose either to compete or cooperate. Which of the two the strategist judges to be most appropriate will usually depend on the specific circumstances.

- As a trade-off. A trade-off is a problem situation in which there are many possible solutions, each striking a different balance between two conflicting pressures. Think of the trade-off between work and leisure time as an example – more of one will necessarily mean less of the other. In a trade-off, many different combinations between the two opposites can be found, each with its own pros and cons, but none of the many solutions is inherently superior to the others. Strategy tensions can also be viewed as trade-offs. If this approach is taken, the conflict between the two opposites is accepted, and the strategist will constantly strive to find the most appropriate balance between them. For instance, the strategist will attempt to balance the pressures for competition and cooperation, depending on the circumstances encountered.

- As a paradox. A paradox is a situation in which two seemingly contradictory, or even mutually exclusive, factors appear to be true at the same time (e.g. Poole and Van de Ven, 1989; Martin, 2007, Reading 1.3). A problem that is a paradox has no real solution, as there is no way to logically integrate the two opposites into an internally consistent understanding of the problem. As opposed to the either–or nature of the dilemma, the paradox can be characterized as a 'both–and' problem – one factor is true and a contradictory factor is simultaneously true (e.g. Collins and Porras, 1994; Lewis, 2000). Hence, a paradox presents the problem-solver with the difficult task of wrestling with the problem, without ever arriving at a definitive solution. At best, the problem-solver can find a workable reconciliation to temporarily cope with the unsolvable paradox. Strategy tensions can also be viewed as paradoxes. If this approach is taken, the conflict between the two opposites is accepted, but the strategist will strive to accommodate both factors at the same time. The strategist will search for new ways of reconciling the opposites as best as possible. To take the same example as above, the strategist faced with the tension between competition and cooperation will attempt to do both as much as possible at the same time, with the intention of reaping the 'best of both worlds'.

Most people are used to solving puzzles, resolving dilemmas and making trade-offs. These ways of understanding and solving problems are common in daily life. They are based on the assumption that, by analysis, one or a number of logical solutions can be identified. It might require a sharp mind and considerable effort, but the answers can be found.

However, most people are not used to, or inclined to, think of a problem as a paradox. A paradox has no answer or set of answers – it can only be coped with as best as possible. Faced with a paradox, one can try to find novel ways of combining opposites, but one will know that none of these creative reconciliations will ever be *the* answer. Paradoxes will always remain surrounded by uncertainty and disagreements on how best to cope.

So, should strategy tensions be seen as puzzles, dilemmas, trade-offs or paradoxes (see Figure 1.7)?

Arguments can be made for all, but viewing strategy tensions as strategy paradoxes is the ultimate intellectual challenge. Looking at the tensions as paradoxes will help readers to avoid 'jumping to solutions' and will encourage the use of creativity to find ways of benefiting from both sides of a tension at the same time. Hence, throughout this book, the strategy tensions will be presented as strategy paradoxes, and readers will be invited to view them as such.

Taking a dialectical approach

As stated earlier, the debate in each chapter has been condensed into its most powerful form – two diametrically opposed perspectives are confronted with one another, each emphasizing one pole of the paradox. These two opposite positions are in fact the thesis and the antithesis of the debate, challenging the reader to search for an appropriate synthesis somewhere between the two extremes. This form of debate is called 'dialectical enquiry' – by using two opposite points of view, the problem-solver attempts to arrive at a better understanding of the issue and a 'higher level resolution' that integrates elements of both the thesis and the antithesis. This approach has a number of advantages:

- Range of ideas. By presenting the two opposite poles in each debate, readers can quickly acquire an understanding of the full range of ideas on the strategy issue. While these two extreme positions do not represent the most widely held views, they do

FIGURE 1.7   Strategy tensions as puzzles, dilemmas, trade-offs and paradoxes

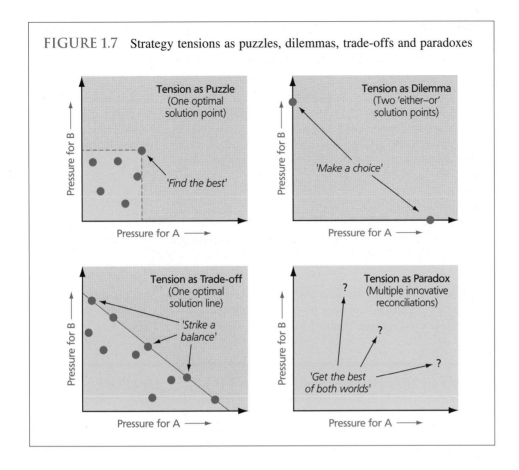

clarify for the reader how diverse the thinking actually is on each strategy issue. This is the *book-end function* of presenting the two opposite perspectives – they 'frame' the full set of views that exist on the topic.

■ Points of contention. Usually there is not across-the-board disagreement between the various approaches to each strategy issue, but opinions tend to diverge on a number of critical points. By presenting the two opposite poles in each debate, readers can rapidly gain insight into these major points of contention. This is the *contrast function* of presenting the two opposite perspectives – they bring the key points of contention into sharper focus.

■ Stimulus for bridging. As the two opposite poles in each debate are presented, readers will be struck by the fact that neither position can be easily dismissed. Both extreme strategy perspectives make a strong case for a particular approach and readers will experience difficulty in simply choosing one over the other. With each extreme position offering certain advantages, readers will feel challenged to incorporate aspects of both into a more sophisticated synthesis. This is the *integrative function* of presenting the two opposite perspectives – they stimulate readers to seek a way of getting the best of both worlds.

■ Stimulus for creativity. Nothing is more creativity evoking than a challenging paradox whereby two opposites seem to be true at the same time. By presenting the two opposite poles of each debate, which both make a realistic claim to being valid, readers are challenged to creatively resolve this paradoxical situation. This is the *generative function* of presenting the two opposite perspectives – they stimulate readers to generate innovative ways of 'transcending' the strategic paradox.

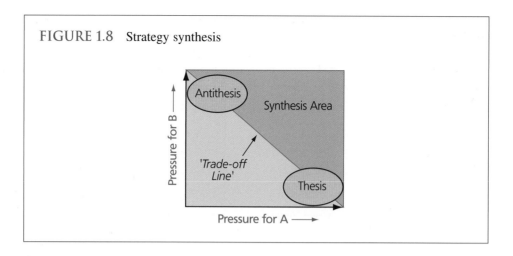

FIGURE 1.8   Strategy synthesis

Each chapter starts with the most traditional pole as the thesis, which is then contrasted with the less established opposite pole as the antithesis. As for the synthesis, that is up to each strategist to find (see Figure 1.8).

DEVELOPING AN INTERNATIONAL PERSPECTIVE

Every man takes the limits of his own field of vision for the limits of the world.
Arthur Schopenhauer (1788–1860); German philosopher

In a highly integrated world economy, in which many firms operate across national boundaries, strategy is by nature an international affair. Some theorists ignore the international arena as irrelevant, uninteresting or too complex, but most theorists, particularly those interested in strategy content, acknowledge the importance of the international context and write extensively on international competition and global strategy. In this book there has been a strong preference to include those authors who explicitly place their arguments within an international setting. Gaining an international perspective is greatly enhanced by reading works that do not take a domestic arena as their default assumption.

To further accentuate the international angle of this book, the international context has been singled out for a closer look in Chapter 10. In this chapter, the conflicting views about developments in the international context will be debated. This, too, should challenge readers to take an international perspective.

However, despite all this attention paid to the international competitive arena, internationalizing companies, cross-border strategies and global products, few authors explicitly question whether their own strategy theories can be globally standardized. Most fail to wonder whether their theories are equally applicable in a variety of national settings. It is seldom asked whether they base themselves on universally valid assumptions, or if they have been severely limited by their domestic 'field of vision'. Yet, there is a very real danger that theories are based on local assumptions that are not true or appropriate in other nations – a threat that could be called 'think local, generalize global'.

Developing an international perspective requires strategists to guard against the indiscriminate export of domestically generated strategy theories across international borders. For international strategists it is important to question whether theories 'travel' as well as the companies they describe. Unfortunately, at the moment, strategizing managers have little to base themselves on. There has been only a modest amount of international comparative research carried out in the field of strategy. National differences in strategic management practices and preferences have occasionally been identified, but in general the topic has received little attention. In practice, the international validity of locally formulated strategy theories has gone largely unquestioned in international journals and forums.

Although there is still so little published material to go on, in this book readers will be encouraged to question the international limitations of strategy theories. Furthermore, they will be challenged to question whether certain strategy perspectives are more popular or appropriate in some countries than in others. To point readers in the right direction, at the end of each chapter a sub-section will be presented that places the strategy topic being debated in an international perspective. In these sub-sections, it will be argued that the strategy paradoxes identified in this book are fundamentally the same around the world, but that there might be international differences in how each paradox is coped with. Strategy perspectives and theories might be more predominant in particular countries because they are based on certain assumptions about dealing with the strategy paradoxes that are more suitable to the national context. In each 'international perspective' sub-section, a number of factors will be discussed that might cause national differences in strategy styles.

Using the cases

An additional way of gaining an international perspective is by trying to employ the strategy perspectives in a variety of national settings. It is especially when trying to deal with concrete strategic problems on an international stage that the limitations of each theory will become more apparent. For this reason, a large number of cases have been included in this book, from many different countries. In each case, readers are encouraged to evaluate the specific national circumstances in which the problem situation is embedded, and to question whether the national context will have an influence on the validity or appropriateness of the various strategy theories and perspectives.

The cases have been selected to cover a wide variety of countries and industries. Furthermore, they have been chosen for their fit with a particular chapter. Each of the following ten chapters in this book has three corresponding cases, in which the paradox under discussion is prominently present. Two of the three cases per chapter are relatively lengthy, and have been grouped together in Section VI of this book. The short case for each chapter has been inserted as an exhibit into the main text. In each case readers will encounter the fact that grappling with strategy paradoxes in 'practice' is just as difficult as dealing with them in 'theory'.

EXHIBIT 1.1   SHORT CASE

DISNEY: IS MAGIC BACK IN THE MOUSE HOUSE?

It is little known that the world's most famous mouse, who goes by such names as Topolino in Italy, Musse Pigg in Sweden and Mi Lao Shu in China, actually used to be a bunny. The main character in Walt Disney's first cartoon was a creature named 'Oswald the Lucky Rabbit', but after Disney was cheated out of his copyrights, he modified the ears and renamed him Mickey Mouse.

What is more widely known is that Walt, together with his brother Roy, subsequently captured the attention of audiences around the world with Mickey as *Steamboat Willie* (1928), in the first cartoon with synchronised sound. After some modest successes with such new characters as Goofy and Donald Duck, the business of Walt Disney Studios really started to accelerate when they moved into full-length animated films, releasing blockbusters such as *Snow White and the Seven Dwarfs* (1937), *Pinocchio* (1940) and *Bambi*

▶

(1942). Soon Disney discovered the lucrative merchandising business, licensing the use of Disney characters for such things as clothing, pencils and soda-cans. On the basis of this success, Disney branched out into TV programmes, film music and live-action movie productions. In 1955, Walt's dream of creating a 'Magical Kingdom' was realized, when Disneyland was opened in Anaheim, California. After Walt's death in 1966, Roy carried on to build Disney World in Orlando, Florida, which was completed just before he passed away in 1971.

While the empire the brothers left behind carried on to entertain billions of children and adults the world over, the creative pipeline dried up completely. After the release of Walt's last project, *Jungle Book,* in 1967, the Disney studios spent the 1970s looking for ways to emulate the founder's magic, but without result. By 1983, only 4% of US moviegoers went to a Disney picture, and the 15-year drought of hit movies was being severely felt in the sales of Disney merchandise and licensing income. In the same year, the Disney Channel was launched in the US, but did not get off to a flying start. Making things worse, the hordes that initially swamped the theme parks were getting bored with Disney's dingy image and visitor numbers began to shrink, while at the same time Disney was incurring heavy costs to finish the Epcot Center at Disney World. To stem the tide, a new management team was hired in 1984, consisting of a brash young executive from Paramount Studios, Michael Eisner, who became CEO, and a level-headed operational man from Warner Brothers, Frank Wells, who became COO.

Together the two worked just like Walt and Roy, with the passionate and outspoken Eisner driving the creative process, and the stable and diplomatic Wells getting things organized. At Paramount, Eisner had produced hit movies such as *Raiders of the Lost Ark* and *Grease,* as well as the successful television shows *Happy Days* and *Cheers.* He was known for his fanatical attention to detail, to the extent of getting involved in reading scripts and selecting costumes. At Disney, he did the same, getting deeply involved in rejuvenating the film business. On the live-action movie side, Eisner and Wells redirected Disney towards lower budget productions, using promising scripts from less established writers and recruiting actors that seemed at the end of their career. Through a new subsidiary, Touchstone Pictures, Disney also entered the attractive market for films for the teen and young adult audience. With hits such as *Good Morning Vietnam* and *Down and Out in Beverly Hills,* Disney reached a 19% US box office share by 1988, causing Eisner to comment that 'nearly overnight, Disney went from nerdy outcast to leader of the popular crowd'. Later Disney was responsible for successes such as *Pretty Woman* (1990) and *Pulp Fiction* (1994) – the latter made by Miramax, an avant-garde movie studio Disney had acquired a year before.

The animation part of the business was also revitalized, with major investments made in new animation technology and new people, in particular a new creative producer, Jeffrey Katzenberg. Eventually, this resulted in a series of very successful films: *The Little Mermaid* (1989), *Beauty and the Beast* (1991), *Aladdin* (1992), and *The Lion King* (1994). To get the new movies back in the limelight, alliances were formed with McDonalds and Coca-Cola, to do promotional tie-ins. And to get spin-off merchandise flowing at greater volumes, Eisner moved beyond mere licensing, building up a global chain of Disney stores. Helped by a little luck, Disney also profited from the new home video trend that was sweeping the world. Not only could Disney release its new movies twice – first in the theatres and then on video – but it could also re-release a steady stream of classic pictures for home audiences.

In the theme park business, the major innovation spearheaded by Eisner and Wells was to make Disneyland and Disney World more appealing to adults. In 1989 the Disney-MGM Studios theme park was opened near Disney World, as well as the Pleasure Island nightlife complex. Based on the success of Tokyo Disneyland, which was opened in 1983, Disney also built a theme park outside of Paris, called Euro Disney in 1992. It turned out that while the Japanese visitors appreciated an almost replica of Disney World in Tokyo, European tastes were very different, requiring a long period of adaptation to the local market conditions and causing Euro Disney (later renamed Disneyland Resort Paris) to suffer significant losses during a number of years.

Then, in 1994, Frank Wells was killed in a helicopter crash, Eisner had bypass heart surgery, and a period of boardroom infighting commenced, leading to the high profile departure of the studio head, Katzenberg, who later teamed up with Steven Spielberg and David Geffen to found a new independent film company, DreamWorks SKG. Other executives also left, pointing to Eisner's overbearing presence. 'People get tired of being second guessed and beaten down', a former studio executive remarked. 'When people came out of Michael's office wounded, Frank was the emergency room', another Disney insider reported to *Fortune,* but with Wells gone, no one was there to repair damaged egos and soothe hurt feelings. However, Eisner viewed the situation differently: 'I've never had a problem with anybody who was truly talented…This autonomy crap? That means you're off working alone. If you want autonomy, be a poet.'

In 1996, Eisner made his biggest move yet, acquiring Capital Cities/ABC for US$ 19.6 billion. This deal included the ABC Television Network (distributing to 224 affiliated stations), the ABC Radio Networks (with 3400 radio outlets) and an 80% share of ESPN, a sport-oriented network, which includes various cable channels and radio stations. Ironically, Eisner had previously worked for ABC as daytime programmer, and felt that he had a lot to add to ABC: 'I would love, every morning, to go over and spend two hours at ABC. Even though my children tell me that I am in the wrong generation and I don't get it anymore, I am totally convinced that I could sit with our guys and make ABC No. 1 in two years.' But the opposite happened, as ABC quickly fell to last place, where it lingered for almost ten years.

After Katzenberg's departure, Disney's animation track record also took a turn for the worse – movies such as *Pocahontas* (1995) and *Tarzan* (1999) didn't do too badly, although soaring costs made them only mildly profitable. Other features, such as *Atlantis* (2001), *Treasure Island* (2002) and *Home on the Range* (2004) were box office fiascos. Disney's real animation successes came from their deal with Pixar, an independent studio specializing in computer-generated animations, owned by Apple CEO, Steve Jobs. Such co-productions as *Toy Story* (1995), *Monsters Inc.* (2000) and *Finding Nemo* (2003) were hits in the cinemas and on DVD. In the area of live-action films, Katzenberg's replacement Joe Roth scrapped the policy of setting a 'financial box' within which the creatives had to operate, leading to bigger budgets, big names and big special effects – and just a few too many big disasters. Illustrative were *Pearl Harbor* (2001) and *Gangs of New York* (2002), both with immense production budgets, yet unable to live up to their promise. The result was a high market share for Disney films, but profitability hovering just above zero.

Although Eisner had taken Disney from US$ 1.5 billion in revenues in 1984 to US$ 30 billion 20 years later, a revolt broke out among shareholders, led by Walt's nephew Roy Disney and director Stanley Gold. They lambasted Eisner's perceived arrogance and inability to foster creativity, calling for his resignation. Eventually, Eisner decided to step down, upon which the board appointed Eisner's right hand man and company president since 2000, Bob Iger, to the position of CEO in 2005. Although Gold called Iger 'a modest man with a lot to be modest about', the new CEO was a popular choice among 'Mouseketeers', because of his calm demeanor and team player mentality.

Iger immediately disbanded the strategic planning department at corporate headquarters in Burbank, California, which was held responsible for blocking many of the divisions' strategic initiatives. Instead, Iger gave the heads of the four divisions – Studio Entertainment (films), Parks & Resorts, Media Networks (TV & radio) and Consumer Products (merchandizing) – more autonomy to make decisions, while at the same time keeping Eisner's emphasis on leveraging Disney characters across all activities. Iger also mended relationships with Stanley Gold and Roy Disney, asking the latter to join the board of directors as consultant. A surprised Gold remarked: 'He's got the company working like a team again. It's very impressive.'

Relations with Katzenberg and DreamWorks were also restored, leading to further cooperation, but most importantly Iger was able to defuse the tense relationship with Pixar's owner, Steve Jobs. As the six-year co-production agreement with Pixar was about to end, Iger needed to find some way to continue the partnership, since Pixar's films were responsible for more than half of Disney's studio profits. The solution turned out to be a classic win–win, with Disney purchasing Pixar for US$ 7.4 billion in Disney shares, while bringing in Steve Jobs as board member. Part of the deal was also that Pixar's president, Ed Catmull, and its top creative executive, John Lasseter, would take over Disney's struggling animation studios. Furthermore, Disney would work together more closely with Apple in making premium content available through Apple's iTunes stores.

Disney's financial results were further strengthened by a renaissance at ABC, where hit shows like *Lost, Desperate Housewives, Grey's Anatomy* and *Ugly Betty* helped to catapult the network to a leading position. Significant growth was also achieved at the Disney Channel, where the traditional focus on the very young was broadened to include 'tweens', nine to 14-year-olds, offering them shows like *Hannah Montana* and *High School Musical*. Not only did these programmes attract a whole new audience, but they led to a wave of new merchandizing opportunities.

Based on Disney's excellent performance and the trust he had built up during the 2005–2008 period, Iger's contract as CEO was extended to 2013. But while the ride had been a bit like the 'Big Thunder Mountain' roller coaster in the first few years, there seemed little reason to believe that the next years would be any less thrilling, as Iger had plenty of strategic issues to deal with. One key strategic challenge for Iger was to continue to reap the synergies between the divisions, by taking movie characters to television, the internet, theme parks and Disney stores. Another example of such cross-media synergy is *High School Musical,* which was leveraged into a live concert tour, a stage musical, a show on ice, and a series of books and video games. Disney now has ten of these 'franchises', ranging from Mickey Mouse to Cars, Winnie the Pooh and Disney Fairies, that it tries to leverage, but the question is how this should be managed, without creating a complex organizational structure and reducing each division's freedom to set its own strategy.

Another issue is internationalization, which Iger has set high on his priority list. If Disney wants to break into non-US markets in a big way, can it do so by leveraging its franchises across borders or must Disney go local, developing local movies and characters? With more or less standardized theme parks in Tokyo, Paris and Hong Kong (2006) and resorts in a variety of locations, there is much to be said for sticking to global franchises. Yet, on the other hand, emerging markets like China, Russia, India and Brazil might be a bit too diverse to cover successfully with globally standardized wares.

Disney's future in interactive media is another issue. So far, its activities in this area have produced a lot of red ink, with a loss in 2008 of approximately US$ 250 million, bringing the total to more than US$ 1 billion. A major question facing Iger was how to know where money could be made in future. Many people had great ideas, but few customers seemed willing to pay for content over the internet. He also wondered whether the future was more in collaboration with digital distributors such as iTunes instead of via Disney's own website. With a clear revenue model lacking, Iger needed to decide whether to keep up the expensive experimentation, or scale back investments until it became more clear where the web-based business was headed.

Probably Iger's biggest challenge, however, was to reinvigorate Disney's heart and soul – its film business. The TV and radio division had done well, growing in revenues from US$ 11 billion in 2004 to US$ 16 billion in 2008, while Parks & Resorts had jumped from US$ 7.7 to 11.5 billion in the same period, with profitability to match. The merchandizing business had also grown a bit, from US$ 2.4 to 2.9 billion, but the core film business had actually shrunk from US$ 8.7 to 7.3 billion. On the animation side, the quality-oriented Pixar people were finding it difficult to increase the level of production, while on the live action side the number of big hits was lagging, which was not helped by the tumultuous departure of the Miramax founders, Bob and Harvey Weinstein. With only *Pirates of the Caribbean* as a highly leverageable recent movie hit, Iger was eagerly looking for new themes around which to build the Disney synergies. One positive reverse example came from Disney's big push into video games, where its partner Ubisoft's hit *Prince of Persia* was actually turned into a movie.

In the 2008 annual report, Iger expressed confidence that 'our brands, products and people will pass the test that lies before them', indicating that he would move ahead 'taking a very pragmatic approach to new investments'. Iger had the trust of the company and of many analysts that he could unleash more magic in the Mouse House. Yet, judging from the wobbly stock price, many investors feared that the clock might strike 12 and the magic might be over.

Co-author: Casper van der Veen

Sources: *Disney Annual Report 2008*; *The Economist*, 26 January 2006 & 17 April 2008; *Fortune*, 23 December 2001; *Business Week*, 5 February 2007 & 9 February 2009; http:/corporate.disney.go.com; *Sunday Times*, 20 February 2005 & 2 October 2005; www.wired.com/gaming/hardware/news/2008/08/portfolio_0806.

READINGS

Unless a variety of opinions are laid before us, we have no opportunity of selection, but are bound of necessity to adopt the particular view which may have been brought forward. The purity of gold cannot be ascertained by a single specimen; but when we have carefully compared it with others, we are able to fix upon the finest ore.

Herodotus (5th century BC); Greek historian

In the following ten chapters the readings will represent the different points of view in the debate. The readings will 'lay the variety of opinions before us'. However, in this opening chapter there is no central debate. Therefore, four readings have been selected that provide a stimulating introduction to the topic of strategy, or reinforce some of the arguments made in the preceding pages. Here, each of the readings will be briefly introduced and its relevance for the discussion will be highlighted.

The opening reading, 'The First Strategists' by Stephen Cummings, places the central question of this book – what is strategy? – in a historical perspective. Cummings takes the reader back to the ancient Greeks, to whom we owe the term 'strategy', in a quest to uncover some fundamental characteristics of military strategy and strategists, which he believes are still important for business strategists today. The charm of this extract lies not only in its clear and concise rendition of Hellenic thought, but also in its ability to place the current state of the art of strategic thinking in the humbling context of history. This reading convincingly points out that many seemingly modern strategy issues are actually millennia old. The development of the business strategy field may be a recent academic trend, stretching no further back than the 1960s, but outside commerce many of the great minds throughout history have occupied themselves with the topic of strategy, especially in the fields of war (see, for instance, the famous Chinese theorist Sun Tzu's *The Art of War* and Karl von Clausewitz's *On War)* and politics (for example, Niccolo Machiavelli's *The Prince* and *The Discourses*). The debate, which Cummings opens with this reading, is to what extent the principles of military strategy can be applied to the business context. Can business strategists learn from military strategists, and vice versa? Stated even more broadly, to what measure are there parallels between strategy in such diverse fields as war, politics, sports, biology and business? Are there universal principles of strategy? The extent to which the strategy principles of one area are valid in another is a recurrent theme in strategy literature.

Reading 1.2, 'Complexity: The Nature of Real World Problems', is the first chapter of Richard Mason and Ian Mitroff's classic book, *Challenging Strategic Planning Assumptions*. This thought-provoking extract has been selected for this chapter to serve as an introduction to the complex nature of the strategic problems addressed in this book. Mason and Mitroff's main argument is that most strategic problems facing organizations are not 'tame' – that is, they are not simple problems that can be separated and reduced to a few variables and relationships, and then quickly solved. Strategic problems are usually 'wicked': strategists are faced with situations of organized complexity in which problems are complicated and interconnected, there is much uncertainty and ambiguity, and they must deal with conflicting views and interests. Therefore, strategic problems have no clearly identifiable correct solutions, but must be tackled by debating the alternatives and selecting the most promising option. Mason and Mitroff call on strategists to systematically doubt the value of all available solutions and to employ dialectics – which is exactly the approach taken in this book. In the context of this chapter, the most important message that Mason and Mitroff have is that the variety of opinions might make things more complex, but is also a useful resource for finding better quality solutions.

In contrast to the more theoretical description of dialectics presented by Mason and Mitroff, the author of Reading 1.3, Roger Martin, offers a hands-on approach to using opposing ideas to reach more effective solutions. This recent *Harvard Business Review* article, 'How Successful Leaders Think' is drawn from his book *The Opposable Mind,* in which he argues that the ability to use opposing ideas is the mental equivalent of having an opposable thumb. Without a thumb opposite to our fingers, we would not be able to create the tension in our hands needed to hold things and perform advanced physical activities. Without the capacity to create a mental tension by holding two opposing ideas in mind, we would not be able to cross-fertilize these ideas to find innovative ways forward. Martin calls this 'integrative thinking' – synthesizing elements from conflicting views to find a third way. It is about avoiding 'either–or' thinking in favour of 'and–and' thinking. In this reading Martin explains in more depth the steps that need to be taken to effectively engage in integrative thinking, which will be of particular use throughout the rest of this book.

The last reading, 'Cultural Constraints in Management Theories' by Geert Hofstede, has been selected to sow seeds of further doubt about the universal validity of strategic management theories. Hofstede is one of the most prominent cross-cultural researchers in the field of management and is known, in particular, for his five dimensions for measuring cultural traits. In this reading he briefly describes the major characteristics of management in Germany, Japan, France, Holland, South-East Asia, Africa, Russia and China, contrasting them all to the United States, to drive home his point that management practices differ from country to country depending on the local culture. Each national style is based on cultural characteristics that differ sharply around the world. Hofstede argues that theories are formulated within these national cultural contexts, and thus reflect the local demands and predispositions. Therefore, he concludes that universal management theories do not exist – each theory is culturally constrained. If Hofstede is right, this re-emphasizes the necessity to view strategic management and strategy theories from an international perspective. Readers must judge which strategy approach is best suited to the national circumstances with which they are confronted.

READING

1.1

The first strategists

By Stephen Cummings[1]

Origin of strategy

The word *strategy* derives from the ancient Athenian position of *strategos*. The title was coined in conjunction with the democratic reforms of Kleisthenes (508–7 BC), who developed a new sociopolitical structure in Athens after leading a popular revolution against a Spartan-supported oligarchy. Kleisthenes instituted 10 new tribal divisions, which acted as both military and political subunits of the district of Athens. At the head of each tribe was elected a strategos. Collectively, the 10 incumbent *strategoi* formed the Athenian war council. This council and its individual members, by virtue of the kudos granted them, also largely controlled nonmilitary politics.

Strategos was a compound of *stratos,* which meant 'army,' or more properly an encamped army *spread out* over ground (in this way *stratos* is also allied to *stratum)* and *agein,* 'to lead.' The emergence of the term paralleled increasing military decision-making complexity. Warfare had evolved to a point where winning sides no longer relied on the deeds of heroic individuals, but on the coordination of many units of men each fighting in close formation. Also, the increasing significance of naval forces in this period multiplied the variables a commander must consider in planning action. Consequently, questions of coordination and synergy among the various emergent units of their organizations became imperative considerations for successful commanders.

Of what interest are the origins of strategy to those engaging in strategic activities and decision making in organizations today? In the words of Adlai Stevenson, we can see our future clearly and wisely only when we know the path that leads to the present. Most involved in corporate strategy have little knowledge of where that path began. A great deal of insight into strategy can be gained from examining those from whom we inherit the term. The first strategists, the Greek strategoi, perhaps practised strategy in its purest sense.

Strategy and strategist as defined by ancient theorists

Aineias the Tactician, who wrote the earliest surviving Western volume on military strategy, *How to Survive under Siege,* in the mid fourth century BC, was primarily concerned with how to deploy available manpower and other resources to best advantage. The term strategy is defined in more detail by Frontinus in the first century AD, as 'everything achieved by a commander, be it characterized by foresight, advantage, enterprise, or resolution.'

Ancient Athenian theorists also had clear ideas about the characteristics that were necessary in an effective strategos. According to Xenophon, a commander 'must be ingenious, energetic, careful, full of stamina and presence of mind, loving and tough, straightforward and crafty, alert and deceptive, ready to gamble everything and wishing to have everything, generous and greedy, trusting, and suspicious.' These criteria for identifying an excellent strategist still ring true.

Xenophon goes on to describe the most important attribute for an aspiring strategos/statement as 'knowing the business which you propose to carry out.' The Athenians in this period were very concerned that their leaders had an awareness of how things worked at the 'coal-face.' Strategoi were publicly elected by their fellow members of the Athenian organization; and to be considered a credible candidate, one had to have worked one's way into this position by demonstrating prowess at both individual combat and hands-on military leadership. Wisdom was considered to be a citizen's ability to combine political acumen and practical intelligence, and strategoi should be the wisest of citizens. The organization's future lay in the hands of these men and, ipso facto, the strategic leadership of the Athenian organization was not to consider itself immune from hardship when times were tough: 'No man was fitted to give fair and honest advice in council if he has not, like his fellows, a family at stake in the hour of the city's danger.'

[1]Source: This article was reprinted from *Long Range Planning,* Vol. 26, No. 3, S. Cummings, 'Brief Case: The First Strategists', pp. 133–135, © 1993. With permission from Elsevier.

To the ancient Athenians strategy was very much a line of function. The formulation of strategy was a leadership task. The Athenian organization developed by Kleisthenes was extremely recursive. The new tribes, and the local communities that these tribes comprised, formed the units and subunits of the army, and were, in their sociopolitical structures, tantamount to the city-state in microcosm. Decision makers at all levels of the corporation were expected to think strategically, in accordance with the behaviour exhibited by those in leadership roles at higher levels of the Athenian system. Strategoi were expected both to direct and take part in the thick of battle, leading their troops into action. For a strategos not to play an active combat role would have resulted in a significant diminution in the morale of those fighting for his tribe.

Practical lessons from the strategoi

If military practice is identified as a metaphor for business competition, the strategic principles of the great strategoi still provide useful guides for those in the business of strategy formulation today. For Pericles, perhaps the greatest of the Athenian strategoi, the goal of military strategies was 'to limit risk while holding fast to essential points and principles.' His often quoted maxims of 'Opportunity waits for no man' and 'Do not make any new conquests during the war' are still applicable advice in a modern business environment.

Epaminondas of Thebes was said to have brought the two arms of his military corporation, infantry and cavalry, together in a 'fruitful organizational blend.' The Theban's strategic principles included economy of force coupled with overwhelming strength at the decisive point; close coordination between units and meticulous staff planning combined with speed of attack; and as the quickest and most economical way of winning a decision, defeat of the competition not at his weakest point but at his strongest. Epaminondas was Philip of Macedon's mentor, and it was largely due to the application of the Theban's innovations that the Macedonian army grew to an extent where it was able to realize Alexander the Great's (Philip's son) vast ambitions. The close integration of all its individual units became the major strength of the Macedonian army organization.

Alexander himself is perhaps the most famous ancient exponent of a contingency approach to strategy. It is often told that as a young man he was asked by his tutor Aristotle what he would do in a given situation. Alexander replied that his answer would depend on the circumstances. Aristotle described a hypothetical set of circumstances and asked his original question again. To this the student answered, 'I cannot tell until the circumstances arise.' In practice Alexander was not often caught without a 'plan B.' An example is related by Frontinus: 'At Arbela, Alexander, fearing the numbers of the enemy, yet confident in the valour of his own troops, drew up a line of battle facing in all directions, in order that the men, if surrounded, might be able to fight from any side.'

Ancient approaches to the learning of strategy

The ancient Greeks took great interest in both the practical and theoretical aspects of strategic leadership. They favored the case method as the best means of passing this knowledge from one generation of strategists to the next. Frontinus argued that 'in this way commanders will be furnished with specimens of wisdom and foresight, which will serve to foster their own power of conceiving and executing like deeds.' Aineias and Xenophon also used and championed such methods in ways that would please any Harvardophile. The best-crafted exposition of the case method, however, belongs to Plutarch, biographer to the ancient world's greatest leaders:

> It is true, of course, that our outward sense cannot avoid apprehending the various objects it encounters, merely by virtue of their impact and regardless of whether they are useful or not: but a man's conscious intellect is something which he may bring to bear or avert as he chooses, and can very easily transfer ... to another object as he sees fit. For this reason, we ought to seek out virtue not merely to contemplate it, but to derive benefit from doing so. A colour, for example, is well suited to the eye if its bright and agreeable tones stimulate and refresh the vision, and in the same way we ought to apply our intellectual vision to those models which can inspire it to attain its own proper virtue through the sense of delight they arouse ... [Such a model is] no sooner seen than it rouses the spectator into action, and yet it does not form his character by mere imitation, but by promoting the understanding of virtuous deeds it provides him with a dominating purpose.

Now, as then, our strategic vision can be refreshed and stimulated through studying the character and deeds of the great strategic leaders of the past.

READING

1.2

Complexity: The nature of real world problems

By Richard Mason and Ian Mitroff[1]

Try a little experiment. Make a short list of the major problems or issues facing policymakers in the world today. Now take your list and arrange it as a matrix like the one in Figure 1.2.1. For each element in the matrix ask yourself the following question: Is the solution to one problem (the row problem) in any way related to the solution of the other problem (the column problem)? If the answer is yes, place a check mark at the point where the row and column intersect; otherwise leave it blank. When you have completed the process, review the matrix and count the number of blanks. Are there any?

'Not fair!' you may say. 'There were a lot of check marks in my matrix because many of these world problems are linked together.' World problems involve all nations. One would not expect to get the same result if the focus was, say, on one's company, city, family, or personal life. Really? Try it and see. Recently, several managers at a major corporation tried this little experiment as part of a strategic planning effort. Among the issues and problem areas they identified were the following:

- Satisfy stockholder dividend and risk requirements.
- Acquire adequate funds for expansion from the capital markets.
- Insure a stable supply of energy at reasonable prices.
- Train a corps of middle managers to assume more responsibility.
- Develop a marketing force capable of handling new product lines.

The managers found that all of these problems and issues were related to each other. Some were only related weakly, but most were related quite strongly. Repeated attempts in other contexts give the same result: *basically, every real world policy problem is related to every other real world problem.* This is an important finding. It means that every time a policymaker attempts to solve a particular policy problem he or she must consider its potential relationship with all other problems. To do this one must have both a comprehensive set of concepts for dealing with any policy and a rich set of tools for acquiring the holistic information needed to guide policy making.

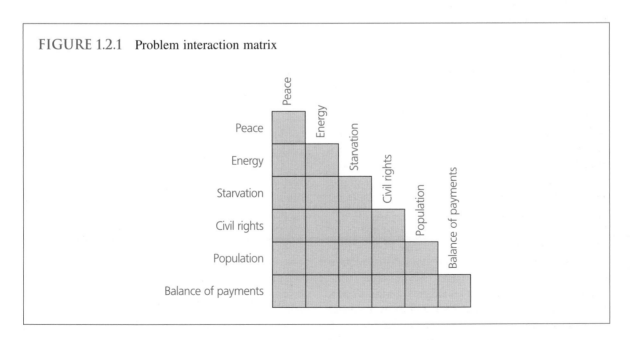

FIGURE 1.2.1   Problem interaction matrix

[1]Source: This article was adapted from Chapter 1 of R. Mason and I. Mitroff, *Challenging Strategic Planning Assumptions,* © John Wiley & Sons, Inc. 1981. This material is used by permission of John Wiley & Sons, Inc.

Characteristics of complexity

There are several characteristics of policy making that the foregoing little experiment is intended to illustrate:

- Any policy-making situation comprises many problems and issues.

- These problems and issues tend to be highly inter-related. Consequently, the solution to one problem requires a solution to all the other problems. At the same time, each solution creates additional dimensions to be incorporated in the solutions to other problems.

- Few, if any, problems can be isolated effectively for separate treatment.

These are the characteristics of complexity. Complexity literally means the condition of being tightly woven or twined together. Most policymakers find that the problems they face today are complex in this sense. Moreover, almost all of today's problems seem to be getting more plentiful and complex.

There is an especially vexing aspect of complexity as it presents itself to policymakers. It is organized. As we have seen in the little experiment, there tends to be an illusive structure underlying problems that gives pattern and organization to the whole. Organization is usually considered the route to the solution of a complex problem. In reality, however, organization in complexity can become an insurmountable barrier to the solution of a problem. This is the major challenge to real world problem solving because we have very few intellectual tools for coping with 'organized complexity.'

The tools we have available seem to work best on simple problems, those that can be separated and reduced to relatively few variables and relationships. These problems of simplicity usually have a one-dimensional value system or goal structure that guides the solution. Three factors – separability, reducibility, and one-dimensional goal structure – mean that simple problems can be bounded, managed, and, as Horst Rittel (1972) puts it, 'tamed.'

Ironically, problems of the utmost complexity can also be tamed as long as the complexity is 'disorganized.' That is, whenever the number of variables is very large and the variables are relatively disconnected, the problem can be tamed with the elegant simplicity of statistical mechanics. For example, there is no known way of predicting how a given individual will vote on a political candidate. However, using polling procedures and statistical techniques it is possible to predict with a fair degree of confidence how an entire population of voters will vote. Similarly, it is difficult to predict whether a given customer will purchase a new product or not. However, using market research methods, a fairly good estimate can be made of a new product's potential market share.

Perhaps one of the greatest insights of the 20th century is the discovery that when a problem situation meets the condition for random sampling – many individual elements exhibiting independent, probabilistic behaviour – there is a potential statistical solution to the problem. In short, disorganized complexity can generally be tamed by statistical means.

One place where the assumption of disorganized complexity has proven invaluable in the past is in the actuarial sciences. Today, however, the insurance industry is discovering that many of the risks once assumed to be reasonably independent and hence analysable according to standard actuarial methods are no longer so. People, organizations, and facilities have become more tightly woven together over wider geographical areas. Consequently, the probabilities of death, accident, fire, or disaster on which the risks and premiums are based are no longer as straightforward as they once were. The result is that the statistical methods that applied under conditions of disorganized complexity have become less reliable as the system has become more organized.

The great difficulty with connected systems of organized complexity is that deviations in one element can be transmitted to other elements. In turn, these deviations can be magnified, modified, and re-verberated so that the system takes on a kind of unpredictable life of its own. Emery and Trist (1965) refer to this condition as 'environmental connectedness' and have labeled this type of environment the 'turbulent' environment.

Emery and Trist cite an interesting case to illustrate the nature of environmental connectedness and the great difficulties it presents to policy makers. In Great Britain after World War II, a large food canning company began to expand. Its main product was a canned vegetable – a staple in the English diet. As part of the expansion plan, the company decided to build a new, automated factory, requiring an investment of several million pounds sterling. For over a decade the company had enjoyed a 65 per cent market share for their product line and saw no reason for this strong market position to deteriorate. Given this large volume, the new plant offered the 'experience curve' advantages of economies to scale and made possible the long production runs required to meet the demand from the traditional market.

After ground was broken, but well before the factory was completed, a series of seemingly detached and isolated socioeconomic events occurred. These relatively insignificant events were to change the destiny of the company. Taken collectively, they rendered the factory economically obsolete and threw the corporate board of directors into a state of turmoil. The scenario of events went something like this. Due to the release of wartime controls on steel strip and tin, a number of new small firms that could economically can imported fruit sprang up. Initially, they in no way competed directly with the large vegetable canner. However, since their business was seasonal, they began to look for ways to keep their machinery and labour employed during the winter. Their answer came from a surprising source – the US quick-frozen food industry. The quick-freezing process requires a substantial degree of consistency in the crop. This consistency is very difficult to achieve. However, it turned out that large crops of the vegetable were grown in the United States and a substantial portion of US crops was unsuitable for quick freezing (a big industry in the United States) but quite suitable for canning. Furthermore, American farmers had been selling this surplus crop at a very low price for animal feed and were only too happy to make it available at an attractive price to the small canners in the United Kingdom. The canners jumped at the opportunity and imported the crop. Using off-season production capacity they began to offer a low-cost product in the large canner's market. The small canners' position was further strengthened as underdeveloped countries began to vie with the United States in an effort to become the cheapest source of supply for the crop.

These untimely events in the large canner's supply market were compounded by events in its product market. Prior to the introduction of quick-freezing, the company featured a high quality, higher price premier brand that dominated the market. This market advantage, however, was diminished by the cascading effect of several more unpredictable events. As the scenario unfolded the quick-frozen product captured the high quality strata of the market, a growing dimension due to increased affluence. The smaller canners stripped off the lower price layers of the market, aided in part by another seemingly unrelated development in retailing – the advent of supermarkets. As supermarkets and large grocery chains developed, they sought to improve their position by establishing their own in-house brand names and by buying in bulk. The small canner filled this need for the supermarket chains. Small canners could undercut the price of the manufacturer's brand product because they had low production costs and almost no marketing expenses. Soon supermarket house brands (which had accounted for less than 1 per cent of the market prior to the war) became the source of 50 per cent of the market sales. The smaller canners were the benefactors of almost all of this growth.

As a result, the company's fancy new automated factory was totally inappropriate for the current market situation. The company's management had failed to appreciate that a number of outside events were becoming connected with each other in a way that was leading up to an inevitable general change. They tried desperately to defend their traditional product lines, but, in the end, this was to no avail. After a series of financial setbacks, the company had to change its mission. It reemerged several years later with a new product mix and a new identity. Management had learned the hard way that their strategy problems were neither problems of simplicity nor problems of disorganized complexity. They were problems of organized complexity.

Many corporate policy planning and strategy issues exhibit this property of organized complexity. The vegetable canning company's automated plant decision clearly was made under conditions of organized complexity. Pricing problems also frequently display this characteristic. Recently, a large pharmaceutical firm addressed the seemingly simple problem of setting a price for its primary drug line. The company's management soon learned, however, that there was an intricate web of corporate relationships woven around this one decision. Below the surface there was a structure of complex relationships between the firm's drug pricing policy and physicians, pharmacists, patients, competitors, suppliers, the FDA, and other parties. These relationships organized the complexity of the firm's pricing decision problem. Purely analytical or statistical methods were rendered inappropriate.

'Wicked' problems

Today, few of the pressing problems are truly problems of simplicity or of disorganized complexity. They are more like the problems described in the illustrative cases above and the ones we uncovered in our little experiment-problems of organized complexity. These problems simply cannot be tamed in the same way that other problems can. For this reason Rittel refers to these problems of organized complexity as 'wicked' problems. Wicked problems are not necessarily wicked in the perverse sense of being evil. Rather, they are wicked like the head of a hydra. They are an ensnarled web of tentacles. The more you attempt to tame them, the more complicated they become.

Rittel (1972) has identified several characteristic properties of wicked problems that distinguish them from tame problems. These properties are:

1   *Ability to formulate the problem*

  a   Tame problems can be exhaustively formulated and written down on a piece of paper.

  b   Wicked problems have no definitive formulation.

2   *Relationship between problem and solution*

  a   Tame problems can be formulated separately from any notion of what their solution might be.

  b   Every formulation of a wicked problem corresponds to a statement of solution and vice versa. Understanding the problem is synonymous with solving it.

3   *Testability*

  a   The solution to a tame problem can be tested. Either it is correct or it is false. Mistakes and errors can be pinpointed.

  b   There is no single criteria system or rule that determines whether the solution to a wicked problem is correct or false. Solutions can only be good or bad relative to one another.

4   *Finality*

  a   Tame problems have closure – a clear solution and ending point. The end can be determined by means of a test.

  b   There is no stopping rule for wicked problems. Like a Faustian bargain, they require eternal vigilance. There is always room for improvement. Moreover, since there is neither an immediate nor ultimate test for the solution to the problem, one never knows when one's work is done. As a result, the potential consequences of the problem are played out indefinitely.

5   *Tractability*

  a   There is an exhaustive list of permissible operations that can be used to solve a tame problem.

  b   There is no exhaustive, enumerable list of permissible operations to be used for solving a wicked problem.

6   *Explanatory characteristics*

  a   A tame problem may be stated as a 'gap' between what 'is' and what 'ought' to be and there is a clear explanation for every gap.

  b   Wicked problems have many possible explanations for the same discrepancy. Depending on which explanation one chooses, the solution takes on a different form.

7   *Level of analysis*

  a   Every tame problem has an identifiable, certain, natural form; there is no need to argue about the level of the problem. The proper level of generality can be found for bounding the problem and identifying its root cause.

  b   Every wicked problem can be considered as a symptom of another problem. It has no identifiable root cause; since curing symptoms does not cure problems, one is never sure the problem is being attacked at the proper level.

8   *Reproducibility*

  a   A tame problem can be abstracted from the real world, and attempts can be made to solve it over and over again until the correct solution is found.

  b   Each wicked problem is a one-shot operation. Once a solution is attempted, you can never undo what you have already done. There is no trial and error.

9   *Replicability*

  a   The same tame problem may repeat itself many times.

  b   Every wicked problem is essentially unique.

10   *Responsibility*

  a   No one can be blamed for failing to solve a tame problem, although solving a tame problem may bring someone acclaim.

  b   The wicked problem solver has 'no right to be wrong.' He is morally responsible for what he is doing and must share the blame when things go wrong. However, since there is no way of knowing when a wicked problem is solved, very few people are praised for grappling with them.

Characteristics of wicked problems.   Most policy planning and strategy problems are wicked problems of organized complexity. These complex wicked problems also exhibit the following characteristics:

1 Interconnectedness. Strong connections link each problem to other problems. As a result, these connections sometimes circle back to form feedback loops. 'Solutions' aimed at the problem seem inevitably to have important opportunity costs and side effects. How they work out depends on events beyond the scope of any one problem.

2 Complicatedness. Wicked problems have numerous important elements with relationships among them, including important 'feedback loops' through which a change tends to multiply itself or perhaps even cancel itself out. Generally, there are various leverage points where analysis and ideas for intervention might focus, as well as many possible approaches and plausible programs of action. There is also a likelihood that different programs should be combined to deal with a given problem.

3 Uncertainty. Wicked problems exist in a dynamic and largely uncertain environment, which creates a need to accept risk, perhaps incalculable risk. Contingency planning and also the flexibility to respond to unimagined and perhaps unimaginable contingencies are both necessary.

4 Ambiguity. The problem can be seen in quite different ways, depending on the viewer's personal characteristics, loyalties, past experiences, and even on accidental circumstances of involvement. There is no single 'correct view' of the problem.

5 Conflict. Because of competing claims, there is often a need to trade off 'goods' against 'bads' within the same value system. Conflicts of interest among persons or organizations with different or even antagonistic value systems are to be expected. How things will work out may depend on interaction among powerful interests that are unlikely to enter into fully cooperative arrangements.

6 Societal constraints. Social, organizational, and political constraints and capabilities, as well as technological ones, are central both to the feasibility and the desirability of solutions.

These characteristics spell difficulty for the policymaker who seeks to serve a social system by changing it for the better. Policymakers must choose the means for securing improvement for the people they serve. They must design, steer, and maintain a stable social system in the context of a complex environment. To do this,

they require new methods of real world problem solving to guide their policy-making activities. Otherwise, they run the risk of setting their social systems adrift.

Implications for policy making. The wicked problems of organized complexity have two major implications for designing processes for making policy:

1 There must be a broader participation of affected parties, directly and indirectly, in the policy-making process.

2 Policy making must be based on a wider spectrum of information gathered from a larger number of diverse sources.

Let us consider each of these implications in turn. The first implication indicates that policy making is increasingly becoming a political process, political in the sense that it involves individuals forming into groups to pursue common interests. Turn again to the results of the little experiment conducted at the outset of this chapter. You will find that in almost every case there are a variety of individual interests at stake in each problem area cited. Furthermore, one of the major factors creating the linkages between problem areas – organizing their complexity – is the number of diverse individual interests that cut across problem areas. Individuals are part of the problem and hence must be part of the solution.

This means that the raw material for forging solutions to wicked problems is not concentrated in a single head, but rather is widely dispersed among the various parties at stake. For any given wicked problem there is a variety of classes of expertise. Every affected party is an expert on some aspect of the problem and its solution. Furthermore, the disparate parties are bound together in a common venture. Thus some form of collective risk sharing is needed in order to deal effectively with the consequences of wicked problems. This suggests the need for a substantial degree of involvement in the policy-making process by those potentially affected by a policy in its formulation process. Effective policy is made *with,* or if adequate representation is present, *for,* but *not at* people. At least those involved should be able to voice their opinion on the relative goodness or badness of proposed solutions.

The diversity of parties at stake is related to the second implication. Since much of the necessary information for coping with wicked problems resides in the heads of several individuals, methods are needed to obtain this information from them and to communicate it to others. This means that as many of the different sources of information as possible must be identified. The relevant information must be obtained from each and stated in an explicit manner.

Contained in the minds of each participant in a wicked problem are powerful notions as to what is, what ought to be, why things are the way they are, how they can be changed, and how to think about their complexity. This represents a much broader class of information than is commonly used to solve problems of simplicity or of disorganized complexity. Also, this participant-based information is less likely to have been stated and recorded in a communicable form. Consequently, this information must be 'objectified' – explicitly, articulated – so that the basis for each party's judgements may be exchanged with others. Objectification has the advantages of being explicit, providing a memory, controlling the delegation of judgements, and raising pertinent issues that might have been ignored otherwise. It also stimulates *doubt.*

To be in doubt about a piece of information is to withhold assent to it. Given the range of diverse information that characterizes a wicked problem, participants in the policy-making process are well advised to develop a healthy respect for the method of doubt. In dealing with problems of organized complexity one should start with Descartes' rule: 'The first precept was never to accept a thing as true until I knew it was such without a single doubt.' This does not mean that one should be a 'nay sayer' or a permanent skeptic. To do so would impede responsible action that must be taken. What it does imply is that one should withhold judgement on things until they have been tested.

All problem-solving methods presuppose some form of guarantor for the correctness of their solutions. Problems of simplicity can be tested and solutions guaranteed by means of repeated solving, just as a theorem is proven in mathematics. This is because simple problems can be stated in closed form. The solutions to problems of disorganized complexity can be guaranteed within some stated confidence interval or degree of risk because the problems are statistical in nature. However, since there are no clearly identifiable correct solutions to problems of organized complexity, neither analytic nor statistical proofs can guarantee results. For solutions to wicked problems, the method of doubt is the best guarantor available.

Dialectics and argumentation are methods of *systematizing* doubt. They entail the processes of

1 making information and its underlying assumptions explicit;

2 raising questions and issues toward which different positions can be taken;

3 gathering evidence and building arguments for and against each position;

4 attempting to arrive at some final conclusion.

Being fundamentally an argumentative process, these four processes are inherent to policy making. For every policy decision there are always at least two alternative choices that can be made. There is an argument for and against each alternative. It is by weighing the pros and cons of each argument that an informed decision can be reached. In policy making these processes of dialectics and argumentation are inescapable.

In addition to the need for participation by a variety of parties and the existence of diverse information sources, two other characteristics of wicked problems should be noted. One is that they must be dealt with in a holistic or synthetic way as well as in an analytic way. Two processes are necessary: to subdivide a complex problem into its elements and to determine the nature of the linkages that give organization to its complexity – the task of analysis; and to understand the problem as a *whole* – the task of synthesis. A critical dimension of wicked problems of organized complexity is that they must ultimately be dealt with in their totality. This calls for holistic thinking. Analysis is only an aid toward reaching a synthesis.

A second characteristic of these problems is that there is some form of latent structure within them. They are organized to some extent. Organization is not an all or nothing phenomenon. Consequently, systems thinking and methods can be used to gain better insight into the structural aspects of wicked problems.

Quest for new methods. The nature and implications of organized complexity suggest some new criteria for the design of real world problem-solving methods. These criteria are:

1 Participative. Since the relevant knowledge necessary to solve a complex problem and also the relevant resources necessary to implement the solution are distributed among many individuals, the methods must incorporate the active involvement of groups of people.

2 Adversarial. We believe that the best judgement on the assumptions in a complex problem is rendered in the context of opposition. Doubt is the guarantor.

3 Integrative. A unified set of assumptions and a coherent plan of action are needed to guide effective policy planning and strategy making. Participation and the adversarial process tend to differentiate and expand the knowledge base. Something else is needed to bring this diverse but relevant knowledge together in the form of a total picture.

4 Managerial mind supporting. Most problem-solving methods and computer aids focus on 'decision support systems,' that is, on systems that provide guidance for choosing a particular course of action to solve a particular decision problem. Problems of organized complexity, as we have seen, are ongoing, ill structured, and generally 'wicked.' The choice of individual courses of action is only a part of the manager's or policymaker's need. More important is the need to achieve insight into the nature of the complexity and to formulate concepts and world views for coping with it. It is the policymaker's thinking process and his or her mind that needs to be supported.

READING 1.3

How successful leaders think

By Roger Martin[1]

The idea in brief

Brilliant leaders excel at integrative thinking. They can hold two opposing ideas in their minds at once. Then, rather than settling for choice A or B, they forge an innovative 'third way' that contains elements of both but improves on each.

Consider Bob Young, cofounder of Red Hat, the dominant distributor of Linux open-source software. The business model Young created for Red Hat transcended the two prevailing software industry models – winning Red Hat entrée into the lucrative corporate market.

How to become an integrative thinker? Resist the simplicity and certainty that comes with conventional 'either–or' thinking. Embrace the messiness and complexity of conflicting options. And emulate great leaders' decision-making approach – looking beyond obvious considerations.

Your reward? Instead of making unattractive trade-offs, you generate a wealth of profitable solutions for your business.

The idea in practice

What does integrative thinking look like in action? Contrast conventional and integrative thinkers' approaches to the four steps of decision-making:

Step 1. Identifying key factors. Conventional thinkers consider only obviously relevant factors while weighing options. Integrative thinkers seek less obvious but potentially more relevant considerations.

■ Example: Bob Young disliked the two prevailing software business models: selling operating software but not source code needed to develop software applications (profitable but anathema to open-source advocates) or selling CD-ROMs containing software and source code (aligned with open-source values but not profitable). Seeking a third choice, he considered the CIOs' reluctance to buy new technology that would be complicated to maintain. Viewing their reluctance as relevant eventually helped Young see that selling software services would be a superior alternative to the existing product-based business models.

Step 2. Analysing causality. Conventional thinkers consider one-way, linear relationships between factors: more of A produces more of B. Integrative thinkers consider multidirectional relationships.

■ Example: Young analysed the complex relationships among pricing, profitability, and distribution channels. He recognized that a product based on freely available components would soon become a commodity. Any electronics retailer could assemble its own Linux product and push it through its

[1]Source: This article is reprinted with permission by permission of Harvard Business Review. From The Opposable Mind: How Successful Leaders Win Through Integrative Thinking 2007 by the Harvard Business School Publishing Corporation, all rights reserved.

well-developed distribution channel – leaving Red Hat stranded. Analysis of these causal relationships yielded a nuanced picture of the industry's future.

Step 3. Envisioning the decision's overall structure.

Conventional thinkers break a problem into pieces and work on them separately. Integrative thinkers see a problem as a whole – examining how its various aspects affect one another.

- Example: Young held several issues in his head simultaneously, including the CIOs' concerns, dynamics of individual and corporate markets for system software, and the evolving economics of the free-software business. Each 'piece' could have pushed him toward a separate decision. But by considering the issues as an interrelated whole, Young began to realize only one player would ultimately dominate the corporate market.

Step 4. Achieving resolution.

Conventional thinkers make either–or choices. Integrative thinkers refuse to accept conventional options.

- Example: To pursue market leadership, Young devised an unconventional business model. The model synthesized two seemingly irreconcilable models by combining low product price with profitable service offerings. Red Hat began helping companies manage the software upgrades available almost daily through Linux's open-source platform. It also gave the software away as a free internet download. Thus, Red Hat acquired the scale and market leadership to attract cautious corporate customers to what became its central offering: service, not software.

We are drawn to the stories of effective leaders in action. Their decisiveness invigorates us. The events that unfold from their bold moves, often culminating in successful outcomes, make for gripping narratives. Perhaps most important, we turn to accounts of their deeds for lessons that we can apply in our own careers. Books like *Jack: Straight from the Gut* and *Execution: The Discipline of Getting Things Done* are compelling in part because they implicitly promise that we can achieve the success of a Jack Welch or a Larry Bossidy – if only we learn to emulate their actions.

But this focus on what a leader does is misplaced. That's because moves that work in one context often make little sense in another, even at the same company or within the experience of a single leader. Recall that Jack Welch, early in his career at General Electric, insisted that each of GE's businesses be number one or number two in market share in its industry; years later he insisted that those same businesses define their markets so that their share was no greater than 10%, thereby forcing managers to look for opportunities beyond the confines of a narrowly conceived market. Trying to learn from what Jack Welch did invites confusion and incoherence, because he pursued – wisely, I might add – diametrically opposed courses at different points in his career and in GE's history.

So where do we look for lessons? A more productive, though more difficult, approach is to focus on how a leader thinks – that is, to examine the antecedent of doing, or the ways in which leaders' cognitive processes produce their actions.

I have spent the past 15 years, first as a management consultant and now as the dean of a business school, studying leaders with exemplary records. Over the past six years, I have interviewed more than 50 such leaders, some for as long as eight hours, and found that most of them share a somewhat unusual trait: They have the predisposition and the capacity to hold in their heads two opposing ideas at once. And then, without panicking or simply settling for one alternative or the other, they're able to creatively resolve the tension between those two ideas by generating a new one that contains elements of the others but is superior to both. This process of consideration and synthesis can be termed integrative thinking. It is this discipline – not superior strategy or faultless execution – that is a defining characteristic of most exceptional businesses and the people who run them.

I don't claim that this is a new idea. More than 60 years ago, F. Scott Fitzgerald saw 'the ability to hold two opposing ideas in mind at the same time and still retain the ability to function' as the sign of a truly intelligent individual. And certainly not every good leader exhibits this capability, nor is it the sole source of success for those who do. But it is clear to me that integrative thinking tremendously improves people's odds.

This insight is easy to miss, though, since the management conversation in recent years has tilted away from thinking and toward doing (witness the popularity of books like *Execution*). Also, many great integrative thinkers aren't even aware of their particular capability and thus don't consciously exercise it. Take Jack Welch, who is among the executives I have interviewed: he is clearly a consummate integrative thinker – but you'd never know it from reading his books.

Indeed, my aim in this article is to deconstruct and describe a capability that seems to come naturally to many successful leaders. To illustrate the concept, I'll concentrate on an executive I talked with at length: Bob Young, the colourful cofounder and former CEO of Red Hat, the dominant distributor of Linux open-source software. The assumption underlying my examination of his and others' integrative thinking is this: It isn't just an ability you're born with – it's something you can hone.

Opposable thumb, opposable mind

In the mid-1990s, Red Hat faced what seemed like two alternative paths to growth. At the time, the company sold packaged versions of Linux open-source software, mainly to computer geeks, periodically bundling together new versions that included the latest upgrades from countless independent developers. As Red Hat looked to grow beyond its $ 1 million in annual sales, it could have chosen one of the two basic business models in the software industry.

One was the classic proprietary software model, employed by big players such as Microsoft, Oracle, and SAP, which sold customers operating software but not the source code. These companies invested heavily in research and development, guarded their intellectual property jealously, charged high prices, and enjoyed wide profit margins because their customers, lacking access to the source code, were essentially locked into purchasing regular upgrades.

The alternative, employed by numerous small companies, including Red Hat itself, was the so-called free-software model, in which suppliers sold CD-ROMs with both the software and the source code. The software products weren't in fact free, but prices were modest – $15 for a packaged version of the Linux operating system versus more than $200 for Microsoft Windows. Suppliers made money each time they assembled a new version from the many free updates by independent developers; but profit margins were narrow and revenue was uncertain. Corporate customers, looking for standardization and predictability, were wary not only of the unfamiliar software but also of its small and idiosyncratic suppliers.

Bob Young – a self-deprecating eccentric in an industry full of eccentrics, who signaled his affiliation with his company by regularly sporting red socks and a red hat – didn't like either of these models. The high-margin proprietary model ran counter to the whole philosophy of Linux and the open-source movement, even if there had been a way to create proprietary

versions of the software. 'Buying proprietary software is like buying a car with the hood welded shut,' Young told me. 'If something goes wrong, you can't even try to fix it.' But the free software model meant scraping a slim profit from the packaging and distribution of a freely available commodity in a fringe market, which might have offered reasonable returns in the short term but wasn't likely to deliver sustained profitable growth.

Young likes to say that he's not 'one of the smart guys' in the industry, that he's a salesman in a world of technical geniuses. Nonetheless, he managed to synthesize two seemingly irreconcilable business models, placing Red Hat on a path to tremendous success. His response to his strategic dilemma was to combine the free-software model's low product price with the proprietary model's profitable service component, in the process creating something new: a corporate market for the Linux operating system. As is often the case with integrative thinking, Young included some twists on both models that made the synthesis work.

Although inspired by the proprietary model, Red Hat's service offering was quite different. 'If you ran into a bug that caused your systems to crash,' Young said of the service you'd buy from the big proprietary shops, 'you would call up the manufacturer and say, "My systems are crashing." And he'd say, "Oh, dear," while he really meant, "Oh, good." He'd send an engineer over at several hundred dollars an hour to fix his software, which was broken when he delivered it to you, and he'd call that customer service.' Red Hat, by contrast, helped companies manage the upgrades and improvements available almost daily through Linux's open-source platform.

Young also made a crucial change to what had been the somewhat misleadingly dubbed free software model: He actually gave the software away, repackaging it as a free download on the internet rather than as an inexpensive but cumbersome CD-ROM. This allowed Red Hat to break away from the multitude of small Linux packagers by acquiring the scale and market leadership to generate faith among cautious corporate customers in what would become Red Hat's central offering – service, not software.

In 1999, Red Hat went public, and Young became a billionaire on the first day of trading. By 2000, Linux had captured 25% of the server operating system market, and Red Hat held more than 50% of the global market for Linux systems. Unlike the vast majority of dot-com era start-ups, Red Hat has continued to grow.

What enabled Young to resolve the apparent choice between two unattractive models? It was his use of an innate but underdeveloped human characteristic, something we might call – in a metaphor that echoes another human trait – the opposable mind.

Human beings are distinguished from nearly every other creature by a physical feature: the opposable thumb. Thanks to the tension that we can create by opposing the thumb and fingers, we can do marvellous things – write, thread a needle, guide a catheter through an artery. Although evolution provided human beings with this potential advantage, it would have gone to waste if our species had not exercised it in ever more sophisticated ways. When we engage in something like writing, we train the muscles involved and the brain that controls them. Without exploring the possibilities of opposition, we wouldn't have developed either its physical properties or the cognition that accompanies and animates it.

Analogously, we were born with opposable minds, which allow us to hold two conflicting ideas in constructive, almost dialectic tension. We can use that tension to think our way toward new, superior ideas. Were we able to hold only one thought or idea in our heads at a time, we wouldn't have access to the insights that the opposable mind can produce.

Unfortunately, because people don't exercise this capability much, great integrative thinkers are fairly rare. Why is this potentially powerful but generally latent tool used so infrequently and to less than full advantage? Because putting it to work makes us anxious. Most of us avoid complexity and ambiguity and seek out the comfort of simplicity and clarity. To cope with the dizzying complexity of the world around us, we simplify where we can. We crave the certainty of choosing between well-defined alternatives and the closure that comes when a decision has been made.

For those reasons, we often don't know what to do with fundamentally opposing and seemingly incommensurable models. Our first impulse is usually to determine which of the two models is 'right' and, by the process of elimination, which is 'wrong'. We may even take sides and try to prove that our chosen model is better than the other one. But in rejecting one model out of hand, we miss out on all the value that we could have realized by considering the opposing two at the same time and finding in the tension clues to a superior model. By forcing a choice between the two, we disengage the opposable mind before it can seek a creative resolution.

This nearly universal personal trait is writ large in most organizations. When a colleague admonishes us to 'quit complicating the issue', it's not just an impatient reminder to get on with the damn job – it's also a plea to keep the complexity at a comfortable level.

To take advantage of our opposable minds, we must resist our natural leaning toward simplicity and certainty. Bob Young recognized from the beginning that he wasn't bound to choose one of the two prevailing software business models. He saw the unpleasant trade-offs he'd have to make if he chose between the two as a signal to rethink the problem from the ground up. And he didn't rest until he found a new model that grew out of the tension between them.

Basically, Young refused to settle for an 'either–or' choice. That phrase has come up time and again in my interviews with successful leaders. When asked whether he thought strategy or execution was more important, Jack Welch responded: 'I don't think it's an "either–or".' Similarly, Procter & Gamble CEO A.G. Lafley – when asked how he came up with a turnaround plan that drew on both cost cutting and investment in innovation – said: 'We weren't going to win if it were an "or". Everybody can do "or".'

The four stages of decision-making

So what does the process of integrative thinking look like? How do integrative thinkers consider their options in a way that leads to new possibilities and not merely back to the same inadequate alternatives? They work through four related but distinct stages. The steps themselves aren't particular to integrative thinking: Everyone goes through them while thinking through a decision. What's distinctive about integrative thinkers is how they approach the steps (see Exhibit 1.3.1).

Determining salience. The first step is figuring out which factors to take into account. The conventional approach is to discard as many as possible – or not even to consider some of them in the first place. In order to reduce our exposure to uncomfortable complexity, we filter out salient features when considering an issue.

We also do this because of how most organizations are structured. Each functional specialty has its own narrow view of what merits consideration. Finance departments haven't traditionally regarded emotional factors as salient; similarly, departments concerned with organizational behaviour have often ignored quantitative questions. Managers pressure employees to limit their view of what's salient to match the department's doctrine, leaving people with only a subset of the factors to which they might otherwise have productively paid attention.

EXHIBIT 1.3.1 CONVENTIONAL VERSUS INTEGRATIVE THINKING

When responding to problems or challenges, leaders work through four steps. Those who are conventional thinkers seek simplicity along the way and are often forced to make unattractive trade-offs. By contrast, integrative thinkers welcome complexity – even if it means repeating one or more of the steps – and this allows them to craft innovative solutions.

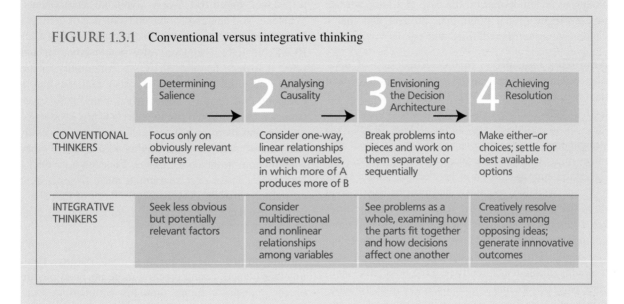

FIGURE 1.3.1   Conventional versus integrative thinking

	1 Determining Salience	**2** Analysing Causality	**3** Envisioning the Decision Architecture	**4** Achieving Resolution
CONVENTIONAL THINKERS	Focus only on obviously relevant features	Consider one-way, linear relationships between variables, in which more of A produces more of B	Break problems into pieces and work on them separately or sequentially	Make either–or choices; settle for best available options
INTEGRATIVE THINKERS	Seek less obvious but potentially relevant factors	Consider multidirectional and nonlinear relationships among variables	See problems as a whole, examining how the parts fit together and how decisions affect one another	Creatively resolve tensions among opposing ideas; generate innnovative outcomes

When our decisions turn out badly, we often recognize after the fact that we've failed to consider factors that are significant to those outside the immediate reach of our jobs or functional specialties. We say to ourselves, 'I should have thought about how the employees in our European operation would have interpreted the wording of that memo' or 'I should have thought about the state's road-repair programme before choosing a site for our new distribution centre.' The integrative thinker, by contrast, actively seeks less obvious but potentially relevant factors. Of course, more salient features make for a messier problem, but integrative thinkers don't mind the mess. In fact, they embrace it because it assures them that they haven't dismissed anything that may illuminate the problem as a whole. They welcome complexity, because that's where the best answers come from. They are confident that they'll find their way through it and emerge on the other side with a clear resolution.

In his thinking about a new business model for Red Hat, Bob Young added into his calculations something ignored both by software companies generally and by Linux suppliers in particular: the day-to-day concerns of corporate CIOs and their systems administrators. Doing this allowed him to envision an innovative model that tapped into an entirely new market for Linux-based products and services.

As a whole, the software industry disdains CIOs' reluctance to buy the newest and best technology, attributing it to timidity or strict adherence to the 'you'll never get fired for buying IBM' mantra. Young not only empathized with the CIOs but found their caution understandable. 'It's not FUD – fear, uncertainty, and doubt,' he said. 'It's sensible.'

Linux software was an entirely new product for corporate buyers, one that didn't follow any familiar rules. It was free. No one supplier controlled it. Thousands of versions were out there, and each one changed nearly every day. From the CIOs' perspective, that Linux was cheaper and better than Windows-based products – the basic sales message delivered by Red Hat's rivals – played a relatively small part in the calculation. The CIOs were thinking about whether their investment would be in a stable and consistent platform that would work across their organizations and whether their suppliers would still be around in ten or 15 years. Systems administrators worried that the complexity of Linux – with its random and almost daily upgrades – would create a management nightmare, since different teams of people throughout the company would have to maintain the software packages.

Viewing these concerns as salient helped lead Young to conclude that, in the case of Linux, service was a bigger selling point than product and that a vendor's long-term credibility was crucial.

Analyzing causality. In the second step of decision-making, you analyse how the numerous salient factors relate to one another. Conventional thinkers tend to take the same narrow view of causality that they do of salience. The simplest type of all is a straight-line causal relationship. It's no accident that linear regression is the business world's preferred tool for establishing relationships between variables. Other tools are available, of course, but most managers shun them because they're harder to use. How many times has a superior scolded you for making a problem more complicated than it needs to be? You protest that you're not trying to complicate anything; you just want to see the problem as it really is. Your boss tells you to stick to your job, and a potentially complex relationship becomes a linear one in which more of A produces more of B.

When we make bad decisions, sometimes it is because we get the causal links between salient features wrong. We may have been right about the direction of a relationship but wrong about the magnitude: 'I thought that our costs would decrease much faster than they actually did as our scale grew.' Or we may have gotten the direction of a relationship wrong: 'I thought that our capacity to serve clients would increase when we hired a new batch of consultants, but it actually shrank, because the experienced consultants had to spend a huge amount of their time training the new ones and fixing their rookie mistakes.'

The integrative thinker isn't afraid to question the validity of apparently obvious links or to consider multidirectional and nonlinear relationships. So, for example, rather than simply thinking, 'That competitor's price-cutting is hurting our bottom line,' the integrative thinker may conclude, 'Our product introduction really upset our rivals. Now they're cutting prices in response, and our profitability is suffering.'

The most interesting causal link that Young identified was the rather subtle one between the free availability of Red Hat software's basic components and the likely – or inevitable, in Young's view – evolution of the industry. The relationships he saw between pricing, profitability, and distribution channel drove his company in a different direction from its Linux competitors, which saw a perfectly good market for their 'free' software. This is what allowed him to create and then lock up the new corporate market.

For example, Young recognized the vulnerability of a product based on freely available components. Whatever you charged for the convenience of getting a Linux operating system bundled together on one CD-ROM, inevitably 'someone else would come in and price it lower', he said. 'It was a commodity in the truest sense of the word.' He also realized that a company that wasn't a current rival – say, a big electronics retailer – could put together a Linux product of its own and then push it through its own well-developed distribution channel, leaving Red Hat and other suppliers out in the cold. 'I knew I needed a product I had some control over so I could make CompUSA a customer' – that is, a corporate purchaser of Red Hat's service package – 'rather than a competitor' with its own CD-ROM product.

The causal relationships spotted by Young weren't earth-shattering on their own, but putting them together helped Young create a more nuanced picture of the industry's future than his competitors were able to.

Envisioning the decision architecture. With a good handle on the causal relationships between salient features, you're ready to turn to the decision itself. But which decision? Even the simple question of whether to go to a movie tonight involves deciding, at the very least, which movie to see, which theatre to go to, and which showing to attend. The order in which you make these decisions will affect the outcome. For example, you may not be able to see your preferred movie if you've already decided you need to be back in time to relieve a babysitter who has plans for later in the evening. When you're trying to invent a new business model, the number of decision-making variables explodes. And with that comes the impulse not only to establish a strict sequence in which issues will be considered but also to dole out pieces of a decision so that various parties – often, different corporate functions – can work on them separately.

What usually happens is that everyone loses sight of the overriding issue, and a mediocre outcome results. Suppose that Bob Young had delegated to different functional heads' questions concerning the pricing, enhancement, and distribution of Red Hat's original software product. Would their individual answers, agglomerated into an overall Red Hat strategy, have produced the spectacularly successful new business model that Young came up with? It doesn't seem all that likely.

Integrative thinkers don't break down a problem into independent pieces and work on them separately or in a certain order. They see the entire architecture of the problem: how the various parts of it fit together, how one decision will affect another. Just as important, they hold all of those pieces suspended in their minds at once. They don't parcel out the elements for others to work on piecemeal or let one element temporarily drop out of sight, only to be taken up again for consideration after everything else has been decided. An architect doesn't ask his subordinates to design a perfect bathroom and a perfect living room and a perfect kitchen, and then hope that the pieces of the house will fit nicely together. A business executive doesn't design a product before considering the costs of manufacturing it.

Young held simultaneously in his head a number of issues: the feelings and the challenges of chief information officers and systems administrators, the dynamics of both the individual and the corporate markets for operating system software, the evolving economics of the free-software business, and the motivations behind the major players in the proprietary software business. Each factor could have pushed him toward a separate decision on how to address the challenge. But he delayed making decisions and considered the relationships between these issues as he slowly moved toward the creation of a new business model, one based on the belief that dominant market share would be critical to Red Hat's success.

Achieving resolution. All of these stages – determining what is salient, analysing the causal relationships between the salient factors, examining the architecture of the problem – lead to an outcome. Too often, we accept an unpleasant trade-off with relatively little complaint, since it appears to be the best alternative. That's because by the time we have reached this stage, our desire for simplicity has led us to ignore opportunities in the previous three steps to discover interesting and novel ways around the trade-off. Instead of rebelling against the meagre and unattractive alternatives, instead of refusing to settle for the best available bad choice, the conventional thinker shrugs and asks, 'What else could we have done?'

'Much else,' the integrative thinker says. A leader who embraces holistic rather than segmented thinking can creatively resolve the tensions that launched the decision-making process. The actions associated

with the search for such resolution – creating delays, sending teams back to examine things more deeply, generating new options at the 11th hour – can appear irresolute from the outside. Indeed, the integrative thinker may even be dissatisfied with the fresh batch of options he's come up with, in which case he may go back and start over. When a satisfactory outcome does emerge, though, it is inevitably due to the leader's refusal to accept trade-offs and conventional options.

The outcome in the case of Red Hat was completely unconventional – not many companies suddenly decide to give away their products – and ultimately successful. Young's gradual realization that only one player in his industry would have leverage with and support from corporate customers – and that such leverage and support could reap attractive service revenues from totally free software – shaped the dramatically creative decision he made.

The thinking that he intuitively engaged in is very different from the thinking that produces most managerial decisions. But, he said, his experience was hardly unique: 'People are often faced with difficult choices – for instance, "Do I want to be the high-quality, high-cost supplier or the low-quality, low-cost supplier?" We're trained to examine the pros and cons of such alternatives and then pick one of them. But really successful businesspeople look at choices like these and say, 'I don't like either one.''' Using that recurring phrase, he added: 'They don't accept that it's an "either–or".'

Born and bred

The consequences of integrative thinking and conventional thinking couldn't be more distinct. Integrative thinking generates options and new solutions. It creates a sense of limitless possibility. Conventional thinking glosses over potential solutions and fosters the illusion that creative solutions don't actually exist. With integrative thinking, aspirations rise over time. With conventional thinking, they wear away with every apparent reinforcement of the lesson that life is about accepting unattractive trade-offs. Fundamentally, the conventional thinker prefers to accept the world just as it is, whereas the integrative thinker welcomes the challenge of shaping the world for the better.

Given the benefits of integrative thinking, you have to ask, 'If I'm not an integrative thinker, can I learn to be one?' In F. Scott Fitzgerald's view, only people with 'first-rate intelligence' can continue to function while holding two opposing ideas in their heads. But I refuse to believe that the ability to use our opposable minds is a gift reserved for a small minority of people. I prefer the view suggested by Thomas C. Chamberlin, a 19th century American geologist and former president of the University of Wisconsin. More than 100 years ago, Chamberlin wrote an article in *Science* magazine proposing the idea of 'multiple working hypotheses' as an improvement over the most commonly employed scientific method of the time: testing the validity of a single hypothesis through trial and error. Chamberlin argued that his approach would provide more accurate explanations of scientific phenomena by taking into account 'the coordination of several agencies, which enter into the combined result in varying proportions'. While acknowledging the cognitive challenges posed by such an approach,

Chamberlin wrote that it 'develops a habit of thought analogous to the method itself, which may be designated a habit of parallel or complex thought. Instead of a simple succession of thoughts in linear order ... the mind appears to become possessed of the power of simultaneous vision from different standpoints'.

Similarly, I believe that integrative thinking is a 'habit of thought' that all of us can consciously develop to arrive at solutions that would otherwise not be evident. First, there needs to be greater general awareness of integrative thinking as a concept. Then, over time, we can teach it in our business schools – an endeavour that colleagues and I are currently working on. At some point, integrative thinking will no longer be just a tacit skill (cultivated knowingly or not) in the heads of a select few.

Cultural constraints in management theories
By Geert Hofstede[1]

Lewis Carroll's *Alice in Wonderland* contains the famous story of Alice's croquet game with the Queen of Hearts. Alice thought she had never seen such a curious croquet ground in all her life; it was all ridges and furrows; the balls were live hedgehogs, the mallets live flamingoes, and the soldiers had to double themselves up and to stand on their hands and feet to make the arches. You probably know how the story goes: Alice's flamingo mallet turns its head whenever she wants to strike with it; her hedgehog ball runs away; and the doubled-up soldier arches walk around all the time. The only rule seems to be that the Queen of Hearts always wins.

Alice's croquet playing problems are good analogies of attempts to build culture-free theories of management. Concepts available for this purpose are themselves alive with culture, having been developed within a particular cultural context. They have a tendency to guide our thinking toward our desired conclusion. As the same reasoning may also be applied to the arguments in this reading, I better tell you my

conclusion before I continue – so that the rules of my game are understood. In this reading we take a trip around the world to demonstrate that there are no such things as universal management theories.

Diversity in management *practices* as we go around the world has been recognized in US management literature for more than 30 years. The term 'comparative management' has been used since the 1960s. However, it has taken much longer for the US academic community to accept that not only practices but also the validity of theories may stop at national borders, and I wonder whether even today everybody would agree with this statement.

The idea that the validity of a theory is constrained by national borders is more obvious in Europe, with all its borders, than in a huge borderless country like the US. Already in the 16th century Michel de Montaigne, a Frenchman, wrote a statement which was made famous by Blaise Pascal about a century later: '*Vérite en-deça des Pyrenées, erreur au-delà*' – 'There are truths on this side of the Pyrenées which are falsehoods on the other'.

[1]Source: This article was adapted from G. Hofstede, 'Cultural Constraints in Management Theories', *Academy of Management Executive*, Vol. 7, No. 1, 1993, pp. 8–21. © Copyright 1993 by Academy of Management. Reproduced with permission of Academy of Management via Copyright Clearance Center.

From Don Armado's love to Taylor's science

According to the comprehensive ten-volume *Oxford English Dictionary,* the words 'manage', 'management', and 'manager' appeared in the English language in the 16th century. The oldest recorded use of the word 'manager' is in Shakespeare's *Love's Labour's Lost,* dating from 1588, in which Don Adriano de Armado, 'a fantastical Spaniard', exclaims (Act I scene ii. 188): 'Adieu, valour! rust, rapier! be still, drum! for your manager is in love; yea, he loveth.'

The linguistic origin of the word is from Latin *manus,* hand, via the Italian *maneggiare,* which is the training of horses in the *manege*; subsequently its meaning was extended to skillful handling in general, like of arms and musical instruments, as Don Armado illustrates. However, the word also became associated with the French *menage,* household, as an equivalent of 'husbandry' in its sense of the art of running a household. The theatre of present-day management contains elements of both *manege* and *menage* and different managers and cultures may use different accents.

The founder of the science of economics, the Scot Adam Smith, in his 1776 book *The Wealth of Nations,* used 'manage', 'management' (even 'bad management') and 'manager' when dealing with the process and the persons involved in operating joint stock companies. British economist John Stuart Mill (1806–1873) followed Smith in this use and clearly expressed his distrust of such hired people who were not driven by ownership. Since the 1880s the word 'management' appeared occasionally in writings by American engineers, until it was canonized as a modern science by Frederick W. Taylor in *Shop Management* in 1903 and in *The Principles of Scientific Management* in 1911.

While Smith and Mill used 'management' to describe a process and 'managers' for the persons involved, 'management' in the American sense – which has since been taken back by the British – refers not only to the process but also to the managers as a class of people. This class (1) does not own a business but sells its skills to act on behalf of the owners and (2) does not produce personally but is indispensable for making others produce, through motivation. Members of this class carry a high status and many American boys and girls aspire to the role. In the US, the manager is a cultural hero.

Let us now turn to other parts of the world. We will look at management in its context in other successful modern economies: Germany, Japan, France, Holland, and among the overseas Chinese. Then we will examine management in the much larger part of the world that is still poor, especially South-East Asia and Africa, and in the new political configurations of Eastern Europe, and Russia in particular. We will then return to the US via mainland China.

Germany

The manager is not a cultural hero in Germany. If anybody, it is the engineer who fills the hero role. Frederick Taylor's scientific management was conceived in a society of immigrants – where a large number of workers with diverse backgrounds and skills had to work together. In Germany this heterogeneity never existed.

Elements of the medieval guild system have survived in historical continuity in Germany until the present day. In particular, a very effective apprenticeship system exists both on the shop floor and in the office, which alternates practical work and classroom courses. At the end of the apprenticeship the worker receives a certificate, the *Facharbeiterbrief,* which is recognized throughout the country. About two thirds of the German worker population holds such a certificate and a corresponding occupational pride. In fact, quite a few German company presidents have worked their way up from the ranks through an apprenticeship. In comparison, two thirds of the worker population in Britain have no occupational qualification at all.

The highly skilled and responsible German workers do not necessarily need a manager, American-style, to 'motivate' them. They expect their boss or *Meister* to assign their tasks and to be the expert in resolving technical problems. Comparisons of similar German, British, and French organizations show the Germans as having the highest rate of personnel in productive roles and the lowest both in leadership and staff roles.

Japan

The American type of manager is also missing in Japan. In the United States, the core of the enterprise is the managerial class. The core of the Japanese enterprise is the permanent worker group: workers who for all practical purposes are tenured and who aspire to life-long employment. They are distinct from the non-permanent employees – most women and subcontracted teams led by gang bosses, to be laid off in slack periods. University graduates in Japan first join the permanent worker group and subsequently fill various positions, moving from line to staff as the need occurs while paid according to seniority rather than position. They take part in Japanese-style group consultation sessions for important decisions, which extend the decision-making period but guarantee fast implementation afterwards. Japanese are to a large extent controlled by their peer group rather than by their manager.

American theories of leadership are ill suited to the Japanese group-controlled situation. During the past two decades, the Japanese have developed their own 'PM' theory of leadership, in which P stands for performance and M for maintenance. The latter is less a concern for individual employees than for maintaining social stability. In view of the amazing success of the Japanese economy in the past 30 years, many Americans have sought the secrets of Japanese management hoping to copy them.

France

The manager, US style, does not exist in France either. The French researcher Philippe d'Iribarne (1990) identifies three kinds of basic principles *(logiques)* of management. In the USA, the principle is *the fair contract* between employer and employee, which gives the manager considerable prerogatives, but within its limits. This is really a labour market in which the worker sells his or her labour for a price. In France, the principle is the *honour* of each class in a society which has always been and remains extremely stratified, in which superiors behave as superior beings and subordinates accept and expect this, conscious of their own lower level in the national hierarchy but also of the honour of their own class. The French do not think in terms of managers versus nonmanagers but in terms of *cadres* versus *non-cadres;* one becomes cadre by attending the proper schools and one remains it forever; regardless of their actual task, cadres have the privileges of a higher social class, and it is very rare for a non-cadre to cross the ranks.

The conflict between French and American theories of management became apparent at the beginning of the 20th century, in a criticism by the great French management pioneer Henri Fayol (1841–1925) of his US colleague and contemporary Frederick W. Taylor (1856–1915). Fayol was a French engineer whose career as a *cadre supérieur* culminated in the position of *Président-Directeur-Général* of a mining company. After his retirement he formulated his experiences in a pathbreaking text on organization: *Administration industrielle et générale,* in which he focused on the sources of authority. Taylor was an American engineer who started his career in industry as a worker and attained his academic qualifications through evening studies. From chief engineer in a steel company he became one of the first management consultants. Taylor was not really concerned with the issue of authority at all; his focus was on efficiency. He proposed to split the task of the first-line boss into eight specialisms, each exercised by a different person; an idea which eventually led to the idea of a matrix organization.

Taylor's work appeared in a French translation in 1913, and Fayol read it and showed himself generally impressed but shocked by Taylor's 'denial of the principle of the Unity of Command' in the case of the eight-boss-system. Seventy years later André Laurent, another of Fayol's compatriots, found that French managers in a survey reacted very strongly against a suggestion that one employee could report to two different bosses, while US managers in the same survey showed fewer misgivings. Matrix organization has never become popular in France as it has in the United States.

Holland

In my own country, Holland or as it is officially called, the Netherlands, the study by Philippe d'Iribarne found the management principle to be a need for consensus among all parties, neither predetermined by a contractual relationship nor by class distinctions, but based on an open-ended exchange of views and a balancing of interests. In terms of the different origins of the word 'manager', the organization in Holland is more *menage* (household) while in the United States it is more *manege* (horse drill).

At my university, the University of Limburg at Maastricht, we asked both the Americans and a matched group of Dutch students to describe their ideal job after graduation, using a list of 22 job characteristics. The Americans attached significantly more importance than the Dutch to earnings, advancement, benefits, a good working relationship with their boss, and security of employment. The Dutch attached more importance to freedom to adopt their own approach to the job, being consulted by their boss in his or her decisions, training opportunities, contributing to the success of their organization, fully using their skills and abilities, and helping others. This list confirms d'Iribarne's findings of a contractual employment relationship in the United States, based on earnings and career opportunities, against a consensual relationship in Holland. The latter has centuries old roots, the Netherlands were the first republic in Western Europe (1609–1810), and a model for the American republic. The country has been and still is governed by a careful balancing of interests in a multi-party system.

In terms of management theories, both motivation and leadership in Holland are different from what they are in the United States. Leadership in Holland presupposes modesty, as opposed to assertiveness in the United States. No US leadership theory has room for that. Working in Holland is not a constant feast, however. There is a built-in premium on mediocrity and jealousy, as well as time-consuming ritual consultations to maintain the appearance of consensus and the pretense of modesty. There is unfortunately another side to every coin.

The overseas Chinese

Among the champions of economic development in the past 30 years we find three countries mainly populated by Chinese living outside the Chinese mainland: Taiwan, Hong Kong and Singapore. Moreover, overseas Chinese play a very important role in the economies of Indonesia, Malaysia, the Philippines and Thailand, where they form an ethnic minority. If anything, the little dragons – Taiwan, Hong Kong and Singapore – have been more economically successful than Japan, moving from rags to riches and now counted among the world's wealthy industrial countries. Yet very little attention has been paid to the way in which their enterprises have been managed.

Overseas Chinese enterprises lack almost all characteristics of modern management. They tend to be small, cooperating for essential functions with other small organizations through networks based on personal relations. They are family owned, without the separation between ownership and management typical in the West, or even in Japan and Korea. They normally focus on one product or market, with growth by opportunistic diversification; in this, they are extremely flexible. Decision-making is centralized in the hands of one dominant family member, but other family members may be given new ventures to try their skills on. They are low-profile and extremely cost-conscious, applying Confucian virtues of thrift and persistence. Their size is kept small by the assumed lack of loyalty of non-family employees, who, if they are any good, will just wait and save until they can start their own family business.

Overseas Chinese prefer economic activities in which great gains can be made with little manpower, like commodity trading and real estate. They employ few professional managers, except their sons and sometimes daughters who have been sent to prestigious business schools abroad, but who upon return continue to run the family business the Chinese way.

The origin of this system, or – in the Western view – this lack of system, is found in the history of Chinese society, in which there were no formal laws, only formal networks of powerful people guided by general principles of Confucian virtue. The favours of the authorities could change daily, so nobody could be trusted except one's kinfolk – of whom, fortunately, there used to be many, in an extended family structure. The overseas Chinese way of doing business is also very well adapted to their position in the countries in which they form ethnic minorities, often envied and threatened by ethnic violence.

Overseas Chinese businesses following this unprofessional approach command a collective gross national product of some 200 to 300 billion US dollars, exceeding the GNP of Australia. There is no denying that it works.

Management transfer to poor countries

Four-fifths of the world population live in countries that are not rich but poor. After World War II and decolonization, the stated purpose of the United Nations and the World Bank has been to promote the development of all the world's countries in a war on poverty. After 40 years it looks very much like we are losing this war. If one thing has become clear, it is that the export of Western – mostly American – management practices and theories to poor countries has contributed little to nothing to their development. There has been no lack of effort and money spent for this purpose: students from poor countries have been trained in this country, and teachers and Peace Corps workers have been sent to the poor countries. If nothing else, the general lack of success in economic development of other countries should be sufficient argument to doubt the validity of Western management theories in non-Western environments.

If we examine different parts of the world, the development picture is not equally bleak, and history is often a better predictor than economic factors for what happens today. There is a broad regional pecking order with East Asia leading. The little dragons have passed into the camp of the wealthy: then follow South-East Asia (with its overseas Chinese minorities), Latin

America (in spite of the debt crisis), South Asia, and Africa always trails behind. Several African countries have only become poorer since decolonization.

Russia and China

The crumbling of the former Eastern bloc has left us with a scattering of states and would-be states for which the political and economic future is extremely uncertain. The best predictions are those based on a knowledge of history, because historical trends have taken revenge on the arrogance of the Soviet rulers who believed they could turn them around by brute power. One obvious fact is that the former bloc is extremely heterogeneous, including countries traditionally closely linked with the West by trade and travel, like the Czech Republic, Hungary, Slovenia, and the Baltic states, as well as others with a Byzantine or Turkish past: some having been prosperous, others always extremely poor. Let me limit myself to the Russian republic, a huge territory with some 140 million inhabitants, mainly Russians. We know quite a bit about the Russians as their country was a world power for several hundreds of years before communism, and in the 19th century it produced some of the greatest writers in world literature. If I want to understand the Russians – including how they could so long support the Soviet regime – I tend to re-read Lev Nikolayevich Tolstoy. In his most famous novel *Anna Karenina* one of the main characters is a landowner, Levin, whom Tolstoy uses to express his own views and convictions about his people. Russian peasants used to be serfs; serfdom had been abolished in 1861, but the peasants, now tenants, remained as passive as before. Levin wanted to break this passivity by dividing the land among his peasants in exchange for a share of the crops; but the peasants only let the land deteriorate further. Here follows a quote:

> *[Levin] read political economy and socialistic works … but, as he had expected, found nothing in them related to his undertaking. In the political economy books – in [John Stuart] Mill, for instance, whom he studied first and with great ardour, hoping every minute to find an answer to the questions that were engrossing him – he found only certain laws deduced from the state of agriculture in Europe; but he could not for the life of him see why these laws, which did not apply to Russia, should be considered universal … Political economy told him that the laws by which Europe had developed and was developing her wealth were universal and absolute. Socialist teaching told him that development along those lines leads to ruin. And neither of them offered the smallest enlightenment as to what he, Levin, and all the Russian peasants and landowners were to do with their millions of hands and millions of acres, to make them as productive as possible for the common good.*

In the summer of 1991, the Russian lands yielded a record harvest, but a large share of it rotted in the fields because no people were to be found for harvesting. The passivity is still there, and not only among the peasants. And the heirs of John Stuart Mill (whom we met before as one of the early analysts of 'management') again present their universal recipes which simply do not apply.

Citing Tolstoy, I implicitly suggest that management theorists cannot neglect the great literature of the countries they want their ideas to apply to. The greatest novel in Chinese literature is considered Cao Xueqin's *The Story of the Stone*, also known as *The Dream of the Red Chamber* which appeared around 1760. It describes the rise and fall of two branches of an aristocratic family in Beijing, who live in adjacent plots in the capital. Their plots are joined by a magnificent garden with several pavilions in it, and the young, mostly female members of both families are allowed to live in them. One day the management of the garden is taken over by a young woman, Tan-Chun, who states:

> *I think we ought to pick out a few experienced trust-worthy old women from among the ones who work in the Garden – women who know something about gardening already – and put the upkeep of the Garden into their hands. We needn't ask them to pay us rent; all we need ask them for is an annual share of the produce. There would be four advantages in this arrangement. In the first place, if we have people whose sole occupation is to look after trees and flowers and so on, the condition of the Garden will improve gradually year after year and there will be no more of those long periods of neglect followed by bursts of feverish activity when things have been allowed to get out of hand. Secondly there won't be the spoiling and wastage we get at present. Thirdly the women themselves will gain a little extra to add to their incomes which will compensate them for the hard work they put in throughout the year. And fourthly, there's no reason why we shouldn't use the money we*

should otherwise have spent on nurserymen, rockery specialists, horticultural cleaners and so on for other purposes.

As the story goes on, the capitalist privatization – because that is what it is – of the Garden is carried through, and it works. When in the 1980s Deng Xiaoping allowed privatization in the Chinese villages, it also worked. If we remember what Chinese entrepreneurs are able to do once they have become overseas Chinese, we shouldn't be too surprised. But what works in China – and worked two centuries ago – does not have to work in Russia, not in Tolstoy's days and not today. I am not offering a solution: I only protest against a naïve universalism that knows only one recipe for development, the one supposed to have worked in the United States.

A theory of culture in management

There is something in all countries called 'management,' but its meaning differs to a larger or smaller extent from one country to the other, and it takes considerable historical and cultural insight into local conditions to understand its processes, philosophies, and problems. If already the word may mean so many different things, how can we expect one country's theories of management to apply abroad? One should be extremely careful in making this assumption, and test it before considering it proven. Management is not a phenomenon that can be isolated from other processes taking place in a society. It interacts with what happens in the family, at school, in politics, and government. It is obviously also related to religion and to beliefs about science. Theories of management always had to be interdisciplinary, but if we cross national borders they should become more interdisciplinary than ever.

As the word culture plays such an important role in my theory, let me give you my definition, which differs from some other very respectable definitions. Culture to me is *the collective programming of the mind which distinguishes one group or category of people from another.* In the part of my work I am referring to now, the category of people is the nation.

Cultural differences between nations can, to some extent, be described using five bipolar dimensions. The position of a country on these dimensions allows us to make some predictions on the way their society operates, including their management processes and the kind of theories applicable to their management.

The first dimension is labelled *power distance*, and it can be defined as the degree of inequality among people which the population of a country considers as normal: from relatively equal (that is, small power distance) to extremely unequal (large power distance). All societies are unequal, but some are more unequal than others.

The second dimension is labelled *individualism*, and it is the degree to which people in a country prefer to act as individuals rather than as members of groups. The opposite of individualism can be called *collectivism*, so collectivism is low individualism. The way I use the word it has no political connotations. In collectivist societies a child learns to respect the group to which it belongs, usually the family, and to differentiate between in-group members and out-group members (that is, all other people). When children grow up they remain members of their group, and they expect the group to protect them when they are in trouble. In return, they have to remain loyal to their group throughout life. In individualist societies, a child learns very early to think of itself as 'I' instead of a part of 'we'. It expects one day to have to stand on its own feet and not to get protection from its group anymore; and therefore it also does not feel a need for strong loyalty.

The third dimension is called *masculinity* and its opposite pole *femininity*. It is the degree to which tough values like assertiveness, performance, success and competition, which in nearly all societies are associated with the role of men, prevail over tender values like the quality of life, maintaining warm personal relationships, service, care for the weak, and solidarity, which in nearly all societies are more associated with women's roles. Women's roles differ from men's roles in all countries; but in tough societies, the differences are larger than in tender ones.

The fourth dimension is labelled *uncertainty avoidance*, and it can be defined as the degree to which people in a country prefer structured over unstructured situations. Structured situations are those in which there are clear rules as to how one should behave. These rules can be written down, but they can also be unwritten and imposed by tradition. In countries that score high on uncertainty avoidance, people tend to show more nervous energy, while in countries that score low, people are more easy-going. A (national) society with strong uncertainty avoidance can be called rigid; one with weak uncertainty avoidance, flexible. In countries where uncertainty avoidance is strong a feeling prevails of 'what is different, is dangerous.' In weak uncertainty avoidance societies, the feeling would rather be 'what is different, is curious.'

The fifth dimension is labelled *long-term versus short-term orientation.* On the long-term side one finds values oriented towards the future, like thrift (saving) and persistence. On the short-term side one finds values rather oriented towards the past and present, like respect for tradition and fulfilling social obligations.

Table 1.4.1 lists the scores on all five dimensions for the United States and for the other countries we just discussed. The table shows that each country has its own configuration on the five dimensions. Some of the values in the table have been estimated based on imperfect replications or personal impressions. The different dimension scores do not 'explain' all the differences in management I described earlier. To understand management in a country, one should have both knowledge of and empathy with the entire local scene. However, the scores should make us aware that people in other countries may think, feel, and act very differently from us when confronted with basic problems of society.

Idiosyncrasies of American management theories

In comparison to other countries, the US culture profile presents itself as below average on power distance and uncertainty avoidance, highly individualistic,

fairly masculine, and short-term oriented. The Germans show a stronger uncertainty avoidance and less extreme individualism; the Japanese are different on all dimensions, least on power distance; the French show larger power distance and uncertainty avoidance, but are less individualistic and somewhat feminine; the Dutch resemble the Americans on the first three dimensions, but score extremely feminine and relatively long-term oriented; Hong Kong Chinese combine large power distance with weak uncertainty avoidance, collectivism, and are very long-term oriented; and so on. The American culture profile is reflected in American management theories. I will just mention three elements not necessarily present in other countries: the stress on market processes, the stress on the individual, and the focus on managers rather than on workers.

The stress on market processes

During the 1970s and 1980s it has become fashionable in the United States to look at organizations from a 'transaction costs' viewpoint. Economist Oliver Williamson has opposed 'hierarchies' to 'markets.' The reasoning is that human social life consists of economic transactions between individuals. We found the same in d'Iribarne's description of the US principle of the contract between employer and employee, the labour market in which the worker sells his or her labour for a price. These individuals will form hierarchical organizations when the cost of the economic

TABLE 1.4.1   Culture dimension scores for 10 countries

	Power Distance	Individualism	Masculinity	Uncertainty Avoidance	Long-Term Orientation
USA	40 L	91 H	62 H	46 L	29 L
Germany	35 L	67 H	66 H	65 M	31 M
Japan	54 M	46 M	95 H	92 H	80 H
France	68 H	71 H	43 M	86 H	30*L
Netherlands	38 L	80 H	14 L	53 M	44 M
Hong Kong	68 H	25 L	57 H	29 L	96 H
Indonesia	78 H	14 L	46 M	48 L	25*L
West Africa	77 H	20 L	46 M	54 M	16 L
Russia	95*H	50*M	40*L	90*H	10*L
China	80*H	20*L	50*M	60*M	118 H

*Estimated

H = top third, M = medium third, L = bottom third (among 53 countries and regions for the first four dimensions; among 23 countries for the fifth).

transactions (such as getting information, finding out whom to trust, etc.) is lower in a hierarchy than when all transactions would take place on a free market.

From a cultural perspective the important point is that the 'market' is the point of departure or base model, and the organization is explained from market failure. A culture that produces such a theory is likely to prefer organizations that internally resemble markets to organizations that internally resemble more structured models, like those in Germany or France. The ideal principle of control in organizations in the market philosophy is competition between individuals. This philosophy fits a society that combines a not-too-large power distance with a not-too-strong uncertainty avoidance and individualism; besides the USA, it will fit all other Anglo countries.

The stress on the individual

I find this constantly in the design of research projects and hypotheses; also in the fact that in the US psychology is clearly a more respectable discipline in management circles than sociology. Culture however is a collective phenomenon. Although we may get our information about culture from individuals, we have to interpret it at the level of collectivities. There are snags here known as the 'ecological fallacy' and the 'reverse ecological fallacy'. None of the US college textbooks on methodology I know deals sufficiently with the problem of multilevel analysis.

A striking example is found in the otherwise excellent book *Organizational Culture and Leadership* by Edgar H. Schein (1985). On the basis of his consulting experience he compares two large companies, nicknamed 'Action' and 'Multi'. He explains the difference in cultures between these companies by the group dynamics in their respective boardrooms. Nowhere in the book are any conclusions drawn from the fact that the first company is an American-based computer firm, and the second a Swiss-based pharmaceutics firm. This information is not even mentioned. A stress on interactions among individuals obviously fits a culture identified as the most individualistic in the world, but it will not be so well understood by the four-fifths of the world population for whom the group prevails over the individual.

One of the conclusions of my own multilevel research has been that culture at the national level and culture at the organizational level – corporate culture – are two very different phenomena and that the use of a common term for both is confusing. If we do use the common term, we should also pay attention to the occupational and the gender level of culture. National cultures differ primarily in the fundamental, invisible values held by a majority of their members, acquired in early childhood, whereas organization cultures are a much more superficial phenomenon residing mainly in the visible practices of the organization, acquired by socialization of the new members who join as young adults. National cultures change only very slowly if at all; organizational cultures may be consciously changed, although this isn't necessarily easy. This difference between the two types of culture is the secret of the existence of multinational corporations that employ employees with extremely different national cultural values. What keeps them together is a corporate culture based on common practices.

The stress on managers rather than workers

The core element of a work organization around the world is the people who do the work. All the rest is superstructure, and I hope to have demonstrated to you that it may take many different shapes. In the US literature on work organization, however, the core element, if not explicitly then implicitly, is considered the manager. This may well be the result of the combination of extreme individualism with fairly strong masculinity, which has turned the manager into a cultural hero of almost mythical proportions. For example, he – not really she – is supposed to make decisions all the time. Those of you who are or have been managers must know that this is a fable. Very few management decisions are just 'made' as the myth suggests it. Managers are much more involved in maintaining networks; if anything, it is the rank-and-file worker who can really make decisions on his or her own, albeit on a relatively simple level.

Conclusion

This article started with *Alice in Wonderland*. In fact, the management theorist who ventures outside his or her own country into other parts of the world is like Alice in Wonderland. He or she will meet strange beings, customs, ways of organizing or disorganizing and theories that are clearly stupid, old-fashioned or even immoral – yet they may work, or at least they may not fail more frequently than corresponding theories do at home. Then, after the first culture shock, the traveller to Wonderland will feel enlightened, and may be able to take his or her experiences home and use them advantageously. All great ideas in science, politics and management have travelled from one country to another, and been enriched by foreign influences. The roots of American management theories are mainly in Europe: with Adam Smith, John Stuart Mill, Lev Tolstoy, Max Weber, Henri Fayol, Sigmund Freud, Kurt Lewin and many others. These theories were replanted here and they developed and bore fruit. The same may happen again. The last thing we need is a Monroe doctrine for management.

FURTHER READING

Woe be to him who reads but one book.
George Herbert (1593–1632); English poet

At the end of each chapter, a number of follow-up books and articles will be suggested for readers who wish to delve deeper into a particular topic and avoid the dangers of reading only one book. These lists of recommended readings will be selective, instead of exhaustive, to assist readers in finding a few key works that can provide a stimulating introduction to the subject and a good starting point for further exploration.

As a follow up to this chapter, readers interested in tensions and paradoxes have a number of stimulating sources to examine. Besides the aforementioned book by Roger Martin, *The Opposable Mind,* another valuable hands-on approach to dealing with paradoxes is provided by Barry Johnson in his book *Polarity Management.* Another highly recommended work is *Building Cross-Cultural Competence: How to Create Wealth from Conflicting Values* by Charles Hampden-Turner and Fons Trompenaars, which looks at cross-cultural management paradoxes.

An older book by Charles Hampden-Turner, *Charting the Corporate Mind: From Dilemma to Strategy,* is also thought provoking in its account of how dialectics can be employed as a problem-solving approach. In the same way, Richard Mason and Ian Mitroff's book *Challenging Strategic Planning Assumptions* makes for very good reading. For a more detailed account of 'wicked' problems, readers should actually go back to Horst Rittel, who coined the term. His article, together with Melvin Webber, entitled 'Dilemmas in a General Theory of Planning', is a particularly readable essay.

For a more academic angle, a relatively recent article by Marianne Lewis in the *Academy of Management Review,* entitled 'Exploring Paradox: Toward a More Comprehensive Guide', is very good, as is an older book by Robert Quinn, *Beyond Rational Management.* The absolute classic, however, is the article 'Using paradox to build management and organization theories', by Michael Poole and Andrew Van de Ven. On the topic of international cultural differences, Geert Hofstede's original book, *Culture's Consequences*, and its more popular follow-up, *Cultures and Organizations: Software of the Mind*, are highly recommended. For a broader discussion of international differences in management and business systems, readers are advised to turn to *The Seven Cultures of Capitalism*, by Charles Hampden-Turner and Fons Trompenaars, *European Management Systems*, by Ronnie Lessem and Fred Neubauer, and *A European Management Model: Beyond Diversity*, by Roland Calori and Philippe de Woot.

REFERENCES

Allison, G. (1971) *Essence of Decision*, Boston: Little Brown.
Astley, W.G., and Van de Ven, A.H. (1983) 'Central Perspectives and Debates in Organization Theory', *Administrative Science Quarterly*, Vol. 28, pp. 245–273.

Barrett, D. (1998) *The Paradox Process: Creative Business Solutions Where You Least Expect to Find Them*, New York: Amacom.

Berger, P.L., and Luckmann, T. (1966) *The Social Construction of Reality*, New York: Doubleday.

Buckley, W.S. (1968) *Sociology and Modern Systems Theory*, Englewood Cliffs, NJ: Prentice Hall.

Burrell, B., and Morgan, G. (1979) *Sociological Paradigms and Organizational Analysis*, London: Heinemann Educational Books.

Calori, R., and de Woot, P. (eds) (1994) *A European Management Model: Beyond Diversity*, London: Prentice Hall.

Cannon, T. (1997) *Welcome to the Revolution: Managing Paradox in the 21st Century*, London: Pitman.

Cicourel, A.V. (1971) *Cognitive Sociology*, New York: Free Press.

Clarke, T., and Clegg, S. (1998) *Changing Paradigms: The Transformation of Management Knowledge for the 21st Century*, London: HarperCollins.

Coleman, J.S. (1986) 'Social Theory, Social Research, and a Theory of Action', *American Journal of Sociology*, Vol. 16, pp. 1309–1335.

Collins, J.C., and Porras, J.I. (1994) *Built to Last: Successful Habits of Visionary Companies*, New York: Harper Business.

Conklin, E.J., and Weil, W. (2002) 'Wicked Problems: Naming the Pain in Organizations', *GPSS Working Paper.*

Cummings, S. (1993) 'Brief Case: The First Strategists', *Long Range Planning*, Vol. 26, No. 3, June, pp. 133–135.

D'Iribarne, P. (1990) *La Logique d'Honneur*, Paris: Editions du Seuil

Eisenhardt, K.M. (2000) 'Paradox, Spirals, Ambivalence: The New Language of Change and Pluralism', *Academy of Management Review*, Vol. 25, No. 4, pp. 703–705.

Emery, F.E., and Trist, E.L. (1965) 'The Causal Texture of Organizational Environments', *Human Relations*, Vol. 18, pp. 21–32.

Fayol, H. (1916/1949) *General and Industrial Management*, London: Pitman.

Fletcher, J.L., and Olwyler, K. (1997) *Paradoxical Thinking: How to Profit from Your Contradictions*, San Fransisco: Berrett-Koehler.

Giddens, A. (1979) *Central Problems in Social Theory*, Berkely, CA: University of California Press.

Glick, W. (1985) 'Conceptualizing and Measuring Organizational and Psychological Climate: Pitfall in Multilevel Research', *Academy of Management Review*, Vol. 10, pp. 601–616.

Glick, W. (1988) 'Response: Organizations are not Central Tendencies: Shadow Boxing in the Dark, Round 2', *Academy of Management Review*, Vol. 13, pp. 133–137.

Hampden-Turner, C. (1990) *Charting the Corporate Mind: From Dilemma to Strategy*, Oxford: Basil Blackwell.

Hampden-Turner, C., and Trompenaars, F. (1990) *The Seven Cultures of Capitalism*, New York: Doubleday.

Hampden-Turner, C., and Trompenaars, F. (2000) *Building Cross-Cultural Competence: How to Create Wealth from Conflicting Values*, New Haven: Yale University Press.

Handy, C. (1994) *The Age of Paradox*, Boston: Harvard Business School Press.

Hernes, G. (1976) 'Structural Change in Social Processes', *American Journal of Sociology*, Vol. 82, pp. 513–545.

Hinterhuber, H.H., and Popp, W (1992) 'Are You a Strategist or Just a Manager?', *Harvard Business Review*, January–February, pp. 105–113.

Hofstede, G. (1980) *Culture's Consequences*, London: Sage.

Hofstede, G. (1991) *Cultures and Organizations: Software of the Mind*, London: McGraw-Hill.

Hofstede, G. (1993) 'Cultural Constraints in Management Theories', *Academy of Management Executive*, Vol. 7, No. 1, pp. 8–21.

James, L., Joyce, W, and Slocum Jr., J.W. (1988) 'Comment: Organizations Do Not Cognize', *Academy of Management Review*, Vol. 13, pp. 129–132.

Johnson, B. (1996) *Polarity Management*, Amherst, MA: HRD Press Inc.

Ketchen, D.J., Thomas, J.B., and McDaniel, R.R (1996) 'Process, Content and Context: Synergistic Effects on Organizational Performance', *Journal of Management*, Vol. 22, pp. 231–257.

Lessem, R., and Neubauer, F.F. (1994) *European Management Systems*, London: McGraw-Hill.

Lewis, M. (2000) 'Exploring Paradox: Toward a More Comprehensive Guide', *Academy of ManagementReview*, Vol. 25, No. 4, pp. 760–776.

Machiavelli, N. (1950) *The Prince and The Discourses*, New York: Modern Library.

Martin, R. (2007) *The Opposable Mind: How Successful Leaders Win through Integrative Thinking*, Harvard Business School Book Press: Cambridge.

Martin, R. (2007) 'How Successful Leaders Think', *Harvard Business Review*.

Mason, R.O., and Mitroff, I.I. (1981) *Challenging Strategic Planning Assumptions*, New York: Wiley.

Merton, R.K. (1948) *Social Theory and Social Structure*, New York: Free Press.

Mintzberg, H. (1990) 'Strategy Formation: Schools of Thought', in: J.W. Frederickson (ed.), *Perspectives on Strategic Management*, New York: Harper & Row.

Mintzberg, H., and Lampel, J. (1999) 'Reflecting on the Strategy Process', *Sloan Management Review*, Vol. 40, No. 3, Spring, pp. 21–30.

Nielsen, H.A. (1967) 'Antinomies', *New Catholic Encyclopedia*, New York: McGraw-Hill, pp. 621–623.

Pettigrew, A. (1992) 'The Character and Significance of Strategy Process Research', *Strategic Management Journal*, Vol. 13, pp. 5–16.

Pettigrew, A., and Whipp, R. (1991) *Managing Change for Competitive Success*, Oxford: Basil Blackwell.

Pfeffer, J. (1982) *Organizations and Organization Theory*, Marshfield, MA: Pitman.

Poole, M.S., and Van de Ven, A.H. (1989) 'Using Paradox to Build Management and Organization Theories', *Academy of Management Review*, Vol. 14, No. 4, pp. 562–578.

Quinn, R.E. (1988) *Beyond Rational Management: Mastering the Paradoxes and Competing Demands of High Performance*, San Francisco: Jossey-Bass.

Quinn, R.E., and Cameron, K.S. (1988) *Paradox and Transformation: Toward a Theory of Change in Organization and Management*, Cambridge, MA: Ballinger Publishing.

Reese, H., and Overton, W.F. (1973) 'Models of Development and Theories of Development', in: J.R. Nessleroade and H.W. Reese (eds), *Life-span Developmental Psychology: Methodological Issues*, New York: Academic Press.

Rescher, N. (2001) *Paradoxes: Their Roots, Range and Resolution*, Chicago: Open Court Publishing.

Rittel, H. (1972) 'On the Planning Crisis: Systems Analysis of the "First and Second Generations"', *Bedriftsokonomen*, No. 8, pp. 390–396.

Rittel, H., and Webber, M. (1973) 'Dilemmas in a General Theory of Planning', *Policy Sciences*, Vol. 4, pp. 155–169.

Ropo, A., and Hunt, J.G. (1995) 'Entrepreneurial Processes as Virtuous and Vicious Spirals in a Changing Opportunity Structure: A Paradoxical Perspective', *Entrepreneurship, Theory and Practice*, Spring, pp. 91–111.

Rumelt, R.P. (1980) 'The Evaluation of Business Strategy', in: W.F. Glueck (ed.), *Business Policy and Strategic Management*, Third Edition, New York: McGraw-Hill.

Schein, E.H. (1985) *Organizational Culture and Leadership*, San Francisco: Jossey-Bass.

Smelser, N. (1962) *Theory of Collective Behavior*, New York: Free Press.

Smith, A. (1776/1986) *The Wealth of Nations*, Harmondsworth: Penguin Books.

Smith, K.K., and Berg, D.N. (1987) *Paradoxes of Group Life*, San Francisco: Jossey-Bass.

Sun Tzu (1983) *The Art of War*, New York: Delacorte Press.

Taylor, F.W (1903) *Shop Management*, New York: Harper.

Taylor, F.W. (1911) *The Principles of Scientific Management*, New York: Harper.

Thurbin, P.J. (1998) *The Influential Strategist: Using the Power of Paradox in Strategic Thinking*, London: Financial Times.

Trompenaars, F., and Hampden-Turner, C. (2001) *21 Leaders for the 21st Century*, Oxford: Capstone Publishing Ltd.

Van de Ven, A.H., and Astley, W.G. (1981) 'Mapping the Field to Create a Dynamic Perspective on Organization Design and Behavior', in: A. Van de Ven and W Joyce (eds.), *Perspectives on Organization Design and Behavior*, New York: Wiley, pp. 427–468.

Van de Ven, A.H., and Poole, M.S. (1988) 'Paradoxical Requirements for a Theory of Organizational Change', in: R. Quinn and K. Cameron (eds.), *Paradox and Transformation: Toward a Theory of Change in Organization and Management*, Cambridge, MA: Ballinger, pp. 19–63.

Van Heigenoort, J. (1958) 'Social Behavior as Exchange', *American Journal of Sociology*, Vol. 63, pp. 597–606.

Van Heigenoort, J. (1972) 'Logical Paradoxes', in: P. Edwards (ed.), *Encyclopedia of Philosophy*, New York: Macmillan, pp. 45–51.

Von Clausewitz, K. (1982) *On War*, Harmondsworth: Penguin.

Wacker, W. and Taylor, J. (2000) *The Visionary's Handbook: Nine Paradoxes That Will Shape the Future of Your Business*, New York: HarperCollins.

Weick, K. (1979) *The Social Psychology of Organizing*, Second Edition, Reading, MA: Addison-Wesley.

Wing, R.L. (1988) *The Art of Strategy: A New Translation of Sun Tzu's Classic 'The Art of War'*, New York: Doubleday.

Whittington, R. (1993) *What Is Strategy and Does It Matter?*, London: Routledge.

STRATEGY PROCESS

Follow the course opposite to custom and you will almost always do well.
Jean Jacques Rousseau (1712–1778); French philosopher

Given the variety of perspectives on strategy, finding a precise definition with which all people agree is probably impossible. Therefore, in this book we will proceed with a very broad conception of strategy as 'a course of action for achieving an organization's purpose'. In this section, it is the intention to gain a better insight into how such a course of action comes about – how is, and should, strategy be made, analyzed, dreamt-up, formulated, implemented, changed and controlled; who is involved; and when do the necessary activities take place?

The process by which strategy comes about can be dissected in many ways. Here, the strategy process has been unravelled into three partially overlapping issues, each of which requires managers to make choices, and each of which is (therefore) controversial (see Figure II.1):

■ Strategic thinking. This issue focuses on the *strategist*. The question is how managers should organize their thinking to achieve a successful strategic reasoning process.

■ Strategy formation. This issue focuses on the *strategy*. The question is how managers should organize their strategizing activities to achieve a successful strategy formation process.

■ Strategic change. This issue focuses on the *organization*. The question is how managers should organize changes to achieve a successful strategic renewal process.

The most important term to remember throughout this section is *process*. In each chapter the discussion is not about one-off activities or outcomes – a strategic thought, a formed strategy or a strategic change – but about the ongoing processes of thinking, forming and changing. These processes need to be organized, structured, stimulated, nurtured and/or facilitated over a prolonged period of time and the question concerns which approach will be successful in the long term, as well as in the short term.

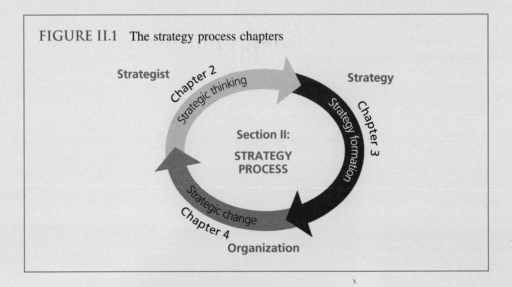

FIGURE II.1   The strategy process chapters

STRATEGIC THINKING

Rational, adj. Devoid of all delusions save those of observation, experience and reflection.

The Devil's Dictionary, Ambrose Bierce (1842–1914); American columnist

INTRODUCTION

What goes on in the mind of the strategist? A fascinating question that is easy to ask, but difficult to answer. Yet, it is a question that is important in two ways – generally and personally. Generally, knowing what goes on in the minds of managers during strategy processes is essential for understanding their choices and behaviours. Opening up the 'black box' of the strategist's mind to see how decisions are made can help to anticipate or influence this thinking. Grasping how managers shape their strategic views and select their preferred actions can be used to develop more effective strategy processes. It is due to this importance of strategic thinking that a separate chapter in this book is devoted to the subject. Yet, for each reader personally, the topic of strategic thinking is also of key importance, as it automatically raises the questions 'what is going on in *my* mind?' and 'how strategic is *my* thinking?' Exploring the subject of strategic thinking triggers each person to explore their own thought processes and critically reflect on their own strategy preferences. Ideally, wondering about the mind of the strategist should inspire readers to constantly question their own assumptions, thoughts, beliefs and ideas, and to sharpen their strategic thinking, as they move through the following chapters. For this reason, it seems only appropriate to start the book with this topic.

So, what goes on in the mind of the strategist? Well, a lot, but if reduced to its bare essentials it can be said that strategists are engaged in the process of dealing with *strategic problems*. Not problems in the negative sense of troublesome conditions that need to be avoided, but in the neutral sense of challenging situations that need to be resolved – a strategic problem is a set of circumstances requiring a reconsideration of the current course of action, either to profit from observed opportunities or to respond to perceived threats. To deal with these strategic problems, managers must not simply think, but they must go through a *strategic reasoning process*, searching for ways to define and resolve the challenges at hand. Managers must structure their individual thinking steps into a reasoning process that will result in effective strategic behaviour. The question is how managers actually go about defining strategic problems (how do they identify and diagnose what is going on?) and how they go about solving strategic problems (how do they generate, evaluate and decide on potential answers?). It is this issue of strategic reasoning, as a string of strategic thinking activities directed at defining and resolving strategic problems, that will be examined in further detail below.

THE ISSUE OF STRATEGIC REASONING

The mind of the strategist is a complex and fascinating apparatus that never fails to astonish and dazzle on the one hand, and disappoint and frustrate on the other. We are often surprised by the power of the human mind, but equally often stunned by its limitations. For the discussion here it is not necessary to unravel all of the mysteries surrounding the functioning of the human brain, but a short overview of the capabilities and limitations of the human mind will help us to understand the issue of strategic reasoning.

The human ability to know is referred to as 'cognition'. As strategists want to know about the strategic problems facing their organizations, they need to engage in *cognitive activities*. These cognitive activities (or strategic thinking activities) need to be structured into a strategic reasoning process. Hence, the first step towards a better understanding of what goes on in the mind of the strategist is to examine the various cognitive activities making up a strategic reasoning process. The four main cognitive activities will be discussed in the first subsection below. To be able to perform these cognitive activities, people need to command certain mental faculties. While very sophisticated, the human brain is still physically strictly limited in what it can do. These limitations to people's *cognitive abilities* will be reviewed in the second sub-section. To deal with its inherent physical shortcomings, the human brain copes by building simplified models of the world, referred to as *cognitive maps*. The functioning of cognitive maps will be addressed in the third sub-section.

In Figure 2.1 the relationship between these three topics is visualized, using the metaphor of a computer. The cognitive abilities of our brains can be seen as a hardware level question – what are the physical limits on our mental faculties? The cognitive maps used by our brains can be seen as an operating system level question – what type of platform/language is 'running' on our brain? The cognitive activities carried out by our brains can be seen as an application level question – what type of program is strategic reasoning?

Cognitive activities

The strategic reasoning process consists of a number of strategic thinking elements or cognitive activities – mental tasks intended to increase the strategist's knowing. A general distinction can be made between cognitive activities directed towards *defining* a strategic problem, and cognitive activities directed at *solving* a strategic problem.

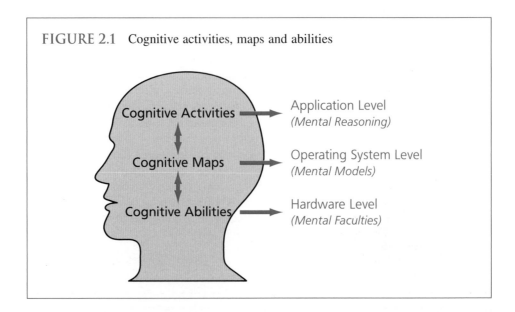

FIGURE 2.1   Cognitive activities, maps and abilities

Cognitive Activities → Application Level *(Mental Reasoning)*

Cognitive Maps → Operating System Level *(Mental Models)*

Cognitive Abilities → Hardware Level *(Mental Faculties)*

Each of these two major categories can be further split in two (see Figure 2.2), leading to the following general elements of a strategic reasoning process:

- **Identifying.** Before strategists can move to benefit from opportunities or to counter threats, they must be aware of these challenges and acknowledge their importance. This part of the reasoning process is variably referred to as identifying, recognizing or sense-making.

- **Diagnosing.** To come to grips with a problem, strategists must try to understand the structure of the problem and its underlying causes. This part of the reasoning process is variably referred to as diagnosing, analyzing or reflecting.

- **Conceiving.** To deal with a strategic problem, strategists must come up with a potential solution. If more than one solution is available, strategists must select the most promising one. This part of the reasoning process is variably referred to as conceiving, formulating or imagining.

- **Realizing.** A strategic problem is only really solved once concrete actions are undertaken that achieve results. Strategists must therefore carry out problem-solving activities and evaluate whether the consequences are positive. This part of the reasoning process is variably referred to as realizing, implementing or acting.

A structured approach to these four cognitive activities is to carry them out in the above order, starting with problem identification and then moving through diagnosis to conceiving solutions and finally realizing them (i.e. clockwise movement in Figure 2.2). In this approach the first step, identifying strategic problems, would require extensive external and internal scanning, thorough sifting of incoming information and the selection of priority issues. In the next reasoning step, the strategic problems recognized would have to be diagnosed by gathering more detailed data, and by further analyzing and refining this information. Once the problem had been properly defined, a strategy could be formulated by evaluating the available options and deciding which solution would be best. In the final phase, realization, the strategist would need to ensure execution of the proposed solution by consciously planning and controlling implementation activities. In this case, the four elements of the strategic reasoning process could actually be labelled recognizing, analyzing, formulating and implementing.

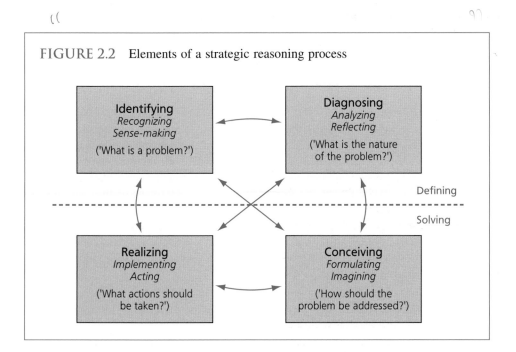

FIGURE 2.2   Elements of a strategic reasoning process

However, strategists do not always reason in this step-by-step fashion. Their thinking is often less orderly, with identifying, diagnosing, conceiving and realizing intermingled with one another – even going on at the same time. Nor are the cognitive activities as straightforward as portrayed above. The identification of strategic problems is often not about objective observation, but rather subjective interpretation – by looking at the world from a particular angle, strategists see and value particular strengths, weaknesses, opportunities and threats. Such sense-making activities (Weick, 1979; Gioia and Chittipeddi, 1991) lead to attention being paid to some issues, while others do not make the strategic agenda (Dutton, 1988; Ocasio, 1997). Likewise, diagnosing strategic problems is not always a structured analytical process. Gaining a deeper understanding of strategic problems may involve explicit analysis, but also intuitive reflecting – by employing unconscious reasoning rules strategists often quickly form a general picture of how key aspects of a strategic problem are interrelated.

Conceiving strategic solutions can be equally 'messy' and subjective. Often, strategic options are not chosen from an available repertoire of potential solutions, but they are invented. In other words, new options are often not selected, discovered or figured out, but are envisioned – strategists imagine how things could be done. Such idea generation can involve reasoning by analogy or metaphor, brainstorming or pure fantasizing. New potential solutions may come to the strategist in a flash (Eureka!) or emerge over time, but usually require a period of incubation beforehand and a period of nurturing afterwards. Furthermore, strategists often find it impossible to objectively prove which new idea would be the best solution. Therefore, the process of deciding on the solution to be pursued may involve more judgement than calculation.

Finally, it must be emphasized that action does not always come last, in the form of solution implementation. Often, strategists do not wait for a problem to be precisely defined and for a solution to be fully conceived before starting to act. On the contrary, strategists often feel they must first act – they must have experience with a problem and know that the current strategy will not be able to overcome the problem. To find a suitable solution it is often also necessary to test certain assumptions in practice and to experiment. Hence, acting regularly precedes, or goes hand in hand with, all other cognitive activities.

Cognitive abilities

People are not omniscient – they do not have infinite knowledge. To some extent this is due to the nature of reality – many future events are inherently unpredictable, due to factors that are uncertain or unknowable. Yet, humans are also burdened with rather imperfect cognitive abilities. The human brain is severely limited in what it can know (Simon, 1957). The limitation to human's cognitive abilities is largely due to three factors:

■ Limited information sensing ability. Humanity's first 'handicap' is a limited information-sensing ability. While the senses – touch, smell, taste, hearing and seeing – are bombarded with stimuli, much of reality remains unobservable to humans. This is partially due to the physical inability to be everywhere, all the time, noticing everything. However, people's limited ability to register the structure of reality is also due to the inherent superficiality of the senses and the complexity of reality. The human senses cannot directly identify the way the world works and the underlying causal relationships. Only the physical consequences of the complex interactions between elements in reality can be picked up by a person's sensory system. Therefore, the mental representations of the world that individuals build up in their minds are necessarily based on circumstantial evidence.

■ Limited information processing capacity. Unfortunately, a second drawback is that humans do not have unlimited data processing abilities. Thinking through problems with many variables, complex relationships and huge amounts of data is a task that people find extremely difficult to perform. Approaching every activity in this way would totally overload a person's brain. For this reason, humans hardly ever think through a problem with full use of all available data, but necessarily make extensive use of mental shortcuts, referred to as 'cognitive heuristics' (Janis, 1989). Cognitive heuristics are mental 'rules of thumb' that simplify a problem, so that it can be more quickly understood and solved. Cognitive heuristics focus a person's attention on a number of key variables that are believed to be most important, and present a number of simple decision rules to rapidly resolve an issue. The set of possible solutions to be considered is also limited in advance.

■ Limited information storage capacity. Another human cognitive shortcoming is poor memory. People have only a limited capacity for storing information. Remembering all individuals, events, dates, places and circumstances is beyond the ability of the human brain. Therefore, people must store information very selectively and organize this information in a way that it can be easily retrieved when necessary. Here again, cognitive heuristics are at play – 'rules of thumb' make the memorization process manageable in the face of severe capacity limitations. Such heuristics help to simplify complex clusters of data into manageable chunks and help to categorize, label and store this information so that it can be recalled at a later time.

To deal with these severe physical limitations, the brain has come up with more than only simple cognitive heuristics. The human mind has come to work with more holistic cognitive maps.

Cognitive maps

Knowledge that people have is stored in their minds in the form of 'cognitive maps' (e.g. McCaskey, 1982; Weick and Bourgnon, 1986), also referred to as 'cognitive schemata' (e.g. Anderson, 1983; Schwenk, 1988), 'mental models' (e.g. Day and Lord, 1992; Knight *et al.,* 1999), 'knowledge structures' (e.g. Lyles and Schwenk, 1992; Walsh, 1995) and 'construed reality' (Finkelstein and Hambrick, 1996). These cognitive maps are representations in a person's mind of how the world works. A cognitive map of a certain situation reflects a person's beliefs about the importance of the issues and about the cause and effect relationships between them.

Cognitive maps are formed over time through education, experience and interaction with others. Based on the inputs of their senses, people will infer causal relationships between phenomena, making guesses about unobservable factors and resolving inconsistencies between the bits of information received. In turn, people's cognitive maps steer their senses; while cognitive maps are built on past sensory data, they will consequently direct which new information will be sought and perceived. A person's cognitive map will focus attention on particular phenomena, while blocking out other data as noise, and will quickly make clear how a situation should be perceived. In this way, a cognitive map provides an interpretive filter or perceptual screen, aiding the senses in selecting and understanding external stimuli (Starbuck and Milliken, 1988). Furthermore, cognitive maps help to direct behaviour, by providing an existing repertoire of 'problem-solving' responses (also referred to as 'scripts' or 'recipes') from which an appropriate action can be derived.

In building their cognitive maps, people acquire a lot of their knowledge by means of direct experience. They learn to communicate, play an instrument, drive a vehicle and solve problems by doing. This knowledge is added to people's cognitive maps without being explicitly articulated. In other words, knowledge gained through experiential learning is usually not codified into formal rules, principles, models or theories, but remains tacit (Polanyi, 1966; Nonaka, 1991). People formulate implicit models and draw conclusions, but do so largely unconsciously. In this way, cognitive maps evolve without people themselves being entirely aware of their own cognitive map. Hence, when people use their 'intuition', this is not a mystical or irrational way of reasoning, but thinking guided by the tacit knowledge they have acquired in the past (Behling and Eckel, 1991). Intuitive thinking is the opposite of analytical thinking – informal and holistic (Von Winterfeldt and Edwards, 1986). Informal means that the thinking is largely unconscious and based on assumptions, variables and causal relationships not explicitly identifiable by those doing the thinking. Holistic means that the thinker does not aim at unravelling phenomena into their constituent parts, but rather maintains a more integrated view of reality.

Yet, people's cognitive maps are not developed independently, but rather in interaction with one another. People tend to construct a shared understanding of the world by interacting with each other within a group over an extended period of time. By exchanging interpretations of what they see, it is said that they *enact* a shared reality (Daft and Weick, 1984; Smircich and Stubbart, 1985). The resulting shared cognitive map is variably referred to as the group's dominant logic (Prahalad and Bettis, 1986), common paradigm (Kuhn, 1970) or belief system (Noorderhaven, 1995). Such a shared worldview can exist within small social units, such as a firm or a family, but also within larger units, such as an industry or a nation.

As individuals can belong to different groups, they can be influenced by different belief systems simultaneously. As members of a national culture, their cognitive maps will to a certain extent be influenced by the beliefs dominant within the nation. As employees of a company, their cognitive maps will be affected by the beliefs common within the firm and the industry as well. In the same manner, people can be impacted by the professional community to which they belong, their religious affiliation, their political party and any other groups in which they interact with others (Hambrick *et al.,* 1993; Sutcliffe and Huber, 1998). Due to the mutually inclusive nature of group membership, an individual's cognitive map will be a complex combination of elements taken from different group-level dominant logics. While these paradigms on which an individual draws can be complementary, or overlapping yet consistent, it is quite possible that inconsistencies arise (Schein, 1985; Trice and Beyer, 1993).

As shared beliefs develop over time through interaction and are passed on through socialization, they remain largely tacit. The shared cognitive map of a group is literally 'common sense' – sense shared by a common group of people. However, where members of different groups come into conflict with one another, or where an individual needs to deal with the inconsistencies brought on by multiple group memberships, beliefs can become more articulated. Different behaviours, based on different cognitive maps, will often lead to the identification and codification of beliefs, either to protect them or to engage in debate with people with other views. As paradigms become more articulated, they also become more mobile, making it possible to transfer ideas to people without direct interaction.

The downside of cognitive maps is that they exhibit a high level of rigidity. People are generally not inclined to change their minds. Once people's cognitive maps have formed, and they have a grip on reality, they become resistant to signals that challenge their conceptions. As McCaskey (1982) remarks, the mind 'strives mightily to bring order, simplicity, consistency, and stability to the world it encounters', and is therefore reluctant to welcome the ambiguity presented by contradicting data. People tend to significantly overestimate the value of information that confirms their cognitive map, underestimate dis-confirming information, and they actively seek out evidence that supports their current beliefs (Schwenk, 1984). Once an interpretive filter is in place, seeing is not believing, but believing is seeing. People might have the impression that they are constantly learning, but they are largely learning within the bounds of a paradigm. When an individual's map is supported by similar beliefs shared within a firm, industry or country, the ability to question key aspects of a paradigm will usually be rather limited. Not only does the individual have no 'intellectual sounding board' for teasing out new ideas, but deviation from the dominant logic might also have adverse social and political ramifications within the group (e.g. DiMaggio and Powell, 1983; Aldrich and Fiol, 1994). Not for nothing the old proverb is: 'old ideas never change; they eventually die out' (Kuhn, 1970).

For strategists, cognitive rigidity is particularly worrying. Strategists should be at the forefront of market developments, identifying changing circumstances and new opportunities before their competitors. Strategic thinking is by its very nature focused on understanding and shaping the future, and therefore strategists must have the ability to challenge current beliefs and change their own mind. They must be able to come up with innovative, but feasible, new strategies that will fit with the unfolding reality. This places extraordinary cognitive demands on strategists – they must be able to overcome the limitations of their own cognitive maps and develop a new understanding.

THE PARADOX OF LOGIC AND CREATIVITY

Information's pretty thin stuff, unless mixed with experience.
Clarence Day (1874–1935); American essayist

Many management theorists have noted that the opposites of intuition and analysis create a tension for managers (e.g. Langley, 1989, 1995; Pondy, 1983). While some researchers make a strong case for more formal analysis (e.g. Isenberg, 1984; Schoemaker and Russo, 1993), there is a broad understanding that managers need to employ both intuitive and analytical thinking, even if they are each other's opposites.

The extensive use of intuitive judgement among managers is understood by most as necessary and beneficial. A manager's intuition is built up through years of experience and contains a vast quantity of tacit knowledge that can only superficially be tapped by formal analysis. Intuition can also give a 'richer' assessment, by blending in all types of qualitative information. Moreover, intuitive thinking is often better at capturing the big picture than analytical thinking. And very practically, intuition is needed to cut corners: without the widespread use of cognitive heuristics, management would grind to a halt, overloaded by the sheer complexity of the analyses that would need to be carried out. Such a situation of rationality gone rampant is referred to as 'paralysis by analysis' (Lenz and Lyles, 1985; Langley, 1995).

However, it is equally clear to most that human intuition is often unreliable. Cognitive heuristics are 'quick and dirty' – efficient, but imprecise. They help people to intuitively jump to conclusions without thorough analysis, which increases speed, but also increases the risk of drawing faulty conclusions. The main danger of cognitive heuristics is that they are inherently biased, as they focus attention on only a few variables and interpret them in a particular way, even when this is not appropriate (e.g. Tversky and Kahneman, 1986; Bazerman, 1990). For this reason, many academics urge practitioners to bolster their intuitive judgements with more explicit rational analysis. Especially in the case of strategic decisions, more time and energy should be made available to avoid falling prey to common cognitive biases. Otherwise the ultimate result might be a 'corporate gravestone' with the epitaph '*extinct by instinct*' (Langley, 1995).

While the tension between intuition and analysis is important, it does not go to the heart of the strategic reasoning issue. For strategists the more fundamental question is how they can escape getting stuck with an outdated cognitive map. How can they avoid the danger of building up a flawed picture of their industry, their markets and themselves? As strategists must be acutely aware of the unfolding opportunities and threats in the environment, and the evolving strengths and weaknesses of the organization, they must be able to constantly re-evaluate their views.

On the one hand, this requires rigorous *logical thinking*. All the key assumptions on which a strategist's cognitive map has been based need to be reviewed and tested against developments in the firm and its environment. On the other hand, strategists must have the ability to engage in *creative thinking*. To be able to see new opportunities and strengths, strategists must be able to think beyond current models of reality. Both demands on strategists will now be reviewed in more detail.

The demand for logical thinking

It is clear that if managers base their strategic decisions only on heavily biased cognitive maps, unconsciously built up through past experience, this will lead to very poor results. Managers need to have the ability to critically reflect on the assumptions they hold, to check whether they are based on actual fact, or on organizational folklore and industry recipes. They must be capable of making their tacit beliefs more explicit, so that the validity of these mental models can be evaluated and they can be further refined. In short, to be successful strategists, managers need to escape the confines of their own cognitive maps – and those of other stakeholders engaged in the strategy process.

Assessing the validity of a cognitive map requires strong logical thinking. Logical thinking is a disciplined and rigorous way of thinking, on the basis of formal rules. When employing logic, each step in an argumentation follows from the previous, based on valid principles. In other words, a logical thinker will draw a conclusion only if it is arrived at by a sound succession of arguments.

Logical thinking can be applied to all four cognitive activities outlined in Figure 2.2. When identifying and diagnosing a strategic problem, logical thinking can help to avoid the emotional interpretations that so often colour people's understanding of environmental opportunities and threats, and organizational strengths and weaknesses. Logical thinking can also expose a person's bullish or bearish bias and can be instrumental in discarding old 'theories' of how the firm and its environment function. By analysing the empirical facts and rigorously testing the hypotheses on which the firm's shared cognitive map has been built, the strategist can prevent building a false model of reality.

When conceiving and realizing a strategic solution, logical thinking can help to avoid the danger of following outdated habits and routines. Routines are programmed courses of action that originally were deliberately conceived, but have been subsequently internalized and are used automatically (March and Simon, 1993). Habits are programmed courses of action that have developed unconsciously. By explicitly formulating strategic options and subjecting them to formal evaluation, the strategist can break away from such established behaviour and develop new approaches to gaining and retaining competitive advantage. Moreover, logical thinking can aid in making a distinction between fantasy and feasibility. Sound logic can serve to weed out strategic options that are flights of fancy, by analysing the factors that will determine success or failure.

The demand for creative thinking

Creative thinking is the opposite of logical thinking. As described above, when employing logic, a thinker bases each step in a train of thought on the previous steps, following formal rules of valid thinking. De Bono (1970) refers to this pattern of thought as 'vertical thinking'. However, when creativity is used, the thinker does not take a valid step, but takes a leap of imagination, without being able to support the validity of the mental jump.

In creative thinking a person abandons the rules governing sound argumentation and draws a conclusion that is not justified based on the previous arguments. In this way the thinker generates a new understanding, but without objective proof that the new idea 'makes sense'. De Bono refers to this pattern of thought as 'lateral thinking'.

In essence, creative thinking takes liberty in following thinking rules. One idea might lead to another idea, without formal logic interfering. One variable might be linked by the thinker to another, without a sound explanation of why a correlation is assumed. Creativity in effect creates a new understanding, with little attention paid to supporting evidence. Often logic is used afterwards to justify an idea that was actually generated by creative means.

When identifying and diagnosing strategic problems, creative thinking is often needed. Old cognitive maps usually have a very compelling logic, locking people into old patterns of thinking. These old cognitive maps are usually tried and tested, and have become immune to external signals that they are no longer fitting. Thinking within the boundaries of a shared cognitive map is generally accepted and people tend to proceed rationally – that is, they try to avoid logical inconsistencies. Challenging a cognitive map's fundamental assumptions, however, cannot be done in a way that is logically consistent with the map itself. Contradicting a paradigm is illogical from the point of view of those who accept the paradigm. Therefore, changing a rigid and subjective cognitive map, rooted in a shared paradigm, requires strategists to imagine new ways of understanding the world that do not logically follow from past beliefs. Strategic thinkers need to be willing and able to break with orthodoxy and make leaps of imagination, that are not logically justified, but needed to generate novel ways of looking at old problems.

The same is true when conceiving and realizing strategic solutions. New strategies often do not follow from the facts, but need to be invented – they are not analyzed into existence, but need to be generated, if they are to be innovative and distinctive. Creative solutions do not follow from the dominant logic, but are the unexpected answers that emerge when the grip of the dominant logic is loosened.

Unfortunately, the conclusion must be that logical thinking and creative thinking are not only opposites, but that they are partially incompatible as well. They are based on methods that are at odds with one another. Strategizing managers would probably love to be fully logical and fully creative at the same time, but both require such a different mindset and range of cognitive skills that in practice it is very difficult to achieve both simultaneously. The demand for logic and creativity is not only contradictory for each individual, but also within teams, departments and the overall firm: while strategizing groups would like to be fully capable of logical and creative thinking, finding ways of incorporating both forms of strategic thinking into a workable strategy process is extremely challenging. Commonly, conflicting styles lead to conflicting people, and therefore a blend between the two is not that simple. It is for this reason that we speak of the 'paradox of logic and creativity' – the two demands on managers seem to be contradictory, yet both are required at the same time.

EXHIBIT 2.1   SHORT CASE

EXACT SOFTWARE: HARD SCIENCE OR IMAGINATIVE ART?

ex.act (ig.zakt) *adj.* Perfectly clear and complete in every detail; precise. That's the ideal name for our new company, thought three young men back in 1984, as they started making bookkeeping software for small and medium-sized enterprises. It remained the perfect name for the company when Exact Software expanded its financial administration software to include all back office functions to become an enterprise resource planning (ERP) software provider. And it is still the best possible name now that Exact offers solutions that integrate all back office and front office information flows into one unified system. The company does precisely what its name promises, offering software that puts exact information at the finger tips of all employees, empowering them to make informed business decisions on the basis of a complete set of data.

Two products are at the heart of the Exact offering. For the back office (or administrative processes) the company has an ERP system called Exact Globe, which integrates the various activities such as stock keeping, ordering, invoicing, payroll and bookkeeping. For the front office (or value-adding processes) they have a package called Exact Synergy, which combines modules for electronic workflow and project management, R&D management, marketing, sales force automation, service management, customer relationship management (CRM), human capital management and quality management. Both products can work together seamlessly, using one central database. On top of this, Exact has a few products that use the database to provide more sophisticated performance management and business analytics. As all these products together give employees and partner firms real-time access to all relevant business process information, Exact calls its combined offering 'Business Empowerment Software'.

Although Exact is one of the world's top 10 business software companies, it is still a David in the land of Goliath. Headquartered in Delft, the Netherlands, Exact has subsidiaries in 40 countries, together employing approximately 2500 people. Its products are sold in more than 125 countries, which in 2008 resulted in revenues of €261 million and an EBITDA of €58.2 million. Yet, compared to its main competitors, SAP (€11.5 billion), Oracle (US$22.4 billion) and Microsoft (US$60.4 billion), Exact is relatively small. But it is this humble size that is also Exact's strength in dealing with its target market, companies with less than 2500 employees. Where the big guys focus on big clients, coming in with huge applications, Exact aims to serve small and medium-sized enterprises (SMEs), as well as similar subsidiaries of multinational companies. Its products are designed to handle up to a few hundred users at a time, but can also be implemented in companies with just a handful of employees.

Being so tailored to the needs of SMEs, Exact's products are easier to implement, while bringing the level of investment in line with what smaller firms can afford. As many of these SMEs don't use English internally, Exact's products are available in 40 languages. Yet, at the same time, internationally operating SMEs and subsidiaries of multinationals can use Exact's products in all countries and just switch between languages where necessary.

'In developing Exact's strategy, not everything followed logically from the data we had,' says CEO Rajesh Patel, who joined the company in 1996 and became head of all activities outside the Netherlands in 2001. In building Exact's international network, Patel's predecessors had emphasized the acquisition of local ERP players, because these had installed bases of ERP clients to which Exact could then offer additional software products. The consequence, however, was that when Patel took over the international network of 14 subsidiaries after the dotcom bubble burst, he found that each was doing their own thing, while the competition had drastically increased. Exact International was a collection of independent fiefdoms, each with different offerings, different pricing schemes and a very local client base, creating almost no joint synergy. After visiting all the subsidiaries and seeing how they hardly worked together, it was clear to Patel that he needed to set international standards and build cross-border bridges. But he felt that he needed a lever to drive the change – something that would create a win–win. Using one of the regular board meetings to brainstorm about possible alternatives, Patel later recalled, it took about half an hour at the flipchart for all the pieces to fall into place – the 'parenting strategy' was born.

This strategy was aimed at leveraging Exact's contacts with the local subsidiaries of large multinationals. The idea was to use the existing contacts with these subsidiaries to approach the parent company and position Exact as a viable alternative in the multinationals' other geographic markets as well. The board immediately agreed that the idea was great and started to draft a change programme that would be needed to get this strategy to work. The biggest hurdle, it was believed, would be to get the buy in of all the Exact subsidiary managers without any hard facts to prove that the strategy would be a commercial success. Therefore, instead of gathering more data to try to convince the country managers with tangible evidence, Patel started a big internal communication campaign to get people to accept 'through the heart, not through the brain'. For the first time in the company's history, all local managers were invited to come to central meetings and trainings, with 'all for one and one for all' as the slogan for the event. People left engaged and energized, and Exact went on to close deals with companies like Siemens, who now run Exact at many of their subsidiaries worldwide. Close to a third of Exact's revenues now comes from such clients.

Reflecting on this episode, marketing director Clemens Riedl concludes that this approach to strategizing is typical for Exact: 'We started from one end without knowing where the other end was.' The emphasis is on having a vision, getting into action, finding things out in practice and adjusting to the unfolding feedback. 'Everything starts with an idea which is then researched and experimented with to prove itself or fail. This is in contrast with what happens at Procter & Gamble, where new ideas come from the marketing department on the basis of market research and analysis', says Riedl. In Patel's words: 'We call ourselves professional mavericks. At Exact everything starts with an idea which is rolled out waiting to be tested by the markets.' The decision to introduce Exact Online, which allows companies to do bookkeeping via the internet, was made in the same way, without extensive analysis or market research, according to Patel. 'If we would have first asked our clients if they wanted to do their bookkeeping on the internet, they would have said no.' But Patel's intuition said yes, so he asked the R&D team to pursue the idea, leading to the important first step of the company in the area of 'software as a service' over the internet.

In 2005, Patel was asked to take over as CEO and to rejuvenate the entire company, as he had done with the international division before. Together with a few trusted advisors, he drew up a strategic roadmap, with three main pillars: Protect, grow and acquire. First, Exact needed to protect its installed base of ERP clients, by investing further in Globe and Exact's local ERP product offerings, while keeping up its high service levels. Second, the company needed to pursue organic growth through its new Exact Synergy offering, largely through enticing its existing clients to complement their ERP system. Third, Exact would be open to selected acquisitions to expand its customer base and/ or add complementary products to its package. But just as importantly, Patel decided to fundamentally alter the organizational culture. As with many IT companies started by technology-oriented entrepreneurs, Exact suffered from a strong product push mentality, supported by a command and control structure at headquarters, with limited room for employee initiative. So, Patel launched an organizational transformation process, directed at building a more empowered and professional organization with a market-driven focus.

To drive the change, some key people were replaced and all managers were brought to Berlin for a global conference to explain the changes and to win hearts *and* minds. By the time Patel got all 400 managers together again in 2007, an enormous cultural change had taken place, as well as a significant improvement in Exact's financial results. Since then, despite the economic recession, results have remained strong, as Exact has been able to capture new customers, not willing to buy one of the Rolls Royce packages due to the market circumstances.

Yet, moving forward Patel had at least two important issues that he needed to address. First was the future of online software. Exact's move to launch a bookkeeping service over the internet had turned out to be successful at the lower end of the market, among relatively small companies. The question for Exact was whether they should invest more heavily in the software-as-a-service approach, providing more offerings and giving more service. Patel's fundamental belief was that the IT industry needed 'more imagination to make breakthroughs', so he was open to taking a leap. Yet, many analysts were expressing doubts about the true potential of online software. According to Gartner, the leading market research firm in the IT field, businesses were showing only a lukewarm response to software-as-a-service, despite an economic climate that would seem to encourage take-up of the technology. Hence, for Patel it seemed a matter of following his instinct or following the market research reports.

The second issue facing Patel was how to stimulate strategic thinking among his managers and what form this thinking should take. As part of the organizational transformation, Patel had encouraged all managers to behave more like leaders and to take more initiative in translating the strategy of the overall company into a strategy for their area of responsibility. Coming from a culture in which they were only asked to implement, this was a huge step for most people. Patel asked himself how he could strengthen their strategic thinking, but also how he would react if they came to him with an investment proposal. Did he want to have firm investment plans, backed up with thorough analyses and corroborating data, or would he be willing to invest based on the creative leap of imagination of his empowered manager? Again, it was a question of whether rational analysis or generative reasoning would be more important.

One thing he was certain about, was that the days of top-down command and control were over. As empowering leader he was intent on deciding less and inspiring more. Only half jokingly he suggested that maybe now it was time to change the meaning of CEO from Chief Executive Officer to Chief Energizing Officer.

Co-author: Martijn Rademakers

Sources: www.exact.com; *Exact Software Annual Report 2008*; company interviews; *The Economist*, 23 October 2008; Gartner Press Release, 8 July 2009.

PERSPECTIVES ON STRATEGIC THINKING

Irrationally held truths may be more harmful than reasoned errors.
T.H. Huxley (1825–1895); English biologist

While the need for both logical and creative thinking is clear, this does place strategists in a rather awkward position of needing to bring two partially contradictory forms of thinking together in one strategic reasoning process. Logical thinking helps to make the strategic reasoning process more *rational* – rigorous, comprehensive and consistent, instead of haphazard, fragmentary and ad hoc. Creative thinking, on the other hand, helps to make the strategic reasoning process more *generative* – producing more unorthodox insights, imaginative ideas and innovative solutions, instead of having a bland, conformist and conservative output. In finding a balance between these opposite forms of thinking, the main question is whether the strategic reasoning process should actually be a predominantly rational affair, or a much more generative process. Is strategizing largely a rational activity, requiring logical thinking to be the dominant modus operandi, with occasional bits of creativity needed here and there to generate new ideas? Or is strategizing largely a generative activity, requiring creative thinking to be the standard operating procedure, with occasional bits of logical analysis needed here and there to weed out unfeasible ideas?

The answer to this question should be found in the strategic management literature. Yet, upon closer inspection, the opinions outlined in both the academic and popular literature show that views vary widely among researchers and managers alike. A wide spectrum of differing perspectives can be recognized, each giving their own angle on how strategic thinking should use logic and creativity – sometimes explicitly mentioning the need for both, but more commonly making implicit assumptions about the role of logic and creativity in strategy processes.

As was outlined in Chapter 1, it is not the intention here to summarize all of the 'schools of thought' on the topic of strategic thinking. Instead, only the two most opposite points of view will be presented in this section. These two poles in the debate are not necessarily the most popular points of view and at times they might seem somewhat extreme, arguing in terms of 'black-and-white' instead of shades of grey. Yet, as the two pure 'archetypes' they do form the ultimate pair for a good debate – a clear-cut thesis and antithesis in a process of dialectical enquiry.

At the one end of the spectrum, there are those who argue that strategic reasoning should be a predominantly rational process, requiring logic to be the main form of thinking in use. This point of view is referred to as the 'rational reasoning perspective'. At the other pole, there are those who argue that the essence of strategic reasoning is the ability to break through orthodox beliefs and generate new insights and behaviours, requiring the extensive use of creativity. This point of view will be referred to as the 'generative reasoning perspective'.

The rational reasoning perspective

 Strategists employing the rational reasoning perspective argue that strategic reasoning is predominantly a 'logical activity' (Andrews, 1987, Reading 2.1). To deal with strategic problems the strategist must first consciously and thoroughly analyze the problem situation. Data must be gathered on all developments external to the organization, and these data must be processed to pinpoint the opportunities and threats in the organization's environment. Furthermore, the organization itself must be appraised, to uncover its strengths and weaknesses and to establish which resources are available. Once the problem has been defined, a number of alternative strategies can be identified by matching external opportunities to internal strengths. Then, the strategic options must be extensively screened, by evaluating them on a number of criteria, such as internal consistency, external consonance, competitive advantage, organizational feasibility, potential return and risks. The best strategy can be selected by comparing the scores of all options and determining the level of risk the strategist is willing to take. The chosen strategy can subsequently be implemented.

This type of intellectual effort requires well-developed analytical skills. Strategists must be able to rigorously, consistently and objectively comb through huge amounts of data, interpreting and combining findings to arrive at a rich picture of the current problem situation. Possible solutions require critical appraisal and all possible contingencies must be logically thought through. Advocates of the rational reasoning perspective argue that such reasoning strongly resembles the problem-solving approach of chess grand masters (Simon, 1987). They also thoroughly assess their competitive position, sift through a variety of options and calculate which course of action brings the best chances of success. Therefore, the reasoning processes of chess grand masters can be used as an analogy for what goes on in the mind of the strategist.

While depicted here as a purely step-by-step process of recognition, analysis, formulation and implementation, proponents of the rational reasoning perspective note that in reality strategists often have to backtrack and redo some of these steps, as new information becomes available or chosen strategies do not work out. Strategists attempt to be as comprehensive, consistent and rigorous as possible in their analyses and calculations, but of course they cannot know everything and their conclusions are not always perfect: even with the most advanced forecasting techniques, not all developments can be foreseen; even with state of the art market research, some trends can be missed; even with cutting edge test marketing, scenario analyses, competitive simulations and net present value calculations, some selected strategies can turn out to be failures. Strategists are not all knowing, and do make mistakes – their rationality is limited by incomplete information and imperfect cognitive abilities. Yet, strategists try to be as rational as possible. Simon (1957) refers to this as 'bounded rationality' – 'people act intentionally rational, but only limitedly so'. This coincides with Ambrose Bierce's famous sarcastic definition of logic as 'the art of thinking and reasoning in strict accordance with the limitations and incapacities of the human misunderstanding'.

The (boundedly) rational strategist must sometimes improvise to make up for a lack of information, but will try to do this as logically as possible. Inferences and speculation will always be based on the facts as known. By articulating assumptions and explicitly stating the facts and arguments on which conclusions have been based, problem definitions and solutions can be debated within the firm to confirm that they have been arrived at using sound reasoning. This strongly resembles the scientific method, in that hypotheses are formulated and tested as a means for obtaining new knowledge. Only by this consistent alignment of mental models with empirical reality can the strategist avoid the danger of becoming stuck with an outdated cognitive map.

The alternative to this rational approach, it is often pointed out, is to be irrational and illogical, which surely cannot be a desirable alternative for the strategist. Non-rational reasoning comes in a variety of forms. For instance, people's thinking can be guided by their emotions. Feelings such as love, hate, guilt, regret, pride, anxiety, frustration and embarrassment can all cloud the strategist's understanding of a problem situation and the possible solutions. Adherents of the rational reasoning perspective do not dispute the importance of emotions – the purpose of an organization is often based on 'personal values, aspirations and ideals', while the motivation to implement strategies is also rooted in human emotions. However, the actual determination of the optimal strategy is a 'rational undertaking' *par excellence* (Andrews, 1987).

Neither is intuitive thinking an appealing alternative for strategists. Of course, intuition can often be useful: decision rules based on extensive experience (cognitive heuristics) are often correct (even if they have been arrived at unconsciously) and they save time and effort. For example, Simon argues that even chess grand masters make many decisions intuitively, based on tacit rules of thumb, formulated through years of experience. Yet, intuitive judgements must be viewed with great suspicion, as they are difficult to verify and infamously unreliable (e.g. Hogarth, 1980; Schwenk, 1984). Where possible, intuitive thinking should be made explicit – the strategist's cognitive map should be captured on paper (e.g. Anthony *et al.*, 1993; Eden, 1989), so that the reasoning of the strategist can be checked for logical inconsistencies.

Creative thinking is equally suspicious. Of course, creativity techniques can be beneficial for triggering some unexpected ideas. Whether it is by means of brainstorming, six thinking caps or action art, creative thinking can spark some unconventional thoughts. Even a rational scientist like Newton has remarked that 'no great discovery was ever made without a bold guess'. But this is usually where the usefulness of creativity ends, and to which it should be limited. In creative thinking anything goes and that can lead to anything between odd and ludicrous. To be able to sift the sane from the zany, logic is needed. To make sense of the multitude of new ideas the logical thinker must analyze and evaluate them. A more serious drawback is that in practice many 'creative ideas' are just someone's unsupported beliefs, dressed up to sound fashionable. 'Creative thinking' is often just an excuse for intellectual laziness.

In conclusion, advocates of the rational reasoning perspective argue that emotions, intuition and creativity have a small place in the strategic reasoning process, but that logical thinking should be the dominant ingredient. It could be said that the rational reasoning process of the strategist strongly resembles that of the scientist. The scientific methods of research, analysis, theorizing and falsification are all directly applicable to the process of strategic reasoning – so much so, that the scientific method can be used as the benchmark for strategy development processes. Consequently, the best preparation for effective strategic reasoning would be to be trained in the scientific tradition.

EXHIBIT 2.2 THE RATIONAL REASONING PERSPECTIVE

BERKSHIRE HATHAWAY: NOT OUTSIDE THE BOX

At the peak of the dotcom boom in September 1999, few people were derided as much as Warren Buffett (1930), chairman of the insurance and investment conglomerate Berkshire Hathaway. Buffett – admiringly nicknamed the Sage of Omaha – had gained a phenomenal reputation as investor during the 1980s and 1990s, but to most it was clear that he hadn't grasped the opportunities presented by the internet. The grand old man might have been the guru of the old economy, but he simply did not understand the new rules of the information age. He was considered a pitiful example of a once brilliant mind that had not been able to make the leap beyond conventional beliefs and comprehend the 'new paradigm'. The investment strategy of Berkshire Hathaway was deemed hopelessly outdated. When almost all funds were rushing into new economy shares, the investment portfolio of Berkshire consisted of companies like Coca-Cola, Walt Disney, Gillette and The Washington Post. The shares of Berkshire traded at the lowest level in years.

The person least perturbed by this new, dubious status was Buffett himself. In his 1999 annual 'Letter to the Berkshire Hathaway Shareholders', he displayed an untouched faith in the fundamentals that had made him one of the richest people in the world: 'If we have a strength, it is in recognizing when we are operating well within our circle of competence and when we are approaching the perimeter. (…) we just stick with what we understand. If we stray, we will have done so inadvertently, not because we got restless and substituted hope for rationality.' He refused to invest in internet stocks, which he considered 'chain letters', in which early participants get rich at the expense of later ones. As the bubble eventually burst, Buffett was more than exonerated.

This famous episode was neither Buffett's first provocative stance against lemming behaviour, nor his last. Following his personal mantra that 'when other investors are greedy be fearful, but when other investors are fearful be greedy', Buffett has always stuck to his analysis and gone against the grain. For instance, during the stock market frenzy of 1969 he was widely ridiculed for not participating in the party. To his shareholders he wrote: 'I am out of step with present conditions. When the game is no longer played your way, it is only human to say the new approach is all wrong, bound to lead to trouble, and so on. On one point, however, I am clear. I will not abandon a previous approach whose logic I understand (although I find it difficult to apply) even though it may mean foregoing large, and apparently easy, profits to embrace an approach which I don't fully understand, have not practiced

successfully, and which possibly could lead to substantial permanent loss of capital.'

Forty years later, during the worst stock market crash since the Great Depression, Warren Buffett was again held to be a fool. With Berkshire Hathaway having lost up to US$25 billion of market value within the span of a year, he was arguing that the time was right to boldly buy: 'I don't like to opine on the stock market, and again I emphasize that I have no idea what the market will do in the short term. Nevertheless, I'll follow the lead of a restaurant that opened in an empty bank building and then advertised: "Put your mouth where your money was." Today my money and my mouth both say equities.' True to his words, Buffett invested US$5 billion in Goldman Sachs in September 2008, as panic about the American financial system was breaking out all around him. In his 2008 shareholder report, he frankly admitted that he had done 'some dumb things in investments', but that overall he was satisfied with the new additions to his portfolio: 'Whether we're talking about socks or stocks, I like buying quality merchandise when it is marked down.'

When valuing companies, Buffett's approach has always been based on a thorough analysis of company fundamentals, 'to separate investment from speculation'. Ultimately, share prices will reflect these fundamentals and therefore nothing can substitute for a meticulous diagnosis of the sustainability of the competitive advantage of a firm. As Buffett puts it: 'I try to buy stock in businesses that are so wonderful that an idiot can run them. Because sooner or later, one will.' Following this logic, he stays away from investing in ill-understood businesses and in fast-changing industries, 'in which the long-term winners are hard to identify'. And when he invests, he keeps his shareholdings for years, or even decades. 'Risk', he states, 'comes from not knowing what you're doing.'

His emphasis on rational reasoning and not following the wisdom of crowds ('a public opinion poll is no substitute for thought'), does not mean that he takes a liking to those who pretend to be scientific and rational ('beware of geeks bearing formulas'). He warns of professionals and academicians talking of efficient markets, dynamic hedging and betas: 'Their interest in such matters is understandable, since techniques shrouded in mystery clearly have value to the purveyor of investment advice. After all, what witch doctor has ever achieved fame and fortune by simply advising "Take two aspirins"?'

While still going strong at his advanced age, many commentators have warned that Berkshire Hathaway is vulnerable due to its dependence on its elderly chairman. Buffett's response so far has been

totally in character: 'I've reluctantly discarded the notion of my continuing to manage the portfolio after my death - abandoning my hope to give new meaning to the term "thinking outside the box".'

Co-author: Martijn Rademakers

Sources: www.berkshirehathaway.com; *The Economist*, 15 March 2001; 18 December 2008; *The Sunday Times*, 1 March 2009; *The New York Times*, 16 October 2008, 1 March 2009.

The generative reasoning perspective

 Strategists taking a generative reasoning perspective are strongly at odds with the unassailable position given to logic in the rational reasoning perspective. They agree that logic is important, but stress that it is often more a hindrance than a help. The heavy emphasis placed on rationality can actually frustrate the main objective of strategic reasoning – to generate novel insights, new ways of defining problems and innovative solutions. Analysis can be a useful tool, but as the aim of strategic reasoning is to tear up outdated cognitive maps and to reinvent the future, creative thinking should be the driving force, and logical thinking a supporting means. For this reason, proponents of the generative reasoning perspective argue that strategists should avoid the false certainty projected by rational approaches to strategic reasoning, but should nurture creativity as their primary cognitive asset.

In the generative reasoning perspective, emphasis is placed on the 'wicked' nature of strategic problems (Rittel, 1972; Mason and Mitroff, 1981). It is argued that strategic problems cannot be easily and objectively defined, but that they are open to interpretation from a limitless variety of angles. The same is true for the possible solutions – there is no fixed set of problem solutions from which the strategist must select the best one. Defining and solving strategic problems, it is believed, is fundamentally a creative activity. As such, strategic reasoning has very little in common with the thought processes of the aforementioned chess grand master, as was presumed by the rationalists. Playing chess is a 'tame' problem. The problem definition is clear and all options are known. In the average game of chess, consisting of 40 moves, 10 120 possibilities have to be considered (Simon, 1972). This makes it a difficult game for humans to play, because of their limited computational capacities. Chess grand masters are better at making these calculations than other people and are particularly good at computational short cuts – recognizing which things to figure out and which not. However, even the best chess grand masters have been beaten at the game by highly logical computers with a superior number crunching capability. For the poor chess grand master, the rules of the game are fixed and there is little room for redefining the problem or introducing innovative approaches.

Engaging in business strategy is an entirely different matter. Strategic problems are wicked. Problem definitions are highly subjective and there are no fixed sets of solutions. It is therefore impossible to 'identify' the problem and 'calculate' an optimal solution. Opportunities and threats do not exist, waiting for the analyst to discover them. A strategist understands that a situation can be 'viewed' as an opportunity and 'believes' that certain factors can be threatening if not approached properly. Neither can strengths and weaknesses be objectively determined – a strategist can employ a company characteristic as a strength, but can also turn a unique company quality into a weakness by a lack of vision. Hence, doing a SWOT analysis (strengths, weaknesses, opportunities and threats) actually has little to do with logical analysis, but in reality is nothing less than a creative interpretation of a problem situation. Likewise, it is a fallacy to believe that strategic options follow more or less logically from the characteristics of the firm and its environment. Strategic options are not 'deduced from the facts' or selected from a 2×2 matrix, but are dreamt up. Strategists must be able to use their imaginations to generate previously unknown solutions. If more than one strategic option emerges from the mind of the strategist, these cannot be simply scored and ranked to choose the optimal one. Some analyses can be done, but ultimately the strategist will have to intuitively judge which vision for the future has the best chance of being created in reality.

Hence, a generative reasoning process is more than just brainstorming or having a wild idea every once in a while. In a generative reasoning process all strategic thinking activities are oriented towards creating, instead of calculating – 'inventing' instead of 'finding' (Liedtka, 2000). This type of creative thinking is very hard work, as strategists must leave the intellectual safety of generally accepted concepts to explore new ideas, guided by little else than their intuition. They must be willing to operate without the security of a dominant logic; experimenting, testing, arguing, challenging, doubting and living amongst the rubble of demolished certainties, without having new certainties to give them shelter. To proponents of the generative reasoning perspective, it is essential for strategists to have a slightly contrarian (Hurst, Rush and White, 1989), revolutionary predisposition (Hamel, 1996). Strategists must enjoy the challenge of thinking 'out of the box', even when this disrupts the status quo and is not much appreciated by those with their two feet (stuck) on the ground. As Picasso once remarked, 'every act of creation is first of all an act of destruction' – strategists must enjoy the task of eroding old paradigms and confronting the defenders of those beliefs. And if some analyses can be done to support this effort, then they can serve a valuable purpose in the overall strategy process.

In conclusion, advocates of the generative reasoning perspective argue that the essence of strategic reasoning is the ability to creatively challenge 'the tyranny of the given' (Kao, 1996) and to generate new and unique ways of understanding and doing things. As such, strategic reasoning closely resembles the frame-breaking behaviour common in the arts. In fields such as painting, music, motion pictures, dancing and architecture, artists are propelled by the drive to challenge convention and to seek out innovative approaches. Many of their methods, such as brainstorming, experimentation, openness to intuition, and the use of metaphors, contradictions and paradoxes, are directly applicable to developing strategy. Consequently, the best preparation for strategic reasoning might actually be to be trained in the artistic tradition of iconoclastic creativity and mental flexibility.

EXHIBIT 2.3   THE GENERATIVE REASONING PERSPECTIVE

GOOGLE: EXPERIMENT IN ANARCHY

Chrome, Streetview, Earth, Android, iGoogle, Maps, Gmail, AdWord, Book Search, Scholar, AdSense, Gtalk, Orkut ... the list goes on and on. While only around since 1998, Google has been able to create an almost endless stream of innovations. These are not just interesting new products, but potential industry rule breakers, many already disrupting the status quo. In each case, Google has taken its overall mission 'to organize the world's information and make it universally accessible and useful', and applied it to specific customer needs, leading to spectacularly novel results. Despite having grown to over 22,000 employees by 2008 and having sales nearing US$22 billion, the company has maintained its ability to be creative and reinvent the way people find and use data. This to the delight of customers around the world and to the increasing anguish of more orthodox competitors.

It is somewhat ironic that a company that was founded on using a logical algorithm to search through mountains of data, relies largely on creativity to come up with new ideas. The reason, according to Google's managing director, Jim Lecinski, is because frame-breaking ideas can't be found, but have to be generated. So, internally Google's product development is not structured like a search engine, rigorously and logically figuring out the best possible answer, but like a laboratory, with many small teams working on ideas and experimenting with a variety of possible answers. This part of the organization is even called Google Labs. The nimble teams at Google Labs make it easier to move fast and get everyone on a team fully involved, but at the same time it is not the intention that each team works in isolation. Sharing and soliciting feedback is the name of the game, both with others inside Google, as with customers. Beta versions are launched early and often to get user inputs, thus truly harnessing the wisdom of crowds. To facilitate internal sharing, special software tracks who is working on what, so that networking within the Google ecosystem is extremely efficient.

When it comes to employees, Google has a preference for generalists over specialists, as they have a broader view and can more easily make intuitive connections between seemingly unconnected ideas. These employees are expected to spend their time according to the 70/20/10 model; 70% of their time should be allocated to Google's mainstream businesses, while 20% should be invested in the development of new services that are already recognized projects. The final 10% is available to pursue their dreams – anything that fits within the mission and respects the core company value to 'do no evil'. In this way, many personal dreams have eventually turned into Google mainstays, amongst others Google Earth.

To make the innovation system work, Google has placed significant emphasis on creating the right culture. Starting with its famous Googleplex headquarters in Mountain View, California, the company has put a lot of effort into nurturing a laid back, fun and collaborative culture, which at the same time is driven by a passion to create, innovate and serve. In that sense, its culture and way of working closely reflect those of the internet – cooperative, irreverent, optimistic, transparent and slightly geeky. When Google CEO Eric Schmidt remarked that 'the internet is the first thing that humanity has built that humanity doesn't understand; the largest experiment in anarchy that we've ever had' he could have also been speaking about Google.

So, what is Google's strategy? According to co-founder Sergey Brin the majority of Google's most successful projects have been bottom-up, not conceived by top management, so it's hard to predict what will happen next. 'We don't have a traditional strategy (...) planning process, like you'd find in traditional technical companies,' says Schmidt, allowing Google 'to innovate very, very quickly, which I think is a real strength of the company.' However, this doesn't mean that at Google everything goes and creativity can run rampant. 'Creativity loves constraint,' says Lecinski. 'Let people explore, but set clear boundaries for that exploration.' And data is certainly not irrelevant; great creative ideas need to be checked against reality and then 'data beats opinion'.

Co-author: Martijn Rademakers

Sources: www.google.com; www.wikipedia.org; *Business Week*, 14 December 2008; *The Economist*, 20 November 2008; *New York Times*, 9 July 2009; *Harvard Business Review*, April 2008 & October 2008.

INTRODUCTION TO THE DEBATE AND READINGS

When you have eliminated the impossible, whatever remains, however improbable, must be the truth.
'Sherlock Holmes', Arthur Conan Doyle (1859–1930); English novelist

Imagination is more important than knowledge.
Albert Einstein (1879–1955); German-American physicist

So, how should managers engage in strategic reasoning processes and how should they encourage fruitful strategic reasoning within their organizations? Should managers view strategic reasoning primarily as a rational and deductive activity or as a more imaginative and generative process? Should strategists train themselves to follow procedural rationality – rigorously analysing problems using scientific methods and calculating the optimal course of action? Or should strategists practice to 'boldly go where no one has gone before' – redefining problems and inventing new courses of action?

As mentioned earlier, the strategic management literature does not offer a clear-cut answer to the question of which strategic reasoning approach is the optimal one. On the contrary, the variety of opinions among strategy theorists is dauntingly large, with many incompatible prescriptions being given. At the centre of the debate on strategic reasoning is the paradox of logic and creativity. Many points of view have been put forward on how to reconcile these opposing demands, but no common perspective has yet emerged. Therefore, it is up to individual strategists to form their own opinion on how best to deal with the topic of strategic thinking.

To help strategists to come to grips with the variety of perspectives on this issue, four readings have been selected that each shed their own light on the debate. As outlined in Chapter 1, the first two readings will be representative of the two poles in this debate (see Table 2.1), while the second set of two readings will bring in extra arguments to add further flavour to the discussion.

Selecting the first reading to represent the rational reasoning perspective was not easy, as few authors make a point of arguing their rational leanings. The position of logical thinking is so entrenched in much of the management literature, that most writers adopt the rational reasoning perspective without making this choice explicit. Hence, it has not proved possible to present a vocal defender of this perspective to get a nicely polarized debate going. Instead, as the first debate reading in this chapter, a classic work has been selected that is a good example of the rational approach to strategic thinking. This reading, 'The Concept of Corporate Strategy', by Kenneth Andrews, has been drawn from one of the most influential textbooks in the field of strategy, *Business Policy: Text and Cases* (Christensen, Andrews, *et al.,* 1987). Andrews is arguably one of the godfathers of strategic management and this chapter from his book has had considerable impact on theorists and practitioners alike. True to the rational reasoning perspective, Andrews argues that strategy analysis and formulation should be conducted consciously, explicitly and rationally. In his view, strategic reasoning is a 'logical activity', while subsequent strategy

TABLE 2.1   Rational reasoning versus generative reasoning perspective

	Rational reasoning perspective	*Generative reasoning perspective*
Emphasis on	Logic over creativity	Creativity over logic
Dominant cognitive style	Analytical	Intuitive
Thinking follows	Formal, fixed rules	Informal, variable rules
Nature of thinking	Deductive and computational	Inductive and imaginative
Direction of thinking	Vertical	Lateral
Problem defining seen as	Recognizing and analyzing activities	Reflecting and sense-making activities
Problem solving seen as	Formulation and implementation activities	Imagining and doing activities
Value placed on	Consistency and rigour	Unorthodoxy and innovativeness
Assumption about reality	Objective, (partially) knowable	Subjective, (partially) creatable
Thinking hindered by	Incomplete information	Adherence to current cognitive map
Decisions based on	Calculation	Judgement
Metaphor	Strategy as science	Strategy as art

implementation 'comprises a series of subactivities that are primarily administrative'. It should be noted that in this article Andrews is positioning himself in opposition to strategic incrementalists (see Chapter 3), not vis-à-vis proponents of the generative reasoning perspective. Therefore, he does not counter any of the major arguments raised by advocates of this perspective.

The second reading in this chapter, highlighting the views of the generative reasoning perspective, is 'The Mind of the Strategist', by Kenichi Ohmae. Ohmae, formerly head of McKinsey's Tokyo office, is one of Japan's best known strategy authors. In this reading, taken from the book of the same name, Ohmae argues that the mind of the strategist is not dominated by linear, logical thinking. On the contrary, a strategist's thought processes are 'basically creative and intuitive rather than rational'. In his view, 'great strategies. . . originate in insights that are beyond the reach of conscious analysis'. He does not dismiss logic as unnecessary, but notes that it is insufficient for arriving at innovative strategies. Yet, he observes that in most large companies creative strategists 'are being pushed to the sidelines in favour of rational, by-the-numbers strategic and financial planners', leading to a withering of strategic thinking ability.

In Reading 2.3, Jeanne Liedtka suggests an alternative metaphor to the rational reasoning's 'strategy as science' and the generative reasoning's 'strategy as art'. Her article is entitled 'Strategy as Design', and her argument is that the process of designing offers a rich metaphor for understanding the process of strategizing – somewhere between the processes of science and art. In describing what designers do, Liedtka points out that there is a fundamental distinction between design and science: designers invent something new, while science investigates that which exists. Designers 'conjure an image of a future reality', which cannot be determined logically, and as such designers resemble artists. Yet, designers are different to artists in that they do not create in a free-flow 'trial-and-error' type of way. Designers, like scientists, formulate hypotheses for testing, build models and check for the internal consistency of the design. Liedtka goes on to describe a number of characteristics of successful 'design thinking' that she believes are also true for effective strategic thinking. Towards the end of her article she responds to concerns about design thinking voiced by Henry Mintzberg (1990, 1991) in a well-known exchange with Igor Ansoff (1991). In subsequent works (1994; 1998, Mintzberg *et al.*), Mintzberg has used the label 'Design School' to refer to people such as Kenneth Andrews, which Liedtka believes does not do justice to the design metaphor. Many of the points made by Liedtka about using design thinking as part of the overall strategy formation process will be examined in more detail in Chapter 3.

The fourth reading, 'Decision-Making: It's Not What You Think', is by Henry Mintzberg and Frances Westley. Mintzberg, in particular, is well known for his critical stabs at the rational reasoning perspective and for challenging managers to move beyond a mechanistic view of strategizing. Yet, in this reading Mintzberg and Westley are more even-handed in looking at different styles of strategizing. This reading has been selected because it neatly summarizes the strengths and weaknesses of starting the strategic reasoning process at different points in Figure 2.2 – either starting with problem identification and diagnosis (which the authors call 'thinking first'), or with solution conception (called 'seeing first'), or with solution realization (called 'doing first'). Mintzberg and Westley argue that the rational approach of starting with identification and diagnosis, and then moving to conception and realization is actually uncommon and only works best for certain types of problems (ones that Mason and Mitroff would call 'tame'). They do not dismiss 'thinking first' outright, but strongly suggest that the other two forms of decision-making should be accorded at least equal prominence. In 'seeing first' the strategic reasoning process is started with conception (new ideas incubate before extensive analysis), after which outcomes are diagnosed and realized. In 'doing first' people start by acting and reflect on what they are doing along the way – putting realization in the lead, with conception, diagnosis and identification trailing behind. In both 'seeing first' and 'doing first' logic plays a much less dominant role, providing space for creativity to blossom and for new solutions to be generated. The authors conclude that 'no organization can do without any one approach', and therefore that the three forms should be combined. Yet, despite Mintzberg and Westley's advice to blend 'thinking first', 'seeing first' and 'doing first', the question remains how this can be achieved in one and the same organization, while the conditions fostering the one approach are so different to the conditions enabling the other.

The concept of corporate strategy

By Kenneth Andrews[1]

What strategy is

Corporate strategy is the pattern of decisions in a company that determines and reveals its objectives, purposes, or goals, produces the principal policies and plans for achieving those goals, and defines the range of business the company is to pursue, the kind of economic and human organization it is or intends to be, and the nature of the economic and noneconomic contribution it intends to make to its shareholders, employees, customers, and communities. In an organization of any size or diversity, *corporate strategy* usually applies to the whole enterprise, while *business strategy,* less comprehensive, defines the choice of product or service and market of individual businesses within the firm. Business strategy is the determination of how a company will compete in a given business and position itself among its competitors. Corporate strategy defines the businesses in which a company will compete, preferably in a way that focuses resources to convert distinctive competence into competitive advantage. Both are outcomes of a continuous process of strategic management that we will later analyze in detail.

The strategic decision contributing to this pattern is one that is effective over long periods of time, affects the company in many different ways, and focuses and commits a significant portion of its resources to the expected outcomes. The pattern resulting from a series of such decisions will probably define the central character and image of a company, the individuality it has for its members and various publics, and the position it will occupy in its industry and markets. It will permit the specification of particular objectives to be attained through a timed sequence of investment and implementation decisions and will govern directly the deployment or redeployment of resources to make these decisions effective.

Some aspects of such a pattern of decisions may be in an established corporation unchanging over long periods of time, like a commitment to quality, or high technology, or certain raw materials, or good labour relations.

Other aspects of a strategy must change as or before the world changes, such as a product line, manufacturing process, or merchandising and styling practices. The basic determinants of company character, if purposefully institutionalized, are likely to persist through and shape the nature of substantial changes in product-market choices and allocation of resources.

It would be possible to extend the definition of strategy for a given company to separate a central character and the core of its special accomplishment from the manifestations of such characteristics in changing product lines, markets, and policies designed to make activities profitable from year to year. *The New York Times,* for example, after many years of being shaped by the values of its owners and staff, is now so self-conscious and respected an institution that its nature is likely to remain unchanged, even if the services it offers are altered drastically in the direction of other outlets for its news-processing capacity.

It is important, however, not to take the idea apart in another way, that is, to separate goals from the policies designed to achieve those goals. The essence of the definition of strategy I have just recorded is pattern. The interdependence of purposes, policies, and organized action is crucial to the particularity of an individual strategy and its opportunity to identify competitive advantage. It is the unity, coherence, and internal consistency of a company's strategic decisions that position the company in its environment and give the firm its identity, its power to mobilize its strengths, and its likelihood of success in the marketplace. It is the interrelationship of a set of goals and policies that crystallizes from the formless reality of a company's environment a set of problems an organization can seize upon and solve.

What you are doing, in short, is never meaningful unless you can say or imply what you are doing it for: the quality of administrative action and the motivation lending it power cannot be appraised without knowing its relationship to purpose. Breaking up the system of corporate goals and the character-determining major policies for attainment leads to narrow and mechanical

[1]Source: This article was adapted with permission from Chapter 2 of *The Concept of Corporate Strategy*, 1987, McGraw-Hill Companies Inc.

conceptions of strategic management and endless logic chopping.

We should get on to understanding the need for strategic decisions and for determining the most satisfactory pattern of goals in concrete instances. Refinement of definition can wait, for you will wish to develop definition in practice in directions useful to you.

Summary statements of strategy

Before we proceed to clarification of this concept by application, we should specify the terms in which strategy is usually expressed. A summary statement of strategy will characterize the product line and services offered or planned by the company, the markets and market segments for which products and services are now or will be designed, and the channels through which these markets will be reached. The means by which the operation is to be financed will be specified, as will the profit objectives and the emphasis to be placed on the safety of capital versus level of return. Major policy in central functions such as marketing, manufacturing, procurement, research and development, labour relations, and personnel, will be stated where they distinguish the company from others, and usually the intended size, form, and climate of the organization will be included.

Each company, if it were to construct a summary strategy from what it understands itself to be aiming at, would have a different statement with different categories of decision emphasized to indicate what it wanted to be or do.

Reasons for not articulating strategy

For a number of reasons companies seldom formulate and publish a complete strategy statement. Conscious planning of the long-term development of companies has been until recently less common than individual executive responses to environmental pressure, competitive threat, or entrepreneurial opportunity. In the latter mode of development, the unity or coherence of corporate effort is unplanned, natural, intuitive, or even nonexistent. Incrementalism in practice sometimes gives the appearance of consciously formulated strategy, but may be the natural result of compromise among coalitions backing contrary policy proposals or skilful improvisatory adaptation to external forces. Practising managers who prefer muddling through to

the strategic process would never commit themselves to an articulate strategy.

Other reasons for the scarcity of concrete statements of strategy include the desirability of keeping strategic plans confidential for security reasons and ambiguous to avoid internal conflict or even final decision. Skilful incrementalists may have plans in their heads that they do not reveal, to avoid resistance and other trouble in their own organization. A company with a large division in an obsolescent business that it intends to drain of cash until operations are discontinued could not expect high morale and cooperation to follow publication of this intent. In a dynamic company, moreover, where strategy is continually evolving, the official statement of strategy, unless couched in very general terms, would be as hard to keep up to date as an organization chart. Finally, a firm that has internalized its strategy does not feel the need to keep saying what it is, valuable as that information might be to new members.

Deducing strategy from behaviour

In your own company you can do what most managements have not done. In the absence of explicit statements and on the basis of your experience, you may deduce from decisions observed what the pattern is and what the company's goals and policies are, on the assumption that some perhaps unspoken consensus lies behind them. Careful examination of the behaviour of competitors will reveal what their strategy must be. At the same time none of us should mistake apparent strategy visible in a pattern of past incremental decisions for conscious planning for the future. What will pass as the current strategy of a company may almost always be deduced from its behaviour, but a strategy for a future of changed circumstances may not always be distinguishable from performance in the present. Strategists who do not look beyond present behaviour to the future are vulnerable to surprise.

Formulation of strategy

Corporate strategy is an organization process, in many ways inseparable from the structure, behaviour, and culture of the company in which it takes place. Nevertheless, we may abstract from the process two important aspects, interrelated in real life but separable for the purposes of analysis. The first of these we may call formulation, the second implementation. Deciding what strategy should be may be approached as a rational undertaking, even if, as in life, emotional attachments (to metal skis or investigative reporting) may complicate choice among future alternatives (for ski manufacturers or alternative newspapers). The principle subactivities of strategy formulation as a logical activity include identifying opportunities and threats in the company's environment and attaching some estimate of risk to the discernible alternatives. Before a choice can be made, the company's strengths and weaknesses should be appraised together with the resources on hand and available. Its actual or potential capacity to take advantage of perceived market needs or to cope with attendant risks should be estimated as objectively as possible. The strategic alternative that results from matching opportunity and corporate capability at an acceptable level of risk is what we may call an *economic strategy*.

The process described thus far assumes that strategists are analytically objective in estimating the relative capacity of their company and the opportunity they see or anticipate in developing markets. The extent to which they wish to undertake low or high risk presumably depends on their profit objectives. The higher they set the latter, the more willing they must be to assume a correspondingly high risk that the market opportunity they see will not develop or that the corporate competence required to excel competition will not be forthcoming.

So far we have described the intellectual processes of ascertaining what a company *might do* in terms of environmental opportunity, of deciding what it *can do* in terms of ability and power, and of bringing these two considerations together in optimal equilibrium. The determination of strategy also requires consideration of what alternatives are preferred by the chief executive and perhaps by his or her immediate associates as well, quite apart from economic considerations. Personal values, aspirations and ideals do, and in our judgement quite properly should, influence the final choice of purposes. Thus what the executives of a company *want to do* must be brought into the strategic decision.

Finally strategic choice has an ethical aspect – a fact much more dramatically illustrated in some industries than in others. Just as alternatives may be ordered in terms of the degree of risk they entail, so may they be examined against the standards of responsiveness to the expectations of society the strategist elects. Some alternatives may seem to the executive considering them more attractive than others when the public good or

service to society is considered. What a company *should do* thus appears as a fourth element of the strategic decision.

The ability to identify the four components of strategy – (a) market opportunity, (b) corporate competence and resources, (c) personal values and aspirations, and (d) acknowledged obligations to segments of society other than stockholders – is easier to exercise than the art of reconciling their implications in a final choice of purpose. Taken by itself each consideration might lead in a different direction.

If you put the various aspirations of individuals in your own organization against this statement you will see what I mean. Even in a single mind contradictory aspirations can survive a long time before the need to calculate trade-offs and integrate divergent inclinations becomes clear. Growth opportunity attracted many companies to the computer business after World War II. The decision to diversify out of typewriters and calculators was encouraged by growth opportunity and excitement that captivated the managements of RCA, General Electric, and Xerox, among others. But the financial, technical, and marketing requirements of this business exceeded the capacity of most of the competitors of IBM. The magnet of opportunity and the incentive of desire obscured the calculations of what resources and competence were required to succeed. Most crucially, where corporate capability leads, executives do not always want to go. Of all the components of strategic choice, the combination of resources and competence is most crucial to success.

The implementation of strategy

Since effective implementation can make a sound strategic decision ineffective or a debatable choice successful, it is as important to examine the processes of implementation as to weigh the advantages of available strategic alternatives. The implementation of strategy comprises a series of subactivities that are primarily administrative. If purpose is determined, then the resources of a company can be mobilized to accomplish it. An organizational structure appropriate for the efficient performance of the required tasks must be made effective by information systems and relationships permitting coordination of subdivided activities. The organizational processes of performance measurement, compensation, management development – all of them enmeshed in systems of incentives and controls – must be directed towards the kind of behaviour required by organizational purpose. The role of personal leadership is important and sometimes decisive in the accomplishment of strategy. Although we know that organizational structure and processes of compensation, incentives, control, and management development influence and constrain the formulation of strategy, we should look first at the logical proposition that structure should follow strategy in order to cope later with the organizational reality that strategy also follows structure. When we have examined both tendencies, we will understand and to some extent be prepared to deal with the interdependence of the formulation and implementation of corporate purpose. Figure 2.1.1 may be useful in understanding the analysis of strategy as a pattern of interrelated decisions.

Criteria for evaluation

How is the actual or proposed strategy to be judged? How are we to know that one strategy is better than another? A number of important questions can regularly be asked. As is already evident, no infallible indicators are available. With practice they will lead to reliable intuitive discriminations.

■ Is the strategy identifiable and has it been made clear either in words or in practice? The degree to which attention has been given to the strategic alternatives available to a company is likely to be basic to the soundness of its strategic decision. To cover in empty phrases ('Our policy is planned profitable growth in any market we can serve well') an absence of analysis of opportunity or actual determination of corporate strength is worse than to remain silent, for it conveys the illusion of a commitment when none has been made. The unstated strategy cannot be tested or contested and is likely therefore to be weak. If it is implicit in the intuition of a strong leader, the organization is likely to be weak and the demands the strategy makes upon it are likely to remain unmet. A strategy must be explicit to be effective and specific enough to require some actions and exclude others.

■ Does the strategy exploit fully domestic and international environmental opportunity? The relation between market opportunity and organizational development is a critical one in the design of future plans. Unless growth is incompatible with the

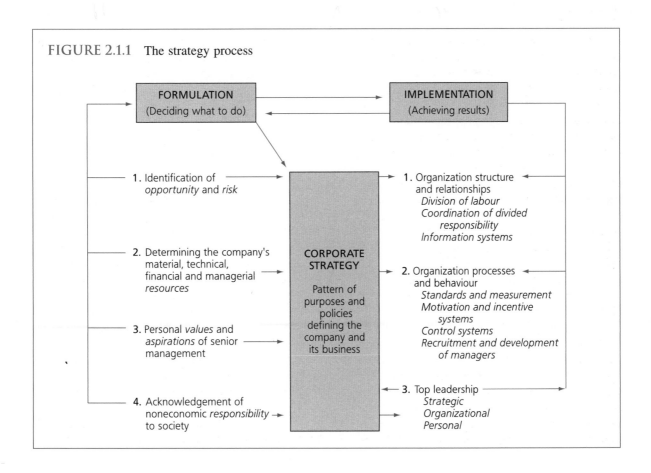

FIGURE 2.1.1   The strategy process

resources of an organization or the aspirations of its management, it is likely that a strategy that does not purport to make full use of market opportunity will be weak also in other aspects. Vulnerability to competition is increased by lack of interest in market share.

■ Is the strategy consistent with corporate competence and resources, both present and projected? Although additional resources, both financial and managerial, are available to companies with genuine opportunity, the availability of each must be finally determined and programmed along a practicable time scale. This may be the most difficult question in this series.

■ Are the major provisions of the strategy and the programme of major policies of which it is comprised internally consistent? One advantage of making as specific a statement of strategy as is practicable is the resultant availability of a careful check on fit, unity, coherence, compatibility, and synergy – the state in which the whole of anything can be viewed as greater than the sum of its parts.

■ Is the chosen level of risk feasible in economic and personal terms? The riskiness of any future plan should be compatible with the economic resources of the organization and the temperament of the managers concerned.

■ Is the strategy appropriate to the personal values and aspirations of the key managers? Conflict between personal preferences, aspirations, and goals of the key members of an organization and the plan for its future is a sign of danger and a harbinger of mediocre performance or failure.

■ Is the strategy appropriate to the desired level of contribution to society? To the extent that the chosen economic opportunity of the firm has social costs, such as air or water pollution, a statement of intention to deal with these is desirable and prudent.

■ Does the strategy constitute a clear stimulus to organizational effort and commitment? Generally speaking, the bolder the choice of goals and the wider the range of human needs they reflect, the more successfully they will appeal to the capable membership of a healthy and energetic organization.

■ Are there early indications of the responsiveness of markets and market segments to the strategy? A strategy may pass with flying colours all the tests so far proposed, and may be in internal consistency and uniqueness an admirable work of art. But if within a time period made reasonable by the company's resources and the original plan the strategy does not work, then it must be weak in some way that has escaped attention.

A business enterprise guided by a clear sense of purpose rationally arrived at and emotionally ratified by commitment is more likely to have a successful outcome, in terms of profit and social good, than a company whose future is left to guesswork and chance. Conscious strategy does not preclude brilliance of improvisation or the welcome consequences of good fortune. Its cost is principally thought and work for which it is hard but not impossible to find time.

READING 2.2

The mind of the strategist

By Kenichi Ohmae[1]

As a consultant I have had the opportunity to work with many large Japanese companies. Among them are many companies whose success you would say must be the result of superb strategies. But when you look more closely, you discover a paradox. They have no big planning staffs, no elaborate, gold-plated strategic planning processes.

Some of them are painfully handicapped by lack of the resources – people, money, and technology – that seemingly would be needed to implement an ambitious strategy. Yet despite all these handicaps, they are outstanding performers in the marketplace. Year after year, they manage to build share and create wealth.

[1]Source: This article was adapted with permission from the Introduction, and Chapters 1 and 17 of *The Mind of the Strategist: The Art of Japanese Busines*, McGraw-Hill, New York, 1982.

How do they do it? The answer is easy. They may not have a strategic planning staff, but they do have a strategist of great natural talent: usually the founder or chief executive. Often – especially in Japan, where there is no business school – these outstanding strategists have had little or no formal business education, at least at the college level. They may never have taken a course or read a book on strategy. But they have an intuitive grasp of the basic elements of strategy. They have an idiosyncratic mode of thinking in which company, customers, and competition merge in a dynamic interaction out of which a comprehensive set of objectives and plans for action eventually crystallizes.

Insight is the key to this process. Because it is creative, partly intuitive, and often disruptive of the status quo, the resulting plans might not even hold water from the analyst's point of view. It is the creative element in these plans and the drive and will of the mind that conceived them that give these strategies their extraordinary competitive impact.

Both in Japan and in the West, this breed of natural or instinctive strategist is dying out or at least being pushed to the sidelines in favour of rational, by-the-numbers strategic and financial planners. Today's giant institutions, both public and private, are by and large not organized for innovation. Their systems and processes are all oriented toward incremental improvement – doing better what they are doing already. In the United States, the pressure of innumerable social and governmental constraints on corporate activities – most notably, perhaps, the proliferation of government regulations during the 1960s and 1970s – has put a premium on the talent for adaptation and reduced still further the incentive to innovate. Advocates of bold and ambitious strategies too often find themselves on the sidelines, labelled as losers, while the rewards go to those more skilled at working within the system. This is especially true in mature industries, where actions and ideas often move in narrow grooves, forcing out innovators. Conversely, venture capital groups tend to attract the flexible, adaptive minds.

In all times and places, large institutions develop cultures of their own, and success is often closely tied to the ability to conform. In our day, the culture of most business corporations exalts logic and rationality; hence, it is analysts rather than innovators who tend to get ahead. It is not unreasonable to say that many large US corporations today are run like the Soviet economy. In order to survive, they must plan ahead comprehensively, controlling an array of critical functions in every detail. They specify policies and procedures in meticulous detail, spelling out for practically everyone

what can and what cannot be done in particular circumstances. They establish hurdle rates, analyze risks, and anticipate contingencies. As strategic planning processes have burgeoned in these companies, strategic thinking has gradually withered away.

My message, as you will have guessed by now, is that successful business strategies result not from rigorous analysis but from a particular state of mind. In what I call the mind of the strategist, insight and a consequent drive for achievement, often amounting to a sense of mission, fuel a thought process which is basically creative and intuitive rather than rational. Strategists do not reject analysis. Indeed they can hardly do without it. But they use it only to stimulate the creative process, to test the ideas that emerge, to work out their strategic implications, or to ensure successful execution of high potential 'wild' ideas that might otherwise never be implemented properly. Great strategies, like great works of art or great scientific discoveries, call for technical mastery in the working out but originate in insights that are beyond the reach of conscious analysis.

If this is so – if the mind of the strategist is so deeply at odds with the culture of the corporation – how can an already institutionalized company recover the capacity to conceive and execute creative business strategies? In a book entitled *The Corporate Strategist* that was published in Japan in 1975, I attempted to answer that question in a specifically Japanese context.

In Japan, a different set of conditions from those in the West inhibits the creation of bold and innovative strategies. In the large Japanese company, promotion is based on tenure; there is no fast track for brilliant performers. No one reaches a senior management post before their mid-fifties, and chief executives are typically over 60 – well past the age when they are likely to be able to generate dynamic strategic ideas. At the same time, the inventive, often aggressive younger people have no means of contributing in a significant way to the strategy of the corporation. The result: strategic stagnation or the strong probability of it.

How, I asked myself, could the mind of the strategist, with its inventive élan, be reproduced in this kind of corporate culture? What were the ingredients of an excellent strategist, and how could they be reproduced in the Japanese context? These were the questions I addressed in my book. The answer I came up with involved the formation within the corporation of a group of young 'samurais' who would play a dual role. On the one hand they would function as real strategists, giving free rein to their imagination and entrepreneurial flair in order to come up with bold and innovative strategic ideas. On the other hand they would serve as staff analysts, testing out, digesting, and assigning priorities to the ideas, and providing staff assistance to line managers in implementing the approved strategies. This 'samurai' concept has since been adopted in several Japanese firms with great success.

Such a solution would not fit the circumstances of the typical American or European company. Yet it seems to me that the central notion of my book and of a sequel published in Japan 18 months later is relevant to the problem of strategic stagnation in any organization. There are ways in which the mind of the strategist can be reproduced, or simulated, by people who may lack a natural talent for strategy. Putting it another way, although there is no secret formula for inventing a successful strategy, there are some specific concepts and approaches that can help anyone develop the kind of mentality that comes up with superior strategic ideas. Thus the reader will find in this reading no formulas for successful business strategy. What I will try to supply in their place is a series of hints that may help him or her develop the capacity for and the habit of strategic thinking.

Analysis: The starting point

Analysis is the critical starting point of strategic thinking. Faced with problems, trends, events, or situations that appear to constitute a harmonious whole or come packaged as a whole by the common sense of the day, the strategic thinker dissects them into their constituent parts. Then, having discovered the significance of these constituents, he reassembles them in a way calculated to maximize his advantage.

In business as on the battlefield, the object of strategy is to bring about the conditions most favourable to one's own side, judging precisely the right moment to attack or withdraw and always assessing the limits of compromise correctly. Besides the habit of analysis, what marks the mind of the strategist is an intellectual elasticity or flexibility that enables him to come up with realistic responses to changing situations, not simply to discriminate with great precision among different shades of grey.

In strategic thinking, one first seeks a clear understanding of the particular character of each element of a situation and then makes the fullest possible use of human brainpower to restructure the elements in the most advantageous way. Phenomena and events in the real world do not always fit a linear model. Hence the most reliable means of dissecting a situation into its constituent parts and reassembling them in the desired pattern is not a step-by-step methodology such as

systems analysis. Rather, it is that ultimate nonlinear thinking tool, the human brain. True strategic thinking thus contrasts sharply with the conventional mechanical systems approach based on linear thinking. But it also contrasts with the approach that stakes everything on intuition, reaching conclusions without any real breakdown or analysis (Figure 2.2.1).

No matter how difficult or unprecedented the problem, a breakthrough to the best possible solution can come only from a combination of rational analysis, based on the real nature of things, and imaginative reintegration of all the different items into a new pattern, using nonlinear brainpower. This is always the most effective approach to devising strategies for dealing successfully with challenges and opportunities, in the market arena as on the battlefield.

Determining the critical issue

The first stage in strategic thinking is to pinpoint the critical issue in the situation. Everyone facing a problem naturally tries in his or her own way to penetrate to the key issue. Some may think that one way is as good as another and that whether their efforts hit the mark is largely a matter of luck. I believe it is not a question of luck at all but of attitude and method. In problem solving, it is vital at the start to formulate the question in a way that will facilitate the discovery of a solution.

Suppose, for example, that overtime work has become chronic in a company, dragging down profitability. If we frame the question as, 'What should be done to reduce overtime?', many answers will suggest themselves:

- work harder during the regular working hours;
- shorten the lunch period and coffee breaks;
- forbid long private telephone conversations.

Such questioning is often employed by companies trying to lower costs and improve product quality by using zero defect campaigns and quality control (QC) circles that involve the participation of all employees. Ideas are gathered, screened, and later incorporated in the improvement program. But this approach has an intrinsic limitation. *The questions are not framed to point toward a solution; rather, they are directed toward finding remedies to symptoms.*

Returning to our overtime problem, suppose we frame the question in a more solution-oriented way: Is this company's work force large enough to do all the work required? To this question there can be only one of

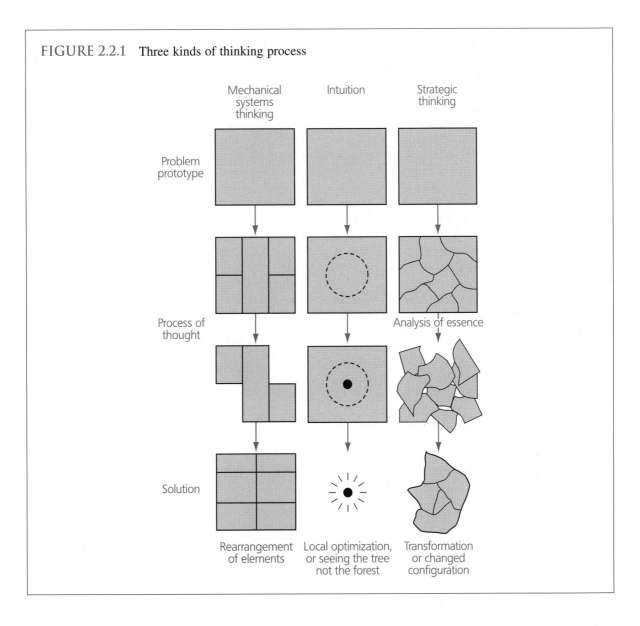

FIGURE 2.2.1   Three kinds of thinking process

two answers – yes or no. To arrive at the answer yes, a great deal of analysis would be needed, probably including a comparison with other companies in the same industries, the historical trend of workload per employee, and the degree of automation and computerization and their economic effectiveness. On the other hand, if – after careful perusal of the sales record, profit per employee, ratio between direct and indirect labour, comparison with other companies, and so on – the answer should turn out to be no (i.e. the company is currently understaffed), this in itself would be tantamount to a solution of the original problem. This solution – an increase in personnel – will be validated by all the usual management indicators. And if the company adopts this

solution, the probability increases that the desired outcome will actually follow. This way, objective analysis can supplant emotional discussions.

That is not the only way the question could have been formulated, however. We might have asked it this way: Do the capabilities of the employees match the nature of the work? This formulation, like the previous one, is oriented toward deriving a possible solution. Here too, a negative answer would imply a shortage of suitable personnel, which would in turn suggest that the solution should be sought either in staff training or in recruiting capable staff from elsewhere. On the other hand, if the answer is yes, this indicates that the problem of chronic overtime lies not in the nature of the work but in the amount of the workload. Thus, not training but adding to the work force would then be the crucial factor in the solution.

If the right questions are asked in a solution-oriented manner, and if the proper analyses are carried out, the final answer is likely to be the same, even though it may have started from a differently phrased question and may have been arrived at by a different route. In either case, a question concerning the nature and amount of work brings the real issue into focus and makes it easy to arrive at a clear-cut verdict.

It is hard to overstate the importance of formulating the question correctly. People who are trained and motivated to formulate the right questions will not offer vague proposals for 'improvements', as are seen in many suggestion boxes. They will come up with concrete, practical ideas.

By failing to grasp the critical issues, too many senior managers today impose great anxiety on themselves and their subordinates, whose efforts end in failure and frustration. Solution-oriented questions can be formulated only if the critical issue is localized and grasped accurately in the first place. A clear common understanding of the nature of a problem that has already been localized provides a critical pressure to

come up with creative solutions. When problems are poorly defined or vaguely comprehended, one's creative mind does not work sharply. The greater one's tolerance for lukewarm solutions, half measures and what the British used to call muddling through, the more loosely the issue is likely to be defined. For this reason, isolating the crucial points of the problem – in other words, determining the critical issue – is most important to the discovery of a solution. The key at this initial stage is to *narrow down the issue by studying the observed phenomena closely.*

Figure 2.2.2 illustrates one method often used by strategists in the process of abstraction, showing how it might work in the case of a large, established company faced with the problem of declining competitive vigour.

The first step in the abstraction process is to use such means as brainstorming and opinion polls to assemble and itemize the respects in which the company is at a disadvantage vis-à-vis its competitors. These points can then be classified under a smaller number of headings (shown in Figure 2.2.2 as Concrete phenomena) according to their common factors.

Next, phenomena sharing some common denominator are themselves combined into groups. Having

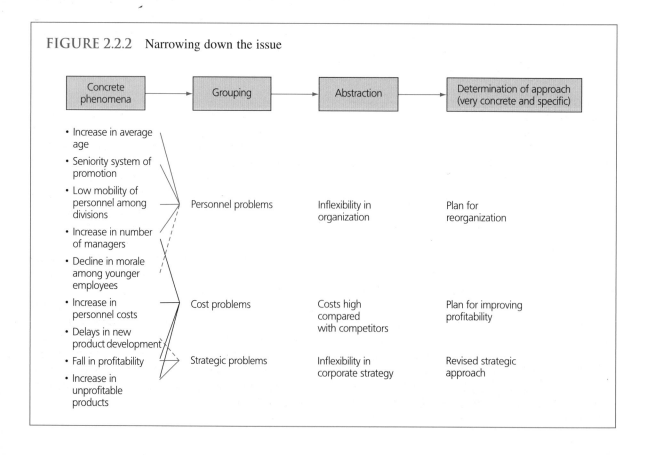

FIGURE 2.2.2   Narrowing down the issue

done this, we look once again at each group as a unit and ask ourselves what crucial issue each unit poses. The source of the problem must be understood before any real solution can be found, and the process of abstraction enables us to bring the crucial issues to light without the risk of overlooking anything important.

Once the abstraction process has been completed, we must next decide on the right approach to finding a solution. Once we have determined the solution in principle, there remains the task of working out implementation programs and then compiling detailed action plans. No solution, however perfectly it may address the critical issue, can be of the slightest use until it is implemented. Too many companies try to short-circuit the necessary steps between identification of critical issues and line implementation of solutions by skipping the intermediate steps: planning for operational improvement and organizing for concrete actions. Even the most brilliant line manager cannot translate an abstract plan into action in a single step.

The art of strategic thinking

Most of us are familiar with Thomas Alva Edison's recipe for inventive genius: '1 percent inspiration, 99 percent perspiration.' The same ratio holds true for creativity in any endeavour, including the development of business strategy. Don't be misled by the ratio. That spark of insight *is* essential. Without it, strategies disintegrate into stereotypes. But to bring insight to fruition as a successful strategy takes method, mental discipline, and plain hard work.

So far we have been exploring the mental processes or thought patterns for the 'grunt' part of the strategy. When we come to creative inspiration, however, our task becomes exceedingly difficult. Insight is far easier to recognize than define. Perhaps we might say that creative insight is the ability to combine, synthesize, or reshuffle previously unrelated phenomena in such a way that you get more out of the emergent whole than you have put in.

What does this all mean to the strategist? Can creativity be taught? Perhaps not. Can it be cultivated consciously? Obviously I believe so, or I wouldn't have written this article. Inventive geniuses such as Thomas Edison or Edwin Land are by definition rare exceptions. For most of us, creative insight is a smouldering ember that must be fanned constantly to glow. I strongly believe that when all the right ingredients are present – sensitivity, will, and receptiveness – they can be nurtured by example, direction,

and conditioning. In short, creativity cannot be taught, but it can be learned.

Putting it more prosaically, we need to identify and stimulate those habits or conditions which nurture creativity and at the same time to crystallize the constraints or boundaries defining our probability of success. In my experience, there are at least three major constraints to which the business strategist needs to be sensitive. I think of them as the essential Rs: reality, ripeness, and resources.

Let's begin with *reality*. Unlike scientific conceptualizers or creative artists, business strategists must always be aware of the customer, the competition, and the company's field of competence. *Ripeness,* or timing, is the second key consideration that the business strategist must address. Unless the time is ripe for the proposed strategy, it is virtually certain to fail. *Resources,* my third R, constitute such an obvious constraint that it is amazing that they should be ignored or neglected by strategists. Yet examples abound of strategies that failed because their authors were not sensitive to their own resource limitations. Take diversification as a case in point. Few food companies trying to move into pharmaceuticals, chemical companies moving into foods, or electronic component manufacturers moving into final assembly have succeeded. The basic reason in most cases has been that the companies involved were not sensitive to the limitations of their own internal resources and skills.

Conditions of creativity

Being attuned to the three Rs is a necessary precondition of creative insight, but in itself it will not fan the spark of creative power within us. For that, other elements are needed. Obviously, there is no single approach that will dependably turn anyone into a superstrategist, but there are certain things we can consciously do to stretch or stimulate our creative prowess. Most important, I believe, we need to cultivate three interrelated conditions – an initial charge, directional antennae, and a capacity to tolerate static.

Call it what you will – vision, focus, inner drive – the initial charge must be there. It is the mainspring of intuitive creativity. We have seen how Yamaha, originally a wood-based furniture company, was transformed into a major force in the leisure industry by just such a vision, born of one man's desire to bring positive enrichment into the lives of the work-oriented Japanese. From this vision he developed a totally new thrust for Yamaha.

An entire family of musical instruments and accessories – organs, trumpets, cornets, trombones, guitars, and so on – was developed to complement Yamaha's pianos. These were followed by stereo equipment, sporting goods, motorcycles and pleasure boats. Music schools were established. Then came the Yamaha Music Camp, complete with a resort lodge complex, a game reserve, an archery range, and other leisure-oriented pursuits. Today, Yamaha plans concerts and is involved with concert hall management as well, reaping profits while enriching the lives of millions of Japanese.

If the initial charge provides the creative impetus, directional antennae are required to recognize phenomena, which, as the saying goes, are in the air. These antennae are the component in the creative process that uncovers and selects, among a welter of facts and existing conditions, potentially profitable ideas that were always there but were visible only to eyes not blinded by habit.

Consider how these directional antennae work for Dr Kazuma Tateishi, founder and chairman of Omron Tateishi Electronics. Tateishi has an uncanny flair for sensing phenomena to which the concept of flow can be applied. He perceived the banking business as a flow of cash, traffic jams and congested train stations as blocked flows of cars and people, and production lines as a physical flow of parts. From these perceptions evolved the development of Japan's first automated banking system, the introduction of sequence controllers that automatically regulate traffic according to road conditions and volume, and the evolution of the world's first unmanned railroad station based on a completely automatic system that can exchange bills for coins, issue tickets and season passes, and adjust fares and operate turnstiles. Today, Omron's automated systems are used in many industrial operations from production to distribution. Dr Tateishi is a remarkable example of a man whose directional antennae have enabled him to implement his youthful creed: 'Man should do only what only man can do.'

Creative concepts often have a disruptive as well as a constructive aspect. They can shatter set patterns of thinking, threaten the status quo, or at the very least stir up people's anxieties. Often when people set out to sell or implement a creative idea, they are taking a big risk of failing, losing money, or simply making fools of themselves. That is why the will to cope with criticism, hostility, and even derision, while not necessarily a condition of creative thinking, does seem to be an important characteristic of successful innovative strategists. To squeeze the last drop out of my original metaphor, I call this the static-tolerance component of creativity.

Witness the static that Soichiro Honda had to tolerate in order to bring his clean-engine car to market. Only corporate insiders can tell how much intracompany interference he had to cope with. That the government vainly brought severe pressure on him to stay out of the auto market is no secret, however. Neither is the public ridicule he bore when industry experts scoffed at his concept.

Dr Koji Kobayashi of NEC tolerated static of a rather different kind. Despite prevailing industry trends, he clung fast to his intuitive belief (some 20 years ahead of its time) that computers and telecommunications would one day be linked. To do so, he had to bear heavy financial burdens, internal dissension, and scorn. All this leads me to a final observation. Strategic success cannot be reduced to a formula, nor can anyone become a strategic thinker merely by reading a book. Nevertheless, there are habits of mind and modes of thinking that can be acquired through practice to help you free the creative power of your subconscious and improve your odds of coming up with winning strategic concepts.

The main purpose of this contribution is to encourage you to do so and to point out the directions you should pursue. The use of Japanese examples to illustrate points and reinforce assertions may at times have given it an exotic flavour, but that is ultimately of no importance. Creativity, mental productivity and the power of strategic insight know no national boundaries. Fortunately for all of us, they are universal.

READING
2.3
Strategy as design

By Jeanne Liedtka[1]

The field of business strategy is in need of new metaphors. We need new metaphors that better capture the challenges of making strategies both real and realizable, metaphors that bring life to the human dimension of creating new futures for institutions. In that spirit, I attempt here to interest the reader in the resuscitation of an old metaphor that I see as offering new possibilities – the metaphor of strategy as a process of design. The metaphor of design offers rich possibilities for helping us to think more deeply about the formation of business strategy, and it is time to liberate the idea of design from its association with outmoded approaches to strategy.

Such liberation would allow us to see one more important goal of strategy formulation as the design of a 'purposeful space' – virtual rather than physical – in which particular activities, capabilities, and relationships are encouraged. These, in turn, produce a particular set of associated behaviours and hence, outcomes in the marketplace. Theories of design have much to teach us about the creation of such spaces.

The idea of design

As we move into the literature of the design field, a set of themes and issues emerges over time in the discussion of the design process. The notion of synthesis – the creation of a coherent harmonious whole emerging with integrity from a collection of specific design choices – constitutes the earliest and most fundamental notion of what constitutes 'good' design, in architecture as well as in business strategy. More recent views have tended to emphasize the concept of the 'best' solution to a stated problem. Perhaps most emblematic of this shift in focus was the emergence of the 'Bauhaus' School in Germany in the 1920s, with its emphasis on flexibility, function, and connecting design to what Walter Gropius called 'the stuff of life'. Together, these themes of beauty and utility illustrate modern design's interest in serving two functions – utilitarian and symbolic.

Models of the design process

Within this context of the goals and principles of design, serious attention to the process of design is a fairly recent phenomena (Bazjanac, 1964) occurring in the middle of this century and in tandem with developments in the fields of mathematics and systems science, which had a major impact on design thinking.

All early models of the design process have one thing in common: they all view the design process as a sequence of well defined activities and are all based on the assumption that the ideas and principles of the scientific method can be applied to it. Design theorists of this era generally describe the design process as consisting of two phases: analysis and synthesis. In the analytical phase, the problem is decomposed into a hierarchy of problem subsets, which in turn produce a set of requirements. In the ensuing stage of synthesis, these individual requirements are grouped and realized in a complete design.

Unlike in business, however, these early models with their emphasis on 'systematic procedures and prescribed techniques' met with immediate criticism for the linearity of their processes and their lack of appreciation for the complexity of design problems. Hörst Rittel (1972) first called attention to what he described as the 'wicked nature' of design problems. Such problems, he asserted, have a unique set of properties. Most importantly, they have no definitive formulation or solution. The definition of the 'problem' itself is open to multiple interpretations (dependent upon the *Weltanschauung,* or worldview, of the observer) and potential solutions are many, with none of them able to be proven to be correct. Writers in the field of business strategy have argued that many issues in strategy formulation are 'wicked' as well, and that traditional approaches to dealing with them are similarly incapable of producing intelligent solutions (Mason and Mitroff, 1981).

Rittel asserted that these 'first generation models' were ill suited for dealing with wicked problems. Instead, he saw design as a process of argumentation,

[1]Source: © 2000, by The Regents of the University of California. Reprinted from the *California Management Review,* Vol. 42, No. 3. By permission of The Regents.

rather than merely analysis and synthesis. Through argumentation, whether as part of a group or solely within the designer's own mind, the designer gained insights, broadened his or her *Weltanschauung*, and continually refined the definition of the problem and its attendant solution. Thus, the design process came to be seen as one of negotiation rather than optimization, fundamentally concerned with learning and the search for emergent opportunities. Rittel's arguments are consistent with recent calls in the strategy literature for more attention to 'strategic conversations' (Liedtka and Rosenblum, 1996), in which a broad group of organizational stakeholders engage in dialogue-based processes out of which shared understanding and, ultimately, shared choices emerge.

The role of hypotheses in the design process

More recently design theorists have explored a number of these issues in greater depth. The issue of the role of the scientific method in the design process has been an on-going focus of discussion. In general, studies of design processes frequently suggest a hypothesis-driven approach similar to the traditional scientific method. Nigel Cross (1995) in reviewing a wide range of studies of design processes in action, notes, 'It becomes clear from these studies that architects, engineers, and other designers adopt a problem-solving strategy based on generating and testing potential solutions.' Donald Schon (1983) after studying architects in action, described design as 'a shaping process' in which the situation 'talks back' continually and 'each move is a local experiment which contributes to the global experiment of reframing the problem'. Schon's designer begins by generating a series of creative 'what if' hypotheses, selecting the most promising one for further enquiry. This enquiry takes the form of a more evaluative 'if then' sequence, in which the logical implications of that particular hypothesis are more fully explored and tested. The scientific method then – with its emphasis on cycles of hypothesis generating and testing and the acquisition of new information to continually open up new possibilities – remains central to design thinking.

However, the nature of 'wicked problems' makes such trial and error learning problematic. Rittel makes this point from the perspective of architecture – a building, once constructed, cannot be easily changed, and so learning through experimentation in practice is undesirable. This is the ultimate source of 'wickedness' in such problems: their indeterminacy places a premium on experimentation, while the high cost of change makes such experimentation problematic. As in business, we know that we might be able or be forced to change our strategies as we go along – but we'd rather not. This apparent paradox is what gives the design process – with its use of constructive forethought – its utility. The designer substitutes mental experiments for physical ones. In this view, design becomes a process of hypothesis generating and testing, whose aim is to provide the builder with a plan that tries to anticipate the general nature of impending changes.

A concern of the design process, however, is the risk of 'entrapment', in which a designer's investment in early hypotheses makes them difficult to give up as the design progresses, despite the presence of disconfirming data. Design is most successful, then, when it creates a virtual world, a 'learning laboratory', where mental experiments can be conducted risk-free and where investments in early choices can be minimized. As Schon (1983) points out:

> *Virtual worlds are contexts for experiment within which practitioners can suspend or control some of the everyday impediments to rigorous reflection–inaction. They are representative worlds of practice in the double sense of 'practice'. And practice in the construction, maintenance, and use of virtual worlds develops the capacity for reflection–inaction which we call artistry.*

Design's value lies in creating a 'virtual' world in which experiments (mental rather than physical) can be conducted on a less costly basis. This offers a very different perspective from which to think about the creation of business strategies. Traditional approaches to strategy have shared the perspective of early design theorists and assumed that planning creates value primarily through a process of controlling, integrating, and coordinating – that the power of planning is in the creation of a systematic approach to problem-solving – de-composing a complex problem into sub-problems to be solved and later integrated back into a whole. While integration, coordination, and control are all potentially important tasks, a focus on these dramatically underestimates the value of planning in a time of change. The metaphor of design calls attention to planning's ability to create a virtual world in which hypotheses can be generated and tested in low cost ways.

Invention versus discovery

Contemporary design theorists have been especially attentive to the areas in which design and science diverge, however, as well as converge. The most fundamental difference between the two, they argue, is that design thinking deals primarily with what does not yet exist; while scientists deal with explaining what is. A common theme is that scientists discover the laws that govern today's reality, while designers invent a different future. Designers are, of course, interested in explanations of current reality to the extent that such understanding reveals patterns in the underlying relationships essential to the process of formulating and executing the new design successfully, but the emphasis remains on the future. Thus, while both methods of thinking are hypothesis-driven, the design hypothesis differs from the scientific hypothesis. Rather than using traditional reasoning modes of induction or deduction, March (1976) argues that design thinking is adductive: 'Science investigates extant forms. Design initiates novel forms. A scientific hypothesis is not the same thing as a design hypothesis . . . A speculative design cannot be determined logically, because the mode of reasoning involved is essentially adductive.'

Adductive reasoning uses the logic of conjecture. Cross borrows from philosopher C.S. Peirce this elaboration of the differences among the modes: 'Deduction proves that something must be; induction shows that something actually is operative; adduction merely suggests that something may be.' Thus, a capacity for creative visualization – the ability to 'conjure' an image of a future reality that does not exist today, an image so vivid that it appears to be real already – is central to design. Successful designers – in business or the arts – are great conjurers, and the design metaphor reminds us of this.

Underlying this emphasis on conjectural thinking and visualization is an on-going enquiry into the relationship between verbal and non-verbal mediums. Design theorists accord a major role to the use of graphic and spatial modelling media – not merely for the purpose of communicating design ideas, but for the generation of ideas as well. 'Designers think with their pencils' is a common refrain. Some theorists have argued that verbalization may in fact 'obstruct intuitive creation', noting that the right side of the brain is mute. Arnheim (1992) asserts that the image 'unfolds' in the mind of the designer as the design process progresses; and that it is, in fact, the unfolding nature of the image that makes creative design possible: As long as the guiding image is still developing it remains tentative, generic, vague. This vagueness, however, is by no means a negative quality. Rather it has the positive quality of a topological shape. As distinguished from geometric shapes, a topological shape stands for a whole range of possibilities without being tangibly committed to any one of them. Being undefined in its specifics, it admits distortions and deviations. Its pregnancy is what the designer requires in the search for a final shape. Thus, the designer begins with what Arnheim calls 'a center, an axis, a direction', from which the design takes on increasing levels of detail and sophistication as it unfolds.

Architect Frank Gehry's description of the Guggenheim Bilbao Museum captures these themes of experimentation in virtual worlds, and the role of sketches and models in the unfolding process (see Exhibit 2.3.1). In the story of Gehry's creation, we witness the designer bringing his or her own previous experiences to the new site and, through a process of iteration that moves back and forth between the general idea and the specific design of its subcomponents, the design evolves, gaining clarity and definition.

EXHIBIT 2.3.1 CASE STUDY

THE DESIGN OF THE GUGGENHEIM BILBAO: AN UNFOLDING PROCESS

In describing this century's 100 'greatest design hits', *New York Times* Architecture Critic Herbert Muschamp included ten buildings, among them Antoni Gaudi's Casa Mila (1906), Mies van der Rohe's Barcelona Pavilion (1929), Frank Lloyd Wright's Fallingwater (1936), Le Corbusier's Chapel at Ronchamp (1950), and I.M. Pei's Bank of China tower in Hong Kong (1982). Number 100, and the only building listed designed in the last decade, was Frank Gehry's Guggenheim Museum in Bilbao. Writing in the *Los Angeles Times,* Architecture Critic Nicolai Ouroussoff effuses:

Gehry has achieved what not so long ago seemed impossible for most architects: the invention of radically new architectural forms that nonetheless speak to the man on the street. Bilbao has become a pilgrimage point for those who, until now, had little interest in architecture. Working class Basque couples arrive toting children on weekends. The cultural elite veer off their regular flight paths so they can tell friends that they, too, have seen the building in the flesh. Gehry has become, in the eyes of a world attuned to celebrity, the great American architect, and, in the process, he has brought hope to an entire profession.

Van Bruggen chronicles the story of the design of the Bilbao Museum, tracing, through a series of interviews with Gehry, the unfolding nature of the design process, with its emphasis on experimentation and iteration, and its comfort with ambiguity. Gehry explains how the design process begins: 'You bring to the table certain things. What's exciting, you tweak them based on the context and the people. . . Krens (Guggenheim Foundation Director), Juan Ignacio (future director of the Bilbao museum site), the Basques, their desire to use culture, to bring the city to the river. And the industrial feeling. . . I knew all of that when I started sketching.'

Gehry's first sketches are on pieces of hotel stationery they are 'fast scrawls and mere annotations. . . the hand functions as an immediate tool of the mind'. Later, on an airplane, as the design evolves, the sketches begin to capture the basics of his scheme for the site. As Van Bruggen notes, he has

begun to take hold of the complexities of the site. . . Allowing the pen to take possession of the space helps him to clarify the program requirements and re-imagine the problem.. . . Elements shift and are regrouped to contribute to a different kind of understanding, a leap from the conditional, technical aspects of building into unrestrained, intuitive sense perception, into sculptural architecture. From here on, a delicate process of cutting apart while holding together takes place, a going back and forth from sketches into models in order to solve problems and refine the plastic shapes of the building.

Gehry explains 'I start drawing sometimes, not knowing where it is going. . . It's like feeling your way along in the dark, anticipating that something will come out usually. I become a voyeur of my own thoughts as they develop, and wander about

them. Sometimes I say "boy here it is, it's coming". I understand it, I get all excited and from there I'll move to the models, and the models drain all of the energy, and need information on scale and relationships that you can't conceive in totality in drawings. The drawings are ephemeral. The models are specific; they then become like the sketches in the next phase.' The models change scale and materials as the project progresses, becoming increasingly detailed, and moving from paper to plastic to wood to industrial foam. In total, six different models were developed over the course of the Bilbao project.

Computer modelling plays a critical role as the physical models evolve. 'The Guggenheim Museum Bilbao would not have stayed within the construction budget allotted by the Basque Administration had it not been for Catia, a computer program originally developed for the French aerospace industry', Van Bruggen observes. Gehry's staff customized the software to model the sculptural shapes, accelerating the layout process and devising more economically buildable designs. These computer models were always translated back into physical models.

Throughout, the process remains iterative. Gehry observes that 'often the models take me down a blind alley, and I go back to sketches again. They become the vehicle for propelling the project forward when I get stuck'. In the end, the process from first sketch into final building remains one of 'unfolding':

In the first sketch, I put a bunch of principles down. Then I become self critical of those images and those principles, and they evoke the next set of responses. And as each piece unfolds, I make the models bigger and bigger, bringing into focus more elements and more pieces of the puzzle: And once I have the beginning, a toehold into where I'm going, I then want to examine the parts in more detail. And those evolve, and at some point I stop, because that's it. I don't come to a conclusion, but I think there's a certain reality of pressure to get the thing done that I accept.

Sources: See H. Muschamp, 'Blueprint: The Shock of the Familiar', *New York Times*, 13 December 1998, section 6, p. 61, col. I; N. Ouroussoff, 'I'm Frank Gehry', *Los Angeles Times*, 25 October 1998, home edition, p. 17; C. Van Bruggen, Frank O. Gehry: *Guggenheim Museum Bilbao* (New York, NY: Guggenheim Museum Publications, 1997, pp. 33, 31, 71, 03, 135, 104, 130).

The general versus the particular

In addition to the prominent role played by conjecture and experimentation in design thinking, there is also a fundamental divergence between the concern of science for generalizable laws and design's interest in the particulars of individual cases. Buchanan and Margolis (1995) argue that there can be no 'science' of design:

> *Designers conceive their subject matter on two levels: general and particular. On a general level, a designer forms an idea or a working hypothesis about the nature of products or the nature of the human-made in the world . . . But such philosophies do not and cannot constitute sciences of design in the sense of the natural, social, or humanistic science. The reason for this is simple: design is fundamentally concerned with the particular, and there is no science of the particular . . . Out of the specific possibilities of a concrete situation, the designer must conceive a design that will lead to this or that particular product . . . (The designer does not begin with) an indeterminate subject waiting to be made determinate. It is an indeterminate subject waiting to be made specific and concrete.*

This quality of indeterminacy has profound implications for the design process. First, the tendency to project determinacy onto past choices – 'prediction after the fact' – is ever present and must be avoided, or it undermines and distorts the true nature of the design process. Second, creative designs do not passively await discovery – designers must actively seek them out. Third, the indeterminacy of the process suggests the possibility for both exceptional diversity and continual evolution in the outcomes produced (even within similar processes). Finally, because design solutions are always matters of invented choice, rather than discovered truth, the judgement of designers is always open to question by the broader public.

Each of these implications resonates with business experiences. Richard Pascale's (1984) contrasting stories of Honda's entry into the US motorcycle market chronicles the kind of retrospective rationalization that can accompany well known business success stories. Similarly the need to seek out the future is one of the most common prescriptions in today's writings on strategy. Similarly, the search for and belief in the ideal of the one right strategy can stifle creativity, cause myopia that misses opportunity and paralyse organizational decision processes.

However, the final implication – this notion of the inevitable need to justify to others the 'rightness' of the design choices made – is perhaps the most significant implication for the design of strategy processes in business organizations. Because strategic choices can never be 'proven' to be right, they remain always contestable and must be made compelling to others in order to be realized. This calls into play Rittel's role of argumentation and focuses attention on others, and the role of rhetoric in bringing them into the design conversation. Participation becomes key to producing a collective learning that both educates individuals and shapes the evolving choices simultaneously. Thus, design becomes a shared process, no longer the province of a single designer.

The role of values in design

Participation is critical, in part, because of the role that values, both individual and institutional, play in the design process. Values drive both the creation of the design and its acceptance.

Successful designs must embody both existing and new values simultaneously. 'Designers persuade', Williamson (1983) argues, 'by referencing accepted values and attributing these to a new subject.' It is the linkage to values already present in the *Weltanschauung* of the observer that allows the new design to find acceptance. The ability to establish and communicate these links is essential to achieving a successfully implemented design. Designs that embody values and purpose that are not shared – however innovative – fail to persuade.

Given the indeterminacy of the choices made, the ability to work with competing interests and values is inevitable in the process of designing. Buchanan and Margolis (1995) note that the question of whose values matter has changed over time, evolving from 1950s beliefs about the 'ability of experts to engineer socially acceptable results' for audiences that were seen as 'passive recipients of preformed messages', towards a view of audiences as 'active participants in reaching conclusions'.

The 'charette' plays a fundamental role in making design processes participative and making collective learning possible. Charettes are intensive brainstorming sessions in which groups of stakeholders come together. Their intention is to share, critique, and invent in a way that accelerates the development of large-scale projects. The charette at the Guggenheim Bilbao, for example, lasted for two months. One of the best known users of charettes is the architectural firm

Duaney Plater-Zyberg, who specialize in the design of new 'traditional towns' like Seaside, Florida, or Disney's Celebration. In their charette for the design of a new town outside of Washington, DC, Duaney Plater-Zyberg brought together architects, builders, engineers, local officials, traffic consultants, utility company representatives, computer experts, architecture professors, shopping mall developers, and townspeople for a discussion/critique that lasted seven days. The more complex the design process, the more critical a role the charette plays.

Design as dialectical

In the design literature, there is clear recognition of the fundamentally paradoxical nature of the design process and its need to mediate between diverging forces. Findeli (1990) notes: 'The discipline of design has got to be considered as paradoxical in essence and an attempt to eliminate one pole to the benefit of the other inevitably distorts its fundamental nature. [The goal becomes] to perceive this dualism as a dialectic, to transform this antagonism into a constructive dynamic.'

Echoing a similar theme, Buchanan and Margolis (1995) situate design as a dialectic at the intersection of constraint, contingency, and possibility. Successful design remains ever mindful of the constraints imposed by the materials and situation at hand, as well as the changing, and contingent, preferences of the audience that it serves. Simultaneously, however, it holds open the promise of the creation of new possibilities – available by challenging the status quo, reframing the problem, connecting the pieces, synthesizing the learning, and improvising as opportunities emerge.

The design of New York's Central Park by Frederick Law Olmsted and Calvert Vaux in the 1850s offers a look at the way in which successful design mediates the tension between constraint, contingency, and possibility. In the competition held to award the contract for the design of the park, only Olmsted and Vaux were able to envision a design that succeeded in meeting all of the requirements set forth – that the park must allow carriages to transverse it, rather than go around it, while retaining a park-like feel – requirements that other designers had seen as impossible to satisfy. They did this by envisioning the park space as three dimensional, rather than two, and proposing the construction of buried roadways that would allow cross-town vehicular traffic, but would be out of sight to those enjoying the park.

This tension created by the often diverging pulls of necessity, uncertainty, and possibility define design's terrain. It is a landscape where a mindset that embraces traditional dichotomies – art versus science, intuition versus analysis, the abstract versus the particular, ambiguity versus precision – find little comfort.

Implied characteristics of design thinking

To summarize, despite the avowed plurality that design theorists use to describe the field more precisely, a set of commonalties does emerge from the recent work on the attributes of design thinking.

First, design thinking is synthetic. Out of the often disparate demands presented by sub-units' requirements, a coherent overall design must be made to emerge. The process through which and the order in which the overall design and its sub-unit designs unfold remains a source of debate. What is clear is that the order in which they are given attention matters, as it determines the givens of subsequent designs, but ultimately successful designs can be expected to exhibit considerable diversity in their specifics.

Second, design thinking is adductive in nature. It is primarily concerned with the process of visualizing what might be, some desired future state, and creating a blueprint for realizing that intention.

Third, design thinking is hypothesis-driven. As such, it is both analytic in its use of data for hypothesis testing and creative in the generation of hypotheses to be tested. The hypotheses are of two types. Primary is the design hypothesis. The design hypothesis is conjectural and, as such, cannot be tested directly. Embedded in the selection of a particular promising design hypothesis, however, are a series of assumptions about a set of cause–effect relationships in today's environment that will support a set of actions aimed at transforming a situation from its current reality to its desired future state. These explanatory hypotheses must be identified and tested directly. Cycles of hypothesis generation and testing are iterative. As successive loops of 'what if' and 'if then' questions are explored, the hypotheses become more sophisticated and the design unfolds.

Fourth, design thinking is opportunistic. As the above cycles iterate, the designer seeks new and emergent possibilities. The power of the design lies in the particular. Thus, it is in the translation from the abstract/global to the particular/local that unforeseen opportunities are most likely to emerge. Sketching and modelling are important tools in the unfolding process, as Gehry's description of the Guggenheim Bilbao design illustrates.

Fifth, design thinking is dialectical. The designer lives at the intersection of often conflicting demands – recognizing the constraints of today's materials and the uncertainties that cannot be defined away, while envisioning tomorrow's possibilities. Olmsted's Central Park testifies to the ability of innovative design to both satisfy and transcend today's constraints to realize new possibilities.

Finally, design thinking is enquiring and value-driven – open to scrutiny, welcoming of enquiry, willing to make its reasoning explicit to a broader audience, and cognizant of the values embedded within the conversation. It recognizes the primacy of the *Weltanschauung* of its audience. The architect imbues the design with his or her own values, as reflected in Gehry's design of the Guggenheim Bilbao. Successful designs, in practice, educate and persuade by connecting with the values of the audience, as well.

Implications for strategy-making as a design process

Having developed a clearer sense of the process of design itself, we can begin to describe the possibilities that the use of such a metaphor might hold for thinking about business strategy, in general, and the design of strategy-making processes, in particular:

■ Strategic thinking is synthetic. It seeks internal alignment and understands interdependencies. It is systemic in its focus. It requires the ability to understand and integrate across levels and elements, both horizontal and vertical, and to align strategies across those levels. Strategic thinking is built on the foundation of a systems perspective. A strategic thinker has a mental model of the complete end-to-end system of value creation, and understands the interdependencies within it. The synthesizing process creates value not only in aligning the components, but also in creatively re-arranging them. The creative solutions produced by many of today's entrepreneurs often rest more with the redesign of aspects of traditional strategies rather than with dramatic breakthroughs.

■ Strategic thinking is adductive. It is future-focused and inventive, as Hamel and Prahalad's (1994) popular concept of strategic intent illustrates. Strategic intent provides the focus that allows individuals within an organization to marshal and leverage their energy, to focus attention, to resist distraction, and to concentrate for as long as it takes to achieve a goal. The creation of a compelling intent, with the sense of 'discovery, direction, and destiny' of which Hamel and Prahalad speak, relies heavily on the skill of alternative generation. As Simon (1993) has noted, alternative generation has received far less attention in the strategic decision-making literature than has alternative evaluation, but is more important in an environment of change. Yet, it is not merely the creation of the intent itself, but the identification of the gap between current reality and the imagined future that drives strategy-making. The ability to link past, present, and future in a process that Neustadt and May (1986) have called 'thinking in time':

> *Thinking in time [has] three components. One is recognition that the future has no place to come from but the past, hence the past has predictive value. Another element is recognition that what matters for the future in the present is departures from the past, alterations, changes, which prospectively or actually divert familiar flows from accustomed channels.... A third component is continuous comparison, an almost constant oscillation from the present to future to past and back, heedful of prospective change, concerned to expedite, limit, guide, counter, or accept it as the fruits of such comparison suggest.*

■ Strategic thinking is hypothesis-driven. In an environment of ever-increasing information availability and decreasing time to think, the ability to develop good hypotheses and to test them efficiently is critical. Because it is hypothesis-driven, strategic thinking avoids the analytic–intuitive dichotomy that has characterized much of the debate about strategic thinking. Strategic thinking is both creative and critical, in nature. Figuring out how to accomplish both types of thinking simultaneously has long troubled cognitive psychologists, since it is necessary to suspend critical judgement in order to think more creatively. Strategic thinking accommodates both creative and analytical thinking sequentially in its use of iterative cycles of hypothesis generating and testing. Hypothesis generation asks the creative question 'what if. . . ?' Hypothesis testing follows with the critical question 'if. . . , then. . . ?' and brings relevant data to bear on the analysis, including an analysis of a hypothetical set of financial flows associated with the idea. Taken together, and repeated over time, this sequence allows us to pose ever-improving hypotheses, without forfeiting the ability to explore new ideas. Such experimentation allows an organization to move beyond simplistic notions of cause and effect to provide on-going learning.

■ Strategic thinking is opportunistic. Within this intent-driven focus, there must be room for opportunism that not only furthers intended strategy, but that also leaves open the possibility of new strategies emerging. In writing about the role of 'strategic dissonance' in the strategy-making process at Intel, Robert Burgelman (1991) has highlighted the dilemma involved in using a well articulated strategy to channel organizational efforts effectively and efficiently against the risks of losing sight of alternative strategies better suited to a changing environment. This requires that an organization be capable of practising 'intelligent opportunism' at lower levels. He concludes: 'One important manifestation of corporate capability is a company's ability to adapt without having to rely on extraordinary top management foresight.'

■ Strategic thinking is dialectical. In the process of inventing the image of the future, the strategist must mediate the tension between constraint, contingency, and possibility. The underlying emphasis of strategic intent is stretch – to reach explicitly for potentially unattainable goals. At the same time, all elements of the firm's environment are not shapeable and those constraints that are real must be acknowledged in designing strategy. Similarly, the 'unknowables' must be recognized and the flexibility to deal with the range of outcomes that they represent must be designed in.

■ Strategic thinking is enquiring and, inevitably, value-driven. Because any particular strategy is invented, rather than discovered – chosen from among a larger set of plausible alternatives – it is contestable and reflective of the values of those making the choice. Its acceptance requires both connection with and movement beyond the existing mindset and value system of the rest of the organization. Such movement relies on inviting the broader community into the argumentation process – the strategic conversation. It is through participation in this dialogue that the strategy itself unfolds, both in the mind of the strategist and in that of the larger community that must come together to make the strategy happen. The conversation is what

allows the strategist to pull his or her colleagues 'through the keyhole' into a new *Weltanschauung*.

Taken together, these characteristics borrowed from the field of design – synthetic, adductive, dialectical, hypothesis-driven, opportunistic, inquiring, and value-driven – describe strategic thinking.

Concerns with the design metaphor

Having delineated the characteristics of design thinking, I will now discuss Mintzberg's (1990, 1994) concerns with the design metaphor. The most prominent of these include:

1 Design suggests that strategy is a process of thought, decoupled from action.

2 Design gives too much emphasis to creativity and uniqueness.

3 In design, implementation must wait for formulation to be completed.

4 Design gives too central a role to the designer – the CEO in the business application of the term.

5 Design is overwhelmingly concerned with fit and focus.

Design as decoupling thought from action

Mintzberg is concerned that the design process is primarily a process of reflection – of cognition rather than action – and that, as such, it precludes learning: 'Our critique of the design school revolves around one central theme: its promotion of thought independent of action, strategy formation above all as a process of conception, rather than as one of learning.'

Mintzberg's preference for action appears to be rooted in a belief that in environments characterized by complexity, change, and uncertainty, learning can only occur in action. The process of constructive forethought that this article suggests, however, is not 'independent of action'. Much of the forethought in the design process is directed specifically at iterative cycles of hypothesis generating and testing whose very purpose is to examine the likely consequences in action of the hypotheses being tested. In support of Mintzberg's point, however, these 'experiments' are conducted mentally rather than physically. Rather than a liability, this is, for design theorists, one of the key benefits of design – the ability to create a virtual environment for risk-reduced, entrapment-minimizing decision-making. Who would choose to construct a building 'as you go along', rather than laying out the design in advance? The likely efficiency, quality coherence, and integrity of the result using the latter process would appear to be far superior to the former. Similarly, to use Mintzberg's own example of the potter at her craft (Mintzberg, 1987), do we want to suggest that it is preferable for the potter to think of her creation only while sitting at the wheel, and never beforehand? The mistakes made at the wheel are clearly more expensive and difficult to undo. The same logic would appear to be compelling for business, especially to the extent to which we accept strategic problems as 'wicked'. Given the ability to do either, would we actively choose to experiment on our customers in the marketplace instead of on 'virtual' customers living in a virtual world? At times, of course, new possibilities may only present themselves at the potter's wheel, necessitating the conduct of actual experiments in the 'real' versus the virtual world. An important aspect of the design process lies with identifying those areas of uncertainty and potential opportunism. The challenge is not to choose correctly between planning and opportunism – an either/or – it is how to develop capabilities to do both in productive ways.

One hypothesizes that it is Mintzberg's assumption that strategists lack, and cannot reasonably be expected to develop, the ability to conduct high quality thought experiments – those that truly model reality. This is an assumption on which disagreement exists. It is one generally not shared by a group of influential learning theorists (Senge, 1990) who have devoted significant attention to the ways in which skills in systems thinking and mental modelling can improve the capability for more effective action. Further, the contention that managers are, in fact, clearly more capable of 'learning from their mistakes' after the fact, rather than at thinking their way to successful choices before the fact, remains unsubstantiated. A review of the design literature suggests that rather than abandoning the process of design, we could more fruitfully turn our attention to enhancing strategists' capabilities to be better designers.

Emphasis on creativity and uniqueness

Here, Mintzberg has two concerns about using the design metaphor: first, design's insistence that the resulting design be 'unique', second that the 'best'

designs emerge from a creative process. There can be no disagreement that a shared emphasis on creative process exists between Mintzberg's design school and the larger design literature, and that this process occurs for both within the context of an emphasis on the particular rather than the generalizable. Where there is less clarity is around what constitutes 'unique' and 'best'. The design literature argues strongly for the possibility of diversity in design, even in the case of similar purpose and circumstance; it does not, however, insist that such diversity, or 'uniqueness', will inevitably be the result of good design. Similarly, 'best' in the design world is strongly linked with purpose – both utilitarian and symbolic – rather than with uniqueness, as it might be in a purely creative process. Thus, we might expect that the 'best' design in situations sharing a common purpose and experiences and in similar circumstances might look a lot alike. Achieving uniqueness might require reducing the emphasis on achieving purpose. While the world of fine arts might view this as a worthy trade-off, the world of design would not.

Formulation precedes implementation

As above, it is literally true in the design field that the act of creation precedes the act of implementation. However, the generative cycle described here is ultimately always repeated and is issue, rather than calendar, driven. For some issues, the loop is continually in motion – a movement back and forth between mental designing and physical implementation that may appear almost simultaneously. Where major new commitments are required, the cycle operates in a more visible, episodic way. It does not insist that the world stand still while lengthy planning cycles operate. Again, though the process of design separates thinking and action, it does not separate 'thinking' from 'thinking about the consequences of action' – these are, in fact, one and the same for design theorists.

What is also clear, however, is that while design theorists talk very little about implementation as an explicit topic, in practice, designers such as Frank Gehry devote tremendous attention to the ultimate reality that their designs represent and what it will take to realize them. In fact, the distinction between formulation and implementation becomes wholly artificial in the practice of designing. What part of design thinking is not fundamentally about implementation – making reality of an image of some future state? The question is not whether implementation precedes, succeeds, or occurs simultaneously with formulation.

Within the design process itself, the distinction simply does not make sense. The important issue behind the formulation/implementation dichotomy is the separation of who is involved in each.

The prominence of the architect/CEO in the design process

Mintzberg equates 'the CEO' with 'the architect' and objects to the extent to which this devalues the role of other organizational members. This is understandable, given the recent history of the architecture field, which has had as much, or perhaps even more, of a 'great man' tenor than the management field. However, the 'great man' obsession of the architecture field should not be confused with the nature of the design process.

In the recent practice of architecture, the roles of designer and builder have, in fact, been made distinct. However, today's notion that architects have the overwhelmingly dominant role in the design process and that builders are mere executors of completed designs only emerged within the last century. In the building of the great cathedrals of Europe, the architects' role was seen as the communication of the general direction, and builders had great latitude in interpreting these design prescriptions, using their knowledge base.

The question of whether design suffers when created by someone who does not understand building as a process, is an important one. Leading architects like Frank Lloyd Wright and Frank Gehry would have answered an emphatic yes. What remains lost, despite an understanding of building, is the opportunity to continually reshape the original design, while under construction, to take advantage of emergent opportunities or to deal with unanticipated constraints. No mental experiments, however carefully conceived and repeated, can anticipate all relevant future developments. Conversely, there is nothing in the idea or process of design itself that suggests that designers ought not to be builders, or vice-versa. While this distinction has emerged in practice in the field of architecture, it is not necessarily an aspect of design practice that we would want to incorporate into business practice, for many of the reasons that Mintzberg reviews. In exploring the transition of the design metaphor to business in a more complete way, the opportunity is to see all managers as designers (and builders as well), each with responsibility for the design of a different piece of the system, within the context of a shared sense of overall purpose.

Design as primarily concerned with focus and fit

Mintzberg's last concern is that design is primarily concerned with the fit between current competencies and external opportunities, that a well-articulated design's likelihood of providing focus impedes change, and that flexibility rather than focus, should be the dominant criteria.

The concept of fit carries with it the same two connotations in the design world that it does in the strategy literature. One is fit as internal cohesion and alignment among sub-systems. The second is fit as what Wright called 'kinship', or harmony, with the surrounding environment. Both are seen as critically important aspects of design. Interestingly, however, both are considered as 'constraints' in the design process. That is, they are important aspects of current reality that must be attended to. The way that they are attended to, however, is in the context of an ever-present tension between them and some different view of a new future. Constraints are not allowed to drive the design process; nor can they be ignored. Instead, they are an important part of the dialectic always underway which the designer tries to mediate through a process of invention. This is a much more powerful view of the natural antagonism between constraint and possibility than has existed in the business strategy field. In business strategy we have tended to capture this tension as a dichotomy that firms must choose between – labelling them the 'strategic fit' and 'strategic intent' perspectives. The design field sets the bar far higher: designers are expected to find creative higher level solutions that honour both the current reality and some different future. Perhaps we should expect the same of business strategists at whatever position they occupy in the organization.

Mintzberg's second point argues that a well-articulated strategy impedes change and that on the focus–flexibility continuum, a design approach locates itself too close to the focus end, forfeiting necessary flexibility to deal with change. Mintzberg's contention that the more articulated the strategy, the harder it is to change and its corollary – the 'fuzzier' the strategy, the more it welcomes change – must be seriously questioned. For several decades, change theorists have argued the opposite – that a clear picture of the desired future state is an essential ingredient in achieving change. In the views of these theorists, the enemy of change is more likely to be the lethargy and lack of action introduced by confusion and 'fuzziness', rather than active resistance mobilized by clarity. In 20 years of work with managers of companies attempting to implement new strategies, I have yet to hear a manager lament, 'if only the strategy was less clear, I would have more freedom to act'. The refrain is universally the opposite – 'if only they would lay out where they think we're headed, I would be happy to do my part!' The goal of achieving clarity in the ultimate design does not imply that such clarity is present throughout the design process. Clearly things start 'fuzzy' and get clearer. They get clearer through a process of iteration, as needed for implementation. Once implemented, things get fuzzy again as the design evolves in a process similar to the cycles of 'chaos' and 'single-minded focus' that Andy Grove describes at Intel (Grove, 1996).

The focus/flexibility conundrum remains one of the central strategic questions of this decade, but the issue here is not primarily one of design versus opportunism. Design, by its nature, is open to emergent opportunity if viewed as an on-going process. Flexibility can, in fact, be designed into systems. In fact, it must be designed into systems in order to be achieved. The mere lack of constructive forethought offers no guarantee of openness to opportunity – quite the opposite, if we believe in the old dictum that 'luck finds the prepared mind.' The trade-off between focused commitment to a particular strategy and an alternative strategy that maximizes flexibility is, instead, often reflected in the former strategy's superior ability to deliver efficiently against a particular purpose and the latter's ability to change purpose. That difference in performance is not a choice made by choosing design, it is a choice made in the process of designing.

Leveraging the design metaphor

The metaphor of design offers a window into a deeper understanding of the process of strategy making. It does this by calling attention to the process of creating a purposeful space. Such space much more than the structures vis work because they create an envi form and function; that builds relat abilities and targets specific outcomes, an emotional and aesthetic level, those to- wards a shared purpose. Values play a v role here, as do hypothesis generating and testing, and the ability to conjure a vivid picture of a set of possibilities that do not yet exist.

What would we do differently in organizations today, if we took seriously the design metaphor? A lot, I believe. It would call for significant changes in the way that strategic planning is approached today, especially in large organizations. The problems with traditional approaches to planning have long been recognized. They include: the attempt to make a science of planning with its subsequent loss of creativity, the excessive emphasis on numbers, the drive for administrative efficiency that standardized inputs and formats at the expense of substance, and the dominance of single techniques, inappropriately applied. Decades later, strategists continue to struggle to propose clear alternatives to traditional processes. Design offers a different approach and would suggest processes that are more widely participative, more dialogue-based, issue-driven rather than calendar-driven, conflict-using rather than conflict-avoiding, all aimed at invention and learning, rather than control. In short, we should involve more members of the organization in two-way strategic conversations. We should view the process as one of iteration and experimentation, and pay sequential attention to idea generation and evaluation in a way that attends first to possibilities before moving onto constraints. Finally and perhaps most importantly, we would recognize that good designs succeed by persuading, and great designs by inspiring.

READING
2.4

Decision-making: It's not what you think

By Henry Mintzberg and Frances Westley[1]

How should decisions be made? Easy, we figured that out long ago. First define the problem, then diagnose its causes, next design possible solutions, and finally decide which is best. And, of course, implement the choice.

But do people always make decisions that way? We propose that this rational, or 'thinking first', model of decision-making should be supplemented with two very different models – a 'seeing first' and a 'doing first' model. When practising managers use all three models, they can improve the quality of their decisions. Healthy organizations, like healthy people, have the capacity for all three.

Consider how a real decision was made, a personal one in this case. It begins with a call from an aunt:

'Hi, kiddo. I want to buy you a housewarming present. What's the colour scheme in your new apartment?'

'Colour scheme? Betty, you've got to be kidding. I'll have to ask Lisa. Lisa, Betty wants to know the colour scheme of the apartment.'

'Black,' daughter Lisa says.

'Black? Lisa, I've got to live there.'

'Black,' she repeats.

A few days later, father and daughter find themselves in a furniture store. They try every desk, every chair: Nothing works. Shopper's lethargy sets in. Then Lisa spots a black stool: 'Wouldn't that look great against the white counter?' And they're off. Within an hour, they have picked out everything – in black, white and steel grey.

The extraordinary thing about this ordinary story is that our conventional theories of decision-making can't explain it. It is not even clear what the final decision was: to buy the stool; to get on with furnishing an apartment; to do so in black and white; to create a new lifestyle? Decision-making can be mysterious.

The limits of 'thinking first'

Rational decision-making has a clearly identified process: define → diagnose → design → decide. However, the rational approach turns out to be uncommon.

Years ago, one of us studied a host of decisions, delineating the steps and then laying them out. A decision process for building a new plant was typical. The process kept cycling back, interrupted by new events, diverted by opportunities and so on, going round and round until finally a solution emerged. The final action was as clear as a wave breaking on the shore, but explaining how it came to be is as hard as tracing the origin of that wave back into the ocean.

Often decisions do not so much emerge as erupt. Here is how Alexander Kotov, the chess master, has described a sudden insight that followed lengthy analysis:

So, I mustn't move the knight. Try the rook move again.. . . At this point you glance at the clock. 'My goodness! Already 30 minutes gone on thinking about whether to move the rook or the knight. It if goes on like this you'll really be in time trouble.' And then suddenly you are struck by the happy idea – why move rook or knight? What about B–QN1? And without any more ado, without analysis at all, you move the bishop. Just like that.

Perhaps, then, decision-making means periods of groping followed by sudden sharp insights that lead to crystallization, as A. Langley and co-authors suggested in a 1995 *Organizational Science* article (see Figure 2.4.1). Or perhaps it is a form of 'organized anarchy', as Stanford professor James March and colleagues have written. They characterize decision-making as 'collections of choices looking for problems, issues and feelings looking for decision situations in which they may be aired, solutions looking for issues to which they might be an answer, and decision-makers looking for work' (see Figure 2.4.2). But is the confusion, as described by those authors, in the process, or is it in the observers? Maybe messy, real-life decision-making makes more sense than we think, precisely because so much of it is beyond conscious thought.

'Seeing first'

Insight – 'seeing into' – suggests that decisions, or at least actions, may be driven as much by what is seen as

[1]Source: This article was adapted with permission from MIT *Sloan Management Review*, Vol. 42, No. 3, Spring 2001, pp. 89–93.

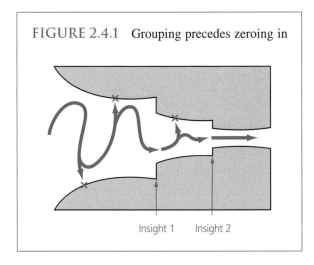

FIGURE 2.4.1   Grouping precedes zeroing in

Insight 1   Insight 2

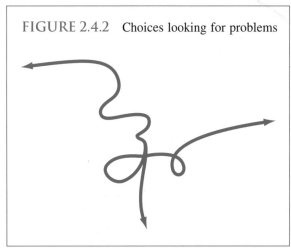

FIGURE 2.4.2   Choices looking for problems

by what is thought. As Mozart said, the best part about creating a symphony was being able to 'see the whole of it at a single glance in my mind'. So, understanding can be visual as well as conceptual.

In W. Koehler's well known 1920s experiment, an ape struggled to reach a banana placed high in its cage. Then it *saw* the box in the corner – not just noticed it, but realized what could be done with it – and its problem was solved. Likewise after Alexander Fleming really *saw* the mould that had killed the bacteria in some of his research samples (in other words, when he realized how that mould could be used), he and his colleagues were able to give us penicillin. The same can be true for strategic vision. Vision requires the courage to see what others do not – and that means having both the confidence and the experience to recognize the sudden insight for what it is.

A theory in Gestalt psychology developed by G. Wallas in the 1920s identifies four steps in creative discovery: preparation → incubation → illumination → verification. Preparation must come first. As Louis Pasteur put it, 'Chance favours only the prepared mind.' Deep knowledge, usually developed over years, is followed by incubation, during which the unconscious mind mulls over the issue. Then with luck (as with Archimedes in the bathtub), there is that flash of illumination. That eureka moment often comes after sleep – because in sleep, rational thinking is turned off, and the unconscious has greater freedom. The conscious mind returns later to make the logical argument. But that verification (reasoning it all out in linear order for purposes of elaboration and proof) takes time. There is a story of a mathematician who solved a formula in his sleep. Holding it in his mind's eye, he was in no rush to write it down. When he did, it took him

four months! Great insights may be rare, but what industry cannot trace its origins to one or more of them? Moreover, little insights occur to all of us all the time. No one should accept any theory of decision-making that ignores insight.

'Doing first'

But what happens when you don't see it and can't think it up? Just do it. That is how pragmatic people function when stymied: They get on with it, believing that if they do 'something', the necessary thinking could follow. It's experimentation – trying something so that you can learn.

A theory for 'doing first', popularized in academia by organizational behaviour professor Karl Weick, goes like this: enactment → selection → retention. That means doing various things, finding out which among them works, making sense of that and repeating the successful behaviours while discarding the rest. Successful people know that when they are stuck, they must experiment. Thinking may drive doing, but doing just as surely drives thinking. We don't just think in order to act, we act in order to think.

Show us almost any company that has diversified successfully, and we will show you a company that has learned by doing, one whose diversification strategy emerged through experience. Such a company at the outset may have laid out a tidy strategy on the basis of assessing its weaknesses and strengths (or, if after 1990, its 'core competencies'), which it almost certainly got wrong. How can you tell a strength from a weakness when you are entering a new sphere? You have no choice but to try things out. Then you can identify the competencies that are really core. Action is important; if you insist on 'thinking first' and, for example, doing formalized strategic planning (which is really part of the same thing), you may in fact discourage learning.

Making decisions through discussion, collage and improvisation

Thus the three major approaches to decision-making are 'thinking first', 'seeing first' and 'doing first'. They correlate with conventional views of science, art and craft. The first is mainly verbal (comprising words in linear order), the second is visual, the third is visceral. Those who favour thinking are people who cherish facts, those who favour seeing cherish ideas and those who favour doing cherish experiences (see Table 2.4.1).

We have for some years conducted workshops on the three approaches with midcareer managers sent by Asian, European and North American companies to our International Masters Program in Practicing Management (www.impm.org). We begin with a general discussion about the relationship between analysis, ideas and action. It soon becomes evident that practising managers recognize the iterative and connected nature of those elements. We then ask small groups first to discuss an issue for about an hour (one of their own or else what we call a 'provocative question'; for example, 'How do you manage customer service when you never see a customer?' or 'How do you organize without structure?'), summarize their conclusions on a flip chart and report back to the full group. Next we give the groups coloured paper, pens, scissors and glue. Each small group must create a collage about the issue they discussed in the thinking-first session. At the end of that second workshop, the groups view one another's images and compare 'see-

ing first' with 'thinking first' – in terms of both process and results. Finally, each group, with only a few minutes of preparation time permitted, improvises a skit to act out its issue. Again, the groups consider the results.

Reactions to the approaches are revealing. Participants note that in the thinking-first workshop, the initial discussions start off easily enough, no matter what the mix of nationalities or work backgrounds. Participants list comments on flip charts and spontaneously use bulleted items and numbers – with the occasional graph thrown in. Almost no time is spent in discussing *how* to go about analysing the problem. Groups quickly converge on one of several conventional analytic frameworks: cause and effect, problem and solution, pros and cons, and so on.

Many participants observe that such frameworks, particularly when adopted early, blunt exploration. Quality and depth of analysis may be sacrificed for process efficiency. Thinking-first workshops encourage linear, rational and rather categorical arguments. All too often, the result is a wish list, with disagreements hidden in the different points. In other words, there may be less discipline in thinking first than we believe. Thinking comes too easily to most of us.

But when a group must make a picture, members have to reach consensus. That requires deeper integration of the ideas. 'We had to think more to do this', a participant reported. The artistic exercise 'really forces you to capture the essence of an issue', another added. People ask more questions in the seeing-first exercise; they become more playful and creative.

'In "thinking first", we focused on the problems; in "seeing first", we focused on the solutions', one person said. One group believed it had agreement on the issue after the thinking-first workshop. Only when the picture making began did its members realize how superficial that agreement was – more of a compromise. In contrast, when you really do see, as someone

TABLE 2.4.1   Characteristics of the three approaches to making decisions

'Thinking first' features the qualities of	'Seeing first' features the qualities of	'Doing first' features the qualities of
Science	Art	Craft
Planning, programming	Visioning, imagining	Venturing, learning
The verbal	The visual	The visceral
Facts	Ideas	Experiences

said, 'The message jumps out at you.' But to achieve that, the group members have to find out more about one another's capabilities and collaborate more closely. 'I felt it became a group project, not just my project', said a participant who had chosen the topic for his group. The seeing-first exercise also draws out more emotions; there is more laughter and a higher energy level. This suggests that being able to see a trajectory – having a vision about what you are doing – energizes people and so stimulates action. In comparing the seeing-first exercise with the thinking-first discussion, a participant remarked, 'We felt more liberated.' The pictures may be more ambiguous than the words, but they are also more involving. A frequent comment: 'They invite interpretation.'

One particularly interesting observation about the pictures was that 'the impression lasts longer'. Studies indicate that we remember pictures much longer and more accurately than words. As R. Haber demonstrated in *Scientific American* in 1970, recall of images, even as many as 10 000 shown at one-second intervals, is nearly 98 per cent – a capability that may be linked to evolution. Humans survived by learning to register danger and safety signals first. Emotion, memory, recall and stimulation are powerfully bundled in 'seeing first'. Contrast that with one comment after the thinking-first workshop: 'Twenty-four hours later, we won't remember what this meant.'

In fact, although many participants have not made a picture since grade school, the art produced in the seeing-first workshops is often remarkable. Creativity flows freely among the managers, suggesting that they could come up with more creative ideas in their home organizations if they more often used symbols beyond words or numbers.

Our multicultural groups may like the art workshop for overcoming language barriers, but groups of managers from the same company, country or language group have responded equally well. One British participant who was working on a joint venture with an American partner found that out. He met with his US counterpart a few days after the workshops. 'We talked past each other for two hours', he reported. When he suggested they create a picture of their common concerns, they finally were able to connect.

The improvisation skits – 'doing first' – generate more spontaneity. Participants respond to one another intuitively and viscerally, letting out concerns held back in conversation and even in artwork. For example, turf battles become evident in the way people stand and talk. Humour, power, fear and anger surface. (M. Crossen and M. Sorrenti discuss improvisation at

length in a helpful article published in 1997 in *Advances in Strategic Management*.)

Weick has suggested that a key aspect of effective action in organizations is the ability to remain open to signals from others, even under extreme pressure. He believes that such heedfulness, as he calls it, is a finely honed skill among group improvisers such as jazz musicians. Organizations that recognize opportunities for improvisation – and hone the skills required – increase their capacity for learning. In improvisation, people have to respond with a speed that eliminates many inhibitions. 'Having to just act gets rid of the fears', a participant said. Another added, after watching a colleague play the role of a frustrated bank customer, 'The output can be scarily real.'

Mere words, in contrast, feel more abstract and disconnected – numbers, even more so – just as the aggregations of marketing are more abstract than the experience of selling. The skits bring out what the words and numbers do not say – indeed, what problems they cause. 'Not everything is unsayable in words', claimed playwright Eugène Ionesco, 'only the living truth.' Or as Isadora Duncan, the modern-dance pioneer, insisted, 'If I could say it, I wouldn't have to dance it.' Thus 'doing first' facilitates the dancing that is so lacking in many of today's organizations.

Enough thinking?

The implications for our large, formalized, thinking-obsessed organizations are clear enough: not to suspend thinking so much as put it in its place, alongside seeing and doing. Isn't it time we got past our obsession with planning and programming, and opened the doors more widely to venturing and visioning? A glance at corporate reports, e-mail and meetings reveals that art is usually something reserved for report covers – or company walls. And when organizations separate the thinking from the doing, with the former coming from the heads of powerful formulators and the latter assigned to the hands of ostensibly docile implementers, those formulators lose the benefits of experimenting – and learning.

Each approach has its own strengths and weaknesses (see Table 2.4.2). 'Thinking first' works best when the issue is clear, the data reliable and the world structured; when thoughts can be pinned down and discipline applied, as in an established production process.

'Seeing first' is necessary when many elements have to be combined into creative solutions and when

TABLE 2.4.2 When each decision-making approach works best

Approach	Works best when	Example
'Thinking first'	■ The issue is clear ■ The data are reliable ■ The context is structured ■ Thoughts can be pinned down ■ Discipline can be applied	As in an established production process
'Seeing first'	■ Many elements have to be combined into creative solutions ■ Commitment to those solutions is key ■ Communication across boundaries is essential	As in new-product development
'Doing first'	■ The situation is novel and confusing ■ Complicated specifications would get in the way ■ A few simple relationship rules can help people move forward	When companies face a disruptive technology

commitment to those solutions is key, as in much new product development. The organization has to break away from the conventional, encourage communication across boundaries, bust up cerebral logjams and engage the heart as well as the head. 'Doing first' is preferred when the situation is novel and confusing, and things need to be worked out. That is often the case in a new industry – or in an old industry thrown into turmoil by a new technology. Under such circumstances, complicated specifications get in the way, and a few simple relationship rules can help people move forward in a coordinated yet spontaneous manner.

That suggests the advantages of combining all three approaches. In order to learn, a company group might tackle a new issue first by craft, which is tied to doing; then, in order to imagine, by art, which is tied to seeing; finally, in order to programme, by science, which is tied to thinking. In ongoing situations, art provides the overview, or vision; science specifies the structure, or plan; and craft produces the action, or energy. In other words, science keeps you straight, art keeps you interested, and craft keeps you going. No organization can do without any one approach. Isn't it time, then, to move beyond our narrow thinking about decision-making: to get in *touch,* to *see* another point of view?

STRATEGIC THINKING IN INTERNATIONAL PERSPECTIVE

Those who judge by their feelings do not understand reasoning, for they wish to get an insight into a matter at a glance, and are not accustomed to look for principles. Contrarily, others, who are accustomed to argue from principles, do not understand the things of the heart, seeking for principles and not being able to see at a glance.

Blaise Pascal (1623–1662); French scientist and philosopher

From the preceding articles it has become clear that opinions differ sharply about what goes on, and should go on, in the mind of the strategist. There are strongly conflicting views on how managers deal with the paradox of logic and creativity. It is up to each reader to judge whether the rational or the generative reasoning perspective is more valuable for understanding strategic thinking. Yet, we hope that readers will feel challenged to consider the possibility that both perspectives may be useful at the same time. Although they are opposites, and partially contradictory, both perspectives might reveal crucial aspects of strategic thinking that need to be combined to achieve superior results. Blending logic and creativity in ingenious ways might allow strategists to get 'the best of both worlds'. What such mixes of logic and creativity in the mind of the strategist could be like will remain a matter for debate – with strategists using their own logical or creative thinking to come up with answers.

Hence, this last part of the chapter is not intended to present a grand synthesis. Readers will have to grapple with the paradox of logic and creativity themselves, by contrasting the thesis (the rational reasoning perspective) and the antithesis (the generative reasoning perspective). In this final part of the chapter it is the intention to view the topic of strategic thinking from an international perspective. The explicit question that must be added to the debate on the mind of the strategist is whether there are discernible national differences in approaches to strategic thinking. Are there specific national preferences for the rational or the generative reasoning perspective, or are the differing views spread randomly across the globe? Are each of the perspectives rooted in a particular national context, making it difficult to extend them to other countries, or are they universally applicable? In short, are views on strategic thinking the same all around the world?

Unfortunately, this question is easier asked than answered. Little cross-cultural research has been done in the field of strategic management and hardly any on this specific topic. This may be partially due to the difficulty of international comparative research, but it probably also reflects the implicit assumption by most that theories on strategic thinking are universally applicable. Few of the authors cited in this chapter suggest that there are international differences or note that their theories might be culturally biased and of limited validity in other national settings.

Yet, the assumption that strategic thinking is viewed in the same way around the world should be questioned. The human inclination to suppose that all others are the same as us is well known – it is a common cognitive bias. In international affairs, however, such an assumption must always be challenged. Strategists operating internationally cannot afford the luxury of assuming that their views are universally accepted and applicable. Therefore, the thought must be entertained that strategists in some countries are more attracted to the rational reasoning perspective, while in other countries the generative reasoning perspective is more pervasive.

As a stimulus to the debate of whether there are such national preferences in perspective on strategic thinking, we would like to bring forward a number of factors that might be of influence on how the paradox of logic and creativity is tackled in different countries. It goes almost without saying that more concrete international comparative research is needed to give this debate a firmer footing.

Position of science

Science and the scientific method do not play the same role, and are not accorded the same value, in all societies. In some countries, science and scientists are held in high esteem, and scientific enquiry is believed to be the most fruitful way of obtaining new knowledge. Typical for these nations is that the scientific method has come to pervade almost all aspects of life. Objective knowledge and skill in analytical reasoning are widely believed to be the critical success factors in most professions – even to become a nurse, a journalist, a sports instructor, an actor or a musician requires a university education. Managers, too, are assumed to be scientifically trained, often specializing in management studies. Much of this education strongly promotes formal, explicit, analytical thinking, and pays little attention to creativity, imagination and intuition. In these nations a more pronounced preference for the rational reasoning perspective might be expected.

In other countries, science holds a less predominant position (Redding, 1980). Scientific methods might shed some light on issues, but other ways of obtaining new insights – such as through experience, intuition, philosophizing, fantasizing, and drawing analogies – are also valued (Keegan, 1983; Kagono *et al.,* 1985). The bounds of socially acceptable reasoning are less constrictive than in more rationalist nations. Leaps of imagination and logical inconsistencies are tolerated, as normal aspects in the messy process of sense-making (Pascale, 1984). In general, thinking is viewed as an art and therefore science has not made deep inroads into most of the professions. Managers, in particular, do not require a specific scientific training, but need to be broadly developed generalists with flexible minds (Nonaka and Johanson, 1985). In these countries, a stronger preference for the generative thinking perspective can be expected.

Level of uncertainty avoidance

National cultures also differ with regard to their tolerance for ambiguity. As Hofstede points out in Reading 1.4 in this book, some societies feel uncomfortable with uncertain situations and strive for security. Countries that score high on Hofstede's 'uncertainty avoidance dimension' typically try to suppress deviant ideas and behaviours, and institute rules that everyone must follow. People in these countries exhibit a strong intellectual need to believe in absolute truths and they place great trust in experts (Schneider, 1989). They have a low tolerance for the ambiguity brought on by creative insights, novel interpretations and 'wild ideas' that are not analytically sound. Therefore, it can be expected that strategists in high uncertainty avoidance cultures will be more inclined towards the rational reasoning perspective than in nations with a low score.

Level of individualism

As stated at the beginning of this chapter, strategists with a generative inclination are slightly rebellious. They show little reverence for the status quo, by continuously questioning existing cognitive maps and launching creative reinterpretations. As the dissenting voice, they often stand alone, and are heavily criticized by the more orthodox. This lonely position is difficult to maintain under the best of circumstances, but is especially taxing in highly collectivist cultures. If strategists wish to be accepted within their group, organization and community, they cannot afford to stick out too much. There will be a strong pressure on the strategist to conform. In more individualist cultures, however, there is usually a higher tolerance for individual variety. People find it easier to have their own ideas, independent of their group, organization and community (see Hofstede's individualism dimension, in Reading 1.4). This gives strategists more intellectual and emotional freedom to be the 'odd man out'. Therefore, it can be expected that strategists in more individualist cultures will be more inclined towards the generative reasoning perspective than those in collectivist cultures.

Position of strategists

Countries also differ sharply with regard to the hierarchical position of the managers engaged in strategy. In many countries strategic problems are largely defined and solved by the upper echelons of management. To reach this hierarchical position requires many years of hands-on experience and climbing through the ranks. Therefore, by the time managers are in the position of being a strategist they are middle-aged and thoroughly familiar with their business – with the danger of being set in their ways. They will also have been promoted several times by senior managers who believe that they will function well within the organization. In general, the effect is that the competent and conformist managers are promoted to strategy positions, while innovative dissidents are selected out along the way. In such countries, creative strategic reasoning often does not take place within large organizations, but within small start-ups, to which the creatively inclined flee.

In cultures that score lower on Hofstede's power distance dimension, managers throughout the organization are often involved in strategy discussions. The responsibility for strategy is spread more widely among the ranks. Younger, less experienced managers are expected to participate in strategy formation processes, together with their senior colleagues. In general, this leads to a more open, messy and lively debate about the organization's strategy and provokes more creative strategic thinking. Therefore, it can be expected that in less hierarchical cultures the generative reasoning perspective will be more popular than in cultures with stronger hierarchical relations.

FURTHER READING

Anyone interested in the topic of strategic thinking will sooner or later run into the work of Herbert Simon. His concept of bounded rationality was originally explored in the book *Models of Man*, which is still interesting reading, but *Organizations*, written together with James March, is a more comprehensive and up-to-date source with which to start. Also, a good introduction to (bounded) rationality is given by Niels Noorderhaven, in his book *Strategic Decision Making*, which additionally covers the topics of emotions, intuition and cognition in relationship to the strategy process. Another excellent book exploring the role of emotions in economic decision-making behaviour and engaging in a debate with rational choice theorists is *Alchemies of the Mind: Rationality and the Emotions*, by Jon Elster.

For a more in-depth discussion on the interplay between cognition and strategic decision-making, a stimulating book is R. Hogarth's *Judgement and Choice: The Psychology of Decision*. Also an excellent book is *The Essence of Strategic Decision Making*, by Charles Schwenk, in particular with regard to the discussion of cognitive biases. A good research article summarizing the role of cognition in (strategic) management is James Walsh's (1995) 'Managerial and Organizational Cognition: Notes from a Trip Down

Memory Lane'. On the topic of the social construction of reality, Karl Weick's *The Social Psychology of Organizing* is still the classic that should be read. A shorter article on the same topic is 'Strategic Management in an Enacted World' by Linda Smircich and Charles Stubbart (1985).

Readers interested in the link between creativity and strategic thinking might want to start with *Creative Management*, an excellent reader edited by John Henry, which contains many classic articles on creativity from a variety of different disciplines. A second step would be to read Gareth Morgan's imaginative book, *Imaginization: The Art of Creative Management*, or John Kao's *Jamming: The Art and Discipline of Business Creativity*, both of which make challenging proposals for improving an organization's creative thinking. Also stimulating is the book *Strategic Innovation*, by Charles Baden-Fuller and Martyn Pitt, which contains a large number of cases on companies exhibiting creative thinking. For a practical guide to creative thinking Stephen Reid's recent book, *How to Think: Building Your Mental Muscle*, is quite useful.

REFERENCES

Aldrich, H.E., and Fiol, C.M. (1994) 'Fools Rush In? The Institutional Context of Industry Creation', *Academy of Management Review*, Vol. 19, No. 4, pp. 645–670.

Anderson, J.R. (1983) *The Architecture of Cognition*, Cambridge, MA: Harvard University Press.

Andrews, K. (1987) *The Concept of Corporate Strategy*, Homewood: Irvin.

Ansoff, H.I. (1965) *Corporate Strategy: An Analytic Approach to Business Policy for Growth and Expansion*, New York: McGraw-Hill.

Ansoff, H.I. (1991) 'Critique of Henry Mintzberg's The "Design School": Reconsidering the Basic Premises of Strategic Management', *Strategic Management Journal*, September, pp. 449–461.

Anthony, W.P, Bennett, R.H., Maddox, E.N., and Wheatley, W.J. (1993) 'Picturing the Future: Using Mental Imagery to Enrich Strategic Environmental Assessment', *Academy of Management Executive*, Vol. 7, No. 2, pp. 43–56.

Archer, L., (1963) 'Systemation Method for Designers', *Design*, pp. 172–188.

Arnheim, R. (1992) 'Sketching and the Psychology of Design', in: V. Margolis and R. Buchanan (eds), *The Idea of Design*, Cambridge, MA: MIT Press.

Baden-Fuller, C, and Pitt, M. (1996) *Strategic Innovation*, London: Routledge.

Bazerman, M.H. (1990) *Judgment in Managerial Decision Making*, Second Edition, New York: Wiley.

Bazjanac, V, 'Architectural Design Theory: Models of the Design Process', in: W Spillers (ed.), *Basic Questions of Design Theory*, New York: American Elsevier, pp. 3–20.

Bazjanac, V. (1964) *The Writings of C. Alexander: Notes on the Synthesis of Form*, Boston, MA: Harvard University Press.

Behling, O., and Eckel, N.L. (1991) 'Making Sense Out of Intuition', *Academy of Management Executive*, Vol. 5, No. 1, pp. 46–54.

Buchanan, R., and Margolis, V. (eds.) (1995) *Discovering Design*, Chicago, IL: University of Chicago Press.

Burgelman, R. (1991) 'Intraorganizational Ecology of Strategy Making and Organizational Adaptation', *Organizational Science*, 213, p. 208, and pp. 239–262.

Calori, R., Johnson, G., and Sarnin, P. (1994) 'CEO's Cognitive Maps and the Scope of the Organization', *Strategic Management Journal*, Vol. 15, No. 6, July, pp. 437–457.

Christensen, C.R., Andrews, K.R., Bower, J.L., Hamermesh, R.G., and Porter, M.E. (1982) *Business Policy: Text and Cases*, IL: Fifth Edition, Homewood: Irwin.

Christensen, C.R., Andrews, K.R., Bower, J.L., Hamermesh, R.G., and Porter, M.E. (1987) *Business Policy: Text and Cases*, IL: Sixth Edition, Homewood: Irwin.

Cross, N. (1995) 'Discovering Design Ability', in: R. Buchanan and V. Margolis (eds.), *Discovering Design*, Chicago, IL: University of Chicago Press.

Daft, R., and Weick, K. (1984) 'Toward a Model of Organizations as Interpretation Systems', *Academy of Management Review*, Vol. 9, pp. 284–295.

Day, D.V., and Lord, R.G. (1992) 'Expertise and Problem Categorization: The Role of Expert Processing in Organizational Sense-Making', *Journal of Management Studies*, Vol. 29, pp. 35–47.

De Bono, E. (1970) *Lateral Thinking*, New York: Harper & Row.

DiMaggio, P., and Powell, W.W. (1983) 'The Iron Cage Revisited: Institutional Isomorphism and Collective Rationality in Organizational Fields', *American Sociological Review*, Vol. 48, pp. 147–160.

Dutton, J.E. (1988) 'Understanding Strategies Agenda Building and its Implications for Managing Change', in: L.R. Pondy, R.J. Boland, Jr., and H. Thomas (eds), *Managing Ambiguity and Change*, Chichester: Wiley.

Eden, C. (1989) 'Using Cognitive Mapping for Strategic Options Development and Analysis (SODA)', in: J. Rosenhead (ed.), *Rational Analysis in a Problematic World*, London: Wiley.

Elster, J. (1999) *Alchemies of the Mind: Rationality and the Emotions*, Cambridge: Cambridge University Press.

Emery, F.E., and Trist, E.L. (1965) 'The Causal Texture of Organizational Environments', *Human Relations*, Vol. 18, pp. 21–32.

Findeli, A. (1990) 'The Methodological and Philosophical Foundations of Moholy-Nagy's Design Pedagogy in Chicago (1927–1946)', *Design Issues*, 711, pp. 4–19, and pp. 32–33.

Finkelstein, S., and Hambrick, D.C. (1996) *Strategic Leadership: Top Executives and Their Effects on Organizations*, St. Paul: West

Gioia, D.A., and Chittipeddi, K. (1991) 'Sensemaking and Sensegiving in Strategic Change Intuition', *Strategic Management Journal*, Vol. 12, pp. 433–448.

Grove, A. (1996) *Only the Paranoid Survive*, New York: Doubleday.

Hambrick, D.C, Geletkanycz, M.A., and Fredrickson, J.W (1993) 'Top Executive Commitment to the Status Quo: Some Tests of Its Determinants', *Strategic Management Journal*, Vol. 14, No. 6, pp. 401–418.

Hamel, G. (1996) 'Strategy as Revolution', *Harvard Business Review*, July–August, Vol. 74, No. 4, pp. 69-82.

Hamel, G., and Prahalad, C.K. (1994) *Competing for the Future*, Boston, MA: Harvard Business School Press.

Henry, J. (ed.) (1991) *Creative Management*, London: Sage in association with the Open University.

Hofstede, G. (1980) *Culture's Consequences*, London: Sage.

Hogarth, R.M. (1980) *Judgement and Choice: The Psychology of Decision*, Chichester: Wiley.

Huff, A.S. (ed.) (1990) *Mapping Strategic Thought*, Chichester: Wiley.

Hurst, D.K., Rush, J.C., and White, R.E. (1989) 'Top Management Teams and Organizational Renewal', *Strategic Management Journal*, Vol. 10, No. 1, pp. 87–105.

Isenberg, D.J. (1984) 'How Senior Managers Think', *Harvard Business Review*, November–December, Vol. 63, No. 6, pp. 81–90.

Janis, I.L. (1989) *Crucial Decisions: Leadership in Policymaking and Crisis Management*, New York: Free Press.

Kagono, T.I., Nonaka, K., Sakakibira, K., and Okumara, A. (1985) *Strategic vs. Evolutionary Management*, North-Holland: Amsterdam.

Kao, J. (1996) *Jamming: The Art and Discipline of Business Creativity*, New York: HarperBusiness.

Keegan, W.J. (1983) 'Strategic Market Planning: The Japanese Approach', *International Marketing Review*, Vol. 1, pp. 5–15.

Knight, D., Pearce, C.L., Smith, K.G., Olian, J.D., Sims, H.P, Smith, K.A., and Flood, P. (1999) 'Top Management Team Diversity, Group Process, and Strategic Consensus', *Strategic Management Journal*, Vol. 20, pp. 445–465.

Kuhn, T.S. (1970) *The Structure of Scientific Revolutions*, Chicago: University of Chicago Press.

Langley, A. (1989) 'In Search of Rationality: The Purposes Behind the Use of Formal Analysis in Organizations', *Administrative Science Quarterly*, Vol. 34, No. 4, pp. 598–631.

Langley, A. (1995) 'Between "Paralysis by Analysis" and "Extinction by Instinct"', *Sloan Management Review*, Vol. 36, No. 3, Spring, pp. 63–76.

Lenz, R.T., and Lyles, M. (1985) 'Paralysis by Analysis: Is Your Planning System Becoming Too Rational?', *Long Range Planning*, Vol. 18, No. 4, pp. 64–72.

Liedtka, J. (2000) 'In defense of strategy as design', *California Management Review*, Vol. 42, No. 3, Spring, pp. 8–30.

Liedtka, J., and Rosenblum, J. (1996) 'Shaping Conversations: Making Strategy, Managing Change', *California Management Review*, Vol. 39, No. 1, Fall, pp. 141–157.

Lyles, M.A., and Schwenk, C.R. (1992) 'Top Management, Strategy and Organizational Knowledge Structures', *Journal of Management Studies*, Vol. 29, pp. 155–174.

March, J.G., and Simon, H.A. (1993) *Organizations*, MA: Second Edition, Blackwell, Cambridge.

March, L. (1976) 'The Logic of Design', in: L. March, (ed.), *The Architecture of Form*, MA: Cambridge University Press, Cambridge.

Mason, R.O., and Mitroff, I.I. (1981) *Challenging Strategic Planning Assumptions*, New York: Wiley.

McCaskey, M.B. (1982) *The Executive Challenge: Managing Change and Ambiguity*, Boston: Pitman.

Mintzberg, H. (1987) 'Crafting Strategy', *Harvard Business Review*, July–August, pp. 66–75.

Mintzberg, H. (1990) 'The Design School: Reconsidering the Basic Premises of Strategic Management', *Strategic Management Journal*, Vol. 11, No. 3, pp. 171–195.

Mintzberg, H. (1991) 'Learning 1, Planning 0: Reply to Igor Ansoff', *Strategic Management Journal*, September, pp. 463–466.

Mintzberg, H. (1994) *The Rise and Fall of Strategic Planning*, New York: The Free Press.

Mintzberg, H., Ahlstrand, B., and Lampel, J. (1998) *Strategy Safari: A Guided Tour through the Wilds of Strategic Management*, New York: The Free Press.

Mintzberg, H.and Westley, F. (2001) 'Decision Making: It's Not What You Think', *Sloan Management Review*, Vol. 42, No. 3, pp. 89–93.

Morgan, G. (1993) *Imaginization: The Art of Creative Management*, Newbury Park, CA: Sage.

Neustadt, R., and May, E. (1986) *Thinking in Time: The Uses of History for Decision-Makers*, New York: The Free Press.

Nonaka, I. (1991) 'The Knowledge-Creating Company', *Harvard Business Review*, Vol. 69, No. 6, November–December, pp. 96–104.

Nonaka, I., and Johanson, J.K. (1985) 'Japanese Management: What about "Hard" Skills?', *Academy of Management Review*, Vol. 10, No. 2, pp. 181–191.

Noorderhaven, N.G. (1995) *Strategic Decision Making*, Wokingham: Addison-Wesley.

Ocasio, W. (1997) 'Towards an Attention-Based View of the Firm', *Strategic Management Journal*, Vol. 18, Special Issue, July, pp. 187–206.

Ohmae, K. (1975) *The Corporate Strategist*, New York: President Inc.

Ohmae, K. (1982) *The Mind of the Strategist*, New York: McGraw-Hill.

Pascale, R.T. (1984) 'Perspectives on Strategy: The Real Story Behind Honda's Success', *California Management Review*, Vol. 26, No. 3, Spring, pp. 47–72.

Pond, L. (1918) *The Meaning of Architecture: An Essay in Constructive Criticism*, Boston, MA: Marshall Jones Company.

Pondy, L.R. (1983) 'Union of Rationality and Intuition in Management Action', in: S. Srivastava (ed.), *The Executive Mind*, San Francisco: Jossey-Bass.

Polanyi, M. (1966) *The Tacit Dimension*, London: Routledge & Kegan Paul.

Prahalad, C.K., and Bettis, R.A. (1986) 'The Dominant Logic: A New Linkage between Diversity and Performance', *Strategic Management Journal*, Vol. 7, No. 6, November–December, pp. 485–601.

Redding, S.G. (1980) 'Cognition as an Aspect of Culture and its Relationship to Management Processes: An Exploratory View of the Chinese Case', *Journal of Management Studies*, Vol. 17, May, pp. 127–148.

Reid, S. (2002) *How to Think: Building Your Mental Muscle*, London: Prentice Hall.

Rittel, H. (1972) 'On the Planning Crisis: Systems Analysis of the "First and Second Generations"', *Bedriftsokonomen*, No. 8, pp. 390–396.

Rittel, H., and Webber, M. (1973) 'Dilemmas in a General Theory of Planning', *Policy Sciences*, Vol. 4, pp. 155–169.

Roos, J., and Victor, B. (1999) 'Towards a New Model of Strategy-making as Serious Play', *European Management Journal*, Vol. 17, No. 4, April, pp. 348–355.

Schein, E.H. (1985) *Organizational Culture and Leadership*, San Francisco: Jossey-Bass.

Schneider, S.C. (1989) 'Strategy Formulation: The Impact of National Culture', *Organization Studies*, Vol. 10, No. 2, pp. 149–168.

Schoemaker, P.J.H., and Russo, J.E. (1993) 'A Pyramid of Decision Approaches', *California Management Review*, Vol. 36, No. 1, Fall, pp. 9–32.

Schon, D. (1983) *The Reflective Practitioner: How Professionals Think in Action*, New York: Basic Books.

Schwenk, C.R. (1984) 'Cognitive Simplification Processes in Strategic Decision-Making', *Strategic Management Journal*, Vol. 5, No. 2, April–June, pp. 111–128.

Schwenk, C.R. (1988) *The Essence of Strategic Decision Making*, Lexington, MA: Lexington Books.

Senge, P. (1990) *The Fifth Discipline*, New York: Doubleday.

Simon, H.A. (1957) *Models of Man*, New York: Wiley.

Simon, H.A. (1969) *The Sciences of the Artificial*, Cambridge, MA: MIT Press.

Simon, H.A. (1972) 'Theories of Bounded Rationality', in: C. McGuire, and R. Radner (eds), *Decision and Organization*, Amsterdam, pp. 161–176.

Simon, H.A. (1987) 'Making Management Decisions: The Role of Intuition and Emotion', *Academy of Management Executive*, Vol. 1, No. 1, pp. 57–64.

Simon, H.A. (1993) 'Strategy and Organizational Evolution', *Strategic Management Journal*, Vol. 14, pp. 131–142.

Smircich, L., and Stubbart, C. (1985) 'Strategic Management in an Enacted World', *Academy of Management Review*, Vol. 10, No. 4, pp. 724–736.

Sutcliffe, K.M., and Huber, G.P. (1998) 'Firm and Industry Determinants of Executive Perceptions of the Environment', *Strategic Management Journal*, Vol. 19, pp. 793–807.

Starbuck, W., and Milliken, F. (1988) 'Challenger: Fine-Tuning the Odds Until Something Breaks', *Journal of Management Studies*, Vol. 25, No. 4, July.

Trice, H.M., and Beyer, J.M. (1993) *The Cultures of Work Organizations*, Englewood Cliffs: Prentice Hall.

Tversky, A., and Kahneman, D. (1986) 'Rational Choice and the Framing of Decisions', *Journal of Business*, Vol. 59, No. 4, pp. 251–278.

Von Ghyczy, T., Von Oetinger, B., and Bassford, C. (2001) *Clausewitz on Strategy*, New York: Wiley.

Von Winterfeldt, D., and Edwards, W (1986) *Decision Analysis and Behavioural Research*, Cambridge: Cambridge University Press.

Walsh, J. (1995) 'Managerial and Organizational Cognition: Notes from a Trip Down Memory Lane', *Organization Science*, Vol. 6, pp. 280–321.

Weick, K.E. (1979) *The Social Psychology of Organizing*, New York: Random House.

Weick, K.E., and Bourgnon, M.G. (1986) 'Organizations as Cognitive Maps', in: H.P Sims Jr. and D.A. Gioia (eds), *The Thinking Organization*, Jossey-Bass, San Francisco. Williamson, J. (1983) *Decoding Advertisements*, New York: Marion Boyars Publishers.

3 STRATEGY FORMATION

To plan, v. To bother about the best method of accomplishing an accidental result.

The Devil's Dictionary, Ambrose Bierce (1842–1914); American columnist

INTRODUCTION

There are many definitions of strategy and many ideas of how strategies should be made. In the introduction to Section II of this book on 'Strategy process', our definition of strategy was kept basic to encompass the large majority of these different views – 'strategy is a course of action for achieving an organization's purpose'. Taking this definition as a starting point, a major distinction can be observed between people who see strategy as an *intended* course of action and those who regard strategy as a *realized* course of action. Mintzberg and Waters (1985) have remarked that these two views of strategy are not contradictory, but complementary. Intended strategy is what individuals or organizations formulate prior to action (a *pattern of decisions),* while realized strategy refers to the strategic behaviour exhibited in practice (a *pattern of actions).* Of course, not all behaviour is necessarily strategic – if the actions do not follow a pattern directed at achieving the organization's purpose, it does not qualify as strategy.

The process by which an intended strategy is created is called 'strategy formulation'. Normally strategy formulation is followed by strategy implementation. However, intentions sometimes end up not being put into practice – plans can be changed or cancelled along the way. The process by which a realized strategy is formed is called 'strategy formation'. What is realized might be based on an intended strategy, but it can also be the result of unplanned actions as time goes by. In other words, the process of strategy formation encompasses both formulation and action. Strategy formation is the entire process leading to strategic behaviour in practice.

For managers with the responsibility for getting results, it would be too limited to only look at the process of strategy formulation and to worry about implementation later. Managers must ask themselves how the entire process of strategy formation should be managed to get their organizations to act strategically. Who should be involved, what activities need to be undertaken and to what extent can strategy be formulated in advance? In short, for managers, finding a way to realize a strategic pattern of actions is the key issue.

THE ISSUE OF REALIZED STRATEGY

Getting an organization to exhibit strategic behaviour is what all strategists aim to achieve. Preparing detailed analyses, drawing up plans, making extensive slide presentations and holding long meetings might all be necessary means to achieve this end, but ultimately it is the organization's actions directed at the market-place that count. The key issue facing managers is, therefore, how this strategic behaviour can be attained. How can a successful course of action be realized in practice?

To answer these questions, it is first necessary to gain a deeper understanding of the 'who' and 'what' of strategy formation – 'what type of strategy formation activities need to be carried out?' and 'what type of strategy formation roles need to be filled by whom?'. Both questions will be examined in the following sections.

Strategy formation activities

In Chapter 2 it was argued that the process of strategic reasoning could be divided into four general categories of activities – identifying, diagnosing, conceiving and realizing. These strategic problem-solving activities, taking place in the mind of the strategist, are in essence the same as those encountered in organizations at large. Organizations also need to 'solve strategic problems' and achieve a successful pattern of actions. The difference is that the organizational context – involving many more people, with different experiences, perspectives, personalities, interests and values – leads to different requirements for structuring the process. Getting people within an organization to exhibit strategic behaviour necessitates the exchange of information and ideas, decision-making procedures, communication channels, the allocation of resources and the coordination of actions.

When translated to an organizational environment, the four general elements of the strategic reasoning process can be further divided into the eight basic building blocks of the strategy formation process, as illustrated in Figure 3.1.

Strategic issue identification activities. If a strategy is seen as an answer to a perceived 'problem' or 'issue', managers must have some idea of what the problem is. 'Identifying' refers to all activities contributing to a better understanding of what should

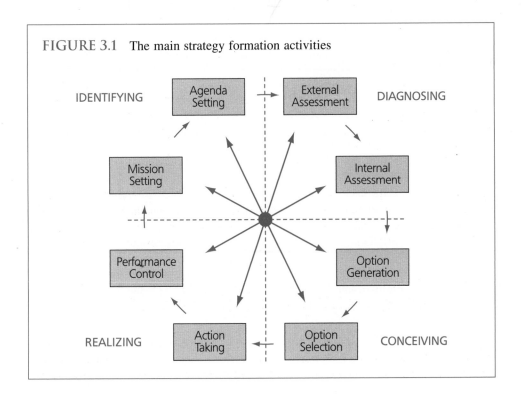

FIGURE 3.1   The main strategy formation activities

IDENTIFYING

Agenda Setting

External Assessment

DIAGNOSING

Mission Setting

Internal Assessment

Performance Control

Option Generation

REALIZING

Action Taking

Option Selection

CONCEIVING

be viewed as problematic – what constitutes an important opportunity or threat that must be attended to if the organization's purpose is to be met. The key activities here are:

- Mission setting. What the organization sees as an issue will in part depend on its mission — the enduring set of fundamental principles outlining what purpose the organization wishes to serve, in what domain and under which conditions. A company's mission, encompassing its core values, beliefs, business definition and purpose, forms the basis of the organization's identity and sets the basic conditions under which the organization wishes to function. Where a company has a clearly developed mission, shared by all key players in the organization, this will strongly colour its filtering of strategic issues. The mission does not necessarily have to be formally captured in a mission statement, but can be informally internalized as a part of the company culture. The topic of mission is discussed at more length in Chapter 11.

- Agenda setting. Besides the organizational mission as screening mechanism, many other factors can contribute to the focusing of organizational attention on specific strategic issues. For instance, the cognitive map of each strategist will influence which environmental and organizational developments are identified as issues. Furthermore, group culture will have an impact on which issues are discussible, which are off-limits to open debate, and under what conditions discussions should take place. Getting people to sit up and take notice will also depend on each actor's communication and political skills, as well as their sources of power, both formal and informal. Together these attention-focusing factors determine which issues are picked up on the 'organizational radar screen', discussed and looked into further. It is said that these issues make it on to the 'organizational agenda', while all other potential problems receive less or no attention. Many of these organizational factors are discussed more extensively in Chapters 4 and 9.

Strategic issue diagnosis activities. To come to grips with a 'problem' or 'issue', managers must try to comprehend its structure and its underlying causes. Especially since most strategic issues are not simple and straightforward, but complex and messy, it is very important to gain a deeper understanding of 'what is going on' – which 'variables' are there and how are they interrelated? This part of the strategy formation processes can be divided into the following activities:

- External assessment. The activity of investigating the structure and dynamics of the environment surrounding the organization is commonly referred to as an external assessment or analysis. Typically such a diagnosis of the outside world includes both a scan of the direct (market) environment and the broader (contextual) environment. In both cases the analyst wants to move beyond observed behaviour, to understand 'what makes the system tick'. What is the underlying structure of the industry and the market that is conditioning each party's behaviour? And what are the characteristics and strategies of each important actor, including customers, competitors, suppliers, distributors, unions, governments and financiers? Furthermore, only understanding the current state of affairs is generally insufficient; it is also necessary to analyse in which direction external circumstances are developing. Which trends can be discerned, which factors seem to be driving the industry and market dynamics, and can these be used to forecast or estimate future developments? In Chapters 5, 7 and 8, these questions surrounding external assessment are discussed in more detail.

- Internal assessment. The activity of investigating the capabilities and functioning of the organization is commonly referred to as an internal assessment or analysis. Typically such a diagnosis of the inner workings of the organization includes an assessment of the *business system* with which the firm creates value and the *organizational system* that has been developed to facilitate the business system. When dissecting the business system, attention is directed at understanding the resources and chain of value-adding activities that enable the firm to offer a set of products and services. To gain insight into the functioning of the organizational system, it is necessary to determine the structure of the organization, the processes used to control and coordinate the various people and units, and the organizational culture. In all these analyses a mere snapshot of the firm is generally insufficient – the direction in which the organization is developing must also be examined, including a consideration of the main change drivers and change inhibitors. Furthermore, for strategy making it is important to compare how the organization scores on all aforementioned factors compared to rival firms. In Chapters 4 and 5 these topics are investigated in more depth.

Strategy conception activities. To deal with a strategic 'problem' or 'issue', managers must come up with a potential solution. A course of action must be found that will allow the organization to relate itself to the environment in such a way that it will be able to achieve its purpose. 'Conceiving' refers to all activities that contribute to determining which course of action should be pursued. In this part of the strategy formation process, the following categories of activities can be discerned:

■ Option generation. Creating potential strategies is what option generation is about. Sometimes managers will immediately jump at one specific course of action, limiting their strategic option generation activities to only one prime candidate. However, many managers will be inclined to explore a number of different avenues for approaching a specific strategic issue, thereby generating multiple strategic options. Each option can range in detail from a general outline of actions to be taken, up to a full-blown strategic plan, specifying goals, actions, tasks, responsibilities, resource allocation, milestones and performance measures. Which questions each strategic option should address is the main focus of discussion in the strategy content section of this book.

■ Option selection. The potential 'solutions' formulated by managers must be evaluated to decide whether they should be acted upon. It must be weighed whether the strategic option generated will actually lead to the results required and then it must be concluded whether to act accordingly. Especially where two or more strategic options have come forward, managers need to judge which one of them is most attractive to act on. This screening of strategic options is done on the basis of evaluation criteria, for instance perceived risk, anticipated benefits, the organization's capacity to execute, expected competitor reactions and follow-up possibilities. Sometimes a number of the evaluation criteria used are formally articulated, but generally the evaluation will at least be partially based on the experience and judgement of the decision-makers involved. Together, these activities of assessing strategic options and arriving at a selected course of action are also referred to as 'strategic decision-making'.

Strategy realization activities. A strategic 'problem' or 'issue' can only be resolved if concrete actions are undertaken that achieve results. Managers must make adjustments to their business or organizational system, or initiate actions in the market – they must not only think, talk and decide, but also do, to have a tangible impact. 'Realizing' refers to all these practical actions performed by the organization. If there is a clear pattern to these actions, it can be said that there is a realized strategy. In this part of the strategy formation process, the following activities can be distinguished:

■ Action taking. A potential problem solution must be carried out – intended actions must be implemented to become realized actions. This performing of tangible actions encompasses all aspects of a firm's functioning. All hands-on activities, more commonly referred to as 'work', fall into this category – everything from setting up and operating the business system to getting the organizational system to function on a day-to-day basis.

- Performance control. Managers must also measure whether the actions being taken in the organization are in line with the option selected and whether the results are in line with what was anticipated. This reflection on the actions being undertaken can be informal, and even unconscious, but it can be formally structured into a performance monitoring and measuring system as well. Such performance measurement can be employed to assess how well certain people and organizational units are doing vis-à-vis set objectives. Incentives can be linked to achieving targets, and corrective steps can be taken to ensure conformance to an intended course of action. However, deviation from the intended strategy can also be a signal to re-evaluate the original solution or even to re-evaluate the problem definition itself. An important issue when engaging in performance control is the determination of which performance indicators will be used – micro-measuring all aspects of the organization's functioning is generally much too unwieldy and time-consuming. Some managers prefer a few simple measures, sometimes quantitative (e.g. financial indicators), sometimes qualitative (e.g. are clients satisfied?), while others prefer more extensive and varied measures, such as a balanced scorecard (Kaplan and Norton, 2001; Simons, 1995).

Note that these strategy formation activities have not been labelled 'steps' or 'phases'. While these eight activities have been presented in an order that seems to suggest a logical sequence of steps, it remains to be seen in which order they should be carried out in practice. In Figure 3.1 the outer arrows represent the logical clockwise sequence, similar to the rational reasoning process discussed in Chapter 2. The inner arrows represent the possibility to jump back and forth between the strategy formation activities, similar to the irregular pattern exhibited in the generative reasoning process in Chapter 2.

Strategy formation roles

In all strategy formation processes the activities discussed above need to be carried out. However, there can be significant differences in who carries out which activities. Roles in the strategy formation process can vary as tasks and responsibilities are divided in alternative ways. The main variations are due to a different division of labour along the following dimensions:

- Top vs. middle vs. bottom roles. Strategy formation activities are rarely the exclusive domain of the CEO. Only in the most extreme cases will a CEO run a 'one-man show', carrying out all activities except realization. Usually some activities will be divided among members of the top management team, while other activities will be pushed further down to divisional managers, business unit managers, and department managers (e.g. Bourgeois and Brodwin, 1983; Floyd and Wooldridge, 2000). Some activities might be delegated or carried out together with people even further down the hierarchy, including employees on the work floor. For activities such as external and internal assessment and option generation it is more common to see participation by people lower in the organization, while top management generally retains the responsibility for selecting, or at least deciding on, which strategic option to follow. The recurrent theme in this question of the vertical division of activities is how far down activities can and should be pushed – how much *empowerment* of middle and lower levels is beneficial for the organization?
- Line vs. staff roles. By definition line managers are responsible for realization of strategic options pertaining to the primary process of the organization. Because they are responsible for achieving results, they are often also given the responsibility to

participate in conceiving the strategies they will have to realize. Potentially, line managers can carry out all strategy formation activities without staff support. However, many organizations do have staff members involved in the strategy formation process. Important staff input can come from all existing departments, while some organizations institute special strategy departments to take care of strategy formation activities. The responsibilities of such strategy departments can vary from general process facilitation, to process ownership to full responsibility for strategy formulation.

■ Internal vs. external roles. Strategy formation activities are generally seen as an important part of every manager's portfolio of tasks. Yet, not all activities need to be carried out by members of the organization, but can be 'outsourced' to outsiders (e.g. Robinson, 1982). It is not uncommon for firms to hire external agencies to perform diagnosis activities or to facilitate the strategy formation process in general. Some organizations have external consultants engaged in all aspects of the process, even to the extent that the outside agency has the final responsibility for drawing up the strategic options.

In organizing the strategy formation process, a key question is how formalized the assignment of activities to the various potential process participants should be. The advantage of formalization is that it structures and disciplines the strategy formation process (e.g. Chakravarthy and Lorange, 1991, Reading 3.1 in this book; Hax and Maljuf, 1984). Especially in large organizations, where many people are involved, it can be valuable to keep the process tightly organized. Formalization can be achieved by the establishment of a strategic planning system. In such a system, strategy formation steps can be scheduled, tasks can be specified, responsibilities can be assigned, decision-making authority can be clarified, budgets can be allocated and evaluation mechanisms can be put in place. Generally, having unambiguous responsibilities, clearer accountability and stricter review of performance will lead to a better functioning organization. The added benefit of formalization is that it gives top management more control over the organization, as all major changes must be part of approved plans and the implementation of plans is checked.

Yet, there is a potential danger in using formal planning systems as a means to make strategy. Formalization strongly emphasizes those aspects that can be neatly organized such as meetings, writing reports, giving presentations, making decisions, allocating resources and reviewing progress, while having difficulty with essential strategy-making activities that are difficult to capture in procedures. Important aspects such as creating new insights, learning, innovation, building political support and entrepreneurship can be sidelined or crushed if rote bureaucratic mechanisms are used to produce strategy. Moreover, planning bureaucracies, once established, can come to live a life of their own, creating rules, regulations, procedures, checks, paperwork, schedules, deadlines and double-checks, making the system inflexible, unresponsive, ineffective and demotivating (e.g. Marx, 1991; Mintzberg, 1994a).

THE PARADOX OF DELIBERATENESS AND EMERGENCE

The ability to foretell what is going to happen tomorrow, next week, next month and next year. And to have the ability afterwards to explain why it didn't happen.

Winston Churchill (1874–1965); British prime minister and writer

Strategy has to do with the future. And the future is unknown. This makes strategy a fascinating, yet frustrating, topic. Fascinating because the future can still be shaped and strategy can be used to achieve this aim. Frustrating because the future is unpredictable, undermining the best of intentions, thus demanding flexibility and adaptability. To managers, the idea of creating the future is highly appealing, yet the prospect of sailing for *terra incognita* without a compass is unsettling at best.

This duality of wanting to intentionally design the future, while needing to gradually explore, learn and adapt to an unfolding reality, is the tension central to the topic of strategy formation. It is the conflicting need to figure things out in advance, versus the need to find things out along the way. On the one hand, managers would like to forecast the future and to orchestrate plans to prepare for it. Yet, on the other hand, managers understand that experimentation, learning and flexibility are needed to deal with the fundamental unpredictability of future events.

In their influential article, 'Of Strategies: Deliberate and Emergent', Mintzberg and Waters (1985) were one of the first to explicitly focus on this tension. They argued that a distinction should be made between deliberate and emergent strategy (see Figure 3.2). Where realized strategies were fully intended, one can speak of 'deliberate strategy'. However, realized strategies can also come about 'despite, or in the absence of, intentions', which Mintzberg and Waters labelled 'emergent strategy'. In their view, few strategies were purely deliberate or emergent, but usually a mix between the two.

FIGURE 3.2   Deliberate and emergent strategy

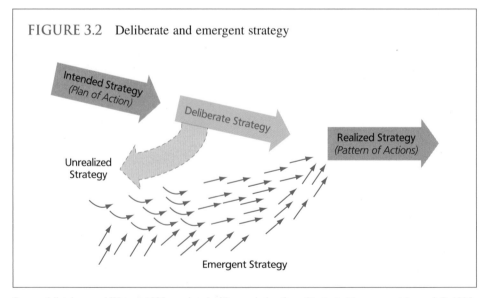

Emergent Strategy

Source: Mintzberg and Waters, 1985; reprinted with permission from *Strategic Management Journal*, © 1985 John Wiley and Sons Ltd.

Hence, in realizing strategic behaviour managers need to blend the conflicting demands for deliberate strategizing and strategy emergence. In the following paragraphs both sides of this paradox of deliberateness and emergence will be examined further.

The demand for deliberate strategizing

Deliberateness refers to the quality of acting intentionally. When people act deliberately, they 'think' before they 'do'. They make a plan and then implement the plan. A plan is an intended course of action, stipulating which measures a person or organization proposes to take. In common usage, plans are assumed to be articulated (made explicit) and documented (written down), although strictly speaking this is not necessary to qualify as a plan.

As an intended course of action, a plan is a means towards an end. A plan details which actions will be undertaken to reach a particular objective. In practice, however, plans can exist without explicit objectives. In such cases, the objectives are implicitly wrapped up in the plan – the plan incorporates both ends and means.

All organizations need to plan. At the operational level, most firms will have some degree of production planning, resource planning, manpower planning and financial planning, to name just a few. When it comes to strategic behaviour, there are also a number of prominent advantages that strongly pressure organizations to engage in deliberate strategizing:

- Direction. Plans give organizations a sense of direction. Without objectives and plans, organizations would be adrift. If organizations did not decide where they wanted to go, any direction and any activity would be fine. People in organizations would not know what they were working towards and therefore would not be able to judge what constitutes effective behaviour (e.g. Ansoff, 1965; Chakravarthy and Lorange, 1991, Reading 3.1).

- Commitment. Plans enable early commitment to a course of action. By setting objectives and drawing up a plan to accomplish these, organizations can invest resources, train people, build up production capacity and take a clear position within their environment. Plans allow organizations to mobilize themselves and to dare to take actions that are difficult to reverse and have a long payback period (e.g. Ghemawat, 1991; Marx, 1991).

- Coordination. Plans have the benefit of coordinating all strategic initiatives within an organization into a single cohesive pattern. An organization-wide master plan can ensure that differences of opinion are ironed out and one consistent course of action is followed throughout the entire organization, avoiding overlapping, conflicting and contradictory behaviour (e.g. Ackoff, 1980; Andrews, 1987).

- Optimization. Plans also facilitate optimal resource allocation. Drawing up a plan disciplines strategizing managers to explicitly consider all available information and consciously evaluate all available options. This allows managers to choose the optimal course of action before committing resources. Moreover, documented plans permit corporate level managers to compare the courses of action proposed by their various business units and to allocate scarce resources to the most promising initiatives (e.g. Ansoff and McDonnell, 1990; Bower, 1970).

- Programming. Last, but not least, plans are a means for programming all organizational activities in advance. Having detailed plans allows organizations to be run with the clockwork precision, reliability and efficiency of a machine. Activities that might otherwise be plagued by poor organization, inconsistencies, redundant routines, random behaviour, helter-skelter fire fighting and chaos, can be programmed and controlled if plans are drawn up (e.g. Grinyer *et al.,* 1986; Steiner, 1979).

Given these major advantages, it can come as no surprise that organizations feel the pressure to engage in deliberate strategizing. Deliberateness is a quality that the strategy formation process cannot do without.

The demand for strategy emergence

Emergence is the process of becoming apparent. A strategy emerges when it comes into being along the way. Where there are no plans, or people divert from their plans but their behaviour is still strategic, it can be said that the strategy is emergent – gradually shaped during an iterative process of 'thinking' and 'doing'.

Emergent strategy differs from ad hoc behaviour in that a coherent pattern of action does evolve. While managers may have no prior intentions, they can explore, learn and piece together a consistent set of behaviours over time. Such an approach of letting strategy emerge has a number of major advantages that organizations also need to consider:

- Opportunism. As the future is unknown and therefore unpredictable, organizations must retain enough mental freedom to grab unforeseen opportunities as they emerge. Organizations must keep an open mind to sense where positive and negative circumstances are unfolding, so that they can respond rapidly to these new conditions – proactively riding the wave of opportunity, using the momentum in the environment and/ or the organization to their advantage. This ability to 'play the field' is an important factor in effective strategy formation (e.g. Quinn, 2002; Stacey, 2001).

- Flexibility. Not only must managers keep an open mind, they must keep their options open as well, by not unnecessarily committing themselves to irreversible actions and investments. Letting strategy emerge means not prematurely locking the organization into a preset course of action, but keeping alternatives open for as long as practically possible. And where commitments must to be made, managers need to select 'robust' options, which permit a lot of leeway to shift along with unfolding events. This pressure to remain flexible is also an important demand on strategizing managers (e.g. Beinhocker, 1999; Evans, 1991).

- Learning. Often, the best way to find out what works is to give it a try – to act before you know. Letting strategy emerge is based on the same principle, that to learn what will be successful in the market must be discovered by experimentation, pilot projects, trial runs and gradual steps. Through the feedback obtained by hands-on 'doing', a rich insight can grow into what really works. As Thomas Alva Edison is well known for remarking, invention is 5% inspiration and 95% perspiration, and this is probably equally true for 'inventing the corporate future'. Learning is hard work, but it is an essential part of strategy formation (e.g. Pascale, 1984; Mintzberg, 1994d).

- Entrepreneurship. Building on the previous point, often the best way to find out what works is to let various people give it a try – to tap into the entrepreneurial spirits within the organization. Different people in the organization will have different strategic ideas and many of them will feel passionately about proving that their idea 'can fly'. By providing individuals, teams and/or entire units with a measure of autonomy to pursue innovative initiatives, firms can use the energy of 'intrapreneurs' within the organization, instead of forcing them to conform or start on their own (e.g. Amabile, 1998; Pinchot, 1985). As true incubators, firms can facilitate various divergent projects simultaneously, increasing commitment or closing them down as their potential unfolds (e.g. Burgelman, 1983, 1991; Lyon, Lumpkin and Dess, 2000).

- Support. A major shift in strategy generally requires a major shift in the political and cultural landscape of an organization – careers will be affected, vested departmental interests will be impacted and cultural values and beliefs will be challenged. Rarely can such shifts be imposed top-down by decree. Getting things done in organizations includes building coalitions, blocking rivals, convincing wavering parties, confronting opposing ideas and letting things 'sink in', all with the intention of gradually building enough support to move forward. Yet, finding out where enough support can be mustered to move forward, and where side steps or even reversals are needed, is an ongoing process and cannot be predicted in advance. Hence, strategizing managers must understand the internal political and cultural dynamics of their organizations and pragmatically shape strategy depending on what is feasible, not on what is ideal (e.g. Allison, 1971; Quinn, 1980).

Each of these points seems to be the opposite counterpart of the advantages of deliberate strategizing – while deliberateness creates commitment, emergence allows for flexibility; while deliberateness gives direction, emergence allows for opportunism; while deliberateness facilitates fixed programming, emergence allows for ongoing learning. This places managers in a paradoxical position. While both deliberate strategizing and strategy emergence seem to have advantageous characteristics, they are each other's opposites and are to a certain extent contradictory – a firm cannot be fully committed to detailed and coordinated long-term plans, while simultaneously adapting itself flexibly and opportunistically to unfolding circumstances, ongoing learning and unpredictable political and cultural processes. With two conflicting demands placed on the strategy formation process at the same time, managers need to choose one at the expense of the other, trying to strike the best possible balance between deliberateness and emergence.

EXHIBIT 3.1 SHORT CASE

SANOMA: SETTING COURSE IN A DIGITAL CLOUD?

Finland is home to a surprising number of global success stories, including handset-maker Nokia, chemical company Kemira, elevator and escalator producer Kone and paper manufacturer Stora Enso. Lesser known, but equally successful, is the media company Sanoma. With its headquarters in downtown Helsinki, Sanoma runs media activities in 20 European countries, employing more than 21 000 people and realizing annual sales exceeding €3 billion in 2008. Having started as a newspaper company in 1889, Sanoma derives its name from its leading newspaper title, *Helsingin Sanomat* (Helsinki News), but has since branched out into a variety of other media. The corporation consists of five divisions: Sanoma News, which includes mostly Finnish newspapers and online news sites (2008 sales of €475 million); Sanoma Entertainment, which encompasses a number of Finnish TV, radio and online operations (2008 sales of €157 million); Sanoma Learning & Literature, with educational and literary publishing activities in seven European countries (2008 sales of €390 million);

Sanoma Trade, which runs kiosks, bookstores, press distribution and movie theaters in another seven European countries (2008 sales of €867 million); and Sanoma Magazines, with a broad range of magazines and online operations in 13 European countries (2008 sales of €1247 million).

The expansion of Sanoma outside of Finland started in earnest in 2001, when former-CEO (and current chairman) Jaakko Rauramo engineered the acquisition of the consumer magazine businesses of the Dutch media group VNU. This portfolio of businesses was partly situated in Belgium and the Netherlands, but also in a range of Eastern Europe countries, as VNU had jumped into this market soon after the fall of the Berlin Wall. A number of intrapreneurs at VNU had realized that countries like Hungary, Slovakia, the Czech Republic, Bulgaria and Romania had enormous potential, but that the media landscape was so entirely different, that only a very localized approach would work. They started local subsidiaries with local magazine titles, as well as licensing international magazine formats such as *Elle, Cosmopolitan* and *Esquire,* but then adapting them to local tastes. In this way, VNU was able to build leading local market positions, while simultaneously nurturing strong local subsidiaries. When Sanoma acquired VNU's consumer magazines, this decentralized organizational model was embraced and all country units under the Sanoma Magazine flag retained a large measure of autonomy to be responsive to their specific local conditions. When in 2005 Sanoma Magazines acquired the largest consumer magazine company in Russia, Independent Media, it too was allowed to be true to its name.

The decentralized approach advocated by VNU actually fits very nicely with the corporate management style within Sanoma. With such diverse activities as newspapers, television, radio, cinemas, magazines and educational publishing, Rauramo preferred to give the divisions significant leeway in setting their strategy and building their organizations. Since taking over as President and CEO in 2007, Hannu Syrjänen has continued this policy, letting each division chart its own growth trajectory and internationalize in its own way. So, while the news and entertainment divisions have decided to focus on growth opportunities in Finland, Sanoma Trade has made significant inroads in Russia and the Baltic states, while Sanoma Learning & Literature has made some big acquisitions in the Netherlands and Poland. In line with this decentralized approach, Sanoma has even encouraged the divisions to set up their headquarters wherever it makes business sense. This has led Sanoma Magazines to select a location close to Amsterdam's Schiphol airport and Sanoma Learning & Literature to pick Den Bosch, in the Netherlands, which was the headquarters of its major acquisition, Malmberg.

In the same way, each division has been reacting to the digital revolution in its own way. So far, the biggest steps have been taken by Sanoma Magazines, which has built on the Dutch online activities that it acquired from VNU, called Ilse Media Group. CEO of Sanoma Magazines, Eija Ailasmaa, has taken a two-pronged approach to the challenge of digitalization, by looking at ways to leverage existing magazine titles and formats in the online world, while at the same time building a portfolio of totally new online businesses. So, on the one hand, the most promising of its 300 magazines have been experimenting at creating companion-sites to build stronger communities, thus offering advertisers both online and offline advertising opportunities. On the other hand, the company has been buying and building a variety of popular websites, in areas such as news, search, product comparison, parenting and weblogs, with the intention of turning the traffic into money. This 'monetization of eyeballs' is done partly by selling advertising, but increasingly also by taking a percentage of the online sales it helps to generate. The ideal type of website is one which not only makes money in its own right, but can be cross-promoted in Sanoma's own magazines, such as it does with www.autotrader.nl and its *AutoWeek* magazine.

As each country has its own 'digital landscape', Ailasmaa leaves the country units in charge of selecting their online growth priorities, but also encourages cross-border sharing. 'We have reached an entirely new level of sharing knowledge and skills within the division', she is quoted as saying in the 2008 annual report, highlighting the systematic collaboration across all 13 operating countries to develop and apply common business models and technologies. Yet, she stresses that while vigorously pursuing growth in the digital arena, she is a strong believer in the staying power of printed magazines. In her view, there will not be a shift from print to online, but the two will be complementary, leaving plenty of room to also grow the printed magazines business in innovative ways, for instance by linking up with television and other media to become a truly multimedia platform.

Driven by its President, Mikael Pentikäinen, Sanoma News has also taken bold steps to develop its online and mobile service offerings. 'Interaction between the print and online media makes both more attractive', says Pentikäinen, explaining why reader-generated content and discussion forums are such important extra features to the newspapers' online and mobile news services. Furthermore, to hold on to its traditional position as job and real estate advertiser, Sanoma News runs online marketplaces for these target audiences. Up until now the newspaper market in Finland has not contracted and Pentikäinen sees it as his challenge to make sure it doesn't happen at all.

At Sanoma Entertainment, President Anu Nissinen has not had to struggle with balancing between old and new media, as its Finnish cable TV infrastructure has enabled it to be a broadband internet access provider from the very beginning. Leveraging this core asset, her strategy has been to develop digital TV and radio channels, while recently also branching out into casual gaming. As for Sanoma Learning & Literature and Sanoma Trade, their digital activities have remained more small scale, such as experimenting with e-learning materials.

Taken together, the initiatives that Sanoma has taken to explore the digital world have been impressive, yet all people involved realize that this is only the beginning. The media industry seems to be at the threshold of a transformation process, of which nobody knows the path or the outcome, yet in which Sanoma needs to find its way. Bold measures will be needed to stake a claim in the digital space before other companies figure out the new rules of the game and beat Sanoma to the best positions. However, with a limited budget to spend, Sanoma cannot afford to fund all initiatives coming out of the decentralized organization simultaneously. Resources will need to be allocated to those digital initiatives that have the highest strategic priority and will be at the centre of the 'Sanoma of the future'. But what will that future be? Can it even be known?

To help the Executive Management Group to deal with these strategic issues, Sven Heistermann was recruited in 2008 to fill the new position of Chief Strategy Officer. One of his key tasks was to guide the strategy formation process within the company, particularly with regard to digitalization. With so many competing digital initiatives and acquisitions coming to the Executive Management Group, he needed to find a way to select priorities among the existing proposals and give direction to the divisions and country units with regard to new investment projects. The question he faced was 'how?' How can a strategy be shaped with so many uncertainties and unknowns, especially in such a decentralized organization?

To Heistermann it was clear that in the unfolding digital world, the rules of the game still need to be discovered. There are many more questions than answers. Will the digital media be largely complementary to Sanoma's existing media, or will there be significant cannibalism? How will future consumers behave in online and mobile environments? For which online content and services will there be demand in the long run? Which business models will prove profitable and which will only burn cash? How much advertising money will migrate to the online world and will it be spent on banners and buttons, or will advertisers only pay-per-click or even pay-per-sale? Will online and mobile markets be global, national or even very local? Who will be Sanoma's new digital competitors and will they operate locally or internationally? And which new technologies will be introduced in the coming years, potentially throwing the whole digital world upside down?

With so many unknowns, tackling Sanoma's strategic issues was not going to be easy. Who should be taking the lead in developing the digital opportunities: the corporate centre, the divisions, the country units, or even the individual operating companies? Should digital activities be linked to magazines, newspapers and the like, or should they be organized separately? Should Sanoma favour building digital add-ons to its current businesses, grow its digital businesses from scratch, or rely on the acquisition of existing digital companies? And how was it going to find the people who understand the new digital reality and are not wedded to the old media rules of the game?

In short, Heistermann not only had to find an effective approach to strategy formation, he also had to determine who should be doing what in the process. Not only how to strategize, but who should strategize. He had heard of cloud computing before, but it was apparent that everything in the digital world is cloudy. So this is how Columbus must have felt, setting a course through the clouds, trying to find his way in an unknown world.

Sources: www.sanoma.com; Sanoma Annual Report 2008, company interviews.

PERSPECTIVES ON STRATEGY FORMATION

It is impossible for a man to learn what he thinks he already knows.

Epictetus (c. 60–120); Roman philosopher

In Hollywood, most directors do not start shooting a movie until the script and storyboard are entirely completed – the script details each actor's words, expression and gestures, while the storyboard graphically depicts how each scene will look in terms of camera angles, lighting, backgrounds and stage props. Together they form a master plan, representing the initial intentions of the director. However, it frequently happens that a director has a new insight, and changes are made to the script or storyboard 'on the fly'. Yet, on the whole, most 'realized movies' are fairly close to directors' initial intentions.

For some directors this is madness. They might have a movie idea, but in their mind's eye they cannot yet picture it in its final form. Some elements might have already crystallized in their thoughts, but other parts of the film can only be worked out once the cameras are rolling and the actors start playing their roles. In this way, directors can let movies emerge without having a detailed script or storyboard in advance to guide them. It can be said that such movies are shaped by gradually blending together a number of small intentional steps over a long period of time, instead of taking one big step of making a master plan and implementing it. This approach of taking many small steps is called 'incrementalism'.

The question is how this works for managers making strategy. Is it best to deliberately draw up a storyboard for the film and trust that the 'actors' are flexible enough to adapt to minor changes in the script as time goes by? Or is the idea of a master plan misplaced, and are the best results achieved by developing a strategy incrementally, emergently responding to opportunities and threats as they unfold along the way? In short, how should strategizing managers strike a balance between deliberateness and emergence?

Unfortunately, the strategic management literature does not offer a clear-cut answer to this question. In both the academic journals and the practitioner-oriented literature, a wide spectrum of views can be observed on how managers should engage in strategy formation. While some writers suggest that there might be different styles in balancing deliberateness and emergence (e.g. Chaffee, 1985; Hart, 1992), most seem intent on offering 'the best way' to approach the issue of strategy formation – which often differs significantly from 'the best way' advised by others.

To come to grips with this variety of views, here the two diametrically opposed pole positions will be identified and discussed. On the basis of these two 'points of departure' the debate on how to deal with the paradox of deliberateness and emergence can be further explored. At one pole we find those managers and theorists who strongly emphasize deliberateness over emergence. They argue that organizations should strive to make strategy in a highly deliberate manner, by first explicitly formulating comprehensive plans, and only then implementing them. In accordance with common usage, this point of view will be referred to as the 'strategic planning perspective'. At the other pole are those who strongly emphasize emergence over deliberateness, arguing that in reality most new strategies emerge over time and that organizations should facilitate this messy, fragmented, piecemeal strategy formation process. This point of view will be referred to as the 'strategic incrementalism perspective'.

The strategic planning perspective

 Advocates of the strategic planning perspective argue that strategies should be deliberately planned and executed. In their view, anything that emerges unplanned is not really strategy. A successful pattern of action that was not intended cannot be called strategy, but should be seen for what it is – brilliant improvisation or just plain luck (Andrews, 1987). However, managers cannot afford to count on their good fortune or skill at muddling through. They must put time and effort into consciously formulating an explicit plan, making use of all available information and weighing all of the strategic alternatives. Tough decisions need to be made and priorities need to be set, before action is taken. 'Think before you act' is the strategic planning perspective's motto. But once a strategic plan has been adopted, action should be swift, efficient and controlled. Implementation must be secured by detailing the activities to be undertaken, assigning responsibilities to managers and holding them accountable for achieving results (e.g. Ansoff and McDonnell, 1990; Chakravarthy and Lorange, 1991, Reading 3.1).

Hence, in the strategic planning perspective, strategies are intentionally designed, much as an engineer designs a bridge. Building a bridge requires a long formulation phase, including extensive analysis of the situation, the drawing up of a number of rough designs, evaluation of these alternatives, choice of a preferred design, and further detailing in the form of a blueprint. Only after the design phase has been completed do the construction companies take over and build according to plan. Characteristic of such a planning approach to producing bridges and strategies is that the entire process can be disassembled into a number of distinct steps that need to be carried out in a sequential and orderly way. Only by going through these steps in a conscious and structured manner will the best results be obtained (e.g. Armstrong, 1982; Powell, 1992).

For advocates of the strategic planning perspective, the whole purpose of strategizing is to give organizations direction, instead of letting them drift. Organizations cannot act rationally without intentions – if you do not know where you are going, any behaviour is fine, which soon degenerates into 'muddling through' (e.g. Ansoff, 1991; Steiner, 1979). By first setting a goal and then choosing a strategy to get there, organizations can get 'organized'. Managers can select actions that are efficient and effective within the context of the strategy. A structure can be chosen, tasks can be assigned, responsibilities can be divided, budgets can be allotted and targets can be set. Not unimportantly, a control system can be created to measure results in comparison to the plan, so that corrective action can be taken.

Another advantage of the planning approach to strategy formation is that it allows for the *formalization* and *differentiation* of strategy tasks. Because of its highly structured and sequential nature, strategic planning lends itself well to formalization. The steps of the strategic planning approach can be captured in planning systems (e.g. Kukalis, 1991; Lorange and Vancil, 1977), and procedures can be developed to further enhance and organize the strategy formation process. In such strategic planning systems, not all elements of strategy formation need to be carried out by one and the same person, but can be divided among a number of people. The most important division of labour is often between those formulating the plans and those implementing them. In many large companies the managers proposing the plans are also the ones implementing them, but deciding on the plans is passed up to a higher level. Often other tasks are spun off as well, or shared with others, such as diagnosis (strategy department or external consultants), implementation (staff departments) and evaluation (corporate planner and controller). Such task differentiation and specialization, it is argued, can lead to a better use of management talent, much as the division of labour has improved the field of production. At the same, having a formalized system allows for sufficient coordination and mutual adjustment, to ensure that all specialized elements are integrated back into a consistent organization-wide strategy (e.g. Grinyer *et al.*, 1986; Jelinek, 1979).

Last, but not least, an advantage of strategic planning is that it encourages long-term thinking and commitment. 'Muddling through' is short-term oriented, dealing with issues of strategic importance as they come up or as a crisis develops. Strategic planning, on the other hand, directs attention to the future. Managers making strategic plans have to take a more long-term view and are stimulated to prepare for, or even create, the future (Ackoff, 1980). Instead of just focusing on small steps, planning challenges managers to define a desirable future and to work towards it. Instead of wavering and opportunism, strategic planning commits the organization to a course of action and allows for investments to be made at the present that may only pay off in the long run (e.g. Ansoff, 1991; Miller and Cardinal, 1994).

One of the difficulties of strategic planning, advocates of this perspective will readily admit, is that plans will always be based on assumptions about how future events will unfold. Plans require forecasts. And as the Danish physicist Niels Bohr once joked, 'prediction is very difficult, especially about the future.'. Even enthusiastic planners acknowledge that forecasts will be inaccurate. As Makridakis, the most prolific writer on the topic of forecasting, writes (1990: 66), 'the future can be predicted only by extrapolating from the past, yet it is fairly certain that the future will be different from the past.' Consequently, it is clear that rigid long-range plans based on such unreliable forecasts would amount to nothing less than Russian roulette. Most proponents of the strategic planning perspective therefore caution for overly deterministic plans. Some argue in favour of 'contingency planning', whereby a number of alternative plans are held in reserve in case key variables in the environment suddenly change. These contingency plans are commonly based on different future 'scenarios' (Van der Heijden, 1996; Wilson, 2000, Reading 3.4 in this book). Others argue that organizations should stage regular reviews, and realign strategic plans to match the altered circumstances. This is usually accomplished by going through the planning cycle every year, and adapting strategic plans to fit with the new forecasts.

The strategic planning perspective shares many of the assumptions underlying the rational reasoning perspective discussed in Chapter 2. Both perspectives value systematic, orderly, consistent, logical reasoning and assume that humans are capable of forming a fairly good understanding of reality. And both are based on a calculative and optimizing view of strategy-making. It is, therefore, not surprising that many managers who are rationally inclined also exhibit a distinct preference for the strategic planning perspective.

EXHIBIT 3.2 THE STRATEGIC PLANNING PERSPECTIVE

SAMSUNG ELECTRONICS: SHOOTING FOR THE STARS

At the end of the 1960s, Byung-Chull Lee was chairman of the Samsung Group, one of the major South Korean *chaebol* – a conglomerate manufacturing a wide array of products, ranging from clothing to ships. Samsung had worked hard to overcome the devastation of the Korean War (1951–1954), but Lee had even more ambitious plans. He wanted to move beyond traditional low value-added industries, into a more attractive industrial sector – electronics. So, in 1969 he launched Samsung Electronics, initially oriented towards the manufacturing of 'white goods' (home appliances), such as refrigerators, stoves and vacuum cleaners. The founding of Samsung Electronics fitted perfectly in the South Korean government's 'Eight-Year Development Plan for Electronics Industries', which provided the firm with significant government support in R&D, the establishment of new plants and access to cheap loans.

Once Samsung Electronics had established a position in white goods by the start of the 1980s, Lee went to Japan to personally investigate where further growth opportunities could be found. Here he observed how the developments in semiconductors were speedily opening up enormous opportunities for new high-tech products. He became convinced that Samsung should not move cautiously in this area, following Sony and Matsushita, but should try to boldly grab a leadership role for itself – becoming an innovative industry shaper instead of remaining a reactive copycat. But for this to be successful, Samsung could not allow its strategy to slowly emerge. Rather, the company would need to set ambitious long-term goals and commit the organization to a disciplined roadmap to go from being a 'nobody' in the electronics industry to becoming 'number one'.

Based on Lee's vision, a business project team for semiconductors was secretly formed in 1982. The team ran a study to find out what the most attractive semiconductor product would be, which resulted in forecasts and strategic options for a range of different electronic components. In 1983, after thorough evaluations, Samsung decided to enter the DRAM (dynamic random access memory) chip industry. A long-term strategic plan was drawn up which would take the company from acquiring relatively simple technologies, to modifying imported technology, to designing new products through reverse engineering, to eventually developing advanced products. Finally, Samsung would become a 'black-belt master' in product and process innovation. To further refine this broad, long-term strategic plan, Samsung hired a group of US-educated South Korean engineers and sent them with a team of managers to the United States to work on the DRAM business project. Their assignment was to write a more detailed business plan and to recruit more engineers. Once this 'blueprint' was completed and approved by Lee, Samsung started DRAM assembly activities for the US-based Micron Technologies.

Over the next ten years, Samsung followed its strategy largely as planned and by the early 1990s had become the industry leader in DRAMs. Its approach of setting extremely ambitious goals and then developing detailed plans to be implemented with a relentless discipline also paid off in the subsequent years. During 1997 and 1998 the industry was hit by a dramatic dip in demand and prices for memory chips. But while some competitors became nervous about short-term profitability and 'adapted' themselves to the unfolding circumstances, slashing capital spending and production capacity, Samsung remained committed to its long-term plans and continued to invest and strengthen its memory chip production operations. When the bust cycle turned into boom again, Samsung was one of the few companies with sufficient DRAM manufacturing capacity to reap the benefit.

Since then, Samsung has gone from strength to strength. It soon became the largest manufacturer of memory chips in the world and, by 2003, the company had become world market leader in LCD screens, monitors, and microwave ovens. In 2005 Samsung surpassed Motorola in mobile telephones, becoming the world's number 2 after Nokia. By 2007 Samsung had reached sales of US$174.2 billion, while employing 263 000 people around the world.

When in 2008 the Samsung strategic planning team (headed by the CEO, Yoon-Woo Lee, and with strong consulting and financial competences on board) faced plummeting worldwide sales due to the global credit crisis, this did not divert the company from substantial R&D efforts to fulfil its strategic objectives. Looking ahead beyond the economic crisis, the company saw the potential to create a leading position in the new arena, where smart phones, communication services and digital media would merge together. It thus restructured its various consumer businesses into a new division, Digital Media and Communications, to both cut costs and facilitate synergies, while at the same time combining the various component businesses into a Device Solutions division.

So far, Samsung's strategic planning approach has been instrumental in making the long-term investments, sustaining the commitment to key technologies and coordinating its various businesses to create vital synergies. Samsung has clearly lived up to its name, meaning 'three stars' in Korean, and written with the characters that translate as 'large, strong and lasting forever'.

Co-author: Martijn Rademakers

Sources: *Far Eastern Economic Review*, 14 September 2002; Yu, 1999; Haour and Cho, 2000; *The Korea Herald*, 16 January 2009; www.samsung.com; www.sciencedirect.com.

The strategic incrementalism perspective

 To advocates of the strategic incrementalism perspective, the planners' faith in deliberateness is misplaced and counter-productive. In reality, incrementalists argue, new strategies largely emerge over time, as managers proactively piece together a viable course of action or reactively adapt to unfolding circumstances. The strategy formation process is not about rigidly *setting* the course of action in advance, but about flexibly *shaping* the course of action by gradually blending together initiatives into a coherent pattern of actions. Making strategy involves sense-making, reflecting, learning, envisioning, experimenting and changing the organization, which cannot be neatly organized and programmed. Strategy formation is messy, fragmented, and piecemeal – much more like the unstructured and unpredictable processes of exploration and invention than like the orderly processes of design and production (e.g. Mintzberg, 1990a; Quinn, 1978, Reading 3.2).

Yet proponents of the strategic planning perspective prefer to press strategy formation into an orderly, mechanistic straightjacket. Strategies must be intentionally designed and executed. According to strategic incrementalists, this excessive emphasis on deliberateness is due to planners' obsession with rationality and control (e.g. Wildavsky, 1979; Mintzberg, 1993). Planners are often compulsive in their desire for order, predictability and efficiency. It is the intention of strategic planning to predict, analysze, optimize and programme – to deliberately fine-tune and control the organization's future behaviour. For them, 'to manage' is 'to control' and therefore only deliberate patterns of action constitute good strategic management.

Incrementalists do not question the value of planning and control as a means for managing some organizational processes, but point out that strategy formation is not one of them. In general, planning and control are valuable for routine activities that need to be efficiently organized (e.g. production or finance). But planning is less suitable for non-routine activities – that is, for doing new things. Planning is not appropriate for innovation (e.g. Hamel, 1996; Kanter, 2002). Just as R&D departments cannot plan the invention of new products, managers cannot plan the development of new strategies. Innovation, whether in products or strategies, is not a process that can be neatly structured and controlled. Novel insights and creative ideas cannot be generated on demand, but surface at unexpected moments, often in unexpected places. Nor are new ideas born full-grown, ready to be evaluated and implemented. In reality, innovation requires brooding, tinkering, experimentation, testing and patience, as new ideas grow and take shape. Throughout the innovation process it remains unclear which ideas might evolve into blockbuster strategies and which will turn out to be miserable disappointments. No one can objectively determine ahead of time which strategic initiatives will 'fly' and which will 'crash'. Therefore, managers engaged in the formation of new strategies must move incrementally, letting novel ideas crystallize over time, and increasing commitment as ideas gradually prove their viability in practice. This demands that managers behave not as planners, but as 'inventors' – searching, experimenting, learning, doubting, and avoiding premature closure and lock- in to one course of action (e.g. Stacey, 1993, Reading 9.2 in this book; Beinhocker, 1999).

Recognizing that strategy formation is essentially an innovation process has more consequences. Innovation is inherently subversive, rebelling against the status quo and challenging those who are emotionally, intellectually or politically wedded to the current state of affairs. Creating new strategies involves confronting people's cognitive maps, questioning the organizational culture, threatening individuals' current interests and disrupting the distribution of power within the organization (e.g. Hamel, 1996; Johnson, 1988). None of these processes can be conducted in an orderly fashion, let alone be incorporated into a planning system. Changing people's cognitive maps requires complex processes of unlearning and learning. Cultural and political changes are also difficult processes to programme. Even for the most powerful CEO, managing cognitive, cultural and political changes is not a matter of deliberate control, but of incremental shaping. Less powerful managers will have an even weaker grip on the unfolding cognitive, cultural and political reality in their organization, and therefore will be even less able to plan. In short, managers who understand that strategy formation is essentially a disruptive process of organizational change will move incrementally, gradually moulding the organization into a satisfactory form. This demands that managers behave not as commanders, but as 'organizational developers' – questioning assumptions, challenging ideas, getting points on the strategic agenda, encouraging learning, championing new initiatives, supporting change and building political support.

Incrementalists point out that planning is particularly inappropriate when dealing with wicked problems. While solving tame problems can often be planned and controlled, strategizing managers rarely have the luxury of using generic solutions to fix clearly recognizable strategic problems. Strategic problems are inherently wicked – they are essentially unique, highly complex, linked to other problems, can be defined and interpreted in many ways, have no correct answer, nor a delimited set of possible solutions. The planning approach of recognizing the problem, fully analyszing the situation, formulating a comprehensive plan and then implementing the solution, is sure to choke on a wicked problem. A number of weaknesses of planning show up when confronted with a wicked problem:

- Problems cannot be simply recognized and analyszed, but can be interpreted and defined in many ways, depending on how the manager looks at it. Therefore, half the work of the strategizing manager is *making sense* out of complex problems. Or, as Rittel and Webber (1973) put it, the definition of a wicked problem is the problem! Managers must search for new ways for understanding old problems and must be aware of how others are reinterpreting what they see (e.g. Liedtka, 2000; Smircich and Stubbart, 1985). This inhibits strategic planning and encourages strategic incrementalism.

- A full analysis of a wicked problem is impossible. Due to a wicked problem's complexity and links to other problems, a full analysis would take, literally, forever. And there would always be more ways of interpreting the problem, requiring more analysis. Strategic planning based on the complete understanding of a problem in advance therefore necessarily leads to paralysis by analysis (e.g. Langley, 1995; Lenz and Lyles, 1985). In reality, however, managers move proactively despite their incomplete understanding of a wicked problem, learning as they go along. By acting and thinking at the same time, strategizing managers can focus their analyses on what seems to be important and realistic in practice, gradually shaping their understanding along the way.

- Developing a comprehensive plan to tackle a wicked problem is asking for trouble. Wicked problems are very complex, consisting of many sub-problems. Formulating a master plan to solve all sub-problems in one blow would require a very high level of planning sophistication and an organization with the ability to implement plans in a highly coordinated manner – much like the circus performers who can keep ten plates twirling at the ends of poles at the same time. Such organizations are rare at best, and the risk of a grand strategy failing is huge – once one plate falls, the rest usually come crashing down. This is also known as Knagg's law: the more complex a plan, the larger the chance of failure. Incrementalists therefore argue that it is wiser to tackle sub-problems individually, and gradually blend these solutions into a cohesive pattern of action.

- Planners who believe that formulation and implementation can be separated underestimate the extent to which wicked problems are interactive. As soon as an organization starts to implement a plan, its actions will induce counteractions. Customers will react, competitors will change behaviour, suppliers will take a different stance, regulatory agencies might come into action, unions will respond, the stock markets will take notice and company employees will draw conclusions. Hence, action by the organization will change the nature of the problem. And since the many counterparties are intelligent players, capable of acting strategically, their responses will not be entirely predictable. Planners will not be able to forecast and incorporate other parties' reactions into the plans. Therefore, plans will be outdated as soon as implementation starts. For this reason, incrementalists argue that action must always be swiftly followed by redefinition of the problem and reconsideration of the course of action being pursued. Over time, this iterative process of action–reaction–reconsideration will lead to the emergence of a pattern of action, which is the best possible result given the interactive nature of wicked problems.

■ This last point, on the unpredictability of external and internal reactions to a plan, leads up to a weakness of strategic planning that is possibly its most obvious one – strategy has to do with the future and the future is inherently *unknown*. Developments cannot be clearly forecast, future opportunities and threats cannot be predicted, nor can future strengths and weaknesses be accurately foreseen. In such unknown terrain, it is foolhardy to commit oneself to a preset course of action unless absolutely necessary. It makes much more sense in new and unpredictable circumstances to remain flexible and adaptive, postponing fixed commitments for as long as possible. An unknown future requires not the mentality of a train conductor, but of an explorer – curious, probing, venturesome and entrepreneurial, yet moving cautiously, step-by-step, ready to shift course when needed.

To proponents of the strategic incrementalism perspective, it is a caricature to call such behaviour ad hoc or muddling through. Rather, it is behaviour that acknowledges the fact that strategy formation is a process of innovation and organizational development in the face of wicked problems in an unknown future. Under these circumstances, strategies must be allowed to emerge and 'strategic planning' must be seen for what it is – a contradiction in terms.

EXHIBIT 3.3   THE STRATEGIC INCREMENTALISM PERSPECTIVE

YOSHINOYA: ONE STORE AT A TIME

The brand Yoshinoya might not be as famous as McDonald's to most diners outside of Japan, but the firm is certainly the country's strongest answer to the 'golden arches' – Yoshinoya serves fast-food Japanese-style. With more than 1000 outlets across Japan and 276 overseas, mainly in the United States, Yoshinoya is only a mid-sized player in the global fast-food industry, but its ongoing growth is phenomenal and its steady financial performance enough to make Ronald McDonald jealous. In 2007 the company recorded sales of ¥135 billion and despite some considerable challenges still showed a ¥2 billion pre-tax profit. Yet its hunger for growth remains undiminished. Shuji Abe, president of Yoshinoya, believes that it should be possible to grow to 1340 outlets in Japan and 560 restaurants abroad by 2012. But, Abe emphasizes, this growth must be realized 'one store at a time' and not on the basis of some pre-set strategic plan.

Yoshinoya was founded in 1899, when it opened its first shop at the famous Tsukiji fish market in Tokyo. The company grew into the first fast-food chain in Japan in the 1960s, serving only *gyudon* – a bowl of rice topped with thinly sliced braised beef. Since then, the slogan has been 'fast, delicious and cheap', and its positioning has been one of stressing the importance of the customer, personal service and quality. Or in Yoshinoya terms, 'for the people'.

Instead of standardizing the fast-food formula and then rolling it out across Japan, the Yoshinoya philosophy has been to avoid a 'cookie-cutter' approach and a rigid expansion blueprint. In Abe's view, such a 'copy–paste' programme of expansion would make insufficient use of the company's ability to learn, improve and adapt along the way. In the food service industry, with its many local characteristics and unfolding rules of the game, much still remains to be discovered 'en route'. Hence, the Japanese fast-food giant considers ongoing experimentation and innovation a crucial and integral part of its strategy development, making extensive use of pilot projects, which are flexibly and rapidly exploited whenever they prove viable.

The company slogan of 'one store at a time' is a reflection of Yoshinoya's dedication to grow organically and in a sure-footed manner, building on its emerging insights into where the fast-food business is headed and can be shaped. Unexpected threats in the business environment are dealt with in the same way. For instance, between 2003 and 2006 Yoshinoya was seriously hindered by the ban on US beef imports into Japan, due to an outbreak of BSE (also known as 'mad cow disease'). Building on previous attempts to alter the menu formula, Yoshinoya turned this threat into an opportunity, swiftly replacing its mainstay *gyudon* with a range of alternative dishes.

Yoshinoya's approach of strategic incrementalism has also worked well for its expansion abroad. Again, Yoshinoya sees internationalization as an ongoing learning process, requiring a pioneering mentality, instead of that of a conqueror, imposing itself on its environment. Yoshinoya gained its first foothold in the US market in Los Angeles in 1979 and gradually expanded its number of outlets in California. Along the way, Yoshinoya gradually reshaped its formula to fit the US market circumstances better. Initially, the company deviated from the franchise method used in Japan, finding out that fully owned restaurants worked better. During this time, management systems were changed and the company found out what type of local items to add to its menu, such as ethnic food and wholesome menu items. Confident in the acquired knowledge about the US market, Yoshinoya started reconsidering their course of action. After expanding to the east coast in 2002 with fully owned restaurants, the company

started a new experiment in 2006 by making franchising opportunities available to US entrepreneurs. By 2008, the number of Yoshinoya outlets in the US passed the 185 mark.

What Yoshinoya will look like in the coming years might not be entirely certain, but the company is likely to keep on expanding and has at least determined one clear long-term intention: 'We are reshaping the fast-food experience.' It might be time for the competition to consider a McRice-Bowl as a response.

Co-author: Martijn Rademakers

Sources: *Look Japan 2003*; *Nation's Restaurant News*, November 2002 and December 2006; *Business Week*, February 2007. Yoshinoya annual report 2007; www.yoshinoyaholding.com; www.yoshinoyafranchise.com

INTRODUCTION TO THE DEBATE AND READINGS

Those who triumph compute at their headquarters a great number of factors prior to a challenge. Little computation brings defeat. How much more so with no computation at all!

Sun Tzu (5th century BC); Chinese military strategist

It is a mistake to look too far ahead. Only one link of the chain of destiny can be handled at a time.

Winston Churchill (1874–1965); British prime minister and writer

So, how should strategies be formed in practice? Should managers strive to formulate and implement strategic plans, supported by a formalized planning and control system? Or should managers move incrementally, behaving as inventors, organizational developers and explorers? As no consensus has yet developed within the field of strategic management on how to balance deliberateness and emergence, it is up to each individual to assess the arguments put forward in the ongoing debate and to form their own opinion.

As an input to the process of assessing the variety of perspectives on this issue, four readings have been selected that each shed their own light on the debate. As in the previous chapter, the first two readings will be representative of the two poles in this debate (see Table 3.1), while the second set of two readings will bring in extra arguments to add further flavour to the discussion.

As opening reading in this debate, 'Managing the Strategy Process', by Balaji Chakravarthy and Peter Lorange, has been selected to represent the strategic planning perspective. Lorange is one of the most well-best known writers on the topic of formal planning systems (Lorange, 1980; Lorange and Vancil, 1977) and this reading is taken from the 1991 textbook he co-authored with Chakravarthy, entitled *Managing the Strategy Process: A Framework for a Multibusiness Firm*. Table 3.1 Strategic planning versus strategic incrementalism perspective As most proponents of the strategic planning

TABLE 3.1 Strategic planning versus strategic incrementalism perspective

	Strategic planning perspective	*Strategic incrementalism perpective*
Emphasis on	Deliberateness over emergence	Emergence over deliberateness
Nature of strategy	Intentionally designed	Gradually shaped
Nature of formation	Figuring out	Finding out
View of future	Forecast and anticipate	Partially unknown and unpredictable
Posture towards the future	Make commtiments, prepare	Postpone commitments, remain flexible
Formation process	Formally structured and comprehensive	Unstructured and fragmented
Formation process steps	First think, then act	Thinking and acting intertwined
Decision-making	Hierarchical	Dispersed
Decision-making focus	Optimal resource allocation and coordination	Experimentation and parallel initiatives
Implementation focused on	Programming (organizational efficiency)	Learning (organizational development)
Strategic change	Implemented top-down	Requires broad cultural and cognitive shifts

perspective, Chakravarthy and Lorange do not actively defend their assumption that formal planning is beneficial. Rather, basing themselves on this supposition, they concentrate on outlining a framework for effectively structuring strategic planning activities. Their ideal is an extensive strategic planning system, comprised of a number of distinct steps, procedures, mechanisms and roles. However, they go further than only structuring strategic planning. In their view, a formal planning system will not lead to effective strategy formation if it is not linked to other organizational systems. In particular, the strategic planning system needs to interact with the monitoring, control and learning system, the incentives system and the staffing system. As such, Chakravarthy and Lorange champion a highly comprehensive and structured approach to strategic planning.

As spokesman for the strategic incrementalism perspective, James Brian Quinn has been chosen. Together with Henry Mintzberg, Quinn has been one of the most influential pioneers on the topic of emergent strategy. Quinn's article, 'Logical Incrementalism', which is reprinted here as Reading 3.2, and his subsequent book *Strategies for Change* (1980), are widely accepted as having been instrumental in developing the strategic incrementalism perspective. In his reading, Quinn explains some of the key shortcomings of formal strategic planning and goes on to make a case for strategic incrementalism. Important in his argumentation is that strategic incrementalism is distinguished from muddling through. Incrementalism is a proactive approach to strategy formation – managers can intentionally choose to let unintended strategies emerge. Muddling through is also incremental in nature, but reactive and ad hoc – improvised decisions are made to deal with unplanned and poorly controllable circumstances. To make this distinction more explicit, Quinn refers to the proactive strain of incremental behaviour as 'logical incrementalism'. By 'logical' he means 'reasonable and well -considered'. However, logical incrementalism is not always logical by the definition used in Chapter 2 – incremental behaviour is not necessarily 'dictated by formal logic'. Therefore, for the sake of accuracy and clarity, the term strategic incrementalism will be used in this book instead of logical incrementalism.

To complement the arguments brought forward by the first authors, a classic study of strategy formation by Graham Allison has been selected, entitled 'Conceptual Models and Decision-Making' (Reading 3.3). In this article and in his famous 1971 book *The Essence of Decision: Explaining the Cuban Missile Crisis*, Allison examines the organizational decision-making surrounding the Cuban missile crisis in 1962 and comes up with three opposing models for explaining the behaviour of the parties involved. His base hypothesis is that people behave rationally and therefore that decision-making is focused on selecting the optimal course of action after a comprehensive analysis. This *rational actor model* largely fits with the rational reasoning and strategic planning perspectives. He carries on to present two other models that explain why suboptimal policies are often pursued. On the one hand, the *organizational process model* suggests that ingrained organizational routines often inhibit rational behaviour. On the other hand, the *bureaucratic politics model* describes how conflicting interests and objectives can result in processes of political maneuvermanoeuvring and positioning within an organization. In the context of this chapter, Allison's contribution is to highlight the importance of these behavioural dynamics on strategy formation. These are the sources of inertia and muddling through with which strategists, both planners and incrementalists, have to struggle.

Reading 3.4 is 'From Scenario Thinking to Strategic Action' by Ian Wilson. This article has been selected to bring the important tool of scenario development into the discussion. Both strategic planners and strategic incrementalists agree that strategizing requires managers to think about the future, and scenario development is one of the most often mentioned methods to take a structured approach to such forward thinking. Scenarios are 'plausible descriptions of alternative futures', requiring managers to envision different directions in which the environment and the firm might develop. Much has been written about scenario use in strategy formation processes, although most of the literature comes from business professionals with experience in its application (e.g. Wack, 1985a; Van der Heijden, 1996). Wilson, too, is a scenario veteran, having spent years as strategic planner at General Electric. In this reading, Wilson does not go into all of the technical details of scenario development, but highlights how scenarios can be used to strengthen strategy formation. He argues that scenarios can be used at four levels of sophistication, ranging from a simple strategy evaluation technique to a full-blown method for developing strategic plans. In his view, scenarios are a valuable means for creating strategic plans that avoid the pitfall of trying to predict the future. Working with various scenarios challenges managers to formulate strategies that are *resilient* (i.e. 'robust') – that fit a variety of future conditions. For proponents of the strategic planning perspective this probably sounds like an excellent refinement of their approach. To strategic incrementalists, however, scenario thinking sounds more like a useful way to assist in mental experimentation and for uncovering cognitive maps (e.g. De Geus, 1988) than as a convincing argument to plan.

READING

3.1

Managing the strategy process

By Balaji Chakravarthy and Peter Lorange[1]

There are five distinct steps in the strategy process (see Figure 3.1.1). The first three steps involve the strategic planning system; the final two steps cover the role of the monitoring, control, and learning system and the incentives and staffing systems, Respectively.

The strategic planning system

The purpose of the first step in the planning system, objectives setting, is to determine a strategic direction for the firm and each of its divisions and business units. Objectives setting calls for an open-ended re-assessment of the firm's business environments and its strengths in dealing with these environments. At the conclusion of this step, there should be agreement at all levels of the organization on the goals that should be pursued and the strategies that will be needed to meet them. It is worth differentiating here between objectives and goals. Objectives refer to the strategic intent of the firm in the long run. Goals, on the other hand, are more specific statements of the achievements targeted for certain deadlines – goals can be accomplished, and when that happens the firm moves closer

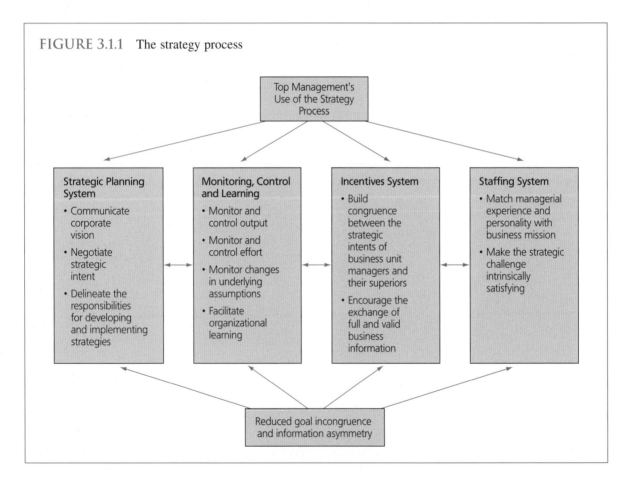

FIGURE 3.1.1   The strategy process

[1] Source: This article was adapted from Chapter 1 of B.S. Chakravarty and P. Lorange, Managing the Strategy Process: A Framework for a Multibusiness Firm, 1991, reprinted by permission of Pearson Education, Inc., Upper Saddle River, NJ

to meeting its objectives. Objectives represent a more enduring challenge.

The second step, *strategic programming*, develops the strategies identified in the first step and defines the cross-functional programmes that will be needed to implement the chosen strategies. Cross-functional co-operation is essential to this step. At the end of the strategic programming step a long-term financial plan is drawn up for the firm as a whole and each of its divisions, business units, and functions. On top of the financial projections from existing operations, the long-term financial plan overlays both the expenditures and revenues associated with the approved strategic programmes of an organizational unit. The time horizon for these financial plans is chosen to cover the typical lead times that are required to implement the firm's strategic programmes. A five-year financial plan is, however, very common. The purpose of the five-year financial plan is to ensure that the approved strategic programmes can be funded through either the firm's internally generated resources or externally financed resources.

The third step, *budgeting*, defines both the strategic and operating budgets of the firm. The strategic budget helps identify the contributions that the firm's functional departments, business units, and divisions will be expected to make in a given fiscal year in support of the firm's approved strategic programmes. It incorporates new product/market initiatives. The operating budget, on the other hand, provides resources to functional departments, business units, and divisions so that they can sustain their existing momentum. It is based on projected short-term activity levels, given past trends. Failure to meet the operating budget will hurt the firm's short-term performance, whereas failure to meet the strategic budget will compromise the firm's future.

The monitoring, control, and learning system

The fourth step in the strategy process is *monitoring, control, and learning*. Here the emphasis is not on output but on meeting key milestones in the strategic budget and on adhering to planned spending schedules. Strategic programmes, like strategic budgets, are monitored for the milestones reached and for adherence to spending schedules. In addition, the key assumptions underlying these programmes are validated periodically. As a natural extension to this validation process, even the agreed-on goals at various levels are reassessed in the light of changes to the resources of the firm and its business environment.

The incentives and staffing systems

The fifth and final step in the strategy process is incentives and staffing. One part of this is the award of incentives as contracted to the firm's managers. If the incentives system is perceived to have failed in inducing the desired performance, redesigning the incentives system and reassessing the staffing of key managerial positions are considered at this step.

Linking organizational levels and steps in strategic planning

An effective strategy process must allow for interactions between the organizational levels and iterations between the process steps. Figure 3.1.2 describes some of the interactions and iterations in the strategic planning steps. The formal interactions in the process are shown in the figure by the solid line that weaves up and down through the organizational levels and across the three steps. The informal interactions that complement the formal interactions are shown by dotted loops.

Objectives setting

The first formal step of the strategy process commences soon after top management reaffirms or modifies the firm's objectives at the beginning of each fiscal year. Embedded in these objectives should be the vision of the chief executive officer (CEO) and his or her top management team. Top management's vision helps specify what will make the firm great. An elaboration of this vision can be done through a formal statement of objectives. However, it is not the formality of a firm's objectives but rather the excitement and challenge that top management's vision can bring to a firm's managers that is important to the strategy process.

Along with its communication of corporate objectives, top management must provide a forecast on key environmental factors. Assumptions on exchange rates, inflation, and other economic factors – as well as projections on the political risks associated with each country – are best compiled centrally so as to ensure objectivity and consistency. These objectives and forecasts are then discussed with a firm's divisional and business unit managers.

Once the corporate objectives are decided, top management negotiates, for each division and business unit in the firm, goals that are consistent with these objectives. The nature of these negotiations can vary. In some firms, top management may wish to set goals in a

FIGURE 3.1.2   Steps in the strategy process

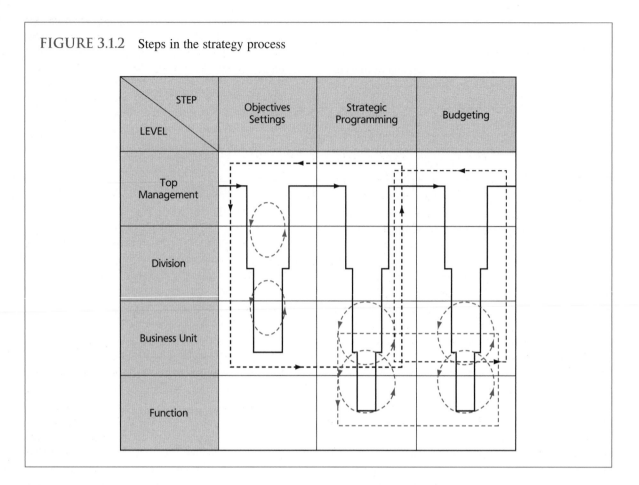

top-down fashion; in others, it may invite subordinate managers to participate in the goal-setting process.

Managers are encouraged to examine new strategies and modify existing ones in order to accomplish their goals. The proposed strategies are approved at each higher level in the organizational hierarchy, then eventually by top management. Top management tries to make certain that the strategies as proposed are consistent with the firm's objectives and can be supported with the resources available to the firm. Modifications, where necessary, are made to the objectives, goals, and strategies in order to bring them in alignment. Another important outcome of the objectives-setting step is to build a common understanding across the firm's managerial hierarchy of the goals and strategies that are intended for each organizational unit.

The objectives-setting step in Figure 3.1.2 does not include the functional departments. As we observed earlier, the primary role of these departments is a supporting one. They do not have a profit or growth responsibility, and their goals cannot be decided until the second step, when strategic programmes in support of approved business unit goals begin to be formed. It is not uncommon, however, for key functional managers to be invited to participate in the objectives-setting step either as experts in a corporate task force or, more informally, as participants in the deliberations that are held at the business unit level.

It is important that divisional proposals be evaluated on an overall basis as elements of a corporate portfolio and not reviewed in a sequential mode. In the latter case, the resulting overall balance in the corporate portfolio would be more or less incidental, representing the accumulated sum of individual approvals. It makes little sense to attempt to judge in isolation whether a particular business family or business strategy is attractive to the corporate portfolio. That will depend on a strategy's fit with the rest of the portfolio and on the competing investment opportunities available to the firm in its business portfolio.

Strategic programming

The second step in the process has two purposes:

1 To forge an agreement between divisional, business unit, and functional managers on the strategic programmes that have to be implemented over the next few years.

2 To deepen the involvement of functional managers in developing the strategies that were tentatively selected in the first step.

The strategic programming step begins with a communication from top management about the goals and strategies that were finally approved for the firm's divisions and business units. The divisional manager then invites his or her business unit and functional managers to identify programme alternatives in support of the approved goals and strategies. Examples of strategic programmes include increasing market share for an existing product, introducing a new product, and launching a joint marketing campaign for a family of divisional products. As in these examples, a strategic programme typically requires the cooperation of multiple functional departments.

However, the functional specialties within a firm often represent different professional cultures that do not necessarily blend easily. Further, day-to-day operating tasks can be so demanding that the functional managers may simply find it difficult to participate in the time-consuming cross-functional teamwork. A key challenge for both divisional and business managers is to bring about this interaction.

The proposed strategic programmes travel up the hierarchy for approval at each level. At the division level, the programmes are evaluated not only for how well they support the approved strategies but also for how they promote synergies within the firm. Synergies can come from two sources: through economies of scale or economies of scope. The creation of synergies based on economies of scale calls for a sharing of common functional activities – such as research and development (R&D), raw materials procurement, production, and distribution – so as to spread over a larger volume the overhead costs associated with these functions. The creation of economies of scope, on the other hand, requires a common approach to the market. Examples of such an approach include the development of a common trademark, the development of products/ services that have a complementary appeal to a customer group, and the ability to offer a common regional service organization for the firm's diverse businesses.

At the corporate level, the proposed strategic programmes provide an estimate of the resources that will be required to support the divisional and business unit goals. These goals, as well as their supporting strategies, are once again reassessed; and where needed, modifications are sought in the proposed strategic programmes. As noted earlier, a long-term financial plan is drawn up at this stage for the firm as a whole and each of its organizational units. The approved strategic programmes are communicated to the divisions, business units, and functional departments at the beginning of the budgeting cycle.

Budgeting

When top management decides on the strategic programmes that the firm should pursue, it has de facto allocated all of the firm's human, technological, and financial resources that are available for internal development. This allocation influences the strategic budgets that may be requested at each level in the organizational hierarchy.

The strategic budgets, together with the operating budgets of the various organizational units, are consolidated and sent up for top management approval. When top management finally approves the budgets of the various organizational units, before the start of a new budget year, it brings to a close what can be a year-long journey through the three steps of the strategy-making subprocess. The strategy implementation subprocess is then set into motion. Even though the two sub-processes are described sequentially here, it is important to mention that even as the budget for a given year is being formed, the one for the prior year will be under implementation. Midcourse corrections to the prior year's budget can have an impact on the formulation of the current budget.

If the actual accomplishments fall short of the strategic budget, in particular, the negative variance may suggest that the firm's managers failed to implement its chosen strategy efficiently. But it can also suggest that the strategic programmes that drive this budget may have been ill conceived or even that the goals underlying these programmes may have been specified incorrectly. The monitoring, control, and learning system provides continuous information on both the appropriateness of a strategic budget and the efficiency with which the budget is implemented. This information, based on the implementation of the prior year's strategic budget, can trigger another set of iterations between the three strategy-making steps, calling into question the goals and strategies on which the current year's budget are based. These iterations are shown by the dotted rectangles in Figure 3.1.2.

READING

3.2

Logical incrementalism

By James Quinn[1]

When I was younger I always conceived of a room where all these [strategic] concepts were worked out for the whole company. Later I didn't find any such room . . . The strategy [of the company] may not even exist in the mind of one man. I certainly don't know where it is written down. It is simply transmitted in the series of decisions made.
Interview quotation

Introduction

When well-managed major organizations make significant changes in strategy, the approaches they use frequently bear little resemblance to the rational-analytical systems so often touted in the planning literature. The full strategy is rarely written down in any one place. The processes used to arrive at the total strategy are typically fragmented, evolutionary, and largely intuitive. Although one can usually find embedded in these fragments some very refined pieces of formal strategic analysis, the real strategy tends to evolve as internal decisions and external events flow together to create a new, widely shared consensus for action among key members of the top management team. Far from being an abrogation of good management practice, the rationale behind this kind of strategy formulation is so powerful that it perhaps provides the normative model for strategic decision-making, rather than the step-by-step 'formal systems planning' approach so often espoused.

The formal systems planning approach

A strong normative literature states what factors should be included in a systematically planned strategy and how to analyse and relate these factors step-by-step. The main elements of this 'formal' planning approach include:

- analysing one's own internal situation: strengths, weaknesses, competencies, problems;
- projecting current product lines, profits, sales, investment needs into the future;
- analysing selected external environments and opponents' actions for opportunities and threats;
- establishing broad goals as targets for subordinate groups' plans;
- identifying the gap between expected and desired results;
- communicating planning assumptions to the divisions;
- requesting proposed plans from subordinate groups with more specific target goals, resource needs, and supporting action plans;
- occasionally asking for special studies of alternatives, contingencies, or longer-term opportunities;
- reviewing and approving divisional plans and summing these for corporate needs;
- developing long-term budgets presumably related to plans;
- implementing plans;
- monitoring and evaluating performance (presumably against plans, but usually against budgets).

While this approach is excellent for some purposes, it tends to focus unduly on measurable quantitative factors and to underemphasize the vital qualitative, organizational, and power-behavioural factors that so often determine strategic success in one situation versus another. In practice, such planning is just one building block in a continuous stream of events that really determine corporate strategy.

The power-behavioural approach

Other investigators have provided important insights on the crucial psychological, power, and behavioural relationships in strategy formulation. Among other things, these have enhanced understanding about the

---

[1]Source: This article was originally published as 'Strategic Change: Logical Incrementalism' in *Sloan Management Review,* Fall, 1978, pp. 7–21. Reproduced by permission.

multiple goal structures of organizations, the politics of strategic decisions, executive bargaining and negotiation processes, 'satisficing' (as opposed to maximizing) in decision making, the role of coalitions in strategic management, and the practice of 'muddling' in the public sphere. Unfortunately, however, many power-behavioural studies have been conducted in settings far removed from the realities of strategy formulation. Others have concentrated solely on human dynamics, power relationships, and organizational processes and ignored the ways in which systematic data analysis shapes and often dominates crucial aspects of strategic decisions. Finally, a few have offered much normative guidance for the strategist.

The study

Recognizing the contributions and limitations of both approaches, I attempted to document the dynamics of actual strategic change processes in some ten major companies as perceived by those most knowledgeably and intimately involved in them. Several important findings have begun to emerge from these investigations:

- Neither the power-behavioral nor the formal systems planning paradigm adequately characterizes the way successful strategic processes operate.

- Effective strategies tend to emerge from a series of 'strategic subsystems', each of which attacks a specific class of strategic issue (e.g. acquisitions, divestitures, or major reorganizations) in a disciplined way, but which blends incrementally and opportunistically into a cohesive pattern that becomes the company's strategy.

- The logic behind each subsystem is so powerful that to some extent it may serve as a normative approach for formulating these key elements of strategy in large companies.

- Because of cognitive and process limits, almost all of these subsystems – and the formal planning activity itself – must be managed and linked together by an approach best described as logical incrementalism.

- Such incrementalism is not muddling. It is a purposeful, effective, proactive management technique for improving and integrating both the analytical and behavioural aspects of strategy formulation.

This article will document these findings, suggest the logic behind several important subsystems for strategy formulation, and outline some of the management and thought processes executives in large organizations use to synthesize them into effective corporate strategies. Such strategies embrace those patterns of high-leverage decisions (on major goals, policies, and action sequences) that affect the viability and direction of the entire enterprise or determine its competitive posture for an extended time period.

Critical strategic issues

Although certain 'hard data' decisions (e.g. on product-market position or resource allocations) tend to dominate the analytical literature, executives identified other 'soft' changes that have at least as much importance in shaping their concern's strategic posture. Most often cited were changes in the company's

- overall organizational structure or its basic management style;

- relationships with the government or other external interest groups;

- acquisition, divestiture, or divisional control practices;

- international posture and relationships;

- innovative capabilities or personnel motivations as affected by growth;

- worker and professional relationships reflecting changed social expectations and values;

- past or anticipated technological environments.

When executives were asked to 'describe the processes through which their company arrived at its new posture' vis-à-vis each of these critical domains, several important points emerged. First, a few of these issues lent themselves to quantitative modelling techniques or perhaps even formal financial analyses. Second, successful companies used a different subsystem to formulate strategy for each major class of strategic issues, yet these subsystems were quite similar among companies even in very different industries. Finally, no single formal analytical process could handle all strategic variables simultaneously on a planned basis. Why?

Precipitating events

Often external or internal events over which managements had essentially no control would precipitate urgent, piecemeal, interim decisions that inexorably shaped the company's future strategic posture. One clearly observes this phenomenon in the decisions forced on General Motors by the 1973–74 oil crisis; the shift in posture pressed upon Exxon by sudden nationalizations; or the dramatic opportunities allowed for Haloid Corporation and Pilkington Brothers Ltd by the unexpected inventions of xerography and float glass.

In these cases, analyses from earlier formal planning cycles did contribute greatly, as long as the general nature of the contingency had been anticipated. They broadened the information base available (as in Exxon's case), extended the options considered (Haloid-Xerox), created shared values to guide decisions about precipitating events in consistent directions (Pilkington), or built up resource bases, management flexibilities, or active search routines for opportunities whose specific nature could not be defined in advance (General Mills, Pillsbury). But no organization – no matter how brilliant, rational, or imaginative – could possibly foresee the timing, severity, or even the nature of all such precipitating events. Further, when these events did occur there might be neither time, resources, nor information enough to undertake a full formal strategic analysis of all possible options and their consequences. Yet early decisions made under stress conditions often meant new thrusts, precedents, or lost opportunities that were difficult to reverse later.

An incremental logic

Recognizing this, top executives usually consciously tried to deal with precipitating events in an incremental fashion. Early commitments were kept broadly formative, tentative, and subject to later review. In some cases neither the company nor the external players could understand the full implications of alternative actions. All parties wanted to test assumptions and have an opportunity to learn from and adapt to the others' responses. For example: Neither the potential producer nor user of a completely new product or process (like xerography or float glass) could fully conceptualize its ramifications without interactive testing. All parties benefited from procedures that purposely delayed decisions and allowed mutual feedback. Some companies, like IBM or Xerox, have formalized this concept into 'phase programme planning' systems. They make concrete decisions only on individual phases (or stages) of new product developments, establish interactive testing procedures with customers, and postpone final configuration commitments until the latest possible moment. Similarly, even under pressure, most top executives were extremely sensitive to organizational and power relationships and

consciously managed decision processes to improve these dynamics. They often purposely delayed initial decisions, or kept such decisions vague, in order to encourage lower-level participation, to gain more information from specialists, or to build commitment to solutions. Even when a crisis atmosphere tended to shorten time horizons and make decisions more goal oriented than political, perceptive executives consciously tried to keep their options open until they understood how the crisis would affect the power bases and needs of their key constituents.

Incrementalism in strategic subsystems

One also finds that an incremental logic applies in attacking many of the critical subsystems of corporate strategy. Those subsystems for considering diversification moves, divestitures, major reorganizations, or government-external relations are typical and will be described here. In each case conscious incrementalism helps to

1 cope with both the cognitive and process limits on each major decision;

2 build the logical-analytical framework these decisions require;

3 create the personal and organizational awareness, understanding, acceptance, and commitment needed to implement the strategies effectively.

The diversification subsystem

Strategies for diversification, either through research and development (R&D) or acquisitions, provide excellent examples. The formal analytical steps needed for successful diversification are well documented. However, the precise directions in which R&D may project the company can only be understood step-by-step as scientists uncover new phenomena, make and amplify discoveries, build prototypes, reduce concepts to practice, and interact with users during product introductions. Similarly, only as each acquisition is sequentially identified, investigated, negotiated for, and integrated into the organization can one predict its ultimate impact on the total enterprise.

A step-by-step approach is clearly necessary to guide and assess the strategic fit of each internal or external diversification candidate. Incremental processes are also required to manage the crucial psychological and power shifts that ultimately determine the programme's overall direction and consequences. These processes help unify both the analytical and behavioural aspects of diversification decisions. They create the broad conceptual consensus, the risk-taking attitudes, the organizational and resource flexibilities, and the adaptive dynamism that determine both the timing and direction of diversification strategies. Most important among these processes are:

- Generating a genuine, top-level psychological commitment to diversification. General Mills, Pillsbury, and Xerox all started their major diversification programmes with broad analytical studies and goal-setting exercises designed both to build top-level consensus around the need to diversify and to establish the general directions for diversification. Without such action, top-level bargaining for resources would have continued to support only more familiar (and hence apparently less risky) old lines, and this could delay or undermine the entire diversification endeavour.

- Consciously preparing to move opportunistically. Organizational and fiscal resources must be built up in advance to exploit candidates as they randomly appear. And a 'credible activist' for ventures must be developed and backed by someone with commitment power. All successful acquirers created the potential for profit-centred divisions within their organizational structures, strengthened their financial-controllership capabilities, took action to create low-cost capital access, and maintained the shortest possible communication lines from the acquisitions activist to the resource-committing authority. All these actions integrally determined which diversifications actually could be made, the timing of their accession, and the pace at which they could be absorbed.

- Building a 'comfort factor' for risk taking. Perceived risk is largely a function of one's knowledge about a field. Hence well-conceived diversification programmes should anticipate a trial-and-error period during which top managers reject early proposed fields or opportunities until they have analyzed enough trial candidates to 'become comfortable' with an initial selection. Early successes tend to be 'sure things' close to the companies' past (real or supposed) expertise. After a few successful diversifications, managements tend to become more confident and accept other candidates – farther from traditional lines – at a faster rate. Again, the way this process is handled affects both the direction and pace of the actual programme.

- Developing a new ethos. If new divisions are more successful than the old – as they should be – they attract relatively more resources and their political power grows. Their most effective line managers move into corporate positions, and slowly the company's special competency and ethos change. Finally, the concepts and products that once dominated the company's culture may decline in importance or even disappear. Acknowledging these ultimate consequences to the organization at the beginning of a diversification programme would clearly be impolitic, even if the manager both desired and could predict the probable new ethos. These factors must be handled adaptively, as opportunities present themselves and as individual leaders and power centres develop.

Each of the above processes interacts with all others (and with the random appearance of diversification candidates) to affect action sequences, elapsed time, and ultimate results in unexpected ways. Complexities are so great that few diversification programmes end up as initially envisioned. Consequently, wise managers recognize the limits to systematic analysis in diversification, and use formal planning to build the 'comfort levels' executives need for risk taking and to guide the programme's early directions and priorities. They then modify these flexibly, step-by-step, as new opportunities, power centres, and developed competencies merge to create new potentials.

The divestiture subsystem

Similar practices govern the handling of divestitures. Divisions often drag along in a less-than-desired condition for years before they can be strategically divested. In some cases, ailing divisions might have just enough yield or potential to offer hoped-for viability. In others, they might represent the company's vital core from earlier years, the creations of a powerful person nearing retirement, or the psychological touchstones of the company's past traditions.

Again, in designing divestiture strategies, top executives had to reinforce vaguely felt concerns with detailed data, build up managers' comfort levels about issues, achieve participation in and commitment to decisions, and move opportunistically to make actual changes. In many cases, the precise nature of the decision was not clear at the outset. Executives often made seemingly unrelated personnel shifts or appointments that changed the value set of critical groups, or started a series of staff studies that generated awareness or acceptance of a potential problem. They might then instigate goal assessment, business review, or 'planning' programmes to provide broader forums for discussion and a wider consensus for action. Even then they might wait for a crisis, a crucial retirement, or an attractive sale opportunity to determine the timing and conditions of divestiture. In some cases, decisions could be direct and analytical. But when divestitures involved the psychological centres of the organization, the process had to be much more oblique and carefully orchestrated.

The major reorganization subsystem

It is well recognized that major organizational changes are an integral part of strategy. Sometimes they constitute a strategy themselves, sometimes they precede and/or precipitate a new strategy, and sometimes they help to implement a strategy. However, like many other important strategic decisions, macro-organizational moves are typically handled incrementally and outside of formal planning processes. Their effects on personal or power relationships preclude discussion in open forums and reports of such processes.

In addition, major organizational changes have timing imperatives (or 'process limits') all their own. In making any significant shifts, executives must think through the new roles, capabilities, and probable individual reactions of the many principals affected. They may have to wait for the promotion or retirement of a valued colleague before consummating any change. They then frequently have to bring in, train, or test new people for substantial periods before they can staff key posts with confidence. During this testing period they may substantially modify their original concept of the reorganization, as they evaluate individuals' potentials, their performance in specific roles, their personal drives, and their relationships with other team members.

Because this chain of decisions affects the career development, power, affluence, and self-image of so many, executives tend to keep close counsel in their discussions, negotiate individually with key people, and make final commitments as late as possible in order to obtain the best matches between people's capabilities, personalities, and aspirations and their new roles. Typically, all these events do not come together at one convenient time, particularly the moment annual plans are due. Instead executives move opportunistically, step-by-step, selectively moving people toward a broadly conceived organizational goal, which is constantly modified and rarely articulated in detail until the last pieces fit together.

The government-external relations subsystem

Almost all companies cited government and other external activist groups as among the most important forces causing significant changes in their strategic postures during the periods examined. However, when asked 'How did your company arrive at its own strategy vis-à-vis these forces?' it became clear that few companies had cohesive strategies (integrated sets of goals, policies, and programmes) for government-external relations, other than lobbying for or against specific legislative actions. To the extent that other strategies did exist, they were piecemeal, ad hoc and had been derived in a very evolutionary manner. Yet there seemed to be very good reasons for such incrementalism. The following are two of the best short explanations of the way these practices develop:

> We are a very large company, and we understand that any massive overt action on our part could easily create more public antagonism than support for our viewpoint. It is also hard to say in advance exactly what public response any particular action might create. So we tend to test a number of different approaches on a small scale with only limited or local company identification. If one approach works, we'll'll test it further and amplify its use. If another bombs, we try to keep it from being used again. Slowly we find a series of advertising, public relations, community relations actions that seem to help. Then along comes another issue and we start all over again. Gradually the successful approaches merge into a pattern of actions that becomes our strategy.

> I [the president] start conversations with a number of knowledgeable people . . . I collect articles and talk to people about how things get done in Washington in this particular field. I collect data from any reasonable source. I begin wide-ranging discussions with people inside and outside the corporation. From these a pattern eventually emerges. It's's like fitting together a jigsaw puzzle. At first the vague outline of an approach appears like the sail of a ship in a puzzle. Then suddenly the rest of the puzzle becomes quite clear. You wonder why you didn't't see it all along. And once it's's crystallized, it's's not difficult to explain to others.

In this realm, uncontrollable forces dominate. Data are very soft, often can be only subjectively sensed, and may be costly to quantify. The possible responses of individuals and groups to different stimuli are difficult to determine in advance. The number of potential opponents with power is very high, and the diversity in their viewpoints and possible modes of attack is so substantial that it is physically impossible to lay out probabilistic decision diagrams that would have much meaning. Results are unpredictable and error costs extreme. Even the best intended and most rational-seeming strategies can be converted into disasters unless they are thoroughly and interactively tested.

Formal planning in corporate strategy

What role do classical formal planning techniques play in strategy formulation? All companies in the sample do have formal planning procedures embedded in their management direction and control systems. These serve certain essential functions. In a process sense, they:

■ provide a discipline forcing managers to take a careful look ahead periodically;

■ require rigorous communications about goals, strategic issues, and resource allocations;

■ stimulate longer-term analyses than would otherwise be made;

■ generate a basis for evaluating and integrating short-term plans;

■ lengthen time horizons and protect long-term investments such as R&D;

■ create a psychological backdrop and an information framework about the future against which managers can calibrate short-term or interim decisions.

In a decision-making sense, they:

■ fine-tune annual commitments;

■ formalize cost-reduction programmes;

■ help implement strategic changes once decided on (for example, coordinating all elements of Exxon's decision to change its corporate name).

Formal plans also 'increment'

Although individual staff planners were often effective in identifying potential problems and bringing them to top management's attention, the annual planning process itself was rarely (if ever) the initiating source of really new key issues or radical departures into new product/market realms. These almost always came from precipitating events, special studies, or conceptions implanted through the kinds of 'logical incremental' processes described above.

In fact, formal planning practices actually institutionalize incrementalism. There are two reasons for this. First, in order to utilize specialized expertise and to obtain executive involvement and commitment, most planning occurs from the bottom up in response to broadly defined assumptions or goals, many of which are longstanding or negotiated well in advance. Of necessity, lower-level groups have only a partial view of the corporation's total strategy, and command only a fragment of its resources. Their power bases, identity, expertise, and rewards also usually depend on their existing products or processes. Hence, these products or processes, rather than entirely new departures, should and do receive their primary attention. Second, most managements purposely design their plans to be 'living' or 'evergreen'. They are intended only as frameworks to guide and provide consistency for future decisions made incrementally. To act otherwise would be to deny that further information could have a value. Thus, properly formulated formal plans are also a part of an incremental logic.

Special studies

Formal planning was most successful in stimulating significant change when it was set up as a special study on some important aspect of corporate strategy. For example, when it became apparent that Pilkington's new float glass process would work, the company formed a Directors' Float Glass Committee consisting of all internal directors associated with float glass 'to consider the broad issues of float glass [strategy] in both the present and the future'. The committee did not attempt detailed plans. Instead, it tried to deal in broad concepts, identify alternate routes, and think through the potential consequences of each route some 10 years ahead. Of some of the key strategic decisions it was later remarked, 'It would be difficult to identify an exact moment when the decision was made … Nevertheless, over a period of time a consensus crystallized with great clarity.'

Such special strategic studies represent a subsystem of strategy formulation distinct from both annual planning activities and the other subsystems exemplified above. Each of these develops some important aspect of strategy, incrementally blending its conclusions with those of other subsystems, and it would be virtually impossible to force all these to-gether to crystallize a completely articulated corporate strategy at any one instant.

Total posture planning

Occasionally, however, managements do attempt very broad assessments of their companies' total posture. Shortly after becoming CEO of General Mills, James McFarland decided that his job was 'to take a very good company and move it to greatness', but that it was up to his management group, not himself alone, to de-cide what a great company was and how to get there. Consequently he took some 35 of the company's top-most managers away for a three-day management re-treat. On the first day, after agreeing to broad financial goals, the group broke up into units of six to eight people. Each unit was to answer the question, 'What is a great company?' from the viewpoints of stockholders, employees, suppliers, the public, and society. Each unit reported back at the end of the day, and the whole group tried to reach a consensus through discussion.

On the second day the groups, in the same format, assessed the company's strengths and weaknesses re-lative to the defined posture of 'greatness.' The third day focused on how to overcome the company's weaknesses and move it toward a great company. This broad consensus led, over the next several years, to the surveys of fields for acquisition, the building of man-agement's initial comfort levels with certain fields, and the acquisition–divestiture strategy that char-acterized the McFarland era at General Mills.

Yet even such a major endeavour is only a portion of a total strategic process. Values that had been built up over decades stimulated or constrained alternatives. Precipitating events, acquisitions, divestitures, external relations, and organizational changes developed im-portant segments of each strategy incrementally. Even the strategies articulated left key elements to be de-fined as new information became available, polities permitted, or particular opportunities appeared. Major product thrusts proved unsuccessful. Actual strategies therefore evolved as each company overextended, consolidated, made errors, and rebalanced various thrusts over time. And it was both logical and expected that this would be the case.

Logical incrementalism

All of the above suggest that strategic decisions do not lend themselves to aggregation into a single massive decision matrix where all factors can be treated relatively simultaneously in order to arrive at a holistic optimum. Many have spoken of the cognitive limits that prevent this. Of equal importance are the process limits – that is, the timing and sequencing imperatives necessary to create awareness, build comfort levels, develop consensus, select and train people, and so forth – that constrain the system yet ultimately de-termine the decision itself. Unlike the preparation of a fine banquet, it is virtually impossible for the manager to orchestrate all internal decisions, external environ-mental events, behavioural and power relationships, technical and informational needs, and actions of in-telligent opponents so that they come together at any precise moment.

Can the process be managed?

Instead, executives usually deal with the logic of each subsystem of strategy formulation largely on its own merits and usually with a different subset of people. They try to develop or maintain in their own minds a consistent pattern among the decisions made in each subsystem. Knowing their own limitations and the un-knowability of the events they face, they consciously try to tap the minds and psychic drives of others. They often purposely keep questions broad and decisions vague in early stages to avoid creating undue rigidities and to stimulate others' creativity. Logic, of course, dictates that they make final commitments as late as possible consistent with the information they have.

Consequently, many successful executives will in-itially set only broad goals and policies that can ac-commodate a variety of specific proposals from below, yet give a sense of guidance to the proposers. As they come forward the proposals automatically and benefi-cially attract the support and identity of their sponsors. Being only proposals, the executives can treat these at less politically charged levels, as specific projects rather than as larger goal or policy precedents. There-fore, they can encourage, discourage, or kill alternatives with considerably less political exposure. As events and opportunities emerge, they can incrementally guide the pattern of escalated or accepted proposals to suit their own purposes without getting prematurely committed to a rigid solution set that unpredictable events might prove wrong or that opponents find sufficiently threa-tening to coalesce against.

A strategy emerges

Successful executives link together and bring order to a series of strategic processes and decisions spanning years. At the beginning of the process it is literally impossible to predict all the events and forces that will shape the future of the company. The best executives can do is to forecast the forces most likely to impinge on the company's affairs and the ranges of their possible impact. They then attempt to build a resource base and a corporate posture so strong in selected areas that the enterprise can survive and prosper despite all but the most devastating events. They consciously select market/technological/product segments the concern can dominate given its resource limits, and place some side bets in order to decrease the risk of catastrophic failure or to increase the company's flexibility for future options.

They then proceed incrementally to handle urgent matters, start longer-term sequences whose specific future branches and consequences are perhaps murky, respond to unforeseen events as they occur, build on successes, and brace up or cut losses on failures. They constantly reassess the future, find new congruencies as events unfurl, and blend the organization's skills and resources into new balances of dominance and risk aversion as various forces intersect to suggest better – but never perfect – alignments. The process is dynamic, with neither a real beginning nor end.

Strategy deals with the unknowable, not the uncertain. It involves forces of such great number, strength, and combinatory powers that one cannot predict events in a probabilistic sense. Hence logic dictates that one proceeds flexibly and experimentally from broad concepts toward specific commitments, making the latter concrete as late as possible in order to narrow the bands of uncertainty and to benefit from the best available information. This is the process of logical incrementalism.

READING 3.3

Conceptual models and decision-making

By Graham Allison[1]

This study proceeds from the premise that marked improvement in our understanding of such events depends critically on more self-consciousness about what observers bring to the analysis. What each analyst sees and judges to be important is a function not only of the evidence about what happened but also of the 'conceptual lenses' through which he looks at the evidence. The principal purpose of this paper is to explore some of the fundamental assumptions and categories employed by analysts in thinking about problems of governmental behaviour, especially in foreign and military affairs. The general argument can be summarized in three propositions:

1 Analysts think about problems of foreign and military policy in terms of largely implicit conceptual models that have significant consequences for the content of their thought. Clusters of related assumptions constitute basic frames of reference or conceptual models in terms of which analysts both ask and answer the questions: What happened? Why did the event happen? What will happen?

Such assumptions are central to the activities of explanation and prediction, for in attempting to explain a particular event, the analyst cannot simply describe the full state of the world leading up to that event. The logic explanation requires that he single out the relevant, important determinants of the occurrence. Moreover, as the logic of prediction underscores, the analyst must summarize the various determinants as they bear on the event in question. Conceptual models both fix the mesh of the nets that the analyst drags through the material in order to explain a particular action of decision and direct him to cast his net in select ponds, at certain depths, in order to catch the fish he is after.

2 Most analysts explain (and predict) the behaviour of national governments in terms of various forms of one basic conceptual model, here entitled the Rational Policy Model (Model I). In terms of this conceptual model, analysts attempt to understand happenings as the more or less purposive acts of unified national governments. For these analysts,

[1]Source: This article was adapted from 'Conceptual Models and the Cuban Missile Crisis', *The American Political Science Review*, No. 3, September 1969, pp. 689–718. Reproduced with permission.

the point of an explanation is to show how the nation or government could have chosen the action in question, given the strategic problem that it faced.

3 Two 'alternative' conceptual models, here labelled an Organizational Process Model (Model II) and a Bureaucratic Politics Model (Model III) provide a base for improved explanation and prediction. Although the standard frame of reference has proved useful for many purposes, there is powerful evidence that it must be supplemented, if not supplanted, by frames of reference which focus upon the large organizations and political actors involved in the policy process. Model I's implication that important events have important causes, i.e. that monoliths perform large actions for big reasons, must be balanced by an appreciation of the facts (a) that monoliths are black boxes covering several gears and levers in a highly differentiated decision-making structure, and (b) that large acts are the consequences of innumerable and often conflicting smaller actions by individuals at various levels of bureaucratic organizations in the service of a variety of only partially compatible conceptions of national goals, organizational goals, and political objectives. Recent developments in the field of organization theory provide the foundation for the second model, what Model I categorizes as 'acts' and 'choices' are instead outputs of large organizations functioning according to certain regular patterns of behaviour. The third model focuses on the internal politics of a government. Happenings in foreign affairs are understood, according to the bureaucratic politics model, neither as choices nor as outputs. Instead, what happens is categorized as outcomes of various overlapping bargaining games among players arranged hierarchically in the national government. A Model III analyst displays the perceptions, motivations, positions, power, and manoeuvres of principal players from which the outcome emerged.

A central metaphor illuminates differences among these models. Foreign policy has often been compared to moves, sequences of moves, and games of chess. If one were limited to observations on a screen upon which moves in the chess game were projected without information as to how the pieces came to be moved, one would assume – as Model I does – that an individual chess player was moving the pieces with reference to plans and manoeuvres toward the goal of winning the game. But a pattern of moves can be imagined that would lead the serious observer, after watching several games, to consider the hypothesis that the chess player was not a single individual but rather a loose alliance of semi-independent organizations, each of which moved its set of pieces according to standard operating procedures. For example, movement of separate sets of pieces might proceed in turn, each according to a routine, the king's rook, bishop, and their pawns repeatedly attacking the opponent according to a fixed plan. Furthermore, it is conceivable that the pattern of play would suggest to an observer that a number of distinct players, with distinct objectives but shared power over the pieces, were determining the moves as the resultant of collegial bargaining. For example, the black rook's move might contribute to the loss of a black knight with no comparable gain for the black team, but with the black rook becoming the principal guardian of the 'palace' on that side of the board.

The space available does not permit full development and support of such a general argument. Rather, the sections that follow simply sketch each conceptual model, articulate it as an analytic paradigm, and apply it to produce an explanation.

Model I: Rational policy

How do analysts account for the coming of the First World War? According to Hans Morgenthau (1960), 'the First World War had its origin exclusively in the fear of a disturbance of the European balance of power.' In the period preceding World War I, the Triple Alliance precariously balanced the Triple Entente. If either power combination could gain a decisive advantage in the Balkans, it would achieve a decisive advantage in the balance of power. 'It was this fear,' Morgenthau asserts, 'that motivated Austria in July 1914 to settle its accounts with Serbia once and for all, and that induced Germany to support Austria unconditionally. It was the same fear that brought Russia to the support of Serbia, and France to the support of Russia.' How is Morgenthau able to resolve this problem so confidently? By imposing on the data a 'rational outline'. The value of this method, according to Morgenthau, is that 'it provides for rational discipline in action and creates astounding continuity in foreign policy which makes American, British, or Russian foreign policy appear as an intelligent, rational continuum … regardless of the different motives, preferences, and intellectual and moral qualities of successive statesmen'.

Deterrence is the cardinal problem of the contemporary strategic literature. Thomas Schelling's

Strategy of Conflict (1960) formulates a number of propositions focused upon the dynamics of deterrence in the nuclear age. One of the major propositions concerns the stability of the balance of terror: in a situation of mutual deterrence, the probability of nuclear war is reduced not by the 'balance' (the sheer equality of the situation) but rather by the *stability* of the balance, i.e. the fact that neither opponent in striking first can destroy the other's ability to strike back. How does Schelling support this proposition? Confidence in the contention stems not from an inductive canvass of a large number of previous cases, but rather from two calculations. In a situation of 'balance' but vulnerability, there are values for which a rational opponent could choose to strike first, e.g. to destroy enemy capabilities to retaliate. In a 'stable balance' where no matter who strikes first, each has an assured capability to retaliate with unacceptable damage, no rational agent could choose such a course of action (since that choice is effectively equivalent to choosing mutual homicide). Whereas most contemporary strategic thinking is driven *implicitly* by the motor upon which this calculation depends, Schelling explicitly recognizes that strategic theory does assume a model. The foundation of a theory of strategy is, he asserts, 'the assumption of rational behaviour – not just of intelligent behaviour, but of behaviour motivated by conscious calculation of advantages, calculation that in turn is based on an explicit and internally consistent value system.'

What is striking about these examples from the literature of foreign policy and international relations are the similarities among analysts of various styles when they are called upon to produce explanations. Each assumes that what must be explained is an action, i.e. the realization of some purpose or intention. Each assumes that the actor is the national government. Each assumes that the action is chosen as a calculated response to a strategic problem. For each, explanation consists of showing what goal the government was pursuing in committing the act and how this action was a reasonable choice, given the nation's objectives. This set of assumptions characterizes the rational policy model. The assertion that Model I is the standard frame of reference implies no denial of highly visible differences among the interests of Sovietologists, diplomatic historians, international relations theorists, and strategists. Indeed, in most respects, differences among the work of Hans Morgenthau and Thomas Schelling could not be more pointed. Appreciation of the extent to which each relies predominantly on Model I, however, reveals basic similarities among Morgenthau's

method of 'rational reenactment,' and Schelling's 'vicarious problem solving'; family resemblances among Morgenthau's 'rational statesman' and Schelling's 'game theorist'.

Most contemporary analysts (as well as laymen) proceed predominantly – albeit most often implicitly – in terms of this model when attempting to explain happenings in foreign affairs. Indeed, that occurrences in foreign affairs are the *acts of nations* seems so fundamental to thinking about such problems that this underlying model has rarely been recognized: to explain an occurrence in foreign policy simply means to show how the government could have rationally chosen that action. To prove that most analysts think largely in terms of the rational policy model is not possible. In this limited space it is not even possible to illustrate the range of employment of the framework. Rather, my purpose is to convey to the reader a grasp of the model and a challenge: let the readers examine the literature with which they are most familiar and make their judgement.

The general characterization can be sharpened by articulating the rational policy model as an 'analytic paradigm'. Systematic statement of basic assumptions, concepts, and propositions employed by Model I analysts highlights the distinctive thrust of this style of analysis. To articulate a largely implicit framework is of necessity to caricature. But caricature can be instructive.

Model I: Basic unit of analysis: Policy as national choice

Happenings in foreign affairs are conceived as actions chosen by the nation or national government. Governments select the action that will maximize strategic goals and objectives. These 'solutions' to strategic problems are the fundamental categories in terms of which the analyst perceives what is to be explained.

Model I: Organizing concepts

National actor. The nation or government, conceived as a rational, unitary decision-maker, is the agent. This actor has one set of specified goals (the equivalent of a consistent utility function), one set of perceived options, and a single estimate of the consequences that follow from each alternative.

The problem. Action is chosen in response to the strategic problem which the nation faces. Threats and opportunities arising in the 'international strategic market place' move the nation to act.

Static selection. The sum of activity of representatives of the government relevant to a problem constitutes what the nation has chosen as its 'solution.' Thus the action is conceived as a steady-state choice among alternative outcomes (rather than, for example, a large number of partial choices in a dynamic stream).

Action as rational choice. The components include:

- Goals and objectives. National security and national interests are the principal categories in which strategic goals are conceived. Nations seek security and a range of further objectives. (Analysts rarely translate strategic goals and objectives into an explicit utility function; nevertheless, analysts do focus on major goals and objectives and trade off side effects in an intuitive fashion.)
- Options. Various courses of action relevant to a strategic problem provide the spectrum of options.
- Consequences. Enactment of each alternative course of action will produce a series of consequences. The relevant consequences constitute benefits and costs in terms of strategic goals and objectives.
- Choice. Rational choice is value-maximizing. The rational agent selects the alternative whose consequences rank highest in terms of his goals and objectives.

Model I: Dominant inference pattern and general propositions

This paradigm leads analysts to rely on the following pattern of inference: if a nation performed a particular action, that nation must have had ends towards which the action constituted an optimal means. The rational policy model's explanatory power stems from this inference pattern. Puzzlement is relieved by revealing the purposive pattern within which the occurrence can be located as a value-maximizing means.

The disgrace of political science is the infrequency with which propositions of any generality are formulated and tested. 'Paradigmatic analysis' argues for explicitness about the terms in which analysis proceeds, and seriousness about the logic of explanation. Simply to illustrate the kind of propositions on which analysts who employ this model rely, the formulation includes several.

The basic assumption of value-maximizing behaviour produces propositions central to most explanations. The general principle can be formulated as follows: the likelihood of any particular action results from a combination of the nation's (1) relevant values and objectives, (2) perceived alternative courses of action, (3) estimates of various sets of consequences (which will follow from each alternative), and (4) net valuation of each set of consequences. This yields two propositions.

- An increase in the cost of an alternative, i.e. a reduction in the value of the set of consequences which will follow from that action, or a reduction in the probability of attaining fixed consequences, reduces the likelihood of that alternative being chosen.
- A decrease in the costs of an alternative, i.e. an increase in the value of the set of consequences which will follow from that alternative or an increase in the probability of attaining fixed consequences, increases the likelihood of that action being chosen.

Model II: Organizational process

For some purposes, governmental behaviour can be usefully summarized as action chosen by a unitary, rational decision-maker: centrally controlled, completely informed, and value maximizing. But this simplification must not be allowed to conceal the fact that a 'government' consists of a conglomerate of semi-feudal, loosely allied organizations, each with a substantial life of its own. Government leaders do sit formally, and to some extent in fact, on top of this conglomerate. But governments perceive problems through organizational sensors. Governments define alternatives and estimate consequences as organizations process information. Governments act as these organizations enact routines. Government behaviour can therefore be understood according to a second conceptual model, less as deliberate choices of leaders and more as *outputs* of large organizations functioning according to standard patterns of behaviour.

To be responsive to a broad spectrum of problems, governments consist of large organizations among which primary responsibility for particular areas is divided. Each organization attends to a special set of problems and acts in quasi-independence on these problems. But few important problems fall exclusively within the domain of a single organization. Thus government behaviour relevant to any important problem reflects the independent output of several organizations, partially coordinated by government leaders. Government leaders can substantially disturb, but not substantially control, the behaviour of these organizations.

To perform complex routines, the behaviour of large numbers of individuals must be coordinated.

Coordination requires standard operating procedures: rules according to which things are done. Assured capability for reliable performance of action that depends upon the behaviour of hundreds of persons requires established 'programmes'. Indeed, if the 11 members of a football team are to perform adequately on any particular down, each player must not 'do what he thinks needs to be done' or 'do what the quarterback tells him to do'. Rather, each player must perform the manoeuvres specified by a previously established play, which the quarterback has simply called in this situation.

At any given time, a government consists of *existing* organizations, each with *a fixed* set of standard operating procedures and programmes. The behaviour of these organizations – and consequently of the government – relevant to an issue in any particular instance is therefore determined primarily by routines established in these organizations prior to that instance. But organizations do change. Learning occurs gradually, over time. Dramatic organizational change occurs in response to major crises. Both learning and change are influenced by existing organizational capabilities.

These loosely formulated propositions amount simply to *tendencies*. Each must be hedged by modifiers like 'other things being equal' and 'under certain conditions'. In particular instances, tendencies hold – more or less. In specific situations the relevant question is: more or less? But this is as it should be. For, on the one hand, 'organizations' are no more homogeneous a class than 'solids'. When scientists tried to generalize about 'solids,' they achieved similar results. Solids tend to expand when heated, but some do and some don't. More adequate categorization of the various elements now lumped under the rubric 'organizations' is thus required. On the other hand, the behaviour of particular organizations seems considerably more complex than the behaviour of solids. Additional information about a particular organization is required for further specification of the tendency statements. In spite of these two caveats, the characterization of government action as organizational output differs distinctly from Model I. Attempts to understand problems of foreign affairs in terms of this frame of reference should produce quite different explanations.

Model II: Basic unit of analysis: Policy as organizational output

The happenings of international politics are, in three critical senses, outputs of organizational processes. First, the actual occurrences are organizational outputs.

Government leaders' decisions trigger organizational routines. Government leaders can trim the edges of this output and exercise some choice in combining outputs. But the mass of behaviour is determined by previously established procedures. Second, existing organizational routines for employing present physical capabilities constitute the effective options open to government leaders confronted with any problem. The fact that fixed programmes (equipment, men, and routines which exist at the particular time) exhaust the range of buttons that leaders can push is not always perceived by these leaders. But in every case it is critical for an understanding of what is actually done. Third, organizational outputs structure the situation within the narrow constraints of which leaders must contribute their 'decision' concerning an issue. Outputs raise the problem, provide the information, and make the initial moves that colour the face of the issue that is turned to the leaders. As Theodore Sorensen has observed: 'Presidents rarely, if ever, make decisions – particularly in foreign affairs – in the sense of writing their conclusions on a clean slate …. The basic decisions, which confine their choices, have all too often been previously made.' If one understands the structure of the situation and the face of the issue – which are determined by the organizational outputs – the formal choice of the leaders is frequently anti-climatic.

Model II: Organizing concepts

Organizational actors. The actor is not a monolithic 'nation' or 'government' but rather a constellation of loosely allied organizations on top of which government leaders sit. This constellation acts only as component organizations perform routines.

Factored problems and fractionated power. Surveillance of the multiple facets of foreign affairs requires that problems be cut up and parcelled out to various organizations. To avoid paralysis, primary power must accompany primary responsibility. But if organizations are permitted to do anything, a large part of what they do will be determined within the organization. Thus each organization perceives problems, processes information, and performs a range of actions in quasi-independence (within broad guidelines of national policy). Factored problems and fractionated power are two edges of the same sword. Factoring permits more specialized attention to particular facets of problems than would be possible if government leaders tried to cope with these problems by themselves. But this additional attention must be paid for in the coin of discretion for what an organization attends to, and how organizational responses are programmed.

Parochial priorities, perceptions, and issues. Primary responsibility for a narrow set of problems encourages organizational parochialism. These tendencies are enhanced by a number of additional factors: (1) selective information available to the organization, (2) recruitment of personnel into the organization, (3) tenure of individuals in the organization, (4) small group pressures within the organization, and (5) distribution of rewards by the organization. Clients, government allies, and extra-national counterparts galvanize this parochialism. Thus organizations develop relatively stable propensities concerning operational priorities, perceptions, and issues.

Action as organizational output. The pre-eminent feature of organizational activity is its programmed character: the extent to which behaviour in any particular case is an enactment of preestablished routines. In producing outputs, the activity of each organization is characterized by:

- Goals: Constraints defining acceptable performance. The operational goals of an organization are seldom revealed by formal mandates. Rather, each organization's operational goals emerge as a set of constraints defining acceptable performance. Central among these constraints is organizational health, defined usually in terms of bodies assigned and dollars appropriated. The set of constraints emerges from a mix of expectations and demands of other organizations in the government, statutory authority, demands from citizens and special interest groups, and bargaining within the organization. These constraints represent a quasi-resolution of conflict – the constraints are relatively stable, so there is some resolution. But conflict among alternative goals is always latent; hence, it is a quasi-resolution. Typically, the constraints are formulated as imperatives to avoid roughly specified discomforts and disasters.

- Sequential attention to goals. The existence of conflict among operational constraints is resolved by the device of sequential attention. As a problem arises, the subunits of the organization most concerned with that problem deal with it in terms of the constraints they take to be most important. When the next problem arises, another cluster of subunits deals with it, focusing on a different set of constraints.

- Standard operating procedures. Organizations perform their 'higher' functions, such as attending to problem areas, monitoring information, and preparing relevant responses for likely contingencies, by doing 'lower' tasks, for example, preparing budgets, producing reports, and developing hardware. Reliable performance of these tasks requires standard operating procedures (hereafter SOPs). Since procedures are 'standard' they do not change quickly or easily. Without these standard procedures, it would not be possible to perform certain concerted tasks. But because of standard procedures, organizational behaviour in particular instances often appears unduly formalized, sluggish, or inappropriate.

- Programmes and repertoires. Organizations must be capable of performing actions in which the behaviour of large numbers of individuals is carefully coordinated. Assured performance requires clusters of rehearsed SOPs for producing specific actions, e.g. fighting enemy units or answering an embassy's cable. Each cluster comprises a 'programme' (in the terms both of drama and computers) which the organization has available for dealing with a situation. The list of programmes relevant to a type of activity, e.g. fighting, constitutes an organizational repertoire. The number of programmes in a repertoire is always quite limited. When properly triggered, organizations execute programmes; programmes cannot be substantially changed in a particular situation. The more complex the action and the greater the number of individuals involved, the more important are programmes and repertoires as determinants of organizational behaviour.

- Uncertainty avoidance. Organizations do not attempt to estimate the probability distribution of future occurrences. Rather, organizations avoid uncertainty. By arranging a *negotiated environment*, organizations regularize the reactions of other actors with whom they have to deal. The primary environment, relations with other organizations that comprise the government, is stabilized by such arrangements as agreed budgetary splits, accepted areas of responsibility, and established conventional practices. The secondary environment, relations with the international world, is stabilized between allies by the establishment of contracts (alliances) and 'club relations' (US State and UK Foreign Office or US Treasury and UK Treasury). Between enemies, contracts and accepted conventional practices perform a similar function, for example, the rules of the 'precarious status quo' which President Kennedy referred to in the missile crisis. Where the international environment cannot be negotiated, organizations deal with remaining uncertainties by establishing a set of *standard scenarios* that constitute the contingencies for which they prepare.

- Problem-directed search. Where situations cannot be construed as standard, organizations engage in search. The style of search and the solution are largely determined by existing routines. Organizational search for alternative courses of action is problem-oriented: it focuses on the atypical discomfort that must be avoided. It is simple-minded: the neighbourhood of the symptom is searched first; then, the neighbourhood of the current alternative. Patterns of search reveal biases which in turn reflect such factors as specialized training or experience and patterns of communication.

- Organizational learning and change. The parameters of organizational behaviour mostly persist. In response to non-standard problems, organizations search and routines evolve, assimilating new situations. Thus learning and change follow in large part from existing procedures. But marked changes in organizations do sometimes occur. Conditions in which dramatic changes are more likely include: (1) Periods of budgetary feast. Typically, organizations devour budgetary feasts by purchasing additional items on the existing shopping list. Nevertheless, if committed to change, leaders who control the budget can use extra funds to effect changes. (2) Periods of prolonged budgetary famine. Though a single year's famine typically results in few changes in organizational structure but a loss of effectiveness in performing some programmes, prolonged famine forces major retrenchment. (3) Dramatic performance failures. Dramatic change occurs (mostly) in response to major disasters. Confronted with an undeniable failure of procedures and repertoires, authorities outside the organization demand change, existing personnel are less resistant to change, and critical members of the organization are replaced by individuals committed to change.

Central coordination and control. Action requires decentralization of responsibility and power. But problems lap over the jurisdictions of several organizations. Thus the necessity for decentralization runs headlong into the requirement for coordination. Both the necessity for coordination and the centrality of foreign policy to national welfare guarantee the involvement of government leaders in the procedures of the organizations among which problems are divided

and power shared. Each organization's propensities and routines can be disturbed by government leaders' intervention. Central direction and persistent control of organizational activity, however, is not possible. The relation among organizations, and between organizations and the government leaders depends critically on a number of structural variables including (1) the nature of the job; (2) the measures and information available to government leaders; (3) the system of rewards and punishments for organizational members; and (4) the procedures by which human and material resources get committed. For example, to the extent that rewards and punishments for the members of an organization are distributed by higher authorities, these authorities can exercise some control by specifying criteria in terms of which organizational output is to be evaluated. These criteria become constraints within which organizational activity proceeds. But constraint is a crude instrument of control. Intervention by government leaders does sometimes change the activity of an organization in an intended direction. But instances are fewer than might be expected. As Franklin Roosevelt, the master manipulator of government organizations, remarked:

The Treasury is so large and far-flung and ingrained in its practices that I find it is almost impossible to get the action and results I want . . . But the Treasury is not to be compared with the State Department. You should go through the experience of trying to get any changes in the thinking, policy, and action of the career diplomats and then you'd know what a real problem was. But the Treasury and the State Department put together are nothing compared with the Na-a-vy . . . To change anything in the Na-a-vy is like punching a feather bed. You punch it with your right and you punch it with your left until you are finally exhausted, and then you find the damn bed just as it was before you started punching.

(Eccles, 1951: 336)

Decisions of government leaders. Organizational persistence does not exclude shifts in governmental behaviour. For government leaders sit atop the conglomerate of organizations. Many important issues of governmental action require that these leaders decide what organizations will play out which programmes where. Thus stability in the parochialisms and SOPs of individual organizations is consistent with some important shifts in the behaviour of governments. The range of these shifts is defined by existing organizational programmes.

Model II: Dominant inference pattern and general propositions

If a nation performs an action of this type today, its organizational components must yesterday have been performing (or have had established routines for performing) an action only marginally different from this action. At any specific point in time, a government consists of an established conglomerate of organizations, each with existing goals, programmes, and repertoires. The characteristics of a government's action in any instance follows from those established routines, and from the choice of government leaders – on the basis of information and estimates provided by existing routines – among existing programmes. The best explanation of an organization's behaviour at t is $t - 1$; the prediction of $t + 1$ is t. Model II's explanatory power is achieved by uncovering the organizational routines and repertoires that produced the outputs that comprise the puzzling occurrence.

A number of general propositions have been stated above. In order to illustrate clearly the type of proposition employed by Model II analysts, this section formulates several more precisely.

Organizational action. Activity according to SOPs and programmes does not constitute far-sighted, flexible adaptation to 'the issue' (as it is conceived by the analyst). Detail and nuance of actions by organizations are determined predominantly by organizational routines, not government leaders' directions.

- SOPs constitute routines for dealing with standard situations. Routines allow large numbers of ordinary individuals to deal with numerous instances, day after day, without considerable thought, by responding to basic stimuli. But this regularized capability for adequate performance is purchased at the price of standardization. If the SOPs are appropriate, average performance, i.e. performance averaged over the range of cases, is better than it would be if each instance were approached individually (given fixed talent, timing, and resource constraints). But specific instances, particularly critical instances that typically do not have 'standard' characteristics, are often handled sluggishly or inappropriately.

- A programme, i.e. a complex action chosen from a short list of programmes in a repertoire, is rarely tailored to the specific situation in which it is executed. Rather, the programme is (at best) the most appropriate of the programmes in a previously developed repertoire.

- Since repertoires are developed by parochial organizations for standard scenarios defined by that organization, programmes available for dealing with a particular situation are often ill-suited.

Limited flexibility and incremental change. Major lines of organizational action are straight, i.e. behaviour at one time is marginally different from that behaviour at $t - 1$. Simpleminded predictions work best: Behaviour at $t + 1$ will be marginally different from behaviour at the present time.

- Organizational budgets change incrementally – both with respect to totals and with respect to intra-organizational splits. Though organizations could divide the money available each year by carving up the pie anew (in the light of changes in objectives or environment), in practice, organizations take last year's budget as a base and adjust incrementally. Predictions that require large budgetary shifts in a single year between organizations or between units within an organization should be hedged.

- Once undertaken, an organizational investment is not dropped at the point where 'objective' costs outweigh benefits. Organizational stakes in adopted projects carry them quite beyond the loss point.

Administrative feasibility. Adequate explanation, analysis, and prediction must include administrative feasibility as a major dimension. A considerable gap separates what leaders choose (or might rationally have chosen) and what organizations implement.

- Organizations are blunt instruments. Projects that require several organizations to act with high degrees of precision and coordination are not likely to succeed.

- Projects that demand that existing organizational units depart from their accustomed functions and perform previously unprogrammed tasks are rarely accomplished in their designed form.

- Government leaders can expect that each organization will do its 'part' in terms of what the organization knows how to do.

- Government leaders can expect incomplete and distorted information from each organization concerning its part of the problem.

- Where an assigned piece of a problem is contrary to the existing goals of an organization, resistance to implementation of that piece will be encountered.

Model III: Bureaucratic politics

The leaders who sit on top of organizations are not a monolithic group. Rather, each is, in his own right, a player in a central, competitive game. The name of the game is bureaucratic politics: bargaining along regularized channels among players positioned hierarchically within the government. Government behaviour can thus be understood according to a third conceptual model not as organizational outputs, but as outcomes of bargaining games. In contrast with Model I, the bureaucratic politics model sees no unitary actor but rather many actors as players, who focus not on a single strategic issue but on many diverse intranational problems as well, in terms of no consistent set of strategic objectives but rather according to various conceptions of national, organizational, and personal goals, making government decisions not by rational choice but by the pulling and hauling that is politics.

The apparatus of each national government constitutes a complex arena for the intra-national game. Political leaders at the top of this apparatus plus the men who occupy positions on top of the critical organizations form the circle of central players. Ascendancy to this circle assures some independent standing. The necessary decentralization of decisions required for action on the broad range of foreign policy problems guarantees that each player has considerable discretion. Thus power is shared.

The nature of problems of foreign policy permits fundamental disagreement among reasonable men concerning what ought to be done. Analyses yield conflicting recommendations. Separate responsibilities laid on the shoulders of individual personalities encourage differences in perceptions and priorities. But the issues are of first order importance. What the nation does really matters. A wrong choice could mean irreparable damage. Thus responsible men are obliged to fight for what they are convinced is right.

Men share power. Men differ concerning what must be done. The differences matter. This milieu necessitates that policy be resolved by politics. What the nation does is sometimes the result of the triumph of one group over others. More often, however, different groups pulling in different directions yield a resultant distinct from what anyone intended. What moves the chess pieces is not simply the reasons which support a course of action, nor the routines of organizations which enact an alternative, but the power and skill of proponents and opponents of the action in question.

This characterization captures the thrust of the bureaucratic politics orientation. If problems of foreign policy arose as discreet issues, and decisions were determined one game at a time, this account would suffice. But most 'issues' emerge piecemeal, over time, one lump in one context, a second in another. Hundreds of issues compete for players' attention every day. Each player is forced to fix upon his issues for that day, fight them on their own terms, and rush on to the next. Thus the character of emerging issues and the pace at which the game is played converge to yield government 'decisions' and 'actions' as collages. Choices by one player, outcomes of minor games, outcomes of central games, and 'foul-ups' – these pieces, when stuck to the same canvas, constitute government behaviour relevant to an issue.

Model III: Basic unit of analysis: Policy as political outcome

The decisions and actions of governments are essentially intra-national political outcomes: outcomes in the sense that what happens is not chosen as a solution to a problem but rather results from compromise, coalition, competition, and confusion among government officials who see different faces of an issue; political in the sense that the activity from which the outcomes emerge is best characterized as bargaining. Following Wittgenstein's use of the concept of a 'game,' national behaviour in international affairs can be conceived as outcomes of intricate and subtle, simultaneous, overlapping games among players located in positions, the hierarchical arrangement of which constitutes the government. These games proceed neither at random nor at leisure. Regular channels structure the game. Deadlines force issues to the attention of busy players. The moves in the chess game are thus to be explained in terms of the bargaining among players with separate and unequal power over particular pieces and with separable objectives in distinguishable subgames.

Model III: Organizing concepts

Players in positions. The actor is neither a unitary nation, nor a conglomerate of organizations, but rather a number of individual players. Groups of these players constitute the agent for particular government decisions and actions. Players are men in jobs.

Individuals become players in the national security policy game by occupying a critical position in an administration. For example, in the US government the players include 'Chiefs': The President, Secretaries of State, Defense, and Treasury, Director of the CIA, Joint Chiefs of Staff and, since 1961, the Special Assistant for National Security Affairs; 'Staffers': the immediate staff of each Chief; 'Indians': the political appointees and permanent government officials within each of the departments and agencies; and 'Ad Hoc Players': actors in the wider government game (especially 'Congressional Influentials'), members of the press, spokesmen for important interest groups (especially the 'bipartisan foreign policy establishment' in and out of Congress), and surrogates for each of these groups. Other members of the Congress, press, interest groups, and public form concentric circles around the central arena – circles which demarcate the permissive limits within which the game is played.

Positions define what players both may and must do. The advantages and handicaps with which each player can enter and play in various games stems from his position. So does a cluster of obligations for the performance of certain tasks.

All of these obligations are his simultaneously. His performance in one affects his credit and power in the others. The perspective stemming from the daily work which he must oversee – the cable traffic by which his department maintains relations with other foreign offices – conflicts with the President's requirement that he serve as a generalist and coordinator of contrasting perspectives. The necessity that he be close to the President restricts the extent to which, and the force with which, he can front for his department. When he defers to the Secretary of Defense rather than fighting for his department's position – as he often must – he strains the loyalty of his officialdom. The Secretary's resolution of these conflicts depends not only upon the position but also upon the player who occupies the position.

For players are also people. Men's metabolisms differ. The core of the bureaucratic politics mix is personality. How each man manages to stand the heat in his kitchen, each player's basic operating style, and the complementarity or contradiction among personalities and styles in the inner circles are irreducible pieces of the policy blend. Moreover, each person comes to his position with baggage in tow, including sensitivities to certain issues, commitments to various programmes, and personal standing and debts with groups in the society.

Parochial priorities, perceptions and issues. Answers to the questions: 'What is the issue?' and 'What must be done?' are coloured by the position from which the questions are considered. For the factors which encourage organizational parochialism also influence the players who occupy positions on top of (or within) these organizations. To motivate members of his organization, a player must be sensitive to the organization's orientation. The games into which the player can enter and the advantages with which he plays enhance these pressures. Thus propensities of perception stemming from position permit reliable prediction about a player's stances in many cases. But these propensities are filtered through the baggage which players bring to positions. Sensitivity to both the pressures and the baggage is thus required for many predictions.

Interests, stakes, and power. Games are played to determine outcomes. But outcomes advance and impede each player's conception of the national interest, specific programmes to which he is committed, the welfare of his friends, and his personal interests. These overlapping interests constitute the stakes for which games are played. Each player's ability to play successfully depends upon his power. Power, i.e. effective influence on policy outcomes, is an elusive blend of at least three elements: bargaining advantages (drawn from formal authority and obligations, institutional backing, constituents, expertise, and status), skill and will in using bargaining advantages, and other players' perceptions of the first two ingredients. Power wisely invested yields an enhanced reputation for effectiveness. Unsuccessful investment depletes both the stock of capital and the reputation. Thus each player must pick the issues on which he can play with a reasonable probability of success. But no player's power is sufficient to guarantee satisfactory outcomes. Each player's needs and fears run to many other players. What ensues is the most intricate and subtle of games known to man.

The problem and the problems. Solutions to strategic problems are not derived by detached analysts focusing coolly on the problem. Instead, deadlines and events raise issues in games, and demand decisions of busy players in contexts that influence the face the issue wears. The problems for the players are both narrower and broader than the strategic problem. For each player focuses not on the total strategic problem but rather on the decision that must be made now. But each decision has critical consequences not only for the strategic problem but for each player's organizational, reputational, and personal stakes. Thus the gap between the problems the player was solving and the problem upon which the analyst focuses is often very wide.

Action-channels.   Bargaining games do not proceed randomly. Action-channels, i.e. regularized ways of producing action concerning types of issues, structure the game by pre-selecting the major players, determining their points of entrance into the game, and distributing particular advantages and disadvantages for each game. Most critically, channels determine 'who's got the action', that is, which department's Indians actually do whatever is chosen.

Action as politics.   Government decisions are made and government actions emerge neither as the calculated choice of a unified group, nor as a formal summary of leaders' preferences. Rather the context of shared power but separate judgements concerning important choices, determines that politics is the mechanism of choice. Note the environment in which the game is played: inordinate uncertainty about what must be done, the necessity that something be done, and crucial consequences of whatever is done. These features force responsible men to become active players. The *pace of the game* – hundreds of issues, numerous games, and multiple channels – compels players to fight to 'get other's attention', to make them 'see the facts', to assure that they 'take the time to think seriously about the broader issue'. The *structure of the game* – power shared by individuals with separate responsibilities – validates each player's feeling that 'others don't see my problem', and 'others must be persuaded to look at the issue from a less parochial perspective'. The *rules of the game* – he who hesitates loses his chance to play at that point, and he who is uncertain about his recommendation is overpowered by others who are sure – pressures players to come down on one side of a 51–49 issue and play. The rewards of the game – effectiveness, i.e. impact on outcomes, as the immediate measure of performance – encourage hard play. Thus, most players come to fight to 'make the government do what is right'.

Streams of outcomes.   Important government decisions or actions emerge as collages composed of individual acts, outcomes of minor and major games, and foul-ups. Outcomes which could never have been chosen by an actor and would never have emerged from bargaining in a single game over the issue are fabricated piece by piece. Understanding of the outcome requires that it be disaggregated.

Model III: Dominant inference pattern and general propositions

If a nation performed an action, that action was the *outcome* of bargaining among individuals and groups within the government. That outcome included *results* achieved by groups committed to a decision or action, *resultants* which emerged from bargaining among groups with quite different positions and *foul-ups*. Model III's explanatory power is achieved by revealing the pulling and hauling of various players, with different perceptions and priorities, focusing on separate problems, which yielded the outcomes that constitute the action in question.

■ Action and intention. Action does not presuppose intention. The sum of behaviour of representatives of a government relevant to an issue was rarely intended by any individual or group. Rather separate individuals with different intentions contributed pieces which compose an outcome distinct from what anyone would have chosen.

■ Where you stand depends on where you sit. Horizontally, the diverse demands upon each player shape his priorities, perceptions, and issues. For large classes of issues, e.g. budgets and procurement decisions, the stance of a particular player can be predicted with high reliability from information concerning his seat.

■ Chiefs and Indians. The aphorism 'where you stand depends on where you sit' has vertical as well as horizontal application. Vertically, the demands upon the President, Chiefs, Staffers, and Indians are quite distinct.

The foreign policy issues with which the President can deal are limited primarily by his crowded schedule: the necessity of dealing first with what comes next. His problem is to probe the special face worn by issues that come to his attention, to preserve his leeway until time has clarified the uncertainties, and to assess the relevant risks.

Foreign policy chiefs deal most often with the hottest issue *de jour,* though they can get the attention of the President and other members of the government for other issues which they judge important. What they cannot guarantee is that 'the President will pay the price' or that 'the others will get on board'. They must build a coalition of the relevant powers that be. They must 'give the President confidence' in the right course of action.

Most problems are framed, alternatives specified, and proposals pushed, however, by Indians. Indians fight with Indians of other departments; for example, struggles between International Security Affairs of the Department of Defense and Political-Military of the State Department are a microcosm of the action at higher levels. But the Indian's major problem is how to get the attention of chiefs, how to get an issue decided, how to get the government 'to do what is right'.

In policy making then, the issue looking *down* is options: how to preserve my leeway until time clarifies uncertainties. The issue looking *sideways* is commitment: how to get others committed to my coalition. The issue looking *upwards* is confidence: how to give the boss confidence in doing what must be done. To paraphrase one of Neustadt's assertions which can be applied down the length of the ladder, the essence of a responsible official's task is to induce others to see that what needs to be done is what their own appraisal of their own responsibilities requires them to do in their own interests.

Conclusion

At a minimum, the intended implications of the argument presented here are four. First, formulation of alternative frames of reference and demonstration that different analysts, relying predominantly on different models, produce quite different explanations should encourage the analyst's self-consciousness about the nets he employs. The effect of these 'spectacles' in sensitizing him to particular aspects of what is going on – framing the puzzle in one way rather than another, encouraging him to examine the problem in terms of certain categories rather than others, directing him to particular kinds of evidence, and relieving puzzlement by one procedure rather than another – must be recognized and explored.

Second, the argument implies a position on the problem of 'the state of the art'. While accepting the commonplace characterization of the present condition of foreign policy analysis – personalistic, non-cumulative, and sometimes insightful – this article rejects both the counsel of despair's justification of this condition as a consequence of the character of the enterprise, and the 'new frontiersmen's' demand for *a priori* theorizing on the frontiers and *ad hoc* appropriation of 'new techniques'. What is required as a first step is non-casual examination of the present product: inspection of existing explanations, articulation of the conceptual models employed in producing them, formulation of the propositions relied upon, specification of the logic of the various intellectual enterprises, and reflection on the questions being asked. Though it is difficult to

overemphasize the need for more systematic processing of more data, these preliminary matters of formulating questions with clarity and sensitivity to categories and assumptions so that fruitful acquisition of large quantities of data is possible are still a major hurdle in considering most important problems.

Third, the preliminary, partial paradigms presented here provide a basis for serious reexamination of many problems of foreign and military policy. Model II and Model III cuts at problems typically treated in Model I terms can permit significant improvements in explanation and prediction. Full Model II and III analyses require large amounts of information. But even in cases where the information base is severely limited, improvements are possible.

Fourth, the present formulation of paradigms is simply an initial step. As such it leaves a long list of critical questions unanswered. Given any action, an imaginative analyst should always be able to construct some rationale for the government's choice. By imposing, and relaxing, constraints on the parameters of rational choice (as in variants of Model I) analysts can construct a large number of accounts of any act as a rational choice. But does a statement of reasons why a rational actor would choose an action constitute an explanation of the *occurrence* of that action? How can Model I analysis be forced to make more systematic contributions to the question of the determinants of occurrences? Model II's explanation of t in terms of $t - 1$ is explanation. The world is contiguous. But governments sometimes make sharp departures. Can an organizational process model be modified to suggest where change is likely? Attention to organizational change should afford greater understanding of why particular programmes and SOPs are maintained by identifiable types of organizations and also how a manager can improve organizational performance. Model III tells a fascinating 'story'. But its complexity is enormous, the information requirements are often overwhelming, and many of the details of the bargaining may be superfluous. How can such a model be made parsimonious? The three models are obviously not exclusive alternatives. Indeed, the paradigms highlight the partial emphasis of the framework – what each emphasizes and what it leaves out. Each concentrates on one class of variables, in effect, relegating other important factors to a *ceteris paribus* clause. Model I concentrates on 'market factors': pressures and incentives created by the 'international strategic marketplace'. Models II and III focus on the internal mechanism of the government that chooses in this environment. But can these relations be more fully specified? Adequate synthesis would require a typology of decisions and actions, some of which are more amenable to treatment in terms of one model and some to another. Government behaviour is but one cluster of factors relevant to occurrences in foreign affairs. Most students of foreign policy adopt this focus

(at least when explaining and predicting). Nevertheless, the dimensions of the chess board, the character of the pieces, and the rules of the game – factors considered by international systems theorists – constitute the context in which the pieces are moved.

READING 3.4

From scenario thinking to strategic action

By Ian Wilson[1]

Introduction

One day in the fall of 1976 I arranged a meeting between Pierre Wack, who at that time headed Royal Dutch/Shell's Business Environment component, and some of my colleagues in General Electric's strategic planning staff. The focus of our discussion was to be the role of scenarios in corporate planning.

At that time, GE had, arguably, the most elaborate and sophisticated strategic planning system in the corporate world, and Shell was enjoying an international reputation for its pioneering scenarios work. Yet in each case something was missing. Wack was convinced that his scenarios needed a tighter linkage to strategic planning and decision-making if they were ever to engage operations managers seriously and continuously. And GE, still shaken and puzzled by the fallout from the first 'oil shock', needed to ground its strategy in an assessment of the future that acknowledged, more explicitly, the inherent uncertainties that then marked the future business environment. The two parties thus came to this discussion from differing points of view, but focused on the same central need: linking perceptions about the future to current decisions.

This meeting marked a turning point in my recognition of the critical importance of strengthening the connection between scenario development and strategic action. From this point forward I recognized that, although developing coherent, imaginative and useful scenarios is certainly important, translating the implications of the scenarios into executive decisions

and, ultimately, into strategic action was the ultimate reason and justification for the exercise.

Cultural barriers to implementation

Scenarios are not an end in themselves. They are a management tool to improve the quality of executive decision making. Yet experience shows that actually using scenarios for this purpose turns out to be a more perplexing problem than the scenario development process itself. As in the larger domain of strategy, implementation – execution – turns out to be the crucial issue.

The causes of this implementation problem, in part practical and procedural, are still largely cultural and psychological. The planning culture in most corporations is still heavily biased toward single-point forecasting. In such a context, the managers' premise is, 'Tell me what the future will be; then I can make my decision.' So their initial reaction, when confronted with the apparent emphasis in scenarios on 'multipoint forecasting', is likely to be one of confusion and disbelief, complaining that three (or four) 'forecasts' are more confusing, and less helpful, than one. The fact that this is a misperception of the nature and role of scenarios does not in any way lessen the implementation problem.

However, the major cultural barrier to scenario implementation stems from the way we define managerial competence. Good managers, we say, *know* where they are, where they're going, and how they'll get there. *We*

[1]Source: This article was reprinted from *Technological Forecasting and Social Change*, Vol. 65, I. Wilson, 'From Scenario Thinking to Strategic Action', pp. 23–29, 2000. With permission from Elsevier.

equate managerial competence with 'knowing', and assume that decisions depend on facts about the present and about the future. Of course, the reality is that *we have no facts about the future*. In a 1975 presentation to the American Association for the Advancement of Science (AAAS), I highlighted this problem in the following way: 'However good our futures research may be, we shall never be able to escape from the ultimate dilemma that all our knowledge is about the past, and all our decisions are about the future.'

Scenarios face up to this dilemma, confronting us with the need to acknowledge that we do not, and cannot, know the future. In the most fundamental way, scenarios seek, as Pierre Wack put it, to change our 'mental maps' of the future. But, in doing so, scenarios also may seem to challenge the way we define managerial competence. That is, by acknowledging uncertainty, scenarios underscore the fact that we cannot know the future, and so we perceive them as challenges to our presumptions of 'knowing', and thus of managerial competence. And because few, if any, corporate cultures reward incompetence, managers have a vested interest in not acknowledging their ignorance, and so in resisting the intrusion of scenario planning into traditional forms of executive decision-making.

Dealing with the dilemma

A starting point for dealing with this dilemma is to establish a clear-cut 'decision focus' for every set of scenarios. The first step in the scenario process is *not* a review of the changing forces affecting the business environment, but rather agreement on the strategic decision(s) that the scenarios should be designed to illuminate. While it is true that scenarios can also be used as a learning tool to explore general areas of risk and opportunity, this use normally leads to the development of more focused scenarios before decisions are taken. This crucial step establishes, at the outset, that the ultimate purpose of the scenarios is not just to develop plausible descriptions of alternative futures – not even to redraw our mental maps of the future, important as that is – but rather to help executives make better, more resilient strategic decisions. By tying scenarios to needed decisions, we effectively link them to specific planning needs, and prevent the process from straying off into overly broad generalizations about the future of society or the global economy.

Usually, the right decisions on which to focus decisions are strategic rather than tactical. This is because scenarios normally deal more with longer term trends and uncertainties, often with a 5 to 10-year time

horizon, rather than short-term developments. Virtually any decision or area of strategic concern in which external factors are complex, changing, and uncertain is a suitable target for the scenario process. However, I have found that the narrower the scope of the decision or strategy (a specific investment or market entry decision, for example), the easier the scenario construction – and interpretation – will be. Developing scenarios for broad strategic concerns – the long-range positioning of a diversified business portfolio, for example – is more difficult.

A word of caution is needed at this point. While clarifying the strategic focus of the scenarios is a critical first step, it is equally important to note that this is not the time for strategizing. Decision-makers, particularly senior executives, have a natural impatience with analysis and a tendency to want to 'cut to the chase'. On many occasions I have had to check this otherwise praiseworthy tendency toward action so that the context for action – the scenarios themselves – can first be established. Once executives see that the process *both begins and ends* with an emphasis on action, they are more easily persuaded of the true value of scenario planning.

What *not* to do

Agreeing that the usefulness of scenarios depends upon their ability to influence executive action is a good first step because at least it focuses attention on what would otherwise be a potential problem. However, it leaves unanswered the questions: What do we do with scenarios once we have developed them? How do we translate what we learn from them into action? Before attempting to answer these questions, there are two things that we should *not* do.

First, we do *not* develop a complete strategy for each of the scenarios, and then by some means – maybe by applying the test of discounted cash value – select the one that appears to give the greatest promise of success and profitability. I know of no management team that would willingly undertake to go through a full-blown strategy development exercise two or three or four times (however, many scenarios have been developed). Such a course would more likely lead to 'paralysis by analysis' than to constructive action. And, in any case, it would be based on a further misunderstanding of scenario planning: the real aim is to develop a resilient strategy within the framework of alternative futures provided by the scenarios.

Before proceeding, a word of explanation – and caution – is needed at this point. In a number of places in this article I refer to the objective of scenario planning as being the development of a resilient strategy. Now, it should be obvious that resilience is not the only quality to be sought in a strategy; and, taken to an extreme, resilience could mean little more than the lowest common denominator of scenario-specific strategies. At a time that calls for bold, even radical, action in many markets, such an interpretation would be a prescription for mediocrity at best, extinction at worst. My point is, rather, that, before taking bold steps, the strategy should be tested against a variety of scenarios so that the management team is forewarned of potential vulnerabilities. Resilience can then be built into the strategy, *not* by reducing its force or boldness, but rather by 'hedging' or contingency planning.

The second thing that we do not do is assign probabilities to the scenarios and then develop a strategy for the 'most probable' one. Of course, in saying this, I am taking a controversial position. Probability has more to do with forecasts than with scenarios; and scenarios are not forecasts, for one cannot, reasonably and at the same time, 'forecast' three or four quite different futures. Scenarios, as a collection of futures, are intended to establish the boundaries of our uncertainty and the limits to plausible futures.

However, I recognize that there is a very powerful human tendency, born of past experience and culture, to assign probabilities at the end of the scenario process. Every individual ends up with his or her own private assessment of probability; and it is almost certainly better to bring these assessments out into the open for group discussion than to leave them suppressed in individual minds. Indeed, doing this usually serves to underscore the wide diversity of opinions – and the consequent foolishness of trying to reach some sort of consensus on this matter. However, whichever course of action one elects – to engage in this group assessment or not – the critical point is to avoid playing the probabilities game to the point of focusing on one 'most probable' scenario to the exclusion of the others. To do so would negate the whole value of the scenario planning exercise.

What to do

Using scenarios to make strategic decisions requires considerable skill and sophistication: and these qualities take time to acquire. Initially, therefore, any organization experimenting with scenario planning needs some sort of a template, a primer, or step-by-step approach to moving from scenarios to strategy.

Some critics will protest that this approach trivializes strategy development, substituting analytical structure for intuitive insight. However, in defense of this utilitarian approach, consider the analogy of learning to play the piano. The beginner has to learn the notes, practice scales, and play rhythmically, paced by a metronome. Only after mastering technique can the piano player perform with feeling and insight. So, too, the beginning scenario player needs to learn some basic techniques that will help to bridge the gap between scenarios and strategy before graduating to a more sophisticated approach.

In this spirit, I offer the following primer of four approaches to this problem, ranging from the most elemental to the more sophisticated.

Sensitivity/risk assessment

This approach can be used to evaluate a specific strategic decision such as a major plant investment or a new business development drive. Here, the need for the decision is known beforehand: the question, therefore, is simply whether or not to proceed, after assessing the strategy's resilience or vulnerability in different business conditions.

A step-by-step approach first identifies the key conditions (such as market growth rate, changes in regulatory climate, technological developments) that the future market or industry environment would have to meet to justify a 'go' decision, and then assesses the state of these conditions in each scenario. It is then possible to compare the scenario conditions with the desired future conditions, and to assess how successful and how resilient or vulnerable, a 'go' decision would be in each scenario. Finally, it is possible to assess the overall resilience of a decision to proceed with the proposed strategy, and to consider the need or desirability of 'hedging' or modifying the original decision in some way in order to increase its resilience.

This approach provides a relatively straightforward application of scenarios to decision-making, using a series of descriptive and judgmental steps. However, it depends on having a very clear and specific decision focus, one which lends itself to a 'go/no go' decision.

An illustration of this approach was provided by a paper company confronted with a decision on whether or not to invest $600 million in a new paper-making facility. The company did not normally use scenarios in its strategic planning, but decided that they would be useful here, given the long life span (30–35 years) of the plant and the corresponding range of uncertainties regarding future electronic technology development, consumer values and time use, prospects for advertising, and general economic conditions.

The scenarios showed, as one might expect, vastly different levels of demand growth, but similar patterns of eventual decline, with the timing of key threats remaining a critical uncertainty. Playing out the investment decision in these different environments suggested that only in the most optimistic conditions would the company meet its 'hurdle rate' for return on investment. As a result, the executives decided on a more incremental approach to the investment, significantly scaling down the initial plant size.

Strategy evaluation

Another relatively straightforward role for scenarios is to act as 'test beds' to evaluate the viability of an existing strategy, usually one that derives from traditional single-point forecasting. By playing a company wide or business unit strategy against the scenarios it is possible to gain some insight into the strategy's effectiveness in a range of business conditions, and so to identify modifications and/or contingency planning that require attention.

First, it is necessary to disaggregate the strategy into its specific thrusts (e.g., 'Focus on upscale consumer market segments', 'Diversify into related services areas') and spell out its goals and objectives. Then it is possible to assess the relevance and likely success (in terms of meeting the desired objectives) of these thrusts in the diverse conditions of the scenarios. Assessing the results of this impact analysis should then enable the management team to identify (a) opportunities that the strategy addresses and those that it misses; (b) threats/risks that the analysis has foreseen or overlooked; and (c) comparative competitive success or failure.

At this point, it is possible to identify options for changes in strategy and the need for contingency planning.

This approach offers a natural and relatively simple first use of scenarios in a corporate strategic planning system. Assessing an existing strategy requires less sophistication than developing a new strategy; nevertheless, assessment provides a quick demonstration of the utility of scenarios in executive decision-making by identifying important 'bottom-line' issues that require immediate attention.

A large department-store chain introduced scenarios this way into its strategic exploration of future patterns of change in the economy, consumer values,

life styles, and the structure and operations of the retail industry. The company used these scenarios in three distinct ways: (1) evaluate the likely payoff from its current strategy; (2) assess and compare the strategies of key competitors (note: this was an interesting – and useful – application of scenario planning, assessing the competitors' as well as one's own strategy); and (3) analyse retail strategy options to identify the most resilient ones for possible inclusion in the company's strategy (the company did, in fact, expand greatly into specialty stores as a result of this exercise).

Strategy development (using a 'planning-focus' scenario)

This approach is an attempt to bridge the 'culture gap' between traditional planning that relies on single-point forecasting and scenario planning. Basically, it consists of selecting one of the scenarios as a starting point and focus for strategy development, and then using the other scenarios to test the strategy's resilience and assess the need for modification, 'hedging' or contingency planning.

The steps involved in this approach are as follows: (a) review the scenarios to identify the key opportunities and threats for the business, looking at each scenario in turn and then looking across all scenarios (to identify common opportunities and threats); (b) determine, based on this review, what the company should do, and should not do, in any case; (c) select a 'planning focus' scenario (usually the 'most probable' one); (d) integrate the strategic elements identified in step b into a coherent strategy for the 'planning focus' scenario; (e) test this strategy against the remaining scenarios to assess its resilience or vulnerability; and (f) review the results of this test to determine the need for strategy modification, 'hedging', and contingency planning.

It should be obvious that this approach flies in the face of my earlier assertion that scenarios should not deal in probabilities. And, while the other scenarios are not discarded, there is still the danger that this approach may close executives' minds to 'unlikely' (which often means 'unpleasant') scenarios and so limits their search for strategy options. However, the approach can be justified as a useful intermediate step (between traditional and scenario planning) in weaning executives away from their reliance on single-point forecasting. It does not commit the ultimate sin of disregarding the other scenarios entirely; and, in its step-by-step process, it does address many of the key questions that scenario-based strategy should ask.

Shell Canada used this approach when it introduced scenarios into its strategic planning system in the early 1980s. As a member of the Royal Dutch/Shell Group, its executives were well aware of the strict interpretation of scenario-based planning, but felt that this modified approach would help the company ease into the new process by making this concession to traditional thinking. In fact, the discussion of probabilities revealed so much uncertainty in executive opinion about future trends, that two scenarios – each with dramatically different drivers – were selected as the 'planning focus'. The company then proceeded to structure its strategic positioning in answer to three questions: (1) What strategies should we pursue no matter which scenario materializes? (2) What strategies should we pursue if either of the 'planning focus' scenarios materializes? (3) How sensitive are base strategies to variations in assumptions under contingent conditions?

In fact, in the end, Shell Canada did succeed, both in bridging the gap between the old and new approaches to strategy development and in preserving the value of considering, and planning for, different business conditions.

Strategy development (without using a 'planning-focus' scenario)

In this approach, executives take all scenarios at face value without judging probabilities, and aim for the development of a resilient strategy that can deal with wide variations in business conditions. The step-by-step process in this approach considers: (1) identifying the key elements of a successful strategy (such as geographic scope, market focus, product range, basis of competition); (2) analysing each scenario to determine the optimal setting for each strategy element (e.g., what would be the best marketing strategy for Scenario A? for Scenario B?); (3) reviewing these scenario-specific settings to determine the most resilient option for each strategy element; and (4) integrating these strategy options into an overall, co-ordinated business strategy.

Without doubt, this is the most sophisticated – and demanding – approach, one that most closely approximates the goal of stategizing within the scenarios framework, and that makes optimal use of the scenarios in strategy development. It provides management with the maximum feasible range of choice, and forces careful evaluation of these options against differing assumptions about the future. It does, however, demand effort, patience, and sophistication, and works best when the decision-makers participate directly throughout the process.

This was the case with a large European financial-services company in which the senior management team was, in effect, both the scenario- and the strategy-development team. After structuring scenarios around their perceptions of the critical uncertainties facing the business, they first identified the strategic opportunities and threats arising from these scenarios. They then used this framework to assess the company's current competitive position and prospective vulnerability. Their approach to strategy development then led them to the following steps: (1) first, to single out 11 key elements of a well-rounded strategy (e.g., product scope, alliances, distribution/delivery, technology); (2) second, to identify the optimal strategic option for each of these 11 elements in each of the four scenarios; and (3) finally, to select the most resilient option for each element, and to integrate the options into a coherent strategy for the company.

Conclusion

I have chosen to emphasize this one aspect of scenario planning – moving from the scenarios themselves to strategy development to action – because, in my experience, it is perhaps the most critical phase of the scenario process. More scenario projects fail because they have no impact on strategy and management decisions rather than because they were unimaginative or poorly constructed.

Moving from traditional planning to scenario-based strategic planning requires a transformation of corporate culture. Scenario planning is not merely a new planning tool, but rather a new way of thinking. Using scenarios on a one-shot basis requires much less investment than instituting them as an integral part of corporate planning. Many, perhaps most, of the problems in introducing scenario planning into an organization stem from a failure to recognize the magnitude and duration of the implementation effort that is required to use this technology to change the prevailing management assumptions.

Like scenarios themselves, this effort has to be tailored to the needs of the organization, but some requirements are constant: senior management commitment, communications, education and guidance, and practice, practice, practice. Like the piano player, the scenarios user will be able to progress from beginning exercises, as outlined here, to intuitive and insightful action only with time, patience, and practice.

STRATEGY FORMATION IN INTERNATIONAL PERSPECTIVE

What we anticipate seldom occurs; what we least expect generally happens.
Benjamin Disraeli (1804–1881); British prime minister and novelist

From the preceding readings it has become evident that views differ sharply as to whether strategies should be formed by means of planning or incrementalism. It is clear that a wide variety of approaches exists to deal with the paradox of deliberateness and emergence. None of the authors, however, suggest that their views may be more appropriate in some countries than in others. Nor do any of them mention the possibility that an organization's choice of approach may be influenced by national circumstances. In other words, so far the international angle has been conspicuously absent. It has generally been assumed that international differences are a non-issue.

Yet, the question of whether there are specific national preferences for the strategic planning or the strategic incrementalism perspective seems quite legitimate. In the past, a few international comparative studies have been carried out that show significantly different levels of formal planning across various industrialized countries. For instance, Steiner and Schollhammer (1975) reported that planning was found to be most common and most formalized in the United States, with other English-speaking countries (Britain, Canada and Australia) also exhibiting a high score. At the other extreme were Italy and Japan, where very little formal planning was witnessed. The low propensity to engage in formal planning in Japan has been noted by a number of other authors as well (e.g. Kagono *et al.*, 1985). Hayashi (1978: 221) remarks that Japanese firms 'distrust corporate planning in general', while Ohmae (1982: 225) characterizes Japanese companies as 'less planned, less rigid, but more vision- and mission-driven' than Western companies. Unfortunately, there are no cross-cultural studies of a more recent date to confirm that these international dissimilarities still exist. However, many observers have suggested that there remain discernible national differences in approaches to strategy formation (e.g. Gilbert and Lorange, 1995; Mintzberg, 1994a; Schneider, 1989).

Although it is difficult to generalize at the national level, since there can be quite a bit of variance within a country, it is challenging to pursue these observed international dissimilarities. Are there really national strategy formation styles and what factors might influence their existence? As a stimulus to the international dimension of this debate, we put forward the following country characteristics as possible influences on how the paradox of deliberateness and emergence is dealt with in different national settings. As we noted at the end of Chapter 2, these propositions are intended to encourage discussion, but more concrete international comparative research is needed to give this debate a firmer footing.

Level of professionalization

The high incidence of formal planning systems in Australia, Britain, Canada, New Zealand and the United States seems odd, given their high level of individualism and their strong preference for a market economy. One might expect that the English-speaking countries' fondness of unplanned markets would be a reflection of a general dislike of planning. Yet, strangely, 'most large US corporations are run like the Soviet economy' of yesteryear, with strong central plans and top-down control, Ohmae concludes (1982: 224).

One explanation might be that formalized planning and control systems are a logical consequence of having professional management (e.g. Mintzberg, 1994a). Nowhere in the industrialized world, with the exception of France, has there been a stronger development of a distinct managerial class than in the English-speaking countries (Hampden-Turner and Trompenaars, 1993; Lessem and Neubauer, 1994). These professional managers run companies on behalf of the owners, who are usually distant from the operations (i.e. often minority shareholders). In the division of labour, the managers perform the 'thinking' tasks – analyzing, planning, coordinating, leading, budgeting, motivating, controlling – while the workforce concentrates on performing the primary activities. This makes it possible for large, complex production processes to be controlled by a hierarchy of professional managers. It is commonly believed that these managers possess general skills that allow them to run a wide variety of different businesses.

In companies with professional management, the split between thinking and doing is made more explicit than in other organizations. The managers are the officers who formulate the strategies and the personnel on the work floor are the troops that must implement them – 'management' has intentions that the 'employees' must realize. This requires formal planning to guide workers' actions and a tight control system to ensure compliance. This mechanism is usually employed all the way up the hierarchy, as higher level managers use a planning and control system to steer and coordinate the behaviour of lower level managers. All the way at the top, senior management must also make plans to win the approval of the shareholders.

This stratified organizational model, that Mintzberg dubs the machine bureaucracy (1979), is also prevalent in France, where the distinction between *cadre* employees and *non-cadre* personnel is also very strong (Hofstede, 1993, Reading 1.4 in this book). In many other countries, however, the split between managerial and non-managerial tasks is not as radical. For instance, in Germany and Japan, senior employees are expected to be involved in operational matters, while junior employees are expected to contribute to strategy formation, by coming up with ideas and passing on information to seniors. In such countries, there is less need to use formal planning and control mechanisms to manage employees, since the 'managers' have direct and informal links with those 'managed'. Usually these managers have risen through the ranks, giving them the richness of information and contacts needed to manage without highly formalized systems. In these nations, consensus-building and personal control are the important management skills, and these are not readily transferable to another industry or even another organization.

In yet other countries, the dominant form of organization is that of direct control by one person or a family. This usually means that organizations remain relatively small, although they can compensate by linking up into networks based on personal connections between the top bosses. This organizational model, common in Italy and among the overseas Chinese (see Hofstede, 1993, Reading 1.4; Weidenbaum and Hughes, 1996) will be further discussed in Chapter 7. Here it is sufficient to conclude that in such organizations there is also little need for formalized planning and control systems to manage employees. The top boss, who is usually also the owner, steers the firm personally, with little regard for 'professional' methods.

The conclusion is that the national propensity to engage in formal planning is probably influenced by the level of professionalization of management within the country. In nations where the machine bureaucracy is the predominant organizational model, a stronger inclination towards formal planning systems can be expected.

Preference for internal control

While the previous section discussed different *types* of internal control, and the related organizational models, it should be noted that countries can also differ with regard to the *level* of internal control their citizens prefer. In some cultures, people have a strong desire for order and structure – clear tasks, responsibilities, powers, rules and procedures. Ambiguous situations and uncertain outcomes are disliked and therefore management strives to control organizational processes. Management can reduce uncertainty in a number of ways. Structure can be offered by strictly following traditions or by imposing top-down paternalistic rule. However, uncertainty can also be reduced by planning (Kagono *et al.*, 1985; Schneider, 1989). By setting direction, coordinating initiatives, committing resources, and programming activities, structure can be brought to the organization. In this way, planning can help to alleviate people's anxiety about 'disorganization'. In cultures that are more tolerant towards ambiguity and uncertainty, one can expect a weaker preference for planning.

The importance of planning as a means for structuring and controlling is particularly important in cultures where there is little confidence in self-organization. This is especially true in individualistic cultures, where organizational members cannot always be counted on to work towards the common good (Hofstede, 1993, Reading 1.4). In these countries, extensive planning and control systems are often used as a formal means for getting people to cooperate, coordinate and serve the organization's interests. Strategic plans function as internal contracts, to limit dysfunctional opportunistic behaviour (Allaire and Firsirotu, 1990; Bungay and Goold, 1991). In cultures with a stronger group-orientation, there is usually more trust that individuals will be team players, making formal control mechanisms redundant (Nonaka and Johansson, 1985). Therefore, in general, one can expect a weaker preference for planning in collectivist cultures.

Preference for external control

Cultures also differ with regard to the level of control that organizational members prefer to have over their environment. At the one extreme are cultures in which people strive to manage or even dominate their surroundings. In these countries, there is a strong desire to create the future and a fear of losing control of one's destiny. George Bernard Shaw's famous remark that 'to be in hell is to drift, to be in heaven is to steer', neatly summarizes these feelings. The consequence is that organizations in these nations are strongly drawn to proactive and deliberate strategy-making, under the motto 'plan or be planned for' (Ackoff, 1980). Drawing up plans to actively engage the outside world meets people's need to determine their own fate. This cultural characteristic is particularly pronounced in Western countries (Trompenaars, 1993).

At the other extreme are cultures in which most people passively accept their destiny. They believe that most external events are out of their hands and that they exert no control over the future. In such fatalistic cultures people tend to approach opportunities and threats reactively, on a day-to-day basis. Such muddling through behaviour rarely leads to emergent strategy, but more often to disjointed, unpatterned action.

In the middle are cultures in which people believe neither in domination of, or submission to, external circumstances. In these cultures people accept that events are unpredictable and that the environment cannot be tightly controlled, yet trust that individuals and organizations can proactively seek their own path among these uncertainties. The environment and the firm, it is thought, co-evolve through interaction and mutual adjustment, often in unforeseen ways. This requires firms to 'develop an attitude of receptivity and high adaptability to changing conditions' (Maruyama, 1984). This way of thinking is particularly pronounced in South-East Asia, and leads to a stronger inclination towards the strategic incrementalism perspective (Kagono *et al.*, 1985; Schneider, 1989).

Time orientation

A culture's time orientation can also be expected to influence national preferences for dealing with the paradox of deliberateness and emergence. There are a number of dimensions along which cultures' perception of time can differ. Cultures can be more involved with the past, the present or the future, whereby some make a strong linear separation between these phases, while others emphasize the continuity of time or even its cyclical nature. With regard to the future, a distinction can also be made between cultures with a more short-term or long-term orientation (Hofstede, 1993, Reading 1.4).

In general, it can be expected that people in cultures that heavily accentuate the past, or the present, over the future, will be less inclined to think and act strategically. In cultures that emphasize the near future, however, it is likely that individuals and organizations will exhibit a preference for planning. A focus on the not-too-distant future, which is more predictable than the long-term future, fits well with a strategic planning approach. In these countries, intentions are formulated, courses of action are determined and resources are committed, but with a relatively short planning horizon. Plans will only be adopted if results can be expected in the 'foreseeable' future. As Hofstede (1993) reports, the English-speaking countries belong to this category of short-term oriented cultures (see also Calori, Valla and de Woot, 1994; Kagono *et al.*, 1985).

In cultures with a stronger long-term orientation, strategic incrementalism can be expected to be a more predominant perspective. Since the long-term future is inherently unknown, planning for the future is seen as an inappropriate response. In these countries, it is generally believed that the unpredictability of the long-term future must be accepted and accommodated. This requires an attitude of caution and flexibility, linked to curiosity, learning and persistence. Actions are often taken that are not optimal in the short run, but point in the right long-term direction. As Hofstede (1993) reports, many South-East Asian countries fall into this category, as do some European countries.

FURTHER READING

For readers interested in an overview of the strategy formation literature, the best place to start is with *Strategy Safari: A Guided Tour Through the Wilds of Strategic Management*, by Henry Mintzberg, B. Ahlstrand and Joseph Lampel. Three other interesting overviews are 'How Strategies Develop in Organizations', by Andy Bailey and Gerry Johnson, 'An Integrative Framework for Strategy-Making Processes', by Stuart Hart and 'Mapping Strategic Diversity: Strategic Thinking from a Variety of Perspectives', by Dany Jacobs.

There are many books that give a detailed rendition of how strategic planning should be conducted within organizations. Igor Ansoff's and E. McDonnell's well-known textbook, *Implanting Strategic Management*, is an excellent, yet taxing, description of strategy-making from a planning perspective, while George Steiner's *Strategic Planning: What Every Manager Must Know* is a more down-to-earth prescription. Between these two extremes is a whole range of widely sold planning-oriented textbooks, such as Arthur Thompson and A.J. Strickland's *Strategic Management: Concepts and Cases*, and Thomas Wheelen and David Hunger's *Strategic Management and Business Policy*. For further reading on formal planning systems, Balaji Chakravarthy and Peter Lorange's book *Managing the Strategy Process: A Framework for a Multibusiness Firm* is a good place to start. On the link between planning and forecasting, the book *Forecasting, Planning and Strategy for the 21st Century*, by Spiro Makridakis, provides a useful introduction. A good book on scenarios is by Kees van der Heyden, entitled *Scenarios: The Art of Strategic Conversation*.

The most articulate critic of planning is probably Henry Mintzberg, whose book *The Rise and Fall of Strategic Planning* makes for thought-provoking reading. David Hurst's article 'Why Strategic Management is Bankrupt' also provides many interesting arguments against strategic planning. For a more extensive description of the strategic incrementalism perspective, James Brian Quinn's book *Strategies for Change* is still a good starting point. The fascinating book *Competing on the Edge: Strategy as Structured Chaos*, by Kathleen Eisenhardt and Shona Brown, also incorporates incrementalist approaches, as does Ralph Stacey's excellent textbook *Strategic Management and Organizational Dynamics*. Also highly recommended are Ikujiro Nonaka's article 'Toward Middle-Up-Down Management: Accelerating Information Creation', Robert Burgelman's article 'Corporate Entrepreneurship and Strategic Management: Insights from a Process Study' and Bjorn Lovas and Sumantra Ghoshal's article 'Strategy as Guided Evolution'.

For a solid research article on how large companies blend planning and incrementalism in practice, Robert Grant's study 'Strategic Planning in a Turbulent Environment: Evidence from the Oil Majors' makes for good reading. For a better understanding of the political processes involved in strategy formation the reader might want to turn to Andrew Pettigrew's article 'Strategy Formulation as a Political Process', or to Jeffrey Pfeffer's book *Power in Organizations*. Graham Allison's classic book *The Essence of Decision: Explaining the Cuban Missile Crisis* is also highly recommended. The cultural processes are vividly described in Gerry Johnson's *Strategic Change and the Management Process*, and more popularly in Rosabeth Moss Kanter's *The Change Masters*. Further articles and books that explore the link between strategy formation and strategic change are presented at the end of Chapter 4.

REFERENCES

Ackoff, R.L. (1980) *Creating the Corporate Future*, Chichester: Wiley.

Allaire, Y., and Firsirotu, M. (1990) 'Strategic Plans as Contracts', *Long Range Planning*, Vol. 23, No. 1, pp. 102–115.

Allison, G.T. (1969) 'Conceptual Models and The Cuban Missile Crisis', *The American Political Science Review*, No. 3, September, pp. 689–718.

Allison, G.T. (1971) *The Essence of Decision: Explaining the Cuban Missile Crisis*, Boston: Little Brown.

Amabile, T.M. (1998) 'How to Kill Creativity', *Harvard Business Review*, Vol. 76, No. 5, September–October, pp. 76–87.

Andrews, K.R. (1987) *The Concept of Corporate Strategy*, Third Edition, Homewood, IL: Irwin.

Ansoff, H.I. (1965) *Corporate Strategy: An Analytic Approach to Business Policy for Growth and Expansion*, New York: McGraw-Hill.

Ansoff, H.I. (1991) 'Critique of Henry Mintzberg's The "Design School": Reconsidering the Basic Premises of Strategic Management', *Strategic Management Journal*, September, pp. 449–461.

Ansoff, H.I., and McDonnell, E. (1990) *Implanting Strategic Management*, Second Edition, New York: Prentice Hall.

Armstrong, J.S. (1982) 'The Value of Formal Planning for Strategic Decisions: Review of Empirical Research', *Strategic Management Journal*, Vol. 3, pp. 197–211.

Bailey, A., and Johnson, G. (1992) 'How Strategies Develop in Organizations', in: D. Faulkner and G. Johnson (eds.), *The Challenge of Strategic Management*, London: Kogan Page.

Beinhocker, E.D. (1999) 'Robust Adaptive Strategies', *Sloan Management Review*, Vol. 40, No. 3, Spring, pp. 95–106.

Bourgeois, L.J., and Brodwin, D.R. (1983) 'Putting Your Strategy into Action', *Strategic Management Planning*, March–May.

Bower, J.L. (1970) *Managing the Resource Allocation Process*, Boston: Harvard Business School Press.

Bungay, S., and Goold, M. (1991) 'Creating a Strategic Control System', *Long Range Planning*, Vol. 24, No. 6, pp. 32–39.

Burgelman, R.A. (1983) 'Corporate Entrepreneurship and Strategic Management: Insights from a Process Study', *Management Science*, Vol. 29, No. 12, pp. 1349–1364.

Burgelman, R.A. (1991) 'Intraorganizational Ecology of Strategy Making and Organizational Adaptation: Theory and Field Research', *Organization Science*, Vol. 2, No. 3, pp. 239–262.

Calori, R., Valla, J.-P, and De Woot, P. (1994) 'Common Characteristics: The Ingredients of European Management', in: R. Calori and P. De Woot (eds.), *A European Management Model: Beyond Diversity*, Hemel Hempstead: Prentice Hall.

Campbell, A., Goold, M., and Alexander M. (1994) *Corporate-Level Strategy: Creating Value in the Multibusiness Company*, New York: Wiley.

Chaffee, E.E. (1985) 'Three Models of Strategy', *Academy of Management Review*, Vol. 10, No. 1, January, pp. 89–98.

Chakravarthy, B.S., and Lorange, P. (1991) *Managing the Strategy Process: A Framework for a Multibusiness Firm*, Englewood Cliffs, NJ: Prentice Hall.

Cohen, M.D., March, J.G., and Olsen, J.P (1972) 'A Garbage Can Model of Organization Choice', *Administrative Science Quarterly*, March, pp. 1–25.

De Geus, A. (1988) 'Planning as Learning', *Harvard Business Review*, March–April, pp. 70–74.

Eccles, M. (1951) *Beckoning Frontiers*, New York: Knopf.

Eisenhardt, K.M., and Brown, S.L. (1998) *Competing on the Edge: Strategy as Structured Chaos*, Boston: Harvard Business School Press.

Evans, J.S. (1991) 'Strategic Flexibility for High Technology Manoeuvres: A Conceptual Framework', *Journal of Management Studies*, Vol. 28, January, pp. 69–89.

Floyd, S.W., and Wooldridge, B. (2000) *Building Strategy from the Middle Reconceptualizing Strategy Process*, Thousand Oaks: Sage.

Ghemawat, P. (1991) *Commitment: The Dynamic of Strategies*, New York: Free Press.

Gilbert, X., and Lorange, P. (1995) 'National Approaches to Strategic Management: A Resource-based Perspective', *International Business Review*, Vol. 3, No. 4, pp. 411–423.

Gluck, F.W, Kaufman, S.P, and Walleck, A.S. (1982) 'The Four Phases of Strategic Management', *Journal of Business Strategy*, Winter, pp. 9–21.

Godet, M. (1987) *Scenarios and Strategic Management*, London: Butterworths.

Grant, R. (2003) 'Strategic Planning in a Turbulent Environment: Evidence from the Oil Majors', *Strategic Management Journal*, Vol. 24, pp. 491–517.

Grinyer, P.H., Al-Bazzaz, S., and Yasai-Ardekani, M. (1986) 'Towards a Contingency Theory of Corporate Planning: Findings in 48 U.K. Companies', *Strategic Management Journal*, Vol. 7, pp. 3–28.

Hamel, G. (1996) 'Strategy as Revolution', *Harvard Business Review*, Vol. 74, No. 4, July–August, pp. 69–82.

Hampden-Turner, C, and Trompenaars, A. (1993) *The Seven Cultures of Capitalism: Value Systems for Creating Wealth in the United States, Japan, Germany, France, Britain, Sweden and the Netherlands*, New York: Doubleday.

Haour, G., and Cho, H.J. (2000) 'Samsung Electronics Co. Ltd in the 1990s: Sustaining Competitiveness', *IMD Business Case*.

Hart, S.L. (1992) 'An Integrative Framework for Strategy-Making Processes', *Academy of Management Review*, Vol. 17, No. 2, pp. 327–351.

Hax, A.C., and Maljuf, N.S. (1984) *Strategic Management: An Integrative Approach*, Englewood Cliffs, NJ: Prentice Hall.

Hayashi, K. (1978) 'Corporate Planning Practices in Japanese Multinationals', *Academy of Management Journal*, Vol. 21, No. 2, pp. 211–226.

Hayes, R.H. (1985) 'Strategic Planning: Forward in Reverse?', *Harvard Business Review*, November–December, pp. 111–119.

Hofstede, G. (1993) 'Cultural Constraints in Management Theories', *Academy of Management Executive*, Vol. 7, No. 1, pp. 81–94.

Hurst, D.K. (1986) 'Why Strategic Management is Bankrupt', *Organizational Dynamics*, Vol. 15, Autumn, pp. 4–27.

Jacobs, D. (2009) *Mapping Strategic Diversity: Strategic Thinking from a Variety of Perspectives*, Oxford: Routledge.

Jelinek, M. (1979) *Institutionalizing Innovation*, New York: Praeger.

Johnson, G. (1987) *Strategic Change and the Management Process*, Oxford: Basil Blackwell.

Johnson, G. (1988) 'Rethinking Incrementalism', *Strategic Management Journal*, Vol. 9, No. 1, January–February, pp. 75–91.

Kagono, T, Nonaka, I., Sakakibara, K., and Okumara, A. (1985) *Strategic vs. Evolutionary Management*, Amsterdam: North-Holland.

Kanter, R. (1983) *The Change Masters: Innovation for Productivity in the American Corporation*, New York: Basic Books.

Kanter, R.M. (2002) 'Strategy as Improvisational Theater', *Sloan Management Review*, Vol. 43, No. 2, pp. 76–81.

Kaplan, R.S., and Norton, D.P. (2001) *The Strategy-Focused Organization: How Balanced Scorecard Thrive in the New Business Environment*, Boston, MA: Harvard Business School Press.

Kiechel, W., III. (1984) 'Sniping at Strategic Planning', *Planning Review*, May, pp. 8–11.

Kukalis, S. (1991) 'Determinants of Strategic Planning Systems in Large Organizations: A Contingency Approach', *Journal of Management Studies*, Vol. 28, pp. 143–160.

Langley, A. (1995) 'Between "Paralysis and Analysis" and "Extinction by Instinct"', *Sloan Management Review*, Vol. 36, No. 3, Spring, pp. 63–76.

Lenz, R.T., and Lyles, M. (1985) 'Paralysis by Analysis: Is Your Planning System Becoming Too Rational?', *Long Range Planning*, Vol. 18, No. 4, pp. 64–72.

Lessem, R., and Neubauer, F.F. (1994) *European Management Systems*, London: McGraw-Hill.

Liedtka, J. (2000) 'In Defense of Strategy as Design', *California Management Review*, Vol. 42, No. 3, pp. 8–30.

Lindblom, C.E. (1959) 'The Science of Muddling Through', *Public Administration Review*, Spring, pp. 79–88.

Lorange, P. (1980) *Corporate Planning: An Executive Viewpoint*, Englewood Cliffs, NJ: Prentice Hall.

Lorange, P., and Vancil, R.F. (1977) *Strategic Planning Systems*, Englewood Cliffs, NJ: Prentice Hall.

Lovas, B., and Ghoshal, S. (2000), 'Strategy as guided evolution', *Strategic Management Journal*, Vol. 21, No. 9, pp. 875–896.

Lyon, D.W., Lumpkin, G.T., and Dess, G.G. (2000) 'Enhancing Entrepreneurial Orientation Research: Operationalizing and Measuring a Key Strategic Decision Making Process', *Journal of Management*, Vol. 26, pp. 1055–1085.

Makridakis, S. (1990) *Forecasting, Planning and Strategy for the 21st Century*, New York: Free Press.

Maruyama, M. (1984) 'Alternative Concepts of Management: Insights from Asia and Africa', *Asia Pacific Journal of Management*, Vol. 1, January, pp. 100–111.

Marx, T.G. (1991) 'Removing the Obstacles to Effective Strategic Planning', *Long Range Planning*, Vol. 24, No. 4, August, pp. 21–28.

Miles, R., Snow, C, Meyer, A., and Coleman, H. (1978) 'Organizational Strategy, Structure, and Process', *Academy of Management Review*, Vol. 3, No. 3, July, pp. 546–562.

Miller, C.C., and Cardinal, L.B. (1994) 'Strategic Planning and Firm Performance: A Synthesis of more than Two Decades of Research', *Academy of Management Journal*, Vol. 37, No. 6, pp. 1649–1665.

Mintzberg, H. (1979) *The Structuring of Organizations: A Synthesis of the Research*, Englewood Cliffs, NJ: Prentice Hall.

Mintzberg, H. (1990a) 'The Design School: Reconsidering the Basic Premises of Strategic Management', *Strategic Management Journal*, Vol. 11, pp. 171–195.

Mintzberg, H. (1990b) 'Strategy Formation: Schools of Thought', in: J. Frederickson (ed.), *Perspectives on Strategic Management*, Boston, MA: Ballinger.

Mintzberg, H. (1991) 'Learning 1. Planning 0: Reply to Igor Ansoff, *Strategic Management Journal*, September, pp. 463–466.

Mintzberg, H. (1993) 'The Pitfalls of Strategic Planning', *California Management Review*, Vol. 36, No. 1, Fall, pp. 32–45.

Mintzberg, H. (1994a) 'The Fall and Rise of Strategic Planning', *Harvard Business Review*, Vol. 73, No. 1, January–February.

Mintzberg, H. (1994b) 'Rethinking Strategic Planning Part I: Pitfalls and Fallacies', *Long Range Planning*, Vol. 27, No. 3, pp. 12–21.

Mintzberg, H. (1994c) 'Rethinking Strategic Planning Part II: New Roles for Planners', *Long Range Planning*, Vol. 27, No. 3, pp. 22–30.

Mintzberg, H. (1994d) *The Rise and Fall of Strategic Planning*, Englewood Cliffs, NJ: Prentice Hall.

Mintzberg, H., Ahlstrand, B., and Lampel, J. (1998) *Strategy Safari: A Guided Tour Through the Wilds of Strategic Management*, New York: The Free Press.

Mintzberg, H., and Waters, J.A. (1985) 'Of Strategy: Deliberate and Emergent', *Strategic Management Journal*, Vol. 6, No. 3, July–September, pp. 257–272.

Morgenthau, H. (1960) *Politics Among Nations*, Third Edition, New York: Knopf.

Nonaka, I. (1988) 'Toward Middle-Up-Down Management: Accelerating Information Creation', *Sloan Management Review*, Vol. 29, No. 3, Spring, pp. 9–18.

Nonaka, I., and Johansson, J.K. (1985) 'Japanese Management: What about "Hard" Skills?', *Academy of Management Review*, Vol. 10, No. 2, pp. 181–191.

Ohmae, K. (1982) *The Mind of the Strategist*, New York: McGraw-Hill.

Pascale, R.T. (1984) 'Perspectives on Strategy: The Real Story Behind Honda's Success', *California Management Review*, Vol. 26, No. 3, pp. 47–72.

Pettigrew, A.M. (1977) 'Strategy Formulation as a Political Process', *International Studies of Management and Organization*, Vol. 7, Summer, pp. 47–72.

Pfeffer, J. (1981) *Power in Organizations*, Marshfield, MA: Pitman.

Pinchot, G., III, (1985) *Intrapreneuring: Why You Don't Have to Leave the Company to Become an Entrepreneur*, New York: Harper & Row.

Porter, M.E. (1987) 'The State of Strategic Thinking', *Economist*, May 23, pp. 21.

Powell, T.C. (1992) 'Strategic Planning as Competitive Advantage', *Strategic Management Journal*, Vol. 13, pp. 551–558.

Quinn, J.B. (1978) 'Strategic Change: "Logical Incrementalism"', *Sloan Management Review*, Fall, pp. 7–21.

Quinn, J.B. (1980) *Strategies for Change*, Homewood, IL: Irwin.

Quinn, J.B. (1985) 'Managing Innovation: Controlled Chaos', *Harvard Business Review*, Vol. 63, No. 3, May–June, pp. 73–84.

Quinn, J.B. (2002) 'Strategy, Science and Management', *Sloan Management Review*, Vol. 43, No. 4.

Rittel, H.W., and Webber, M.M. (1973) 'Dilemmas in a General Theory of Planning', *Policy Sciences*, Vol. 4, pp. 155–169.

Robinson, R.B. (1982) 'The Importance of Outsiders in Small Firm Strategic Planning', *Academy of Management Journal*, Vol. 25, pp. 80–93.

Schein, E.H. (1985) *Organizational Culture and Leadership*, San Francisco: Jossey-Bass.

Schelling, T. (1960) *The Strategy of Conflict*, Cambridge, MA: Harvard University Press.

Schneider, S.C. (1989) 'Strategy Formulation: The Impact of National Culture', *Organization Studies*, Vol. 10, No. 2, pp. 149–168.

Shrivastava, P., and Grant, J. (1985) 'Empirically Derived Models of Strategic Decision-Making Processes', *Strategic Management Journal*, Vol. 6, pp. 97–113.

Simons, R. (1995) *Levers of Control: How Managers Use Innovative Control Systems to Drive Strategic Renewal*, Boston, MA: HBS Press.

Smircich, L., and Stubbart, C. (1985) 'Strategic Management in an Enacted World', *Academy of Management Review*, Vol. 10, No. 4, pp. 724–736.

Stacey, R.D. (1993) 'Strategy as Order Emerging from Chaos', *Long Range Planning*, Vol. 26, No. 1, pp. 10–17.

Stacey, R.D. (1996) *Strategic Management and Organizational Dynamics*, Second Edition, London: Pitman.

Stacey, R.D. (2001) *Complex Responsive Processes in Organizations: Learning and Knowledge Creation*, London: Routledge.

Steiner, G.A. (1979) *Strategic Planning: What Every Manager Must Know*, New York: Free Press.

Steiner, G.A., and Schollhammer, H. (1975) 'Pitfalls in Multi-National Long-Range Planning', *Long Range Planning*, Vol. 8, No. 2, April, pp. 2–12.

Thompson, A.A., and Strickland III, A.J. (1995) *Strategic Management: Concepts and Cases*, Eighth Edition, Chicago: Irwin.

Trompenaars, A. (1993) *Riding the Waves of Culture: Understanding Cultural Diversity in Business*, London: The Economist Books.

Van der Heyden, K. (1996) *Scenarios: The Art of Strategic Conversation*, New York: Wiley.

Wack, P. (1985a) 'Scenarios: Unchartered Waters Ahead', *Harvard Business Review*, Vol. 64, No. 5, September–October, pp. 73–89.

Wack, P. (1985b) 'Scenarios: Shooting the Rapids', *Harvard Business Review*, Vol. 64, No. 6, November–December, pp. 139–150.

Weidenbaum, M., and Hughes, S. (1996) *The Bamboo Network: How Expatriate Chinese Entrepreneurs Are Creating a New Economic Superpower in Asia*, New York: Free Press.

Wheelen, T.L., and Hunger, J.D. (1992) *Strategic Management and Business Policy*, Fourth Edition, Boston, MA: Addison-Wesley.

Wildavsky, A. (1979) *Speaking Truth to Power: The Art and Craft of Policy Analysis*, Toronto: Little, Brown & Co..

Wilson, I. (2000) 'From Scenario Thinking to Strategic Action', *Technological Forecasting and Social Change*, Vol. 65, No. 1, September, pp. 23–29.

Yu, S. (1999) 'The Growth Pattern of Samsung Electronics: A Strategy Perspective', *International Studies of Management Organization*, Vol. 28, No. 4, pp. 57–72.

4 STRATEGIC CHANGE

There is nothing more difficult to take in hand, more perilous to conduct, or more uncertain in its success, than to take the lead in the introduction of a new order of things. Because the innovator has for enemies all those who have done well under the old conditions, and lukewarm defenders in those who may do well under the new.

Niccolo Machiavelli (1469–1527); Florentine statesman and political philosopher

INTRODUCTION

In a world of new technologies, transforming economies, shifting demographics, reforming governments, fluctuating consumer preferences and dynamic competition, it is not a question of whether firms *should* change, but of where, how and in what direction they *must* change. For 'living' organizations, change is a given. Firms must constantly be aligned with their environments, either by reacting to external events, or by proactively shaping the businesses in which they operate.

While change is pervasive, not all change in firms is strategic in nature. Much of the change witnessed is actually the ongoing operational kind. To remain efficient and effective, firms constantly make 'fine-tuning' alterations, whereby existing procedures are upgraded, activities are improved and people are reassigned. Such operational changes are directed at increasing the performance of the firm within the confines of the existing system – within the current basic set-up used to align the firm with the environment. Strategic changes, on the contrary, are directed at creating a new type of alignment – a new fit between the basic set-up of the firm and the characteristics of the environment. Strategic changes have an impact on the way the firm does business (its 'business system') and on the way the organization has been configured (its 'organizational system'). In short, while operational changes are necessary to maintain the business and organizational systems, strategic changes are directed at renewing them.

For managers the challenge is to implement strategic changes on time, to keep the firm in step with the shifting opportunities and threats in the environment. Some parts of the firm's business system and organizational system can be preserved, while others need to be transformed for the firm to stay up-to-date and competitive. This process of constantly enacting strategic changes to remain in harmony with external conditions is called 'strategic renewal'. This chapter examines the issue of the series of strategic change steps required in order to bring about a process of ongoing strategic renewal.

THE ISSUE OF STRATEGIC RENEWAL

There are many actions that constitute a strategic change – a reorganization, a diversification move, a shift in core technology, a business process redesign and a product portfolio reshuffle, to name a few. Each one of these changes is fascinating in itself. Yet, here the discussion will be broader than just a single strategic change, looking instead at the process of how a series of strategic changes can be used to keep the firm in sync with its surroundings (see Figure 4.1). How can 'a path of strategic changes' be followed to constantly renew the firm and avoid a situation whereby the firm 'drifts' too far away from the demands of the environment (Johnson, 1988).

To come to a deeper understanding of the issue of strategic renewal, the first step that must be taken is to examine what is actually being renewed during a process of strategic renewal. The areas of strategic renewal will be explored in the next section. After this initial analysis of 'what' is being changed, a distinction will be made between the magnitude and the pace of change. The magnitude of change refers to the size of the steps being undertaken, whereby the question is whether managers should move in bold and dramatic strides, or in moderate and undramatic ones. The pace of change refers to the relative speed at which the steps are being taken, whereby the question is whether managers should move quickly in a short period of time, or more gradually over a longer time span.

Areas of strategic renewal

Firms are complex systems, consisting of many different elements, each of which can be changed. Therefore, to gain more insight into the various areas of potential change, firms need to be analytically disassembled into a number of component parts. The most fundamental distinction that can be made within a firm, is between the business system and the organizational system:

- Business system. The term 'business system' refers to the way a firm conducts its business. A simple definition would be 'how a firm makes money'. A more formal

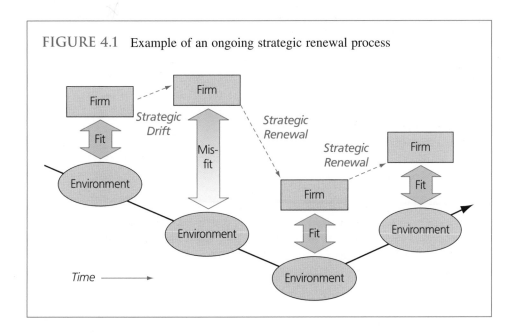

FIGURE 4.1   Example of an ongoing strategic renewal process

definition of business system is 'the specific configuration of resources, value-adding activities and product/service offerings directed at creating value for customers'. Each firm has its own specific system for taking certain resources as inputs (e.g. materials and know-how), adding value to them in some type of manner (e.g. production and branding) and then selling a particular package of products and/or services as output. As such, a firm's business system (or 'value creation system') is particular to the type of business that the firm is in – an airplane manufacturer conducts its business differently from an airline.

■ Organizational system. The term 'organizational system' refers to the way a firm gets its people to work together to carry out the business. A simple definition would be 'how a firm is organized'. A more formal definition of the organizational system would be 'how the individuals populating a firm have been configured, and relate to one another, with the intention of facilitating the business system'. Every firm needs to determine some type of organizational structure, dividing the tasks and responsibilities among the organizational members, thereby instituting differing functions and units. Firms also require numerous organizational processes to link individual members to each other, to ensure that their separate tasks are coordinated into an integrated whole. And firms necessarily have organizational cultures, and sub-cultures, as organizational members interact with one another and build up joint beliefs, values and norms.

In Figure 4.2 the relationship between the business system and the major components of the organizational system is depicted. As this figure illustrates, the business system is 'supported' by the organizational system, with the organizational members 'at its base'. While each firm's business and organizational systems are essentially unique, their general configuration can be fairly similar to that of other firms. Where firms have a comparable business 'formula', it is said that they share the same business model. Likewise, where firms have a similar organizational 'form', they are said to subscribe to the same organizational model.

Both the business system and the organizational system can be further disaggregated into component parts and examined in more detail. With this aim in mind, the business system will be at the centre of attention in Chapter 5. Here the organizational system will be further dissected. Actually, the term 'dissection' conjures up images of the

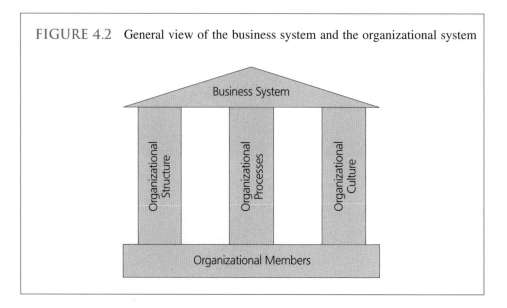

FIGURE 4.2   General view of the business system and the organizational system

organizational system as 'corporate body', which is a useful metaphor for distinguishing the various components of an organizational system (Morgan, 1986).

Following Bartlett and Ghoshal (1995) the organizational system can be divided into its anatomy (structure), physiology (processes) and psychology (culture). Each of these components, summarized in Figure 4.3, will be examined in the following sub-section.

Organizational structure. Organizational structure refers to the clustering of tasks and people into smaller groups. All organizations need at least some division of labour in order to function efficiently and effectively, requiring them to structure the organization into smaller parts. The main question when determining the organizational structure is which criteria will be used to differentiate tasks and to cluster people into particular units. While there are numerous structuring (or decomposition) criteria, the most common ones are summarized in Figure 4.4. In a simple organization tasks might be divided according to just one criterion, but in most organizations multiple criteria are used (either sequentially or simultaneously).

To balance this horizontal differentiation of tasks and responsibilities, all organizations also have integration mechanisms, intended to get the parts to function well within the organizational whole (Lawrence and Lorsch, 1967). While some of these integration mechanisms are found in the categories of organizational processes and culture, the most fundamental mechanism is usually built into the organizational structure – formal authority. In organizations, managers are appointed with the specific task of supervising the activities of various people or units and to report to managers higher up in the hierarchy.

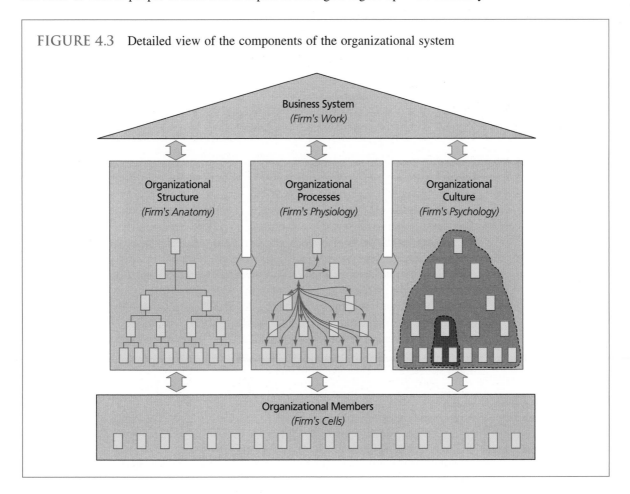

FIGURE 4.3 Detailed view of the components of the organizational system

FIGURE 4.4   Organizational structuring criteria

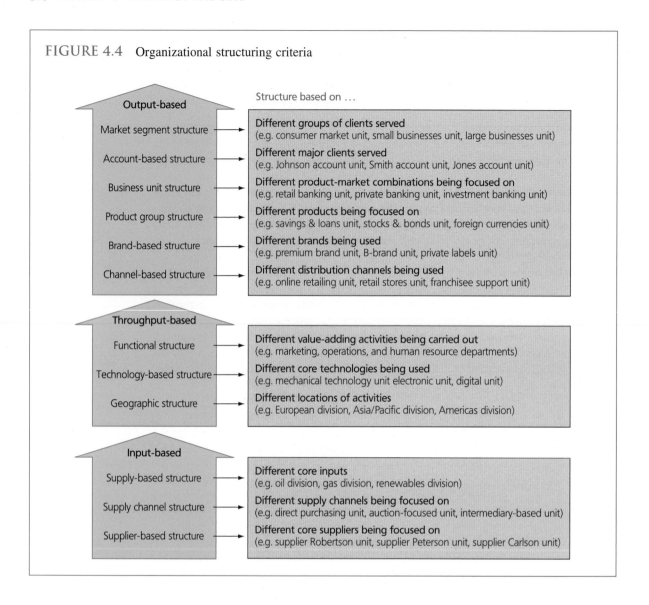

Depending on the span of control of each manager (the number of people or units reporting to him/her) an organizational structure will consist of one or more layers of management. At the apex of this vertical structure is the board of directors, with the ultimate authority to make decisions or ratify decisions made at lower levels in the hierarchy. The most important questions in this context are the number of management layers needed and the amount of authority delegated to lower levels of management. It should be noted that the organizational charts used to represent the formal structure of an organization (see Figure 4.3) need not be an accurate reflection of the informal organizational structure as it operates in reality.

Organizational processes.   Organizational processes refer to the arrangements, procedures and routines used to control and coordinate the various people and units within the organization. Some formalized processes span the entire organization, such as business planning and control procedures, and financial budgeting and reporting processes. Other control and coordination processes have a more limited scope, such as new product development meetings, yearly sales conferences, weekly quality circles, web-based expert panels and quarterly meetings with the board of directors. But not all organizational processes are institutionalized as ongoing integration mechanisms. Often, integration across units and departments is needed for a short period, making it useful to employ task forces, committees, working groups, project teams and even joint lunches as means for ensuring coordination.

While all of these processes are formalized to a certain degree, many more informal organizational processes exist, such as communicating via hallway gossip, building support through personal networking, influencing decision-making through informal negotiations and solving conflicts by means of impromptu meetings.

Organizational culture.   Organizational culture refers to the worldview and behavioural patterns shared by the members of the same organization (e.g. Schein, 1985; Trice and Beyer, 1993). As people within a group interact and share experiences with one another over an extended period of time, they construct a joint understanding of the world around them. This shared belief system will be emotionally charged, as it encompasses the values and norms of the organizational members and offers them an interpretive filter with which to make sense of the constant stream of uncertain and ambiguous events around them. As this common ideology grows stronger and becomes more engrained, it will channel members' actions into more narrowly defined patterns of behaviour. As such, the organizational culture can strongly influence everything, from how to behave during meetings to what is viewed as ethical behaviour.

As part of the organizational system, culture can act as a strong integration mechanism, controlling and coordinating people's behaviour, by getting them to abide by 'the way we do things around here'. Having a common 'language', frame of reference and set of values also makes it easier to communicate and work together. However, an organizational culture is not always homogeneous – in fact, strongly divergent sub-cultures might arise in certain units, creating 'psychological' barriers within the organization.

The magnitude of change

Strategic change is by definition far-reaching. We speak of strategic change when fundamental alterations are made to the business system or the organizational system. Adding a lemon-flavoured Coke to the product portfolio is interesting, maybe important, but not a strategic change, while branching out into bottled water was – it was a major departure from Coca-Cola's traditional business system. Hiring a new CEO, like Raj Patel at Exact Software (see Chapter 2), is also important, but is in itself not a strategic change, while his consequent reorientation towards integrated front office and back office software was – it was a major shift from Exact Software's traditional back office focus.

Strategic renewal is often even more far-reaching, as a number of strategic changes are executed in a variety of areas to keep the firm aligned with market demands. But while the result of all of these strategic changes is far-reaching, this says nothing about the size of the steps along the way. The strategic renewal process might consist of a few large change steps or numerous small ones. This distinction is illustrated in Figure 4.5. The total amount of strategic change envisaged is measured along the Y-axis. Change Path A shows the change path taken by a firm that has implemented all changes in two big steps, while Change Path B shows the change path followed by a firm taking numerous smaller steps. Both organizations have completed the same renewal, but via distinctly different routes.

The size of the change steps is referred to as the magnitude of change. This issue of change magnitude can be divided into two component parts:

- Scope of change. The scope of change in a firm can vary from broad to narrow. Change is broad when many aspects and parts of the firm are altered at the same time. In the

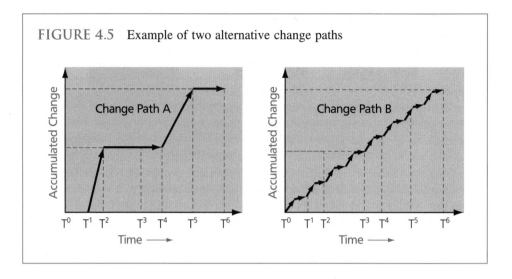

FIGURE 4.5   Example of two alternative change paths

most extreme case the changes might be comprehensive, whereby the business system is entirely revised, and the organizational structure, processes, culture and people are changed in unison. However, change can also be much more narrowly focused on a specific organizational aspect (e.g. new product development processes) or department (e.g. marketing). If many changes are narrowly targeted, the total result will be a more piecemeal change process.

■ Amplitude of organizational changes. The amplitude of change in firms can vary from high to low. The amplitude of change is high when the new business system, organizational culture, structure, processes or people are a radical departure from the previous situation. The amplitude of change is low when the step proposed is a moderate adjustment to the previous circumstances.

Where a change is comprehensive and radical, the magnitude of the change step is large. In Figure 4.5 this is represented as a large jump along the Y-axis. Where a change is narrow and moderate, the magnitude of the step is small. However, the above distinction also clarifies that there are two rather different types of medium-sized change steps – a focused radical change (narrow scope, high amplitude) and a comprehensive moderate change (broad scope, low amplitude). Both changes are 'mid-sized', yet significantly different to manage in practice.

The pace of change

Strategic renewal takes time. Yet, there is a variety of ways by which the strategic renewal process can take place over time. Strategic change measures can be evenly spread out over an extended period, allowing the organization to follow a relatively steady pace of strategic renewal. However, it is also possible to cluster all changes into a few short irregular bursts, giving the renewal process an unsteady, stop-and-go pace.

This distinction is seen in Figure 4.5 as well. The total time period needed for achieving a strategic change is measured along the X-axis. Change Path A shows the change path taken by a firm that has had an unsteady pace of change, while Change Path B tracks the path taken by a firm on a more steady change trajectory. Both organizations have completed the same strategic renewal process by T^3 and by T^6, but have distributed their change activities differently during the period.

In Figure 4.5 it can also be seen that the pace of organizational changes can be decomposed into two related parts:

■ Timing of change. First, the pace of change depends on the moment at which changes are initiated. The timing of change can vary from intermittent to constant. Where change is intermittent, it is important for a firm to determine the right moment for launching a new initiative (for example, T^1 and T^4 in Change Path A). The need to 'wait for the right timing' is often a reason for spreading change activities unevenly over time. On the other hand, change can be constant, so that the exact moment for kicking off any new set of measures is less important, as long as there is no peak at any one moment in time (see Change Path B).

■ Speed of change. The pace of change also depends on the time span within which changes take place. The speed of change can vary from high to low. Where a major change needs to be implemented within a short period of time, the speed of change must be high. A short burst of fast action can bring about the intended changes. In Figure 4.5, the speed can be seen by the slope of the arrow (in Change Path A, the speed between T^1 and T^2 is higher than between T^4 and T^5). On the other hand, where the change measures are less formidable and the time span for implementation is longer, the speed of change can be lower.

The variables of timing and speed of change, together with the variables of scope and amplitude of change, create a wide range of possible strategic renewal paths. Firms have many different ways of bringing about strategic change. Unavoidably, this raises the question of which route is best. Why should a firm choose one trajectory over another?

THE PARADOX OF REVOLUTION AND EVOLUTION

Nothing in progression can rest on its original plan.
We may as well think of rocking a grown man in the cradle of an infant.
Edmund Burke (1729–1797); Irish-born politician and man of letters

In selecting an approach to strategic change, most managers struggle with the question of how bold they should be. On the one hand, they usually realize that to fundamentally transform the organization, a break with the past is needed. To achieve strategic renewal it is essential to turn away from the firm's heritage and to start with a clean slate. On the other hand, they also recognize the value of continuity, building on past experiences, investments and loyalties. To achieve lasting strategic renewal, people in the organization will need time to learn, adapt and grow into a new organizational reality.

This distinction between disruptive change and gradual change has long been recognized in the strategic management and organizational behaviour literature (e.g. Greiner, 1972; Tushman and O'Reilly, 1996, Reading 4.3 in this book). Disruptive change is variably referred to as 'frame-breaking' (e.g. Baden-Fuller and Stopford, 1992; Grinyer, Mayes and McKiernan, 1987), 'radical' (e.g. Stinchcombe, 1965; Greenwood and Hinings, 1996) and 'revolutionary' (e.g. Gersick, 1991; Tushman, Newman and Romanelli, 1986). Gradual change is variably referred to as 'incremental' (e.g. Quinn, 1980; Johnson, 1987) and 'evolutionary' (e.g. Nelson and Winter, 1982; Tushman and O'Reilly, 1996, Reading 4.3 in this book). Here the labels revolutionary and evolutionary change will be used, in keeping with the terminology used by Greiner (1972) in his classic work.

It is widely accepted among researchers that firms need to balance revolutionary and evolutionary change processes. However, most authors see this as a balancing of strategic (revolutionary) change and operational (evolutionary) change. As strategic change is far-reaching, it is often automatically equated with radical means, while gradual means are reserved for smaller-scale operational changes. Yet, in the previous section it was made clear that a radical result (a strategic change) can be pursued by both revolutionary and evolutionary means (e.g. Hayes, 1985; Krüger, 1996, Reading 4.4 in this book; Nonaka, 1988; Strebel, 1994).

While these two change processes are each other's opposites, and they seem to be at least partially contradictory, both approaches are needed within firms. In practice both change processes have valuable, but conflicting, qualities. The tension that this creates between revolution and evolution will be explored in the following sections.

The demand for revolutionary change processes

Revolution is a process whereby an abrupt and radical change takes place within a short period of time. Revolutionary change processes are those that do not build on the status quo, but overthrow it. 'Revolutionaries' revolt against the existing business system and organizational system, and attempt to push through changes that will reinvent the firm. Thus, revolution leads to a clear break with the past – a discontinuity in the firm's development path.

Such a 'big bang' approach to strategic change is generally needed when organizational rigidity is so deeply rooted that smaller pushes do not bring the firm into movement. If the firm threatens to become paralysed by these inherited rigidities in the business system and organizational system, the only way to get moving can be to radically break with the past. Typical sources of organizational rigidity include:

■ Psychological resistance to change. Many people resist change, because of the uncertainty and ambiguity that unavoidably accompanies any shift in the old way of doing business (e.g. Argyris, 1990; Pondy, Boland and Thomas, 1988). As people become accustomed to fixed organizational routines and established habits, their ability to learn and gradually adapt invariably recedes. New business methods or job descriptions are not seen as a challenging opportunity to learn, but as an unwelcome interference in the existing system. It can be necessary to break through this psychological resistance to change by imposing a new business system and/or organizational system on people (e.g. Hammer, 1990, Reading 4.1 in this book; Powell, 1991).

■ Cultural resistance to change. As discussed in Chapter 2, people can easily become immune to signals that their cognitive maps are outdated, especially if they are surrounded by others with the same flawed belief system. Once an organizational culture develops that perpetuates a number of obsolete assumptions about the market or the organization, it is very difficult for organizational members to challenge and gradually reshape the organizational belief system. It can be necessary to break through this cultural resistance to change by exposing the organization to a shocking crisis or by imposing a new organizational system (e.g. Tushman, Newman and Romanelli, 1986, Senge, 1990, Reading 9.3 in this book).

■ Political resistance to change. Change is hardly ever to everyone's advantage, as Machiavelli pointed out at the start of this chapter. Each organizational change leads to a different constellation of winners and losers. Generally, the potential losers reject a strategic change, although they are likely to think of some seemingly objective reasons for their opposition. Even a situation in which a person or department thinks that it might run the risk of losing power to others can be enough to block a change. Since strategic changes invariably have a significant impact on all people within an organization, there will always be a number of open, and hidden, opponents. It can be necessary to break through this political resistance by imposing a new business system and reshuffling management positions (e.g. Allison, 1969, Reading 3.3 in this book; Krüger, 1996, Reading 4.4 in this book).

■ Investment lock-in. Once a firm has committed a large amount of money and time to a certain product portfolio, activity system or technology, it will find that this fixed investment locks the organization in. Any gradual movement away from the past investment will increase the risk of not earning back the sunk cost. Therefore, it can be necessary to break through the lock-in by radically restructuring or disposing of the investment (e.g. Ghemawat, 1991; Bower and Christensen, 1995).

■ Competence lock-in. The better a firm becomes at something, the more a firm becomes focused on becoming even better still – which is also known as the virtuous circle of competence-building. Once a competitive advantage has been built on a particular type of competence, the natural tendency of firms is to favour external opportunities based on these competences. New people are hired that fit with the corporate competence profile and R&D spending further hones the firm's skill. But if the firm's competence base threatens to become outdated due to market or technological changes, its former advantage could become its downfall – the firm could become caught in a vicious 'competence trap', unable to gradually shift the organization to an alternative set of competences, because the entire business system and organizational system have been aligned to the old set (e.g. Leonard-Barton, 1995; Teece, Pisano and Shuen, 1997). Changing the core competence of the corporation in a comprehensive and radical manner can be the only way to 'migrate' from one competence profile to another.

■ Systems lock-in. Firms can also become locked into an open standard (e.g. sizes in inches, GAAP accounting rules) or a proprietary system (e.g. Windows operating system, SAP enterprise resource planning software). Once the firm has implemented a standard or system, switching to another platform cannot be done gradually or at low cost. Therefore, the lock-in can usually only be overcome by a big bang transition to another platform (e.g. Arthur, 1996; Shapiro and Varian, 1998).

■ Stakeholder lock-in. Highly restrictive commitments can also be made towards the firm's stakeholders. Long-term contracts with buyers and suppliers, warranties, commitments to governments and local communities and promises to shareholders can all lock firms into a certain strategic direction. To break through the stakeholders' resistance to change it can be necessary to court a crisis and aim for a radical restructuring of the firm's external relationships (e.g. Freeman, 1984; Oliver, 1991).

Besides the use of revolutionary change to overcome organizational rigidity, such a radical approach to strategic renewal is often also necessary given the short time span available for a large change. The 'window of opportunity' for achieving a strategic change can be small for a number of reasons. Some of the most common triggers for revolutionary strategic change are:

■ Competitive pressure. When a firm is under intense competitive pressure and its market position starts to erode quickly, a rapid and dramatic response might be the only approach possible. Especially when the organization threatens to slip into a downward spiral towards insolvency, a bold turnaround can be the only option left to the firm.

■ Regulatory pressure. Firms can also be put under pressure by the government or regulatory agencies to push through major changes within a short period of time. Such externally imposed revolutions can be witnessed among public sector organizations (e.g. hospitals and schools) and highly regulated industries (e.g. utilities and telecommunications), but in other sectors of the economy as well (e.g. antitrust break-ups, public health regulations).

■ First mover advantage. A more proactive reason for instigating revolutionary change, is to be the first firm to introduce a new product, service or technology and to build up barriers to entry for late movers. Especially for know-how that is dissipation-sensitive, or for which the patent period is limited, it can be important to cash in quickly before others arrive on the market (e.g. Kessler and Chakrabarthi, 1996; Lieberman and Montgomery, 1988, 1998).

To some extent all managers recognize that their organizations are prone to inertia, and most will acknowledge that it is often vital to move quickly, either in response to external pressures or to cash in on a potential first mover advantage. It should therefore come as no surprise that most managers would like their organizations to have the ability to successfully pull off revolutionary strategic changes.

The demand for evolutionary change processes

Evolution is a process whereby a constant stream of moderate changes gradually accumulates over a longer period of time. Each change is in itself small, but the cumulative result can be large. Evolutionary change processes take the current firm as a starting point, constantly modifying aspects through extension and adaptation. Some 'mutations' to the firm prove valuable and are retained, while other changes are discarded as dysfunctional. Thus, a new business system and/or organizational system can steadily evolve out of the old, as if the organization were shedding its old skin to grow a new one (e.g. Aldrich, 1999; Kagono *et al.*, 1985).

This 'metamorphosis' approach to strategic change is particularly important where the strategic renewal hinges on widespread organizational learning. Learning is not a process that is easily compressed into a few short bursts of activity (as anyone who has studied knows). Learning is a relatively slow process, whereby know-how is accumulated over an extended period of time. It can take years to learn things, especially if the necessary knowledge is not readily available, but must be acquired 'on the job' (e.g. Agryris, 1990; Senge, 1990, Reading 9.3 in this book). This is true for both individuals and firms. When groups of people in a firm need to develop new routines, new competences, new processes, as well as new ways of understanding the world, time is needed to experiment, reflect, discuss, test and internalize. Even in the circumstances where individuals or departments are merely asked to adjust their behaviours to new norms, the learning process is often protracted and difficult (e.g. Nelson and Winter, 1982; Pfeffer and Sutton, 1999, Reading 9.4).

While the evolutionary nature of learning is a positive factor stimulating gradual change, the organizational reality is often also that power is too dispersed for revolutionary changes to be imposed upon the firm. Where no one has enough sway in the organization to push through radical changes, a more evolutionary approach can be the only viable route forward.

To some extent all managers recognize that their firms need to continuously learn and adapt, while most will acknowledge that they do not have the absolute power to impose revolutionary changes at will. For these reasons managers generally would like their organizations to have the ability to pursue evolutionary changes.

Yet, engaging in evolutionary change is the opposite of revolutionary change. On the one hand, being opposites might make revolution and evolution complementary. Some authors suggest that organizations should be 'ambidextrous', using both revolution and evolution, contingent upon internal and external conditions (e.g. Duncan, 1976; Krüger, 1996, Reading 4.4; Tushman and O'Reilly, 1996, Reading 4.3). On the other hand, the above discussion makes clear that the two are, to a certain extent, mutually incompatible. Once the one form of change has been chosen, this will seriously limit the ability of the strategist to simultaneously, or even subsequently, use the other. Hence, managers are once again faced with a paradox, between revolution and evolution.

EXHIBIT 4.1 SHORT CASE

HILTI: CUT OR FASTEN?

Mention Liechtenstein in a conversation and you will either get an empty look from your discussion partners, or they will start about downhill skiing, postage stamps or tax evasion, depending on how they spend their spare time. As one of the smallest countries in the world, with only 35 000 inhabitants, the Principality of Liechtenstein doesn't show up on most people's radar screen, yet one of its firms frequently does – Hilti. This company is a global market leader in drilling, sawing and fastening products, systems and services for the construction industry. Hilti's range of power tools vary from diamond-tipped drills, to demolition hammers, circular saws, sanders and screwdrivers, while they also have a broad range of construction accessories, such as anchors, coatings, sealants, and foams, as well as products for fastening pipes, cables and conduits. While some of their competitors like Black & Decker and Bosch also service the consumer market, Hilti is strongly focused on the professional user willing to pay for their superior products.

Founded in 1941 by Martin Hilti, the company has grown from being a small mechanical workshop with five employees to a corporation employing more than 21 000 people in 120 countries by 2009. Almost from the outset, Hilti's growth and internationalization have been driven by its combination of innovation and quality. The firm's first big breakthrough came in the early 1950s, when Martin Hilti invented a safe nail-driving tool, called the DX. As this tool needed to be demonstrated to get the conservatively inclined construction industry to adopt it, Hilti was forced to hire a direct sales force that could actively spread the word. This start-up problem turned out to be formative for the Hilti business model and culture. To this day, Hilti's direct sales force is at the core of the company's strategy, while its culture is much more market-oriented than many of its competitors.

To lessen dependence on one blockbuster product, Martin Hilti was also early in diversifying into related products, that could also be sold via the direct sales channel. But as his company grew, Martin Hilti found it increasingly difficult to make most decisions himself in Liechtenstein. So, by the 1970s, he switched from being sole managing director to being chairman of a management board including non-family members. He also created new corporate departments, including finance, marketing and engineering. Regional managers were endowed with more autonomy and in order to counter the effects of currency exchange fluctuations, sourcing was regionalized and part of the production was moved to the US. What did not change – and never has – is the family ownership of the company.

Hilti's darkest hour was in the early 1980s, when a deep economic recession hit the construction industries in Europe and the US. In response to lower sales and crumbling profitability, the management board decided to dramatically decrease overhead and personnel costs, increase investment in marketing efforts and restructure the organization from a functional organization into a regional one. The three regions – the Americas, Europe and Asia-Pacific – were given responsibility for innovation, production and sales, in an effort to speed up time-to-market and adapt better to regional needs. Along with the new organizational structure, Hilti launched a leadership programme to rejuvenate the corporate culture. The result of these workshops was the formulation of the four principles that are still the cornerstones of the Hilti corporate culture today – integrity, courage, teamwork and commitment.

In 1990, Martin Hilti's son Michael took over as chairman, emphasizing continuity with the direction set by his father, who passed away in 1997. In that same year, Hilti presented a refined strategy, called Champion 3C, referring to the three key pillars of success, namely Customer, Competence and Concentration. To this day, these are the three pillars on which the company bases its actions. In the area of customers, Hilti stretched the definition of its target audience to encompass all construction professionals, not only construction companies, thus bringing the large segment of self-employed craftsmen within scope. To serve these customers, Hilti set about to broaden its competences beyond direct sales, for instance in the area of e-business and shop-in-shop retailing. It also looked for growth by providing services to complement its products. The third C, concentration, referred to the need for Hilti to keep its diversification in check and only remain in product categories in which it could build a dominant market position.

To underpin the Champion 3C strategy, Michael Hilti also invested heavily in getting the right people on board and fortifying the company culture. In the area of recruitment, Hilti placed significantly more emphasis on close ties to universities and technical schools, with the intention of drawing in the best young talent. Simultaneously, having the right values and attitude were given more prominence in recruiting, over mere technical ability. To strengthen the company culture, virtually all Hilti employees attended a programme called Team Camp, reinforcing the key Hilti principles of teamwork, great customer service and continuous innovation. Upon receiving the Carl Bertelsmann Prize for Excellence in Corporate Culture in 2003, Michael Hilti explained: 'I view corporate culture as a very significant, if not the most significant, driver of corporate success. A clear orientation is required to harmonize personal development and corporate growth, and to be able to focus on common values and goals.'

By 2009, Michael Hilti had 18 great years of phenomenal growth behind him, with sales skyrocketing to CHF 4.7 billion (€2.8 billion). Hilti had continued to innovate and branch out to supply markets neighbouring the construction industry, such as making drills for the mining industry and fastening systems for solar energy panels. Budgets for R&D had been more than doubled, while the sales network had been further internationalized and strengthened with more technical sales people, better online customer service systems and more professional call centres. Hilti had also introduced a novel tool rental business, called 'fleet management', in which Hilti manages a customer's 'fleet of tools', including maintenance and repair, so that they always have the right tools at the right time. Besides growth initiatives, Hilti had also improved its efficiency and operational excellence. The supply chain was integrated globally, a new logistics centre was built in Liechtenstein, production was expanded in China and the biggest reorganization project in the company's history was launched in 2003, with the introduction of a new global ERP system, standardizing IT systems and organizational processes worldwide. In 2006 Michael Hilti took a step back, allowing the Swiss Pius Baschera to become chairman of the Board of Directors, while at the same time promoting the Swede Bo Risberg to the position of CEO.

But in early 2009, the global recession had started to hurt, as economic recovery seemed far off and with the construction industry hit even harder due to real estate bubbles in many key countries.

However, in the 2008 Company Report, published in the spring of 2009, Risberg had still sounded extremely confident, accepting that 2009 would hardly show any growth, yet pushing ahead with major investments. 'In 2009 our goal is to maintain our sales and profitability at the same level as last year', he stated. 'Of course, in today's environment it is difficult to assess the impact the financial crisis will have on building activities,' he warned, but 'it goes without saying that we will continue to pursue the course necessary to achieve our "Vision 2015".' This vision, he explained, 'is to be a great company. We want to fill our customers and employees with enthusiasm and double our sales profitability. We will achieve this vision by concentrating on our four focal points within the "Champion 3C" strategy: growth, differentiation, productivity and employee development.' He also highlighted that Hilti planned to build a new Innovation Center in Liechtenstein, construct a new plant in Mexico and expand three plants in Europe. 'Last, but not least,' Risberg concluded, 'in 2008 we recruited 1500 additional employees – in spite of the difficult times.'

Then in April 2009 the first quarterly sales figures were compiled, showing a global sales decline of 16%, while the bottom of the recession was nowhere in sight. With the downturn obviously much worse than he had anticipated, Risberg was faced with the question how to respond. He was not particularly enthusiastic about postponing investments and innovations, as he believed this was the moment to gain the upper hand against the likes of Bosch, Würth and Black & Decker. He also did not like the idea of cutting the workforce he had so carefully built up. Moreover, he felt a strong sense of responsibility towards his employees and was anxious what a headcount reduction would do to the company culture and overall morale. Hilti could always try to fasten its buckles and ride out the storm, accepting the potential losses as an investment towards a stronger starting position after the recession.

But as it became clearer that the recession would probably be long and deep, Risberg started to consider his change options. He could follow a more evolutionary path, taking the time to find the best places to cut cost and allow downsizing by attrition, or he could go for a more revolutionary approach and slash costs more radically. He could ask the Hilti family for a financial sacrifice to lessen the cost reductions or he could boldly wield a circular saw and cut deeply. He could ask his own organization to look for ways to trim cost and raise sales themselves, or he could call in the consultants to take a tougher angle. With all these possible approaches to the issue of change, he was reminded of the famous words of the 26-year-old Martin Hilti in 1941: 'One cannot take anything for granted, the only constant is change.'

Co-authors: Martijn Rademakers and Marc Sniukas

Source: Hilti Annual Reports 2000–2008; www.hilti.com; Baschera and Risch, 2006

PERSPECTIVES ON STRATEGIC CHANGE

No great thing is created suddenly, any more than a bunch of grapes or a fig. If you tell me that you desire a fig, I answer that there must be time. Let it first blossom, then bear fruit, then ripen.
Epictetus (c. 60–120); Roman philosopher

Although the demand for both revolutionary and evolutionary change is clear, this does place managers in the difficult position of having to determine how these two must be combined and balanced in a process of ongoing strategic renewal. Revolutionary change is necessary to create *discontinuity* in the renewal process – radical and swift breaks with the past. Evolutionary change is necessary to ensure *continuity* in the renewal process – moderate and gradual metamorphosis from one state into another. In finding a balance between these two demands, the question is which of the two must play a leading role and what type of change path this leads to. Does successful strategic renewal hinge on a few infrequent big bangs, with some minor evolutionary changes in the intervening time span, or is successful strategic renewal essentially a gradual process of mutation and selection, where revolutionary changes are used only in case of emergency?

Yet, as in previous chapters, we see that the strategic management literature comes up with a wide variety of answers to this question. Both among business practitioners and strategy researchers, views differ sharply about the best way of dealing with the paradox of revolution and evolution. To gain insight into the major points of disagreement between people on the issue of strategic renewal, we will again outline the two diametrically opposed perspectives here.

At one end of the virtual continuum of views, are the strategists who argue that real strategic renewal can only be achieved by radical means. Revolutionary change, although difficult to achieve, is at the heart of renewal, while evolutionary changes can only figure in a supporting role. This point of view will be referred to as the 'discontinuous renewal perspective'. At the other end of the spectrum are the strategists who argue that real strategic renewal is not brought about by an 'axe', but must grow out of the existing firm, in a constant stream of small adjustments. Evolutionary change, although difficult to sustain, is at the heart of renewal, while revolutionary changes are a fall-back alternative, if all else fails. This point of view will be referred to as the 'continuous renewal perspective'.

The discontinuous renewal perspective

According to advocates of the discontinuous renewal perspective, it is a common misconception that firms develop gradually. It is often assumed that organizations move fluidly from one state to the next, encountering minimal friction. In reality, however, strategic change is arduous and encounters significant resistance. Pressure must be exerted, and tension must mount, before a major shift can be accomplished. Movement, therefore, is not steady and constant, as a current in the sea, but abrupt and dramatic, as in an earthquake, where resistance gives way and tension is released in a short shock. In general, the more significant a change is, the more intense the shock will be.

Proponents of this perspective argue that people and organizations exhibit a natural reluctance to change. Humans have a strong preference for stability. Once general policy has been determined, most firms are inclined to settle into a fixed way of working. The organizational structure will solidify, formal processes will be installed, standard operating procedures will be defined, key competence areas will be identified, a distribution of power will emerge and a corporate culture will become established. The stability of an organization will be especially high if all of these elements form a consistent and cohesive configuration (e.g. Mintzberg, 1991; Waterman, Peters and Philips, 1982). Moreover, if a firm experiences a period of success, this usually strongly reinforces the existing way of working (e.g. Markides, 1998; Miller, 1990).

It must be emphasized that stability is not inherently harmful, as it allows people to 'get to work'. A level of stability is required to function efficiently (e.g. March and Simon, 1958; Thompson, 1967). Constant upheaval would only create an organizational mess. There would be prolonged confusion about tasks and authority, poorly structured internal communication and coordination, and a lack of clear standards and routines. The instability brought on by such continuously changing processes and structures would lead to widespread insecurity, political manoeuvring and inter-departmental conflicts.

Advocates of the discontinuous renewal perspective, therefore, argue that long periods of relative stability are necessary for the proper functioning of firms. However, the downside of stability is rigidity – the unwillingness and/or inability to change, even when it is urgently required. To overcome rigidity and get the firm in motion, a series of small nudges will by no means be sufficient. A big shove will be needed. For strategic changes to really happen, measures must be radical and comprehensive. A coordinated assault is usually required to decisively break through organizational defences and 'shock therapy' is needed to fundamentally change people's cognitive maps. Solving lock-in problems generally also demands a quick, firm-wide switchover to a new system. For instance, business process reengineering must involve all aspects of the value chain at once (e.g. Hammer, 1990, Reading 4.1; Hammer and Champy, 1993). However, proponents of the discontinuous renewal perspective emphasize that the period of turmoil must not take too long. People cannot be indefinitely confronted with high levels of uncertainty and ambiguity, and a new equilibrium is vital for a new period of efficient operations.

Therefore, the long-term pattern of strategic renewal is not gradual, but episodic. Periods of relative stability are interrupted by short and dramatic periods of instability, during which revolutionary changes take place (e.g. Greiner, 1972; Tushman, Newman and Romanelli, 1986). This pattern of development has been recognized in a variety of other sciences as well (Gersick, 1991). Following the natural historians Eldredge and Gould, this discontinuous pattern of strategic renewal is often called 'punctuated equilibrium' – stability punctuated by episodes of revolutionary change.

Some proponents of this view argue that episodes of revolutionary change are generally not chosen freely, but are triggered by crises. A major environmental jolt can be the reason for a sudden crisis (e.g. Meyer, 1982; Meyer, Brooks and Goes, 1990) – for example, the introduction of a new technology, a major economic recession, new government regulations, a novel market entrant or a dramatic event in international political affairs. However, often a misalignment between the firm and its environment grows over a longer period of time, causing a mounting sense of impending crisis (e.g. Johnson, 1988; Strebel, 1992). As tension increases, people in the firm become more receptive to submitting to the painful changes that are necessary. This increased willingness to change under crisis circumstances coincides with the physical law that 'under pressure things become fluid'. As long as the pressure persists, revolutionary change is possible, but as soon as the pressure lets up the firm will resolidify in a new form, inhibiting any further major changes (e.g. Lewin, 1947; Miller and Friesen, 1984). For this reason, managers often feel impelled to heighten and prolong the sense of crisis, to keep organization members receptive to the changes being pushed through. And where a crisis is lacking, some managers will induce one, to create the sense of urgency and determination needed to get people in the change mind-set.

Other authors argue that revolutionary changes are not always reactive responses to crisis conditions. Revolutionary change can also be proactively pursued to gain a competitive advantage, or even to change the rules of the game in the industry in which the firm is competing. If a firm decides to use a breakthrough technology or a new business model to improve its competitive position vis-à-vis rivals, this does entail that it will need to execute some major changes in a short period of time. Such innovations to the business system are inherently revolutionary. Creating novel products and developing a unique business formula requires a sharp break with the past. Old ways must be discarded before new methods can be adopted. This is the essence of what Schumpeter (1950) referred to as the process of 'creative destruction', inherent in the capitalist system. This process is not orderly and protracted, but disruptive and intense. Therefore, it is argued, to be a competitive success, firms must learn to master the skill of ongoing revolutionary change (e.g. D'Aveni, 1994; Hamel, 1996). Rapid implementation of system-wide change is an essential organizational capability – the firm needs to be able to run faster than its competitors.

It can be concluded that strategic changes, whether proactive or reactive, require an abrupt break with the status quo. Change management demands strong leadership to rapidly push through stressful, discomforting and risky shifts in the business and organizational system. Battling the sources of rigidity and turning crisis into opportunity are the key qualities needed by managers implementing strategic change. Ultimately, strategizing managers should know when to change and when it is more wise to seek stability – they should know when to trigger an 'earthquake' and when to avoid one.

EXHIBIT 4.2   THE DISCONTINUOUS RENEWAL PERSPECTIVE

GROHE: PRODUCTIVE LOCUST

In April 2005 a political controversy started in Germany in the run up to the regional elections in the state of North Rhine-Westphalia, when the chairman of the national Social Democratic Party (SPD), Franz Müntefering, compared private equity companies to locust. Pointing to the radical restructuring being planned at the world-famous sanitary fittings manufacturer, Grohe, Müntefering warned that private equity firms swarming in from the US and the UK were destroying jobs and companies. They would outsource jobs to low cost countries, get rich themselves and leave only an empty shell in Germany, was the fear he entrusted to the newspaper, *Bild am Sonntag*. The ensuing political storm lasted for more than a year, with over 600 negative newspaper articles being written about Grohe in May and June 2005 alone.

What had happened? Grohe, known for its sophisticated faucets, thermostats and showers, had made great strides in export markets throughout the 1980s and 1990s, but was increasingly unable to pass on its high German costs to its international clients. As the euro gained in strength compared to most currencies and steel prices increased, Grohe was simultaneously faced by tougher competition, particularly from China. In 1999 Grohe had been purchased by BC Partners, a private equity company, who encouraged CEO Körfer-Schün to work on lowering Grohe's cost structure. He concluded that with more than 75% of sales coming from outside of Germany, it would make sense to internationalize production as well, gradually building up its factories in Portugal and Canada. These plants would be able to supply the high international growth he intended to achieve. Yet, with an eye to the very strong IG Metall union and the outspoken workers' council, Körfer-Schün emphasized that he did not plan to reduce the number of plants and employees in Germany, while production process improvement would be done incrementally.

As Grohe's financial position grew worse after 2001, with its home market also stalling after the dotcom crash, plans to list the company on the stock exchange were scrapped and all shares were sold to Texas Pacific Group and Credit Suisse Private Equity in 2004. This change in ownership brought a change in management as well. David Haines, a British manager with considerable experience in Germany, was brought in as CEO and he quickly changed most of the top management team. Extensive plans were prepared to make a complete overhaul of Grohe and re-establish the company as the undisputed leader in the premium segment of the sanitary fittings market. It was these plans that were leaked to Müntefering and caused the big commotion in the German media.

Haines' plan was to transform Grohe's German operations into the innovation and competence hub of the company, while transferring straightforward manufacturing activities to low cost locations in Portugal and Thailand. This would involve the closing of one of the four German plants and the total reengineering of the remaining ones, to take them from the 1960s straight to the 21st century. Approximately one thousand people, a third of the Grohe workforce in Germany, would lose their jobs. In an effort to reduce complexity, the product range would also be cut from 17 000 to 6000 products and the number of suppliers reduced from 7500 to 1500. Furthermore, company headquarters would be shifted from the small town of Hemer, where the company had started in 1911, to Düsseldorf, which would make Grohe a much more attractive employer for non-German managers. The total plan would require an investment of € 200 million up until 2008, of which approximately 70% would be in Germany. The intended result was a structural reduction in cost of € 150 million per year.

Despite the political storm and the extremely critical media coverage, the discontinuous renewal of Grohe has been a phenomenal success. Exactly one year after announcing the restructuring, Haines could declare in June 2006 that Grohe was growing and profitable again. Since then, the going has remained tough against strong rivals, but Grohe has continued to grow faster than the market, breaking through the € 1 billion sales mark in 2008. Out of its 5100 employees, 2600 are still located in Germany, working in headquarters, the new design centre and the three remaining plants. The renewed plant in Hemer has received the best factory award from INSEAD and the WHU Otto Beisheim School of Management in 2009. In addition, product development has been revitalized, with 54 per cent of the 2008 turnover coming from products less than three years old. With the development of the new Blue technology, a tap water purification system, the company has started to diversify into the kitchen. Furthermore, the campaigns 'Grohe – enjoy water' and 'Perfect flow. Always' have won awards and helped to strengthen the Grohe brand.

Surprisingly, the entire revolution happened without a strike or a rise in absenteeism, partly due to the enormous efforts taken by Haines to communicate with, and involve, all major stakeholders, including the union. Moreover, considerable time went into formulating an extensive 'social plan', to support ex-employees with coaching, training and money as they looked for other jobs. The union IG Metall later called this plan the best Germany has ever seen. Not bad for a bunch of locust.

Co-author: Marc Sniukas

Sources: *Kommunikations Manager*, March 2008; *Wirtschaftswoche*, 20 April 2009; www.grohe.com; www.handelsblatt.com various issues.

The continuous renewal perspective

 According to proponents of the continuous renewal perspective, if firms shift by 'earthquake' it is usually their own 'fault'. The problem with revolution is that it commonly leads to the need for further revolution at a later time – discontinuous change creates its own boom-and-bust cycle. Revolutionary change is generally followed by a strong organizational yearning for stability. The massive, firm-wide efforts to implement agonizing changes can often be sustained for only a short period of time, after which change momentum collapses. Any positive inclination towards change among employees will have totally disappeared by the time the re-organizations are over. Consequently, the firm lapses back into a stable state in which only minor changes occur. This stable situation is maintained until the next round of shock therapy becomes necessary, to jolt the organization out of its ossified state.

To supporters of the continuous renewal perspective, the boom-and-bust approach to strategic change is like running a marathon by sprinting and then standing still to catch one's breath. Yet, marathons are not won by good sprinters, but by runners with endurance and persistence, who can keep a steady pace – runners who are more inspired by the tortoise than by the hare. The same is true for companies in the marathon of competition. Some companies behave like the hare in Aesop's fable, showing off their ability to take great leaps, but burdened by a short span of attention. Other companies behave more like the tortoise, moving gradually and undramatically, but unrelentingly and without interruption, focusing on the long-term goal. In the short run, the hares might dash ahead, suggesting that making big leaps forward is the best way to compete. But in the long run, the most formidable contenders will be the diligent tortoises, whose ability to maintain a constant speed will help them to win the race.

Therefore, the 'big ideas', 'frame-breaking innovations' and 'quantum leaps' that so mesmerize proponents of the discontinuous renewal perspective are viewed with suspicion by supporters of continuous renewal. Revolution not only causes unnecessary disruption and dysfunctional crises, but also is usually the substitute for diligence. If organizations do not have the stamina to continuously improve themselves, quick fix radical change can be used as a short-term remedy. Where firms do not exhibit the drive to permanently upgrade their capabilities, revolutionary innovations can be used as the short cut to renewed competitiveness. In other words, the lure of revolutionary change is that of short-term results. By abruptly and dramatically making major changes, managers hope to rapidly book tangible progress – and instantly win recognition and promotion (Imai, 1986, Reading 4.2 in this book).

To advocates of the continuous renewal perspective, a preference for revolution usually reflects an unhealthy obsession with the short term. Continuous renewal, on the other hand, is more long term in orientation. Development is gradual, piecemeal and undramatic, but as it is constantly maintained over a longer period of time, the aggregate level of change can still be significant. Three organizational characteristics are important for keeping up a steady pace of change. First, all employees within the firm should be committed to *continuously improve*. Everyone within the firm should be driven by constructive dissatisfaction with the status quo. This attitude, that things can always be done better, reflects a rejection of stability and the acceptance of bounded instability (e.g. Beinhocker, 1999; Stacey, 1993a, Reading 9.2) – everything is open to change.

Secondly, everyone in the firm must be motivated to *continuously learn*. People within the organization must constantly update their knowledge base, which not only means acquiring new information, but challenging accepted company wisdom as well. Learning goes hand in hand with unlearning – changing the cognitive maps shared within the organization. In this respect, it is argued that an atmosphere of crisis actually inhibits continuous renewal. In a situation of crisis, it is not a matter of 'under pressure things become fluid', but 'in the cold everything freezes'. Crisis circumstances might lower people's resistance to imposed change, but it also blunts their motivation for experimenting and learning, as they brace themselves for the imminent shock. Crisis encourages people to seek security and to focus on the short term, instead of opening up and working towards long-term development (e.g. Bate, 1994; Senge, 1990, Reading 9.3).

Thirdly, everyone in the firm must be motivated to *continuously adapt.* Constant adjustment to external change and fluid internal realignment should be pursued. To this end, the organization must actively avoid inertia, by combating the forces of ossification. Managers should strive to create flexible structures and processes (e.g. Bartlett and Ghoshal, 1995; Eisenhardt and Brown, 1997), to encourage an open and tolerant corporate culture, and to provide sufficient job and career security for employees to accept other forms of ambiguity and uncertainty (e.g. Kagono *et al.*, 1985; Nonaka, 1988).

These three characteristics of an evolutionary firm – continuous improvement, learning and adaptation – have in common that basically everyone in the organization is involved. Revolutionary change can be initiated by top management, possibly assisted and urged on by a few external consultants, and carried by a handful of change agents or champions (e.g. Maidique, 1980; Day, 1994). Evolutionary change, on the other hand, requires a firm-wide effort. Leaders cannot learn on behalf of their organizations, nor can they orchestrate all of the small improvements and adaptations needed for continuous renewal. Managers must realize that evolution can be led from the top, but not be imposed from the top. For strategizing managers to realize change, hands-on guidance of organizational developments is more important than commanding organizational actions.

EXHIBIT 4.3 THE CONTINUOUS RENEWAL PERSPECTIVE

MCKINSEY & COMPANY: 'THE FIRM' REMAINS FIRM

Ise Jingu is Japan's most sacred Shinto shrine and in the eyes of many also its most aesthetically pure and serene one. The shrine compound consists of more than 200 buildings that are constructed using 13 600 Japanese cypress trees, special Kaya straw, and not a single nail. Every 20 years, Ise Jingu is completely razed to the ground and the priests move to an exact replica that has been built in the meantime on a parallel site. Here they will stay for the next 20 years, until it is time to move back again. In 1993, the shrine was moved for the 61st time since the year 690, a ceremony that has been maintained with only one exception, in Japan's war-torn 16th century.

Why tear down such elaborate structures only to rebuild exact replicas? The high priests of Shinto realized at the time, that the only way to maintain the know-how for constructing the shrine was to rebuild it once every 20 years, thus handing down the skills from one generation to the next. Moreover, by continuously rebuilding the shrine, the relentless process of deterioration is mastered. Ise Jingu remains eternally young – visitors enter brand new buildings that are 1300 years old. The symbolic importance of this ritual reaches very deep. As with the construction know-how of the shrine, the

insight into the Shinto belief system must also be passed on to the young. By making each new generation 'rebuild' it, Shintoism evolves successfully with the challenges and opportunities of the present day, without changing what is at its core.

A similar approach to change can be observed at McKinsey & Company, the international management consulting company that has such a solid position in corporate markets that it is often simply referred to as 'the Firm'. McKinsey was founded in 1926 by James McKinsey, but started its spectacular growth in the 1930s after the arrival of Marvin Bower, who remained active in the company until his death in January 2003. From the outset, Bower imprinted a set of principles and values to guide the functioning of McKinsey and these have remained virtually unchanged over the years. He also devised a business model that is basically the same today as it was 50 years ago. Few expect this situation to change after the election in February 2009 of the 11th worldwide managing director, the Canadian Dominic Barton, who is known as 'someone steeped in the McKinsey tradition'.

McKinsey's profile has remained fundamentally consistent, as the firm has grabbed a position of leadership across all continents, and many industries. A McKinsey consultant in Mumbai today would easily recognize the Düsseldorf operations of the 1980s or New York of the 1970s. Similarly, the profile and image of McKinsey consultants has stayed remarkably stable, independent of time and place. But how can a company that does not seem to change continuously achieve the highest recognition across such a wide range of countries, industries and times? Doesn't the fast changing world require the firm to constantly reinvent itself? In reality, McKinsey does change, only fluidly, in a continuous stream of small steps.

One of its most notorious management practices bringing about that continuous renewal is McKinsey's 'up or out policy', or more politely its 'grow or go' system. This policy forces every consultant in the firm to constantly rise through the ranks, or else to leave. Even the speed at which each career step should be taken is fixed at about a year and a half, give or take a few months. The effect of this policy is that nobody in the company can ever build a nesting place. Even senior directors must move on, leaving an open space for a rising newcomer to occupy and to learn the necessary skills for this level anew. The effect is also that as an open space

is reoccupied, it is reshaped to take account of the then somewhat different external business environment, different business cycle, and change in industry or shift in regional focus. Newcomers may be in the same slot as their predecessors, and they will adhere to the same McKinsey values of 'Client First, Firm Second, everything else Third', but their job will be a changed one. Since the long-term reliance on a fixed skill base is made impossible through the 'grow or go' system, the McKinsey consultants, and with them the entire company, evolve seamlessly over time and across borders, even while remaining the same at their core. Hence, while McKinsey often advises its clients to radically restructure, for itself the firm prefers to stick to a process of continual adjustment.

Co-authors: Peer Ederer and Martijn Rademakers

Sources: Coaldrake, W. (1996); *The Economist*, 1 March 2003; *Financial Times*, 4 February 2009; alumni.mckinsey.com/alumni; www.isejingu.or.jp.

INTRODUCTION TO THE DEBATE AND READINGS

Every act of creation is first of all an act of destruction.
Pablo Picasso (1881–1973); Spanish artist

Slow and steady wins the race.
The Hare and the Tortoise, Aesop
(c. 620–560 BC); Greek writer

So, how should managers go about renewing their organizations? Should managers strive to bring about renewal abruptly, by emphasizing radical, comprehensive and dramatic changes? Or should they try to make renewal a more continuous process, accentuating ongoing improvement, learning and adaptation? As no consensus has yet developed within the field of strategic management on how to balance revolution and evolution, it is once again up to each individual to assess the arguments put forward in the debate and to form their own opinion.

As an input to the process of assessing the variety of perspectives on this issue, four readings have been selected that each can help readers to make up their own minds. Again, the first two readings will be representative of the two poles in this debate (see Table 4.1), while the second set of two readings will highlight additional arguments that are of relevance to finding a balance between the opposing demands.

As the opening reading, Michael Hammer's 'Reengineering Work: Don't Automate, Obliterate' has been selected to represent the discontinuous renewal perspective. This paper was published in *Harvard Business Review* in 1990 and was followed in 1993 by the highly influential book *Reengineering the Corporation: A Manifesto for Business Revolution*, that Hammer co-authored with James Champy. In this article, Hammer explains the concept of reengineering in much the same way as in the best-selling book.

TABLE 4.1 Discontinuous renewal versus continuous renewal perspective

	Discontinuous renewal perspective	*Continuous renewal perspective*
Emphasis on	Revolution over evolution	Evolution over revolution
Strategic renewal as	Disruptive innovation/turnaround	Uninterrupted improvement
Strategic renewal process	Creative destruction	Organic adaptation
Magnitude of change	Radical, comprehensive and dramatic	Moderate, piecemeal and undramatic
Pace of change	Abrupt, unsteady and intermittent	Gradual, steady and constant
Lasting renewal requires	Sudden break with status quo	Permanent learning and flexibility
Reaction to external jolts	Shock therapy	Continuous adjustment
View of organizational crises	Under pressure things becomes fluid	In the cold everything freezes
Long-term renewal dynamics	Stable and unstable states alternate	Persistent transient state
Long-term renewal pattern	Punctuated equilibrium	Gradual development

'At the heart of reengineering,' he writes, 'is the notion of discontinuous thinking – of recognizing and breaking away from the outdated rules and fundamental assumptions that underlie operations.' In his view, radically redesigning business processes 'cannot be planned meticulously and accomplished in small and cautious steps. It's an all-or-nothing proposition with an uncertain result.' He exhorts managers to 'think big', by setting high goals, taking bold steps and daring to accept a high risk. In short, he preaches business revolution, and the tone of his article is truly that of a manifesto – impassioned, fervent, with here and there 'a touch of fanaticism'.

Equally impassioned is the argumentation in the second reading, 'Kaizen', by Masaaki Imai, which has been selected to represent the continuous renewal perspective. This article has been taken from Imai's famous book *Kaizen: The Key to Japan's Competitive Success*. Kaizen (pronounced Ky'zen) is a Japanese term that is best translated as continuous improvement. Imai argues that it is this continuous improvement philosophy that best explains the competitive strength of so many Japanese companies. In his view, Western companies have an unhealthy obsession with one-shot innovations and revolutionary change. They are fixated on the great leap forward, while disregarding the power of accumulated small changes. Imai believes that innovations are also important for competitive success, but that they should be embedded in an organization that is driven to continuously improve.

While the articles by Hammer and Imai clearly illustrate the fundamentals of revolution and evolution, both are strongly focused on operational instead of strategic changes. To rectify this imbalance, two readings have been included that emphasize the strategic level. The first is a classic from 1996, by Michael Tushman and Charles O'Reilly, 'Ambidextrous Organizations: Managing Evolutionary and Revolutionary Change'. While Hammer presents revolution as the radical measure needed to break the shackles of antiquated business systems, it is unclear what the corporation must do after it is re-engineered. Tushman and O'Reilly look beyond a single episode of revolution, to the longer-term pattern of development. In their view, short periods of revolutionary change are usually followed by longer periods of gradual change, similar to the pattern found in nature, which scientists have dubbed 'punctuated equilibrium'. They argue that to be successful during periods of relative stability, firms need to commit themselves to a certain strategy, structure and culture, to create a strong fit with the environment. During such periods the emphasis should be on evolutionary adaptation to the always changing demands in the market. But as soon as discontinuous changes happen in the environment, firms need to be able to be revolutionary as well. Hence they conclude that the paradox of revolution and evolution needs to be managed by being ambidextrous, i.e. being able to do both, sometimes sequentially, sometimes even at the same time. This can be achieved by stimulating internal diversity, allowing different strategies, structures and cultures to blossom side-by-side, making a firm more robust in adapting to whatever external change comes its way.

Reading 4.4 is by one of the leading German theorists on strategic change, Wilfried Krüger, whose work is unfortunately not particularly well known outside of his native country. In this article, entitled 'Implementation: The Core Task of Change Management', Krüger provides a thorough review of the challenges and approaches to strategy implementation and change, presenting many useful analytical tools and practical solutions along the way. Although he explicitly recognizes the value of both revolution and evolution (acknowledging the contributions of Hammer and Imai), his main point is that they should be explicitly combined to ensure ongoing implementation – renewal might not be entirely *continuous* (uninterrupted), but it should be *continual* (ongoing). In his words, 'change is a permanent task and challenge for general management and implementation is an integral element thereof'. Although this does not place Krüger fully in the continuous renewal 'camp', its does echo the thrust of their argumentation that managers should be constantly working towards renewal, instead of letting it erupt periodically. Krüger's emphasis on the importance of political and cultural acceptance to achieve successful strategic change and his belief that 'the overcoming of acceptance barriers must be designed as an individual and organizational learning process', fits very closely with the basic premises of the continuous renewal perspective.

Discontinuous or continuous renewal? It is now up to readers to decide whether they sympathize more with the tortoise or the hare.

READING

4.1

Reengineering work: Don't automate, obliterate

By Michael Hammer[1]

Despite a decade or more of restructuring and downsizing, many US companies are still unprepared to operate in the 1990s. In a time of rapidly changing technologies and ever-shorter product life cycles, product development often proceeds at a glacial pace. In an age of the customer, order fulfilment has high error rates and customer enquiries go unanswered for weeks. In a period when asset utilization is critical, inventory levels exceed many months of demand.

The usual methods for boosting performance – process rationalization and automation – haven't yielded the dramatic improvements companies need. In particular, heavy investments in information technology have delivered disappointing results – largely because companies tend to use technology to mechanize old ways of doing business. They leave the existing processes intact and use computers simply to speed them up.

But speeding up those processes cannot address their fundamental performance deficiencies. Many of our job designs, workflows, control mechanisms, and organizational structures came of age in a different competitive environment and before the advent of the computer. They are geared toward efficiency and control. Yet the watchwords of the new decade are innovation and speed, service and quality.

It is time to stop paving the cow paths. Instead of embedding outdated processes in silicon and software, we should obliterate them and start over. We should 'reengineer' our businesses: use the power of modern information technology to radically redesign our business processes in order to achieve dramatic improvements in their performance.

Every company operates according to a great many unarticulated rules. 'Credit decisions are made by the credit department.' 'Local inventory is needed for good customer service.' 'Forms must be filled in completely and in order.' Reengineering strives to break away from the old rules about how we organize and conduct business. It involves recognizing and rejecting some of them and then finding imaginative new ways to accomplish work. From our redesigned processes, new rules will emerge that fit the times. Only then can we hope to achieve quantum leaps in performance.

Reengineering cannot be planned meticulously and accomplished in small and cautious steps. It's an all-or-nothing proposition with an uncertain result. Still, most companies have no choice but to muster the courage to do it. For many, reengineering is the only hope for breaking away from the antiquated processes that threaten to drag them down. Fortunately, managers are not without help. Enough businesses have successfully reengineered their processes to provide some rules of thumb for others.

What Ford and MBL did

Japanese competitors and young entrepreneurial ventures prove every day that drastically better levels of process performance are possible. They develop products twice as fast, utilize assets eight times more productively, respond to customers ten times faster. Some large, established companies also show what can be done. Businesses like Ford Motor Company and Mutual Benefit Life Insurance have reengineered their processes and achieved competitive leadership as a result. Ford has reengineered its accounts payable processes, and Mutual Benefit Life its processing of applications for insurance.

In the early 1980s, when the American automotive industry was in a depression, Ford's top management put accounts payable – along with many other departments – under the microscope in search of ways to cut costs. Accounts payable in North America alone employed more than 500 people. Management thought that by rationalizing processes and installing new computer systems, it could reduce the head count by some 20 per cent.

Ford was enthusiastic about its plan to tighten accounts payable – until it looked at Mazda. While Ford was aspiring to a 400-person department, Mazda's accounts payable organization consisted of a total of five people. The difference in absolute numbers was astounding, and even after adjusting for Mazda's smaller size, Ford figured that its accounts payable organization was five times the size it should be. The Ford team knew better than to attribute the discrepancy to callisthenics, company songs, or low interest rates.

Ford managers ratcheted up their goal: accounts payable would perform with not just a hundred but many hundreds fewer clerks. It then set out to achieve it. First, managers analysed the existing system. When Ford's purchasing department wrote a purchase order, it sent a copy to accounts payable. Later, when material control received the goods, it sent a copy of the receiving document to accounts payable. Meanwhile, the vendor sent an invoice to accounts payable. It was up to accounts payable, then, to match the purchase order against the receiving document and the invoice. If they matched, the department issued payment.

The department spent most of its time on mismatches, instances where the purchase order, receiving document, and invoice disagreed. In these cases, an accounts payable clerk would investigate the discrepancy, hold up payment, generate documents, and all-in-all gum up the works.

One way to improve things might have been to help the accounts payable clerk investigate more efficiently, but a better choice was to prevent the mismatches in the first place. To this end, Ford instituted 'invoiceless processing'. Now when the purchasing department initiates an order, it enters the information into an on-line database. It doesn't send a copy of the purchase order to anyone. When the goods arrive at the receiving dock, the receiving clerk checks the database to see if they correspond to an outstanding purchase order. If so, he or she accepts them and enters the transaction into the computer system. (If receiving can't find a database entry for the received goods, it simply returns the order.)

Under the old procedures, the accounting department had to match 14 data items between the receipt record, the purchase order, and the invoice before it could issue payment to the vendor. The new approach requires matching only three items – part number, unit of measure, and supplier code – between the purchase order and the receipt record. The matching is done automatically, and the computer prepares the check, which accounts payable sends to the vendor. There are no invoices to worry about since Ford has asked its vendors not to send them.

Ford didn't settle for the modest increases it first envisioned. It opted for radical change – and achieved dramatic improvement. Where it has instituted this new process, Ford has achieved a 75 per cent reduction in head count, not the 20 per cent it would have gotten with a conventional programme. And since there are no discrepancies between the financial record and the physical record, material control is simpler and financial information is more accurate.

Mutual Benefit Life, the country's eighteenth largest life carrier, has reengineered its processing of insurance applications. Prior to this, MBL handled customers' applications much as its competitors did. The long, multistep process involved credit checking, quoting, rating, underwriting, and so on. An application would have to go through as many as 30 discrete steps, spanning five departments and involving 19 people. At the very best, MBL could process an application in 24 hours, but more typical turnarounds ranged from five to 25 days – most of the time spent passing information from one department to the next. (Another insurer estimated that while an application spent 22 days in process, it was actually worked on for just 17 minutes.)

MBL's rigid, sequential process led to many complications. For instance, when a customer wanted to cash in an existing policy and purchase a new one, the old business department first had to authorize the treasury department to issue a check made payable to MBL. The check would then accompany the paperwork to the new business department.

The president of MBL, intent on improving customer service, decided that this nonsense had to stop and demanded a 60 per cent improvement in productivity. It was clear that such an ambitious goal would require more than tinkering with the existing process. Strong measures were in order, and the management team assigned to the task looked to technology as a means of achieving them. The team realized that shared databases and computer networks could make many different kinds of information available to a single person, while expert systems could help people with limited experience make sound decisions. Applying these insights led to a new approach to the application-handling process, one with wide organizational implications and little resemblance to the old way of doing business.

MBL swept away existing job definitions and departmental boundaries and created a new position called a case manager. Case managers have total responsibility for an application from the time it is received to the time a policy is issued. Unlike clerks, who performed a fixed task repeatedly under the watchful gaze of a supervisor, case managers work autonomously. No more handoffs of files and responsibility, no more shuffling of customer enquiries.

Case managers are able to perform all the tasks associated with an insurance application because they are supported by powerful PC-based workstations that run an expert system and connect to a range of automated systems on a mainframe. In particularly tough cases, the case manager calls for assistance from a senior underwriter or physician, but these specialists work only as consultants and advisers to the case manager, who never relinquishes control.

Empowering individuals to process entire applications has had a tremendous impact on operations. MBL can now complete an application in as little as four hours, and average turnaround takes only two to five days. The company has eliminated 100 field office positions, and case managers can handle more than twice the volume of new applications the company previously could process.

The essence of reengineering

At the heart of reengineering is the notion of discontinuous thinking – of recognizing and breaking away from the outdated rules and fundamental assumptions that underlie operations. Unless we change these rules, we are merely rearranging the deckchairs on the *Titanic*. We cannot achieve breakthroughs in performance by cutting fat or automating existing processes. Rather, we must challenge old assumptions and shed the old rules that made the business underperform in the first place.

Every business is replete with implicit rules left over from earlier decades. 'Customers don't repair their own equipment.' 'Local warehouses are necessary for good service.' 'Merchandising decisions are made at headquarters.' These rules of work design are based on assumptions about technology, people, and organizational goals that no longer hold. The contemporary repertoire of available information technologies is vast and quickly expanding. Quality, innovation, and service are now more important than cost, growth, and control. A large portion of the population is educated and capable of assuming responsibility, and workers cherish their autonomy and expect to have a say in how the business is run.

It should come as no surprise that our business processes and structures are outmoded and obsolete: our work structures and processes have not kept pace with the changes in technology, demographics, and business objectives. For the most part, we have organized work as a sequence of separate tasks and employed complex mechanisms to track its progress.

This arrangement can be traced to the Industrial Revolution, when specialization of labour and economies of scale promised to overcome the inefficiencies of cottage industries. Businesses disaggregated work into narrowly defined tasks, reaggregated the people performing those tasks into departments, and installed managers to administer them.

Our elaborate systems for imposing control and discipline on those who actually do the work stem from the post-war period. In that halcyon period of expansion, the main concern was growing fast without going broke, so businesses focused on cost, growth, and control. And since literate, entry-level people were abundant but well-educated professionals hard to come by, the control systems funnelled information up the hierarchy to the few who presumably knew what to do with it.

These patterns of organizing work have become so ingrained that, despite their serious drawbacks, it's hard to conceive of work being accomplished any other way. Conventional process structures are fragmented and piecemeal, and they lack the integration necessary to maintain quality and service. They are breeding grounds for tunnel vision, as people tend to substitute the narrow goals of their particular department for the larger goals of the process as a whole. When work is handed off from person to person and unit to unit, delays and errors are inevitable. Accountability blurs, and critical issues fall between the cracks. Moreover, no one sees enough of the big picture to be able to respond quickly to new situations. Managers desperately try, like all the king's horses and all the king's men, to piece together the fragmented pieces of business processes.

Managers have tried to adapt their processes to new circumstances, but usually in ways that just create more problems. If, say, customer service is poor, they create a mechanism to deliver service but overlay it on the existing organization. Bureaucracy thickens, costs rise, and enterprising competitors gain market share.

In reengineering, managers break loose from outmoded business processes and the design principles underlying them and create new ones. Ford had operated under the old rule that 'we pay when we receive the invoice.' While no one had ever articulated or recorded it, that rule determined how the accounts payable process was organized. Ford's reengineering effort challenged and ultimately replaced the rule with a new one: 'We pay when we receive the goods.'

Reengineering requires looking at the fundamental processes of the business from a cross-functional perspective. Ford discovered that reengineering only the accounts payable department was futile. The appropriate focus of the effort was what might be called the goods acquisition process, which included purchasing and receiving as well as accounts payable.

One way to ensure that reengineering has a cross-functional perspective is to assemble a team that represents the functional units involved in the process being reengineered and all the units that depend on it. The team must analyse and scrutinize the existing process until it really understands what the process is trying to accomplish. The point is not to learn what happens to form 73B in its peregrinations through the company but to understand the purpose of having form 73B in the first place. Rather than looking for opportunities to improve the current process, the team should determine which of its steps really add value and search for new ways to achieve the result.

The reengineering team must keep asking Why? and What if? Why do we need to get a manager's signature on a requisition? Is it a control mechanism or a decision point? What if the manager reviews only requisitions above $500? What if he or she doesn't see them at all? Raising and resolving heretical questions can separate what is fundamental to the process from what is superficial. The regional offices of an East Coast insurance company had long produced a series of reports that they regularly sent to the home office. No one in the field realized that these reports were simply filed and never used. The process outlasted the circumstances that had created the need for it. The reengineering study team should push to discover situations like this.

In short, a reengineering effort strives for dramatic levels of improvement. It must break away from conventional wisdom and the constraints of organizational boundaries and should be broad and cross-functional in scope. It should use information technology not to automate an existing process but to enable a new one.

Principles of reengineering

Creating new rules tailored to the modern environment ultimately requires a new conceptualization of the business process – which comes down to someone having a great idea. But reengineering need not be haphazard. In fact, some of the principles that companies have already discovered while reengineering their business processes can help jump start the effort for others.

Organize around outcomes, not tasks

This principle says to have one person perform all the steps in a process. Design that person's job around an objective or outcome instead of a single task. The redesign at Mutual Benefit Life, where individual case managers perform the entire application approval process, is the quintessential example of this.

The redesign of an electronics company is another example. It had separate organizations performing each of the five steps between selling and installing the equipment. One group determined customer requirements, another translated those requirements into internal product codes, a third conveyed that information to various plants and warehouses, a fourth received and assembled the components, and a fifth delivered and installed the equipment. The process was based on the centuries-old notion of specialized labour and on the limitations inherent in paper files. The departments each possessed a specific set of skills, and only one department at a time could do its work.

The customer order moved systematically from step to step. But this sequential processing caused problems. The people getting the information from the customer in step one had to get all the data anyone would need throughout the process, even if it wasn't needed until step five. In addition, the many handoffs were responsible for numerous errors and misunderstandings. Finally, any questions about customer requirements that arose late in the process had to be referred back to the people doing step one, resulting in delay and rework.

When the company reengineered, it eliminated the assembly-line approach. It compressed responsibility for the various steps and assigned it to one person, the 'customer service representative'. That person now oversees the whole process – taking the order, translating it into product codes, getting the components assembled, and seeing the product delivered and installed. The customer service rep expedites and co-ordinates the process, much like a general contractor. And the customer has just one contact, who always knows the status of the order.

Have those who use the output of the process perform the process

In an effort to capitalize on the benefits of specialization and scale, many organizations established specialized departments to handle specialized processes. Each department does only one type of work and is a 'customer' of other groups' processes. Accounting does only accounting. If it needs new pencils, it goes to the purchasing department, the group specially equipped with the information and expertise to perform that role. Purchasing finds vendors, negotiates price, places the order, inspects the goods, and pays the invoice – and eventually the accountants get their pencils. The process works (after a fashion), but it's slow and bureaucratic.

Now that computer-based data and expertise are more readily available, departments, units, and individuals can do more for themselves. Opportunities exist to reengineer processes so that the individuals who need the result of a process can do it themselves. For example, by using expert systems and databases, departments can make their own purchases without sacrificing the benefits of specialized purchasers. One manufacturer has reengineered its purchasing process along just these lines. The company's old system, whereby the operating departments submitted requisitions and let purchasing do the rest, worked well for controlling expensive and important items like raw materials and capital equipment. But for inexpensive and nonstrategic purchases, which constituted some 35 per cent of total orders, the system was slow and cumbersome; it was not uncommon for the cost of the purchasing process to exceed the cost of the goods being purchased.

The new process compresses the purchase of sundry items and pushes it on to the customers of the process. Using a database of approved vendors, an operating unit can directly place an order with a vendor and charge it on a bank credit card. At the end of the month, the bank gives the manufacturer a tape of all credit card transactions, which the company runs against its internal accounting system.

When an electronics equipment manufacturer reengineered its field service process, it pushed some of the steps of the process on to its customers. The manufacturer's field service had been plagued by the usual problems: technicians were often unable to do a particular repair because the right part wasn't on the van, response to customer calls was slow, and spare-parts inventory was excessive.

Now customers make simple repairs themselves. Spare parts are stored at each customer's site and managed through a computerized inventory-management system. When a problem arises, the customer calls the manufacturer's field-service hot line and describes the symptoms to a diagnostician, who accesses a diagnosis support system. If the problem appears to be something the customer can fix, the diagnostician tells the customer what part to replace and how to install it. The old part is picked up and a new part left in its place at a later time. Only for complex problems is a service technician dispatched to the site, this time without having to make a stop at the warehouse to pick up parts.

When the people closest to the process perform it, there is little need for the overhead associated with managing it. Interfaces and liaisons can be eliminated, as can the mechanisms used to coordinate those who perform the process with those who use it. Moreover, the problem of capacity planning for the process performers is greatly reduced.

Subsume information-processing work into the real work that produces the information

The previous two principles compress linear processes. This principle suggests moving work from one person or department to another. Why doesn't an organization that produces information also process it? In the past, people didn't have the time or weren't trusted to do both. Most companies established units to do nothing but collect and process information that other departments created. This arrangement reflects the old rule about specialized labour and the belief that people at lower organizational levels are incapable of acting on information they generate. An accounts payable department collects information from purchasing and receiving and reconciles it with data that the vendor provides. Quality assurance gathers and analyses information it gets from production.

Ford's redesigned accounts payable process embodies the new rule. With the new system, receiving, which produces the information about the goods received, processes this information instead of sending it to accounts payable. The new computer system can easily compare the delivery with the order and trigger the appropriate action.

Treat geographically dispersed resources as though they were centralized

The conflict between centralization and decentralization is a classic one. Decentralizing a resource (whether people, equipment, or inventory) gives better service to those who use it, but at the cost of redundancy, bureaucracy, and missed economies of scale. Companies no longer have to make such trade-offs. They can use databases, telecommunications networks, and standardized processing systems to get the benefits of scale and coordination while maintaining the benefits of flexibility and service.

At Hewlett-Packard, for instance, each of the more than 50 manufacturing units had its own separate purchasing department. While this arrangement provided excellent responsiveness and service to the plants, it prevented H-P from realizing the benefits of its scale, particularly with regard to quantity discounts. H-P's solution is to maintain the divisional purchasing organizations and to introduce a corporate unit to coordinate them. Each purchasing unit has access to a shared database on vendors and their performance and issues its own purchase orders. Corporate purchasing maintains this database and uses it to negotiate contracts for the corporation and to monitor the units. The payoffs have come in a 150 per cent improvement in on-time deliveries, 50 per cent reduction in lead times, 75 per cent reduction in failure rates, and a significantly lower cost of goods purchased.

Link parallel activities instead of integrating their results

H-P's decentralized purchasing operations represent one kind of parallel processing in which separate units perform the same function. Another common kind of parallel processing is when separate units perform different activities that must eventually come together. Product development typically operates this way. In the development of a photocopier, for example, independent units develop the various subsystems of the copier. One group works on the optics, another on the mechanical paper-handling device, another on the power supply, and so on. Having people do development work simultaneously saves time, but at the dreaded integration and testing phase, the pieces often fail to work together. Then the costly redesign begins.

Or consider a bank that sells different kinds of credit – loans, letters of credit, asset-based financing – through separate units. These groups may have no way of knowing whether another group has already extended credit to a particular customer. Each unit could extend the full $ 10 million credit limit.

The new principle says to forge links between parallel functions and to coordinate them while their activities are in process rather than after they are completed. Communications networks, shared databases, and teleconferencing can bring the independent groups together so that coordination is ongoing. One large electronics company has cut its product development cycle by more than 50 per cent by implementing this principle.

Put the decision point where the work is performed, and build control into the process

In most organizations, those who do the work are distinguished from those who monitor the work and make decisions about it. The tacit assumption is that the people actually doing the work have neither the time nor the inclination to monitor and control it and that they lack the knowledge and scope to make decisions about it. The entire hierarchical management structure is built on this assumption. Accountants, auditors, and supervisors check, record, and monitor work. Managers handle any exceptions.

The new principle suggests that the people who do the work should make the decisions and that the process itself can have built-in controls. Pyramidal management layers can therefore be compressed and the organization flattened.

Information technology can capture and process data, and expert systems can to some extent supply knowledge, enabling people to make their own decisions. As the doers become self-managing and self-controlling, hierarchy – and the slowness and bureaucracy associated with it – disappears.

When Mutual Benefit Life reengineered the insurance application process, it not only compressed the linear sequence but also eliminated the need for layers of managers. These two kinds of compression – vertical and horizontal – often go together; the very fact that a worker sees only one piece of the process calls for a manager with a broader vision. The case managers at MBL provide end-to-end management of the process, reducing the need for traditional managers. The managerial role is changing from one of controller and supervisor to one of supporter and facilitator.

Capture information once and at the source

This last rule is simple. When information was difficult to transmit, it made sense to collect information repeatedly. Each person, department, or unit had its own requirements and forms. Companies simply had to live with the associated delays, entry errors, and costly overhead. But why do we have to live with those problems now? Today when we collect a piece of information, we can store it in an on-line database for all who need it. Bar coding, relational databases, and electronic data interchange (EDI) make it easy to collect, store, and transmit information. One insurance company found that its application review process required that certain items be entered into 'stovepipe' computer systems supporting different functions as many as five times. By integrating and connecting these systems, the company was able to eliminate this redundant data entry along with the attendant checking functions and inevitable errors.

Think big

Reengineering triggers changes of many kinds, not just of the business process itself. Job designs, organizational structures, management systems – anything associated with the process must be refashioned in an integrated way. In other words, reengineering is a tremendous effort that mandates change in many areas of the organization.

When Ford reengineered its payables, receiving clerks on the dock had to learn to use computer terminals to check shipments, and they had to make decisions about whether to accept the goods. Purchasing agents also had to assume new responsibilities – like making sure the purchase orders they entered into the database had the correct information about where to send the check. Attitudes toward vendors also had to change: vendors could no longer be seen as adversaries; they had to become partners in a shared business process. Vendors too had to adjust. In many cases, invoices formed the basis of their accounting systems. At least one Ford supplier adapted by continuing to print invoices, but instead of sending them to Ford threw them away, reconciling cash received against invoices never sent.

The changes at Mutual Benefit Life were also widespread. The company's job-rating scheme could not accommodate the case manager position, which had a lot of responsibility but no direct reports. MBL had to devise new job-rating schemes and compensation policies. It also had to develop a culture in which people doing work are perceived as more important than those supervising work. Career paths, recruitment and training programs, promotion policies – these and many other management systems are being revised to support the new process design.

The extent of these changes suggests one factor that is necessary for reengineering to succeed: executive leadership with real vision. No one in an organization wants reengineering. It is confusing and disruptive and affects everything people have grown accustomed to. Only if top-level managers back the effort and outlast the company cynics will people take reengineering seriously. As one wag at an electronics equipment manufacturer has commented, 'Every few months, our senior managers find a new religion. One time it was quality, another it was customer service, another it was flattening the organization. We just hold our breath until they get over it and things get back to normal.' Commitment, consistency – maybe even a touch of fanaticism – are needed to enlist those who would prefer the status quo.

Considering the inertia of old processes and structures, the strain of implementing a reengineering plan can hardly be overestimated. But by the same token, it is hard to overestimate the opportunities, especially for established companies. Big, traditional organizations aren't necessarily dinosaurs doomed to extinction, but they are burdened with layers of unproductive overhead and armies of unproductive workers. Shedding them a layer at a time will not be good enough to stand up against sleek start-ups or streamlined Japanese companies. US companies need fast change and dramatic improvements.

We have the tools to do what we need to do. Information technology offers many options for reorganizing work. But our imaginations must guide our decisions about technology – not the other way around. We must have the boldness to imagine taking 78 days out of an 80-day turnaround time, cutting 75 per cent of overhead, and eliminating 80 per cent of errors. These are not unrealistic goals. If managers have the vision, reengineering will provide a way.

READING

4.2

Kaizen

By Masaaki Imai[1]

B ack in the 1950s, I was working with the Japan Productivity Center in Washington, DC. My job mainly consisted of escorting groups of Japanese businessmen who were visiting American companies to study 'the secret of American industrial productivity'. Toshiro Yamada, now Professor Emeritus of the Faculty of Engineering at Kyoto University, was a member of one such study team visiting the United States to study the industrial vehicle industry. Recently, the members of his team gathered to celebrate the silver anniversary of their trip.

At the banquet table, Yamada said he had recently been back to the United States in a 'sentimental journey' to some of the plants he had visited, among them the River Rouge steelworks in Dearborn, Michigan. Shaking his head in disbelief, he said, 'You know, the plant was exactly the same as it had been 25 years ago.'

These conversations set me to thinking about the great differences in the ways Japanese and Western managers approach their work. It is inconceivable that a Japanese plant would remain virtually unchanged for over a quarter of a century.

I had long been looking for a key concept to explain these two very different management approaches, one that might also help explain why many Japanese companies have come to gain their increasingly conspicuous competitive edge. For instance, how do we explain the fact that while most new ideas come from the West and some of the most advanced plants, institutions, and technologies are found there, there are also many plants there that have changed little since the 1950s?

Change is something which everybody takes for granted. Recently, an American executive at a large multinational firm told me his company chairman had said at the start of an executive committee meeting: 'Gentlemen, our job is to manage change. If we fail, we must change management.' The executive smiled and said, 'We all got the message!'

In Japan, change is a way of life, too. But are we talking about the same change when we talk about managing change or else changing management? It dawned on me that there might be different kinds of change: gradual and abrupt. While we can easily observe both gradual and abrupt changes in Japan, gradual change is not so obvious a part of the Western way of life. How are we to explain this difference?

This question led me to consider the question of values. Could it be that differences between the value systems in Japan and the West account for their different attitudes toward gradual change and abrupt change? Abrupt changes are easily grasped by everyone concerned, and people are usually elated to see them. This is generally true in both Japan and the West. Yet what about the gradual changes? My earlier statement that it is inconceivable that a Japanese plant would remain unchanged for years refers to gradual change as well as abrupt change.

Thinking all this over, I came to the conclusion that the key difference between how change is understood in Japan and how it is viewed in the West lies in the Kaizen concept – a concept that is so natural and obvious to many Japanese managers that they often do not even realize that they possess it! The Kaizen concept explains why companies cannot remain the same for long in Japan. Moreover, after many years of studying Western business practices, I have reached the conclusion that this Kaizen concept is non-existent, or at least very weak, in most Western companies today. Worse yet, they reject it without knowing what it really entails. It's the old 'not invented here' syndrome. And this lack of Kaizen helps explain why an American or European factory can remain exactly the same for a quarter of a century.

The essence of Kaizen is simple and straightforward: Kaizen means improvement. Moreover, Kaizen means ongoing improvement involving everyone, including both managers and workers. The Kaizen philosophy assumes that our way of life – be it our working life, our social life, or our home life – deserves to be constantly improved.

In trying to understand Japan's post-war 'economic miracle,' scholars, journalists, and businesspeople alike have dutifully studied such factors as the productivity

[1]Source: This article was adapted with permission from Chapters 1 and 2 of *Kaizen: The Key to Japan's Competitive Success*, McGraw-Hill, New York, 1986.

movement, total quality control (TQC), small-group activities, the suggestion system, automation, industrial robots, and labour relations. They have given much attention to some of Japan's unique management practices, among them the lifetime employment system, seniority-based wages, and enterprise unions. Yet I feel they have failed to grasp the very simple truth that lies behind the many myths concerning Japanese management.

The essence of most 'uniquely Japanese' management practices – be they productivity improvement, TQC (total quality control) activities, QC (quality control) circles, or labour relations – can be reduced to one word: Kaizen. Using the term Kaizen in place of such words as productivity, TQC, ZD (zero defects), *kamban,* and the suggestion system paints a far clearer picture of what has been going on in Japanese industry. Kaizen is an umbrella concept covering most of those 'uniquely Japanese' practices that have recently achieved such world-wide fame.

The implications of TQC or CWQC (company-wide quality control) in Japan have been that these concepts have helped Japanese companies generate a process-oriented way of thinking and develop strategies that assure continuous improvement involving people at all levels of the organizational hierarchy. The message of the Kaizen strategy is that not a day should go by without some kind of improvement being made somewhere in the company.

The belief that there should be unending improvement is deeply ingrained in the Japanese mentality. As the old Japanese saying goes, 'If a man has not been seen for three days, his friends should take a good look at him to see what changes have befallen him.' The implication is that he must have changed in three days, so his friends should be attentive enough to notice the changes.

After World War II, most Japanese companies had to start literally from the ground up. Every day brought new challenges to managers and workers alike, and every day meant progress. Simply staying in business

required unending progress, and Kaizen has become a way of life. It was also fortunate that the various tools that helped elevate this Kaizen concept to new heights were introduced to Japan in the late 1950s and early 1960s by such experts as W.E. Deming and J.M. Juran.

However, most new concepts, systems, and tools that are widely used in Japan today have subsequently been developed in Japan and represent qualitative improvements upon the statistical quality control and total quality control of the 1960s.

Kaizen and management

Figure 4.2.1 shows how job functions are perceived in Japan. As indicated, management has two major components: maintenance and improvement. Maintenance refers to activities directed toward maintaining current technological, managerial, and operating standards; improvement refers to those directed toward improving current standards.

Under its maintenance functions, management performs its assigned tasks so that everybody in the company can follow the established SOP (Standard Operating Procedure). This means that management must first establish policies, rules, directives, and procedures for all major operations and then see to it that everybody follows SOP. If people are able to follow the standard but do not, management must introduce discipline. If people are unable to follow the standard, management must either provide training or review and revise the standard so that people can follow it.

In any business, an employee's work is based on existing standards, either explicit or implicit, imposed by management. Maintenance refers to maintaining such standards through training and discipline. By contrast, improvement refers to improving the standards. The Japanese perception of management boils down to one precept: maintain and improve standards.

The higher up the manager is, the more he is concerned with improvement. At the bottom level, an

---

FIGURE 4.2.1 Japanese perceptions of job functions

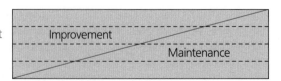

Top Management
Middle Management
Supervisors
Workers

Improvement

Maintenance

unskilled worker working at a machine may spend all his time following instructions. However, as he becomes more proficient at his work, he begins to think about improvement. He begins to contribute to improvements in the way his work is done, either through individual suggestions or through group suggestions.

Ask any manager at a successful Japanese company what top management is pressing for, and the answer will be, 'Kaizen' (improvement). Improving standards means establishing higher standards. Once this is done, it becomes management's maintenance job to see that the new standards are observed. Lasting improvement is achieved only when people work to higher standards. Maintenance and improvement have thus become inseparable for most Japanese managers.

What is improvement? Improvement can be broken down between Kaizen and innovation. Kaizen signifies small improvements made in the status quo as a result of ongoing efforts. Innovation involves a drastic improvement in the status quo as a result of a large investment in new technology or equipment. Figure 4.2.2 shows the breakdown among maintenance, Kaizen, and innovation as perceived by Japanese management.

On the other hand, most Western managers' perceptions of job functions are as shown in Figure 4.2.2. There is little room in Western management for the Kaizen concept.

Sometimes, another type of management is found in the high-technology industries. These are the companies that are born running, grow rapidly, and then disappear just as rapidly when their initial success wanes or markets change.

The worst companies are those which do nothing but maintenance, meaning there is no internal drive for Kaizen or innovation, change is forced on management by market conditions and competition and management does not know where it wants to go.

Implications of QC for Kaizen

While management is usually concerned with such issues as productivity and quality, the thrust of this article is to look at the other side of the picture – at Kaizen.

The starting point for improvement is to recognize the need. This comes from recognition of a problem. If no problem is recognized, there is no recognition of the need for improvement. Complacency is the archenemy of Kaizen. Therefore, Kaizen emphasizes problem-awareness and provides clues for identifying problems.

Once identified, problems must be solved. Thus Kaizen is also a problem-solving process. In fact, Kaizen requires the use of various problem-solving tools. Improvement reaches new heights with every problem that is solved. In order to consolidate the new level, however, the improvement must be standardized. Thus Kaizen also requires standardization.

Such terms as QC (quality control), SQC (statistical quality control), QC circles, and TQC (or CWQC) often appear in connection with Kaizen. To avoid unnecessary confusion, it may be helpful to clarify these terms here. The word *quality* has been interpreted in many different ways, and there is no agreement on what actually constitutes quality. In its broadest sense, quality is anything that can be improved. In this context, quality is associated not only with products and services but also with the way people work, the way machines are operated, and the way systems and procedures are dealt with. It includes all aspects of human behaviour. This is why it is more useful to talk about Kaizen than about quality or productivity.

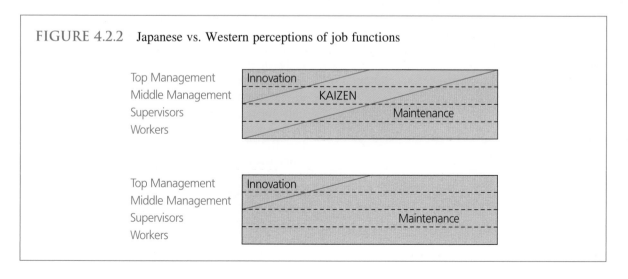

FIGURE 4.2.2   Japanese vs. Western perceptions of job functions

The English term *improvement* as used in the Western context more often than not means improvement in equipment, thus excluding the human elements. By contrast, Kaizen is generic and can be applied to every aspect of everybody's activities. This said, however, it must be admitted that such terms as quality and quality control have played a vital role in the development of Kaizen in Japan.

In March 1950, the Union of Japanese Scientists and Engineers (JUSE) started publishing its magazine *Statistical Quality Control*. In July of the same year, W.E. Deming was invited to Japan to teach statistical quality control at an eight-day seminar organized by JUSE. Deming visited Japan several times in the 1950s, and it was during one of those visits that he made his famous prediction that Japan would soon be flooding the world market with quality products.

Deming also introduced the 'Deming cycle', one of the crucial QC tools for assuring continuous improvement, to Japan. The Deming cycle is also called the Deming wheel or the PDCA (Plan-Do-Check-Action) cycle (see Figure 4.2.3.) Deming stressed the importance of constant interaction among research, design, production, and sales in order for a company to arrive at better quality that satisfies customers. He taught that this wheel should be rotated on the ground of quality-first perceptions and quality-first responsibility. With this process, he argued, the company could win consumer confidence and acceptance and prosper.

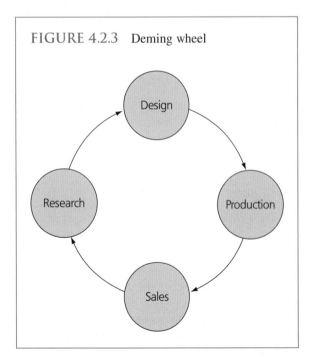

FIGURE 4.2.3   Deming wheel

In July 1954, J.M. Juran was invited to Japan to conduct a JUSE seminar on quality-control management. This was the first time QC was dealt with from the overall management perspective.

In 1956, Japan Shortwave Radio included a course on quality control as part of its educational programming. In November 1960, the first national quality month was inaugurated. It was also in 1960 that Q-marks and Q-flags were formally adopted. Then in April 1962 the magazine *Quality Control for the Foreman* was launched by JUSE, and the first QC circle was started that same year.

A QC circle is defined as a small group that *voluntarily* performs quality-control activities within the shop. The small group carries out its work continuously as part of a company-wide programme of quality control, self-development, mutual education, and flow-control and improvement within the workshop. The QC circle is only *part* of a company-wide programme; it is never the whole of TQC or CWQC.

Those who have followed QC circles in Japan know that they often focus on such areas as cost, safety, and productivity, and that their activities sometimes relate only indirectly to product-quality improvement. For the most part, these activities are aimed at making improvements in the workshop.

There is no doubt that QC circles have played an important part in improving product quality and productivity in Japan. However, their role has often been blown out of proportion by overseas observers who believe that QC circles are the mainstay of TQC activities in Japan. Nothing could be further from the truth, especially when it comes to Japanese management. Efforts related to QC circles generally account for only 10 per cent to 30 per cent of the overall TQC effort in Japanese companies.

What is less visible behind these developments is the transformation of the term quality control, or QC, in Japan. As is the case in many Western companies, quality control initially meant quality control applied to the manufacturing process, particularly the inspections for rejecting defective incoming material or defective outgoing products at the end of the production line. But very soon the realization set in that inspection alone does nothing to improve the quality of the product, and that product quality should be built at the production stage. 'Build quality into the process' was (and still is) a popular phrase in Japanese quality control. It is at this stage that control charts and the other tools for statistical quality control were introduced after Deming's lectures.

Juran's lectures in 1954 opened up another aspect of quality control: the managerial approach to quality control. This was the first time the term QC was positioned as a vital management tool in Japan. From then on, the term QC has been used to mean both quality control and the tools for overall improvement in managerial performance.

At a later stage, other industries started to introduce QC for such products as consumer durables and home appliances. In these industries, the interest was in building quality in at the design stage to meet changing and increasingly stringent customer requirements. Today, management has gone beyond the design stage and has begun to stress the importance of quality product development, which means taking customer-related information and market research into account from the very start.

All this while, QC has grown into a full-fledged management tool for Kaizen involving everyone in the company. Such company-wide activities are often referred to as TQC (total quality control) or CWQC (company-wide quality control). No matter which name is used, TQC and CWQC mean company-wide Kaizen activities involving everyone in the company, managers and workers alike. Over the years, QC has been elevated to SQC and then to TQC or CWQC, improving managerial performance at every level. Thus it is that such words as QC and TQC have come to be almost synonymous with Kaizen. This is also why I constantly refer to QC, TQC, and CWQC in explaining Kaizen.

On the other hand, the function of quality control in its original sense remains valid. Quality assurance remains a vital part of management, and most companies have a QA (quality assurance) department for this.

To confuse matters, TQC or CWQC activities are sometimes administered by the QA department and sometimes by a separate TQC office. Thus it is important that these QC-related words be understood in the context in which they appear.

Kaizen and TQC

Considering the TQC movement in Japan as part of the Kaizen movement gives us a clearer perspective on the Japanese approach. First of all, it should be pointed out that TQC activities in Japan are not concerned solely with quality control. People have been fooled by the term 'quality control' and have often construed it within the narrow discipline of product-quality control. In the West, the term QC is mostly associated with inspection of finished products, and when QC is brought up in discussion, top managers, who generally assume they have very little to do with quality control, lose interest immediately.

It is unfortunate that in the West TQC has been dealt with mainly in technical journals when it is more properly the focus of management journals. Japan has developed an elaborate system of Kaizen strategies as management tools within the TQC movement. These rank among this century's most outstanding management achievements. Yet because of the limited way in which QC is understood in the West, most Western students of Japanese QC activities have failed to grasp their real significance and challenge. At the same time, new TQC methods and tools are constantly being studied and tested.

TQC in Japan is a movement centered on the improvement of managerial performance at all levels. As such, it has typically dealt with:

1 quality assurance;
2 cost reduction;
3 meeting production quotas;
4 meeting delivery schedules;
5 safety;
6 new-product development;
7 productivity improvement;
8 supplier management.

More recently, TQC has come to include marketing, sales, and service as well. Furthermore, TQC has dealt with such crucial management concerns as organizational development, cross-functional management, policy deployment, and quality deployment. In other words, management has been using TQC as a tool for improving overall performance.

Those who have closely followed QC circles in Japan know that their activities are often focused on such areas as cost, safety and productivity, and that their activities may only indirectly relate to product-quality improvement. For the most part, these activities are aimed at making improvements in the workplace.

Management efforts for TQC have been directed mostly at such areas as education, systems development, policy deployment, cross-functional management and, more recently, quality deployment.

Kaizen and the suggestion system

Japanese management makes a concerted effort to involve employees in Kaizen through suggestions. Thus, the suggestion system is an integral part of the established management system, and the number of workers' suggestions is regarded as an important criterion in reviewing the performance of these workers' supervisor. The manager of the supervisors is in turn expected to assist them so that they can help workers generate more suggestions.

Most Japanese companies active in Kaizen programmes have a quality-control system and a suggestion system working in concert. The role of QC circles may be better understood if we regard them collectively as a group-oriented suggestion system for making improvements.

One of the outstanding features of Japanese management is that it generates a great number of suggestions from workers and that management works hard to consider these suggestions, often incorporating them into the overall Kaizen strategy. It is not uncommon for top management of a leading Japanese company to spend a whole day listening to presentations of activities by QC circles, and giving awards based on predetermined criteria. Management is willing to give recognition to employees' efforts for improvements and makes its concern visible wherever possible. Often, the number of suggestions is posted individually on the wall of the workplace in order to encourage competition among workers and among groups.

Another important aspect of the suggestion system is that each suggestion, once implemented, leads to a revised standard. For instance, when a special foolproof device has been installed on a machine at a worker's suggestion, this may require the worker to work differently and, at times, more attentively.

However, inasmuch as the new standard has been set up by the worker's own volition, he takes pride in the new standard and is willing to follow it. If, on the contrary, he is told to follow a standard imposed by management, he may not be as willing to follow it.

Thus, through suggestions, employees can participate in Kaizen in the workplace and play a vital role in upgrading standards. In a recent interview, Toyota Motor chairman Eiji Toyoda said, 'One of the features of the Japanese workers is that they use their brains as well as their hands. Our workers provide 1.5 million suggestions a year, and 95 per cent of them are put to practical use. There is an almost tangible concern for improvement in the air at Toyota.'

Kaizen vs. innovation

There are two contrasting approaches to progress: the gradualist approach and the great-leap-forward approach. Japanese companies generally favour the

gradualist approach and Western companies the great-leap approach – an approach epitomized by the term 'innovation'.

Western management worships at the altar of innovation. This innovation is seen as major changes in the wake of technological breakthroughs, or the introduction of the latest management concepts or production techniques. Innovation is dramatic, a real attention-getter. Kaizen, on the other hand, is often undramatic and subtle, and its results are seldom immediately visible. While Kaizen is a continuous process, innovation is generally a one-shot phenomenon.

In the West, for example, a middle manager can usually obtain top management support for such projects as CAD (computer-aided design), CAM (computer-aided manufacture), and MRP (materials requirements planning), since these are innovative projects that have a way of revolutionizing existing systems. As such, they offer ROI (return on investment) benefits that managers can hardly resist.

However, when a factory manager wishes, for example, to make small changes in the way his workers use the machinery, such as working out multiple job assignments or realigning production processes (both of which may require lengthy discussions with the union as well as reeducation and retraining of workers), obtaining management support can be difficult indeed.

Table 4.2.1 compares the main features of Kaizen and of innovation. One of the beautiful things about Kaizen is that it does not necessarily require sophisticated technique or state-of-the-art technology. To implement Kaizen, you need only simple, conventional techniques. Often, common sense is all that is needed. On the other hand, innovation usually requires highly sophisticated technology, as well as a huge investment.

Kaizen is like a hotbed that nurtures small and ongoing changes, while innovation is like magma that appears in abrupt eruptions from time to time. One big difference between Kaizen and innovation is that while Kaizen does not necessarily call for a large investment to implement it, it does call for a great deal of continuous effort and commitment. The difference between the two opposing concepts may thus be likened to that of a staircase and a slope. The innovation strategy is supposed to bring about progress in a staircase progression. On the other hand, the Kaizen strategy brings about gradual progress. I say the innovation strategy 'is supposed to' bring about progress in a staircase progression, because it usually does not. Instead of following the staircase pattern, the actual progress achieved through innovation will generally follow the pattern shown in Figure 4.2.4, if it lacks the

TABLE 4.2.1   Features of Kaizen and innovation

	Kaizen	*Innovation*
1. Effect	Long-term and long-lasting but undramatic	Short-term but dramatic
2. Pace	Small steps	Big steps
3. Timeframe	Continuous and incremental	Intermittent and non-incremental
4. Change	Gradual and constant	Abrupt and volatile
5. Involvement	Everybody	Select few 'champions'
6. Approach	Collectivism, group efforts, systems approach	Rugged individualism, individual ideas and efforts
7. Mode	Maintenance and improvement	Scrap and rebuild
8. Spark	Conventional know-how and state of the art	Technological break-throughs, new inventions, new theories
9. Practical requirements	Requires little investment but great effort to maintain it	Requires large investment but little effort to maintain it
10. Effort orientation	People	Technology
11. Evaluation criteria	Process and efforts for better results	Results and profits
12. Advantage	Works well in slow-growth economy	Better suited to fast-growth economy

Kaizen strategy to go along with it. This happens because a system, once it has been installed as a result of new innovation, is subject to steady deterioration unless continuing efforts are made first to maintain it and then to improve on it.

In reality, there can be no such thing as a static constant. All systems are destined to deteriorate once they have been established. One of the famous Parkinson's Laws is that an organization, once it has built its edifice, begins its decline. In other words, there must be a continuing effort for improvement to even maintain the status quo.

When such effort is lacking, decline is inevitable (see Figure 4.2.4). Therefore, even when an innovation makes a revolutionary standard of performance attainable, the new performance level will decline unless the standard is constantly challenged and upgraded. Thus, whenever an innovation is achieved, it must be followed by a series of Kaizen efforts to maintain and improve it (see Figure 4.2.5).

Whereas innovation is a one-shot deal whose effects are gradually eroded by intense competition and deteriorating standards, Kaizen is an ongoing effort with cumulative effects marking a steady rise as the years go by. If standards exist only in order to maintain the status quo, they will not be challenged so long as the level of performance is acceptable. Kaizen, on the other hand, means a constant effort not only to

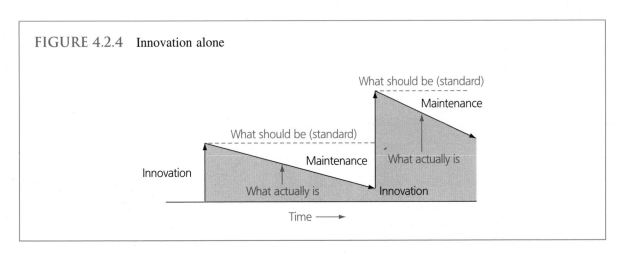

FIGURE 4.2.4   Innovation alone

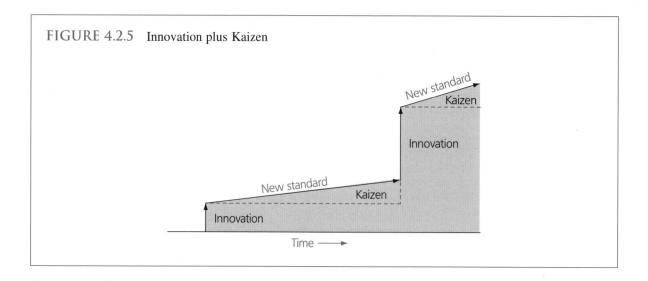

FIGURE 4.2.5   Innovation plus Kaizen

maintain but also to upgrade standards. Kaizen strat-egists believe that standards are by nature tentative, akin to stepping stones, with one standard leading to another as continuing improvement efforts are made. This is the reason why QC circles no sooner solve one problem than they move on to tackle a new problem. This is also the reason why the so-called PDCA (plan–do–check–action) cycle receives so much emphasis in Japan's TQC movement.

Another feature of Kaizen is that it requires vir-tually everyone's personal efforts. In order for the Kaizen spirit to survive, management must make a conscious and continuous effort to support it. Such support is quite different from the fanfare recognition that management accords to people who have achieved a striking success or breakthrough. Kaizen is con-cerned more with the process than with the result. The strength of Japanese management lies in its successful development and implementation of a system that ac-knowledges the ends while emphasizing the means.

Thus Kaizen calls for a substantial management commitment of time and effort. Infusions of capital are no substitute for this investment in time and effort.

Investing in Kaizen means investing in people. In short, Kaizen is people-oriented, whereas innovation is technology- and money-oriented.

Finally, the Kaizen philosophy is better suited to a slow-growth economy, while innovation is better suited to a fast-growth economy. While Kaizen advances inch-by-inch on the strength of many small efforts, in-novation leaps upward in hopes of landing at a much higher plateau in spite of gravitational inertia and the weight of investment costs. In a slow-growth economy characterized by high costs of energy and materials,

overcapacity, and stagnant markets, Kaizen often has a better payoff than innovation does. As one Japanese executive recently remarked, 'It is extremely difficult to increase sales by 10 per cent. But it is not so difficult to cut manufacturing costs by 10 per cent to even better effect.'

I argued that the concept of Kaizen is nonexistent or at best weak in most Western companies today. How-ever, there was a time, not so long ago, when Western management also placed a high priority on Kaizen-like improvement-consciousness. Older executives may recall that before the phenomenal economic growth of the late 1950s and early 1960s, management attended assiduously to improving all aspects of the business, particularly the factory. In those days, every small improvement was counted and was seen as effective in terms of building success.

People who worked with small, privately owned companies may recall with a touch of nostalgia that there was a genuine concern for improvement 'in the air' before the company was bought out or went pub-lic. As soon as that happened, the quarterly P/L (profit/loss) figures suddenly became the most important cri-terion, and management became obsessed with the bottom line, often at the expense of pressing for con-stant and unspectacular improvements.

For many other companies, the greatly increased market opportunities and technological innovations that appeared during the first two decades after World War II meant that developing new products based on the new technology was much more attractive or 'sexier' than slow, patient efforts for improvement. In trying to catch up with the ever-increasing market de-mand, managers boldly introduced one innovation after another, and they were content to ignore the seemingly minor benefits of improvement.

Most Western managers who joined the ranks during or after those heady days do not have the slightest concern for improvement. Instead, they take an offensive posture, armed with professional expertise geared toward making big changes in the name of innovation, bringing about immediate gains, and winning instant recognition and promotion. Before they knew it, Western managers had lost sight of improvement and put all their eggs in the innovation basket.

Another factor that has abetted the innovation approach has been the increasing emphasis on financial controls and accounting. By now, the more sophisticated companies have succeeded in establishing elaborate accounting and reporting systems that force managers to account for every action they take and to spell out the precise payout or ROI of every

managerial decision. Such a system does not lend itself to building a favourable climate for improvement.

Improvement is by definition slow, gradual, and often invisible, with effects that are felt over the long run. In my opinion, the most glaring and significant shortcoming of Western management today is the lack of improvement philosophy. There is no internal system in Western management to reward efforts for improvement; instead, everyone's job performance is reviewed strictly on the basis of results. Thus it is not uncommon for Western managers to chide people with, 'I don't care what you do or how you do it. I want the results – and now!' This emphasis on results has led to the innovation-dominated approach of the West. This is not to say that Japanese management does not care about innovation. But Japanese managers have enthusiastically pursued Kaizen even when they were involved in innovation.

READING 4.3

Ambidextrous organizations: Managing evolutionary and revolutionary change

By Michael L. Tushman and Charles A. O'Reilly III[1]

All managers face problems in overcoming inertia and implementing innovation and change. But why is this problem such an enduring one? Organizations are filled with sensible people and usually led by smart managers. Why is anything but incremental change often so difficult for the most successful organizations? And why are the patterns of success and failure so prevalent across industries and over time? To remain successful over long periods, managers and organizations must be ambidextrous – able to implement both incremental and revolutionary change.

Patterns in organization evolution

Across industries there is a pattern in which success often precedes failure. But industry-level studies aren't very helpful for illustrating what actually went wrong. Why are managers sometimes ineffective in making

the transition from strength to strength? To understand this we need to look inside firms and understand the forces impinging on management as they wrestle with managing innovation and change. To do this, let's examine the history of two firms, RCA semiconductors and Seiko watches, as they dealt with the syndrome of success followed by failure.

The stark reality of the challenge of discontinuous change can be seen in Figure 4.3.1. This is a listing of the leading semiconductor firms over a 40-year period. In the mid-1950s, vacuum tubes represented roughly a $ 700 million market. At this time, the leading firms in the then state-of-the-art technology of vacuum tubes included great technology companies such as RCA, Sylvania, Raytheon, and Westinghouse. Yet between 1955 and 1995, there was almost a complete turnover in industry leadership. With the advent of the transistor, a major technological discontinuity, we see the

[1]Source: This article © 1996. Tushman, M.L., and O'Reilly III, C.A. (1996) 'Ambidextrous Organizations: Managing Evolutionary and Revolutionary Change', *California Management Review*, Vol. 38, No. 4, Summer, pp. 8–30.

beginnings of a remarkable shake-out. By 1965, new firms such as Motorola and Texas Instruments had become important players while Sylvania and RCA had begun to fade. Over the next 20 years still other upstart companies like Intel, Toshiba, and Hitachi became the new leaders while Sylvania and RCA exited the product class.

Why should this pattern emerge? Is it that managers and technologists in 1955 in firms like Westinghouse, RCA, and Sylvania didn't understand the technology? This seems implausible. In fact, many vacuum tube producers did enter the transistor market, suggesting that they not only understood the technology, but saw it as important. RCA was initially successful at making the transition. While from the outside it appeared that they had committed themselves to transistors, the inside picture was very different.

Within RCA, there were bitter disputes about whether the company should enter the transistor business and cannibalize their profitable tube business. On one side, there were reasonable arguments that the transistor business was new and the profits uncertain. Others, without knowing whether transistors would be successful, felt that it was too risky not to pursue the new technology. But even if RCA were to enter the solid-state business, there were thorny issues about how to organize it within the company. How could they manage both technologies? Should the solid-state division report to the head of the electronics group, a person steeped in vacuum tube expertise?

With its great wealth of marketing, financial, and technological resources, RCA decided to enter the business. Historically, it is common for successful firms to experiment with new technologies. Xerox, for example, developed user-interface and software technologies, yet left it to Apple and Microsoft to implement them. Western Union developed the technology for telephony and allowed American Bell (AT&T) to capture the benefits. Almost all relatively wealthy firms can afford to explore new technologies. Like many firms before them, RCA management recognized the problems of trying to play two different technological games but were ultimately unable to resolve them. In the absence of a clear strategy and the cultural differences required to compete in both markets, RCA failed.

In his study of this industry, Richard Foster (then a Director at McKinsey & Company) notes, 'Of the 10 leaders in vacuum tubes in 1955 only two were left in 1975. There were three variants of error in these case histories. First is the decision not to invest in the new technology. The second is to invest but picking the wrong technology. The third variant is cultural. Companies failed because of their inability to play two games at once: To be both effective defenders of what quickly became old technologies and effective attackers with new technologies.' Senior managers in these firms fell victim to their previous success and their inability to play two games simultaneously. New firms, like Intel and Motorola, were not saddled with this internal conflict and inertia. As they grew, they

---

FIGURE 4.3.1 Semiconductor industry 1955–1995

	1955 (Vacuum Tubes)	1955 (Transistors)	1965 (Semi-conductors)	1975 (Integrated Circuits)	1982 (VLSI)	1995 (Submicron)
1.	RCA	Hughes	TI	TI	Motorola	Intel
2.	Sylvania	Transitron	Fairchild	Fairchild	TI	NEC
3.	General Electric	Philco	Motorola	National	NEC	Toshiba
4.	Raytheon	Sylvania	GI	Intel	Hitachi	Hitachi
5.	Westinghouse	TI	GE	Motorola	National	Motorola
6.	Amperex	GE	RCA	Rockwell	Toshiba	Samsung
7.	National Video	RCA	Sprague	GI	Lntel	TI
8.	Rawland	Westinghouse	Philco	RCA	Philips	Fujitsu
9.	Eimac	Motorola	Transitron	Philips	Fujitsu	Mitsubishi
10.	Lansdale	Clevite	Raytheon	AMD	Fairchild	Philips

Source: Adapted from R. Foster, *Innovation: The Attacker's Advantage* (New York, NY 1986).

were able to re-create themselves, while other firms remained trapped.

In contrast to RCA, consider Hattori-Seiko's watch business. While Seiko was the dominant Japanese watch producer in the 1960s, they were a small player in global markets. Bolstered by an aspiration to be a global leader in the watch business, and informed by internal experimentation between alternative oscillation technologies (quartz, mechanical, and tuning fork), Seiko's senior management team made a bold bet. In the mid-1960s, Seiko transformed itself from being merely a mechanical watch firm into being both a quartz and mechanical watch company. This move into low-cost, high-quality watches triggered wholesale change within Seiko and, in turn, within the world-wide watch industry. As transistors replaced vacuum tubes (to RCA's chagrin), quartz movement watches replaced mechanical watches. Even though the Swiss had invented both the quartz and tuning fork movements, at this juncture in history they moved to reinvest in mechanical movements. As Seiko and other Japanese firms prospered, the Swiss watch industry drastically suffered. By 1980, SSIH, the largest Swiss watch firm, was less than half the size of Seiko. Eventually, SSIH and Asuag, the two largest Swiss firms, went bankrupt. It would not be until after these firms were taken over by the Swiss banks and transformed by Nicholas Hayek that the Swiss would move to recapture the watch market.

The real test of leadership, then, is to be able to compete successfully by both increasing the alignment or fit among strategy, structure, culture, and processes, while simultaneously preparing for the inevitable revolutions required by discontinuous environmental change. This requires organizational and management skills to compete in a mature market (where cost, efficiency, and incremental innovation are key) *and* to develop new products and services (where radical innovation, speed, and flexibility are critical). A focus on either one of these skill sets is conceptually easy. Unfortunately, focusing on only one guarantees short-term success but long-term failure. Managers need to be able to do both at the same time, that is, they need to be ambidextrous. Juggling provides a metaphor. A juggler who is very good at manipulating a single ball is not interesting. It is only when the juggler can handle multiple balls at one time that his or her skill is respected.

These short examples are only two illustrations of the pattern by which organizations evolve: periods of incremental change punctuated by discontinuous or revolutionary change. Long-term success is marked by increasing alignment among strategy, structure, people, and culture through incremental or evolutionary change punctuated by discontinuous or revolutionary change that requires the simultaneous shift in strategy, structure, people, and culture. These discontinuous changes are almost always driven either by organizational performance problems or by major shifts in the organization's environment, such as technological or competitive shifts. Where those less successful firms (e.g., SSIH, RCA) react to environmental jolts, those more successful firms proactively initiate innovations that reshape their market (e.g., Seiko).

What's happening? Understanding patterns of organizational evolution

These patterns in organization evolution are not unique. Almost all successful organizations evolve through relatively long periods of incremental change punctuated by environmental shifts and revolutionary change. These discontinuities may be driven by technology, competitors, regulatory events, or significant changes in economic and political conditions. For example, deregulation in the financial services and airline industries led to waves of mergers and failures as firms scrambled to reorient themselves to the new competitive environment. Major political changes in Eastern Europe and South Africa have had a similar impact. The combination of the European Union and the emergence of global competition in the automobile and electronics industries has shifted the basis of competition in these markets. Technological change in microprocessors has altered the face of the computer industry.

The sobering fact is that the cliché about the increasing pace of change seems to be true. Sooner or later, discontinuities upset the congruence that has been a part of the organization's success. Unless their competitive environment remains stable – an increasingly unlikely condition in today's world – firms must confront revolutionary change. The underlying cause of this pattern can be found in an unlikely place: evolutionary biology.

Innovation patterns over time

For many years, biological evolutionary theory proposed that the process of adaptation occurred gradually over long time periods. The process was assumed to be one of variation, selection, and retention. Variations occurred naturally within species across generations. Those variations that were most adapted to the environment would, over time, enable a species to survive and reproduce. This form would be selected in that it endured while less adaptable forms reproduced less productively and would diminish over time. For instance, if the world became colder and snowier, animals who were whiter and had heavier coats would be advantaged and more likely to survive. As climatic changes affected vegetation, those species with longer necks or stronger beaks might do better. In this way, variation led to adaptation and fitness, which was subsequently retained across generations. In this early view, the environment changed gradually and species adapted slowly to these changes. There is ample evidence that this view has validity.

But this perspective missed a crucial question: What happened if the environment was characterized, not by gradual change, but periodic discontinuities? What about rapid changes in temperature, or dramatic shifts in the availability of food? Under these conditions, a reliance on gradual change was a one-way ticket to extinction. Instead of slow change, discontinuities required a different version of Darwinian theory – that of punctuated equilibria in which long periods of gradual change were interrupted periodically by massive discontinuities. What then? Under these conditions, survival or selection goes to those species with the characteristics needed to exploit the new environment. Evolution progresses through long periods of incremental change punctuated by brief periods of revolutionary or discontinuous change.

So it seems to be with organizations. An entire subfield of research on organizations has demonstrated many similarities between populations of insects and animals and populations of organizations. This field, known as 'organizational ecology', has successfully applied models of population ecology to the study of sets of organizations in areas as diverse as wineries, newspapers, automobiles, biotech companies, and restaurants. The results confirm that populations of organizations are subject to ecological pressures in which they evolve through periods of incremental adaptation punctuated by discontinuities. Variations in organizational strategy and form are more or less suitable for different environmental conditions. Those organizations and managers who are most able to adapt to a given market or competitive environment will prosper. Over time, the fittest survive – until there is a major discontinuity. At that point, managers of firms are faced with the challenge of reconstituting their organizations to adjust to the new environment. Managers who try to adapt to discontinuities through incremental adjustment are unlikely to succeed. The

processes of variation, selection, and retention that winnow the fittest of animal populations seem to apply to organizations as well.

To understand how this dynamic affects organizations, we need to consider two fundamental ideas; how organizations grow and evolve, and how discontinuities affect this process. Armed with this understanding, we can then show how managers can cope with evolutionary and revolutionary change.

Organizational growth and evolution. There is a pattern that describes organizational growth. All organizations evolve following the familiar S-curve. For instance, consider the history of Apple Computer and how it grew. In its inception, Apple was not so much an organization as a small group of people trying to design, produce, and sell a new product, the personal computer. With success, came the beginnings of a formal organization, assigned roles and responsibilities, some rudimentary systems for accounting and payroll, and a culture based on the shared expectations among employees about innovation, commitment, and speed. Success at this stage was seen in terms of congruence among the strategy, structure, people, and culture. Those who fit the Apple values and subscribed to the cultural norms stayed. Those who found the Jobs and Wozniak vision too cultish left. This early structure was aligned with the strategy and the critical tasks needed to implement it. Success flowed not only from having a new product with desirable features, but also from the ability of the organization to design, manufacture, market, and distribute the new PC. The systems in place tracked those outcomes and processes that were important for the implementation of a single product strategy. Congruence among the elements of the organization is a key to high performance across industries.

As the firm continued its successful growth, several inexorable changes occurred. First, it got larger. As this occurred, more structure and systems were added. Although this trend toward professionalization was resisted by Jobs (who referred to professional managers as 'bozos'), the new structures and procedures were required for efficiency and control. Without them, chaos would have reigned. As Apple got older, new norms were developed about what was important and acceptable and what would not be tolerated. The culture changed to reflect the new challenges. Success at Apple and at other firms is based on learning what works and what doesn't.

Inevitably, even Apple's strategy had to change. What used to be a single-product firm (selling the Apple PC and then its successor, the Apple II) now sold a broader range of products in increasingly competitive markets. Instead of a focused strategy, the emphasis shifted to a market-wide emphasis. Not only was Apple selling to personal computer users, but also to the educational and industrial markets. This strategic shift required further adjustment to the structure, people, culture, and critical tasks. What worked in a smaller, more focused firm was no longer adequate for the larger, more differentiated Apple. Success at this phase of evolution required management's ability to realign the organization to insure congruence with the strategy. The well-publicized ouster of Steve Jobs by Apple's board of directors reflected the board's judgement that John Sculley had the skills necessary to lead a larger, more diversified company. Jobs's approach was fine for a smaller, more focused firm but inappropriate for the challenges Apple faced in the mid-1980s.

Over an even longer period of success, there are inevitably more changes – sometimes driven by technology, sometimes by competition, customers, or regulation, sometimes by new strategies and ways of competing. As the product class matures, the basis of competition shifts. While in the early stages of a product class, competition is based on product variation, in the later stages competition shifts to features, efficiency, and cost. In the evolution of Apple, this can be seen as the IBM PC and the clones emerged. The Windows operating system loosened the grip Apple had maintained on the easy-to-use graphical interface and triggered a battle between three incompatible operating systems – the Mac, IBM's OS/2, and Microsoft Windows. Once Windows became the industry standard in operating systems, the basis of competition shifted to cost, quality and efficiency. Faced with these realities, Apple managers once again had to re-balance the congruence among strategy, structure, people, and culture. Success comes from being able to outdo the competition in this new environment. So the board of directors replaced Sculley as CEO in 1994 with Michael Spindler, who was seen as having the operational skills needed to run the company in a mature market. Spindler's task was to emphasize the efficiencies and lower margins required in today's markets and reshape Apple to compete in this new market. With Apple's performance stagnant, its board chose a turnaround expert, Gil Amelio, to finish what Spindler could not do.

Notice how Apple evolved over a 20-year period. Incremental or evolutionary change was punctuated by discontinuous or revolutionary change as the firm moved through the three stages of growth in the product class; innovation, differentiation, and maturity. Each of these stages required different competencies, strategies, structures, cultures, and leadership skills. These changes are what drives performance. But while absolutely necessary for short-term success, incremental change is not sufficient for long-term success. It is not by chance that Steve Jobs was successful at Apple until the market became more differentiated and demanded the skills of John Sculley. Nor is it surprising that, as the industry consolidated and competition emphasized costs, operations-oriented managers such as Michael Spindler and, in turn, Gil Amelio were selected to reorient Apple.

To succeed over the long haul, firms have to periodically reorient themselves by adopting new strategies and structures that are necessary to accommodate changing environmental conditions. These shifts often occur through discontinuous changes – simultaneous shifts in strategy, structures, skills, and culture. If an environment is stable and changes only gradually, as is the case in industries such as cement, it is possible for an organization to evolve slowly through continuous incremental change. But, many managers have learned (to their stockholders' chagrin) that slow evolutionary change in a fast-changing world is, as it was for the dinosaurs, a path to the boneyard.

Technology cycles. Although organizational growth by itself can lead to a periodic need for discontinuous change, there is another more fundamental process occurring that results in punctuated change. This is a pervasive phenomenon that occurs across industries and is not widely appreciated by managers. Yet it is critical to understanding when and why revolutionary change is necessary: This is the dynamic of product, service, and process innovation, dominant designs, and substitution events which together make up technology cycles. Figure 4.3.2 shows the general outline of this process.

In any product or service class (e.g., microprocessors, automobiles, baby diapers, cash management accounts) there is a common pattern of competition that describes the development of the class over time. As shown in Figure 4.3.2, technology cycles begin with a proliferation of innovation in products or services as the new product or service gains acceptance. Think, for example, of the introduction of VCRs. Initially, only a few customers bought them. Over time, as demand increased, there was increasing competition between Beta and VHS. At some point, a design emerged that became the standard preferred by customers (i.e., VHS). Once this occurred, the basis of competition shifted to price and features, not basic product or service design. The emergence of this *dominant design* transforms

FIGURE 4.3.2 Two invisible forces: technology cycles and evolution

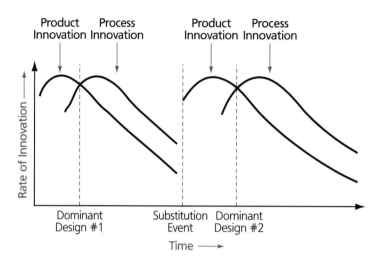

Source: Adapted from J. Utterback, *Mastering the Dynamics of Innovation* (Boston, MA; Harvard Business School Press, 1994).

competition in the product class. Once it is clear that a dominant design has emerged, the basis of competition shifts to process innovation, driving down costs, and adding features. Instead of competing through product or service innovation, successful strategies now emphasize compatibility with the standard and productivity improvement. This competition continues until there is a major new product, service, or process substitution event and the technology cycle kicks off again as the basis of competition shifts back again to product or service variation (e.g., CDs replacing audio tapes). As technology cycles evolve, bases of competition shift within the market. As organizations change their strategies, they must also realign their organizations to accomplish the new strategic objectives. This usually requires a revolutionary change.

A short illustration from the development of the automobile will help show how dramatic these changes can be for organizations. At the turn of the century, bicycles and horse-driven carriages were threatened by the 'horseless carriage', soon to be called the automobile. Early in this new product class there was substantial competition among alternative technologies. For instance, there were several competing alternative energy sources – steam, battery, and internal combustion engines. There were also different steering mechanisms and arrangements for passenger compartments. In a fairly short period of time, however, there emerged a consensus that certain features were to be standard – that is, a dominant design emerged. This

consisted of an internal combustion engine, steering wheel on the left (in the US), brake pedal on the right, and clutch on the left (this dominant design was epitomized in the Ford Model T). Once this standard emerged, the basis of competition shifted from variations in what an automobile looked like and how it was powered to features and cost. The new competitive arena emphasized lower prices and differentiated market segments, not product variation. The imperative for managers was to change their strategies and organizations to compete in this market. Those that were unable to manage this transition failed. Similar patterns can be seen in almost all product classes (e.g., computers, telephones, fast foods, retail stores).

With a little imagination, it is easy to feel what the managerial challenges are in this environment. Holding aside the pressures of growth and success, managers must continually readjust their strategies and realign their organizations to reflect the underlying dynamics of technological change in their markets. These changes are not driven by fad or fashion but reflect the imperatives of fundamental change in the technology. This dynamic is a powerful cause of punctuated equilibria and can demand revolutionary rather than incremental change. This pattern occurs across industries as diverse as computers and cement, the only issue is the frequency with which these cycles repeat themselves. Faced with a discontinuity, the option of incremental change is not likely to be viable. The danger is that, facing a discontinuous change, firms that have been successful may suffer from life-threatening inertia – inertia that results from the very congruence that made the firm successful in the first place.

The success syndrome: Congruence as a managerial trap

Successful companies learn what works well and incorporate this into their operations. This is what organizational learning is about; using feedback from the market to continually refine the organization to get better and better at accomplishing its mission. A lack of congruence (or internal inconsistency in strategy, structure, culture, and people) is usually associated with a firm's current performance problems. Further, since the fit between strategy, structure, people, and processes is never perfect, achieving congruence is an ongoing process requiring continuous improvement and incremental change. With evolutionary change, managers are able to incrementally alter their organizations. Given that these changes are comparatively small, the incongruence injected by the change is controllable. The process of making incremental changes is well known and the uncertainly created for people affected by such changes is within tolerable limits. The overall system adapts, but it is not transformed.

When done effectively, evolutionary change of this sort is a crucial part of short-term success. But there is a dark side to this success. As we described with Apple, success resulted in the company becoming larger and older. Older, larger firms develop structural and cultural inertia – the organizational equivalent of high cholesterol. As companies grow, they develop structures and systems to handle the increased complexity of the work. These structures and systems are interlinked so that proposed changes become more difficult, more costly, and require more time to implement, especially if they are more than small, incremental modifications. This results in *structural inertia* – a resistance to change rooted in the size, complexity, and interdependence in the organization's structures, systems, procedures, and processes.

Quite different and significantly more pervasive than structural inertia is the *cultural inertia* that comes from age and success. As organizations get older, part of their learning is embedded in the shared expectations about how things are to be done. These are sometimes seen in the informal norms, values, social networks and in myths, stories, and heroes that have evolved over time. The more successful an organization has been, the more institutionalized or ingrained these norms, values, and lessons become. The more institutionalized these norms, values, and stories are, the greater the cultural inertia – the greater the organizational complacency and arrogance. In relatively stable environments, the firm's culture is a critical component of its success. Culture is an effective way of controlling and coordinating people without elaborate and rigid formal control systems. Yet, when confronted with discontinuous change, the very culture that fostered success can quickly become a significant barrier to change. When Lou Gerstner took over as CEO at IBM, he recognized that simply crafting a new strategy was not the solution to IBM's predicament. In his view, 'Fixing the culture is the most critical – and the most difficult – part of a corporate transformation.' Cultural inertia, because it is so ephemeral and difficult to attack directly, is a key reason managers often fail to successfully introduce revolutionary change – even when they know that it is needed.

Ambidextrous organizations: Mastering evolutionary and revolutionary change

The dilemma confronting managers and organizations is clear. In the short run they must constantly increase the fit or alignment of strategy, structure, and culture. This is the world of evolutionary change. But this is not enough for sustained success. In the long run, managers may be required to destroy the very alignment that has made their organizations successful. For managers, this means operating part of the time in a world characterized by periods of relative stability and incremental innovation, and part of the time in a world characterized by revolutionary change. These contrasting managerial demands require that managers periodically destroy what has been created in order to reconstruct a new organization better suited for the next wave of competition or technology.

Ambidextrous organizations are needed if the success paradox is to be overcome. The ability to simultaneously pursue both incremental and discontinuous innovation and change results from hosting multiple contradictory structures, processes, and cultures within the same firm. There are good examples of companies and managers who have succeeded in balancing these tensions. To illustrate more concretely how firms can do this, consider three successful ambidextrous organizations, Hewlett-Packard, Johnson & Johnson, and ABB (Asea Brown Boveri). Each of these has been able to compete in mature market segments through incremental innovation and in emerging markets and technologies through discontinuous innovation. Each has been successful at winning by engaging in both evolutionary and revolutionary change.

At one level they are very different companies. HP competes in markets like instruments, computers, and networks. J&J is in consumer products, pharmaceuticals, and professional medical products ranging from sutures to endoscopic surgical equipment. ABB sells power plants, electrical transmission equipment, transportation systems, and environmental controls. Yet each of them has been able to periodically renew itself and to produce streams of innovation. HP has gone from an instrument company to a minicomputer firm to a personal computer and network company. J&J has moved from consumer products to pharmaceuticals. ABB transformed itself from a slow heavy engineering company based primarily in Sweden and Switzerland to an aggressive global competitor with major investments in Eastern Europe and the Far East. In spite of their differences, each has been ambidextrous in similar ways.

Organizational architectures

Although the combined size of these three companies represents over 350 000 employees, each has found a common way to remain small by emphasizing autonomous groups. For instance, J&J has over 165 separate operating companies that scramble relentlessly for new products and markets. ABB relies on over 5,000 profit centres with an average of 50 people in each. These centres operate like small businesses. HP has over 50 separate divisions and a policy of splitting divisions whenever a unit gets larger than a thousand or so people. The logic in these organizations is to keep units small and autonomous so that employees feel a sense of ownership and are responsible for their own results. This encourages a culture of autonomy and risk taking that could not exist in a large, centralized organization. In the words of Ralph Larsen, CEO of J&J, this approach 'provides a sense of ownership and responsibility for a business you simply cannot get any other way'.

But the reliance on small, autonomous units are not gained at the expense of firm size or speed in execution. These companies also retain the benefits of size, especially in marketing and manufacturing. ABB continually reevaluates where it locates its worldwide manufacturing sites. J&J uses its brand name and marketing might to leverage new products and

technologies. HP uses its relationships with retailers developed from its printer business to market and distribute its new personal computer line. But these firms accomplish this without the top-heavy staffs found at other firms. Barnevik reduced ABB's hierarchy to four levels and a headquarters staff of 150 and purposely keeps the structure fluid. At J&J headquarters, there are roughly a thousand people, but no strategic planning is done by corporate. The role of the centre is to set the vision and review the performance of the 165 operating companies. At HP, the former CEO, John Young, recognized in the early 1990s that the more centralized structure that HP had adopted in the 1980s to coordinate their minicomputer business had resulted in a suffocating bureaucracy that was no longer appropriate. He wiped it out, flattening the hierarchy and dramatically reducing the role of the centre.

In these companies, size is used to leverage economies of scale and scope, not to become a checker and controller that slows the organization down. The focus is on keeping decisions as close to the customer or the technology as possible. The role of headquarters is to facilitate operations and make them go faster and better. Staff have only the expertise that the field wants and needs. Reward systems are designed to be appropriate to the nature of the business unit and emphasize results and risk taking. Barnevik characterizes this as his 7–3 formula; better to make decisions quickly and be right seven out of ten times than waste time trying to find a perfect solution. At J&J this is expressed as a tolerance for certain types of failure; a tolerance that extends to congratulating managers who take informed risks, even if they fail. There is a delicate balance among size, autonomy, teamwork, and speed which these ambidextrous organizations are able to engineer. An important part of the solution is massive decentralization of decision-making, but with consistency attained through individual accountability, information sharing, and strong financial control. But why doesn't this result in fragmentation and a loss of synergy? The answer is found in the use of social control.

Multiple cultures

A second commonality across these firms is their reliance on strong social controls. They are simultaneously tight and loose. They are tight in that the corporate culture in each is broadly shared and emphasizes norms critical for innovation such as openness, autonomy, initiative, and risk taking. The culture is loose in that the manner in which these common values are expressed varies according to the type of innovation required. At HP, managers value the openness and consensus needed to develop new technologies. Yet, when implementation is critical, managers recognize that this consensus can be fatal. One senior manager in charge of bringing out a new workstation prominently posted a sign saying, 'This is not a democracy.' At J&J, the emphasis on autonomy allows managers to routinely go against the wishes of senior management, sometimes with big successes and sometimes with failures. Yet, in the changing hospital supply sector of their business, managers recognized that the cherished J&J autonomy was stopping these companies from coordinating the service demanded by their hospital customers. So, in this part of J&J, a decision was made to take away some of the autonomy and centralize services. CEO Larsen refers to this as J&J companies having common standards but unique personalities.

A common overall culture is the glue that holds these companies together. The key in these firms is a reliance on a strong, widely shared corporate culture to promote integration across the company and to encourage identification and sharing of information and resources – something that would never occur without shared values. The culture also provides consistency and promotes trust and predictability. Whether it is the Credo at J&J, the HP Way, or ABB's Policy Bible, these norms and values provide the glue that keeps these organizations together. Yet, at the same time, individual units entertain widely varying subcultures appropriate to their particular businesses. For example, although the HP Way is visible in all HP units worldwide, there are distinct differences between the new video server unit and an old line instrument division. What constitutes risk taking at a mature division is different than the risk taking emphasized at a unit struggling with a brand new technology. At J&J, the Credo's emphasis on customers and employees can be seen as easily in the Philippines as in corporate headquarters in New Brunswick, New Jersey. But the operating culture in the Tylenol division is distinctly more conservative than the culture in a new medical products company.

This tight–loose aspect of the culture is crucial for ambidextrous organizations. It is supported by a -common vision and by supportive leaders who both encourage the culture and know enough to allow appropriate variations to occur across business units. These companies promote both local autonomy and risk taking and ensure local responsibility and accountability through strong, consistent financial control systems. Managers aren't second-guessed by headquarters. Strategy flows from the bottom up. Thus, at HP the $ 7 billion printer business emerged not because of strategic foresight and planning at HP's headquarters, but rather due to the entrepreneurial flair of a small group of managers who had the freedom to pursue what was believed to be a small market. The same approach allows J&J and ABB to enter small niche markets or develop unproven technologies without the burdens of a centralized bureaucratic control system. On the other hand, in return for the autonomy they are granted, there are strong expectations of performance. Managers who don't deliver are replaced.

Ambidextrous managers

Managing units that pursue widely different strategies and that have varied structures and cultures is a juggling act not all managers are comfortable with. At ABB, this role is described as 'preaching and persuading'. At HP, managers are low-key, modest, team players who have learned how to manage this tension over their long tenures with the company. At HP, they also lead by persuasion. 'As CEO my job is to encourage people to work together, to experiment, to try things, but I can't order them to do it', says Lew Platt. Larsen at J&J echoes this theme, emphasizing the need for lower level managers to come up with solutions and encouraging reasonable failures. Larsen claims that the role is one of a symphony conductor rather than a general.

One of the explanations for this special ability is the relatively long tenure managers have in these organizations and the continual reinforcement of the social control system. Often, these leaders are low-keyed but embody the culture and act as visible symbols of it. As a group the senior team continually reinforces the core values of autonomy, teamwork, initiative, accountability, and innovation. They ensure that the organization avoids becoming arrogant and remains willing to learn from its competitors. Observers of all three of these companies have commented on their modesty or humility in constantly striving to renew themselves. Rather than becoming complacent, these organizations are guided by leaders who venerate the past but are willing to change continuously to meet the future.

The bottom-line is that ambidextrous organizations learn by the same mechanism that sometimes kills successful firms: variation, selection, and retention. They promote variation through strong efforts to decentralize, to eliminate bureaucracy, to encourage individual autonomy and accountability, and to experiment and take risks. This promotes wide variations in products, technologies, and markets. It is what allows the managers of an old HP instrument division to push their technology and establish a new division dedicated to video servers. These firms also select 'winners' in markets and technologies by staying close to their customers, by being quick to respond to market signals, and by having clear mechanisms to 'kill' products and projects. This selection process allowed the development of computer printers at HP to move from a venture that was begun without formal approval to the point where it now accounts for almost 40% of HP's profits. Finally, technologies, products, markets, and even senior managers are retained by the market, not by a remote, inwardly focused central staff many hierarchical levels removed from real customers. The corporate vision provides the compass by which senior managers can make decisions about which of the many alternative businesses and technologies to invest in, but the market is the ultimate arbiter of the winners and losers. Just as success or failure in the marketplace is Darwinian, so too is the method by which ambidextrous organizations learn. They have figured out how to harness this power within their companies and organize and manage accordingly.

Summary

Managers must be prepared to cannibalize their own business at times of industry transitions. While this is easy in concept, these organizational transitions are quite difficult in practice. Success brings with it inertia and dynamic conservatism. Four hundred years ago, Niccolo Machiavelli noted, 'There is no more delicate matter to take in hand, nor more dangerous to conduct, nor more doubtful in its success, than to be a leader in the introduction of changes. For he who innovates will have for enemies all those who are well off under the old order of things, and only lukewarm supporters in those who might be better off under the new.'

While there are clear benefits to proactive change, only a small minority of farsighted firms initiate discontinuous change before a performance decline. Part of this stems from the risks of proactive change. One reason for RCA's failure to compete in the solid-state market or for SSIH's inability to compete in quartz movements came from the divisive internal disputes over the risks of sacrificing a certain revenue stream from vacuum tubes and mechanical watches for the uncertain profits from transistors and quartz watches. However, great managers are willing to take this step. Andy Grove of Intel puts it succinctly, 'There is at least one point in the history of any company when you have to change dramatically to rise to the next performance level. Miss the moment and you start to decline.'

READING 4.4

Implementation: The core task of change management

By Wilfried Krüger[1]

Change processes do not achieve objectives or even fail. This is caused by a widespread and systematic underestimation of implementation problems. Managers tend to regard implementation as a separate stage of a standardized project procedure which comes last in the project life cycle. The corresponding activities are called 'introduction', 'realization' or 'application'. In the worst case, implementation is reduced to a single management directive with which the people concerned just have to comply, whether they like it or not. In most cases implementation also comprises information and training activities.

This project-management type of implementation is endangered by various change barriers which have their origin in individual uncertainty and fear of disadvantages. Such problems do not just arise when people are told to follow an application directive. They also appear in early stages of change projects such as project definition and design. They are often caused by issues which are not directly related to the change programme or are hidden by day-to-day business.

[1]Source: W. Krüger, 'Implementation: the Core Task of Change Management', *CEMS Business Review*, Vol. 1, 1996, Kluwer Academic/Plenum Publishers. Reproduced by permission.

Therefore, a phase-oriented concept of implementation reaches its limits at lest in comprehensive and fundamental change processes. In these cases implementation has to begin at or even before the project definition, where needs and intentions are identified and then goals are established. People concerned have to be taken into account when identifying the project team, and everybody should be convinced of the need for change before the project start.

At present change management mainly concentrates on the goals of the strategic triangle 'cost, time, and quality (customer benefit)'. Conventional project solutions usually only cover a part of this triangle due to the typical conflict inherent to these three goals.

Business reengineering as a new concept tries to overcome this goal-conflict by forcing the development of innovative solutions. For example the dramatic shortening of a procedure reduces processing-time and costs and at the same time yields lower failure rates (i.e. higher quality) due to a smaller number of interfaces.

However, according to Michael Hammer (the inventor and leading protagonist of business reengineering), more than 70% of all business reengineering projects fail. We suggest this happens because of the negligence of change acceptance. Conceptually 'good' solutions fail during application because they are not accepted by the people concerned. 'Giants' of conceptualization and design are 'dwarfs' when it comes to application. Therefore, we introduce acceptance as a fourth, separate goal of change. Only if 'sufficient' acceptance is aimed for will change management realize the difficulties to be expected in time and only then can problems be solved by active implementation management. Unfortunately the acceptance goal requires activities which counteract the other goals and the strategic triangle thus assumes the form of a 'vicious square'.

Management of change

Which type of conflict and barriers arise and consequently, which kind of implementation management is appropriate depends on the kind of change and the applied change strategy. Therefore, we first introduce dimensions of change before considering tasks and tools of implementation management. The content of implementation activities depends first of all on the depth of change. It can be said that a change of 'hard facts' like strategy or information systems as well as the adjustment of structures and processes just scratches the surface of a company, whereas a change of 'soft facts' like shared values, mindsets and capabilities is comparatively profound.

Strategies for change

The implementation strategy cannot be chosen separately from the strategy for change. In the literature on the subject two main approaches to the problem are discussed: corporate transformation either as revolutionary, quantum, dramatic change ('quantum leaps') or as evolutionary, piecemeal, incremental change ('small steps'). The evolutionary model emphasizes the possibility of a learning organization and its capability to create something new step by step. Any change brings confusion and resistance, and therefore 'all but incremental change is resisted' (Pettigrew, 1985). Miller and Friesen (1984) describe a revolutionary model with a concerted quantum change in situations of crisis. A concerted quantum change is necessary because of the various interdependencies between a company's elements of structure. Here change should be rare, but then quick and dramatic.

From an analytic standpoint there are arguments in favour of and against both conceptual models of change.

The approach of *continuous improvement processes* ('Kaizen', Imai, 1993) seems to correspond to the *evolutionary model*. Here the employees' experience and ideas are used and the starting point is the 'operating company base'. In contrast, attempts at fundamental process optimization ('business reengineering', Hammer and Champy, 1994) demand a radical turning away from the status quo and strict directives by corporate management. This approach follows the revolutionary change model. At present both forms can be observed in German companies.

We will now turn to strategies for implementation. In practice many attempts at change are planned and prepared under the 'top secret' label and carried out with strict 'top-down' directives. Kirsch, Esser and Gabele (1979) refer to this implementation strategy as 'bombing' or as 'air raid'. Bombing implies fundamental change and corresponds to the revolutionary change model. This does not necessarily mean that revolutionary change always has to be implemented by bombing. Nevertheless, even fundamental change can be an open and participative process. For successful bombing the effect of surprise and the mastering of subsequent resistance are crucial. The apparent advantage of a quick introduction is accompanied by the disadvantage of a high acceptance risk.

The possibility of a hidden change also exists for cooperative change processes initiated by the operating company base. This concept, less often considered in the literature, can be characterized as 'guerrilla tactics'. It can only be applied up to the limits of the autonomous powers of decision enjoyed by subunits. This occurrence of informal networks which prepare for change and transform their plans into action when the time has come is also known as 'bootlegging'. Guerrilla tactics may be an evasive answer to bombing or an attempt to dilute its consequences. In this case the 'revolution ex machina' (bombing) triggers off a 'counterrevolution of the operating base' (guerrilla tactics). On the other hand the guerrilla tactics of lower and middle management could also be a sign of need for change which has been ignored by corporate management.

The special difficulty and challenge of change management is to choose the right time for action. Anticyclical change demands particular strategic courage. The public in Germany was baffled and could not understand when BMW made 3000 employees redundant in the middle of a car production boom (1991/92). Later, in the 1993 recession, its 'lean' staff helped BMW to achieve by far the best results of the German car-industry. In particular cases it may be advantageous to combine evolution and revolution in a countercurrent process (Figure 4.4.1; Krüger, 1994a). With regard to process optimization, which at present is the focus of change management, 'kaizen' and 'business reengineering' could be combined. The framework of conditions and the direction of change are determined 'top-down' by corporate management,

whereas the contents of change are rooted 'bottom-up' on impacts from the operating base. This approach can be regarded as *'controlled evolution'* (Marr, 1987; Kirsch, 1992).

Personnel barriers as the core problem of change

The core problem of change is the existence of various factual and personnel change barriers which have to be identified and handled by implementation. Implementation management is *barrier management* and comprises all three dimensions of change management we have considered. Subsequently we will discuss the regularly underestimated and neglected *personnel barriers*. With regard to the people concerned, these barriers can be roughly classified into *company-wide barriers*, *management barriers* and *employee barriers* (Krüger, 1994a).

Company-wide barriers. The imaginary sum of values shared by all company members, their mindsets and behavioural patterns form the central elements of corporate culture. The stronger the corporate culture, the more effective it is, but also the more difficult to change. Values and beliefs can solidify to form the 'genetic code' of a company. This code may even comprise beliefs about the structure of the industry, the basis of competitive advantage, promising strategies and the best organizational structure. If environment demands change, a strong code can militate against or even prevent change. Corporate culture assumes the

FIGURE 4.4.1 Corporate transformation as a countercurrent process

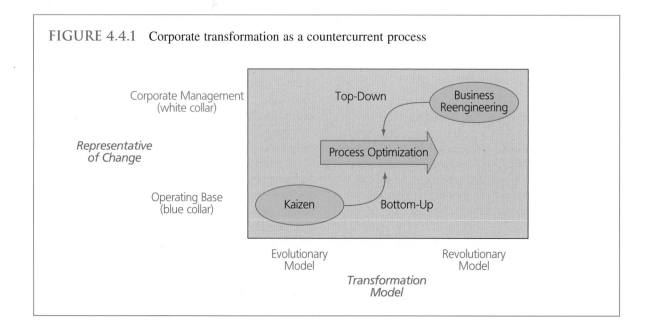

characteristics of a 'flat tyre' or even 'fossilization' (Figure 4.4.2). This may be the reason why previously successful companies often go into decline and why many change processes are so dramatic.

Considerable external pressure (e.g. exerted by stakeholders) leading to a real crisis or even the intervention of external constitutional bodies (e.g. the supervisory board) is needed to trigger off change processes. An additional barrier lies in the fact that positions in the external constitutional bodies are typically held by people who share the values of corporate management (e.g. in Germany former chief executives 'retire' into the supervisory board).

Management barriers. Specific management barriers lie in the field of *problem awareness* and *problem solution.* Problem awareness is often impeded by day-to-day business. Urgent issues are dealt with instead of the important ones. Here an effect referred to as the *'expert-doer syndrome'* (Krüger and Ebeling, 1991) can be observed. The need for rethinking is not seen. When new problems occur the 'expert' tries to apply previously successful solutions without realizing that the situation has changed. When success fails to materialize, the expert puts even more effort into his 'reliable' solution, which cannot lead to success since it is a solution to the wrong problem. A vicious circle of effort, failure and intensification of efforts arises. In this situation neglecting the need for rethinking constitutes an *attitude barrier* to change. Often the people responsible for a solution to a problem fear loss of position and personal standing. Insecurity and a fear to assume responsibility also have to be taken into account. An *'authority fear syndrome'* can be diagnosed which yields cautious, reactive rather than proactive

behaviour. These motivational barriers are *behavioural barriers* to change. In companies where lower and middle management have extensive powers of decision, management barriers have a special significance. Initiatives and impacts 'from below' must be amplified, and change within one's own area of competence must be set in motion. At times even guerrilla tactics may be appropriate if needed for the survival of the company. This means that lower and middle management walk a thin line between obedience and the refusal to carry out commands.

Employee barriers. Even when top management has opted for change, this decision still has to be executed, and the employees concerned, often including lower and middle management, must be convinced of the need for change. Various additional barriers have their root here. Psychologically these barriers, like management barriers, can be explained by individual insecurity and fear of negative consequences. These interests are articulated, represented and negotiated either by direct organizational participation or on the basis of legal rights of participation, for example by co-determination executed through workers' councils or through the workers' representatives in the supervisory board.

Change processes as fields of force

Considering the personnel barriers described above, the change process can be seen as a field of forces on which the various change participants interact (Figure 4.4.3). The promoters, clearly in favour of change, represent the proactive forces. They face a group of opponents with an aversion to change representing the opposing reactive forces, and an 'indecisive' group, that has not yet decided on its final attitude towards change. Change management has to detect the causes for the development of change barriers and, with it, the opposition or indecisiveness; then appropriate activities for implementation, namely the overcoming of barriers, can be organised.

In general, the individual employee will judge the forthcoming change according to the consequences for his own job and whether the results are obvious or uncertain. The following items will be taken into consideration:

- job security;
- working place, working time, income;
- tasks, authority, responsibility;
- requirements (qualification, motivation, behaviour);

FIGURE 4.4.2 Possible effects of individual corporate cultures

Corporate culture is:	Up to date	Not up to date
Strong	'Accelerator'	'Fossilization'
Weak	'Mild Breeze'	'Flat Tyre'

FIGURE 4.4.3   Actors of change and their attitudes

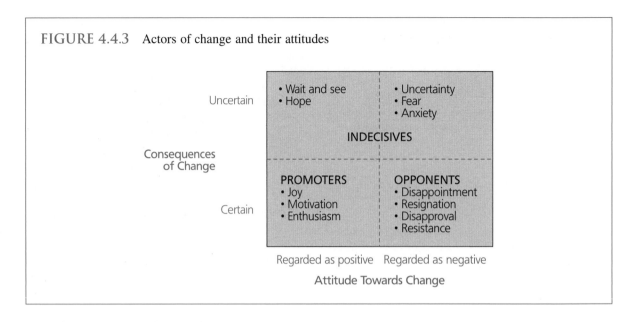

- symbols of position and status;
- organizational environment of the position;
- peer groups;
- private relations.

On the basis of the expected advantages and disadvantages of change and the certainty or uncertainty of their occurrence, a cost–benefit analysis is performed. If the consequences can be foreseen clearly, those who expect to benefit are likely to act as promoters of change, whereas those expecting to suffer disadvantages become opponents (Figure 4.4.3). If the consequences are uncertain, it does not really matter whether they are regarded as positive or negative. Due to anxiety, fear, or possibly hope, employees will remain indecisive.

The net consequence is the result of processing the available information. This cognitive process only leads to a positive or negative (internal) *attitude* towards change. In order to acquire an insight into the (external) *behaviour* of the actors of change we use two different models: the *attitude–behaviour hypothesis,* which has proved to be a helpful tool in marketing science (Kroeber-Riel, 1992), and the consideration of *attitude* and *behaviour acceptance.*

First the *attitude–behaviour hypothesis* is discussed, splitting the attitude into an 'attitude towards change in general' and an 'attitude towards personal change'. If the two attitudes match, a clear position is taken, either as promoter (positive attitudes) or as opponent (negative attitudes). Diverging attitudes result in indecisiveness, which now can be examined in more detail. Individual behaviour can be derived from the attitude

towards personal change, since we expect it to be dominant. This may be different in cultures where employees may value the benefit of their social system (e.g. the company 'family') higher than individual consequences. Somebody will behave as a *potential promoter* (Figure 4.4.4) if his attitude towards change in general is positive, but due to expected disadvantages his attitude towards personal change is negative. Often a negative attitude towards personal change can be explained by *motivational barriers* and *capability barriers.* Likewise, *hidden opponents* can be explained by a negative attitude towards change in general, but a positive attitude towards personal change due to expected advantages ('opportunists').

As research on technology acceptance has shown, there are often gaps between (internal) attitude and (external) behaviour (Wiendieck, 1992). Hence, the behaviour of potential promoters and hidden opponents can be explained by distinguishing between *attitude acceptance* and *behaviour acceptance* towards change. Opponents have negative attitude acceptance and behaviour acceptance, whereas in the case of promoters, both forms of acceptance are positive. When the two categories of acceptance diverge, the situation is less obvious. An actor whose behaviour is positive (positive behaviour acceptance) does not necessarily have a positive attitude as well. Either he helps to carry the change process more or less voluntarily or apathetically ('opportunist', 'fellow traveller'), ready to change his behaviour when necessary, or for tactical reasons he acts positively without really being convinced ('hidden opponent', Figure 4.4.4).

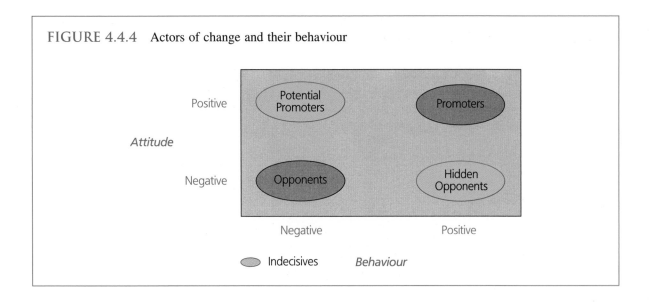

FIGURE 4.4.4   Actors of change and their behaviour

The counterpart is the 'potential promoter', somebody who is generally in favour of change but lacks the final conviction to act in support of change. Insufficient behaviour acceptance can be explained by lack of motivation *(motivational barriers)* and/or by insufficient know-how and skills *(capability barriers).*

Implementation management

Figure 4.4.5 shows the underlying framework for implementation management. The starting point for the internal or external actor who wants to influence and direct the 'implementation force field' is an assessment of attitude and behaviour acceptance and, with it, the classification of the four groups, promoters, potential promoters, opponents and hidden opponents. Usually the numbers of clearly identifiable promoters will be fairly small, whereas the indecisive and opposed groups will be comparatively large. Though the search for the respective groups can be quite tedious, this offers new possibilities for 'impacting' and controlling the change process.

First the three dimensions of change and implementation management (the management of perceptions and beliefs, power and politics management, and issue management) are roughly assigned to the four target groups. Here the task focus of each activity dimension can already be seen. In the first step *opponents* have to be controlled via the management of perceptions and beliefs in order to change their attitudes as far as possible in the direction of change acceptance. This 'mind forming' is supported by activities such as inducements, incentives and countertrading as well as

negative sanctions. If there is no chance of overcoming the negative attitudes of opponents, it might even be necessary to consider their dismissal. For implementation management tasks involving *promoters* constitute the counterfocus. Promoters do not need to be convinced and little persuasion is needed, since they take advantage of change and, therefore, support it.

Hidden opponents are characterized by negative attitudes and positive behaviour. Here management of perceptions and beliefs supported by information (issue management) is needed to change their attitude. *Potential promoters* show the reverse attitude constellation. They behave in negative or passive ways although their attitude is positive. Power and politics management seems to be appropriate in this case, especially for creating stimuli. Depending on the situation, information and training activities may also help to change behaviour.

The common basis of all the implementation activities proposed here is a comprehensive concept of *integration* (Krüger, 1994a). The individual should become integrated in the change process in different ways in order to ensure efficiency and the effectiveness of change. Losses due to friction and stalemates have to be avoided. The general forms of integration can be used for implementation management, for example, integration by shared values *(value-based integration),* which often yields real commitment. In the same way more conventional forms usually associated with integration, such as the participation of the people affected in project teams, groups or steering committees *(structural integration),* may be applied.

FIGURE 4.4.5 Framework for implementation management

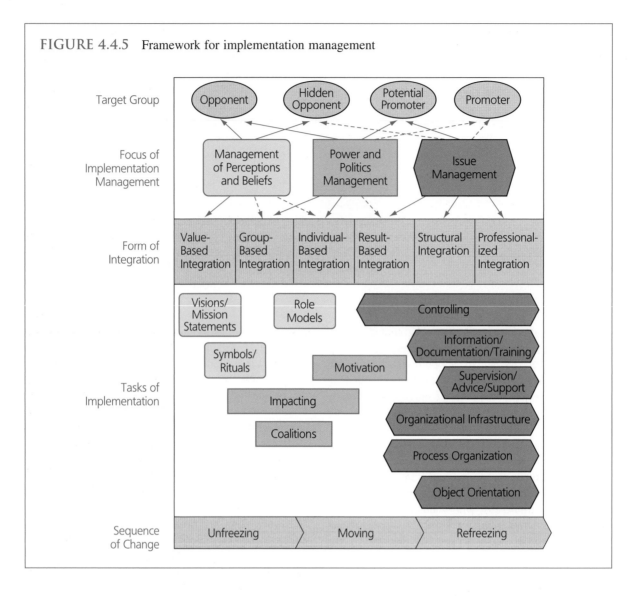

In the lower part of Figure 4.4.5 the tasks of implementation management are assigned to the six forms of integration. From left to right the diagram shows the sequence of change according to Kurt Lewin: *unfreezing*, *moving*, and *refreezing* (1947). It can be clearly seen that the beginning of the process is dominated by management of perceptions and beliefs, represented by, for example, the formulation of new visions and mission statements. This helps to defreeze patterns of thinking and behaviour. In the middle of the process, organizational units and individuals are set in motion (moving) by power and politics management, represented by motivation and impacting activities. Finally, issue management with activities such as information and training, but also supervision and control takes over. New solutions have to be learned and practised until they are rooted deeply enough for the final application (refreezing).

Management of perceptions and beliefs

Management of perceptions and beliefs aims primarily at *attitude acceptance* – target groups are identified and hidden opponents. It aims at changing existing and creating new values and beliefs. The need for change and the way in which change is to occur must be communicated. The more profound, long-lasting and important the change process is and the more development originates in the organizational units involved, the more pervasive will be the change in awareness.

A change of attitudes constitutes the *beginning* of the change process. It precedes the various activities in the area of power and politics and the discussion of single issues. The process-triggering change of attitudes can be compared with 'defreezing' or 'defrosting'. The formulation of 'inspiring' and 'thought-provoking' visions and mission statements often constitutes the first step. A good example is provided by BMW, where the board of directors proclaimed the motto 'enterprise mobility'. From the external standpoint this does not focus attention on the product 'cars', but on mobility as a specific customer need. From the internal standpoint, 'enterprise mobility' challenges every single employee and organizational unit in their behaviour. This visionary 'battle cry' is supported by a number of *action maxims* which form the mission statement. Here values, norms and behavioural patterns are anchored, as well as the employees' ability both to formulate and accept positive criticism.

But visions and mission statements in themselves are not enough. They must be lived as well. In this context *symbols* and *rituals* are of more importance than written directives. Deeply rooted and widely accepted values and norms and each employee's permanent personal commitment to these values should be the objective. This can be illustrated by an example taken from total quality management. In order to achieve fundamental quality improvements Hewlett Packard organized a steamboat trip for all employees of the units concerned. A huge rock, in which all quality faults had been engraved symbolized the 'obstacle' which had to be removed. In the middle of the lake the boat stopped and with a joint effort the rock was pushed overboard. Certainly this was an unforgettable and unequivocal ritual symbolizing commitment to quality.

In practice, role models have proved to be of great importance. Individuals, teams or groups can serve as models. Sceptics can be convinced and opponents be won over by working together and sharing experiences with exemplary colleagues. A good example of this practice is Porche's employment of Japanese experts in its production line. On the other hand, top management must not only announce, but also live the values they are striving for. Real models prove the feasibility of the desired change and constitute a bridge between an ambitious concept and its application in practice. This analysis demonstrates that the management of perceptions and beliefs primarily uses *value-based integration*. The individual is offered many opportunities to identify with values. When role models are used, value-based integration is supported by *group-based* and *individual-based* integration.

Power and politics management

Power and politics management aims at *behaviour acceptance* and tries to have an impact on open opponents and potential promoters, both of which are groups with behaviour barriers. Power and politics can be exerted by individuals as well as by groups. Therefore, power and politics management primarily works with group-based and individual-based integration. *Vertical* integration is carried out by higher ranks including direct superiors as well as heads of central units and project managers. *Horizontally,* power and politics are managed by single colleagues or groups of colleagues who act as peers or peer groups. In this situation promoters who have already been identified can be used as tools to achieve multiplication effects.

Key variables and at the same time tools for integration are specific forms of power (influence) and authority (Krüger, 1994a). First, the power to *reward* and *coerce* are explained. The power to reward (e.g. appreciation, praise, bonuses, compensations) helps to diminish possible disadvantages. In this case the effects of power are *compensatory.* Coercive power (e.g. withdrawal of support, financial disadvantages, transfers, dismissals and strikes) mainly works through threats and the repression of doubt and resistance. Here the effects of power can be regarded as *repressive.* The use of coercive power is restricted by strict legal limits.

From the standpoint of motivation theory rewards and coercion mean the granting or withdrawing of stimuli and therefore are linked to satisfaction and performance. Motivation and impacting by power and politics go hand in hand. Even the isolated change of an incentive system may be enough to trigger behavioural change. Better effects will be achieved if the activities of power and politics management and those of management of perceptions and beliefs are harmonized in an *implementation mix,* similar to marketing mix.

Witte (1973) identified a tandem structure of *promoters by power* and *promoters by know-how* as the most efficient. The *power* to *reward* and *coerce* constitute the basis for *promoters by power.* This kind of promoter mainly acts at the beginning and at the end of a change process. *Promoters by know-how* base their power mainly on *information*, i.e. knowledge and capabilities relevant for change. They usually act in the middle part of the process (moving). This expert power above all helps to emphasize the need for change and to legitimize it. From this point of view it has a *conditioning* impact, similar to the results of value-based integration. At the same time promoters by know-how and information power play an important role in issue management. The tandem structure may be supported by a process-promoter, who typically uses various forms of impacting during the whole change process (Hauschildt, 1993). Apart from reward, coercive and expert power, the process promoters relies on the power rooted in his personality which can be described as *personality power.*

Power and politics management not only means influencing single employees but managing whole systems of influence within a company (Mintzberg, 1983; Krüger, 1994a). Therefore, from the standpoint of coalition theory, implementation can be regarded as building up a *change supporting coalition.* Depending on how far-reaching the change process is, not only internal but also external coalition partners have to be considered and integrated. Quite often, a stable *bureaucratic system of influence* based on formal authority impedes change. The counterpart could be formed by *a personalized system of influence* based on the personality power of the peers and/or a *professionalized influence* based on expert power. The categories of promoters and opponents can be identified in the respective systems of influence. Active and reactive forces develop. The specific constellation of forces determines the course and the results of implementation. There is either a positive response to pressures for change or they are ignored.

Issue management

The management of issues, which is usually considered first in the discussion of change, is intentionally the last point to be examined here. The various tasks and tools are familiar from project management. In larger companies many different documents and handbooks exist in which issue management is discussed in detail. Obviously the failure of change projects and processes is not a matter of inadequate issue management, but a consequence of underestimating power and politics management and the management of perception and beliefs.

Issue management focuses on *factual barriers* to change, and the strategic triangle 'cost, time, and quality' enjoys first priority. We shall now show that there are many interrelations with personnel change barriers and the acceptance problem. Issue management and the conventional understanding of implementation typically concentrate on activities like *informing*, *training*, *documenting*, *supervising* and *consulting* the people concerned. These activities are designed to adapt employees to the new requirements of their jobs resulting from changed tasks, structures

and procedures. The desired result can be described as *professionalized integration.* The individual employee is given the opportunity to meet new work requirements and to develop his professional skills by means of information and training activities. Hence, issue management is closely interrelated to the problem of *personnel change barriers.* Possible worries and fears about 'being left behind' can be eased by information, training and supervision. This also has a positive impact on attitudes and behaviour acceptance. First *capability barriers,* which are directly rooted in a lack of knowledge and skills, can be reduced and overcome. However, anybody's potential to develop is limited. This has been made clear by attempts to introduce lean management and modern manufacturing organization. As job requirements partly exceeded the workers' capacity, the failure rate increased considerably after the introduction of work centres in the Rüsselsheim Opel factory. Now production is reverted to the conventional process flow, based on the division of labour.

Information, training, supervision and other professionalized integration activities are initiated either partly or entirely *after* the decision has been taken to adopt a certain change concept. More fundamental forms of integration actively involve those concerned in the change process. Partial self-control replaces uniform top-down control. The various forms of *participation* ranging from, for example, consultation and participation in decision-making, to quality circles, project team or even self-controlled work centres must be institutionalized. The most advanced forms of self-control correspond to the idea of a *learning organization.* Corporate management must break the ground and prepare a foundation for the concept. Then a process of continuous learning must be set in motion and maintained. 'Implementation' can no longer be a separate task or stage. Once an awareness of change has been created it has to be maintained. Implementation integrates those involved by means of organizational rules. Such approaches are forms of *structural integration.* Implementation management has to establish structures and procedures which form the *organizational implementation infrastructure.*

Process organization is another organizational task of implementation. It is not only relevant for implementation but moulds the change process as a whole. More complex processes cannot be mastered simply by a more detailed planning which takes longer. The integration and overlapping of 'stages' associated with 'simultaneous engineering' must replace the conventional sequential project life cycle approach. Then forms of 'realization', such as prototypes or pilot projects, can begin within the 'planning and design' stage. With shorter planning intervals and faster realization, change and its consequences can be foreseen earlier. For those concerned the period of uncertainty is reduced while rapid improvement provides both a taste of success and learning experience. This results in higher motivation and better quality. Small first steps bringing success significantly raises the acceptance for second steps. Therefore, solutions on the level of rational decision-making like pilot projects or partial results should be used to reduce acceptance problems.

What must be done when optimising business processes is also necessary for the organization of change processes: the dominance of functional specialization – represented by the stages of 'feasibility', 'planning and design', 'realization' and 'implementation' in the project life cycle – must be replaced or supplemented by an *object orientation*. In business, process organization objects are modules or parts of a product, e.g. BMW, where all experts needed for the design of the body or the engine are brought together in 'module-teams'. For change processes in the surface layer (issue management) the objects are the corresponding subjects of change. A change team could be responsible for a new information system or technological equipment, for example. More radical change demands power and politics management and the management of perceptions and beliefs as well.

Implementation processes also need *control* and *supervision*. Deadlines, costs and the desired quantitative and qualitative results of change must be determined. Performance has to be controlled and checked. This is necessary to check results and to assess and gratify those responsible. Managing by results is very important, especially where wide powers of decision and self-control have been granted to operating units. Full commitment can only be expected if those concerned benefit personally from success. In this way the reduction of other forms of integration inherent to self-control can be compensated by *result-based integration*.

Tools for implementation

A number of tools can be used to inspire readiness for change and to achieve change acceptance (Krüger, 1994b). Their application can be seen in an analogy to marketing science. Those affected by change can be regarded as internal customers and change management as customer-oriented. From this point of view, implementation has to be regarded as project marketing with marketing-mix instruments as tools (Reiss, 1993). A customer-oriented implementation mix replaces an

'introduction-directive'. Figure 4.4.6 shows a selection of tools which have proved to be efficient in practice. We have deliberately refrained from a separate systematization of these very different approaches. Instead, the diagram shows the areas of implementation management on which the tools focus, which enables us to compile an implementation toolbox. Most of the tools have a clearly identifiable position in this implementation portfolio although the position may vary depending on the specific form of the instrument. However, for each project or process the tools chosen have to be combined in an appropriate implementation mix.

Some instruments can be used for the conceptualization of change as well as for its application and these are of special interest. For example *workshops* can detect the need for change and at the same time help to classify and structure the identified problem. In the next step *project teams* may consider the question in more detail. They can take into account the best practices already in existence *(benchmarking)*, the feasibility of which improves change acceptance. Meetings with *conference* character (e.g. kick-off meetings and information markets) can be used to present the authorized results and to communicate further details. *Pilot projects* and *prototypes* accelerate the change process and reduce the risk of failure. All these instruments not only have evident advantages but also improve change acceptance.

Conclusions

Figure 4.4.7 illustrates the main results of this study. Change is a permanent task and challenge for general management and implementation is an integral element thereof. It can be conceived as an iceberg with a small part above the surface of the water and the main part below the surface. The visible tip represents the rational and factual dimension of change management. Issue management concentrates on the goals of the strategic triangle 'cost, time and quality' but can only achieve results, i.e. 'float', at a level consistent with the buoyancy provided by acceptance.

The supporting base is rooted in both the interpersonal and behavioural dimension and the normative and cultural dimension, and is subject to power and politics management and to the management of perceptions and beliefs. Without this support, the rational and factual tip would sink and thereby render cost, time and quality goals unachievable. To conclude, we have derived seven propositions concerning implementation management.

FIGURE 4.4.6   Implementation toolbox

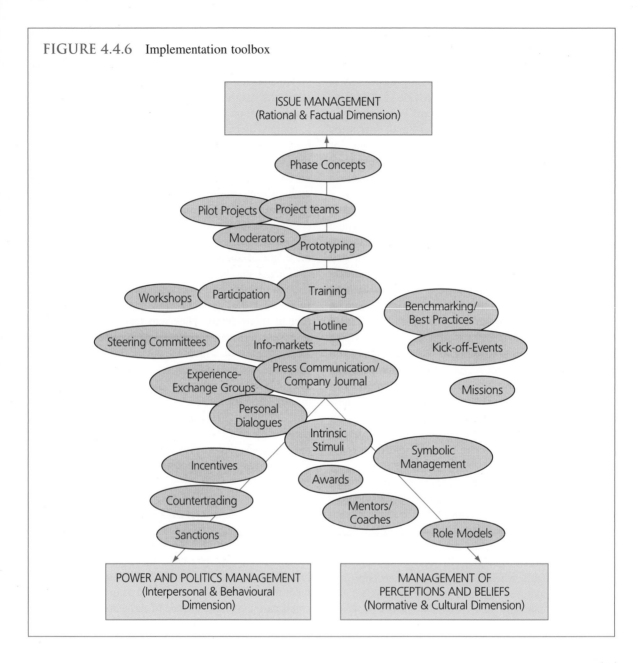

(1) Implementation as an integrative element of change processes

Implementation is more than a segregated stage between 'planning' and 'realization' in a project life-cycle. The 'introduction of a ready made solution' often merely results in the rejection of the transplant instead of the change integrated in and accepted by its environment. Implementation activities must encompass the entire change process. The raising of change awareness and the strengthening of existing forces for change are just as much part of implementation as the building up of acceptance towards results already achieved.

(2) Developing a contingency implementation concept

There is no 'master plan' for implementation. Instead, an implementation concept must be designed which is contingent upon the current situation. In addition to the rational and factual dimension (issue management), the interpersonal and behavioural dimension (power and politics management), as well as the

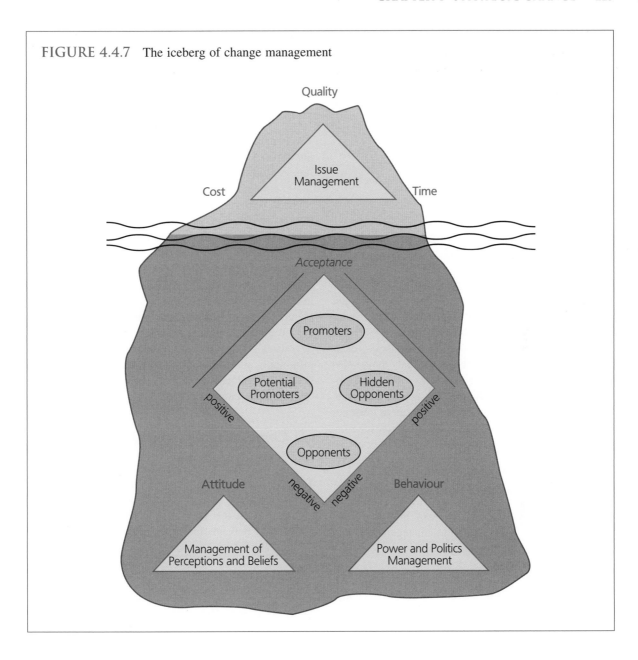

FIGURE 4.4.7   The iceberg of change management

normative and cultural dimension (management of perceptions and beliefs) become more and more important with increasing depth and breadth of change. Strategies must be determined for change and implementation – quantum revolution vs. evolution in steps, bombing or guerrilla tactics. Finally, the attitude and behaviour of those concerned, the interaction between promoters, opponents and indecisive groups as well as the structure and relevance of the corresponding influence systems must be taken into account when designing and combining tasks and tools for implementation management.

(3) Acceptance as a separate implementation goal

Behavioural attitude to change can be positive or negative. It is the task of implementation management to induce or support positive and diminish negative attitudes and behavioural patterns among those concerned. The key problem is to identify and overcome acceptance barriers. Neither a quick and cheap nor a technically perfect solution without considering acceptance is a guarantee for success. Results can only be seen after application and maintenance or rejection and delay. Hence, a highly accepted 'imperfect patch' is better than a completely rejected 'perfect solution'. There is truth in the maxim that we should 'meet people where they are'. We understand implementation as an integrative element in change processes and, therefore, the overcoming of acceptance barriers must be designed as an individual and organizational learning process. In the best of cases the company as a whole acquires the ability to learn – a necessary condition for building up core competencies in the competition for the future!

(4) Management of perceptions and beliefs to secure attitude acceptance

The change of attitudes – necessary above all for open and hidden opponents – occurs in the normative and cultural dimension of change. It is a task for the management of perceptions and beliefs to provide a frame of reference in the form of striking visions and clear mission statements. Symbols and rituals have also proved helpful. Finally, the feasibility of desired objectives can be demonstrated by appropriate role models and their behaviour. Top management must not only proclaim, but embody the values striven for.

(5) Power and politics management to secure behaviour acceptance

Change processes are force fields of promoters and opponents which implementation management must impact and control on the individual as well as on the group level. Opponents and potential promoters must be influenced by power and politics management. Promoters by power, promoters by know-how and process-promoters can be used, as well as specific influence coalitions.

(6) Issue management to achieve the strategic triangle 'cost, time, quality'

The management of perceptions and beliefs and power and politics management aim at acceptance as a separate goal. Issue management concentrates on the goals 'cost, time, and quality'. Activities like informing, training, supervising and consulting help to develop the required knowledge and skills, while at the same time capability barriers are overcome. Integration by structures and procedures can actively involve those concerned by allowing them to take over responsibility: people affected must become active participants in change. The organizational infrastructure of implementation should be accompanied by modern process organization. This implies the integration and overlapping of 'phases' as well as prototyping and pilot-applications. Finally, functional specialization should be replaced or supported by object orientation (e.g. module teams).

(7) Combining tools in an implementation mix

There are various tools for implementation. Those responsible must devise a tool combination in accordance with the prevailing situational constraints, taking into account the main tasks to be performed. Change should be treated as a market product which has to be 'sold' to 'change customers'. The needs and problems of the change target group must be met with the appropriate implementation mix.

STRATEGIC CHANGE IN INTERNATIONAL PERSPECTIVE

Wisdom lies neither in fixity nor in change, but in the dialectic between the two.

Octavio Paz (1914–1998); Mexican poet and essayist

Again it has become clear that there is little consensus within the field of strategic management. Views on the best way to accomplish strategic renewal differ sharply. Even authors from one and the same country exhibit strikingly divergent perspectives on how to deal with the paradox of revolution and evolution.

Provocatively, Reading 4.2 by Imai explicitly introduced the international dimension, suggesting that there are specific national preferences in approach to strategic change. He argues that 'Japanese companies generally favour the gradualist approach and Western companies the great-leap approach – an approach epitomized by the term innovation. Western management worships at the altar of innovation.' This general, yet fundamental, distinction is supported by other researchers such as Ouchi (1981), Pascale and Athos (1981) and Kagono *et al.* (1985), although all of these international comparative studies concentrate only on US–Japanese differences and are relatively old. The extensive study by Kagono and his colleagues among the top 1000 American and Japanese companies concludes that there are clearly different national change styles: 'The US-style elite-guided, logical, deductive approach achieves major innovation in strategies geared to surpass other companies. In contrast, the Japanese inductive, step-wise gradual adjustment approach seeks to steadily build upon the existing strengths to *evolve* strategy' (Kagono *et al.*, 1985: 89–90). Other authors suggest that the United States and Japan seem to represent the two extremes, while most other industrialized countries seem to be somewhere in between (e.g. Calori and De Woot, 1994; Krüger, 1996, Reading 4.4 in this book).

Such pronounced international variance raises the question of cause. Why do firms in different countries prefer such significantly different approaches to strategic change? Which factors determine the existence of national strategic change styles? Answers to these questions might assist in defining the most appropriate context for revolutionary change, as opposed to circumstances in which evolutionary change would be more fitting. Understanding international dissimilarities and their roots should help to clarify whether firms in different countries can borrow practices from one another or are limited by their national context.

As a stimulus to the international dimension of this debate, a short overview will be given of the country characteristics mentioned in the literature as the major influences on how the paradox of revolution and evolution is dealt with in different national settings. It should be noted, however, that cross-cultural research on this topic has not been extensive. Therefore, the propositions brought forward here should be viewed as tentative explanations, intended to encourage further discussion and research.

Prevalence of mechanistic organizations

At the end of Chapter 3, the international differences in organizing work were briefly discussed. It was argued that in some countries the machine bureaucracy is a particularly dominant form of organization, while in other countries organizations are more organic. The machine bureaucracy, that is more predominant in English-speaking countries and France, is characterized by clear hierarchical authority relationships, strict differentiation of tasks, and highly formalized communication, reporting, budgeting, planning and decision-making processes. In such organizations, there is a relatively clear line separating the officers (management) from the troops, and internal relationships are depersonalized and calculative. In more organic forms of organization, management and production activities are not strictly separated, leading to less emphasis on top-down decision-making, and more on bottom-up initiatives. Job descriptions are less strictly defined and control systems are less sophisticated. Integration within the organization is not achieved by these formal systems, but by extensive informal communication and consultation, both horizontally and vertically, and by a strong common set of beliefs and a shared corporate vision. Internal relationships are based on trust, cooperation and a sense of community, leading Ouchi (1981) to call such organizations 'clans'. This type of organization is more prevalent in Japan, and to a lesser extent in, for example, Germany, the Netherlands and the Nordic countries.

Various researchers have suggested that machine bureaucracies exhibit a high level of inertia (e.g. Kanter, 1989; Mintzberg, 1994). Once formal systems have been created, they become difficult to change. As soon as particular tasks are specified and assigned to a person or group, it becomes their turf, while all else is 'not their business'. Once created, hierarchical positions, giving status and power, are not easily abolished. The consequence, it is argued, is that machine bureaucracies are inherently more resistant to change than clanlike organizations (Kagono *et al.*, 1985). Therefore, revolution is usually the potent mode of change needed to make any significant alterations. It can be expected that in countries where organizations are more strongly mechanistic, the preference for the discontinuous renewal perspective will be more pronounced.

Clan-like organizations, on the other hand, are characterized by a strong capacity for self-organization – the ability to exhibit organized behaviour without a boss being in control (Nonaka, 1988; Stacey, 1993a, Reading 9.2). They are better at fluidly, and spontaneously, reorganizing around new issues because of a lack of rigid structure, the close links between management and production tasks, the high level of group-oriented information-sharing and consensual decision-making, and the strong commitment of individuals to the organization, and vice versa. In countries where organizations are more organic in this way, a stronger preference for the continuous renewal perspective can be expected. This issue will be discussed at greater length in Chapter 9.

Position of employees

This second factor is linked to the first. A mechanistic organization, it could be said, is a system, into which groups of people have been brought, while an organic organization is a group of people, into which some system has been brought. In a machine bureaucracy, people are human resources *for* the organization, while in a clan, people *are* the organization. These two conceptions of organization represent radically different views on the position and roles of employees within organizations.

In mechanistic organizations, employees are seen as valuable, yet expendable, resources utilized by the organization. Salaries are determined by prices on the labour market and the value added by the individual employee. In the contractual relationship between employer and employee, it is a shrewd bargaining tactic for employers to minimize their dependence on employees. Organizational learning should, therefore, be captured in formalized systems and procedures, to avoid the irreplaceability of their people. Employees, on the other hand, will strive to make themselves indispensable for the organization, for instance by not sharing their learning. Furthermore, calculating employees will not tie themselves too strongly to the organization, but will keep their options open to job-hop to a better-paying employer. None of these factors contribute to the long-term commitment and receptiveness for ambiguity and uncertainty needed for continuous renewal.

In clan-like organizations the tolerance for ambiguity and uncertainty is higher, because employees' position within the organization is more secure. Information is more readily shared, as it does not need to be used as a bargaining chip and acceptance within the group demands being a team player. Employers can invest in people instead of systems, since employees are committed and loyal to the organization. These better-trained people can consequently be given more decision-making power and more responsibility to organize their own work to fit with changing circumstances. Therefore, clan-like organizations, with their emphasis on employees as permanent co-producers, instead of temporary contractors, are more conducive to evolutionary change. It is in this context that Imai concludes that 'investing in Kaizen means investing in people ... Kaizen is people-oriented, whereas innovation is technology- and money-oriented'.

A number of factors have been brought forward to explain these international differences in the structuring of work and the position of employees. Some authors emphasize cultural aspects, particularly the level of individualism. It is argued that the mechanistic–organic distinction largely coincides with the individualism–collectivism division (e.g. Ouchi, 1981; Pascale and Athos, 1981). In this view, machine bureaucracies are the logical response to calculative individuals, while clans are more predominant in group-oriented cultures. Other authors point to international differences in labour markets (e.g. Kagono et al., 1985; Calori, Valla and De Woot, 1994). High mobility of personnel would coincide with the existence of mechanistic organizations, while low mobility (e.g. life time employment) fits with organic forms. Yet others suggest that the abundance of skilled workers is important. Machine bureaucracies are suited to dealing with narrowly trained individuals requiring extensive supervision. Clan-like organizations, however, need skilled, self-managing workers, who can handle a wide variety of tasks with relative autonomy. Kogut (1993: 11) reports that the level of workers within a country with these qualifications 'has been found to rest significantly upon the quality of education, the existence of programs of apprenticeship and worker qualifications, and the elimination of occupational distinctions'.

On the basis of these arguments it can be proposed that the discontinuous renewal perspective will be more prevalent in countries with a more individualistic culture, high labour mobility and less skilled workers. Conversely, the continuous renewal perspective will be more strongly rooted in countries with a group-oriented culture, low labour mobility and skilled, self-managing workers.

Role of top management

The third factor is also related to the previous points. Various researchers have observed important international differences in leadership styles and the role of top management. In some countries, top management is looked on as the 'central processing unit' of the company, making the key decisions and commanding the behaviour of the rest of the organizational machine. Visible top-down leadership is the norm, and therefore, strategic innovation and change are viewed as top management responsibilities (e.g. Hambrick and Mason, 1984; Hitt et al., 1997). Strategic changes are formulated by top managers and then implemented by lower levels. Top managers are given significant power and discretion to develop bold new initiatives and to overcome organizational resistance to change. If organizational advances are judged to be insufficient or if an organization ends up in a crisis situation, a change of top management is often viewed as a necessary measure to transform or turn around the company (e.g. Boeker, 1992; Fredrickson, Hambrick and Baumrin, 1988). In nations where people exhibit a strong preference for this commander type of leadership, an inclination towards the discontinuous renewal perspective can be expected. In other countries, top managers are viewed as the captains of the team and leadership is less direct and less visible (e.g. Kagono et al., 1985; Hofstede, 1993, Reading 1.4). The role of top managers is to facilitate change and innovation among the members of the group. It is not necessarily the intention that top managers initiate entrepreneurial activities themselves. Change comes from within the body of the organization, instead of being imposed upon it by top management. Therefore, change under this type of leadership will usually be more evolutionary than revolutionary. In nations where people exhibit a strong preference for this servant type of leadership, an inclination towards the continuous renewal perspective is more likely.

Time orientation

At the end of Chapter 3 a distinction was made between cultures that are more oriented towards the past, the present and the future. Obviously, it can be expected that cultures with a past or present orientation will be much less inclined towards change than future-oriented cultures. Among these future-minded cultures, a further division was made between those with a long-term and a short-term orientation.

Various researchers have argued that short-term oriented cultures exhibit a much stronger preference for fast, radical change than cultures with a longer time horizon. In short-term oriented cultures, such as the English-speaking countries, there are significant pressures for rapid results, which predisposes managers towards revolutionary change. Especially the sensitivity to stock prices is often cited as a major factor encouraging firms to focus on short spurts of massive change and pay much less attention to efforts and investments with undramatic long-term benefits. Other contributing factors mentioned include short-term oriented bonus systems, stock option plans and frequent job-hopping (e.g. Calori, Valla and De Woot, 1994; Kagono *et al.*, 1985).

In long-term oriented cultures, such as Japan, China and South Korea, there is much less pressure to achieve short-term results. There is broad awareness that firms are running a competitive marathon and that a high, but steady, pace of motion is needed. Generally, more emphasis is placed on facilitating long-term change processes, instead of intermittently moving from short-term change to short-term change. Frequently mentioned factors contributing to this long-term orientation include long-term employment relationships, the lack of short-term bonus systems, and most importantly, the accent on growth, as opposed to profit, as firms' prime objective (e.g. Abegglen and Stalk, 1985; Hitt *et al.*, 1997). This topic will be discussed at more length in Chapter 11.

FURTHER READING

Many excellent writings on the topic of strategic change are available, although most carry other labels, such as innovation, entrepreneurship, reengineering, revitalization, rejuvenation and learning. For a good overview of the literature, readers can consult 'Environmental Jolts and Industry Revolutions: Organizational Responses to Discontinuous Change', by Alan Meyer, Geoffry Brooks and James Goes. Paul Strebel's book *Breakpoints: How Managers Exploit Radical Business Change* also provides broad introduction to much of the work on change.

In the discontinuous renewal literature, Larry Greiner's article 'Evolution and Revolution as Organizations Grow' is a classic well worth reading. Danny Miller and Peter Friesen's landmark book *Organizations: A Quantum View* is also stimulating, although not easily accessible. More readable books on radical change are *Rejuvenating the Mature Business*, by Charles Baden-Fuller and John Stopford, *Sharpbenders: The Secrets of Unleashing Corporate Potential*, by Peter Grinyer, David Mayes and Peter McKiernan, and *Crisis and Renewal*, by David Hurst. More 'hands-on' is Rosabeth Moss Kanter's *When Giants Learn to Dance*, and of course *Reengineering the Corporation: A Manifesto for Business Revolution*, by Michael Hammer and James Champy, which expands on the ideas discussed in Hammer's article in this chapter (Reading 4.1).

On the topic of innovation, Jim Utterback's book *Mastering the Dynamics of Innovation* provides a good overview, as does *Managing Innovation: Integrating Technological, Market and Organizational Change*, by Joe Tidd, John Bessant and Keith Pavitt. An excellent collection of cases is provided by Charles Baden-Fuller and Martin Pitt in their book *Strategic Innovation*.

Literature taking a continuous renewal perspective is less abundant, but no less interesting. Masaaki Imai's article in this chapter (Reading 4.2) has been reprinted from his book *Kaizen: The Key to Japan's Competitive Success*, which is highly recommended. A more academic work that explains the continuous renewal view in detail is 'The Art of Continuous Change: Linking Complexity Theory and Time-Paced Evolution in Relentlessly Shifting Organizations', by Kathleen Eisenhardt and Shona Brown. Their excellent book *Competing on the Edge: Strategy as Structured Chaos* (Brown and Eisenhardt, 1998) is also a good source. Another good academic work is *Strategic vs. Evolutionary Management: A US-Japan Comparison of Strategy and Organization*, by Tadao Kagono, Ikujiro Nonaka, Kiyonori Sakakibara and Akihiro Okumura. Ikujiro Nonaka's article 'Creating Organizational Order Out of Chaos: Self-Renewal in Japanese Firms' gives a good summary of this way of thinking.

Finally, the award-winning article 'Ambidextrous Organizations: Managing Evolutionary and Revolutionary Change', by Michael Tushman and Charles O'Reilly (Reading 4.3) must be mentioned as a delightful article, in particular with regard to the way in which the authors explicitly wrestle with the paradox of revolution and evolution. Their book *Winning Through Innovation: A Practical Guide to Leading Organizational Change and Renewal* is equally stimulating.

REFERENCES

Abegglen, J.C., and Stalk, G. (1985) *Kaisha, The Japanese Corporation*, New York: Basic Books.

Aldrich, H. (1999) *Organizations Evolving*, London: Sage.

Allaire, Y., and Firsirotu, M. (1985) 'How to Implement Radical Strategies in Large Organizations', *Sloan Management Review*, Vol. 26, No. 3, Spring, pp. 19–34.

Allison, G.T. (1969) 'Conceptual Models and The Cuban Missile Crisis', *The American Political Science Review*, No. 3, September, pp. 689–718.

Argyris, C. (1990) *Overcoming Organizational Defenses: Facilitating Organizational Learning*, Boston, MA: Prentice Hall.

Arthur, W.B. (1996) 'Increasing Returns and the New World of Business', *Harvard Business Review*, Vol. 74, No. 4, July–August, pp. 100–109.

Baden-Fuller, C., and Pitt, M. (1996) *Strategic Innovation*, London: Routledge.

Baden-Fuller, C., and Stopford, J.M. (1992) *Rejuvenating the Mature Business*, London: Routledge.

Bartlett, C.A., and Ghoshal, S. (1995) *Transnational Management: Text, Cases, and Readings in Cross-Border Management*, Second Edition, , Homewood, IL: R.D. Irwin Inc.

Bate, P. (1994) *Strategies for Cultural Change*, Oxford: Butterworth-Heinemann.

Beinhocker, E.D. (1999) 'Robust Adaptive Strategies', *Sloan Management Review*, Vol. 40, No. 3, Spring, pp. 95–106.

Boeker, W. (1992) 'Power and Managerial Dismissal: Scapegoating at the Top', *Administrative Science Quarterly*, Vol. 37, No. 4, pp. 538–547.

Bower, J.L., and Christensen, C.M. (1995) 'Disruptive Technologies: Catching the Wave', *Harvard Business Review*, Vol. 73, No. 1, January–February, pp. 43–53.

Brown, S.L., and Eisenhardt, K.M. (1998) *Competing on the Edge: Strategy as Structured Chaos*, Boston, MA: Harvard Business School Press.

Calori, R., and de Woot, P. (eds) (1994) *A European Management Model: Beyond Diversity*, Hemel: Prentice Hall.

Calori, R., Valla, J.-P, and de Woot, P. (1994) 'Common Characteristics: The Ingredients of European Management', in: R. Calori and P. de Woot (eds), *A European Management Model: Beyond Diversity*, Hemel Hempstead: Prentice Hall.

Christensen, C.M. (1997) *The Innovator's Dilemma*, New York: HarperBusiness.

Christensen, C.M., and Overdorf, M. (2000) 'Meeting the Challenge of Disruptive Change', *Harvard Business Review*, Vol. 78, No. 2, March–April, pp. 66–76.

D'Aveni, R. (1994) *Hypercompetition: Managing the Dynamics of Strategic Maneuvering*, New York: Free Press.

Day, D.L. (1994) 'Raising Radicals: Different Processes for Championing Innovative Corporate Ventures', *Organization Science*, Vol. 5, No. 2, May, pp. 148–172.

Duncan, R.B. (1976) 'The Ambidextrous Organization: Designing Dual Structures for Innovation', in: R.H. Kilmann, L.R. Pondy, and D.P Slevin (eds), *The Management of Organizational Design*, New York: Elsevier North Holland, pp. 167–188.

Eisenhardt, K.M., and Brown, S.L. (1997) 'The Art of Continuous Change: Linking Complexity Theory and Time-Paced Evolution in Relentlessly Shifting Organizations', *Administrative Science Quarterly*, Vol. 42, No. 1, March, pp. 1–34.

Eisenhardt, K.M., and Brown, S.L. (1998) 'Time Pacing: Competing in Markets That Won't Stand Still', *Harvard Business Review*, March–April, Vol. 77, No. 2, pp. 8–18.

Fredrickson, J.W., Hambrick, D.C., and Baumrin, S. (1988) 'A Model of CEO Dismissal', *Academy of Management Review*, Vol. 13, No. 2, April, pp. 255–270.

Freeman, R.E. (1984) *Strategic Management: A Stakeholder Approach*, Boston: Pitman/Ballinger.

Gersick, C.J.G. (1991) 'Revolutionary Change Theories: A Multilevel Exploration of the Punctuated Equilibrium Paradigm', *Academy of Management Review*, Vol. 17, No. 1, January, pp. 10–36.

Ghemawat, P. (1991) *Commitment: The Dynamic of Strategy*, New York: Free Press.

Greenwood, R., and Hinings, C.R. (1996) 'Understanding Radical Organizational Change: Bringing Together the Old and the New Institutionalism', *Academy of Management Review*, Vol. 21, No. 4, October, pp. 1022–1054.

Greiner, L.E. (1972) 'Evolution and Revolution as Organizations Grow', *Harvard Business Review*, Vol. 50, No. 4, July–August, pp. 37–46.

Greiner, L.E., and Bhambri, A. (1989) 'New CEO Intervention and Dynamics of Deliberate Strategic Change', *Strategic Management Journal*, Vol. 10, Special issue, Summer, pp. 67–86.

Grinyer, P.H., Mayes, D., and McKiernan, P. (1987) *Sharpbenders: The Secrets of Unleashing Corporate Potential*, Oxford: Blackwell.

Hambrick, D.C., and Mason, P. (1984) 'Upper Echelons: The Organization as a Reflection of Its Top Managers', *Academy of Management Review*, Vol. 9, No. 2, April, pp. 193–206.

Hamel, G. (1996) 'Strategy as Revolution', *Harvard Business Review*, Vol. 74, No. 4, July–August, pp. 69–82.

Hammer, M. (1990) 'Reengineering Work: Don't Automate, Obliterate', *Harvard Business Review*, Vol. 68, No. 4, July–August, pp. 104–111.

Hammer, M., and Champy, J. (1993) *Reengineering the Corporation: A Manifesto for Business Revolution*, New York: HarperCollins.

Hammer, M., and Champy, J. (1994) *Business Reengineering: Die Radikalkur für das Unternehmen*, Frankfurt am Main–New York: Nicholas Brealey Publishing.

Hannan, M.T., and Freeman, J. (1984) 'Structural Inertia and Organizational Change', *American Sociological Review*, Vol. 49, No. 2, April, pp. 149–164.

Hauschildt, J. (1993) *Innovationsmanagement*, München: Vahlen.

Hayes, R.H. (1985) 'Strategic Planning: Forward in Reverse?', *Harvard Business Review*, Vol. 63, No. 6, November–December, pp. 111–119.

Hitt, M.A., Dacin, M.T., Tyler, B.B, and Park, D. (1997) 'Understanding the Differences in Korean and U.S. Executives' Strategic Orientations', *Strategic Management Journal*, Vol. 18, pp. 159–167.

Hofstede, G. (1993) 'Cultural Constraints in Management Theories', *Academy of Management Executive*, Vol. 7, No. 1, pp. 8–21.

Hurst, D. (1995) *Crisis and Renewal*, Boston: Harvard Business School Press.

Imai, M. (1986) *Kaizen: The Key to Japan's Competitive Success*, McGraw-Hill, New York.

Imai, M. (1993) *Kaizen: Der Schlüssel zum Erfolg der Japaner im Wettbewerb*, Third Edition, Berlin: Wirtschaftsverlag.

Ireland, R.D., and Hitt, M.A. (1999) 'Achieving and Maintaining Strategic Competitiveness in the 21st Century: The Role of Strategic Leadership', *Academy of Management Executive*, Vol. 13, No. 1, February, pp. 43–57.

Johnson, G. (1987) *Strategic Change and the Management Process*, Oxford: Basil Blackwell.

Johnson, G. (1988) 'Rethinking Incrementalism', *Strategic Management Journal*, Vol. 9, No. 1, January–February, pp. 75–91.

Kagono, T, Nonaka, I., Sakakibara, K., and Okumura, A. (1985) *Strategic vs. Evolutionary Management: A US-Japan Comparison of Strategy and Organization*, Amsterdam: North Holland.

Kanter, R.M. (1983) *The Change Masters: Innovation for Productivity in the American Corporation*, New York: Basic Books.

Kanter, R.M. (1989) *When Giants Learn to Dance*, New York: Simon & Schuster.

Kanter, R.M. (1991) 'Championing Change: An Interview With Bell Atlantic's CEO Raymond Smith', *Harvard Business Review*, Vol. 69, No. 1, January–February, pp. 119–130.

Kessler, E.H., and Chakrabarthi, A.K. (1996) 'Innovation Speed: A Conceptual Model of Context, Antecedents, and Outcomes', *Academy of Management Review*, Vol. 21, No. 4, October, pp. 1143–1191.

Kirsch, W. (1992) *Kommunikatives Handeln, Autopoesie, Rationalität. Sondierungen z,u einer evolutionären Führungslehre*, München.

Kirsch, W., Esser, W.N., and Gabele, E. (1979) *Das Management des geplanten Wandels von Organisationen*, Stuttgart.

Kogut, B. (ed.) (1993) *Country Competitiveness: Technology and the Organizing of Work*, Oxford: Oxford University Press, Oxford.

Kroeber-Riel, W. (1992) *Konsumentenverhalten*, Fifth Edition, München: Vahlen.

Krüger, W. (1994a) *Organisation der Unternehmung*, Third Edition, Stuttgart.

Krüger, W. (1994b) 'Umsetzung neuer Organisationsstrategien: Das Implementierungsproblem', *zfbf*, Vol. 33, pp. 197–221.

Krüger, W. (1996) 'Implementation: The Core Task of Change Management', *CEMS Business Review*, Vol. 1, pp. 77–96.

Krüger, W., and Ebeling, F. (1991) 'Psychologik: Topmanager müssen lernen, politisch zu handeln', *HARVARDmanager*, Vol. 2, pp. 47–56.

Lawrence, P.R., and Lorsch, J.W. (1967) *Organization and the Environment*, Boston, MA: Harvard Business School.

Leonard-Barton, D. (1992) 'Core Capabilities and Core Rigidities: A Paradox in Managing New Product Development', *Strategic Management Journal*, Vol. 13, Special Issue, Summer, pp. 111–125.

Leonard-Barton, D. (1995) *Wellsprings of Knowledge*, Boston, MA: Harvard Business School Press.

Lewin, K. (1947) 'Frontiers in Group Dynamics: Social Equilbria and Social Change', *Human Relations*, Vol. 1, pp. 5–41.

Lieberman, M.B., and Montgomery, D.B. (1988) 'First Mover Adavantages', *Strategic Management Journal*, Vol. 9, No. 1, January–February, pp. 41–58.

Lieberman, M.B., and Montgomery, D.B. (1998) 'First-Mover (Dis)Advantages: Retrospective and Link with the Resource-Based View', *Strategic Management Journal*, Vol. 19, No. 12, December, pp. 1111–1126.

Maidique, M.A. (1980) 'Entrepreneurs, Champions, and Technological Innovation', *Sloan Management Review*, Vol. 21, pp. 18–31.

March, J.G., and Simon, H.A. (1958) *Organizations*, New York: Wiley.

Markides, C. (1998) 'Strategic Innovation in Established Companies', *Sloan Management Review*, Vol. 39, No. 3, pp. 31–42.

Marr, R. (1987) 'Die Implementierung eines flexiblen Arbeitszeitsystems als Prozess organisatorischer Entwicklung', in: R. Marr (ed.), *Arbeitszeitmanagement*, Berlin, pp. 339–355.

McCaskey, M.B. (1982) *The Executive Challenge: Managing Change and Ambiguity*, Boston: Pitman.

Meyer, A.D. (1982) 'Adapting to Environmental Jolts', *Administrative Science Quarterly*, Vol. 27, No. 4, December, pp. 515–537.

Meyer, A., Brooks, G., and Goes, J. (1990) 'Environmental Jolts and Industry Revolutions: Organizational Responses to Discontinuous Change', *Strategic Management Journal*, Vol. 11, No. 2, February, pp. 93–110.

Miller, D. (1990) *The Icarus Paradox: How Excellent Companies Bring About Their Own Downfall*, New York: Harper Business.

Miller, D., and Friesen, P. (1984) *Organizations: A Quantum View*, Englewood Cliffs, NJ: Prentice Hall.

Mintzberg, H. (1983) *Power In and Around Organizations*, Englewood Cliffs, NJ: Prentice Hall.

Mintzberg, H. (1991) 'The Effective Organization: Forces and Forms', *Sloan Management Review*, Vol. 32, No. 2, Winter, pp. 54–67.

Mintzberg, H. (1994) *The Rise and Fall of Strategic Planning*, Englewood Cliffs, NJ: Prentice Hall.

Mintzberg, H., and Westley, F. (1992) 'Cycles of Organizational Change', *Strategic Management Journal*, Vol. 13, pp. 39–59.

Morgan, G. (1986) *Images of Organization*, London: Sage.

Nelson, R.R., and Winter, S.G. (1982) *An Evolutionary Theory of Economic Change*, Cambridge, MA: Harvard University Press.

Nonaka, I. (1988) 'Creating Organizational Order Out of Chaos: Self-Renewal in Japanese Firms', *California Management Review*, Vol. 30, No. 3, Spring, pp. 9–18.

Oliver, C. (1991) 'Strategic Responses to Institutional Processes', *Academy of Management Review*, Vol. 16, No. 1, January, pp. 145–179.

Ouchi, W. (1981) *Theory Z: How American Business Can Meet the Japanese Challenge*, Reading, MA: Addison-Wesley.

Pascale, R.T., and Athos, A.G. (1981) *The Art of Japanese Management*, New York: Simon & Schuster.

Pettigrew, A.M. (1985) *The Awakening Giant: Continuity and Change in Imperial Chemical Industries*, Oxford: Blackwell.

Pettigrew, A.M. (1988) *The Management of Strategic Change*, Oxford: Basil Blackwell.

Pfeffer, J., and Sutton, R.I. (1999) 'Knowing "What" to Do is Not Enough: Turning Knowledge Into Action', *California Management Review*, Vol. 42, No. 1, Fall, pp. 83–108.

Pondy, L.R., Boland, J.R., and Thomas, H. (eds) (1988) *Managing Ambiguity and Change*, New York: Wiley.

Powell, W.W. (1991) 'Expanding the scope of Institutional Analysis', in: W.W. Powell and P.J. Di-Maggio (eds), *The New Institutionalism in Organizational Analysis*, Chicago: University of Chicago Press, pp. 183–123.

Quinn, J.B. (1980) *Strategies for Change*, Homewood, IL: Irwin.

Reiss, M. (1993) 'Führungsaufgabe Implementierung', *Personal*, Vol. 12, pp. 551–555.

Schein, E.H. (1985) *Organizational Culture and Leadership*, San Francisco: Jossey-Bass.

Schumpeter, J.A. (1950) *Capitalism, Socialism and Democracy*, Third Edition, New York: Harper and Brothers.

Senge, P.M. (1990) 'The Leader's New Work: Building Learning Organizations', *Sloan Management Review*, Vol. 32, No. 1, Fall, pp. 7–23.

Shapiro, C., and Varian, H. (1998) *Information Rules: A Strategic Guide to the Network Economy*, Cambridge, MA: Harvard Business School Press.

Stacey, R.D. (1993a) 'Strategy as Order Emerging from Chaos', *Long Range Planning*, Vol. 26, No. 1, pp. 10–17.

Stacey, R.D. (1993b) *Strategic Management and Organizational Dynamics*, London: Pitman Publishing.

Stinchcombe, A.L. (1965) 'Social Structure and Organizations', in: J.G. March (ed.), *Handbook of Organizations*, Chicago: Rand McNally, pp. 142–193.

Stopford, J.M., and Baden-Fuller, C.W.F. (1994) 'Creating Corporate Entrepreneurship', *Strategic Management Journal*, Vol. 15, No. 7, September, pp. 521–536.

Strebel, P. (1992) *Breakpoints: How Managers Exploit Radical Business Change*, Boston: Harvard Business School Press.

Strebel, P. (1994) 'Choosing the Right Change Path', *California Management Review*, Vol. 36, No. 2, Winter, pp. 29–51.

Teece, D.J., Pisano, G., and Shuen, A. (1997) 'Dynamic Capabilities and Strategic Management', *Strategic Management Journal*, Vol. 18, No. 7, August, pp. 509–533.

Thompson, J.D. (1967) *Organizations in Action*, New York: McGraw-Hill.

Tidd, J., Bessant, J., and Pavitt, K. (1997) *Managing Innovation: Integrating Technological, Market and Organizational Change*, Chichester: Wiley.

Trice, H.M., and Beyer, J.M. (1993) *The Cultures of Work Organizations*, Englewood Cliffs, NJ: Prentice Hall.

Tushman, M.L., Newman, W.H., and Romanelli, E. (1986) 'Convergence and Upheaval: Managing the Unsteady Pace of Organizational Evolution', *California Management Review*, Vol. 29, No. 1, Fall, pp. 29–44.

Tushman, M.L., and O'Reilly III, C.A. (1996) 'Ambidextrous Organizations: Managing Evolutionary and Revolutionary Change', *California Management Review*, Vol. 38, No. 4, Summer, pp. 8–30.

Tushman, M.L., and O'Reilly III, C.A. (1997) *Winning Through Innovation: A Practical Guide to Leading Organizational Change and Renewal*, Boston, MA: Harvard Business School Press.

Tushman, M., and Romanelli, E. (1985) 'Organizational Evolution: A Metamorphosis Model of Convergence and Reorientation', in: L.L. Cummings and B.M. Staw (eds), *Research in Organizational Behavior*, Greenwich, CT: JAI Press. Vol. 7, pp. 171–222.

Utterback, J. (1994) *Mastering the Dynamics of Innovation*, Boston, MA: Harvard Business School Press.

Waterman, R.H., Peters, T.J., and Phillips, J.R. (1980) 'Structure is Not Organization', *Business Horizons*, Vol. 23, June, pp. 14–26.

Wiendieck, G. (1992) 'Akzeptanz', in: E. Frese (ed.), *Handwörter-buch der Organisation*, Third Edition, Stuttgart, pp. 89–98.

Witte, E. (1973) *Organisation für Innovationsentscheidungen: Das Promotorenmodell*, Göttingen: Schartz & Co.

iii

STRATEGY CONTENT

Every generation laughs at the old fashions but religiously follows the new.
Henry David Thoreau (1817–1862); American philosopher

The output of the strategy process is a particular strategy that an organization follows – this is called the strategy content. 'Strategy content' is another way of saying 'the strategy itself, with all its specific characteristics'. While the strategy process section dealt with the questions of *how* strategy should be formed, *who* should be involved and *when* it should be made, the strategy content section deals with the question of *what* the strategy should be – what should be the course of action the firm should follow to achieve its purpose?

In determining what the strategy should be, two types of 'fit' are of central concern to managers. First, as discussed in Chapter 4, there needs to be a fit between the firm and its environment. If the two become misaligned, the firm will be unable to meet the demands of the environment and will start to underperform, which can eventually lead to bankruptcy or takeover. This type of fit is also referred to as 'external consonance'. At the same time, managers are also concerned with achieving an internal fit between the various parts of the firm. If various units become misaligned, the organization will suffer from inefficiency, conflict and poor external performance, which can eventually lead to its demise as well. This type of fit is also referred to as 'internal consistency'.

As external consonance and internal consistency are prerequisites for a successful strategy, they need to be achieved for each organizational unit. Most organizations have various levels, making it necessary to ensure internal and external fit at each level of aggregation within the firm. In Figure III.1 all these possible levels within a corporation have been reduced to just three general categories, and a fourth, supra-organizational level has been added. At each level the strategy followed should meet the requirements of external consonance and internal consistency:

- Functional level strategy. For each functional area, such as marketing, operations, finance, logistics, human resources, procurement and R&D, a strategy needs to be developed. At this level, internal consistency means having an overarching functional strategy that integrates various functional sub-strategies (e.g. a marketing strategy that aligns branding, distribution, pricing, product and communication strategies). External consonance means that the strategy must be aligned with the demands in the relevant external arena (e.g. the logistics or procurement environment).

- Business level strategy. At the business level, an organization can only be effective if it can integrate functional level strategies into an internally consistent whole. To achieve external consonance the business unit must be aligned with the specific demands in the relevant business area.

- Corporate level strategy. Where a company operates in two or more business areas, the business level strategies need to be aligned to form an internally consistent corporate level strategy. Between business and corporate levels there can also be divisions, but for most strategy purposes they can be approached as mini-corporations (both divisional and corporate level strategy are technically speaking 'multi-business level'). Achieving external consonance at this level of aggregation means that a corporation must be able to act as one tightly integrated unit or as many autonomous, differentiated units, depending on the demands of the relevant environment.

- Network level strategy. Where various firms work together to create economic value, it sometimes is deemed necessary to align business and/or corporate level strategies to shape an internally consistent network level strategy. Such a network, or multi-company, level strategy can involve anywhere between two and thousands of companies. Here, too, the group must develop a strategy that fits with the demands in the relevant environment.

As the strategy content issues differ greatly depending on the level of aggregation under discussion, this section has been divided along the following lines. Chapter 5 will

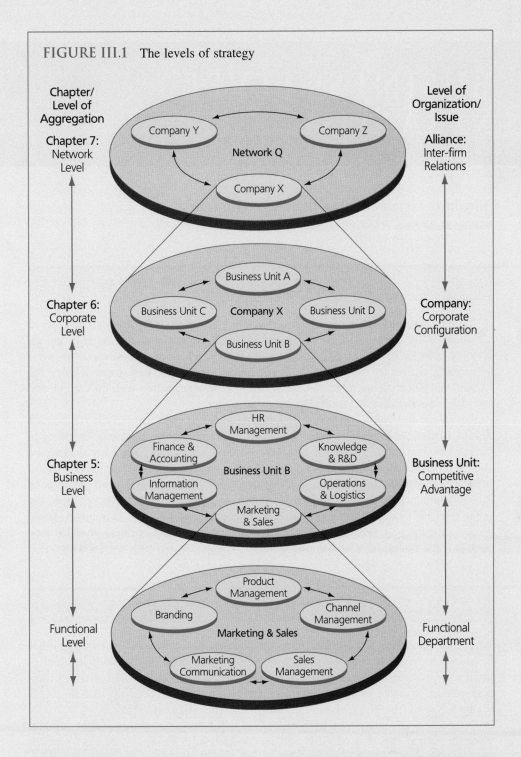

FIGURE III.1 The levels of strategy

Chapter/
Level of
Aggregation

Level of
Organization/
Issue

Chapter 7:
Network
Level

Company Y

Company Z

Network Q

Company X

Alliance:
Inter-firm
Relations

Chapter 6:
Corporate
Level

Business Unit A

Business Unit C   **Company X**   Business Unit D

Business Unit B

Company:
Corporate
Configuration

Chapter 5:
Business
Level

HR
Management

Finance &
Accounting

Knowledge
& R&D

Business Unit B

Information
Management

Operations
& Logistics

Marketing
& Sales

Business Unit:
Competitive
Advantage

Functional
Level

Product
Management

Branding

Channel
Management

Marketing & Sales

Marketing
Communication

Sales
Management

Functional
Department

focus on business level strategy, Chapter 6 on corporate level strategy and Chapter 7 on network level strategy. Only the functional level strategies will be given no extensive coverage, as they are usually explored in great detail in functionally oriented books. It must be noted, however, that the aggregation levels used here are an analytical distinction and not an empirical reality that can always be found in practice – where one level stops and the other starts is more a matter of definition than of thick demarcation lines. Hence, when discussing strategy issues at any level, it is important to understand how they fit with higher and lower level strategy questions.

BUSINESS LEVEL STRATEGY

Advantage is a better soldier than rashness.
William Shakespeare (1564–1616); English dramatist and poet

INTRODUCTION

Strategic management is concerned with relating a firm to its environment in order to successfully meet long-term objectives. As both the business environment and individual firms are dynamic systems, constantly in flux, achieving a fit between the two is an ongoing challenge. Managers are continuously looking for new ways to align the current, and potential, strengths and weaknesses of the organization with the current, and potential, opportunities and threats in the environment.

Part of the difficulty lies in the competitive nature of the environment. To be successful, firms need to gain a competitive advantage over rival organizations operating in the same business area. Within the competitive arena chosen by a firm, it needs to accrue enough power to counterbalance the demands of buyers and suppliers, to outperform rival producers, to discourage new firms from entering the business and to fend off the threat of substitute products or services. Preferably this competitive advantage over other players in the business should be sustainable over a prolonged period of time. How firms should go about creating a (sustainable) competitive advantage in each business in which they operate is the central issue concerning managers engaged in business level strategy.

THE ISSUE OF COMPETITIVE ADVANTAGE

Whether a firm has a competitive advantage depends on the business system that it has developed to relate itself to its business environment. A business system is the configuration of resources (inputs), activities (throughput) and product/service offerings (output) intended to create value for customers – it is the way a firm conducts its business. In Figure 5.1 an overview is given of the components of a business system.

Competitive advantage can be achieved only if a business system creates superior value for buyers. Therefore, the first element in a successful business system is a superior 'value proposition'. A firm must be able to supply a product or service more closely fitted to client needs than rival firms. To be attractive, each element of a firm's 'product offering' needs to be targeted at a particular segment of the market and have a superior mix of attributes (e.g. price, availability, reliability, technical specifications, image, colour, taste, ease of use, etc.). Secondly, a successful company must also have the ability to actually develop and supply the superior product offering. It needs to have the capability to perform the necessary value-adding activities in an effective and efficient manner.

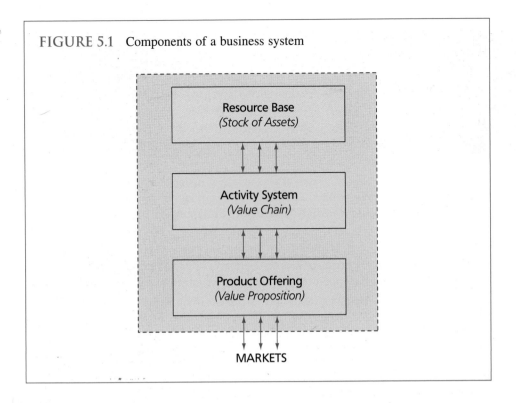

FIGURE 5.1 Components of a business system

These value-adding activities, such as R&D, production, logistics, marketing and sales, are jointly referred to as a firm's activity system (or value chain). The third component of a business system consists of the resource base required to perform the value-adding activities. Resources such as know-how, patents, facilities, money, brands and relationships make up the stock of assets that can be employed to create the product offering. If these firm-specific assets are distinctive and useful, they can form the basis of a superior value proposition. To create a competitive advantage, alignment must be achieved between all three elements of a business system. In the following pages all three elements will be discussed in more detail.

Product offering

At the intersection between a firm and its environment, transactions take place whereby the firm supplies goods or performs services for clients in the market-place. It is here that the alignment of the firm and its environment is put to the test. If the products and services offered by the firm are more highly valued by customers than alternatives, a profitable transaction could take place. In other words, for sales to be achieved a firm must have a competitive value proposition – a cluster of physical goods, services or additional attributes with a superior fit to customer needs.

For the strategizing manager the key question is which products should be developed and which markets should be served. In many cases the temptation is to be everything to everybody – making a wide range of products and serving as many clients as possible. However, a number of practical constraints inhibit companies from taking such an unfocused approach to the market. Companies that do not focus on a limited set of product–market combinations run the risk of encountering a number of major problems:

- Low economies of scale. Being unfocused is expensive, because of the low economies of scale that can be achieved. In general, the less specialized the company, the lower the opportunities to organize the activity system efficiently and leverage the resource base.

- Slow organizational learning. Being involved in a multitude of products and markets generally slows the organization's ability to build up specific knowledge and capabilities. In general, the less specialized the company, the lower the opportunity to develop a distinctive activity system and resource base.

- Unclear brand image. Unfocused companies have the added disadvantage of having a fuzzy image in the market. In general, companies that stand for everything tend to stand out in nothing.

- Unclear corporate image. The lack of clear external image is usually compounded by a lack of internal identity within unfocused organizations. In general, a company with highly diversified activities will have difficulty explaining why its people are together in the same company.

- High organizational complexity. Highly diverse products and customers also create an exponential increase in organizational complexity. In general, the less specialized the company, the lower the opportunity to keep the organization simple and manageable.

- Limits to flexibility. Being all things to all people is often physically impossible due to the need to specify procedures, routines, systems and tools. In general, less specialized firms are often forced into certain choices due to operational necessity.

For these reasons, companies need to focus on a limited number of businesses and within each business on a limited group of customers and a limited set of products. This focus should not be arbitrary – the challenge for strategizing managers is to understand which businesses are (or can be made to be) structurally attractive and how their firm can gain a competitive advantage within each business, by offering specific value propositions to selected customer segments.

Determining a focus starts by looking for the 'boundaries' of a business – how can managers draw meaningful delineation lines in the environment, distinguishing one arena of competition from another, so that they can select some and ignore others? Ideally, the environment would be made up of neatly compartmentalized businesses, with clear borders separating them. In reality, however, the picture is much more messy. While there are usually certain clusters of buyers and suppliers interacting more intensely with one another, suggesting that they are operating in the same business, there are often numerous exceptions to any neat classification scheme. To explore how a business can be defined, it is first necessary to specify how a business differs from an 'industry' and a 'market'.

Delineating industries. An industry is defined as a group of firms making a similar type of product or employing a similar set of value-adding processes or resources. In other words, an industry consists of producers that are much alike–there is *supply side similarity* (Kay, 1993). The simplest way to draw an industry boundary is to use product similarity as the delineation criterion. For instance, British Airways can be said to be in the airline industry, along with many other providers of the same product, such as Singapore Airlines and Ryanair. However, an industry can also be defined on the basis of activity system similarity (e.g. consulting industry and mining industry) or resource similarity (e.g. information technology industry and oil industry).

Economic statisticians tend to favour fixed industry categories based on product similarity and therefore most figures available about industries are product-category based, often making use of Standard Industrial Classification (SIC) codes. Strategists, on the contrary, like to challenge existing definitions of an industry, for instance by regrouping them on the basis of underlying value-adding activities or resources. Take the example of Swatch – how did it conceptualize which industry it was in? If they had focused on the physical product and the production process, then they would have been inclined to situate Swatch in the watch industry. However, Swatch also viewed its products as fashion accessories, placing emphasis on the key value-adding activities of fashion design and marketing. On this basis, Swatch could just as well be categorized as a member of the fashion industry (Porac, Thomas and Baden-Fuller, 1989). For the strategizing manager, the realization that Swatch can be viewed in both ways is an important insight. As creating a competitive advantage often comes from doing things differently, rethinking the definition of an industry can be a powerful way to develop a unique product offering.

Figure 5.2 gives four examples of traditionally defined 'industry columns', which Porter (1980, Reading 5.1 in this book) draws not top-down, but left-right, using the term 'value system'. These columns start with upstream industries, which are involved in the extraction/growing of raw materials and their conversion into inputs for the manufacturing sector. Downstream industries take the output of manufacturing companies and bring them to clients, often adding a variety of services into the product mix. In practice, industry columns are not as simple as depicted in Figure 5.2, as each industry has many different industries as suppliers and usually many different industries as buyers.

A second limitation of the industry columns shown in Figure 5.2 is that they are materials-flow oriented – industry boundaries are drawn on the basis of product

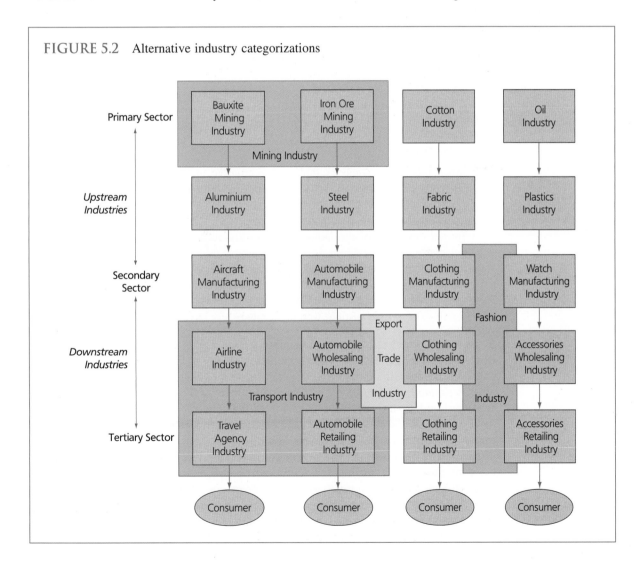

FIGURE 5.2 Alternative industry categorizations

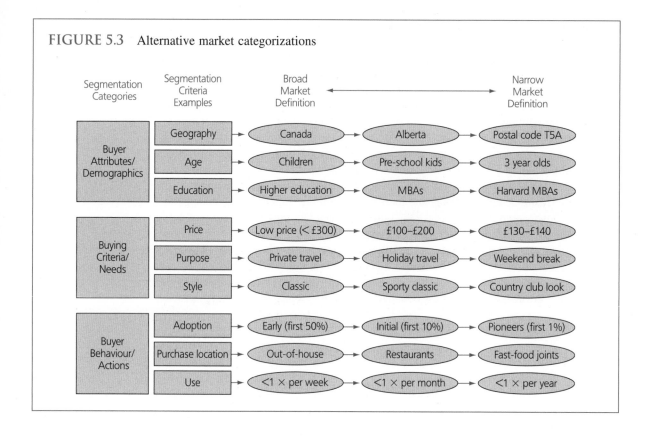

FIGURE 5.3   Alternative market categorizations

similarity, while strategists might want to take a different angle on defining the industry. The brown blocks are some examples of alternative industry definitions, but one can imagine many more; not only broader definitions, but also more narrow ones. For instance, it could be argued that clothing retailers with physical stores are in a distinct industry as opposed to internet/mail-order retailers.

A further downside of the industry column figure is that the 'materials-flow' angle does not really suit the two-thirds of the economy that is involved in services. Understanding who are the buyers and the suppliers of insurance, education, consultancy, advertising and healthcare requires a different way of conceiving the industry column than looking at the flow of goods. Generally, for each different type of service a different value system will exist, with a distinct web of suppliers and buyers.

Segmenting markets.   While economists see the market as a place where supply and demand meet, in the business world a market is usually defined as a group of customers with similar needs. In other words, a market consists of buyers whose demands are much alike – *demand side similarity*. For instance, there is a market for air transportation between London and Jamaica, which is a different market than for air transportation between London and Paris – the customer needs are different and therefore these products cannot be substituted for one another. But customers can substitute a British Airways London–Paris flight for one by Air France, indicating that both companies are serving the same market. Yet, this market definition (London–Paris air transport) might not be the most appropriate, if in reality many customers are willing to substitute air travel by rail travel through the Channel tunnel, or by ferry. In this case, there is a broader London–Paris transportation market, and air transportation is a specific *market segment*. If many customers are willing to substitute physical travel by teleconferencing or other telecommunications methods, the market might need to be defined as the 'London–Paris meeting market'.

As with industries, there are many ways of defining markets, depending on which buyer characteristics are used to make a clustering. In Figure 5.3, a number of examples are given of segmentation criteria. The first group of segmentation criteria is based on buyer attributes that are frequently thought to be important predictors of actual buying criteria and buyer behaviour. Such customer characteristics are commonly used to group potential clients because this information is objective and easily available. However, the pitfall of segmenting on the basis of buyer attributes is that the causal link between characteristics and actual needs and behaviours is often rather tenuous – not all Canadians need hockey sticks and not all three-year-olds nag their parents while shopping. In other words, the market can be segmented on the basis of any demographic characteristic (e.g. income, family composition, employment), but this might not lead to meaningful groups of customers with similar needs and buying behaviour.

Therefore, instead of using buyer attributes as *indirect* – predictive – measures of what clients probably want, segments can also be *directly* defined on the basis of buying criteria employed or buyer behaviours exhibited. The advantage is that segments can then be identified with clearly similar wishes or behaviours. The disadvantage is that it is very difficult to gather and interpret information on what specific people want and how they really act.

For strategists, one of the key challenges is to look at existing categorizations of buyers and to wonder whether a different segmentation would offer new insights and new opportunities for developing a product offering specifically tailored to their needs. As with the redefining of industry boundaries, it is often in the reconceptualization of market segments that a unique approach to the market can be found.

Defining and selecting businesses. A business is a set of related product–market combinations. The term 'business' refers neither to a set of producers nor a group of customers, but to the domain where the two meet. In other words, a business is a competitive arena where companies offering similar products serving similar needs compete against one another for the favour of the buyers. Hence, a business is delineated in both industry and market terms (see Figure 5.4). Typically, a business is narrower than the entire industry and the set of markets served is also limited. For instance, within the

FIGURE 5.4   Industries, markets and businesses

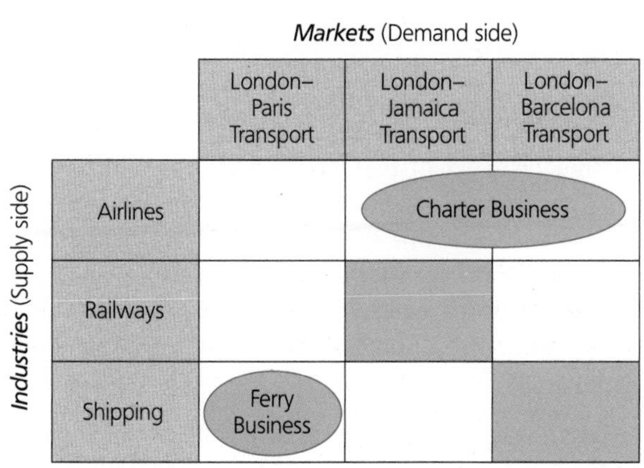

airline industry the charter business is usually recognized as rather distinct. In the charter business, a sub-set of the airline services is offered to a number of tourist markets. Cheap flights from London to Jamaica and from London to Barcelona fall within this business, while service levels will be different than in other parts of the airline industry. It should be noted, though, that just as with industries and markets, there is no best way to define the boundaries of a business (Abell, 1980).

As stated earlier, companies cannot afford to be unfocused, operating superficially in a whole range of businesses. They must direct their efforts by focusing in two ways:

1 Selecting a limited number of businesses. The first constraint that companies need to impose on themselves is to choose a limited array of businesses within which they wish to be successful. This essential strategic challenge is referred to as the issue of corporate configuration and will be examined in more detail in Chapter 6 (multi-business level strategy). Here it suffices to say that firms need to analyse the structural characteristics of interesting businesses to be able to judge whether they are attractive enough for the firm, or can be made to be attractive. In Reading 5.1 Porter presents the 'five forces analysis' as a framework for mapping the structure of industries and businesses.

2 Focusing within each selected business. Even within the limited set of businesses selected, firms need to determine what they want to be and what they want to leave aside. To be competitive, it is necessary to choose a number of distinct market segments and to target a few special product offerings to meet these customers' needs. As illustrated in Figure 5.1, these specific product offerings in turn need to be aligned with a focused activity system and resource base.

This act of focusing the overall business system to serve the particular needs of a targeted group of buyers, in a way that distinguishes the firm vis-à-vis rivals, is called positioning. This positioning of the firm in the business requires a clearly tailored product offering (product positioning), but also an activity system and resource base that closely fit with the demands of the specific group of customers and competitors being targeted.

Positioning within a business. Positioning is concerned with both the questions of 'where to compete' and 'how to compete' (Porter, 1980, Reading 5.1). Determining in which product–market combinations within a business a firm wants to be involved is referred to as the issue of competitive scope. Finding a way to beat rivals and win over customers for a product offering is the issue of competitive advantage. The two questions are tightly linked, because firms need to develop a specific advantage to be competitive within a specific product–market domain. If they try to use the same competitive advantage for too many dissimilar products and customers, they run the risk of becoming unfocused.

In selecting a competitive scope, firms can vary anywhere between being widely oriented and very tightly focused. Firms with a broad scope compete in a large number of segments within a business, with varied product offerings. Firms with a narrow scope target only one, or just a few, customer segments and have a more limited product line (see Figure 5.5). If there is a small part of the business with very specific demands, requiring a distinct approach, firms can narrowly focus on this niche as their competitive scope. In between these two extremes are firms with a segment focus and firms with a product focus, but in practice many other profiles are also possible.

In developing a competitive advantage, firms have many dimensions along which they can attempt to outdo their rivals. Some of the most important bases of competitive advantage are the following:

- Price. The most straightforward advantage a firm can have in a competitive situation is the ability to charge a lower price. All things being equal, buyers generally prefer to

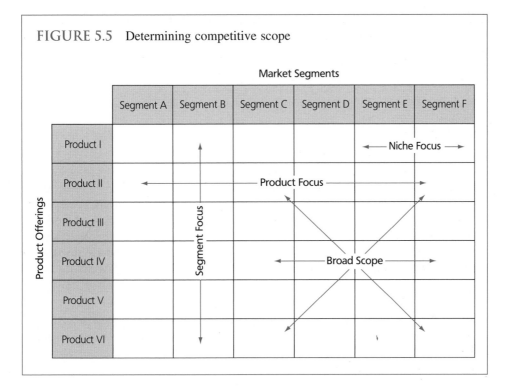

FIGURE 5.5 Determining competitive scope

pay the lowest amount necessary. Hence, when purchasing a commodity product or service, most customers will be partial to the lowest priced supplier. And even when selecting among differentiated products, many customers will be inclined to buy the cheapest or at least the cheapest within a sub-group of more comparable products. For a firm wanting to compete on price, the essential point is that it should have a *low cost* product offering, activity system and resource base to match the price positioning. After all, in the long run a firm can survive at a lower price level only if it has developed a business system that can sustainably operate at a lower cost level.

■ Features. Firms can also distinguish their product offerings by having different intrinsic functional characteristics than competing offerings. There are many ways to make a product or service different, for instance by changing its size, smell, taste, colour, functionality, compatibility, content, design or style. An ice cream manufacturer can introduce a new flavour and more chunky texture, a motorcycle producer can design a special low rider model for women, a pay TV company can develop special channels for dog owners and science fiction addicts, and a utility company can offer environmentally friendly electricity. To be able to compete on each of these product features, firms need to command different specialized resources and activity systems. In some cases, they require significant technological knowledge and a technically sophisticated activity system, while in other cases design capabilities, marketing prowess or a satellite infrastructure are essential to the functioning of the business system.

■ Bundling. Another way to offer a uniquely different value proposition is to sell a package of products or services 'wrapped together'. By bundling a number of separate elements into a package, the customer can have the convenience of 'one stop shopping', while also having a family of related products or services that fit together well. So, for instance, many customers prefer to purchase their software from one supplier because this raises the chance of compatibility. In the chocolate industry, the leading manufacturer of chocolate making machines, Rademakers, was able to gain a competitive advantage by bundling its machines with various services, such as installation, repair, spare parts and financing.

- Quality. When competing with others, a firm's product offering doesn't necessarily have to be fundamentally different, it can just be better. Customers generally appreciate products and services that exhibit superior performance in terms of usability, reliability and durability, and are often willing to pay a premium price for such quality. Excellent quality can be secured on many fronts, for instance through the materials used, the people involved, the manufacturing process employed, the quality assurance procedures followed or the distribution system used.

- Availability. The method of distribution can in itself be the main competitive edge on which a firm bases its positioning. Having a product available at the right place, at the right moment and in the right way, can be much more important to customers than features and quality. Just ask successful ice cream manufacturers – most of their revenues are from out-of-doors impulse sales, so they need to have their products available in individually wrapped portions at all locations where people have the urge to indulge. In the same way, Avon's cosmetics are not primarily sold because of their uniqueness or low price, but because of the strength of their three million sales force, who can be at the right place at the right time.

- Image. In the competition for customers' preference, firms can also gain an advantage by having a more appealing image than their rivals. In business-to-consumer markets this is particularly clear when looking at the impact of brands. Consumers often feel attracted to brands that project a certain image of the company or the products it sells. Brands can communicate specific values that consumers want to be associated with (Nike's 'just do it'), or can help to build trust among consumers who have too little information on which to base their product choices (GE's 'we bring good things to life'). But even in business-to-business markets buyers often suffer from a shortage of information about the available product offerings or lack the time to research all possible suppliers. Therefore, the image of suppliers, mostly in terms of their standing ('a leading global player') and reputation ('high quality service') can be essential to be considered at all (to be 'shortlisted') and to be trusted as business partner.

- Relations. Good branding can give customers the impression that they know the supplier, without actually being in direct contact. Yet, having a direct relation with customers can in itself be a potent source of competitive advantage. In general, customers prefer to know their suppliers well, as this gives them a more intimate knowledge of the product offering being provided. Having a relationship with a supplier can also give the customer more influence on what is offered. But besides these rational points, customers often value the personal contact, the trust and the convenience of having a longstanding relationship as well. For suppliers this means that they might acquire a competitive edge by managing their customer relationships well. To do so, however, does imply that the activity system and resource base are fit to fulfil this task.

The type of competitive advantage that a firm chooses to pursue will be influenced by what the targeted group of buyers find important. These factors of importance to potential clients are referred to as 'value drivers' – they are the elements responsible for creating value in the eyes of the customer. Which value drivers a firm will want to base its value proposition on is a matter of positioning.

According to Porter (1980, Reading 5.1 in this book) all the specific forms of competitive advantage listed above can be reduced to two broad categories, namely lower cost and differentiation. On the one hand, firms can organize their business systems in such a manner that, while their products or services are largely the same as other manufacturers, their overall cost structure is lower, allowing them to compete on price. On the other hand, firms can organize their business systems to supply a product or service that has distinctive qualities compared to rival offerings. According to Porter, these two forms of competitive advantage demand fundamentally different types of business systems and therefore are next to impossible to combine. Firms that do try to realize both at the same time run the risk of getting 'stuck in the middle' – not being able to do either properly.

Treacy and Wiersema (1995) argue that there are actually three generic competitive advantages, each requiring a fundamentally different type of business system (they speak of three distinctive 'value disciplines'). They, too, warn firms to develop an internally consistent business system focused on one of these types of competitive advantage, avoiding a 'mix-and-match' approach to business strategy:

■ Operational excellence. Firms striving for operational excellence meet the buyers' need for a reliable, low cost product offering. The activity system required to provide such no-frills, standardized, staple products emphasizes a 'lean and mean' approach to production and distribution, with simple service.

■ Product leadership. Firms taking the route of product leadership meet the buyers' need for special features and advanced product performance. The activity system required to provide such differentiated, state-of-the-art products emphasizes innovation and the creative collaboration between marketing and R&D.

■ Customer intimacy. Firms deciding to focus on customer intimacy meet the buyers' need for a tailored solution to their particular problem. The activity system required to provide such a client-specific, made-to-measure offering emphasizes flexibility and empowerment of the employees close to the customer.

Other strategy researchers, however, argue that there is no such thing as generic competitive strategies that follow from two or three broad categories of competitive advantage (e.g. Baden-Fuller and Stopford, 1992). In their view, there is an endless variety of ways in which companies can develop a competitive advantage, many of which do not fit into the categories outlined by Porter or Treacy and Wiersema – in fact, finding a new type of competitive advantage might be the best way of obtaining a unique position in a business.

Activity system

To be able to actually make what it wants to sell, a firm needs to have an activity system in place. An activity system is an integrated set of value creation processes leading to the supply of product or service offerings. Whether goods are being manufactured or services are being provided, each firm needs to perform a number of activities to successfully fill the customer's wants. As these value-adding activities need to be coordinated and linked together, this part of the business system is also frequently referred to as the 'value chain' (Porter, 1985).

Activity systems can vary widely from industry to industry. The activity system of a car manufacturer is quite distinct from that of an advertising agency. Yet even within an industry there can be significant differences. Most 'bricks and mortar' bookstores have organized their value chain differently than on-line book retailers like Amazon.com. The activity systems of most 'hub-and-spoke' airline companies hardly resemble that of 'no-frills' carriers such as Southwest in the United States and easyJet in Europe.

While these examples point to radically different activity systems, even firms that subscribe to the same basic model can apply it in their own particular way. Fast-food restaurants such as McDonald's and Burger King may employ the same basic model, but their actual activity systems differ in quite a few ways. The same goes for the PC manufacturers HP and Lenovo, which share a similar type of activity system, but which still differ on many fronts. 'On-line mass-customization' PC manufacturer Dell, on the other hand, has a different model and consequently a more strongly differing activity system than HP and Lenovo.

Having such a distinct activity system often provides the basis for a competitive advantage. A unique value chain allows a firm to offer customers a unique value proposition, by doing things better, faster, cheaper, nicer or more tailored than competing firms. Developing the firm's activity system is therefore just as strategically important as developing new products and services.

Although activity systems can differ quite significantly, some attempts have been made to develop a general taxonomy of value-adding activities that could be used as an analytical framework (e.g. Day, 1990; Norman and Ramirez, 1993). By far the most influential framework is Porter's value chain, which distinguishes primary activities and support activities (see Figure 5.6). Primary activities 'are the activities involved in the physical creation of the product and its sale and transfer to the buyer, as well as after-sale assistance' (Porter, 1985: 16). Support activities facilitate the primary process, by providing purchased inputs, technology, human resources and various firm-wide functions. The generic categories of primary activities identified by Porter are:

- Inbound logistics. Activities associated with receiving, storing, and disseminating inputs, including material handling, warehousing, inventory control, vehicle scheduling and returns to suppliers.

- Operations. Activities associated with transforming inputs into final products, including machining, packaging, assembly, equipment maintenance, testing, printing and facility operations.

- Outbound logistics. Activities associated with collecting, storing and physically distributing products to buyers, including warehousing, material handling, delivery, order processing and scheduling.

- Marketing and sales. Activities associated with providing a means by which buyers can purchase the product and inducing them to do so, including advertising, promotion, sales force, quoting, channel selection, channel relations and pricing.

- Service. Activities associated with providing service to enhance or maintain the value of products, including installation, repair, training, parts supply and product adjustment.

For service industries Porter argues that the specific activities will be different, and might be performed in a different order, but can still be subdivided into these five generic

FIGURE 5.6   The generic value chain (Porter, 1985)

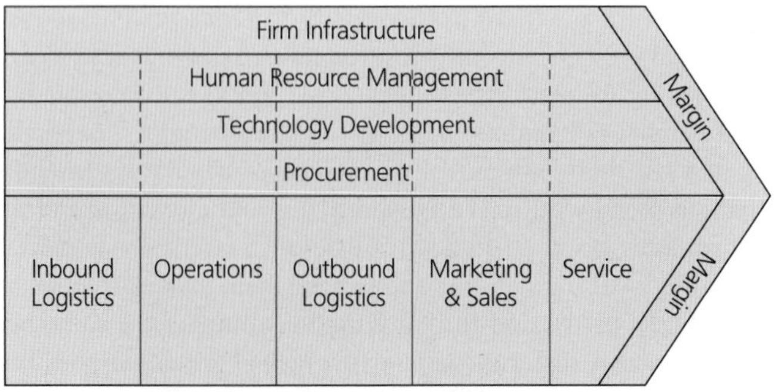

categories. To ensure that the primary activities can be carried out, each firm also needs to organize four types of support activities:

- Procurement. Activities associated with the purchasing of inputs to facilitate all other activities, including vendor selection, negotiations, contracting and invoice administration.
- Technology development. Activities associated with the improvement of technologies throughout the firm, including basic research, product and process design, and procedure development.
- Human resource management. Activities associated with the management of personnel throughout the organization, including recruiting, hiring, training, development and compensation.
- Firm infrastructure. Firm infrastructure consists of all general activities that support the entire value chain, including general management, planning, finance, accounting, legal, government affairs and quality management.

The uniqueness of the activity system, and its strength as the source of competitive advantage, will usually not depend on only a few specialized activities, but on the extraordinary configuration of the entire activity system. An extraordinary configuration multiplies the distinctness of a particular activity system, while often raising the barrier to imitation (Porter, 1996; Amit and Zott, 2001).

Resource base

To carry out activities and to produce goods and services, firms need resources. A firm's resource base includes all means at the disposal of the organization for the performance of value-adding activities. Other authors prefer the term 'assets', to emphasize that the resources belong to the firm (e.g. Dierickx and Cool, 1989; Itami, 1987).

Under the broad umbrella of resource-based view of the firm, there has been much research into the importance of resources for the success and even existence of firms (e.g. Penrose, 1959; Wernerfelt, 1984; Barney, 1991, Reading 5.4). No generally accepted classification of firm resources has yet emerged in the field of strategic management, however the following major distinctions (see Figure 5.7) are commonly made:

- Tangible vs. intangible resources. Tangible resources are all means available to the firm that can physically be observed (touched), such as buildings, machines, materials,

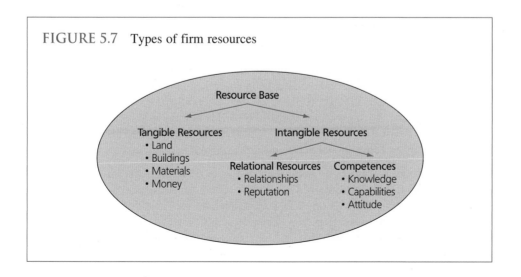

FIGURE 5.7   Types of firm resources

land and money. Tangibles can be referred to as the 'hardware' of the organization. Intangibles, on the other hand, are the 'software' of the organization. Intangible resources cannot be touched, but are largely carried within the people in the organization. In general, tangible resources need to be purchased, while intangibles need to be developed. Therefore, tangible resources are often more readily transferable, easier to price and usually are placed on the balance sheet.

■ Relational resources vs. competences. Within the category of intangible resources, relational resources and competences can be distinguished. Relational resources are all of the means available to the firm derived from the firm's interaction with its environment (Lowendahl, 1997). The firm can cultivate specific relationships with individuals and organizations in the environment, such as buyers, suppliers, competitors and government agencies, which can be instrumental in achieving the firm's goals. As attested by the old saying, 'it's not what you know, but whom you know', relationships can often be an essential resource (see Chapter 7 for a further discussion). Besides direct relationships, a firm's reputation among other parties in the environment can also be an important resource. Competence, on the other hand, refers to the firm's fitness to perform in a particular field. A firm has a competence if it has the knowledge, capabilities and attitude needed to successfully operate in a specific area.

This description of competences is somewhat broad and therefore difficult to employ. However, a distinction between knowledge, capability and attitude (Durand, 1996) can be used to shed more light on the nature of competences:

■ Knowledge. Knowledge can be defined as the whole of rules (know-how, know-what, know-where and know-when) and insights (know-why) that can be extracted from, and help make sense of, information. In other words, knowledge flows from, and influences, the interpretation of information (Dretske, 1981). Examples of knowledge that a firm can possess are market insight, competitive intelligence, technological expertise, and understanding of political and economic developments.

■ Capability. Capability refers to the organization's potential for carrying out a specific activity or set of activities. Sometimes the term 'skill' is used to refer to the ability to carry out a narrow (functional) task or activity, while the term 'capability' is reserved for the quality of combining a number of skills. For instance, a firm's capability base can include narrower abilities such as market research, advertising and production skills, that if coordinated could result in a capability for new product development (Stalk, Evans and Shulman, 1992).

■ Attitude. Attitude refers to the mind-set prevalent within an organization. Sometimes the terms 'disposition' and 'will' are used in the same sense, to indicate how an organization views and relates to the world. Although ignored by some writers, every sports coach will acknowledge the importance of attitude as a resource. A healthy body (tangible resource), insight into the game (knowledge), speed and dexterity (capabilities) – all are important, but without the winning mentality a team will not get to the top. Some attitudes may change rapidly within firms, yet others may be entrenched within the cultural fabric of the organization – these in particular can be important resources for the firm. A company's attitude can, for instance, be characterized as quality-driven, internationally oriented, innovation-minded or competitively aggressive.

It must be noted that the term 'competences' is used in many different ways, partially due to the ambiguous definition given by its early proponents (Prahalad and Hamel, 1990, Reading 6.2 in this book). It is often used as a synonym for capabilities, while Prahalad and Hamel seem to focus more on technologically oriented capabilities ('how to coordinate diverse production skills and integrate multiple streams of technologies').

Others (e.g. Durand, 1996) have suggested that a firm has a competence in a certain area, when the firm's underlying knowledge base, capabilities and attitude are all aligned. So, Honda's engine competence is built on specific knowledge, development capabilities and the right predisposition. Wal-Mart's inventory control competence depends on specific information technology knowledge, coordination capabilities and a conducive state of mind. Virgin's service competence combines customer knowledge, adaptation capabilities and a customer-oriented attitude.

As in the case of industries, markets and businesses, employing the concepts of tangible and intangible resources is quite difficult in practice. Two problems need to be overcome – resources are difficult to categorize, but worse yet, often difficult to recognize. The issue of categorization is a minor one. For some resources it is unclear how they should be classified. Are human resources tangible or intangible? Problematically, both. In humans, hardware and software are intertwined – if an engineer's expertise is required, the physical person usually needs to be hired. Knowledge, capabilities and attitudes need human carriers. Sometimes it is possible to separate hardware and software, by making the intangibles more tangible. This is done by 'writing the software down'. In such a manner, knowledge can be codified, for instance in a patent, a capability can be captured in a computer program and a relationship can be formalized in a contract. Sometimes intangibles become more tangible, as they become attached to physical carriers – for instance, attitude can be embodied by a person or a symbol, while reputation becomes attached to a brand.

More important is the problem of resource identification. Tangible resources, by their very nature, are relatively easy to observe. Accountants keep track of the financial resources, production managers usually know the quality of their machinery and stock levels, while the personnel department will have an overview of all people on the payroll. Intangible resources, on the other hand, are far more difficult to identify (e.g. Grant, 1991; Itami, 1987). With whom does the firm have a relationship and what is the state of this relationship? What is the firm's reputation? These relational resources are hard to pin down. Competences are probably even more difficult to determine. How do you know what you know? Even for an individual it is a formidable task to outline areas of expertise, let alone for a more complex organization. Especially the *tacit* (non-articulated) nature of much organizational knowledge makes it difficult to identify the firm's knowledge base (Polanyi, 1958; Nonaka and Konno, 1998). The same is true for a firm's capabilities, which have developed in the form of organizational routines (Nelson and Winter, 1982). Likewise, the firm's attitudes are difficult to discern, because all people sharing the same disposition will tend to consider themselves normal and will tend to believe that their outlook is 'a matter of common sense' (see Chapter 2). Hence, firms intent on identifying their competences find that this is not an easy task.

While an overview of the firm's resource base is important in itself, a strategizing manager will want to compare the firm's resources to other companies to determine their relative strength. In other words, are the firm's resources unique, superior to or inferior to the resources of (potential) competitors? This type of analysis is particularly difficult, as comparison requires insight into other firms' resource bases. Especially the identification of other firms' intangible resources can be quite arduous.

Sustaining competitive advantage

A firm has a competitive advantage when it has the means to edge out rivals when vying for the favour of customers. In the previous sub-sections it was argued that competitive advantage is rooted in a unique business system, whereby the resource base, activity system and product–market position are all aligned to provide goods and/or services with a superior fit to customer needs.

A competitive advantage is said to be sustainable if it cannot be copied, substituted or eroded by the actions of rivals, and is not made redundant by developments in the environment (Porter, 1980). In other words, sustainability depends on two main factors, competitive defendability and environmental consonance:

■ Competitive defendability. Some competitive advantages are intrinsically easier to defend than others, either because they are difficult for rivals to imitate, or because rivals find it next to impossible to find an alternative route of attack. In general, a firm's competitive advantage is more vulnerable when it is based on only a limited number of distinct elements (e.g. a different packaging technology, a different delivery system or different product colours). For rivals, imitating or substituting a few elements is comparatively easy. If, however, a firm's business system has an entirely different configuration altogether, the barriers to imitation and substitution are much higher. In such a case, it is said that a firm has a distinct 'business model'. So, for instance, in the airline industry the traditional firms have tried to imitate some parts of the low cost service of Southwest in the United States, and Ryanair and easyJet in Europe, but have been largely unsuccessful because their business model as a whole is based on a different logic. Yet, many strategists note that the best defence is not to build walls around a competitive position to 'keep the barbarians out', but to have the ability to run faster than rivals – to be able to upgrade one's resources, activity system and product offering more rapidly than competitors. In this view, a competitive advantage is sustainable due to a company's capacity to stay one step ahead of rivals, *outpacing* them in a race to stay ahead (e.g. Gilbert and Strebel, 1989; Stalk, Evans and Shulman, 1992).

■ Environmental consonance. The sustainability of a firm's competitive advantage is also threatened by developments in the market. Customer needs and wants are in constant flux, distribution channels can change, government regulations can be altered, innovative technologies can be introduced and new entrants can come into the competitive arena. All of these developments can undermine the fit between the firm's competitive advantage and the environment, weakening the firm's position (Rumelt, 1980).

Yet, these two factors for sustaining competitive advantage seem to pose opposite demands on the organization. Building a distinctive business system to fend off competition would suggest that a firm should remain true to its fundamental *strengths,* especially when it comes to unique resources and activities that it has built up over a prolonged period of time. On the other hand, environmental consonance requires a firm to continually adapt its business system to the demands and new *opportunities* in the market place. The tension created by these opposite pressures will be discussed in the following section.

THE PARADOX OF MARKETS AND RESOURCES

Sell where you can, you are not for all markets.

As You Like It, William Shakespeare (1564–1616); English dramatist and poet

There must be a fit between an organization and its environment. This point is often expressed in terms of the classic SWOT analysis tool, which suggests that a sound strategy should match a firm's strengths (S) and weaknesses (W) to the opportunities (O) and threats (T) encountered in the firm's environment. The key to success is *alignment* of the two sides. Yet, fitting internal strengths and weaknesses to external opportunities and threats is often frustrated by the fact that the two sides pull in opposite directions – the distinctive resource base and activity system of a firm can point in a totally different direction compared with the developments in their current markets. Take the example of Bally, in the 1990s the worldwide market leader in pinball machines. Their strength in the manufacturing of electromechanical games was no longer aligned with developments in the market, where young people were turning to video games produced by companies such as Nintendo, Sega and Sony. As sales of pinball machines were quickly deteriorating, it was clear that Bally had to find a new fit with the market to survive. On the one hand, this meant that there was a strong pressure on Bally to adapt to market developments, for instance by upgrading its technology to also produce video games. On the other hand, Bally felt a strong pressure to exploit its current strength in electromechanical manufacturing, instead of building a new competence base from scratch. It was not self-evident for Bally how the demands for market adaptation and resource leveraging could be met simultaneously, as they seemed to be tugging the firm in diametrically opposite directions.

This tension arising from the partially conflicting demands of market adaptation and resource leveraging is referred to as the paradox of markets and resources. In the following sub-sections both sides of the paradox will be examined in more detail.

The demand for market adaptation

While adaptation to the environment is a vital requirement for the success of any organization, Bally had been very slow in responding to external developments ever since the introduction of Pac-Man. Bally had not exhibited the ability to shift its product offering to follow changing customer preferences and to respond to new entrants in the gaming market. It had lost its leading position because it no longer fully understood 'the rules of the game' in its own market. As Bally drifted further and further away from developments in the market, the misalignment was threatening the survival of its business. 'Game over' was impending.

To counter this downward trend, Bally needed to identify an attractive market opportunity that it could exploit. Not a short-term sales opportunity, but a market position that could be defended against rival firms and potential new entrants over a longer period. Ideally, this market position would serve buyers willing and able to pay a premium price, and whose loyalty could be won, despite the efforts of the competition. This market position would also need to be largely immune to substitute products and should not make the firm overly dependent on strong suppliers. Once such an opportunity had been identified, it would be essential for Bally to reorganize itself to fully meet the demands of this new positioning.

Adapting to a new market position and subsequently following the many shifts in such factors as customer preferences, competitor moves, government regulations and distribution structures, can have a significant impact on a firm. It requires significant agility in changing the product offering, activity system and resource base to remain in constant alignment with the fluctuating external circumstances. For Bally, adapting to the digital technology and software environment of the current gaming industry would have had far-reaching consequences for its entire business system. Even if Bally decided to stick to electromechanical pinball machines and to target the home market of aging pinball wizards, the company would need to make significant alterations to its business system, getting to know new distribution channels and developing new marketing competences.

The demand for resource leveraging

Yet, for Bally it was essential to build on the resource base and activity system that it had already developed. It did not want to write off the investments it had made in building up a distinctive profile – it had taken years of acquiring and nurturing resources and fine-tuning the activity system to reach its level of expertise. Its strength in electromechanical manufacturing and the development of large 'moving parts' games was much too valuable to casually throw away just because video games were currently in fashion.

However, building a new area of competence, it was understood, should not be considered lightly. It would take a considerable amount of time, effort and money to shift the resource base and reconfigure the activity system, while there would be many risks associated with this transformation process as well. On the other hand, the danger of attempting to exploit the firm's current resources would be to excel at something of increasing irrelevance. The pinball machine might be joining the buggy whip and the vacuum tube as a museum exhibit, with a real threat that Bally too could become history.

Eventually, the solution found by Bally was to give up on pinball machines altogether and to redirect its existing resources towards a much more attractive market opportunity– slot machines. This move allowed Bally to exploit its electromechanical manufacturing capability and game-making expertise, while building a strong market position in a fast growing market. But while Bally was able to find a synthesis, reconciling the two conflicting demands, not all companies are as successful. Nor do all managers agree on how the paradox of markets and resources can best be tackled.

EXHIBIT 5.1 SHORT CASE

AVON: KEEP THOSE DOORBELLS RINGING?

Few powers in the world can field an army of 5.8 million, with the ability to reach every corner of the globe. Yet one organization has such a legion, spread across 110 countries, equipped to engage in close-range encounters, toting little more than lipstick, some samples and a few brochures. This superpower is Avon, the world's largest direct sales company. With 2008 sales of almost US$10.7 billion, of which roughly 78% outside of North America, Avon is a huge player in the global market for beauty products, such as cosmetics, fragrances, creams, shampoos and soaps. The New York-based company has approximately half a million independent sales representatives in the US and Canada, with the other 5.3 million spread across Latin America (US$3.9 billion sales), Central and Eastern Europe (US$1.7 billion), Asia Pacific (US$0.9 billion), China (US$350 million), and Western Europe, Africa and the Middle East (US$1.4 billion). While Avon is generally known for its beauty products, 18% of its sales come from fashion apparel, jewellery and accessories, with another 10% realized in the areas of decorative items, home entertainment and gifts.

From its start in 1886 as the California Perfume Company, Avon has been based on the concept of independent sales representatives selling directly to women. These sales reps, commonly referred to as Avon Ladies, are independent intermediaries, who buy from Avon at a discount and then resell to their clients at list price. While men are not excluded, only a small fraction of the Avon Ladies are not female. In the early years most of the sales were done door-to-door, making the 1950s slogan 'Ding Dong, Avon Calling' quite appropriate. Since then, large numbers of women have shifted to paid employment in most of Avon's major markets and the company has followed them, making about a third of all sales at work. Yet, Avon's positioning has remained basically the same as at the outset – quality beauty products are provided to women of average and below average income at competitive prices, while offering personal attention and advice.

In 1999 Andrea Jung became Avon's CEO the first female in the company's history to occupy the top job, but reflective of a management pyramid composed of more than 50% women. With years of experience in the company, Jung was acutely aware that Avon was facing a difficult battle on many fronts, particularly in its mature North American and Western European markets. While growth was high in many developing economies in Latin America and Eastern Europe, where the retailing infrastructure was weak and jobs for women were few, results in the developed economies were extremely lacklustre. Avon's brand was perceived as stale and down market, particularly by fashion-conscious younger women. Despite years of efforts to revitalize the brand, for many women Avon retained the connotation of the 1950s housewife. As Jung's predecessor, James Preston, had earlier confessed: 'I am well aware that there are many women who would not want to open their purses and pull out Avon lipstick.'

To compound the image problem, Avon was finding it increasingly difficult to find new, younger recruits as Avon Ladies. For years the sales force in the mature markets had been shrinking, as younger women no longer had plenty of spare time to sell beauty products, or had better-paying alternatives open to them. Moreover, younger women seem to prefer to go out shopping, not only purchasing products from Avon's traditional department store competitors, but increasingly from the new breed of cosmetics specialists, such as The Body Shop (by 2009, 2400 stores in 61 countries), Sephora (515 stores in 14 mature markets, of which more than 250 stores in Canada and the US) and Douglas (1200 stores in 22 European countries and just starting in the US). And if they are not out shopping, these young women are behind their computers, where they can purchase beauty products directly and cheaply from a whole string of internet retailers.

To counter these strategic weaknesses, Jung set out to unleash a 'thoughtful transformation' of Avon. Her first priority was to rejuvenate the Avon brand. A new advertising campaign was launched around the slogan 'Let's Talk' and a new tag line was added to the Avon logo – The Company for Women. Packaging was upgraded, to create a Lancôme or Estée Lauder type luxury feel to the products and brochures were restyled to fit the new image. Jung also carried through some drastic business processes redesigning activities and streamlining production and logistics.

Another important move Jung set out to implement was to strengthen the sales force, both in numbers and in quality. To improve the quality, Jung initiated the Beauty Advisor programme, aimed at training tens of thousands of salespeople each year in the areas of beauty product knowledge and consultative selling skills. To increase the number of sales women was much more difficult since Avon, like most direct sales companies, experienced a nearly 100% turnover of its sales force each year. A core group of sales representatives – the President's Club – form the backbone of the system, generally selling full-time for many years, while the other 80% are part-timers that on average stay less than one year. To recruit almost five million salespeople each year is quite an effort, especially since Avon is not a 'network marketing' organization in which each sales representative can recruit their own resellers (multi-level sales structure). As Avon has a single level sales organization, more management time must be spent finding and training new recruits. To get the existing salespeople to assist with this task, Jung introduced a 'Sales Leadership' programme, offering significant bonuses for contributing to the expansion of the sales force.

But with pressure to grow and to improve profitability, more was needed than these realignment measures. Jung was convinced that organic growth through the direct sales channels would be too limited in scale and would not catapult Avon into the top league. Therefore, Jung introduced the slogan, 'The brand is bigger than the channel', and started to look for ways to become a multi-channel company. An early experiment was to have free-standing beauty kiosks in more than 50 American shopping malls, to bring shoppers into contact with Avon products. More surprising was Avon's move in 2001 to start selling an entirely new, upmarket product line called beComing at 92 J.C. Penney department stores across the United States. Both initiatives were not a success and were discontinued within a few years.

Other growth options were also pursued, such as launching a range of wellness products in 2002 and establishing a new brand for females between 16 and 24 called 'mark' in 2003. For the latter, Jung not only had a new product range developed, but also a separate website and separate network of young saleswomen, to visit colleges, high schools, shopping malls and other youth-oriented spots. Both activities were a moderate success, but not enough to stop the slow decay of Avon's position in its key mature markets.

When in 2005 sales even began to decline in these markets and Avon's share price took a beating, Jung accepted that more radical action was required. A turnaround plan was formulated, costing approximately US$500 million, to restructure the supply chain, improve market intelligence, increase the advertising budget and stimulate product innovation. At the same time, multiple management layers were cut and many activities centralized in New York, leaving 25% of senior staff without a job. The first ever global advertising campaign was launched themed 'Hello Tomorrow', for which actress Reece Witherspoon was recruited as global ambassador. A centrally managed Global Direct Selling function was established to accelerate the worldwide rollout of the Avon Sales Leadership programme and to run a new Avon Direct Selling university. Internet sales were also targeted, by encouraging sales reps to not only order online themselves, but to create their own pages on the Avon website, through which their clients could place orders.

With these measures, and the new innovative products coming out of Avon's previously planned US$100 million state-of-the-art research and development facility in Suffern, New York, Avon's sales and profits took a turn for the better in 2006. They remained positive until hit by the economic crisis starting in 2008. Although this global contraction in consumer spending effected all retailers of beauty products, Avon had a relative advantage, as it had less expensive products to push, while many new women were willing to sign up as Avon Ladies to supplement their incomes. Avon actually redoubled its recruitment efforts, focusing on the many newly unemployed, offering them the opportunity to start their own business.

Yet, despite all these initiatives, the company's stock price was still performing below the S&P 500 average, suggesting that investors were not convinced that Avon had significant upside potential. To many it seemed that Avon was at a crossroads, with two distinctly different directions in which it could develop itself. On the one hand, Avon could focus on growing and leveraging its direct sales organization, by carrying more products and reaching new market segments. Take men, for instance. Although they account for about 20% of the global cosmetics market, they make up only 1% of Avon's sales. If Avon were to build on this traditional strength, Avon would remain a direct sales organization, but on a much larger scale.

On the other hand, Jung could fulfil her dream to become *the* Company for Women. Many times she has advocated that Avon should be the trusted partner of women, catering for their needs and helping them to succeed. As the new generation of women have new needs, maybe Avon needed to rethink how women can best be served, instead of only focusing on a direct sales model. Jung's earlier belief that the brand is more than the channel might need to be revisited. This would fit well with Avon's long-standing commitment to improving the position of females around the world, as it does through the Avon Foundation for Women, the largest corporate-affiliated philanthropy for women in the world, which has spent US$660 million so far on such causes as breast cancer, domestic violence and emergency disaster relief.

Whichever focus was pursued, the challenges for the coming years seemed large, calling for Jung to make some clear strategic choices and not be satisfied with a mere cosmetic touch up.

Sources: www.avoncompany.com; *Avon annual reports* 2005–2008; *Business Week*, 20 August 2002 and 13 January 2003; *New York Times*, 29 June 2006, 31 October 2008; *Business Week*, 27 August 2008; *The Economist*, 30 May 2009

PERSPECTIVES ON BUSINESS LEVEL STRATEGY

Always to be best, and to be distinguished above the rest.
The Iliad, Homer (8th century BC); Greek poet

Firms need to adapt themselves to market developments and they need to build on the strengths of their resource bases and activity systems. The main question dividing managers is 'who should be fitted to whom' – should an organization adapt itself to its environment or should it attempt to adapt the environment to itself? What should be the dominant factor driving a firm, its strengths or the opportunities? Should managers take the environment as the starting point, choose an advantageous market position and then build the resource base and activity system necessary to implement this choice? Or should managers take the organization's resource base (and possibly also its activity system) as the starting point, selecting and/or adapting an environment to fit with these strengths?

As before, the strategic management literature comes with strongly different views on how managers should proceed. The variety of opinions among strategy theorists is dauntingly large, with many incompatible prescriptions being given. Here the two diametrically opposed positions will be identified and discussed in order to show the richness of differing opinions. On the one side of the spectrum, there are those managers who argue that the market opportunities should be leading, while implying that the organization should adapt itself to the market position envisioned. This point of view is called the 'outside-in perspective'. At the other end of the spectrum, many managers believe that competition eventually revolves around rival resource bases and that firms must focus their strategies on the development of unique resources and activity systems. They argue that product-market positioning is a tactical decision that can be taken later. This view is referred to as the 'inside-out perspective'.

The outside-in perspective

Managers with an outside-in perspective believe that firms should not be self-centred, but should continuously take their environment as the starting point when determining their strategy. Successful companies, it is argued, are externally oriented and market-driven (e.g. Day, 1990; Webster, 1994). They have their sights clearly set on developments in the market place and are determined to adapt to the unfolding opportunities and threats encountered. They take their cues from customers and competitors, and use these signals to determine their own game plan (Jaworski and Kohli, 1993). For these successful companies, markets are leading, resources are following.

Therefore, for the outside-in directed manager, developing strategy begins with an analysis of the environment to identify attractive market opportunities. Potential customers must be sought, whose needs can be satisfied more adequately than currently done by other firms. Once these customers have been won over and a market position has been established, the firm must consistently defend or build on this position by adapting itself to changes in the environment. Shifts in customers' demands must be met, challenges from rival firms must be countered, impending market entries by outside firms must be rebuffed and excessive pricing by suppliers must be resisted. In short, to the outside-in manager the game of strategy is about market positioning and understanding and responding to external developments. For this reason, the outside-in perspective is sometimes also referred to as the 'positioning approach' (Mintzberg, Ahlstrand and Lampel, 1998).

Positioning is not short-term, opportunistic behaviour, but requires a strategic perspective, because superior market positions are difficult to attain, but once conquered can be the source of sustained profitability. Some proponents of the outside-in perspective argue that in each market a number of different positions can yield sustained profitability. For instance, Porter suggests that companies that focus on a particular niche, and companies that strongly differentiate their product offering, can achieve strong and profitable market positions, even if another company has the lowest cost position (Porter, 1980, 1985; Reading 5.1). Other authors emphasize that the position of being market leader is particularly important (e.g. Buzzell and Gale, 1987). Companies with a high market share profit more from economies of scale, benefit from risk aversion among customers, have more bargaining power towards buyers and suppliers, and can more easily flex their muscles to prevent new entrants and block competitive attacks.

Unsurprisingly, proponents of the outside-in perspective argue that insight into markets and industries is essential. Not only the general structure of markets and industries needs to be analysed, but also the specific demands, strengths, positions and intentions of all major forces need to be determined. For instance, buyers must be understood with regard to their needs, wants, perceptions, decision-making processes and bargaining chips. The same holds true for suppliers, competitors, potential market and/or industry entrants and providers of substitute products (Porter, 1980, 1985; Reading 5.1). Once a manager knows 'what makes the market tick' – sometimes referred to as the 'rules of the game' – a position can be identified within the market that could give the firm bargaining power vis-à-vis suppliers and buyers, while keeping competitors at bay. Of course, the wise manager will not only emphasize winning under the current rules with the current players, but will attempt to anticipate market and industry developments, and position the firm to benefit from these. Many outside-in advocates even advise firms to initiate market and industry changes, so that they can be the first to benefit from the altered rules of the game (this issue will be discussed further in Chapter 8).

Proponents of the outside-in perspective readily acknowledge the importance of firm resources and activities for cashing in on market opportunities the firm has identified. If the firm does not have, or is not able to develop or obtain, the necessary resources to implement a particular strategy, then specific opportunities will be unrealizable. Therefore, managers should always keep the firm's strengths and weaknesses in mind when choosing an external position, to ensure that it remains feasible. Yet, to the outside-in strategist, the firm's current resource base should not be the starting point when determining strategy, but should merely be acknowledged as a potentially limiting condition on the firm's ability to implement the best business strategy.

Actually, firms that are market-driven are often the first ones to realize that new resources and/or activities need to be developed and, therefore, are better positioned to build up a 'first mover advantage' (Lieberman and Montgomery, 1988, 1998). Where the firm does not have the ability to catch up with other firms' superior resources, it can always enter into an alliance with a leading organization, offering its partner a crack at a new market opportunity.

EXHIBIT 5.2 THE OUTSIDE-IN PERSPECTIVE

STOKKE: FOLLOW THAT BABY

Who has never seen the famed Tripp Trapp chair by the Norwegian designer Peter Opsvik, with its characteristic Z-shaped frame? Millions have been sold around the world, since it was introduced in 1972. The company behind this icon of Scandinavian furniture design is Stokke, a family-owned business headquartered in Ålesund, Norway, about 500 kilometers northwest of Oslo. Established in 1932, Stokke has long been known for its innovative seating designs, such as the zero gravity chair, which have often been developed with the help of famous names in the Norwegian design world.

In the late 1990s, looking for new growth possibilities, this long-standing chair company took a strategic change of direction. Instead of only designing seating furniture for a variety of market segments, they focused more closely on one segment in which they were doing particularly well and which held great growth potential – babies. Or actually, the affluent parents of babies, who had an eye for ergonomics and style, who were willing to invest heavily in junior. Their Tripp Trapp chairs, which are adjustable for children ranging from 6 months until adulthood, were already big sellers in the baby segment. On the basis of this experience, they had an adjustable bed designed, that could be used from birth to old age. The Sleepi bed system was a baby crib, that could be converted into a toddler bed, then into a child's sofa, to be eventually transformed into two chairs. As with the Tripp Trapp, they found that when it comes to their babies, parents are discerning customers and willing to pay a premium for a quality product that is beautiful, intelligent and environmentally friendly. They also found that competition was very thin in this upscale part of the market.

After this success in 1999, Stokke added a matching changing table in 2001. But their big step came in 2003, when after five years of extensive research, design and field testing, they introduced the Xplory baby stroller. This was a huge leap for a furniture maker to take, but the market opportunity they had identified was just too good to leave unexploited. A big advantage of coming into a totally new product category was that Stokke could entirely rethink the business, without any preconceived notions about the market and without the pressure to use existing technologies or facilities.

To compensate for their lack on product knowhow, Stokke started the design process by inviting a number of designers in various countries to submit initial proposals. The briefing they were given was to come up with an innovative baby stroller, that fit with Stokke's design philosophy, meaning adjustable, with modern styling and ergonomically-optimized. Based on their first screening, Stokke

selected the Norwegian firm K8 Industridesign to do further development, eventually finishing the product in close cooperation with Bård Eker Industrial Design. In the same way, Stokke also found an external partner to manufacture the product to their specifications.

Building on this enormous success, Stokke has added more baby furniture, such as closets, to their product line, but also an entirely new set of items, baby table top playing/eating mats. At the same time, to help them to focus on following opportunities in the premium segment of the baby market, Stokke decided to exit its traditional chair business. In 2006, all chairs not intended for children (their 'Movement Collection') were brought into a separate company, still owned by the Stokke family for 40%, and are now sold under the brand name Variér.

While the sales of Xplory strollers are booming in almost all of the 50 countries in which Stokke has authorized dealers, people without babies might still have no idea what this Porsche-for-babies looks like. If by now you are curious, but aren't surrounded by trendy parents, you can always rent the *Sex and the City* movie – Charlotte has one, of course.

Sources: www.stokke.com; www.wikipedia.org/wiki/Tripp_Trapp; *Fast Company*, 19 December 2007; www.norskdesign.no/case/stokke; www.credopartners.no

The inside-out perspective

Managers adopting an inside-out perspective believe that strategies should not be built around external opportunities, but around a company's strengths. Successful companies, it is argued, build up a strong resource base over an extended period of time, which offers them access to unfolding market opportunities in the medium and short term. For such companies, the starting point of the strategy formation process is the question of which resource base it wants to have. The fundamental strategic issue is which difficult-to-imitate competences and exclusive assets should be acquired and/or further refined. Creating such a resource platform requires major investments and a long breath, and to a large extent will determine the culture and identity of the organization. Hence, it is of the utmost importance and should be the central tenet of a firm's strategy. Once the long-term direction for the building of the resource infrastructure has been set, attention can be turned to identifying market opportunities where these specific strengths can be exploited. To the inside-out oriented manager the issue of market positioning is essential, as only a strong competitive position in the market will result in above-average profitability. However, market positioning must take place within the context of the broader resource-based strategy and not contradict the main thrust of the firm – selected market positions must leverage the existing resource base, not ignore it. In other words, market positioning is vital, but tactical, taking place within the boundaries set by the resource-driven strategy. For success, resources should be leading, and markets following.

Many managers taking an inside-out perspective tend to emphasize the importance of a firm's competences over its tangible resources (physical assets). Their way of looking at strategy is referred to as the competence-based view (e.g. Prahalad and Hamel, 1990, Reading 6.2; Sanchez, Heene and Thomas, 1996) or capabilities-based view (e.g. Stalk, Evans and Shulman, 1992; Teece, Pisano and Shuen, 1997). These managers point out that it is especially the development of unique abilities that is such a strenuous and lengthy process, more so than the acquisition of physical resources, such as production facilities and computer systems. Some companies might be able to achieve a competitive advantage based on physical assets, but usually such tangible infrastructure is easily copied or purchased. However, competences are not readily for sale on the open market as 'plug-and-play' components, but need to be painstakingly built up by an organization through hard work and experience. Even where a company takes a short cut by buying another organization or engaging in an alliance, it takes significant time and effort to internalize the competences in such a way that they can be put to productive use. Hence, having distinctive competences can be a very attractive basis for competitive advantage, as rival firms generally require a long time to catch up (e.g. Collis and Montgomery, 1995; Barney, 1991, Reading 5.4). And even if competitors are successful at identifying embedded competences and imitating them, the company with an initial lead can work at upgrading its competences in a race to stay ahead – this is often referred to as the dynamic capabilities view (Teece, Pisano and Shuen, 1997).

To proponents of the inside-out perspective the 'dynamic capabilities' argument accentuates the importance of committing the organization to the long-term development of a limited set of competences in which it can stay ahead of rivals. The 'nightmare scenario' for inside-out oriented strategists is where the firm flexibly shifts from one market demand to the next, building up an eclectic collection of unrelated competences, none of which are distinctive compared to competence-focused companies. In this scenario, a firm is fabulously market-driven, adaptively responding to shifts in the environment, but incapable of concentrating itself on forming the distinctive competence base needed for a robust competitive advantage over the longer term.

Most inside-out oriented managers also recognize the 'shadow side' of competences – they are not only difficult to learn, but difficult to unlearn as well. The laborious task of building up competences makes it hard to switch to new competences, even if that is what the market demands (e.g. Christensen, 1997; Rumelt, 1996). Companies far down the route of competence specialization, find themselves locked in by the choices made in the past. In the same way as few concert pianists are able (and willing) to switch to playing saxophone when they are out of a job, few companies are able and willing to scrap their competence base, just because the market is taking a turn for the worse. Becoming a concert pianist not only costs years of practice but is a way of life, with a specific way of working, network and career path, making it very unattractive to make a mid-career shift towards a more marketable trade. Likewise, companies experience that their core competences can simultaneously be their core rigidities, locking them out of new opportunities (Leonard-Barton, 1995). From an inside-out perspective, both companies and concert pianists should therefore first try to build on their unique competences and attempt to find or create a more suitable market, instead of reactively adapting to the unpredictable whims of the current environment (see Figure 5.8).

FIGURE 5.8   Two perspectives on shaping the business system

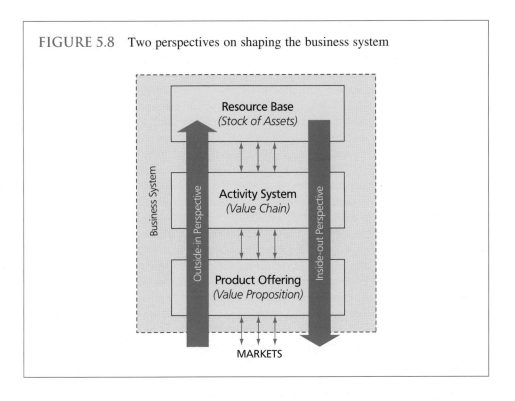

EXHIBIT 5.3   THE INSIDE-OUT PERSPECTIVE

FABER-CASTELL: HARD CORE

If you throw a Faber-Castell pencil from a 30 metre high tower on to the street, you can rest assured that the graphite 'lead' will not break. Count Anton Wolfgang von Faber-Castell, CEO of the company, can say this with authority, as he once threw a box of 144 pencils out the window of his ancestral castle near Nuremberg in Germany, and not one of them broke. This is because the lead core is tightly squeezed and glued into its pinewood sleeve, unlike cheaper pencils. As discerning hobbyists and artists know, Faber-Castells are the Rolls Royce of pencils, with such fans as designer Karl Lagerfeld and architect Lord Foster. And this status is not new – Vincent van Gogh once wrote that 'they produce a capital black and are most agreeable for large studies'.

Started by cabinet maker Kaspar Faber in 1761, the company has been a leading pencil maker for near to 250 years, while remaining in family hands the entire time. It was the fourth generation Faber, Lothar, who after taking over in 1839 expanded the business internationally and transformed the company into a major industrial corporation. He bought a graphite mine in Siberia to secure the best supplies and established the first overseas production facility in New York in 1849. For his contribution to the economy he was made baron by the king of Bavaria, becoming Lothar *von* Faber. It was his granddaughter who married Count zu Castell-Rüdenhausen, later changing the family name to Faber-Castell to acquire title to the pencil firm. The current CEO, Anton, is the eighth generation, while his son is being trained to eventually take over.

When Anton Wolfgang became chairman in 1978, Faber-Castell had diversified into a number of related products, such as pens, rulers, technical drawing instruments and slide rules, used for mathematical calculations. At first he assumed he could leave day-to-day operations to non-family professionals, but soon the firm's slide rule business was being decimated by the introduction of electronic calculators, while the technical drawing instruments were being eclipsed by computer programs. As he got more involved, he was advised by consultants to follow the market trends and also develop electronic capabilities. He was told to 'embrace the digital age'. Yet his intuition said 'no'. With such a long history of craftsmanship and emphasis on deep know-how, he felt that a strategy built on exploiting the firm's core competences made much more sense. Now he says that 'if back then I had listened to the consultants, we wouldn't be here anymore.'

He decided to take over as CEO and began to re-structure the company, focusing on Faber-Castell's core competence in designing high quality writing instruments. He accepted that products like slide rules and technical drawing instruments would die out, and that most 'writing' in future would be done on computers, but he felt that sufficient new appli-cations could be found for the firm's existing cap-abilities. So he divided the product range into five focus areas, looking for growth in each: Playing and Learning, Art and Graphic, Premium Writing Instruments, General Writing Instruments and Marking. International multidisciplinary teams were formed, leading to a flood of product and process innovations. One of the brilliant ideas was to take Faber-Castell's core pencil product into the luxury market. Instead of taking luxury pen makers Mont Blanc and Omas directly, Faber-Castell first focused on developing the ultimate luxury pencil, thus more easily gaining access to luxury product distributors and upgrading the company's image. Later, fountain pens, ball points and leather accessories were added to the product line. Another innovation was the triangular *Grip* pencil, embossed with its novel anti-slip dots, launched in 2000.

A second moment of truth came during the late 1990s, Count von Faber-Castell told reporters in 2005, while shaking his head. Again 'I got such dumb advice' from consultants, 'as they tried to convince me that I had to get into the internet and dotcom business.' He didn't, instead expanding the traditional business internationally, to become the largest pencil maker in the world, producing more than two billion per year. But pencils only made up 30% of Faber-Castell's annual sales of €428 million in 2008/9, with the rest coming from pens and markers, but also from private label cosmetics, which the company entered to leverage its core competence into eye liner pencils. It employs some 7000 people at 15 production sites, in countries like Brazil, Peru, Indonesia, China and Malaysia, and at 23 sales subsidiaries.

In the meantime, Count von Faber-Castell has also been collecting awards for socially and ecologically responsible behaviour. Following Lothar's lead, who established a health care plan in 1844, Anton Wolfgang launched a social charter in 2000 to se-cure worldwide employee work-related welfare. He also started a huge forestry project on 10 000 hec-tares of pastureland in southeastern Brazil in 1981, to ensure a long-term supply of sustainable pencil wood. The company even developed an environ-ment-friendly paint technology to coat its pencils, making them more healthy as well. So, if you are a notorious pencil-chewer, you needn't worry – just get yourself a Rolls Royce.

Sources: www.faber-castell.de; *The Economist*, 3 March 2007; *Bilanz*, 25 September 2005; *Financial Times*, 1 January 2008; *Wirtschaftsblatt*, 20 June 2008; *Frankfurter Rundschau*, 16 August 2008.

INTRODUCTION TO THE DEBATE AND READINGS

One does not gain much by mere cleverness.
Marquis de Vauvenargues (1715–1747);
French soldier and moralist

Drive thy business; let it not drive thee.
Benjamin Franklin (1706–1790);
American writer and statesman

So, how can a sustainable competitive advantage be created? Should generals create a sustainable competitive advantage by first selecting a superior position in the environment (e.g. a mountain pass) and then adapt their military resources to this position, or should generals develop armies with unique resources and then try to let the battle take place where these resources can best be employed? Should football coaches first determine how they want the game to be played on the field and then attract and train players to fit with this style, or should coaches develop uniquely talented players and then adapt the team's playing style to make the best use of these resources? Whether a military, sports or business strategist, an approach to creating competitive advantage must be chosen.

As no consensus has yet developed within the field of strategic management on how to balance markets and resources, it is once again up to each individual to assess the arguments put forward in the debate and to form their own opinion. To help strategists to come to grips with the variety of perspectives on this issue, four readings have been selected that each shed their own light on the debate. As in previous chapters, the first two readings will be representative of the two poles in this debate (see Table 5.1), while the second set of two readings will bring in extra arguments to add further flavour to the discussion.

Reading 5.1, 'Competitive Strategy', has been taken from Michael Porter's 1985 book *Competitive Advantage,* but its central concepts were originally introduced in his 1980 book, *Competitive Strategy.* Since Porter is considered by all to be the most important theorist in the positioning tradition, it is only logical to start with him as representative of the outside-in perspective. In his contribution Porter argues that 'two central questions underlie the choice of competitive strategy'. First, managers must select a competitive domain with attractive characteristics and then they must position the firm vis-à-vis the five competitive forces encountered. These five forces impinging on the firm's profit potential are 'the entry of new competitors, the threat of substitutes, the bargaining power of buyers, the bargaining power of suppliers, and the rivalry among the existing competitors'. Long run above-average performance results from selecting one of the three defensible positions available to the strategist: cost leadership, differentiation or focus.

According to Porter, these three options, or 'generic strategies', are the only feasible ways of achieving a sustainable competitive advantage. A firm that does not make a clear choice between one of the three generic strategies, is 'stuck in the middle' and will suffer below-average performance. For the debate in this chapter it is important to note that Porter does not explicitly advocate an exclusively outside-in approach. However, he strongly emphasizes competitive positioning as a leading strategy principle and treats the development of firm resources as a derivative activity. Indirectly, therefore, his message to managers is that in the game of strategy it is essential to be focused on the external dynamics.

As representative of the inside-out perspective, a recent article (Reading 5.2) by Danny Miller, Russell Eisenstat and Nathaniel Foote has been selected, with the telling title 'Strategy From the Inside Out: Building Capability-Creating Organizations'. In this reading the authors start by emphasizing the value of 'skills, knowledge, processes, relationships, or outputs an organization possesses or produces' that are unique and difficult

TABLE 5.1 Outside-in versus inside-out perspective

	Outside-in perspective	*Inside-out perspective*
Emphasis on	Markets over resources	Resources over markets
Orientation	Opportunity-driven (external potential)	Strength-driven (internal potential)
Starting point	Market demand and industry structure	Resource base and activity system
Fit through	Adaptation to environment	Adaptation of environment
Strategic focus	Attaining advantageous position	Attaining distinctive resources
Strategic moves	External positioning	Building resource base
Tactical moves	Acquiring necessary resources	External positioning
Competitive weapons	Bargaining power and mobility barriers	Superior resources and imitation barriers

for competitors to copy or acquire – which in this book are called 'resources', but which Miller, Eisenstat and Foote prefer to call 'asymmetries', to accentuate that they encompass all differences, even those that have not yet been turned to economic use. The thrust of the authors' argumentation is that 'by continually identifying and building on asymmetries, by nurturing and exploiting these within a complementary organizational design, and by leveraging them via an appropriate market focus, companies may be able to aspire realistically to attain sustainable competitive advantage'. To make this inside-out approach work they believe that companies must do three things well. First, they must be able to discover asymmetries and to recognize their potential. Secondly, these asymmetries must be developed into a cohesive set of capabilities. Thirdly, market opportunities must be pursued that build on and leverage these capabilities. On this last point Miller, Eisenstat and Foote recognize that in the tension between markets and resources one cannot fully dominate over the other: 'Managers need to find opportunities tailored to their capabilities. Opportunities also must ultimately shape capabilities.' Yet, while they underline the value of mutual adjustment between markets and resources, they do reiterate that asymmetries and capabilities should be the drivers of this processes, not created somewhere along the line on the basis of a perceived opportunity. An important additional point brought up by the authors is that capabilities can be leveraged across two or more business units. This makes capability-based approaches to strategy equally relevant to corporate level strategy as to business level strategy (in Chapter 6, Prahalad and Hamel will pick up on this issue in Reading 6.2).

Since the early 1990s, the resource-based view of the firm has increasingly come to dominate the field of strategic management. Consequently, implicit support of the inside-out perspective on business strategy has also grown strongly. Interestingly, on the other side of the fence, in the field of marketing, the outside-in perspective is still widely expounded. Almost simultaneously with the strategy field's emphasis on resource-driven strategies, the marketing field has huddled around the concept of market-driven strategy (e.g. Jaworski and Kohli, 1993; Slater and Narver, 1998; Webster, 1994). In an effort to avoid disciplinary myopia and to keep the debate on the paradox of markets and resources open to all challenging points of view, one of the best contributions from the field of marketing has been incorporated into the chapter as Reading 5.3. In this paper, 'The Capabilities of Market-Driven Organizations', George Day argues that not all capabilities are inside-out in orientation. Capabilities in the areas of manufacturing, logistics, technology development, finances and human resource management are deployed from the inside-out, but likewise there are outside-in capabilities, such as market sensing, customer linking, channel bonding and technology monitoring. He also distinguishes spanning capabilities, such as purchasing, new product development and strategy development, that link inside-out and outside-in capabilities. According to Day, in a market-driven organization outside-in capabilities should 'inform and guide both spanning and inside-out capabilities'. Although he just stops short of advocating a dominant role for outside-in capabilities, it is clear that he believes that in a market-driven organization all activities become more externally oriented. In the context of the discussion in this chapter, Day's article makes more tangible what an outside-in oriented company is like, and indirectly what the profile is of an inside-out oriented company.

While much of the theoretical underpinning of the inside-out perspective comes from a stream of literature known under the umbrella term 'resource-based view of the firm', little attention has so far been paid to its fundamentals. Miller, Eisenstat and Foote also use some of the key ideas of this body of literature to build up their argument, but do not really explain the essence of this school of thought. Therefore, to add further depth to the discussion, an often-cited article by Jay Barney has been selected as a more thorough introduction to the resource-based view. In Reading 5.4, 'Firm Resources and Sustained Competitive Advantage', Barney differentiates resource-based models of competitive advantage from the Porter-like environmental models. He does not dismiss externally oriented explanations of profitability, but wishes to explore the internally oriented explanation that idiosyncratic firm resources are at the base of superior performance. He sets out on this task by pinpointing the two fundamental assumptions on which the resource-based view rests – that firms have different resources *(resource heterogeneity)* and that these resources cannot be easily transferred to, or copied by, other firms *(resource immobility)*. He goes on to argue that these resources can be the basis of competitive advantage if they meet four criteria: they must be valuable and rare, while being difficult to imitate and substitute.

For readers the challenge now is to turn the arguments 'inside-out' and 'outside-in', and to determine themselves how to approach the topic of business level strategy.

Competitive strategy

By Michael Porter[1]

Competition is at the core of the success or failure of firms. Competition determines the appropriateness of a firm's activities that can contribute to its performance, such as innovations, a cohesive culture, or good implementation. Competitive strategy is the search for a favourable competitive position in an industry, the fundamental arena in which competition occurs. Competitive strategy aims to establish a profitable and sustainable position against the forces that determine industry competition.

Two central questions underlie the choice of competitive strategy. The first is the attractiveness of industries for long-term profitability and the factors that determine it. Not all industries offer equal opportunities for sustained profitability, and the inherent profitability of its industry is one essential ingredient in determining the profitability of a firm. The second central question in competitive strategy is the determinants of relative competitive position within an industry. In most industries, some firms are much more profitable than others, regardless of what the average profitability of the industry may be.

Neither question is sufficient by itself to guide the choice of competitive strategy. A firm in a very attractive industry may still not earn attractive profits if it has chosen a poor competitive position. Conversely, a firm in an excellent competitive position may be in such a poor industry that it is not very profitable, and further efforts to enhance its position will be of little benefit. Both questions are dynamic; industry attractiveness and competitive position change. Industries become more or less attractive over time, and competitive position reflects an unending battle among competitors. Even long periods of stability can be abruptly ended by competitive moves.

Both industry attractiveness and competitive position can be shaped by a firm, and this is what makes the choice of competitive strategy both challenging and exciting. While industry attractiveness is partly a reflection of factors over which a firm has little influence, competitive strategy has considerable power to make an industry more or less attractive. At the same time, a firm can clearly improve or erode its position within an industry through its choice of strategy. Competitive strategy, then, not only responds to the environment but also attempts to shape that environment in a firm's favour.

The structural analysis of industries

The first fundamental determinant of a firm's profitability is industry attractiveness. Competitive strategy must grow out of a sophisticated understanding of the rules of competition that determine an industry's attractiveness. The ultimate aim of competitive strategy is to cope with and, ideally, to change those rules in the firm's favour. In any industry, whether it is domestic or international or produces a product or a service, the rules of competition are embodied in five competitive forces: the entry of new competitors, the threat of substitutes, the bargaining power of buyers, the bargaining power of suppliers, and the rivalry among the existing competitors.

The collective strength of these five competitive forces determines the ability of firms in an industry to earn, on average, rates of return on investment in excess of the cost of capital. The strength of the five forces varies from industry to industry, and can change as an industry evolves. The result is that all industries are not alike from the standpoint of inherent profitability. In industries where the five forces are favourable, such as pharmaceuticals, soft drinks, and database publishing, many competitors earn attractive returns. But in industries where pressure from one or more of the forces is intense, such as rubber, steel, and video games, few firms command attractive returns despite the best efforts of management. Industry profitability is not a function of what the product looks like or whether it embodies high or low technology, but of industry structure. Some very mundane industries such as postage meters and grain trading are extremely profitable, while some more glamorous, high-technology industries such as personal

[1]Source: This article was adapted with the permission of the Free Press, a Division of Simon and Schuster Adult Publishing Group, from *Competitive Advantage: Creating and Sustaining Superior Performance* by Michael E. Porter. © 1985, 1998 by Michael E. Porter.

computers and cable television are not profitable for many participants.

The five forces determine industry profitability because they influence the prices, costs, and required investment of firms in an industry – the elements of return on investment. Buyer power influences the prices that firms can charge, for example, as does the threat of substitution. The power of buyers can also influence cost and investment, because powerful buyers demand costly service. The bargaining power of suppliers determines the costs of raw materials and other inputs. The intensity of rivalry influences prices as well as the costs of competing in areas such as plant, product development, advertising, and sales force. The threat of entry places a limit on prices, and shapes the investment required to deter entrants.

The strength of each of the five competitive forces is a function of *industry structure,* or the underlying economic and technical characteristics of an industry. Its important elements are shown in Figure 5.1.1. Industry structure is relatively stable, but can change over time as an industry evolves. Structural change shifts the overall and relative strength of the competitive forces, and can thus positively or negatively influence industry profitability. The industry trends that are the most important for strategy are those that affect industry structure.

If the five competitive forces and their structural determinants were solely a function of intrinsic industry characteristics, then competitive strategy would rest heavily on picking the right industry and understanding the five forces better than competitors. But while these are surely important tasks for any firm, and are the essence of competitive strategy in some industries, a firm is usually not a prisoner of its industry's structure. Firms, through their strategies, can influence the five forces. If a firm can shape structure, it can fundamentally change an industry's attractiveness for better or for worse. Many successful strategies have shifted the rules of competition in this way.

Figure 5.1.1 highlights all the elements of industry structure that may drive competition in an industry. In any particular industry, not all of the five forces will be equally important and the particular structural factors that are important will differ. Every industry is unique and has its own unique structure. The five-forces framework allows a firm to see through the complexity and pinpoint those factors that are critical to competition in its industry, as well as to identify those strategic innovations that would most improve the industry's – and its own – profitability. The five-forces framework does not eliminate the need for creativity in finding new ways of competing in an industry. Instead, it directs managers' creative energies toward those aspects of industry structure that are most important to long-run profitability. The framework aims, in the process, to raise the odds of discovering a desirable strategic innovation.

Strategies that change industry structure can be a double-edged sword, because a firm can destroy industry structure and profitability as readily as it can improve it. A new product design that undercuts entry barriers or increases the volatility of rivalry, for example, may undermine the long-run profitability of an industry, though the initiator may enjoy higher profits temporarily. Or a sustained period of price-cutting can undermine differentiation. In the tobacco industry, for example, generic cigarettes are a potentially serious threat to industry structure. Generics may enhance the price sensitivity of buyers, trigger price competition, and erode the high advertising barriers that have kept out new entrants. Joint ventures entered into by major aluminium producers to spread risk and lower capital cost may have similarly undermined industry structure. The majors invited a number of potentially dangerous new competitors into the industry and helped them overcome the significant entry barriers to doing so. Joint ventures also can raise exit barriers because all the participants in a plant must agree before it can be closed down.

Often firms make strategic choices without considering the long-term consequences for industry structure. They see a gain in the competitive position if a move is successful, but they fail to anticipate the consequences of competitive reaction. If imitation of a move by major competitors has the effect of wrecking industry structure, then everyone is worse off. Such industry 'destroyers' are usually second-tier firms that are searching for ways to overcome major competitive disadvantages, firms that have encountered serious problems and are desperately seeking solutions, or 'dumb' competitors that do not know their costs or have unrealistic assumptions about the future. In the tobacco industry, for example, the Liggett Group (a distant follower) has encouraged the trend toward generics.

The ability of firms to shape industry structure places a particular burden on industry leaders. Leaders' actions can have a disproportionate impact on structure, because of their size and influence over buyers, suppliers, and other competitors. At the same time, leaders' large market shares guarantee that anything that changes overall industry structure will affect them as well. A leader, then, must constantly balance its own competitive position against the health of the industry as a

FIGURE 5.1.1   Elements of industry structure

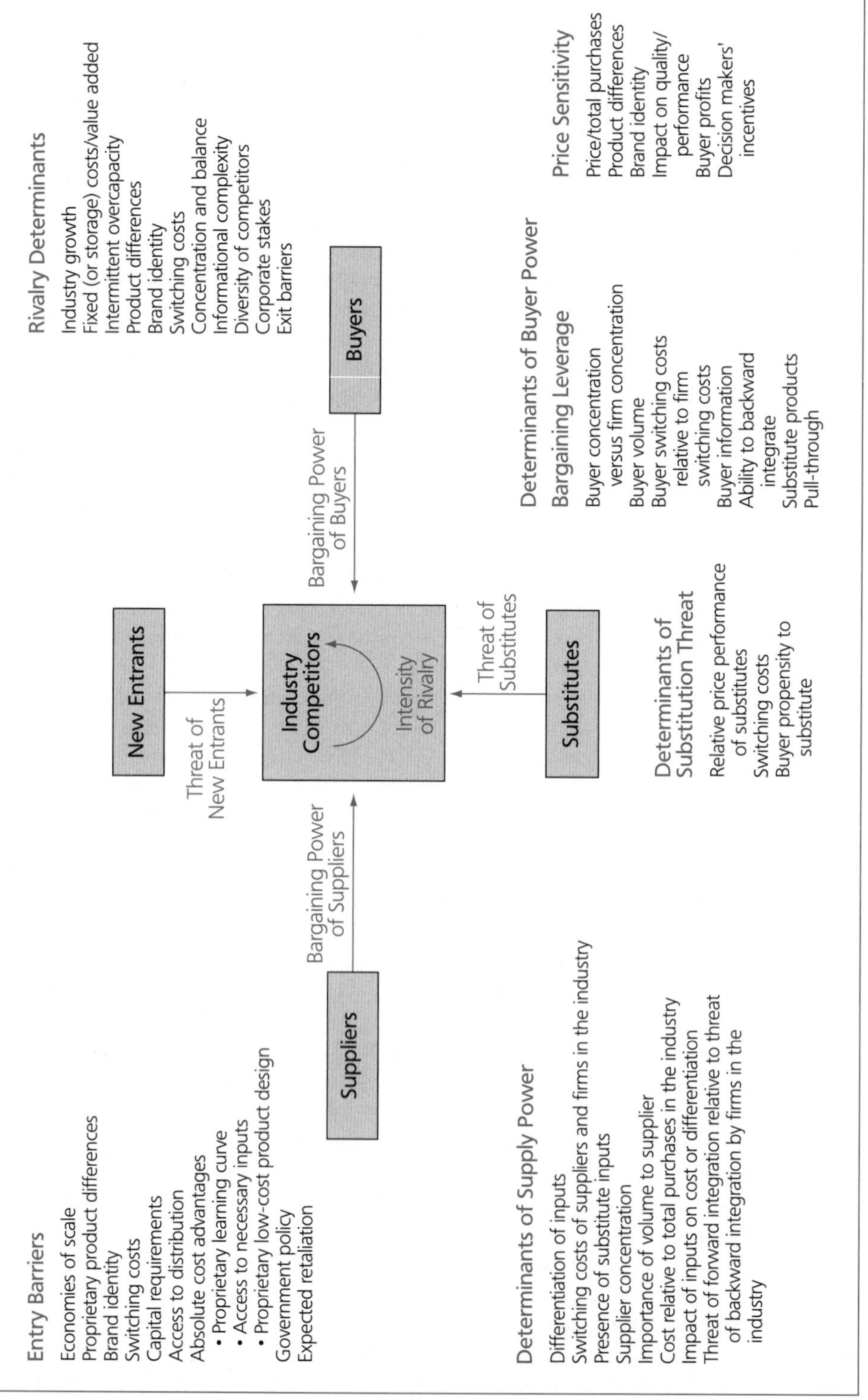

Entry Barriers

Economies of scale
Proprietary product differences
Brand identity
Switching costs
Capital requirements
Access to distribution
Absolute cost advantages
  • Proprietary learning curve
  • Access to necessary inputs
  • Proprietary low-cost product design
Government policy
Expected retaliation

Rivalry Determinants

Industry growth
Fixed (or storage) costs/value added
Intermittent overcapacity
Product differences
Brand identity
Switching costs
Concentration and balance
Informational complexity
Diversity of competitors
Corporate stakes
Exit barriers

Determinants of Supply Power

Differentiation of inputs
Switching costs of suppliers and firms in the industry
Presence of substitute inputs
Supplier concentration
Importance of volume to supplier
Cost relative to total purchases in the industry
Impact of inputs on cost or differentiation
Threat of forward integration relative to threat
  of backward integration by firms in the
  industry

Determinants of Buyer Power

Bargaining Leverage

Buyer concentration
  versus firm concentration
Buyer volume
Buyer switching costs
  relative to firm
  switching costs
Buyer information
Ability to backward
  integrate
Substitute products
Pull-through

Price Sensitivity

Price/total purchases
Product differences
Brand identity
Impact on quality/
  performance
Buyer profits
Decision makers'
  incentives

**Determinants of
Substitution Threat**

Relative price performance
  of substitutes
Switching costs
Buyer propensity to
  substitute

Suppliers

New Entrants

**Industry
Competitors**

Intensity
of Rivalry

Substitutes

Buyers

Bargaining Power
of Suppliers

Threat of
New Entrants

Threat of
Substitutes

Bargaining Power
of Buyers

whole. Often leaders are better off taking actions to improve or protect industry structure rather than seeking greater competitive advantage for themselves. Such industry leaders as Coca-Cola and Campbell's Soup appear to have followed this principle.

Industry structure and buyer needs

It has often been said that satisfying buyer needs is at the core of success in business endeavour. How does this relate to the concept of industry structural analysis? Satisfying buyer needs is indeed a prerequisite to the viability of an industry and the firms within it. Buyers must be willing to pay a price for a product that exceeds its cost of production, or an industry will not survive in the long run.

Satisfying buyer needs may be a prerequisite for industry profitability, but in itself is not sufficient. The crucial question in determining profitability is whether firms can capture the value they create for buyers, or whether this value is competed away to others. Industry structure determines who captures the value. The threat of entry determines the likelihood that new firms will enter an industry and compete away the value, either passing it on to buyers in the form of lower prices or dissipating it by raising the costs of competing. The power of buyers determines the extent to which they retain most of the value created for themselves, leaving firms in an industry only modest returns. The threat of substitutes determines the extent to which some other product can meet the same buyer needs, and thus places a ceiling on the amount a buyer is willing to pay for an industry's product. The power of suppliers determines the extent to which value created for buyers will be appropriated by suppliers rather than by firms in an industry. Finally, the intensity of rivalry acts similarly to the threat of entry. It determines the extent to which firms already in an industry will compete away the value they create for buyers among themselves, passing it on to buyers in lower prices or dissipating it in higher costs of competing.

Industry structure, then, determines who keeps what proportion of the value a product creates for buyers. If an industry's product does not create much value for its buyers, there is little value to be captured by firms regardless of the other elements of structure. If the product creates a lot of value, structure becomes crucial. In some industries such as automobiles and heavy trucks, firms create enormous value for their buyers but, on average, capture very little of it for themselves through profits. In other industries such as bond rating services, medical equipment, and oil field services and equipment, firms also create high value for their buyers but have historically captured a good proportion of it. In oil field services and equipment, for example, many products can significantly reduce the cost of drilling. Because industry structure has been favourable, many firms in the oil field service and equipment sector have been able to retain a share of these savings in the form of high returns. Recently, however, the structural attractiveness of many industries in the oil field services and equipment sector has eroded as a result of falling demand, new entrants, eroding product differentiation, and greater buyer price sensitivity. Despite the fact that products offered still create enormous value for the buyer, both firm and industry profits have fallen significantly.

Industry structure and the supply/demand balance

Another commonly held view about industry profitability is that profits are a function of the balance between supply and demand. If demand is greater than supply, this leads to high profitability. Yet, the long-term supply/demand balance is strongly influenced by industry structure, as are the consequences of a supply/demand imbalance for profitability. Hence, even though short-term fluctuations in supply and demand can affect short-term profitability, industry structure underlies long-term profitability.

Supply and demand change constantly, adjusting to each other. Industry structure determines how rapidly competitors add new supply. The height of entry barriers underpins the likelihood that new entrants will enter an industry and bid down prices. The intensity of rivalry plays a major role in determining whether existing firms will expand capacity aggressively or choose to maintain profitability. Industry structure also determines how rapidly competitors will retire excess supply. Exit barriers keep firms from leaving an industry when there is too much capacity, and prolong periods of excess capacity. In oil tanker shipping, for example, the exit barriers are very high because of the specialization of assets. This has translated into short peaks and long troughs of prices. Thus industry structure shapes the supply/demand balance and the duration of imbalances.

The consequences of an imbalance between supply and demand for industry profitability also differs widely depending on industry structure. In some industries, a small amount of excess capacity triggers price wars and low profitability. These are industries where there are structural pressures for intense rivalry or powerful buyers. In other industries, periods of excess capacity have relatively little impact on profitability because of favourable structure. In oil tools, ball valves, and many other oil field equipment products, for example, there has been intense price-cutting during the recent sharp downturn. In drill bits, however, there has been relatively little discounting. Hughes Tool, Smith International, and Baker International are good competitors operating in a favourable industry structure. Industry structure also determines the profitability of excess demand. In a boom, for example, favourable structure allows firms to reap extraordinary profits, while a poor structure restricts the ability to capitalize on it. The presence of powerful suppliers or the presence of substitutes, for example, can mean that the fruits of a boom pass to others. Thus industry structure is fundamental to both the speed of adjustment of supply to demand and the relationship between capacity utilization and profitability.

Generic competitive strategies

The second central question in competitive strategy is a firm's relative position within its industry. Positioning determines whether a firm's profitability is above or below the industry average. A firm that can position itself well may earn high rates of return even though industry structure is unfavourable and the average profitability of the industry is therefore modest.

The fundamental basis of above-average performance in the long run is *sustainable competitive advantage.* Though a firm can have a myriad strengths and weaknesses vis-à-vis its competitors, there are two basic types of competitive advantage a firm can possess: low cost or differentiation. The significance of any strength or weakness a firm possesses is ultimately a function of its impact on relative cost or differentiation. Cost advantage and differentiation in turn stem from industry structure. They result from a firm's ability to cope with the five forces better than its rivals.

The two basic types of competitive advantage combined with the scope of activities for which a firm seeks to achieve them lead to three *generic strategies* for achieving above-average performance in an industry: cost leadership, differentiation, and focus. The focus strategy has two variants, cost focus and differentiation focus. The generic strategies are shown in Figure 5.1.2.

Each of the generic strategies involves a fundamentally different route to competitive advantage, combining a choice about the type of competitive advantage sought with the scope of the strategic target in which competitive advantage is to be achieved. The cost leadership and differentiation strategies seek competitive advantage in a broad range of industry segments, while focus strategies aim at cost advantage (cost focus) or differentiation (differentiation focus) in a narrow segment. The specific actions required to implement each generic strategy vary widely from industry to industry, as do the feasible generic strategies in a particular industry. While selecting and implementing a generic strategy is far from simple, they are the logical routes to competitive advantage that must be probed in any industry.

FIGURE 5.1.2   Three generic strategies

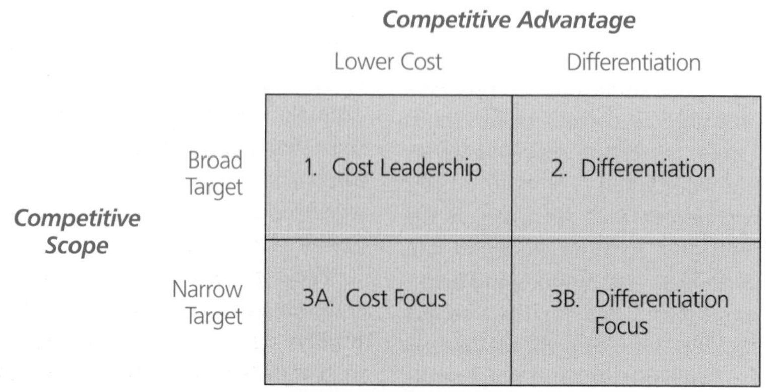

The notion underlying the concept of generic strategies is that competitive advantage is at the heart of any strategy, and achieving competitive advantage requires a firm to make a choice – if a firm is to attain a competitive advantage, it must make a choice about the type of competitive advantage it seeks to attain and the scope within which it will attain it. Being all things to all people is a recipe for strategic mediocrity and below-average performance, because it often means that a firm has no competitive advantage at all.

" Cost leadership "

Cost leadership is perhaps the clearest of the three generic strategies. In it, a firm sets out to become *the* low-cost producer in its industry. The firm has a broad scope and serves many industry segments, and may even operate in related industries – the firm's breadth is often important to its cost advantage. The sources of cost advantage are varied and depend on the structure of the industry. They may include the pursuit of economies of scale, proprietary technology, preferential access to raw materials, and other factors. In TV sets, for example, cost leadership requires efficient-size picture tube facilities, a low-cost design, automated assembly, and global scale over which to amortize research and development (R&D). In security guard services, cost advantage requires extremely low overhead, a plentiful source of low-cost labour, and efficient training procedures because of high turnover. Low-cost producer status involves more than just going down the learning curve. A low-cost producer must find and exploit all sources of cost advantage. Low-cost producers typically sell a standard, or no-frills, product and place considerable emphasis on reaping scale or absolute cost advantages from all sources.

If a firm can achieve and sustain overall cost leadership, then it will be an above-average performer in its industry provided it can command prices at or near the industry average. At equivalent or lower prices than its rivals, a cost leader's low-cost position translates into higher returns. A cost leader, however, cannot ignore the bases of differentiation. If its product is not perceived as comparable or acceptable by buyers, a cost leader will be forced to discount prices well below competitors' to gain sales. This may nullify the benefits of its favourable cost position. Texas Instruments (in watches) and Northwest Airlines (in air transportation) are two low-cost firms that fell into this trap. Texas Instruments could not overcome its disadvantage in differentiation and exited the watch industry. Northwest

Airlines recognized its problem in time, and has instituted efforts to improve marketing, passenger service, and service to travel agents to make its product more comparable to those of its competitors.

A cost leader must achieve *parity or proximity* in the bases of differentiation relative to its competitors to be an above-average performer, even though it relies on cost leadership for its competitive advantage. Parity in the bases of differentiation allows a cost leader to translate its cost advantage directly into higher profits than competitors'. Proximity in differentiation means that the price discount necessary to achieve an acceptable market share does not offset a cost leader's cost advantage and hence the cost leader earns above-average returns.

The strategic logic of cost leadership usually requires that a firm be *the* cost leader, not one of several firms vying for this position. Many firms have made serious strategic errors by failing to recognize this. When there is more than one aspiring cost leader, rivalry among them is usually fierce because every point of market share is viewed as crucial. Unless one firm can gain a cost lead and 'persuade' others to abandon their strategies, the consequences for profitability (and long-run industry structure) can be disastrous, as has been the case in a number of petrochemical industries. Thus cost leadership is a strategy particularly dependent on pre-emption, unless major technological change allows a firm to radically change its cost position.

Differentiation

The second generic strategy is differentiation. In a differentiation strategy, a firm seeks to be unique in its industry along some dimensions that are widely valued by buyers. It selects one or more attributes that many buyers in an industry perceive as important, and uniquely positions itself to meet those needs. It is rewarded for its uniqueness with a premium price. "

" The means for differentiation are peculiar to each industry. Differentiation can be based on the product itself, the delivery system by which it is sold, the marketing approach, and a broad range of other factors. In construction equipment, for example, Caterpillar Tractor's differentiation is based on product durability, service, spare parts availability, and an excellent dealer network. In cosmetics, differentiation tends to be based more on product image and the positioning of counters in the stores. "

A firm that can achieve and sustain differentiation will be an above-average performer in its industry if its price premium exceeds the extra costs incurred in being unique. A differentiator, therefore, must always seek ways of differentiating that lead to a price premium greater than the cost of differentiating. A differentiator cannot ignore its cost position, because its premium prices will be nullified by a markedly inferior cost position. A differentiator thus aims at cost parity or proximity relative to its competitors by reducing cost in all areas that do not affect differentiation.

The logic of the differentiation strategy requires that a firm choose attributes in which to differentiate itself that are *different* from its rivals'. A firm must truly be unique at something or be perceived as unique if it is to expect a premium price. In contrast to cost leadership, however, there can be more than one successful differentiation strategy in an industry if there are a number of attributes that are widely valued by buyers.

Focus

The third generic strategy is focus. This strategy is quite different from the others because it rests on the choice of a narrow competitive scope within an industry. The focuser selects a segment or group of segments in the industry and tailors its strategy to serving them to the exclusion of others. By optimizing its strategy for the target segments, the focuser seeks to achieve a competitive advantage in its target segments even though it does not possess a competitive advantage overall.

The focus strategy has two variants. In *cost focus* a firm seeks a cost advantage in its target segment, while in *differentiation focus* a firm seeks differentiation in its target segment. Both variants of the focus strategy rest on *differences* between a focuser's target segments and other segments in the industry. The target segments must either have buyers with unusual needs or else the production and delivery system that best serves the target segment must differ from that of other industry segments. Cost focus exploits differences in cost behaviour in some segments, while differentiation focus exploits the special needs of buyers in certain segments. Such differences imply that the segments are poorly served by broadly targeted competitors who serve them at the same time as they serve others. The focuser can thus achieve competitive advantage by dedicating itself to the segments exclusively. Breadth of target is clearly a matter of degree, but the essence of focus is the exploitation of a narrow target's differences from the balance of the industry. Narrow focus in and of itself is not sufficient for above-average performance.

A good example of a focuser who has exploited differences in the production process that best serves different segments is Hammermill Paper. Hammermill has increasingly been moving toward relatively low-volume, high-quality speciality papers, where the larger paper companies with higher volume machines face a stiff cost penalty for short production runs. Hammermill's equipment is more suited to shorter runs with frequent setups.

A focuser takes advantage of suboptimization in either direction by broadly targeted competitors. Competitors may be *underperforming* in meeting the needs of a particular segment, which opens the possibility for differentiation focus. Broadly targeted competitors may also be *overperforming* in meeting the needs of a segment, which means that they are bearing higher than necessary cost in serving it. An opportunity for cost focus may be present in just meeting the needs of such a segment and no more.

If a focuser's target segment is not different from other segments, then the focus strategy will not succeed. In soft drinks, for example, Royal Crown has focused on cola drinks, while Coca-Cola and Pepsi have broad product lines with many flavoured drinks. Royal Crown's segment, however, can be well served by Coke and Pepsi at the same time they are serving other segments. Hence Coke and Pepsi enjoy competitive advantages over Royal Crown in the cola segment due to the economies of having a broader line.

If a firm can achieve sustainable cost leadership (cost focus) or differentiation (differentiation focus) in its segment and the segment is structurally attractive, then the focuser will be an above-average performer in its industry. Segment structural attractiveness is a necessary condition because some segments in an industry are much less profitable than others. There is often room for several sustainable focus strategies in an industry, provided that focusers choose different target segments. Most industries have a variety of segments, and each one that involves a different buyer need or a different optimal production or delivery system is a candidate for a focus strategy.

Stuck in the middle

A firm that engages in each generic strategy but fails to achieve any of them is 'stuck in the middle.' It possesses no competitive advantage. This strategic position is usually a recipe for below-average performance. A firm that is stuck in the middle will compete at a disadvantage because the cost leader, differentiators, or focusers will be better positioned to compete in any segment. If a firm that is stuck in the middle is lucky enough to discover a profitable product or buyer, competitors with a sustainable competitive advantage will quickly eliminate the spoils. In most industries, quite a few competitors are stuck in the middle.

A firm that is stuck in the middle will earn attractive profits only if the structure of its industry is highly favourable, or if the firm is fortunate enough to have competitors that are also stuck in the middle. Usually, however, such a firm will be much less profitable than rivals achieving one of the generic strategies. Industry maturity tends to widen the performance differences between firms with a generic strategy and those that are stuck in the middle, because it exposes ill-conceived strategies that have been carried along by rapid growth.

Becoming stuck in the middle is often a manifestation of a firm's unwillingness to make *choices* about how to compete. It tries for competitive advantage through every means and achieves none, because achieving different types of competitive advantage usually requires inconsistent actions. Becoming stuck in the middle also afflicts successful firms, who compromise their generic strategy for the sake of growth or prestige. A classic example is Laker Airways, which began with a clear cost-focus strategy based on no-frills operation in the North Atlantic market, aimed at a particular segment of the travelling public that was extremely price sensitive. Over time, however, Laker began adding frills, new services, and new routes. It blurred its image, and suboptimized its service and delivery system. The consequences were disastrous, and Laker eventually went bankrupt.

The temptation to blur a generic strategy, and therefore become stuck in the middle, is particularly great for a focuser once it has dominated its target segments. Focus involves deliberately limiting potential sales volume. Success can lead a focuser to lose sight of the reasons for its success and compromise its focus strategy for growth's sake. Rather than compromise its generic strategy, a firm is usually better off finding new industries in which to grow where it can use its generic strategy again or exploit interrelationships.

Pursuit of more than one generic strategy

Each generic strategy is a fundamentally different approach to creating and sustaining a competitive advantage, combining the type of competitive advantage a firm seeks and the scope of its strategic target. Usually a firm must make a choice among

them, or it will become stuck in the middle. The benefits of optimizing the firm's strategy for a particular target segment (focus) cannot be gained if a firm is simultaneously serving a broad range of segments (cost leadership or differentiation). Sometimes a firm may be able to create two largely separate business units within the same corporate entity, each with a different generic strategy. A good example is the British hotel firm Trusthouse Forte, which operates five separate hotel chains each targeted at a different segment. However, unless a firm strictly separates the units pursuing different generic strategies, it may compromise the ability of any of them to achieve its competitive advantage. A suboptimized approach to competing, made likely by the spillover among units of corporate policies and culture, will lead to becoming stuck in the middle.

Achieving cost leadership and differentiation is also usually inconsistent, because differentiation is usually costly. To be unique and command a price premium, a differentiator deliberately elevates costs, as Caterpillar has done in construction equipment. Conversely, cost leadership often requires a firm to forego some differentiation by standardizing its product, reducing marketing overhead, and the like.

Reducing cost does not always involve a sacrifice in differentiation. Many firms have discovered ways to reduce cost not only without hurting their differentiation but while actually raising it, by using practices that are both more efficient and effective or employing a different technology. Sometimes dramatic cost savings can be achieved with no impact on differentiation at all if a firm has not concentrated on cost reduction previously. However, cost reduction is not the same as achieving a cost advantage. When faced with capable competitors also striving for cost leadership, a firm will ultimately reach the point where further cost reduction requires a sacrifice in differentiation. It is at this point that the generic strategies become inconsistent and a firm must make a choice.

If a firm can achieve cost leadership and differentiation simultaneously, the rewards are great because the benefits are additive – differentiation leads to premium prices at the same time that cost leadership implies lower costs. An example of a firm that has achieved both a cost advantage and differentiation in its segments is Crown Cork and Seal in the metal container industry. Crown has targeted the so-called hard-to-hold uses of cans in the beer, soft drink, and aerosol industries. It manufactures only steel cans rather than both steel and aluminium. In its target segments, Crown has differentiated itself based on service, technological assistance, and offering a full line of steel cans, crowns, and canning machinery. Differentiation of this type would be much more difficult to achieve in other industry segments that have different needs. At the same time, Crown has dedicated its facilities to producing only the types of cans demanded by buyers in its chosen segments and has aggressively invested in modern two-piece steel-canning technology. As a result, Crown has probably also achieved low-cost producer status in its segments.

Sustainability

A generic strategy does not lead to above-average performance unless it is sustainable vis-à-vis competitors, though actions that improve industry structure may improve industrywide profitability even if they are imitated. The sustainability of the three generic strategies demands that a firm's competitive advantage resist erosion by competitor behaviour or industry evolution. Each generic strategy involves different risks, which are shown in Table 5.1.1.

The sustainability of a generic strategy requires that a firm possess some barriers that make imitation of the strategy difficult. Since barriers to imitation are never insurmountable, however, it is usually necessary for a firm to offer a moving target to its competitors by investing in order to continually improve its position.

Each generic strategy is also a potential threat to the others-as Table 5.1.1 shows, for example, focusers must worry about broadly targeted competitors and vice versa.

Table 5.1.1 can be used to analyse how to attack a competitor that employs any of the generic strategies. A firm pursuing overall differentiation, for example, can be attacked by firms that open up a large cost gap, narrow the extent of differentiation, shift the differentiation desired by buyers to other dimensions, or focus. Each generic strategy is vulnerable to different types of attacks.

In some industries, industry structure or the strategies of competitors eliminate the possibility of achieving one or more of the generic strategies. Occasionally no feasible way for one firm to gain a significant cost advantage exists, for example, because several firms are equally placed with respect to scale economies, access to raw materials, or other cost drivers. Similarly, an industry with few segments or only minor differences among segments, such as low-density polyethylene, may offer few opportunities for focus. Thus the mix of generic strategies will vary from industry to industry.

In many industries, however, the three generic strategies can profitably coexist as long as firms pursue different ones or select different bases for differentiation or focus. Industries in which several strong firms are pursuing differentiation strategies based on

TABLE 5.1.1   Risks of the generic strategies

Risks of cost leadership	Risks of differentiation	Risks of focus
Cost leadership is not sustained	Differentiation is not sustained	The focus strategy is imitated
■ competitors imitate ■ technology changes ■ other bases for cost leadership erode	■ competitors imitate ■ bases for differentiation become less important to buyers	The target segment becomes structurally unattractive ■ structure erodes ■ demand disappears
Proximity in differentiation is lost	Cost proximity is lost	Broadly targeted competitors overwhelm the segment ■ the segment's differences from other segments narrow ■ the advantages of a broad line increase
Cost focusers achieve even lower cost in segments	Differentiation focusers achieve even greater differentiation in segments	New focusers subsegment the industry

different sources of buyer value are often particularly profitable. This tends to improve industry structure and lead to stable industry competition. If two or more firms choose to pursue the same generic strategy on the same basis, however, the result can be a protracted and unprofitable battle. The worst situation is where several firms are vying for overall cost leadership. The past and present choice of generic strategies by competitors, then, has an impact on the choices available to a firm and the cost of changing its position.

The concept of generic strategies is based on the premise that there are a number of ways in which competitive advantage can be achieved, depending on industry structure. If all firms in an industry followed the principles of competitive strategy, each would pick different bases for competitive advantage. While not all would succeed, the generic strategies provide alternate routes to superior performance. Some strategic planning concepts have been narrowly based on only one route to competitive advantage, most notably cost. Such concepts not only fail to explain the success of many firms, but they can also lead all firms in an industry to pursue the same type of competitive advantage in the same way – with predictably disastrous results.

READING 5.2	# Strategy from the inside out: Building capability-creating organizations

By Danny Miller, Russell Eisenstat and Nathaniel Foote[1]

For Citibank CEO John Reed, 1991 was a very tough year. Citi's stock had plummeted, in no small part because of its trouble-ridden global corporate bank. Some problems, such as non-performing Latin American loans, were shared by competitors. However, Citi was especially hobbled. Paradoxically, although it had banks in over 100 countries, many of these were weak. Local rivals with better ties to customers and government were strangling Citi's revenues and eroding its margins.

The choices confronting Reed seemed bleak. On the one hand, he could try to strengthen Citi's presence in lucrative markets such as Germany or Japan by copying regional rivals like Deutsche Bank. He might, for example, try to build deeper relationships with local businesses. However, Citi would always be at a disadvantage vis-à-vis local rivals, who had better government and industry contacts – relationships that for historical and political reasons Citi was unlikely to duplicate. A more feasible strategy would be to offer new services and try to become more efficient. However, there was nothing to stop competitors from following suit and neutralizing Citi's efforts. Reed, like so many of today's CEOs, was facing a quandary.

Citibank (now Citigroup) and some two dozen other firms we studied have managed, quite craftily, to escape this predicament of how to grow sustainable capabilities. They began not emulating best practices, but by delving constantly within themselves to discover and build on their unique, hard-to-copy assets, knowledge, relationships, and experiences. We call these emergent, potential, or hidden resources 'asymmetries'. Over time, the firms we studied evolved a set of explicit organizational processes and designs to find these asymmetries, turn them into capabilities, and leverage them across the appropriate market opportunities.

At Citi, John Reed realized that his extensive network of international banks could be of immense service to large multinationals (MNCs). This was no commonplace observation as the scattered network was at the time a liability in serving MNCs. Citi's local banks gave service priority to local clients, offered products unsuitable to MNCs, and did not cooperate to facilitate cross-border business. Nor were MNCs the most profitable customers. However, Reed had a three-pronged epiphany. He realized first that no rival had Citi's global reach or could attain it easily. He also saw that by redesigning his organization, processes, and performance management systems he could make the network more responsive to MNCs. Finally, he envisioned how the international bank network could be redeployed to great advantage to serve not local firms but large clients doing extensive – and lucrative-cross – border business. In short, Reed saw how his bank was different, figured out

[1]Source: This article © 2002, by the Regents of the University of California. Adapted from the *California Management Review*, Vol. 33, No. 3. By permission of the Regents. All rights reserved.

how to make that difference an asset, and found a market that would most value that asset.

It is vital to point out that it is not only large firms such as Citi that may have potentially valuable asymmetries. The example of Shana Corp. (Exhibit 5.2.1) shows a very similar path of asymmetry identification and capability development unfolding even within a small and new firm with nowhere near the assets or relationships of a Citigroup.

The lessons from Citi and Shana are much the same: competitive advantage comes not from imitation but from using organizational processes and designs to identify emerging asymmetries and build them into capabilities. Again, asymmetries are hard-to-copy ways in which a firm differs from its rivals – ways that may ultimately bring advantage (see Exhibit 5.2.2 for

the definitions of our key terms). They may consist of outputs (such as products or solutions), relationships and alliances, systems (such as Citi's global network or contacts), processes and routines, and nascent skills and knowledge (such as Shana's) – all provided that rivals cannot imitate these within practical time and cost constraints. In fact, asymmetries, because of their subtlety or uniqueness, confer a head start and discourage imitation – and that sustains their edge.

Another advantage is their accessibility. Due to accidents of history and normal variations in the skills and experiences of organizations, many companies will find that they possess asymmetries. While the capabilities or best practices of other enterprises may be almost impossible to duplicate, managers begin the hunt for asymmetries in their own back yard.

EXHIBIT 5.2.1

MOLEHILLS INTO MOUNTAINS: THE CASE OF SHANA CORP.

Shana Corp is a private Canadian software company. Some of Shana's product development efforts, combined with a few technologically related contracts, had allowed the company, over several years, to develop special expertise. It acquired the capability to create sophisticated forms completion software that was compatible between two popular operating systems. This occurred, quite fortuitously, because of the kinds of jobs Shana had worked on. However, the top managers of Shana soon became quite conscious of this emerging capability. Their firm, they realized, had learned to artfully and economically do some valuable kinds of work that its competitors simply could not do as well or as fast. Also, some natural affinities began to occur among the software developers as each began to realize more fully one another's strengths and weaknesses, and each began to specialize on certain subroutines. What had been a work group became a real team, with all of the synergies and efficiencies that entails. Soon Shana's managers began to develop training routines, work procedures, and compensation and incentive policies to further improve team performance. Shana also began to use its growing body of specialized knowledge and its effective development teams to concentrate on particular clients that required its special abilities. These were clients that used the

two popular operating systems but wanted the same forms software for both. The new market focus and additional product development and marketing experience it brought sharpened Shana's expertise still further, widening the skill gap between it and its rivals. This gradual convergence of the company around its capabilities and target market helped to focus new selection and training programmes, project management protocols, and marketing campaigns. These allowed Shana to exploit and extend its competitive advantage.

Note that Shana did not set out to master a special capability. Nor did it perform a competitive analysis to look for promising niches. Rather, Shana's managers noticed retrospectively what their firm was unusually good at, reflected on and developed it, and pursued those clients that would most benefit from Shana's emerging talents. The firm, moreover, did not set out to emulate the competitive advantages and competences of its most successful rivals. First, it did not have the financial or technological logical wherewithal to accomplish this, nor could it reasonably expect to develop it. Second, even if Shana were able to develop those competencies, by the time it did its competitors most likely would have moved ahead. Shana's managers realized that emulation would cede to rivals product and market leadership – no competitor was a sitting target. Finally, had it attempted to do what its rivals do well, Shana would have had to share a market with a host of other imitators.

Unfortunately, *asymmetries are not resources or core competencies.* Like personal characteristics such as shyness or aggressiveness, they can serve as advantages or disadvantages. As with Citi's network they tend to be under-explored, under-funded, and unconnected to a firm's engine of value creation. However, where carefully fostered and directed, asymmetries may come to underlie the most important capabilities in a firm's competitive arsenal. By continually identifying and building on asymmetries, by nurturing and exploiting these within a complementary organizational design, and by leveraging them via an appropriate market focus, companies may be able to aspire realistically to attain sustainable advantage.

Paradoxically, a continual and intimate connection with the market environment is vital to this 'inside-out approach'. First, firms have to understand their rivals in order to know how they themselves are unique. More importantly, they need to track market reactions to discover which asymmetries are relevant. It is this ongoing ability to find the intersection between a firm's emerging asymmetries and the opportunities in the environment that is the fundamental strength of the organizations we describe here.

The three imperatives of inside-out strategy

Three imperatives are especially central to our approach. Although our presentation is necessarily linear, the process of developing inside-out strategy is emergent – full of trial and error, iteration between imperatives, and exploitation of chance.

Imperative 1: Discover asymmetries and their potential

To do well, firms need to develop important capabilities or resources that their rivals cannot. As

indicated, however, it is hard for them to develop these resources unless they already have some realized or potential edge. The first step is *discovering* the asymmetries that underlie that edge, as unrecognized resources or capabilities are of little advantage.

Asymmetries can arise in a number of ways. Some, such as Citi's banking network, develop as a result of the vagaries of corporate history. Others, such as long-term contracts and distinctive patents, are consciously created. In all cases, asymmetries serve as useful starting points for creating advantage precisely because they cannot be easily copied. The search for asymmetries is the search for these inimitable differences.

The inimitability of an asymmetry may be due to legal barriers, as in the case of patents. More often, however, it is because asymmetries represent subtle and interrelated attributes and skills that have co-evolved over a significant interval – as in the case of Shana. The subtle and tacit nature of these attributes, and in some cases their lack of connection to success, keeps these asymmetries beneath the radar screens of rivals (and sometimes those of the firm itself).

Because of this subtlety, the search for asymmetries cannot be a casual process. It demands thorough and persistent enquiry across the breadth of an organization. The search must lead to an understanding of how a firm differs from its competitors in the assets it possesses, the execution processes it uses, and the combinations of these things. It should also provide insights into how these asymmetries are currently generating or may potentially generate the resources or capabilities that produce advantage. Having discovered these resources, they must be evaluated for their potential contributions to performance.

Outside search.   A good place to begin the search for internal asymmetries is to find the more obvious *external* ones – the kinds of clients and business that gravitate to a firm rather than its competitors. Managers might look for the kinds of opportunities they can capture that their competitors cannot. The types of customers and the peculiarities of their product and service demands are key clues. Asymmetries can also be spotted by asking why a company beats its rivals in capturing a particular client or market. Answers may be found in the breadth of offerings or geographic reach, reputation with a client, or intimate market knowledge.

Learning demands action as well as reflection. In fact, one of the surest ways of revealing valuable asymmetries is to launch a set of entrepreneurial initiatives, determine which ones show promise, and then try to discover why. These can be viewed as experiments and may include broaching new kinds of customers or market segments, combining existing products with services, and altering the mix of products. Such experiments bring out new fans of the firm and make clearer *emerging* asymmetries. Shana's particular talents became clearer to its managers both as it pursued different clients and new software projects. In fact, in highly emergent contexts – in e-commerce, for example, or a newly deregulated industry – required capabilities are highly ambiguous and first mover advantages are central to ultimate success. Here firms are better off moving quickly to seize opportunities. Only after carrying out their market experiments can they determine where their advantages lie.

Inside search. Search also must take place inside a company. In many cases, the most useful asymmetries are buried deep within a firm and have to be traced back from surface abilities. Willamette Inc. is a successful medium-sized paper manufacturer. One of Willamette's apparent strengths was its ability to track the paper market by making the right grade of paper at the right time. However, the knowledge of what to make is widely available – many competitors have it. The most basic capability is an ability to convert production processes quickly and cheaply enough to take advantage of industry price changes. The reason Willamette could do this was because of its flexible equipment. The reason it had such equipment when its competitors did not was because of the experience Willamette's engineers had built up over the years converting the dilapidated plants of rivals into some of the most flexible and efficient factories in the industry. Willamette's fundamental asymmetry and its primary source of advantage was its state-of-the-art plant conversion and operating capabilities – capabilities, it turned out, that usually could not even be duplicated by the nation's top engineering consultants. It was this profound recognition of its capabilities that then allowed Willamette to allocate the human and financial resources and gear its hiring, training, promotion, and compensation approaches to support them.

Discovering asymmetries that represent *latent* resources or capabilities is particularly challenging. The case of Citigroup's global relationship banking unit was instructive because its crucial asymmetry – unrivalled geographic presence – for many years represented as much a liability as an asset. By 1980, Citi had developed a system of banks in 100 countries. Its nearest rival, Hong Kong Shanghai Bank Corp., had offices in 40 countries. However, many of Citi's banks were weak, and margins were being squeezed in developed countries by competing local banks with better ties to customers and government. Meanwhile in developing countries, market volatility and political instability were real and costly hazards. Despite these problems, then-CEO John Reed realized that the international network could *potentially* put it in a unique position to do business with far-flung multinationals that desired further globalization. Also, it was unlikely that rivals could easily imitate this resource.

Thus, asymmetry identification can take at least two forms. The first is a re-framing insight, spotting preexisting but unexploited assets – as at Citi. The second is evolutionary and requires managers to recognize an emerging edge, frequently in intangible assets such as knowledge, relationships, and reputation. This was the case at Shana and Willamette.

Table 5.2.1 provides suggestions on how a firm can identify its own key asymmetries and capabilities. An Assessment Audit is available from the authors to guide this process.

Imperative 2: Create capability configurations – by design

Asymmetries evolve into sustainable core capabilities largely through organization design – which builds and supports capabilities by embedding them in a cohesive configuration. Design also energizes these configurations by setting up 'virtuous circles' of capability enhancement.

There are two aspects to capability configurations. First, they are made up of a *cohesive combination of resources and capabilities* that is hard to imitate. Simple resources such as patents or proprietary processes can be contrasted with more complex bundles of elements such as a distribution system. Citi's bank network, for example, encompassed a set of mutually reinforcing elements that made it easier to serve multinational clients – many banks in many countries, business and political contacts connected to and shared

TABLE 5.2.1   Discovering asymmetries and capabilities

Questions	Information sought	Possible data sources
What are the differences in observable outputs between a firm and its rivals: where is the firm superior? Hints from: ■ What kinds of customers are more apt to choose this firm than its rivals and why? ■ What do they ask from the firm – and value most from its offerings?	Comparison of outputs along dimensions such as design attractiveness or functionality, service, price, solutions tailoring, reputation, guarantees, and quality. Also relevant may be the scale, scope, and reach of the firm and its EDI and logistical connections to clients.	Market facing units or key account managers; customer reactions; and data on kinds of clients drawn to firm and their reactions to firm. Indexes of performance and quality by product, geography, and plant.
Which resources and capabilities appear to underlie the above sources of superiority – and where in the firm do they reside? Which asymmetries between a firm and its rivals ultimately can be *built* into sources of superiority?	**Resources** may include those that are *property-based:* patents, control over unique supplies or channels, talent under long-term contract; *knowledge-based:* unique information about customers, segments, and tecnologies; and *relationship-based:* partnerships, alliances, reputation, and customer ties. **Capabilities** include process and product design, product development, operations, value chain integration, all aspects of marketing and customer service, and organization design.	Managers in product and process development units, market and client-facing units, and geographic units.
Which resources and capabilities would be hardest for rivals to nullify?	Target for analysis especially those resources and competencies identified above.	Market-facing managers and customers, studies of rivals' products, communications, and what is written about them.
Which capabilities and resources are most central now and for the future to a firm's competitive advantage?	Consider the degree to which each of the resources and capabilities are sustainable, drive growth and profitability, underlie other capabilities, complement other capabilities, can be enhanced and developed, and can be leveraged across a wide range of market opportunities.	Managers from different functions and SBUs.

among the banks, and a set of common product and service standards across banks. Such resource or capability configurations tend to be far more powerful, distinctive, and tough to copy than single capabilities. Advantages of capability configurations include:

1 Configurations develop powerful complementarities around core capabilities and among resources, often by using an array of design levers.

2 Configurations embed and empower resources within a design, thereby more firmly capturing those resources, and making them more valuable to an organization than to its rivals (a condition economists call asset specificity).

3 Configurations organize capabilities into socially complex systems that are difficult for rivals to imitate.

4 Configurations embody virtuous cycles that enhance capabilities.

5 Points 2 to 4 all help to turn capabilities into sustainable competitive advantages.

However, capability configurations have an even more valuable property – they are *embedded within a design infrastructure* that leverages, sustains, and develops them. At Citicorp, the international bank network at first was just a *potentially* valuable resource, not an actual one. The network only became a sustainable capability within the context of a supportive organizational design. As long as Citi was organized as a set of geographically based profit centres, local managers refused to give good service to multinationals that demanded bargain interest rates and service fees. John Reed was only able to unlock the value of the international network for multinationals through a new organization design. The design incorporated a group of very powerful key account managers and the multifunctional, multi-product teams needed to serve them. A flexible resource allocation system was set up to provide human, product, and knowledge resources to each multinational client – to serve that client in a globally coordinated and integrated way anywhere in the world, for a vast array of products and on demand. Reed reinforced the configuration with information systems that give all key account team members access to all client information and with a dynamic planning process that makes team members commit to specific objectives for each customer. He extracted support from local managers by having them assessed and rewarded against their ability to serve the multinationals. At Citi, then, the design of the organization was a core enabler and key component of the capability configuration (Table 5.2.2), one that dramatically enhanced its business with multinationals.

The Citi case is a good example of a firm that identified a key asymmetry (the international bank system and web of connections), realized that it could be an important resource, and developed that resource into a capability configuration by embedding it in an effective organization design. Without the configuration, the bank system resource could not be exploited or leveraged. In fact, the reason so many potentially valuable resources go undetected is because they only take on value when deployed within a complementary design configuration.

Building molehills into mountains: Virtuous cycles that enhance capabilities. One of the most advantageous aspects of design configurations is that they create 'virtuous cycles' of capability enhancement – cycles that turn the potential of an asymmetry into a real and growing capability. Virtuous cycles are simply chains of influence in which one good outcome promotes another. Companies, for example, may possess a capability that attracts talented new employees and partners whose enlistment then augments that capability. Well-managed capabilities also raise performance, which in turn fuels them with additional resources and attention.

The emergence of Denmark's International Service System (ISS), illustrates the powerful role of virtuous circles in building what is now one of the largest service firms in the world. Early in its history, ISS began to accept contracts for cleaning slaughterhouses. This was a demanding task as equipment had to be disassembled for cleaning, and it was necessary to use special detergents and pressurized cleaning techniques to eradicate harmful bacteria. Also needed was expertise in testing for sterility. The experience gained with various types of clients allowed ISS to develop highly effective and efficient routines for doing the work, as well as enough financial expertise to be able to cost and price cleaning services by the machine, square metre, type of food, and so on. The proprietary technical knowledge gained in food hygiene enabled ISS to form partnerships with customers to jointly develop techniques for new products and evolving types of bacteria. This enhanced ISS's skills still further, giving them an even greater competitive advantage and an expanding client base. Eventually, ISS's expertise grew to encompass related hygiene-food businesses, including poultry and fish.

Such virtuous cycles do not happen by themselves. Design and leaders play a key role. At ISS, both executive action and the levers of design convert experience gained in a capability into policy priorities and market targets, codified knowledge, and efficient routines – which in turn extend those capabilities. For example, ISS's leadership strives to acquire 'customer density' in various segments. Scale in a segment leads not only to buying power but greater specialization, with resulting learning and customer intimacy advantages. Leaders also prioritize new opportunities that are becoming realizable because of growing skills or reputation. Information systems then build databases on costs and customers that facilitate better pricing, costing, and scheduling: this improves the capture rate of the most prized kinds of customers. Also, human resource systems codify criteria for selection and training, thereby sharpening the most important capabilities. Finally, structural mechanisms bring managers together to share knowledge across clients so that additional services can be sold to existing clients and ideas are shared around picking up additional business. Each of these design levers shapes the virtuous cycle as they help accumulate 'stocks of

TABLE 5.2.2 How designs build and exploit capability

Design enablers	Leadership/ governance	Values and culture	Structural mechanisms	Systems and policies
Embedding capabilities within the organization	Leaders create context to prioritize, fund, and build strategy around capabilities. TMT ensures synergy among resources and capabilities. TMT establishes policies to bring front and back units together to develop and adapt capabilities.	Corporate culture celebrates capabilities and accords prestige to units and people most central in creating those capabilities. Collaborative culture to bring together front and back units. Emphasis is on knowledge building and knowledge sharing among units.	Capability-based units such as task forces and cross-SBU teams are established to create and share knowledge. Multi-SBU, multi-function coordinating committees build and adapt capabilities. High-level management committees oversee long-term development of a specific capability.	Information and planning systems target and track capabilities by unit versus competitors. HR systems select, reward, and promote based on capabilities. Knowledge systems codify proprietary information on technologies, customers, and so on.
Enhancing capabilities	Governance bodies describe a trajectory for core capability extension and leveraging.	Informal networks bring front and back units and people together to develop capabilities.	Multi-unit teams and strategic alliances build knowledge. Communities of practice grow capabilities.	Information systems feed learning efforts: e.g., report results according to segments and customers. Training programmes.
Shaping capabilities to market opportunities	Leaders link capabilities to target markets and define policy parameters for identification and sequencing of opportunities.	Entrepreneurial culture encourages managers to identify opportunities that exploit capabilities.	Opportunity-based units help shape capabilities to market segments.	HR, planning, and incentive systems create resources that can be easily leveraged across opportunities. Rewards based on firm-wide objectives to get front and back to collaborate.

assets' such as reputation, technical, managerial and customer knowledge, cohesive teams and team skills, and distinctive systems and infrastructures.

Virtuous cycles have a number of things in common. They engender good performance and thus create resources to plow back into capability development. They enhance reputation, which brings opportunities. They elicit positive feedback from the market that reinforces the right kinds of people, skills, and products. Design serves as a powerful governor and amplifier of these cycles in identifying and prioritizing a capability; in assembling and coordinating the resources, people, systems, and mechanisms to develop it; in disseminating the capability within the organization; and in leveraging the capability across the right market opportunities.

Imperative 3: Pursue market opportunities that build on and leverage capabilities

The deepest capabilities and most integrated configurations are of no value unless they extract superior returns. So they have to satisfy the needs of a large enough audience who will pay amply to have that done. At the same time, emerging capabilities must be constantly unearthed and evaluated so they can be leveraged across a wider audience and set of opportunities.

A market can be looked at as a set of niches and opportunities that a firm must choose from to best leverage its capabilities. Managers must ask not only where are the opportunities, but also why should their firm be able to capture and exploit them better than potential competitors. The attractiveness of a niche must be evaluated in the context of a firm's uniqueness and the capabilities it can attain more readily than its rivals.

It is also vital that *market niches and opportunities be related or complementary in that they benefit from the same kinds of capabilities.* This consideration guided some of our most successful firms. Citi's global corporate clients, for example, are similar in that they are large, do plenty of cross-border business, and benefit from Citi's global presence and international banking services. In fact, Citi changed its pricing strategy to attract *only* those types of clients. Without this relatedness, Citi's capabilities would be underutilized or underdeveloped. Note that it is not similarity of outputs or industry boundaries that define complementarity: Citi's global clients were in many different industries and locations, and Citi sold lots of different products. Rather, complementarity is defined in terms of the ability of different opportunities to benefit from the same asymmetries and capabilities.

Citi also pursued complementarity among opportunities in developing multi-product international banking solutions tailored to specific industries. It created product packages or 'industry templates' that would appeal to *many* clients within an industry – and thus give Citi economies of product development and market knowledge. Citi's product packages built not only on the similar needs of global clients in the same industry, but also on its banking contacts and expertise in foreign exchange, global cash management, and investment banking.

Inevitably, managers will have to shape capabilities according to such related opportunities. Recall that Citi made many changes to render its international bank network valuable to global clients – for example, abolishing regional profit centres to get local managers to serve multinationals. Citi also organized its global bank into industry groups to develop its tailored product solutions and increase market penetration. Because market focus was so clear, the bank could afford to develop industry- and client-based planning and information systems. These incorporated detailed information on *each* targeted client's potential banking business, which enabled representatives to home in on the best business opportunities and develop tailored approaches to capture that business. As the examples show, when adapting asymmetries and capabilities to market opportunities, the design configuration again plays a central role.

Leveraging capabilities across new opportunities. Capabilities are especially valuable when they can be leveraged across a broadening set of market opportunities. Such leveraging must become a never-ending process. Here again virtuous cycles are useful. They strengthen current capabilities, but they also push asymmetries and capabilities into new areas. As learning occurs, a firm is able to employ capabilities or resources garnered in one situation to serve a different one. This can happen in several ways.

- The same capabilities can be applied across different products and industries. ISS leveraged its special capabilities in cleaning and sterilizing slaughterhouses to enter the hospital services field. A deep knowledge of bacteria, chemicals, sterilization, cleaning, and testing techniques allowed ISS to enter a completely different industry, with similar capability requirements.

- Customer-related expertise and reputation developed around one output can be used to sell others to the same customer. ISS-Mediclean used the reputation and customer-specific knowledge it garnered in cleaning a given hospital to get other types of service contracts with that same institution. 'Knowledge of a specific customer and a broader range of services gains Mediclean access to the customer's senior management. … It is this access that leads to the deepening and expanding of the relationship.'

- Segment-related expertise developed with one customer can be used with others in the same segment. ISS leveraged its knowledge across different health care institutions based on its extensive segment-specific knowledge. The company is successful in part because it thoroughly understands the needs of the British hospital customer, and because its capabilities span a comprehensive array of hospital cleaning and facilitates management services.

ISS excels at all three kinds of leverage, in part because of an organization design that encompasses entrepreneurial, opportunity-seeking leadership as well as systems that gather and disseminate information on both capabilities and market opportunities. ISS's culture ensures that knowledge is easily shared across organizational boundaries, and its flexible administrative structure can manage capabilities and exploit new opportunities.

Ultimately, most capabilities become obsolete. Major sources of obsolescence include rival imitators eroding value, product lines reaching maturity, and major transformations in industry technology. The threat of imitation can often be countered by our virtuous cycles that build on capabilities fast enough to stay ahead of competitors. The threat of product obsolescence can be reduced by leveraging capabilities across new or related product areas. However, the only way to deal with technological or knowledge obsolescence is to continually look for *new* asymmetries that can be developed into capabilities that can be connected with a new set of opportunities (Christensen, 1997). This involves all three of our imperatives.

Implications for managers

In pursuing strategy from the inside out managers must learn both to pursue and trade off seeming opposites. Specifically, in discovering, building and leveraging capability they must balance reflection and action, selection and variation, resources and opportunities. Moreover, to make these tradeoffs in a quick and superior way, firms must make organizational design their source of competitive advantage. They must significantly empower their units to discover and develop the right capabilities and leverage them across the right opportunities; and they must create strong leadership and infrastructure at the centre to get those units to collaborate to do this rapidly and effectively.

Three tradeoffs

Balance reflection and action: Discovering asymmetries and capabilities.   Knowledge about capabilities comes in part from reflection. Managers must critically evaluate their resources and talents in looking for hidden gems – trying to determine which

are the best employees, which people and units work together best, which technologies show promise, what types of projects and products succeed, and what sorts of customers are attracted to the firm. The best outcomes of reflection are imaginative 're-framings' of the value of different resources, experiences, and relationships. At Shana, for example, they led managers to see that the really valuable capabilities were not in building forms software but in bridging operating systems.

Reflection, however, is not enough. True self-knowledge demands action and experimentation. Asymmetries and capabilities are always changing and the best way to keep track is by trying things and assessing the results. At ISS experiments might include working with different types of customers, trying a new process, or changing offerings for a new market segment. These experiments provide good information on what works – cues that then can be used to shape more focused experiments that converge on capabilities and launch virtuous circles.

Given the job pressures, managers must put time aside to reflect on capabilities and initiate experiments. They might launch quarterly sessions with top management, venture teams, or 'capability teams' to explore emerging competencies and the opportunities they bring. These discussions may work especially well when members of different business or technical units or functions get together. 'Outsider' units often see creative uses for resources their counterparts deem commonplace. Gathering to address a specific market challenge or opportunity may bring some urgency to the task of surfacing capabilities.

Balance variation and selection: Developing and embedding capabilities.   Leaders must determine *which* emerging capabilities are most promising and then 'select' or embed them as priorities for development. If the targeted set of capabilities is overly large or varied, resources will be too thinly spread to achieve critical mass and competitive superiority. Core or fundamental capabilities must take the lion's share of funds, talent, and visibility – even where this hurts other activities. However, to commandeer resources from 'secondary' activities, priorities must be reflected in accountabilities, performance criteria, rewards and promotions, and also in dedicated units and teams and in planning and information systems. ISS and Willamette use their planning and resource-allocation processes to drive resources towards the most promising asymmetries and capabilities. They also designate top priority capabilities and constitute teams that are appraised and rewarded according to capability development.

Variation in capabilities must also be restricted over time. Core capabilities have the highest yields when developed cumulatively over the long run and varied 'around the edges'. This requires top-level, long-term resource planning, coupled with regular follow-ups to determine how to elaborate, adapt, and fund a capability. In many of our firms, multi-functional, multi-SBU units and top-management committees assured continuity in developing longstanding capabilities. At the same time, firms searched for and experimented with capability variations – emerging but related relationships, client knowledge, expertise, and technologies. Without this exploration and 'playfulness' at the edges, a capability set narrows and loses relevance.

Balance capabilities and opportunities: Leveraging capabilities in the market. Managers need to find opportunities tailored to their capabilities. Opportunities also must ultimately shape capabilities. The faster these mutual adjustments occur, the more likely the virtuous circles, and the longer a firm is able to sustain competitive advantage. Of course, such speed is only possible when organizational designs and processes foster an ongoing, enriching dialogue between capability managers and opportunity managers.

Advantage by design

Different parts of the firm bring to bear different perspectives in building capabilities and making these tradeoffs. Units dealing with customers and markets ('front-end' units) look to leverage asymmetries in customer relationships, perhaps by broadening the product set. Units charged with engineering, R&D, and operations ('back-end' units) seek to leverage functional capabilities or products across different market opportunities. Both these pursuits are essential. Unfortunately, some product variations will unduly stretch capabilities, and some capabilities will not find a market. It is only by getting the front and back of an organization to work together that complementarity can be quickly realized between capabilities and market opportunities. This calls for organizational designs that not only empower front- and back-end units to develop opportunities and capabilities, but also create a strong centre and infrastructure to get these units to collaborate.

Strong front, strong back. Back-end units must have fungible resources: flexible resources they can use to discover and develop capabilities, and ones that are free from the day-to-day pull of operations. They also require the clout to call upon resources from the front to discover the needs of customers and the strengths of the competition. Typically, this requires that some front-end resources be accountable for capability development. Front-end units also need fungible resources to identify and pursue opportunities. Moreover, they need access to resources from the back to help them adapt capabilities to the new opportunities. Back-end resources, therefore, may have to be made accountable for realizing front-end opportunities. At Citi, for example, back-end functional and product specialists were appraised according to their service to large clients.

Strong-centre: Leadership and collaborative infrastructure. A strong centre is needed to make front and back collaborate. This involves myriad organizational levers and processes (see Table 5.2.2), with strong leadership being primary. Leaders must establish objectives, policies, and even transfer prices for determining how front and back can work together. They need to prioritize capabilities and opportunities, or at least delineate their scope. Leaders also may act as final arbiters in disputes between front and back, the way John Reed was called to do at Citi.

However, firms do even better where front and back can work together without a leader's intervention. This is more apt to happen where corporate cultures encourage collaboration, as at Willamette, or where extensive informal networks exist, as at Citi and ISS. Such cultures are fostered by strong and clear corporate values and by grapevines that widely disseminate reputational information so that managers can assemble effective teams. Other useful integrators are clear conflict resolution protocols, job rotation and training programmes that reduce parochialism, and even virtual communities on the internet.

Structural mechanisms such as multi-functional, multi-SBU task forces, standing committees, and integrative positions and roles can also bring together front and back. Finally, in all of the firms we studied, important roles were played by a variety of organizational systems and processes. Information and resource allocation systems, for example, identified the best human resources to serve capabilities and opportunities. Incentive systems rewarded organization-wide goals rather than departmental goals, and ensured that collaboration around capabilities and opportunities would be in the long-run interests of the firm.

Final words

Well-conceived organization processes and designs can help managers constantly identify asymmetries and potential capabilities, embed these in a configuration that grows and exploits them, and leverage those capabilities across complementary sets of market opportunities. Indeed, effective design provides the vehicle for bringing together developing resources and emerging opportunities in an ongoing process that sustains advantage.

READING

5.3

The capabilities of market-driven organizations

By George Day[1]

The marketing concept has been a paradox in the field of management. For over 40 years managers have been exhorted to 'stay close to the customer', 'put the customer at the top of the organizational chart,' and define the purpose of a business as the creation and retention of satisfied customers. Companies that are better equipped to respond to market requirements and anticipate changing conditions are expected to enjoy long-run competitive advantage and superior profitability.

Throughout much of its history, however, the marketing concept has been more an article of faith than a practical basis for managing a business. Little was known about the defining features or attributes of this organizational orientation, and evidence as to the antecedents and performance consequences was mainly anecdotal. Consequently, managers had little guidance on how to improve or redirect their organizations' external orientation toward their markets.

Fortunately, this situation is changing following a 'rediscovery' in the late 1980s (Dickson 1992; Webster 1992). In the last five years, a number of conceptual and empirical studies have appeared that more clearly describe what a market orientation is and what it consists of. According to this emerging literature market orientation represents superior skills in understanding and satisfying customers (Day 1990). Its principal features are the following:

- a set of beliefs that puts the customer's interest first;
- the ability of the organization to generate, disseminate, and use superior information about customers and competitors;

- the coordinated application of interfunctional resources to the creation of superior customer value.

In addition, a modest but growing body of empirical evidence supports the proposition that a market orientation is positively associated with superior performance. Despite the recent progress in understanding what a market-driven organization does and identifying who they are, troubling gaps and shortcomings remain. Little is known, for example, about the characteristics of successful programmes for building market orientation. How should these programmes be designed? Should management emphasize fundamental culture change, revised work processes, organizational restructuring, new systems, redirected incentives, or some other set of plausible initiatives?

I address these issues by examining the role of capabilities in creating a market-oriented organization. Capabilities are complex bundles of skills and collective learning, exercised through organizational processes, that ensure superior coordination of functional activities. I propose that organizations can become more market oriented by identifying and building the special capabilities that set market-driven organizations apart.

Classifying capabilities

It is not possible to enumerate all possible capabilities, because every business develops its own configuration of capabilities that is rooted in the realities of its competitive market, past commitments, and anticipated requirements. None the less, certain types of capabilities

[1]Source: This article was adapted from G.S. Day, 'The Capabilities of Market-Driven Organizations', *Journal of Marketing*, October, 1994, Vol. 58, No. 4, pp. 37–52. Reprinted with permission from the *Journal of Marketing*, published by the American Marketing Association.

can be recognized in all businesses, corresponding to the core processes for creating economic value.

Some capabilities are easier to identify than others, usually because their activities are contained within the organization. Thus, Pitney-Bowes's ability to solve customers' mail-handling problems and McDonald's Corporation's achievement of unparalleled consistency of service delivery in dispersed outlets are pointed to as distinctive capabilities that explain their durable advantages. The visibility and prevalence of these examples of capabilities that have been successfully deployed from the inside out have led some observers to argue that firms should be defined by what they are capable of doing, rather than by the needs they seek to satisfy. This perspective is unbalanced, because it is the ability of the business to use these inside-out capabilities to exploit external possibilities that matters. Thus, there has to be a matching 'outside-in' capability to sense these possibilities and decide how best to serve them.

Consider the Corning, Inc. division that manufactures fibre optic products. Its challenge was to balance demands for increased product customization and faster delivery while reducing costs to stay ahead of aggressive competition. Originally, its objective was to be the most efficient mass producer of standard fibre optics. As the fibre optic market evolved and customers began to demand more specialized products, it was necessary to convert the manufacturing capabilities from a rigid, standard-production system to a flexible manufacturing platform capable of building customized fibre products to order. This transition required both an inside-out capability to produce the low-cost, custom products on a timely basis and an outside-in capability for understanding the evolving requirements of customers and energizing the organization to respond to them.

Capabilities can be usefully sorted into three categories, depending on the orientation and focus of the defining processes (see Figure 5.3.1). At one end of the spectrum are those that are deployed from the *inside-out* and activated by market requirements, competitive challenges, and external opportunities. Examples are manufacturing and other transformation activities, logistics, and human resource management, including recruiting, training, and motivating employees. At the other end of the spectrum are those capabilities whose focal point is almost exclusively outside the organization. The purpose of these *outside-in* capabilities is to connect the processes that define the other organizational capabilities to the external environment and enable the business to compete by anticipating market requirements ahead of competitors and creating durable relationships with customers, channel members, and suppliers. Finally, spanning capabilities are needed to integrate the inside-out and outside-in

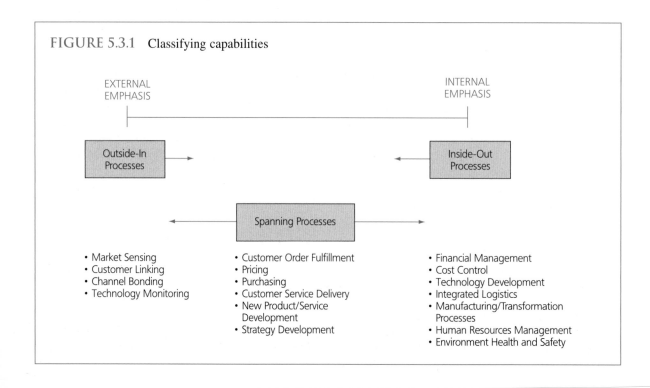

FIGURE 5.3.1   Classifying capabilities

EXTERNAL EMPHASIS

INTERNAL EMPHASIS

Outside-In Processes

Inside-Out Processes

Spanning Processes

- Market Sensing
- Customer Linking
- Channel Bonding
- Technology Monitoring

- Customer Order Fulfillment
- Pricing
- Purchasing
- Customer Service Delivery
- New Product/Service Development
- Strategy Development

- Financial Management
- Cost Control
- Technology Development
- Integrated Logistics
- Manufacturing/Transformation Processes
- Human Resources Management
- Environment Health and Safety

capabilities. Strategy development, new product/service development, price setting, purchasing, and customer order fulfilment are critical activities that must be informed by both external (outside-in) and internal (inside-out) analyses.

Market-driven organizations have superior market sensing, customer linking, and channel bonding capabilities. The processes underlying their superior capabilities are well understood and effectively managed and deliver superior insights that inform and guide both spanning and inside-out capabilities. The effect is to shift the span of all processes further toward the external end of the orientation dimension. Consider what happens when human resources are managed by the belief that customer satisfaction is both a cause and a consequence of employee satisfaction. Key policies become market oriented: rewards are based on measurable improvements in customer satisfaction and retention, employees are empowered to resolve customer problems without approvals, recruiting is based on customer problem-solving skills, and so forth. By contrast, the spanning and inside-out capabilities of internally oriented firms will be poorly guided by market considerations, which confines them to a narrow band toward the internal end of the orientation dimension. One reason is that the necessary outside-in processes that comprise the market sensing, customer linking, and channel bonding capabilities are likely to be poorly understood, badly managed, or deficient.

The role of spanning capabilities

Spanning capabilities are exercised through the sequences of activities that comprise the processes used to satisfy the anticipated needs of customers identified by the outside-in capabilities and meet the commitments that have been made to enhance relationships. Order fulfilment, new product development, and service delivery processes all play this role. Managing these horizontal processes so they become distinctive capabilities that competitors cannot readily match is very different from managing a vertical function in a traditional hierarchical organization.

First, process management emphasizes external objectives. These objectives may involve customers' satisfaction with the outcome of the process, whether quality, delivery time, or installation assistance, or may be based on competitive performance benchmarks (e.g. cycle time, order processing time). This helps ensure that all those involved with the process are focused on providing superior value to external or internal customers. These objectives become the basis

for a measurement and control system that monitors progress toward the objective. Second, in coordinating the activities of a complex process, several jurisdictional boundaries must be crossed and horizontal connections made. These interactions require an identifiable owner of the process who can isolate sources of delay and take action to eliminate them. When no one understands the total flow of activities in an order-entry process, for example, critical time-consuming steps such as credit checks may be undertaken separately in sequence when they could have been done in parallel to save time.

Third, information is readily available to all team members, unfiltered by a hierarchy. If a question arises concerning order requirements, delivery status, or parts availability, everyone who is affected by the answer can get the information directly without having to go through an intermediary.

The order fulfilment process in Figure 5.3.2 illustrates both the problems and benefits of managing a process so it becomes a distinctive capability rather than simply a sequential series of necessary activities. Often this process is obscured from top management view because it links activities that take place routinely as sales forecasts are made, orders are received and scheduled, products are shipped, and services are provided. Things can go awry if unrealistic promises are made to customers, these promises are not kept, blame is passed around, and inventories expand as each function seeks to protect itself from the shortcomings of another (in part because no one incurs a cost for holding excess inventories).

Furthermore, the order fulfilment process has a wealth of connections to other processes. It brings together information from the outside-in processes and depends on their ability to forecast and generate a flow of orders. It depends even more on the inside-out manufacturing and logistics processes to fulfil the scheduled orders or have capacity in place to service requests and transactions. Finally, there is the allied process of cost estimation and pricing of orders. The management of this activity will significantly improve profitability, if the customer value of each order is clearly recognized and the costs of filling each order are known.

Market sensing as a distinctive capability

Every discussion of market orientation emphasizes the ability of the firm to learn about customers, competitors, and channel members in order to continuously

FIGURE 5.3.2   Order fulfilment processes: Basis of a critical spanning capability

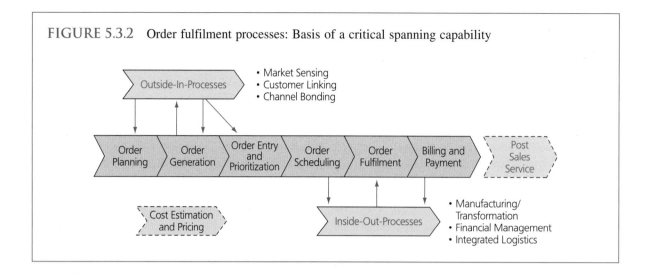

sense and act on events and trends in present and prospective markets. In market-driven firms the processes for gathering, interpreting, and using market information are more systematic, thoughtful, and anticipatory than in other firms. They readily surpass the ad hoc, reactive, constrained, and diffused efforts of their internally focused rivals.

A behavioural definition of a market orientation as 'the organization-wide generation of market intelligence, dissemination of its intelligence across departments, and organization-wide responsiveness to it' (Kohli and Jaworski, 1990), captures the essence of a market sensing capability. Each element of this definition describes a distinct activity having to do with collecting and acting on information about customer needs and the influence of technology, competition, and other environmental forces. Narver and Slater (1990) offer another definition in the same spirit. They distinguish three behavioural components: customer orientation – the firm's understanding of the target market; competitor orientation – the firm's understanding of the longrun capabilities of present and prospective competitors; and interfunctional coordination – the coordinated utilization of company resources to create superior customer value.

An alternative to this behavioural perspective holds that a market orientation is part of a more deeply rooted and pervasive culture. For this purpose, Deshpandé and Webster (1989) define culture as 'the pattern of shared values and beliefs that gives the members of an organization meaning, and provides them with the rules for behaviour'. A market-driven culture supports the value of thorough market intelligence and the necessity of

functionally coordinated actions directed at gaining a competitive advantage. An absence of these shared beliefs and values would surely compromise the activity patterns advocated by the behavioural perspective.

The process of market sensing follows the usual sequence of information processing activities that organizations use to learn. The stylized sequence in Figure 5.3.3 can be initiated by a forthcoming decision or an emerging problem, such as explaining why performance is declining. In addition, established procedures for collecting secondary information may prompt further market-sensing activity. This step leads to the active acquisition and distribution of information about the needs and responses of the market, how it is segmented, how relationships are sustained, the intentions and capabilities of competitors, and the evolving role of channel partners. Before this information can be acted on, it has to be interpreted through a process of sorting, classification, and simplification to reveal coherent patterns. This interpretation is facilitated by the mental models of managers, which contain decision rules for filtering information and useful heuristics for deciding how to act on the information in light of anticipated outcomes. Further learning comes from observing and evaluating the results of the decisions taken on the basis of the prior information. Did the market respond as expected, and if not, why not? Organizational memory plays several roles in this process: it serves as a repository for collective insights contained within policies, procedures, routines, and rules that can be retrieved when needed; a source of answers to ongoing enquiries; and a major determinant of the ability to ask appropriate questions.

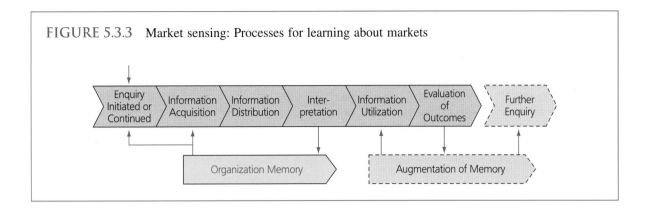

FIGURE 5.3.3   Market sensing: Processes for learning about markets

Market-driven firms are distinguished by an ability to sense events and trends in their markets ahead of their competitors. They can anticipate more accurately the responses to actions designed to retain or attract customers, improve channel relations, or thwart competitors. They can act on information in a timely, coherent manner because the assumptions about the market are broadly shared. This anticipatory capability is based on superiority in each step of the process. It is achieved through opened-minded enquiry, synergistic information distribution, mutually informed interpretations, and accessible memories.

Open-minded enquiry

All organizations acquire information about trends, events, opportunities, and threats in their market environment through scanning, direct experience, imitation, or problem-solving enquiries. Market-driven organizations approach these activities in a more thoughtful and systematic fashion, in the belief that all decisions start with the market. The most distinctive features of their approach to enquiry are the following:

- Active scanning. All organizations track key market conditions and activities and try to learn from the departures from what is normal and expected. However, this learning is usually a top-down effort because information from the front-line employees is blocked. In market-driven organizations, these front-line contacts, who hear complaints or requests for new services and see the consequences of competitive activity, are motivated to inform management systematically.
- Self-critical benchmarking. Most firms do regular tear-down analyses of competitors' products and

occasionally study firms for insights into how to perform discrete functions and activities better. Market-driven firms study attitudes, values, and management processes of nonpareils.

- Continuous experimentation and improvement. All organizations tinker with their procedures and practices and take actions aimed at improving productivity and customer satisfaction. However, most are not very serious about systematically planning and observing the outcomes of these ongoing changes, so those that improve performance are adopted and others are dropped.
- Informed imitation. Market-driven firms study their direct competitors so they can emulate successful moves before the competition gets too far ahead. This investigation requires thoughtful efforts to understand why the competitor succeeded, as well as further probes for problems and shortcomings to identify improvements that would be welcomed by customers. Here the emphasis is more on what the competitor was able to achieve in terms of superior performance, features, and so forth, and less on understanding the capabilities of the competitor that resulted in the outcome.

Synergistic information distribution

Firms often do not know what they know. They may have good systems for storing and locating 'hard' routine accounting and sales data, but otherwise managers have problems figuring out where in the organization a certain piece of information is known or assembling all the needed pieces in one place. This is especially true of competitor information, in which, for example, manufacturing may be aware of certain activities through common equipment suppliers, sales may hear about initiatives from distributors and collect rumours from customers, and the engineering department may have hired recently from a competitor.

Market-driven firms do not suffer unduly from organizational chimneys, silos, or smokestacks, which restrict information flows to vertical movements within functions. Instead, information is widely distributed, its value is mutually appreciated, and those functions with potentially synergistic information know where else it could be used beneficially.

Mutually informed interpretations

The simplifications inherent in the mental models used by managers facilitate learning when they are based on undistorted information about important relationships and are widely shared throughout the organization. These mental models can impede learning when they are incomplete, unfounded, or seriously distorted by functioning below the level of awareness, they are never examined. A market-driven organization avoids these pitfalls by using scenarios and other devices to force managers to articulate, examine, and eventually modify their mental models of how their markets work, how competitors and suppliers will react, and the parameters of the response coefficients in their marketing programs.

Accessible memory

Market-driven enquiry, distribution, and interpretation will not have a lasting effect unless what is learned is lodged in the collective memory. Organizations without practical mechanisms to remember what has worked and why will have to repeat their failures and rediscover their success formulas over and over again. Collective recall capabilities are most quickly eroded by turnover through transfers and rapid disbanding of teams. Data banks that are inaccessible to the entire organization can also contribute to amnesia. Here is where information technology can play an especially useful role.

Customer linking as a distinctive capability

As buyer–seller relationships continue their transformation, a customer-linking capability – creating and managing close customer relationships – is becoming increasingly important. At one time, standard purchasing practice emphasized arm's length adversarial bargaining with suppliers, aimed at achieving the lowest price for each transaction or contract. Not surprisingly, suppliers focused on individual transactions and gave little attention to the quality of the interface with the customer. They had little incentive to be open with buyers or develop superior or dedicated capabilities because they could easily lose the business to a competitor. The buyer, in turn, was unlikely to be aware of a supplier's costs and capabilities.

Now customers, as well as major channel members such as Ikea and Wal-Mart, are seeking closer, more collaborative relationships with suppliers based on a high level of coordination, participation in joint programmes, and close communication links. They want to replace the adversarial model, which assumes that advantages are gained through cutting input costs, with a cooperative model that seeks advantage through total quality improvement and reduced time to market. This way of doing business suits their better suppliers, who confront intense competition that quickly nullifies their product advantages and powerful channels that control access to the market.

Despite recent emphasis on the establishment, maintenance, and enhancement of collaborative relationships, few firms have mastered this capability and made it a competitive advantage. Successful collaboration requires a high level of purposeful cooperation aimed at maintaining a trading relationship over time. The activities to be managed start with the coordination of inside-out and spanning capabilities, although these are not the means by which the relationship is managed. Instead, new skills, abilities, and processes must be mastered to achieve mutually satisfactory collaboration. These include the close communication and joint problem solving, and coordinating activities.

Close communication and joint problem solving

Suppliers must be prepared to develop team-based mechanisms for continuously exchanging information about needs, problems, and emerging requirements and then taking action. In a successful collaborative relationship, joint problem solving displaces negotiations. Suppliers must also be prepared to participate in the customer's development processes, even before the product specifications are established.

Communications occur at many levels and across many functions of the customer and supplier organizations, requiring a high level of internal coordination and a new role for the sales function. When the focus is on transactions, the salesperson is pivotal and the emphasis is on persuading the customer through features, price, terms, and the maintenance of a presence. The sales function adopts a very different – and possibly subordinate – role in a collaborative relationship. It is responsible for coordinating other functions, anticipating needs, demonstrating responsiveness, and building credibility and trust.

Coordinating activities

In addition to the scheduling of deliveries, new management processes are needed for (1) joint production planning and scheduling; (2) management of information system links so each knows the other's requirements and status and orders can be communicated electronically; and (3) mutual commitments to the improvement of quality and reliability.

Manufacturer–reseller relations has become a fertile area for the development of collaborative management capabilities, with the major grocery product firms taking the lead. The objective of each party used to be to transfer as much of their cost to the other as possible. This approach leads to dysfunctional practices such as forward buying to take advantage of manufacturer's promotional offers, resulting in excessive warehousing expenses and costly spikes in production levels. Traditionally, contacts between parties were limited to lower-level sales representatives calling on buyers who emphasized prices, quantities, and deals. Increasingly, manufacturers like Procter & Gamble and retailers like KMart are assigning multifunctional teams to deal with each other at many levels, including harmonizing systems, sharing logistics and product movement information, and jointly planning for promotional activity and product changes. The objectives of this collaborative activity are to cut total system costs while helping retailers improve sales.

Firms that have developed a distinctive capability for managing collaborative relationships find they have more integrated strategies. The integration begins with a broad-based agreement on which customers serve collaboratively. No longer is this choice left to the sales function, without regard to the impact on the manufacturing and service functions. The cross-functional coordination and information sharing required to work collaboratively with customers enhances shared understanding of the strategy and role of the different functions.

Although collaborative relationships are becoming increasingly important, they are not appropriate for every market or customer. Some customers want nothing more than the timely exchange of the product or service with minimum hassle and a competitive price. And because of the effort and resources required to support a tightly linked relationship, it may not be possible to do this with more than a few critical customers. Yet even when most relationships are purely transactional, there are still possibilities for gaining advantages by nurturing some elements of a linking capability within the organization. This process begins by analysing which customers are more loyal or easier to retain and proceeds by seeking ways to maintain continuity with these customers through customized services or incentives.

Developing the capabilities of market-driven organizations

Initiatives to enhance market sensing and customer linking capabilities are integral to broader efforts to build a market-driven organization. The overall objective is to demonstrate a pervasive commitment to a set of processes, beliefs, and values, reflecting the philosophy that all decisions start with the customer and are guided by a deep and shared understanding of the customer's needs and behaviour and competitors' capabilities and intentions, for the purpose of realizing superior performance by satisfying customers better than competitors.

Many firms have aspired to become market driven but have failed to instil and sustain this orientation. Often these aspirants underestimate how difficult a task it is to shift an organization's focus from internal to external concerns. They apparently assume that marginal changes, a few management workshops, and proclamations of intent will do the job, when in fact a wide-ranging cultural shift is necessary. To have any chance for success, change programmes will have to match the magnitude of the cultural shift.

Preliminary insights into how to design change programmes come from empirical research on why some organizations are more market oriented than others. For example, Jaworski and Kohli (1993) confirm the long-standing belief that top management commitment is essential. Strong affirmation of the notion that market-driven organizations have superior capabilities comes from three of their findings. First, they found that formal and informal connectedness of functions facilitates the exchange of information whereas interdepartmental conflicts inhibit the communications that are necessary to effective market sensing. This confirms the desirability of managing this capability as a set of organization-spanning activities. Second, there was solid evidence that centralization was antithetical to market orientation. This mind-set appears to flourish when there is delegation of decision-making authority and extensive participation in decision making. Finally, the use of market-based factors such as customer satisfaction for evaluating and rewarding managers was the single most influential determinant of market orientation.

Summary and conclusions

It is almost an article of faith within marketing that superior business performance is the result of superior skills in understanding and satisfying customers. This proposition has been partially validated by a growing body of research on the impact of a market orientation on business performance. This work has helped give a fuller picture of the attributes of market-driven organizations, highlighting the roles of culture, information utilization, and interfunctional coordination. These insights are not sufficient for managers, because they do not reveal how the superior skills were developed. All we see is the results of the organizational transformation. Now managers seek guidance on how to enhance the market orientation of their organization.

The emerging capabilities approach to strategy offers a valuable new perspective on how to achieve and sustain a market orientation. This approach seeks the sources of defensible competitive positions in the distinctive, difficult-to-imitate capabilities the organization has developed. The shift in emphasis to capabilities does not mean that strategic positioning is any less important. On the contrary, the choice of which capabilities to nurture and which investment commitments to make must be guided by a shared understanding of the industry structure, the needs of the target customer segments, the positional advantages being sought, and the trends in the environment.

Two capabilities are especially important in bringing these external realities to the attention of the organization. One is the market sensing capability, which determines how well the organization is equipped to continuously sense changes in its market and to anticipate the responses to marketing actions. The second is a customer-linking capability, which comprises the skills, abilities, and processes needed to achieve collaborative customer relationships so individual customer needs are quickly apparent to all functions and well-defined procedures are in place for responding to them.

READING 5.4

Firm resources and sustained competitive advantage

By Jay Barney[1]

Understanding sources of sustained competitive advantage for firms has become a major area of research in the field of strategic management. Since the 1960s, a single organizing framework has been used to structure much of this research. This framework, summarized in Figure 5.4.1, suggests that firms obtain sustained competitive advantages by implementing strategies that exploit their internal strengths, through responding to environmental opportunities, while neutralizing external threats and avoiding internal weaknesses. Most research on sources of sustained competitive advantage has focused either on isolating a firm's opportunities and threats (Porter, 1980, 1985), describing its strengths and

weaknesses (Hofer and Schendel, 1978; Penrose, 1958), or analysing how these are matched to choose strategies.

Research by Porter and his colleagues (Caves and Porter, 1977; Porter, 1980, 1985) has attempted to describe the environmental conditions that favour high levels of firm performance. Porter's 'five forces model', for example, describes the attributes of an attractive industry and thus suggests that opportunities will be greater, and threats less, in these kinds of industries.

To help focus the analysis of the impact of a firm's environment on its competitive position, much of this type of strategic research has placed little emphasis on

[1]Source: This article was adapted with permission from J.B. Barney, 'Firm Resources and Sustained Competitive Advantage', *Journal of Management*, Vol. 17, No. 1, 1991, pp. 99–120, © 1991 Oklahoma State University. Reprinted by permission of SAGE Publications.

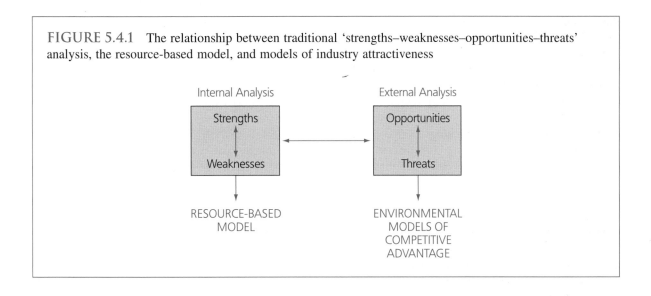

FIGURE 5.4.1 The relationship between traditional 'strengths–weaknesses–opportunities–threats' analysis, the resource-based model, and models of industry attractiveness

the impact of idiosyncratic firm attributes on a firm's competitive position. Implicitly, this work has adopted two simplifying assumptions. First, these environmental models of competitive advantage have assumed that firms within an industry (or firms within a strategic group) are identical in terms of the strategically relevant resources they control and the strategies they pursue. Second, these models assume that should resource heterogeneity develop in an industry or group (perhaps through new entry) that this heterogeneity will be very short lived because the resources that firms use to implement their strategies are highly mobile (i.e. they can be bought and sold in factor markets).

There is little doubt that these two assumptions have been very fruitful in clarifying our understanding of the impact of a firm's environment on performance. However, the resource-based view of competitive advantage, because it examines the link between a firm's internal characteristics and performance, obviously cannot build on these same assumptions. These assumptions effectively eliminate firm resource heterogeneity and immobility as possible sources of competitive advantage. The resource-based view of the firm substitutes two alternate assumptions in analysing sources of competitive advantage. First, this model assumes that firms within an industry (or group) may be heterogeneous with respect to the strategic resources they control. Second, this model assumes that these resources may not be perfectly mobile across firms, and thus heterogeneity can be long lasting. The resource-based model of the firm examines the implications of these two assumptions for the analysis of sources of sustained competitive advantage.

Defining key concepts

To avoid possible confusion, three concepts that are central to the perspective developed in this reading are defined in this section. These concepts are firm resources, competitive advantage, and sustained competitive advantage.

Firm resources

In this reading, firm resources include all assets, capabilities, organizational processes, firm attributes, information, knowledge, etc. controlled by a firm that enable the firm to conceive of and implement strategies that improve its efficiency and effectiveness. In the language of traditional strategic analysis, firm resources are strengths that firms can use to conceive of and implement their strategies.

A variety of authors have generated lists of firm attributes that may enable firms to conceive of and implement value-creating strategies. For purposes of this discussion, these numerous possible firm resources can be conveniently classified into three categories: physical capital resources, human capital resources, and organizational capital resources. Those attributes of a firm's physical, human, and organizational capital that do enable a firm to conceive of and implement strategies that improve its efficiency and effectiveness are, for purposes of this discussion, firm resources. The purpose of this reading is to specify the conditions under which such firm resources can be a source of sustained competitive advantage for a firm.

Competitive advantage and sustained competitive advantage

A firm is said to have a competitive advantage when it is implementing a value creating strategy not simultaneously being implemented by any current or potential competitors. It is said to have a sustained competitive advantage when it is implementing a value creating strategy not simultaneously being implemented by any current or potential competitors and when these other firms are unable to duplicate the benefits of this strategy. That a competitive advantage is sustained does not imply that it will 'last forever'. It only suggests that it will not be competed away through the duplication efforts of other firms. Unanticipated changes in the economic structure of an industry may make what was, at one time, a source of sustained competitive advantage, no longer valuable for a firm, and thus not a source of any competitive advantage. These structural revolutions in an industry redefine which of a firm's attributes are resources and which are not. Some of these resources, in turn, may be sources of sustained competitive advantage in the newly defined industry structure. However, what were resources in a previous industry setting may be weaknesses, or simply irrelevant, in a new industry setting. A firm enjoying a sustained competitive advantage may experience these major shifts in the structure of competition, and may see its competitive advantages nullified by such changes. However, a sustained competitive advantage is not nullified through competing firms duplicating the benefits of that competitive advantage.

Competition with homogeneous and perfectly mobile resources

Armed with these definitions, it is now possible to explore the impact of resource heterogeneity and immobility on sustained competitive advantage. This is done by examining the nature of competition when firm resources are perfectly homogeneous and mobile.

Resource homogeneity and mobility and sustained competitive advantage

Imagine an industry where firms possess exactly the same resources. This condition suggests that firms all have the same amount and kinds of strategically relevant physical, human, and organizational capital. Is there a strategy that could be conceived of and implemented by any one of these firms that could not also be conceived of and implemented by all other firms in this industry? The answer to this question must be no. The conception and implementation of strategies employs various firm resources. That one firm in an industry populated by identical firms has the resources to conceive of and implement a strategy means that these other firms, because they possess the same resources, can also conceive of and implement this strategy. Because these firms all implement the same strategies, they all will improve their efficiency and effectiveness in the same way, and to the same extent. Thus, in this kind of industry, it is not possible for firms to enjoy a sustained competitive advantage.

Resource homogeneity and mobility and first-mover advantages

One objection to this conclusion concerns so-called 'first-mover advantages' (Lieberman and Montgomery, 1988). In some circumstances, the first firm in an industry to implement a strategy can obtain a sustained competitive advantage over other firms. These firms may gain access to distribution channels, develop goodwill with customers, or develop a positive reputation, all before firms that implement their strategies later. Thus, first-moving firms may obtain a sustained competitive advantage.

However, upon reflection, it seems clear that if competing firms are identical in the resources they control, it is not possible for any one firm to obtain a competitive advantage from first moving. To be a first mover by implementing a strategy before any competing firms, a particular firm must have insights about the opportunities associated with implementing a strategy that are not possessed by other firms in the industry, or by potentially entering firms (Lieberman and Montgomery, 1988). This unique firm resource (information about an opportunity) makes it possible for the better informed firm to implement its strategy before others. However, by definition, there are no unique firm resources in this kind of industry. If one firm in this type of industry is able to conceive of and implement a strategy, then all other firms will also be able to conceive of and implement that strategy, and these strategies will be conceived of and implemented in parallel, as identical firms become aware of the same opportunities and exploit that opportunity in the same way.

It is not being suggested that there can never be first-mover advantages in industries. It is being suggested that in order for there to be a first-mover advantage, firms in an industry must be heterogeneous in terms of the resources they control.

Resource homogeneity and mobility and entry/mobility barriers

A second objection to the conclusion that sustained competitive advantages cannot exist when firm resources in an industry are perfectly homogeneous and mobile concerns the existence of 'barriers to entry' (Bain, 1956), or more generally, 'mobility barriers' (Caves and Porter, 1977). The argument here is that even if firms within an industry (group) are perfectly homogeneous, if there are strong entry or mobility barriers, these firms may be able to obtain a sustained competitive advantage vis-à-vis firms that are not in their industry (group). This sustained competitive advantage will be reflected in above normal economic performance for those firms protected by the entry or mobility barrier (Porter, 1980).

However, from another point of view, barriers to entry or mobility are only possible if current and potentially competing firms are heterogeneous in terms of the resources they control and if these resources are not perfectly mobile. The heterogeneity requirement is self-evident. For a barrier to entry or mobility to exist, firms protected by these barriers must be implementing different strategies than firms seeking to enter these protected areas of competition. Firms restricted from entry are unable to implement the same strategies as firms within the industry or group. Because the implementation of strategy requires the application of firm resources, the inability of firms seeking to enter an industry or group to implement the same strategies as firms within that industry or group suggests that firms seeking to enter must not have the same strategically relevant resources as firms within the industry or group. Thus, barriers to entry and mobility only exist when competing firms are heterogeneous in terms of the strategically relevant resources they control.

The requirement that firm resources be immobile in order for barriers to entry or mobility to exist is also clear. If firm resources are perfectly mobile, then any resource that allows some firms to implement a strategy protected by entry or mobility barriers can easily be acquired by firms seeking to enter into this industry or group. Once these resources are acquired, the strategy in question can be conceived of and implemented in the same way that other firms have conceived of and

implemented their strategies. These strategies are thus not a source of sustained competitive advantage.

Again, it is not being suggested that entry or mobility barriers do not exist. However, it is being suggested that these barriers only become sources of sustained competitive advantage when firm resources are not homogeneously distributed across competing firms and when these resources are not perfectly mobile.

Firm resources and sustained competitive advantage

Thus far, it has been suggested that in order to understand sources of sustained competitive advantage, it is necessary to build a theoretical model that begins with the assumption that firm resources may be heterogeneous and immobile. Of course, not all firm resources hold the potential of sustained competitive advantages. To have this potential, a firm resource must have four attributes:

- it must be valuable, in the sense that it exploits opportunities and/or neutralizes threats in a firm's environment;
- it must be rare among a firm's current and potential competition;
- it must be imperfectly imitable;
- there cannot be strategically equivalent substitutes for this resource that are valuable but neither rare nor imperfectly imitable.

These attributes of firm resources can be thought of as empirical indicators of how heterogeneous and immobile a firm's resources are and thus how useful these resources are for generating sustained competitive advantages. Each of these attributes of a firm's resources is discussed in more detail below.

Valuable resources

Firm resources can only be a source of competitive advantage or sustained competitive advantage when they are valuable. As suggested earlier, resources are valuable when they enable a firm to conceive of or implement strategies that improve its efficiency and effectiveness. The traditional 'strengths–weaknesses–opportunities–threats' model of firm performance suggests that firms are able to improve their performance only when their strategies exploit opportunities or neutralize threats. Firm attributes may have the other characteristics that could qualify them as sources of competitive advantage (e.g. rareness, inimitability, non-substitutability), but these attributes only become resources when they exploit opportunities or neutralize threats in a firm's environment.

That firm attributes must be valuable in order to be considered resources (and thus as possible sources of sustained competitive advantage) points to an important complementarity between environmental models of competitive advantage and the resource-based model. These environmental models help isolate those firm attributes that exploit opportunities or neutralize threats, and thus specify which firm attributes can be considered as resources. The resource-based model then suggests what additional characteristics that these resources must possess if they are to generate sustained competitive advantage.

Rare resources

By definition, valuable firm resources possessed by large numbers of competing or potentially competing firms cannot be sources of either a competitive advantage or a sustained competitive advantage. A firm enjoys a competitive advantage when it is implementing a value-creating strategy not simultaneously implemented by large numbers of other firms. If a particular valuable firm resource is possessed by large numbers of firms, then each of these firms have the capability of exploiting that resource in the same way, thereby implementing a common strategy that gives no one firm a competitive advantage.

The same analysis applies to bundles of valuable firm resources used to conceive of and implement strategies. Some strategies require a particular mix of physical capital, human capital, and organizational capital resources to implement. One firm resource required in the implementation of almost all strategies is managerial talent (Hambrick, 1987). If this particular bundle of firm resources is not rare, then large numbers of firms will be able to conceive of and implement the strategies in question, and these strategies will not be a source of competitive advantage, even though the resources in question may be valuable.

To observe that competitive advantages (sustained or otherwise) only accrue to firms that have valuable and rare resources is not to dismiss common (i.e. not rare) firm resources as unimportant. Instead, these valuable but common firm resources can help ensure a firm's survival when they are exploited to create competitive parity in an industry. Under conditions of competitive parity, though no one firm obtains a competitive advantage, firms do increase their probability of economic survival.

How rare a valuable firm resource must be in order to have the potential for generating a competitive advantage is a difficult question. It is not difficult to see that if a firm's valuable resources are absolutely unique among a set of competing and potentially competing firms, those resources will generate at least a competitive advantage and may have the potential of generating a sustained competitive advantage. However, it may be possible for a small number of firms in an industry to possess a particular valuable resource and still generate a competitive advantage. In general, as long as the number of firms that possess a particular valuable resource (or a bundle of valuable resources) is less than the number of firms needed to generate perfect competition dynamics in an industry, that resource has the potential of generating a competitive advantage.

Imperfectly imitable resources

It is not difficult to see that valuable and rare organizational resources may be a source of competitive advantage. Indeed, firms with such resources will often be strategic innovators, for they will be able to conceive of and engage in strategies that other firms could either not conceive of, or not implement, or both, because these other firms lacked the relevant firm resources. The observation that valuable and rare organizational resources can be a source of competitive advantage is another way of describing first-mover advantages accruing to firms with resource advantages.

However, valuable and rare organizational resources can only be sources of sustained competitive advantage if firms that do not possess these resources cannot obtain them. These firm resources are imperfectly imitable. Firm resources can be imperfectly imitable for one or a combination of three reasons: (a) the ability of a firm to obtain a resource is dependent upon *unique historical conditions*, (b) the link between the resources possessed by a firm and a firm's sustained competitive advantage is *causally ambiguous*, or (c) the resource generating a firm's advantage is *socially complex*. Each of these sources of the imperfect imitability of firm resources are examined below.

Unique historical conditions and imperfectly imitable resources. Another assumption of most environmental models of firm competitive advantage, besides resource homogeneity and mobility, is that the performance of firms can be understood independent of the particular history and other idiosyncratic attributes of firms. These researchers seldom argue that firms do not vary in terms of their unique histories, but rather that these unique histories are not relevant to understanding a firm's performance (Porter, 1980).

The resource-based view of competitive advantage developed here relaxes this assumption. Indeed, this approach asserts that not only are firms intrinsically historical and social entities, but that their ability to acquire and exploit some resources depends upon their place in time and space. Once this particular unique time in history passes, firms that do not have space-and time-dependent resources cannot obtain them, and thus these resources are imperfectly imitable.

Resource-based theorists are not alone in recognizing the importance of history as a determinant of firm performance and competitive advantage. Traditional strategy researchers often cited the unique historical circumstances of a firm's founding, or the unique circumstances under which a new management team takes over a firm, as important determinants of a firm's long-term performance. More recently, several economists (e.g. Arthur, Ermoliev and Kaniovsky, 1987; David, 1985) have developed models of firm performance that rely heavily on unique historical events as determinants of subsequent actions. Employing path-dependent models of economic performance these authors suggest that the performance of a firm does not depend simply on the industry structure within which a firm finds itself at a particular point in time, but also on the path a firm followed through history to arrive where it is. If a firm obtains valuable and rare resources because of its unique path through history, it will be able to exploit those resources in implementing value-creating strategies that cannot be duplicated by other firms, for firms without that particular path through history cannot obtain the resources necessary to implement the strategy.

The acquisition of all the types of firm resources examined in this article can depend upon the unique historical position of a firm. A firm that locates its facilities on what turns out to be a much more valuable location than was anticipated when the location was chosen possesses an imperfectly imitable physical capital resource. A firm with scientists who are uniquely positioned to create or exploit a significant scientific breakthrough may obtain an imperfectly imitable resource from the history-dependent nature of these scientists' individual human capital. Finally, a firm with a unique and valuable organizational culture that

emerged in the early stages of a firm's history may have an imperfectly imitable advantage over firms founded in another historical period, where different (and perhaps less valuable) organizational values and beliefs come to dominate.

Causal ambiguity and imperfectly imitable resources. Unlike the relationship between a firm's unique history and the imitability of its resources, the relationship between the causal ambiguity of a firm's resources and imperfect imitability has received systematic attention in the literature. In this context, causal ambiguity exists when the link between the resources controlled by a firm and a firm's sustained competitive advantage is not understood or understood only very imperfectly.

When the link between a firm's resources and its sustained competitive advantage is poorly understood, it is difficult for firms that are attempting to duplicate a successful firm's strategies through imitation of its resources to know which resources it should imitate. Imitating firms may be able to describe some of the resources controlled by a successful firm. However, under conditions of causal ambiguity, it is not clear that the resources that can be described are the same resources that generate a sustained competitive advantage, or whether that advantage reflects some other non-described firm resource. Sometimes it is difficult to understand why one firm consistently outperforms other firms. Causal ambiguity is at the heart of this difficulty. In the face of such causal ambiguity, imitating firms cannot know the actions they should take in order to duplicate the strategies of firms with a sustained competitive advantage.

To be a source of sustained competitive advantage, both the firms that possess resources that generate a competitive advantage and the firms that do not possess these resources but seek to imitate them must be faced with the same level of causal ambiguity (Lippman and Rumelt, 1982). If firms that control these resources have a better understanding of their impact on competitive advantage than firms without these resources, then firms without these resources can engage in activities to reduce their knowledge disadvantage. They can do this, for example, by hiring away well placed knowledgeable managers in a firm with a competitive advantage or by engaging in a careful systematic study of the other firm's success. Although acquiring this knowledge may take some time and effort, once knowledge of the link between a firm's resources and its ability to implement certain strategies is diffused throughout competing firms, causal ambiguity no longer exists, and thus cannot be a source of imperfect imitability. In other words, if a firm with a competitive advantage understands the link between the resources it controls and its advantages, then other firms can also learn about that link, acquire the necessary resources (assuming they are not imperfectly imitable for other reasons), and implement the relevant strategies. In such a setting, a firm's competitive advantages are not sustained because they can be duplicated.

At first, it may seem unlikely that a firm with a sustained competitive advantage will not fully understand the source of that advantage. However, given the very complex relationship between firm resources and competitive advantage, such an incomplete understanding is not implausible. The resources controlled by a firm are very complex and interdependent. Often, they are implicit, taken for granted by managers, rather than being subject to explicit analysis. Numerous resources, taken by themselves or in combination with other resources, may yield sustained competitive advantage. Although managers may have numerous hypotheses about which resources generate their firm's advantages, it is rarely possible to rigorously test these hypotheses. As long as numerous plausible explanations of the sources of sustained competitive advantage exist within a firm, the link between the resources controlled by a firm and sustained competitive advantage remains somewhat ambiguous, and thus which of a firm's resources to imitate remains uncertain.

Social complexity. A final reason that a firm's resources may be imperfectly imitable is that they may be very complex social phenomena, beyond the ability of firms to systematically manage and influence. When competitive advantages are based in such complex social phenomena, the ability of other firms to imitate these resources is significantly constrained.

A wide variety of firm resources may be socially complex. Examples include the interpersonal relations among managers in a firm, a firm's culture (Barney, 1986), a firm's reputation among suppliers and customers. Notice that in most of these cases it is possible to specify how these socially complex resources add value to a firm. Thus, there is little or no causal ambiguity surrounding the link between these firm resources and competitive advantage. However, understanding that, say, an organizational culture with certain attributes or quality relations among managers can improve a firm's efficiency and effectiveness does not necessarily imply that firms without these attributes can engage in systematic efforts to create them. Such social engineering

may be, for the time being at least, beyond the capabilities of most firms. To the extent that socially complex firm resources are not subject to such direct management, these resources are imperfectly imitable.

Notice that complex physical technology is not included in this category of sources of imperfectly imitable. In general, physical technology, whether it takes the form of machine tools or robots in factories or complex information management system, is by itself typically imitable. If one firm can purchase these physical tools of production and thereby implement some strategies, then other firms should also be able to purchase these physical tools, and thus such tools should not be a source of sustained competitive advantage.

On the other hand, the exploitation of physical technology in a firm often involves the use of socially complex firm resources. Several firms may all possess the same physical technology, but only one of these firms may possess the social relations, culture, traditions, etc. to fully exploit this technology in implementing strategies. If these complex social resources are not subject to imitation (and assuming they are valuable and rare and no substitutes exist), these firms may obtain a sustained competitive advantage from exploiting their physical technology more completely than other firms, even though competing firms do not vary in terms of the physical technology they possess.

Substitutability

The last requirement for a firm resource to be a source of sustained competitive advantage is that there must be no strategically equivalent valuable resources that are themselves either not rare or imitable. Two valuable firm resources (or two bundles of firm resources) are strategically equivalent when they each can be exploited separately to implement the same strategies. Suppose that one of these valuable firm resources is rare and imperfectly imitable, but the other is not. Firms with this first resource will be able to conceive of and implement certain strategies. If there were no strategically equivalent firm resources, these strategies would generate a sustained competitive advantage (because the resources used to conceive and implement them are valuable, rare, and imperfectly imitable). However, that there are strategically equivalent resources suggests that other current or potentially competing firms can implement the same strategies, but in a different way, using different resources. If these alternative resources are either not rare or imitable, then numerous firms will be able to conceive of and implement the strategies in question, and those strategies will not generate a sustained competitive advantage. This will be the case even though one approach to implementing these strategies exploits valuable, rare, and imperfectly imitable firm resources.

Substitutability can take at least two forms. First, though it may not be possible for a firm to imitate another firm's resources exactly, it may be able to substitute a similar resource that enables it to conceive of and implement the same strategies. For example, a firm seeking to duplicate the competitive advantages of another firm by imitating that other firm's high quality top management team will often be unable to copy that team exactly. However, it may be possible for this firm to develop its own unique top management team. Though these two teams will be different (different people, different operating practices, a different history, etc.), they may likely be strategically equivalent and thus be substitutes for one another. If different top management teams are strategically equivalent (and if these substitute teams are common or highly imitable), then a high quality top management team is not a source of sustained competitive advantage, even though a particular management team of a particular firm is valuable, rare and imperfectly imitable.

Second, very different firm resources can also be strategic substitutes. For example, managers in one firm may have a very clear vision of the future of their company because of a charismatic leader in their firm. Managers in competing firms may also have a very clear vision of the future of their companies, but this common vision may reflect these firms' systematic, company-wide strategic planning process. From the point of view of managers having a clear vision of the future of their company, the firm resource of a charismatic leader and the firm resource of a formal planning system may be strategically equivalent, and thus substitutes for one another. If large numbers of competing firms have a formal planning system that generates this common vision (or if such a formal planning is highly imitable), then firms with such a vision derived from a charismatic leader will not have a sustained competitive advantage, even though the firm resource of a charismatic leader is probably rare and imperfectly imitable.

Of course, the strategic substitutability of firm resources is always a matter of degree. It is the case, however, that substitute firm resources need not have exactly the same implications for an organization in order for those resources to be equivalent from the point of view of the strategies that firms can conceive of and implement. If enough firms have these valuable substitute resources (i.e. they are not rare), or if enough firms can acquire them (i.e. they are imitable), then none of these firms (including firms whose resources are being substituted for) can expect to obtain a sustained competitive advantage.

The framework

The relationship between resource heterogeneity and immobility; value, rareness, imitability, and substitutability; and sustained competitive advantage is summarized in Figure 5.4.2. This framework can be applied in analysing the potential of a broad range of firm resources to be sources of sustained competitive advantage. These analyses not only specify the theoretical conditions under which sustained competitive advantage might exist, they also suggest specific

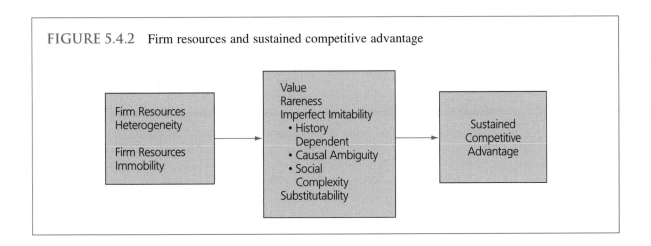

FIGURE 5.4.2   Firm resources and sustained competitive advantage

empirical questions that need to be addressed before the relationship between a particular firm resource and sustained competitive advantage can be understood.

That the study of sources of sustained competitive advantage focuses on valuable, rare, imperfectly imitable, and non-substitutable resource endowments does not suggest – as some population ecologists would have it (e.g., Hannan and Freeman, 1977) – that managers are irrelevant in the study of such advantages. In fact, managers are important in this model, for it is managers that are able to understand and describe the economic performance potential of a firm's endowments. Without such managerial analyses, sustained competitive advantage is not likely. This is the case even though the skills needed to describe the rare,

imperfectly imitable, and non-substitutable resources of a firm may themselves not be rare, imperfectly imitable, or non-substitutable.

Indeed, it may be the case that a manager or a managerial team is a firm resource that has the potential for generating sustained competitive advantages. The conditions under which this will be the case can be outlined using the framework presented in Figure 5.4.2. However, in the end, what becomes clear is that firms cannot expect to 'purchase' sustained competitive advantages on open markets. Rather, such advantages must be found in the rare, imperfectly imitable, and non-substitutable resources already controlled by a firm.

BUSINESS LEVEL STRATEGY IN INTERNATIONAL PERSPECTIVE

Whoever is winning at the moment will always seem to be invincible.
George Orwell (1903–1950); English novelist

Just as in the previous debates, it has become clear that there are various ways of dealing with the paradox of markets and resources. Each of the authors has argued a particular point of view, and it is the reader's task to judge which approach will yield the highest strategic dividends, under which set of circumstances. And as before, the chapter is concluded by explicitly looking at the issue from an international angle.

The difference between this and other chapters is that comparative management researchers have not reported specific national preferences for an inside-out or an outside-in perspective. This may be due to the fact that there actually are no distinct national inclinations when dealing with this paradox. However, it might also be the case that the late emergence of resource-based theories (starting in the early 1990s) has not yet allowed for cross-national comparisons.

As a stimulus to the debate on whether there are national differences in the approach to business level strategies, we would like to bring forward a number of factors that might be of influence on how the paradox of markets and resources is tackled in different countries. It goes almost without saying that more international research is needed to give this issue a firmer footing.

Mobility barriers

In general, industry and market positions will be of more value if there are high mobility barriers within the environment (Porter, 1980). Some of these mobility barriers can be specifically national in origin. Government regulation, in particular, can be an important source of mobility barriers. For instance, import quotas and duties, restrictive licensing systems, and fiscal regulations and subsidies, can all – knowingly or unknowingly – result in protection of incumbent firms. Such government intervention enhances the importance of obtained positions.

Other national sources of mobility barriers can be unions' resistance to change and high customer loyalty. In some economies high mobility barriers might also be imposed by powerful groups or families.

In such economies, which are more rigid due to high mobility barriers, strategists might have a strong preference to think in terms of market positions first, because these are more difficult to obtain than the necessary resources. The opposite would be true in more dynamic economies, where market positions might easily be challenged by competitors, unless they are based on distinctive and difficult to imitate resources.

Resource mobility

A second international difference might be found in the types of resources employed across countries. In nations where the dominant industries are populated by firms using relatively simple and abundant resources, market positions are far more important, since acquisition of the necessary resources is hardly a worry. However, if a national economy is composed of industries using complex bundles of resources, requiring many years of painstaking development, there might be a tendency to emphasize the importance of resources over market positions.

FURTHER READING

Although many textbooks give an overview of the variety of approaches to the topic of business level strategy, none of these introductions are as crisp as John Kay's book, *Foundations of Corporate Success: How Business Strategies Add Value*, which can be highly recommended as further reading. For a clear summary of the competing perspectives on business level strategy, see Robert Hoskisson's article 'Theory and Research in Strategic Management: Swings of a Pendulum'.

Most of what has been published on the topic of business level strategy has implicitly or explicitly made reference to the work of Michael Porter. Therefore, any follow-up readings should include his benchmark works *Competitive Strategy* and *Competitive Advantage*. It is also interesting to see how his thinking has developed and has embraced some of the resource-based concepts. In particular his articles 'Towards a Dynamic Theory of Strategy', and 'What is Strategy?' are stimulating works. Also highly recommended is the book by Robert Buzzell and Bradley Gale, *The PIMS Principles: Linking Strategy to Performance*, which has had a big impact by clarifying how market share and profitability are closely linked.

For a better insight into the resource-based approach, readers might want to go back to Edith Penrose's classic book *The Theory of the Growth of the Firm*. For a more recent introduction, the follow-up to Jay Barney's original article (Reading 5.4) is recommended. This article, written together with Mike Wright and David Ketchen, is titled 'The Resource-Based View of the Firm: Ten Years After 1991' and was part of an insightful special issue of the *Journal of Management*. David Collis and Cynthia Montgomery have also written an accessible article explaining the resource-based view, entitled 'Competing on Resources: Strategy in the 1990s'. Other important works that are more academically oriented are 'Dynamic Capabilities and Strategic Management' by David Teece, Garry Pisano and Amy Shuen, and 'The Cornerstones of Competitive Advantage: A Resource-Based View' by Margaret Peteraf. A very stimulating article bringing together outside-in and inside-out arguments is 'Strategic Integration:

Competing in the Age of Capabilities', by Peter Fuchs, Kenneth Mifflin, Danny Miller and John Whitney.

Last, but not least, the works of Garry Hamel and C.K. Prahalad should be mentioned. Many of their articles in *Harvard Business Review*, such as 'Strategic Intent,' 'Strategy as Stretch and Leverage' and 'The Core Competence of the Corporation' (Reading 6.2 in this book) have had a major impact, both on practitioners and academics, and are well worth reading. Many of the ideas expressed in these articles have been brought together in their book *Competing for the Future*, which is therefore highly recommended.

REFERENCES

Abell, D. (1980) *Defining the Business: The Starting Point of Strategic Planning*, Englewood Cliffs, NJ: Prentice Hall.

Amit, R., and Zott, C. (2001) 'Value Creation in E-business', *Strategic Management Journal*, Vol. 22, pp. 493–520.

Arthur, W.B., Ermoliev, Y.M., and Kaniovsky, Y.M. (1987) 'Path Dependent Processes and the Emergence of Macro Structure', *European Journal of Operations Research*, Vol. 30, pp. 294–303.

Ashkenas, R. (1995) *The Boundaryless Organization*, San Francisco, CA: Jossey-Bass.

Baden-Fuller, C., and Stopford, J.M. (1992) *Rejuvenating the Mature Business*, London: Routledge.

Bain, J. (1956) *Barriers to New Competition*, Harvard University Press, Cambridge, MA.

Barney, J.B. (1986) 'Organizational Culture: Can It Be a Source of Sustained Competitive Advantage?', *Academy of Management Review*, Vol. 11, pp. 656–665.

Barney, J.B. (1991) 'Firm Resources and Sustained Competitive Advantage', *Journal of Management*, Vol. 17, No. 1, pp. 99–120.

Barney, J.B., Wright, M., and Ketchen, D.J. (2001) 'The Resource-Based View of the Firm: Ten Years After 1991', *Journal of Management*, Vol.27, Issue 6, pp. 625–641.

Buzzell, R.D., and Gale, B.T (1987) *The PIMS Principles: Linking Strategy to Performance*, New York: Free Press.

Caves, R.E., and Porter, M.E. (1977) 'From Entry Barriers to Mobility Barriers: Conjectural Decisions and Contrived Deterrence to New Competition', *Quarterly Journal of Economics*, Vol. 91, pp. 241–262.

Christensen, C. (1997) *The Innovator's Dilemma*, New York: HarperBusiness.

Collis, D.J., and Montgomery, C.A. (1995) 'Competing on Resources: Strategy in the 1990s', *Harvard Business Review*, Vol. 73, No. 4, July–August, pp. 118–128.

David, P.A. (1985) 'Clio and the Economics of QWERTY', *American Economic Review Proceedings*, Vol. 75, pp. 332–337.

Day, G.S. (1990) *Market Driven Strategy, Processes for Creating Value*, New York: The Free Press.

Day, G.S. (1994) 'The Capabilities of Market-Driven Organizations', *Journal of Marketing*, Vol. 58, No. 4, October, pp. 37–52.

Deshpandé, R., and Webster Jr., F.E. (1989) 'Organizational Culture and Marketing: Defining the Research Agenda', *Journal of Marketing*, Vol. 53, pp. 3–15.

Dickson, P.R. (1992) 'Toward A General Theory of Competitive Rationality', *Journal of Marketing*, Vol. 56, pp. 69–83.

Dierickx, I., and Cool, K. (1989) 'Asset Stock Accumulation and Sustainability of Competitive Advantage', *Management Science*, Vol. 35, No. 12, December, pp. 1504–1511.

Dretske, F. (1981) *Knowledge and the Flow of Information*, Cambridge, MA: MIT Press.

Durand, T. (1996) *Revisiting Key Dimensions of Competence*, Paper presented to the SMS Conference, Phoenix.

Eisenstat, R., Foote, N., Galbraith, J., and Miller, D. (2001) 'Beyond the Business Unit', *McKinsey Quarterly*, No. 1, January, pp. 54–63.

Fuchs, P.H., Mifflin, K.E., Miller, D., and Whitney, J.O. (2000) 'Strategic Integration: Competing in the Age of Capabilities', *California Management Review*, Vol. 42, No. 3, Spring, pp. 118–147.

Gilbert, X., and Strebel, P. (1989) 'From Innovation to Outpacing', *Business Quarterly*, Summer, pp. 19–22.

Grant, R.M. (2002) *Contemporary Strategy Analysis: Concepts, Techniques, Applications*, Fourth Edition, Oxford: Blackwell Publishers.

Hambrick, D. (1987) 'Top Management Teams: Key to Strategic Success', *California Management Review*, Vol. 30, pp. 88–108.

Hamel, G., and Prahalad, C.K. (1989) 'Strategic Intent', *Harvard Business Review*, May–June, pp. 63–77.

Hamel, G., and Prahalad, C.K. (1993) 'Strategy as Stretch and Leverage', *Harvard Business Review*, Vol. 71, No. 2, March–April, pp. 75–84.

Hamel, G., and Prahalad, C.K. (1994) *Competing for the Future*, Boston, MA: Harvard Business School Press.

Hannan, M.T., and Freeman, J. (1977) 'The Population Ecology of Organizations', *American Journal of Sociology*, Vol. 82, No. 5, March, pp. 929–964.

Hofer, C., and Schendel, D. (1978) *Strategy Formulation: Analytical Concepts*, St. Paul, MN: West.

Hoskisson, R.E. (1999) 'Theory and Research in Strategic Management: Swings of a Pendulum', *Journal of Management*, May–June, pp. 1–50.

Itami, H. (1987) *Mobilizing Invisible Assets*, Cambridge, MA: Harvard University Press.

Jaworski, B., and Kohli, A.K. (1993) 'Market Orientation: Antecedents and Consequences', *Journal of Marketing*, Vol. 57, No. 3, July, pp. 53–70.

Kay, J. (1993) *Foundations of Corporate Success: How Business Strategies Add Value*, Oxford: Oxford University Press.

Kohli, A.K., and Jaworski, B. (1990) 'Market Orientation: The Construct, Research Propositions, and Managerial Implications', *Journal of Marketing*, Vol. 54, pp. 1–18.

Leonard-Barton, D. (1995) *Wellsprings of Knowledge*, Boston, MA: Harvard Business School Press.

Lieberman, M.B., and Montgomery, D.B. (1988) 'First Mover Adavantages', *Strategic Management Journal*, Vol. 9, No. 1, January–February, pp. 41–58.

Lieberman, M.B., and Montgomery, D.B. (1998) 'First-Mover (Dis)Advantages: Retrospective and Link with the Resource-Based View', *Strategic Management Journal*, Vol. 19, No. 12, December, pp. 1111–1126.

Lippman, S., and Rumelt, R. (1982) 'Uncertain Imitability: An Analysis of Interfirm Differences in Efficiency under Competition', *Bell Journal of Economics*, Vol. 13, pp. 418–438.

Lowendahl, B.R. (1997) *Strategic Management of Professional Business Service Firms*, Copenhagen: Copenhagen Business School Press.

Miller, D. (1990) *The Icarus Paradox*, New York: Harper Business.

Miller, D., Eisenstat, R., and Foote, N. (2002) 'Strategy from the Inside-Out: Building Capability-Creating Organizations', *California Management Review*, Vol. 44, No. 3, Spring, pp. 37–54.

Mintzberg, H., Ahlstrand, B., and Lampel, J. (1998) *Strategy Safari: A Guided Tour Through the Wilds of Strategic Management*, New York: The Free Press.

Narver, J.C., and Slater, S.F. (1990) 'The Effect of a Marketing Orientation on Business Profitability', *Journal of Marketing*, Vol. 54, October, pp. 20–35.

Nelson, R., and Winter, S. (1982) *An Evolutionary Theory of Economic Change*, Cambridge, MA: Harvard University Press.

Nonaka, I. (1991) 'The Knowledge-Creating Company', *Harvard Business Review*, Vol. 69, No. 6, November–December, pp. 96–104.

Nonaka, I., and Konno, N. (1998) 'The Concept of Ba: Building a Foundation for Knowledge Creation', *California Management Review*, Vol. 40, No. 3, Spring, pp. 40–54.

Norman, R., and Ramirez, R. (1993) 'From Value Chain to Value Constellation: Designing Interactive Strategy', *Harvard Business Review*, July–August, pp. 65–77.

Penrose, E.T. (1958) *The Theory of the Growth of the Firm*, New York: Wiley.

Peteraf, M.A. (1993) 'The Cornerstones of Competitive Advantage: A Resource-Based View', *Strategic Management Journal*, Vol. 14, pp. 179–191.

Polanyi, M. (1958) *Personal Knowledge*, Chicago: University of Chicago Press.

Porac, J.F., Thomas, H., and Baden-Fuller, C. (1989) 'Competitive Groups as Cognitive Communities: The Case of Scottish Knitwear Manufacturers', *Journal of Management Studies*, Vol. 26, pp. 397–416.

Porter, M.E. (1980) *Competitive Strategy: Techniques for Analyzing Industries and Competitors*, New York: Free Press.

Porter, M.E. (1985) *Competitive Advantage: Creating and Sustaining Superior Performance*, New York: Free Press.

Porter, M.E. (1991) 'Towards a Dynamic Theory of Strategy', *Strategic Management Journal*, Vol. 12, pp. 95–117.

Porter, M.E. (1996) 'What is Strategy?', *Harvard Business Review*, Vol. 74, No. 6, November–December, pp. 61–78.

Prahalad, C.K., and Hamel, G. (1990) 'The Core Competence of the Corporation', *Harvard Business Review*, Vol. 68, No. 3, May–June, pp. 79–91.

Rumelt, R.P. (1980) 'The Evaluation of Business Strategy', in: WF. Glueck (ed.), *Business Policy and Strategic Management*, Third Edition, New York: McGraw-Hill.

Rumelt, R.P. (1996) 'Inertia and Transformation', in: C.A. Montgomery (ed.), *Resource-based and Evolutionary Theories of the Firm: Towards a Synthesis*, Boston, MA: Kluwer Academic Publishers, pp. 101–132.

Sanchez, R., Heene, A., and Thomas, H. (eds) (1996) *Dynamics of Competence-Based Competition*, London: Elsevier.

Shay, J.P., and Rothaermel, R.T. (1999) 'Dynamic Competitive Strategy: Towards a Multi-perspective Conceptual Framework', *Long Range Planning*, Vol. 32, No. 6, pp. 559–572.

Slater, S.F., and Narver, J.C. (1998) 'Customer-led and Market-oriented: Let's Not Confuse the Two', *Strategic Management Journal*, Vol. 19, No. 10, pp. 1001–1006.

Stalk, G., Evans, P., and Schulman, L.E. (1992) 'Competing on Capabilities: The New Rules of Corporate Strategy', *Harvard Business Review*, Vol. 70, No. 2, March–April, pp. 57–69.

Teece, D.J., Pisano, G., and Shuen, A. (1997) 'Dynamic Capabilities and Strategic Management', *Strategic Management Journal*, Vol. 18, No. 7, August, pp. 509–533.

Treacy, M., and Wiersema, F. (1995) *The Discipline of Market Leaders*, Reading, MA: Addison-Wesley.

Webster, F.E., Jr. (1992) 'The Changing Role of Marketing in the Corporation', *Journal of Marketing*, Vol. 56, October, pp. 1–17.

Webster, F. (1994) *Market Driven Management: Using the New Marketing Concept to Create a Customer-oriented Company*, New York: Wiley.

Wernerfelt, B. (1984) 'A Resource-Based View of the Firm', *Strategic Management Journal*, Vol. 5, No. 2, April–June, pp. 171–180.

CORPORATE LEVEL STRATEGY

We are not all capable of everything.

Virgil (70–19 BC); Roman philosopher

INTRODUCTION

As firms seek growth, they have a number of directions in which they can expand. The most direct source of increased revenue is to enlarge their market share, selling more of their current product offerings in their current market segments. Besides this growth through focused market penetration, firms can also broaden their scope by extending their product range (product development) or move into neighbouring market segments and geographic areas (market development). All of these growth options can be pursued while staying within the 'boundaries' of a single business (see Figure 6.1). However, firms can broaden their scope even further, venturing into other lines of business, thus becoming multi-business corporations. Some multi-business firms are involved in only two or three businesses, but there are numerous corporations spanning 20, 30, or more, business areas.

This chapter deals with the specific strategic questions facing firms as they work on determining their multi-business scope. At this level, strategists must not only consider how to gain a competitive advantage in each line of business the firm has entered, but also which businesses they should be in at all. Corporate level strategy is about selecting an optimal set of businesses and determining how they should be integrated into the corporate whole. This issue of deciding on the best array of businesses and relating them to one another is referred to as the issue of 'corporate configuration'.

THE ISSUE OF CORPORATE CONFIGURATION

All multi-business firms have a particular configuration, either intentionally designed or as the result of emergent formation. Determining the configuration of a corporation can be disentangled into two main questions: (a) What businesses should the corporation be active in? and (b) How should this group of businesses be managed? This first question of deciding on the business areas that will be covered by the company is called the topic of 'corporate composition'. The second question, of deciding on the organizational system necessary to run the cluster of businesses, is labelled as the issue of 'corporate management'. In the following pages both questions will be explored in more detail.

Corporate composition

A multi-business firm is composed of two or more businesses. When a corporation enters yet another line of business, either by starting up new activities (internal growth) or by

FIGURE 6.1   Corporate growth directions

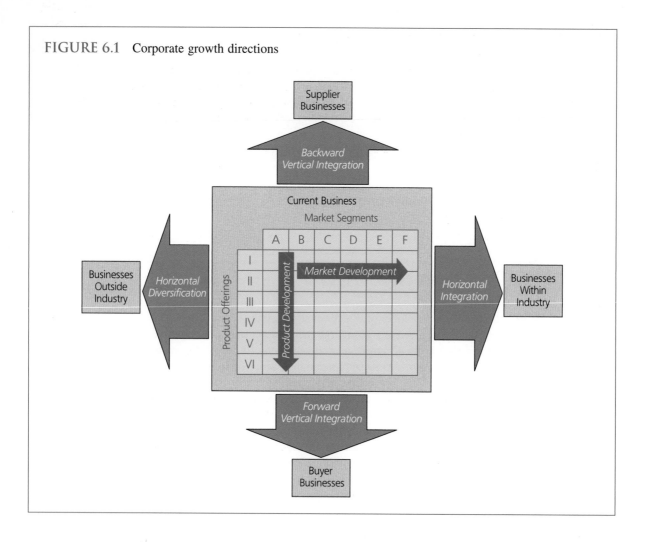

buying another firm (acquisition), this is called diversification. There are two general categories of diversification moves, vertical and horizontal. Vertical diversification, usually called vertical integration, is when a firm enters other businesses upstream or downstream within its own industry column (see Chapter 5) – it can strive for backward integration by getting involved in supplier businesses or it can initiate forward integration by entering the businesses of its buyers. The firm can also integrate related businesses at the same tier in the industry column – an example of such horizontal integration is when a newspaper and magazine publisher moves into educational publishing, as Thomson did. If a firm expands outside of its current industry, the term 'integration' is no longer employed, and the step is referred to as straightforward (horizontal) diversification (see Figure 6.1).

The issue of corporate composition deals with the question of where the firm wants to have which level of involvement. Corporate level strategists must decide where to allocate resources, build up activities and try to achieve market sales. The issue of corporate composition can be further subdivided into two parts:

■ Corporate scope. First, the composition of the corporation depends on the business areas selected. The more 'business components' chosen, the broader the scope of the corporation. Deciding on the corporate scope is not only a matter of choosing out of the diversification options depicted in Figure 6.1, but can also work in the opposite direction, as a firm can withdraw from a certain line of business, either by divesting, or closing down, its activities.

■ Corporate distribution. The composition of the corporation also depends on the relative size of the activities in each business area covered. The distribution within the corporation is determined by the relative weight of each business component. Some corporations are equally active in all of their selected businesses, while other firms are more asymmetrical, placing more emphasis on just a few of their business activities. Deciding on the corporate distribution is a matter of determining which lines of business will receive more attention than others. Corporate level strategists need to decide which activities will be the focus of further growth and increased weight within the firm, allocating resources accordingly. However, they must also keep in mind that a certain balance within the corporation might be beneficial.

A common way of depicting the corporate composition is to plot all of the businesses in a 'portfolio matrix'. The term 'portfolio' refers to the set of business activities carried out by the corporation. In a portfolio matrix each business activity is represented as a 'bubble' in a two-dimensional grid, with the size of the bubble reflecting the revenue generated with that activity. The number of bubbles indicates the corporate scope, while the corporate distribution can be seen in the relative size of the bubbles. The intention of a portfolio matrix is not merely to give an overview of the corporate scope and distribution, but also to provide insight into the growth and profitability potential of each of the corporation's business activities and to judge the balance between the various business activities.

There are different types of portfolio matrices in use, the most well known of which (see Figure 6.2) are the Boston Consulting Group (BCG) matrix (Hedley, 1977, Reading 6.1 in this book) and the General Electric (GE) business screen (Hofer and Schendel, 1978). All of these portfolio matrices are based on the same analytical format. Each business activity is mapped along two dimensions – one measuring the attractiveness of the business itself, the other measuring the strength of the corporation to compete in the business. In other words, one axis is a measure of external *opportunity*, while the other

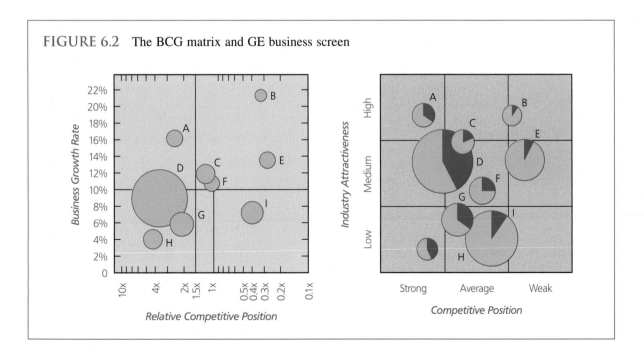

FIGURE 6.2   The BCG matrix and GE business screen

axis is a measure of internal *strength* in comparison to rival firms. The major difference between the portfolio matrices is which measures are used along the axes. The BCG matrix employs two simple variables: business growth to determine attractiveness and relative market share to reflect competitive strength. The GE business screen, on the other hand, uses composite measures: both industry attractiveness and competitive position are determined by analysing and weighing a number of different factors. Industry attractiveness will be impacted by such variables as sales growth, demand cyclicality, buyer power, supplier power, the threat of new entrants, the threat of substitutes and competitive intensity. Competitive position often reflects such factors as market share, technological know-how, brand image, customer loyalty, cost structure and distinctive competences. Another difference between the two matrices is that in the BCG portfolio grid the bubbles represent the company's sales in a line of business, while in the GE business screen the bubbles reflect the total business size, with the pie slices indicating the firm's share of the business.

Deciding which portfolio of businesses to pursue, both in terms of corporate scope and corporate distribution, will depend on how the corporate strategist intends to create value – or as Porter (1987) puts it, how the corporate strategist wants to make 'the corporate whole add up to more than the sum of its business unit parts'. After all, there must be some benefit to having the various business activities together in one corporation, otherwise each business activity could just as easily (and with less overhead) be carried out by autonomous firms. This added value of having two or more business activities under one corporate umbrella is called 'multi-business synergy' and it strongly determines the corporate composition the strategist will prefer. But before turning to the topic of synergy, the counterpart of corporate composition, namely corporate management, needs to be reviewed first.

Corporate management

It has become a widespread policy to organize multi-business firms into strategic business units (SBUs). This organizational structure is often referred to as the M-form (Williamson, 1975). Each strategic business unit is given the responsibility to serve the particular demands of one business area. The business units are labelled 'strategic', because each is driven by its own business level strategy.

This dominant approach to structuring multi-business firms does present managers with the issue of how to bring together the separate parts into a cohesive corporate whole. The corporation can be divided into business units with the intent of focusing each on separate business areas, but this *differentiation* must be offset by a certain degree of *integration* to be able to address common issues and realize synergies (Lawrence and Lorsch, 1967). The challenge for managers is to find the most effective and efficient forms of integration between two or more separate business units. Three key integration mechanisms can be distinguished:

- Centralization. The most straightforward form of integration is to bring resources and activities physically together into one organizational unit. In other words, where the 'division of labour' between the business units has not been applied, resources and activities will be kept together in one department. Such a centralized department can be situated at the corporate centre, but can also reside at one of the business units or at another location.

- Coordination. Even where resources, activities and product offerings have been split along business unit lines, integration can be achieved by ensuring that coordination is carried out between business units. Such orchestration of work across business unit boundaries should result in the ability to operate as if the various parts were actually one unit.

- Standardization. Integration can also be realized by standardizing resources, activities and/or product offering characteristics across business unit boundaries. By having similar resources (e.g. technologies, people), standardized activities (e.g. R&D, human resource management) and common product features (e.g. operating system, high-tech positioning) such advantages as economies of scale and rapid competence development can be achieved without the need to physically centralize or continuously coordinate.

These three integration mechanisms are the tools available to managers to achieve a certain level of harmonization between the various parts of the corporate whole. Yet often the question is, who should take the initiative to realize integration – where in the management system is the responsibility vested to ensure that centralization, coordination and standardization are considered and carried out? If all business unit managers are looking after their own backyard, who is taking care of the joint issues and cross-business synergies? Basically there are two organizational means available to secure the effective deployment of the integration mechanisms (see Figure 6.3):

- Control. A straightforward way to manage activities that cross the boundaries of an individual business unit is to give someone the formal power to enforce centralization, coordination and standardization. Such a division level or corporate level manager can exert control in many ways. It can be by direct supervision (telling business units what to do), but often it is indirect, by giving business units objectives that must be met and discussing initiatives. The formal authority to secure integration does not always have to be given to a manager at the corporate centre, but can be assigned to a manager within one of the business units as well. There are also various levels of authority that can be defined, ranging from full final decision-making power to 'coordinator' or 'liaison officer', who have only limited formal means at their disposal.

- Cooperation. Centralization, coordination and standardization between business units can also be achieved without the use of hierarchical authority. Business units might be willing to cooperate because it is in their interest to do so, or because they recognize the overall corporate interests. If business units believe in the importance of certain joint activities, this can be a powerful impetus to collaborate. Corporate strategists interested in such integration by mutual adjustment will focus on creating the organizational circumstances under which such self-organization can take place (See Chapter 9 for a further discussion). For instance, they might strengthen formal and informal ties between the business units in order to enhance mutual understanding and

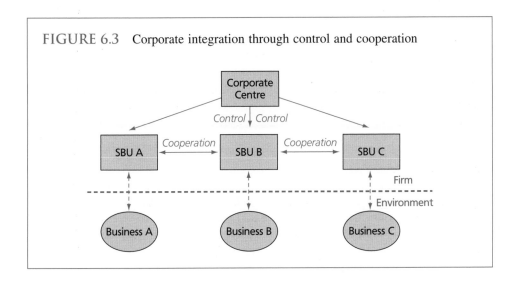

FIGURE 6.3   Corporate integration through control and cooperation

encourage the exchange of ideas and joint initiatives. They may also support cross-business career paths and try to instil a corporation-wide culture, to facilitate the communication between business units (Eisenhardt and Galunic, 2000).

It is the task of the corporate level strategist to determine the mix of control and cooperation needed to manage the corporation. In their seminal research, Goold and Campbell (1987) distinguish three general corporate control styles, each emphasizing different levels of centralization, coordination and standardization:

- Financial control style. In the financial control style the strategic business units are highly autonomous from the corporate centre. Few activities are centralized or standardized (except for the financial reporting system) and the corporate centre does not explicitly attempt to coordinate activities across business unit boundaries. Control is exerted by negotiating, setting and monitoring financial objectives.

- Strategic control style. In the strategic control style the strategic business units have a closer relationship with the corporate centre. A number of central services exist, some systems and activities are standardized and the corporate centre explicitly tries to co-ordinate activities that reach beyond the boundaries of only one business unit. Control is exerted by negotiating, setting and monitoring strategic objectives.

- Strategic planning style. In the strategic planning style the strategic business units have relatively little autonomy from the corporate centre. Many key activities are centralized or standardized, and the corporate centre is also heavily involved in securing cross-business coordination. Control is exerted by means of direct supervision.

Which corporate management style is adopted depends strongly on what the corporate strategist wishes to achieve. The preferred corporate management style will be determined by the type of multi-business synergies that the corporate strategist envisages, but also on the level of autonomy that the business units require. On the one hand, strategists will want to encourage integration to reap the benefits of having various business units together under one corporate roof and will therefore have a strong motivation to exert strong corporate centre control and stimulate inter-business cooperation. On the other hand, strategists will be wary of heavy-handed head office intervention, blunt centralization, rigid standardization, paralysing coordination meetings and excessive overhead. Recognizing that the business units need to be highly responsive to the specific demands of their own business area, corporate strategists will also be inclined to give business units the freedom to manoeuvre and to emphasize their own entrepreneurship. Yet, these two demands on the corporate level strategy – *multi-business synergy* and *business responsiveness* – are to a certain extent at odds with one another. How corporate strategists deal with the tension created by these conflicting demands will be examined more closely in the following section.

THE PARADOX OF RESPONSIVENESS AND SYNERGY

Nihil est ab omni parte beatum (nothing is an unmixed blessing).
Horace (65–8 BC); Roman poet

When Cor Boonstra took over as CEO of Philips Electronics in 1996, after a long career at the fast-moving consumer goods company Sara Lee, one of his first remarks to the business press was that Philips reminded him of 'a plate of spaghetti' – the company's more than 60 business units were intertwined in many different ways, sharing technologies, facilities, sales forces and customers, leading to excessive complexity, abundant bureaucracy, turf wars and a lack of accountability. To Boonstra the pursuit of multi-business synergy had spiralled into an overkill of centralization, coordination and standardization, requiring direct rectification. Thus Boonstra set out to restructure Philips into, in his own words, 'a plate of asparagus', with business units neatly lined up, one next to the other. Over a period of five years he disposed of numerous business units and made sure that the others were independent enough 'to hold up their own pants'. The result was a loss of some valuable synergies, but a significant increase in the business units' responsiveness to the demands in their own business. Then, in 2001, Boonstra handed over the reigns to a Philips insider, Gerard Kleisterlee, who during one of his first media encounters as new CEO stated that the business units within Philips had become too insular and narrowly focused, thereby missing opportunities to capture important synergies. Therefore, he indicated that it would be his priority to get Philips to work more like a team.

What this example of Philips illustrates is that corporate level strategists constantly struggle with the balance between realizing synergies and defending business unit responsiveness. To achieve synergies, a firm must to some extent integrate the activities carried out in its various business units. The autonomy of the business units must be partially limited, in the interest of concerted action. However, integration comes with a price tag. An extra level of management is often required, more meetings, extra complexity, potential conflicts of interest, additional bureaucracy–harmonization of operations costs money and diminishes a business unit's ability to precisely tailor its strategy to its specific business environment. Hence, for the corporate strategist the challenge is to realize more *value creation* through multi-business synergies than *value destruction* through the loss of business responsiveness (e.g. Campbell, Goold and Alexander, 1995; Prahalad and Doz, 1987).

This tension arising from the partially conflicting demands of business responsiveness and multi-business synergy is called the paradox of responsiveness and synergy. In the following sub-sections both sides of the paradox will be examined in more detail.

The demand for multi-business synergy

Diversification into new business areas can only be economically justified if it leads to value creation. According to Porter (1987) entering into another business (by acquisition or internal growth) can only result in increased shareholder value if three essential tests are passed:

- The attractiveness test. The business 'must be structurally attractive, or capable of being made attractive'. In other words, firms should only enter businesses where there is a possibility to build up a profitable competitive position (see Chapter 5). Each new business area must be judged in terms of its competitive forces and the opportunities available to the firm to sustain a competitive business model.

- The cost-of-entry test. 'The cost of entry must not capitalize all the future profits.' In other words, firms should only enter new businesses if it is possible to recoup the investments made. This is important for internally generated new business ventures, but even more so for external acquisitions. Many researchers argue that, on average, firms significantly overpay for acquisitions, making it next to impossible to compensate for the value given away during the purchase (e.g. Sirower, 1997).

- The better-off test. 'Either the new unit must gain competitive advantage from its link with the corporation or vice versa.' In other words, firms should only enter new businesses if it is possible to create significant synergies. If not, then the new unit would be better off as an independent firm or with a different parent company, and should be cut loose from the corporation.

It is this last test that reveals one of the key demands of corporate level strategy. Multi-business level firms need to be more than the sum of their parts. They need to create more added value than the extra costs of managing a more complex organization. They need to identify opportunities for synergy between business areas and manage the organization in such a way that the synergies can be realized.

But what are the sources of synergy? For quite some time, strategists have known that potential for synergy has something to do with 'relatedness' (Rumelt, 1974). Diversification moves that were unrelated (or 'conglomerate'), for example a food company's entrance into the bicycle rental business, were deemed to be less profitable, in general, than moves that were related (or 'concentric'), such as a car-maker's diversification into the car rental business (e.g. Chatterjee, 1986; Rumelt, 1982). However, the problem has been to determine the nature of 'relatedness'. Superficial signs of relatedness do not indicate that there is potential for synergy. Drilling for oil and mining might seem highly related (both are 'extraction businesses'), but Shell found out the hard way that they were not related, selling the acquired mining company Billiton to Gencor after they were unable to create synergy (see the Shell case in Section VI). Chemicals and pharmaceuticals seem like similar businesses (especially if pharmaceuticals are labelled 'specialty chemicals'), but ICI decided to split itself in two (into ICI and Zeneca), because it could not achieve sufficient synergy between these two business areas.

Strategy researchers have therefore attempted to pin down the exact nature of relatedness (e.g. Prahalad and Bettis, 1986; Ramanujam and Varadarajan, 1989). Following the business model framework outlined in Chapter 5, the areas of relatedness that have the potential for creating synergy can be organized into three categories (see Figure 6.4): resource relatedness, product offering relatedness and activity relatedness.

FIGURE 6.4   Forms of multi-business synergy

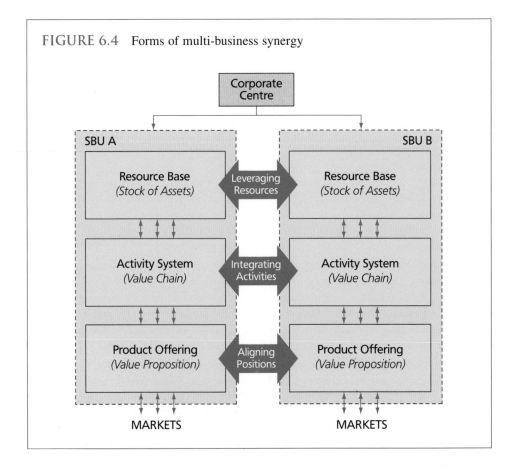

Synergy by leveraging resources. The first area of relatedness is at the level of the businesses' resource bases. Two or more businesses are related if their resources can be productively shared between them. In principle, all types of resources can be shared, both the tangible and the intangible, although in practice some resources are easier to share than others – for example, it is easier to transfer money than knowledge. Such 'resource leveraging' (Hamel and Prahalad, 1993) can be achieved by physically reallocating resources from one business area to another, or by replicating them so they can be used in a variety of businesses simultaneously:

- Achieving resource reallocation. Instead of leaving firm resources in the business unit where they happen to be located, a corporation can create synergy by transferring resources to other business units, where better use can be made of them (Helfat and Eisenhardt, 2004). For instance, money and personnel are often shifted between business units, depending on where they are needed and the potential return is highest.

- Achieving resource replication. While physical resources can only be used in one place at a time, intangible resources can often be copied from one business unit to another, so that the same resource can be used many times over. This happens, for example, when knowledge and capabilities are copied and reused in other business units.

Synergy by aligning positions. A second area of relatedness is at the level of product offerings. Two or more businesses are related if they can help each other by aligning their positioning in the market. Such coordination between product–market combinations can both improve the businesses' bargaining position vis-à-vis buyers, as well as improve the businesses' competitive position vis-à-vis rival firms:

- Improving bargaining position. Business units can improve their bargaining power vis-à-vis buyers by offering a broad package of related products or services to specific customer groups. Especially when the products being offered are complementary, share a common brand and have a comparable reputation, will they support each other in the market.

- Improving competitive position. Coordination of product offerings within one firm can also prevent a number of business units from fighting fiercely amongst one another, which might have happened if all units were independent companies. Moreover, it is even possible for multiple business units to support each other in attacking a third party, for example by setting a common standard or aggressively pricing selected products. Similarly, business units can team up to protect each other from attack and create barriers to entry into the industry/market (Baum and Greve, 2001; Jayachandran, Gimeno and Varadarajan, 1999).

Synergy by integrating activities. The third area of relatedness is at the level of activity systems. Two or more businesses are related if an integration of their value chains is more efficient and/or more effective than if they were totally separated. Such integration of value-creation activities can focus on the sharing of similar activities or the linking up of sequential activities:

- Sharing value-adding activities. Business units often combine some of their value-adding activities, such as logistics, production or marketing, if this leads to significant scale advantages or quality improvements. It is also common to see that the corporate centre organizes certain support activities centrally. These 'shared services' often include functions such as human resource management, procurement, quality control, legal affairs, research and development, finance and corporate communication.

- Linking value-adding activities. Business units that are not horizontally but vertically related (see Figure 6.1) can have an internal customer–supplier relationship. Such vertical integration of sequential value-adding activities in one firm can be more efficient than operating independently where supplies need to be highly tailored to a specific type of customer demand.

Much attention in the literature has been paid to this issue of vertical integration of activities. It is also referred to as 'internalization' because firms decide to perform activities inside the firm, instead of dealing with outside suppliers and buyers. In general, companies will strive to integrate upstream or downstream activities where one or more of the following conditions are deemed important (e.g. Harrigan 1985; Mahoney, 1992):

- Operational coordination. It can be necessary for various parts of the value system to be tightly coordinated or even physically integrated, to ensure that the right components, meeting the right specifications, are available in the right quantities, at the right moment, so that high quality, low cost or timely delivery can be achieved. To realize this level of coordination it can be necessary to gain control over a number of key activities in the value system, instead of trying to get suppliers and buyers to cooperate.

- Avoidance of transaction costs. Reaching a deal with a supplier or buyer and transferring the goods or services to the required location may be accompanied by significant direct costs. These contracting costs can include the expenses of negotiations, drawing up a contract, financial transfers, packaging, distribution and insurance. Add to these the search costs, required to locate and analyse potential new suppliers or buyers, as well as the policing costs, which are incurred to check whether the contract is being met according to expectations and to take actions against those parties not living up to their contractual responsibilities. If a firm vertically integrates, many of these costs can be avoided, leading to potential savings (Williamson, 1975).

- Increased bargaining power. If a firm is facing a supplier or buyer with a disproportionately high level of bargaining power (for instance, a monopolist), vertical integration can be used to weaken or neutralize such a party. By fully or partially performing the activities in-house, the firm can lessen its dependence on a strong buyer or supplier. The firm can also strive to acquire the other party, to avoid the bargaining situation altogether.

- Learning curve advantages. Where vertically linked business units work closely together, exchanging knowledge and personnel, they might also learn more quickly and more efficiently than if the business units were independent. Especially where they initiate joint R&D projects and collaborate on business process improvement efforts then significant learning curve advantages can be realized.

- Implementing system-wide changes. Besides continual operational coordination and ongoing learning, there may be a need to coordinate strategic changes throughout the value system. Switching over to new technologies, new production methods and new standards can sometimes only be implemented if there is commitment and a concerted effort in various parts of the value system. Sometimes even neighbouring value systems need to be involved in the changes. Vertical integration and horizontal diversification can give a firm the formal control needed to push through such changes.

Corporate level strategy is about determining the corporate configuration that offers the best opportunities for synergy, and implementing a corporate management system capable of realizing the intended synergies. However, what types of synergies can realistically be achieved, without paying a heavier penalty in terms of integration costs? Recognizing the possible benefits of bringing together various businesses under one corporate umbrella is one thing, but developing a corporate management system that does not cost more than it yields is another. Therefore, corporate strategists need to carefully consider the potential downside of resource leveraging, activity integration and position alignment – the loss of business responsiveness.

The demand for business responsiveness

Responsiveness is defined as the ability to respond to the competitive demands of a specific business area in a timely and adequate manner. A business unit is responsive if it has the capability to tightly match its strategic behaviour to the competitive dynamics in its business. If a business unit does not focus its strategy on the conditions in its direct environment and does not organize its value-adding activities and management systems to fit with the business characteristics, it will soon be at a competitive disadvantage compared to more responsive rivals. Business responsiveness is therefore a key demand for successful corporate level strategy.

Yet, in multi-business firms the responsiveness of the business units is constantly under pressure. Various scope disadvantages limit the ability of the corporation to ensure business responsiveness. The major problems encountered by multi-business firms are the following:

- High governance costs. Coordinating activities within a firm requires managers. Layers of management, and the bureaucratic processes that might entail, can lead to escalating costs.

- Slower decision-making. Business units must usually deal with more layers of management, more meetings for coordination purposes, more participants in meetings, more conflicts of interest and more political infighting. This not only increases governance costs, but also slows down decision-making and action.

- Strategy incongruence. The resource leveraging, activity integration and position alignment envisioned in the corporate strategy can be more suited to the conditions in some businesses than to others. Consequently, some business units might need to compromise, adapting their business strategy to fit with the corporate strategy. However, such internal adaptation might lead to a misfit with the business demands.

- Dysfunctional control. The corporate centre might not have the specific business know-how needed to judge business unit strategies, activities and results. However, the corporate centre might feel the need to exert some control over business units, potentially steering them in an inappropriate direction.

- Dulled incentives. Limited autonomy combined with the aforementioned problems can have a significant negative impact on the motivation to perform optimally. This dulled incentive to be entrepreneurial and to excel can be compounded by poorly delineated responsibilities, a lack of clear accountability and the existence of 'captive' internal customers. Together these factors limit the business units' drive to be responsive.

These threats make clear that multi-business firms must determine their composition and management systems in a way that enables business units to be responsive. Yet, simultaneously, corporate strategists need to strive towards the identification and realization of synergies. The question is how these two conflicting demands can be reconciled – how can corporate level strategists deal with the paradox of responsiveness and synergy?

EXHIBIT 6.1 SHORT CASE

DANONE: DIGESTIVE PROBLEMS?

In 1919, Isaac Carusso, a Spanish physician of Greek origin, came up with a unique treatment for patients with digestive problems. Inspired by groundbreaking medical research at the Institut Pasteur in Paris, Carusso developed a product that he distributed through pharmacies and drug stores, and which soon became a big success – yoghurt.

The company he founded was named after his son Daniel, who in true Catalan tradition was usually called 'Little Daniel' – Danone. After a study as bacteriologist, Daniel Carusso took over the company in 1929, later merging it with the French maker of dairy products, Gervais. By the time of Daniel's death in 2009, at the age of 103, Danone had grown to become a Fortune 500 company and one of the most successful health food firms in the world. As honorary chairman until the very end, Daniel Carusso had seen Danone expand to 120 countries around the globe, employing around 80 000 people and achieving sales of €15.2 billion. Following its mission to bring health through tasty, nutritious and affordable food and beverage products to as many people as possible, Danone had become the largest maker of fresh dairy products in the world. It had also built up strong positions in bottled water (no. 2 worldwide), baby food (also no. 2 worldwide) and medical nutrition (no. 3 worldwide).

Yet, the growth of the Groupe Danone has not been a simple story of straightforward expansion. It could be said that the true founding father of the current group is not Daniel Carusso, but Antoine Riboud, who engineered the merger between his firm BSN and Gervais Danone in 1973, to form BSN-Gervais-Danone. Starting in 1966, Riboud had aggressively grown the family business into a large glass and packaging corporation, which had subsequently begun to forward integrate, buying such customers as beer brewer Kronenbourg and mineral water company Evian. Not long after the merger with Gervais Danone, the new company sold its glass works, to focus fully on food and food packaging. In 1987 Riboud bought the French manufacturer of LU cookies, Général Biscuit, followed by the European biscuit operations of Nabisco in 1989. It was only in 1994 that Riboud decided to change the company name from BSN-Gervais-Danone into Groupe Danone.

After taking over from his father as chairman and CEO in 1996, Franck Riboud continued to divest businesses outside of Danone's three core product groups, dairy, beverages and cereals. The food packaging businesses were sold between 1999 and 2003, its European and Chinese beer activities in 2000 and 2002 respectively, its Italian cheese and meats activities in 2002, its British and Irish biscuit operations in 2004 and its sauces in 2005 and 2006.

But Franck Riboud's biggest move came in 2007, when within the space of one busy week, the company first announced the intention to sell its entire Biscuits and Cereals Division (16% of the annual sales in 2006) to Kraft Foods for €5.3 billion, followed by an all-cash offer of approximately €12.3 billion for Royal Numico, a global leader in baby food and medical nutrition (18% of the merged company sales).

In a press release on 9th July 2007, Riboud proudly proclaimed that with the acquisition of Numico, Groupe Danone had become 'a unique food company – the one with the clearest and most powerful health positioning in the world.' He explained that by boldly divesting slow growing regular food products and focusing on faster growing health foods, Danone had positioned itself to become an outperformer in the food business. According to Riboud, 'our business model is unashamedly designed for growth and it enjoys our full, unqualified attention.' He assured employees of Numico that while their CEO and CFO would not be staying after the acquisition, the headquarters of the new baby food and medical nutrition division would remain in Amsterdam and no job losses were foreseen. Investors were told that the acquisition would result in €45–60 million worth of annual cost savings and eventually also produce approximately €120 million worth of revenue synergies.

While some commentators were impressed by Danone's transformation into a focused healthy food corporation, others expressed doubts about the price tag. At €55 per share, Danone was paying a premium of 44% over the average share price in the preceding months. The total bill of €12.3 billion was almost four times the estimated sales of Numico over 2007 and 23 times the projected operating profit. To justify a price in this range, Danone would have to create an enormous amount of added value from this acquisition, it was argued. More critical commentators suggested that the acquisition was in fact defensive, as the slimmed down and weakly leveraged Danone had become a likely acquisition target itself. In 2005 it had already been rumoured that PepsiCo was contemplating a bid, prompting then prime minister of France, Dominique de Villepin, to call Danone one of the country's national 'jewels' that needed to be defended from foreign attack.

However, Riboud brushed these arguments aside. The price 'reflects the growth potential and the results the firm has achieved during the past few years'. He was confident that Danone would be able to integrate Numico successfully into the corporation and create significant added value in the process. One of the key areas where he saw synergy was in research and development, in which both companies have a strong tradition. 'Numico is strong in prebiotics, Danone in probiotics. That is why here one plus one is more than two', Riboud explained. The prebiotics that Numico's researchers were specialized in consist of non-digestible food ingredients that stimulate the growth or activity of bacteria in the digestive system. The probiotics that Danone's researchers have focused on are bacteria that are purposely added to food to improve the health of the recipient. Danone keeps the largest lactic bacteria bank in the world with 3600 strands. What both companies have in common is their scientific mindset and standards, which put them on par with the pharmaceutical industry. Together they would have the largest R&D network of any major food company, comprising 900 professionals, as well as sponsoring an international not-for–profit laboratory network called Danone Institutes.

Besides the complementarity in R&D, Danone also saw synergy in leveraging its marketing approach. It had built up considerable expertise in launching blockbuster platforms, with sales in excess of €1 billion. If this knowhow could be applied to Numico's product range significant growth could be realized.

The question was how to attain these synergies without demotivating the Numico people in the process. Having paid so much to acquire the prized asset, it would be foolhardy to march in and impose the Danone way of doing things, scaring away top talent in the process. Yet leaving the baby food and medical nutrition activities as stand-alone divisions would not create the additional value required to justify the premium price.

There was also the issue of the overlapping country-based sales organizations. How would Numico's more than three-dozen national sales units fit into the broader Danone organizational structure? Should local sales subsidiaries be forced to merge in countries where both Danone and Numico units existed, or left to operate in parallel? And what to do in countries with only one sales subsidiary? Get them to sell the entire range of products? Danone had a fairly decentralized, almost federative set-up, with fiercely independent country managers and product managers. All were given significant leeway on how to run their business – as long as they hit their financial targets. Product managers decided which new offerings to develop in negotiation with the country managers who indicated which products they required. To suddenly impose on country managers that they must also sell baby food and medical nutrition would be completely against previous corporate practice.

Also on the mind of Numico managers was whether there was going to be enough financial resources to go around. With a portfolio made up of only 'stars' and a corporate balance sheet that did not allow for very much additional borrowing, there was a concern that internal competition for resources could heat up over time. In Danone's fresh dairy products division, which accounts for half the company, it was already proving difficult to prioritize the various growth opportunities. Besides the existing blockbuster platforms Activia, Actimel, Taillefine/Vitalinea, and Danonino, more were under development, requiring major investments. Internationalization was also demanding increased attention. In 2002 Danone had started a 'new frontiers' programme, focused on markets identified as having the highest growth potential, like China, Indonesia, Russia, Mexico and the US. By 2007, these markets accounted for 25% of Danone sales, while growing at an annual rate of 20%, which involved major commitments in terms of money and people. Yet at the same time, many managers were pointing to the untapped opportunities in Latin America, North Africa and the Middle East.

Danone also had a sea of opportunities in the water business, where besides the globally leading spring water brand Evian, it owns Badoit, Volvic, Bonafont and Aqua, the market leader in Indonesia and the world's largest bottled water brand. In its closely contested battle with Nestlé for the global top position (Danone leading by volume, Nestlé by value), Danone had plenty of room to grow by adding more value to its basic water product.

However, the Numico product lines also needed capital to grow further. In 2006 its baby food business had almost €1.9 billion in sales and a health operating profit of €340 million, but was also growing at an annual rate of 12.2%. It was either market leader or in second place in 26 out of 33 countries in which it operated, including being biggest in fast-growing China. The clinical nutrition business had sales of €743 million sales, with an operating profit of €192 million, but was also growing at a rate of 10.9% per year. It was first or second placed in 25 out of the 29 markets in which it was present. Danone could not afford to under-fund this growth, or maybe worse, lose key people in a messy integration process. Riboud had to keep the growth engine running, while at the same time realizing the synergy potential he had identified.

As Riboud knew all too well, taking big bites is easy – it is the subsequent digestion that is usually the problem. Yet this was a challenge in which he was willing to sink his teeth.

Co-author: Peer Ederer

Sources: www.danone.com; Groupe Danone Annual Report 2008, www.evmi.nl/danone; *The New York Times*, 9 July 2007; European Food and Agribusiness Seminar 2009, Wageningen University.

PERSPECTIVES ON CORPORATE LEVEL STRATEGY

We must indeed all hang together, or, most assuredly, we shall all hang separately.

Benjamin Franklin (1706–1790); American politician, inventor and scientist

Corporations need to capture multi-business synergies and they need to ensure each business unit's responsiveness to its competitive environment. In other words, corporations need to be integrated and differentiated at the same time – emphasizing the *whole* and respecting the *part*. Striving towards synergy is a centripetal force, pulling the firm together into an integrated whole, while being responsive to business demands is a centrifugal force, pulling the firm apart into autonomous market-focused units (Ghoshal and Mintzberg, 1994). The main question dividing strategists is whether a corporation should primarily be a collection of parts or an integrated whole. Should corporations be loose federations of business units or tightly knit teams? Should corporations be business groups made up of distinctive parts, where only modest synergies can be realized and business units should be accorded a large measure of leeway to be responsive to their specific market conditions? Or should corporations actually be unitary organizations, with the parts serving the whole, allowing for significant synergies to be achieved, with the challenge of being responsive enough to varied business demands.

As before, the strategic management literature comes with strongly different views on how strategists should proceed. Here the two diametrically opposed positions will be identified and discussed to show the richness of differing opinions. On the one side of the spectrum, there are those strategists who believe that multi-business firms should be viewed as portfolios of autonomous business units in which the corporation has a financial stake. They argue that business responsiveness is crucial and that only a limited set of financial synergies should be pursued. This point of view is referred to as the 'portfolio organization perspective'. At the other end of the spectrum, there are strategists who believe that corporations should be tightly integrated, with a strong central core of shared resources, activities and/or product offerings keeping the firm together. They argue that corporations built up around these strong synergy opportunities can create significantly more value than is lost through limitations to responsiveness. This point of view is referred to as the 'integrated organization perspective'.

The portfolio organization perspective

In the portfolio organization perspective, responsiveness is strongly emphasized over synergy. Managers taking this perspective usually argue that each business

has its own unique characteristics and demands. Firms operating in different businesses must therefore develop a specific strategy for each business and assign the responsibility for each business strategy to a separate strategic business unit. In this manner, the (strategic) business units can be highly responsive to the competitive dynamics in the business, while being a clear unit of accountability towards the corporate centre. High responsiveness, however, requires freedom from corporate centre interference and freedom from cross-business coordination. Hence, a high level of business unit autonomy is required, with the corporate centre's influence limited to arm's length financial control.

In the portfolio organization perspective, the main reason for a number of highly autonomous business units to be in one firm is to leverage financial resources. The only synergies emphasized are financial synergies (e.g. Lubatkin and Chatterjee, 1994; Trautwein, 1990). Actually, the term 'portfolio' entered the business vocabulary via the financial sector, where it refers to an investor's collection of shareholdings in different companies, purchased to spread investment risks. Transferred to corporate strategy, the portfolio organization perspective views the corporate centre as an active investor with financial stakes in a number of stand-alone business units. The role of the centre is one of selecting a promising portfolio of businesses, keeping tight financial control, and allocating available capital – redirecting flows of cash from business units where prospects are dim ('cash cows' or 'dogs'), to other business units where higher returns can be expected ('stars' or 'question marks'). The strategic objective of each business unit is, therefore, also financial in orientation – grow, hold, milk or divest, depending on the business unit's position on the portfolio grid (e.g. Henderson, 1979; Hedley, 1977). A good corporate strategy strives for a balanced portfolio of mature cash producers and high potential ROI cash users, at an acceptable level of overall risk.

The financial synergies can be gained in a number of different ways (e.g. Chatterjee, 1986; Weston, Chung and Hoag, 1990). First, by having various businesses within one firm, the corporate centre can economize on external financing. By internally shifting funds from one business unit to another the corporation can avoid the transaction costs and taxation associated with external capital markets. Secondly, the corporation can limit dependence on the whims of external capital providers, who might be less inclined to finance some ventures (e.g. new businesses or high risk turnarounds) at acceptable levels of capital cost. Thirdly, where the corporation does want to secure external financing, the firm's larger size, debt capacity and creditworthiness can improve its bargaining position in the financial markets. Finally, by having revenue and earning streams from two or more different businesses, the corporation can reduce its exposure to the risk of a single business. This risk balancing, or co-insurance, effect is largest where the portfolio is made up of counter-cyclical businesses. In turn, the stability and predictability of revenue and earning flows enable the corporation to plan and function more effectively and efficiently (e.g. Amit and Livnat, 1988; Seth, 1990).

The business units do not necessarily need to be 'related' in any other way than financial. In practice, the business units can be related, that is, there can be resource leveraging, activity integration and position alignment opportunities that are seized. The portfolio organization perspective does not reject the pursuit of other forms of synergy, but neither does it accommodate such efforts (Haspeslagh, 1982). Responsiveness is not compromised to achieve these synergy opportunities.

New businesses can be entered by means of internal growth, but the portfolio approach to corporate strategy is particularly well suited to diversification through acquisition. In a multi-business firm run on portfolio principles, acquired companies are simple to integrate into the corporation, because they can be largely left as stand-alone units and only need to be linked to corporate financial reporting and control systems. Proponents of the portfolio organization perspective argue that such 'non-synergistic' acquisitions can be highly profitable (Kaplan, 1989; Long and Ravenscraft, 1993). Excess cash can be routed to more attractive investment opportunities than the corporation has internally. Moreover, the acquiring corporation can shake up the management of the acquired company and can function as a strategic sounding board for the new people. In this way, the acquirer can release the untapped value potential of underperforming stand-alone businesses (Anslinger and Copeland, 1996).

The portfolio organization perspective is particularly well known for the analytical techniques that have been developed to support it. As was mentioned before, a large number of portfolio grids are in widespread use as graphical tools for visualizing corporate composition and for determining the position of each of the business units. These portfolio analysis tools have proven to be popular and much used (Goold and Lansdell, 1997), even among strategists who are not proponents of the portfolio organization perspective.

In conclusion, the basic assumption of the portfolio organization perspective is that business units must be responsible for their own competitive strategy. Business units are the main locus of strategic attention and the corporate centre should understand their limited ability to get involved and stimulate synergy. Corporate centres should be modest in ambition and size, taking heed of the words of the famous 'business philosopher' Groucho Marx that 'the most difficult thing about business is minding your own'.

EXHIBIT 6.2   THE PORTFOLIO ORGANIZATION PERSPECTIVE

VIRGIN: PLENTY OF CHILDREN

'I thought that Virgin was the most stupid name ever for an airline, and I told him that his plan [for business class only] was not a good idea and explained why. But with Richard, you never let the facts get in the way of a good idea!' This is how David Tait recalled his initial discussions with Richard Branson, before the two of them went on to launch the successful Virgin Atlantic Airways company in 1984. But Tait was not the first or the last one to be stunned by Branson's brash rule breaking style and the company's unconventional name. Since starting his first firm in 1970 and provocatively calling it Virgin Records, Branson has continued to shock and amaze, gaining millions of admirers, while being mocked and ridiculed by many others. Yet, whether loved or derided, famous he is. And the Virgin brand, which the registration authorities almost rejected because it was deemed to be in bad taste, is highly recognized around the world and is closely associated with words such as fun, innovation and success.

And successful Virgin can definitely be called. Since its humble beginnings as a record label, signing young unknowns such as Mike Oldfield, the Sex Pistols, Simple Minds and Culture Club in the 1970s and 1980s, the Virgin Group has grown into a family of 200 companies worldwide, employing approximately 50 000 people in 29 countries. As a privately held company, its financial results are not precisely known, but revenues in 2008 were reported to be in excess of £ 11 billion. The company is grouped into six sectors: travel, lifestyle, media & mobile, money, music and green. Travel includes airlines like Virgin Atlantic, Virgin Blue, Virgin America and V Australia, but also tour operator Virgin Holidays, Virgin Trains, Virgin Limobike, Virgin Limousines and space flight company Virgin Galactic. Lifestyle runs from Virgin Active health clubs to Virgin Books, Virgin Games, Virgin Wines, Virgin Balloon Flights and Virgin Drinks. Media & Mobile spans a number of Virgin Mobile companies in various countries as well as Virgin Media, the channel Virgin 1 and Virgin Connect. Money includes operations in the UK, the US, Australia and South Africa, while music includes Virgin Megastores, Virgin Radio International and Virgin Festivals. And the new green sector includes Virgin Green Fund, which focuses on investing in environment-friendly technologies.

Characteristically, Branson sold his first company, Virgin Records, in 1992 to fund the expansion of Virgin Atlantic and to get into more lines of business where he saw the opportunity to be the consumer champion by taking on powerful, but plodding incumbents. 'We look for opportunities where we can offer something better, fresher, and more valuable, and we seize them', says Branson of his approach. 'We often move into areas where the customer has traditionally received a poor deal, and where the competition is complacent. And with our growing e-commerce activities, we also look to deliver "old" products in new ways. We are proactive and quick to act, often leaving bigger and more cumbersome organizations in our wake … Typically, we review the industry and put ourselves in the customer's shoes to see what could make it better.'

Virgin labels itself a 'branded venture capital organization', explaining on its website that 'contrary to what some people may think, our constantly expanding and eclectic empire is neither random nor reckless. Each successive venture demonstrates our devotion to picking the right market and the right opportunity.' Once an opportunity has been identified, knowledgeable people from around the Virgin Group are brought in to start the venture and where competencies are lacking, partnerships are created with other firms. Great strengths that Virgin can bring to new ventures are the Virgin brand name, Richard Branson's personal reputation, Virgin's network of friends, contacts and partners, as well as the Virgin management style.

This Virgin management style can be summarized as entrepreneurial. Despite Branson's quip that 'I believe in benevolent dictatorship provided I am the dictator', in practice he delegates decision-making to the team running each company, with a minimum of central guidance. Virgin has a tiny central office, called Virgin Management Ltd (VML), which provides advisory and managerial support to all of the Virgin companies and the six sector teams. As Virgin itself explains it: 'VML's fastidious number-crunchers get to manage Virgin's financial assets in the group, our cheeky marketeers and spin doctors get to protect and maximize the value of the Virgin brand and our touchy-feely people teams ensure Virgin is an employer of choice.' There are also regional support offices in London, New York and Sydney, but these are

small. 'Our companies are part of a family rather than a hierarchy', according to Virgin. 'They are empowered to run their own affairs, yet the companies help one another, and solutions to problems often come from within the Group somewhere. In a sense we are a commonwealth, with shared ideas, values, interests and goals.'

Describing his style of leadership Branson says: 'As much as you need a strong personality to build a business from scratch, you also must understand the art of delegation. I have to be good at helping people run the individual businesses, and I have to be willing to step back. The company must be set up so it can continue without me.' But also run without too much interference from headquarters. 'Seeing as the Virgin businesses are all so diverse and independent, we pretty much practise a collaborative and supportive style of custodianship', VML reports. 'We give birth to new Virgin companies, encourage them to walk, hold their hands and then watch them on their way as they become fully-fledged members of the Virgin family. It can sometimes get quite emotional.'

About the future Branson is also clear: 'I'm inquisitive. … and I love a new challenge … and if I feel that we can do it better than it's been done by other people, we'll have a go. Some people call that "brand stretching" and say that this is not the way business should be done, and in the Western world generally it's not the way business is done. And I think to be perfectly frank the reason it's not done that way is that most big companies are public … they have fund managers who only specialize in one area … and so if you go and stray outside that fund manager's arena, the company gets criticized. Fortunately we're not a public company – we're a private group of companies, and I can do what I want.' And what he wants to do is keep on building his 'eclectic' portfolio and keep on pursuing new opportunities. Because, as Branson has famously said, 'business opportunities are like buses, there's always another one coming.'

Sources: www.virgin.com; Dick, Kets de Vries and Vitry d'Avaucourt (2000); *The Economist*, 25 September 2008.

The integrated organization perspective

 The integrated organization perspective is fundamentally at odds with the portfolio organization perspective's minimalist interpretation of corporate level strategy. To proponents of the integrated organization perspective, a multi-business firm should be more than a loose federation of businesses held together by a common investor. Actually, a corporation should be quite the opposite – a tightly knit team of business units grouped around a common core. Having various businesses together in one corporation, it is argued, can only be justified if the corporate centre has a clear conception of how strategically relevant multi-business synergies can be realized. It is not enough to capture a few operational synergies here and there – a compelling logic must lie at the heart of the corporation, creating a significant competitive advantage over rivals who operate on a business-by-business basis. The multi-business synergies generated at the core of the organization should enable the corporation to beat its competitors in a variety of business areas.

As corporate level strategists 'lead from the centre' (Raynor and Bower, 2001) and develop a joint competitive strategy together with business level strategists, they must make very clear which multi-business synergies they intend to foster as the nucleus of the corporation. It is their task to determine what the core of the organization should be and to take the lead in building it. To be successful, it is necessary for them to work closely together with business level managers, whose main task it is to apply the core strengths of the corporation to their specific business area. The consequence of this joint strategy development and synergy realization is that all business units are highly interdependent, requiring continual coordination.

Many different multi-business synergies can form the core of the corporation. In the strategic management literature one specific form has received a large amount of attention – the *core competence* centred corporation (Prahalad and Hamel, 1990, Reading 6.2 in this book). In such an organization a few competences are at the heart of the corporation and are leveraged across various business units. Prahalad and Hamel's metaphor for the corporation is not an investor's portfolio, but a large tree: 'the trunk and major limbs are core products, the smaller branches are business units, the leaves, flowers and fruit are end products; the root system that provides nourishment, sustenance and stability is the core competence.' Business unit branches can be cut off and new ones can grow on, but all spring from the same tree. It is the corporate centre's role to nurture this tree, building up the core competences and ensuring that the firm's competence carriers can easily be redeployed across business unit boundaries. The strategic logic behind leveraging these intangible resources is that high investments in competence development can then be spread over a number of different businesses. Moreover, by using these competences in different business settings they can be further refined, leading to a virtuous circle of rapid learning, profiting the entire corporation. In line with the arguments of the inside-out perspective (see Chapter 5), it is pointed out that in the long run inter-firm rivalries are often won by the corporation who has been able to upgrade its competences fastest – skirmishes in particular markets are only battles in this broader war. From this angle, building the corporation's core competences is strategic, while engaging other corporations in specific business areas is tactical. The corporate centre is therefore at the forefront of competitive strategy, instead of the business units, that are literally divisions in the overall campaign (e.g. Kono, 1999; Stalk, Evans and Schulman, 1992).

As all business units should both tap into, and contribute to, the corporation's core competences, the business units' autonomy is necessarily limited. Unavoidably, the responsiveness to the specific characteristics of each business does suffer from this emphasis on coordination. Yet, to advocates of the core competence model, the loss of business responsiveness is more than compensated for by the strategic benefits gained.

Besides competences as the core of the corporation, other synergies can also be at the heart of a multi-business firm. For instance, corporations can focus on aligning a variety of product offerings for a group of 'core customers'. Many professional service firms, such as PricewaterhouseCoopers and Cap Gemini, are involved in a broad range of businesses, with the intention of offering an integrated package of services to their selected market segments. Another type of core is where a multi-business firm is built around shared activities. Many of the large airlines, for example, have one 'core process', flying planes, but operate in the very different businesses of passenger travel and cargo transport. Yet another central synergy can be the leveraging of the firm's 'software'. For instance, Disney is such a 'core content' corporation, letting Cinderella work hard selling Disney videos, luring families to Disney theme parks, getting kids to buy Disney merchandise and enticing people to watch the Disney channel. Whichever synergy is placed centre stage, to the proponents of the integrated organization perspective it should not be trivial, as such minor value-creation efforts do not provide the driving motivation to keep a corporation together. The 'glue' of the corporation must be strong enough to convince all involved that they are much better off as part of the whole than on their own.

The flip side of having a tightly knit group of businesses arranged around a common core is that growth through acquisition is generally much more difficult than in the 'plug and play' set-up of a portfolio organization. To make an acquisition fit into the corporate family and to establish all of the necessary links to let the new recruits profit from, and contribute to, the core synergies, can be very challenging. Taking the previous metaphor a step further, the corporate centre will find it quite difficult to graft oak roots and elm branches on to an existing olive tree. Consequently, acquisitions will be infrequent, as the firm will prefer internal growth.

EXHIBIT 6.3   THE INTEGRATED ORGANIZATION PERSPECTIVE

CARL ZEISS: CLEAR FOCUS

'That's one small step for man, one giant leap for' … Carl Zeiss! Few companies can claim that they went to the moon and even fewer that one of their products is still there, but Carl Zeiss can. The snapshots that the Apollo 11 astronauts Armstrong and Aldrin took on the moon were made with a Carl Zeiss Biogon lens, fitted onto a Hasselblad 500EL camera. To reduce weight on the way back, they left the camera on the moon, where it has been ever since, waiting to be collected for a future space flight museum. But Carl Zeiss products can be found in many more places – research laboratories, hospitals, shooting ranges, semiconductor factories, planetariums and Hollywood film sets, to name just a few.

While not a household name, technological enthusiasts know Carl Zeiss as the leading global firm in the optical industry. Their core competence is in manufacturing state-of-the-art lenses and linking these to fine mechanical and electronic systems, to achieve amazing technological results. As their company slogan summarizes it, 'we make it visible.'

This core competence has been applied to numerous areas. In the medical field, Carl Zeiss Meditec makes surgical microscopes and digital visualization equipment, while for researchers and educational institutions, Carl Zeiss MicroImaging can provide similar microscopes and imaging systems. In the industrial field, Carl Zeiss SMT uses its lenses to focus laser beams for semiconductor chip manufacturing (lithography), but also employs its electron microscope technology to materials analysis and nanotechnology applications. Consumers might bump into the Zeiss brand name if they visit a planetarium, where the company uses its lenses and projectors to provide entire planetarium systems. But you might also know the company from their binoculars, riflescopes or eyeglasses. However, for most, the name Zeiss remains linked to camera lenses, for amateur and professional movie cameras, as well as for photography. Zeiss lenses have even been integrated into a whole range of Nokia phones.

The company was established by Carl Zeiss in 1846 in the German city of Jena to produce microscopes and blossomed when the leading optical scientist, Ernst Abbe, joined in 1866. To ensure top quality glass for their lenses, Zeiss and Abbe got together with Otto Schott to found a glass manufacturing company, which today is the high-tech glass specialist Schott AG, with annual sales of over €2 billion and employing 17 000 people worldwide. Being a farsighted man, Abbe ensured that all shares of the Carl Zeiss and Schott companies were given to a foundation, which he named after his friend Zeiss. Since then the Carl Zeiss Foundation has remained owner of both companies and has used the proceeds to fund worthy causes. After the Second World War, the American occupying forces helped Carl Zeiss to reallocate from Jena in the Soviet zone, to Oberkochen in West Germany, where the headquarters has remained since. As some activities stayed in Eastern Germany, for many years there were two Zeiss companies, but they were reunited soon after the fall of the Berlin Wall.

By 2008, Carl Zeiss had grown to a company with annual sales of €2.7 billion, employing 13 000 people at approximately 20 production sites in Germany, France, Hungary, the US, China and Belarus, and sales offices in 30 countries. In almost all of its product markets, it fills the number one or two spot. The current CEO, Dr. Dieter Kurz, ascribes a large part of the company's success to its relentless pursuit of innovation. Of its 2008 sales, more than 60% was from products less than five years old. In the same year, it applied for 422 new patents, which is about two per working day. These

were generated by a research and development army of more than 2000 people, making up 16% of the company's workforce. The total R&D budget was €321 million, which is 12% of sales. And to supplement the company's know-how, Zeiss had partnerships with more than 400 universities, research organizations and companies around the world.

While only a part of Carl Zeiss's R&D is conducted centrally in Oberkochen, the corporate centre plays a key role in coordinating R&D activities and exchanging know-how across the 12 business units. Four areas of core competence have been selected; lithography optics, microstructured optics, life science-oriented optical technology and imaging technology. As all units are configured around these same core competences, enormous synergies have been gained by sharing advances in basic and applied research, while also helping to speed up developments. To further support the translation of invention to innovation, head office also has an Innovation Management Team, with the CEO playing a hands-on role.

Ranging from nanotubes to the movement of planets, a broad spectrum of nature's secrets have been probed by a variety of Carl Zeiss instruments. But while seemingly diverse products, all were born of a shared focus and a clear vision.

Sources: www.zeiss.com; *New York Times*, 18 March 2004, 2 February 2006; www.wikipedia.com.

INTRODUCTION TO THE DEBATE AND READINGS

Consider the little mouse, how sagacious an animal it is which never entrusts its life to one hole only.
Plautus (254–184 BC); Roman playwright

None ever got ahead of me except the man of one task.
Azariah Rossi (1513–1578); Italian physician

So, how should the corporate configuration be determined? Should corporate strategists limit themselves to achieving financial synergies, leaving SBU managers to 'mind their own business'? Or should corporate strategists strive to build a multi-business firm around a common core, intricately weaving all business units into a highly integrated whole? As before, the strategic management literature does not offer a clear-cut answer to the question of which corporate level strategies are the most successful. Many points of view have been put forward on how to reconcile the opposing demands of responsiveness and synergy, but no common perspective has yet emerged. Therefore, it is up to individual strategists to form their own opinion once again.

To help strategists to come to grips with the variety of perspectives on this issue, four readings have been selected that each shed their own light on the debate. As in previous chapters, the first two readings will be representative of the two poles in this debate (see Table 6.1), while the second set of two readings will bring extra arguments into the discussion.

To open the debate on behalf of the portfolio organization perspective, Barry Hedley's article 'Strategy and the Business Portfolio' has been selected as Reading 6.1. Hedley was an early proponent of the portfolio perspective, together with other consultants from the Boston Consulting Group (BCG), such as Bruce Henderson (1979). In this article, he explains the strategic principles underlying the famed growth-share grid that is commonly known as the BCG matrix. His argument is based on the premise that a complex corporation can be viewed as a portfolio of businesses, which each have their own competitive arena to which they must be responsive. By disaggregating a corporation into its business unit components, separate strategies can be devised for each. The overarching role of the corporate level can then be defined as that of portfolio manager. The major task of the corporate headquarters is to manage the allocation of scarce financial resources over the business units, to achieve the highest returns at an acceptable level of risk. Each business unit can be given a strategic mission to grow, hold or milk, depending on their prospects compared to the businesses in the corporate portfolio. This is where portfolio analysis comes in. Hedley argues that the profit and growth potential of each business unit depends on two key variables: the growth rate of the total business and the relative market share of the business unit within its business. When these two variables are put together in a grid, this forms the BCG matrix. For the discussion in this chapter, the precise details of the BCG portfolio technique are less relevant than the basic corporate strategy perspective that Hedley advocates – running the multi-business firm as a hands-on investor.

Selecting a representative for the integrated organization perspective for Reading 6.2 was a simple choice. In 1990, C.K. Prahalad and Gary Hamel published an article in *Harvard Business Review* with the title 'The Core Competence of the Corporation'. This article has had a profound impact on the debate surrounding the topic of corporate level strategy, and has inspired a considerable amount of research and writing investigating resource-based synergies. In this article, and in their subsequent book, *Competing for the*

TABLE 6.1 Portfolio organization versus integrated organization perspective

	Portfolio organization perspective	*Integrated organization perspective*
Emphasis on	Responsiveness over synergy	Synergy over responsiveness
Conception of corporation	Collection of business shareholdings	Common core with business applications
Corporate composition	Potentially unrelated (diverse)	Tightly related (focused)
Key success factor	Business unit responsiveness	Multi-business synergy
Focal type of synergy	Cash flow optimization and risk balance	Integrating resources, activities and positions
Corporate management style	Exerting financial control	Joint strategy development
Primary task corporate centre	Capital allocation and performance control	Setting direction and managing synergies
Position of business units	Highly autonomous (independent)	Highly integrated (interdependent)
Coordination between BUs	Low, incidental	High, structural
Growth through acquisitions	Simple to accommodate	Difficult to integrate

Future, Prahalad and Hamel explicitly dismiss the portfolio organization perspective as a viable approach to corporate strategy. Prahalad and Hamel acknowledge that diversified corporations have a portfolio of businesses, but they do not believe that this implies the need for a portfolio organization approach, in which the business units are highly autonomous. In their view, 'the primacy of the SBU – an organizational dogma for a generation – is now clearly an anachronism'. Drawing mainly on Japanese examples, they carry on to argue that corporations should be built around a core of shared competences. Business units should use and help to further develop these core competences. The consequence is that the role of corporate level management is much more far-reaching than in the portfolio organization perspective. The corporate centre must 'establish objectives for competence building' and must ensure that this 'strategic architecture' is carried through.

The third reading has been selected to highlight a very important subject in the debate, which has only been touched on indirectly so far in this chapter – the role of acquisitions in corporate level strategy. In discussing the issue of corporate configuration, it is almost impossible not to take a view on the possibilities and impossibilities of growing the corporation by means of acquisition. Therefore, Reading 6.3, 'Understanding Acquisition Integration Approaches', by Philippe Haspeslagh and David Jemison, has been included in this chapter. This reading is a key chapter from their well known book *Managing Acquisitions: Creating Value Through Corporate Renewal*, in which they outline three generic approaches to the integration of acquired companies. Haspeslagh and Jemison's main argument is that the integration of acquisitions depends on the levels of responsiveness and synergy that are necessary – in the terminology of Haspeslagh and Jemison these opposing forces are called the 'need for organizational autonomy' and the 'need for strategic interdependence'. This gives three different types of acquisition integration approach. Where an acquired company requires high responsiveness/autonomy and low synergy/interdependence, Haspeslagh and Jemison advise a 'preservation acquisition', in which the acquiree can retain much separate identity and freedom. In the opposite case of a high need for synergy and low responsiveness, an 'absorption acquisition' is preferred. The most difficult situation, according to the authors, is where the needs for responsiveness and synergy are both high. In such a situation they suggest a 'symbiotic acquisition', in which 'the two organizations first coexist and then gradually become increasingly interdependent'. However, they acknowledge that this approach is fraught with difficulties and it can be debated what the chances of success are likely to be.

Reading 6.4 is 'Seeking Synergies' by Andrew Campbell and Michael Goold. These researchers from the Ashridge Strategic Management Centre have been responsible for a constant stream of insightful work on corporate level strategy. One of their most recent publications has been the book *Synergy: Why Links Between Business Units Often Fail and How to Make Them Work*, from which this is the summary chapter. This reading has been selected for this chapter in order to pay more attention to the issue of realizing synergies. As a large part of the debate revolves around different views on whether synergies can actually be captured or not, it is valuable to get some more input on approaches to synergy creation and a better insight into 'synergy killers'. Campbell and Goold give a structured and practical framework for analysing a corporation's synergy opportunities and synergy approach, followed by an analysis of the most important policies and characteristics that systematically inhibit attempts at reaping synergy advantages. In the context of this debate, it is important to note that Campbell and Goold do not necessarily side with either of the two perspectives. In their view, there are different styles of corporate strategy and different levels of synergy that can be achieved, as long as the 'parent company' develops the matching parenting capabilities and synergy parenting approach.

Strategy and the business portfolio

By Barry Hedley[1]

All except the smallest and simplest companies comprise more than one business. Even when a company operates within a single broad business area, analysis normally reveals that it is, in practice, involved in a number of product-market segments which are distinct economically. These must be considered separately for purposes of strategy development.

The fundamental determinant of strategy success for each individual business segment is relative competitive position. As a result of the experience curve effect the competitor with high market share in the segment relative to competition should be able to develop the lowest cost position and hence the highest and most stable profits. This will be true regardless of changes in the economic environment. Hence relative competitive position in the appropriately defined business segment forms a simple but sound strategic goal. Almost invariably, any company which reviews its various businesses carefully in this light will discover that they occupy widely differing relative competitive positions. Some businesses will be competitively strong already, and may appear to present no strategic problem; others will be weak, and the company must face the question of whether it would be worthwhile to attempt to improve their position, making whatever investments might be required to achieve this; if this is not done, the company can only expect poor performance from the business and the best option economically will be divestment.

Even in quite small companies, the total number of possible combinations of individual business strategies can be extremely large. The difficulty of making a firm final choice on strategy for each business is normally compounded by the fact that most companies must operate within constraints established by limited resources, particularly cash resources.

The business portfolio concept

At its most basic, the importance of growth in shaping strategy choice is two-fold. First, the growth of a business is a major factor influencing the likely ease – and hence cost – of gaining market share. In low-growth businesses, any market share gained will tend to require an actual volume reduction in competitors' sales. This will be very obvious to the competitors and they are likely to fight to prevent the throughput in their plants dropping. In high-growth businesses, on the other hand, market share can be gained steadily merely by securing the largest share of the growth in the business: expanding capacity earlier than the competitors, ensuring product availability and effective selling support despite the strains imposed by the *growth*, and so forth. Meanwhile competitors may even be unaware of their share loss because their actual volume of throughput has been well maintained. Even if aware of their loss of share, the competitors may be unconcerned by it given that their plants are still well loaded. This is particularly true of competitors who do not understand the strategic importance of market share for long term profitability resulting from the experience curve effect.

An unfortunate example of this is given by the history of the British motorcycle industry. British market share was allowed to erode in motorcycles world-wide for more than a decade, throughout which the British factories were still fairly full: British motorcycle production volumes held up at around 80 000 units per year throughout the sixties; in sharp contrast, Japanese export volumes leapt from only about 60 000 in 1960 to 2.5 million in 1973; their total production volumes roughly tripled in the same period. The long-term effect was that while Japanese real costs were falling rapidly British costs were not: somewhat over-simplified, this is why the British motorcycle industry faced bankruptcy in the early seventies.

The second important factor concerning growth is the opportunity it provides for investment. Growth businesses provide the ideal vehicles for investment, for ploughing cash into a business in order to see it compound and return even larger amounts of cash at a later point in time. Of course this opportunity is also a need: the faster a business grows, the more investment

[1]Source: This article was adapted from B. Hedley, 'Strategy and the Business Portfolio', *Long Range Planning*, February 1977, Vol. 10, No. 1, pp. 9–15, © 1977. With permission from Elsevier.

it will require just to maintain market share. Yet the experience curve effect means that this is essential if its profitability is not to decline over time.

Whilst these growth considerations affect the rate at which a business will use cash, the relative competitive position of the business will determine the rate at which the business will generate cash: the stronger the company's position relative to its competitors the higher its margins should be, as a result of the experience curve effect. The simplest measure of relative competitive position is, of course, relative market share. A company's relative market share in a business can be defined as its market share in the business divided by that of the largest other competitor. Thus only the biggest competitor has a relative market share greater than one. All the other competitors should enjoy lower profitability and cash generation than the leader.

The growth – share matrix

Individual businesses can have very different financial characteristics and face different strategic options depending on how they are placed in terms of growth and relative competitive position. Businesses can basically fall into any one of four broad strategic categories, as depicted schematically in the growth – share matrix in Figure 6.1.1.

- Stars. High growth, high share – are in the upper left quadrant. Growing rapidly, they use large amounts

of cash to maintain position. They are also leaders in the business, however, and should generate large amounts of cash. As a result, star businesses are frequently roughly in balance on net cash flow, and can be self-sustaining in growth terms. They represent probably the best profit growth and investment opportunities available to the company, and every effort should therefore be made to maintain and consolidate their competitive position. This will sometimes require heavy investment beyond their own generation capabilities and low margins may be essential at times to deter competition, but this is almost invariably worthwhile for the longer term: when the growth slows, as it ultimately does in all businesses, very large cash returns will be obtained if share has been maintained so that the business drops into the lower left quadrant of the matrix, becoming a cash cow. If star businesses fail to hold share, which frequently happens if the attempt is made to net large amounts of cash from them in the short and medium term (e.g. by cutting back on investment and raising prices, creating an 'umbrella' for competitors), they will ultimately become dogs (lower right quadrant). These are certain losers.

- Cash cows. Low growth, high share – should have an entrenched superior market position and low costs. Hence profits and cash generation should be high, and because of the low growth reinvestment needs should be light. Thus large cash surpluses should be generated by these businesses. Cash cows

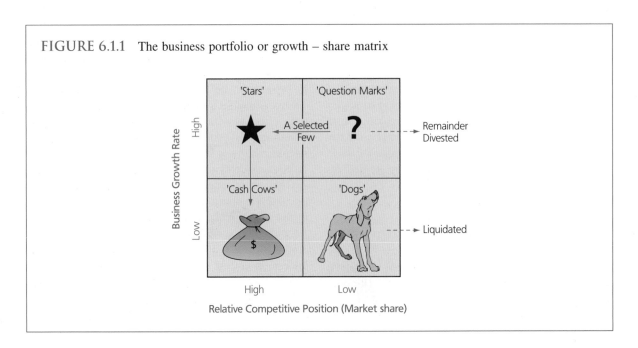

FIGURE 6.1.1   The business portfolio or growth – share matrix

pay the dividends and interest, provide the debt capacity, pay for the company overhead and provide the cash for investment elsewhere in the company's portfolio of businesses. They are the foundation on which the company rests.

- Dogs. Low growth, low share – represent a tremendous contrast. Their poor competitive position condemns them to poor profits. Because the growth is low, there is little potential for gaining sufficient share to achieve a viable cost position at anything approaching a reasonable cost. Unfortunately, the cash required for investment in the business just to maintain competitive position, though low, frequently exceeds that generated, especially under conditions of high inflation. The business therefore becomes a 'cash trap' likely to absorb cash perpetually unless further investment in the business is rigorously avoided. The colloquial term dog describing these businesses, though undoubtedly pejorative, is thus rather apt. A company should take every precaution to minimize the proportion of its assets that remain in this category.

- Question marks. High growth, low share – have the worst cash characteristics of all. In the upper right quadrant, their cash needs are high because of their growth, but their cash generation is small because of their low share. If nothing is done to change its market share, the question mark will simply absorb large amounts of cash in the short term and later, as the growth slows, become a dog. Following this sort of strategy, the question mark is a cash loser throughout its existence. Managed this way, a question mark becomes the ultimate cash trap.

In fact there is a clear choice between only two strategy alternatives for a question mark, hence the name. Because growth is high, it should be easier and less costly to gain share here than it would be in a lower growth business. One strategy is therefore to make whatever investments are necessary to gain share, to try to fund the business to dominance so that it can become a star and, ultimately a cash cow when the business matures. This strategy will be very costly in the short term – growth rates will be even higher than if share were merely being maintained, and additional marketing and other investments will be required to make the share actually change hands – but it offers the only way of developing a sound business from the question mark over the long term. The only logical alternative is divestment. Outright sale is preferable; but if this is not possible, then a firm decision

must be taken not to invest further in the business and it must be allowed simply to generate whatever cash it can while none is reinvested. The business will then decline, possibly quite rapidly if market growth is high, and will have to be shut down at some point. But it will produce cash in the short term and this is greatly preferable to the error of sinking cash into it perpetually without improving its competitive position.

These then, are the four basic categories to which businesses can belong. Some companies tend to fit almost entirely into a single quadrant. General Motors and English China Clays are examples of predominantly cash cow companies. Chrysler, by comparison, is a dog which compounded its fundamental problem of low share in its domestic US market by acquiring further mature low share competitors in other countries (e.g. Rootes which became Chrysler UK). IBM in computers, Xerox in photocopiers, BSR in low cost record autochangers, are all examples of predominantly star businesses. Xerox's computer operation, XDS, was clearly a question mark, however, and it is not surprising that Xerox recently effectively gave it away free to Honeywell, and considered itself lucky to escape at that price! When RCA closed down its computer operation, it had to sustain a write-off of about $490m. Question marks are costly.

Portfolio strategy

Most companies have their portfolio of businesses scattered through all four quadrants of the matrix. It is possible to outline quite briefly and simply what the appropriate overall portfolio strategy for such a company should be. The first goal should be to maintain position in the cash cows, but to guard against the frequent temptation to reinvest in them excessively. The cash generated by the cash cows should be used as a first priority to maintain or consolidate position in those stars which are not self-sustaining. Any surplus remaining can be used to fund a selected number of question marks to dominance. Most companies will find they have inadequate cash generation to finance market share-gaining strategies in all their question marks. Those which are not funded should be divested either by sale or liquidation over time.

Finally, virtually all companies have at least some dog businesses. There is nothing reprehensible about this, indeed on the contrary, an absence of dogs probably indicates that the company has not been sufficiently adventurous in the past. It is essential, however, that the fundamentally weak strategic position of the dog be recognized for what it is. Occasionally it is possible to restore a dog to viability by a creative business segmentation strategy, rationalizing and specializing the business into a small niche which it can dominate. If this is impossible, however, the only thing which could rescue the dog would be an increase in share taking it to a position comparable to the leading competitors in the segment. This is likely to be unreasonably costly in a mature business, and therefore the only prospect for obtaining a return from a dog is to manage it for cash, cutting off all investment in the business. Management should be particularly wary of expensive 'turn around' plans developed for a dog if these do not involve a significant change in fundamental competitive position. Without this, the dog is a sure loser. An indictment of many corporate managements is not the fact that their companies have dogs in the portfolio, but rather that these dogs are not managed according to logical strategies. The decision to liquidate a business is usually even harder to take than that of entering a new business. It is essential, however, for the long-term vitality and performance of the company overall that it be prepared to do both as the need arises.

Thus the appropriate strategy for a multibusiness company involves striking a balance in the portfolio such that the cash generated by the cash cows, and by those question marks and dogs which are being liquidated, is sufficient to support the company's stars and to fund the selected question marks through to dominance. This pattern of strategies is indicated by the arrows in Figure 6.1.1. Understanding this pattern conceptually is, however, a far cry from being able to implement it in practice. What any company should do with its own specific businesses is of course a function of the precise shape of the company's portfolio, and the particular opportunities and problems it presents. But how can a clear picture of the company's portfolio be developed?

The matrix quantified

Based on careful analysis and research it is normally possible to divide a company into its various business segments appropriately defined for purposes of strategy development. Following this critical first step, it is usually relatively straightforward to determine the overall growth rate of each individual business (i.e. the growth of the market, not the growth of the company within the market), and the company's size (in terms of turnover or assets) and relative competitive position (market share) within the business.

Armed with these data it is possible to develop a precise overall picture of the company's portfolio of businesses graphically. This can greatly facilitate the identification and resolution of the key strategic issues facing the company. It is a particularly useful approach where companies are large, comprising many separate businesses. Such complex portfolios often defy description in more conventional ways.

The nature of the graphical portfolio display is illustrated by the example in Figure 6.1.2. In this chart, growth rate and relative competitive position are plotted on continuous scales. Each circle in the display represents a single business or business segment, appropriately defined. To convey an impression of the relative significance of each business, size is indicated by the area of the circle, which can be made proportional to either turnover or assets employed. Relative competitive position is plotted on a logarithmic scale, in order to be consistent with the experience curve effect, which implies that profit margin or rate of cash generation differences between competitors will tend to be related to the ratio of their relative competitive positions (market shares). A linear axis is used for growth, for which the most generally useful measure is volume growth of the business concerned, as, in general, rates of cash use should be directly proportional to growth.

The lines dividing the portfolio into four quadrants are inevitably somewhat arbitrary. 'High growth', for example, is taken to include all businesses growing in excess of 10 per cent per annum in volume terms. Certainly, above this growth rate market share tends to become fairly fluid and can be made to change hands quite readily. In addition many companies have traditionally employed a figure of 10 per cent for their discount rate in times of low inflation, and so this also tends to be the growth rate above which investment in market share becomes particularly attractive financially.

The line separating areas of high and low relative competitive position is set at 1.5 times. Experience in using this display has been that in high-growth businesses relative strengths of this magnitude or greater are necessary in order to ensure a sufficiently dominant position that the business will have the characteristic of a star in practice. On the other hand, in low-growth businesses acceptable cash generation characteristics are occasionally, but not always, observed at relative strengths as low as 1 times; hence the addition of a second separating line at 1 times in the low growth

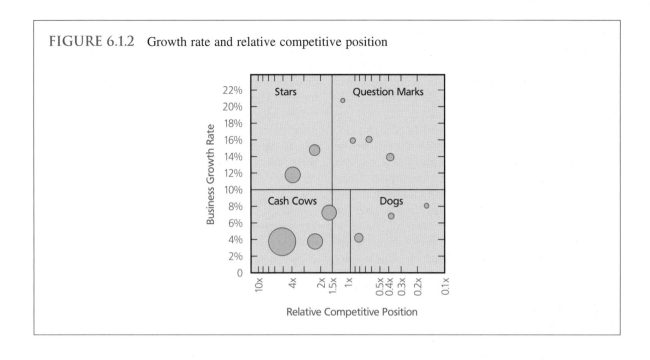

FIGURE 6.1.2 Growth rate and relative competitive position

area, to reflect this. These lines should, of course, be taken only as approximate guides in characterizing businesses in the portfolio as dogs and question marks, cash cows and stars. In actuality, businesses cover a smooth spectrum across both axes of the matrix. There is obviously no 'magic' which transforms a star into a cash cow as its growth declines from 10.5 to 9.5 per cent. It is undeniably useful, however, to have some device for broadly indicating where the transition points occur within the matrix, and the lines suggested here have worked well in practical applications of the matrix in a large number of companies.

Portfolio approaches in practice

The company shown in Figure 6.1.2 would be a good example of a potentially well-balanced portfolio. With a firm foundation in the form of two or three substantial cash cows, this company has some well-placed stars to provide growth and to yield high cash returns in the future when they mature. The company also has some question marks, at least two of which are probably sufficiently well placed that they offer a good chance of being funded into star positions at a reasonable cost, not out of proportion to the company's resources. The company is not without dogs, but properly managed there is no reason why these should be a drain on cash.

The sound portfolio, unsoundly managed

Companies with an attractive portfolio of this kind are not rare in practice. In fact Figure 6.1.2 is a disguised version of a representation of an actual UK company analysed in the course of a Boston Consulting Group assignment. What is much rarer, however, is to find that the company has made a clear assessment of the matrix positioning and appropriate strategy for each business in the portfolio.

Ideally, one would hope that the company in Figure 6.1.2 would develop strategy along the following lines. For the stars, the key objectives should be the maintenance of market share; current profitability should be accorded a lower priority. For the cash cows, however, current profitability may well be the primary goal. Dogs would not be expected to be as profitable as the cash cows, but would be expected to yield cash. Some question marks would be set objectives in terms of increased market share; others, where gaining dominance appeared too costly, would be managed instead for cash.

The essence of the portfolio approach is therefore that strategy objectives must vary between businesses. The strategy developed for each business must fit its own matrix position and the needs and capabilities of the company's overall portfolio of businesses. In practice, however, it is much more common to find all businesses within a company being operated with a common overall goal in mind. 'Our target in this company is to grow at 10 per cent per annum and achieve a return of 10 per cent on capital.' This type of overall target is then taken to apply to every business in the company. Cash cows beat the profit target easily, though they frequently miss on growth. Nevertheless, their managements are praised and they are normally rewarded by being allowed to plough back what only too frequently amounts to an excess of cash into their 'obviously attractive' businesses. Attractive businesses, yes: but not for growth investment. Dogs on the other hand rarely meet the profit target. But how often is it accepted that it is in fact unreasonable for them ever to hit the target? On the contrary, the most common strategic mistake is that major investments are made in dogs from time to time in hopeless attempts to turn the business around without actually shifting market share. Unfortunately, only too often question marks are regarded very much as dogs, and get insufficient investment funds ever to bring them to dominance. The question marks usually do receive some investment, however, possibly even enough to maintain share. This is throwing money away into a cash trap. These businesses should either receive enough support to enable them to achieve segment dominance, or none at all.

These are some of the strategic errors which are regularly committed even by companies which have basically sound portfolios. The result is a serious sub-optimization of potential performance in which some businesses (e.g. cash cows) are not being called on to produce the full results of which they are actually capable, and resources are being mistakenly squandered on other businesses (dogs, question marks) in an attempt to make them achieve performance of which they are intrinsically incapable without a fundamental improvement in market share. Where mismanagement of this kind becomes positively dangerous, is when it is applied within the context of a basically unbalanced portfolio.

The unbalanced portfolio

The disguised example in Figure 6.1.3 is another actual company. This portfolio is seriously out of balance. As shown in Figure 6.1.3(a), the company has a very high proportion of question marks in its portfolio, and an inadequate base of cash cows. Yet at the time of investigation this company was in fact taking such cash as was being generated by its mature businesses and spreading it out amongst all the high-growth businesses, only one of which was actually receiving sufficient investment to enable it even to maintain share! Thus the overall relative competitive position of the portfolio was on average declining. At the same time, the balance in the portfolio was shifting: as shown in the projected portfolio in Figure 6.1.3(b), because of the higher relative growth of the question marks their overall weight in the portfolio was

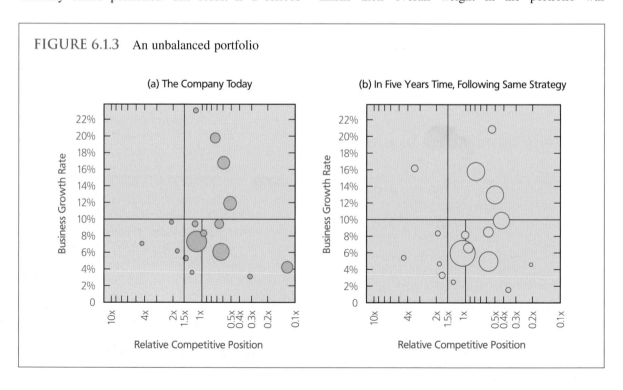

FIGURE 6.1.3   An unbalanced portfolio

increasing, making them even harder to fund from the limited resources of the mature businesses.

If the company continued to follow the same strategy of spreading available funds between all the businesses, then the rate of decline could only increase over time leading ultimately to disaster.

This company was caught in a vicious circle of decline. To break out of the circle would require firm discipline and the strength of will to select only one or two of the question marks and finance those, whilst cutting off investment in the remainder. Obviously the choice of which should receive investment involves rather more than selection at random from the portfolio chart. It requires careful analysis of the actual nature of the businesses concerned and particularly the characteristics and behaviour of the competitors faced in those businesses. However, the nature of the strategic choice facing the company is quite clear, when viewed in portfolio terms. Without the clarity of view provided by the matrix display, which focuses on the real fundamentals of the businesses and their relationships to each other within the portfolio, it is impossible to develop strategy effectively in any multibusiness company.

READING

6.2

The core competence of the corporation

By C.K. Prahalad and Gary Hamel[1]

The most powerful way to prevail in global competition is still invisible to many companies. During the 1980s, top executives were judged on their ability to restructure, declutter, and delayer their corporations. In the 1990s, they'll be judged on their ability to identify, cultivate, and exploit the core competencies that make growth possible – indeed, they'll have to rethink the concept of the corporation itself.

Rethinking the corporation

Once, the diversified corporation could simply point its business units at particular end-product markets and admonish them to become world leaders. But with market boundaries changing ever more quickly, targets are elusive and capture is at best temporary. A few companies have proven themselves adept at inventing new markets, quickly entering emerging markets, and dramatically shifting patterns of customer choice in established markets. These are the ones to emulate. The critical task for management is to create an organization capable of infusing products with irresistible functionality or, better yet, creating products that customers need but have not yet even imagined.

This is a deceptively difficult task. Ultimately, it requires radical change in the management of major companies. It means, first of all, that top managements of western companies must assume responsibility for competitive decline. Everyone knows about high interest rates, Japanese protectionism, outdated antitrust laws, obstreperous unions, and impatient investors. What is harder to see, or harder to acknowledge, is how little added momentum companies actually get from political or macroeconomic 'relief'. Both the theory and practice of western management have created a drag on our forward motion. It is the principles of management that are in need of reform.

The roots of competitive advantage

In the short run, a company's competitiveness derives from the price/performance attributes of current products. But the survivors of the first wave of global competition, western and Japanese alike, are all converging on similar and formidable standards for product cost and quality – minimum hurdles for continued competition, but less and less important as sources of differential advantage. In the long run, competitiveness derives from an ability to build, at lower cost and more speedily than competitors, the core competencies that spawn unanticipated products. The real sources of advantage are to be found in management's ability to consolidate corporate-wide technologies and

[1]Source: This article was reprinted by permission of *Harvard Business Review*. From 'The Core Competence of the Corporation' by C.K. Prahalad and G. Hamel, May–June 1990, Vol. 68. © 1990 by the Harvard Business School Publishing Corporation, all rights reserved.

production skills into competencies that empower individual businesses to adapt quickly to changing opportunities.

Senior executives who claim that they cannot build core competencies either because they feel the autonomy of business units is sacrosanct or because their feet are held to the quarterly budget fire should think again. The problem in many western companies is not that their senior executives are any less capable than those in Japan or that Japanese companies possess greater technical capabilities. Instead, it is their adherence to a concept of the corporation that unnecessarily limits the ability of individual businesses to fully exploit the deep reservoir of technological capability that many American and European companies possess.

The diversified corporation is a large tree. The trunk and major limbs are core products, the smaller branches are business units; the leaves, flowers, and fruit are end products. The root system that provides nourishment, sustenance, and stability is the core competence. You can miss the strength of competitors by looking only at their end products, in the same way you miss the strength of a tree if you look only at its leaves (see Figure 6.2.1).

Core competencies are the collective learning in the organization, especially how to coordinate diverse production skills and integrate multiple streams of technologies. Consider Sony's capacity to miniaturize or Philips's optical-media expertise. The theoretical knowledge to put a radio on a chip does not in itself assure a company the skill to produce a miniature radio no bigger than a business card. To bring off this feat, Casio must harmonize know-how in miniaturization, microprocessor design, materials science, and ultrathin precision casing – the same skills it applies in its miniature card calculators, pocket TVs, and digital watches.

If core competence is about harmonizing streams of technology, it is also about the organization of work and the delivery of value. Among Sony's competencies is miniaturization. To bring miniaturization to its products, Sony must ensure that technologists, engineers, and marketers have a shared understanding of customer needs and of technological possibilities. The force of core competence is felt as decisively in services as in manufacturing. Citicorp was ahead of others investing in an operating system that allowed it to participate in world markets 24 hours a day. Its competence in systems has provided the company with the means to differentiate itself from many financial service institutions.

Core competence is communication, involvement, and a deep commitment to working across organizational boundaries. It involves many levels of people and all functions. World-class research in, for example, lasers or ceramics can take place in corporate laboratories without having an impact on any of the businesses of the company. The skills that together constitute core competence must coalesce around individuals whose efforts are not so narrowly focused that they cannot recognize the opportunities for

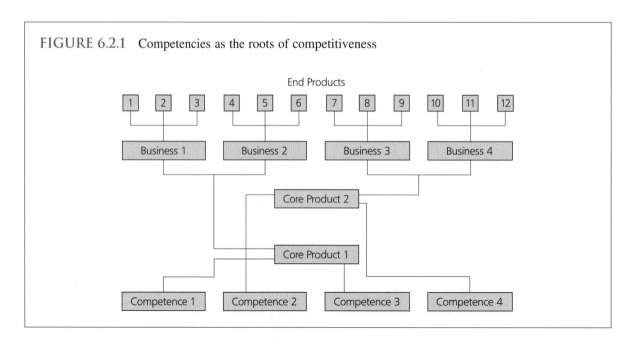

FIGURE 6.2.1 Competencies as the roots of competitiveness

blending their functional expertise with those of others in new and interesting ways.

Core competence does not diminish with use. Unlike physical assets, which do deteriorate over time, competencies are enhanced as they are applied and shared. But competencies still need to be nurtured and protected; knowledge fades if it is not used. Competencies are the glue that binds existing businesses. They are also the engine for new business development. Patterns of diversification and market entry may be guided by them, not just by the attractiveness of markets.

Consider 3M's competence with sticky tape. In dreaming up businesses as diverse as 'Post-it' note pads, magnetic tape, photographic film, pressure-sensitive tapes, and coated abrasives, the company has brought to bear widely shared competencies in substrates, coatings, and adhesives and devised various ways to combine them. Indeed, 3M has invested consistently in them. What seems to be an extremely diversified portfolio of businesses belies a few shared core competencies.

In contrast, there are major companies that have had the potential to build core competencies but failed to do so because top management was unable to conceive of the company as anything other than a collection of discrete businesses. General Electric sold much of its consumer electronics business to Thomson of France, arguing that it was becoming increasingly difficult to maintain its competitiveness in this sector. That was undoubtedly so, but it is ironic that it sold several key businesses to competitors who were already competence leaders – Black & Decker in small electrical motors, and Thomson, which was eager to build its competence in microelectronics and had learned from the Japanese that a position in consumer electronics was vital to this challenge.

Management trapped in the strategic business unit (SBU) mind-set almost inevitably finds its individual businesses dependent on external sources for critical components, such as motors or compressors. But these are not just components. They are core products that contribute to the competitiveness of a wide range of end products. They are the physical embodiments of core competencies.

How not to think of competence

Since companies are in a race to build the competencies that determine global leadership, successful companies have stopped imagining themselves as bundles of businesses making products. Canon, Honda, Casio, or NEC may seem to preside over portfolios of businesses unrelated in terms of customers, distribution channels, and merchandising strategy. Indeed, they have portfolios that may seem idiosyncratic at times: NEC is the only global company to be among leaders in computing, telecommunications, and semiconductors *and* to have a thriving consumer electronics business.

But looks are deceiving. In NEC, digital technology, especially VLSI and systems integration skills, is fundamental. In the core competencies underlying them, disparate businesses become coherent. It is Honda's core competence in engines and power trains that gives it a distinctive advantage in car, motorcycle, lawn mower, and generator businesses. Canon's core competencies in optics, imaging, and microprocessor controls have enabled it to enter, even dominate, markets as seemingly diverse as copiers, laser printers, cameras, and image scanners. Philips worked for more than 15 years to perfect its optical-media (laser disc) competence, as did JVC in building a leading position in video recording. Other examples of core competencies might include mechantronics (the ability to marry mechanical and electronic engineering), video displays, bioengineering, and microelectronics. In the early stages of its competence building, Philips could not have imagined all the products that would be spawned by its optical-media competence, nor could JVC have anticipated miniature camcorders when it first began exploring videotape technologies.

Unlike the battle for global brand dominance, which is visible in the world's broadcast and print media and is aimed at building global 'share of mind', the battle to build world-class competencies is invisible to people who aren't deliberately looking for it. Top management often tracks the cost and quality of competitors' products, yet how many managers untangle the web of alliances their Japanese competitors have constructed to acquire competencies at low cost? In how many western boardrooms is there an explicit, shared understanding of the competencies the company must build for world leadership? Indeed, how many senior executives discuss the crucial distinction between competitive strategy at the level of a business and competitive strategy at the level of an entire company?

Let us be clear. Cultivating core competence does not mean outspending rivals on research and development. In 1983, when Canon surpassed Xerox in worldwide unit market share in the copier business, its R&D budget in reprographics was but a small fraction of

Xerox's. Over the past 20 years, NEC has spent less on R&D as a percentage of sales than almost all of its American and European competitors.

Nor does core competence mean shared costs, as when two or more SBUs use a common facility – a plant, service facility, or sales force – or share a common component. The gains of sharing may be substantial, but the search for shared costs is typically a post hoc effort to rationalize production across existing businesses, not a premeditated effort to build the competencies out of which the businesses themselves grow.

Building core competencies is more ambitious and different than integrating vertically, moreover. Managers deciding whether to make or buy will start with end products and look upstream to the efficiencies of the supply chain and downstream toward distribution and customers. They do not take inventory of skills and look forward to applying them in nontraditional ways. (Of course, decisions about competencies *do* provide a logic for vertical integration. Canon is not particularly integrated in its copier business, except in those aspects of the vertical chain that support the competencies it regards as critical.)

Identifying core competencies – and losing them

At least three tests can be applied to identify core competencies in a company. First, a core competence provides potential access to a wide variety of markets. Competence in display systems, for example, enables a company to participate in such diverse businesses as calculators, miniature TV sets, monitors for laptop computers, and automotive dashboards – which is why Casio's entry into the handheld TV market was predictable. Second, a core competence should make a significant contribution to the perceived customer benefits of the end product. Clearly, Honda's engine expertise fills this bill.

Finally, a core competence should be difficult for competitors to imitate. And it will be difficult if it is a complex harmonization of individual technologies and production skills. A rival might acquire some of the technologies that comprise the core competence, but it will find it more difficult to duplicate the more-or-less comprehensive pattern of internal coordination and learning. JVC's decision in the early 1960s to pursue the development of a videotape competence passed the three tests outlined here. RCA's decision in the late

1970s to develop a stylus-based video turntable system did not.

Few companies are likely to build world leadership in more than five or six fundamental competencies. A company that compiles a list of 20 to 30 capabilities has probably not produced a list of core competencies. Still, it is probably a good discipline to generate a list of this sort and to see aggregate capabilities as building blocks. This tends to prompt the search for licensing deals and alliances through which the company may acquire, at low cost, the missing pieces.

Most western companies hardly think about competitiveness in these terms at all. It is time to take a tough-minded look at the risks they are running. Companies that judge competitiveness, their own and their competitors', primarily in terms of the price/performance of end products are courting the erosion of core competencies – or making too little effort to enhance them. The embedded skills that give rise to the next generation of competitive products cannot be 'rented in' by outsourcing and original equipment manufacturer (OEM) supply relationships. In our view, too many companies have unwittingly surrendered core competencies when they cut internal investment in what they mistakenly thought were just 'cost centres' in favour of outside suppliers.

Of course, it is perfectly possible for a company to have a competitive product line up but be a laggard in developing core competencies – at least for a while. If a company wanted to enter the copier business today, it would find a dozen Japanese companies more than willing to supply copiers on the basis of an OEM private label. But when fundamental technologies changed or if its supplier decided to enter the market directly and become a competitor, that company's product line, along with all of its investments in marketing and distribution, could be vulnerable. Outsourcing can provide a shortcut to a more competitive product, but it typically contributes little to building the people-embodied skills that are needed to sustain product leadership.

Nor is it possible for a company to have an intelligent alliance or sourcing strategy if it has not made a choice about where it will build competence leadership. Clearly, Japanese companies have benefited from alliances. They've used them to learn from western partners who were not fully committed to preserving core competencies of their own. Learning within an alliance takes a positive commitment of resources– travel, a pool of dedicated people, test-bed facilities, time to internalize and test what has been learned.

A company may not make this effort if it doesn't have clear goals for competence building.

Another way of losing is forgoing opportunities to establish competencies that are evolving in existing businesses. In the 1970s and 1980s, many American and European companies – like General Electric, Motorola, GTE, Thorn, and General Electric Company (GEC) – chose to exit the colour television business, which they regard as mature. If by 'mature' they meant that they had run out of new product ideas at precisely the moment global rivals had targeted the TV business for entry, then yes, the industry was mature. But it certainly wasn't mature in the sense that all opportunities to enhance and apply video-based competencies had been exhausted.

In ridding themselves of their television businesses, these companies failed to distinguish between divesting the business and destroying their video media-based competencies. They not only got out of the TV business but they also closed the door on a whole stream of future opportunities reliant on video-based competencies.

There are two clear lessons here. First, the costs of losing a core competence can be only partly calculated in advance. The baby may be thrown out with the bath water in divestment decisions. Second, since core competencies are built through a process of continuous improvement and enhancement that may span a decade or longer, a company that has failed to invest in core competence building will find it very difficult to enter an emerging market, unless, of course, it will be content simply to serve as a distribution channel.

American semiconductor companies like Motorola learned this painful lesson when they elected to forgo direct participation in the 256k generation of DRAM chips. Having skipped this round, Motorola, like most of its American competitors, needed a large infusion of technical help from Japanese partners to rejoin the battle in the 1-megabyte generation. When it comes to core competencies, it is difficult to get off the train, walk to the next station, and then reboard.

From core competencies to core products

The tangible link between identified core competencies and end products is what we call the core products – the physical embodiments of one or more core competencies. Honda's engines, for example, are core products, linchpins between design and development skills that ultimately lead to a proliferation of end products. Core products are the components or subassemblies that actually contribute to the value of the end products. Thinking in terms of core products forces a company to distinguish between the brand share it achieves in end product markets (for example, 40 per cent of the US refrigerator market) and the manufacturing share it achieves in any particular core product (for example, 5 per cent of the world share of compressor output).

It is essential to make this distinction between core competencies, core products, and end products because global competition is played out by different rules and for different stakes at each level. To build or defend leadership over the long term, a corporation will probably be a winner at each level. At the level of core competence, the goal is to build world leadership in the design and development of a particular class of product functionality – be it compact data storage and retrieval, as with Philips's optical-media competence, or compactness and ease of use, as with Sony's micromotors and microprocessor controls.

To sustain leadership in their chosen core competence areas, these companies *seek to maximize their world manufacturing share in core products.* The manufacture of core products for a wide variety of external (and internal) customers yields the revenue and market feedback that, at least partly, determines the pace at which core competencies can be enhanced and extended. This thinking was behind JVC's decision in the mid-1970s to establish VCR supply relationships with leading national consumer electronics companies in Europe and the United States. In supplying Thomson, Thorn, and Telefunken (all independent companies at that time) as well as US partners, JVC was able to gain the cash and the diversity of market experience that ultimately enabled it to outpace Philips and Sony. (Philips developed videotape competencies in parallel with JVC, but it failed to build a world-wide network of OEM relationships that would have allowed it to accelerate the refinement of its videotape competence through the sale of core products.)

JVC's success has not been lost on Korean companies like Goldstar, Samsung, Kia, and Daewoo, who are building core product leadership in areas as diverse as displays, semiconductors, and automotive engines through their OEM-supply contracts with western companies. Their avowed goal is to capture investment initiative away from potential competitors, often US companies. In doing so, they accelerate their competence-building efforts while 'hollowing out' their competitors. By focusing on competence and embedding it in core products, Asian competitors have built up advantages in component markets first and have then leveraged off their superior products to move downstream to build brand share. And they are not likely to remain the low-cost suppliers forever. As their reputation for brand leadership is consolidated, they may well gain price leadership. Honda has proven this with its Acura line, and other Japanese carmakers are following suit.

Control over core products is critical for other reasons. A dominant position in core products allows a company to shape the evolution of applications and end markets. Such compact audio disc-related core products as data drives and lasers have enabled Sony and Philips to influence the evolution of the computer-peripheral business in optical-media storage. As a company multiplies the number of application arenas for its core products, it can consistently reduce the cost, time, and risk in new product development. In short, well-targeted core products can lead to economies of scale and scope.

The tyranny of the SBU

The new terms of competitive engagement cannot be understood using analytical tools devised to manage the diversified corporation of 20 years ago, when competition was primarily domestic (GE versus Westinghouse, General Motors versus Ford) and all the key players were speaking the language of the same business schools and consultancies. Old prescriptions have potentially toxic side effects. The need for new principles is most obvious in companies organized

exclusively according to the logic of SBUs. The implications of the two alternate concepts of the corporation are summarized in Table 6.2.1.

Obviously, diversified corporations have a portfolio of products and a portfolio of businesses. But we believe in a view of the company as a portfolio of competencies as well. United States companies do not lack the technical resources to build competencies, but their top management often lacks the vision to build them and the administrative means for assembling resources spread across multiple businesses. A shift in commitment will inevitably influence patterns of diversification, skill deployment, resource allocation priorities, and approaches to alliances and outsourcing.

We have described the three different planes on which battles for global leadership are waged: core competence, core products, and end products. A corporation has to know whether it is winning or losing on each plane. By sheer weight of investment, a company might be able to beat its rivals to blue-sky technologies yet still lose the race to build core competence leadership. If a company is winning the race to build core competencies (as opposed to building leadership in a few technologies), it will almost certainly outpace rivals in new business development. If a company is winning the race to capture world manufacturing share in core products, it will probably outpace rivals in improving product features and the price/performance ratio.

Determining whether one is winning or losing end-product battles is more difficult because measures of

TABLE 6.2.1 Two concepts of the corporation

	SBU	Core competence
Basis for competition	Competiveness of today's products	Interfirm competition to build competencies
Corporate structure	Portfolio of businesses related in product-market terms	Portfolio of competencies, core products, and businesses
Status of the business unit	Autonomy is sacrosanct; the SBU 'owns' all resources other than cash	SBU is a potential reservoir of core competencies
Resource allocation	Discrete businesses are the unit of analysis; capital is allocated business by business	Businesses and competencies are the unit of analysis: top management allocates capital and talent
Value added of top management	Optimizing corporate returns through capital allocation trade-offs among businesses	Enunciating strategic architecture and building competencies to secure the future

product market share do not necessarily reflect various companies' underlying competitiveness. Indeed, companies that attempt to build market share by relying on the competitiveness of others, rather than investing in core competencies and world core-product leadership, may be treading on quicksand. In the race for global brand dominance, companies like 3M, Black & Decker, Canon, Honda, NEC, and Citicorp have built global brand umbrellas by proliferating products out of their core competencies. This has allowed their individual businesses to build image, customer loyalty, and access to distribution channels.

When you think about this reconceptualization of the corporation, the primacy of the SBU – an organizational dogma for a generation – is now clearly an anachronism. Where the SBU is an article of faith, resistance to the seductions of decentralization can seem heretical. In many companies, the SBU prism means that only one plane of the global competitive battle, the battle to put competitive products on the shelf *today*, is visible to top management. What are the costs of this distortion?

Underinvestment in developing core competencies and core products

When the organization is conceived of as a multiplicity of SBUs, no single business may feel responsible for maintaining a viable position in core products or be able to justify the investment required to build world leadership in some core competence. In the absence of a more comprehensive view imposed by corporate management, SBU managers will tend to underinvest. Recently, companies such as Kodak and Philips have recognized this as a potential problem and have begun searching for new organizational forms that will allow them to develop and manufacture core products for both internal and external customers.

SBU managers have traditionally conceived of competitors in the same way they've seen themselves. On the whole, they've failed to note the emphasis Asian competitors were placing on building leadership in core products or to understand the critical linkage between world manufacturing leadership and the ability to sustain development pace in core competence. They've failed to pursue OEM-supply opportunities or to look across their various product divisions in an attempt to identify opportunities for coordinated initiatives.

Imprisoned resources

As an SBU evolves, it often develops unique competencies. Typically, the people who embody this competence are seen as the sole property of the business in which they grew up. The manager of another SBU who asks to borrow talented people is likely to get a cold rebuff. SBU managers are not only unwilling to lend their competence carriers but they may actually hide talent to prevent its redeployment in the pursuit of new opportunities. This may be compared to residents of an underdeveloped country hiding most of their cash under their mattresses. The benefits of competencies, like the benefits of the money supply, depend on the velocity of their circulation as well as on the size of the stock the company holds.

Western companies have traditionally had an advantage in the stock of skills they possess. But have they been able to reconfigure them quickly to respond to new opportunities? Canon, NEC, and Honda have had a lesser stock of the people and technologies that compose core competencies but could move them much quicker from one business unit to another. Corporate R&D spending at Canon is not fully indicative of the size of Canon's core competence stock and tells the casual observer nothing about the velocity with which Canon is able to move core competencies to exploit opportunities.

When competencies become imprisoned, the people who carry the competencies do not get assigned to the most exciting opportunities, and their skills begin to atrophy. Only by fully leveraging core competencies can small companies like Canon afford to compete with industry giants like Xerox. How strange that SBU managers, who are perfectly willing to compete for cash in the capital budgeting process, are unwilling to compete for people – the company's most precious asset. We find it ironic that top management devotes so much attention to the capital budgeting process yet typically has no comparable mechanism for allocating the human skills that embody core competencies. Top managers are seldom able to look four or five levels down into the organization, identify the people who embody critical competencies, and move them across organizational boundaries.

Bounded innovation

If core competencies are not recognized, individual SBUs will pursue only those innovation opportunities that are close at hand – marginal product-line extensions or geographic expansions. Hybrid opportunities like fax machines, laptop computers, handheld televisions, or portable music keyboards will emerge only when managers take off their SBU blinkers. Remember, Canon appeared to be in the camera business at the time it was preparing to become a world leader in copiers. Conceiving of the corporation in terms of core competencies widens the domain of innovation.

Developing strategic architecture

The fragmentation of core competencies becomes inevitable when a diversified company's information systems, patterns of communication, career paths, managerial rewards, and processes of strategy development do not transcend SBU lines. We believe that senior management should spend a significant amount of its time developing a corporate-wide strategic architecture that establishes objectives for competence-building. A strategic architecture is a road map of the future that identifies which core competencies to build and their constituent technologies.

By providing an impetus for learning from alliances and a focus for internal development efforts, a strategic architecture like NEC's C&C (computers and communication) can dramatically reduce the investment needed to secure future market leadership. How can a company make partnerships intelligently without a clear understanding of the core competencies it is trying to build and those it is attempting to prevent from being unintentionally transferred?

Of course, all of this begs the question of what a strategic architecture should look like. The answer will be different for every company. But it is helpful to think again of that tree, of the corporation organized around core products and, ultimately, core competencies. To sink sufficiently strong roots, a company must answer some fundamental questions: How long could we preserve our competitiveness in this business if we did not control this particular core competence? How central is this core competence to perceived customer benefits? What future opportunities would be foreclosed if we were to lose this particular competence?

The architecture provides a logic for product and market diversification, moreover. An SBU manager would be asked: Does the new market opportunity add to the overall goal of becoming the best player in the world? Does it exploit or add to the core competence? At Vickers, for example, diversification options have been judged in the context of becoming the best power and motion control company in the world.

The strategic architecture should make resource allocation priorities transparent to the entire organization. It provides a template for allocation decisions by top management. It helps lower-level managers understand the logic of allocation priorities and disciplines senior management to maintain consistency. In short, it yields a definition of the company and the markets it serves. 3M, Vickers, NEC, Canon, and Honda all qualify on this score. Honda knew it was exploiting what it had learned from motorcycles – how to make high-revving, smooth-running, lightweight engines – when it entered the car business. The task of creating a strategic architecture forces the organization to identify and commit to the technical and production linkages across SBUs that will provide a distinct competitive advantage.

It is consistency of resource allocation and the development of an administrative infrastructure appropriate to it that breathes life into a strategic architecture and creates a managerial culture, teamwork, a capacity to change, and a willingness to share resources, to protect proprietary skills, and to think long term. That is also the reason the specific architecture cannot be copied easily or overnight by competitors. Strategic architecture is a tool for communicating with customers and other external constituents. It reveals the broad direction without giving away every step.

Redeploying to exploit competencies

If the company's core competencies are its critical resource and if top management must ensure that competence carriers are not held hostage by some particular business, then it follows that SBUs should bid for core competencies in the same way they bid for capital. We've made this point glancingly. It is important enough to consider more deeply.

Once top management (with the help of divisional and SBU managers) has identified overarching competencies, it must ask businesses to identify the projects and people closely connected with them. Corporate officers should direct an audit of the location, number, and quality of the people who embody competence.

This sends an important signal to middle managers: core competencies are corporate resources and may be reallocated by *corporate* management. An individual business doesn't own anybody. SBUs are entitled to the services of individual employees so long as SBU management can demonstrate that the opportunity it is pursuing yields the highest possible payoff on the investment in their skills. This message is further underlined if each year in the strategic planning or budgeting process, unit managers must justify their hold on the people who carry the company's core competencies.

Also, reward systems that focus only on product-line results and career paths that seldom cross SBU boundaries engender patterns of behaviour among unit managers that are destructively competitive. At NEC, divisional managers come together to identify next-generation competencies. Together they decide how much investment needs to be made to build up each future competence and the contribution in capital and staff support that each division will need to make. There is also a sense of equitable exchange. One division may make a disproportionate contribution or may benefit less from the progress made, but such short-term inequalities will balance out over the long term.

Incidentally, the positive contribution of the SBU manager should be made visible across the company. An SBU manager is unlikely to surrender key people if only the other business (or the general manager of that business who may be a competitor for promotion) is going to benefit from the redeployment. Cooperative SBU managers should be celebrated as team players. Where priorities are clear, transfers are less likely to be seen as idiosyncratic and politically motivated.

Transfers for the sake of building core competence must be recorded and appreciated in the corporate memory. It is reasonable to expect a business that has surrendered core skills on behalf of corporate opportunities in other areas to lose, for a time, some of its competitiveness. If these losses in performance bring immediate censure, SBUs will be unlikely to assent to skills transfers next time.

Finally, there are ways to wean key employees off the idea that they belong in perpetuity to any particular business. Early in their careers, people may be exposed to a variety of businesses through a carefully planned rotation programme.

Competence carriers should be regularly brought together from across the corporation to trade notes and ideas. The goal is to build a strong feeling of community among these people. To a great extent, their loyalty should be to the integrity of the core competence area they represent and not just to particular businesses. In travelling regularly, talking frequently to customers, and meeting with peers, competence carriers may be encouraged to discover new market opportunities.

Core competencies are the wellspring of new business development. They should constitute the focus for strategy at the corporate level. Managers have to win manufacturing leadership in core products and capture global share through brand-building programmes aimed at exploiting economies of scope. Only if the company is conceived of as a hierarchy of core competencies, core products, and market-focused business units will it be fit to fight.

Nor can top management be just another layer of accounting consolidation, which it often is in a regime of radical decentralization. Top management must add value by enunciating the strategic architecture that guides the competence acquisition process. We believe an obsession with competence building will characterize the global winners of the 1990s. With the decade underway, the time for rethinking the concept of the corporation is already overdue.

READING
6.3

Understanding acquisition integration approaches

By Philippe Haspeslagh and David Jemison[1]

The senior members of a management team of an historically successful firm were discussing their experiences in integrating acquisitions outside their base business. When the chairman asked the

[1]Source: This article was adapted with permission from with permission *Managing Acquisitions: Creating Value Through Corporate Renewal* by Philippe C. Haspeslagh and David B. Jemison. 1991.

management team what integration meant, the consensus answer was, 'Integrating an acquisition means making them like us.' Although that approach may be appropriate in a few instances, the chairman's reaction reflected the frustration felt by many senior executives involved in diversification activities: 'How can we do anything different with an attitude like this?'

Integration clearly means different things to different people. Most importantly, it means different things in different situations. While there are common ingredients in the process, each acquisition presents managers with a different situation and forces a choice of integration approach. Earlier writers on acquisitions have suggested several distinctions that affect the type of integration approach. For example, it has been argued that differences in the integration task are based on the relative size of the acquired firm, the acquired firm's profitability, whether the synergies are in marketing or manufacturing, and whether the cultures are similar or not. But when we compared the detailed observations from our research with such distinctions, none by itself provided a sufficient explanation of the range of integration phenomena we observed.

Our research identified two key dimensions that led to a broad logic for choosing an integration approach. This reading examines those dimensions and presents the three integration approaches that correspond to these contexts. We do not suggest that there is one best way to integrate each acquisition. Good performance is also affected by consistency and discipline in execution of what is ultimately a managerial choice. But we do advocate carefully choosing an integration approach based on the analysis of a number of key factors and then remaining flexible to adapt the approach as events unfold. In this reading we will emphasize a logic to guide integration choices and the analysis on which it can be based.

Key dimensions in acquisition integration

A firm's approach to integration can be understood by considering two central dimensions of the acquisition – its relationship to the acquiring firm and the way in which value is expected to be created. The first dimension relates to the nature of the interdependence that needs to be established between the firms to make possible the type of strategic capability transfer that is expected. The other dimension is associated with the need to preserve intact the acquired strategic capabilities after the acquisition.

Strategic interdependence need

The essential task in any acquisition is to create the value that becomes possible when the two organizations are combined, value that would not exist if the firms operated separately. The analysis, negotiation, and internal selling of an acquisition candidate and ultimately the premium offered are all predicated on this central idea. Yet managers often shy away from the integration task because of uncertainties about the fundamentals of the acquired business, because of organizational or cultural differences, or because of a fear that they will be resisted.

Capability transfer requires creating and managing interdependencies between both organizations. These interdependencies disturb the 'boundary' of the acquired company, that invisible line that distinguishes them from the acquirer. This disturbance is likely to be resented, if not resisted, by managers in the acquired firm, who want to keep their identity and their way of doing things. To transfer capabilities between firms and overcome possible resistance requires that the interdependence between the two firms be carefully managed. Thus, a key determinant of the integration task is the nature of the interdependence between the two firms and how that interdependence is to be managed.

The nature of the interdependence in an acquisition depends on how value will be created. We discuss three types of capability transfer (resource sharing, functional skill transfer, and general management capability transfer), as well as a number of combination benefits. Each of these four benefits implies different requirements for interdependence and, thus, for the degree to which the boundary of the acquired organization will have to be disturbed and eliminated, and, conversely, the degree to which the organizational identity of the original company should be maintained.

Some acquisitions are based primarily on *resource sharing*, which involves the combination and rationalization of operating assets. Resource sharing implies an integration process that completely dissolves the boundaries between the two subparts of the organizations that are to be rationalized. In resource sharing, value is created by combining the entities at the operating level, so that functional overlaps and duplication are eliminated. The greater efficiency of the streamlined operations is supposed to outweigh any costs associated with the rationalization. Such costs include not only those of a one-time rationalization of the firms, but also the harder-to-measure ongoing consequences of a loss of specialized focus and commitment that might derive from combining both operations.

The integration process is inherently different if the strategic capability transfer involves the *transfer of functional skills.* Skills reside in individuals, groups of people, and their procedures and practices, not in assets. They can be transferred only as people are moved across organizational boundaries or when information, knowledge, and know-how are shared. For example, the R&D capability of a chemical firm can be transferred to an acquired firm through a variety of mechanisms, including coordinated management of the R&D functions, transfer of R&D scientists in both directions, or transfer of the products or processes that are the outcome of such R&D. Although each organization retains a distinct presence in the function in question, continuing interference and involvement (or potential interference) from the acquiring company's corresponding functional managers impinge on the acquired company managers' autonomy. Because that boundary disruption comes about through essentially horizontal rather than hierarchical interactions, it is often regarded as illegitimate by the acquired managers, who want to preserve the integrity of what they still see as their firm. The transfer of *general management capability* can create value through improved strategic or operational insight, coordination, or control. These improvements can be achieved partly through direct, substantive involvement in general management decisions, or on a more permanent basis through the installation and use of systems, controls, budgets, and plans that improve both the strategic decision making and the operational efficiency of acquired management.

General management capability transfer was seen as somewhat less disruptive than the other types of strategic capability transfer. Direct involvement by hierarchical superiors was considered more legitimate than the involvement of functional counterparts from the acquirer, and after the one-time disruption of changes in systems, life inside the acquired unit could go on without further boundary disruption. Nevertheless, disruption did occur. For example, managers in the acquired firms typically regarded being subjected to the discipline of formal investment approval as a loss of freedom, even when no projects had been turned down or, to the contrary, accelerated investment had been encouraged.

Finally, any acquisition brings with it a number of *combination benefits* that are available automatically as a result of the combination and are not related to

capability transfer. Some acquisitions may yield excess cash resources or borrowing capacity between the firms. In others, benefits may come from greater size, whether through the added purchasing power it provides, or through the greater market power that size brings. The merger between Metal Box of the UK and Carnaud of France, for example, to create CMB, one of the larger packaging firms in the world, had a clear impact on the bargaining position of Metal Box vis-à-vis British Steel, its main source of tin-plated steel. Not only did the combined firm become the largest European customer for a product that had long been cartelized by suppliers, but it also gave Metal Box access to Carnaud's integrated capacity. Given Metal Box's prior size, the immediate cost savings on its existing volume were not dramatic, but it was able to channel its new bargaining power into obtaining much more important quality and on-time delivery benefits. At the same time CMB is continuing to make acquisitions of smaller firms, and with them opportunities for a significant raw materials cost saving.

Any individual acquisition may involve benefits from several of these sources. Yet our research suggests that in most cases, independent of the variety and number of possible synergies, it is possible, and advisable, to recognize one type of capability transfer as the *dominant* source of initial value creation.

Formally assessing the strategic interdependence needs of an acquisition has several important benefits. It helps managers develop a more unbiased, objective view of the strategic task involved in creating value with the acquisition irrespective of the ease or difficulty of implementation. At the same time, by categorizing these strategic tasks in a way that reflects the required extent of interdependence, managers can go beyond identifying potential areas of synergy and examine the organizational tasks that will be needed to bring out the expected benefits. Finally, by considering only those interdependencies regarded as critical for achieving the benefits upon which the acquisition was originally justified, managers can begin to develop a clearer sense of the strategic and organizational tradeoffs involved. Before making these trade-offs, however, the organizational factors that are central to the integration process must be addressed.

Organizational autonomy need

Because we regard strategic capability transfer as the precursor to value creation, it is clearly vital to preserve the strategic capability that is to be transferred. Yet one of the paradoxes in acquisitions is that the pursuit of capability transfer itself may lead to the destruction of the capability being transferred. Whereas capability transfer requires different degrees of boundary disruption or dissolution, the preservation of capabilities requires boundary protection and, hence, organizational autonomy.

This paradox is especially evident in acquisitions where the acquired capabilities reside in people or groups of people. The disintegration of many of the financial firms that were acquired in London during the build-up to 'Big Bang' in 1986 is an example of this problem. Key people may decide to leave simply because, as we discussed earlier, they feel that value has been destroyed for them. At the heart of this problem is the issue of boundary management. Demands for organizational autonomy and 'no change' are present in every acquisition. They come from the deep-seated identification of managers, employees, and other organizational stakeholders with their original organization.

All too often, acquiring managers respond to these demands for autonomy by promising whatever it takes to make acquired managers 'accept' the takeover. They then often shroud their promises in the illusion that all expected benefits of an acquisition will be realized without any disruptive changes. For example, a dispute over the integration of Blue Arrow, the British temporary services company, with its American acquisition of Manpower, Inc. in the United States led to the resignation of Manpower's CEO. The chairman of Blue Arrow said that it was time to look for 'back office synergies and cost savings'. At the same time, he hastily added that he would not change Manpower's culture or the way its services were marketed (*New York Times*, 6 December 1998, p. 23). Statements such as this are often made for public consumption or to soothe the apprehensions of acquired managers and employees. But, as experienced acquirers well know, this sort of schizophrenic attitude often paves the way for the reverse: organizational upheaval with synergies left unrealized.

We indicated earlier that most of the organizational behaviour and corporate culture research on acquisitions has focused on the issue of the impact on people and their acceptance of the acquisition. The assumption often seems to be that in an acquisition no one should be disturbed or have 'bad' things happen to them. We, too, believe that people are important in an acquisition and we believe they should be treated fairly and with dignity. But if managers lose sight of the fact that the strategic task of an acquisition is to create

value, they may either grant autonomy too quickly or fall into the perilous 'no change-all synergies expected' syndrome described above. Managers and employees in acquired firms are too smart to be fooled by this syndrome.

Dealing with the perceived need for autonomy after an acquisition is one of the most important challenges a manager will face. The manager should not deviate from the strategic task – transferring capabilities to create value – unless the argument for autonomy corresponds to a real need for boundary protection. Such a real need exists when the strategic capabilities whose transfer is key to the acquisition are embedded in a distinct organization and culture and that distinction is central to the preservation of those capabilities. That is, the other firm may have been acquired precisely because it is different.

Managers in acquiring firms can consider the need for organizational autonomy in more practical terms by examining three questions: Is autonomy essential to preserve the strategic capability we bought? If so, how much autonomy should be allowed? In which areas specifically is autonomy important?

Regarding the first question, our research suggests that autonomy should be provided the acquired unit if the survival of the strategic capabilities on which the acquisition is based depends on preservation of the organizational culture from which they came. The important question, thus, is *not* how different the two cultures are, but whether *maintaining that difference* in the long term will serve a useful purpose. For example, when BASF, the German chemical giant, bought American Enka's petrochemical operations from Akzo in 1985, its main purpose was to improve the raw materials supply position of its fibre business through acquisition of the Enka plant. The economics of that facility depended very little on the organizational culture of American Akzo.

On the other hand, when BASF bought the Celanese advanced composites materials businesses in that same year, the situation was very different. The very success of that acquisition depended on BASF's ability to keep intact both the entrepreneurial culture of the former Celanese organization and its links with important aerospace and defence clients – substantial challenges for a large foreign acquirer. In such cases, allowing sufficient autonomy to preserve the acquired capabilities constitutes more than a tactic to gain acceptance and placate employees. It is vital to the success of the acquisition.

If there is a genuine need to maintain autonomy, managers must next consider whether the capabilities are widely spread or fairly isolated in the acquired organization. At one end of the spectrum the strategic capability may be embedded in a particular subunit of the organization. For example, a particular firm's value for the acquirer may derive from a specific R&D capability that, although highly dependent on a sub-culture within the R&D department, is fairly unrelated to the rest of the organization, from which it can be 'extracted'. In contrast, an acquired firm's value may depend on more generalized capabilities that extend well beyond a particular department to involve the entire organization. In the acquisition of the Beatrice companies by ICI, for example, the value of companies like LNP and Fiberite was based on the fact that they were close to the (leading edge) US market, solution oriented, and entrepreneurial, properties that were spread throughout the organization. Another illustration is seen in the comment of the managing director of BP Nutrition, who, in the purchase of Hendrix, a Dutch animal feed company, realized that Hendrix had a very different dynamic and was most concerned about 'keeping their flywheel going', because BP would not be able to start it again.

These considerations allowed us to distinguish among the acquisitions we studied in terms of their need for autonomy. In some situations, company-wide autonomy was needed because the acquirer had virtually no experience in the business and the particular skills sought were inseparable from the culture in which they were rooted. In others, the protection of important, functionally embedded capabilities was needed, whereas other parts of the organization were less sensitive to change. Finally, in some situations the organizational differences were not at the root of the targeted benefits and hence change would not prejudice the realization of the benefits.

Managers may not always have the information to judge how different the cultures and subcultures of both organizations are before they experience those differences. Yet, we suggest, an early focus on which strategic capabilities need to be preserved, to what extent they depend on maintaining a cultural difference, and to what extent they can be contained in a subpart of the organization focus will be of critical importance in choosing an integration approach. This focus can help managers distinguish between the strategic needs of the situation and the desire of the acquired firm's management to retain its independence. It can also help to clarify the trade-offs at stake in granting or refusing autonomy to an acquired firm and help managers define decision rules for action in each setting.

Types of integration approaches

While understanding the distinctive needs for strategic interdependence and organizational autonomy can offer insights, considering them in a combined fashion helps suggest specific approaches to integration. Figure 6.3.1 positions integration approaches in light of the relationships between these two key factors. Some acquisitions have a high need for strategic interdependence, and a low need for organizational autonomy. These acquisitions call for what we label an *absorption* approach to integration. Other acquisitions, to the contrary, present a low need for strategic interdependence but a high need for organizational autonomy. We will call the integration approach associated with these acquisitions *preservation*. Other acquisitions are characterized by high needs for interdependence and high needs for organizational autonomy. We will use the term *symbiosis* to describe the integration approach called for in such acquisitions.

These three acquisition integration approaches represent, in our experience, useful metaphors to guide the integration task. In practice, of course, the degree of strategic interdependence and of organizational autonomy present in an acquisition integration depends on the choices managers make about how they perceive those respective needs.

The usefulness of choosing an overall metaphor for an acquisition integration does not change the fact that acquisitions bring with them many positions and capabilities, the integration of which, seen in more detailed perspective, might be best served by a different approach. A detailed analysis of the autonomy needs and interdependence needs of the main components of the acquisition helps a company determine how, within the dominant metaphor, they can try to differentiate the approach to each capability. The choice between the compromise of a fairly blanket approach and a tailor-made differentiation depends on the capability of the organization to implement the integration approach it chooses. We will describe each of these approaches more fully.

None of the acquisitions in our sample fell into the fourth quadrant in Figure 6.3.1, which could be labelled as 'holding' acquisitions: These would be acquisitions where the firm has no intention of integrating and creating value through anything except financial transfers, risk-sharing, or general management capability, even though the two firms are presumably in such similar businesses that there is no need for organizational autonomy. The only integration in such

---

FIGURE 6.3.1   Types of acquisition integration approaches

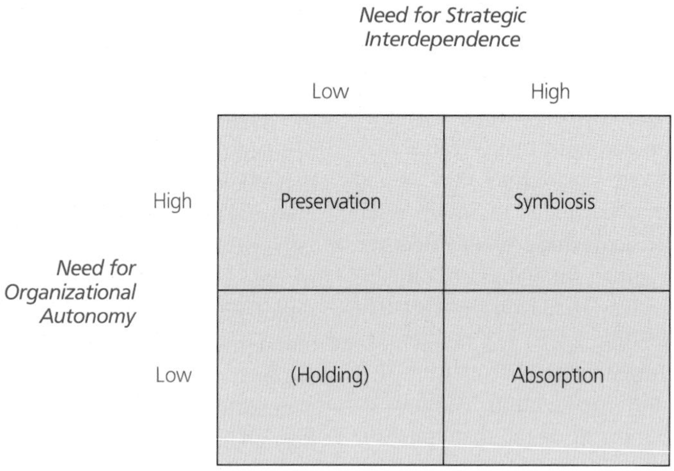

---

acquisitions would, in a sense, be a mere holding activity. Given our research focus on strategic acquirers, it is not surprising that we did not encounter such acquisitions. Nevertheless, it is conceivable that such acquisitions exist. The situation of Triangle Industries, which had acquired both National Can and American Can before selling them off to the French company, Pechiney, is an example. Another is the acquisition and simultaneous holding by the financial firm McAndrews and Forbes of Revlon, Max Factor, and Barnes-Hinds, three firms in similar businesses, which were kept completely at arm's-length from each other. Such acquisitions would be made in a value-capturing perspective, as in the example of Triangle, or value creation would be based solely on the introduction of better general management.

Understanding these differences is a precondition to managing them successfully.

Absorption acquisitions

Absorption acquisitions are those in which the strategic task requires a high degree of interdependence to create the value expected but has a low need for organizational autonomy to achieve that interdependence. Integration in this case implies a full consolidation, over time, of the operations, organization, and culture of both organizations.

To eliminate all differences between both original companies may take a very long time indeed, especially if one is not just folding a small unit into a large one, but combining two sizable companies in the same businesses. The distinction that matters is one of intent at the outset: in absorption acquisitions the objective is ultimately to dissolve the boundary between both units. In this light, the key integration issue becomes a question of timing rather than how much integration should take place. In absorption acquisitions the acquiring company needs the courage of its convictions to ensure that its vision for the acquisition is carried out. Wavering because of extreme sensitivity to cultural issues is likely to limit the firm's ability to get the value expected, because the management task is to bring about the interdependence of the firms.

A recognition that the decisions can be tough but necessary is illustrated by the challenge facing ICI's Agrochemicals division after the acquisition of Stauffer. The two companies had a large degree of overlap in their sales territory in the United States. Each was set up to sell and market different products to essentially the same farmers. One company had a very direct sales approach, using its own sales force, whereas the other used independent wholesalers to provide sales and service to farmers. Whether and how to integrate the sales function and according to which model were clearly crucial and complex questions, worthy of detailed analysis. Yet a decision about whether to integrate or not had to be made very quickly. In this seasonal business, product turmoil during the crucial ordering period could mean the loss of an entire year.

Preservation acquisitions

In the preservation acquisitions there is a high need for autonomy and a low need for interdependence among the combining firms. In such situations the primary task of management is to keep the source of the acquired benefits intact, because deterioration in the acquired (and sometimes acquiring) company's ways of managing, practices, or even motivation would endanger success. Even though needs for interdependence are low in preservation acquisitions, this sort of autonomy and the protection it implies are often difficult to provide. In these situations the acquired operations are managed at arm's-length beyond those specific areas in which interdependence is to be pursued. The latter typically consist of financial/risk sharing and general management capability transfer to the extent that such capability is not industry-dependent.

In preservation acquisitions it is important to understand how sufficient value can be created to off-set the acquisition premiums paid. The typical conception is that the main benefit is to be derived from the ability to bring funding to the acquired company. However, in the successful preservation cases we studied, money was not the main factor. In fact, all were successful enough to finance their own development completely. In these cases, value was created through a series of interactions that brought about positive changes in the ambition, risk-taking, and professionalism of the acquired company's management group. The metaphor that best captures the way value is created in preservation acquisitions is that of *nurturing*.

Nurturing the acquired firm represents only part of the value-creation potential that may be realized through a preservation approach. Another important source of value creation, which we will discuss later, is the *learning* that for the acquiring company might derive, both in terms of making further acquisitions in the newly explored area and in terms of learning for its base businesses. This learning is typically central to the purpose in the case of platform acquisitions. Exxon's ill-fated acquisitions in electronics companies; BP's entry into the nutrition business; the acquisition of Burndy, the American connector manufacturer, by Framatome, the French nuclear company; and the acquisitive development of Lafarge-Coppée New Materials' division into decorative paints are all examples of situations requiring preservation.

Symbiotic acquisitions

The third type of acquisition integration approach presents the most complex managerial challenges. Symbiotic acquisitions involve high needs for both strategic interdependence (because substantial capability transfer must take place) and organizational autonomy (because the acquired capabilities need to be preserved in an organizational context that is different from the acquirer's).

In symbiotic acquisitions the two organizations first coexist and then gradually become increasingly interdependent. This coexistence and mutual dependency are slowly achieved despite the tension arising from the conflicting needs for strategic capability transfer and the maintenance of each organization's autonomy and culture. Symbiotic acquisitions need simultaneous boundary preservation and boundary permeability. These needs can be kept in balance by protecting the boundary between both firms that shields the broad identity and character of the acquired firm at the same time that it is becoming increasingly permeable to a whole series of interactions aimed at functional as well as general management skill transfer.

The needs to preserve autonomy in symbiotic acquisitions can be gradually lifted only to the extent that the acquired company itself changes its own organizational practices to adapt to the new situation. To succeed in truly amalgamating the organizations symbiotically, each firm must take on the original qualities of the other.

Impact of other differences

The dual needs for strategic interdependence and organizational autonomy captured were by far the most important factors that we observed determining the integration approach. Two other factors, the quality and size of the acquired firm, were also found important. But, we suggest, the role these factors play in shaping the nature of the integration process is not as great as the pressures that arise from the need for strategic interdependence and the need for organizational autonomy.

Seeking synergies

By Andrew Campbell and Michael Goold[1]

A review of synergy management can be triggered in a number of ways. A parent manager may suspect that co-ordination opportunities are being missed, but may not be sure what is being missed, how important it is, or what to do about it. A new chief executive may sense that his predecessor's emphasis on decentralization has led unit managers to overlook sharing opportunities. A visit to other companies that sing the praises of co-ordination may raise concerns about what is being missed. Critical press comments about the company's failure to achieve synergies across its portfolio may prompt questions about what more could be achieved. Given our concern about 'synergy bias', we counsel caution in following up vague disquiets. But an audit of how well synergy management is working can be a useful step in allaying fears or pinpointing areas that need to be addressed.

A review can also be triggered by grumbles at lower levels in the company that current co-ordination efforts are pointless or damaging or contradictory. Business managers may complain that short-term budget targets prevent them from exploring potentially valuable synergy opportunities or about the pointlessness of corporate-wide conferences at expensive resorts to promote 'family feeling'. Corridor gossip about the negative influence of the parent may percolate up to the chief executive. More direct complaints may be received from frustrated business managers. Bottom-up pressures to think again about a company's approach to synergies should be taken seriously, and, if there are widespread or deep-seated concerns, a systematic and objective stock-taking may be in order.

Some companies build a periodic review of their cross-company initiatives into their regular planning processes. We are less enthusiastic about this practice, since it can easily lead either to superficial, year-by-year reiteration of what everyone already knows about the areas of overlap between businesses or to vain attempts to come up with new ideas. Unless there is a particular reason to review linkage management, it will probably cause more frustration than enlightenment. On the whole, therefore, we believe that a review should only be undertaken when there are identifiable reasons for doing so.

Good reasons to take stock of the current approach include:

- a belief that a major category of synergies such as international rationalization, sharing technical know-how or joint development of new business opportunities, is being systematically missed;
- visible and costly failures of several recent synergy initiatives;
- evidence that business units are favouring links with third parties in preference to internal links.

While it would be useful to have a way of objectively deciding when a stock take is necessary, our experience suggests that it is best judged subjectively by thinking about how well the current organization is working.

The purpose of a review should be to decide whether changes are needed in the overall corporate approach to synergies; to identify any specific opportunities that merit closer investigations; and to propose possible new linkage mechanisms or interventions.

A framework for a review

Our review framework is shown in Figure 6.4.1. It involves taking stock of both synergy opportunities available and the current corporate approach to cross-company linkages. The effectiveness of the approach can be assessed by testing how well it fits with the opportunities. The assessment can then be used to pinpoint new initiatives that may be worth considering. The framework will bring out aspects of the overall approach that are working well or badly, and lead to proposals for changes.

[1]Source: This article was adapted from Chapter 7 of *Synergy: Why Links Between Business Units Often Fail and How to Make Them Work*. Reproduced with permission from John Wiley & Sons Ltd.

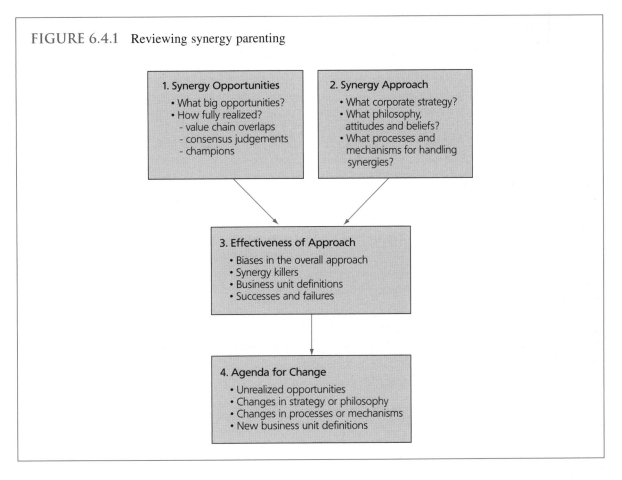

FIGURE 6.4.1 Reviewing synergy parenting

The value of the framework is that it obliges companies to address some fundamental questions:

■ What is our current attitude to co-ordination between our business units, and how do we go about managing it?

■ What do we believe are the main synergy opportunities in our portfolio, and how fully are we grasping them?

■ How well suited is our current approach, including structures, processes and staff support, to the opportunities we believe are on offer?

■ What current synergy initiatives should we drop, what new opportunities should we go for, and what changes in processes and mechanisms should we consider?

These questions can be asked of the whole company or of a multi-business division within a larger company. The framework is equally applicable when applied to any level above that of the individual business unit. However, when working at a division level, it is valuable to understand some of the broader corporate context in which the division is operating.

Although the framework provides a systematic means of tackling these questions, it should not be treated either as a straitjacket or a panacea. The emphasis of a review should depend on the concerns that prompted it. Is it primarily a matter of fine-tuning the current mechanisms and processes to work more smoothly, or are we more concerned with the underlying philosophy or structure of the company? Did we get into the review to beat the bushes to create a wide agenda of all possible new opportunities, or was it really a means of legitimizing a fresh look at one or two specific issues? With different motivations for the review, the weight given to different areas of analysis will vary, the order in which activities take place will be different, and the level of effort and speed of the review will change.

We also recognize that the structured framework we suggest may not appeal to all companies. Some may have a culture that stresses a more intuitive assessment of issues, and may find the analytical approach we propose too constraining. Others may have their own preferred analyses that we have not included in our framework. We recognize that our approach is not the only way to undertake a review of linkage parenting, and we advise each company to tailor its approach to its own needs, culture and preferences.

As we discuss the different steps in the framework, readers should accordingly view our proposals as building blocks from which to construct their own review process, rather than as an inflexible 'how to do it' manual. We have found the steps useful in our work with companies, but we are not dogmatic about the framework we put forward.

Synergy opportunities

The first step in the review involves developing a list of major synergy opportunities and judging how fully they are being realized. The purpose is to unearth any important opportunities that are not currently being successfully grasped. This may prompt ideas for changes in the overall approach or for specific new interventions.

To undertake detailed analysis for every linkage opportunity as part of a general review is clearly not feasible. It would take too long and cost too much. The challenge is to find efficient ways of homing in quickly on possible areas of high unexploited potential.

In our research, we have identified three useful prompts that can help to reveal neglected potential: rough modelling of value chain overlaps; interviews, focus groups or questionnaires designed to draw out consensus from business unit and parent managers; and identification of pet projects or initiatives that are being strongly championed by individual managers.

Value chain overlaps

Businesses with value chains that overlap, or could overlap, are obvious candidates for linkage opportunities. If two businesses purchase similar components, what benefits might be available by co-ordinating their purchases? If two businesses have overseas offices in the same country, what could be saved by sharing premises, salesforces, or management? We have found that rough modelling of the extent of overlaps and of the economies of scale or utilization available from sharing can rapidly yield a broad sizing of the benefits available in different areas. For example, a retail group was able to prioritize opportunities for joint purchasing

by assessing the extent of overlaps in different product ranges between two of their chains, and estimating the level of extra purchase discounts that would be available from combined buying. Back-of-the-envelope calculations showed that there were only two product ranges with significant overlaps and, thus, real prospects for achieving better terms. More detailed analysis then focussed on these prime candidates. Although there was nothing precise or sophisticated about the modelling that led to this conclusion, it was highly effective in narrowing down the opportunities to consider.

Even rough value chain modelling can, however, be hard to do or too time consuming at the review stage. The benefits may not yet be sufficiently well defined, or may be made up of several different component parts, or may be too numerous to analyse. An alternative is to rely on consensus judgements of informed managers.

Consensus judgement

When experienced managers agree that there is probably a worthwhile benefit to go for, their views deserve to be heard. If most of the marketing managers in different countries believe that they could benefit from sharing best practice in advertising, it is almost certainly worth trying to understand more about the opportunity. If, on the other hand, the corporate marketing director has suggested more sharing but the national marketing managers are lukewarm, it should probably be put on the backburner – at least unless the corporate director can argue convincingly that the national managers may be misjudging the opportunity. In the difficult field of synergies, the gut-feel and intuitive judgement of experienced managers should carry considerable weight.

In companies where information flows freely and managers are encouraged to express their views, it is comparatively easy for parent managers to discern an emerging consensus. In other companies, it can be much more difficult. Managers from different units may not meet together often enough to share views, or may not feel empowered to express their views to each other. They may also be constrained to follow prevailing corporate policies rather than challenge them. Whatever the reason, a structured approach to eliciting the consensus is frequently needed.

There are a variety of ways to draw out consensus judgements, ranging from questionnaires, through focus groups, to some form of systematic interviewing process. The method chosen needs to be tailored to the circumstances of the company – and we have adopted somewhat different methods in each of the companies we have worked with. In all cases, however, the objective is to discover whether informed managers generally feel that there are important unexplored opportunities going begging, and, if so, what priorities they should receive.

Championing

A third valuable prompt comes from championing. Strong and enthusiastic champions are important for the effective implementation of new interventions. We believe that they can also provide a short cut to identifying priority opportunity areas. If a manager feels so powerfully that an opportunity is worthwhile that he is willing to lobby for it, devote personal sweat equity to it, and risk the displeasure of his colleagues and bosses by repeatedly advocating it, it is usually worth taking notice.

There is little danger that strong champions will not be heard by the corporate parent. The danger is more that they will be too readily discounted. Persistent champions, particularly if their ideas challenge vested interests, can face strong opposition. Their views may be dismissed as unrealistic or irrelevant, or they may be labelled eccentrics or troublemakers. Prudent managers then pipe down, and learn to live with their frustrations. However, frustrated champions welcome any chance to promote their pet projects. A review of linkage parenting is a good opportunity to give them an objective hearing. Our advice is to listen carefully to what they have to say – even if the rest of the organization has long ago decided not to.

Creativity and realism

In drawing up the short-list of opportunities that merit detailed consideration, we need to balance creativity and open-mindedness with realism. We want managers with new ideas to come forward, we want to encourage brainstorming that will generate fresh thinking, we want to give a hearing to highly motivated champions. Especially if the purpose of the review is to make sure we're not missing something, we should be positive about new suggestions and supportive of 'thinking the unthinkable'.

We should also be willing to accept that some promising ideas may be clouded by considerable uncertainty. In Consco, for example, there was

widespread support for more sharing of best practice in training and management development. But the benefits available were somewhat nebulous. Some managers had fairly specific ideas about how course designs or materials could be shared better. Others were simply reflecting a sense that this was an increasingly important area, in which they did not feel that their units were doing a very good job. Some had anecdotes or examples to support their views. But there was considerable uncertainty about where the real opportunities lay and how they should be pursued. And, in some situations, there is intrinsic uncertainty about the nature of the benefits. In businesses in the middle of rapid technological change, such as media and communications, the benefits of collaborating to develop new businesses to some extent depend on market and technology developments that are simply not predictable. The review should encourage managers to put forward speculative or uncertain opportunities: on closer examination they may turn out to contain real nuggets of gold. But any interventions to pursue them will probably have to be exploratory, designed to find out whether there are solid benefits to be obtained or not.

In creating a short-list of ideas to examine more closely, we should, however, guard against pursuing mirages, and question whether there really are likely to be parenting opportunities to address. When we assess the short-listed ideas, we shall need to be rigorous in applying the mental disciplines to them. In drawing up the short-list, we should therefore reject ideas if there is insufficient logic or evidence to support them. For example, if the champion of a shared salesforce appears to have given little serious consideration to important details, such as salesmen's calling patterns or the purchase criteria of customers, his proposal should receive less weight. Or if, on reflection, no-one can see any possible parenting opportunities associated with the targeted benefit, we should avoid wasting time with further investigation of it. We need to blend support for fresh thinking with the reality checks and tough-mindedness that the mental disciplines provide. It is the ideas that will stand up under closer analysis that we are interested in.

Synergy approach

The next step in the review is to lay out the main features of the company's approach to synergy management. It should cover the role that synergies play within the corporate strategy. It should bring out the company's underlying philosophy, attitudes and beliefs concerning the units' relationships to each other and to the centre. And it should make explicit the mechanisms and processes that the company typically uses to deal with these issues.

Corporate strategy

In our research on corporate strategy, we have found that different companies place very different emphases on the horizontal and vertical linkages that they foster. Some companies, such as Hanson (before the break-up), Emerson, RTZ and BTR (prior to 1995), place much more weight on the value that they add through stand-alone parenting than through linkage parenting. Others, such as Banc One, Unilever, 3M, ABB and Canon, have always seen the management of synergies as a key part of their corporate strategies. Business managers in organizations such as Hanson know that the main focus of the parent's attention will be on opportunities to improve the performance of each business as a stand-alone entity, and that they will receive few brownie points for collaborative efforts with other units. By contrast, business managers in Canon or Unilever know that their bosses expect and require them to seek out and participate in opportunities for working together with other units. Furthermore, they know what sorts of synergies the parent typically promotes most energetically. In Canon, for example, the strongest drive is for new product developments that require co-operation across business unit boundaries, while in Unilever the transfer of product and market information across geographic boundaries is critical.

Exhibit 6.4.1 summarizes the main sources of value creation identified in one international manufacturing and marketing company. This way of summarizing the corporate strategy into a list of parenting tasks helps position the importance of synergy initiatives versus other forms of parenting.

In summary, the review should document the priority given to linkage issues versus other forms of parenting and record the types of linkages that feature most prominently as key sources of added value. The review should also record the direction of movement in the corporate strategy. Is the company looking to build more synergies in the future or unwind some of the links and co-ordinated activities that currently exist? The current corporate strategy and the perceived direction of movement influences the sort of synergies that managers are likely to pursue and the priority they give them.

Philosophy, attitudes and beliefs

Companies also have different underlying attitudes and beliefs about how best to handle linkages. Often these differences concern the advantages of centralization or decentralization. To achieve benefits from pooled purchasing power, for example, a parent with a belief in the efficacy of central initiatives may set up a central purchasing department and insist that

EXHIBIT 6.4.1 SOURCES OF PARENTING VALUE CREATION

- Transferring know-how about products, markets, marketing, manufacturing and other functions from/to business units around the world.
- Helping businesses (mainly in developed economies) avoid the pitfall of under investment in new product development and consumer understanding.
- Creating a value-based performance culture that has low tolerance of unnecessary costs or weak performance, yet is capable of investing where necessary.
- Orchestrating pools of mobile management talent so that businesses can draw on them in times of need.

- Developing and appointing outstanding managers to lead each business, with skills appropriate to the particular challenges of that business.
- Helping businesses (mainly in emerging markets) to avoid common pitfalls, such as insufficient investment in local management or poor timing of major commitments.
- Developing valuable relationships with potential partners and influential governments, and building the company brand into one of the world's leading corporate brands.
- Providing cost effective central services and corporate governance activities.

all purchases of certain items are handled by this department. Conversely, a parent that favours decentralized networking may simply circulate data on the purchasing terms and conditions being achieved by each unit, maintaining strong pressure on the businesses to reduce their individual unit costs. Such an intervention leaves the businesses much freer to determine whether and how they wish to work with other businesses to improve their purchasing power, but gives them no direct help or guidance about what to do. Between these extremes, there are a variety of other possibilities, such as establishing joint purchasing teams with members from different businesses, nominating selected businesses to act as lead units in purchasing for different items, centralizing certain aspects of negotiations on terms and conditions but allowing each business to make its own buying decisions, and hiring a central purchasing expert who is available to the businesses, but need only be used by them if they choose.

For any synergy benefit, a range of possible intervention options can be arrayed along a spectrum of more versus less centralist interventions (see Table 6.4.1). Some companies, such as Mars and Unilever, are philosophically committed to the decentralized, networking end of the spectrum. They believe that it is vital to preserve business-unit autonomy and leave decisions to business-unit managements. Wary of central interference, they prefer to rely on the 'enlightened self-interest' of unit managers to guide linkages. Other companies, such as Canon or Rentokil, are more comfortable mandating policies or decisions

TABLE 6.4.1 Differences in linkage philosophy

	Belief in decentralization	Mixed	Belief in central direction
Know-how sharing	■ Network facilitation	■ Some central policies ■ Centres of excellence ■ Lead units ■ Franchise	■ Mandatory central policies/directives
Tangible resources sharing	■ Internal JVs/contracts ■ Voluntary use of shared resource units ■ set up as profit centres	■ Limited central functions and resources ■ Service level agreements	■ Mandatory central functions and resources ■ Incomplete SBUs
Pooled negotiating power	■ Information sharing ■ Joint SBU teams and initiatives	■ Lead units	■ Central functions experts
Vertical integration	■ Third party trading relationships, but first refusal in-house	■ Negotiated transfer prices ■ In-house preference ■ Centre influences relationship	■ Centre sets transfer prices and manages relationships for corporate benefit
Co-ordinated strategies	■ Centre arbitrates ■ Minimal constraints on scope/strategy	■ Restrained central role ■ Matrix structure ■ Task forces ■ Franchise	■ Centre directs ■ Low SBU autonomy
New business creation	■ SBU driven	■ Task forces drawn from centre and SBUs	■ Centrally driven

from the centre on a range of issues. Although they accept the importance of unit motivation and initiative, they believe that there are many important benefits that will not be realized unless the parent makes the decisions.

Differences in attitudes concerning the appropriate degree of centralization affect the range of intervention options that a parent is likely to perceive. Those who favour decentralized solutions will tend to give little or no consideration to more mandatory central interventions. Those who typically mandate central policies and decisions will be less sensitive to how much can be accomplished through a variety of measures that encourage networking. Corporate linkage philosophies represent blinkers that constrain the options that receive attention.

Another important factor is the corporate parent's attitude to central staff resources. Should large, heavyweight staff groups be set up or not? Should the businesses be forced to work with the corporate staffs, or should their use by the businesses be voluntary? As with centralization/decentralization choices, companies tend to have a dominant philosophy which governs the role of staff in managing linkages. Companies such as ABB are strenuously opposed to the use of corporate staffs, wherever possible relying on decisions and resources in the business units. They fear that, lacking direct profit responsibility, staffs can easily lose touch with the needs of the businesses and take on a life of their own, in which power and empire-building take precedence over the benefits delivered to the corporation. Other companies, 3M or Cooper for instance, believe that corporate staffs, at least in selected areas, are the best way to ensure that specialist expertise is developed and shared among units. They are therefore a source of valuable linkages. These beliefs will be reflected in the synergy interventions that the parent makes.

Different philosophies therefore influence the sorts of synergies that will be pursued and the means which will be used to pursue them. Take, for example, a new product-development initiative involving joint work between two or more business units. At one extreme, a 'Hanson' approach, suspicious of shared responsibilities of this sort, would likely press for the initiative to be pursued within one of the businesses or else dropped. By contrast, a 'Unilever' approach would be to provide encouragement and, if necessary, expert assistance, while allowing the businesses to pursue the matter in their own way, within a framework of strong corporate cultural norms to guide decision-making. A 'Canon' approach would be different again, entailing

willingness to give high corporate priority to the project, including assignment of numbers of both corporate and business staff to work full-time on the project to see it through to commercialization. Some assessment of the underlying corporate attitudes and beliefs about linkages should therefore form part of the review.

Mechanisms and processes

Companies also differ in the nature of the specific mechanisms and processes that they typically use to manage co-ordination. The review should identify the mechanisms and processes that are most frequently used, and should articulate the impact that they have on synergy management. What is the nature and importance of the budget and planning processes and how, if at all, do they affect cross-company initiatives? What sort of cross-business committees are in place and how do they work? What staff groups exist and what role do they play in linkages?

We argue that 'well-grooved' mechanisms are an important factor in gauging the ease with which a company's synergy intervention will be implemented. Equally, ineffective or ill-suited mechanisms and processes can account for failure to realize some opportunities.

'Five lenses analysis'

As a means of describing and analysing the parent's approach to synergy issues, we have found that a display that views the characteristics of the parent through five inter-linked lenses is useful (see Goold, Campbell and Alexander, 1994 and Figure 6.4.2). The five lenses are:

■ The beliefs, knowledge or mental maps that guide the behaviour and decisions of senior managers in the parent organization. These mental maps determine the corporate linkage strategy and philosophy, and guide the parent's thinking about the selection and implementation of linkage mechanisms and interventions.

■ The structure of the company, including the way in which the business units are defined and the nature of parenting structures to which they report, and the systems and processes through which parent managers mainly exercise influence, pressure and control. The business-unit definitions determine what links between units need to be managed; the nature of the parenting structure, for example whether

FIGURE 6.4.2   Parenting characteristics

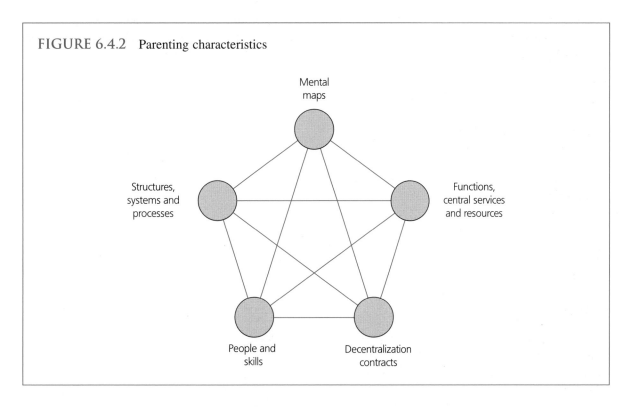

there are product divisions, geographical divisions, or a matrix structure, influences the parenting opportunities that will be pursued; and the systems and processes that are in place determine how they are most likely to be handled.

- The functional staffs, central service groups, and corporate resources that are important in synergy management. The size, composition and strengths of the corporate staff and the way in which they operate are key components of the overall approach to cross-company working.

- The people in the parent organization. The experience, skills and biases of key individuals in the parent have a major impact on synergy management.

- The extent to which authority is delegated to business managers, together with the criteria by which their performance is judged and the rewards or sanctions for good or poor performance; we refer to this as the 'decentralization contract' for each business. The manner in which decentralization contracts are defined influences the sorts of linkage intervention that the parent is likely to make and that the businesses are likely to accept.

We have found that these five lenses provide a useful checklist for itemizing those features of the corporate parent's approach to the management of

synergies that matter most. By running through each of these headings and taking stock of the key features under each, a picture of the overall approach can be built up and made explicit. The five lenses can also be used to bring out ways in which the approach is changing, giving a direction of movement as well as a static picture.

Effectiveness of approach

The third step is to assess the effectiveness of the current synergy approach. How well does the approach match up with the opportunities? Is it working reasonably well, apart from a few specific problems? Are there any fundamental shortcomings that need to be tackled? Once the approach and the opportunities have been laid out in the first two steps of the review, the answers to these questions may be readily apparent. There are, however, some more structured questions that it may be useful to ask. These include:

- Are there biases in the overall approach that condition which opportunities will be realized?

- Are there any aspects of the approach which are impeding linkages; are there any 'synergy killers'?

- Do any business unit definitions need to be changed?

■ What have been the successes and failures of the approach, and what problems need addressing?

Biases in the overall approach

Earlier in this reading, we contrasted the corporate strategies and philosophies of different companies, including Hanson, Unilever, ABB and Canon. The differences in these companies' approaches to synergies mean that they will each steer away from certain sorts of interventions and towards others: their approaches bias both the types of linkages they are likely to emphasize and the means by which they will be pursued.

Nearly all companies have biases in their linkage parenting, and a value of the review is to lay out what they are. What does the corporate strategy emphasize? What are the dominant mental maps that are driving the linkage interventions that the parent chooses to make? What are the well-grooved processes that are usually chosen as the preferred way to intervene? If we can make these biases explicit, we may be able to see why certain synergy opportunities are grasped, while others are systematically overlooked; why some initiatives run smoothly, while others are always contentious and difficult.

■ In one manufacturer of automotive components, the corporate strategy stressed the importance of global co-ordination across different national companies. This strategy led to cost savings and superior customer service in many areas. However, it also led to pressure for rationalization of the product range that carried high opportunity costs in some countries. The basic presumption in favour of international coordination made it very difficult for the countries in question to get a fair hearing on these costs. Instead, they were accused of NIH thinking and told to fall into line with global policy. The bias in favour of international co-ordination in the corporate strategy prevented the parent from taking a balanced view of the advantages and disadvantages of product-range rationalization.

■ In a building products company, there was a strong commitment to decentralized networking as the best way to capture synergies, based partly on history and partly on a belief in the need to respect differences in each business unit's markets. When the corporate parent wanted to encourage all the businesses to adopt a common MIS system, the networking bias resulted in an endless sequence of

project-team meetings, in which it was impossible to reach agreement on a new standard system for all the businesses. It was only after literally years of delay that the parent insisted on a choice being made and pushed it through. The bias in favour of networking prevented a stronger corporate lead from being taken earlier.

The biases in a company's overall approach will make it specially effective at handling certain sorts of linkages, but ineffective at others. For example, there are some parenting opportunities that require mandated central decisions and are unlikely to be grasped through interventions that simply aim to promote networking between the businesses. Hence, a parent with a bias in favour of decentralized networking is unlikely to be successful at realizing these sorts of parenting opportunities. Similarly, a staff-averse company that always tends to use cross-business project teams to handle linkages will find it difficult to push through parenting opportunities for which central staffs are needed. By making explicit any biases in the approach, we may be able to understand better why some opportunities are being successfully realized while others are proving problematic. We can then decide whether to maintain the approach and endorse its biases or to consider making changes.

Synergy killers

Most discussions of synergy concern ways in which the corporate parent can make linkages between business units work better. Unfortunately, the harsh reality is that the corporate parent often inadvertently makes these connections more difficult, not easier. We need to recognize this fact, and can use a review of linkage parenting as a means of rooting out things that are impeding linkages. We refer to policies or characteristics of the parent that are systematically inhibiting linkages as 'synergy killers'.

The effectiveness of the approach to linkages will be compromised if any of the following synergy killers are present:

■ Inhibiting corporate strategy. The most common way in which the corporate-level strategy can work against synergy is through lack of clarity. Lack of clarity about corporate priorities leads managers to be excessively cautious about when they collaborate and with whom. If managers in the businesses are unsure whether the corporate parent expects them to be co-ordinating their technical efforts or looking for cost savings in marketing, the uncertainty can leave them paralysed. A more obvious, if rarer, problem stems from corporate strategies that actively discourage linkages of any sort. In a notorious memorandum written after GEC's acquisition of English Electric, Lord Weinstock informed the managers of the English Electric businesses that all cross-unit committees and projects were to be disbanded forthwith. In future, they would have only one responsibility: the performance of their own units. Though few companies today take such a radical stance against synergies between businesses, some corporate-level strategies still discourage co-operation. 'In my view', stated one chief executive, 'synergy is always an illusion. What is more, it fatally damages accountability.' Not surprisingly, this attitude had a dampening effect on unit managers' attempts to work together.

■ Infighting between the barons. In some companies, there are battles raging between senior managers. The battles may be about differences in corporate strategy or management philosophy. They may be about competition between managers for the top job. They may be due to personality clashes. They may be due to previous collaborations where one party felt let down. Whatever the reason, these battles have a huge negative impact on co-operation. Managers lower down are often aware of lost opportunities, but the climate of hostility between their bosses means that co-operation to pursue them is stifled. It is simply not acceptable to be seen to be 'working with the enemy'.

■ Culture of secrecy. In secretive companies, people play their cards close to their chests. Information about business unit performance, new product plans, operating issues, and organization structures is given out reluctantly. In these circumstances, co-operation is hard, not only because it is difficult to find out what is going on in other units, but also because the free flow of information and communication that is needed to oil the wheels of synergies is inhibited. Why do these cultures occur? Sometimes it is fear of competitor espionage. Sometimes it is a result of resisting corporate information requests and interference. Sometimes it is associated with baronial infighting. Whatever the cause, a culture of secrecy reduces synergy.

■ Misaligned incentives. In many companies, bonus systems and promotion criteria depend largely or exclusively on the results managers achieve in their own businesses, and give no credit for contributions to other businesses or the corporate whole. The personal incentive system then makes it more difficult for business managers to co-operate, unless they can structure a deal that rewards all the units involved. Where the synergy involves a sacrifice by one unit to help others, and there is no ready process by which to compensate the loser, the incentive system will block progress. Again and again, we encountered situations in which this prevented managers from helping colleagues in other businesses, even though there was a clear net benefit. Where win/lose trade-offs exist, reward systems should aim to make it easier for business managers to co-operate; all too often, they have precisely the reverse effect.

■ Excessive performance pressure. When managers are hounded by close-to-impossible targets, they are apt to become defensive and inward-looking. In companies where business unit performance is paramount and where targets are set too high, managers often concentrate exclusively on things within their own immediate control and cease to be comfortable with situations where they must rely on their colleagues' co-operation. Oppressive targets damp down the spirit of mutuality and collaboration from which synergies flow.

■ Insulation from performance pressure. At the opposite end of the spectrum from excessive performance pressure is insulation from performance pressure. If business units are insulated from performance pressures, the basic drive of enlightened self-interest, on which so many beneficial sharing initiatives depend, will be weakened. In companies where synergies thrive, such as Mars or Canon, senior managers keep up the pressure for constant improvement, knowing that this leads to more energy from working together. In companies where the parent insulates the businesses from such pressures, the businesses are less likely to seek out mutually rewarding synergies.

■ Domineering corporate staff. If corporate staff groups have domineering or insensitive attitudes, business managers will automatically reject their ideas for improving linkages, however sound they may be. In a major chemical company with old-established functional baronies, the heads of the corporate staff departments were inclined to issue policies and guidelines to the businesses with little consultation or recognition of inter-company differences. Over time, the business heads became adept at passive resistance and non-co-operation, spending much more time on the tactics of opposition than on assessing whether the proposed policies were, in fact, beneficial. As a result, genuine synergy opportunities were resisted as strenuously as misguided attempts at standardization.

■ Mistrust. An atmosphere of mistrust undermines cooperation. If the businesses believe that their sister units are out to take advantage of them, or are always unwilling to put themselves out to help, relations are quickly soured to the point where even well-intentioned initiatives are blocked. Equally, if a climate of opinion has grown up where business managers believe that corporate management or staff are incompetent or untrustworthy, synergy interventions are likely to be resisted in principle. Expensive, high profile failures seriously undermine the credibility and prospects of any future proposal. Particular problems arise when the parent is suspected of having a hidden agenda, since all initiatives will be scrutinized for ulterior motives, and interpreted in the worst possible light.

All companies have some synergy killers. Our concern should be with pathological characteristics that may be causing widespread damage, not with minor irritants. Is there a strong sense that some of the parent's characteristics are really preventing collaboration? Can we see evidence from the unrealized opportunities that indicates that these synergy killers are having a real impact? How can the parent adjust the corporate context to make linkages work better?

While synergy killers inhibit linkages, their opposites create the sort of fertile ground in which co-operation flourishes. Clear corporate strategies that support high priority synergies; good personal relationships between senior managers in the businesses; an open culture that promotes sharing; incentive systems that reward attempts to create synergies; corporate pressure to raise performance through sharing best practices; competent staff units that are sensitive in their relationships with the businesses; and an atmosphere of mutual trust and support are all conducive to perceiving synergy opportunities and implementing them successfully. The parent should aim to nurture synergies through creating these fertile ground conditions. Hence, even if no real synergy killers exist, the review may still pinpoint ways in which the corporate context could be made more fertile for synergies.

Business unit definitions

The boundaries established around a group's business units are fundamental for the approach to synergies. By changing the definition of the business units, the parent automatically changes the nature of the potential links between business units. If a new European unit is set up out of previously separate national units, issues of manufacturing co-ordination that used to be handled as linkages between separate units are now managed within a single larger entity. 'Internalizing' the linkages in this way makes a big difference, because there is now a single general manager for the combined business who is in a position to decide on trade-offs between the sub-units and who will be held responsible for the results of the integrated entity. This makes certain interventions much easier to push through, although it may involve some reduction in focus on the product-market niches within the larger entity.

The trade-offs between breadth and focus in business-unit definition are complex. There are, however, some business-unit definition issues that should be addressed in a review of synergy management. In particular, it is important to raise the following questions:

■ Are there some important synergies that are never likely to be realized with the current business-unit definitions? If so, are there alternative definitions that should be considered?

■ Are certain synergies harder to achieve because of the manner in which the boundaries around the business units are set up and managed?

There are some circumstances in which coordination between separate businesses is never likely to be achieved, however beneficial it may be for the group. If, for example, the collective net benefits involve costs to one or more units that are hard or impossible to compensate for, the initiative is likely to be blocked. Thus, it may be almost impossible to bring about co-ordinated production planning between separate units if it involves one or more units shutting their factories and transferring production to another. To avoid the consequent reduction in power and status, the general managers of the units in question will be likely to go to any lengths to block or undermine the initiative. Conclusion: the best way to achieve this synergy benefit will probably be to redefine the business to encompass all the previously separate units, giving responsibility for optimizing performance to a single management team.

Other situations in which managers should consider a redefinition of the businesses to achieve desirable synergies include the following:

- **Deeply embedded hostility and mistrust between senior managers in the different units.** If the rivalry between the general managers of the units is intense, they may simply be unwilling to work together, whatever the benefits. The solution may be to redefine the business units and give responsibility for both of them to one or other of the managers.

- **Hard-to-allocate costs and revenues.** If shared production facilities or the lack of an open third-party market for products traded between the units make it difficult to agree a split of costs and revenues, any form of co-operation is likely to suffer, since underlying disputes about transfer prices and allocated costs will dominate everything else. In such circumstances, it is often better to expand the business definition to include both units, with a single bottom line. Co-ordination issues then become a means to maximize aggregate profitability rather than the pretext for haggling over how to divide up the results.

- **Need for speedy and continuous resolution of tradeoff judgements.** Concerns about contamination and lack of focus have led many companies to create more and more separate profit centres, each with its own management and strategy. This drive for business focus creates major difficulties if the separate businesses need to be in constant touch with each other and have to resolve a series of difficult day-to-day trade-offs. For example, if two petrochemical businesses share a process plant and continuous decisions about output mix are needed to achieve the optimum overall profitability, taking account of the shifting relative prices of different inputs and of different end products, the two businesses will be locked in constant complex negotiations about how to run the plant. A structure in which a single management team is responsible for optimizing both businesses is likely to work more smoothly.

The underlying issue is whether, for whatever reason, co-ordination between the separate businesses' management teams will always be much less effective than co-ordination under a single management team. Managers should therefore examine the current business-unit boundaries to see if they are preventing any important synergies from taking place. If they are, consider altering the boundaries.

Judgements about whether a redefinition of the businesses is necessary should also reflect the nature of the boundaries. If decentralization contracts emphasize the autonomy of the business heads and provide few incentives or opportunities for them to work together, potential problems resulting from separate business definitions will be magnified. If, however, business heads do not expect to have full control over all the functions and resources they need in their businesses, and work in a context that encourages and requires frequent liaison with colleagues from other businesses and from central functions, the boundaries around the separate businesses will be more naturally permeable. In Canon, for example, business managers are very ready to work on cross-business project teams, to draw on corporate staff support, and to co-ordinate with other businesses: the corporate approach to coordination stresses the connections between the businesses, not the boundaries that separate them. With more permeable boundaries around the businesses, there is more flexibility to make different business definitions work well. With more separation between businesses, there is a greater premium on drawing the boundaries in ways that will internalize linkages that would otherwise become problematic.

Successes and failures

Last, but not least, the effectiveness of the overall approach can be tested in terms of evident successes and failures: well and poorly rated mechanisms and processes, fully and less fully realized synergy opportunities, patterns of success and failure that cast light on organizational strengths and weaknesses.

As part of the audit of the current approach, it is essential to canvas opinion about the effectiveness of the main systems and processes for managing synergies, and of the key staff groups that promote them. Surveys, in-depth discussions or focus groups can bring well-grooved and successful mechanisms into relief and pinpoint areas of friction or dissatisfaction. Poorly rated mechanisms should then be examined more carefully. What are the causes of dissatisfaction? Is it a mechanism for chasing mirages? Are the parenting opportunities on which it is targeted clear, or is it being driven by parenting bias? Is it wasting the time of managers at the centre or in the businesses? Should we consider other ways of intervening to realize the target benefits, or should we simply discontinue our efforts if they are not working?

Another way into the successes and failures analysis is via the synergy opportunities review. Do the unrealized opportunities indicate some underlying gap or shortcoming in our approach? Is there some mismatch between the processes or interventions we use for getting at the opportunities and the nature of the opportunities? If, for example, we are consistently failing to achieve the benefits of better capacity utilization that vertical integration should provide, is this because there is something wrong with our transfer-pricing processes or with our approach to combined investment planning? Or are our business-specific performance measures to blame? Our quest should be to unearth new or different mechanisms for intervening that are better suited for the parenting opportunities open to us, in order to reduce the number of important unrealized opportunities.

We have also found that a retrospective analysis of patterns of success and failure with previous synergy interventions can be useful. Which synergies have we managed well – and probably taken for granted? What notorious initiatives have caused the most trouble and yielded the least benefit? What can we learn from these successes and failures?

By examining the successes, we will be able to see more clearly what mechanisms work best for us. What opportunities have we derived most benefit from? By what means did we realize these opportunities? Answers to these questions will reveal what the organization's well-grooved mechanisms and processes are, and will help to shape thinking about how to tackle new opportunities. By examining the failures, we may discover underlying weaknesses in our skills or processes, or organizational blockages and synergy killers that lie behind our inability to implement certain types of synergies successfully. A sense of these underlying patterns is useful in assessing the effectiveness of the approach.

Agenda for change

The output from the review should be a short-list of possible new initiatives for more detailed consideration. Since the review is a broadly based stock take, the purpose is to create an agenda of possible changes, not to arrive at firm conclusions about how to move forward. Each of the possible initiatives that emerge from the review will then need to be subjected to detailed scrutiny.

The short-list should embrace:

- high priority unrealized synergy opportunities, including ways to address them;

- changes in underlying strategy or philosophy that may increase the effectiveness of the overall approach;

- changes in specific co-ordination processes or mechanisms, including elements that should be discontinued because they may be having a damaging effect, as well as new initiatives that should be considered;

- possible changes in business unit definitions.

Prioritization of the ideas that emerge from the review is essential. The front-runners normally select themselves, either because of the size of the potential benefits (or disbenefits) or the strength of feeling among managers. But the cut-off on what to take forward is more a matter for judgement. We have four pieces of advice in forming the judgement.

First, be selective. A focused follow-through on three or four key initiatives is much more likely to yield tangible benefits than a long-drawn-out survey of a couple of dozen possibly attractive options. And if the review is not seen to lead on fairly quickly to action, its creditability will suffer and managers will lose enthusiasm.

Second, look forward, not back. Give preference to ideas that anticipate breaking trends and build links that will become increasingly valuable in the future. Avoid focusing on initiatives that deal with yesterday's problems or with issues that are likely to become less significant. Concentrate, for example, on putting in place pricing co-ordination mechanisms to avoid arbitrage in what will become an increasingly integrated European marketplace. Don't struggle to promote common design and manufacturing of components that more and more of the business units are already tending to outsource.

Third, use your rivals and competitors to guide your sense of priorities. If your main competitors are deriving much more benefit from sharing know-how than you are, move it up your priority list, unless there are good reasons why it is always likely to be less important to you than to them. If others have tried and failed with a shared-purchasing initiative, be cautious about pushing ahead with it. The concern should be with the specific achievements of known competitors, not with current general management fads and fashions. Of course, this presumes a certain level of competitive intelligence, which is not always present. However, we believe that efforts to find out about competitors' initiatives can play a valuable role in establishing a final short-list.

Fourth, recognize system effects. The five-lenses analysis brings out the connections between different aspects of the synergy approach. Successes and failures often stem from deeply rooted attitudes that underlie the use of certain mechanisms rather than others. Proposals to make changes in a given process or to address a specific opportunity may therefore entail consequential changes in other areas. Consider whether specific initiatives will work in the whole context in which they will be taken; assess the possibility that a systematic change programme to shift the overall culture may be required as a precondition for success in specific areas.

CORPORATE LEVEL STRATEGY IN INTERNATIONAL PERSPECTIVE

Growth for the sake of growth is the ideology of the cancer cell.
Edward Abbey (1927–1989); American author

As with the topic in the previous chapter, scarce attention has been paid to international differences in multi-business level strategies. Despite the high media profile of major corporations from different countries and despite researchers' fascination with large companies, little comparative research has been done. Yet, it seems not unlikely that corporate strategy practices and preferences vary across national boundaries, although these differences are not blatant. Casual observation of the major corporations around the globe quickly makes clear that one cannot easily divide the world into portfolio-oriented and integration-oriented countries. However, Goold, Campbell and Alexander do observe that in their research they have found 'there are relatively few companies in the United Kingdom, the United States, and other Western countries that pursue a full-fledged Strategic Planning style', while it is 'the most popular style among leading Japanese companies' (1994: 413). This observation has also been made by Kono (1999).

As an input to the debate of whether there are international differences in corporate strategy perspectives, we would like to put forward a number of factors that might be of influence on how the paradox of responsiveness and synergy is managed in different countries. It should be noted, however, that these propositions must be viewed as tentative explanations, intended to encourage further discussion and research.

Functioning of capital and labour markets

One of the arguments levelled against the portfolio organization perspective is that there is no need for corporations that merely act as investors. With efficiently operating capital markets, investing should be left to 'real' investors. Stock markets are an excellent place for investors to spread their risks and for growing firms to raise capital. Start-up companies with viable plans can easily find venture capitalists to assist them. And all these capital providers can perform the task of financial control – portfolio-oriented corporations have nothing else to add but overhead costs. Add to this the argument that large corporations no longer have an advantage in terms of professional management skills. While in the past large firms could add value to smaller units by injecting more sophisticated managers, flexible labour markets now allow small firms to attract the same talent themselves.

Even if this general line of argumentation is true, the extent to which capital and labour markets are 'efficient' varies widely across countries. Porter (1987), an outspoken detractor of the portfolio organization perspective, acknowledges that 'in developing countries, where large companies are few, capital markets are undeveloped, and professional management is scarce, portfolio management still works'. However, he quickly adds that portfolio thinking 'is no longer a valid model for corporate strategy in advanced economies'. But are capital and labour markets equally efficient across all so-called advanced economies? Few observers would argue that venture capital markets in Asia and Europe work as well as in the United States, and the terms under which large corporations can raise capital on these continents are usually far better than for smaller companies. Neither does holding shares of a company through the stock markets of Asia and Europe give investors as much influence over the company as in the United States. In short, even in the group of developed economies, various gradations of capital market efficiency seem to exist, suggesting varying degrees to which corporations can create value by adopting the role of investors.

The same argument can be put forward for the efficiency of 'managerial labour' markets. Even if Porter is right when stating that smaller companies can attract excellent professional managers through flexible labour markets, this conclusion is not equally true across advanced economies. Lifetime employment might be a declining phenomenon in most of these countries, but not to the same extent. Job-hopping between larger and smaller companies is far more common in the United States, than in many European and Asian countries (e.g. Calori and de Woot, 1994). In many advanced economies large corporations still command a more sophisticated core of professional managers, through superior recruiting and training practices, higher compensation and status, and greater perceived career opportunities and job security. Hence, even within this group of countries, different degrees of labour market flexibility exist, suggesting that corporations in some countries might be able to create more value as developers and allocators of management talent than in other countries.

Leveraging of relational resources

With the portfolio organization perspective favouring the leveraging of financial resources and the integrated organization perspective often focusing on the leveraging of competence, the leveraging of relational resources is a topic receiving far less attention within the field of strategic management. It is widely acknowledged that 'umbrella' brands can often be stretched to include more product categories and that the corporation's reputation can commonly be employed to the business units' benefit. However, in the areas of political science and industrial organization much more attention is paid to the corporation as leverager of contacts and power. In many circumstances knowing the right people, being able to bring parties together, being able to force compliance and having the power to influence government regulations, are essential aspects of doing business. Often, corporations, either by their sheer size, or by their involvement in many businesses, will have more clout and essential contacts than can be mustered by individual businesses.

Here the international differences come in. As put forward at the end of Chapter 5, in some countries relational resources are more important than in others. Influence over government policy-making, contacts with the bureaucrats applying the rules, power over local authorities and institutions, connections with the ruling elite, access to informal networks of companies – the importance of these factors can differ from country to country. Therefore, it stands to reason that the clustering of businesses around key external relationships and power bases will vary strongly across nations. In some countries 'core contacts' centred corporations are more likely to be encountered than in others.

Costs of coordination

Coordination comes at a cost, it is argued. Individual business units usually have to participate in all types of corporate systems, file reports, ask permission, attend meetings and adapt their strategy to fit with the corporate profile. This can result in time delays, lack of fit with the market, less entrepreneurial action, a lack of accountability and a low morale. On top of this, business units have to pay a part of corporate overhead as well. The benefits of coordination should be higher than these costs.

This argument might be suffering from a cultural bias, as it assumes that individuals and businesses are not naturally inclined to coordinate. However, control by the corporate centre and cooperation with other business units is not universally viewed as a negative curtailment of individual autonomy. In many countries coordination is not an unfortunate fact of life, but a natural state of affairs. Coordination within the corporate whole is often welcomed as motivating, not demotivating, especially in cultures that are more group-oriented (Hofstede, 1993, Reading 1.4 in this book). As observed in Chapter 4, if the common form of organization in a country resembles a clan, coordination might not be as difficult and costly as in other nations. Therefore, on the basis of this argument, it is reasonable to expect a stronger preference for the portfolio perspective in countries that favour mechanistic organizations.

Preference for control

The last point of international difference ties into the discussion in the next chapter. If the essence of corporate strategy is about realizing synergies between businesses, is it not possible for these businesses to coordinate with one another and achieve synergies without being a part of the same corporation? In other words, is it necessary to be owned and controlled by the same parent in order to leverage resources, integrate activities and align product offerings? Or could individual businesses band together and work as if they were one company – acting as a 'virtual corporation'?

In Chapter 7 it will be argued that there are significant international differences on this account. In some countries there is a strong preference to have hierarchical control over two businesses that need to be coordinated. In other countries there is a preference for businesses to use various forms of cooperation to achieve synergies with other businesses, while retaining the flexibility of independent ownership. Preference for control, it will be argued, depends on how managers deal with the paradox of competition and cooperation.

FURTHER READING

Readers who would like to gain a better overview of the literature on the topic of corporate level strategy have a number of good sources from which to choose. Two scholarly reviews are 'Strategy and Structure in the Multiproduct Firm' by Charles Hill and Robert Hoskisson, and 'Research on Corporate Diversification: A Synthesis', by Vasudevan Ramanujam and P. Varadarajan, although both have become somewhat dated. A more recent review is 'Why Diversify? Four Decades of Management Thinking', by Michael Goold and Kathleen Luchs. Mark Sirower's book *The Synergy Trap: How Companies Lose the Acqusition Game* also has an excellent overview of the literature as an appendix.

Much of the strategy literature taking a portfolio organization perspective is from the end of the 1970s and the beginning of the 1980s. Bruce Henderson's popular book, *On Corporate Strategy*, which explains the basic principles of the portfolio organization perspective, is from this period. However, a better review of the portfolio approach, and especially portfolio techniques, is given by Charles Hofer and Dan Schendel in *Strategy Formulation: Analytical Concepts.* Recently, there has been renewed interest in viewing the corporation as investor and restructurer. In this crop, the article 'Growth Through

Acquisitions: A Fresh Look', by Patricia Anslinger and Thomas Copeland is particularly provocative.

For further reading on the integrated organization perspective, Gary Hamel and C.K. Prahalad's book *Competing for the Future* is an obvious choice. The literature on the resource-based view of the firm mentioned in the 'Further reading' section at the end of Chapter 5 is also interesting in the context of this chapter. Highly stimulating is Hiroyuk Itami's book *Mobilizing Invisible Assets*, in which he also argues for sharing intangible resources throughout a multi-business firm.

On the topic of acquisitions, a good overview of the arguments and quantitative research is provided by Anju Seth, in his article 'Value Creation in Acquisitions: A Re-Examination of Performance Issues'. Mark Sirower's earlier mentioned book is also an excellent choice. When it comes to issues in the area of post-acquisition integration, Philippe Haspeslagh and David Jemison's book *Managing Acquisitions: Creating Value Through Corporate Renewal* from which Reading 6.3 was reprinted is a good start. The more recent book by Michael Hitt, J. Harrison, and R. Ireland, *Mergers and Acquisitions: A Guide to Creating Value for Shareholders*, is also well worth reading.

On the role of the corporate centre, *Corporate-Level Strategy: Creating Value in the Multibusiness Company*, by Michael Goold, Andrew Campbell and Marcus Alexander, is highly recommended. Also stimulating is Charles Hill's article 'The Functions of the Headquarters Unit in Multibusiness Firms'. For a more academic analysis, readers are advised to turn to Vijay Govindarajan's article 'A Contingency Approach to Strategy Implementation at the Business-Unit Level: Integrating Administrative Mechanisms with Strategy'. And last but not least, for those who enjoyed Reading 6.4 by Andrew Campbell and Michael Goold, the book from which it was taken, *Synergy: Why Links Between Business Units Often Fail and How to Make Them Work*, offers more interesting insights.

REFERENCES

Amit, R., and Livnat, J. (1988) 'Diversification and the Risk-Return Trade-off', *Academy of Management Journal*, Vol. 31, No. 1, March, pp. 154–165.

Anslinger, P.L., and Copeland, T.E. (1996) 'Growth Through Acquisitions: A Fresh Look', *Harvard Business Review,* Vol. 74, No. 1, January–February, pp. 126–135.

Baum, J.A.C., and Greve, H.R. (eds) (2001) *Multiunit Organization and Multimarket Strategy*, vol. 18, Stamford, CT: JAI Press.

Calori, R., and CESMA (1988) 'How Successful Companies Manage Diverse Businesses', *Long Range Planning*, Vol. 21, No. 3, pp. 80–89.

Calori, R., and de Woot, P. (eds) (1994) *A European Management Model: Beyond Diversity*, Hemel Hempstead: Prentice Hall.

Campbell, A., and Goold, M. (1998) *Synergy: Why Links Between Business Units Often Fail and How to Make Them Work*, Oxford: Capstone Publishing.

Campbell, A., Goold, M., and Alexander, M. (1995) 'The Value of the Parent Company', *California Management Review*, Vol. 38, No. 1, Fall, pp. 79–97.

Campbell, A., and Luchs, K. (1992) *Strategic Synergy,* London: Butterworth Heinemann.

Chatterjee, S. (1986) 'Types of Synergy and Economic Value: The Impact of Acquisitions on Merging and Rival Firms', *Strategic Management Journal*, Vol. 7, No. 2, March–April, pp. 119–139.

Dundas, K.N.M., and Richardson, P.R. (1980) 'Corporate Strategy and the Concept of Market Failure', *Strategic Management Journal*, Vol. 1, pp. 177–188.

Eisenhardt, K.M., and Galunic, D.C. (2000) 'Coevolving: At Last, a Way to Make Synergies Work', *Harvard Business Review*, Vol. 78, No. 1, January–February, pp. 91–101.

Ghoshal, S., and Mintzberg, H. (1994) 'Diversification and Diversifact', *California Management Review*, Vol. 37, No. 1, Fall, pp. 8–27.

Goold, M., and Campbell, A. (1987) *Strategies and Styles: The Role of the Centre in Managing Diverse Corporations*, Oxford: Basil Blackwell.

Goold, M., Campbell, A., and Alexander, M. (1994) *Corporate-Level Strategy: Creating Value in the Multibusiness Company*, New York: Wiley.

Goold, M., and Lansdell, S. (1997) *Survey of Corporate Strategy Objectives, Concepts and Tools*, Ashridge Strategic Management Centre.

Goold, M., and Luchs, K. (1993) 'Why Diversify? Four Decades of Management Thinking', *Academy of Management Executive*, Vol. 7, No. 3, August, pp. 7–25.

Govindarajan, V. (1988) 'A Contingency Approach to Strategy Implementation at the Business-Unit Level: Integrating Administrative Mechanisms with Strategy', *Academy of Management Journal*, Vol. 31, No. 4, December, pp. 828–853.

Hamel, G., and Prahalad, C.K. (1993) 'Strategy as Stretch and Leverage', *Harvard Business Review*, Vol. 71, No. 2, March–April, pp. 75–84.

Hamel, G., and Prahalad, C.K. (1994) *Competing for the Future*, Boston, MA: Harvard Business School Press.

Harrigan, K.R. (1985) 'Vertical Integration and Corporate Strategy', *Academy of Management Journal*, Vol. 28, No. 2, June, pp. 397–425.

Haspeslagh, P. (1982) 'Portfolio Planning: Uses and Limits', *Harvard Business Review*, Vol. 60, No. 1, January–February, pp. 58–73.

Haspeslagh, P., and Jemison, D. (1991) *Managing Acquisitions: Creating Value Through Corporate Renewal*, New York: Free Press.

Hedley, B. (1977) 'Strategy and the "Business Portfolio"', *Long Range Planning*, Vol. 10, No. 1, February, pp. 9–15.

Helfat, C.E., and Eisenhardt, K.M. (2004) 'Inter-temporal Economies of Scope, Organizational Modularity, and the Dynamics of Diversification', *Strategic Management Journal*, Vol. 25, No. 13, pp. 1217–1296.

Henderson, B.D. (1979) *On Corporate Strategy*, Cambridge, MA: Abt Books.

Hill, C.W.L. (1994) 'The Functions of the Headquarters Unit in Multibusiness Firms', in: R. Rumelt, D. Teece, and D. Schendel (eds), *Fundamental Issues in Strategy Research*, Cambridge, MA: Harvard University Press.

Hill, C.W.L., and Hoskisson, R.E. (1987) 'Strategy and Structure in the Multiproduct Firm', *Academy of Management Review*, Vol. 12, No. 2, April, pp. 331–341.

Hitt, M., Harrison, J., and Ireland, R. (2001) *Mergers and Acquisitions: A Guide to Creating Value for Shareholders*, New York: Oxford Press.

Hofer, C, and Schendel, D. (1978) *Strategy Formulation: Analytical Concepts*, St. Paul: West.

Hofstede, G. (1993) 'Cultural Constraints in Management Theories', *Academy of Management Executive*, Vol. 7, No. 1, pp. 8–21.

Itami, H. (1987) *Mobilizing Invisible Assets*, Cambridge, MA: Harvard University Press.

Jayachandran, S., Gimeno, J., and Varadarajan, P.R. (1999) 'Theory of Multimarket Competition: A Synthesis and Implications for Marketing Strategy', *Journal of Marketing*, Vol. 63, No. 3, pp. 49–66.

Kaplan, S. (1989) 'The Effects of Management Buyouts on Operating Performance and Value', *Journal of Financial Economics*, Vol. 24, No. 2, October, pp. 217–254.

Kogut, B., and Zander, U. (1993) 'Knowledge of the Firm and the Evolutionary Theory of the Multinational Corporation', *Journal of International Business Studies*, Vol. 24, No. 4, pp. 625–646.

Kono, T. (1999) 'A Strong Head Office Makes a Strong Company', *Long Range Planning*, Vol. 32, No. 2, pp. 225–236.

Lawrence, P.R., and Lorsch, J.W. (1967) *Organization and Environment*, Cambridge, MA: Harvard University Press.

Long, W.F., and Ravenscraft, D.J. (1993) 'Decade of Debt: Lessons from LBOs in the 1980s', in: M.M. Blair (ed.), *The Deal Decade: What Takeovers and Leveraged Buyouts Mean for Corporate Governance*, Washington: Brookings Institution.

Lubatkin, M., and Chatterjee, S. (1994) 'Extending Modern Portfolio Theory into the Domain of Corporate Diversification: Does It Apply?', *Academy of Management Journal*, Vol. 37, No. 1, pp. 109–136.

Mahoney, J.T. (1992) 'The Choice of Organizational Form: Vertical Financial Ownership versus Other Methods of Vertical Integration', *Strategic Management Journal*, Vol. 13, No. 8, pp. 559–584.

Porter, M.E. (1987) 'From Competitive Advantage to Corporate Strategy', *Harvard Business Review*, Vol. 65, No. 3, May–June, pp. 43–59.

Prahalad, C.K., and Bettis, R.A. (1986) 'The Dominant Logic: A New Linkage Between Diversity and Performance', *Strategic Management Journal*, Vol. 7, No. 6, November–December, pp. 485–601.

Prahalad, C.K., and Doz, Y. (1987) *The Multinational Mission: Balancing Local Demands and Global Vision*, New York: Free Press.

Prahalad, C.K., and Hamel, G. (1990) 'The Core Competence of the Corporation', *Harvard Business Review*, Vol. 68, No. 3, May–June, pp. 79–91.

Ramanujam, V., and Varadarajan, P. (1989) 'Research on Corporate Diversification: A Synthesis', *Strategic Management Journal*, Vol. 10, No. 6, November–December, pp. 523–551.

Raynor, M.E., and Bower, J.L. (2001) 'Lead from the Center: How to Manager Diverse Businesses', *Harvard Business Review*, Vol. 80, No. 5, May, pp. 93–100.

Rumelt, R.P. (1974) *Strategy, Structure, and Economic Performance*, Cambridge, MA: Harvard University Press.

Rumelt, R.P. (1982) 'Diversification Strategy and Profitability', *Strategic Management Journal*, Vol. 3, No. 4, October–December, pp. 359–369.

Seth, A. (1990) 'Value Creation in Acquisitions: A Re-Examination of Performance Issues', *Strategic Management Journal*, Vol. 11, No. 2, February, pp. 99–115.

Sirower, M.L. (1997) *The Synergy Trap: How Companies Lose the Acquisition Game*, New York: Free Press.

Stalk, G., Evans, P., and Schulman, L.E. (1992) 'Competing on Capabilities: The New Rules of Corporate Strategy', *Harvard Business Review*, Vol. 70, No. 2, March–April, pp. 57–69.

Trautwein, F. (1990) 'Merger Motives and Merger Prescriptions', *Strategic Management Journal*, Vol. 11, No. 4, May–June, pp. 283–295.

Weston, J.F., Chung, K.S., and Hoag, S.E. (1990) *Mergers, Restructuring, and Corporate Control*, Englewood Cliffs, NJ: Prentice Hall.

Williamson, O.E. (1975) *Markets and Hierarchies: Analysis and Antitrust Implications*, New York: Free Press.

NETWORK LEVEL STRATEGY

Alliance, n. In international politics, the union of two thieves who have their hands so deeply inserted in each other's pocket that they cannot separately plunder a third.

The Devil's Dictionary, Ambrose Bierce (1842–1914); American columnist

INTRODUCTION

A business unit can have a strategy, while a group of business units can also have a strategy together – this joint course of action at the divisional or corporate level was discussed in the previous chapter. What has not been examined yet is whether a group of companies can also have a strategy together. Is it possible that companies do not develop their strategies in 'splendid isolation', but rather coordinate their strategies to operate as a team? And is it a good idea for firms to link up with others for a prolonged period of time to try to achieve shared objectives together?

Where two or more firms move beyond a mere transactional relationship and work jointly towards a common goal, they form an alliance, partnership or network. Their shared strategy is referred to as a network level strategy. In such a case, strategy is not only 'concerned with relating a firm to its environment', as was stated in Chapter 5, but also with relating a network to its broader environment.

The existence of networks does raise a range of questions, not the least of which is whether they make strategic sense or not. Is it beneficial to engage in long-term collaborative relationships with other firms or is it more advantageous for firms to 'keep their distance' and to interact with one another in a more market-like, transactional way? Is it viable to manage a web of partnership relations or is it preferable to keep it simple, by having the firm operate more or less independently? To address these questions is to raise the issue of inter-organizational relationships – what should be the nature of the relationship between a firm and other organizations in its surroundings? This issue will be the focus of the further discussion in this chapter.

THE ISSUE OF INTER-ORGANIZATIONAL RELATIONSHIPS

No firm exists that is autarchic. All firms must necessarily interact with other organizations (and individuals) in their environment and therefore they have inter-organizational (or inter-firm) relationships. These relationships can evolve without any clear strategic intent or tactical calculation, but most managers agree that actively determining the nature of their external relations is a significant part of what strategizing is about. Even avoiding relations with some external parties can be an important strategic choice.

To gain a better understanding of the interaction between firms, four aspects are of particular importance and will be reviewed here – the who, why, what and how of inter-organizational relationships (see Figure 7.1). The first aspect is the question of who – who are the potential counterparts with whom a firm can actually have a relationship? This is referred to as the topic of 'relational actors'. The second aspect is the question of why – why do the parties want to enter into a relationship with one another? This is referred to as the topic of 'relational objectives'. The third aspect is the question of what – what type of influences determine the nature of the relationship? This is referred to as the topic of 'relational factors'. The fourth aspect is the question of how – how can relationships be structured into a particular organizational form to let them function in the manner intended? This is referred to as the topic of 'relational arrangements'.

Relational actors

In Figure 7.2 an overview is given of the eight major groups of external parties with whom the firm can, or must, interact. A distinction has been made between industry and contextual actors. The industry actors are those individuals and organizations that perform value-adding activities or consume the outputs of these activities. The contextual actors are those parties whose behaviour, intentionally or unintentionally, sets the conditions under which the industry actors must operate. The four main categories of relationships between the firm and other industry parties are the following (e.g. Porter, 1980; Reve, 1990):

- Upstream vertical (supplier) relations. Every company has suppliers of some sort. In a narrow definition these include the providers of raw materials, parts, machinery and business services. In a broader definition the providers of all production factors (land, capital, labour, technology, information and entrepreneurship) can be seen as suppliers, if they are not part of the firm itself. All these suppliers can either be the actual producers of the input, or an intermediary (distributor or agent) trading in the product or service. Besides the suppliers with which the firm transacts directly (first-tier suppliers), the firm may also have relationships with suppliers further upstream in the industry. All these relationships are traditionally referred to as upstream vertical relations, because economists commonly draw the industry system as a column.

- Downstream vertical (buyer) relations. On the output side, the firm has relationships with its customers. These clients can either be the actual users of the product or service, or intermediaries trading the output. Besides the buyers with which the firm transacts directly, it may also have relationships with parties further downstream in the industry column.

- Direct horizontal (industry insider) relations. This category includes the relations between the firm and other industry incumbents. Because these competitors produce similar goods or services, they are said to be at the same horizontal level in the industry column.

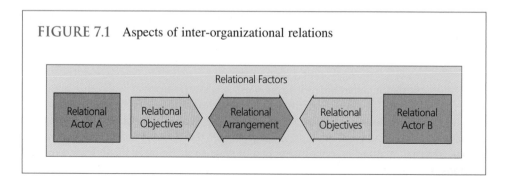

FIGURE 7.1   Aspects of inter-organizational relations

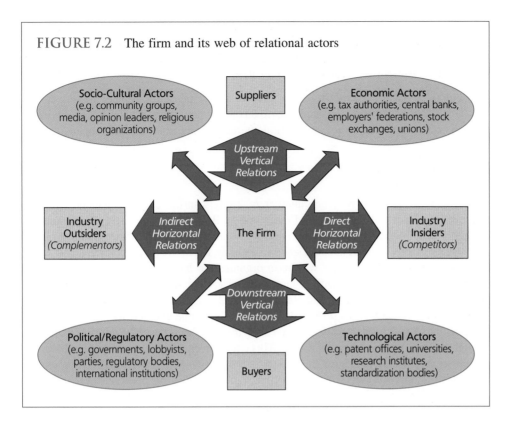

FIGURE 7.2   The firm and its web of relational actors

■ Indirect horizontal (industry outsider) relations. Where a firm has a relationship with a company outside its industry, this is referred to as an indirect horizontal relation. Commonly, companies will have relationships with the producers of complementary goods and services (e.g. hardware manufacturers with software developers). Such a relationship can develop with the producer of a substitute good or service, either as an adversary or as an ally. A relation can also exist between a firm and a potential industry entrant, whereby the incumbent firm can assist or attempt to block the entry of the industry outsider. Furthermore, a firm can establish a relationship with a firm in another industry, with the intention of diversifying into that, or a third, industry. In reality, where industry boundaries are not clear, the distinction between direct and indirect horizontal relations is equally blurry.

Besides relationships with these industry actors, there can be many contacts with condition-setting parties in the broader environment. Employing the classic SEPTember distinction, the following rough categories of contextual actors can be identified:

■ Socio-cultural actors. Individuals or organizations that have a significant impact on societal values, norms, beliefs and behaviours may interact with the firm. These could include the media, community groups, charities, religious organizations and opinion leaders

■ Economic actors. There can also be organizations influencing the general economic state of affairs, with which the firm interacts. Among others, tax authorities, central banks, employers' federations, stock exchanges and unions may be of importance.

■ Political/legal actors. The firm may also interact with organizations setting or influencing the regulations under which companies must operate. These could include governments, political parties, special interest groups, regulatory bodies and international institutions.

■ Technological actors. There are also many organizations that influence the pace and direction of technological development and the creation of new knowledge. Among others, universities, research institutes, patent offices, government agencies and standardization bodies may be important to deal with.

As Figure 7.2 visualizes, companies can choose, but are often also forced, to interact with a large number of organizations and individuals in the environment. This configuration of external actors with which the organization interacts is referred to as the company's group of 'external stakeholders'.

Relational objectives

How organizations deal with one another is strongly influenced by what they hope to achieve (e.g. Dyer and Singh, 1998; Preece, 1995). Both parties may have clear, open and mutually beneficial objectives, but it is also possible that one or both actors have poorly defined intentions, hidden agendas and/or mutually exclusive goals. Moreover, it is not uncommon that various people within an organization have different, even conflicting, objectives and expectations with regard to an external relationship (e.g. Allison, 1969, Reading 3.3 in this book; Doz and Hamel, 1998).

Where two or more firms seek to work together with one another, they generally do so because they expect some value added – they assume more benefit from the interaction than if they had proceeded on their own. This expectation of value creation as a driver for cooperation was also discussed in Chapter 6, where two or more business units worked together to reap synergies. In fact, the same logic is at play between business units and between companies. In both cases, managers are oriented towards finding sources of added value in a potential relationship with another – either across business unit boundaries or across company boundaries. Hence, the same sources of synergy identified in the discussion on corporate level strategy are just as relevant when examining the objectives for inter-organizational cooperation (see Figure 7.3).

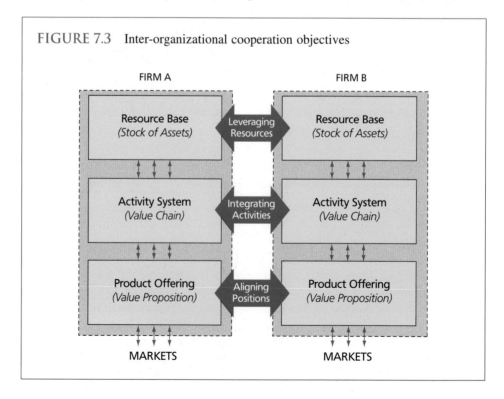

FIGURE 7.3   Inter-organizational cooperation objectives

Relations oriented towards leveraging resources.   The first area where companies can cooperate is at the level of their resource bases. By sharing resources with one another, companies can improve either the quantity or quality of the resources they have at their disposal. There are two general ways for firms to leverage resources to reap mutual benefit:

■ Learning. When the objective is to exchange knowledge and skills, or to engage in the joint pursuit of new know-how, the relationship is said to be learning-oriented. Firms can enter into new learning relationships with industry outsiders, but can also team up with industry incumbents, for instance to develop new technologies or standards (e.g. Hamel, Doz and Prahalad, 1989, Reading 7.1; Shapiro and Varian, 1998). However, firms can add a learning objective to an already existing relationship with a buyer or supplier as well.

■ Lending. Where one firm owns specific resources that it cannot make full use of, or another firm can make better use of, it can be attractive for both to lend the resource to the other. Lending relationships happen frequently in the areas of technology, copyrights and trademarks, where licensing is commonplace. But physical resources can also be lent, usually in the form of lease contracts. In all cases the benefit to lenders can be financial or they receive other resources in return.

Relations oriented towards integrating activities.   The second area where companies can cooperate is at the level of their activity systems. Few companies can span an entire industry column from top to bottom and excel at every type of activity. Usually, by integrating their value chains with other organizations, firms can be much more efficient and effective than if they were totally separated. There are two general ways for firms to integrate their activities with others:

■ Linking. The most common type of relationship in business is the vertical link between a buyer and a seller. All relationships in which products or services are exchanged fall into this category. Most firms have many linking relationships, both upstream and downstream, because they want to focus on only a limited number of value-adding activities, but need a variety of inputs, as well as clients to purchase their finished goods.

■ Lumping. Where firms bring together their similar activities to gain economies of scale, the relationship is said to be oriented towards lumping. Sharing operations (e.g. airline alliances), sales infrastructure (e.g. software cross-selling deals), logistics systems (e.g. postal partnerships) or payment facilities (e.g. inter-bank settlement agreements) are examples of where firms can lump their activities together. Because the activities need to be more or less the same to be able to reap scale economies, lumping relationships are usually found between two or more industry insiders.

Relations oriented towards aligning positions.   The third area where companies can cooperate is at the level of their market positions. Even where companies want to keep their value-adding activities separate, they can coordinate their moves in the environment with the intention of strengthening each other's position. Usually, this type of coalition-building is directed at improving the joint bargaining power of the cooperating parties. These position-enhancing relationships can be further subdivided into two categories:

■ Leaning. Where two or more firms get together to improve their bargaining position vis-à-vis other industry actors, it is said that they lean on each other to stand stronger. Leaning can be directed at building up a more powerful negotiation position towards suppliers, or to offer a more attractive package of products and services towards buyers. Getting together with other companies to form a consortium to launch a new industry standard can also bolster the position of all companies involved. At the same time, the cooperation can be directed at weakening the position of an alternative group of companies or even heightening the entry barriers for interested industry outsiders.

- Lobbying. Firms can also cooperate with one another with the objective of gaining a stronger position vis-à-vis contextual actors. Such lobbying relationships are often directed at strengthening the firms' voice towards political and regulatory actors, such as governments and regulatory agencies. However, firms can get together to put pressure on various other contextual actors, such as standard setting bodies, universities, tax authorities and stock exchanges as well.

In practice, cooperative relationships between organizations can involve a number of these objectives simultaneously. Moreover, it is not uncommon for objectives to shift over time and for various participants in the relationship to have different objectives.

Relational factors

How inter-organizational relationships develop is strongly influenced by the objectives pursued by the parties involved. However, a number of other factors also have an impact on how relationships unfold. These relational factors can be grouped into four general categories (e.g. Mitchell, Agle and Wood, 1997; Gulati, 1998):

- Legitimacy. Relationships are highly impacted by what is deemed to be legitimate. Written and unwritten codes of conduct give direction to what is viewed as acceptable behaviour. Which topics are allowed on the agenda, who has a valid claim, how interaction should take place and how conflicts should be resolved, are often decided by what both parties accept as 'the rules of engagement'. There is said to be 'trust', where it is expected that the other organization or individual will adhere to these rules. However, organizations do not always agree on 'appropriate behaviour', while what is viewed as legitimate can shift over time as well. It can also be (seen as) advantageous to act opportunistically by not behaving according to the unwritten rules (e.g. Gambetta, 1988; Williamson, 1991).

- Urgency. Inter-organizational relations are also shaped by the factor 'timing'. Relationships develop differently when one or both parties are under time pressure to achieve results, as opposed to a situation where both organizations can interact without experiencing a sense of urgency (e.g. Pfeffer and Salancik, 1978; James, 1985).

- Frequency. Inter-organizational relations also depend on the frequency of interaction and the expectation of future interactions. Where parties expect to engage in a one-off transaction they usually behave differently than when they anticipate a more structural relationship extending over multiple interactions. Moreover, a relationship with a low rate of interaction tends to develop differently than one with a high regularity of interaction (e.g. Axelrod, 1984; Dixit and Nalebuff, 1991).

- Power. Last but not least, relations between organizations are strongly shaped by the power held by both parties. Power is the ability to influence others' behaviour and organizations can have many sources of power. Most importantly for inter-organizational relationships, a firm can derive power from having resources that the other organization requires. In relationships with a very high level of resource dependence, firms tend to behave differently towards each other than when they are interdependent or relatively independent of one another (e.g. Pfeffer and Salancik, 1978; Porter, 1980).

Especially the impact of power differences on inter-organizational relationships is given extensive attention in the strategic management literature. Many authors (e.g. Chandler,

1990; Kay, 1993; Pfeffer and Salancik, 1978; Porter, 1980; Schelling, 1960) stress that for understanding the interaction between firms it is of the utmost importance to gain insight into their relative power positions. One way of measuring relative power in a relationship is portrayed in Figure 7.4, where a distinction is made between the closeness of the relationship (loose vs. tight) and the distribution of power between the two parties involved (balanced vs. unbalanced). This leads to a categorization of four specific types of inter-firm relationships from the perspective of relative power position. These four categories (adapted from Ruigrok and Van Tulder, 1995) are:

A Mutual independence. Organizations are independent in a relationship if they have full freedom to act according to their own objectives. Independence in an inter-organizational relationship means that organizations will only interact on their own terms and that they have the ability to break off the relationship without any penalty. In a situation of mutual independence, neither organization has significant influence over the other.

B Unbalanced independence. When two organizations work together in a loose relationship, one side (Firm A) can have more power than the other (Firm B). In such a case, it is said that Firm A is more independent than Firm B – Firm A's power gives it more freedom to act, while Firm B can be influenced by the powerful Firm A. This situation is called unbalanced independence, as both sides are independent, but one more so than the other.

C Mutual dependence. Two organizations can have a tight relationship, in which they are mutually dependent, while having an equal amount of sway over their counterpart. This type of situation, where there is a substantial, yet balanced, relationship between two or more parties, is also called interdependence.

D Unbalanced dependence. Where a tight relationship is characterized by asymmetrical dependence, one party will be able to dominate the other. In this situation of unbalanced dependence, the organization with the lower level of dependence will have more freedom to manoeuvre and impose its conditions than its counterpart.

The first category, mutual independence, is what is typically expected of a *market* relationship, although it is not strange to also witness market relationships that fit more in the second category, unbalanced independence. At the other extreme, unbalanced

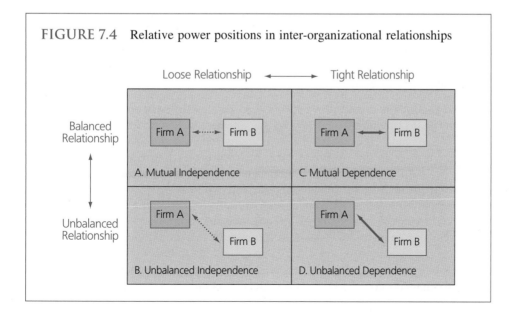

FIGURE 7.4 Relative power positions in inter-organizational relationships

dependence is very close to the situation that would occur if the dominant firm acquired its counterpart. Whether acquired or fully dependent, the dominant firm controls its behaviour. For this reason it is said that in cases of unbalanced dependence the inter-organizational relationship comes close to resembling the *hierarchy-type* relationship found within a firm. Interdependence seems to be somewhere between market and hierarchy-type relationships. What this means for the structuring of these relationships will be examined below.

Relational arrangements

In the classic dichotomy, the firm and its environment are presented as rather distinct entities. Within a firm coordination is achieved by means of direct control, leading transaction cost economists to refer to this organizational form as a 'hierarchy' (Williamson, 1975, 1985). In a hierarchy a central authority governs internal relationships and has the formal power to coordinate strategy and solve inter-departmental disputes. In the environment, relationships between firms are non-hierarchical, as they interact with one another without any explicit coordination or dispute settlement mechanism. This organizational form is referred to as a 'market'.

In Chapter 6 it was argued that there are all types of activities that companies should not want to internalize and run themselves, but should leave up to the marketplace. In many situations, it is much more efficient to buy inputs in the market than to make them yourself – where activities are performed by autonomous parties and outputs are sold in the marketplace, costs will often be lowest. As summarized by Ouchi (1980, p. 130), 'in a market relationship, the transaction takes place between the two parties and is mediated by a price mechanism in which the existence of a competitive market reassures both parties that the terms of exchange are equitable'.

Integration of activities into the firm is only necessary where 'markets do not function properly' – where doing it yourself is cheaper or better. The firm must internalize activities, despite the disadvantages of hierarchy, where the 'invisible hand' of the market cannot be trusted to be equitable and effective. Control over activities by means of formal authority – the 'visible hand' – is needed under these conditions. This is particularly true of all of the synergy advantages mentioned in Chapter 6, that the corporation would not be able to reap if the various business activities were not brought together under one 'corporate roof'.

In reality, however, there are many organizational forms between markets and hierarchies (e.g. Håkansson and Johanson, 1993; Powell, 1990; Thorelli, 1986). These are the networks, partnerships, or alliances introduced at the start of this chapter. In networks, strategies are coordinated and disputes resolved, not through formal top-down power, but by mutual adaptation. To extend the above metaphor, networks rely neither on the visible nor invisible hand to guide relationships, but rather employ the 'continuous handshake' (Gerlach, 1992).

The organizations involved in networks can employ different sorts of collaborative arrangements to structure their ties with one another. In Figure 7.5, an overview of a number of common types of collaborative arrangements is presented. Two major distinctions are made in this overview. First, between bilateral arrangements, which only involve two parties, and multilateral arrangements, which involve three or more. Commonly, only the multilateral arrangements are referred to as networks, although here the term is employed to cover all groupings of two or more cooperating firms. The second distinction is between non-contractual, contractual and equity-based arrangements. Non-contractual arrangements are cooperative agreements that are not binding by law, while contractual arrangements do have a clear legal enforceability. Both, however, do not involve taking a financial stake in each other or in a new joint venture, while the equity-based arrangements do.

FIGURE 7.5   Examples of collaborative arrangements

	Non-Contractual Arrangements	Contractual Arrangements	Equity-based Arrangements
Multilateral Arrangements	• Lobbying coalition (e.g. European Roundtable of Industrialists) • Joint standard setting (e.g. Linux coalition) • Learning communities (e.g. Strategic Management Society)	• Research consortium (e.g. Symbian in PDAs) • International marketing alliance (e.g. Star Alliance in airlines) • Export partnership (e.g. Netherlands Export Combination)	• Shared payment system (e.g. Visa) • Construction consortium (e.g. Eurotunnel) • Joint reservation system (e.g. Galileo)
Bilateral Arrangements	• Cross-selling deal (e.g. between pharmaceutical firms) • R&D staff exchange (e.g. between IT firms) • Market information sharing agreement (e.g. between hardware and software makers)	• Licensing agreement (e.g. Disney and Coca-Cola) • Co-development contract (e.g. Disney and Pixar in movies) • Co-branding alliance (e.g. Coca-Cola and McDonald's)	• New product joint venture (e.g. Sony and Ericsson in cellphones) • Cross-border joint venture (e.g. Daimler Chrysler and Beijing Automotive) • Local joint venture (e.g. CNN Turk in Turkey)

The intent of these collaborative arrangements is to profit from some of the advantages of vertical and horizontal integration, without incurring their costs. Networks are actually hybrid organizational forms that attempt to combine the benefits of hierarchy with the benefits of the market. The main benefits of hierarchy are those associated with the structural coordination of activities. In non-market relational arrangements, all parties collaborate on a more long-term basis with the intent of realizing a common goal. They will organize procedures, routines and control systems to ensure effective and efficient functioning of their joint activities and a smooth transition at their organizational inter-faces. The benefits of the market that these collaborative arrangements retain are flexibility and motivation. By not being entirely locked into a fixed hierarchy, individual firms can flexibly have multiple relationships, of varying length and intensity, and can change these relationships more easily where circumstances require adaptation. The market also provides the motivation to be efficient and to optimize the pursuit of the organization's self-interest. This entrepreneurial incentive can be a strong spur for risk-taking, innovation and change.

A significant advantage of collaborative arrangements is that such relationships facilitate the process of 'co-specialization'. Much of humanity's economic progress is based on the principle of specialization by means of a division of labour. As people and firms focus more closely on performing a limited set of value-adding activities, they become more effective and efficient in their work. This division of labour assumes, however, that the value-adding activities that are outsourced by one become the specialization of another, hence co-specialization. Yet, many activities cannot be outsourced to outsiders on the basis of normal market relations, either due to the risk of dependence or because of the need for the structural coordination of activities. Under these conditions, collaborative arrangements can act as a synthesis of hierarchy and market relations, thus catalysing the process of specialization (e.g. Best, 1990; Axelsson and Easton, 1992).

Such co-specialization can progress to such an extent that clusters of firms work to-gether in more of less permanent networks. Such symbiotic groups of collaborating firms can actually function as 'virtual corporations' (e.g. Chesbrough and Teece, 1996; Quinn, 1992). In such networks, the relationships between the participating firms are often very tight and durable, based on a high level of trust and perceived mutual interest. While each organization retains its individual identity, the boundaries between them become fuzzy, blurring the clear distinction between 'the organization' and 'its environment'. When a high level of trust and reciprocity has been achieved, relations can move far beyond simple contractual obligations. The collaborative relations can become more open-ended, with objectives, responsibilities, authority and results not fully determined in advance in a written contract, but evolving over time, given all parties' sincere willingness to 'work on their relationship' (e.g. Jarillo, 1988; Kanter, 1994).

While the intention of collaborative arrangements may be to blend the advantages of hierarchy with the qualities of the market, it is also possible that the weaknesses of both are actually combined. The main weakness of hierarchy is bureaucracy – creating red tape, unnecessary coordination activities and dulling the incentive to perform. In reality, collaborative arrangements might be mechanisms for structuring static relationships and dampening entrepreneurial behaviour. A further danger is that the mutual dependence might become skewed, shifting the balance of power to one of the partners. Under such conditions, one or more organizations can become dependent on a dominant party, without much influence (voice) or the possibility to break off the relationship (exit). Such unbalanced dependency relationships (see Figure 7.4) might be a great benefit for the stronger party, but can easily lead to the predominance of its interests over the interests of the weaker partners (e.g. Oliver and Wilkinson, 1988; Ruigrok and Van Tulder, 1995).

Simultaneously such partnerships are vulnerable to the main disadvantage of the market, namely opportunism. Companies run the risk of opportunism, that is (according to Williamson, 1985: 47):

self-interest seeking with guile. This includes but is scarcely limited to more blatant forms, such as lying, stealing and cheating.... More generally, opportunism refers to the incomplete or distorted disclosure of information, especially to calculated efforts to mislead, distort, disguise, obfuscate, or otherwise confuse.

Such behaviour can be limited by clearly defining objectives, responsibilities, authority and expected results ahead of time, preferably in an explicit contract. Even then colla-borative arrangements expose companies to the risk of deception, the abuse of trust and the exploitation of dependence, making their use by no means undisputed.

THE PARADOX OF COMPETITION AND COOPERATION

We have no eternal allies and we have no perpetual enemies. Our interests are eternal and perpetual, and those interests it is our duty to follow.
Lord Palmerston (Henry John Temple) (1784–1865); British prime minister

When former CEO of KLM Royal Dutch Airlines, Pieter Bouw, teamed up with North-west Airlines in 1989, he was thrilled to have the first major transatlantic strategic alli-ance in the industry, involving joint flights, marketing and sales activities, catering, ground handling, maintenance and purchasing. Northwest was the fourth largest

American carrier at that time, but was in 'Chapter 11', balancing on the verge of bank-ruptcy, and in dire need of cash. To help their new ally out, KLM gave a US$400 million capital injection, in return for 20% of the shares and the option to increase this to a majority stake within a few years. KLM and Northwest were on their way to becoming a virtual transatlantic company – a marriage 'made in the heavens'.

Commercially the deal was a success, but relationally the alliance was a Shakespear-ean drama. KLM gave up its hopes of an alliance with Swissair, SAS and Delta, to remain loyal to Northwest, but as soon as Northwest emerged from Chapter 11, it blocked KLM's efforts to increase its shareholding. In the resulting two-year legal shooting match be-tween 1995 and 1997, relations deteriorated sharply and the goose laying the golden eggs was threatened to be killed in the cross fire. Disappointed and dismayed, Bouw decided to give in, selling Northwest back its shares, in return for a prolongation of the alliance, after which he immediately resigned. His successor, and current CEO, Leo van Wijk, has managed the alliance since then and it is still 'up in the air', in both senses of the ex-pression. His most important conclusion has been that a collaborative alliance is not only about working together towards a common interest, but equally about being assertive with regard to one's own interests. Alliances are not only *cooperative*, but also have *compe-titive* aspects.

What this example of KLM and Northwest illustrates is that firms constantly struggle with the tension created by the need to work together with others, while simultaneously needing to pursue their own interests. Firms cannot isolate themselves from their en-vironments, but must actively engage in relationships with suppliers and buyers, while selectively teaming up with other firms inside and outside their industry to attain mutual benefit. But while they are collaborating to create joint value, firms are also each other's rivals when it comes to dividing the benefits. These opposite demands placed on organ-izations are widely referred to as the pressures for competition and cooperation (e.g. Brandenburger and Nalebuff, 1996; Lado, Boyd and Hanlon, 1997). In the following sections both pressures will be examined in more detail.

The demand for inter-organizational competition

Competition can be defined as the act of working against others, where two or more organizations' goals are mutually exclusive. In other words, competition is the rivalry behaviour exhibited by organizations or individuals where one's win is the other's loss.

Organizations need to be competitive in their relationships with others. As the interests or objectives of different organizations are often mutually exclusive, each organization needs to be determined and assertive in pursuing its own agenda. Each organization needs to be willing to confront others to secure its own interests. Without the will to engage in competitive interaction, the organization will be at the mercy of more aggressive coun-terparts, e.g. suppliers will charge excessively for products, buyers will express stiff de-mands for low prices, governments will require special efforts without compensation, and rival firms will poach among existing customers. Taking a competitive posture towards these external parties means that the organization is determined to assert its own interests and fight where necessary.

The resulting competitive relations can vary between open antagonism and conflict on the one hand, and more subtle forms of friction, tension and strain on the other. Blatant competitive behaviour is often exhibited towards organizations whose objectives are fully in conflict – most clearly other producers of the same goods, attempting to serve the same markets (aptly referred to as 'the competition'). Highly competitive behaviour can also be witnessed where a supplier and a buyer confront each other for dominance in the industry value chain (e.g. Porter, 1980; Van Tulder and Junne, 1988). A more restrained competitive stance can be observed where organizations' objectives are less at odds, but assertiveness is still important to protect the organization's interests. Negotiation and bargaining will commonly be employed under these circumstances.

To be competitive an organization must have the power to overcome its rivals and it must have the ability and will to use its power. Many factors shape the power of an organization, but its relative level of resource dependence is one of the most important determining elements. The more independent the organization, and the more others are dependent on it, the more power the organization will wield. In competitive relationships manoeuvring the other party into a relatively dependent position is a common approach. In general, calculation, bargaining, manoeuvring, building coalitions and outright conflict are all characteristic for the competitive interaction between organizations.

The demand for inter-organizational cooperation

Cooperation can be defined as the act of working together with others, where two or more organizations' goals are mutually beneficial. In other words, cooperation is the collaborative behaviour exhibited by organizations or individuals where both sides need each other to succeed.

Organizations need to be cooperative in their relationships with others. The interests or objectives of different organizations are often complementary and working together can be mutually beneficial. Therefore, organizations must be willing to behave as partners, striving towards their common good. Without the will to engage in cooperative interaction, the organization will miss the opportunity to reap the advantages of joint efforts, e.g. developing new products together with suppliers, creating a better service offering together with buyers, improving the knowledge infrastructure together with government and setting new technical standards together with other firms in the industry. Taking a cooperative posture towards these external parties means that the organization is determined to leverage its abilities through teamwork.

The resulting cooperative relations can vary between occasional alliances on the one hand, to tight-knit, virtual integration on the other. Strongly cooperative behaviour can be witnessed where the long-term interests of all parties are highly intertwined. This type of symbiotic relationship can be found between the producers of complementary goods and services, where success by one organization will positively impact its partners – aptly referred to as the 'network effect' (Arthur, 1994; Shapiro and Varian, 1998). Highly cooperative behaviour can also be observed where suppliers and buyers face a joint challenge (such as government regulation, an innovative technology or a new market entrant) that can only be tackled by significant mutual commitment to a shared objective.

More restrained cooperative behaviour is common where there is potential for a 'positive sum game', but some parties seek to optimize their own returns to the detriment of others. Under such circumstances, exhibiting cooperative behaviour does not mean being naïve or weak, but creating conditions under which the long-term shared interests prevail over the short-term temptation by some to cheat their partners. An important ingredient for overcoming the lure of opportunism is to build long-term commitment to one another, not only in words and mentality, but also practically, through a high level of interdependence. Where organizations are tightly linked to one another, the pay-off for cooperative behaviour is usually much more enticing than the possibility to profit from the dependence of one's partner. But to be willing to commit to such a high level of interdependence, people on both sides of a relationship need to trust each other's intentions and actions, while there must be coordination and conflict-resolution mechanisms in place to solve evolving issues (e.g. Dyer, Kale and Singh, 2001, Reading 7.4 in this book; Simonin, 1997).

EXHIBIT 7.1   SHORT CASE

MERCK: A MEDICINE AGAINST ANOREXIA?

Name an industry in which the average product takes 10 to 15 years to develop, at a cost of more than US$1 billion a shot. Aerospace? Robotics? Logical choices, but the right answer is pharmaceuticals. Developing new drugs does not come easily or cheaply. The R&D budgets of the large pharmaceutical companies are approximately 18% of sales, placing some of them among the biggest R&D spenders in the world. With such high investments and long lead times, the pharmaceutical industry is a competitive arena that should be avoided by the short-winded and faint-hearted. Richard Clark, however, does not need to reach for a box of the hypertension medicine Cozaar just yet – he only needs to sell the product and is doing so quite successfully. Clark has been CEO of the New Jersey headquartered pharmaceutical giant Merck & Co. since 2005 and was the architect of its acquisition of Schering-Plough in 2009. This US$41.1 billion deal catapulted Merck from the 7th spot in the worldwide rankings to a 3rd position, just behind Roche and Pfizer. With sales of US$46.9 billion in 2008 and more than 100 000 employees, Clark has created a pharmaceutical heavyweight, but one faced with the challenge of maintaining its weight and not slowly shrivelling under competitive pressure.

Merck has competed in this high-stakes industry for more than 100 years, initially as the US subsidiary of the German company, Merck. During World War I the Merck subsidiary became separated from its parent company in Darmstadt, and to this day both companies use the Merck name (the German E. Merck has sales of approximately €7.5 billion, two thirds of which are in pharmaceuticals). For decades, the pharmaceutical industry has enjoyed double-digit revenue growth and recession-proof high profitability, making it a stock market favourite despite the risk involved in the drug development process. But since the end of the 1990s, the industry conditions have taken a turn for the worse. After years of unchallenged price hikes, governments have started to look at the drug firms as partially responsible for the soaring cost of healthcare, and have been taking measures to lower prices of prescribed drugs. In the US, the rise of

'managed care' organizations that can buy in bulk has further enhanced the bargaining power of buyers, placing more pressure on prices. In many other countries, healthcare insurance companies have become major players in searching for ways to clamp down on spiralling pharmaceutical expenditures.

At the same time, the highly profitable 'monopoly' period after the launch of a new drug is becoming ever shorter – successful products are soon joined by competitors' me-too products, which skilfully circumvent patent protection. And as soon as the patents actually expire, aggressive generic drug manufacturers quickly enter the market with products at cut-rate prices, often largely wiping out the sales of the patent holder. In the period 2008–2011, the world's largest pharmaceutical companies are slated to see more than 70 of their blockbuster drugs lose their patent protection. This represents a collective loss of US$100 billion in annual sales, on worldwide revenues of approximately US$600 billion. To extend their monopoly period, the research-based pharmaceutical companies have tried to devise all types of ways of getting new patents for modifications to existing drugs – only 15% of newly approved major drugs are based on 'new chemical entities' or treat illnesses in novel ways. However, some generic drug companies have responded by making court battles their standard operating procedure, sometimes fighting up to 100 cases a year. Most research-based drug companies realize that their best defence is to forge ahead and develop new blockbuster products. The result has been a significant growth in R&D investments, yet the stream of new products has slowed, remaining far behind what is needed to keep sales steady.

The US$1 billion price tag and 10–15 year time span for getting the scientists' chemical compounds out of the test tube and onto the pharmacists' shelves is only partially attributable to the process of actually discovering a potential new drug. In general it takes about one to three years for a new preparation to be synthesized and tested. But once a preparation is in the pipeline, many further steps need to be taken before it becomes a sellable product. First, the preparation enters the pre-clinical development phase, which might involve animal testing. If after a few years of tests, the results are promising, permission can be gained to proceed with clinical trials on human volunteers. At first, these are conducted on small groups, but if successful, they are enlarged to full-scale tests. The clinical trials can take five to ten years before a drug is approved for broader use and sales can begin. On average, of the 20 preparations entering pre-clinical development, only one comes out of the pipeline as a marketable drug. Obviously, pharmaceutical companies would like to increase this yield and shorten the process, but this will not be easy in the face of strict regulations and demands for approval by agencies like the Food and Drug Administration (FDA) in the US. Moreover, shortening the testing phase can seriously backfire, as Merck found out in 2004, when a drug called Vioxx proved to have unforeseen negative side effects, leading to serious health problems in patients and resulting in a US$4.5 billion settlement agreement in the US alone.

While some firms, such as Sanofi-Aventis, have decided to descend into the low-margin generic drug business, most have tried to supplement their half-empty pipelines with promising drugs from other companies, either through mergers and acquisitions, or through alliances. There have been many headline grabbing deals, such as Pfizer's acquisition of Wyeth for US$68 billion in 2009, followed by Roche's purchase of Genentech for US$46.8 billion just a few months later, making them the world's number one and two. But this is just the tip of the deal-making iceberg, with hundreds of other acquisitions leading to a major consolidation in the industry. The added benefit of these acquisitions has been to achieve significant cost savings in administration, marketing and sales.

In stark contrast to the scarcity of new products in the traditional pharmaceutical firms, many promising new drugs have been emerging from small biotech firms, often started as spin-offs from universities – thousands of them are scattered across the world, and many hundreds are clustered in hotspots, most prominently in the US, Singapore, France (Paris), Germany (Munich) and the UK (London). All of these firms are so specialized, that at any one moment at least one of them will be ahead of any given big firm in any given technology. Most pharmaceutical giants believe that it is wise to tap into this source of new products, especially if this speeds up the process of getting newly developed drugs into their pipeline. Moreover, licensing in new drugs from the small biotech firms can usually be achieved at a fraction of the cost of doing it in-house. Most biotech firms do not have the financial stamina to shepherd their products through the years of development and trials, nor do they have the marketing and distribution infrastructure needed to reap the benefits of their labours. This gives the big firms the negotiating position to snap up promising products for considerably less than they are worth. Alternatively, they can also purchase the entire biotech firm, if they feel that more interesting products can be expected.

The enthusiasm of Merck's competitors for alliances with (or the acquisition of) the creative independents has been based on the view 'if you can't beat them, let them join you'. However, for a long time Merck was rather reluctant to become dependent on outside research to fill its pipeline, strongly favouring self-sufficiency and organic growth. Only in 2002 did Merck's Vice President and CFO, Judy Lewent, announce that the company would consider more alliances with small bio-tech companies, both in R&D and marketing. But the company's approach has been hesitant, with not more than 5% of Merck's total research spending ending up outside of its own laboratories. This emphasis on doing most R&D in-house contrasts sharply with the direction taken by many others in the industry. Most of Merck's rivals reserve between 10 and 20 per cent of their R&D budgets for external work. In some cases only the laborious task of conducting clinical trials is outsourced, but increasingly the pharmaceutical giants are contracting out the development of new drugs to specialist firms, or licensing in the new products created by small biotech start-ups. Some analysts are predicting that the proportion of R&D performed outside of the big companies could reach 80%. Sir Richard Sykes, former CEO of GlaxoSmithKline, has even suggested that the major drug firms will increasingly become 'virtual' companies, as they concentrate on the marketing of drugs developed by the legions of small independent biotech firms.

While embarking on the path of outsourcing, alliances and joint ventures, it is doubtful Merck will ever go that far. There is a strong sense within the firm that outsourcing could easily lead to hollowing out – a type of 'R&D anorexia'. It is believed that without first class in-house scientific talent a drug firm will have problems to rapidly identify the best biotech ideas worth buying. The president of Merck Research Laboratories, Peter Kim, has indicated that if Merck does lack certain key knowledge, he would prefer to selectively acquire smaller companies and integrate them into his research community. In this way, Merck has acquired the biotech company GlycoFi in 2006, in the field of yeast glycol-engineering and optimization of biologic drug molecules, and has transformed it into a new biotech division, Merck BioVentures.

So, how far should Richard Clark go in linking up with biotech companies? And should he buy and integrate them, or cooperate with them in some type of way? Or does it make more sense to focus attention on the internal challenge of getting the Merck and Schering-Plough R&D teams to

integrate and cut overhead, leaving the additional complexity of pursuing more external relationships aside for the moment? Given the uncertainty and stress of answering these questions, maybe Clark should keep some Cozaar handy, just in case.

Co-author: Martijn Rademakers

Sources: www.fiercebiotech.com; www.ims-global.com. www. merck.com; *The Economist*, 16 August 2008; 26 January and 5 February 2009; *Business Week*, 30 July 2007; *Wall Street Journal*, 5 December 2008; *Bloomberg*, 3 February 2009; *The Washington Times*, 13 March 2009

PERSPECTIVES ON NETWORK LEVEL STRATEGY

Concordia discors (discordant harmony).

Horace (65–8 BC); Roman poet

Firms need to be able to engage in competition and cooperation simultaneously, even though these demands are each other's opposites. Firms need to exhibit a strongly cooperative posture to reap the benefits of collaboration, and they need to take a strongly competitive stance to ensure that others do not block their interests. Some theorists conclude that what is required is 'co-opetition' (Brandenburger and Nalebuff, 1996). But while a catchy word, managers are still left with the difficult question of how to deal with these conflicting demands. To meet the pressure for cooperation, firms must actually become part of a broader 'team', spinning a web of close collaborative relationships. But to meet the pressure for competition, firms must not become too entangled in restrictive relationships, but rather remain free to manoeuvre, bargain and attack, with the intention of securing their own interests. In other words, firms must be *embedded* and *independent* at the same time – embedded in a network of cooperative interactions, while independent enough to wield their power to their own advantage.

The question dividing strategizing managers is whether firms should be more embedded or more independent. Should firms immerse themselves in broader networks to create strong groups, or should they stand on their own? Should firms willingly engage in long-term interdependence relationships or should they strive to remain as independent as possible? Should firms develop network level strategies at all, or should the whole concept of multi-firm strategy-making be directed to the garbage heap?

While strategy writers generally agree about the need to manage the paradox of competition and cooperation, they come to widely differing prescriptions on how to do so. Views within the field of strategic management are strongly at odds with regard to the best approach to inter-organizational relations. As before, here the two diametrically opposed positions will be identified and discussed, to show the scope of differing ideas. On one side of the spectrum, there are strategists who believe that it is best for companies to be primarily competitive in their relationships to all outside forces. They argue that firms should remain independent and interact with other companies under market conditions as much as possible. As these strategists emphasize the discrete boundaries separating the firm from its 'competitive environment', this point of view is called the 'discrete organization perspective'. At the other end of the spectrum, there are strategists who believe that companies should strive to build up more long-term cooperative relationships with key organizations in their environment. They argue that firms can reap significant benefits by surrendering a part of their independence and developing close collaborative arrangements with a group of other organizations. This point of view will be referred to as the 'embedded organization perspective'.

The discrete organization perspective

Managers taking the discrete organization perspective view companies as independent entities competing with other organizations in a hostile market environment. In line with neoclassical economics, this perspective commonly emphasizes that individuals, and the organizations they form, are fundamentally motivated by aggressive self-interest and therefore that competition is the natural state of affairs. Suppliers will try to enhance their bargaining power vis-à-vis buyers with the aim of getting a better price, while conversely buyers will attempt to improve their negotiation position to attain better quality at lower cost. Competing firms will endeavour to gain the upper hand against their rivals if the opportunity arises, while new market entrants and manufacturers of substitute products will consistently strive to displace incumbent firms (e.g. Porter, 1980, 1985, Reading 5.1).

In such a hostile environment it is a strategic necessity for companies to strengthen their competitive position in relation to the external forces. The best strategy for each organization is to obtain the market power required to get good price/quality deals, ward off competitive threats, limit government demands and even determine the development of the industry. Effective power requires independence and therefore heavy reliance on specific suppliers, buyers, financiers or public organizations should be avoided.

The label 'discrete organization' given to this perspective refers to the fact that each organization is seen as being detached from its environment, with sharp boundaries demarcating where the outside world begins. The competitive situation is believed to be *atomistic*, that is, each self-interested firm strives to satisfy its own objectives, leading to rivalry and conflict with other organizations. Vertical interactions between firms in the industry column tend to be transactional, with an emphasis on getting the best possible deal. It is generally assumed that under such market conditions the interaction will be of a zero-sum nature, that is, a fight for who gets how much of the pie. The firm with the strongest bargaining power will usually be able to appropriate a larger portion of the 'economic rent' than will the less potent party. Therefore, advocates of the discrete organization perspective emphasize that the key to competitive success is the ability to build a powerful position and to wield this power in a calculated and efficient manner. This might sound Machiavellian to the faint-hearted, but it is the reality of the marketplace that is denied at one's own peril.

Essential for organizational power is the avoidance of resource dependence. Where a firm is forced to lean on a handful of suppliers or buyers, this can place the organization in a precariously exposed position. To managers taking a discrete organization perspective, such dependence on a few external parties is extremely risky, as the other firm will be tempted to exploit their position of relative power to their own advantage. Wise firms will therefore not let themselves become overly dependent on any external organization, certainly not for any essential resources. This includes keeping the option open to exit from the relationship at will – with low barriers to exit the negotiating position of the firm is significantly stronger. Therefore the firm must never become so entangled with outsiders that it cannot rid themselves of them at the drop of a hat. The firm must be careful that in a web of relationships it is the spider, not the fly (e.g. Pfeffer & Salancik, 1978; Ruigrok and Van Tulder, 1995).

Keeping other organizations at arm's length also facilitates clear and business-like interactions. Where goods and services are bought or sold, distinct organizational boundaries help to distinguish tasks, responsibilities, authority and accountability. But as other firms will always seek to do as little as possible for the highest possible price, having clear contracts and a believable threat to enforce them, will serve as a method to ensure discipline. Arm's-length relations are equally useful in avoiding the danger of vital information leaking to the party with whom the firm must (re)negotiate.

In their relationships with other firms in the industry it is even clearer that companies' interests are mutually exclusive. More market share for one company must necessarily come at the expense of another. Coalitions are occasionally formed to create power blocks, if individual companies are not strong enough to compete on their own. Such tactical alliances bring together weaker firms, not capable of doing things independently. But 'competitive collaboration' is usually short lived – either the alliance is unsuccessful and collapses, or it is successful against the common enemy, after which the alliance partners become each other's most important rivals.

Proponents of the discrete organization perspective argue that collaborative arrangements are always second best to doing things independently. Under certain conditions, weakness might force a firm to choose an alliance, but it is always a tactical necessity, never a strategic preference. Collaborative arrangements are inherently risky, fraught with the hazard of opportunism. Due to the ultimately competitive nature of relationships, allies will be tempted to serve their own interests to the detriment of the others, by manoeuvring, manipulating or cheating. The collaboration might even be a useful ploy, to cloak the company's aggressive intentions and moves. Collaboration, it is therefore concluded, is merely 'competition in a different form' (Hamel, Doz and Prahalad, 1989, Reading 7.1). Hence, where collaboration between firms really offers long-term advantages, a merger or acquisition is preferable to the uncertainty of an alliance.

Where collaboration is not the tool of the weak, it is often a conspiracy of the strong to inhibit competition. If two or more formidable companies collaborate, chances are that the alliance is actually ganging up on a third party – for instance on buyers. In such cases the term 'collaboration' is just a euphemism for collusion and not in the interest of the economy at large.

Worse yet, collaboration is usually also bad for a company's long-term health. A highly competitive environment is beneficial for a firm, because it provides the necessary stimulus for companies to continually improve and innovate. Strong adversaries push companies towards competitive fitness. A more benevolent environment, cushioned by competition-inhibiting collaboration, might actually make a firm more content and less eager to implement tough changes. In the long run this will make firms vulnerable to more aggressive companies, battle-hardened by years of rivalry in more competitive environments.

In conclusion, the basic assumption of the discrete organization perspective is that companies should not develop network level strategies, but should strive for 'strategic self-sufficiency'. Collaborative arrangements are a tactical tool, to be selectively employed. The sentiment of this perspective has been clearly summarized by Porter (1990; 224): 'alliances are rarely a solution … no firm can depend on another independent firm for skills and assets that are central to its competitive advantage … Alliances tend to ensure mediocrity, not create world leadership.'

EXHIBIT 7.2   THE DISCRETE ORGANIZATION PERSPECTIVE

MCCAIN: NO SMALL FRY

Which *Belgian* invention was spread around the world by *American* fast-food restaurants and is dominated by a *Canadian* multinational? Well, a product English-speakers accidentally call *French* fries. The Canadian firm leading the international market for this golden crispy delicacy is McCain, headquartered in the small town of Florenceville in the province of New Brunswick. With worldwide annual sales of over US$6 billion, more than 20 000 employees scattered around the globe and producing over one thousand tons of potato products every hour, McCain is no 'small fry'. As producer of one third of all frozen French fries in the world, McCain is worldwide market leader, ahead of its major US-based rivals Simplot and Lamb Weston.

While most people know McCain from its chilled and frozen potato products found in supermarket freezers, most of its sales are in the B2B market, which includes fast-food restaurants such as McDonald's, KFC, Wendy's and Burger King. This market in particular is a low margin, high volume business with very demanding customers. Achieving a stable supply of potatoes at a uniform quality level is key to keeping customers happy and margins up – which is easier said than done, as potatoes are highly susceptible to the influences of the weather and natural pests. The first step in getting a good supply of quality potatoes is in breeding 'seed potatoes' that are free of diseases and suited to local growing conditions. The second step is the actual growing and harvesting of the edible potatoes. Then come the industrialized processing steps of grading, skinning, slicing and packaging. Most companies in the industry column are specialized in either breeding, growing or processing, as each step requires significantly different competences. Breeding is highly R&D intensive, oriented towards developing new, patented varieties that taste different, or have lower growing or processing costs. Potato growing has also become increasingly knowledge intensive, but can still be carried out efficiently even by relatively small-sized farms. Potato processing, by contrast, is a highly industrialized process where economies of scale matter.

In striking contrast with its specialized competitors, McCain's strategy has long been to control the entire value chain. Or as one key manager recently put it, McCain's perspective is that 'competitive strength comes from having control over every aspect of the business'. While its competitors are dependent on others in the value chain for their success, McCain has gained a high level of independence by building a substantial power base in all stages of the industry column.

At the breeding stage, McCain develops its own varieties, which ensures its independence from external breeders. The company also seeks to buy patents of promising varieties before others get access to them. At the growing stage, McCain maintains a limited in-house farming capacity, yet leaves most potato production to independent farmers, because potato growing has low economies of scale and a high level of risk, due to unpredictable harvests. An important part of the potato supplies that keep McCain's factories running are secured via 'pre-harvest' contracts. The contract conditions tend to be very favourable to McCain – the many individual potato growers dealt with are relatively small players, giving McCain a powerful bargaining position. To secure uniform, high quality supplies for its factories, tightly specified contracts are used that set standards and strict delivery times. Furthermore, the firm has an 'agronomy' team that closely monitors and supports contract farmers on a day-to-day basis. Besides these contract suppliers, McCain also purchases additional supplies on the postharvest spot market, in which large price fluctuations can occur. For this reason (but also to keep in touch with the art of potato production), McCain grows a small part of its own potato supply – just enough to counter speculative 'trade strikes' by growers and traders. Well-timed trade strikes, whereby suppliers refuse to sell their produce, can drive up the spot market potato price, just when processors need new supplies to keep their factories running. Applying the same rationale of independence, McCain operates its own transportation business to ensure flawless distribution of its products, instead of leaving this to specialists from outside.

The discrete organization perspective, which drives McCain's vertical relationships within the value chain, is also at the basis of their horizontal relationships (with competitors and trade associations for potato firms). McCain prefers to stand alone – avoiding any dependence on the trade associations that populate the potato industry. These associations, jointly paid and run by the competing firms, are mainly aimed at promoting common interests vis-à-vis national and supranational (e.g. the European Union) regulatory agencies and pressure groups. Apart from the occasional short-term coalition, McCain has sought to pursue its interests on its own.

Co-author: Martijn Rademakers

Sources: *Rademakers*, 1999; www.mccain.com; www.refrigeratedfrozenfood.com; *New York Times*, 26 October 2008.

The embedded organization perspective

Strategists taking an embedded organization perspective are fundamentally at odds with the assumption that competition is the predominant factor determining the interaction between organizations. Business isn't war, so to approach all interactions from an antagonistic angle is seen as overly pessimistic, even cynical. On the contrary, it is argued that business is about value creation, which is inherently a positive-sum activity. Creating value brings together organizations towards a common goal, as they can achieve more by working together than by behaving autonomously. In the modern economy, no organization can efficiently perform all activities in-house, as the division of labour has encouraged companies to specialize and outsource as many non-core activities as possible. Companies are necessarily cogs in the larger industrial machine and they can achieve little without working in unison with the other parts of the system. In the embedded organization perspective, atomistic competition is a neoclassical theoretical abstraction that seriously mischaracterizes the nature of relationships between organizations. In reality, cooperation is the predominant factor determining inter-organizational relations. Symbiosis, not aggression, is the fundamental nature of economic functioning (e.g. Jarillo, 1988; Moore, 1996, Reading 7.3).

A company can always find many organizations in its environment with which it shares an interest and whose objectives are largely parallel to its own (Child and Faulkner, 1998). A company might want to develop new products together with its buyers, optimize the logistical system together with its suppliers, expand the industry's potential together with other manufacturers, link technological standards with other industries and improve employment conditions together with the government. In general, most organizations have a stronger interest in increasing the size of the pie, than in deciding who gets what – keeping the focus on making a success of value creation eases the process of finding an equitable solution to the issue of value distribution.

The label 'embedded organization' given to this perspective refers to the fact that firms are becoming increasingly integrated into webs of mutually dependent organizations (e.g. Gnyawali and Madhavan, 2001; Granovetter, 1985). As companies strive to focus on a limited set of core competences and core business processes, they have moved to outsource as many non-core activities as possible. But as firms have attempted to further specialize by outsourcing activities that are close to their core business, they have become more vulnerable to outside suppliers and the need for explicit coordination of activities has often remained high. The outsourcing of such essential and coordination-intensive activities can only take place where the other party can be trusted to closely collaborate with the joint interests in mind. Of course, a company will not quickly move to such dependence on an outside supplier. But as experience and trust build over time, a strategic partnership can develop, where both sides come to accept the value of the close cooperation (e.g. Axelsson and Easton, 1992; Lorenzoni and Baden-Fuller, 1995, Reading 7.2).

For a firm to willingly surrender a part of its independence, it must be certain that its partners are also willing to invest in the relationship and will not behave opportunistically. Ideally, therefore, durable partnerships are based on mutual dependence and reciprocity. Both sides of the relationship must need each other, which gives an important incentive for both to find solutions to the disputes that will inevitably pop up. A balance in the benefits to be gained and the efforts to be exerted will also contribute to the success of a long-term collaborative relationship.

While such close collaborative relationships place a firm in a position of resource dependence, the benefits are much larger. By specializing in a certain area, the firm can gain scale and experience advantages much faster. Specialization helps the firm to focus on a more limited set of core competences, which can be developed more efficiently and rapidly than if the firm were a 'conglomerate' of activities. At the same time the firm can tap into the complementary resources (Richardson, 1972) developed by its co-specialized partners. These complementary resources will usually be of higher quality and lower price than if the firm had built them up independently.

Specialized firms also use collaborative arrangements to quickly combine their resources with industry outsiders, to create new products and services. As product and business innovation is high paced and usually requires the combination of various types of resources, developing everything in isolation is unworkable for most firms. By teaming up with other firms that have complementary resources, a company can make the most of its own resource base, without having to build up other resources from scratch. But again trust is needed to engage in such a joint venture, as there are significant downside risks that the firm needs to take into account.

So, from the embedded organization perspective, collaboration is not competition in disguise, but a real alternative means of dealing with other organizations (e.g. Contractor and Lorange, 1988; Piore and Sabel, 1984). Successful firms embed themselves in webs of cooperative relationships, developing strategies together with their partners. These networks might compete against other networks (e.g. Gomes-Casseres, 1994; Hamilton and Woolsey Biggart, 1988; Weidenbaum and Hughes, 1996), but even here the relationships need not be fundamentally antagonistic. Proponents of the embedded organization perspective do not believe that firms should become obsessed with 'putting the competition out of business', as this again reduces business to a win–lose, zero-sum game. Firms should be focused on creating value and avoiding direct confrontation with other manufacturers, emphasizing the opportunity for a win–win, positive-sum game (e.g. Kim and Mauborgne, 2004, Reading 8.4; Moore, 1996, Reading 7.3). With this approach, firms in the same industry will recognize that they often have parallel interests as well. Setting industry standards, lobbying the government, finding solutions to joint environmental problems, improving the image of the industry, investing in fundamental research and negotiating with the unions are just a few of the issues where cooperation can be fruitful.

EXHIBIT 7.3   THE EMBEDDED ORGANIZATION PERSPECTIVE

DUCATI: RIDING WITH THE PACK

Few sights are more breathtaking and few roars more exhilarating than a Ducati streaking down the road. Whether in elegant motion or just standing still, Ducati motorcycles always make heads turn. Distinctively designed and engineered for appearance, sound, and performance, Ducatis are all modern icons on wheels – ranging from their Hypermotard sports bike, of Terminator movie fame, to their Monster, Multistrada, Streetfighter, Superbike and Desmosedici models. And they are fast, as proved by their numerous wins in the MotoGP and Superbike World Championships. They are truly a motorcycle enthusiast's motorcycle.

Founded by the Ducati brothers in Bologna, Italy, in 1926, the Ducati company hit a slippery patch during the 1990s, as the big Japanese competitors Honda, Yamaha, Suzuki and Kawasaki became so dominant, that only a few niche players like BMW and Harley-Davidson were able to survive. In 1996, Ducati was purchased by US-based Texas-Pacific Group, which nursed the company back to health, eventually selling it to Investindustrial Holdings SpA in 2006. In 2008 Ducati racked up annual sales of about 42 000 bikes, worth approximately €470 million.

So, how does Ducati manage to stay ahead of its much larger Japanese competitors? An important part of the answer lies in the extensive network of specialized companies in which Ducati is embedded, enabling it to be cost-effective, innovative and flexible. As Ducati President and CEO Gabriele Del Torchio puts it: 'We are a small company with just about 1000 people on the payroll. We do not have the budgets that the Japanese giants have. They sell up to 250 times more motorbikes than we do. And we do not have the synergy advantages that some of them reap from their car business. So we need to work closely with our network of partners to be competitive.' The Ducati family, as this network is called, consists of approximately 180 suppliers, responsible for more than 90% of the cost of each bike. Ducati itself focuses on managing the network and integrating the parts. Its in-house activities are limited to R&D, design, the machining of crank cases and camshafts, assembly, quality control and marketing. While some of the suppliers are on short-term contracts, most relationships are long-term strategic partnerships, based on mutual trust and commitment to being a winning team. Del Torchio: 'We believe in making the pie bigger for all of us, instead of just fighting for a slice of the current pie.' More than 80% of the Ducati network partners are located within the Bologna industrial district, called Borgo Panigale, making communication and cooperation even easier.

As the company switched to lean manufacturing in the 1990s, it became even more important to work closely with its suppliers. As the former supply chain manager explained: 'To get them on board, we introduced an integration programme that involved Ducati people and supplier staff working in teams. We wanted to consider our suppliers as extensions of Ducati, and that meant connecting them via the web so we could exchange and accelerate the flow of information, like production planning, parts price lists, invoices, quality reports and so on.' The resulting levels of cost, quality and reliability of the products are known in the industry to be highly competitive.

On the distribution and sales side, Ducati has taken the same approach, working with strategic partners as opposed to doing things itself.

Transport, warehousing and packaging are entirely outsourced to network partners, while the exclusive Ducati Stores are owned by independent entrepreneurs, rather than by Ducati. These stores are equipped with real-time information systems connecting them with Ducati and the network of suppliers, enabling smooth and fast customer order management. Moreover, the Ducati network does not stop at the stores. The company also engages in networking activities with Ducatisti (as its customers are known), using internet based forums and community platforms, to allow discussions and to invite customers to give their views on issues such as advertising campaigns, improving product features, and designing new models.

When it comes to staying abreast of the latest technological developments, Ducati has its own R&D, but also teams up with partners in and beyond the motorcycle industry. The company works with several universities and firms like Magneti Marelli in the field of engine technology and also with a host of specialists in system performance engineering, such as SKF. Öhlins, Brembo, and Bridgestone are deeply involved as partners in developing the newest shock absorber, brake and tyre technologies – often proving their value on the racing tracks first. In the field of fuel consumption and emissions, Shell is an important research ally.

On the marketing side, Ducati also has an eye for the win–win partnership. It has struck joint marketing deals with Telecom Italia, insurance giant Generali and energy company Enel, while also linking up to create joint products with sports gear maker Puma and sunglass company Oakley of the Luxottica Group. Ducati even reinforces its premium positioning with selective alliances in the area of luxury goods, such as fragrances, jewellery and art, with its bikes playing a prominent role in advertising.

For Ducati, its approach to strategy is clear: Why ride alone, when there is strength in numbers?

Co-authors: Martijn Rademakers and Roger Cook

Sources: www.motorcyclenews.com; www.univ-evry.fr/labos/gerpisa/rencontre/S21Bardi-Garibaldo.pdf; www.oracle.com/oramag/profit/05-nov/p45ducati.html; www.ducati.com; company interviews; company documents.

INTRODUCTION TO THE DEBATE AND READINGS

The strong one is most powerful alone.
Friedrich von Schiller (1759–1805); German writer

All for one, one for all.
The Three Musketeers, Alexandre Dumas Jr. (1824–1895); French novelist

So, should managers form network level strategies or not? Should firms consciously embed themselves in a web of durable collaborative relationships, emphasizing the value of cooperative inter-organizational interactions for realizing their long-term aims? Or should firms try to remain as independent as possible, emphasizing the value of competitive power in achieving their strategic objectives? Is it 'all for one, one for all' or must the strong truly stand alone?

The debate on this issue within the field of strategy is far from being concluded. Many perspectives exist on how to reconcile the conflicting demands of competition and co-operation, and many 'best practices' have been put forward, but no consensus has thus far emerged. Therefore, individual strategists are once again in the position of needing to determine their own point of view.

To help strategists to gain more insight into the variety of perspectives on this issue, four readings have been selected that each takes a different angle on the debate. As in previous chapters, the first two readings will be representative of the two poles in this debate (see Table 7.1), while the second set of two readings will bring in additional factors to add further depth to the discussion.

To open on behalf of the discrete organization perspective, Michael Porter's reading in Chapter 5 could easily have been selected. In Reading 5.1, Porter states that 'the essence of strategy formulation is coping with competition', and that there are five sources of competitive pressure, all impinging on a firm's profit potential. These competitive forces are the threat of new entrants, powerful buyers and suppliers, rivalry among existing competitors and the threat of substitute products. Porter asserts that a company's profitability depends on how well it is able to defend itself against these 'opponents'. It is this view of the firm, as a lone organization surrounded by hostile forces, which places this reading clearly within the discrete organization perspective. While Porter does not denounce or warn against cooperative arrangements in this reading (as he does in Reading 10.3), neither does

TABLE 7.1   Discrete organization versus embedded organization perspective

	Discrete organization perspective	Embedded organization perspective
Emphasis on	Competition over cooperation	Cooperation over competition
Preferred position	Independence	Interdependence
Environment structure	Discrete organizations (atomistic)	Embedded organizations (networked)
Firm boundaries	Distinct and defended	Fuzzy and open
Inter-organizational relations	Arm's-length and transactional	Close and structural
Interaction outcomes	Mainly zero-sum (win/lose)	Mainly positive-sum (win/win)
Interaction based on	Bargaining power and calculation	Trust and reciprocity
Network level strategy	No	Yes
Use of collaboration	Temporary coalitions (tactical alliance)	Durable partnerships (strategic alliance)
Collaborative arrangements	Limited, well-defined, contract-based	Broad, open, relationship-based

he recognize cooperation as a possibility. His message is that of *realpolitik* – in inter-organizational relationships, conflict and power are the name of the game.

Because Porter's reading is already included in Chapter 5, another classic, 'Collaborate with Your Competitors – and Win', has been selected as Reading 7.1 for this chapter to represent the discrete organization perspective. In this piece, the authors, Gary Hamel, Yves Doz and C.K. Prahalad, basically take the same stance as Porter, in assuming that inter-firm relations are largely competitive and governed by power and calculation. However, while Porter makes little mention of, or is apprehensive about, collaboration with other organizations, Hamel, Doz and Prahalad see collaboration as a useful tool for improving the firm's competitive profile. They argue that alliances with competitors 'can strengthen both companies against outsiders even if it weakens one partner vis-à-vis the other', and therefore that the net result can be positive. Yet they emphasize that companies should not be naïve about the real nature of alliances –– 'collaboration is competition in a different form'. An alliance is 'a constantly evolving bargain', in which each firm will be fending for itself, trying to learn as much as possible from the other, while attempting to limit the partner's access to its knowledge and skills.

The authors advise firms to procede cautiously with alliances, only when they have clear objectives of what they wish to learn from their allies, a well-developed capacity to learn, and defences against their allies' probing of their skills and technologies. While Hamel, Doz and Prahalad only focus on horizontal relationships in this reading, their message is similar to that of Porter – competition in the environment is paramount and cooperation is merely an opportunistic move in the overall competitive game.

As representative of the embedded organization perspective, an article by Gianni Lorenzoni and Charles Baden-Fuller has been selected for Reading 7.2, entitled 'Creating a Strategic Centre to Manage a Web of Partners'. Lorenzoni and Baden-Fuller are particularly interested in how companies structure their vertical relationships, balancing pressures for competition and cooperation. In their view, where a group of firms works together closely, they can form a 'virtual company'. This type of network can benefit from most of the advantages of being a large vertically integrated company, while avoiding most of the pitfalls of integration. But Lorenzoni and Baden-Fuller articulate that it is necessary for a network of firms to have a strategic centre that can act as builder and coordinator. As builder, the strategic centre can deliberately design and assemble the network components, and as coordinator it can regulate activities and resolve disputes. The authors carry on to specify the conditions under which a network of firms can be an advantageous organizational form and what is required to make them work. Overall, their main message is that durable partnerships between multiple firms are not easy, but if this interdependence can be managed well, it can give the group a strong competitive edge against others.

Reading 7.3, 'Coevolution in Business Ecosystems', by James Moore, is intended to further detail a key aspect of the debate, which both perspectives make important assumptions about – the nature of the business environment. This reading is from Moore's best-selling book *The Death of Competition*, in which he places the paradox of competition and cooperation in the broader context of 'business ecosystems'. He defines a business ecosystem as a part of the business environment where a variety of firms co-exist with one another and co-evolve on the basis of their ongoing interaction. He explains the functioning of a business ecosystem by drawing a parallel with biological ecosystems – plants and animals cannot be understood in isolation, as they co-evolve with one another in an endless cycle of change and selection. So too, the success or failure of companies cannot be understood without understanding how they have been able to nestle into the business ecosystem and how well the entire system is doing. Great companies, like great animal species, will still face extinction if their ecosystem goes into decline. Similarly, companies that want to create a new market must recognize that they actually need to create a new business ecosystem, with a lush variety of suppliers, distributors, service-providers and customers. If a firm only 'plants' its new product without engendering a broader ecosystem, it will be just as successful as a new species of tropical tree in the desert. Moore's point is that you should try to 'understand the economic systems evolving around you and find ways to contribute'. He concludes that 'competitive advantage stems principally from ... cooperative, co-evolving relationships with a network of other contributors to the overall economic scene'. In other words, cooperation and systems level thinking are essential to the strategist – however, not to substitute competitive behaviour, but rather to complement it.

Reading 7.4, 'How to Make Strategic Alliances Work', by Jeffrey Dyer, Prashant Kale and Harbir Singh, does exactly what its title suggests – it gives a thorough run-down of the necessary management systems and activities needed to make strategic alliances work. This reading has been added to serve as starting point for a discussion on how to manage cooperative relationships in practice. The main argument put forward by Dyer, Kale and Singh is that managing alliances is an essential expertise, but difficult to master, and therefore that firms should build a dedicated strategic alliance function – 'a vice president or director of strategic alliance with his or her own staff and resources'. Not only can such a department help to build up the necessary know-how, but it can also provide internal coordination, assist in setting strategic priorities, draw on resources across the company and ensure clear accountability. Furthermore, having a dedicated alliance function offers internal legitimacy to alliances and signals commitment to external partners and interested parties. Dyer, Kale and Singh enthusiastically conclude that the company that 'builds a successful dedicated strategic alliance function will reap substantial rewards'. Yet, the question open for discussion is whether managing strategic alliances requires a new staff department, or whether alternative organizational forms would be better – for instance, having alliance responsibility dispersed among the line managers who need to make the relationships function 'on the work floor'.

Collaborate with your competitors – and win

By Gary Hamel, Yves Doz and C.K. Prahalad[1]

Collaboration between competitors is in fashion. General Motors and Toyota assemble automobiles, Siemens and Philips develop semiconductors, Canon supplies photocopiers to Kodak, France's Thomson and Japan's JVC manufacture videocassette recorders. But the spread of what we call 'competitive collaboration' – joint ventures, outsourcing agreements, product licensings, cooperative research – has triggered unease about the long-term consequences. A strategic alliance can strengthen both companies against outsiders even as it weakens one partner vis-à-vis the other. In particular, alliances between Asian companies and western rivals seem to work against the western partner. Cooperation becomes a low-cost route for new competitors to gain technology and market access.

Yet the case for collaboration is stronger than ever. It takes so much money to develop new products and to penetrate new markets that few companies can go it alone in every situation. ICL, the British computer company, could not have developed its current generation of mainframes without Fujitsu. Motorola needs Toshiba's distribution capacity to break into the Japanese semiconductor market. Time is another critical factor. Alliances can provide shortcuts for western companies racing to improve their production efficiency and quality control.

We have spent more than five years studying the inner workings of 15 strategic alliances and monitoring scores of others. Our research involves cooperative ventures between competitors from the United States and Japan, Europe and Japan, and the United States and Europe. We did not judge the success or failure of each partnership by its longevity – a common mistake when evaluating strategic alliances – but by the shifts in competitive strength on each side. We focused on how companies use competitive collaboration to enhance their internal skills and technologies while they guard against transferring competitive advantages to ambitious partners.

There is no immutable law that strategic alliances *must* be a windfall for Japanese or Korean partners. Many western companies do give away more than they gain – but that's because they enter partnerships without knowing what it takes to win. Companies that benefit most from competitive collaboration adhere to a set of simple but powerful principles.

- Collaboration is competition in a different form. Successful companies never forget that their new partners may be out to disarm them. They enter alliances with clear strategic objectives, and they also understand how their partners' objectives will affect their success.

- Harmony is not the most important measure of success. Indeed, occasional conflict may be the best evidence of mutually beneficial collaboration. Few alliances remain win–win undertakings forever. A partner may be content even as it unknowingly surrenders core skills.

- Cooperation has limits. Companies must defend against competitive compromise. A strategic alliance is a constantly evolving bargain whose real terms go beyond the legal agreement or the aims of top management. What information gets traded is determined day to day, often by engineers and operating managers. Successful companies inform employees at all levels about what skills and technologies are off-limits to the partner and monitor what the partner requests and receives.

- Learning from partners is paramount. Successful companies view each alliance as a window on their partners' broad capabilities. They use the alliance to build skills in areas outside the formal agreement and systematically diffuse new knowledge throughout their organizations.

Why collaborate?

Using an alliance with a competitor to acquire new technologies or skills is not devious. It reflects the commitment and capacity of each partner to absorb the skills of the other. We found that in every case in which a Japanese company emerged from an alliance stronger than its western partner, the Japanese company had made a greater effort to learn.

Strategic intent is an essential ingredient in the commitment to learning. The willingness of Asian companies to enter alliances represents a change in competitive tactics, not competitive goals. NEC, for example, has used a series of collaborative ventures to enhance its technology and product competences. NEC is the only company in the world with a leading position in telecommunications, computers, and semiconductors – despite its investing less in research and development (R&D) (as a percentage of revenues) than competitors like Texas Instruments, Northern Telecom, and L.M. Ericsson. Its string of partnerships, most notably with Honeywell, allowed NEC to leverage its in-house R&D over the last two decades.

Western companies, on the other hand, often enter alliances to avoid investments. They are more interested in reducing the costs and risks of entering new businesses or markets than in acquiring new skills. A senior US manager offered this analysis of his company's venture with a Japanese rival: 'We complement each other well – our distribution capability and their manufacturing skill. I see no reason to invest upstream if we can find a secure source of product. This is a comfortable relationship for us.'

An executive from this company's Japanese partner offered a different perspective: 'When it is necessary to collaborate, I go to my employees and say, "This is bad, I wish we had these skills ourselves. Collaboration is second best. But I will feel worse if after four years we do not know how to do what our partner knows how to do." We must digest their skills.'

The problem here is not that the US company wants to share investment risk (its Japanese partner does too) but that the US company has no ambition beyond avoidance. When the commitment to learning is so one-sided, collaboration invariably leads to competitive compromise.

Many so-called alliances between western companies and their Asian rivals are little more than sophisticated outsourcing arrangements. General Motors buys cars and components from Korea's Daewoo. Siemens buys computers from Fujitsu. Apple buys laser printer engines from Canon. The traffic is almost entirely one way. These original equipment manufacturer (OEM) deals offer Asian partners a way to capture investment initiative from western competitors and displace customer-competitors from value-creating activities. In many cases this goal meshes with that of the western partner: to regain competitiveness quickly and with minimum effort.

Consider the joint venture between Rover, the British automaker, and Honda. Some 25 years ago, Rover's forerunners were world leaders in small car design. Honda had not even entered the automobile business. But in the mid-1970s, after failing to penetrate foreign markets, Rover turned to Honda for technology and product development support. Rover has used the alliance to avoid investments to design and build new cars. Honda has cultivated skills in European styling and marketing as well as multinational manufacturing. There is little doubt which company will emerge stronger over the long term.

Troubled laggards like Rover often strike alliances with surging latecomers like Honda. Having fallen behind in a key skills area (in this case, manufacturing small cars), the laggard attempts to compensate for past failures. The latecomer uses the alliance to close a specific skills gap (in this case, learning to build cars for a regional market). But a laggard that forges a partnership for short-term gain may find itself in a dependency spiral: as it contributes fewer and fewer distinctive skills, it must reveal more and more of its internal operations to keep the partner interested. For the weaker company, the issue shifts from, 'Should we collaborate?' to 'With whom should we collaborate?' to 'How do we keep our partner interested as we lose the advantages that made us attractive to them in the first place?'

There's a certain paradox here. When both partners are equally intent on internalizing the other's skills, distrust and conflict may spoil the alliance and threaten its very survival. That's one reason joint ventures between Korean and Japanese companies have been few and tempestuous. Neither side wants to 'open the kimono'. Alliances seem to run most smoothly when one partner is intent on learning and the other is intent on avoidance – in essence, when one partner is willing to grow dependent on the other. But running smoothly is not the point; the point is for a company to emerge from an alliance more competitive than when it entered it.

One partner does not always have to give up more than it gains to ensure the survival of an alliance. There are certain conditions under which mutual gain is possible, at least for a time:

- The partners' strategic goals converge while their competitive goals diverge. That is, each partner allows for the other's continued prosperity in the shared business. Philips and Du Pont collaborate to develop and manufacture compact discs, but neither side invades the other's market. There is a clear upstream/downstream division of effort.

- The size and market power of both partners is modest compared with industry leaders. This forces each side to accept that mutual dependence may have to continue for many years. Long-term collaboration may be so critical to both partners that neither will risk antagonizing the other by an overtly competitive bid to appropriate skills or competences. Fujitsu's 1 to 5 size disadvantage with IBM means it will be a long time, if ever, before Fujitsu can break away from its foreign partners and go it alone.

- Each partner believes it can learn from the other and at the same time limit access to proprietary skills. JVC and Thomson, both of whom make VCRs, know that they are trading skills. But the two companies are looking for very different things. Thomson needs product technology and manufacturing prowess; JVC needs to learn how to succeed in the fragmented European market. Both sides believe there is an equitable chance for gain.

How to build secure defences

For collaboration to succeed, each partner must contribute something distinctive: basic research, product development skills, manufacturing capacity, access to distribution. The challenge is to share enough skills to create advantage vis-à-vis companies outside the alliance while preventing a wholesale transfer of core skills to the partner. This is a very thin line to walk. Companies must carefully select what skills and technologies they pass to their partners. They must develop safeguards against unintended, informal transfers of information. The goal is to limit the transparency of their operations.

The type of skill a company contributes is an important factor in how easily its partner can internalize the skills. The potential for transfer is greatest when a partner's contribution is easily transported (in engineering drawings, on computer tapes, or in the heads of a few technical experts); easily interpreted (it can be reduced to commonly understood equations or symbols); and easily absorbed (the skill or competence is independent of any particular cultural context).

Western companies face an inherent disadvantage because their skills are generally more vulnerable to transfer. The magnet that attracts so many companies to alliances with Asian competitors is their manufacturing excellence – a competence that is less transferable than most. Just-in-time inventory systems and quality circles can be imitated, but this is like pulling a few threads out of an oriental carpet. Manufacturing excellence is a complex web of employee training, integration with suppliers, statistical process controls, employee involvement, value engineering, and design for manufacture. It is difficult to extract such a subtle competence in any way but a piecemeal fashion.

So companies must take steps to limit transparency. One approach is to limit the scope of the formal agreement. It might cover a single technology rather than an entire range of technologies; part of a product line rather than the entire line; distribution in a limited number of markets or for a limited period of time. The objective is to circumscribe a partner's opportunities to learn.

Moreover, agreements should establish specific performance requirements. Motorola, for example, takes an incremental, incentive-based approach to technology transfer in its venture with Toshiba. The agreement calls for Motorola to release its microprocessor technology incrementally as Toshiba delivers on its promise to increase Motorola's penetration in the Japanese semiconductor market. The greater Motorola's market share, the greater Toshiba's access to Motorola's technology.

Many of the skills that migrate between companies are not covered in the formal terms of collaboration. Top management puts together strategic alliances and sets the legal parameters for exchange. But what actually gets traded is determined by day-to-day interactions of engineers, marketers, and product developers: who says what to whom, who gets access to what facilities, who sits on what joint committees. The most important deals ('I'll share this with you if you share that with me') may be struck four or five organizational levels below where the deal was signed. Here lurks the greatest risk of unintended transfers of important skills.

Consider one technology-sharing alliance between European and Japanese competitors. The European company valued the partnership as a way to acquire a specific technology. The Japanese company considered it a window on its partner's entire range of competences and interacted with a broad spectrum of its partner's marketing and product development staff. The company mined each contact for as much information as possible.

For example, every time the European company requested a new feature on a product being sourced from its partner, the Japanese company asked for detailed customer and competitor analyses to justify the request. Over time, it developed a sophisticated picture of the European market that would assist its own entry strategy. The technology acquired by the European partner through the formal agreement had a useful life of three to five years. The competitive insights acquired informally by the Japanese company will probably endure longer.

Limiting unintended transfers at the operating level requires careful attention to the role of gatekeepers, the people who control what information flows to a partner. A gatekeeper can be effective only if there are a limited number of gateways through which a partner can access people and facilities. Fujitsu's many partners all go through a single office, the 'collaboration section,' to request information and assistance from different divisions. This way the company can monitor and control access to critical skills and technologies.

We studied one partnership between European and US competitors that involved several divisions of each company. While the US company could only access its partner through a single gateway, its partner had unfettered access to all participating divisions. The European company took advantage of its free rein. If one division refused to provide certain information, the European partner made the same request of another division. No single manager in the US company could tell how much information had been transferred or was in a position to piece together patterns in the requests.

Collegiality is a prerequisite for collaborative success. But *too much* collegiality should set off warning bells to senior managers. CEOs or division presidents should expect occasional complaints from their counterparts about the reluctance of lower level employees to share information. That's a sign that the gatekeepers are doing their jobs. And senior management should regularly debrief operating personnel to find out what information the partner is requesting and what requests are being granted.

Limiting unintended transfers ultimately depends on employee loyalty and self-discipline. This was a real issue for many of the western companies we studied. In their excitement and pride over technical achievements, engineering staffs sometimes shared information that top management considered sensitive. Japanese engineers were less likely to share proprietary information.

There are a host of cultural and professional reasons for the relative openness of western technicians. Japanese engineers and scientists are more loyal to their company than to their profession. They are less steeped in the open give-and-take of university research since they receive much of their training from employers. They consider themselves team members more than individual scientific contributors. As one Japanese manager noted, 'We don't feel any need to reveal what we know. It is not an issue of pride for us. We're glad to sit and listen. If we're patient we usually learn what we want to know.'

Controlling unintended transfers may require restricting access to facilities as well as to people. Companies should declare sensitive laboratories and factories off-limits to their partners. Better yet, they might house the collaborative venture in an entirely new facility. IBM is building a special site in Japan where Fujitsu can review its forthcoming mainframe software before deciding whether to license it. IBM will be able to control exactly what Fujitsu sees and what information leaves the facility.

Finally, which country serves as 'home' to the alliance affects transparency. If the collaborative team is located near one partner's major facilities, the other partner will have more opportunities to learn – but less control over what information gets traded. When the partner houses, feeds, and looks after engineers and operating managers, there is a danger they will 'go native'. Expatriate personnel need frequent visits from headquarters as well as regular furloughs home.

Enhance the capacity to learn

Whether collaboration leads to competitive surrender or revitalization depends foremost on what employees believe the purpose of the alliance to be. It is self-evident: to learn, one must want to learn. Western companies won't realize the full benefits of competitive collaboration until they overcome an arrogance borne of decades of leadership. In short, western companies must be more receptive.

We asked a senior executive in a Japanese electronics company about the perception that Japanese companies learn more from their foreign partners than vice versa. 'Our western partners approach us with the attitude of teachers', he told us. 'We are quite happy with this, because we have the attitude of students.'

Learning begins at the top. Senior management must be committed to enhancing their companies' skills as well as to avoiding financial risk. But most learning takes place at the lower levels of an alliance. Operating employees not only represent the front lines in an effective defence but also play a vital role in acquiring knowledge. They must be well briefed on the partner's strengths and weaknesses and understand how acquiring particular skills will bolster their company's competitive position.

This is already standard practice among Asian companies. We accompanied a Japanese development engineer on a tour through a partner's factory. This engineer dutifully took notes on plant layout, the number of production stages, the rate at which the line was running, and the number of employees. He recorded all this despite the fact that he had no manufacturing responsibility in his own company, and that the alliance didn't encompass joint manufacturing. Such dedication greatly enhances learning.

Collaboration doesn't always provide an opportunity to fully internalize a partner's skills. Yet just acquiring new and more precise benchmarks of a partner's performance can be of great value. A new benchmark can provoke a thorough review of internal performance levels and may spur a round of competitive innovation. Asking questions like, 'Why do their semiconductor logic designs have fewer errors than ours?' and 'Why are they investing in this technology and we're not?' may provide the incentive for a vigorous catch-up programme.

Competitive benchmarking is a tradition in most of the Japanese companies we studied. It requires many of the same skills associated with competitor analysis: systematically calibrating performance against external targets; learning to use rough estimates to determine where a competitor (or partner) is better, faster, or cheaper; translating those estimates into new internal targets; and recalibrating to establish the rate of improvement in a competitor's performance. The great advantage of competitive collaboration is that proximity makes benchmarking easier.

Indeed, some analysts argue that one of Toyota's motivations in collaborating with GM in the much-publicized NUMMI venture is to gauge the quality of GM's manufacturing technology. GM's top manufacturing people get a close look at Toyota, but the reverse is true as well. Toyota may be learning whether its giant US competitor is capable of closing the productivity gap with Japan.

Competitive collaboration also provides a way of getting close enough to rivals to predict how they will behave when the alliance unravels or runs its course. How does the partner respond to price changes? How does it measure and reward executives? How does it prepare to launch a new product? By revealing a competitor's management orthodoxies, collaboration

can increase the chances of success in future head-to-head battles.

Knowledge acquired from a competitor-partner is only valuable after it is diffused through the organization. Several companies we studied had established internal clearinghouses to collect and disseminate information. The collaborations manager at one Japanese company regularly made the rounds of all employees involved in alliances. He identified what information had been collected by whom and then passed it on to appropriate departments. Another company held regular meetings where employees shared new knowledge and determined who was best positioned to acquire additional information.

Proceed with care – but proceed

After World War II, Japanese and Korean companies entered alliances with western rivals from weak positions. But they worked steadfastly toward independence. In the early 1960s, NEC's computer business was one-quarter the size of Honeywell's, its primary foreign partner. It took only two decades for NEC to grow larger than Honeywell, which eventually sold its computer operations to an alliance between NEC and Group Bull of France. The NEC experience demonstrates that dependence on a foreign partner doesn't automatically condemn a company to also-ran status. Collaboration may sometimes be unavoidable; surrender is not.

Managers are too often obsessed with the ownership structure of an alliance. Whether a company controls 51 per cent or 49 per cent of a joint venture may be much less important than the rate at which each partner learns from the other. Companies that are confident of their ability to learn may even prefer some ambiguity in the alliance's legal structure. Ambiguity creates more potential to acquire skills and technologies. The challenge for western companies is not to write tighter legal agreements but to become better learners.

Running away from collaboration is no answer. Even the largest western companies can no longer outspend their global rivals. With leadership in many industries shifting toward the east, companies in the United States and Europe must become good borrowers – much like Asian companies did in the 1960s and 1970s. Competitive renewal depends on building new process capabilities and winning new product and technology battles. Collaboration can be a low-cost strategy for doing both.

READING

7.2

Creating a strategic centre to manage a web of partners

By Gianni Lorenzoni and Charles Baden-Fuller[1]

Strategic alliances and inter-firm networks have been gaining popularity with many firms for their lower overhead costs, increased responsiveness and flexibility, and greater efficiency of operations. Networks that are *strategically guided* are often fast-growing and on the leading edge. In 10 years, Sun Microsystems (founded in 1982) grew to $3.2 billion in sales and $284 million in profits. This remarkable growth has been achieved by Sun's strategic direction of a web of alliances.

Few would expect such rapid growth and technological success in an older and mature industry such as textiles. Yet Benetton, the famous global textile empire, is in many ways like Sun. Founded in 1964, it had by 1991 achieved more than $2 billion in sales and $235 million in profits. Benetton is widely admired in Europe and the Far East for its rapid growth and ability to change the industry's rules of the game through its strategy of 'mass fashion to young people'.

What creates and guides the successful, innovative, leading-edge interfirm network? Most research into inter-firm networks has emphasized how they can reconcile the flexibility of market relationships with the long-term commitment of hierarchically centralized management. Although all networks reflect the conscious decisions of some managers, it is becoming increasingly apparent that those networks that are not guided strategically by a 'centre' are unable to meet the demanding challenges of today's markets. In this reading, we are concerned with those strategic centres that have had a very significant impact on their sectors, especially as regards innovation. They are not confined to just a few isolated sectors, but have been observed in a wide variety of circumstances, some of which are listed in Table 7.2.1.

In this reading, we examine three dimensions of the strategic centre:

- as a creator of value for its partners;
- as leader, rule setter, and capability builder;
- as simultaneously structuring and strategizing.

The role of the strategic centre

The strategic centre (or central firm) plays a critical role as a creator of value. The main features of this role are:

- Strategic outsourcing. Outsource and share with more partners than the normal broker and traditional firm. Require partners to be more than doers, expect them to be problem-solvers and initiators.

- Capability. Develop the core skills and competencies of partners to make them more effective and competitive. Force members of the network to share their expertise with others in the network, and with the central firm.

- Technology. Borrow ideas from others which are developed and exploited as a means of creating and mastering new technologies.

- Competition. Explain to partners that the principle dimension of competition is between value chains and networks. The network is only as strong as its weakest link. Encourage rivalry between firms inside the network, in a positive manner.

From subcontracting to strategic outsourcing

All firms that act as brokers or operate networks play only a limited role in undertaking the production and delivery of the good or service to the markets in which the system is involved. What distinguishes central firms is both the extent to which they subcontract, and the way that they collect together partners who contribute to the whole system and whose roles are clearly defined in a positive and creative way.

Many organizations see their sub-contractors and partners as passive doers or actors in their quest for competitive advantage. They typically specify exactly what they want the partners to do, and leave little to the creative skills of others. They reserve a special creative role for only a few 'critical' partners. In

[1]Source: This article ©1995, by the Regents of the University of California. Adapted from the *California Management Review*, Vol. 37, No. 3. By permission of the Regents. All rights reserved.

TABLE 7.2.1   Some central firms and their activities

Name of company and its industry	Activities of strategic centre	Activities of the network
Apple *(computers)*	■ Hardware design ■ Software design ■ Distribution	■ Principal subcontractors manufacture ■ 3000 software developers
Benetton *(apparel)*	■ Designing collections ■ Selected production ■ Developing new technology systems	■ 6000 shops ■ 400 subcontractors in production ■ Principal joint ventures in Japan, Egypt, India, and others
Corning *(glass, medical products and optical fibers)*	■ Technology innovation ■ Production	■ More than 30 joint ventures world-wide
Genentech *(biotechnology/DNA)*	■ Technology innovation	■ JVs with drug companies for production and distribution, licensing in from universities
McDonald's *(fast food)*	■ Marketing ■ Prototyping technology and systems	■ 9000 outlets, joint ventures in many foreign countries
McKesson *(drug distribution)*	■ Systems ■ Marketing ■ Logistics ■ Consulting advice	■ Thousands of retail drug outlets, and ties with drug companies, and government institutions
Nike *(shoes and sportswear)*	■ Design ■ Marketing	■ Principal subcontractors
Nintendo *(video games)*	■ Design ■ Prototyping ■ Marketing	■ 30 principal hardware subcontractors ■ 150 software developers
Sun *(computers and computer systems)*	■ Innovation of technology ■ Software ■ Assembly	■ Licensor/licensees for software and hardware
Toyota *(automobiles)*	■ Design ■ Assembly ■ Marketing	■ Principal subcontractors for complex components ■ Second tier for other components ■ Network of agents for distribution

strategic networks, it is the norm rather than an exception for partners to be innovators.

Typically each of these partnerships extends beyond a simple subcontracting relationship. Strategic centres expect their partners to do more than follow the rules, they expect them to be creative. For example,

Apple worked with Canon and Adobe to design and create a laser jet printer which then gave Apple an important position in its industry. In all the cases we studied, the strategic centre looked to the partners to be creative in solving problems and being proactive in the relationships. They demanded more – and obtained more – from their partners than did their less effective counterparts that used traditional subcontracting.

Developing the competencies of the partners

How should the central firm see its own competencies vis-à-vis its partners? Most writers ague that current competences should guide future decisions. Many have warned of the dangers in allowing the other partners in a joint venture or alliance to exploit the skills of the host organization. For example, Reich and Mankin (1986) noted that joint ventures between Japanese and US firms often result in one side (typically the Japanese) gaining at the expense of the other. Bleeke and Ernst (1991) found similar disappointment in that in only 51 per cent of the cases they studied did both firms gain from alliances. In a study of cross border alliances, Hamel (1991) found that the unwary partner typically found that its competencies were 'hollowed out' and that its collaborator became a more powerful competitor. Badaracco (1991) examined the experiences of GM and IBM, who have signed multiple agreements, and explored the difficulties they face.

Traditional brokers and large integrated firms do not 'hand out' core skills, but the central firms we studied have ignored this advice and won. While keeping a very few skills and assets to themselves, the central firms were remarkable in their desire to transfer skill and knowledge adding value to their partners. Typically, they set out to build up the partners' ability and competencies. At Benetton, site selection and sample selection were skills which Benetton would offer to the new retail partners, either directly or through the agents. Skill transfers were also evident in the machinery networks and at Apple.

Nike brings its partners to its research site at Beaverton to show them the latest developments in materials, product designs, technologies, and markets. Sometimes the partners share some of the costs, but the prime benefit is to shorten cycle times and create a more vibrant system. Toyota's subcontractors may receive training from Toyota and are helped in their development of expertise in solving problems pertaining to their particular component. Not only does this encourage them to deliver better quality parts to the Toyota factories, but it also allows the Toyota system to generate an advantage over other car manufacturers.

In contrast to these companies, the less successful organizations we studied did not have groups of specialists to transfer knowledge to partners – nor, it seems, did they appreciate its importance. They did not enlist all their suppliers and customers to fight a common enemy. Moreover, their experiences did not encourage exploration of this approach. They spoke of past difficulties in alliances. Skill transfers between parties did not always result in mutual benefit. One defence contractor explained that their experience of skill transfers nearly always meant that the partner was strengthened and became a stronger rival.

Borrowing–developing–lending new ideas

While all firms bring in new ideas from outside, the central firms we studied have adopted an unusual and aggressive perspective in this sphere. They scan their horizons for all sorts of opportunities and utilize a formula we call *borrow–develop–lend*. 'Borrow' means that the strategic centre deliberately buys or licenses some existing technological ideas from a third party; 'develop' means that it takes these outside ideas and adds value by developing them further in its own organization. This commercialization can then be exploited or 'lent' with great rapidity through its stellar system, creating new adjuncts to leverage to the greatest advantage. Borrowing ideas, which are subsequently developed and exploited, stretches the organization and forces it to grow its capabilities and competencies. It demands a new way of thinking.

In the Italian packaging machinery sector, lead producers follow this strategy. They borrow designs of a new machine from specialist designers or customers. These designs are then prototyped. From these prototypes, small and medium-sized partners or specialists often improve the design in a unique way, such as improving the flows and linkages. The focal firm then repurchases and exploits the modified design, licensing to producers for the final development and marketing phase. Thus we see a ' to-and-fro' pattern of development between the central firm and its many partners.

Sun also used the borrow-develop-lend approach in their project to build a new workstation delivering 'more power with less cost'. They borrowed existing technology from other parties, recombined and developed them further inside Sun, and then licensed them to third parties for development and sale under the Sun brand.

The borrow-develop-lend principle helps the central firm reduce the cost of development, make progress more quickly, and, most importantly, undertake projects which would normally lie outside its scope. This approach contrasts with the procedures used by other large firms. Although these firms may buy ideas from other sources, large firms usually have a slower pace of development and rarely match the speed of exploitation achieved through networking and re-lending the idea to third parties. The strategic centre seems to avoid the *not-invented-here* syndrome, where innovations and ideas are rejected because they are not internally created and developed.

From the view of independent inventors, the strategic centre is an attractive organization with which to do business. The central firms have a track record of rapid commercialization (usually offering large incentives to those with ideas). They emphasize moving quickly from ideas to market by a simultaneous learning process with partners, thereby offering a competitive advantage over other developers. Finally, the willingness to involve others means rapid diffusion with fast payback, thus lessening the risks.

Perceptions of the competitive process

Firms in the same industry experience varying degrees of competitive rivalry. The joint venture, formal agreements, or the use of cross shareholdings are mechanisms used to create common ties, encourage a common view, and unite firms against others in the industry. Strategic centres also create this sense of cooperation across competing enterprises.

Competitive success requires the integration of multiple capabilities (e.g. innovation, productivity, quality, responsiveness to customers) across internal and external organizational boundaries. Such integration is a big challenge to most organizations. Strategic centres rise to this challenge and create a sense of common purpose across multiple levels in the value chain and across different sectors. They achieve a combination of specialized capability and large-scale integration at the same time, despite the often destructive rivalry between buyers and customers. Strategic purchasing partnerships are commonly used to moderate this rivalry, but few firms are able to combine both horizontal and vertical linkages.

In building up their partner's capabilities and competencies, strategic centres convey an unusual perspective to their partners on the nature of the competitive process. This perspective permits the partners to take a holistic view of the network, seeing the collective as a unit that can achieve competitive advantage. In this respect, the whole network acts like a complex integrated firm spanning many markets.

Table 7.2.2 illustrates how the actions of the strategic centre differ from other organizations. Chain stores are a good example of organizations that coordinate activities across many actors, yet at a single stage of the value chain. In contrast, the narrowly defined, vertically integrated firm coordinates across many stages but not across many markets or actors. Only the strategic centre and the large multi-market, vertically integrated organization are able to coordinate across many markets and many stages of the value chain.

Beyond the hollow organization

Although the strategic centre outsources more activities than most organizations, it is not hollow. Unlike the traditional broker that is merely a glorified arranger, the central firms we studied understand that they have to develop some critical core competencies. These competencies are, in general, quite different from those stressed by most managers in traditional firms. The agenda for the central firm consists of:

■ The idea. Creating a vision in which partners play a critical role.

TABLE 7.2.2 Different kinds of competition across sectors and stages of the value chain

	Single units within the sector	Multiple units within the sector or across related sectors
Multiple stages of the value chain	■ Vertical integration; or ■ Value-added partnerships	■ Strategic centres and their webs of partners; or ■ Large integrated multi-market organizations
Single stages of the value chain	■ Traditional adversarial firm	■ Chain stores; or ■ Simple networks

- The investment. A strong brand image and effective systems and support.
- The climate. Creating an atmosphere of trust and reciprocity.
- The partners. Developing mechanisms for attracting and selecting partners.

Sharing a business idea

Most of the central firms we studied are small, lean, and focused operations. They employ comparatively few people and are very selective in what they do. Yet, they have an unusual ability to conceptualize a business idea that can be shared not only internally, but with other partners. In the case of Benetton, this idea has a few key elements such as: mass fashion for young people, and the notion of a strategic network to orchestrate and fulfil this vision. In food-machinery, the key idea of the central firms is to solve the client's problems, rather than selling existing competencies, while new partners are developed in response to customer needs – a novel notion in this sector. These simple ideas are not easy to create or sustain.

These ideas have been able to capture the imagination of the employees and their partners. They also encapsulate strategy and so contain, in the language of Prahalad and Hamel (1990, Reading 7.2 in this book), the features of a clear strategic intent. Common to all the business ideas we studied, there is a notion of partnership which includes the creation of a learning culture and the promotion of systems experiments so as to outpace rival competing organizations. The strategic centres view their role as one of leading and orchestrating their systems. Their distinctive characteristics lie in their ability to perceive the full business idea and understand the role of all the different parties in many different locations across the whole value chain. The managers in the strategic centre have a dream and they orchestrate others to fulfil that dream.

This vision of the organization is not just an idea in the minds of a few managers, it is a feature that is shared throughout the organization. Many of the strategic centres we studied admit that their visions have emerged over time, they are not the work of a moment. Their vision is dynamic, for as their network grows and as the environment changes, the organizational vision also changes. This is not the case in the less successful alliances. They showed the typical characteristics of most organizations, multifaceted views of the world and a less-than-clear expression of their vision.

Clearly, vision is reinforced by success. The ability of central firms to deliver profits and growth for the partners helps cement a vision in their minds and makes their claims credible. It creates a cycle where success breeds clarity, which in turn helps breed more success.

Brand power and other support

To maintain the balance of power in the network, all central firms retain certain activities. The control of the brand names and the development of the systems that integrate the network are two activities that give the organization a pivotal role and allow it to exercise power over the system.

Some of the firms we observed were involved in consumer markets where branding is important. The brand name, owned by the central firm, was promoted by the activities of the partners, who saw the brand as a shared resource. They were encouraged to ensure its success, and quite often these efforts helped the brand become famous in a short period of time. While the brand and marketing are not so vital in producer goods markets, they are still important – and the strategic centre neglects these at its peril. Its importance is highlighted by the experiences of one of the less successful organizations we studied. This aerospace firm had problems as a result of the inability of its members to relinquish many of the aspects of marketing to a single central firm.

To retain its power, the central firm must ensure that the information between partners flows freely and is not filtered. Communication is a costly activity, and developing effective communication systems is always the responsibility of the strategic centre. These systems are not only electronically based, but include all other methods of communication. Often there is a style for meeting among the partners, which is set and monitored by the central firm. The quality of information is a key requirement if the central firm is to mandate effectively the stream of activities scattered among different firms.

Trust and reciprocity

Leveraging the skills of partners is easy to conceive but hard to implement. The difficulties occur because it takes many partners operating effectively to make the system work, but the negative behaviour of only a few can bring the whole system to a halt. The strategic vision requires all its members to contribute all the time without fail. This is a considerable demand. The typical organizational response to such a need is to circumscribe the contracts with outsiders in a tight legalistic manner. But this is not always wise; contract making and policing can be difficult and expensive. Formal contracts are relatively inflexible and are suitable only where the behaviour is easy to describe and is relatively inflexible. But the relationships are creative and flexible and so very difficult to capture and enforce contractually.

The approach of the central firms we studied is to develop a sense of trust and reciprocity in the system. This trust and reciprocity is a dynamic concept and it can be very tight. The tightness is apparent in each party agreeing to perform its known obligations. This aspect has similarities to contracts in the sense that obligations are precisely understood. But Anglo-Saxon contracts are typically limited in the sense that partners are not expected to go beyond the contract. In contrast, in a network perspective, the behaviour is prescribed for the unknown, each promising to work in a particular manner to resolve future challenges and difficulties as they arise. This means that each partner will promise to deliver what is expected, and that future challenges will also be addressed positively. If there are uncertainties and difficulties in the relationships, these will be resolved after the work is done. If one party goes beyond (in the positive sense) the traditional contract, others will remember and reciprocate at a later date.

Trust and reciprocity are complements, not substitutes, to other obligations. If partners do not subscribe to the trust system, they can hold the whole system hostage whenever they are asked to do something out of the ordinary, or even in the normal course of events. Such behaviour will cause damage to all, and the system will break up. Only with trust can the system work in unison.

The Benetton franchising system is perhaps an extreme version of this trust system. On the continent of Europe, Benetton does not use legal contracts, rather it relies on the unwritten agreement. This, it claims, focuses everyone's attention on making the expectations clear. It also saves a great deal of time and expense. Many other strategic centres also rely on trust, but utilize contracts and formal controls as a complement. Central firms develop rules for settling disputes (for there will be disputes even in a trust system). The central firm also ensures that rewards are distributed in a manner which encourages partners to reinforce the positive circle. Benetton has encountered limits to its approach in the US, where the cultural emphasis on law and contracts has come into conflict with Benetton's strategy.

In sharp contrast are the other less successful systems we studied. There, trust was used on a very limited scale, since most organizations had difficulty in getting partners to deliver even that which was promised. Broken promises and failed expectations were common in the defence systems. Very low anticipated expectations of partner reciprocity were a common feature of the Scottish network and appliance sectors. Most organizations believed that anything crucial had to be undertaken in-house.

Trust is delicate, and it needs fostering and underpinning. One of the ways in which positive behaviour is encouraged is to ensure that the profit-sharing relationships give substantial rewards to the partners. None of the central firms we studied seeks to be the most profitable firm in the system; they are happy for others to take the bulk of the profit. In Benetton, a retailer may find his or her capital investment paid back in three years. In Corning, some partners have seen exceptional returns. This seemingly altruistic behaviour, however, does not mean that the rewards to the central firm are small.

Partner selection

The central firms we studied recognize that creating success and a long-term perspective must begin with the partner selection process. In building a network, partners must be selected with great care. Initially, the central firms followed a pattern of trial and error, but following successful identification of the key points in the selection process, they became more deliberate. The many new styles of operation and new ways of doing things are not easy to grasp, and they are quite difficult to codify – especially at the early stages of the selection process. As time passes, a partner profile emerges together with a selection procedure aimed at creating the correct conditions for the relationships. These relationships require coordination among all the partners, a common long-term perspective, an acceptance of mutual adaptation, and incremental innovation. When we looked at the details of the selection procedure, there was a difference between those central firms that had a few large partners and those that had many small-scale partners. In the case of the network composed of a few, large firm alliances, the selection criterion is typically based on careful strategic considerations. There is the question of matching capabilities and resources, as well as considerations of competition. However, most important are the organizational features based on a compatibility of management systems, decision processes, and perspectives – in short, a cultural fit.

The selection process must also be tempered by availability. Typically, there are few potential partners to fit the ideal picture. Perhaps it is for this reason that some Japanese and European firms start the process early on by deliberately spinning off some of their internal units to create potential partners. Typically these units will contain some of their best talents. However, these units will have a cultural affinity and a mutual understanding, which makes the partnership easier.

In the case of the large network composed of many small partners, the centre acts as a developer of the community. Its managers must assume a different role. Apple called some of its managers 'evangelists' because they managed the relationships with 3000 third-party developers. So that they could keep constant contact with them, they used images of the 'Figure-head' and the 'Guiding Light'.

Simultaneous structuring and strategizing

Of all the battles firms face, the most difficult is not the battle for position, nor is it even the battle between strong firms and weak firms following the same strategic approaches. Rather, it is the battle between firms adopting different strategies and different approaches to the market. In these battles, the winners are usually those who use fewer and different resources in novel combinations. The central firms we studied fit this category, for they have typically dominated their sectors by stretching and leveraging modest resources to great effect. In trying to understand these battles of stretch and leverage, others have stressed the technical achievements of central firms such as lean production, technical innovation, or flexible manufacturing and service delivery. To be sure, these advances are important and provide partial explanations for the success of Sun, Nintendo, Benetton, Apple, and others. Equally important, if not more important, are new ideas on the nature of strategizing and structuring. Strategizing is a shared process between the strategic centre and its partners; structuring of the relationships between the partners goes hand in hand and is seen as a key part of the strategy.

Strategy conception and implementation of ideas is shared between central firms and their webs of partners. Here they differ from most conventional organizations, which neither share their conceptions of strategy with other organizations nor insist that their partners share their ideas with them in a constructive dialogue. While all firms form partnerships with some of their suppliers and customers, these linkages rarely involve sharing ideas systematically. Subcontracting relationships are usually deeper and more complex,

and many firms share their notions of strategy with their subcontractors, but the sharing is nearly always limited. Alliances demand even greater levels of commitment and interchange, and it is common for firms involved in alliances to exchange ideas about strategy and to look for strategic fit and even reshaping of strategic directions. Networks can be thought of as a higher stage of alliances, for in the strategic centre there is a conscious desire to influence and shape the strategies of the partners, and to obtain from partners ideas and influences in return.

This conscious desire to share strategy is reflected in the way in which central firms conceive of the boundaries of their operations. Most organizations view their joint ventures and subcontractors as beyond the boundaries of their firm, and even those involved in alliances do not think of partners as an integral part of the organization. Even firms that are part of a franchise system (and thus have a more holistic perspective) do not view their relationships as a pattern of multilateral contracts. Going beyond the franchise view, central firms and their participants communicate multilaterally across the whole of the value chain. In the words of Johanson and Mattsson (1992), they have a 'network theory,' a perception of governing a whole system.

Strategizing and structuring in the central firms we studied reverses Chandler's famous dictum about structure following strategy. When partner's competencies are so crucial to the developments of the business idea of the strategic centre, the winners are building strategy and structure simultaneously whereas the losers are signing agreements without changing their organizational forms to match them. When each partner's resources and competencies are so essential to the success of the enterprise, new forms must be designed. To achieve this, structuring must come earlier, alongside strategizing, and both require an interaction among partners to create a platform of flexibility and capability. This behaviour challenges much of what is received managerial practice and avoids some of the traps that webs of alliances face.

Like the large integrated cohesive organization, networked firms are able to behave as a single competitive entity which can draw on considerable resources.

However, the network form avoids many of the problems of large integrated firms, who typically find themselves paralysed in the struggle between freedom and control. By focusing attention on the matters where commonality is important (e.g. product design) and by allowing each unit to have freedom elsewhere, cooperation is fostered, time and energy spent in monitoring is reduced, and resources are optimized. In this way, the networked organization succeeds in bridging the gap between centralization and decentralization. But cooperation can dull the edge of progress, and the organizations in our study have avoided this trap by fostering a highly competitive spirit.

Marketing and information sharing

The way in which information is collected and shared in the system reveals how structure and strategy go hand in hand. The gathering of information is a central activity in any organization. A strategic feature of a network of alliances is that the firms in the system are closely linked for the sharing of information. Members of the network exchange not only hard data about best practice, but also ideas, feelings, and thoughts about customers, other suppliers, and general market trends.

The central firm structures the information system so that knowledge is funnelled to the areas that need it the most. Members specializing in a particular function have access to others in the system performing similar tasks, and share their knowledge. This creates a level playing field within the network system. It also provides the opportunity for the members to focus and encourage the development of competitive advantage over rivals.

One of the basic premises in our network view is that new information leading to new ways of doing things emerges in a process of interaction with people and real-life situations. It follows that the 'information ability' of the firm depends critically on a scheme of interactions. The difficulty is that the generation of new information cannot be planned, but has to emerge. Thus, the task of the manager is one of designing a structure which provides an environment favourable for interactions to form, and for new information to be generated. Such a structure is a network.

Our study found, as have others, that the availability of large amounts of high quality information on many aspects of the business facilitated more rapid responses to market opportunities. Information condensed through the network is ' thicker' than that condensed through the brokerage market, but is 'freer' than in the hierarchy.

The need for a sophisticated system was clear when we contrasted the central firms we studied with other firms. In these other firms, we often found that critical information was guarded, not shared. As is so common among organizations, individual players are either afraid of being exploited or they have a desire to exploit the power they have through knowledge. Even in traditional franchise systems, information is typically passed to the centre for filtering before being shared. In the large integrated firm, centralization also causes unnecessary filtering. With centralization, the process of collecting and distributing information can be cumbersome and slow. Moreover, power to manipulate the information can be accidentally or intentionally misused by a small central group.

Some of the 'control group' of firms we studied did share their information, with adverse consequences. For example, defence contractors, unable to create an effective strategic network, found the partners sometimes used the shared information to their own advantage, and then did not reciprocate. The knowledge was exploited by partners to create superior bargaining positions. Opportunities to foster collective interest were missed, and in extreme cases, partners used the information to bolster a rival alliance to the detriment of the original information provider.

Learning races

Whereas identifying opportunities for growth is facilitated by information sharing, responding to the opportunity is more difficult. Here we see some of the clearest evidence that structure and strategy go hand in hand. First and foremost, the central firms we studied reject the idea of doing everything themselves. Instead, they seek help from others to respond to the opportunities they face. When the knowledge and capabilities exist within the network, the role of the centre is to orchestrate the response so that the whole system capitalizes on the opportunity.

It frequently happens that opportunities require an innovative response, and it is common for strategic centres to set up 'learning races'. Here, partners are given a common goal (say a new product or process development) with a prize for the first to achieve the target. The prize may be monetary, but more commonly it is the opportunity to lead off the exploitation of the new development. There is a catch, the development must be shared with others in the network. Learning races create a sense of competition and rivalry, but within an overall common purpose.

Nintendo uses carefully nurtured learning races with its partners to create high quality rapid innovation. Partners are typically restricted in the number of contributions they can make. In the case of software design, the limit may be three ideas a year. These restrictions force a striving for excellence, and the consequence is a formidable pace of progress.

Learning races can be destructive rather than constructive if the partners do not have the skills and resources. The strategic centres we studied get around these difficulties by sharing knowledge and in effect allowing the whole network to 'borrow' skills and competencies from each other.

It is important to understand the role of new members in the process of creating innovations. Many central firms follow the twin strategies of internal and external development. Internal development involves offering existing partners a possibility of sharing in the growth markets. External development involves the finding of new partners to fill the gaps and accelerate the possibilities. New partners typically fit the pattern set by existing partners. These newly found 'look alike' firms allow the strategic centre to truncate development of the necessary capabilities, leveraging off earlier experiences developed by the existing partners. By making growth a race between old and new partners, speed is assured and scale effects exploited. Our strategic centres fostered positive rivalry rather than hostility by ensuring that both old and new partners share in the final gains. When pursuing rapid growth, the twin tracks of internal and external development can lessen tensions. Because they are independent, existing members can respond to the new demands as they wish. But, if they do not respond positively, the central firm can sign up new partners to fill the gaps. The stresses and strains of growth can thus be reduced for each of the members of the network.

Conclusions

The strategically minded central firms in our study view the boundaries of the organization differently because their conception and implementation of strategy are shared with a web of partners. This attitude contrasts sharply with most organizations, which view their joint ventures and subcontractors as existing beyond the boundaries of their firm. Even those involved in alliances typically do not think of partners as an integral part of their organization; they rarely share their conceptions of strategy and even fewer insist that their partners share their strategy with them in a constructive dialogue. In contrast, strategic centres communicate strategic ideas and intent multilaterally across the whole of the value chain. They have a network view of governing a whole system.

Strategic centres reach out to resolve classic organizational paradoxes. Many subcontracting and alliance relationships seemed to be mired in the inability to reconcile the advantages of the market with those of the hierarchy. Strategic centres are able to create a system that has the flexibility and freedom of the market coupled with long-term holistic relationships, ensuring the requisite strategic capabilities across the whole system. Another paradox exists between creativity and discipline. Most organizations oscillate between having ample creativity and little discipline, or too much discipline and not enough creativity. Through their unusual attitude to structuring and strategizing, strategic centres attain leading-edge technological and market developments while retaining rapid decision making processes.

All organizations have much to learn from studying strategic centres and their unusual conception of the managerial task. Strategic centres have taken modest resources and won leadership positions in a wide variety of sectors. They have brought a new way of thinking about business and organizing. Much of what they do is at the cutting edge, and they are shining examples of how firms can change the rules of the game by creative and imaginative thinking.

READING

7.3

Coevolution in business ecosystems

By James F. Moore[1]

During the past decade, a great deal of insight has been gleaned about complex biological communities – illuminated by biologists poking around in Central American jungles, collecting insects in Asia, and observing birds in the Arctic. Much of this work has focused on the intricate and far-reaching

[1]Source: This article © 1996 by James F. Moore. Adapted from Chapter One of James F. Moore, *The Death of Competition: Leadership and Strategy in the Age of Business Ecosystems*, by permission of HarperCollins Publishers Inc.

relationships among species: predator and prey, pollinator and plant, protector and herd. What has become clear is that some ecosystems, notably those besieged by wave after wave of potential settlers, develop a special resiliency, flexibility, and resistance to catastrophes. In contrast, those that develop in isolation like Hawaii can become highly vulnerable to ecological disasters, and may even face mass extinctions.

Recent work in community ecology has dwelled on topics like 'keystone' species, the most critical of the species in an ecosystem. When they disappear from an ecosystem, life within the system itself changes radically. One example is the sea otter. Sea otters on the California coast prey on sea urchins. The urchins feast on kelp beds and other seaweeds along the ocean floor. When the otters were hunted almost to extinction during the nineteenth century, urchin populations grew exponentially and consumed much of the kelp beds, diminishing the biodiversity of the ecosystem. The ocean floor became almost barren. Through aggressive efforts, conservationists reintroduced the sea otter to the area. The urchins have now been harvested and the rich complexity along the coast restored.

Biologists have also concentrated on highly aggressive 'exotic' species that can have a particularly disruptive effect when injected into an ecosystem. The hydrilla plant, for instance, was introduced into Florida from Asia in the 1950s. Today hydrilla infests over 40 per cent of the waterways in the state – choking lakes and rivers, killing native fish and other wildlife. The hydrilla is almost impossible to control and seems destined to have a permanently damaging effect on biological diversity and robustness in the region.

Unfortunately, the study of business communities lags well behind the biological. Yet close examination of the history of business innovation and the creation of wealth shows that there are important parallels between these two seemingly dissimilar worlds.

While biological analogies are often applied to the study of business, they are frequently applied much too narrowly. Almost invariably, the recurring focus is on the evolution of species. For example, some argue that in a market economy a Darwinian selection occurs in which the fittest products and companies survive. More recently, as businesses have been dissected into processes through the quality and reengineering movements, some now maintain that the fittest processes and systems of processes drive out the weak. In either instance, the ' species' are seen to be subject to genetic mutation and selection that gradually transforms them.

I have become convinced that the world is more complicated than that, and that we must think in grander terms. Species-level improvement of business processes is unquestionably crucial for keeping companies successful, and creates unmistakable value for society. But there are complementary forms of evolution that play vital but grossly underrated roles in both biology and business. They encompass the ecological and evolutionary interactions that occur across an entire ecosystem, comprising all the organisms of a particular habitat as well as the physical environment itself. Leaders who learn to understand these dimensions of ecology and evolution will find themselves equipped with a new model for devising strategy, and critical new options for shaping the future of their companies.

In biological ecosystems, changes take place over different time scales: many ecological changes occur within the lifetime of the individual organism, whereas evolutionary changes transpire over numerous generations. In business ecosystems, these two time scales collapse into one, because, unlike biological species, a business can guide its own evolution and effect dramatic evolutionary changes during its lifetime. A leader in a business ecosystem has an important edge over the species in a biological ecosystem: the ability to see the big picture and understand the dynamics of the ecosystem as a whole. This enables a business to alter its traits to better fit its ecosystem. What is more, a business can anticipate future changes in its ecosystem and evolve now so that it is well prepared to face future challenges.

Coevolution: Working together to create the future

The late anthropologist Gregory Bateson, who had a lifelong obsession with the workings of complex systems, greatly influenced my thinking. His thought-provoking theories of coevolution, culture, and addiction as they applied to natural and social systems are very intriguing, and I was struck by how he often studied systems in biological terms and then tried to understand how consciousness played its part in those systems.

In his thinking, Bateson focused on patterns. One of his observations was that behaviours within systems – companies, societies, species, families – coevolve. What does 'coevolve' mean in this context? In his book *Mind and Nature*, Bateson (1979) describes coevolution as a process in which interdependent species evolve in an endless reciprocal cycle – 'changes in species A set the stage for the natural selection of changes in species B', and vice versa. Take the caribou and the wolf. The wolf culls the weaker caribou, which strengthens the herd. But with a stronger herd, it is imperative for wolves to evolve and become stronger themselves to succeed. And so the pattern is not simply competition or cooperation, but coevolution. Over time, as coevolution proceeds, the whole system becomes more hardy.

From Bateson's standpoint, coevolution is more important a concept than simply competition or cooperation. The same holds true in business. Too many executives focus their time primarily on day-to-day product and service-level struggles with direct competitors. Over the past few years, more managers have also emphasized cooperation: strengthening key customer and supplier relationships, and in some cases working with direct competitors on initiatives like technical standards and shared research to improve conditions for everyone.

A small number of the most effective firms in the world develop new business advantages by learning to lead economic coevolution. These companies – such as Intel, Hewlett-Packard, Shell, Wal-Mart, Creative Artists Agency, and others – recognize that they live in a rich and dynamic environment of opportunities. The job of their top management is to seek out potential centres of innovation where, by orchestrating the contributions of a network of players, they can bring powerful benefits to bear for customers and producers alike. Their executives must not only lead their current competitors and industries – whether by competition or cooperation – but hasten the coming together of disparate business elements into new economic wholes from which new businesses, new rules of competition and cooperation, and new industries can emerge.

Obliterating industry boundaries

There are certain spots on the earth – Amazon rain forests, for instance – where biological evolution proceeds at madcap speed. In these hyperdomains, nature brazenly experiments with new evolutionary loops and wrinkles, as well as new strategies for genetic invention. As a consequence, new organisms are spawned that, in due course, crawl out and populate the rest of the world.

Similar and unprecedented upheaval is astir in the world of business. There are certain identifiable hot spots of rapidly accelerating evolutionary activity in the global economy, places where the speed of business is exceedingly fast and loose. New technologies, deregulation, and changes in customer behaviour are the metaphorical equivalent of floods and fires, opening up new competitive landscapes. On such newly cleared and fertile grounds, embryonic or transformed businesses are sprouting.

These new renditions are businesses with an edge. In a sense, they are renegades. In their marauding ways, they do not respect traditional industry paradigms and partitions. Indeed, what they share is a tendency to upend business and industry models and to redraw increasingly porous boundaries.

What we are seeing, in fact, is the end of industry. That's not to say that we now need to mourn the dissolution of the airline industry or the cement industry. Rather, it means the end of industry as a useful concept in contemplating business. The notion of 'industry' is really an artifact of the slowly paced business evolution during the middle of this century. The presumption that there are distinct, immutable businesses within which players scramble for supremacy is a tired idea whose time is past. It has little to do with what is shaping the world. The designation itself is simplistic, describing certain players better than others. But, in truth, the label is not much more than a crude grid used to compare and contrast businesses, a fiction conjured up by policymakers and regulators, investment analysts, and even academic students of business strategy.

There has been a profound change in management thinking of senior executives over recent years. Earlier, many senior managers could rightfully be accused of living in denial about the structural transformations of the world economy and its impact on their businesses. Today, nearly no senior management team can really be charged with living in such a state. There is no need to argue that the economic times have shifted - there is widespread agreement that this is true. The traditional industry boundaries that we've all taken for granted throughout our careers are blurring – and in may cases crumbling.

Enter a new logic to guide action

The important question for management today is not whether such changes are upon us but how to make strategy in this new world. Few management teams have been able to put together systematic approaches for dealing with the new business reality. Most find themselves struggling with varying degrees of effectiveness, but with no clear way to think about and communicate, let alone confront, the new strategic issues.

What is most needed is a new language, a logic for strategy, and new methods for implementation. Many of the old ideas simply don't work anymore. For instance, diversification strategies that emphasize finding 'attractive' industries often assume the fixedness of industry structure, yet our experience tells us that industry structures evolve very rapidly. Our traditional notions of vertical and horizontal integration fail us in the new world of cooperating communities. Competitive advantage no longer accrues necessarily from economies of scale and scope. Many firms can attain the volume of production to be efficient. Flexible systems are widely available that enable firms to customize their offers, proliferate variety, and do so at little additional cost. In the new world, scale and scope matter, but only as they contribute to a continuing innovation trajectory so that a company continually lowers its costs while increasing its performance.

Companies agitating to be leaders in the volatile new world order must transform themselves profoundly and perpetually so as to defy categorization. Is Wal-Mart a retailer, a wholesaler, or an information services and logistics company? Is Intel governed by the economic realities of the semiconductor industry, or does it lead one of several coevolving, competing personal computer-centred ecosystems? Are its competitors Texas Instruments and NEC or Microsoft and Compaq?

In place of 'industry', I suggest an alternative, more appropriate term: *business ecosystem*. The term circumscribes the microeconomies of intense coevolution coalescing around innovative ideas. Business ecosystems span a variety of industries. The companies within them coevolve capabilities around the innovation and work cooperatively and competitively to support new products, satisfy customer needs, and incorporate the next round of innovation. Microsoft, for example, anchors an ecosystem that traverses at least four major industries: personal computers, consumer electronics, information, and communications. Centred on innovation in microprocessing, the Microsoft ecosystem encompasses an extended web of suppliers including Intel and Hewlett-Packard and myriad customers across market segments.

A second new term is 'opportunity environment,' a space of business possibility characterized by unmet customer needs, unharnessed technologies, potential regulatory openings, prominent investors, and many other untapped resources. Just as biological ecosystems thrive within a larger environment, so do business ecosystems. As traditional industry boundaries erode around us, companies often unexpectedly find themselves in fierce competition with the most unlikely of rivals. At the same time, the most creative and aggressive companies exploit these wider territories, transforming the landscape with new ecosystems. Thus, shaping cohesive strategy in the new order starts by defining an opportunity environment. Within such an environment, strategy-making revolves around devising novel ways to seize opportunities and create viable networks with other business ecosystems.

Unfortunately, most prevailing ideas on strategy today begin with the wrongheaded assumption that competition is bounded by clearly defined industries. As a result, these ideas are nearly useless in the current business climate and are sure to be even less valid in the future. Can one understand the economic events of tomorrow relying on these ideas? I very much doubt it. It is more important to see a company within its food web than in competition with superficially similar firms bundled together in an industry.

We compete in a bifurcated world. Executives today really must view strategy from two perspectives: They must pay attention to the wider opportunity environment and strive to lead in establishing the business ecosystems that will best utilize it. The dominant new ecosystems will likely consist of networks of organizations stretching across several different industries, and they will joust with similar networks, spread across still other industries.

At the same time, executives must continue to see their companies in the traditional sense, as members of homogenous industries clawing away at rivals for market share and growth. In terms of strategy, it no longer matters if the industries are old and venerable like banking and automobiles, or frisky new ones like cable television and personal computers. So understanding one's industry will be only the first step to pursuing customers, innovation, and the creation of wealth.

Learn from companies investing in the new approach

I believe that this change in conceptualizing is vitally important for three reasons. First, the conditions and challenges prevalent in the fastest-moving sectors of the global economy are spreading inexorably to all the others. The dynamics of these centres, and the challenges confronting their feistiest companies and leaders, are now relevant to us all.

Second, some of the hottest centres of economic competition – computers, communications, media, retailing, health care – are now devising fresh approaches to strategy and leadership. These approaches are not very well understood, even by many of their creators, and they surely are not appreciated by the wider public. Nevertheless, the scope of the strategic ambitions are truly breathtaking. If their creators succeed in their endeavours, their initiatives will have profound implications in our daily lives. What it already means is the end of competition as we know it.

Third, these ideas are already propagating across the general business landscape and thus are guaranteed to have a dramatic and irreversible impact on how we do business from now on. Because of these reasons, business people, no matter what business they conduct, must comprehend at least the broad outlines of what is afoot.

The special task of business leadership: Creating communities of shared imagination

In one significant respect, a strictly biological metaphor does not apply to business. Unlike biological communities of coevolving organisms, business communities are social systems. And social systems are composed of real people who make decisions. A powerful shared imagination, focused on envisioning the future, evolves in a business ecosystem that is unlike anything in biology. Conscious choice does play an important role in ecology. Animals often choose their habitats, their mates, and their behaviour. In the economic world, however, strategists and policymakers and investors spend a great deal of time trying to understand the overall game and find fruitful ways to play it or change it. This consciousness is central to economic relationships.

Even more, shared imagination is what holds together economies, societies and companies. Therefore, a great deal of leadership and business strategy relies on creating shared meaning, which in turn shapes the future. For example, during 1995 millions of people from diverse backgrounds became convinced that the internet would become a major locus for commerce, entertainment, and personal communication. They rushed to become involved and, in the act of so doing, established a foundation for the very reality they believed was coming about. While many other factors encouraged the exponential growth of interest in the internet, Sun Microsystems played a powerful role by introducing a software language called Java. Java made it possible to create appealing animated experiences across the internet.

Sun makes a wide range of computers. Java was the result of a small research project, outside the company mainstream. Nonetheless, Sun executives saw Java's potential to enliven the community. Sun executives chose not to treat Java as just another product. Instead, they essentially gave away Java to the rest of the world in order to feed the internet frenzy and reinforce Sun's image as a leader of the movement. What mattered was Java the campaign – not Java the product. A widespread perception formed that Sun was prescient and well positioned for the future. Sun's sales rose, its stock appreciated, and it became more able to get other stakeholders to follow its lead.

It is the mind that imparts the harmony and the sense and the syncopation to the business ecosystem. The larger patterns of business coevolution are maintained by a complex network of choices, which depend, at least in part, on what participants are aware of. As Gregory Bateson stressed, if you change the ideas in a social system, you change the system itself. We are seeing the birth of ideas. The very fact that new ideas are coming into existence is changing the conditions. If you don't follow these new ideas, you will be totally lost.

As companies get more sophisticated in creating new ecosystems, become more like the guiding hand of a forester or gardener in an ecological environment, the more this new level of consciousness will become the dominant reality of business strategy. The game of leadership will evolve to new levels. There is a wonderful book of business history by Alfred Chandler (1977) called *The Visible Hand*. It chronicles the rise of the multidivisional organization between 1900 and 1930 and the consciousness of people like Alfred Sloane who made the development of this then new organization possible. We are witnessing the next revolution beyond multidivisional organizations and beyond the visible hand. It is the ability in an environment of immense resources, immense plasticity, and powerful information systems to make and break microeconomic relationships with enormous subtlety and velocity. We are entering an age of imagination.

In an age of imagination, the ultimate struggle among companies is for the souls of customers and the hearts of vast communities of suppliers and other associated companies. Strange things can happen in the new world of virtual organizations. In the new world, strategy based on conventional competition and cooperation gives way to strategy based on coevolution – which in turn defines a new level of competition. At this higher level, competition defines attractive futures and galvanizes concerted action. We can vividly see the tremendous power of a company like Microsoft, which leads and shapes the collective behaviour of thousands of associated suppliers, even though during most of the years of its most powerful influence, Microsoft never had more than $6 billion in sales.

But heightened consciousness of the benefits of ecosystem power and influence can also make prospective partners wary of committing to a leader. Competition to lead coevolution can bring its own peculiar paranoia – and fragment a community of companies. We already see this sort of effect within the PC business, where the heightened consciousness of Microsoft's role in overturning IBM's dominion has put all participants in the computer, communications, and even the entertainment business on notice.

Now prospective allies and partners of Microsoft appreciate the costs as well as the benefits of allegiance to the company from Redmond. Many of them have become reluctant coadventurers. Worries over Microsoft's motives and leadership outweighed the genuine benefits that appeared to be achieved by working together. Such worries also helped Sun Microsystems and Java. Java appealed to some stakeholders in part because it did not originate from Microsoft. The success of Sun and Java was welcomed as a limiter of Microsoft's influence on the future.

The new ecology of business

The heart of strategy is understanding these evolutionary patterns. What is consistent from business to business is the process of coevolution, the complex interplay between competitive and cooperative business strategies.

The immense changes that have taken place in business are minor compared to what is yet to come. When an ecological approach to management becomes more common, and when an increasing number of executives become conscious of coevolution, the pace of business change will accelerate at an exponential rate. Executives whose horizons are bounded by traditional industry perspectives will miss the real challenges and opportunities facing their companies. Shareholders and directors, who perceive the new reality, will eventually oust them. For companies caught up in dynamic business ecosystems, the stakes are considerable, but the rewards are commensurate and the challenges exhilarating as never before.

READING
7.4

How to make strategic alliances work

By Jeffrey H. Dyer, Prashant Kale and Harbir Singh[1]

Strategic alliances – a fast and flexible way to access complementary resources and skills that reside in other companies – have become an important tool for achieving sustainable competitive advantage. Indeed, the past decade has witnessed an extraordinary increase in alliances (Anand and Khanna, 2000). Currently, the top 500 global businesses have an average of 60 major strategic alliances each.

Yet alliances are fraught with risks, and almost half fail. Hence the ability to form and manage them more effectively than competitors can become an important source of competitive advantage. We conducted an in-depth study of 200 corporations and their 1572 alliances. We found that a company's stock price jumped roughly 1% with each announcement of a new alliance, which translated into an increase in market value of $54 million per alliance (Kale, Dyer and Singh, 2000). And although all companies seemed to create some value through alliances, certain companies – for example, Hewlett-Packard, Oracle, Eli Lilly & Co. and Parke-Davis (a division of Pfizer Inc.) – showed themselves capable of systematically generating more alliance value than others. (See Figure 7.4.1.) How do they do it? By building a dedicated strategic-alliance function. The companies and others like them appoint a vice president or director of strategic

[1]Source: This article was adapted from J.H. Dyer, P. Kale and H. Singh, 'How to Make Strategic Alliances Work' in *Sloan Management Review*, 2001, Vol. 23, No. 4, pp. 37–43. Reproduced by permission.

FIGURE 7.4.1   A dedicated function improves the success of strategic alliances, 1993–1997

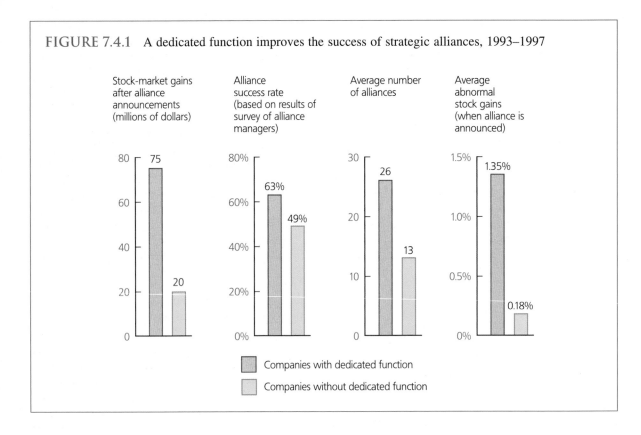

alliances with his or her own staff and resources. The dedicated function coordinates all alliance-related activity within the organization and is charged with institutionalizing processes and systems to teach, share and leverage prior alliance-management experience and know-how throughout the company.

And it is effective. Enterprises with a dedicated function achieved a 25% higher long-term success rate with their alliances than those without such a function – and generated almost four times the market wealth whenever they announced the formation of a new alliance. (See Exhibit 7.4.1.)

EXHIBIT 7.4.1

RESEARCH DESIGN AND METHODOLOGY

We conducted two types of research. From 1996 to 2000, we interviewed at companies such as Hewlett-Packard, Warner-Lambert (now part of Pfizer), Oracle, Corning, Lilly, GlaxoSmithKline and others that were reputed to have effective alliance capabilities. We also interviewed executives at companies that did not have a dedicated strategic alliance function, many of which have had relatively poor success with alliances. We conducted a survey-based study of 203 companies (from a variety of industries) with average revenues of $3.05

billion in 1998. The analysis of alliance success and stock market gain from alliance announcements is based on data from 1572 alliances formed by the companies between 1993 and 1997.

To assess the long-term success of the alliances, we collected survey data on the primary reasons that each of the alliances was formed. We then asked managers to evaluate each alliance on the following dimensions:

- the extent to which the alliance met its stated objectives;

- the extent to which the alliance enhanced the competitive position of the parent company;

- the extent to which the alliance enabled each parent company to learn some critical skills from the alliance partner; and
- the level of harmony the partners involved in the alliance exhibited.

Managers used a standard 1–7 (1 = low and 7 = high) survey scale. Alliances that received an above-average score on the four dimensions were rated 'successes', and those that received scores below average were rated 'failures'. Assessments of the alliance success and failure then were used to calculate an overall alliance success rate for each company. The alliance success rate is essentially a ratio of each company's 'successful' alliances to all its alliances during the study period.

In recent years, academics have begun using a market-based measure of alliance value creation and success based on abnormal stock-market gains. To estimate incremental value creation for each company, we built a model to predict stock price based on daily firm stock prices for 180 days before an alliance announcement. The model also includes daily market returns on the value-weighted S&P 500. Abnormal stock-market gains reflect the daily unanticipated movements in the stock price for each firm after an alliance announcement.

How a dedicated alliance function creates value

An effective dedicated strategic-alliance function performs four key roles: It improves knowledge-management efforts, increases external visibility, provides internal coordination, and eliminates both accountability problems and intervention problems. (See Figure 7.4.2.)

Improving knowledge management

A dedicated function acts as a focal point for learning and for leveraging lessons and feedback from prior and ongoing alliances. It systematically establishes a series of routine processes to articulate, document, codify and share alliance know-how about the key phases of the alliance life cycle. There are five key phrases, and companies that have been successful with alliances have tools and templates to manage each. (See Figure 7.4.3.)

Many companies with dedicated alliance functions have codified explicit alliance-management knowledge by creating guidelines and manuals to help them manage specific aspects of the alliance life cycle, such as partner selection and alliance negotiation and contracting. For example, Lotus Corp. created what it calls its '35 rules of thumb' to manage each phase of an alliance, from formation to termination. Hewlett-Packard developed 60 different tools and templates, included in a 300-page manual for guiding decision

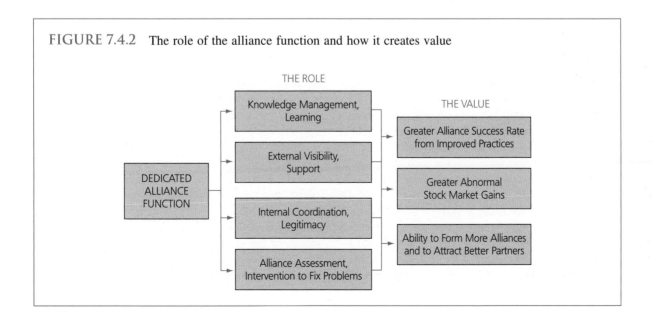

FIGURE 7.4.2 The role of the alliance function and how it creates value

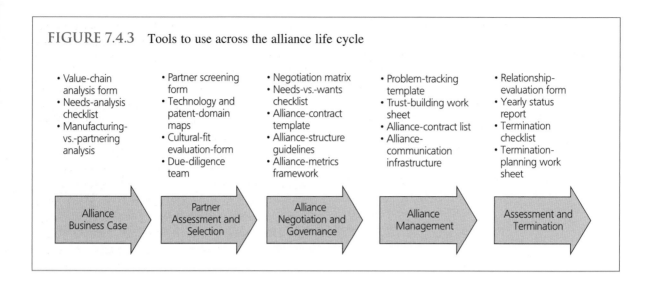

FIGURE 7.4.3   Tools to use across the alliance life cycle

- Value-chain analysis form
- Needs-analysis checklist
- Manufacturing-vs.-partnering analysis

Alliance Business Case

- Partner screening form
- Technology and patent-domain maps
- Cultural-fit evaluation-form
- Due-diligence team

Partner Assessment and Selection

- Negotiation matrix
- Needs-vs.-wants checklist
- Alliance-contract template
- Alliance-structure guidelines
- Alliance-metrics framework

Alliance Negotiation and Governance

- Problem-tracking template
- Trust-building work sheet
- Alliance-contract list
- Alliance-communication infrastructure

Alliance Management

- Relationship-evaluation form
- Yearly status report
- Termination checklist
- Termination-planning work sheet

Assessment and Termination

making in specific alliance situations. The manual included such tools as a template outlining the roles and responsibilities of different departments, a list of ways to measure alliance performance and an alliance-termination checklist.

Other companies, too, have found that creating tools, templates and processes is valuable. For example, using the Spatial Paradigm for Information Retrieval and Exploration, or SPIRE, database, Dow Chemical developed a process for identifying potential alliance partners. The company was able to create a topographical map pinpointing the overlap between its patent domains and the patent domains of possible alliance partners. With this tool, the company discovered the potential for an alliance with Lucent Technologies in the area of optical communications. The companies subsequently formed a broad-based alliance between three Dow businesses and three Lucent businesses that had complementary technologies.

After identifying potential partners, companies need to assess whether or not they will be able to work together effectively. Lilly developed a process of sending a due-diligence team to the potential alliance partner to evaluate the partner's resources and capabilities and to assess its culture. The team looks at such things as the partner's financial condition, information technology, research capabilities, and health and safety record. Of particular importance is the evaluation of the partner's culture. In Lilly's experience, culture clashes are one of the main reasons alliances fail. During the cultural assessment, the team examines the potential partner's corporate values and expectations, organizational

structure, reward systems and incentives, leadership styles, decision-making processes, patterns of human interaction, work practices, history of partnerships, and human-resources practices. Nelson M. Sims, Lilly's executive director of alliance management, states that the evaluation is used both as a screening mechanism and as a tool to assist Lilly in organizing, staffing and governing the alliance.

Dedicated alliance functions also facilitate the sharing of tacit knowledge through training programmes and internal networks of alliance managers. For example, HP developed a two-day course on alliance management that it offered three times a year. The company also provided short three-hour courses on alliance management and made its alliance materials available on the internal HP alliance web site. HP also created opportunities for internal networking among managers through internal training programmes, companywide alliance summits and 'virtual meetings' with executives involved in managing alliances. And the company regularly sent its alliance managers to alliance-management programmes at business schools to help its managers develop external networks of contacts.

Formal training programmes are one route; informal programmes are another. Many companies with alliance functions have created roundtables with opportunities for alliance managers to get together and informally share their alliance experience. To that end, Nortel initiated a three-day workshop and networking initiative for alliance managers. BellSouth and Motorola have conducted similar two-day workshops for people to meet and learn from one another.

Increasing external visibility

A dedicated alliance function can play an important role in keeping the market apprised of both new alliances and successful events in ongoing alliances. Such external visibility can enhance the reputation of the company in the marketplace and support the perception that alliances are adding value. The creation of a dedicated alliance function sends a signal to the marketplace and to potential partners that the company is committed both to its alliances and to managing them effectively. And when a potential partner wants to contact a company about establishing an alliance, a dedicated function offers an easy, highly visible point of contact. In essence, it provides a place to screen potential partners and bring in the appropriate internal parties if a partnership looks attractive.

For instance, Oracle put the partnering process on the web with Alliance Online (now Oracle Partners Program) and offered terms and conditions of different 'tiers' of partnership. Potential partners could choose the level that fit them best. At the tier I level (mostly resellers, integrators and application developers), companies could sign up for a specific type of agreement online and not have to talk with someone in Oracle's strategic alliance function. Oracle also used its web site to gather information on its partners' products and services, thereby developing detailed partner profiles. Accessing those profiles, customers easily matched the products and services they desired with those provided by Oracle partners. The web site allowed the company to enhance its external visibility, and it emerged as the primary means of recruiting and developing partnerships with more than 7000 tier I partners. It also allowed Oracle's strategic alliance function to focus the majority of its human resources on its higher-profile, more strategically important partners.

Providing internal coordination

One reason that alliances fail is the inability of one partner or another to mobilize internal resources to support the initiative. Visionary alliance leaders may lack the organizational authority to access key resources necessary to ensure alliance success. An alliance executive at a company without such a function observed: 'We have a difficult time supporting our alliance initiatives, because many times the various resources and skills needed to support a particular alliance are located in different functions around the company. Unless it is a very high-profile alliance, no one person has the power to make sure the company's full resources are utilized to help the alliance succeed. You have to go begging to each unit and hope that they will support you. But that's time-consuming, and we don't always get the support we should.'

A dedicated alliance function helps solve that problem in two ways. First, it has the organizational legitimacy to reach across divisions and functions and request the resources necessary to support the company's alliance initiatives. When particular functions are not responsive, it can quickly elevate the issue through the organization's hierarchy and ask the appropriate executives to make a decision on whether a particular function or division should support an alliance initiative. Second, over time, individuals within the alliance function develop networks of contacts throughout the organization. They come to know where to find useful resources within the organization. Such networks also help develop trust between alliance managers and employees throughout the organization – and thereby lead to reciprocal exchanges.

A dedicated alliance function also can provide internal coordination for the organization's strategic priorities. Some studies suggest that one of the main reasons alliances fail is that the partnership's objectives no longer match one or both partners' strategic priorities (Bleeke and Ernst, 1993, 1998). As one alliance executive complained:

> We will sometimes get far along in an alliance, only to find that another company initiative is in conflict with the alliance. For example, in one case, an internal group started to develop a similar technology that our partner already had developed. Should they have developed it? I don't know. But we needed some process for communicating internally the strategic priorities of our alliances and how they fit with our overall strategy.

Companies need to have a mechanism for communicating which alliance initiatives are most important to achieving the overall strategy – as well as which alliance partners are the most important. The alliance function ensures that such issues are constantly addressed in the company's strategy-making sessions and then are communicated throughout the organization.

Facilitating intervention and accountability

A 1999 survey by Anderson Consulting (now Accenture) found that only 51 per cent of companies that form alliances had any kind of formal metrics in place to assess performance. Of those, only about 20 per cent believed that the metrics they had in place were really the appropriate ones to use. In our research, we found that 76 per cent of companies with dedicated alliance function had implemented formal alliance metrics. In contrast, only 30 per cent of the companies without a dedicated function had done so.

Many executives we interviewed indicated that an important benefit of creating an alliance function was that it compelled the company to develop alliance metrics and to evaluate the performance of its alliances systematically. Moreover, doing so compelled senior managers to intervene when an alliance was struggling. Lilly established a yearly 'health check' process for each of its key alliances, using surveys of both Lilly employees and the partner's alliance managers. After the survey, an alliance manager from the dedicated function could sit down with the leader of a particular alliance to discuss the results and offer recommendations. In some cases, Lilly's dedicated strategic-alliance group found that it needed to replace the leader of a particular Lilly alliance.

When serious conflicts arise, the alliance function can help resolve them. One executive commented, 'Sometimes an alliance has lived beyond its useful life. You need someone to step in and either pull the plug or push it in new directions.' Alliance failure is the culmination of a chain of events. Not surprisingly, signs of distress are often visible early on, and with monitoring, the alliance function can step in and intervene appropriately.

How to organize an effective strategic-alliance function

One of the major challenges of creating an alliance function is knowing how to organize it. It is possible to organize the function around key partners, industries, business units, geographic areas or a combination of all four. How an alliance function is organized influences its strategy and effectiveness. For instance, if the alliance function is organized by business unit, then the function will reflect the idiosyncrasies of each business unit and the industry in which it operates. If the alliance function is organized geographically, then knowledge about partners and coordination mechanisms, for example, will be accumulated primarily with a geographic focus.

Identify key strategic parameters and organize around them

Organizing around key strategic parameters enhances the probability of alliance success. For example, a company with a large number of alliances and a few

central players may identify partner-specific knowledge and partner-specific strategic priorities as critical. As a result, it may decide to organize the dedicated alliance function around central alliance partners.

Hewlett-Packard is a good example of a company that created processes to share knowledge on how to work with a specific alliance partner. (See Figure 7.4.4.) It identified a few key strategic partners with which it had numerous alliances, such as Microsoft, Cisco, Oracle and America Online and Netscape (now part of AOL Time Warner) among others. HP created a partner-level alliance-manager position to oversee all its alliances with each partner. The strategic-partner-level alliance managers had the responsibility of working with the managers and teams of the individual alliances to ensure that each of the partner's alliances would be as successful as possible. Because HP had numerous marketing and technical alliances with partners such as Microsoft, it also assigned some marketing and technical program managers to the alliance function. The managers supported the individual alliance managers and teams on specific marketing and technical issues relevant to their respective alliances. Thus HP became good at sharing partner-specific experiences and developing partner-specific priorities.

Citicorp developed a different approach. Rather than organize around key partners, the company organized its alliance function around business units and geographic areas. In some divisions, the company also used an alliance board – similar to a board of directors – to oversee many alliances. The corporate alliance function was assigned a research-and-development and co-ordinating role for the alliance functions that resided in each division. For instance, the e-business-solutions division engaged in alliances that were typically different from those of the retail-banking division; therefore, the alliance function needed to create alliance-management knowledge relevant to that specific division. Furthermore, to respond to differences among geographic regions, each of Citicorp's divisions created an alliance function within each region. For example, the e-business-solutions alliance group in Latin America would oversee all Citicorp's Latin American alliances in the e-business sector. The e-business division's Latin American alliance board would review potential Latin American alliances – and approve or reject them.

Organize to facilitate the exchange of knowledge on specific topics

The strategic-alliance function should be organized to make it easy for individuals throughout the organization

FIGURE 7.4.4 Hewlett-Packard alliance structure for key alliance partners

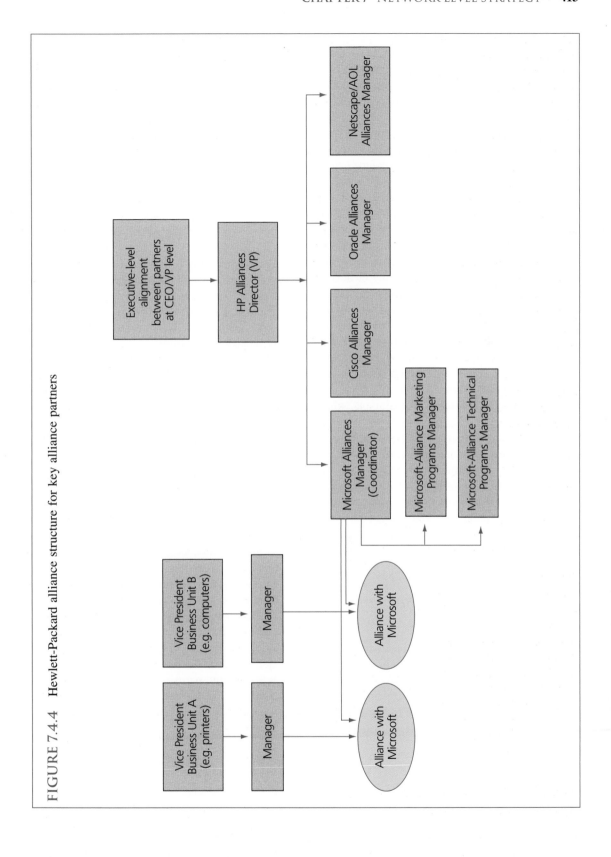

to locate codified or tacit knowledge on a particular issue, type of alliance or phase of the alliance life cycle. In other words, in addition to developing partner-specific, business-specific or geography-specific knowledge, companies should charge certain individuals with responsibility for developing *topic-specific* knowledge. For example, when people within the organization want to know the best way to negotiate a strategic alliance agreement, what contractual provisions and governance arrangements are most appropriate, which metrics should be used, or the most effective way to resolve disagreements with partners, they should be able to access that information easily through the strategic-alliance function. In most cases, someone within the alliance function acts as the internal expert and is assigned the responsibility of developing and acquiring knowledge on a particular element of the alliance life cycle. For some companies, it may be important to develop expertise on specific types of alliances – for example, those tied to research and development, marketing and cobranding, manufacturing, standard setting, consolidation joint ventures or new joint ventures. The issues involved in setting up such alliances can be very different. For example, whenever the success of an alliance depends on the exchange of knowledge – as is the case in R&D alliances – equity-sharing governance arrangements are preferable because they give both parties the incentives necessary for them to bring all relevant knowledge to the table. But when each party brings to the alliance an 'easy to value' resource – as with most marketing and cobranding alliances – contractual governance arrangements tend to be more suitable.

Locate the function at an appropriate level of the organization

When done properly, dedicated alliance functions offer internal legitimacy to alliances, assist in setting strategic priorities and draw on resources across the company. That is why the function cannot be buried within a particular division or be relegated to low-level support within business development. It is critical that the director or vice president of the strategic-alliance function report to the COO or president of the company. Because alliances play an increasingly important role in overall corporate strategy, the person in charge of alliances should participate in the strategy-making processes at the highest level of the company. Moreover, if the alliance function's director reports to the company president or COO, the function will have the visibility and reach to cut across boundaries and draw on the company's resources in support of its alliance initiatives.

A critical competence

Companies with a dedicated alliance function have been more successful than their counterparts at finding ways to solve problems regarding knowledge management, external visibility, internal coordination, and accountability – the underpinnings of an alliance management capability.

But although a dedicated alliance function can create value, success does not come without challenges. First, setting up such a function requires a serious investment of the company's resources and its people's time. Businesses must be large enough or enter into enough alliances to cover that investment. Second, deciding where to locate the function in the organization – and how to get line managers to appreciate the role of such a function and recognize its value – can be difficult. Finally, establishing codified and consistent procedures may mean inappropriately emphasizing process over speed in decision-making.

Such challenges exist. But the company that surmounts them and builds a successful dedicated strategic alliance function will reap substantial rewards. Companies with a well-developed alliance function generate greater stock-market wealth through their alliances and better long-term strategic alliance success rates. Over time, investment in an alliance-management capability enhances the reputation of a company as a preferred partner. Hence an alliance management capability can be thought of as a competence in itself, one that can reap rich rewards for the organization that knows its worth.

NETWORK LEVEL STRATEGY IN INTERNATIONAL PERSPECTIVE

Do as adversaries in law, strive mightily, but eat and drink as friends.
William Shakespeare (1564–1616); English dramatist and poet

Of all the debates in the field of strategic management, this one has received the most attention from comparative management researchers. Almost all of these researchers have concluded that firms from different countries display widely divergent propensities to compete and cooperate. Many authors suggest that there are recognizable national inclinations, even national styles, when it comes to establishing inter-firm relationships. For instance, Kanter (1994) notes that:

> *North American companies, more than others in the world, take a narrow, opportunistic view of relationships, evaluating them strictly in financial terms or seeing them as barely tolerable alternatives to outright acquisition. Preoccupied with the economics of the deal, North American companies frequently neglect the political, cultural, organizational, and human aspects of the partnership. Asian companies are the most comfortable with relationships, and therefore they are the most adept at using and exploiting them. European companies fall somewhere in the middle.*

Although Kanter's 'classification' is somewhat rough, most strategic management researchers who have done international comparative studies agree with the broad lines of her remark (e.g. Contractor and Lorange, 1988; Kagono *et al.*, 1985).

While it is difficult to generalize at the national level, since there can be quite a bit of variance within a country, it is challenging to debate these observed international dissimilarities. Are there really national inter-organizational relationship styles and what factors might influence their existence? As a stimulus to the international dimension of this debate, a number of country characteristics are put forward as possible influences on how the paradox of competition and cooperation is dealt with in different national settings. As noted before, it is the intention of these propositions to encourage further discussion and cross-cultural research on the topic of inter-organizational relationships.

Level of individualism

At the most fundamental level, cultural values can place more emphasis on competition or cooperation. Some researchers (e.g. Hofstede, 1993, Reading 1.4; Hampden Turner and Trompenaars, 1993) point out that this has much to do with a culture's orientation toward individuals or groups. More individualist cultures accentuate the position of each single person as a distinct entity, while more collectivist cultures stress people's group affiliations. In Hofstede's research, the United States surfaced as highest scoring nation in the world on the individualism scale, closely followed by the other English-speaking countries, Australia, Great Britain, Canada and New Zealand respectively. Hofstede argues that 'in the US individualist conception, the relationship between the individual and the organization is essentially calculative, being based on enlightened self-interest', while in more collectivist cultures the relationship 'is not calculative, but moral: It is based not on self interest, but on the individual's loyalty toward the clan, organization, or society – which is supposedly the best guarantee of that individual's ultimate interest'. The willingness of individuals to forgo self-interested behavior for the good of the group is believed to be the same cultural value spurring individual firms to cooperate for the good of an entire network (e.g. Gerlach, 1992). Pascale and Athos (1981) agree that in the highly group- oriented culture of Japan, interdependence is valued, while the 'self' is regarded as an obstacle to joint development. Group members feel indebted and obligated toward one another, and trust results from a shared understanding and acceptance of interdependence.

The strong orientation of the English-speaking ('Anglo-Saxon') cultures toward individualism and the Japanese cultural emphasis on group affiliation, is also recognized by Lessem and Neubauer (1994), who place these two cultures at the extreme ends of a continuum. In the socially atomistic Anglo-Saxon nations, individuals are seen as the building blocks of society and each person is inclined to optimize her/his own interests. In the socially symbiotic Japanese culture, the whole is more important than the individual parts, so that individuals are more likely to strive towards a group's common good. Interestingly, Lessem and Neubauer (following Albert, 1991) argue that, on this point, the German and Japanese cultures are strikingly similar. Both cultures exhibit a 'wholist' worldview, in which 'management and banker, employer and employee, government and industry combine forces rather than engage in adversarial relations', to the benefit of the entire system. This collectivist bent can be observed at the multi-company level (industrial networks/ *keiretsu*), but also at the industry and national levels of aggregation, leading many analysts to speak of Japan Incorporated and Deutschland AG.

Other cultures fall somewhere between these two extremes. Italy, for instance, is often cited for its high number of networked companies (Piore and Sabel, 1984). Besides the well-known example of Benetton, there are many networks in the textile industry of Prato, the ceramics industry of Sassuolo, the farm machine industry of Reggio Emilia and the motorcycle industry of Bologna. Similar to the Germans and Japanese, Italian culture is also characterized by a strong group orientation, but the affiliations valued by Italians tend to be mostly family-like, based on blood-ties, friendships or ideological bonds between individuals. There is often a strong loyalty and trust within these family-like communities, but distrust toward the outside world. Therefore, cooperation tends to be high within these communities, but competition prevails beyond.

In France the situation is again different. In French culture, according to Lessem and Neubauer (1994), there is 'an ingrained mistrust of the natural play of forces of a free economy'. People have a strong sense that cooperation in economic affairs is important, similar to the Japanese, Germans and Italians. However, the French are unwilling to depend on the evolution of cooperation between (semi-) independent firms. Generally, there is a preference to impose cooperation top-down, by integrating companies into efficiently working bureaucracies. Such structuring of the economy usually takes place under influence, or by direct intervention, of the French government. Such *dirigisme* is based on the opposite assumption to Williamson's work (1975, 1985): hierarchical coordination is usually preferable to market transactions. Former prime minister, Edouard Balladur, summarized this assumption far more graciously, when he remarked: 'What is the market? It is the law of the jungle, the law of nature. And what is civilization? It is the struggle against nature' (*The Economist,* March 15 1997). Based on this view, even relationships with firms not absorbed into the hierarchy are of a bureaucratic nature – that is, formal, rational and depersonalized.

Type of institutional environment

Of course, the cultural values described above are intertwined with the institutional structures that have developed in each country. Some comparative management researchers focus on these institutional forces, such as governments, banks, universities and unions, to explain the divergent national views on competition and cooperation. It is generally argued that most countries have developed an idiosyncratic economic system – that is, their own distinct brand of capitalism – with a different emphasis on competition and cooperation.

One prominent analysis is that of business historian Chandler (1986, 1990), who has described the historical development of 'personal capitalism' in the United Kingdom, 'managerial capitalism' in the United States, 'cooperative capitalism' in Germany and 'group capitalism' in Japan from 1850 to 1950. The legacy of these separately evolving forms of capitalism is that, to this day, there are significantly different institutional philosophies, roles and behaviors in each of these countries. In the English-speaking nations, governments have generally limited their role to the establishment and maintenance of competitive markets (Hampden-Turner and Trompenaars, 1993). A shared belief in the basic tenets of classical economies has led these governments to be suspicious of competition-undermining collusion masquerading under the term 'cooperation'. For instance, in the United States the Sherman Antitrust Act was passed in 1890 and has been applied with vigor since then to guard the functioning of the market. Many companies that would like to cooperate have been discouraged from doing so (e.g. Teece, 1992; Dyer and Ouchi, 1993).

In the German 'cooperative capitalism' system, the situation has been quite different. The government has major shareholdings in hundreds of companies outside the public services. According to Lessem and Neubauer (1994) 'the attitude to government participation in industry is based not on ideology but on a sense of partnership with the business community. It extends to the local level where local authorities, schools, banks and businesses combine to establish policies of mutual benefit.' Especially the large German banks have played an important role in guiding industrial development, promoting cooperation and defusing potentially damaging conflicts between companies. They have had an intimate knowledge of the business and have had a long-term stake in each relationship, often expressed by a minority shareholding of the bank in the client company and/or a seat on its supervisory board. The offices of the largest bank, Deutsche Bank, hold hundreds of seats on other companies' supervisory boards, although this system has been unraveling since the late 1990s. The trade associations and unions, it should be noted, also employ a long-term, cooperative perspective.

The Japanese 'group capitalism' system is somewhat akin to the German model. In Japan, too, business and social institutions have formed a partnership to promote mutually beneficial developments. However, in Japan, the government has played a more prominent role than in Germany, through its national industrial strategies (Best, 1990). As Thurow (1991) points out, the Japanese government has been actively involved in the indirect protection of some domestic industries, the selection of other sectors as development priorities and the funding of related research and development. Furthermore, the *keiretsu* industry groups, such as Mitsui, Mitsubishi, Sanwa, Hitachi and Sumitomo, have also formed long-term networks of cooperating companies. While some consortia have been formed to deal with a particular task at hand, firms within a *keiretsu* are familiar with one another through long historical association and have had durable, open-ended relationships, partially cemented by multilateral minority shareholdings.

In France, the dirigiste state planners play an even more prominent role than in Japan. The French model, which could be dubbed 'bureaucratic capitalism', focuses sharply on the state as industrial strategist, coordinating many major developments in the economy. It is the planners' job 'to maintain a constant pressure on industry – as part industrial consultant, part banker, part plain bully – to keep it moving in some desired direction' (Lessem and Neubauer, 1994). The unions, on the other hand, tend to be more antagonistic, particularly in their relationship to the government. On the work floor, however, a more cooperative attitude prevails.

In the 'familial capitalism' system of Italy, on the contrary, the central government plays a very small role. Instead, local networks of economic, political and social actors cooperate to create a mutually beneficial environment. Trade associations, purchasing cooperatives, educational institutions and cooperative marketing are often created to support a large number of small, specialized firms working together as a loose federation. Trust within the network is often extensive, but institutions outside of these closed communities are mistrusted, especially the central government, tax authorities, bankers and the trade unions.

Market for corporate control

Linked to the general institutional environment, is how the issue of mergers, acquisitions and takeovers is viewed in each nation. In countries such as the United States and Britain, companies whose shares are traded on the stock exchange are exposed to the threat of a takeover. This relatively open market for corporate control facilitates vertical and horizontal integration. Companies can contemplate acquiring another firm, if they believe that internal coordination is preferable to a market-based relationship. In other countries, however, the market for corporate control is less open, if not entirely absent. Where horizontal or vertical integration is difficult to achieve, but working together is still beneficial, potential acquirers often only have collaborative arrangements as an alternative.

Type of career paths

Finally, a more down to earth reason why competition or cooperation might be more prevalent in a particular country may be found at the level of personnel policy. In general, the longer people know each other and the more they interact, the more trust and cooperation that evolves (e.g. Axelrod, 1984; Teece, 1992). In countries such as Japan and Germany, where stable, long-term employment is still common, individuals are in a better position to build up durable personal relationships with people in other firms. In nations where employees frequently shift between positions and companies, establishing personal ties and gradually building mutual trust is more difficult to achieve.

Another relationship-building mechanism can be the exchange of personnel, on a temporary or permanent basis. In Japan, for instance, it is not unusual to send an employee 'on assignment' to a partner firm for a long period of time, often simultaneously accepting 'external' employees in return. In some countries, the transfer of employees between partner organizations is more permanent. France and Japan are known for their public servants' mid-career shifts to the private sector (*pantouflage* and *amakudari*, respectively), which makes building public–private partnerships much easier.

FURTHER READING

No one who wishes to delve more deeply into the topic of organizational boundaries and inter-organizational relationships can avoid running into references to the classic in this area. Oliver Williamson's *Markets and Hierarchies: Analysis and Antitrust Implications*. Williamson's writings have inspired many researchers, especially economists. Others have remarked that Williamson's transaction cost economics largely ignores the political, social and psychological aspects of business relationships. As an antidote to Williamson's strongly rationalist view of the world, another classic can be recommended. Jeffrey Pfeffer and Gerald Salancik's *The External Control of Organizations: A Resource Dependency Perspective* is an excellent book that emphasizes the political aspects of inter-organizational relationships. However, both books are quite academic and not for the faint-hearted.

A shorter and more accessible, theoretical overview of the topic of inter-organizational cooperation is provided by Ranjay Gulati, Nitin Nohria and Akbar Zaheer, in their article 'Strategic Networks', in which they also compare the networking literature with the positioning school (Porter, 1980, Reading 5.1) and the resource-based view of the firm (Barney, 1991, Reading 5.4). For the more practice-oriented reader, Yves Doz and Gary Hamel's book *The Alliance Advantage: The Art of Creating Value Through Partnering*, is a good starting point, while *Smart Alliances: A Practical Guide to Repeatable Success*, by John Harbison and Peter Pekar, is even more hands-on.

For further reading on the subject of vertical relationships, Michael Best's *The New Competition,* and Carlos Jarillo's 'On Strategic Networks', are both excellent choices. For horizontal relationships a good starting point would be *Strategic Alliances: Formation, Implementation and Evolution*, by Peter Lorange and Johan Roos, or *The Knowledge Link: How Firms Compete Through Strategic Alliances*, by J. Badaracco. If the reader is interested in a broader view of the business ecosystem and liked James Moore's reading, then his book, *The Death of Competition: Leadership and Strategy in the Age of Business Ecosystems,* can also be recommended.

All of the above works are positively inclined towards collaboration, largely adopting the embedded organization perspective. For a more critical appraisal of networks, alliances and close relationships, by authors taking the discrete organization perspective, readers are advised to start with the article 'Outsourcing and Industrial Decline', by Richard Bettis, Stephen Bradley and Gary Hamel. Other critical accounts are John Hendry's article 'Culture, Community and Networks: The Hidden Cost of Outsourcing', and S. MacDonald's 'Too Close for Comfort?: The Strategic Implications of Getting Close to the Customer'.

For a more thorough understanding of networks within the Japanese context, Michael Gerlach's *Alliance Capitalism: The Social Organization of Japanese Business* is a good book to begin with. T. Nishiguchi's book *Strategic Industrial Sourcing: The Japanese Advantage* is particularly interesting on the topic of Japanese supplier relationships. For the Chinese view on networks, Murray Weidenbaum and Samuel Hughes book *The Bamboo Network: How Expatriate Chinese Entrepreneurs Are Creating a New Economic Superpower in Asia* is recommended, as is S. Redding's *The Spirit of Chinese Capitalism.* For an overview of European views, Ronnie Lessem and Fred Neubauer's *European Management Systems* is an excellent book, but also Roland Calori and Philippe de Woot's collection *A European Management Model: Beyond Diversity* provides challenging insights.

REFERENCES

Albert, M. (1991) *Capitalisme contre Capitalisme*, Paris: Seuil.

Allison, G.T. (1969) 'Conceptual Models and The Cuban Missile Crisis', *The American Political ScienceReview*, No. 3, September, pp. 689–718.

Anand, B., and Khanna, T. (2000) 'Do Companies Learn to Create Value?', *Strategic Management Journal*, Vol. 21, No. 3, March, pp. 295–316.

Anderson Consulting (1999) 'Dispelling the Myths of Alliances', *Outlook*, pp. 28.

Aoki, M., Gustafsson, B., and Williamson, O.E. (1990) *The Firm as a Nexus of Treaties*, London: Sage.

Arthur, W.B. (1994) *Increasing Returns and Path Dependence in the Economy*, Ann Arbor, MI: University of Michigan Press.

Axelrod, R. (1984) *The Evolution of Cooperation*, New York: Basic Books.

Axelsson, B., and Easton, G. (1992) *Industrial Networks: A New View of Reality*, New York: Wiley.

Badaracco, J.L. (1991) *The Knowledge Link: How Firms Compete Through Strategic Alliances*, Boston, MA: Harvard Business School Press.

Bateson, G. (1979) *Mind and Nature: A Necessary Unity*, New York: Dutton.

Best, M.H. (1990) *The New Competition: Institutions of Industrial Restructuring*, Cambridge: Polity.

Bettis, R.A., Bradley, S.P., and Hamel, G. (1992) 'Outsourcing and Industrial Decline', *Academy of Management Executive*, Vol. 6, No. 1, pp. 7–22.

Bleeke, J., and Ernst, D. (1991) 'The Way to Win in Cross Border Alliances', *Harvard Business Review*, Vol. 69, No. 6, November–December, pp. 127–135.

Bleeke, J., and Ernst, D. (1993) *Collaborating To Compete*, New York: Wiley.

Bleeke, J., and Ernst, D. (1998) 'The Way To Win in Cross-Border Alliances', *The Alliance Analyst*, March, pp. 1–4.

Brandenburger, A.M., and Nalebuff, B.J. (1996) *Co-opetition*, New York: Currency Doubleday.

Calori, R., and de Woot, P. (eds) (1994) *A European Management Model: Beyond Diversity*, Hemel Hempstead: Prentice Hall.

Chandler, A.D. Jr. (1977) *The Visible Hand: The Managerial Revolution in American Business*, Cambridge, MA: Harvard University Press.

Chandler, A.D. (1986) 'The Evolution of Modern Global Competition', in: Porter, M.E. (ed.), *Competition in Global Industries*, Boston: Harvard Business School Press, pp. 405–448.

Chandler, A.D. (1990) *Scale and Scope*, Cambridge, MA: Belknap.

Chesbrough, H.W., and Teece, D.J. (1996) 'Organizing for Innovation: When is Virtual Virtuous?', *Harvard Business Review*, Vol. 74, No. 1, January–February, pp. 65–73.

Child, J., and Faulkner, D. (1998) *Strategies for Cooperation: Managing Alliances, Networks, and Joint Ventures*, Oxford: Oxford University Press.

Contractor, F.J., and Lorange, P. (1988) *Cooperative Strategies in International Business*, Lexington, MA: Lexington Books.

Dixit, A.K., and Nalebuff, B.J. (1991) *Thinking Strategically: The Competitive Edge in Business, Politics, and Everyday Life*, New York: WW Norton.

Doz, Y., and Hamel, G. (1998) *The Alliance Advantage: The Art of Creating Value Through Partnering*, Boston, MA: Harvard Business School Press.

Dyer, J.H. (1996) 'Specialized Supplier Networks as a Source of Competitive Advantage: Evidence from the Auto Industry', *Strategic Management Journal*, Vol. 17, No. 4, pp. 271–291.

Dyer, J.H., Kale, P., and Singh, H. (2001) 'How to Make Strategic Alliances Work', *Sloan Management Review*, Vol. 42, No. 4, Summer, pp. 37–43.

Dyer, J.H., and Ouchi, W.G. (1993) 'Japanese-Style Partnerships: Giving Companies a Competitive Edge', *Sloan Management Review*, Fall, pp. 51–63.

Dyer, J.H., and Singh, H. (1998) 'The Relational View: Cooperative Strategy and Sources of Interorganizational Competitive Advantage', *Academy of Management Review*, Vol. 23, No. 4, pp. 660–679.

Feldstein, J., Flanagan, C.S., and Holloway, C.A. (2001) *Handspring – Partnerships*, Case #SM-79, Stanford Graduate School of Business.

Gambetta, D. (ed.) (1988) *Trust: Making and Breaking Cooperative Relations*, New York: Blackwell.

Gerlach, M. (1992) *Alliance Capitalism: The Social Organization of Japanese Business*, Berkeley, CA: University of California Press.

Gnyawali, D.R., and Madhavan, R. (2001) 'Cooperative Networks and Competitive Dynamics: A Structural Embeddedness Perspective', *Academy of Management Review*, Vol. 26, No. 3, pp. 431–445.

Gomes-Casseres, B. (1994) 'Group versus Group: How Alliance Networks Compete', *Harvard Business Review*, Vol. 72, No. 4, July–August, pp. 62–74.

Grabher, G. (ed.) (1993) *The Embedded Firm: On the Socioeconomics of Industrial Networks*, London: Routledge.

Granovetter, M.S. (1985) 'Economic Action and Social Structure: The Problem of Embeddedness', *American Journal of Sociology*, Vol. 91, pp. 481–501.

Greenhalgh, L. (2001) *Managing Strategic Relationships*, New York: The Free Press.

Gulati, R. (1998) 'Alliances and Networks', *Strategic Management Journal*, Vol. 19, No. 4, pp. 293–317.

Gulati, R., Nohria, N., and Zaheer, A. (2000) 'Strategic Networks', *Strategic Management Journal*, Vol. 21, pp. 203–215.

Håkansson, H., and Johanson, J. (1993) 'The Network as a Governance Structure: Interfirm Cooperation beyond Markets and Hierarchies', in: Grabner, G. (ed.), *The Embedded Firm: On the Socioeconomics of Industrial Networks*, London: Routledge, pp. 35–51.

Hamel, G. (1991) 'Competition for Competence and Inter-Partner Learning Within International Strategic Alliances', *Strategic Management Journal*, Vol. 12, Special Issue, Summer, pp. 83–103.

Hamel, G., Doz, Y.L., and Prahalad, C.K. (1989) 'Collaborate with Your Competitors – and Win', *Harvard Business Review*, Vol. 67, No. 1, January–February, pp. 133–139.

Hamilton, G.G., and Woolsey Biggart, N. (1988) 'Market, Culture and Authority: A Comparative Analysis of Management and Organization in the Far East', *American Journal of Sociology*, Vol. 94, pp. 52.

Hampden-Turner, C., and Trompenaars, A. (1993) *The Seven Cultures of Capitalism: Value Systems for Creating Wealth in the United States, Japan, Germany, France, Britain, Sweden and the Netherlands*, New York: Doubleday.

Handy, C. (1989) *The Age of Unreason*, London: Business Books.

Harbison, J., and Pekar, P. (2000) *Smart Alliances: A Practical Guide to Repeatable Success*, San Francisco: Jossey-Bass.

Harrigan, K.R. (1985) *Strategies for Joint Ventures*, D.C. Lexington, MA: Heath.

Hendry, J. (1995) 'Culture, Community and Networks: The Hidden Cost of Outsourcing', *European Management Journal*, Vol. 13, No. 2, pp. 193–200.

Hill, C.W.L. (1990) 'Cooperation, Opportunism, and the Invisible Hand: Implications for Transaction Cost Theory', *Academy of Management Review*, Vol. 15, No. 3, pp. 500–513.

Hofstede, G. (1993) 'Cultural Constraints in Management Theories', *Academy of Management Executive*, Vol. 7, No. 1, pp. 8–21.

James, B.G. (1985) *Business Wargames*, Harmondsworth: Penguin.

Jarillo, J.C. (1988) 'On Strategic Networks', *Strategic Management Journal*, Vol. 9, No. 1, January–February, pp. 31–41.

Johanson, J., and Mattson, L.G. (1987) 'Interorganisational Relations in Industrial Systems: A Network Approach Compared with the Transaction Cost Approach', *International Studies in Management and Organisation*, Vol. 17, No. 1, pp. 34–48.

Johanson, J., and Mattson, L.G. (1992) 'Network Position and Strategic Action: An Analytical Framework', in: Axelsson, B., and Easton, G. (eds), *Industrial Networks: A New View of Reality*, London: Routledge.

Kagono, T., Nonaka, I., Sakakibara, K., and Okumara, A. (1985) *Strategic vs. Evolutionary Management*, Amsterdam: North-Holland.

Kale, P., Dyer, J., and Singh, H. (2000) 'Alliance Capability, Stock Market Response and Long-Term Alliance Success', *Academy of Management Proceedings*, August.

Kanter, R.M. (1994) 'Collaborative Advantage: The Art of Alliances', *Harvard Business Review*, Vol. 72, No. 4, July–August, pp. 96–108.

Kay, J.A. (1993) *Foundations of Corporate Success*, Oxford: Oxford University Press.

Kim, W.C., and Mauborgne, R. (2004) 'Blue Ocean Strategy', *Harvard Business Review*, October, pp. 2–11.

Kogut, B. (1988) 'Joint Ventures: Theoretical and Empirical Perspectives', *Strategic Management Journal*, Vol. 9, pp. 319–332.

Lado, A.A., Boyd, N.G., and Hanlon, S.C. (1997) 'Competition, Cooperation and the Search for Economic Rents: A Syncretic Model', *Academy of Management Review*, Vol. 22, No. 1, January, pp. 110–141.

Lessem, R., and Neubauer, F.F. (1994) *European Management Systems*, London: McGraw-Hill.

Lorange, P., and Roos, J. (1992) *Strategic Alliances: Formation, Implementation and Evolution*, Cambridge, MA: Blackwell.

Lorenzoni, G., and Baden-Fuller, C., (1995) 'Creating a Strategic Centre to Manage a Web of Partners', *California Management Review*, Vol. 37, No. 3, Spring, pp. 146–163.

MacDonald, S. (1995) 'Too Close for Comfort? The Strategic Implications of Getting Close to the Customer', *California Management Review*, Vol. 37, Summer, pp. 8–27.

Mahoney, J.T. (1992) 'The Choice of Organizational Form: Vertical Financial Ownership versus Other Methods of Vertical Integration', *Strategic Management Journal*, Vol. 13, No. 8, pp. 559–584.

Miles, R.E., and Snow, C.C. (1986) 'Network Organizations: New Concepts for New Forms', *California Management Review*, Vol. 28, Spring, pp. 62–73.

Mitchell, R.K., Agle, B.R., and Wood, D.J. (1997) 'Toward a Theory of Stakeholder Identification and Salience: Defining the Principle of Who and What Really Counts', *Academy of Management Review*, Vol. 22, No. 4, October, pp. 853–886.

Moore, J.F. (1993) 'Predators and Prey: A New Ecology of Competition', *Harvard Business Review*, Vol. 71, No. 3, pp. 75–86.

Moore, J.F. (1996) *The Death of Competition: Leadership and Strategy in the Age of Business Ecosystems*, New York: HarperBusiness.

Nalebuff, B.J., and Brandenburger, A.M. (1997) 'Co-opetition: Competitive and Cooperative Business Strategies for the Digital Economy', *Strategy and Leadership*, Vol. 25, No. 6, November–December, pp. 28–35.

Nishiguchi, T. (1994) *Strategic Industrial Sourcing: The Japanese Advantage*, New York: Oxford University Press.

Oliver, N., and Wilkinson, B. (1988) *The Japanization of British Industry*, London: Basil Blackwell.

Ouchi, W.G. (1980) 'Markets, Bureaucracies, and Clans', *Administrative Science Quarterly*, Vol. 25, No. 1, pp. 129–142.

Parolini, C. (1999) *The Value Net*, Chichester: Wiley.

Pascale, R.T., and Athos, A.G. (1981) *The Art of Japanese Management*, New York: Simon & Schuster.

Pfeffer, J., and Salancik, G.R. (1978) *The External Control of Organizations: A Resource Dependency Perspective*, New York: Harper & Row.

Piore, M., and Sabel, C.F (1984) *The Second Industrial Divide*, New York: Basic Books.

Porter, M.E. (1979) 'How Competitive Forces Shape Strategy', *Harvard Business Review*, March–May, pp. 137–145.

Porter, M.E. (1980) *Competitive Strategy: Techniques for Analyzing Industries and Competitors*, New York: Free Press.

Porter, M.E. (1985) *Competitive Advantage*, New York: Free Press.

Porter, M.E. (1990) *The Competitive Advantage of Nations*, London: Macmillan.

Powell, W. (1990) 'Neither Market nor Hierarchy: Network Forms of Organization', *Research in Organizational Behavior*, Vol. 12, pp. 295–336.

Prahalad, C.K., and Hamel, G. (1990) 'The Core Competence of the Corporation', *Harvard Business Review*, Vol. 68, No. 3, May–June, pp. 79–91.

Preece, S.B. (1995) 'Incorporating International Strategic Alliances into Overall Firm Strategy: A Typology of Six Managerial Objectives', *The International Executive*, Vol. 37, No. 3, May–June, pp. 261–277.

Quinn, J.B. (1992) *The Intelligent Enterprise: A Knowledge and Service Based Paradigm for Industry*, New York: Free Press.

Rademakers, M.F.L. (1999) *Managing Inter-Firm Cooperation in Different Institutional Environments: A Comparison of the Dutch and UK Potato Industries*, PhD Series in General Management, Rotterdam School of Management, Rotterdam.

Redding, S.G. (1990) *The Spirit of Chinese Capitalism*, Berlin: Walter de Gruyter.

Reich, R., and Mankin, E. (1986) 'Joint Ventures with Japan Give Away Our Future', *Harvard Business Review*, Vol. 64, No. 2, March–April, pp. 78–86.

Reve, T. (1990) 'The Firm as a Nexus of Internal and External Contracts', in: Aoki, M., Gustafsson, B., and Williamson, O.E. (eds), *The Firm as a Nexus of Treaties*, London: Sage.

Richardson, G. (1972) 'The Organization of Industry', *Economic Journal*, Vol. 82, pp. 833–896.

Ruigrok, W, and Van Tulder, R. (1995) *The Logic of International Restructuring*, London: Routledge.

Schelling, T. (1960) *The Strategy of Conflict*, Cambridge, MA: Harvard University Press.

Shapiro, C., and Varian, H. (1998) *Information Rules: A Strategic Guide to the Network Economy*, Cambridge, MA: Harvard Business School Press.

Simonin, B. (1997) 'The Importance of Collaborative Know-How', *Academy of Management Journal*, Vol. 40, No. 5, pp. 1150–1174.

Teece, D.J. (1992) 'Competition, Cooperation, and Innovation: Organizational Arrangements for Regimes of Rapid Technological Progress', *Journal of Economic Behavior and Organization*, Vol. 18, pp. 1–25.

Thorelli, H.B. (1986) 'Networks: Between Markets and Hierarchies', *Strategic Management Journal*, Vol. 7, No. 1, January–February, pp. 37–51.

Thurow, L. (1991) *Head to Head*, Cambridge, MA: MIT Press.

Van Tulder, R., and Junne, G. (1988) *European Multinationals and Core Technologies*, London: Wiley.

Weidenbaum, M., and Hughes, S. (1996) *The Bamboo Network: How Expatriate Chinese Entrepreneurs Are Creating a New Economic Superpower in Asia*, New York: Free Press.

Williamson, O.E. (1975) *Markets and Hierarchies: Analysis and Antitrust Implications*, New York: Free Press.

Williamson, O.E. (1979) 'Transaction Cost Economics: The Governance of Contractual Relations', *Journal of Law and Economics*, Vol. 22, pp. 223–261.

Williamson, O.E. (1985) *The Economic Institutions of Capitalism*, New York: Free Press.

Williamson, O.E. (1991) 'Strategizing, Economizing, and Economic Organization', *Strategic Management Journal*, Vol. 12, Winter: Special Issue, pp. 75–94.

STRATEGY CONTEXT

Circumstances? I make circumstances!

Napoleon Bonaparte (1769–1821); French emperor

The strategy context is the set of circumstances surrounding strategy-making – the conditions under which both the strategy process and the strategy content are formed. It could be said that strategy context is concerned with the *where* of strategy – where (i.e. in which firm and which environment) the strategy process and strategy content are embedded.

Most strategizing managers have an ambivalent relationship with their strategy context. On the one hand, strategizing is about creating something new, and for this a healthy level of disregard, or even disrespect, for the present circumstances is required. Much like Napoleon, managers do not want to hear about current conditions limiting their capability to shape the future – they want to create their own circumstances. On the other hand, managers recognize that many contextual limitations are real and that wise strategists must take these circumstances into account. In this section, this fundamental tension between *shaping* the context and *adapting* to it will be at the centre of attention.

As visualized in Figure IV.1, the strategy context can be dissected along two different dimensions: industry versus organization, and national versus international. This gives the three key contexts that will be explored in Chapters 8, 9 and 10:

- The industry context. The key issue here is how industry development takes place. Can the individual firm influence its industry and to what extent does the industry context dictate particular types of firm behaviour?

- The organizational context. The key issue here is how organizational development takes place. Can strategizing managers influence their own organizational conditions and to what extent does the organizational context determine particular types of firm behaviour?

- The international context. The key issue here is how the international context is developing. Must firms adapt to ongoing global convergence or will international diversity remain a characteristic with which firms will need to cope?

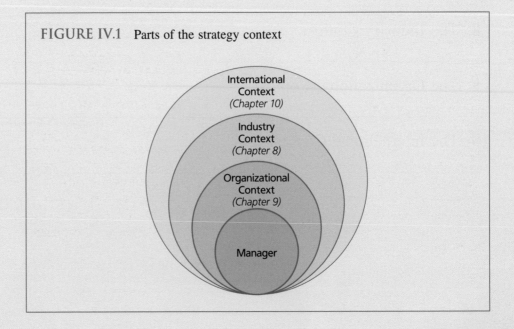

FIGURE IV.1 Parts of the strategy context

THE INDUSTRY CONTEXT

Know the other and know yourself: Triumph without peril.
Know nature and know the situation: Triumph completely.

Sun Tzu (5th century BC); Chinese military strategist

INTRODUCTION

If strategic management is concerned with relating a firm to its environment, then it is essential to know this environment well. In the previous chapters the factors and actors that shape the external context of the firm have been thoroughly reviewed. While the entire outside world was taken into consideration, emphasis was placed on the direct environment in which a firm needs to compete – its industry context. It was concluded that an understanding of competitors, buyers, suppliers, substitutes and potential new entrants, as well as the structural factors that influence their behaviour, is invaluable for determining a successful strategy.

A constant theme in the strategy process and strategy content sections was industry change. Knowing the current industry context, it became clear, is not enough to secure an ongoing alignment between a firm and its environment. Strategizing managers need to recognize in which direction the industry is developing to be able to maintain a healthy fit. However, what was not addressed in these discussions is how industry development actually takes place. Important questions such as 'what are the drivers propelling industry development?' and 'what patterns of development do industries exhibit?' have not yet been examined. Nor has it been established whether industries develop in the same way and at the same speed, and whether change is always accompanied by the same opportunities and threats. In this chapter, these questions surrounding the issue of industry development will be at the centre of attention.

For strategizing managers, however, the most important question linked to the issue of industry development is how a firm can move beyond *adapting* to *shaping*. How can a firm, or a group of collaborating firms, modify the structure and competitive dynamics in their industry to gain an advantageous position? How can the industry's evolutionary path be proactively diverted into a particular direction? If a firm would be capable of shaping its industry environment instead of following it, this would give them the potential for creating a strong competitive advantage – they could 'set the rules of the competitive game' instead of having to 'play by the rules' set by others. This topic of industry leadership-shaping events as opposed to following them – will be the key focus throughout this chapter.

THE ISSUE OF INDUSTRY DEVELOPMENT

When strategists look at an industry, they are interested in understanding 'the rules of the game' (e.g. Prahalad and Doz, 1987; Hamel, 1996). The industry rules are the demands dictated to the firm by the industry context, which limit the scope of potential strategic behaviours. In other words, industry rules stipulate what must be done to survive and thrive in the chosen line of business – they determine under what conditions the competitive game will be played. For example, an industry rule could be 'must have significant scale economies', 'must have certain technology' or 'must have strong brand'. Failure to adhere to the rules leads to being selected out.

The industry rules arise from the structure of the industry (e.g. Porter, 1980; Tirole, 1988). All of Porter's five forces can impose constraints on a firm's freedom of action. Where the rules are strict, the degrees of freedom available to the strategist are limited. Strict rules imply that only very specific behaviour is allowed – firms must closely follow the rules of the game or face severe consequences. Where the rules are looser, firms have more room to manoeuvre and exhibit distinctive behaviour – the level of managerial discretion is higher (e.g. Hambrick and Abrahamson, 1995; Carpenter and Golden, 1997).

As industries develop, the rules of competition change – vertical integration becomes necessary, certain competences become vital or having a global presence becomes a basic requirement. To be able to play the competitive game well, strategizing managers need to identify which characteristics in the industry structure and which aspects of competitive interaction are changing. This is the topic of 'dimensions of industry development', which will be reviewed in more detail below. To determine their response, it is also essential to understand the nature of the change. Are the industry rules gradually shifting or is there a major break with the past? Is the industry development more evolutionary or more revolutionary? A process of slow and moderate industry change will demand a different strategic reaction than a process of sudden and dramatic disruption of the industry rules. This topic of 'paths of industry development' will also be examined more closely.

As strategists generally like to have the option to shape instead of always being shaped, they need to recognize the determinants of industry development as well. What are the factors that cause the industry rules to change? This subject can be divided into two parts. First, the question of what the drivers of industry development are, pushing the industry in a certain direction. Secondly, the question of what the inhibitors of industry development are, placing a brake on changes. Together, these forces of change and forces for stability will determine the actual path of development that the industry will follow. How these four topics are interrelated is outlined in Figure 8.1.

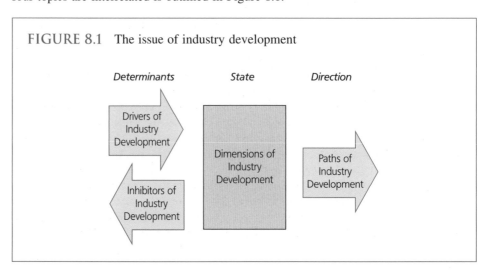

FIGURE 8.1   The issue of industry development

Dimensions of industry development

Industry development means that the structure of the industry changes. In Chapter 5, the key aspects of the industry structure have already been discussed. Following Porter (1980), five important groups of industry actors were identified (i.e. competitors, buyers, suppliers, new entrants and substitutes) and the underlying factors determining their behaviour were reviewed. Industry development (which Porter calls 'industry evolution', see Reading 8.1) is the result of a change in one or more of these underlying factors.

As Porter already indicates, the industry structure can be decomposed into dozens of elements, each of which can change, causing a shift in industry rules. Here it is not the intention to go through all of these elements, but to pick out a number of important structural characteristics that require special attention. Each one of these structural characteristics represents a dimension along which significant industry developments can take place:

- Convergence–divergence. Where the business models that firms employ increasingly start to resemble each other, the industry is said to be moving towards convergence (e.g. insurance and airline industries). In contrast, where many firms introduce new business models, the industry is said to be developing towards more diversity (e.g. car retailing and restaurant industries). Higher diversity can be due to the 'mutation' of existing firms, as they strive to compete on a different basis, or the result of new entrants with their own distinct business model. Convergence is the consequence of adaptation by less successful firms to a 'dominant design' in the industry and the selecting out of unfit firms incapable of adequate and timely adaptation (e.g. Hannan and Freeman, 1977; Porter, 1980). Generally, patterns of divergence and convergence can be witnessed in all industries, although the amount of mutation and the pressure for convergence can greatly differ, as can the overall cycle time of an 'evolutionary phase' of mutation and selection (e.g. Aldrich, 1999; Baum and Singh, 1994).

- Concentration–fragmentation. Where an increasing share of the market is in the hands of only a few companies, the industry is said to be developing towards a more concentrated structure (e.g. aircraft and food retailing industries). Conversely, where the average market share of the largest companies starts to decrease, the industry is said to be moving towards a more fragmented structure (e.g. airline and telecom services industries). Concentration can be due to mergers and acquisitions, or the result of companies exiting the business. Fragmentation can happen when new companies are formed and grab a part of the market, or through the entry of existing companies into the industry. In a concentrated industry it is much more likely that only one or two firms will be dominant than in a fragmented industry, but it is also possible that the industry structure is more balanced.

- Vertical integration–fragmentation. Where firms in the industry are becoming involved in more value-adding activities in the industry column, the industry is said to be developing towards a more vertically integrated structure (e.g. media and IT service providers). Conversely, where firms in the industry are withdrawing from various value-adding activities and 'going back to the core', the industry is said to be moving towards a more disintegrated, layered or vertically fragmented structure (e.g. telecom and automotive industries). It is even possible that the entire vertical structure changes if a new business model has major consequences upstream and/or downstream. In recent years, technological changes surrounding IT and the internet have triggered a number of such instances of industry reconfiguration (e.g. travel and encyclopaedia industries). However, even though we are now equipped with more fashionable terms (e.g. 'deconstruction'), such industry-wide transformations of the value-creation process are in themselves not new (e.g. PCs and the computer industry in the 1980s; airplanes and the travel industry in the 1950s) (e.g. Evans and Wurster, 1997; Porter, 2001).

■ Horizontal integration–fragmentation. Where the boundaries between different businesses in an industry become increasingly fuzzy, the industry is said to be developing towards a more horizontally integrated structure (e.g. consumer electronics and defence industries). Conversely, where firms become more strictly confined to their own business, the industry is said to be moving towards a more segmented or horizontally fragmented structure (e.g. construction and airline industries). Links between businesses can intensify or wane, depending on the mobility barriers and potential cross-business synergies. However, horizontal integration and fragmentation are not limited to the intra-industry domain. Inter-industry integration between two or more industries can also increase, creating a more or less open competitive space (Hamel and Prahalad, 1994) with few mobility barriers (e.g. the digital industries). Inter-industry integration can also occur where the producers of different products and services are complementary or converge on a common standard or platform (e.g. Palm OS and Linux), making them 'complementors' (e.g. Cusumano and Gawer, 2002; Moore, 1996, Reading 7.3). Yet, the opposite trend is possible as well, whereby an industry becomes more isolated from neighbouring sectors (e.g. accountancy).

■ International integration–fragmentation. Where the international boundaries separating various geographic segments of an industry become increasingly less important, the industry is said to be developing towards a more internationally integrated structure (e.g. food retailing and business education industries). Conversely, where the competitive interactions in an industry are increasingly confined to a region (e.g. Europe) or country, the industry is said to be moving towards a more internationally fragmented structure (e.g. satellite television and internet retailing). These developments will be more thoroughly examined in Chapter 10, which deals with the international context.

■ Expansion–contraction. Industries can also differ with regard to the structural nature of the demand for their products and/or services. Where an industry is experiencing an ongoing increase in demand, the industry is said to be in growth or expansion. Where demand is constantly receding, the industry is said to be in decline or contraction. If periods of expansion are followed by periods of contraction, and vice versa, the industry is said to be cyclical. A prolonged period of expansion is usually linked to the growth phase of the industry life cycle (e.g. Moore, 2000; Porter, 1980, Reading 8.1), while contraction is linked to the decline phase, but often it is rather difficult to apply the 'life cycle' concept to an entire industry (as opposed to a product or technology). As industry growth (expansion) can easily follow a period of industry decline (contraction), the life cycle model has little descriptive value – what does it mean to be mature? – and even less predictive value.

Paths of industry development

The development of an industry can be mapped along any one of the dimensions listed above. The most popular is to track the pattern of expansion and contraction, to gain some indication of the life cycle phase in which the industry might have arrived. Another frequently analysed characteristic is the level of concentration, commonly using a concentration index to measure the market share of the four or eight largest companies. But it is equally viable to trace the trajectory of vertical, horizontal or international integration. In Figure 8.2 examples of these paths of industry development are given.

In Figure 8.3 one particular element of the convergence–divergence dimension has been selected for further magnification. As discussed above, in the development of an industry a particular business model can become the dominant design around which the rest of the industry converges. A strategically relevant development occurs when the dominant business model is replaced by a new business model that offers customers

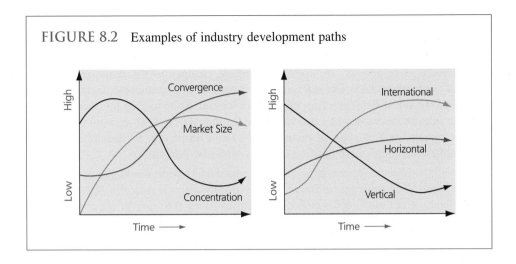

FIGURE 8.2   Examples of industry development paths

higher value. In Figure 8.3, four generic patterns of industry development are outlined, each describing a different type of transition from the old dominant model to the new (Burgelman and Grove, 1996; D'Aveni, 1999):

■ Gradual development. In an industry where one business model is dominant for a long period of time and is slowly replaced by an alternative that is a slight improvement, the development process is gradual. The firms adhering to the dominant design will generally have little trouble adapting to the new rules of the game, leading to a situation of

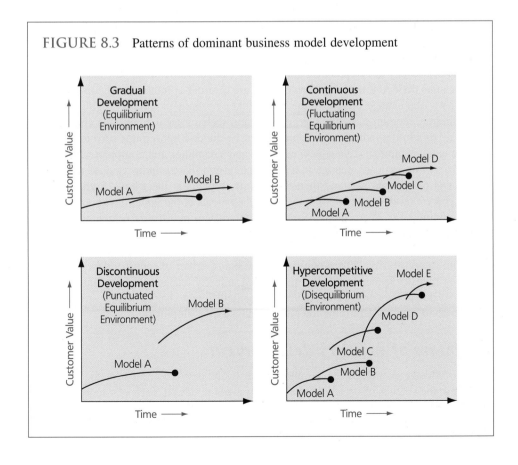

FIGURE 8.3   Patterns of dominant business model development

relative stability. Competition can be weak or fierce, depending on the circumstances, but will take place on the basis of the shared rules of the game. In this type of environment, companies with an established position have a strong advantage.

■ Continuous development. In an industry where changes to the dominant business model are more frequent, but still relatively modest in size, the development process is continuous. While firms need not have difficulties adjusting to each individual change to the rules of the game, they can fall behind if they do not keep up with the pace of improvement. In this type of environment, rapid adaptation to developments will strengthen the competitive position of firms vis-à-vis slow movers.

■ Discontinuous development. In an industry where one business model is dominant for a long period of time and is then suddenly displaced by a radically better one, the development process is discontinuous. The firms riding the wave of the new business model will generally have a large advantage over the companies that need to adjust to an entirely different set of industry rules. Where industry incumbents are themselves the 'rule breakers' (Hamel, 1996), they can strongly improve their position vis-à-vis the 'rule takers' in the industry. But the business model innovator can also be an industry outsider, who gains entrance by avoiding competition with established players on their terms (e.g. Bower and Christensen, 1995; Slywotsky, 1996).

■ Hypercompetitive development. In an industry where business models are frequently pushed aside by radically better ones, the development process is hypercompetitive (D'Aveni, 1994). The rules of the game are constantly changing, making it impossible for firms to build up a sustainably dominant position. The only defence in this type of environment is offence – being able to outrun existing competitors, being innovative first and being able to outperform new rule breakers at their own game.

Drivers of industry development

There is an endless list of factors in the environment that can change and can influence the direction of industry development. Following the categorization made in Chapter 7, these factors can be divided into change drivers that are external or internal to the industry (see Figure 8.4). The change drivers in the contextual environment can be roughly split into socio-cultural, economic, political/regulatory and technological forces for change. The change drivers in the industry environment can be divided into groups surrounding suppliers, buyers, incumbent rivals, new entrants, and substitutes and complementors.

As the arrows indicate, change in a complex system like an industry does not always start in one discernible part and then reverberate throughout the whole. Rather, change can also be the result of the interplay of various elements in the system, without any clear start or ending point. Yet, for the discussion on shaping industry development it is important to recognize the distinction between industry changes that are largely triggered by an individual firm, as opposed to broader, system-wide changes, for which no one actor can claim responsibility. Where one firm is the major driver of industry development, it can claim industry leadership. But if there is no industry leader and the evolution of the industry is due to the complex interaction of many different change drivers, it is said that the industry dynamics determine the path of industry development.

Inhibitors of industry development

Forces of change do not always go unopposed. In the discussion on strategic change in Chapter 4, the sources of organizational rigidity were reviewed, each of which acts as an inhibitor to organizational change. In the same way, there are many sources of industry rigidity, making the industry rules much more difficult to bend or break. Industry rigidity can be defined as the lack of susceptibility to change. If an industry is rigid, the rules of

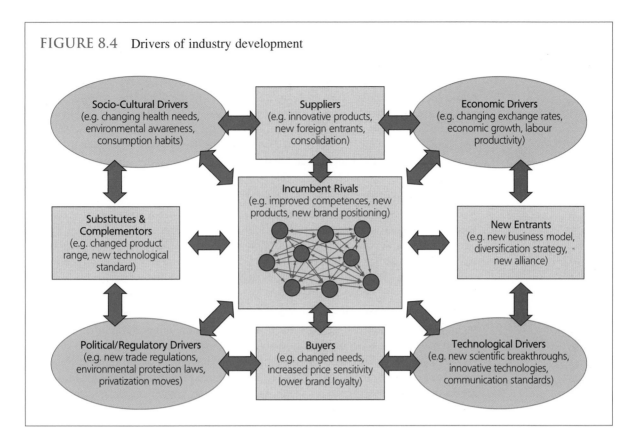

FIGURE 8.4   Drivers of industry development

the game cannot be altered and competitive positions are relatively fixed. The opposite term is industry plasticity – an industry's susceptibility to change.

A large number of factors can contribute to rigidity, thereby inhibiting industry development. Some of the most important ones are the following:

- Underlying conditions. Basically, some rules might be immutable because the underlying industry conditions cannot be changed. In some industries economies of scale are essential (e.g. airplane manufacturing, merchant shipping), while in others economies of scale are not of importance (e.g. wedding services, dentistry services). In some industries buyers are fragmented (e.g. newspapers, moving services), while in others they are highly concentrated (e.g. defence systems, harbour construction). In some industries buyers value product differentiation (e.g. clothing, restaurants), while in others bulk producers must compete on price (e.g. chemicals, general construction). Many of these structural factors are inherent to the industry and defy any attempts to change them (e.g. Bain, 1959; Porter, 1980).

- Industry integration. Besides the limited plasticity of individual aspects of the industry context, it is also important to recognize that some industries are particularly rigid because of the complex linkages between various aspects of the industry. For example, to be a rule-breaking music company not only requires developing new delivery methods via the internet, but also getting electronics manufacturers to adopt the new standards, finding ways to safeguard copyrights, working together with governments to find new policing methods, and not least to change the buying behaviour of consumers. Such interrelations between various elements of the industry can make it particularly difficult to actually influence the direction of events over time. The industry can become 'locked in' to a specific structure for a long period of time (e.g. Arthur, 1994; Shapiro and Varian, 1998).

■ Power structures. The industry rules can also be kept in place by those who feel they are better off with the status quo. Powerful industry incumbents often have little to gain and much to lose. They have established positions and considerable sunk costs, in the form of historical investments in technology, competences, facilities and relationships, which makes them reluctant to support changes to the rules of the game. Hence, rule changers are usually vehemently resisted by existing firms and denied support by potential suppliers and buyers. For example, rivals might attack a rule breaker by lowering prices, launching a media campaign, or even lobbying government regulators to impose legal rules. Especially where a rule breaker needs allies to secure supplies, distribution or a new standard it will be vulnerable to the counter-moves of parties with a vested interest in the current structure (e.g. Ghemawat, 1991; Moore, 2000, Reading 8.3).

■ Risk averseness. Challenging the industry rules is not only a risky step for the rule breaker, but also for many other parties involved. Customers might be hesitant about a new product or service until it has a firmer track record. Suppliers and distributors might worry whether the initial investments will pay off and what the countermoves will be of the established companies. The more risk averse the parties in the industry, the more rigid will be the industry rules (e.g. Christensen, 1997; Parolini, 1999).

■ Industry recipes. An industry recipe is a widely held perception among industry incumbents regarding the actual rules of the game in the industry. In other words, an industry recipe is the cognitive map shared by industry incumbents about the structure and demands of an industry. Such a common understanding of the rules of the game can develop over time through shared experiences and interaction – the longer people are in the industry and converse with each other, the greater the chance that a consensus will grow about 'what makes the industry tick'. Thus, the industry recipe can limit people's openness to rule changers who challenge the industry orthodoxy (e.g. Baden-Fuller and Stopford, 1992, Reading 8.2; Spender, 1989).

■ Institutional pressures. While the industry recipe is a shared understanding of how the industry actually functions, industry incumbents usually also share norms of what constitutes socially acceptable economic behaviour. Companies experience strong pressures from government, professional associations, customers, consultants, trade unions, pressure groups and other industry incumbents prescribing permissible strategies and actions, and generally internalize these behavioural standards. Such conformity to institutional pressures gives companies legitimacy, but makes them less willing to question industry conventions, let alone work together with a maverick rule breaker (e.g. Aldrich and Fiol, 1994; Oliver, 1997).

Taken together, these historically determined factors inhibit developments in the industry. It is said that industry evolution is path dependent – the path that the industry has travelled in the past will strongly limit how and in which direction it can develop in the future. In other words, 'history matters', setting bounds on the freedom to shape the future.

THE PARADOX OF COMPLIANCE AND CHOICE

When people are free to do as they please, they usually imitate each other.
Eric Hoffer (1902–1983); American philosopher

Yet, the question is whether firms should attempt to shape their industries at all, given the required effort and apparent risk of failure. There might be attractive rewards if a firm can lead industry developments, but trying to break industry rules that turn out to be immutable can be a quick way to achieve bankruptcy. Being an industry leader might sound very proactive, and even heroic, but it is potentially suicidal if the industry context defies being shaped.

This duality of wanting to change the industry rules that are malleable, while needing to adapt to the industry rules that are fixed, is the tension central to dealing with the industry context. On the one hand, managers must be willing to irreverently transgress widely acknowledged industry rules, going against what they see as the industry recipe. On the other hand, managers must respectfully accept many characteristics of the industry structure and play according to existing rules of the competitive game. Yet, these conflicting demands of being irreverent and respectful towards the industry rules are difficult for strategists to meet at the same time.

Where firms cannot influence the structure of their industry, *compliance* to the rules of the game is the strategic imperative. Under these circumstances, the strategic demand is for managers to adapt the firm to the industry context. Where firms do have the ability to manipulate the industry structure, they should exercise their freedom of *choice* to break the industry rules. In such a case, the strategic demand is for managers to try to change the terms of competition in their own favour.

This tension between compliance and choice has been widely acknowledged in the strategic management literature (e.g. Porter, 1980, Reading 8.1; Hrebiniak and Joyce, 1985). The pressure for compliance has usually been presented as a form of environmental determinism, as the industry developments force firms to adapt or be selected out (e.g. Astley and Van der Ven, 1983; Wilson, 1992). The freedom of choice has often been labelled as organizational voluntarism, to convey the notion that industry developments can be the result of the wilful actions of individual organizations (e.g. Bettis and Donaldson, 1990; Child, 1972). In the following sections both compliance and choice will be further examined.

The demand for firm compliance

It goes almost without saying that organizations must, to a large extent, adapt themselves to their environments. No organization has the ability to shape the entire world to fit its needs. Therefore, to be successful, all organizations need to understand the context in which they operate and need to play by most of the rules of the game.

After all, the alternative of ignoring the rules is fraught with danger. Probably the most common cause of 'corporate death' is misalignment between the organization and its environment. And misalignment can happen very quickly, as most industries are constantly in flux. Companies can misinterpret the direction of the changes, can fail to take appropriate corrective action, or can be plainly self-centred, paying insufficient attention to external developments. Most companies have enough difficulty just staying attuned to the current rules of the competitive game, let alone anticipating how the industry context will change in the future.

To achieve compliance with the industry rules, firms must develop structures, processes and a culture in which listening and adapting to the environment becomes engrained. Firms must learn to become customer and market-oriented, reacting to the 'pull' of the market instead of 'pushing' their standard approach and pet projects at an unwilling audience. Firm compliance means avoiding the pitfall of organizational arrogance – knowing better than the market and imposing an approach that no one is waiting for (e.g. Miller, 1990; Whitley, 1999).

The demand for strategic choice

While compliance to the industry rules can be very beneficial, contradicting them can also be strategically valuable. If firms only play by the current rules, it is generally very difficult for them to gain a significant competitive advantage over their rivals. After all, adapting to the current industry structure means doing business in more or less the same way as competitors, with few possibilities to distinguish the organization. In other words, 'compliance' might be another way of saying 'follow a me-too strategy'.

To be unique and develop a competitive advantage, firms need to do something different, something that does not fit within the current rules of the game. The more innovative the rule breaker, the larger will be the competitive advantage over rivals stuck with outdated business models. The more radical the departure from the old industry recipe, the more difficult it will be for competitors to imitate and catch up. Where companies are capable of constantly leading industry developments, they will have the benefit of capturing attractive industry positions before less proactive competitors eventually follow. In other words, there is a strong pressure for firms to attempt to shape the industry rules.

To achieve organizational choice, firms must find ways of escaping the pitfall of organizational conformity – the strict adherence to current industry rules. Firms must develop structures, processes and a culture in which the current industry recipe is constantly questioned, challenged and changed. Managers must come to see that in the long run the easy path of following the industry rules will be less productive than the rocky road of innovation and change (e.g. Hamel and Prahalad, 1994; Kim and Mauborgne, 2005, Reading 8.4).

EXHIBIT 8.1 SHORT CASE

CARMAX VS. AUTONATION VS. ZAG: AMERICA'S NEXT TOP MODEL?

Picture this. After 150 000 miles (240 000 kilometres) of faithful service, your old car is ready to roll over and die. So you drive down the road to the local car dealer to look at the used cars on offer. As you kick the tires on the 50 vehicles on the lot, you suddenly hear a voice behind you: 'That one belonged to a little old lady. She hardly drove over 30 miles per hour with it.' Great, a used car salesman. You're thrilled by the prospect of spending the rest of the day visiting other dealers, listening to more unlikely stories and haggling over prices.

Tom Folliard is counting on this story sending a shiver down your spine. He is President and CEO of CarMax, the American used car retailer with a twist. Realizing that most people hate the hassle and uncertainty that seem so inherent to buying a second hand car, CarMax was launched in 1993 based on a totally different retailing concept: the auto superstore. Similar to food and electronics big box stores, the giant CarMax outlets offer an enormous choice of 500 to 1500 cars of all brands, most no more than six model years old, with a past of no more than 70 000 miles (112 000 km). To be sales-worthy, a car must pass an extensive 125-point inspection programme, allowing CarMax to subsequently offer a free 30-day warranty and a relatively inexpensive extended service plan. While the potential buyers make a test drive in the vehicle of their choice, the salesperson checks a range of financing and insurance options from which the clients can choose. But probably the most important difference with traditional dealers is that CarMax outlets offer no room for haggling, by using fixed prices for their vehicles. The salespersons receive a fixed commission per car, independent of the price of the vehicle. That is why CarMax calls them 'consultants', using their time to smooth the process for the customer, instead of using it for bargaining over prices.

Since opening its first outlet near its headquarters in Richmond, Virginia, CarMax has grown to 100 stores in 46 metropolitan markets across the US, selling 350 000 used cars in 2008 alone, making it the largest in the world and a Fortune 500 company. This size gives CarMax a number of significant advantages. Not only can it leverage its advertising, IT systems and central services across a great number of units, but CarMax can also offer the customer even more choice, by shipping vehicles over from neighbouring stores if not available locally. Nearly 25% of CarMax's sales are generated by such inter-store transfers. At the same time, CarMax has considerable negotiation power when buying used cars from lease companies and rental agencies. Besides such fleet purchases, CarMax buys approximately half of its vehicles from private individuals, independent of whether they buy their next car from CarMax or not.

As the growth of the company suggests, customer response has been very positive, with satisfaction ratings generally topping 90%. In 2008 CarMax was one of North America's two winners of the Better Business Bureau's prestigious International Torch Award for Marketplace Excellence, in recognition of their ethical business practices. But employees, too, have been pleased, as can be seen from CarMax's fifth consecutive ranking as one of Fortune's 'Best Companies to Work for'. Despite the implosion of the US car market during the recession, sales only dropped from 8 to 7 billion dollars between 2007 and 2008, while disciplined cost cutting kept the company profitable. In the annual report 2009, Folliard announced that the high pace of store openings would be temporarily scaled back until the economy recovered, but that his long-term strategy was still directed at significant growth. While CarMax is twice the size as the next largest used car retailer, its market share was barely 2% in the US, with a world beyond, offering the company plenty of growth potential for the foreseeable future.

Yet, CarMax's 100 big box stores didn't make much of an impression on the largest car retailer in the world, AutoNation. With 239 sales locations in 15 states and annual sales of US$13.7 billion in 2008, AutoNation was approximately twice the size of CarMax. Back in 1996, CarMax had initially inspired AutoNation's founder Wayne Huizenga to also enter the car retail market with superstores. Like CarMax, he saw that the huge car retailing sector, with sales exceeding US$1 trillion per year, was populated by relatively small local or regional dealers carrying one or two brands. Prior to launching AutoNation, Huizenga had cut his teeth as entrepreneur by setting up two other overwhelmingly successful industry leaders, Waste Management in garbage collection and Blockbuster Video in the video rental business. In both cases, the contrarian Huizenga had come into a fragmented industry wedded to outdated business recipes, in which he introduced innovative business practices and drove consolidation. In auto sales, he planned to be the same rule breaker and industry leader.

However, when by 1999 the AutoNation superstores were still not profitable, Huizenga attracted the head of Mercedes-Benz USA, Mike Jackson, to become CEO, as he had significant car retailing experience and was equally motivated to revolutionize the business. Within a few months Jackson decided to close all the superstores and exit the car rental business that Huizenga had also entered. All energy was directed at transforming the hundreds of car dealerships that the company had acquired into a large-scale professional retailing organization. The retail formula that emerged has some commonalities with CarMax, particularly its 'one-price, no-hassle' car selling process, removing many buyers' frustration of having to deal with high-pressure salespeople. Likewise, AutoNation combines low operational costs with a great buying experience. An example of this combination is the firm's Smart Choice software, whereby customers' needs are analysed within two minutes, leading to a selection of the appropriate vehicle, with the price and financing options included. This programme cuts transaction times by 50%, saving the customer time and effort, while reducing AutoNation's costs per sale. As at CarMax, there is a drive to leverage scale advantages, to benchmark stores against one another and to share best practices between locations.

Yet, unlike CarMax, AutoNation does not have multi-brand supermarkets, but single brand dealerships, just as the car manufacturers want it. This makes it possible to work together with the manufacturers, instead of as adversaries. AutoNation has dealership agreements with 35 car brands, ranging from Rolls Royce and Porsche to Kia and Honda, each with their own dedicated outlets. AutoNation's added value is not in bringing various brands together under one roof, but in providing the know-how, infrastructure and people needed to make each dealership excellent.

AutoNation's approach has been to strive for at least a 15% share of each local market, allowing them to attract more professional management and have a larger marketing budget than rivals, while still having a competitive cost structure. To gain such a large market share quickly, AutoNation has acquired the top two or three car dealerships in many of the most lucrative market areas in the US. Generally, these dealerships already had the best management teams, good reputations, excellent market knowledge, reasonable retail capabilities, and clean operations, making it easier for Auto-Nation to quickly go from good to great. Additional benefits of this acquisition policy have been that no extra capacity has been added to the market spoiling prices and that potential copycats will have to settle for buying the third or fourth best dealerships if they want to take on AutoNation.

While about 60 per cent of sales are new cars and 30 per cent are used vehicles, approximately 70 per cent of gross profit is generated by the remaining 10 per cent of sales, namely parts, service, insurance and financing. Therefore, for AutoNation, it is extremely important to win their customers trust, to be allowed to offer the entire package. Besides an excellent customer experience, branding is also important. Therefore, AutoNation has created regional retail brands such as Champion in Houston, Desert in Las Vegas, Team in Atlanta and Courtesy in Orlando, each spanning multiple car brands and dealer locations. Its initial intention was to create one AutoNation brand, but the major car manufacturers expressed their discontent about one such powerful brand, so AutoNation was forced to accept a regional brand compromise.

Being a large professional car retailer, Auto-Nation has been able to attract top talent that otherwise would never have considered becoming car salespeople. AutoNation supplies them with excellent training through its corporate university and offers them plenty of career opportunities and entrepreneurial leeway. As COO, Mike Maroone puts it: 'We try to provide a frame that they have to operate within. If they stay inside that frame, they have lots of room for creativity and flexibility. We want them to possess a true entrepreneurial spirit.' CEO Jackson notes the company culture that he has nurtured as his most satisfying achievement.

The outcome of AutoNation's strategy has not only been excellent financial results compared to most car retailers, but high customer loyalty and widespread public recognition. In 2003 the Automotive Hall of Fame selected Jackson as Automotive Industry Leader of the Year, while AutoNation has been named America's Most Admired Automotive Retailer five times by Fortune Magazine.

AutoNation has also been the largest seller of cars through the fastest growing sales channel – the internet – generating more than 25% of its sales. But not for long, if it is up to Zag. Started in 2006 by internet veteran Scott Painter, Zag offers a platform for buyer groups to purchase cars from 2000 selected dealers at a fixed price. Zag provides its technology platform on a private label basis to companies and associations that can bundle purchasing power, such as Parenting.com and 14 AAA motoring clubs. Users also include some of the biggest providers of car loans in the US, including Capital One and American Express. Instead of wiping out dealers, Zag intends to work with them to make car buying more pleasurable and to drive down costs. Dealers can join if they are willing to be transparent about prices, give sizable discounts, ensure quick delivery and offer excellent service. According to David Bohne, President of USAA, the Fortune 200 financial services company with 6.8 million members among the American military and their families, joining Zag in 2009 was obvious: 'Zag's online car-buying platform is convenient and cost-effective, saves our members money and improves the experience of searching for and buying a car. It's a valuable service for our members.'

Despite the recession, growth was fast, with the 50 000th car sold in June 2009. While Chrysler and GM were announcing the closure of about 2000 dealerships, among them 6 owned by AutoNation, Zag was looking for more buyer groups interested in joining. As Painter remarked: 'Zag is thriving and growing even as both the auto industry and the economy as a whole are struggling. What the auto industry needs right now is innovation – not only in the products themselves, but also in the way they're sold.' He was convinced that everyone could 'clearly see the value of what Zag is doing – challenging the status quo and giving consumers a much better way to buy a car.'

But would Zag be the new industry leader? Or were the business models of AutoNation or CarMax better suited to become 'America's next top model'? And would the transformation of car retailing stop at the borders of the US or spread around the world? It was clear that the economic recession was going to trigger a big shake-out among dealers, but it was unclear who would emerge from the struggle as strongest. Quite an appropriate ending to the year that Darwin would have turned 200.

Sources: www.carmax.com; http://corp.AutoNation.com; www.zag.com; Sexton (2001), *St. Petersburg Times*, 1 March 2005; *Business Week*, 10 April 2007, 29 June 2007; *The Economist*, 25 May 2006; *Reuters*, 5 February 2009, 15 May 2009.

PERSPECTIVES ON THE INDUSTRY CONTEXT

A wise man will make more opportunity than he finds.

Francis Bacon (1561–1624); Lord Chancellor of England

Once again the strategizing manager seems 'stuck between a rock and a hard place'. The pressures for both compliance and choice are clear, but as opposites they are at least partially incompatible. Developing an organizational culture, structure and processes attuned to compliance will to some extent be at odds with the culture, structure and processes needed to shape an industry. An organization well rehearsed in the art of adaptation and skilful imitation is usually quite different than one geared towards business innovation and contrarian behaviour. How should managers actually deal with the issue of industry development – should they lead or follow?

In the strategic management literature many answers to this question are given – unfortunately, many contradictory ones. The views among management theorists differ sharply, as they emphasize a different balance between the need to comply and the need to choose. To gain a better overview of the range of conflicting opinions, here the two diametrically opposed positions will be identified and discussed. On the one hand, there are strategists who argue that industry development is an autonomous process, which individual firms can hardly hope to shape. They believe that compliance to shifting industry characteristics is mandatory – adjust or risk being selected out. This point of view will be referred to as the 'industry dynamics perspective'. On the other hand, many strategists believe that the industry context can be shaped in an infinite variety of ways by innovative firms. Therefore, industry development can be driven by firms willing and able to take a leading role. This point of view will be referred to as the 'industry leadership perspective'.

The industry dynamics perspective

 To those taking an industry dynamics perspective, the popular notion that individual firms have the power to shape their industry is an understandable, but quite misplaced, belief. Of course, the illusion of control is tempting – most people, especially managers, would like to control their own destiny. Most individuals assume they have a free will and can decide their own future. Many governments suppose that they can shape society and many cultures assume that they control nature. In the same way, it is seductive to believe that the individual firm can matter, by influencing the development of its industry.

Unfortunately, this belief is largely a fallacy, brought on by a poor understanding of the underlying industry dynamics. In reality, according to advocates of the industry dynamics perspective, industries are complex systems, with a large number of forces interacting simultaneously, none of which can significantly direct the long-term development of the whole. Firms are relatively small players in a very large game – their behaviours may have some impact on industry development, but none can fundamentally shape the direction of changes. On the contrary, as industries evolve, all firms that do not meet the changing demands of the environment are weeded out. Firms not suited to the new circumstances die, while firms complying with the changing rules prosper. Hence, through selection the industry context determines the group of industry survivors and through the pressures for adaptation the behaviour of the remaining firms is determined. In short, the industry shapes the firm, not the other way around.

The industry dynamics perspective is often also referred to as the industry evolution perspective, due to the strong parallel with biological evolution. Both evolutionary processes, it is argued, share a number of basic characteristics. In nature, as in business, the survival and growth of entities depends on their fit with the environment. Within each environment variations to a successful theme might come about. These new individuals will thrive, as long as they suit the existing circumstances, but as the environment changes, only those that meet the new demands will not be selected out. Hence, Darwin's well-known principle of 'survival of the fittest' is based on a cycle of variation and environmental selection. Many proponents of the industry dynamics perspective think that this biological view of evolution is a good model for what happens in industries – new organizations arise as mutations and only the fittest mutations survive. However, it is usually pointed out that in a business environment, organizations do not vary 'at random', but purposefully, and they possess the ability to adapt to selection pressures during the evolution process (e.g. Nelson and Winter, 1982; Baum and Singh, 1994). Therefore, organizations have much more flexibility to evolve along with the unfolding industry dynamics than life forms generally do. This process of mutual adaptation and development between entities in the system is called 'co-evolution' (e.g. Aldrich, 1999; Moore, 1996, Reading 7.3). To proponents of the industry dynamics perspective, the objective of a firm should be to co-evolve with its environment, instead of trying to conquer it.

Supporters of the industry dynamics perspective do not deny that every once in a while a rule breaker comes along, turning an industry upside down and spawning dozens of case studies by admiring business professors and hours of television interviews. But these successes must be put into perspective, just as a lottery winner should not encourage everyone to invest their life savings into buying lottery tickets. Yes, some business innovators are successful, but we have no idea of how many challengers were weeded out along the way – only the most spectacular failures make it into the media, but most go unreported. This is called the 'survivor's bias', and the emphasis on case-based reasoning in the field of strategy makes theorists and practitioners equally susceptible to fall into this trap. But even where a firm has been able to pull off a major industry change once, this does not make them the industry leader going into the future. They might have been the right company in the right place at the right time, able to push the industry in a certain direction once, but to assume that they will win the lottery twice is not particularly realistic.

The conclusion drawn by advocates of the industry dynamics perspective is that 'winning big' by changing the rules of the game sounds easy, fast and spectacular – but isn't. If one thing has been learnt from the internet bubble, it is that changing the rules of the game is extremely difficult, slow and hazardous, and should be left up to those 'high rollers' willing to play for 'high stakes' with only a low chance of success (i.e. venture capitalists and entrepreneurs). For regular companies, such an approach cannot be the mainstay of their strategy. Their basic approach must be to stick close to the shifting currents in their industry, which is challenging enough in most cases. Competitive advantage can be sought, but through hard work within the rules of the game.

The bad news is that this leaves limited freedom to manoeuvre and that the general level of profitability that a firm can achieve is largely predetermined. Once in a poor industry, a firm's growth and profit potential are significantly limited (Porter, 1980). The good news is that this still leaves plenty of room for a firm to score above the industry average, by positioning better than competitors, but also by adapting better to the on-going industry changes, or even anticipating changes more skilfully and reacting appropriately.

EXHIBIT 8.2 THE INDUSTRY DYNAMICS PERSPECTIVE

WESTJET: GO WITH THE FLOW

Everyone visiting the world's largest rodeo, the Calgary Stampede, knows that it doesn't matter who gets out of the gate first – the winner is the one who stays on the wild horse's back longest. This lesson has not been lost on the entrepreneurs David Neeleman and Clive Beddoe, who started their airline, WestJet, in Calgary in 1996. WestJet was by no means the first Southwest Airlines clone in Canada, offering low fare, no-frills, point-to-point air travel. But while they were not first movers, and did not attempt to rewrite the rules of the game in the airline industry, they are still on the bronco's back, while many of their competitors have been sent flying to the ground. Within only a few years, WestJet has become Canada's second largest, and most profitable airline, not by being more innovative than its rivals, but by steadfastly rolling out its business model in accordance with the emerging industry rules.

WestJet did not take off immediately. In the first few years, WestJet was a small pioneering outfit, with three Boeing 737-200s, struggling to overcome initial barriers, such as strict safety-related licensing regulations and the need to build up a good reputation and route structure. Raising capital, however, turned out to be relatively easy, Beddoe later reflected: 'It was one of the simplest things I ever did. I just told the story of Southwest Airlines – it was just staggering what they had achieved in an industry that never makes money. So, we said, "We're going to do the same thing in Canada."'

WestJet's growth was disciplined, and after 1999 expansion started in earnest. When in 2002 one of WestJet's main competitors, Canada 3000, went bankrupt, WestJet was propelled into the position of Canada's second largest airline after Air Canada, with 35 aircraft. By 2009, the company was operating 76 Boeing 737s and it planned to grow its fleet to 120 aircraft by 2013, making use of Air Canada's continued inability to come close to its cost structure. Besides overtaking Air Canada domestically, growing Canadian market share from 35% to 50% within 5 years, WestJet planned to boldly expand international flights.

Looking back over the past few years, it can be seen that WestJet's business model has evolved along with the developments in the industry. Being different sometimes means imitating someone else in a different market. Starting as a straightforward Southwest Airlines clone, WestJet has gradually moved away from point-to-point services, towards the hub-and-spoke model typical of the industry incumbents. Its home base, Calgary, already was a mini-hub and nearby Edmonton was soon given the same function. Another change, whereby WestJet has moved along with shifting external circumstances, has been to refocus on more long-haul routes. Initially WestJet had targeted car travellers, luring them to switch to air travel for shorter distances. But with more security charges, fuel surcharges and rising airport taxes, short hops became less competitive compared to driving.

The WestJet 'go with the flow' approach is also reflected in its late conversion to the Sabre global ticket reservation system in 2002 and its reluctant joining of the OneWorld alliance in 2008. In both cases, WestJet only cautiously adopted these common practices when they were convinced that these rules of the game could no longer be ignored and the firm was satisfied that these changes would not undermine their business model.

The skies look bright for WestJet. Clearly, the competitive rules in the Canadian airline industry have tilted in favour of genuine low-cost, no-frills carriers. Despite avid attempts by Air Canada to strike back by starting its own low-cost airlines, Tango and Zip, both imitators have crash landed after a few years of losses. Apparently, playing by the industry rules is more demanding to do 'on the fly' than it looks. Referring to Air Canada's copycat attempts, Beddoe wryly stated: 'Imitation is the greatest form of flattery.' He should know, as WestJet was no stranger to the practice of flattering the right examples.

Co-author: Martijn Rademakers

Sources: *Financial Times*, 2 August 2006; 26 August and 21 October 2002; *Airline Business*, 1 October 2002; *Financial Post*, 5 November 2008 and 5 February 2009; www.atwonline.com.

The industry leadership perspective

Strategists taking an industry leadership perspective fundamentally disagree with the determinism inherent in the industry dynamics perspective. Even in biology, breeders and genetic engineers consistently attempt to shape the natural world. Of course, in industries, as in biology, some rules are immutable. Certain economic, technological, social and political factors have to be accepted as hardly changeable. But the remaining environmental factors that can be manipulated leave strategists with an enormous scope for moulding the industry of the future. This belief is reflected in the remark by the Dutch poet Jules Deelder that 'even within the limits of the possible, the possibilities are limitless'. It is up to the strategist to identify which rules of the game must be respected and which can be ignored in the search for new strategic options. The strategist must recognize both the limits on the possible and the limitless possibilities.

Advocates of the industry leadership perspective do not deny that in many industries the developments are largely an evolutionary result of industry dynamics. For an understanding of the development paths of these 'leaderless' industries, the industry dynamics perspective offers a powerful explanatory 'lens' – many industries do evolve without a clear industry leader. However, these industries only followed this path because no firm was creative and powerful enough to actively shape the direction of change. A lack of leadership is not the 'natural state of affairs', but simply weakness on behalf of the industry incumbents. Industry developments can be shaped, but it does require innovative companies willing to take on the leadership role (e.g. Baden-Fuller and Stopford, 1992, Reading 8.2; Hamel and Prahalad, 1994).

A leadership role, supporters of this perspective argue, starts with envisioning what the industry of tomorrow might look like. The firm's strategists must be capable of challenging the existing industry recipe and building a new conception of how the industry could function in the future. They must test their own assumptions about which industry rules can be changed and must, in fact, think of ways of 'destroying their current business'. Hamel and Prahalad (1994) refer to this as intellectual leadership, noting that smart strategists also develop 'industry foresight', anticipating which trends are likely to emerge, so that they can be used to the firm's advantage.

Not only must a firm have the intellectual ability to envision the industry's future, but it must also be able to communicate this vision in a manner that other firms and individuals will be willing to buy into. If a vision of the industry of tomorrow is compelling enough, people inside and outside the company will start to anticipate, and will become committed to, that future, making it a self-fulfilling prophecy. This 'inevitableness' of an industry vision can be important in overcoming risk averseness and resistance from industry incumbents (e.g. Levenhagen, Porac and Thomas, 1993; Moore, 2000, Reading 8.3).

To actually change the rules of the competitive game in an industry, a firm must move beyond a compelling vision, and work out a new competitive business model. If this new business model is put into operation and seems to offer a competitive advantage, this can attract sufficient customers and support to gain 'critical mass' and break through as a viable alternative to the older business models. To shape the industry, the firm will also need to develop the new competences and standards required to make the new business model function properly. The better the firm is at building new competences and setting new standards, alone or in cooperation with others, the more power it will have to determine the direction of industry development (e.g. D'Aveni, 1999; Hamel, 1996).

All of the above points together add up to quite a considerable task. But then, industry leadership is not easy and changing the industry rules rarely happens overnight. Rather, it can take years, figuring out which rules can be broken and which cannot. It can be a marathon, trying to get the business model right, while building competences and support. Therefore, organizations require perseverance and commitment if they are to be successful as industry shapers (Hamel and Prahalad, 1994).

EXHIBIT 8.3 THE INDUSTRY LEADERSHIP PERSPECTIVE

METROPOLITAN OPERA: DRAMATIC INNOVATION

If you think that Rigoletto is a type of pasta, that Plácido Domingo plays for Real Madrid, that Puccini is a breed of Italian dogs and that the Ring Cycle has something to do with Tolkien's novels, you are obviously not an opera buff. However, you are by no means alone. Opera houses the world over are experiencing dwindling audiences and a general lack of interest from the broader public. Likewise the world famous Metropolitan Opera in New York, which for many years saw ticket sales decline and the average age of its audience shuffle upwards to over 65. So when in 2006 general manager Joseph Volpe retired, it was clear to the board of the Met that something more than the excellence of its long time musical director, James Levine, was needed to avoid eventual extinction. Much to the surprise of almost everyone, the board reached outside the opera world to bring in a 'young' fresh perspective. Peter Gelb, 53, was recruited from Sony Records, where he headed the classical music division.

'When I took over, the Met was on a declining slope toward extermination', Gelb later recalled, pointing to rising production costs, intense competition for sponsoring and falling attendance levels. Yet what disturbed Gelb most was the nature of the product itself – opera had become increasingly elitist and had lost touch with mainstream audiences. And the Met was probably the stuffiest of them all. Founded in 1883 by the leading families of New York, such as the Vanderbilts, the Astors, the Morgans and the Roosevelts, the Met had a long tradition of catering to the well-to-do. By ensuring the financial support of a few rich patrons, the Met could take great liberty to set its own artistic direction, without needing to bow to the taste of the masses. As a record executive, Gelb had already warned against this elitism: 'There is a danger, whether you are running a record label or an orchestra or an opera house, of not understanding who the public is. It doesn't mean you should pander to the public, but you should understand that there *is* a public. You can't operate an opera house in a vacuum, and I think more often than not that is how opera houses operate.'

At Sony, Gelb had built a reputation as innovator and popularizer, to the dismay of the many conservatives and purists in the classical music industry. He had teamed up the classical cellist Yo-Yo Ma with the country fiddle player, Marc O'Connor to record American folk dances, while getting pop singer Michael Bolton to record famous opera arias. So, when his appointment at the Met was announced, *The New York Times* pleaded for him to stay away from 'crossover opera'. Only a year later, in the same newspaper, the Met was heralded as 'perhaps the most exciting cultural institution in New York'. And since then the praise has kept on coming.

What Gelb did was to reconsider every rule in the book and open the windows to innovation, while at the same time keeping rich patrons on board. He started by strengthening his marketing team and launching an outreach programme to attract a bigger and younger audience. Dress rehearsals were opened to the public, opening nights were broadcast live to the plaza in front of the Met at Lincoln Center and in Times Square, and heavily discounted seats were sold for weekday performances. The number of new productions per season was also increased from three or four to six or seven.

Artistically, Gelb shifted productions away from static scenes emphasizing the singing (the 'park and bark' school of opera), to more dramatic action and emphasis on theatricality, which younger audiences prefer. Another of Gelb's innovations was to mount co-productions with other opera companies, giving the Met, in effect, the advantage of out-of-town tryouts.

However, his most revolutionary move has been to offer people around the world the opportunity to see the Met's live performances up close via high-definition telecasts to cinemas around the world. During the 2007–2008 season over 600 cinemas in 23 countries in North America, Australia, Europe and Japan showed these 'simulcasts', reaching an audience of almost a million people, while in the 2008–2009 season cinema ticket sales surpassed the 1.5 million mark. These simulcasts are expensive, costing about US$1.1 million each, as they require a production team of about 60, with 15 cameras filming the action. But with the Met getting 50% of the box-office revenue from simulcast tickets, which are sold at an average price of US$22, they still made a small profit, while the main objective is to promote opera in general and the Met in particular.

Having broken so many rules and taken on the industry leadership, it was clear to Gelb that others would follow. Unworried, he looked forward to new seasons and ongoing innovation. Confident that he could continue to stay at least one step ahead, he remarked to the *New Yorker:* 'I don't have a lot of preconceived ideas about how you do things. To be successful (…) you have to be able to think about lots of different aspects. Most people in the arts are either businesspeople or they are artistic people. Rarely are they both.'

Sources: www.metoperafamily.org; *The New Yorker*, 22 October 2007; *The Economist*, 3 July 2008; *Economist.com*, 27 March 2009.

INTRODUCTION TO THE DEBATE AND READINGS

The pilot cannot mitigate the billows or calm the winds.
Plutarch (c. 46–c. 120); Greek biographer and philosopher

The reasonable man adapts himself to the world; the unreasonable one persists in trying to adapt the world to himself. Therefore, all progress depends on the unreasonable man.
George Bernard Shaw (1856–1950); Irish playwright and critic

So, how should managers deal with the industry context? Should they concentrate on adapting to the dynamics in the industry, honing their ability to respond to changing demands and to adjust their business model to meet new requirements? Or should they take a more proactive role in shaping the future of the industry, changing the rules of the competitive game to suit their own needs? As the views within the field of strategic management are so far apart and no consensus seems to be emerging, managers must once again determine their own view on the topic, finding some way of balancing compliance and choice.

As an input to the process of assessing the variety of perspectives on this issue, four readings have been selected that each shed their own light on the debate. As in previous chapters, the first two readings will be representative of the two poles in this debate (see Table 8.1), while the second pair has been chosen to bring additional arguments into the discussion.

Actually, Reading 8.1 is not entirely representative of the industry dynamics perspective. In selecting a reading, we were faced by the problem that almost all contributions to the strategic management literature by researchers taking an industry dynamics perspective have been written in academic journals and do not make for easy reading. There are many excellent works, but none that are accessible enough to act as the opening article in this debate. Few strategists like to hear that they have little influence over their industry and that they should play by the rules – this message is hardly inspiring, if not outright frustrating, and it definitely does not sell books, which might partially explain why few proponents of the industry dynamics perspective have written for an audience of practising managers.

As a compromise, therefore, the debate in this chapter will be started off by an author who is strongly affiliated with the industry dynamics perspective, but who is not fully in their camp. This author is Michael Porter, and the article selected is appropriately titled 'Industry Evolution'. In this reading, taken from his classic book *Competitive Strategy*, Porter expands on his basic premises, which were discussed in Chapter 5. In his view, a company's profitability is heavily influenced by the structure of the industry in which it competes. Some industries have a poor structure, making it difficult for even the best firms to make a profit. Other industries, however, have a more advantageous structure, making it much easier to show a good performance. In Porter's opinion, how the game of competition

TABLE 8.1   Industry dynamics versus industry leadership perspective

	Industry dynamics perspective	Industry leadership perspective
Emphasis on	Compliance over choice	Choice over compliance
Industry development	Uncontrollable evolutionary process	Controllable creation process
Change dynamics	Environment selects fit firms	Firm creates fitting environment
Firm success due to	Fitness to industry demands	Manipulation of industry demands
Ability to shape industry	Low, slow	High, fast
Normative implication	Play by the rules (adapt)	Change the rules (innovate)
Development path	Convergence towards dominant design	Divergence, create new design
Firm profitability	Largely industry-dependent	Largely firm-dependent

is played in each industry is largely determined by the underlying economics. The industry structure presents the strict rules with which companies must comply. As an industry's structure evolves, Porter sees two processes at work that determine which companies will survive and profit over the longer term. On the one hand, Porter recognizes 'natural selection' processes, whereby only the fittest survive and firms that are not suited to the new environment become extinct. For instance, Porter argues that the selection of fit companies is particularly strong as industries move into a mature phase of development: 'when growth levels off in an industry ... there is a period of turmoil as intensified rivalry weeds out the weaker firms'. On the other hand, Porter also believes that companies can adapt themselves to changes in the industry's structure, although he emphasizes that they first must understand the drivers of change. So far, Porter's arguments fully coincide with the industry dynamics perspective. However, besides compliance with the industry context, Porter mentions the possibility of 'co-makership' as well. Or, in his own terms, he believes that firms can have some influence on the evolution of the industry's structure. Thus, each company does have a certain degree of strategic freedom to determine its own fate, but ultimately the autonomous development of the industry structure is crucially important to the survival and profitability of the company.

To open the debate on behalf of the industry leadership perspective, Reading 8.2 by Charles Baden-Fuller and John Stopford has been selected, with the telling title 'The Firm Matters, Not the Industry'. In a direct reference to Porter, they state that their view 'contrasts sharply with the popular, but misguided, school of thought that believes that the fortune of a business is closely tied to its industry'. They point out that only a fraction of the differences in profitability between companies can be attributed to industry char-acteristics, while more than half of the profit variations are due to the choice of strategy. Their conclusion is that the given industry circumstances are largely unimportant – it's how a firm plays the game that matters. In their opinion, high profitability is not the consequence of complying with some preset rules, but the result of acting creatively and imaginatively. For instance, they challenge the widely held belief that high market share is important for profitability. Nor do they agree that the competitive game dictates generic strategies, as Porter suggested in Chapter 5. They do not even believe that there is such a thing as a mature industry. In their view, the industry context does not present any fixed rules that cannot be avoided or changed by innovative companies. Their advice, therefore, is to remain imaginative and to adopt approaches that counter traditional solutions.

The second set of two readings starts with a recent work by Geoffrey Moore entitled 'Living on the Fault Line', which has been taken from the book of the same name (note that there are more Moores; Geoffrey's namesake in the previous chapter was James Moore). This reading has been added to bring in an issue of vital importance to industry development – the introduction of new technology. Of all the drivers of industry development, the adoption of disruptive technologies is probably the most prominent. Disruptive technologies are those that do not complement established technologies, but displace them. As such, Moore points out, disruptive technologies can cause dramatic shifts in an industry as 'competitive advantage positions that once seemed secure are abruptly overthrown and management teams … must scramble to recover'. Moore's central thesis is that for the innovators, championing a new technology, creating a mainstream market requires going through a number of phases, each with its own inherent strategic logic. He describes these phases of market development, making use of the widely known technology adoption life cycle. The first phase, or 'early market', is where technology enthusiasts and visionaries adopt the innovation. This phase is generally followed by a 'chasm', which is a period of no adoption, which needs to be bridged to get to the second phase, called the 'bowling alley', where early pragmatists 'knock' others into also adopting the new technology. Once adoption starts picking up speed, the third phase is entered, the 'tornado', where high growth is experienced. Finally, the technology achieves the fourth phase of broad acceptance, called 'Main Street'. Key to success in each phase, Moore concludes, is realizing that the strategy of the previous phase is no longer appropriate and that a new strategy must be developed. In his argumentation Moore focuses his attention on customer acceptance, paying less attention to the reactions of competitors and other industry actors. As such, his contribution is more to understanding market development and less to highlighting overall industry development. However, this reading still provides invaluable insight into the difficult process of changing the rules of the game based on technological innovation.

The last article (Reading 8.4) is 'Blue Ocean Strategy', by W. Chan Kim and Renée Mauborgne. This relatively recent *Harvard Business Review* article is a summary of the arguments they put forward in their successful book of the same name. Their core idea is that companies should not focus on competing in existing overcrowded markets, which they call red oceans, bloodied by battle, but should create new uncontested market spaces – blue oceans. Staying in a red ocean means accepting the existing industry conditions and finding a way to survive in this harsh environment, while breaking out into blue oceans means leaving competition behind and having a sea all to yourself. As such, Kim and Mauborgne are fully in line with the industry leadership perspective, that rule breaking is superior to rule taking. Yet, they introduce two additional arguments not often heard in the 'choice' camp. First, they contradict many of the points made by Moore in the previous reading about the nature of innovation and industry development. Looking at a wide range of industries, stretching from automobiles and computers to movie theatres and circuses, Kim and Mauborgne conclude that much of the business innovation witnessed is not based on technology pioneering as Moore suggests, but actually uses existing technologies. The innovativeness they see comes from fundamentally new and superior ways of creating value for buyers, which they call 'value innovation'. While Moore places a lot of emphasis on disruptive technologies as driver of industry development, Kim and Mauborgne are much more impressed by the way companies innovate their business models to create superior value in the eyes of customers. Building on this, Kim and Mauborgne make a second infrequently heard point, namely that industry incumbents can also be rule breakers. The headline grabbing innovators are often new entrants that disrupt the existing industry pecking order, but many of the value innovators reviewed by Kim and Mauborgne are actually industry incumbents who have been able to revolutionize their industries from the inside.

With so many competing opinions on the nature of the industry context, readers may now want to 'select the fittest one'. Or maybe readers will have to conclude that one view has rewritten the rules of competition in the strategy industry. Whichever way, it is up to each individual reader to form their own judgement on how to deal with the paradox of compliance and choice.

READING

8.1
Industry evolution
By Michael Porter[1]

Structural analysis gives us a framework for understanding the competitive forces operating in an industry that are crucial to developing competitive strategy. It is clear, however, that industries' structures change, often in fundamental ways. Entry barriers and concentration have gone up significantly in the US brewing industry, for example, and the threat of substitutes has risen to put a severe squeeze on acetylene producers.

Industry evolution takes on critical importance for formulation of strategy. It can increase or decrease the basic attractiveness of an industry as an investment opportunity, and it often requires the firm to make strategic adjustments. Understanding the process of industry evolution and being able to predict change are important because the cost of reacting strategically usually increases as the need for change becomes more obvious and the benefit from the best strategy is the highest for the first firm to select it. For example, in the early post-war farm equipment business, structural change elevated the importance of a strong exclusive dealer network backed by company support and credit. The firms that recognized this change first had their pick of dealers to choose from.

This article will present analytical tools for predicting the evolutionary process in an industry and understanding its significance for the formulation of competitive strategy.

Basic concepts in industry evolution

The starting point for analysing industry evolution is the framework of structural analysis (see Chapter 5). Industry changes will carry strategic significance if they promise to affect the underlying sources of the five competitive forces; otherwise changes are important only in a tactical sense. The simplest approach to analysing evolution is to ask the following question: Are there any changes occurring in the industry that will affect each element of structure? For example, do any of the industry trends imply an increase or decrease in mobility barriers? An increase or decrease in the relative power of buyers or suppliers? If this question is asked in a disciplined way for each competitive force and the economic causes underlying it, a profile of the significant issues in the evolution of an industry will result.

Although this industry-specific approach is the place to start, it may not be sufficient, because it is not always clear what industry changes are occurring currently, much less which changes might occur in the future. Given the importance of being able to predict evolution, it is desirable to have some analytical techniques that will aid in anticipating the pattern of industry changes we might expect to occur.

The product life cycle

The grandfather of concepts for predicting the probable course of industry evolution is the familiar product life cycle. The hypothesis is that an industry passes through a number of phases or stages – introduction, growth, maturity, and decline – illustrated in Figure 8.1.1. These stages are defined by inflection points in the rate of growth of industry sales. Industry growth follows an S-shaped curve because of the process of innovation and diffusion of a new product. The flat introductory phase of industry growth reflects the difficulty of overcoming buyer inertia and stimulating trials of the new product. Rapid growth occurs as many buyers rush into the market once the product has proven itself successful. Penetration of the product's potential buyers is eventually reached, causing the rapid growth to stop and to level off to the underlying rate of growth of the relevant buyer group. Finally, growth will eventually taper off as new substitute products appear.

As the industry goes through its life cycle, the nature of competition will shift. I have summarized in Table 8.1.1 the most common predictions about how

[1]Source: Reprinted with the permission of the Free Press, a Division of Simon and Schuster Adult Publishing Group, from *Competitive Strategy: Techniques for Analyzing Industries and Competitors* by Michael E. Porter. © 1980, 1988 by The Free Press.

FIGURE 8.1.1 Stages of the life cycle

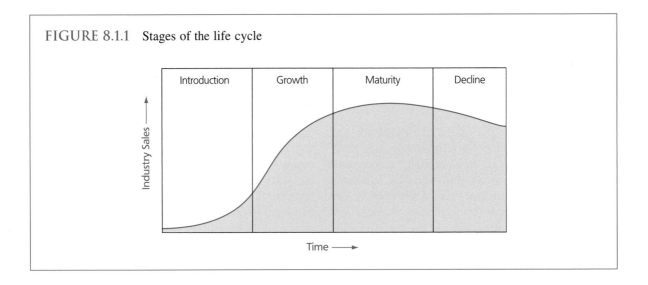

TABLE 8.1.1 Predictions of product life cycle growth theories

	Introduction	*Growth*	*Maturity*	*Decline*
Buyers and buyer behaviour	■ High-income purchaser ■ Buyer inertia ■ Buyers must be convinced to try the product	■ Widening buyer group ■ Consurner will accept uneven quality	■ Mass market ■ Saturation ■ Repeat buying ■ Choosing among brands is the rule	■ Customers are sophisiticated buyers of the product
Products and product change	■ Poor quality ■ Product design and development key ■ Many different product variations; no standards ■ Frequent design changes ■ Basic product designs	■ Products have technical and performance differentiation ■ Reliability key for complex products ■ Competitive product improvements ■ Good quality	■ Superior quality ■ Less product differentiation ■ Standardization ■ Less rapid product changes – more minor annual model changes ■ Trade-ins become significant	■ Little product ■ Spotty product quality
Marketing	■ Very high advertising/sales ■ Creaming price strategy ■ High marketing costs	■ High advertising, but lower percent of sales than introductory ■ Most promotion of ethical drugs ■ Advertising and distribution key for nontechnical products	■ Market segmentation ■ Efforts to extend life cycle ■ Broaden line ■ Service and deals more prevalent ■ Packaging important ■ Advertising competition ■ Lower advertising/sales	■ Low advertising/ sales and other marketing

	Introduction	Growth	Maturity	Decline
Manufacturing and distribution	■ Overcapacity ■ Short production runs ■ High skilled-labour content ■ High production costs ■ Specialized channels	■ Undercapacity ■ Shift toward mass production ■ Scramble for distribution ■ Mass channels	■ Some overcapacity ■ Optimum capacity ■ Increasing stability of manufacturing process ■ Lower labour skills ■ Long production runs with stable techniques ■ Distribution channels pae down their lines to improve their margins ■ High physical distribution costs due to broad lines ■ Mass channels	■ Substantial overcapacity ■ Mass production ■ Specialty channels
R&D	■ Changing production techniques			
Foreign trade	■ Some exports	■ Significant exports ■ Few imports	■ Falling exports ■ Significant imports	■ No exports ■ Significant imports
Overall strategy	■ Best period to increase market share ■ R&D, engineering are key functions	■ Pratical to change price or quality image ■ Marketing the key function	■ Bad time to increase market share, particularly if low-share company ■ Having competitive costs becomes key ■ Bad time to change price image or quality image ■ 'Marketing effectiveness' key	■ No exports ■ Significant imports ■ Cost control key
Competition	■ Few companies	■ Entry ■ Many competitors ■ Lots of mergers and casualties	■ Price competition ■ Shakeout ■ Increase in private brands	■ Exits ■ Fewer competitors
Risk	■ High risk	■ Risks can be taken here because growth covers them up	■ Cyclicality sets in	
Margins and profits	■ High prices and margins ■ Low profits ■ Price elasticity to individual seller not as great as in maturity	■ High profits ■ Highest profits ■ Fairly high prices ■ Lower prices than introductory phase ■ Recession resistant ■ High P/Es ■ Good acquisition climate	■ Falling prices ■ Lower profits ■ Lower margins ■ Lower dealer margins ■ Increased stability of market shares and price structure ■ Poor acquisition climate – tough to sell companies ■ Lowest prices and margins	■ Low prices and margins ■ Falling prices ■ Prices might rise in late decline

an industry will change over the life cycle and how this should affect strategy.

The product life cycle has attracted some legitimate criticism:

- The duration of the stages varies widely from industry to industry, and it is often not clear what stage of the life cycle an industry is in. This problem diminishes the usefulness of the concept as a planning tool.

- Industry growth does not always go through the S-shaped pattern at all. Sometimes industries skip maturity, passing straight from growth to decline. Sometimes industry growth revitalizes after a period of decline, as has occurred in the motorcycle and bicycle industries and recently in the radio broadcasting industry. Some industries seem to skip the slow takeoff of the introductory phase altogether.

- Companies can *affect* the shape of the growth curve through product innovation and repositioning, extending it in a variety of ways. If a company takes the life cycle as given, it becomes an undesirable self-fulfilling prophesy.

- The nature of competition associated with each stage of the life cycle is *different* for different industries. For example, some industries start out highly concentrated and stay that way. Others, like bank cash dispensers, are concentrated for a significant period and then become less so. Still others begin highly fragmented; of these some consolidate (automobiles) and some do not (electronic component distribution). The same divergent patterns apply to advertising, research and development (R&D) expenditures, degree of price competition, and most other industry characteristics. Divergent patterns such as these call into serious question the strategic implications ascribed to the life cycle.

The real problem with the product life cycle as a predictor of industry evolution is that it attempts to describe *one* pattern of evolution that will invariably occur. And except for the industry growth rate, there is little or no underlying rationale for why the competitive changes associated with the life cycle will happen. Since actual industry evolution takes so many different paths, the life cycle pattern does not always hold, even if it is a common or even the most common pattern of evolution. Nothing in the concept allows us to predict when it will hold and when it will not.

A framework for forecasting evolution

Instead of attempting to describe industry evolution, it will prove more fruitful to look underneath the process to see what really drives it. Like any evolution, industries evolve because some forces are in motion that create incentives or pressures for change. These can be called *evolutionary processes.*

Every industry begins with an *initial structure* – the entry barriers, buyer and supplier power, and so on that exist when the industry comes into existence. This structure is usually (though not always) a far cry from the configuration the industry will take later in its development. The initial structure results from a combination of underlying economic and technical characteristics of the industry, the initial constraints of small industry size, and the skills and resources of the companies that are early entrants. For example, even an industry like automobiles with enormous possibilities for economies of scale started out with labour-intensive, job-shop production operations because of the small volumes of cars produced during the early years.

The evolutionary processes work to push the industry toward its *potential structure,* which is rarely known completely as an industry evolves. Embedded in the underlying technology, product characteristics, and nature of present and potential buyers, however, there is a range of structures the industry might possibly achieve, depending on the direction and success of research and development, marketing innovations, and the like.

It is important to realize that instrumental in much industry evolution are the investment decisions by both existing firms in the industry and new entrants. In response to pressures or incentives created by the evolutionary process, firms invest to take advantage of possibilities for new marketing approaches, new manufacturing facilities, and the like, which shift entry barriers, alter relative power against suppliers and buyers, and so on. The luck, skills, resources, and orientation of firms in the industry can shape the evolutionary path the industry will actually take. Despite potential for structural change, an industry may not actually change because no firm happens to discover a feasible new marketing approach; or potential scale economies may go unrealized because no firm possesses the financial resources to construct a fully integrated facility or simply because no firm is inclined to think about costs. Because innovation, technological developments, and the identities (and resources) of the particular firms either in the industry or considering entry into it are so important to evolution, industry evolution will not only be hard to forecast with certainty but also an industry can potentially evolve in a variety of ways at a variety of different speeds, depending on the luck of the draw.

Evolutionary processes

Although initial structure, structural potential, and particular firms' investment decisions will be industry-specific, we can generalize about what the important evolutionary processes are. There are some predictable (and interacting) dynamic processes that occur in every industry in one form or another, though their speed and direction will differ from industry to industry:

- long-run changes in growth;
- changes in buyer segments served;
- buyer's learning;
- reduction of uncertainty;
- diffusion of proprietary knowledge;
- accumulation of experience;
- expansion (or contraction) in scale;
- changes in input and currency costs;
- product innovation;
- marketing innovation;
- process innovation;
- structural change in adjacent industries;
- government policy change;
- entries and exits.

Key relationships in industry evolution

In the context of this analysis, *how* do industries change? They do not change in a piecemeal fashion, because an industry is an *interrelated system*. Change in one element of an industry's structure tends to trigger changes in other areas. For example, an innovation in marketing might develop a new buyer segment, but serving this new segment may trigger changes in manufacturing methods, thereby increasing economies of scale. The firm reaping these economies first will also be in a position to start backward integration, which will affect power with suppliers – and so on. One industry change, therefore, often sets off a chain reaction leading to many other changes.

It should be clear from the discussion here that whereas industry evolution is always occurring in nearly every business and requires a strategic response, there is no one way in which industries evolve. Any single model for evolution such as the product life cycle should therefore be rejected. However, there are some particularly important relationships in the evolutionary process that I will examine here.

Will the industry consolidate?

It seems to be an accepted fact that industries tend to consolidate over time, but as a general statement, it simply is not true. In a broad sample of 151 four-digit US manufacturing industries in the 1963–1972 time period, for example, 69 increased in four-firm concentration more than two percentage points, whereas 52 decreased more than two percentage points in the same period. The question of whether consolidation will occur in an industry exposes perhaps the most important interrelationships among elements of industry structure – those involving competitive rivalry, mobility barriers, and exit barriers.

Industry concentration and mobility barriers move together

If mobility barriers are high or especially if they increase, concentration almost always increases. For example, concentration has increased in the US wine industry. In the standard-quality segment of the market, which represents much of the volume, the strategic changes (high advertising, national distribution, rapid brand innovation, and so on) have greatly increased barriers to mobility. As a result, the larger firms have gotten further ahead of smaller ones, and few new firms have entered to challenge them.

No concentration takes place if mobility barriers are low or falling

Where barriers are low, unsuccessful firms that exit will be replaced by new firms. If a wave of exit has occurred because of an economic downturn or some other general adversity, there may be a temporary increase in industry concentration. But at the first signs that profits and sales in the industry are picking up, new entrants will appear. Thus a shakeout when an industry reaches maturity does not necessarily imply long-run consolidation.

Exit barriers deter consolidation

Exit barriers keep companies operating in an industry even though they are earning subnormal returns on investment. Even in an industry with relatively high mobility barriers, the leading firms cannot count on reaping the benefits of consolidation if high exit barriers hold unsuccessful firms in the market.

Long-run profit potential depends on future structure

In the period of very rapid growth early in the life of an industry (especially after initial product acceptance has been achieved), profit levels are usually high. For example, growth in sales of skiing equipment was in excess of 20 per cent per year in the late 1960s, and nearly all firms in the industry enjoyed strong financial results. When growth levels off in an industry, however, there is a period of turmoil as intensified rivalry weeds out the weaker firms. All firms in the industry may suffer financially during this adjustment period. Whether or not the remaining firms will enjoy above-average profitability will depend on the level of mobility barriers, as well as the other structural features of the industry. If mobility barriers are high or have increased as the industry has matured, the remaining firms in the industry may enjoy healthy financial results even in the new era of slower growth. If mobility barriers are low, however, slower growth probably means the end of above-average profits for the industry. Thus mature industries may or may not be as profitable as they were in their developmental period.

Changes in industry boundaries

Structural change in an industry is often accompanied by changes in industry boundaries. Industry evolution has a strong tendency to shift these boundaries. Innovations in the industry or those involving substitutes may effectively enlarge the industry by placing more firms into direct competition. Reduction in transportation cost relative to timber cost, for example, has made timber supply a world market rather than one restricted to continents. Innovations increasing the reliability and lowering the cost of electronic surveillance devices have put them into effective competition with security guard services. Structural changes making it easier for suppliers to integrate forward into the industry may well mean that suppliers effectively become competitors. Or buyers purchasing private label goods in large quantities and dictating product design criteria may become effective competitors in the manufacturing industry. Part of the analysis of the strategic significance of industry evolution is clearly an analysis of how industry boundaries may be affected.

Firms can influence industry structure

Industry structural change can be influenced by firms' strategic behaviour. If it understands the significance of structural change for its position, the firm can seek to influence industry change in ways favourable to it, either through the way it reacts to strategic changes of competitors or in the strategic changes it initiates.

Another way a company can influence structural change is to be very sensitive to external forces that can cause the industry to evolve. With a head start, it is often possible to direct such forces in ways appropriate to the firm's position. For example, the specific form of regulatory changes can be influenced; the diffusion of innovations coming from outside the industry can be altered by the form that licensing or other agreements with innovating firms take; positive action can be initiated to improve the cost or supply of complementary products through providing direct assistance and help in forming trade associations or in stating their case to the government; and so on for the other important forces causing structural change. Industry evolution should not be greeted as a fait accompli to be reacted to, but as an opportunity.

READING

8.2

The firm matters, not the industry

By Charles Baden-Fuller and John Stopford[1]

Introduction

It is the firm that matters, not the industry. Successful businesses ride the waves of industry misfortunes; less successful businesses are sunk by them. This view contrasts sharply with the popular, but misguided, school of thought that believes that the fortune of a business is closely tied to its industry. Those who adhere to this view believe that some industries are intrinsically more attractive for investment than others. They (wrongly) believe that if a business is in a profitable industry, then its profits will be greater than if the business is in an unprofitable industry.

The role of the industry in determining profitability

Old views can be summarized as follows:

- Some industries are intrinsically more profitable than others.
- In mature environments it is difficult to sustain high profits.
- It is environmental factors that determine whether an industry is successful, not the firms in the industry.

New views can be summarized as follows:

- There is little difference in the profitability of one industry versus another.

- There is no such thing as a mature industry, only mature firms; industries inhabited by mature firms often present great opportunities for the innovative.
- Profitable industries are those populated by imaginative and profitable firms; unprofitable industries have unusually large numbers of uncreative firms.

This notion that there are 'good' and 'bad' industries is a theme that has permeated many strategy books. As one famous strategy writer (Porter, 1980) put it:

The state of competition in an industry depends on five basic competitive forces. ... The collective strength of these forces determines the ultimate profit potential in the industry, where profit potential is measured in terms of long-run return on invested capital. ... The forces range from intense in industries like tires, paper and steel – where no firm earns spectacular returns – to relatively mild like oil-field equipment and services, cosmetics and toiletries – where high returns are quite common.

Unfortunately, the writer overstates his case, for the evidence does not easily support his claim. Choosing good industries may be a foolish strategy; choosing good firms is far more sensible. As noted in Table 8.2.1, recent statistical evidence does not support the view that the choice of industry is important. At best only 10 per cent of the differences in profitability between one business unit and another can be related to

TABLE 8.2.1   The role of industry factors determining firm performance

Percentage of business units' profitability explained by	
Choice of industry	8.3 per cent
Choice of strategy	46.4 per cent
Parent company	0.8 per cent
Not explained – random	44.5 per cent

Source: Adapted from Rumelt (1991).

[1]Source: This article has been adapted from Chapter 2 of *Rejuvenating the Mature Business*, Routledge, 1992, pp. 13–14. Used with permission.

their choice of industry. By implication, nearly 90 per cent of profitability variations are not explained by the choice of industry, and *at least half appear to be attributable to the choice of strategy*. Put simply, the correct choice of strategy appears to be at least five times more important than the correct choice of industry.

Mature industries offer good prospects for success

It is often stated that market opportunities are created rather than found. Thus market research would never have predicted the large potential of xerography, laptop computers, or the pocket cassette recorder. Leaps of faith may be required. By analogy, low-growth mature markets or troubled industries are arguably ones that may offer greater chances of rewards than ones that appear to be glamorous and profitable. Our reasoning is simple. In general, profitable industries are more profitable because they are populated by more imaginative and more creative businesses. These businesses create an environment that attracts customers, grows the industry revenues, and makes the industry attractive. But creative and innovative businesses are also more fiercely competitive. To win in such environments may be difficult, as the pace of change may be rapid and the minimum standards high. In contrast, many less profitable industries are populated by sleepy, uncreative businesses that fail to innovate. In such environments, the potential for success by a creative newcomer is greater. The demands of competition may be less exacting and the potential for attracting customers is better.

We do not wish to overstate our case, but rather to force the reader to focus attention away from the mentality of labelling and prejudging opportunities based only on industry profitability. For example, outsiders often point to low-growth industries and suggest that the opportunities are less than those in high-growth industries. Yet the difference in growth rates may be dependent on the ability of businesses in these industries to be creative and innovative. Until Honda came, the motorcycle market was in steady decline. By their innovations – of new bicycles with attractive features sold at reasonable prices – the market was once again revived. Thus we suggest that the growth rate of the industry is a reflection of the kinds of businesses in the industry, not the intrinsic nature of the environment.

Large market share is the reward, not the cause of success

We believe that many managers are mistaken in the value they ascribe to market share. A large share of the market is often the symptom of success, but it is not always its cause. Banc One and Cook achieved significant positions in their industries because they were successful. For these organizations the sequence of events was success followed by growth, which was then cemented into greater success. Banc One has been doing things differently from many of its competitors for many years. It emphasized operational efficiency and it quickly captured a significant position as a low cost, high quality data processor for other banks and financial service companies. It also emphasized service, in particular service to retail and commercial customers, which contrasted with the approach of many other banks that sought to compete solely on price or failed to appreciate what the customer really wanted. Mergers and growth have been an important part of Banc One's strategy, but in every case, the merged organizations have been changed to fit the philosophy of Banc One.

Market share and profitability

Old views can be summarized as follows:

- Large market share brings lower costs and higher prices and so yields greater profits.
- Small-share firms cannot challenge leaders.

New views can be summarized as follows:

- Large market share is the reward for efficiency and effectiveness.
- If they do things better, small-share firms can challenge the leaders.

For creative organizations we see an upward spiral (Figure 8.2.1), and for organizations that are not creative, we see the cycles shown in Figure 8.2.2.

Our assertions run counter to much of what has been written in conventional books on strategy, and what is believed in many corporate boardrooms (see Exhibit 8.2.1). There is a common but incorrect belief among managers that being number one or number two in an industry gives the business unique advantages and that these are greatest in industries characterized by slow growth. With a large market share, it is often argued, the business can achieve lower costs and

FIGURE 8.2.1   Upward spiral of creative business

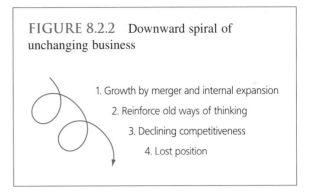

5. Number one position
4. Greater profitability
3. More change
2. Merger and internal growth
1. Internal change and growth in profits

FIGURE 8.2.2   Downward spiral of unchanging business

1. Growth by merger and internal expansion
2. Reinforce old ways of thinking
3. Declining competitiveness
4. Lost position

EXHIBIT 8.2.1   MARKET SHARE AND PROFITABILITY

There is a lively debate on the importance of market share in *explaining* business unit profitability. By *explaining* we do not mean *causing*. High market share could be the consequence of profitability, or the cause of both.

Those who advocate that large market share *leads* to greater profits point to the importance of several causal factors. First, large market share gives rise to the need to deliver large volumes of the service or good. These increased volumes in turn give rise to opportunities for costs savings by exploiting scale economies in production, service delivery, logistics, and marketing. Second, large market share permits the firm to benefit from experience or learning effects that also lower costs. Third, larger market share may allow the firm to charge higher prices. A product or service with a large share may seem intrinsically less risky to consumers. Finally, with a large market share, new entrants may be discouraged because they perceive the incumbent to have a substantial commitment to the industry through perceived or actual sunk costs.

In contrast, there are several who argue that these supposed benefits of large share are overrated. It is innovation that matters, innovators that realize new ways of competing can achieve their advantages by new approaches that do not necessarily need large market shares. However, those with new approaches may win market share, in which case large share is a reward for success. This Darwinian view of the market suggests that the competitive process is one where success goes to the firm that successfully innovates.

The strongest proponents of the importance of market share as a cause of success are Buzzell and Gale. Using the PIMS database drawn from a very large sample of business units across a range of industries, they asserted the existence of a strong relationship between relative market share and profitability. The figures below (Buzzell and Gale, 1987) suggest that a firm that has first rank in an industry will be more than twice as profitable as one of fourth rank.

Industry rank (by market share)	1	2	3	4	≤5
Pretax profits/sales (per cent)	12.7	9.1	7.1	5.5	4.5

However, these figures are misleading, for in a very large proportion of the industries studied, the firm with largest rank was *not* the most profitable. Often the picture is quite different; indeed according to the statistics published in Buzzell and Gale (1987) only 4 per cent of the differences in profitability of one business unit versus another could be explained by differences in market share. Schmalensee (1985), in his extensive study of more than 400 firms in US manufacturing, found that less than 2 per cent of the variations in profitability between one business and another could be explained by differences in market share. Market share effects appear to be relatively unimportant across a wide sample of industries. Of course, market share may be important in specific instances, but this only goes to reinforce our basic point that the critical success is dependent on getting the right strategy.

charge higher prices than its rivals. In slow-growth markets, it is argued, this may prove to be a decisive factor. This thinking ignores the importance of innovation, and believes that it is the size of the business that confers the advantage, not the new ways of doing things.

These false beliefs are widespread. They appear in many guises. At one extreme there are chief executives who say, 'We are only interested in industries where we hold a number one or number two position.' Such statements, if unaccompanied by an emphasis on innovation, will give out the wrong signal that high share will lead to success. At a more mundane level, managers are encouraged to write in their plans, 'We should dominate the industry and seek success by capturing a number one position.' Again, such statements are dangerous where the writer and reader believe that share by itself will bring success.

Growing market share is not the panacea for an organization's ills, not even in mature slow-growing markets. The belief that gaining market share will lead to greater profitability comes from confusing cause and effect. Many successful businesses do have a large market share, but the causality is usually from success to share, not the other way. Successful businesses often (but not always) grow because they have discovered an overwhelming source of competitive advantage, such as quality at low cost. Such advantages can be used to displace the market share of even the most entrenched incumbents.

Competing recipes

The crucial battles amongst firms in an industry are often centred around differing approaches to the market. Even in the so-called mature industries, where incumbent strategies have evolved and been honed over long time periods, it is new ideas that displace the existing leaders. Traditional wisdom has overstated the power of the generic approach (see Exhibit 8.2.2) and underplayed the role of innovation. Banc One established its premier position by rejecting conventional orthodoxy and emphasizing aspects hitherto neglected by industry leaders. Cook won in the steel castings industry by emphasizing quality and service to the customer. Hotpoint emphasized variety and quality in its approach to both the retailers and the final consumers. No single approach works well in all industries, but rather a multiple set of approaches. Here we emphasize the more fundamental point: the real competitive battles are fought out between firms with a diversity of approaches to the market.

The dynamics of competition in traditional industries

The old view is:

- Competition is based on firms following well-defined traditional (or generic) approaches to the market.

EXHIBIT 8.2.2 THE FALLACY OF THE GENERIC STRATEGY

It has been fashionable to suggest that there are a few *stable generic strategies* that offer fundamental choices to the organization. Typically these are described as a choice between a *low cost strategy* or a *differentiated strategy*. The low cost strategy involves the sacrifice of something – speed, variety, fashion, or even quality – in order to keep costs low, the lowest in the industry. In contrast, the high cost, differentiated strategy involves the focus on the very factors ignored by the others. The advocates of generic strategy make an (implicit or explicit) assertion: that the opposites cannot be reconciled. According to the generic strategists, it is not possible to be both low cost and high quality, or low cost and fashionable, or low cost and speedy. Trying to reconcile the opposites means being *stuck*

in the middle. This, it is suggested, is the worst of both worlds.

Generic strategies are a fallacy. The best firms are striving all the time to reconcile the opposites. Cook did find a way to be both high quality and low cost, so, too, many of the other creative firms we studied. At any point in time, there are some combinations that have not yet been resolved, but firms strive to resolve them. Until McDonald's, the idea of consistency and low price for fast food had not been achieved on a large scale. McDonald's solved that problem. Benetton was but one of many firms that resolved the dilemma of fashion at low cost. Given the enormous rewards that accrue to those who can resolve the dilemmas of the opposites, it is not surprising that there are no *lasting or enduring generic strategies.*

The new view is:

■ The real battles are fought among firms taking different approaches, especially those that counter yesterday's ideas.

Conclusions

Organizations that have become mature and suffer from poor performance typically view themselves as prisoners of their environment. Often their managers blame everyone but themselves for their poor performance. Labelling their environment as mature or hostile, they identify excess capacity, unfair competition, adverse exchange rates, absence of demand, and a host of other factors to explain why they are doing badly. Alas, too often these external factors are not really the causes of their demise but rather the symptoms of their failure. This conclusion is not so new; others have made the point before, yet their words appear to have been forgotten. Hall (1980) in an article in the *Harvard Business Review* noted:

Even a cursory analysis of the leading companies in the eight basic industries leads to an important observation: survival and prosperity are possible even when the business environment turns hostile and industry trends change from favourable to unfavourable. In this regard, the casual advice frequently offered to competitors in basic industries – that is diversify, dissolve or be prepared for below average returns – seems oversimplified and even erroneous.

Of course all industries experience the roller coaster of economic upswings and downswings, but there are organizations that appear to ride the waves and others that appear to be submerged by them.

Those who are submerged all too often clutch at the wrong things in trying to escape their drowning. Seeking simple solutions such as industry recipes, the value of market share, or the need to amass large resources, they fail to appreciate the extent to which the rules of the game in an industry are always changing.

Living on the fault line

By Geoffrey Moore[1]

The technology adoption life cycle models the response of any given population to the offer of a discontinuous innovation, one that forces the abandonment of traditional infrastructure and systems for the promise of a heretofore unavailable set of benefits. It represents this response as a bell curve, separating out five sub-populations, as illustrated in Figure 8.3.1.

The bell curve represents the total population of people exposed to a new technology offer. The various segments of the curve represent the percentage of people predicted to adopt one or another of the five different strategies for determining when and why to switch allegiance from the old to the new. The five strategies unfold sequentially as follows:

1 The *technology enthusiast strategy* is to adopt the new technology upon its first appearance, in large part just to explore its properties to determine if it is

'cool'. The actual benefits provided may not even be of interest to this constituency, but the mechanism by which they are provided is of great interest. If they are entertained by the mechanism, they often adopt the product just to be able to show it off.

2 The *visionary strategy* is to adopt the new technology as a means for capturing a dramatic advantage over competitors who do not adopt it. The goal here is to be first to deploy an advantaged system and use that head start to leapfrog over the competition, establishing a position so far out in front that the sector realigns around its new leader. Visionaries are mavericks who want to break away from the herd and differentiate themselves dramatically.

3 The *pragmatist strategy* is directly opposed to the visionary. It wants to stay with the herd, adopting the new technology if and only if everyone else

[1]Source: © 2000 Geoffrey Moore.

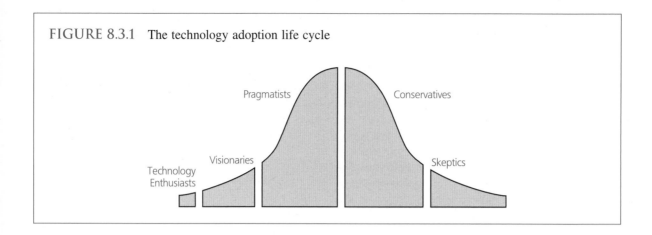

FIGURE 8.3.1 The technology adoption life cycle

does as well. The goal here is to use the wisdom of the marketplace to sort out what's valuable and then to be a fast follower once the new direction has clearly emerged. Pragmatists consult each other frequently about who's adopting what in an effort to stay current but do not commit to any major change without seeing successful implementations elsewhere first.

4 The *conservative strategy* is to stick with the old technology for as long as possible (a) because it works, (b) because it is familiar, and (c) because it is paid for. By putting off the transition to the new platform, conservatives conserve cash and avoid hitting the learning curve, making themselves more productive in the short run. Long term, when they do switch, the system is more completely debugged, and that works to their advantage as well. The downside of the strategy is that they grow increasingly out of touch for the period they don't adopt and can, if they wait too long, get isolated in old technology that simply will not map to the new world.

5 Finally, the *skeptic strategy* is to debunk the entire technology as a false start and refuse to adopt it at all. This is a winning tactic for those technologies that never do gain mainstream market acceptance. For those that do, however, it creates extreme versions of the isolation problems conservatives face.

Each of these strategies has validity in its own right, and a single individual is perfectly capable of choosing different strategies for different offers. But for any given technology, the market will develop in a characteristic pattern due to the aggregate effects of a population distributing its choices in the proportions outlined by the bell curve. The resulting market development model is shown in Figure 8.3.2.

The model segments the evolution of a technology-based market as follows:

■ The first phase, or *early market,* is a time when early adopters (technology enthusiasts and visionaries) take up the innovation while the pragmatic majority holds back. The market development goal at this stage is to gain a few prestigious flagship customers who help publicize the technology and celebrate its potential benefits.

■ The early market is followed by a *chasm,* a period of no adoption, when the early adopters have already made their choices, but the pragmatist majority is still holding back. The barrier to further progress is that pragmatists are looking to other pragmatists to be references, but no one wants to go first. The market development goal at this stage is to target an initial beachhead segment of pragmatists who can lead the second wave of adoption.

■ In the development of most technology-enabled markets, specific niches of pragmatic customers adopt the new technology before the general pragmatist population. We call this period the *bowling alley* because the market development goal is to use the first group of adopters as references to help win over the next group, and the next, and so on. Typically the 'head bowling pin' is a niche of pragmatists who have a major business problem that cannot be solved with current technology but that does respond to a solution built around the new innovation. These are the *department managers in charge of a broken, mission-critical process.* Once this first group starts to move it takes much less of a motive to overcome the inertia of the next group.

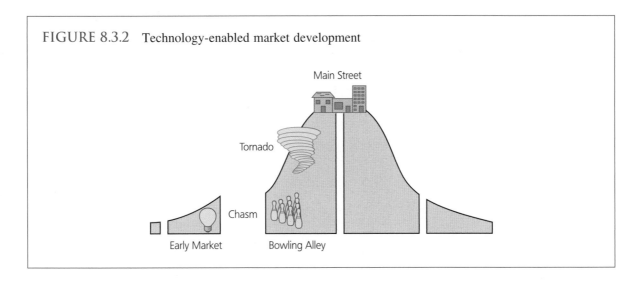

FIGURE 8.3.2   Technology-enabled market development

■ As pragmatist adoption builds in niches, one of two futures emerges. In one, adoption continues to remain localized to niche markets, creating a pattern we call 'bowling alley forever'. In this pattern, each niche's solution is relatively complex and differentiated from every other niche's. As a result, no mass market emerges, and the market development goal is simply to expand existing niches and create new ones as the opportunity arises. In the other pattern, a 'killer app' emerges – a single application of the innovative technology that provides a compelling benefit that can be standardized across multiple niches. The killer app transforms niche adoption into mass adoption, creating an enormous uptick in demand for the new technology across a wide range of sectors. We call this period the *tornado* because the onrush of mass demand is so swift it creates a vortex that sucks the supply out of the market and puts the category into hypergrowth for a number of years. The market development goal here is to win as much market share as possible during a period when the entire market is choosing its supplier for the new class of technology-enabled offering.

■ Once the supply side of the market finally catches up with the backlog of demand, the tornado phase subsides, and the market reaches a state we call *Main Street*. The new technology has been broadly deployed and, with the support of conservatives, now settles down to a (hopefully) long engagement as the incumbent technology. The market development goal here is to continuously improve the value of the offering, decreasing its base costs, and recouping margins by increasing the number of value-adding extensions that can supplement it. The ultimate extension in many cases is to convert the offering from a product sale to a services subscription, allowing the customer to gain the benefit of the product without having to take on the responsibility for maintaining it.

It is important to note that the end of the technology adoption life cycle does not represent the end of technology's productive market life. The category of offering can be sustained indefinitely on Main Street, coming to an end only when the next discontinuous innovation renders the prior technology obsolete. Indeed, despite all the emphasis on shortening life cycles, Main Street markets normally last for decades after complete absorption of the enabling technology – witness the car, the telephone, the television, the personal computer, and the cell phone. Importantly, however, the marketplace pecking order set by market share that emerges during the bowling alley and tornado phases tends to persist for the life of Main Street. That is, while Main Street represents the final and lasting distribution of competitive advantage, its boundaries get set prior to arrival. Thus success in every prior stage in the life cycle is key to building sustainable Main Street market success.

Stage-one adoption: The early market

The early market begins with the ambitions of two constituencies who live at opposite ends of the value chain (see Figure 8.3.3). On the left is the *technology*

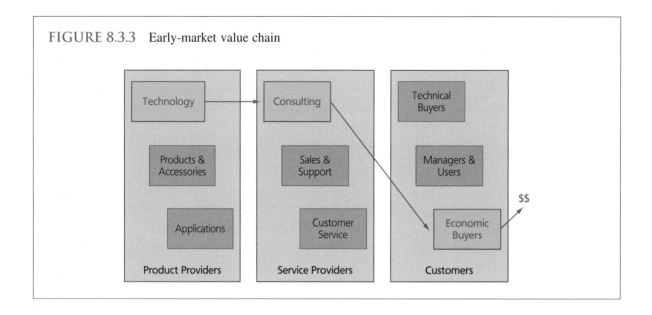

FIGURE 8.3.3 Early-market value chain

provider, the supplier of the discontinuous innovation, with ambitions of constructing an entirely new marketplace based on a new platform. On the right are one or more visionary executives, in the role of *economic buyer,* who also have ambitions of their own. They want to rearchitect the marketplaces they participate in to install their company as the new market leader – and they want to do it fast. They see in the new technology an opportunity to disrupt the established order and insert themselves into the lead.

Between these two poles, however, there is at present no existing value chain that can link their ambitions. Indeed, the existing value chain is appalled by them. There is, however, one institution in the market that can bridge the gulf between the two, can transform the technology provider's magic into the economic buyer's dream, and that is the *consulting firm.* Rather than try to incubate a value chain in the marketplace, this consultancy will instead create a temporary value chain to serve a single project's specific needs. That is, they will pull together the products, the applications, the sales and support, the customer service, and in extreme cases even substitute their own people for the customer's technical buyer (and even for the customer's end users), all to make the value chain work *in a single instance for a single customer.*

Needless to say, this is an expensive proposition. But if it pays off, if the sponsoring company really does leapfrog over its competition in a new market order, then the visionary becomes a hero, and whatever money was spent was pocket change by comparison to the appreciation in the customer company's stock price.

Competitive advantage in the early market

The primary competitive advantage strategy for the early market consists of being first to catch the new technology wave. This is often called *first-mover advantage.* Amazon.com, by catching the Web retail wave first, has created a powerful brand that its competitors cannot hope to replicate, regardless of how much they spend. By being first to introduce auctions onto the Web, eBay gained first-mover advantage also, so that even when assaulted by an alliance of extremely powerful companies – Microsoft, Dell, Lycos, Excite – it has been able to sustain market share. Four years into Web advertising, the top ten sites, with Yahoo! leading the list, garner as much as 85 per cent of the total spending – largely because of first-mover advantage. The Sabre system for airline and other travel-related reservations has had a similar track record, even as Apollo and Galileo and others have entered the market. Same with United Airlines' and American Airlines' frequent-flyer systems.

In every case, first-mover advantage equates to getting the market started around your unique approach and making the others play catch-up. It is a great strategy – when it works. The risk, of course, is that the market never goes forward to adopt the paradigm. At the time when the visionaries make their moves, this is a high probability. Visionaries are always bucking the odds in that most markets, like most mutations, die out before they can reproduce themselves sufficiently to gain persistence. Indeed, market creation is very much like the origin of species in nature, with the early market equating to the emergence of at least a few vital representatives of the new order.

The key metric of competitive advantage at this stage is simply the existence of proof of having one or more such representatives. For the technology provider, the test is one or more major corporate commitments from prestigious customers who champion the new paradigm as a platform for change in their industries. For the customer, the test is whether on top of this new platform an industry-changing offer can be promulgated. Neither measure is financial. Neither measure uses market share. The goal in both cases is just to validate the category. That puts the new wave on the map, enters it in the race.

The benefit to the company sponsoring this new initiative is that it gets a lot of attention. This attracts prospective customers to it at no additional cost of marketing. It also positions it as something of a thought leader in its industry. At the same time, however, it starts a timer ticking, with the expectation that within some definable period dramatic results will appear. If they do not, then the customers lose face, and the technology providers lose their company.

Value disciplines for the early market

In order to execute on a winning agenda, management teams must understand that the early market rewards discontinuous innovation and product leadership and penalizes customer intimacy and operational excellence. Thus optimal results are gained by elevating the former and suppressing the latter, as follows:

- Elevate discontinuous innovation and product leadership. The early market is driven by the demands of visionaries for offerings that create dramatic competitive advantages of the sort that would allow them to leapfrog over the other players in their industry. Only discontinuous innovation offers such advantage. In order to field that innovation, however, it must be transformed into a product offering that can be put to work in the real world. Hence the need for product leadership.

- Suppress customer intimacy and operational excellence. When technologies are this new, there are no target markets as yet and thus customer intimacy is not practical. Moreover, discontinuous

innovations demand enormous customer tolerance and sacrifice as they get debugged, again not a time for celebrating putting the customer first. At the same time, because everything is so new and so much is yet to be discovered, it is equally impractical to target operational excellence. There is just too much new product, process, and procedure to invent and then shake out before pursuing this value discipline would be reasonable. Instead, one has to make peace with the strategy 'Go ugly early.'

Looking at the above, it is not surprising that engineering-led organizations, who resonate with the value disciplines in favour, are much more successful at early-market initiatives than marketing-led or operations-led organizations, who lean toward the value disciplines that should be suppressed. Going forward, as we look at each subsequent phase of the life cycle, we will see that the rewarded and penalized disciplines change and so will the types of organizations that can be most successful.

Stage-two adoption: Crossing the chasm into the bowling alley

For technologies to gain persistent marketplace acceptance, they must cross the chasm and take up a position on the other side. Now we are in the realm of the pragmatists. To get pragmatists to move at all, companies must rethink their marketing objective from the early market. There the goal was to win a customer, and then another, and another. To cross the chasm, however, you have to *win a herd*. Here's why:

- Pragmatists only feel comfortable moving in herds. That's why they ask for references and use word of mouth as their primary source of advice on technology purchase decisions. Selling individual pragmatists on acting ahead of the herd is possible but very painful, and the cost of sales more than eats up the margin in the sale itself.

- Pragmatists evaluate the entire value chain, not just the specific product offer, when buying into a new technology. Value chains form around herds, not individual customers. There has to be enough repeatable business in the pipeline to reward an investment in specializing in the new technology. Sporadic deals, regardless of how big they are, do not create persistent value chains.

The visible metric for crossing the chasm, therefore, is to *make a market* and *create a value chain* where there were no market and no value chain before. This is a difficult undertaking. To increase its chances for success, and to decrease the time it takes to achieve, it is best to focus the effort on creating a niche market first before trying to create a mass market. It is simply prudent to minimize the number of variables at risk.

Think of a niche market as a self-contained system of commerce with its own local set of specialized needs and wants. Isolated from the mainstream market, which does not serve these special needs, it offers a *value-chain incubator* for emerging technology-enabled markets. That is, its isolation protects the fragile new chain from direct competitive attacks from the incumbent value chain. The customer community, in effect, nurtures the fledgling enterprise because it hopes to gain great benefit from it.

Value-chain strategy

To visualize the changes in moving from the early market to the bowling alley, let us return to our value-chain diagram, this time focusing on a new set of market makers (see Figure 8.3.4).

At the right-hand end of the chain, the *managers* in the customer domain represent the preassembled herd, an aggregation of relatively homogeneous demand. These are the department managers in charge of a broken, mission-critical process, all huddled in a mass. At the other end, the *application provider* in the product domain offers a relatively homogeneous solution to this herd's problem. It will bring its solution to

market through a sales and support organization where it is the *support function* that really counts. That is because at the outset of a market the remaining value-chain partners are just getting recruited and cannot be relied upon to assemble the whole product correctly on their own. Later on these same partners will compete to take over the support function – and the enlightened application provider will let them, as it will greatly expand its market and its reach – but for now it is all just too new. So the application provider's support team must take the lead in working through all the glitches until a working whole product is in place, even when the problem is with someone else's part of the offering and not their own.

Note that the money-recycling arrow has now been restored to the diagram. This is the whole point of the niche-market strategy. We are now creating for the first time a self-funding persistent market where the economic gains of the customer lead to increasing and ongoing investment in the products and services that bring them about. Even if no other market ever adopts this technology, it will still be economically viable to maintain this niche. To be sure, the returns will not be all that the investors hoped for, but it will not be a total bust either. That is because niche markets have persistent competitive advantages that allow them to sustain themselves even when the marketplace in general is unsupportive of their efforts. Moreover, if the value chain extends its reach into additional niches, then it can add market growth to its already attractive price margins to produce highly attractive returns indeed.

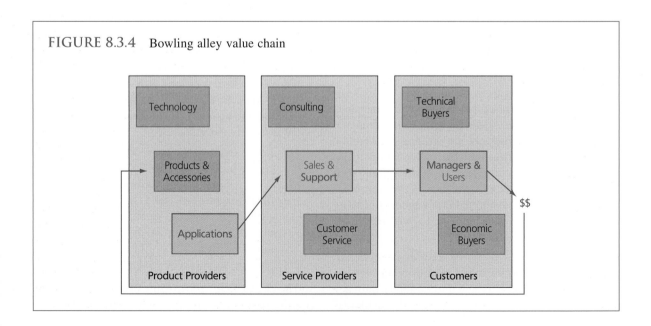

FIGURE 8.3.4 Bowling alley value chain

The major beneficiaries of this strategy are the application providers. It is they who harness the new wave of technology to the specific needs of the target segment, and they who rally the rest of the value chain to support this effort. Because the application provider is the company that really does 'make the market', it gains a dominant market-specific competitive advantage during this market formation period. This advantage will persist indefinitely, even after the technology adoption life cycle goes forward, since once any market falls into a particular pecking order, it is loath to change.

Everyone else in the value chain – the core technology providers, the hardware and software product companies, the business consultants and the systems integrators, the customer service staff, and even the client's own technical staff – all happily take a backseat. That's because they will all be operating primarily as cost-effective generalists, making relatively minor modifications to their way of doing business, whereas the application vendor, interacting intimately with the problem-owning department managers, must operate as a value-creating specialist and invest significantly to be able to do so effectively.

Competitive advantage in the bowling alley

The ability to harness the technology wave to solve the critical problem of one or more specific niche markets is what creates power at this stage, and that power goes primarily to the application provider. As more and more of the pragmatist department managers in the niches see their colleagues getting out of the soup, they, too, will come forward and insist on buying this vendor's application. Thus every other company in the value chain becomes dependent on that one vendor's good graces to get into the good deals. In effect, this creates a form of value-chain domination, but it is restricted solely to the niches served, and so it has very different properties – and a very different valuation – from the kind of broad horizontal-market domination we will see develop inside the tornado.

Because they reap the bulk of the rewards, it is relatively easy for application providers to understand and adopt niche marketing, especially if the alternative is to spend another year in the chasm. It is much more problematic, however, for a platform product or a transaction services company to embrace it. Their business plans are normally predicated on either broad horizontal adoption across a multitude of business segments or a broad cross-section of consumers. They are not well positioned to go after niche markets. Vertical industry domain expertise holds little value for them, and voluntarily subordinating themselves to an application vendor just to gain entry into one little niche seems like a huge price to pay. Moreover, even if the tactic proves successful, the resulting order stream will be relatively modest, and worse, may inappropriately cause the rest of the market to misperceive the company as a niche player. For all these very good reasons, platform-products and transaction-services vendors tend to shy away from taking the niche approach to crossing the chasm. And yet it is still a mistake. Here's why.

As we shall see shortly, platform products are optimized for tornado markets, and transaction-services offers are optimized for Main Street markets. Those are the phases of the life cycle in which they will shine. So their strategy should be to accelerate technology adoption to get to 'their' phase as quickly as possible. Time spent in the chasm for either strategy represents a huge opportunity cost, giving their competitors a chance to catch up to first-mover advantage while making no progress for themselves at all. This makes exiting the chasm as quickly as possible their top strategic imperative – hence their need to perform the admittedly unnatural act of niche marketing. To be sure, it is a little bit like asking a caterpillar who has a stated goal to be a butterfly to first spin itself into a cocoon and melt – the intermediate step is so disconnected from the end result that it is hard to warrant taking it. But there is now sufficient history to show that not taking the step is fatal – as demonstrated by the market development failures of ISDN networking, object-oriented databases, IBM's OS/2 operating system, pen-based PCs, infrared connectivity protocols, and artificial intelligence.

To be sure, once an initial niche market is established, the winning strategy for platform products and transaction services does indeed split off from the application providers. For the latter, the most powerful path forward is to stay in the bowling alley – this is their sweet spot – expanding niche to niche, following a bowling pin strategy. In this manner, such companies can chew their way through multiple markets with a very high probability of securing dominant positions in the majority of their niches. It is a 'bowling alley forever' strategy focused on *preserving complexity* in order to create a source of profit margins for themselves and their service partners. It ends up trading off massive scale in favour of locally dominant roles and eventually makes the transition to Main Street as a leader in a set of mature vertical markets.

By contrast, for platform-product and transaction-services companies, the goal should be to get beyond niches altogether as soon as possible. Their quest instead should be for a single, general-purpose 'killer app' – a word-processing program, a spreadsheet, e-mail, voice-mail, a Web site, an e-commerce server – something that can be adopted by whole sectors of the economy all at once, thereby leveraging their horizontal business models' strength in being able to scale rapidly. But students of the life cycle should note that in the era prior to pervasive word processing, there were segment-specific solutions for lawyers, doctors, consultants, and governmental functions. These were a critical stepping stone toward getting to a mass market.

Value disciplines for the bowling alley

To execute on a niche strategy in an emerging technology-enabled market, companies must realign their value discipline orientation to meet a new set of market priorities, as follows:

■ Elevate product leadership and customer intimacy. The bowling alley is driven by the demands of pragmatists for a whole product that will fix a broken mission-critical business process. The fact that the process will not respond to conventional treatment calls out the need for product leadership. The fact that the required whole product will have to integrate elements specific to a particular vertical segment calls out the need for customer intimacy.

■ Suppress discontinuous innovation and operational excellence. Pragmatist department managers under pressure to fix a broken process have neither the time nor the resources to support debugging a discontinuous innovation. At the same time, their need for special attention is incompatible with the kind of standardization needed for operational excellence.

Marketing-led organizations are best at crossing the chasm, specifically those that combine strong domain expertise in the targeted market segment with a solutions orientation. Operations-led organizations struggle with the amount of customization required that cannot be amortized across other segments, all of which offends their sense of efficiency. Engineering-led organizations struggle with the lack of product symmetry resulting from heavily privileging one niche's set of issues over a whole raft of other needed enhancements.

To win with this strategy, the critical success factor is focus – specifically, focus on doing whatever it takes to get that first herd of pragmatist customers to adopt en masse the new technology. Hedging one's bet by sponsoring forays targeted at additional herds at the same time is bad strategy. Both engineering- and operations-oriented organizations, however, are drawn to this approach because they fear that the company is putting all its eggs into one basket. Of course, that is precisely what it *is* doing. The reason it is good strategy to do so is that only by creating critical mass can one move a market and bring into existence a new value chain. Unless they can leverage tornado winds blowing in other markets, alternative initiatives subtract from the needed mass and, ironically, increase rather than decrease market risk.

Stage-three adoption: inside the tornado

A tornado occurs whenever pragmatists across a variety of market sectors all decide simultaneously that it is time to adopt a new paradigm – in other words, when the pragmatist herd stampedes. This creates a dramatic spike in demand, vastly exceeding the currently available supply, calling entire categories of vendors to reconfigure their offerings to meet the needs of a new value chain.

Value-chain strategy

The overriding market force that is shaping the tornado value chain is the desire for everyone in the market, beginning with the customer but quickly passing through to all vendors, to drive the transition to a new paradigm as quickly as possible. That calls to the fore the three constituencies highlighted in Figure 8.3.5.

Each of these constituencies is well positioned to benefit from standardization for rapid deployment.

■ In the product sphere, it is *products,* not technology and not applications, that get the privileged position. The problem with technology is that it is too malleable to be mass-produced and thus does not lend itself to rapid proliferation of common, standard infrastructure. The problem with applications is that they must be customized to sector-specific processes, and so again they do not deploy as rapidly as desired. By contrast, products, and specifically those that serve as platforms for a broad range of applications, are the ideal engine for paradigm proliferation.

FIGURE 8.3.5   Tornado value chain

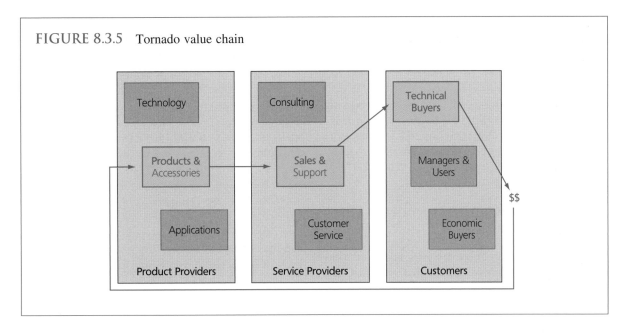

- Now, to be sure, there must be at least one application that warrants the purchase of the platform in the first place, but in a tornado that application must be essentially the same for every sector. Such an application is called 'the killer app', and it becomes the focus for horizontal expansion across multiple sectors of the economy. *Accounting* was the killer app for mainframes, *manufacturing automation* for minicomputers, *word processing* for PCs, *computer-aided design* for workstations, and *electronic mail* for local area networks. But in every case, it was the platform product providers, not the killer app vendors, who were ultimately the big tornado winners because as other applications came on-line, they created still more demand for their platforms.

- In the services sphere, it is the sales and support function, with the emphasis on *sales,* that carries the day. The drawback with consulting is that its projects are too complex, take too long, and require resources that are too scarce to ever permit a tornado to go forward. The drawback with customer service is that it is too focused on serving existing customers at a time when the overwhelming emphasis has to be on acquiring new customers.

- Generating sales in the tornado is not a problem of winning over the customer so much as it is of beating the competition. It is critical, therefore, to field the most competitive sales force you can at this time. Because so much wealth is changing hands, and because the long-term consequences of market share are so great, tornado sales tactics are brutal, and sales aggressiveness is the core discipline. This is the time when nice guys do finish last.

- On the support side, the key issue is to get new customers up and running on a minimal system as quickly as possible and then move on to the next new customer. The more cookie-cutter the process, the faster it replicates, and the more new customers you can absorb. The push is for operational excellence, not customer intimacy. This is not a normal support profile, so once again focusing the team on the right value discipline is a critical executive responsibility.

- On the customer side of the value chain, it is the *technical buyer,* not the end-user departments and not the economic buyer, who becomes the key focus. The problem with end users is that they inevitably seek customization to meet their department-specific needs. Not only is such complexity contrary to the vendor's wishes, it also works against the host institution's imperative to roll out the new infrastructure to everyone in the company as quickly as possible. Such rapid deployment requires a one-size-fits-all approach for the initial roll-out, something that the technical buyer understands far better than the end user. It is also not the time to court senior executives in their role as economic buyers. Once the tornado is under way, they sense the need to get over to the new infrastructure and delegate the task, including the selection process, to their technical staff.

■ When technical buyers become the target customer, their compelling reason to buy drives sales outcomes. High on their list is conformance to common standards, followed by market leadership status, which initially is signalled by partnerships with other market leaders, and later on confirmed by market share. The technical buyers' biggest challenge is systems integration, and this is where the support function can contribute to faster roll-outs by building standard interfaces to the most prevalent legacy systems.

The tornado, in essence, is one big land grab – a fierce struggle to capture as many new customers as possible during the pragmatist stampede to the new paradigm. Increasing shareholder value revolves entirely around maximizing market share, and to that end there are three sources of competitive-advantage leverage to exploit.

Competitive advantage in the tornado

The primary source of competitive advantage is simply to be riding the new technology wave as it enters into its tornado phase. Mass-market adoption is an awesome market creation force that wreaks havoc on installed bases rooted in old technology. As the incumbents retreat under the impact of this force to protect their increasingly conservative installed bases, your company advances with the new wave of adoption to occupy their lost ground. This is *category advantage* at work, and it alone will enhance your stock price – hence the scramble of every vendor in the sector to position themselves on the bandwagon of whatever this hot new category is.

The second element of competitive advantage derives from the potential institutionalization of key market-making companies as value-chain leaders or dominators. That is, for each element in the value chain, tornado markets seek out a single market-leading provider to set the de facto standards for that component. That role normally goes to the company that garners the most new customers early in the race. In addition, when a single company can gain power over the rest of the value chain, typically by leveraging the power to withhold its proprietary technology and thereby stymie the entire offer, the market accords even more privilege to it.

The power of market-share leadership is rooted in the pragmatist preference to make the safe buy by going with the market leader. That is, rather than rely on their own judgement, pragmatists prefer to rely on

the group's. Once that judgement has been made clear, once one vendor has emerged as the favourite, then pragmatists naturally gravitate to that choice, which of course further increases that company's market share, intensifying its gravitational attraction.

This cycle of positive feedback not only spontaneously generates market leaders, but once they are generated, works to keep them in place. That is, the value chain advantage a market leader gains over its direct competitors is that it has become the default choice for any other company in the chain to round out its offers. Thus the company gains sales that it never initiated and gets invited into deals its competitors never see. Such sales not only add to revenues but to margins, since the absence of competition removes much of the pressure to discount price. In short, winning the market-share prize is a very sweet deal, which, if it is not working for you, is working against you. Hence the need to focus all guns on market share.

Thus the essence of tornado strategy is simply to capture the maximum number of customers in the minimum amount of time and to minimize all other efforts. At each moment the winning strategy is to strike and move on, strike and move on. Anything you can do to slow down a competitor along the way is gravy. What you must not do is voluntarily slow yourself down, not even for a customer. That is, during the tornado *customer acquisition* takes temporary priority over *customer satisfaction*. The entire pragmatist herd is switching from the old to the new – not a frequent event. As customers, in other words, they are temporarily 'up for grabs'. Once they choose their new vendor, they will be highly reluctant to consider changing yet again. So either you win these customers now, or you risk losing them *for the life of the paradigm*.

And then there is the super grand prize bonanza of tornado market development to which we have already alluded, namely, gaining *value-chain power over the other vendors in the value chain*. As noted, this occurs when a single vendor has monopoly control of a crucial element in the value chain, the way Microsoft and Intel each do for the personal computer, the way Cisco does for the internet, the way Qualcomm appears to do for the future of wireless telephony. In such cases, as the market tornado unfolds, the standard whole product that forms around the killer app incorporates a piece of your proprietary technology. Going forward, for the value-chain offering as a whole to evolve, it must take your technology along with it – and there is no substitute for it. This makes everyone in the chain dependent upon you, which in turn allows you to orchestrate the behaviour of the rest of the chain. This can include pressuring value-chain partners to adopt or support some of your less successful products so that you gain power across a much broader portion of your product line than its actual features and benefits would normally merit.

Value disciplines for the tornado

Elevate product leadership and operational excellence. Whatever position one achieves during the tornado market depends largely on your company's ability to execute a market-share land-grab strategy. To this end, the market rewards a third alignment of value disciplines, as follows:

- Elevate product leadership and operational excellence. The tornado is driven by the demands of infrastructure buyers for standard, reliable offerings suitable for rapid mass deployment. Here product leadership gets translated into shipping the next release with the new set of features ahead of the competition and thereby grabbing additional market share from them. Operational excellence is critical to this effort because if there is any hiccup in the process, the market can still shift to an alternative vendor, with major market-share consequences that will last for the duration of the paradigm.

- Suppress discontinuous innovation and customer intimacy. Any form of discontinuous innovation during a tornado creates opportunity for error, putting rapid mass deployment at risk, and is thus anathema. Customer intimacy is also suppressed for the duration of the roll-out for the same reason, sacrificed to the end of achieving reliable, consistent deployment. Once the infrastructure is set in place, then there will be time to come back and meet customer-specific requests.

Operations-led organizations tend to have the edge in a tornado, where meeting deadlines, shipping in quantity, and minimizing returns all take priority over innovation and customer delight. Marketing-led organizations, by contrast, typically flounder because they cannot bear to relinquish their commitment to customer intimacy and customer satisfaction. They need to realize that, in a tornado, just getting the new systems installed and working properly is grounds for customer satisfaction.

Stage-four adoption: On Main Street

Main Street begins as the market-share frenzy that drives tornado winds subsides. The overwhelming bulk of the pragmatists in the market have chosen their vendor, made their initial purchases, and rolled out the first phase of a multiphase deployment. Only a fraction of the total forecastable sales in the segment has actually been made at this point, but from here on out the market-share boundaries are relatively fixed. This has significant implications for the value chain.

Value-chain strategy

Here is the fourth and final mutation in the value chain. This one will endure for the life of the paradigm. In effect, it is the value chain we have been setting up all along (see Figure 8.3.6).

There is a key change underlying this entire value chain, which is that the technology adoption life cycle as a whole has evolved from the pragmatist to the conservative agenda, and every constituency in the value chain is affected by this change. Let's start with the customer.

When companies adopt new paradigms, conservative customers at first hang back, preferring to eke out some last bit of value from the old system. But once it is clear that the new system must supplant the old one, then they seek to put their stamp on the new vendor relationship. They remind all these new arrivals that most of the promises that were made on behalf of their products and services are as yet far from true, and they work to keep everyone focused on making incremental improvements going forward. In effect, they transform what heretofore was a discontinuous innovation into what will from now on be a system of continuous innovation.

In mature – or maturing – markets, both the economic buyer and the technical buyer recede in importance. The economic buyer is no longer looking for competitive advantage or to support a manager in fixing a broken business process; now the issue is simply staying within budget, and that can be delegated. And the technical buyer is no longer concerned about how to either manage or postpone the introduction of a disruptive technology; now the concern is simply to stay compliant with established standards, and that, too, can be delegated. Even within the user community, the managers are now taking the new systems for granted, assuming that it must be doing pretty much what it was bought to do (a naïve, but all too frequent point of view). Thus it is only *end users*, the people who actually interact with the system on a frequent basis, that (a) know anything about how it really works, and (b) have a stake in sponsoring improvements to it.

If these end users do not voice their desires, then the offering becomes a complete commodity, with the

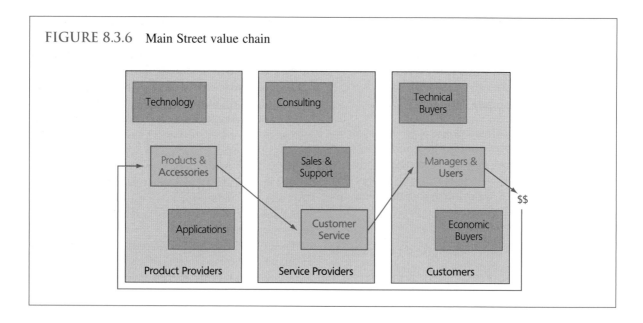

FIGURE 8.3.6 Main Street value chain

purchasing department driving a *supplier relationship* going forward. If they do voice their desires, however, and gain their managers' approval, then end users can drive a *vendor relationship*, a condition that allows a company to earn margins above commodity levels. We are long past the time for customers to embrace you in a *strategic partner relationship*, something that is confined to earlier phases in the life cycle.

To earn preferred margins from end-user sponsorship, focus shifts to those aspects of the value chain that end users can directly experience. On the product side, this suppresses the importance of technology, platform products, and even the core of the application. All these are still important, but they are more directly experienced by the technical buyer than the end user. By contrast, any product element that is consumable, is highly user visible. It is here that minor enhancements for a modest increase in price can generate dramatic changes in gross profit margin, the way, for example, the cup holder has done in the automotive industry.

Lucrative as the accessories and consumables business is on Main Street, however, an even bigger opportunity lies in the product-service shift. What customers used to value and buy as products becomes reconceived as service offerings – shifting the burden of system maintenance from the customer back to the vendor. Thus the move from answering machine to voice-mail, from videotapes to pay-per-view, from bar bells to health clubs.

The primary organization tasked with masterminding this shift is *customer service*. Historically this has been a challenge because that organization

was not constructed nor were its personnel recruited with the thought that it would eventually become a lead contributor to the P&L and market valuation of the company. In the age of the internet, however, investors are now actively pursuing companies that have been founded from day one with just such an agenda in mind.

Competitive advantage on Main Street

The technology wave has crested and broken and no longer provides market development leverage. The value chain is already formed, and whatever place you have in it is not going to change without massive and usually unwarranted investment. There is always the possibility of you finding an underserved market segment here or there, but the speed of market penetration now will be much slower, the impact on any local value chain much less, and thus the rewards more modest than they would have been during the bowling alley phase. And so it is that we get to the domain of company execution, to which we shall turn in a moment, and differentiated offerings.

There are classically two types of differentiation strategies that succeed on Main Street. The first is being the low-cost provider, a strategy that works best in commodity markets where it is not the end user but the purchasing manager acting as economic buyer who is the real decision maker. The other type is a customer-delight strategy, which works best in consumer markets or in business markets where the end user is permitted to behave as a consumer. The more a market matures, the more opportunity your company has to deliver on both of these propositions to be competitive. To do so it must gravitate toward a product or service deployment strategy called *mass customization.*

Mass customization separates any offering into a *surface* and a *substructure.* The surface is what the end user experiences. It is here that changes are made to enhance that experience. This is the *customization* portion of the offer. By contrast, the substructure is the necessary delivery vehicle for the entire performance, but it is not directly experienced by the end user. The goal here is to provide maximum reliability at the lowest possible cost, and the preferred tactic is to reduce variability and increase standardization to achieve high volume. This is the *mass* portion of the offer.

To combine the two without sacrificing the benefits of either, the customizing portion must often be done downstream in the value chain in a separate step from the mass portion. This typically leads to a need to redesign the value chain, creating new opportunities for service providers to create customization value at the point of customer contact. Think of how cell phones are provided, and you get the idea. Everything upstream from the retail outlet is totally standardized; everything downstream is customizable – the phone itself, its accessories, service options, program pricing, and the like. Prior to retail, everything is sold as a commodity; after retail, it is a value-added offering.

The implications of this restructuring of the market are far-reaching, and not just for service providers. Consumables have the same potential to deliver customized value. Consider, for example, the razor-to-razor-blade transition in Gillette's history, or Kodak's move from cameras to film, or HP's transition from inkjet printers to inkjet cartridges. In every case once Main Street is reached, it is the consumable at the surface, and not the underlying engine at the core, that becomes the basis of differentiation and the locus of high profit margins.

Alternatively, service transactions can also replace the serviced commodity as the locus of value creation. This has been the case in the automobile industry, where the bulk of the profits are made not from selling new cars but from financing the purchase, insuring the vehicle, supplying the consumables, and providing the maintenance services. In every case margins are affected by the end user's experience during these transactions. That is why companies like Lexus have been so successful with their customer-care offers. It is also why traditional car dealerships are failing with their customer-unfriendly approach to purchase and financing, driving their customers to brokers and to the Web instead.

In large part the promise of the internet is based on it being a universal platform for value-adding customization in Main Street value chains. The systems are not yet completely in place to fulfil this proposition today, but forward-thinking executives and enlightened investors can see how with incremental improvements they will be able to generate scaleable, low-cost, high-touch offerings of the sort that create attractive profit margins on Main Street.

Value disciplines

To execute on this strategy of mass customization, companies as elsewhere in the life cycle must learn to elevate one pair of value disciplines and suppress the other:

- Elevate operational excellence and customer intimacy. Main Street markets are supported by conservative customers seeking incremental gains in value. These can be achieved either through decreasing the costs of the current set of offers – the domain of operational excellence – or by introducing a new set of offers improved through readily absorbed continuous innovations – the domain of customer intimacy.

- Suppress discontinuous innovation and product leadership. Discontinuous innovation runs directly contrary to the interests of Main Street customers and is simply not welcome. Even offers based on product leadership are problematic. If they require retooling the existing infrastructure, they usually just aren't worth it. What development teams must realize is that now product improvements should be focused either on keeping the core product viable, with operational excellence as a guide, or on making cosmetic changes at the surface, with customer intimacy providing the direction.

Of all the pairings, this particular set should be the most familiar to established companies in mature markets. They should see themselves as the champions of the first pair, and those wretched dotcoms assaulting their marketplace as the purveyors of the second. Note that in this pairing the established company's existing customers are very much on its side, not on the dotcoms'. That's because they, like the company itself, are ruled by conservative interests. It is instead the flock of new customers who are entering the tornado for the next big thing that are undermining this company's stock price going forward.

TABLE 8.3.1 Comparison of market states

	Early market	*Bowling alley*	*Tornado*	*Main Street*
Primary competitive advantage	Catching technology wave	Market-segment domination	Market-share leadership	Differentiated offerings
Product focus	Technology	Applications	Platform products	Consumables
Service focus	Consulting	Support	Sales	Customer service
Customer focus	Economic buyer	Department manager	Technical buyer	End user

Implications of living on the fault line

The four market states are set out in a side-by-side comparison in Table 8.3.1. The table maps the working out of the competitive advantage hierarchy over the course of a technology-enabled market's development. The columns lay out the life-cycle phases these markets evolve through. The rows lay out the changes in focus that organizations must make to adapt to this evolution. The first row sets forth the layer in the competitive-advantage hierarchy that has the most impact during each phase. The next three rows highlight the value-chain elements that create the most impact during the phase because they are best suited to leveraging the type of competitive advantage available.

Even a cursory glance, shows that the changes companies have to make in order to adapt to these forces are dramatic indeed. Moreover, the time allotted to make them is painfully short. As a result, it should surprise no one that few real-world organizations are very good at actually making them. Indeed, the larger and more successful a company becomes, the less likely it is to attempt making them at all.

READING 8.4

Blue ocean strategy

By W. Chan Kim and Renée Mauborgne[1]

A onetime accordion player, stilt walker, and fire-eater, Guy Laliberté is now CEO of one of Canada's largest cultural exports, Cirque du Soleil. Founded in 1984 by a group of street performers, Cirque has staged dozens of productions seen by some 40 million people in 90 cities around the world. In 20 years, Cirque has achieved revenues that Ringling Bros. and Barnum & Bailey – the world's leading circus – took more than a century to attain.

Cirque's rapid growth occurred in an unlikely setting. The circus business was (and still is) in long-term decline. Alternative forms of entertainment – sporting events, TV, and video games – were casting a growing shadow. Children, the mainstay of the circus audience, preferred PlayStations to circus acts. There was also rising sentiment, fuelled by animal rights groups, against the use of animals, traditionally an integral part of the circus. On the supply side, the star performers that Ringling and the other circuses relied on to draw in the crowds could often name their own terms. As a result, the industry was hit by steadily decreasing audiences and increasing costs. What's more, any new entrant to this business would be competing against a formidable incumbent that for most of the last century had set the industry standard.

How did Cirque profitably increase revenues by a factor of 22 over the last ten years in such an un-attractive environment? The tagline for one of the first Cirque productions is revealing: 'We reinvent the circus.' Cirque did not make its money by competing within the confines of the existing industry or by stealing customers from Ringling and the others. In-stead it created uncontested market space that made the competition irrelevant. It pulled in a whole new group of customers who were traditionally non-customers of the industry – adults and corporate clients who had turned to theatre, opera, or ballet and were, therefore, prepared to pay several times more than the price of a conventional circus ticket for an un-precedented entertainment experience.

To understand the nature of Cirque's achievement, you have to realize that the business universe consists of two distinct kinds of space, which we think of as red and blue oceans. Red oceans represent all the in-dustries in existence today – the known market space. In red oceans, industry boundaries are defined and accepted, and the competitive rules of the game are well understood. Here, companies try to outperform their rivals in order to grab a greater share of existing demand. As the space gets more and more crowded, prospects for profits and growth are reduced. Products turn into commodities, and increasing competition turns the water bloody.

Blue oceans denote all the industries *not* in ex-istence today – the unknown market space, untainted by competition. In blue oceans, demand is created ra-ther than fought over. There is ample opportunity for growth that is both profitable and rapid. There are two ways to create blue oceans. In a few cases, companies can give rise to completely new industries, as eBay did with the online auction industry. But in most cases, a blue ocean is created from within a red ocean when a company alters the boundaries of an existing industry. As will become evident later, this is what Cirque did. In breaking through the boundary traditionally separating circus and theatre, it made a new and profitable blue ocean from within the red ocean of the circus industry.

Cirque is just one of more than 150 blue ocean creations that we have studied in over 30 industries, using data stretching back more than 100 years. We analysed companies that created those blue oceans and their less successful competitors, which were caught in red oceans. In studying these data, we have observed a consistent pattern of strategic thinking behind the creation of new markets and industries, what we call blue ocean strategy. The logic behind blue ocean strategy parts with traditional models focused on competing in existing market space. Indeed, it can be argued that managers' failure to realize the differences between red and blue ocean strategy lies behind the difficulties many companies encounter as they try to break from the competition.

In this article, we present the concept of blue ocean strategy and describe its defining characteristics. We assess the profit and growth consequences of blue oceans and discuss why their creation is a rising im-perative for companies in the future. We believe that an understanding of blue ocean strategy will help today's companies as they struggle to thrive in an accelerating and expanding business universe.

Blue and red oceans

Although the term may be new, blue oceans have al-ways been with us. Look back 100 years and ask yourself which industries known today were then un-known. The answer: Industries as basic as auto-mobiles, music recording, aviation, petrochemicals, pharmaceuticals, and management consulting were unheard-of or had just begun to emerge. Now turn the clock back only 30 years and ask yourself the same question. Again, a plethora of multibillion-dollar in-dustries jump out: mutual funds, cellular telephones, biotechnology, discount retailing, express package delivery, snowboards, coffee bars, and home videos, to name a few. Just three decades ago, none of these industries existed in a meaningful way.

This time, put the clock forward 20 years. Ask yourself: How many industries that are unknown today will exist then? If history is any predictor of the future, the answer is many. Companies have a huge capacity to create new industries and re-create existing ones, a fact that is reflected in the deep changes that have been necessary in the way industries are classified. The half-century-old Standard Industrial Classification (SIC) system was replaced in 1997 by the North American Industry Classification System (NAICS). The new system expanded the ten SIC industry sectors into 20 to reflect the emerging realities of new industry territ-ories – blue oceans. The services sector under the old system, for example, is now seven sectors ranging from information to health care and social assistance. Given that these classification systems are designed for standardization and continuity, such a replacement shows how significant a source of economic growth the creation of blue oceans has been.

Looking forward, it seems clear to us that blue oceans will remain the engine of growth. Prospects in most established market spaces – red oceans – are shrinking steadily. Technological advances have substantially improved industrial productivity, permitting suppliers to produce an unprecedented array of products and services. And as trade barriers between nations and regions fall and information on products and prices becomes instantly and globally available, niche markets and monopoly havens are continuing to disappear. At the same time, there is little evidence of any increase in demand, at least in the developed markets, where recent United Nations statistics even point to declining populations. The result is that in more and more industries, supply is overtaking demand.

This situation has inevitably hastened the commoditization of products and services, stoked price wars, and shrunk profit margins. According to recent studies, major American brands in a variety of product and service categories have become more and more alike. And as brands become more similar, people increasingly base purchase choices on price. People no longer insist, as in the past, that their laundry detergent be Tide. Nor do they necessarily stick to Colgate when there is a special promotion for Crest, and vice versa. In overcrowded industries, differentiating brands becomes harder both in economic upturns and in downturns.

The paradox of strategy

Unfortunately, most companies seem becalmed in their red oceans. In a study of business launches in 108 companies, we found that 86% of those new ventures were line extensions – incremental improvements to existing industry offerings – and a mere 14% were aimed at creating new markets or industries. While line extensions did account for 62% of the total revenues, they delivered only 39% of the total profits. By contrast, the 14% invested in creating new markets and industries delivered 38% of total revenues and a startling 61% of total profits.

So why the dramatic imbalance in favour of red oceans? Part of the explanation is that corporate strategy is heavily influenced by its roots in military strategy. The very language of strategy is deeply imbued with military references – chief executive 'officers' in 'headquarters', 'troops' on the 'front lines'. Described this way, strategy is all about red ocean competition. It is about confronting an opponent and driving him off a battlefield of limited territory. Blue ocean strategy, by contrast, is about doing business where there is no competitor. It is about creating new land, not dividing up existing land. Focusing on the red ocean therefore

means accepting the key constraining factors of war – limited terrain and the need to beat an enemy to succeed. And it means denying the distinctive strength of the business world – the capacity to create new market space that is uncontested.

The tendency of corporate strategy to focus on winning against rivals was exacerbated by the meteoric rise of Japanese companies in the 1970s and 1980s. For the first time in corporate history, customers were deserting Western companies in droves. As competition mounted in the global marketplace, a slew of red ocean strategies emerged, all arguing that competition was at the core of corporate success and failure. Today, one hardly talks about strategy without using the language of competition. The term that best symbolizes this is 'competitive advantage'. In the competitive-advantage worldview, companies are often driven to outperform rivals and capture greater shares of existing market space.

Of course competition matters. But by focusing on competition, scholars, companies, and consultants have ignored two very important – and, we would argue, far more lucrative – aspects of strategy: One is to find and develop markets where there is little or no competition – blue oceans – and the other is to exploit and protect blue oceans. These challenges are very different from those to which strategists have devoted most of their attention.

Toward blue ocean strategy

What kind of strategic logic is needed to guide the creation of blue oceans? To answer that question, we looked back over 100 years of data on blue ocean creation to see what patterns could be discerned. Some of our data are presented in Exhibit 8.4.1 'A Snapshot of Blue Ocean Creation'. It shows an overview of key blue ocean creations in three industries that closely touch people's lives: autos – how people get to work; computers – what people use at work; and movie theatres – where people go after work for enjoyment. We found that:

Blue oceans are not about technology innovation. Leading-edge technology is sometimes involved in the creation of blue oceans, but it is not a defining feature of them. This is often true even in industries that are technology intensive. As the exhibit reveals, across all three representative industries, blue oceans were seldom the result of technological innovation per se; the underlying technology was often already in existence. Even Ford's revolutionary assembly line can be traced to the meatpacking industry

EXHIBIT 8.4.1   A SNAPSHOT OF BLUE OCEAN CREATION

Key blue ocean creations	Was the blue ocean created by a new entrant or an incumbent?	Was it driven by technology pioneering or value pioneering?*	At the time of the blue ocean creation, was the industry attractive or unattractive?
Automobiles			
Ford Model T Unveiled in 1908, the Model T was the first mass-produced car, priced so that many Americans could afford it.	New entrant	Value pioneering (mostly existing technologies)	Unattractive
GM's 'car for every purse and purpose' GM created a blue ocean in 1924 by injecting fun and fashion into the car.	Incumbent	Value pioneering (some new technologies)	Attractive
Japanese fuel-efficient autos Japanese automakers created a blue ocean in the mid-1970s with small, reliable lines of cars.	Incumbent	Value pioneering (some new technologies)	Unattractive
Chrysler minivan With its 1984 minivan, Chrysler created a new class of automobile that was as easy to use as a car but had the passenger space of a van.	Incumbent	Value pioneering (mostly existing technologies)	Unattractive
Computers			
CTR's tabulating machine In 1914, CTR created the business machine industry by simplifying, modularizing, and leasing tabulating machines. CTR later changed its name to IBM.	Incumbent	Value pioneering (some new technologies)	Unattractive
IBM 650 electronic computer and System/360 In 1952, IBM created the business computer industry by simplifying and reducing the power and price of existing technology. And it exploded the blue ocean created by the 650 when in 1964 it unveiled the System/360, the first modularized computer system.	Incumbent	Value pioneering (650: mostly existing technologies) Value and technology pioneering (System/360: new and existing technologies)	Nonexistent
Apple personal computer Although it was not the first home computer, the all-in-one, simple-to-use Apple II was a blue ocean creation when it appeared in 1978.	New entrant	Value pioneering (mostly existing technologies)	Unattractive
Compaq PC servers Compaq created a blue ocean in 1992 with its ProSignia server, which gave buyers twice the file and print capability of the minicomputer at one-third the price.	Incumbent	Value pioneering (mostly existing technologies)	Nonexistent
Dell built to order computers In the mid-1990s, Dell created a blue ocean in a highly competitive industry by creating a new purchase and delivery experience for buyers.	New entrant	Value pioneering (mostly existing technologies)	Unattractive

Key blue ocean creations	Was the blue ocean created by a new entrant or an incumbent?	Was it driven by technology pioneering or value pioneering?*	At the time of the blue ocean creation, was the industry attractive or unattractive?
Movie Theatres			
Nickelodeon The first Nickelodeon opened its doors in 1905, showing short films around the clock to working class audiences for five cents.	New entrant	Value pioneering (mostly existing technologies)	Nonexistent
Palace theatres Created by Roxy Rothapfel in 1914, these theateres provided an opera-like environment for cinema viewing at an affordable price.	Incumbent	Value pioneering (mostly existing technologies)	Attractive
AMC multiplex In the 1960s, the number of multiplexes in America's suburban shopping malls mushroomed. The multiplex gave viewers greater choice while reducing owners' costs.	Incumbent	Value pioneering (mostly existing technologies)	Unattractive
AMC megaplex Megaplexes, introduced in 1995, offered every current blockbuster and provided spectacular viewing experiences in theatere complexes as big as stadiums, at a lower cost to theatere owners.	Incumbent	Value pioneering (mostly existing technologies)	Unattractive

*Driven by value pioneering does not mean that technologies were not involved. Rather, it means that the defining technologies used had largely been in existence, whether in that industry or elsewhere.

in America. Like those within the auto industry, the blue oceans within the computer industry did not come about through technology innovations alone but by linking technology to what buyers valued. As with the IBM 650 and the Compaq PC server, this often involved simplifying the technology.

Incumbents often create blue oceans – and usually within their core businesses. GM, the Japanese automakers, and Chrysler were established players when they created blue oceans in the auto industry. So were CTR and its later incarnation, IBM, and Compaq in the computer industry. And in the cinema industry, the same can be said of palace theatres and AMC. Of the companies listed here, only Ford, Apple, Dell, and Nickelodeon were new entrants in their industries; the first three were start-ups, and the fourth was an established player entering an industry that was new to it. This suggests that incumbents are not at a disadvantage in creating new market spaces. Moreover, the blue oceans made by incumbents were usually

within their core businesses. In fact, as the exhibit shows, most blue oceans are created from within, not beyond, red oceans of existing industries. This challenges the view that new markets are in distant waters. Blue oceans are right next to you in every industry.

Company and industry are the wrong units of analysis. The traditional units of strategic analysis – company and industry – have little explanatory power when it comes to analyzing how and why blue oceans are created. There is no consistently excellent company; the same company can be brilliant at one time and wrongheaded at another. Every company rises and falls over time. Likewise, there is no perpetually excellent industry; relative attractiveness is driven largely by the creation of blue oceans from within them.

The most appropriate unit of analysis for explaining the creation of blue oceans is the strategic move – the set of managerial actions and decisions involved in making a major market-creating business offering. Compaq, for example, is considered by many people to be 'unsuccessful' because it was acquired by Hewlett-Packard in 2001 and ceased to be a company. But the firm's ultimate fate does not invalidate the smart strategic move Compaq made that led to the creation of the multibillion-dollar market in PC servers, a move that was a key cause of the company's powerful comeback in the 1990s.

Creating blue oceans builds brands. So powerful is blue ocean strategy that a blue ocean strategic move can create brand equity that lasts for decades. Almost all of the companies listed in the exhibit are remembered in no small part for the blue oceans they created long ago. Very few people alive today were around when the first Model T rolled off Henry Ford's assembly line in 1908, but the company's brand still benefits from that blue ocean move. IBM, too, is often regarded as an 'American institution' largely for the blue oceans it created in computing; the 360 series was its equivalent of the Model T.

Our findings are encouraging for executives at the large, established corporations that are traditionally seen as the victims of new market space creation. For what they reveal is that large R&D budgets are not the key to creating new market space. The key is making the right strategic moves. What's more, companies that understand what drives a good strategic move will be well placed to create multiple blue oceans over time, thereby continuing to deliver high growth and profits over a sustained period. The creation of blue oceans, in other words, is a product of strategy and as such is very much a product of managerial action.

The defining characteristics

Our research shows several common characteristics across strategic moves that create blue oceans. We found that the creators of blue oceans, in sharp contrast to companies playing by traditional rules, never use the competition as a benchmark. Instead they make it irrelevant by creating a leap in value for both buyers and the company itself. (Exhibit 8.4.2 compares the chief characteristics of these two strategy models.)

Perhaps the most important feature of blue ocean strategy is that it rejects the fundamental tenet of conventional strategy: that a trade-off exists between value and cost. According to this thesis, companies can either create greater value for customers at a higher cost or create reasonable value at a lower cost. In other words, strategy is essentially a choice between differentiation and low cost. But when it comes to creating blue oceans, the evidence shows that successful companies pursue differentiation and low cost simultaneously.

To see how this is done, let us go back to Cirque du Soleil. At the time of Cirque's debut, circuses focused on benchmarking one another and maximizing their shares of shrinking demand by tweaking traditional circus acts. This included trying to secure more and better-known clowns and lion tamers, efforts that raised circuses' cost structure without substantially altering the circus experience. The result was rising costs without rising revenues and a downward spiral in overall circus demand. Enter Cirque. Instead of following the conventional logic of outpacing the competition by offering a better solution to the given problem – creating a circus with even greater fun and thrills – it redefined the problem itself by offering people the fun and thrill of the circus *and* the intellectual sophistication and artistic richness of the theatre.

In designing performances that landed both these punches, Cirque had to reevaluate the components of the traditional circus offering. What the company found was that many of the elements considered essential to the fun and thrill of the circus were unnecessary and in many cases costly. For instance, most circuses offer animal acts. These are a heavy economic burden, because circuses have to shell out not only for the animals but also for their training, medical care, housing,

EXHIBIT 8.4.2   RED OCEAN VERSUS BLUE OCEAN STRATEGY

Red ocean strategy	Blue ocean strategy
■ Compete in existing market space. ■ Beat the competition. ■ Exploit existing demand. ■ Make the value/cost trade-off. ■ Align the whole system of a company's activities with its strategic choice of differentiation or low cost.	■ Create uncontested market space. ■ Make the competition irrelevant. ■ Create and capture new demand. ■ Break the value/cost trade-off. ■ Align the whole system of a company's activities in pursuit of differentiation and low cost.

insurance, and transportation. Yet Cirque found that the appetite for animal shows was rapidly diminishing because of rising public concern about the treatment of circus animals and the ethics of exhibiting them.

Similarly, although traditional circuses promoted their performers as stars, Cirque realized that the public no longer thought of circus artists as stars, at least not in the movie star sense. Cirque did away with traditional three-ring shows, too. Not only did these create confusion among spectators forced to switch their attention from one ring to another, they also increased the number of performers needed, with obvious cost implications. And while aisle concession sales appeared to be a good way to generate revenue, the high prices discouraged parents from making purchases and made them feel they were being taken for a ride.

Cirque found that the lasting allure of the traditional circus came down to just three factors: the clowns, the tent, and the classic acrobatic acts. So Cirque kept the clowns, while shifting their humour away from slapstick to a more enchanting, sophisticated style. It glamorized the tent, which many circuses had abandoned in favour of rented venues. Realizing that the tent, more than anything else, captured the magic of the circus, Cirque designed this classic symbol with a glorious external finish and a high level of audience comfort. Gone were the sawdust and hard benches. Acrobats and other thrilling performers were retained, but Cirque reduced their roles and made their acts more elegant by adding artistic flair.

Even as Cirque stripped away some of the traditional circus offerings, it injected new elements drawn from the world of theatre. For instance, unlike traditional circuses featuring a series of unrelated acts, each Cirque creation resembles a theatre performance in that it has a theme and story line. Although the themes are intentionally vague, they bring harmony and an intellectual element to the acts. Cirque also borrows ideas from Broadway. For example, rather than putting on the traditional 'once and for all' show, Cirque mounts multiple productions based on different themes and story lines. As with Broadway productions, too, each Cirque show has an original musical score, which drives the performance, lighting, and timing of the acts, rather than the other way around. The productions feature abstract and spiritual dance, an idea derived from theatre and ballet. By introducing these factors, Cirque has created highly sophisticated entertainments. And by staging multiple productions, Cirque gives people reason to come to the circus more often, thereby increasing revenues.

Cirque offers the best of both circus and theatre. And by eliminating many of the most expensive elements of the circus, it has been able to dramatically reduce its cost structure, achieving both differentiation and low cost.

By driving down costs while simultaneously driving up value for buyers, a company can achieve a leap in value for both itself and its customers. Since buyer value comes from the utility and price a company offers, and a company generates value for itself through cost structure and price, blue ocean strategy is achieved only when the whole system of a company's utility, price, and cost activities is properly aligned. It is this whole-system approach that makes the creation of blue oceans a sustainable strategy. Blue ocean strategy integrates the range of a firm's functional and operational activities.

A rejection of the trade-off between low cost and differentiation implies a fundamental change in strategic mind-set – we cannot emphasize enough how fundamental a shift it is. The red ocean assumption that industry structural conditions are a given and firms are forced to compete within them is based on an intellectual worldview that academics call the *structuralist* view, or *environmental determinism.* According to this view, companies and managers are largely at the mercy of economic forces greater than themselves. Blue ocean strategies, by contrast, are based on a worldview in which market boundaries and industries can be reconstructed by the actions and beliefs of industry players. We call this the *reconstructionist* view.

The founders of Cirque du Soleil clearly did not feel constrained to act within the confines of their industry. Indeed, is Cirque really a circus with all that it has eliminated, reduced, raised, and created? Or is it theatre? If it is theatre, then what genre – Broadway show, opera, ballet? The magic of Cirque was created through a reconstruction of elements drawn from all of these alternatives. In the end, Cirque is none of them and a little of all of them. From within the red oceans of theatre and circus, Cirque has created a blue ocean of uncontested market space that has, as yet, no name.

Barriers to imitation

Companies that create blue oceans usually reap the benefits without credible challenges for ten to 15 years, as was the case with Cirque du Soleil, Home Depot, Federal Express, Southwest Airlines, and CNN, to name just a few. The reason is that blue ocean strategy creates considerable economic and cognitive barriers to imitation.

For a start, adopting a blue ocean creator's business model is easier to imagine than to do. Because blue ocean creators immediately attract customers in large volumes, they are able to generate scale economies very rapidly, putting would-be imitators at an immediate and continuing cost disadvantage. The huge economies of scale in purchasing that Wal-Mart enjoys, for example, have significantly discouraged other companies from imitating its business model. The immediate attraction of large numbers of customers can also create network externalities. The more customers eBay has online, the more attractive the auction site becomes for both sellers and buyers of wares, giving users few incentives to go elsewhere.

When imitation requires companies to make changes to their whole system of activities, organizational politics may impede a would-be competitor's ability to switch to the divergent business model of a blue ocean strategy. For instance, airlines trying to follow Southwest's example of offering the speed of air travel with the flexibility and cost of driving would have faced major revisions in routing, training, marketing, and pricing, not to mention culture. Few established airlines had the flexibility to make such extensive organizational and operating changes overnight. Imitating a whole-system approach is not an easy feat.

The cognitive barriers can be just as effective. When a company offers a leap in value, it rapidly earns brand buzz and a loyal following in the marketplace. Experience shows that even the most expensive marketing campaigns struggle to unseat a blue ocean creator. Microsoft, for example, has been trying for more than ten years to occupy the centre of the blue ocean that Intuit created with its financial software product Quicken. Despite all of its efforts and all of its investment, Microsoft has not been able to unseat Intuit as the industry leader.

In other situations, attempts to imitate a blue ocean creator conflict with the imitator's existing brand image. The Body Shop, for example, shuns top models and makes no promises of eternal youth and beauty. For the established cosmetic brands like Estée Lauder and L'Oréal, imitation was very difficult, because it would have signalled a complete invalidation of their current images, which are based on promises of eternal youth and beauty.

A consistent pattern

While our conceptual articulation of the pattern may be new, blue ocean strategy has always existed, whether or not companies have been conscious of the fact.

Just consider the striking parallels between the Cirque du Soleil theatre-circus experience and Ford's creation of the Model T.

At the end of the nineteenth century, the automobile industry was small and unattractive. More than 500 automakers in America competed in turning out handmade luxury cars that cost around $1500 and were enormously *un*popular with all but the very rich. Anticar activists tore up roads, ringed parked cars with barbed wire, and organized boycotts of car-driving businessmen and politicians. Woodrow Wilson caught the spirit of the times when he said in 1906 that 'nothing has spread socialistic feeling more than the automobile'. He called it 'a picture of the arrogance of wealth'.

Instead of trying to beat the competition and steal a share of existing demand from other automakers, Ford reconstructed the industry boundaries of cars and horse-drawn carriages to create a blue ocean. At the time, horse-drawn carriages were the primary means of local transportation across America. The carriage had two distinct advantages over cars. Horses could easily negotiate the bumps and mud that stymied cars – especially in rain and snow – on the nation's ubiquitous dirt roads. And horses and carriages were much easier to maintain than the luxurious autos of the time, which frequently broke down, requiring expert repairmen who were expensive and in short supply. It was Henry Ford's understanding of these advantages that showed him how he could break away from the competition and unlock enormous untapped demand.

Ford called the Model T the car 'for the great multitude, constructed of the best materials'. Like Cirque, the Ford Motor Company made the competition irrelevant. Instead of creating fashionable, customized cars for weekends in the countryside, a luxury few could justify, Ford built a car that, like the horse-drawn carriage, was for everyday use. The Model T came in just one colour, black, and there were few optional extras. It was reliable and durable, designed to travel effortlessly over dirt roads in rain, snow, or sunshine. It was easy to use and fix. People could learn to drive it in a day. And like Cirque, Ford went outside the industry for a price point, looking at horse-drawn carriages ($400), not other autos. In 1908, the first Model T cost $850; in 1909, the price dropped to $609, and by 1924 it was down to $290. In this way, Ford converted buyers of horse-drawn carriages into car buyers – just as Cirque turned theatregoers into circusgoers. Sales of the Model T boomed. Ford's market share surged from 9% in 1908 to 61% in 1921, and by 1923, a majority of American households had a car.

Even as Ford offered the mass of buyers a leap in value, the company also achieved the lowest cost structure in the industry, much as Cirque did later. By keeping the cars highly standardized with limited options and interchangeable parts, Ford was able to scrap the prevailing manufacturing system in which cars were constructed by skilled craftsmen who swarmed around one workstation and built a car piece by piece from start to finish. Ford's revolutionary assembly line replaced craftsmen with unskilled labourers, each of whom worked quickly and efficiently on one small task. This allowed Ford to make a car in just four days – 21 days was the industry norm – creating huge cost savings.

Blue and red oceans have always coexisted and always will. Practical reality, therefore, demands that companies understand the strategic logic of both types of oceans. At present, competing in red oceans dominates the field of strategy in theory and in practice, even as businesses' need to create blue oceans intensifies. It is time to even the scales in the field of strategy with a better balance of efforts across both oceans. For although blue ocean strategists have always existed, for the most part their strategies have been largely unconscious. But once corporations realize that the strategies for creating and capturing blue oceans have a different underlying logic from red ocean strategies, they will be able to create many more blue oceans in the future.

THE INDUSTRY CONTEXT IN INTERNATIONAL PERSPECTIVE

How many things are looked upon as quite impossible until they have been actually effected?

Pliny the Elder (23–79); Roman writer

In the field of strategy, views differ sharply on whether the industry context can be shaped or not, although these differences of opinion usually remain implicit – few practising managers or strategy theorists make a point of expounding their assumptions about the nature of the environment. For this reason, it is difficult to identify whether there are national preferences when it comes to industry context perspective. Yet, it seems not unlikely that strategists in different countries have different inclinations on this issue. Although it is always difficult to generalize, it seems that strategists in some nations gravitate more towards an industry leadership perspective than in other nations.

As an input to the debate whether there are international differences in industry context perspective, we would like to put forward a number of factors that might be of influence on how the paradox of compliance and choice is viewed in different countries. It should be noted, however, that these propositions are intended to encourage discussion and constitute only tentative explanations for cross-cultural differences in perspective. More specific international research is needed to give this debate a firmer basis.

Locus of control

Culture researchers have long recognized international differences in how people perceive the power of individuals to shape their environment. In some cultures the view that an individual is at the mercy of external events is more predominant, while in other cultures there is a stronger belief in the freedom of individuals to act independent of the environment and even to create their own circumstances. Psychologists refer to this as the perceived 'locus of control' (e.g. Miller, Kets de Vries and Toulouse, 1982). People with an internal locus of control believe that they largely control their own fate. Their efforts will shape their circumstances – success is earned and failure is one's own fault. People with an external locus of control, on the other hand, believe that their fate is largely the result of circumstances beyond their control. Any effort to improve one's position, if at all possible, should be directed towards complying with external demands – fortune favours those who go with the flow. In the most extreme case, however, people with an external locus of control are fatalistic, that is, they assume no efforts will change that which is inevitable.

Obviously, in countries where the culture is more inclined towards an internal locus of control, it is reasonable to expect that the industry leadership perspective will be more widespread. It is in such nations that one might expect remarks, such as that by the 19th century English essayist Sydney Smith: 'When I hear any man talk of an unalterable law, the only effect it produces on me is to convince me that he is an unalterable fool.' In cultures with a strong emphasis on external locus of control, the industry dynamics perspective is likely to be more predominant.

Time orientation

As was identified in Chapter 4, cultures can also differ with respect to their time orientation. Some cultures are directed towards the past, while others are more focused on the present or on the future. In countries with a future orientation, the belief is widespread that change is progress. People generally welcome change as an opportunity for advancement. Therefore, in future-oriented cultures, people are even willing to initiate painful change processes, in the expectation that this will lead to future benefits. In these countries a stronger inclination towards the industry leadership perspective is most likely.

In past-oriented cultures, the belief is widespread that change is decay. People generally actively resist change and protect the status quo. In these cultures, external changes will only be adapted to if strictly necessary. In present-oriented cultures, the belief is widespread that change is relatively unimportant. People live for the day and adapt to changes as they come. In both types of culture, the industry dynamics perspective is more likely to be more predominant.

Role of government

Internationally, opinions also differ on the role that governments can play in encouraging the shaping of industries. In some countries the predominant view is that governments should facilitate industry change by creating good business circumstances and then staying out of the way of company initiatives. Governments are needed to set basic rules of business conduct, but firms should not be impeded by other governmental intervention in the functioning of industries and markets. Individual companies are seen as the primary drivers of industry development and if companies are given enough leeway, excellent ones can significantly shape their industry context. Such economic liberalism is particularly strong in the English-speaking nations, and it is here that governments attempt to actually facilitate firms' industry shaping efforts. Unsurprisingly, the industry leadership perspective is rather pronounced in these countries.

In other nations the predominant view is that Adam Smith's free market ideal often proves to be dysfunctional. A fully liberal market, it is believed, can lead to short-termism, negative social consequences, mutually destructive competition, and an inability to implement industry-wide changes. Governments must therefore assume a more proactive role. They must protect weaker parties, such as workers and the environment, against the negative side effects of the market system, and actively create a shared infrastructure for all companies. Furthermore, the government can develop an industrial policy to encourage the development of new industries, force companies to work together where this is more effective, and push through industry-wide changes, if otherwise a stalemate would occur. Such a 'managed competition' view has been prevalent in Japan and France, and to a lesser extent in Germany (e.g. Hampden-Turner and Trompenaars, 1993; Lessem and Neubauer, 1994). In these countries the industry leadership perspective is not as strongly held as in the English-speaking nations – industries can be shaped, but few companies have the power to do so without a good industrial policy and government backing.

Network of relationships

This factor is linked to the discussion in the previous chapter. In countries where the discrete organization perspective is predominant, companies often strive to retain their independence and power position vis-à-vis other companies. As these firms are not embedded in complex networks, but operate free from these constraining relationships, they are more at liberty to challenge the existing rules of the game. In other words, where firms are not entangled in a web of long-term relationships, they are better positioned for rule breaking behaviour – every firm can make a difference. In these countries an industry leadership perspective is more prevalent.

However, in nations where firms are more inclined to operate in networks, each individual firm surrenders a part of its freedom in exchange for long-term relationships. The ability of the individual firm to shape its industry thus declines, as all changes must be discussed and negotiated with its partners. Hence, in these countries, the industry leadership perspective is generally less strongly held than in the countries favouring discrete organizations. It should be noted that a group of firms, once in agreement, is often more powerful than each individual firm and therefore more capable of shaping the industry. However, it is acknowledged that getting the network partners to agree is a formidable task and a significant limit on the firm's ability to shape its environment.

FURTHER READING

For a good academic overview of the debate on 'who shapes whom' readers are advised to consult the special edition of *Academy of Management Review* (July 1990) that focused on this issue. In particular, the article 'Market Discipline and the Discipline of Management' by Richard Bettis and Lex Donaldson is very insightful. For a broader discussion on the issue of determinism and voluntarism, good readings are 'Central Perspective and Debates in Organization Theory', by W. Graham Astley and Andrew van der Ven, and 'Organizational Adaptation: Strategic Choice and Environmental Determinism', by Lawrence Hrebiniak and William Joyce. Also useful is the recent work on managerial discretion, which attempts to measure how much leeway top managers have in shaping the future of their firm in different industries. Of these, the article 'Managerial Discretion: A Bridge Between Polar Views of Organizational Outcomes', by Donald Hambrick and Sydney Finkelstein, is interesting for its theoretical base, while, Assessing the Amount of Managerial Discretion in Different Industries: A Multi-Method Approach', by Donald Hambrick and Eric Abrahamson is interesting for its analysis of various industry environments. All of these studies, it should be mentioned, do not have an audience of practitioners in mind.

The same is true for all further literature taking an industry dynamics perspective. A good book outlining the population ecology view of industry and firm development is the classic *Organizational Ecology* by Michael Hannan and John Freeman. For an excellent overview of the work in the area of industry and organizational evolution see Howard

Aldrich's recent book, *Organizations Evolving*. Other constraints on the freedom of firms to shape their own fate are brought forward by institutional theory and resource dependence theory, both of which have not been represented in this debate. Christine Oliver gives a good overview of these two approaches in her article 'Strategic Responses to Institutional Processes'. The classic in the field of institutional theory is Paul DiMaggio and Walter Powell's article 'The Iron Cage Revisited: Institutional Isomorphism and Collective Rationality in Organizational Fields', while Scott's book *Institutions and Organizations* is a good, more recent work. The classic in the field of resource dependence is Jeffrey Pfeffer and Gerald Salancik's book *The External Control of Organizations*.

Readers interested in the industry leadership perspective might want to start by looking at J.C. Spender's book *Industry Recipe: An Enquiry into the Nature and Sources of Managerial Judgement*. The book from which Charles Baden-Fuller and John Stopford's article was taken, *Rejuvenating the Mature Business,* is also excellent follow-up reading. The same is true of Gary Hamel and C.K. Prahalad's book *Competing for the Future*. In this context, Richard D'Aveni's book *Hypercompetition* is also worth reviewing. For a more complete view of Geoffrey Moore's line of argumentation, his book *Living on the Fault Line* is an interesting and entertaining read.

For those who want to understand what happened during the internet bubble and whether there was anything to the New Economy, we advise starting with Michael Porter's article 'Strategy and the Internet'. Also valuable is Michael Cusumano and Annabelle Gawer's article 'The Elements of Platform Leadership' which describes the functioning of industry standards, as does Carl Shapiro and Hal Varian's excellent book, *Information Rules*.

REFERENCES

Aldrich, H.E. (1979) *Organizations and Environments*, Englewood Cliffs, NJ: Prentice Hall.

Aldrich, H.E. (1999) *Organizations Evolving*, London: Sage.

Aldrich, H.E., and Fiol, C.M. (1994) 'Fools Rush In? The Institutional Context of Industry Creation', *Academy of Management Review*, Vol. 19, No. 4, pp. 645–670.

Arrow, K.J. (1962) 'Economic Welfare and the Allocation of Resources for Inventions', in: R.R. Nelson (ed.), *The Rate and Direction of Inventive Activity*, Princeton, NJ: Princeton University Press.

Arthur, W.B. (1994) *Increasing Returns and Path Dependence in the Economy*, Ann Arbor, MI: University of Michigan Press.

Arthur, W.B. (1996) 'Increasing Returns and the New World of Business', *Harvard Business Review*, Vol. 74, No. 4, July–August, pp. 100–109.

Astley, W.G., and van der Ven, A.H. (1983) 'Central Perspectives and Debates in Organization Theory', *Administrative Science Quarterly*, Vol. 28, No. 2, June, pp. 245–273.

Baden-Fuller, C.W.F., and Stopford, J.M. (1992) *Rejuvenating the Mature Business*, London: Routledge.

Bain, J.S. (1959) *Industrial Organizations*, New York: Wiley.

Baum, A.C., and Singh, J.V (eds) (1994) *Evolutionary Dynamics of Organizations*, New York: Oxford University Press.

Beinhocker, E.D. (1997) 'Strategy at the Edge of Chaos', *The McKinsey Quarterly*, No. 1, pp. 24–39.

Bettis, R.A., and Donaldson, L. (1990) 'Market Discipline and the Discipline of Management', *Academy of Management Review*, Vol. 15, No. 3, July, pp. 367–368.

Bower, J.L., and Christensen, C.M. (1995) 'Disruptive Technologies: Cathing the Wave', *Harvard Business Review*, Vol. 73, No. 1, January–February, pp. 43–53.

Burgelman, R.A., and Grove, A.S. (1996) 'Strategic Dissonance', *California Management Review*, Vol. 38, No. 2, pp. 106–131.

Buzzell, R.D., and Gale, B.T. (1987) *The PIMS Principles: Linking Strategy to Performance*, New York: Free Press.

Carpenter, M.A., and Golden, B.R. (1997) 'Perceived Managerial Discretion: A Study of Cause and Effect', *Strategic Management Journal*, Vol. 18, No. 3, March, pp. 187–206.

Child, J. (1972) 'Organizational Structure, Environment, and Performance: The Role of Strategic Choice', *Sociology*, January, pp. 2–22.

Christensen, C.M. (1997) *The Innovator's Dilemma*, New York: HarperBusiness.

Cusumano, M.A., and Gawer, A. (2002) 'The Elements of Platform Leadership', *Sloan Management Review*, Vol. 43, No. 3, Spring, pp. 51–58.

D'Aveni, R.A. (1994) *Hypercompetition: Managing the Dynamics of Strategic Maneuvering*, New York: Free Press.

D'Aveni, R.A. (1999) 'Strategic Supremacy through Disruption and Dominance', *Sloan Management Review*, Vol. 40, No. 3, pp. 127–135.

DiMaggio, P.J., and Powell, W.W. (1983) 'The Iron Cage Revisited: Institutional Isomorphism and Collective Rationality in Organizational Fields', *American Sociological Review*, Vol. 48, No. 2, April, pp. 147–160.

Evans, P.B., and Wurster, T.S. (1997) 'Strategy and the New Economics of Information', *Harvard Business Review*, Vol. 76, No. 5, September–October, pp. 71–82.

Finkelstein, S., and Hambrick, D.C. (1996) *Strategic Leadership: Top Executives and Their Effects on Organizations*, St. Paul: West.

Freeman, J., and Boeker, W. (1984) 'The Ecological Analysis of Business Strategy', *California Management Review*, Spring, pp. 73–86.

Ghemawat, P. (1991) *Commitment: The Dynamic of Strategy*, New York: Free Press.

Gilbert, X., and Strebel, P. (1989) 'Taking Advantage of Industry Shifts', *European Management Journal*, December, pp. 398–402.

Hall, W.K. (1980) 'Survival Strategies in a Hostile Environment', *Harvard Business Review*, Vol. 58, No. 5, September–October, pp. 75–85.

Hambrick, D.C., and Abrahamson, E. (1995) 'Assessing the Amount of Managerial Discretion in Different Industries: A Multi-Method Approach', *Academy of Management Journal*, Vol. 38, No. 5, October, pp. 1427–1441.

Hambrick, D.C., and Finkelstein, S. (1987) 'Managerial Discretion: A Bridge Between Polar Views of Organizational Outcomes', in: B.M. Staw and L.L. Cummings (eds), *Research in Organizational Behavior*, Vol. 9, Greenwich, CT: JAI, pp. 369–406.

Hamel, G. (1996) 'Strategy as Revolution', *Harvard Business Review*, Vol. 74, No. 4, July–August, pp. 69–82.

Hamel, G., and Prahalad, C.K. (1994) *Competing for the Future*, Boston: Harvard Business School Press.

Hampden-Turner, C., and Trompenaars, A. (1993) *The Seven Cultures of Capitalism: Value Systems for Creating Wealth in the United States, Japan, Germany, France, Britain, Sweden and the Netherlands*, New York: Doubleday.

Hannan, M.T., and Freeman, J. (1977) 'The Population Ecology of Organizations', *American Journal of Sociology*, Vol. 82, No. 5, March, pp. 929–964.

Hannan, M.T., and Freeman, J. (1989) *Organizational Ecology*, Cambridge, MA: Harvard University Press.

Hill, C.W.L. (1988) 'Differentiation Versus Low Cost or Differentiation and Low Cost', *Academy of Management Review*, Vol. 13, July, pp. 401–412.

Hrebiniak, L.G., and Joyce, W.F. (1985) 'Organizational Adaptation: Strategic Choice and Environmental Determinism', *Administrative Science Quarterly*, Vol. 30, No. 3, September, pp. 336–349.

Kanter, R.M. (1996) 'When a Thousand Flowers Bloom: Structural, Collective, and Social Conditions, for Innovation in Organizations', in: P.S. Myers (ed.), *Knowledge Management and Organization Design*, Boston: Butterworth-Heinemann, pp. 169–211.

Kim, W.C. and Mauborgne, R. (2004) 'Blue Ocean Strategy'. *Harvard Business Review*. October.

Lawrence, P.R., and Lorsch, J.W. (1967) *Organization and Environment*, Cambridge, MA: Harvard University Press.

Lessem, R., and Neubauer, F.F. (1994) *European Management Systems*, London: McGraw-Hill.

Levenhagen, M., Porac, J.F., and Thomas, H. (1993) 'Emergent Industry Leadership and the Selling of Technological Visions: A Social Constructionist View', in: J. Hendry, G. Johnson, and J. Newton (eds), *Strategic Thinking: Leadership and the Management of Change*, Chichester: Wiley.

Markides, C. (1997) 'Strategic Innovation', *Sloan Management Review*, Vol. 38, No. 3, Spring, pp. 9–23.

Markides, C. (1998) 'Strategic Innovation in Established Companies', *Sloan Management Review*, Vol. 39, No. 3, Spring, pp. 31–42.

Miles, R.E., and Snow, C.C. (1978) *Organizational Strategy: Structure and Process*, New York: McGraw-Hill.

Miller, D. (1990) *The Icarus Paradox: How Excellent Companies Bring About Their Own Downfall*, New York: Harper Business.

Miller, D., Kets de Vries, M., and Toulouse, J.M. (1982) 'Top Executive Locus of Control and its Relationship to Strategy-making, Structure and Environment', *Academy of Management Journal*, Vol. 25, pp. 237–253.

Moore, G.A. (2000) *Living on the Fault Line: Managing for Shareholder Value in the Age of the Internet*, New York: HarperBusiness.

Moore, J.F. (1993) 'Predators and Prey: A New Ecology of Competition', *Harvard Business Review*, May–June, pp. 75–86.

Moore, J.F. (1996) *The Death of Competition: Leadership & Strategy in the Age of Business Ecosystems*, New York: HarperBusiness.

Nelson, R.R., and Winter, S.G. (1982) *An Evolutionary Theory of Economic Change*, Reading, MA: Harvard University Press.

Oliver, C. (1991) 'Strategic Responses to Institutional Processes', *Academy of Management Review*, Vol. 16, No. 1, January, pp. 145–179.

Oliver, C. (1997) 'Sustainable Competitive Advantage: Combining Institutional and Resource-based Views', *Strategic Management Journal*, Vol. 18, No. 9, October, pp. 697–713.

Parolini, C. (1999) *The Value Net*, Chichester: Wiley.

Pfeffer, J., and Salancik, G. (1978) *The External Control of Organizations: A Resource Dependency Perspective*, New York: Harper & Row.

Porter, M.E. (1980) *Competitive Strategy: Techniques for Analyzing Industries and Competitors*, New York: Free Press.

Porter, M.E. (1985) *Competitive Advantage: Creating and Sustaining Superior Performance*, New York: Free Press.

Porter, M.E. (1996) 'What is Strategy?', *Harvard Business Review*, Vol. 74, No. 6, November–December, pp. 61–78.

Porter, M.E. (2001) 'Strategy and the Internet', *Harvard Business Review*, Vol. 80, No. 3, March, pp. 62–78.

Prahalad, C.K., and Doz, Y.L. (1987) *The Multinational Mission: Balancing Local Demands and Global Vision*, New York: Free Press.

Rumelt, R. (1991) 'How Much Does Industry Matter?', *Strategic Management Journal*, Vol. 12, No. 3, March, pp. 167–186.

Schmalensee, R. (1985) 'Do Markets Differ Much?', *American Economic Review*, June, pp. 341–351.

Schumpeter, J.A. (1934) *The Theory of Economic Development*, Cambridge, MA: Harvard University Press.

Scott, W.R. (1995) *Institutions and Organizations*, Thousand Oaks, CA: Sage.

Sexton, D.L. (2001) 'Wayne Huizenga: Entrepreneur and Wealth Creator', *Academy of Management Executive*, Vol. 15, No. 1, pp. 40–48.

Shapiro, C.E., and Varian, H.R. (1998) *Information Rules*, Boston, MA: HBS Press.

Shapiro, C.E., and Varian, H.R. (1999) 'The Art of Standard Wars', *California Management Review*, Vol. 41, No. 2, Winter, pp. 8–32.

Slywotsky, A.J. (1996) *Value Migration*, Boston: Harvard Business School Press.

Spender, J.C. (1989) *Industry Recipe: An Enquiry into the Nature and Sources of Managerial Judgement*, New York: Basil Blackwell.

Tirole, J. (1988) *The Theory of Industrial Organization*, Cambridge, MA: MIT Press.

Whitley, R.D. (1999) *Divergent Capitalisms: The Social Structuring and Change of Business Systems*, Oxford: Oxford University Press.

Wilson, D.C. (1992) *A Strategy of Change*, London: Routledge.

Yoffie, D.B., and Kwak, M. (2001) 'Mastering Strategic Movement at Palm', *Sloan Management Review*, Vol. 43, No. 1, pp. 55–63.

THE ORGANIZATIONAL CONTEXT

We shape our environments, then our environments shape us.

Winston Churchill (1874–1965); British statesman and writer

INTRODUCTION

In organizations, just as in families, each new generation does not start from scratch but inherits properties belonging to their predecessors. In families, a part of this inheritance is in the form of genetic properties, but other attributes are also passed down such as family traditions, myths, habits, connections, feuds, titles and possessions. People might think of themselves as unique individuals, but to some degree they are an extension of the family line, and their behaviour is influenced by this inheritance. In firms the same phenomenon is observable. New top managers may arrive on the scene, but they inherit a great deal from the previous generation. They inherit traditions and myths in the form of an organizational culture. Habits are passed along in the form of established organizational processes, while internal and external relationships and rivalries shape the political constellation in which new managers must function. They are also handed the family jewels – brands, competences and other key resources.

In Chapter 4 it was pointed out that such inheritance is often the source of organizational rigidity and inertia (e.g. Hannan and Freeman, 1977; Rumelt, 1995). Inheritance limits 'organizational plasticity' – the capacity of the organization to change shape. As such, organizational inheritance can partially predetermine a firm's future path of development – which is referred to as path dependency, or sometimes simply summed up as 'history matters' (e.g. Aldrich, 1999; Nelson and Winter, 1982). Therefore, it was concluded that for strategic renewal to take place, some inherited characteristics could be preserved, but others needed to be changed, by either evolutionary or revolutionary means.

What was not discussed in Chapter 4 was *who* should trigger the required strategic changes. Who should initiate adaptations to the firm's business system and who should take steps to reshape the organizational system? Typically, managers will have some role to play in all developments in the organizational context, but the question is what role. It is unlikely that any manager will have complete influence over all organizational developments, or would even want to exert absolute control. Inheritance and other organizational factors limit 'organizational malleability' – the capacity of the organization to be shaped by someone. As such, managers need to determine what power they do have and where this power should be applied to achieve the best results. At the same time, managers will generally also look for opportunities to tap into the capabilities of other people in the firm to contribute to ongoing organizational adaptation.

So, the question can be summarized as, 'what is the role of managers in achieving a new alignment with the environment and what input can be garnered from other organizational members?' This question is also referred to as the issue of organizational development and will be the central topic of further discussion in this chapter.

THE ISSUE OF ORGANIZATIONAL DEVELOPMENT

When it comes to realizing organizational development, managers generally acknowledge that they have some type of leadership role to play. Leadership refers to the act of influencing the views and behaviours of organizational members with the intention of accomplishing a particular organizational aim (e.g. Selznick, 1957; Bass, 1990). Stated differently, leadership is the act of getting organizational members to follow. From this definition it can be concluded that not all managers are necessarily leaders, and not all leaders are necessarily managers. Managers are individuals with a formal position in the organizational hierarchy, with associated authority and responsibilities. Leaders are individuals who have the ability to sway other people in the organization to get something done.

To be able to lead organizational developments, managers need power. Power is the capability to influence. They also need to know how to get power, and how and where to exert it. In the following sections, these three topics will be examined in more detail. First, the sources of leadership influence will be described, followed by the levers of leadership influence. Finally, the arenas of leadership influence will be explored.

Sources of leadership influence

To lead means to use power to influence others. Leaders can derive their potential influence from two general sources – their position and their person (Etzioni, 1961). 'Position power' comes from a leader's formal function in the organization. 'Personal power' is rooted in the specific character, knowledge, skills and relationships of the leader. Managers always have some level of position power, but they do not necessarily have the personal power needed to get organizational members to follow them. These two main types of power can be further subdivided into the following categories (French and Raven, 1959):

- Legitimate power. Legitimate power exists when a person has the formal authority to determine certain organizational behaviours and other employees agree to comply with this situation. Examples of legitimate power are the authority to assign work, spend money and demand information.
- Coercive power. People have coercive power when they have the capability to punish or withhold rewards to achieve compliance. Examples of coercive power include giving a poor performance review, withholding a bonus and dismissing employees.
- Reward power. Reward power is derived from the ability to offer something of value to a person in return for compliance. Examples of reward power include giving praise, awarding wage raises and promoting employees.
- Expert power. Expert power exists when organizational members are willing to comply because of a person's superior knowledge or skills in an important area. Such expert power can be based on specific knowledge of functional areas (e.g. marketing, finance), technologies (e.g. pharmaceuticals, information technology), geographic areas (e.g. South-East Asia, Florida) or businesses (e.g. mining, automotive).
- Referent power. When organizational members let themselves be influenced by a person's charismatic appeal, this is called referent power. This personal attraction can be based on many attributes, such as likeableness, forcefulness, persuasiveness, visionary qualities and image of success.

The first three types of power are largely determined by the organizational position of leaders and their willingness to exert them – coercive and reward capabilities without the credibility of use are not a viable source of power. The last two sources of power, expert and referent power, are largely personal in nature, and also more subjective. Whether someone is seen as an expert and therefore accorded a certain level of respect and influence depends strongly on the perceptions of the people being lead. Expert power can be made more tangible by wearing a white lab coat, putting three pens in your breast pocket or writing a book, but still perceived expertise will be in the eyes of the beholder. The same is true for referent power, as people do not find the same characteristics equally charismatic. What is forceful to one follower might seem pushy to someone else; what is visionary to one person might sound like the murmurings of a madman to others (e.g. Klein and House, 1998; Waldman and Yammarino, 1999).

In practice, leaders will employ a mix of all five types of power to achieve the influence they desire. However, leadership styles can differ greatly depending on the relative weight placed on the various sources of power within the mix.

Levers of leadership influence

The sources of power available to the leader need to be used to have influence. There are three generic ways for leaders to seek influence, each focused on a different point in the activities of the people being influenced. These levers of leadership influence are:

- Throughput control. Leaders can focus their attention directly at the actions being taken by others in the organization. Throughput control implies getting involved hands-on in the activities of others, either by suggesting ways of working, engaging in a discussion on how things should be done, leading by example or simply by telling others what to do. This form of direct influence does require sufficiently detailed knowledge about the activities of others to be able to point out what should be done.

- Output control. Instead of directly supervising how things should be done, leaders can set objectives that should be met. Output control implies reaching agreement on certain performance targets and then monitoring how well they are being lived up to. The targets can be quantitative or qualitative, financial or strategic, simple or complex, realistic or stretch-oriented. And they can be arrived at by mutual consent or imposed by the leader. The very act of setting objectives can have an important influence on people in the organization, but the ability to check ongoing performance and to link results with punishment and rewards can further improve a person's impact.

- Input control. Leaders can also choose to influence the general conditions under which activities are carried out. Input control implies shaping the circumstances preceding and surrounding the actual work. Before activities start a leader can influence who is assigned to a task, which teams are formed, who is hired, where they will work and in what type of environment. During the execution of activities the leader can supply physical and financial resources, mobilize relationships and provide support. Not unimportantly, the leader can also be a source of enthusiasm, inspiration, ambition, vision and mission.

Of these three, throughput control is the most direct in its impact and input control the least. However, throughput control offers the lowest leverage and input control the highest, allowing a leader to influence many people over a longer period of time, while leaving more room for organizational members to take on their own responsibilities as well. In practice, leaders can combine elements of all three of the above, although leadership styles differ greatly with regard to the specific mix.

Arenas of leadership influence

As leaders attempt to guide organizational development, there are three main organizational arenas where they need to direct their influence to achieve strategic changes. These three overlapping arenas are the parts in the organization most resistant to change – they are the sub-systems of the firm where organizational inheritance creates its own momentum, resisting a shift into another direction (e.g. Miller and Friesen, 1980; Tushman, Newman and Romanelli, 1986):

■ The political arena. While most top managers have considerable position power with which they can try to influence the strategic decision-making process within their organization, very few top managers can impose their strategic agenda on the organization without building widespread political support. Even the most autocratic CEO will need to gain the commitment and compliance of key figures within the organization to be able to successfully push through significant changes. In practice, however, there are not many organizations where the 'officers and the troops' unquestioningly follow the general into battle. Usually, power is more dispersed throughout organizations, with different people and units having different ideas and interests, as well as the assertiveness to pursue their own agenda. Ironically, the more leaders that are developed throughout the organization, the more complex it becomes for any one leader to get the entire organization to follow – broad leadership can easily become fragmented leadership, with a host of strong people all pointing in different directions. For top management to gain control of the organization they must therefore build coalitions of supporters, not only to get favourable strategic decisions made, but also to ensure acceptance and compliance during the period of implementation. Otherwise strategic plans will be half-heartedly executed, opposed or silently sabotaged. However, gaining the necessary political support in the organization can be very difficult if the strategic views and interests of powerful individuals and departments differ significantly. Cultural and personality clashes can add to the complexity. Yet, top managers cannot recoil from the political arena, for it is here that new strategic directions are set (e.g. Allison, 1969, Reading 3.3 in this book; Pfeffer, 1992).

■ The cultural arena. Intertwined with the process of gaining political influence in the organization, there is the process of gaining cultural influence. After all, to be able to change the organization, a leader must be able to change people's beliefs and associated behavioural patterns. Yet, affecting cultural change is far from simple. A leader must be capable of questioning the shared values, ideas and habits prevalent in the organization, even though the leader has usually been immersed in the very same culture for years. Leaders must also offer an alternative worldview and set of behaviours to supercede the old. All of this requires exceptional skills as visionary – to develop a new image of a desired future state for the firm – and as missionary – to develop a new set of beliefs and values to guide the firm. Furthermore, the leader needs to be an excellent teacher to engage the organizational members in a learning process to adapt their beliefs, values and norms to the new circumstances. In practice, this means that leaders often have to 'sell' their view of the new culture, using a mix of rational persuasion, inspirational appeal, symbolic actions, motivational incentives and subtle pressure (e.g. Senge, 1990b, Reading 9.3; Ireland and Hitt, 1999).

■ The psychological arena. While leaders need to influence the political process and the cultural identity of the organization, attention also needs to be paid to the psychological needs of individuals. To affect organizational change, leaders must win both the hearts and minds of the members of the organization. People must be willing to, literally, 'follow the leader' – preferably not passively, but actively, with commitment, courage and even passion (e.g. Bennis and Nanus, 1985; Kelley, 1988). To achieve such 'followership', leaders must gain the respect and trust of their colleagues. Another important factor in winning people over is the ability to meet their emotional need for certainty, clarity and continuity, to offset the uncertainties, ambiguities and discontinuities surrounding them (e.g. Argyris, 1990; Pfeffer and Sutton, 1999b, Reading 9.4).

Even where political, cultural and psychological processes make the organization difficult to lead, managers might still be able to gain a certain level of control over their organizations. Yet, there will always remain aspects of the organizational system that managers cannot control, and should not even want to control, and this will be discussed in the following section.

THE PARADOX OF CONTROL AND CHAOS

Of all men's miseries the bitterest is this, to know so much and to have control over nothing.

Herodotus (5th century BC); Greek historian

In general, managers like to be in control. Managers like to be able to shape their own future, and by extension, to shape the future of their firm. Managers do not shy away from power – they build their power base to be able to influence events and steer the development of their organization. In short, to be a manager is to have the desire to be in charge.

Yet, at the same time, most managers understand that their firms do not resemble machines, where one person can sit at the control panel and steer the entire system. Organizations are complex social systems, populated by numerous self-thinking human beings, each with their own feelings, ideas and interests. These people need to decide and act for themselves on a daily basis, without the direct intervention of the manager. They must be empowered to weigh situations, take initiatives, solve problems and grab opportunities. They must be given a certain measure of autonomy to experiment, do things differently and even constructively disagree with the manager. In other words, managers must also be willing to 'let go' of some control for the organization to function at its best.

Moreover, managers must accept that in a complex system, like an organization, trying to control everything would be a futile endeavour. With so many people and so many interactions going on in a firm, any attempt to run the entire system top-down would be an impossible task. Therefore, letting go of some control is a pure necessity for normal organizational functioning.

This duality of wanting to control the development of the organization, while understanding that letting go of control is often beneficial, is the key strategic tension when dealing with the organizational context. On the one hand, managers must be willing to act as benevolent 'philosopher kings', autocratically imposing on the company what they see as best. On the other hand, managers must be willing to act as constitutional monarchs, democratically empowering organizational citizens to take their own responsibilities and behave more as entrepreneurs. The strategic paradox arises from the fact that the need for top-down *imposition* and bottom-up *initiative* are conflicting demands that are difficult for managers to meet at the same time.

On one side of this strategy paradox is 'control', which can be defined as the power to direct and impose order. On the other side of the paradox is the need for 'chaos', which can be defined as disorder or the lack of fixed organization. The paradox of control and chaos is a recurrent theme in the literature on strategy, organization, leadership and governance.

In most writings the need for control is presented as a pressure for a directive leadership style or an autocratic governance system (e.g. Tannenbaum and Schmidt, 1958; Vroom and Jago, 1988). The need for chaos is presented as a pressure for a participative leadership style and/or a democratic governance system (e.g. Ackoff, 1980; Stacey, 1992). In the following sub-sections both control and chaos will be further examined.

The demand for top management control

As Herodotus remarked, it would be bitter indeed to have control over nothing. Not only would it be a misery for the frustrated managers, who would be little more than mere administrators or caretakers. It would also be a misery for their organizations, which would need to constantly adjust course without a helmsman to guide the ship. Managers cannot afford to let their organizations drift on the existing momentum. It is a manager's task and responsibility to ensure that the organization changes in accordance to the environment, so that the organizational purpose can still be achieved.

Top management cannot realize this objective without some level of control. They need to be able to direct developments in the organization. They need to have the power to make the necessary changes in the organizational structure, processes and culture, to realign the organization with the demands of the environment. This power, whether positional or personal, needs to be applied towards gaining sufficient support in the political arena, challenging existing beliefs and behaviours in the cultural arena, and winning the hearts and minds of the organizational members in the psychological arena.

The control that top management needs is different from the day-to-day control built in to the organizational structure and processes – they need *strategic control* as opposed to *operational control*. While operational control gives managers influence over activities within the current organizational system, strategic control gives managers influence over changes to the organizational system itself (e.g. Goold and Quinn, 1990; Simons, 1994). It is this power that managers require to be able to steer the development of their organization.

The demand for organizational chaos

To managers the term 'chaos' sounds quite menacing – it carries connotations of rampant anarchy, total pandemonium and a hopeless mess. Yet, chaos only means disorder, coming from the Greek term for the unformed original state of the universe. In the organizational context chaos refers to situations of disorder, where phenomena have not yet been organized, or where parts of an organizational system have become 'unfreezed'. In other words, something is chaotic if it is unformed or has become 'disorganized'.

While this still does not sound particularly appealing to most managers, it should, because a period of disorganization is often a prerequisite for strategic renewal. Unfreezing existing structures, processes, routines and beliefs, and opening people up to different possibilities might be inefficient in the short run, as well as making people feel uncomfortable, but it is usually necessary to provoke creativity and to invent new ways of seeing and doing things. By allowing experimentation, skunk works, pilot projects and out-of-the-ordinary initiatives, managers accept a certain amount of disorder in the organization, which they hope will pay off in terms of organizational innovations.

But the most appealing effect of chaos is that it encourages 'self-organization'. To illustrate this phenomenon, one should first think back to the old Soviet 'command economy', which was based on the principle of control. It was believed that a rational, centrally planned economic system, with strong top-down leadership, would be the most efficient and effective way to organize industrial development. In the West, on the other hand, the 'market economy' was chaotic – no one was in control and could impose order. Everyone could go ahead and start a company. They could set their own production levels and even set their own prices! As entrepreneurs made use of the freedom offered to them, the economy 'self-organized' bottom-up. Instead of the 'visible hand' of the central planner controlling and regulating the economy, it was the 'invisible hand' of the market that created relative order out of chaos.

As the market economy example illustrates, chaos does not necessarily lead to pandemonium, but can result in a self-regulating interplay of forces. A lack of top-down control frees the way for a rich diversity of bottom-up ventures. Managers who also want to release the energy, creativity and entrepreneurial potential pent up in their organizations must therefore be willing to let go and allow some chaos to exist. In this context, the role of top management is comparable to that of governments in market economies – creating suitable conditions, encouraging activities and enforcing basic rules.

EXHIBIT 9.1   SHORT CASE

KPMG: BEING ONE?

According to Wikipedia, *The Big Four* is a novel by Agatha Christie, but also an Indian snake, a place in West Virginia and a problem you can have with ten pin bowling. The big four can also refer to Manchester United, Chelsea, Liverpool and Arsenal if you are a soccer/football fan; Paris, Milan, New York and London if you are into fashion; or Anthrax, Megadeath, Metallica and Slayer, if thrash metal is more your thing. Yet to most people in the business world the big four are Pricewaterhouse-Coopers, Deloitte, Ernst & Young and KPMG. These four firms together dominate the global auditing market, with an overwhelming share of the auditing done for large international companies, but also with a major slice of the local business in most countries around the world. Interestingly, all four have a very similar service offering, combining a core auditing business with financial, tax and organizational advice. While roughly equal in size, each has its own strengths, in certain industry sectors, geographies, technical competencies and service offerings.

By a nose length difference, the smallest of the four is KPMG. It operates in more than 140 countries and employs approximately 135 000 people, realizing revenues in excess of US$22 billion in 2008. Like its peers, KPMG is named after its founders, although most people have no idea what the initials stand for. The K is for Pieter Klynveld, who started the Dutch office in 1917, the P is for Sir William Barclay Peat, who started an accountancy firm in London in 1870, the M is for James Marwick, who together with Roger Mitchell founded Marwick, Mitchell & Co. in New York in 1897, and G is for Dr Reinhardt Goerdeler, who was chairman of the German firm Deutsche Treuhandgesellschaft. After a string of earlier mergers, Peat Marwick International and Klynveld Main Goerdeler got together in 1987 to form KPMG. However, this international consolidation was never a full integration in a legal sense. To this day, KPMG is a federation of legally independent companies that synchronize their activities via a joint body, KPMG International.

The role of KPMG International, which is structured as a Swiss cooperative, is to coordinate and support the global network of national, independent firms. It does not provide clients services, but rather makes sure that all companies in the group implement the international strategy and abide by the jointly formulated set of values and principles governing daily work. Each member company is responsible for formulating its own strategy under the joint umbrella and for running its own day-to-day business.

Decision-making within KPMG International is structured into three separate bodies. The largest group is the Global Council, which 'focuses on high-level governance tasks and provides a forum for open discussion and communication among KPMG member firms'. It includes representation from 54 member firms. The principal governance and oversight body of KPMG International is the Global Board. Chairman of the Global Board is

Timothy Flynn, from the US organization, while John Harrison from KPMG China acts as Deputy Chairman. Also on the board is the CEO, Michael Wareing, originally from the UK, and the chairmen of each of the three regions; John Veihmeyer for the Americas; Carlson Tong for Asia-Pacific; and John Griffith Jones for Europe, the Middle East, Africa and India. Furthermore, senior partners representing 19 countries are also members of this decision-making body. Key responsibilities of the Global Board are 'the approval of the KPMG strategy, the protection and enhancement of the brand, oversight of the management of KPMG International, as well as the approval of policies and procedures'. The third body is the Global Executive Team, which is the principal management body of KPMG International. It is led by the Chairman, and includes the Deputy Chairman, the CEO, global practice heads, regional leaders and a number of country senior partners. The Global Executive Team 'drives the execution of the strategy approved by the Global Board and establishes processes to monitor and enforce policy compliance. By including executive members as well as regional and country representation, the Global Executive Team is able to make decisions that represent the best interests of member firms and ensure implementation of those decisions in a timely, efficient manner'. The Global Executive Team is supported by Global Steering Groups that focus on executing the global strategy and the business plans in their respective areas.

One of the big strategic moves made during the last ten years was the decision in 2001 to divest the bulk of the advisory activities in a number of countries, under regulatory pressure in the wake of the demise of Arthur Anderson. In the US these advisory services were separated and brought to the stock market as a new company, BearingPoint, while the UK and Dutch activities were sold to Atos Origin. However, since then, KPMG has decided to rebuild its advisory services, once again becoming an important player in this market. In 2008, advisory services achieved sales of US$7.27 billion, focusing on areas such as restructuring, mergers and acquisitions, corporate finance, risk and compliance, performance management and IT services. Sales on the auditing side amounted to US$10.67 billion, while in the third core area, tax, sales totalled US$4.73 billion.

Within this context, Herman Dijkhuizen was appointed head of the Dutch organization in October 2008, taking over from Ben van der Veer, who had been chairman for over ten years. KPMG Netherlands is headquartered near Amsterdam and employs approximately 4500 people. Together they realized revenues of € 715 million, more or less - with the same 50/30/20 split between audit, advisory and tax services as within the broader KPMG network. Although working in a country the size of a postage stamp, KPMG has 17 offices in the Netherlands, as being close to local clients is seen as extremely important, particularly for the audit services. An oddity of the Dutch organization is that the tax activities are organized into a separate entity, KPMG Meijburg & Co., which is an association of 49 private limited liability companies. KPMG Netherlands and KPMG Meijburg share some facilities, but are separate members of KPMG International, and Dijkhuizen has no formal authority over the tax activities.

Although a relatively young man (47), Dijkhuizen had been with KPMG for almost 20 years, having started his career as accountant straight out of high school. During this period he had got to know the company as highly professional, hard working and performance-driven. He was particularly attracted to the type of people working for the company; friendly, extremely competent and dedicated to their work and clients. Dijkhuizen had probably been chosen for the position of chairman of the board because he combined outspokenness and firmness with charm and the ability to mobilize others to get things done. Moreover, he had been a member of the board since 2006, giving him the opportunity to shape his opinion about the direction in which he would like to lead the company.

He summarized his vision as 'one by being one'; by working as one team he believed that KPMG could reach the number one spot in the Dutch market. Much to his dislike, KPMG was the number three in the Netherlands, just behind Deloitte and PwC. For Dijkhuizen it was a stimulating goal to pull ahead of these competitors and build a sustainable leading position for KPMG. But this could only be achieved, he believed, by working together more closely within the company. For instance, to offer clients a more integrated solution to their problems, it was often necessary to get people from audit, consultancy and even tax to coordinate their activities. Other clients required more coordination across regions in the Netherlands and across borders internationally. Furthermore, sharing leads and introducing colleagues to prospective clients was an area where more cooperation could result in extra business. On the competence side, Dijkhuizen also recognized significant room for sharing across industry sector units and across countries.

Yet sharing and coordinating were not deeply engrained in the culture. As a firm with over 200 partners, each with their own targets and area of responsibility, the natural tendency had always been to literally 'mind your own business'. KPMG Netherlands, much like the other country organizations, had been structured into a variety of specialist units, centring around a particular competence, product, industry sector or geographic area, and run by one or a few partners. Each unit had a high level of internal cohesion and joint sense of mission, but this mutual commitment was not necessarily felt towards the broader Dutch organization, let alone the international firm. Working in relatively small units had the additional advantage of being flexible and responsive to client needs, while having the freedom to experiment with innovative service offerings. Moreover, each unit was accountable for their own results and rewards could be distributed accordingly.

It was clear to Dijkhuizen that a majority of the partners agreed that more coordination was needed. In 2007 a vote had been held among the Dutch partners on whether to engage in a cross-border merger with the KPMG organizations in the UK, Germany and Switzerland. This vote was just short of the required two-thirds majority needed to be adopted, leaving the other three country organizations to proceed without the participation of the Dutch. This episode made clear to Dijkhuizen that while many partners agreed with the direction he had in mind, many others still needed to be brought

on board. The question was how to convince these partners, and many other doubters in the organization, that the merger was the best way forward. Of course, he could force the issue and try for a second vote, but even if this were a success he ran the risk of losing dissatisfied partners, who could take their clients and their people elsewhere. Yet, giving up and accepting the status quo of a loose federation was not really an option he was willing to consider.

The broader issue raised by his conundrum was whether this was the best way to develop strategy within KPMG. Needing to get the buy in of so many partners was time consuming and there was a real threat that the resulting strategy would be a bland compromise. Maybe a stronger top-down decision-making structure would be more efficient and effective, both inside the Dutch organization as within the international KPMG network. Perhaps it was time for the Global Executive Teams to be given more power to make decisions on the strategy and structure of KPMG. Yet, on the other hand, the question was whether existing partners would be willing to work in a more top-down organization. But not only partners; the new generation of recruits were asking for even higher levels of empowerment and involvement in the strategy-making process. More than previous generations, they didn't want to be 'foot soldiers', but wanted to participate in decision-making and setting the direction of the organization.

For Dijkhuizen it was an interesting start to his new job. Lucky for him, he had plenty of consultants around that could help him.

Sources: www.kpmg.com; *KPMG International Annual Review 2008*; *Accountancynieuws*, 20 September 2007, 7 November 2008; *The Economist*, 19 July 2007; *Memory Magazine*, October 2008.

PERSPECTIVES ON THE ORGANIZATIONAL CONTEXT

I claim not to have controlled events, but confess plainly that events have controlled me.

Abraham Lincoln (1809–1865); American president

While the pressures for both control and chaos are clear, this does leave managers with the challenging question of how they must reconcile two opposite, and at least partially incompatible, demands. Gaining a considerable level of top management control over the development of the organization will to some extent be at odds with a policy of accepting, or even encouraging, organizational chaos. To control or not to control, that is the question.

And yet again managers should not hope to find widespread consensus in the strategic management literature on what the optimal answer is for dealing with these two conflicting pressures. For among strategy academics and business practitioners alike, opinions differ strongly with regard to the best balance between control and chaos. Although many writers do indicate that there may be different styles in dealing with the paradox and that these different styles might be more effective under different circumstances (e.g. Strebel, 1994; Vroom and Jago, 1988), most authors still exhibit a strong preference for a particular approach – which is duly called the 'modern' or 'new' style, or better yet, '21st century practices' (Ireland and Hitt, 1999).

Following the dialectical enquiry method used in previous chapters, here the two diametrically opposed positions will be identified and discussed. On the one hand, there are those who argue that top managers should lead from the front. Top managers should dare to take on the responsibility of imposing a new strategic agenda on the organization and should be at the forefront in breaking away from organizational inheritance where necessary. This point of view, with its strong emphasis on control and leading top-down, will be referred to as the 'organizational leadership perspective'. This view is also known as the strategic leadership perspective (e.g. Cannella and Monroe, 1997; Rowe, 2001), but to avoid confusion with the industry leadership perspective discussed in Chapter 8, here the prefix 'organizational' is preferred. On the other hand, there are people who believe that managers rarely have the ability to shape their organizations at will, but rather that organizations develop according to their own dynamics. These strategists argue that in most organizations no one is really in control and that managers should not focus their energy on attempting to impose developments top-down, but rather focus on facilitating processes of self-organization. This point of view, with its strong emphasis on chaos and facilitating bottom-up processes, will be referred to as the 'organizational dynamics perspective'.

The organizational leadership perspective

 To proponents of the organizational leadership perspective, top management can – and should – take charge of the organization. In their view, organizational inertia and a growing misfit between the organization and its environment are not an inevitable state of affairs, but result from a failure of leadership. Bureaucracy, organizational fiefdoms, hostile relationships, inflexible corporate cultures, rigid competences and resistance to change – all of these organizational diseases exist, but they are not unavoidable facts of organizational life. 'Healthy' organizations guard against falling prey to such degenerative illnesses, and when symptoms do arise it is a task of the leader to address them. If organizations do go 'out of control', it is because weak leadership has failed to deal with a creeping ailment. The fact that there are many sick, poorly controllable companies does not mean that sickness should be accepted as the natural condition.

At the basis of the organizational leadership perspective lies the belief that if people in organizations are left to 'sort things out' by themselves, this will inevitably degenerate into a situation of strategic drift (see Chapter 4). Without somebody to quell political infighting, set a clear strategic direction, force through tough decisions, and supervise disciplined implementation, the organization will get bogged down in protracted internal bickering. Without somebody to champion a new vision, rally the troops and lead from the front, the organization will never get its heavy mass in motion. Without somebody who radiates confidence and cajoles people into action, the organization will not be able to overcome its risk averseness and conservatism. In short, leaders are needed to counteract the inherent inertia characteristic of human organization.

As organizational order and direction do not happen spontaneously, the 'visible hand' of management is indispensable for the proper functioning of the organization (e.g. Child, 1972; Cyert, 1990, Reading 9.1). And this hand must be firm. Managers cannot afford to take a *laissez-faire* attitude towards their task as leader – to lead means to get the organizational members to follow, and this is usually plain hard work (e.g. Bennis and Nanus, 1985; Kelley, 1988). To convince people in the organization to let themselves be led, managers cannot simply fall back on their position power. To be able to steer organizational developments managers need considerable personal power. To be successful, managers must be trusted, admired and respected. The forcefulness of their personality and the persuasiveness of their vision must be capable of capturing people's attention and commitment. And as leaders, managers must also be politically agile, able to build coalitions where necessary to get their way.

Of course, not all managers have the qualities needed to be effective leaders – either by nature or nurture. Some theorists emphasize the importance of 'nature', arguing that managers require specific personality traits to be successful leaders (e.g. House and Aditya, 1997; Tucker, 1968). Yet, other theorists place more emphasis on 'nurture', arguing that most effective leadership behaviour can be learned if enough effort is exerted (e.g. Kotter, 1990; Nanus, 1992). Either way, the importance of having good leadership makes finding and developing new leaders one of the highest priorities of the existing top management team.

To proponents of the organizational leadership perspective, being a leader does not mean engaging in simple top-down, command-and-control management. There are circumstances where the CEO or the top management team design strategies in isolation and then impose them on the rest of the organization. This type of direct control is sometimes necessary to push through reorganizations or to make major acquisitions. In other circumstances, however, the top managers can control organizational behaviour more indirectly. Proposals can be allowed to emerge bottom-up, as long as top management retains its power to approve or terminate projects as soon as they become serious plans (e.g. Bourgeois and Brodwin, 1983; Quinn, 1980, Reading 3.2). Some authors suggest that top management might even delegate some decision-making powers to lower level managers, but still control outcomes by setting clear goals, developing a conducive incentive system and fostering a particular culture (e.g. Senge, 1990b, Reading 9.3; Tichy and Cohen, 1997).

What leaders should not do, however, is to relinquish control over the direction of the organization. The strategies do not have to be their own ideas, nor do they have to carry out everything themselves. But they should take upon themselves the responsibility for leading the organization in a certain direction and achieving results. If leaders let go of the helm, organizations will be set adrift, and will be carried by the prevailing winds and currents in directions unknown. Someone has to be in control of the organization, otherwise its behaviour will be erratic. Leadership is needed to ensure that the best strategy is followed.

In conclusion, the organizational leadership perspective holds that the upper echelons of management can, and should, control the strategy process and by extension the strategy content. The CEO, or the top management team (e.g. Finkelstein and Hambrick, 1996; Hambrick and Mason, 1984), should have a grip on the organization's process of strategy formation and should be able to impose their will on the organization. Leaders should strive to overcome organizational inertia and adapt the organization to the strategic direction they intend. This type of controlled strategic behaviour is what Chandler (1962) had in mind when he coined the aphorism 'structure follows strategy' – the organizational structure should be adapted to the strategy intended by the decision-maker. In the organizational leadership perspective it would be more fitting to expand Chandler's maxim to 'organization follows strategy' – all aspects of the company should be matched to the strategist's intentions.

EXHIBIT 9.2   THE ORGANIZATIONAL LEADERSHIP PERSPECTIVE

NATIONAL AUSTRALIA BANK: NEW STEWART-SHIP

In January 2004 Australia's largest retail bank, National Australia Bank (NAB), was in a crisis. For years it had been criticized as bureaucratic and complacent, while many business commentators seriously questioned its stated ambition of becoming a global player. In 2001 its reputation had already suffered a severe blow when huge errors in interest rate calculations at its US HomeSide unit became known, eventually leading to a loss of US$3.6 billion. Although NAB conducted an internal investigation to identify the source of the errors, no findings were made public and no executives were fired, which did not boost confidence that such mishaps would not happen again. So when in late 2003 it was announced that four members of the foreign exchange options trading desk had lost a hefty AUS$360 million through unauthorized trading in currency options, this was one scandal too many, making CEO Frank Cicutto's exit unavoidable and the crisis complete. His replacement would have the Herculean task of 'cleaning out the stables'; changing the organizational processes to avoid more mishaps, but more fundamentally transforming the inward-looking bureaucratic culture to a more customer-centric open one. The new CEO would have to salvage NAB's dented reputation and show how the bank could be put back on track to becoming a serious actor on the global stage.

Just five years later, the task was completed. NAB had been spectacularly transformed and was weathering the credit crisis with flying colours. The source of the radical rejuvenation of this 150-year-old institution? New stewardship, or actually Stewart-ship. In February 2004 the Scotsman John Stewart had been appointed CEO, barely six months after having been hired to revitalize NAB's lacklustre UK operations. He was selected because his fresh management style – easy going, open,

forthright and customer-focused – contrasted starkly with the old formal, bureaucratic, Melbourne-head-office-centric culture. It was his leadership that drove the transformation.

One of his first acts on becoming CEO was to write an open letter to all NAB customers saying that he was committed to 'listening and observing, so that I can fully understand our great potential and address our shortcomings'. In contrast to NAB tradition, as soon as the investigators reported that they found 'excessive focus on process, documentation and manuals rather than on substance, along with arrogance in dealing with the warning signs', Stewart immediately opened up to the media. He criticized the 'complacent and arrogant' corporate culture and vowed to 'weed out the cultural misfits' by cleaning out top management and to introduce strict new risk controls. In just four weeks, a vision with a clear strategic agenda began to take shape – change the culture, hire a new, talented leadership team and return to customer-focused banking rather than corporate instrument trading as the basis for profits.

By the end of 2004, there were six new non-executive directors and two additional executive directors and within two years, not a single member of the bank's previous top management team, internally nicknamed the pharaohs, had survived. At the same time, he established a new set of corporate principles, to set the platform for cultural change. In a series of sweeping operational changes in his first year, Stewart restructured NAB's information technology operations, cutting staff and costs, and he overhauled NAB's performance-based, short-term focused, remuneration system which he said led to 'bad behaviour'. Furthermore, he got rid of consultants and NAB's focus on 'consultantitis' for decision-making. He also put more business bankers into the branch networks, removed dozens of restrictions on their practices and adopted more aggressive lending practices to investment property borrowers to rebuild market share.

▶

Big changes continued through 2005 and 2006, including the sale of many non-core assets and a reorganization into three regional businesses: National Australia Bank (Australia), Yorkshire Bank and Clydesdale Bank (United Kingdom) and Bank of New Zealand (New Zealand). The internal transformation was mirrored by a new external look, with a quirky lower-case 'nab' logo to reflect the friendlier and more accessible face of the bank. But most importantly, the cultural change continued apace, with Stewart committed to breaking down silos, and what he called the delusion, hubris and incompetence that he felt had led to the bank's slide. CEO of the Australian business, Ahmed Fahour, warned that there would be 'public hangings' if the cultural change programme at the heart of NAB's recovery programme did not take hold.

By the end of 2008, Stewart felt that the cultural transformation had made significant progress and that the company's international ambitions could be revisited. Despite 2008 being the stormiest in the history of the global financial system, NAB had performed relatively well, declaring a profit of AUS$3.9 billion, down only 11% on the previous year. In the coming years many banks would be available at very reasonable prices. But Stewart decided that this challenge should be left to a successor and that it was time for him to retire to his other Stewart-ship – one floating in the Mediterranean.

Co-authors: Graham Hubbard and Judy Hubbard

Sources: NAB Annual Reports 2007, 2008; *Australian Financial Review*, 14 February, 12 May and 29 September 2005; *The Australian*, 6 December 2008.

The organizational dynamics perspective

To proponents of the organizational dynamics perspective, such an heroic depiction of leadership is understandable, but usually more myth than reality. There might be a few great, wise, charismatic managers that rise to the apex of organizations, but unfortunately, all other organizations have to settle for regular mortals. Strong leaders are an exception, not the norm, and even their ability to mould the organization at will is highly exaggerated – good stories for best-selling autobiographies, but legend nevertheless (e.g. Chen and Meindl, 1991; Kets de Vries, 1994). Yet, the belief in the power of leadership is quite popular, among managers and the managed alike (e.g. Meindl, Ehrlich and Dukerich, 1985; Pfeffer, 1977). Managers like the idea that as leaders of an organization or organizational unit, they can make a difference. To most, 'being in control' is what management is all about. They have a penchant for attributing organizational results to their own efforts (e.g. Hayward, Rindova and Pollock, 2004; Sims and Lorenzi, 1992). As for 'the managed', they too often ascribe organizational success or failure to the figurehead leader, whatever that person's real influence has been – after all, they too like the idea that somebody is in control. In fact, both parties are subscribing to a seductively simple 'great person model' of how organizations work. The implicit assumption is that an individual leader, by the strength of personality, can steer large groups of people, like a present-day Alexander the Great.

However seductive, this view of organizational functioning is rarely a satisfactory model. A top manager does not resemble a commander leading the troops into battle, but rather a diplomat trying to negotiate a peace. The top manager is not like a jockey riding a thoroughbred horse, but more like a cowboy herding mules. Organizations are complex social systems, made up of many 'stubborn individuals' with their own ideas, interests and agendas (e.g. Greenwood and Hinings, 1996; Stacey, 1993a). Strategy formation is therefore an inherently political process, that leaders can only influence depending on their power base. The more dispersed the political power, the more difficult it is for a leader to control the organization's behaviour. Even if leaders are granted, or acquire, significant political power to push through their favoured measures, there may still be considerable resistance and guerrilla activities. Political processes within organizations do not signify the derailment of strategic decision-making – politics is the normal state of affairs and few leaders have real control over these political dynamics.

Besides such political limitations, a top manager's ability to control the direction of a company is also severely constrained by the organization's culture. Social norms will have evolved, relationships will have been formed, aspirations will have taken root and cognitive maps will have been shaped. A leader cannot ignore the cultural legacy of the organization's history, as this will be deeply etched into the minds of the organization's members. Any top manager attempting to radically alter the direction of a company will find out that changing the underlying values, perceptions, beliefs and expectations is extremely difficult, if not next to impossible. As Weick (1979) puts it, an organization does not have a culture, it is a culture – shared values and norms are what make an organization. And just as it is difficult to change someone's identity, it is difficult to change an organization's culture (e.g. Schein, 1993; Smircich and Stubbart, 1985). Moreover, as most top managers rise through the ranks to the upper echelons, they themselves are a product of the existing organizational culture. Changing your own culture is like pulling yourself up by your own bootstraps – a great trick, too bad that nobody can do it.

In Chapters 5 and 6, a related argument was put forward, as part of the resource-based view of the firm. One of the basic assumptions of the resource-based view is that building up competences is an arduous task, requiring a relatively long period of time. Learning is a slow process under the best of circumstances, but even more difficult if learning one thing means unlearning something else. The stronger the existing cognitive maps (knowledge), routines (capabilities) and disposition (attitude), the more challenging it is to 'teach an old dog new tricks'. The leader's power to direct and speed up such processes, it was argued, is quite limited (e.g. Barney, 1991, Reading 5.4; Leonard-Barton, 1995).

Taken together, the political, cultural and learning dynamics leave top managers with relatively little direct power over the system they want to steer. Generally, they can react to this limited ability to control in one of two basic ways – they can squeeze tighter or let go. Many managers follow the first route, desperately trying to acquire more power, to gain a tighter grip on the organization, in the vain attempt to become the heroic leader of popular legend. Such a move to accumulate more power commonly results in actions to assert control, including stricter reporting structures, more disciplined accountability, harsher punishment for non-conformists and a shakeout among managers. In this manner, control comes to mean restriction, subordination or even subjugation. Yet, such a step towards authoritarian management will still not bring managers very much further towards having a lasting impact on organizational development.

The alternative route is for managers to accept that they cannot, but also should not try to, tightly control the organization. As they cannot really control organizational dynamics, all heavy-handed control approaches will have little more result than making the organization an unpleasant and oppressive place to work. If managers emphasize control, all they will do is run the risk of killing the organization's ability to innovate and learn. Innovation and learning are very difficult to control, especially the business innovation and learning happening outside of R&D labs. Much of this innovation and learning is sparked by organizational members, out in the markets or on the work floor, questioning the status quo. New ideas often start 'in the margins' of the organization and grow due to the room granted to offbeat opinions. Fragile new initiatives often need to be championed by their owners lower down in the hierarchy and only survive if there is a tolerance for unintended 'misfits' in the organization's portfolio of activities. Only if employees have a certain measure of freedom and are willing to act as intrapreneurs, will learning and innovation be an integral part of the organization's functioning (e.g. Amabile, 1998; Quinn, 1985).

In other words, if managers move beyond their instinctive desire for control and recognize the creative and entrepreneurial potential of self-organization, they will not bemoan their lack of control. They will see that a certain level of organizational chaos can create the conditions for development (e.g. Levy, 1994; Stacey, 1993a, Reading 9.2). According to the organizational dynamics perspective, the task for managers is to use their limited powers to facilitate self-organization (e.g. Beinhocker, 1999; Wheatley and Kellner-Rogers, 1996). Managers can encourage empowerment, stimulate learning and innovation, bring people together, take away bureaucratic hurdles – all very much like the approach by most governments in market economies, who try to establish conditions conducive to entrepreneurial behaviour instead of trying to control economic activity. Managers' most important task is to ensure that the 'invisible hand of self-organization' functions properly, and does not lead to 'out-of-hand disorganization'.

So, does the manager matter? Yes, but in a different sense than is usually assumed. The manager cannot shape the organization – it shapes itself. Organizational developments are the result of complex internal dynamics, which can be summarized as strategy follows organization, instead of the other way around. Managers can facilitate processes of self-organization and thus indirectly influence the direction of development, but at the same time managers are also shaped by the organization they are in.

EXHIBIT 9.3 THE ORGANIZATIONAL DYNAMICS PERSPECTIVE

SEMCO: NEVER UNDER CONTROL

When Ricardo Semler took over his father's pump-making business in 1980, Semco was a US$4 million company, focused on the domestic Brazilian market, and heading for bankruptcy in a severe recession that was to last for most of the decade. By 2007, Semco had expanded beyond pumps to dishwashers, digital scanners, cooling units, mixers, real estate and environmental consultancy, operating as a federation of autonomous businesses, with revenues over US$240 million and about 3000 employees. While a fascinating business success, Semco's turnaround is all the more interesting because it was achieved without the leadership of a charismatic CEO – actually, it was achieved without having a CEO at all. 'I do nothing and see what happens. The company has never been under my control', says Semler.

According to Semler most companies use 'formats that are basically legacies of military hierarchies', which neglect or deny the power of human intuition and democratic participation. Therefore, at Semco major decisions affecting the entire organization, such as the purchase of a new plant site or an acquisition, are put to a democratic vote, while other decisions are taken consensually by all employees involved. Provocatively Semler says of this approach: 'We'll send our sons anywhere in the world to die for democracy, but don't seem to apply the concept to our own companies.'

The alternative organizational configuration of Semco is made up of four concentric circles. The innermost circle consists of six Counselors, who serve as the executive team and take turns as chairperson every six months. Despite being the 90% owner of the company, Semler is only one of these six. Around the Counselors is a circle of Partners, who act as business unit managers. Around them is a circle of Coordinators, who function as first-line supervisors. Everybody else is in the fourth circle, and is called Associate. Additionally there are 'Nucleuses of Technology Innovation', which are 'no-boss' temporary project teams who are freed from their day-to-day work in order to focus on some kind of business improvement project, a new product, a cost reduction programme, a new business plan or the like. And then there is the 'Out of your Mind!' committee, where really crazy ideas can be fielded.

To stimulate information exchange, the offices at Semco have no walls and all memos must be kept to one page, without exception. Furthermore, everyone is trained to read financial statements, and everybody knows the profit and loss statements of the company and their business unit. There are no internal audit groups and no controls on travel expenses, while inventory and storage rooms remain unlocked. But all information is made available to everyone, encouraging self-control. According to Semler, 'freedom is no easy thing. It does not make life carefree, because it introduces difficult choices.'

The members of Semco decide among themselves what their pay will be. The amount is made transparent to all others by regular participation in salary surveys, thus everybody knows what the pay is of everyone else. Furthermore, every member is part of the company-wide profit sharing programme that pays out 23% of a business unit's profits per quarter to the employees. In fact, the payout ratio of 23% was also decided by the employees. Members of a Nucleus of Technology Innovation receive royalties on the achievements of their projects.

As for strategy, Semco has no grand design. Semler readily admits that he has no idea what the company will be making in ten years time: 'I think that strategic planning and vision are often barriers to success.' Semco's approach is largely to let strategy emerge on the basis of opportunities identified by employees close to the market. Where new initiatives can muster enough support among colleagues, they are awarded more time and money to bring them to fruition. In this way, Semco can make the best possible use of the engagement and entrepreneurship of its employees.

'A company full of crazy people?' the Semco website asks. 'A group of nutters? If you think that Semco is something along these lines, you're not entirely wrong.' The website goes on to explain how this culture actually helps Semco to be so innovative. It also summarizes the key elements of the Semco Way: saying what you really think, participation, no formalities, flexible working hours, mandatory vacations, job rotation and no mandatory retirement age. During the last 25 years, employee turnover has been approximately 2% per year.

Summing up the Semco philosophy, Semler told the *Financial Times*:

> At Semco, the basic question we work on is: how do you get people to come to work on a grey Monday morning? This is the only parameter we care about, which is a 100% motivation issue. Everything else – quality, profits, growth – will fall into place, if enough people are interested in coming to work on Monday morning.

Co-author: Peer Ederer

Sources: http://semco.locaweb.com.br; Semler (1994, 1995, 2003); *Financial Times*, 15 May 1997; *Guardian Unlimited*, 17 April 2003; http://mitworld.mit.edu/video/308/; *The Independent Financial Review*, 14 March 2007; *Strategy & Business*, Winter 2005.

INTRODUCTION TO THE DEBATE AND READINGS

An institution is the lengthened shadow of one man.
Ralph Waldo Emerson (1803–1882);
American essayist and poet

Chaos often breeds life, when order breeds habit.
Henry Brooks Adams (1838–1919);
American writer and historian

So, how should organizational development be encouraged? Can the top management of a firm shape the organization to fit with their intended strategy or does the organizational context determine the strategy that is actually followed? And should top management strive to have a tight grip on the organization, or should they leave plenty of room for self-organization?

As before, views differ strongly, both in business practice and in academia; not only in the field of strategy, but also in neighbouring fields such as organizational behaviour, human resource management and innovation management. And not only in the management sciences, but more broadly in the humanities, including sociology, economics, political science and psychology as well. The economic sociologist Duesenberry once remarked that 'economics is all about how people make choices; sociology is all about how they don't have any choices to make'. Although half in jest, his comment does ring true. Much of the literature within the field of economics assumes that people in organizations can freely make choices and have the power to shape their strategy, while possible restraints on their freedom usually come from the environment. Sociological literature, but also psychological and political science work, often features the limitations on individual's freedom. These different disciplinary inclinations are not absolute, but can be clearly recognized in the debate.

With so many conflicting views and incompatible prescriptions on the issue of organizational development, it is again up to each individual strategist to form their own opinion on how best to deal with the paradox of control and chaos. But to help strategists to come to grips with the variety of perspectives on this issue, four readings have been selected that each shed their own light on the topic. As in previous chapters, the first two readings will be representative of the two poles in this debate (see Table 9.1), while the second set of two readings will bring in extra angles to add further depth to the discussion.

To open the debate on behalf of the organizational leadership perspective, Reading 9.1 has been selected entitled 'Defining Leadership and Explicating the Process', which is by one of the 'godfathers' of organizational theory, Richard Cyert. In this article, Cyert starts by summarizing the functions of a leader: determining the organizational structure, selecting managers, setting strategic objectives, controlling internal and external information flows, maintaining morale and making important decisions. But while some authors who take an organizational leadership perspective tend to conjure up an image of the leader as an octopus, with many long arms performing all of these tasks at the same time, Cyert has a more human, two-armed individual in mind. His view of the leader is not the control freak who wants to run the organization single-handedly, but a person who can 'heavily influence the process of determining the goals of the organization', and then can 'have the participants in the organization behave in the ways that the leader believes are desirable'. This definition of leadership has two important ingredients. First, Cyert argues that leaders need to take the initiative in determining a vision and organizational goals,

TABLE 9.1 Organizational leadership versus organizational dynamics perspective

	Organizational leadership perspective	*Organizational dynamics perspective*
Emphasis on	Control over chaos	Chaos over control
Organizational development	Controllable creation process	Uncontrollable evolutionary process
Development metaphor	The visible hand	The invisible hand
Development direction	Top-down, imposed organization	Bottom-up, self-organization
Decision-making	Authoritarian (rule of the few)	Democratic (rule of the many)
Change process	Leader shapes new behaviour	New behaviour emerges from interactions
Change determinants	Leader's vision and skill	Political, cultural and learning dynamics
Organizational malleability	High, fast	Low, slow
Development driver	Organization follows strategy	Strategy follows organization
Normative implication	Strategize, then organize	Strategizing and organizing intertwined

although they do this in interaction with other organizational members. Secondly, Cyert argues that leaders need to focus on modifying the people's behaviours. To get people to move in the desired direction, he states that it is not so important what a leader decides or tells people to do. Rather, an effective leader 'controls the allocation of the attention focus of the participants in the organization . . . so that their attention is allocated to the areas that the leader considers important'. In this way, Cyert believes, organizational members will voluntarily align their behaviours with where the leader wants to go. He admits that 'this conception of leadership might strike some as making the leader a manipulative person', but feels that if leaders have a genuine belief in what they are doing and have an honest dedication to the people in the organization, exerting this type of leadership is justified. Although Cyert is well aware that organizations are complex systems of interacting human beings, his unquestioned supposition throughout the reading is that leadership is *possible* and *necessary*. As many writers taking an organizational leadership perspective, the demand for top management control is an implicit assumption – the main issue discussed is how to get power and how to exert control. Cyert's preference is for more indirect control, implicitly leaving some room for bottom-up self-organization.

As the opening reading to represent the organizational dynamics perspective (Reading 9.2), an article by Ralph Stacey has been selected, entitled 'Strategy as Order Emerging from Chaos'. Stacey argues that top managers cannot, and should not even try, to control the organization and its strategy. In his view, the organizational dynamics involved in strategy formation, learning and change are too complex to simply be controlled by managers. He states that 'sometimes the best thing a manager can do is to let go and allow things to happen'. The resulting chaos, he argues, does not mean that the organization will be a mess – a lack of control, he assures, does not mean that the organization will be adrift. His reasoning is that non-linear feedback systems, such as organizations, have a self-organizing ability, which 'can produce controlled behaviour, even though no one is in control'. In his view, real strategic change requires the chaos of contention and conflict to destroy old recipes and to encourage the quest for new solutions. The 'self-organizing processes of political interaction and complex learning' ensure that chaos does not result in disintegration. Hence, in Stacey's opinion, it is management's task to help create a situation of bounded instability in which strategy can emerge. Managers do have a role in organizations, but it can hardly be called leadership – 'leaders' must direct their efforts at influencing the organizational context in such a way that the right conditions prevail for self-organization to take place. 'Leaders' are largely facilitators, making it possible for new and unexpected strategies to develop spontaneously.

To complement the two 'opening statements' in the debate, two additional readings have been selected for this chapter that shed more light on aspects of the organizational context that have not yet been sufficiently accentuated. Reading 9.3 is 'Building Learning Organizations' by Peter Senge. This reading summarizes many of the major points of Senge's (1990a) acclaimed book *The Fifth Discipline: The Art and Practice of the Learning Organization*. This reading has been selected to delve more deeply into the role of learning in the organizational development process. Both the organizational leadership perspective and the organizational dynamics perspective acknowledge that learning is an important part of ongoing organizational adaptation, but the two sides emphasize different aspects of the learning process. Proponents of the organizational leadership perspective, like Cyert, highlight the role of leaders in guiding organizational learning and stress how learning needs to be channelled in the most appropriate direction to be valuable. However, advocates of the organizational dynamics perspective, like Stacey, point to the need for organizational members to think for themselves and to strike out in bold new directions, unlimited by rigid organizational paradigms or corporate 'thought police'. In his contribution Senge takes arguments from both sides in an attempt to find a way to 'build a learning organization'. Senge agrees with Stacey that leaders cannot learn on behalf of their organizations and then push through the strategic changes they believe should be made. In his view, leaders must facilitate organizational learning – leaders 'are responsible for building organizations where people are continually expanding their capabilities to shape their future'. Creating organizations that want to adapt, learn and evolve means avoiding the traditional sources of inertia. Senge believes that one of the keys to continuous learning is motivation. He suggests that the drive to learn can best be stimulated by establishing a creative tension between the current reality and a compelling vision of the future. But, Senge points out, creating a shared vision and designing the organization in a way that enables learning, instead of impeding it, are clearly leadership tasks. This is where he swings more to Cyert's point of view. In his opinion, leaders are needed to perform these important formative tasks, as well as to act as organizational teachers. A teacher is not someone with all the right answers, but a leader who can ask challenging questions and can shake up existing cognitive maps. Together, these 'new tasks' of leaders give them plenty of scope to influence the future direction of the firm, while at the same time leaving enough room for organizational members to also contribute to the organization's development.

The final reading is 'The Knowing-Doing Gap', by Jeffrey Pfeffer and Robert Sutton, an article based on their (1999b) book *The Knowing-Doing Gap: How Smart Companies Turn Knowledge Into Action*. This reading has been selected to review many of the sources of inertia that frustrate organizational development and to highlight the role of knowledge management, both as a driver and a major inhibitor of organizational development. The main thesis of Pfeffer and Sutton is that most organizations actually know what they should do, but somehow don't do it – most organizations don't suffer from *ignorance*, but only from a lack of *implementation*. And where there is a gap between 'ignorance and knowing', this is easier to bridge than the gap between 'knowing and doing'. This observation does not fit well with the conception of strong top management control put forward by the organizational leadership perspective, because implementation should in theory be something that is easily controllable, using either throughput or output controls. Yet, Pfeffer and Sutton argue that various organizational processes are at work, which interfere with the translation of organizational knowledge into concrete organizational action. In their view, managers can play an important role in solving the knowing-doing problem, but not by engaging in traditional control-oriented behaviour, imposing programmes on docile employees. Their practical advice for managers is to create conditions for *knowing through doing* – emphasizing action and getting organizational members to learn along the way. In this approach, managers have influence on what is going on in the organization, by outlining a vision, teaching others hands-on, rewarding action, encouraging cooperation and measuring progress, but the engagement of all organizational members is required to shape the firm together. Pfeffer and Sutton do not use the word self-organization, but their advocacy of active participation of all people in the firm in realizing organizational development shows that they clearly appreciate the importance of organizational chaos as well.

READING

9.1

Defining leadership and explicating the process

By Richard M. Cyert[1]

It is true that organizations, whether for-profit or not-for-profit, are in need of leadership. Most people in leadership positions in organizations tend to be managers rather than leaders. They administer, allocate resources, resolve conflicts, and go home at night convinced that they have done a good day's work. They may have, but they have not provided the organization with the critical ingredient that every organization needs – leadership (Zalesnik, 1977; Bavelas, 1964).

It is possible to generalize three broad functions that a leader performs. I specify these functions as organizational, interpersonal, and decisional. The organizational function involves the development of the organizational structure and the selection of people to manage the various segments of an organization. It involves the determination of the goal structure and the control of the internal and external information flows. This function requires the leader to make certain that the participants in the organization and the relevant groups external to the organization are knowledgeable about the organization.

The interpersonal function involves the maintenance of morale in the organization. It reflects the degree of concern about the humanness of the organization. It requires the leader to pay attention to individual concerns.

The decision function involves the making of decisions that must be made in order for the organization to progress toward the achievement of its goals. This is the function that has traditionally been associated with leadership.

Nature of leadership

Although there is little agreement on the definition of leadership, most students of leadership would agree that the three functions just described are clearly a part of the definition. In a broad sense, the leader is attempting to have the participants in the organization behave in the ways that the leader believes are desirable. A major step in performing the organizational function is to define desirable behaviour.

Desirability is determined by the goals of the organization. The leader should heavily influence the process of determining the goals of the organization. The determination of a goal structure for an organization is the result of a series of interactions among the participants and between the participants and the leader. The goal structure represents the vision of the leader and of the organization's other members. Projecting a vision for the organization is another characteristic that is commonly associated with leadership.

The vision embedded in the goal structure is essentially a map that is used as a guide for the direction of the organization. Clearly, the map is more detailed as one's view shifts to sub-units within the organization. At the top leadership position, a number of broad principles are specified to guide the overall construction of the vision.

These principles relate to the process by which the organization's vision can be constantly modified and reshaped. The specification of strategic principles and of the process by which the vision is modified is another characteristic of leadership. The leader is the helmsman, and the goal structure, together with the strategic principle, is the means by which the leader steers the organization. But, an organization is an interactive system of human beings, and its performance depends on the behaviour of individuals. Regardless of the policies that are promulgated, the participants in the organization will determine the destiny of the organization by their productivity.

The goal structure is important in the leading of an organization. However, organizations can have conflicting goals (Cyert and March, 1963), primarily because they tend to goals sequentially. Also, each unit in an organization can focus on different goals. These goals may conflict, but they can all be embraced by the organization (Birnbaum, 1988).

---

[1]Source: This article was adapted from 'Defining Leadership and Explicating the Process', R.M. Cyert: © 1990 Jossey-Bass Inc. Publishers. This material is used by permission of John Wiley & Sons, Ltd.

A definition of leadership

The concept of attention focus is one of the most important variables in organization theory (March and Simon, 1958; Cyert and March, 1963). Participants in an organization allocate their attention to a variety of matters. The amount of attention allocated to each matter has been a subject of study. It can affect the organization in crucial ways. For example, if attention is not given to problems concerned with the future, the organization may flounder from myopia – too much attention to immediate problems. Clearly, the problems, concerns, ideas, concepts, and so on to which the participants pay attention will determine the long-run viability of the organization. The control of this allocation of attention is vital to the organization.

In discussing the formation of the organizational coalition, Cyert and March (1963, p. 39) argue that one of the five basic mechanisms for a theory of coalition formation is 'an attention-focus mechanism'; however, 'we know rather little about the actual mechanisms that control this attention factor.' In this paper, I argue that the leadership function is one of the mechanisms that controls the attention factor.

In fact, my definition of leadership is that the leader controls the allocation of the attention focus of the participants in the organization. The leader of any organization, no matter how small or large it is, affects the allocation of attention by participants. In a decentralized, structured organization, standard operating procedures determine the allocation of attention if the leader does not intervene. In general, in any organization where managers dominate, structured rules tend to influence the allocation of attention, but the leader will try to capture the attention focus of the participants so that their attention is allocated to the areas that the leader considers important.

The issues or problems on which the leader attempts to focus attention reflect, at least in part, the vision of the organization that exists in the leader's mind. This vision will generally have been developed from discussions with relevant participants, from the leader's experience and knowledge, and from his or her assessment of the organization's future in the light of existing information. This vision will change over time as the leader gets feedback from the organization's performance. As the vision changes, so does the priority of individual issues and problems to which the leader wishes to allocate the attention of participants. Organizations are dynamic, and attention allocation is an ongoing and always necessary process. Leadership, in the sense in which I have defined it here, must also be continuous.

Leadership, as I define it here, must also have substance. A leader cannot succeed in allocating attention without a strong intellectual position for a particular attention focus. This position can only come from a knowledge of the organization and of the area in which it functions. This need for specific knowledge is one of the reasons why it is difficult for executives to move from an organization in one industry to an organization in a different industry. The executive may be able to function as a manager, but he or she will have more difficulty functioning as a leader.

A second definition of leadership

Subgroups develop in every organization. Participants involved in the same department or in similar endeavours form a natural alliance (March and Simon, 1958). Important individuals in an organization can constitute subgroups in and of themselves. The point is that subgroups can develop a goal structure of their own, and this goal structure may conflict with that of the central organization.

The leader must bring about conformity between subgroup goals and the goals of the central organization. In other words, the leader must convince the members of the subgroup to give up or modify their goals and adopt the central organization's goals. In some cases, of course, the leader may decide that the central goals should be changed in the direction of the subgroup's goals. The point is that the leader cannot tolerate conflicting goals in the organization (Vroom and Jago, 1988). There must be a single goal structure, and everyone in the organization must accept it if the organization's goals are to be achieved. The concept of teamwork – of everyone working together – is a necessity for any organization.

Definitions of leadership and the three leadership functions

Having defined leadership, it is now logical for us to discuss the methods that one uses in the act of leadership. However, before we move to that topic, it will be useful to relate our two definitions of leadership – which really are essentially one – to the three functions of leadership discussed earlier.

In order to understand the leader's role, we need to go back to the distinction between managers and leaders. Every leader must perform some managerial functions, even though every manager cannot take a leadership role.

For example, in an effort to change organizational performance, many managers attempt to change the structure of their organizations. Currently, in an effort to reduce costs, many managers are attempting to reduce the number of hierarchical levels. Sometimes, the structure is changed by modifying the reporting relationship among units. The level at which decisions are made can also be changed. The organization can become more centralized or more decentralized with respect to decision making. Yet, changes in organizational structure alone are not likely to have any lasting impact on the organization's performance unless the structure affects the basic desire of participants to improve their performance.

The leader recognizes that it is necessary to focus the attention of participants on factors that will change performance. Thus, the leader makes changes in structure for their effect on attention focus, not because he or she believes that organizational structure alone can change the performance of participants. If the leader wishes to focus attention on costs, he or she looks at changes in the organization's structure that will encourage participants to allocate their attention to costs. Increased decentralization will often accomplish such a shift. The point is that leaders look at organizational tasks with a view to the impact that their actions will have on the attention focus of participants. Attention focus is central to the performance of the organizational function of leadership.

A similar statement can be made about the interpersonal function. The leader's role is to relate to the participants in ways that will affect their attention focus. The interpersonal function of leadership is sometimes viewed as one that holds the leader responsible for making everyone in the organization feel good. Friendliness and openness can be good for an organization if they help participants to focus their attention on the elements that the leader deems to be important. The interpersonal function is extremely important, but the leader must relate his or her actions in this area to the desired impact on attention focus. There is ample evidence that there is a low correlation between high morale and high productivity (Misumi, 1985).

The relation between the decisional function and attention focus is perhaps the most interesting of the three. Bavelas (1964, p. 206) defined leadership in terms of decision-making: 'leadership consists of the continuous choice-making process that permits the organization as a whole to proceed toward its objectives despite all sorts of internal and external perturbations.' More explicitly, he regards leadership as

consisting of the reduction of uncertainty; this reduction is achieved by making choices.

This definition, which is close to the commonly accepted view of leadership, is quite different from those propounded here. My definitions focus on the leader's responsibility for modifying the behaviour of participants in the organization. They assume that behaviour is affected by the items to which individuals allocate their attention. The leader is able to capture the attention focus of participants. The leader gets participants to allocate attention to the items that he or she deems to be important. There is no question that the decisions that a leader makes are ways of making the priorities for attention clear. That is the aspect of decision-making that in my view is part of leadership, not the fact that decision-making reduces uncertainty. Nevertheless, it could be argued that influencing the allocation of attention tends to reduce uncertainty.

Studies of decision-making tend to show that decisions are rarely made by a single individual without regard to the views of the members of the organization. Leadership in an organization has to be less individualistic than it is in a combat situation where the leader may single-handedly eliminate a machine gun nest. Decision-making in an organization must take into account the fact that members of the organization are interested in the direction that the organization takes. If the leader has captured the attention focus of the members, then it is possible to demonstrate 'the highest expressions of personal leadership' (Bavelas, 1964) and carry the organization along with those expressions.

Methods of leadership

If leadership is adequately encompassed by my definitions, we may ask how leadership is actually implemented in an organization. How does a person act in an organization when he or she plays a leadership role and wants to exert leadership?

There are at least three general approaches that are taken. They can be classified as communication, role modelling, and reward systems. I will discuss each of these approaches.

Communication

The first action that influences attention focus is oral interaction. These talks are ways of capturing the attention focus of participants. The ultimate aim is to change the behaviour of people in the organization by influencing their focus. The underlying theory is that individuals' behaviour is controlled by their attention focus. Put another way, the leader brings about the behaviour that he or she desires by convincing participants to focus their attention on the ideas and actions that the leader considers important.

The interesting and difficult problem is that the methods of communication in organizations, are not well defined (March and Simon, 1958). In general, it is best to use a variety of communication channels. These channels can vary from one-on-one discussions to departmental meetings and meetings of the whole faculty and staff.

The leader also uses written communication. Again, different approaches must be found. Written communications can vary from personal letters to letters to the whole organization and formal reports. Even articles written for newspapers or other publications can be used to explicate the leader's desired priorities for the allocation of attention among participants.

Communication is perhaps the most important mechanism of leadership. The leader must have a clear understanding of the message that he or she is communicating, and he or she must be aware that the goal of communication is to influence the allocation of attention of the organization's members.

Role model

As a way of continuing to communicate with members of the organization, the leader must take into account the impact of his or her behaviour on the attention focus of participants. The actions of the leader clearly represent the ideas that he or she considers to be important. If a university president is trying to emphasize research as an activity of importance, he or she should engage in research activity as well as emphasize research in the direct communications that he or she makes. Role modelling is a case in which actions speak as loudly as words.

The leader's activities are widely known among the members of any organization. Thus, the leader has ample opportunity to affect the attention focus of participants by demonstrating the factors that are important in his or her own behaviour. In other words, role modelling is a form of communication. The leader's behaviour exerts leadership whether the leader intends it or not.

Reward system

The reward system that the leader establishes is another way of reinforcing the attention focus of members. The relationship between particular rewards and performance is not well established. An organization cannot offer a specific monetary award and achieve a particular performance. However, a leader can use rewards to reinforce the priority system for attention allocation that he or she has established. The reward system can lead to both honour and money for recipients. The reward system is also a means of communicating the leader's priorities to participants. Obviously, a reward system cannot guarantee that performance in teaching will improve, but it can supplement the leader's effort to capture the attention focus of participants and allocate attention to areas that the leader considers important.

Conclusion

The theory of leadership just outlined is essentially a simple one. It assumes that participants in an organization behave in accordance with their focus attention. Behaviour follows from the items on which they focus. From this perspective, leadership is the effort to capture the attention focus of the members of an organization. Three mechanisms help to perform the leadership function: communication between leader and participants, role modelling, and reward systems. The three mechanisms are alike in that all are ways of communicating the matters on which the leader wants members to focus their attention. There are other, related mechanisms. My list is not exhaustive. In all cases, the effort is to capture the attention focus of participants.

This conception of leadership might strike some as making the leader a manipulative person (Glassman, 1986). The key is that the leader must believe in what he or she is expressing. Mintzberg (1989) has put it exactly right: 'To my mind, key to the development of an organization ideology, in a new or existing organization, is a leadership with a genuine belief in mission and an honest dedication to the people who must carry it out.'

It is obvious, although I have not emphasized it, that a leader must have the ability and the knowledge needed to select the right items for the attention focus of participants (Mintzberg, 1982). That is, the items singled out for attention must enable the organization to attain its goals. The process of capturing the attention focus is also a dynamic one. The items on which the leader wishes participants to focus will change, and the leader must be perceptive enough to select the new items properly.

Although I have simplified the nature of leadership and the methods by which leadership can be exerted, I do not mean to imply that leadership is anything but complex. In any organization of significant size, the leader uses a system composed of many variables. To attend to the appropriate constituencies and focus their attention on the appropriate items requires thought, planning, energy, conviction, and an ability to persuade.

READING

9.2

Strategy as order emerging from chaos

By Ralph Stacey[1]

There are four important points to make on the recent discoveries about the complex behaviour of dynamic systems, all of which have direct application to human organizations.

Chaos is a form of instability where the specific long-term future is unknowable

Chaos in its scientific sense is an irregular pattern of behaviour generated by well defined nonlinear feedback rules commonly found in nature and human society. When systems driven by such rules operate away from equilibrium, they are highly sensitive to selected tiny changes in their environments, amplifying them into self-reinforcing virtuous and vicious circles that completely alter the behaviour of the system. In other words, the system's future unfolds in a manner dependent upon the precise detail of what it does, what the systems constituting its environments do, and upon chance. As a result of this fundamental property of the system itself, specific links between cause and effect are lost in the history of its development, and the specific path of its long-term future development is completely unpredictable. Over the short term, however, it is possible to predict behaviour because it takes time for the consequences of small changes to build up.

Is there evidence of chaos in business systems? We would conclude that there was if we could point to small changes escalating into large consequences; if we could point to self-reinforcing vicious and virtuous circles; if we could point to feedback that alternates between the amplifying and the damping. It is not difficult to find such evidence.

Creative managers seize on small differences in customer requirements and perceptions to build significant differentiators for their products. Customers may respond to this by switching from other product offerings, leading to a virtuous circle; or they may switch away, causing the kind of vicious circle that Coca-Cola found itself caught up in when it made that famous soft drink slightly sweeter.

Managers create, or at the very least shape, the requirements of their customers through the product offerings they make. Sony created a requirement for personal hi-fi systems through its Walkman offering, and manufacturers and operators have created requirements for portable telephones. Sony and Matsushita created the requirement for video recorders, and when companies supply information systems to their clients, they rarely do so according to a complete specification – instead, the supplier shapes the requirement. When managers intentionally shape customer demands through the offerings they make, this feeds back into customer responses, and managers may increase the impact by intentionally using the copying and spreading effects through which responses to product offerings feed back into other customers' responses. When managers do this, they are deliberately using positive feedback – along with negative feedback controls to meet cost and quality targets, for example – to create business success.

A successful business is also affected by many amplifying feedback processes that are outside the control of its managers and produce effects that they did not intend. Successful businesses are quite clearly characterized by feedback processes that flip between the negative and the positive, the damping and the

[1]Source: This article was reprinted from *Long Range Planning*, Vol. 26, No. 1, R. Stacey, 'Strategy as Order Emerging from Chaos', pp. 23–29, © 1993. With permission from Elsevier.

amplifying; that is, they are characterized by feedback patterns that produce chaos. The long-term future of a creative organization is absolutely unknowable, and no one can intend its future direction over the long term or be in control of it. In such a system long-term plans and visions of future states can be only illusions.

But in chaos there are boundaries around the instability

While chaos means disorder and randomness in the behaviour of a system at the specific level, it also means that there is a qualitative pattern at a general, overall level. The future unfolds unpredictably, but it always does so according to recognizable family-like resemblances. This is what we mean when we say that history repeats itself, but never in the same way. We see this combination of unpredictable specific behaviour within an overall pattern in snowflakes. As two nearby snowflakes fall to the earth, they experience tiny differences in temperature and air impurities. Each snowflake amplifies those differences as they form, and by the time they reach the earth they have different shapes – but they are still clearly snowflakes. We cannot predict the shape of each snowflake, but we can predict that they will be snowflakes. In business, we recognize patterns of boom and recession, but each time they are different in specific terms, defying all attempts to predict them.

Chaos is unpredictable variety within recognizable categories defined by irregular features, that is, an inseparable intertwining of order and disorder. It is this property of being bounded by recognizable qualitative patterns that makes it possible for humans to cope with chaos. Numerous tests have shown that our memories do not normally store information in units representing the precise characteristics of the individual shapes or events we perceive. Instead, we store information about the strength of connection between individual units perceived. We combine information together into categories or concepts using family resemblance-type features. Memory emphasizes general structure, irregular category features, rather than specific content. We remember the irregular patterns rather than the specific features and we design our next actions on the basis of these memorized patterns. And since we design our actions in this manner, chaotic behaviour presents us with no real problem. Furthermore, we are adept at using analogical reasoning and intuition to reflect upon experience and adapt it to new situations, all of which is ideally suited to handling chaos.

Unpredictable new order can emerge from chaos through a process of spontaneous self-organization

When nonlinear feedback systems in nature are pushed far from equilibrium into chaos, they are capable of creating a complex new order. For example, at some low temperature the atoms of a particular gas are arranged in a particular pattern and the gas emits no light. Then, as heat is applied, it agitates the atoms causing them to move, and as this movement is amplified through the gas it emits a dull glow. Small changes in heat are thus amplified, causing instability, or chaos, that breaks the symmetry of the atoms' original behaviour. Then at a critical point, the atoms in the gas suddenly all point in the same direction to produce a laser beam. Thus, the system uses chaos to shatter old patterns of behaviour, creating the opportunity for the new. And as the system proceeds through chaos, it is confronted with critical points where it, so to speak, makes a choice between different options for further development. Some options represent yet further chaos and others lead to more complex forms of orderly behaviour, but which will occur is inherently unpredictable. The choice itself is made by spontaneous self-organization amongst the components of the system in which they, in effect, communicate with each other, reach a consensus, and commit to a new form of behaviour. If a more complex form of orderly behaviour is reached, it has what scientists call a dissipative structure, because continual attention and energy must be applied if it is to be sustained – for example, heat has to be continually pumped into the gas if the laser beam is to continue. If the system is to develop further, then the dissipative structure must be short-lived; to reach an even more complex state, the system will have to pass through chaos once more.

It is striking how similar the process of dealing with strategic issues in an organization is to the self-organizing phenomenon just outlined. The key to the effectiveness with which organizations change and develop new strategic directions lies in the manner in which managers handle what might be called their strategic issue agenda. That agenda is a dynamic, unwritten list of issues, aspirations, and challenges that key groups of managers are attending to. Consider the steps managers can be observed to follow as they handle their strategic issue agenda:

- Detecting and selecting small disturbances. In open-ended strategic situations, change is typically the result of many small events and actions that are unclear, ambiguous, and confusing, with consequences that are unknowable. The key difficulty is to identify what the real issues, problems, or opportunities are, and the challenge is to find an appropriate and creative aspiration or objective. In these circumstances the organization has no alternative but to rely on the initiative of individuals to notice and pursue some issue, aspiration, or challenge. In order to do this, those individuals have to rely on their experience-based intuition and ability to detect analogies between one set of ambiguous circumstances and another.

- Amplifying the issues and building political support. Once some individual detects some potential issue, that individual begins to push for organizational attention to it. A complex political process of building special interest groups to support an issue is required before it gains organizational attention and can thus be said to be on the strategic issue agenda.

- Breaking symmetries. As they build and progress strategic issue agendas, managers are in effect altering old mental models, existing company and industry recipes, to come up with new ways of doing things. They are destroying existing perceptions and structures.

- Critical points and unpredictable outcomes. Some issues on the agenda may be dealt with quickly, while others may attract attention, continuous or periodic, for a very long time. How quickly an issue is dealt with depends upon the time required to reach enough consensus and commitment to proceed to action. At some critical point, an external or internal pressure in effect forces a choice. The outcome on whether and how to proceed to action over the issue is unpredictable because it depends upon the context of power, personality, and group dynamic within which it is being handled. The result may or may not be action, and action will usually be experimental at first.

- Changing the frame of reference. Managers in a business come to share memories of what worked and what did not work in the past – the organizational memory. In this way they build up a business philosophy, or culture, establishing a company recipe and in common with their rivals an industry recipe too. These recipes have a powerful effect on what issues will subsequently be detected and attended to; that is, they constitute a frame of reference within which managers interpret what to do next. The frame of reference has to be continually

challenged and changed because it can easily become inappropriate to new circumstances. The dissipative structure of consensus and commitment is therefore necessarily short-lived if an organization is to be innovative.

These phases constitute a political and learning process through which managers deal with strategic issues, and the key point about these processes is that they are spontaneous and self-organizing: no central authority can direct anyone to detect and select an open-ended issue for attention, simply because no one knows what it is until someone has detected it; no one can centrally organize the factions that form around specific issues; nor can anyone intend the destruction of old recipes and the substitution of new ones since it is impossible to know what the appropriate new ones are until they are discovered. The development of new strategic direction requires the chaos of contention and conflict, and the self-organizing processes of political interaction and complex learning.

Chaos is a fundamental property of nonlinear feedback systems, a category that includes human organizations

Feedback simply means that one action or event feeds into another; that is, one action or event determines the next according to some relationship. For example, one firm repackages its product and its rival responds in some way, leading to a further action on the part of the first, provoking in turn yet another response from the second, and so on. The feedback relationship may be linear, or proportional, and when this is the case, the first firm will repackage its product and the second will respond by doing much the same. The feedback relationship could be nonlinear, or nonproportional, however, so that when the first firm repackages its product, the second introduces a new product at a lower price; this could lead the first to cut prices even further, so touching off a price war. In other words, nonlinear systems are those that use amplifying (positive) feedback in some way. To see the significance of positive feedback, compare it with negative feedback.

All effective businesses use negative or damping feedback systems to control and regulate their day-to-day activities. Managers fix short-term targets for profits and then prepare annual plans or budgets, setting out the time path to reach the target. As the business moves through time, outcomes are measured and compared with annual plan projections to yield variances. Frequent monitoring of those variances prompts corrective action to bring performance indicators back onto their planned paths; that is, variances feed back into corrective action and the feedback takes a negative form, so that when profit is below target, for example, offsetting action is taken to restore it. Scheduling, budgetary, and planning systems utilize negative feedback to keep an organization close to a predictable, stable equilibrium path in which it is adapted to its environment. While negative feedback controls a system according to prior intention, positive feedback produces explosively unstable equilibrium where changes are amplified, eventually putting intolerable pressure on the system until it runs out of control.

The key discovery about the operation of nonlinear feedback systems, however, is that there is a third choice. When a nonlinear feedback system is driven away from stable equilibrium toward explosive unstable equilibrium, it passes through a phase of bounded instability – there is a border between stability and instability where feedback flips autonomously between the amplifying and the damping to produce chaotic behaviour; a paradoxical state that combines both stability and instability.

All human interactions take the form of feedback loops simply because the consequences of one action always feed back to affect a subsequent one. Furthermore, all human interactions constitute nonlinear feedback loops because people under- and overreact. Since organizations are simply a vast web of feedback loops between people, they must be capable of chaotic, as well as stable and explosively unstable, behaviour. The key question is which of these kinds of behaviours leads an organization to success. We can see the answer to this question if we reflect upon the fundamental forces operating on an organization.

All organizations are powerfully pulled in two fundamentally different directions:

- Disintegration. Organizations can become more efficient and effective if they divide tasks, segment markets, appeal to individual motivators, empower people, promote informal communication, and separate production processes in geographic and other terms. These steps lead to fragmenting cultures and dispersed power that pull an organization toward disintegration, a phenomenon that can be seen in practice as companies split into more and more business units and find it harder and harder to maintain control.

- Ossification. To avoid this pull to disintegration, and to reap the advantages of synergy and coordination, all organizations are also pulled to a state in which tasks are integrated, overlaps in market segments and production processes managed, group goals stressed above individual ones, power concentrated, communication and procedures formalized, and strongly shared cultures established. As an organization moves in this direction it develops more and more rigid structures, rules, procedures, and systems until it eventually ossifies, consequences that are easy to observe as organizations centralize.

Thus, one powerful set of forces pulls every organization toward a stable equilibrium (ossification) and another powerful set of forces pulls it toward an explosively unstable equilibrium (disintegration). Success lies at the border between these states, where managers continually alter systems and structures to avoid attraction either to disintegration or to ossification. For example, organizations typically swing to centralization in one period, to decentralization in another, and back again later on. Success clearly lies in a nonequilibrium state between stable and unstable equilibria; and for a nonlinear feedback system, that is chaos.

Eight steps to create order out of chaos

When managers believe that they must pull together harmoniously in pursuit of a shared organizational intention established before they act, they are inevitably confined to the predictable – existing strategic directions will simply be continued or innovations made by others will simply be imitated. When, instead of this, managers create the chaos that flows from challenging existing perceptions and promote the conditions in which spontaneous self-organization can occur, they make it possible for innovation and new strategic direction to emerge. Managers create such conditions when they undertake actions of the following kind.

Develop new perspectives on the meaning of control

The activity of learning in a group is a form of control that managers do not normally recognize as such. It is a self-organizing, self-policing form of control in which the group itself discovers intention and exercises control. Furthermore, we are all perfectly accustomed to the idea that the strategic direction of local communities, nation-states, and international communities is developed and controlled through the operation of political systems, but we rarely apply this notion to organizations. When we do, we see that a sequence of choices and actions will continue in a particular direction only while those espousing that direction continue to enjoy sufficient support. This constitutes a form of control that is as applicable to an organization when it faces the conflicts around open-ended change, as it is to a nation. The lesson is that self-organizing processes can produce controlled behaviour even though no one is in control – sometimes the best thing a manager can do is to let go and allow things to happen.

Design the use of power

The distribution of power and the way in which it is used provide very important boundaries around the group learning process from which new strategic directions emerge. The application of power in particular forms has fairly predictable consequences for group dynamics. Where power is applied as force and consented to out of fear, the group dynamic will be one of submission, or where such power is not consented to, the group dynamic will be one of rebellion, either covert or overt. Power may be applied as authority, and the predictable group dynamic here is one in which members of the group suspend their critical faculties and accept instructions from those above them. Groups in states of submission, rebellion, or conformity are incapable of complex learning, that is, the development of new perspectives and new mental models.

The kind of group dynamics that are conducive to complex learning occur when highly competitive win/ lose polarization is removed, and open questioning and public testing of assertions encouraged. When this happens, people use argument and conflict to move toward periodic consensus and commitment to a particular issue. That consensus and commitment cannot, however, be the norm when people are searching for new perspectives – rather, they must alternate between conflict and consensus, between confusion and clarity. This kind of dynamic is likely to occur when they most powerfully alternate the form in which they use their power: sometimes withdrawing and allowing conflict; sometimes intervening with suggestions; sometimes exerting authority.

Encourage self-organizing groups

A group will be self-organizing only if it discovers its own challenges, goals, and objectives. Mostly, such groups need to form spontaneously – the role of top managers is simply to create the atmosphere in which this can happen. When top managers do set up a group to deal with strategic issues, however, they must avoid the temptation to write terms of reference, set objectives, or prod the group to reach some predetermined view. Instead top managers must present ambiguous challenges and take the chance that the group may produce proposals they do not approve of. For a group of managers to be self-organizing, it has to be free to operate as its members jointly choose, within the boundaries provided by their work together. This means that when they work together in this way, the normal hierarchy must be suspended for most of the time. Members are there because of the contributions they are able to make and the influence they can exert through those contributions and their own personalities. This suspension of the normal hierarchy can take place only if those on higher levels behave in a manner that indicates that they attach little importance to their position for the duration of the work of the group.

Provoke multiple cultures

One way of developing the conflicting countercultures required to provoke new perspectives is to rotate people between functions and business units. The motive here is to create cultural diversity as opposed to the current practice of using rotation to build a cadre of managers with the same management philosophy. Another effective way of promoting countercultures is that practised by Canon and Honda, where significant numbers of managers are hired at the same time, midway through their careers in other organizations, to create sizeable pockets of different cultures that conflict with the predominant one.

Present ambiguous challenges instead of clear long-term objectives or visions

Agendas of strategic issues evolve out of the clash between different cultures in self-organizing groups. Top managers can provoke this activity by setting ambiguous challenges and presenting half-formed issues for others to develop, instead of trying to set clear long-term objectives. Problems without objectives should be intentionally posed to provoke the emotion and conflict that lead to active search for new ways of doing things. This activity of presenting challenges should also be a two-way one, where top executives hold themselves open to challenge from subordinates.

Expose the business to challenging situations

Managers who avoid taking chances face the certainty of stagnation and therefore the high probability of collapse in the long term, simply because innovation depends significantly on chance. Running for cover because the future is unknowable is in the long run the riskiest response of all. Instead, managers must intentionally expose themselves to the most challenging of situations. In his study of international companies, Michael Porter concludes that those who position themselves to serve the world's most sophisticated and demanding customers, who seek the challenge of competing with the most imaginative and competent competitors, are the ones who build sustainable competitive advantage on a global scale.

Devote explicit attention to improving group learning skills

New strategic directions emerge when groups of managers learn together in the sense of questioning deeply held beliefs and altering existing mental models rather than simply absorbing existing bodies of knowledge and sets of techniques. Such a learning process may well be personally threatening and so arouse anxiety that leads to bizarre group dynamics – this is perhaps the major obstacle to effective organizational learning. To overcome it, managers must spend time explicitly exploring how they interact and learn together – the route to superior learning is self-reflection in groups.

Create resource slack

New strategic directions emerge when the attitudes and behaviour of managers create an atmosphere favourable to individual initiative and intuition, to political interaction, and to learning in groups. Learning and political interaction are hard work, and they cannot occur without investment in spare management resources. A vital precondition for emergent strategy is thus investment in management resources to allow it to happen.

Conclusion

Practising managers and academics have been debating the merits of organizational learning as opposed to the planning conceptualization of strategic management. That debate has not, however, focused clearly on the critical unquestioned assumptions upon which the planning approach is based, namely, the nature of causality. Recent discoveries about the nature of dynamic feedback systems make it clear that cause and effect links disappear in innovative human organizations, making it impossible to envision or plan their long-term futures. Because of this lack of causal connection between specific actions and specific outcomes, new strategic directions can only emerge through a spontaneous, self-organizing political and learning process. The planning approach can be seen as a specific approach applicable to the short-term management of an organization's existing activities, a task as vital as the development of a new strategic direction.

READING

9.3 Building learning organizations

By Peter Senge[1]

Over the past two years, business academics and senior managers have begun talking about the notion of the learning organization. Ray Stata of Analog Devices put the idea succinctly in these pages last spring: 'The rate at which organizations learn may become the only substantial source of competitive advantage.' And in late May of this year, at an MIT-sponsored conference entitled 'Transforming Organizations', two questions arose again and again: How can we build organizations in which continuous learning occurs? and, What kind of person can best lead the learning organization? This article, based on Senge's recently published book, *The Fifth Discipline: The Art and Practice of the Learning Organization*,

[1]Source: This article was reprinted from 'The Leader's New Work: Building Learning Organizations', *Sloan Management Review*, Fall, 1990. Reproduced by permission.

begins to chart this new territory, describing new roles, skills, and tools for leaders who wish to develop learning organizations.

Human beings are designed for learning. No one has to teach an infant to walk, or talk, or master the spatial relationships needed to stack eight building blocks that don't topple. Children come fully equipped with an insatiable drive to explore and experiment. Unfortunately, the primary institutions of our society are oriented predominantly toward controlling rather than learning, rewarding individuals for performing for others rather than for cultivating their natural curiosity and impulse to learn. The young child entering school discovers quickly that the name of the game is getting the right answer and avoiding mistakes – a mandate no less compelling to the aspiring manager.

'Our prevailing system of management has destroyed our people', writes W. Edwards Deming, leader in the quality movement. 'People are born with intrinsic motivation, self-esteem, dignity, curiosity to learn, joy in learning. The forces of destruction begin with toddlers – a prize for the best Halloween costume, grades in school, gold stars, and on up through university. On the job, people, teams, divisions are ranked – reward for the one at the top, punishment at the bottom. Management by Objectives (MBO), quotas, incentive pay, business plans, put together separately, division by division, cause further loss, unknown and unknowable.'

Ironically, by focusing on performing for someone else's approval, corporations create the very conditions that predestine them to mediocre performance. Over the long run, superior performance depends on superior learning.

If anything, the need for understanding how organizations learn and accelerating that learning is greater today than ever before. The old days when a Henry Ford, Alfred Sloan, or Tom Watson learned for the organization are gone. In an increasingly dynamic, interdependent, and unpredictable world, it is simply no longer possible for anyone to 'figure it all out at the top'. The old model, 'the top thinks and the local acts', must now give way to integrating thinking and acting at all levels. While the challenge is great, so is the potential payoff.

Adaptive learning and generative learning

The prevailing view of learning organizations emphasizes increased adaptability. Given the accelerating pace of change, or so the standard view goes, 'the most successful corporation of the 1990s', according to *Fortune* magazine, 'will be something called a learning organization, a consummately adaptive enterprise'.

But increasing adaptiveness is only the first stage in moving toward learning organizations. The impulse to learn in children goes deeper than desires to respond and adapt more effectively to environmental change. The impulse to learn, at its heart, is an impulse to be generative, to expand our capability. This is why leading corporations are focusing on *generative* learning, which is about creating, as well as *adaptive* learning, which is about coping.

The total quality movement in Japan illustrates the evolution from adaptive to generative learning. With its emphasis on continuous experimentation and feedback, the total quality movement has been the first wave in building learning organizations. But Japanese firms' view of serving the customer has evolved. In the early years of total quality, the focus was on 'fitness to standard', making a product reliably so that it would do what its designers intended it to do and what the firm told its customers it would do. Then came a focus on 'fitness to need', understanding better what the customer wanted and then providing products that reliably met those needs. Today, leading-edge firms seek to understand and meet the 'latent need' of the customer – what customers might truly value but have never experienced or would never think to ask for.

Generative learning, unlike adaptive learning, requires new ways of looking at the world, whether in understanding customers or in understanding how to better manage a business. For years, US manufacturers sought competitive advantage in aggressive controls on inventories, incentives against overproduction, and rigid adherence to production forecasts. Despite these incentives, their performance was eventually eclipsed by Japanese firms who saw the challenges of manufacturing differently. They realized that eliminating delays in the production process was the key to reducing instability and improving cost, productivity, and service. They worked to build networks of relationships with trusted suppliers and to redesign physical production processes to reduce delays in materials procurement, production setup, and in-process inventory – a much higher-leverage approach to improving both cost and customer loyalty.

As Boston Consulting Group's George Stalk has observed (Stalk, Evans and Shulman, 1992), the Japanese saw the significance of delays because they saw the process of order entry, production scheduling, materials procurement, production, and distribution as an integrated system. 'What distorts the system so badly is time', observes Stalk – the multiple delays between events and responses. 'These distortions reverberate throughout the system, producing disruptions, waste, and inefficiency.' Generative learning requires seeing the systems that control events. When we fail to grasp the systemic source of problems, we are left to 'push on' symptoms rather than eliminate underlying causes. The best we can ever do is adaptive learning.

The leader's new work

Our traditional view of leaders – as special people who set the direction, make the key decisions, and energize the troops – is deeply rooted in an individualistic and nonsystemic worldview. Especially in the West, leaders are heroes – great men (and occasionally women) who rise to the fore in times of crisis. So long as such myths prevail, they reinforce a focus on short-term events and charismatic heroes rather than on systemic forces and collective learning.

Leadership in learning organizations centres on subtler and ultimately more important work. In a learning organization, leaders' roles differ dramatically from that of the charismatic decision maker. Leaders are designers, teachers, and stewards. These roles require new skills: the ability to build shared vision, to bring to the surface and challenge prevailing mental models, and to foster more systemic patterns of thinking. In short, leaders in learning organizations are responsible for building organizations where people are continually expanding their capabilities to shape their future – that is, leaders are responsible for learning.

Creative tension: The integrating principle

Leadership in a learning organization starts with the principle of creative tension. Creative tension comes from seeing clearly where we want to be, our 'vision', and telling the truth about where we are, our 'current reality'. The gap between the two generates a natural tension.

Creative tension can be resolved in two basic ways: by raising current reality toward the vision, or by lowering the vision toward current reality. Individuals, groups, and organizations who learn how to work with creative tension learn how to use the energy it generates to move reality more reliably toward their visions.

Without vision there is no creative tension. Creative tension cannot be generated from current reality alone.

All the analysis in the world will never generate a vision. Many who are otherwise qualified to lead fail to do so because they try to substitute analysis for vision. They believe that, if only people understood current reality, they would surely feel the motivation to change. They are then disappointed to discover that people resist the personal and organizational changes that must be made to alter reality. What they never grasp is that the natural energy for changing reality comes from holding a picture of what might be that is more important to people than what is.

But creative tension cannot be generated from vision alone; it demands an accurate picture of current reality as well. Vision without an understanding of current reality will more likely foster cynicism than creativity. The principle of creative tension teaches that *an accurate picture of current reality is just as important as a compelling picture of a desired future.*

Leading through creative tension is different from solving problems. In problem solving, the energy for change comes from attempting to get away from an aspect of current reality that is undesirable. With creative tension, the energy for change comes from the vision, from what we want to create, juxtaposed with current reality. While the distinction may seem small, the consequences are not. Many people and organizations find themselves motivated to change only when their problems are bad enough to cause them to change. This works for a while, but the change process runs out of steam as soon as the problems driving the change become less pressing. With problem solving, the motivation for change is extrinsic. With creative tension, the motivation is intrinsic. The distinction mirrors the distinction between adaptive and generative learning.

New roles

The traditional authoritarian image of the leader as 'the boss calling the shots' has been recognized as over-simplified and inadequate for some time. According to Edgar Schein (1985), 'Leadership is intertwined with culture formation.' Building an organization's culture and shaping its evolution is the 'unique and essential function' of leadership. In a learning organization, the critical roles of leadership – designer, teacher, and steward – have antecedents in the ways leaders have contributed to building organizations in the past. But each role takes on new meaning in the learning organization and, as will be seen in the following sections, demands new skills and tools.

Leader as designer

The functions of design, or what some have called social architecture, are rarely visible; they take place behind the scenes. The consequences that appear today are the result of work done long in the past, and work today will show its benefits far in the future. Those who aspire to lead out of a desire to control, or gain fame, or simply to be at the centre of the action will find little to attract them to the quiet design work of leadership.

But what, specifically, is involved in organizational design? 'Organization design is widely misconstrued as moving around boxes and lines', says Hanover's O'Brien. 'The first task of organization design concerns designing the governing ideas of purpose, vision, and core values by which people will live.' Few acts of leadership have a more enduring impact on an organization than building a foundation of purpose and core values.

If governing ideas constitute the first design task of leadership, the second design task involves the policies, strategies, and structures that translate guiding ideas into business decisions. Leadership theorist Philip Selznick calls policy and structure the 'institutional embodiment of purpose.' 'Policy making (the rules that guide decisions) ought to be separated from decision making', says Jay Forrester. 'Otherwise, short-term pressures will usurp time from policy creation.'

Traditionally, writers like Selznick and Forrester have tended to see policy-making and implementation as the work of a small number of senior managers. But that view is changing. Both the dynamic business environment and the mandate of the learning organization to engage people at all levels now make it clear that this second design task is more subtle. Henry Mintzberg has argued that strategy is less a rational plan arrived at in the abstract and implemented throughout the organization than an 'emergent phenomenon'. Successful organizations 'craft strategy' according to Mintzberg, as they continually learn about shifting business conditions and balance what is desired and what is possible. The key is not getting the right strategy but fostering strategic thinking.

Behind appropriate policies, strategies, and structures are effective learning processes; their creation is the third key design responsibility in learning organizations. This does not absolve senior managers of their strategic responsibilities. Actually, it deepens and extends those responsibilities. Now they are not only responsible for ensuring that an organization has well developed strategies and policies but also for ensuring that processes exist whereby these are continually improved.

In the early 1970s, Shell was the weakest of the big seven oil companies. Today, Shell and Exxon are arguably the strongest, both in size and financial health. Shell's ascendance began with frustration. Around 1971 members of Shell's Group Planning in London began to foresee dramatic change and unpredictability in world oil markets. However, it proved impossible to persuade managers that the stable world of steady growth in oil demand and supply they had known for 20 years was about to change. Despite brilliant analysis and artful presentation, Shell's planners realized, in the words of Pierre Wack (1985), that they 'had failed to change behaviour in much of the Shell organization'. Progress would probably have ended there, had the frustration not given way to a radically new view of corporate planning.

As they pondered this failure, the planners' view of their basic task shifted: 'We no longer saw our task as producing a documented view of the future business environment five or ten years ahead. Our real target was the microcosm (the "mental model") of our decision makers.' Only when the planners reconceptualized their basic task as fostering learning rather than devising plans did their insights begin to have an impact. The initial tool used was 'scenario analysis', through which planners encouraged operating managers to think through how they would manage in the future under different possible scenarios. It mattered not that the managers believed the planners' scenarios absolutely, only that they became engaged in ferreting out the implications. In this way, Shell's planners conditioned managers to be mentally prepared for a shift from low prices to high prices and from stability to instability. The results were significant. When the Organisation of Petroleum Exporting Countries (OPEC) became a reality, Shell quickly responded by increasing local operating company control (to enhance manoeuvrability in the new political environment), building buffer stocks, and accelerating development of non-OPEC sources – actions that its competitors took much more slowly or not at all.

Somewhat inadvertently, Shell planners had discovered the leverage of designing institutional learning processes whereby, in the words of former planning director De Geus, 'Management teams change their shared mental models of their company, their markets, and their competitors.' Since then, 'planning as learning' has become a byword at Shell, and Group Planning has continually sought out new learning tools that can be integrated into the planning process. Some of these are described below.

Leader as teacher

Leader as teacher does *not* mean leader as authoritarian expert whose job it is to teach people the 'correct' view of reality. Rather, it is about helping everyone in the organization, oneself included, to gain more insightful views of current reality. This is in line with a popular emerging view of leaders as coaches, guides, or facilitators. In learning organizations, this teaching role is developed further by virtue of explicit attention to people's mental models and by the influence of the systems perspective.

The role of leader as teacher starts with bringing to the surface people's mental models of important issues. No one carries an organization, a market, or a state of technology in his or her head. What we carry in our heads are assumptions. These mental pictures of how the world works have a significant influence on how we perceive problems and opportunities, identify courses of action, and make choices.

One reason that mental models are so deeply entrenched is that they are largely tacit. Ian Mitroff, in his study of General Motors, argues that an assumption that prevailed for years was that, in the United States, 'Cars are status symbols. Styling is therefore more important than quality.' The Detroit automakers didn't say, 'We have a mental model that all people care about is styling.' Few actual managers would even say publicly that all people care about is styling. So long as the view remained unexpressed, there was little possibility of challenging its validity or forming more accurate assumptions.

But working with mental models goes beyond revealing hidden assumptions. Reality, as perceived by most people in most organizations, means pressures that must be borne, crises that must be reacted to, and limitations that must be accepted. Leaders as teachers help people *restructure their views of reality* to see beyond the superficial conditions and events into the underlying causes of problems and therefore to see new possibilities for shaping the future.

Specifically, leaders can influence people to view reality at three distinct levels: events, patterns of behaviour, and systemic structure.

Systemic Structure (Generative)

↓

Patterns of Behaviour (Responsive)

↓

Events (Reactive)

The key question becomes 'Where do leaders predominantly focus their own and their organization's attention?'

Contemporary society focuses predominantly on events. The media reinforces this perspective, with almost exclusive attention to short-term, dramatic events. This focus leads naturally to explaining what happens in terms of those events: 'The Dow Jones average went up 16 points because high fourth-quarter profits were announced yesterday.'

Pattern-of-behaviour explanations are rarer in contemporary culture than event explanations, but they do occur. Trend analysis is an example of seeing patterns of behaviour. A good editorial that interprets a set of current events in the context of long-term historical changes is another example. Systemic, structural explanations go even further by addressing the question 'What causes the patterns of behaviour?'

In some sense, all three levels of explanation are equally true. But their usefulness is quite different. Event explanations – who did what to whom – doom their holders to a reactive stance toward change. Pattern-of-behaviour explanations focus on identifying long-term trends and assessing their implications. They at least suggest how, over time, we can respond to shifting conditions. Structural explanations are the most powerful. Only they address the underlying causes of behaviour at a level such that patterns of behaviour can be changed.

By and large, leaders of our current institutions focus their attention on events and patterns of behaviour, and under their influence, their organizations do likewise. That is why contemporary organizations are predominantly reactive, or at best responsive – rarely generative. On the other hand, leaders in learning organizations pay attention to all three levels, but focus especially on systemic structure; largely by example, they teach people throughout the organization to do likewise.

Leader as steward

This is the subtlest role of leadership. Unlike the roles of designer and teacher, it is almost solely a matter of attitude. It is an attitude critical to learning organizations.

While stewardship has long been recognized as an aspect of leadership, its source is still not widely understood. I believe Robert Greenleaf (1977) came closest to explaining real stewardship, in his seminal book *Servant Leadership*. There, Greenleaf argues that 'the servant leader *is* servant first . . . . It begins with the natural feeling that one wants to serve, to serve *first*. This conscious choice brings one to aspire to lead. That person is sharply different from one who is leader first, perhaps because of the need to assuage an unusual power drive or to acquire material possessions.'

Leaders' sense of stewardship operates on two levels: stewardship for the people they lead and stewardship for the larger purpose or mission that underlies the enterprise. The first type arises from a keen appreciation of the impact one's leadership can have on others. People can suffer economically, emotionally, and spiritually under inept leadership. If anything, people in a learning organization are more vulnerable because of their commitment and sense of shared ownership. Appreciating this naturally instils a sense of responsibility in leaders. The second type of stewardship arises from a leader's sense of personal purpose and commitment to the organization's larger mission. People's natural impulse to learn is unleashed when they are engaged in an endeavour they consider worthy of their fullest commitment. Or, as Lawrence Miller puts it, 'Achieving return on equity does not, as a goal, mobilize the most noble forces of our soul.'

New skills

New leadership roles require new leadership skills. These skills can only be developed, in my judgement, through a lifelong commitment. It is not enough for one or two individuals to develop these skills. They must be distributed widely throughout the organization. This is one reason that understanding the disciplines of a learning organization is so important. These disciplines embody the principles and practices that can widely foster leadership development.

Three critical areas of skills (disciplines) are building shared vision, surfacing and challenging mental models, and engaging in systems thinking.

Building shared vision

The skills involved in building shared vision include the following:

■ Encouraging personal vision. Shared visions emerge from personal visions. It is not that people only care about their own self-interest – in fact, people's values usually include dimensions that concern family, organization, community, and even the world. Rather, it is that people's capacity for caring is personal.

■ Communicating and asking for support. Leaders must be willing to continually share their own vision, rather than being the official representative of the corporate vision. They also must be prepared to ask, 'Is this vision worthy of your commitment?'

This can be difficult for a person used to setting goals and presuming compliance.

■ Visioning as an ongoing process. Building shared vision is a never-ending process. At any one point there will be a particular image of the future that is predominant, but that image will evolve. Today, too many managers want to dispense with the 'vision business' by going off and writing the Official Vision Statement. Such statements almost always lack the vitality, freshness, and excitement of a genuine vision that comes from people asking, 'What do we really want to achieve?'

■ Blending extrinsic and intrinsic visions. Many energizing visions are extrinsic – that is, they focus on achieving something relative to an outsider, such as a competitor. But a goal that is limited to defeating an opponent can, once the vision is achieved, easily become a defensive posture. In contrast, intrinsic goals like creating a new type of product, taking an established product to a new level, or setting a new standard for customer satisfaction can call forth a new level of creativity and innovation. Intrinsic and extrinsic visions need to coexist; a vision solely predicated on defeating an adversary will eventually weaken an organization.

■ Distinguishing positive from negative visions. Many organizations only truly pull together when their survival is threatened. Similarly, most social movements aim at eliminating what people don't want: for example, anti-drug, anti-smoking, or anti-nuclear arms movements. Negative visions carry a subtle message of powerlessness: people will only pull together when there is sufficient threat. Negative visions also tend to be short term. Two fundamental sources of energy can motivate organizations: fear and aspiration. Fear, the energy source behind negative visions, can produce extraordinary changes in short periods, but aspiration endures as a continuing source of learning and growth.

Surfacing and testing mental models

Many of the best ideas in organizations never get put into practice. One reason is that new insights and initiatives often conflict with established mental models. The leadership task of challenging assumptions without invoking defensiveness requires reflection and inquiry skills possessed by few leaders in traditional controlling organizations.

■ Seeing leaps of abstraction. Our minds literally move at lightning speed. Ironically, this often slows our learning, because we leap to generalizations so quickly that we never think to test them. We then confuse our generalizations with the observable data upon which they are based, treating the generalizations as if they were data.

- Balancing enquiry and advocacy. Most managers are skilled at articulating their views and presenting them persuasively. While important, advocacy skills can become counterproductive as managers rise in responsibility and confront increasingly complex issues that require collaborative learning among different, equally knowledgeable people. Leaders in learning organizations need to have both enquiry and advocacy skills.

- Distinguishing espoused theory from theory in use. We all like to think that we hold certain views, but often our actions reveal deeper views. For example, I may proclaim that people are trustworthy, but never lend friends money and jealously guard my possessions. Obviously, my deeper mental model (my theory in use), differs from my espoused theory. Recognizing gaps between espoused views and theories in use (which often requires the help of others) can be pivotal to deeper learning.

- Recognizing and defusing defensive routines. As one CEO (chief executive officer) in our research programme puts it, 'Nobody ever talks about an issue at the eight o'clock business meeting exactly the same way they talk about it at home that evening or over drinks at the end of the day.' The reason is what Chris Argyris calls defensive routines, entrenched habits used to protect ourselves from the embarrassment and threat that come with exposing our thinking. For most of us, such defences began to build early in life in response to pressures to have the right answers in school or at home. Organizations add new levels of performance anxiety and thereby amplify and exacerbate this defensiveness. Ironically, this makes it even more difficult to expose hidden mental models, and thereby lessens learning. The first challenge is to recognize defensive routines, then to enquire into their operation. Those who are best at revealing and defusing defensive routines operate with a high degree of self-disclosure regarding their own defensiveness.

Systems thinking

We all know that leaders should help people see the big picture. But the actual skills whereby leaders are supposed to achieve this are not well understood. In my experience, successful leaders often are 'systems thinkers' to a considerable extent. They focus less on day-to-day events and more on underlying trends and forces of change. But they do this almost completely intuitively. The consequence is that they are often unable to explain their intuitions to others and feel frustrated that others cannot see the world the way they do. One of the most significant developments in management science today is the gradual coalescence of managerial systems thinking as a field of study and practice. This field suggests some key skills for future leaders:

- Seeing interrelationships, not things, and processes, not snapshots. Most of us have been conditioned throughout our lives to focus on things and to see the world in static images. This leads us to linear explanations of systemic phenomenon.

- Moving beyond blame. We tend to blame each other or outside circumstances for our problems. But it is poorly designed systems, not incompetent or unmotivated individuals, that cause most organizational problems. Systems thinking shows us that there is no outside – that you and the cause of your problems are part of a single system.

- Distinguishing detail complexity from dynamic complexity. Some types of complexity are more important strategically than others. Detail complexity arises when there are many variables. Dynamic complexity arises when cause and effect are distant in time and space, and when the consequences over time of interventions are subtle and not obvious to many participants in the system. The leverage in most management situations lies in understanding dynamic complexity, not detail complexity.

- Focusing on areas of high leverage. Some have called systems thinking the 'new dismal science' because it teaches that most obvious solutions don't work – at best, they improve matters in the short run, only to make things worse in the long run. But there is another side to the story. Systems thinking also shows that small, well-focused actions can produce significant, enduring improvements, if they are in the right place. Systems thinkers refer to this idea as the principle of leverage. Tackling a difficult problem is often a matter of seeing where the high leverage lies, where a change – with a minimum of effort – would lead to lasting, significant improvement.

- Avoiding symptomatic solutions. The pressures to intervene in management systems that are going awry can be overwhelming. Unfortunately, given the linear thinking that predominates in most organizations, interventions usually focus on symptomatic fixes, not underlying causes. This results in only temporary relief, and it tends to create still more pressures later on for further, low-leverage intervention. If leaders acquiesce to these pressures, they can be sucked into an endless spiral of increasing intervention. Sometimes the most difficult leadership acts are to refrain from intervening through popular quick fixes and to keep the pressure on everyone to identify more enduring solutions.

The consequences of leaders who lack systems-thinking skills can be devastating. Many charismatic leaders manage almost exclusively at the level of events. They deal in visions and in crises, and little in-between. Under their leadership, an organization hurtles from crisis to crisis. Eventually, the worldview of people in the organization becomes dominated by events and reactiveness. Many, especially those who are deeply committed, become burned out. Eventually, cynicism comes to pervade the organization. People have no control over their time, let alone their destiny.

Similar problems arise with the 'visionary strategist', the leader with vision who sees both patterns of change and events. This leader is better prepared to manage change. He or she can explain strategies in terms of emerging trends, and thereby foster a climate that is less reactive. But such leaders still impart a responsive orientation rather than a generative one.

Many talented leaders have rich, highly systemic intuitions but cannot explain those intuitions to others. Ironically, they often end up being authoritarian leaders, even if they don't want to, because only they see the decisions that need to be made. They are unable to conceptualize their strategic insights so that these can become public knowledge, open to challenge and further improvement.

Developing leaders and learning organizations

In a recently published retrospective on organization development in the 1980s, Marshall Sashkin and N. Warner Burke observe the return of an emphasis on developing leaders who can develop organizations. They also note Schein's critique that most top executives are not qualified for the task of developing culture. Learning organizations represent a potentially significant evolution of organizational culture. So it should come as no surprise that such organizations will remain a distant vision until the leadership capabilities they demand are developed. 'The 1990s may be the period', suggest Sashkin and Burke, 'during which organization development and (a new sort of) management development are reconnected.'

I believe that this new sort of management development will focus on the roles, skills, and tools for leadership in learning organizations. Undoubtedly, the ideas offered above are only a rough approximation of this new territory. The sooner we begin seriously exploring the territory, the sooner the initial map can be improved – and the sooner we will realize an age-old vision of leadership:

The wicked leader is he who the people despise. The good leader is he who the people revere. The great leader is he who the people say, 'We did it ourselves.'

Lao Tsu

READING

9.4

The knowing-doing gap

By Jeffrey Pfeffer and Robert I. Sutton[1]

Why do so much education and training, management consulting, and business research and so many books and articles produce so little change in what managers and organizations actually do? In 1996, more than 1700 business books were published in the United States, and more are published each year. Many of these books are filled with the same analyses and prescriptions, albeit using different language and

---

[1]Source: This article was adapted from *The Knowing–Doing Gap* by J. Pfeffer and R.I. Sutton, 1999, Chapter 1, by permission of Harvard Business School Press. © 1999 by the Harvard Business School Publishing Corporation, all rights reserved.

graphics, as could be found in similar books published the year before. In fact, many of the ideas proclaimed as new each year can be found in similar books printed decades earlier. Yet these books find a ready market because the ideas, although often widely known and proven to be useful and valid, remain unimplemented. So, authors try, in part through repackaging and updating, to somehow get managers to not only *know* but to *do* something with what they know. And managers continue to buy the books filled with ideas they already know because they intuitively understand that knowing isn't enough. They hope that by somehow buying and reading one more book they will finally be able to translate this performance knowledge into organizational action.

Each year, more than $60 billion is spent on training in and by organizations, particularly management training. Much of this training, on subjects such as Total Quality Management (TQM), customer service and building customer loyalty, leadership, and organizational change is based on knowledge and principles that are fundamentally timeless – unchanged and unchanging. Nevertheless, the training often is repeated. Regardless of the quality of the content, the delivery, or the frequency of repetition, management education is often ineffective in changing organizational practices.

Professor Mark Zbaracki (1998) studied Total Quality Management training in five organizations in which senior executives believed that TQM methods could enhance the quality of their products and services and that the training had changed how people performed their jobs. Zbaracki found, however, that the quantitative TQM methods were not used *at all* in four of the organizations and only on a limited basis in the fifth. This result is not unique to TQM – we observed it repeatedly during our research.

Each year, billions of dollars are spent on management consultants by organizations seeking advice – one estimate for 1996 was $43 billion. But that advice is seldom implemented. One consultant, making a presentation to obtain work from a large US bank, showed an overhead slide that had the recommendations from four previous consulting studies conducted in just the prior six years for that bank. All four studies had come to the same conclusions, which is not surprising given that smart people from four different firms looked at essentially the same data. The presenter, selling implementation and change rather than analytical services, asked the assembled executives, 'Why do you want to pay for the same answer a fifth time?' He and his firm got the job. As another example of knowing but not doing in the world of management

consulting, two consultants from one of the leading firms worked on a project for a large electrical utility in Latin America that was facing deregulation. They were chagrined to discover that management already had a four-year-old, 500-page document with extensive plans and recommendations produced by a different consulting firm in a previous engagement. They reported:

> *The old document was very good. It had benchmarking cost studies from best-practice utilities all around the world, summaries of the most successful training systems in other industrial companies, and pretty detailed implementation calendars. . . . As our analysis was based on the same . . . information that was given to the last consultants four years before . . . our recommendations were basically the same. The problem was not analysis. It was implementation. Although we could identify some new areas for improvement, the core was almost a copy of the old document. . . . The client already had the basic information we were giving them.*

Each year the hundreds of business schools in the United States graduate more than 80 000 MBAs and conduct numerous research studies on business topics. Business education and research are growing in scope and prominence in countries around the world. Yet the translation of this research and management education into practice proceeds slowly and fitfully. There is little evidence that being staffed with people who have an advanced education in business is consistently related to outstanding organizational performance. Many top-performing firms – Southwest Airlines, Wal-Mart, The Men's Wearhouse, Service-Master, PSS/World Medical, SAS Institute, AES, Whole Foods Market, and Starbucks – don't recruit at the leading business schools and don't emphasize business degree credentials in their staffing practices. Numerous researchers have found that 'little of what is taught in college or even business schools really prepares would-be managers for the realities of managing'. One study reported that 73 per cent of the surveyed MBA programme graduates said, 'that their MBA skills were used "only marginally or not at all" in their first managerial assignments'.

Did you ever wonder why so much education and training, management consultation, organizational research, and so many books and articles produce so few changes in actual management practice? Did you ever wonder why the little change that does occur often happens with such great difficulty? Why is it that, at the end of so many books and seminars, leaders report being enlightened and wiser, but not much happens in their organizations?

Implementation or ignorance: Does a knowing-doing gap really exist?

How do we know that knowledge isn't always implemented and that this is a problem affecting organizational performance? And perhaps even more important, how can organizations discover to what degree they are not actually doing what they think they should? These are important, but relatively straightforward, issues.

Evidence of knowing-doing gaps

There are a number of studies within single industries demonstrating that there are superior ways of managing people and organizing their work. Yet although these superior management practices are reasonably well known, diffusion proceeds slowly and fitfully, and backsliding is common. A study of apparel manufacturing demonstrated that modular production, with an emphasis on team-based production, produced far superior economic performance along a number of dimensions compared with the traditional bundle system of manufacturing using individual piece work and limited training. Trade publications, industry associations, and the relevant unions have favoured modular production since the early 1980s. Nonetheless, in 1992 about 80 per cent of all garments were still sewn using the bundle method, and some plants that had adopted modular production abandoned it and returned to the bundle system.

Similarly, evidence for the advantages of flexible or lean production in automobile assembly is compelling. This knowledge is widely diffused within the industry and has been for some time. Nevertheless, a five-year follow-up study of the diffusion of flexible manufacturing systems found that there was only modest implementation of flexible arrangements and that 'some plants undertook only minor changes in their use of high-involvement work practices . . . and still others showed modest decreases'. And a large-scale study of semi-conductor fabrication revealed substantial differences in performance, as measured by cycle time, line yield, and defect density, based on the

management practices used. Yet the study found substantial variation in these practices, even in an industry that was characterized by geographic concentration, particularly of corporate headquarters, and substantial movement of personnel between firms. In these and other studies the evidence seems compelling that, although there are better ways of managing and organizing, these superior practices are not necessarily quickly or readily adopted.

Some other examples illustrate the frequently large gap between knowing that something is important and actually doing it. For instance, the Association of Executive Search Consultants conducted a survey in which 'three-quarters of the responding CEOs said companies should have "fast track" programmes, [but] fewer than half have one at their own companies'. As noted in a *Fortune* article commenting on this study, 'Maybe chief executives don't say what they mean, and maybe they have trouble implementing what they say.' Our research indicates that it is the latter problem – implementing what leaders say and know – that is more pervasive.

Evidence from various industry studies, and from studies of firms in multiple industries, shows that knowledge of how to enhance performance is not readily or easily transferred *across* firms. Moreover, there is evidence that knowledge of how to enhance performance doesn't transfer readily even *within* firms. There are persistent and substantial differences in performance within facilities in the same company. One study of 42 food plants in a single company doing essentially the same manufacturing tasks with similar technologies found differences in performance of 300 per cent between the best- and worst-performing plants. The best plant earned 80 per cent more than the mean, and the worst plant earned 40 per cent less than the mean for all the plants. A study of oil refineries reported little consistency in performance in multirefinery organizations. There was no evidence of a 'company effect' on performance, indicating that there was not much consistency in management practices or philosophy across different facilities within the same company.

An intensive study of an effort to make a Hewlett-Packard (HP) manufacturing unit more effective reported: 'By interviewing thirteen such stakeholders from other departments, including procurement, process generation, engineering, and finance, design team members discovered that communication between departments was poor, thus limiting the degree to which they learned from each other. . . . Opportunities to share innovative process technologies or other sources of competitive advantage were being overlooked.' The problems associated with transferring knowledge within HP have led Lew Platt, the CEO, to lament, 'I wish we knew what we know at HP.' Another study of the transfer of best practices, or knowledge, within firms, noted:

You would think that . . . better practices would spread like wildfire in the entire organization. They don't. As William Buehler, senior vice president at Xerox, said, 'You can see a high-performance factor or office, but it just doesn't spread.' . . . One Baldrige winner [said], 'We can have two plants right across the street from one another, and it's the damnedest thing to get them to transfer best practices.'

Does the knowing-doing gap matter?

The answer to the question of whether the knowing-doing gap actually matters for organizational performance is not as obvious as it might at first seem. It is possible that differences in organizational performance come from differences in what firms *know* – the quality and depth of their insights about business strategy, technologies, products, customers, and operations -rather than from their ability to translate that knowledge into action. There are, however, numerous reasons to doubt this is the case. We do not deny that there are important differences in knowledge across firms, such as differences in the sophistication of their understanding of management and operations. But we argue that such differences are only part of the reason for differences in firm performance, and that a much larger source of variation in performance stems from the ability to turn knowledge into action.

Why do we argue that the gap between knowing and doing is more important than the gap between ignorance and knowing? First, because there are too many activities and organizations involved in acquiring and disseminating knowledge to plausibly maintain that there are many important performance 'secrets'. Consider the plethora of books, articles, consultants, and training programs we have already described. All of these have as one of their objectives the transmission of information. There are organizations that specialize in collecting knowledge about management practices, storing it, and then transferring the information to those who need such information about enhancing performance. These organizations, sometimes called *knowledge brokers*, make a business of transferring performance knowledge.

Major consulting firms have units that specialize in transferring knowledge about best practices learned from work with past clients to current clients who did not know, or at least did not use, such information (Hargadon, 1998).

Although the market for information about 'best practices' may not be as efficient as financial or capital markets are reputed to be, it is nonetheless implausible to presume that better ways of doing things can remain secret for long. There are few managers who can resist the temptation to tell their counterparts at other firms or the business press about what they are doing to achieve organizational success. Managers of successful firms are also frequently interviewed and hired by competing firms in the same industry and by firms in other industries that hope to learn and implement the practices of these firms.

Southwest Airlines is a firm that uses fairly simple business practices that are widely known, but it continues to have the best financial performance in the airline industry. Numerous books, case studies, and television shows have described Southwest's management approach, but the firm's competitors have either not tried to imitate what it does or, when they have, like the United Shuttle did, they have not been nearly as successful as Southwest.

Second, research demonstrates that the success of most interventions designed to improve organizational performance depends largely on implementing what is already known, rather than from adopting new or previously unknown ways of doing things. Consider one representative study. A field experiment was conducted with an electrical wholesale company with headquarters in Melbourne, Australia. The experiment compared sales changes in branches that used benchmarking with branches that set high performance goals. In the more-effective benchmarking treatment, 'at the beginning of each month . . . each branch was sent a "League Ladder" showing the percentage improvement [in sales] and ranking of all the branches in that group for the past month. In addition, they were sent a list of "Best Practices" hints compiled . . . from information provided by managers of the best-performing branches' (Mann, Samson & Dow, 1998). Over a three-month period, these branches improved their sales performance by almost 6 per cent.

The 'Best Practice' hints were actually:

well-known practices, with the extra dimension that they were reinforced and carried out reliably in the better performing branches. . . . Most managers agreed with the hints, but claimed they were already aware of and employing most of them. . . . Given the nature of the 'Best Practice' hints, we can rule out discovery and communication of highly original and effective practices as the reason for improvement in the benchmarking group.

Using regular schedules to plan weekly activities, conducting meetings of branch staff to review and discuss branch staff performance, training sales representatives in understanding and interpreting sales trend reports, and using practices that ensure fast and reliable customer service are far from rocket science. They are, in fact, common sense. It is interesting how uncommon common sense is in its implementation.

Or consider Honda's efforts to enhance the performance of its suppliers, which resulted in productivity increases averaging 50 per cent at the 53 suppliers participating in Honda's BP (Best Practice, Best Process, Best Performance) programme. A study of Honda's process noted that 'the underlying scientific knowledge for the reengineering of production lines was primarily concrete and simple rather than abstract and complex' (MacDuffie and Helper, 1997). The changes were consistent with the idea of *kaizan*, or continuous improvement, most of them being small, simple, and in many cases, quite commonsensical given the particular manufacturing process. The genius of the Honda system was in its implementation, not in particularly novel or complicated technical ideas for enhancing productivity.

If there is widespread diffusion of information on 'best' (or at least 'better') practices, and if the evidence suggests that many successful interventions rely more on implementation of simple knowledge than on creating new insights or discovering obscure or secret practices used by other firms, then our position that the gap between knowing and doing is important for firm performance follows logically. This conclusion means that although knowledge creation, benchmarking, and knowledge management may be important, transforming knowledge into organizational action is at least as important to organizational success.

How knowledge management contributes to the knowing-doing problem

One might think that with the current interest in 'knowledge management' and intellectual capital,

there wouldn't be a knowing–doing problem. After all, there is general acceptance that 'knowledge has become increasingly important as a contributor to a country's and individual firm's success in industrial competition'. Tomas Stewart's conclusion (1998) is typical: 'The new economy is about the growing value of knowledge as an input and output, making it the most important ingredient of what people buy and sell.' But the view of knowledge taken by many consultants, organizations, and management writers is of something to be acquired, measured, and distributed – something reasonably tangible, such as patents. There are two problems with this conception of knowledge or know-how. First, the conception of knowledge as something explicit and quantifiable draws a problematic distinction between knowledge as a tangible good and the use of that good in ongoing practice. The emphasis that has resulted has been to build the stock of knowledge, acquiring or developing intellectual property (note the use of the term *property)* under the presumption that knowledge, once possessed, will be used appropriately and efficiently. As we have seen, this presumption is often not valid.

There is some attention in both the management literature and in management practice to knowledge in use, but this perspective is comparatively rare. Commenting on the papers at a conference on knowledge management, Don Cohen (1998) noted, 'In the US, most knowledge practice focuses on collecting, distributing, re-using, and measuring existing codified knowledge and information. Practitioners often look to information technology to capture and distribute this explicit knowledge; firms measure success by near-term economic returns on knowledge investment.' An Ernst & Young survey of 431 firms conducted in 1997 is quite revealing about why most firms' efforts in knowledge management are not likely to do much good and may even be counterproductive regarding turning knowledge into organizational action. According to data from that survey (see Figure 9.4.1), most firms' efforts consist of investing in knowledge repositories such as intranets and data warehouses, building networks so that people can find each other, and implementing technologies to facilitate collaboration. These are all activities that treat knowledge pretty much like steel or any other resource, to be gathered, shared, and distributed. What firms haven't done very much is build knowledge into products and services, or develop new products and services based on knowledge. Furthermore, there is no item on this list of knowledge management projects that reflects implementing knowledge on an ongoing basis.

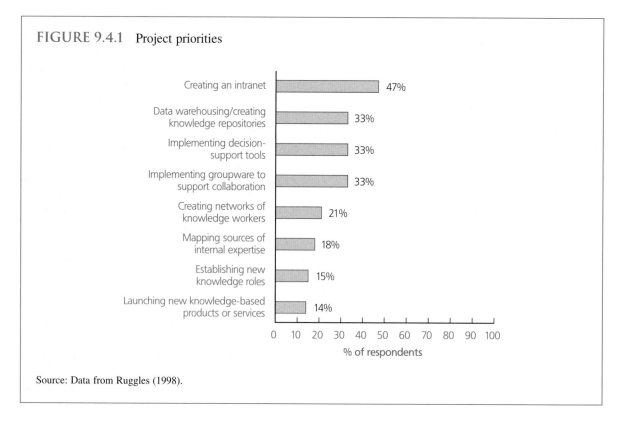

FIGURE 9.4.1   Project priorities

% of respondents

Source: Data from Ruggles (1998).

One of the main reasons that knowledge management efforts are often divorced from day-to-day activities is that the managers, consulting firms, and information technologists who design and build the systems for collecting, storing, and retrieving knowledge have limited, often inaccurate, views of how people actually use knowledge in their jobs.

Sociologists call this 'working knowledge' (Harper, 1987). Knowledge management systems rarely reflect the fact that essential knowledge, including technical knowledge, is often transferred between people by stories, gossip, and by watching one another work. This is a process in which social interaction is often crucial. A recent study of 1000 employees in business, government, and non-profit organizations reported that 'most workplace learning goes on unbudgeted, unplanned, and uncaptured by the organization. . . . Up to 70 per cent of workplace learning is informal.' This study by the Center for Workforce Development found that informal learning occurs in dozens of daily activities, including participating in meetings, interacting with customers, supervising or being supervised, mentoring others, communicating informally with peers, and training others on the job.

Yet, most knowledge management efforts emphasize technology and the storage and transfer of codified information such as facts, statistics, canned presentations, and written reports. A June 1997 Conference Board conference on creating and leveraging intellectual capital reported: 'Most corporate initiatives to manage intellectual capital are focused on specific projects, the most common of which deploy technology to share and leverage knowledge and best practices.' There is an unfortunate emphasis on technology, particularly information technology, in these efforts. For instance, one recent article on making knowledge management a reality asserted that 'it's clear that an intranet is one of the most powerful tools for achieving results within this [knowledge management] arena'. Another article asserted that 'knowledge management starts with technology'. We believe that this is precisely wrong. As the Conference Board report noted, 'Dumping technology on a problem is rarely an effective solution.' When knowledge is transferred by stories and gossip instead of solely through formal data systems, it comes along with information about the process that was used to develop that knowledge. When just reading reports or seeing presentations, people don't learn about the subtle nuances of work methods – the failures, the tasks that were fun, the tasks that were boring, the people who were helpful, and the people who undermined the work.

Formal systems can't store knowledge that isn't easily described or codified but is nonetheless essential for doing the work, called *tacit knowledge*. So, while firms keep investing millions of dollars to set up knowledge management groups, most of the knowledge that is actually used and useful is transferred by the stories people tell to each other, by the trials and errors that occur as people develop knowledge and skill, by inexperienced people watching those more experienced, and by experienced people providing close and constant coaching to newcomers.

The Ernst & Young survey described earlier also asked executives to rate their organizations on how well they were doing in the various dimensions of knowledge management. These results are reproduced in Figure 9.4.2. Managers seem to believe they are doing a good job in generating new knowledge and even doing pretty well in obtaining knowledge from the environment. What they aren't doing very well at all, by their own assessments, is transferring knowledge *within* the organization. And perhaps most important, Ernst & Young didn't even ask if the knowledge in these firms was being used by the firms – not just in decision making which was covered in the survey, but in day-to-day operations and management practices.

Knowledge management systems seem to work best when the people who generate the knowledge are also those who store it, explain it to others, and coach them as they try to implement the knowledge. For example, Hewlett-Packard's Strategic Planning, Analysis, and Modeling group has had success transferring knowledge about supply chain management that has been implemented in many HP divisions. One of the reasons the group has been successful is that the same people who do this internal consulting are also responsible for storing and disseminating knowledge about it within the company. Corey Billington, the head of this group, describes his job as 'part librarian, part consultant, and part coach'. He is responsible for knowing the technical solutions and the stories surrounding the 150 or so consulting jobs his group has done within HP so that he and others in his group can suggest ideas to help new internal clients and can actually coach the clients as they implement the ideas.

The second problem with much of the existing literature and practice in knowledge management is that it conceptualizes knowledge as something tangible and explicit that is quite distinct from philosophy or values. As Don Cohen (1998), a writer specializing on knowledge issues, put it, 'The noun "knowledge"

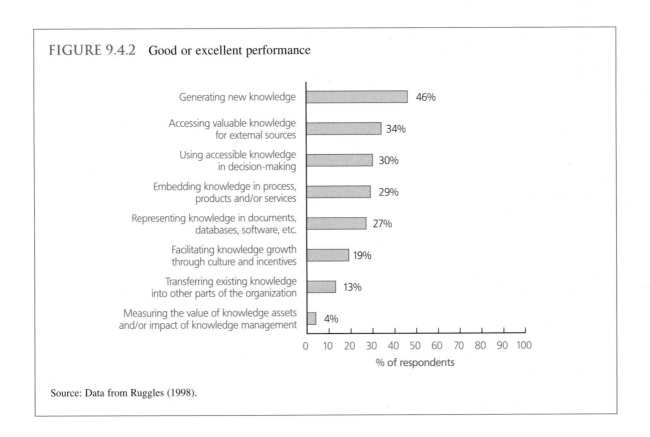

FIGURE 9.4.2   Good or excellent performance

Generating new knowledge — 46%
Accessing valuable knowledge for external sources — 34%
Using accessible knowledge in decision-making — 30%
Embedding knowledge in process, products and/or services — 29%
Representing knowledge in documents, databases, software, etc. — 27%
Facilitating knowledge growth through culture and incentives — 19%
Transferring existing knowledge into other parts of the organization — 13%
Measuring the value of knowledge assets and/or impact of knowledge management — 4%

% of respondents

Source: Data from Ruggles (1998).

implies that knowledge is a thing that can be located and manipulated as an independent object or stock. It seems possible to "capture" knowledge, to "distribute," "measure," and "manage" it. The gerund "knowing" suggests instead a process, the action of knowers and inseparable from them.' A leading Japanese scholar in the area of knowledge in organizations made a simple but important point (Nonaka and Konno, 1998): 'Knowledge is embedded in . . . these shared spaces, where it is then acquired through one's own experience or reflections on the experiences of others. . . . Knowledge is intangible.'

The fact that knowledge is acquired through experience and is often intangible and tacit produces a third problem in turning knowledge into action. One important reason we uncovered for the knowing-doing gap is that companies overestimate the importance of the tangible, specific, programmatic aspects of what competitors, for instance, do, and underestimate the importance of the underlying philosophy that guides what they do and why they do it. Although specific practices are obviously important, such practices evolve and make sense only as part of some system that is often organized according to some philosophy or meta-theory of performance. As such, there is a knowing-doing gap in part because firms have misconstrued what they should be knowing or seeking to know in the first place.

Why has it been so difficult for other automobile manufacturers to copy the Toyota Production System (TPS), even though the details have been described in books and Toyota actually gives tours of its manufacturing facilities? Because 'the TPS techniques that visitors see on their tours – the *kanban* cards, *andon* cords, and quality circles – represent the surface of TPS but not its soul' (Taylor, 1997). The Toyota Production System is about philosophy and perspective, about such things as people, processes, quality, and continuous improvement. It is not just a set of techniques or practices:

> On the surface, TPS appears simple. . . . Mike DaPrile, who runs Toyota's assembly facilities in Kentucky, describes it as having three levels: techniques, systems, and philosophy. Says he: Many plants have put in an andon cord that you pull to stop the assembly line if there is a problem. A 5-year-old can pull the cord. But it takes a lot of effort to drive the right philosophies down to the plant floor.

A similar perspective is evident in the study examining how Honda creates lean suppliers. Honda chooses its supplier-partners in large part based on the attitudes of the companies' management. In the words of Rick Mayo, the Honda engineer directing these activities, 'We are a philosophy-driven company . . . Honda felt it was easier to teach the technical knowledge associated with a different product or process technology than to find a technically capable supplier possessing the combination of risk-taking attitude, motivation to improve, responsiveness to future needs, and overall competence that is valued so highly' (MacDuffie and Helper, 1997).

Nor is this emphasis on philosophy just the view of some Japanese automobile companies. The importance of values and philosophy is a theme that was repeated by Howard Behar, president of Starbucks International, the coffee company; David Russo, vice president of human resources for SAS Institute, a software firm recently ranked by *Fortune* as the third-best company to work for in the United States; and George Zimmer, founder and chairman of The Men's Wearhouse, a rapidly growing, extremely profitable off-price retailer of tailored and casual men's clothing. All three of these organizations have been financially successful, and all are renowned for their people management practices. In all three instances, the message was the same: What is important is not so much what we do – the specific people management techniques and practices – but *why* we do it – the underlying philosophy and view of people and the business that provides a foundation for the practices. Attempting to copy just *what* is done – the explicit practices and policies – without holding the underlying philosophy is at once a more difficult task and an approach that is less likely to be successful. Because of the importance of values and philosophy in the management processes of many successful companies, the emphasis on the tangible, explicit aspects of knowledge that characterizes most knowledge management projects is unlikely to provide much value and may be, at worst, a diversion from where and how companies should be focusing their attention.

Turning knowledge into action

Knowledge and information are obviously crucial to performance. But we now live in a world where knowledge transfer and information exchange are tremendously efficient, and where there are numerous organizations in the business of collecting and transferring best practices. So, there are fewer and smaller differences in *what firms know* than in their *ability to act* on

> ## EXHIBIT 9.4.1 WHY TYPICAL KNOWLEDGE MANAGEMENT PRACTICES MAKE KNOWING – DOING GAPS WORSE
>
> - Knowledge management efforts mostly emphasize technology and the transfer of codified information.
> - Knowledge management tends to treat knowledge as a tangible thing, as a stock or quantity, and therefore separates knowledge as some thing from the use of that thing.
> - Formal systems cannot easily store or transfer tacit knowledge.
> - The people responsible for transferring and implementing knowledge management frequently don't understand the actual work being documented.
> - Knowledge management tends to focus on specific practices and ignores the importance of philosophy.

that knowledge. It is widely recognized that many firms have gaps between what they know and what they do, but the causes have not been fully understood. Harlow Cohen (1998) has called this gap between knowing and doing the performance paradox: 'Managers know what to do to improve performance, but actually ignore or act in contradiction to either their strongest instincts or to the data available to them.'

There are no simple analyses or easy answers for the knowing–doing problem. The problem is not just costs, or leadership, or some single organizational practice that can be changed to remedy the problem. The knowing-doing gap arises from a constellation of factors and it is essential that organizational leaders understand them all and how they interrelate. Nonetheless, there are some recurring themes that help us understand the source of the problem and, by extension, some ways of addressing it.

1. Why before how: Philosophy is important.   Why has General Motors in the past had so much difficulty learning from Saturn or NUMMI? Why have executives from so many firms toured Toyota's facilities but failed to comprehend the essence of the Toyota Production System? Why have so few firms copied The Men's Wearhouse, SAS Institute, Whole Foods Market, AES, PSS/World Medical, Kingston Technology, or the many other successful firms that people read about, visit, but then fail to learn from? One reason is that too many managers want to learn 'how' in terms of detailed practices and behaviours and techniques, rather than 'why' in terms of philosophy and general guidance for action.

Saturn, Toyota, Honda, IDEO Product Development, AES, the SAS Institute, The Men's Wearhouse, and many of the other organizations we have discussed begin not with specific techniques or practices but rather with some basic principles – a philosophy or set of guidelines about how they will operate. AES has a set of four core values – fun, fairness, integrity, and social responsibility – that guide its behaviour. It also has a set of core assumptions about people that it tries to implement in its management approach: that people (1) are creative, thinking individuals, capable of learning; (2) are responsible and can be held accountable; (3) are fallible; (4) desire to make positive contributions to society and like a challenge; and (5) are unique individuals, deserving of respect, not numbers or machines (Pfeffer, 1997a). SAS Institute has a philosophy of treating everyone fairly, equally, and with trust and respect – treating people in accordance with the firm's stated belief in their importance to the organization. The Men's Wearhouse philosophy comes from founder George Zimmer's background: 'He'd grown up in the mid-sixties to early seventies . . . and was definitely interested in alternative forms of social organization, (Pfeffer, 1997b). Zimmer believes very strongly that there is tremendous untapped human potential and that it is his company's job to help people realize that potential. 'What creates longevity in a company is whether you look at the assets of your company as the untapped human potential that is dormant within thousands of employees, or is it the plant and equipment? . . . If you ask me how I measure the results of my training program, I can't. I have to do it on . . . trust in the value of human potential.' That is why Zimmer has stated that the company is in the people business, not the suit business.

These firms learn and change and do things consistent with implementing their general principles to enhance organizational performance. Operating on the basis of a general business model or theory of organizational performance, a set of core values, and an underlying philosophy permits these organizations to avoid the problem of becoming stuck in the past or mired in ineffective ways of doing things just because they have done it that way before. They don't let precedent or memory substitute for thinking. No particular practice, in and of itself, is sacred. What is constant and fundamental are some basic business and operating principles. Consequently, these firms are able to learn and adapt, to communicate with new-comers and across large geographic distances, and to do so in ways consistent with their basic understanding of what creates success and high performance in their particular business.

2. Knowing comes from doing and teaching others how. In a world of conceptual frameworks, fancy graphics presentations, and, in general, lots of *words*, there is much too little appreciation for the power, and indeed the necessity of not just talking and thinking but of *doing* – and this includes explaining and teaching – as a way of knowing. Rajat Gupta, managing director of McKinsey since 1994, had this to say about the importance of apprenticeship and experience in developing leadership within the firm: 'The notion of apprenticeship and mentoring is that you learn by ob-servation, learn from doing together with someone who's done it before. . . . You [also] learn a lot when you're thrown into a situation and you don't have a lot of help.'

Teaching is a way of knowing, and so is doing the work, trying different things, experimenting. As David Sun of Kingston Technology said, 'If you do it, then you will know.' Honda's emphasis on putting people where they could see the actual part and the actual si-tuation reflects the idea that seeing and touching, being closely involved in the actual process, is imperative for real understanding and learning.

The notion that learning is best done by trying a lot of things, learning from what works and what does not, thinking about what was learned, and trying again is practiced with religious zeal at IDEO Product Devel-opment, the largest and most successful product design consulting firm in the world. CEO David Kelley likes to say that 'enlightened trial and error outperforms the planning of flawless intellects'. As in the other action-oriented firms we studied, Kelley doesn't just talk about the virtues of learning through trial and error. They live it at IDEO. As engineer Peter Skillman puts it, 'Rapid prototyping is our religion. When we get an idea, we make it right away so we can see it, try it, and learn from it.' Kelley, Skillman, and many others at

IDEO also regularly teach classes to managers, engineers, and artists in which they explain their phi-losophy and have students enact it by designing, building, demonstrating, and pitching their inventions to others.

What an out-of-fashion idea – being in proximity to what you are learning, using experience as a teacher, learning by doing and teaching! We live in an era of distance learning. We have companies that sell CD-ROMs so that people can learn things alone by inter-acting with their computers. We have a plethora of seminars in which people sit and listen to ideas and concepts. We human beings can learn some things those ways – mostly specific cognitive content. But many things, about organizations, operations, and people, can only be learned by firsthand experience. The tangible, physical, material aspects of knowledge acquisition and knowledge transfer, learning by doing, learning by coaching and teaching, are critical.

Knowing by doing is, unfortunately, a less cost-efficient way of transmitting knowledge. There is less ability to leverage the Internet or to put lots of people in a large room with one instructor, which are, un-fortunately, the modes of instruction at most business schools today. But both the evidence and the logic seem clear: Knowing by doing develops a deeper and more profound level of knowledge and virtually by definition eliminates the knowing – doing gap.

3. Action counts more than elegant plans and concepts. A number of years ago, Tom Peters and Robert Waterman (1982) talked about the virtues of a 'ready, fire, aim' approach to running organizations. We have seen that this principle of acting even if you haven't had the time to fully plan the action has two advantages. First, it creates opportunities for learning by doing. Without taking some action, without being in the actual setting and confronting the actual 'part', learning is more difficult and less efficient because it is not grounded in real experience. Second, the idea of 'firing' and then 'aiming' – or doing and then planning – helps to establish a cultural tone that action is valued and that talk and analysis without action are unacceptable.

Greg Brenneman, the COO of Continental Airlines and one of the architects of its successful turnaround, attributed the turnaround to an action orientation: 'If you sit around devising elegant and complex strategies and then try to execute them through a series of flawless decisions, you're doomed. We saved Continental be-cause we acted and we never looked back.' In a world where sounding smart has too often come to substitute for doing something smart, there is a tendency to let planning, decision making, meetings, and talk come to substitute for implementation. People achieve status through their words, not their deeds. Managers come to believe that just because a decision has been made and there was discussion and analysis, something will happen. As we have seen, that is often not the case.

A while ago we worked with the World Bank as it was trying to transform its culture. One of the problems that the bank faced was a set of human resource policies and practices that clashed with the culture the bank thought it wanted and that it needed to implement to fulfil its evolving role in the world economy. So the bank embarked on an effort to change those practices. But what this particular change effort largely entailed, and this was true in many other instances of change in the bank, was preparing a white paper laying out options, providing rationales, talking about implementation plans, and providing supporting data. The white paper on human resource practices was then critiqued by senior officials and revised on the basis of those critiques. And the process continued – analysis, writing, critique, and revision. There was great concern to produce an outstanding paper about human resource policies and practices, but much less concern with actually making any changes. This sort of process came naturally in an environment of people with advanced degrees who had learned to write journal articles in precisely this way – write, get comments, revise, and produce yet another draft. But behaviour that may be useful for writing articles in scientific journals can be quite unproductive for organizations trying to change. In the time it took the people at the bank to analyse, document, propose, and revise descriptions of possible changes to management practices, they could have implemented many actual changes, learned what worked and what did not and why, and could have made revisions based on that experience numerous times.

4. There is no doing without mistakes. What is the company's response? In building a culture of action, one of the most critical elements is what happens when things go wrong. Actions, even those that are well planned, inevitably entail the risk of being wrong. What is the company's response? Does it provide, as PSS/World Medical does, 'soft landings'? Or does it treat failure and error so harshly that people are encouraged to engage in perpetual analysis, discussion, and meetings but not to do anything because they are afraid of failure?

Warren Bennis and Burt Nanus (1997) defined learning as an extension of the word trying and asserted that 'all learning involves some "failure," something from which one can continue to learn'. They proposed a general rule for all organizations: 'Reasonable failure should never be received with anger', which they illustrated with the following story about Thomas Watson Sr, IBM's founder and CEO for many decades:

> *A promising junior executive of IBM was involved in a risky venture for the company and managed to lose over $10 million in the gamble. It was a disaster. When Watson called the nervous executive into his office, the young man blurted out, 'I guess you want my resignation?' Watson said, 'You can't be serious. We just spent $10 million dollars educating you!'*

5. Fear fosters knowing-doing gaps, so drive out fear. Fear in organizations causes all kinds of problems. Greg Brenneman, COO of Continental Airlines, noted: 'Pressure and fear often make managers do erratic, inconsistent, even irrational things.' No one is going to try something new if the reward is likely to be a career disaster. The idea of rapid prototyping – trying things out to see if they work and then modifying them on the basis of that experience – requires a culture in which failure is not punished because failure provides an opportunity for learning. Clayton Christensen, a professor at Harvard Business School, has said, 'What companies need is a forgiveness framework and not a failure framework, to encourage risk taking and empower employees to be thinking leaders rather than passive executives.' Fear produces sentiments like the following, which we often hear when we teach executives about high-performance work cultures and ask why their firms don't implement these ideas: 'We may not be doing very well, but at least our performance is predictable. And, no one has gotten fired for doing what we're doing. So why should we try something new that has risk involved?'

That is why firms that are better able to turn knowledge into action drive out fear. They don't go on missions to find who has erred, but rather attempt to build cultures in which even the concept of failure is not particularly relevant. Livio DeSimone, Minnesota Mining and Manufacturing's CEO, commented: 'We don't find it useful to look at things in terms of success or failure. Even if an idea isn't successful initially, we can learn from it.' Such firms put people first and act as if they really care about their people. If they have too many people – as the New Zealand Post did or as Continental Airlines did when it began paring back its routes – those who are redundant are treated humanely, with dignity and respect. At Continental, many managers had come in under Frank Lorenzo, CEO and hostile takeover king. Many of these managers were replaced because they drove fear in rather than out of the organization, clashing with the new culture. As routes were restructured, other people had to leave. But, 'cleaning house needn't be a brutal or humiliating experience. . . . If you fire people inhumanely, you'll be left with a bunch of employees who don't trust the company or their coworkers.'

Putting people first and driving out fear are not just ideas to be implemented when times are good. You can downsize, you can even close a facility; but do it in a way that maintains employee dignity and well-being and, as a consequence, productivity and performance. The people at the Newcastle Steelworks of the Australian firm BHP learned in April 1997 that the works would have to be closed. There was over-capacity in steel making within BHP and this particular plant required excessive capital for modernization. Extensive evidence suggests that 'at least half of the plants facing closure experience between limited to extreme productivity losses'. A case study of the Newcastle plant, however, revealed that in the time after the closing announcement, the plant enjoyed *higher* productivity, better quality, and better safety. Why did this occur? The plant management did a number of things right, many of the same things that Levi Strauss did when it implemented plant closings. One of the most important was to make and keep a commitment to look after the employees. The company implemented a program called Pathways, 'a structured set of initiatives aimed at assessing employees both to decide their future direction (path) after leaving . . . and to receive intensive support to achieve it.' That programme, coupled with open communication and lots of employee and union involvement, created an atmosphere of trust and mutual respect. If this success in both performance and maintaining employee morale and spirit can be achieved under the difficult and demanding experience of a plant closure, think what can be achieved under more favourable circumstances by organizations committed to building a workplace in which people aren't afraid of the future.

Fear starts, or stops, at the top. It is unfortunate, but true, that a formal hierarchy gives people at the top the power to fire or harm the careers of people at lower levels. Fear of job loss reflects not only the reality of whether or not one can readily find another job, but also the personal embarrassment that any form of rebuke causes. Organizations that are successful in turning knowledge into action are frequently characterized by leaders who inspire respect, affection, or admiration, but not fear.

Hierarchy and power differences are real. But firms can do things to make power differences less visible and, as a consequence, less fear-inducing. This is possibly one of the reasons why removing status markers and other symbols that reinforce the hierarchy can be so useful and important. Those symbols of hierarchy serve as reminders that those farther down have their jobs, their salaries, and their futures within the firm mostly at the sufferance of those in superior positions. Although to some extent this is always true, removing visible signs of hierarchy – things such as reserved parking spaces, private dining rooms, elaborate, separate offices, differences in dress - removes physical reminders of a difference in hierarchical power that can easily inspire fear among those not in the highest-level positions.

6. Beware of false analogies: Fight the competition, not each other. Cooperation has somehow developed a bad reputation in many organizations. Collaborative, cooperative organizations, where people worry about the welfare of each other and the whole instead of just themselves, seem to remind some people of socialism. Yet, cooperation means that 'the result is the product of common effort, the goal is shared, and each member's success is linked with every other's. . . . Ideas and materials, too, will be shared, labour will sometimes be divided, and everyone in the group will be rewarded for successful completion of the task' (Kohn, 1992). There is a mistaken idea that because competition has apparently triumphed as an economic system, competition *within* organizations is a similarly superior way of managing. This is not just a sloppy use of analogies, but has real consequences that hurt real people and real organizations. Following this suspect logic, firms establish all sorts of practices that intensify internal rivalry: forced-curve performance rankings, prizes and recognition for relatively few employees, raises given out in a zero-sum fashion, and individual rewards and measurements that set people against each other.

We have shown that these ideas and the practices they produce almost certainly undermine organizational performance as well as employee well being. British Petroleum enjoyed a turnaround in the 1990s because it encouraged business units to learn from each other and had senior leaders that worked to build a culture of cooperation that made doing so possible. The Men's Wearhouse has succeeded in selling clothes by emphasizing team selling and the fact that employees succeed only as their colleagues succeed. 'The customer doesn't care about who gets the commission. All he remembers is the store's atmosphere. That's why we use "team selling". One wardrobe consultant can offer the customer a cup of coffee; another can offer to press his clothing while he's in our dressing rooms; and another can take his kids to watch the videos we keep in some of our stores.' One of the reasons that SAS Institute's turnover is so low is that people actually prefer working in a place where they don't have to always look over their shoulder to see who is doing them in. In contrast, learning within Fresh Choice, particularly following the Zoopa acquisition, was inhibited by the competition for internal status and related feelings of insecurity and fearfulness. Learning with General Motors was similarly hampered by unproductive internal competition that left people reluctant to learn from each other or to share their knowledge with internal competitors.

There is also much evidence that people prefer collaborative and cooperative work arrangements. For instance, a study of 180 people from five organizations found that 'employees with compatible goals had high expectations, exchanged resources, and managed conflicts. Cooperative interactions improved the work relationship, employee morale, and task completion' (Tjosvold, 1986).

Turning knowledge into action is easier in organizations that have driven fear and internal competition out of the culture. The idea that the stress of internal competition is necessary for high levels of performance confuses *motivation* with *competition*. It is a perspective that mistakes internal competition and conflict, accompanied by a focus on 'winning' internal contests, for an interest in enhancing *organizational* performance and winning the battle in the marketplace.

7. Measure what matters and what can help turn knowledge into action.

'The foundation of any successfully run business is a strategy everyone understands coupled with a few key measures that are routinely tracked.' But this simple notion is frequently ignored in practice. Organizations proliferate measures. 'Mark Graham Brown (1998) reports working with a telecommunications company that expected its managers to review 100 to 200 pages of data a week.' The readily available computer hardware and software that make data capture and analysis easy also make it hard to resist the temptation to confuse data with information and to measure more and more things.

The dictum that what is measured is what gets done has led to the apparent belief that if a company measures more things, more will get done. But that is not at all the case. Southwest Airlines focuses on the critical measures of lost bags, customer complaints, and on-time performance – keys to customer satisfaction and therefore to success in the airline industry. AES focuses on plant utilization (uptime), new business development, and environmental and safety compliance, the factors that are critical to success in the electric power generation business. SAS Institute measures employee retention, important in an intellectual capital business. A few measures that are directly related to the basic business model are better than a plethora of measures that produce a lack of focus and confusion about what is important and what is not.

Organizations tend to measure the past. Typical information systems can tell you what has happened – how much has been sold, what costs have been, how much has been invested in capital equipment – but the systems seldom provide information that is helpful in determining *why* results have been as they have or what is going to happen in the near future. We sit in too many meetings in which too much time is spent discussing what has occurred but too little time is spent on discussing why or, more important, what is going to be done to create a different and better future.

Organizations tend to measure outcomes instead of processes. We know what the quality of our output is, but we don't know why it is so good or so bad. One of the important lessons of the quality movement is the importance of measuring processes so that process improvement is possible. As we saw, when General Motors became more serious about implementing lean or flexible manufacturing, attention switched to enhancing measures of intermediate outcomes and in-process indicators.

Even fewer organizations measure knowledge implementation. Typical knowledge management systems and processes focus instead on the stock of knowledge, the number of patents, the compilation of skills inventories, and knowledge captured on overheads or reports and made available over some form of groupware. Holding aside whether these systems even capture the tacit, experiential knowledge that is probably more important than what can be easily written down, such systems certainly don't capture whether or not this knowledge is actually being used. Organizations that are serious about turning knowledge into action should measure the knowing–doing gap itself and do something about it.

8. What leaders do, how they spend their time and how they allocate resources, matters. The difference between Barclays Global Investors, IDEO, or British Petroleum in the late 1990s and the many organizations that have greater difficulty in turning knowledge into action is not that one set of firms is populated by smarter, better, or nicer people than the other. The difference is in the systems and the day-to-day management practices that create and embody a culture that values the building and transfer of knowledge and, most important, acting on that knowledge. Leaders of companies that experience smaller gaps between what they know and what they do understand that their most important task is not necessarily to make strategic decisions or, for that matter, many decisions at all. Their task is to help build systems of practice that produce a more reliable transformation of knowledge into action. When Dennis Bakke of AES says that in 1997 he only made one decision, he is not being cute or facetious. He understands that his job is not to know everything and decide everything, but rather to create an environment in which there are *lots* of people who both know and do. Leaders create environments, reinforce norms, and help set expectations through what they do, through their actions and not just their words.

When Dave House left Intel to become CEO of Bay Networks, a company that was experiencing extremely poor performance, he knew he had to change the existing culture and do so quickly. The company suffered from its creation through a merger of two competitors. Synoptics and Wellfleet Communications, two firms of about equal size, one headquartered on the East Coast and one on the West. Following the merger, the company had tried to take on the best products and ideas of both companies, but what had resulted was product proliferation and slow decision making in a rapidly moving market. 'Bay engineers were working on twice as many new products as the company had the resources to ship.' What House did was create a set of courses to teach business practices he believed could help the company, and House taught many of the sessions himself. By actually delivering the material, House showed he was serious about the ideas and about making change happen. Larry Crook, Bay's director of global logistics, described the impact of House's training sessions: 'They blew my mind. . . . He showed us that he was serious about how we conducted ourselves – and that if we wanted to be successful, we had to get down to basics.'

Skip LeFauve told us that the CEO of General Motors teaches in GM University, reinforcing the importance of the knowledge building and sharing activity. David Kearns, when he was CEO at Xerox, applied quality principles to the top management team as he encouraged their implementation throughout the company. For instance, he and his colleagues thought about who their customers were and realized that these were managers one and two levels below who looked to them for advice and for strategic direction. So Kearns instituted practices to gather information on how well the senior leadership was actually helping executives below them to do their jobs.

The remarkable success of the product development firm IDEO is not simply because the firm has somehow been able to attract 'better' designers. Its success is dependent in large measure on a set of management practices that come from a philosophy that values an 'attitude of action' and the importance of learning by trying new things. For instance, David Kelley believes that, even when a designer knows a lot about a product, there are advantages in trying to feel and act 'stupid'. By pretending to be naïve and asking 'dumb' questions, and even trying to design solutions that are known to be wrong, product designers can overcome the hazards of being too knowledgeable. The ability of product designers at IDEO to think and act in this fashion comes from the fact that this is how Kelley himself behaves, and from his efforts to create consistent norms for management behaviour throughout the company.

Knowing about the knowing-doing gap is not enough

We now have a better understanding of some of the organizational processes and factors that hinder efforts to turn knowledge into action. But even if we do understand something more about why organizations fail to turn knowledge into action, these insights are insufficient to solve the problem. *Knowing* about the knowing-doing gap is different from *doing* something about it. Understanding causes is helpful because such understanding can guide action. But by itself, this knowing is insufficient – action must occur.

THE ORGANIZATIONAL CONTEXT IN INTERNATIONAL PERSPECTIVE

So long as men worship the Caesars and Napoleons, Caesars and Napoleons will duly arise and make them miserable.

Aldous Huxley (1894–1963); English novelist

Again it has become clear that there is little consensus in the field of strategy. Views on the nature of the organizational context vary sharply. Even authors from one and the same country have contrasting opinions on the paradox of control and chaos. However, looking back on the readings in the sections on strategy process and strategy content, it is striking how few of the authors make a point of expounding their outlook on organizational development. The assumptions on which their theories are built are largely left implicit.

For this reason, it is difficult to identify whether there are national preferences when it comes to organizational context perspective. Yet, it seems not unlikely that strategists in different countries have different inclinations on this issue. In large-scale field work carried out by researchers at Cranfield Business School in the United Kingdom (Kakabadse *et al.*, 1995), significantly different 'leadership styles' were recognized among European executives. The predominant approach in Sweden and Finland was typified as the 'consensus' style (low power distance, low masculinity), while executives in Germany and Austria had a style that was labelled 'working towards a common goal' (specialists working together within a rule-bound structure). In France, the most popular style was 'managing from a distance' (focus on planning, high power distance), while executives from the United Kingdom, Ireland, and Spain preferred 'leading from the front'. This last leadership style, according to the researchers, relies 'on the belief that the charisma and skills of some particular individuals will lead to either the success or the failure of their organizations'. This finding suggests that the organizational leadership perspective will be more popular in these three countries (as well as in other 'Anglo-Saxon' and 'Latin' cultures), than in the rest of Europe. Other cross-cultural theorists also support this supposition (e.g. Hampden-Turner and Trompenaars, 1993; Lessem and Neubauer, 1994).

As an input to the debate whether there are international differences in perspective, we would like to put forward a number of factors that might be of influence on how the paradox of control and chaos is viewed in different countries. It should be noted, however, that these propositions are intended to encourage discussion and constitute only tentative explanations for cross-cultural differences in perspective. More specific international research is needed to give this debate a firm footing.

Locus of control

This point can be kept short, as it was also raised in Chapter 8. People with an internal locus of control believe that they can shape events and have an impact on their environment. People with an external locus of control believe that they are caught up in events that they can hardly influence. Cross-cultural researchers have argued that cultures can differ significantly with regard to the perceived locus of control that is predominant among the population.

Obviously, in countries where the culture is more inclined towards an internal locus of control, it is reasonable to expect that the organizational leadership perspective will be more widespread. Managers in such 'just do it' cultures will be more strongly predisposed to believe that they can shape organizational circumstances. In cultures that are characterized by a predominantly external locus of control, more support for the organizational dynamics perspective can be expected.

Level of uncertainty avoidance

A cultural characteristic related to the previous point, is the preference for order and structure that prevails in some countries. Hofstede (1993, Reading 1.4) refers to this issue as uncertainty avoidance. In some cultures, there is a low tolerance for unstructured situations, poorly defined tasks and responsibilities, ambiguous relationships and unclear rules. People in these nations exhibit a distinct preference for order, predictability and security – they need to feel that things are 'in control'. In other cultures, however, people are less nervous about uncertain settings. The tolerance for situations that are 'unorganized' or 'self-organizing', is much higher – even in relatively chaotic circumstances, the call for 'law and order' will not be particularly strong. It can be expected that there will be a more pronounced preference for the organizational leadership perspective in countries that score high on uncertainty avoidance, than in nations with a low score.

Prevalence of mechanistic organizations

In Chapters 3 and 4, different international views on the nature of organizations were discussed. A simple distinction was made between mechanistic and organic conceptions of organizations. In the mechanistic view, organizations exist as systems that are staffed with people, while in the organic view organizations exist as groups of people into which some system has been brought.

When it comes to organizational development, people taking a mechanistic view will see leaders as mechanics – the organizational system can be redesigned, reengineered and restructured to pursue another course of action where necessary. Success will depend on leaders' design, engineering and structuring skills, and their ability to overcome resistance to change by the system's inhabitants. If a leader does not function well, a new one can be installed, and if employees are too resistant, then they can be replaced. In countries where the mechanistic view of organizations is more predominant, a leaning towards the organizational leadership perspective can be expected.

People taking an organic view will see a leader as the head of the clan, bound by tradition and loyalty, but able to count on the emotional commitment of the members. Success in reshaping the organization will depend on reshaping the people – changing beliefs, ideas, visions, skills and interests. Important in reorienting and rejuvenating the organization is the leader's ability to challenge orthodox ideas, motivate people and manage the political processes. In countries where the organic view of organizations is more predominant, a leaning towards the organizational dynamics perspective can be expected.

FURTHER READING

Readers interested in pursuing the topics of leadership and organizational dynamics have a rich body of literature from which to choose. An excellent overview of the subject is provided by Sydney Finkelstein and Donald Hambrick, in their book *Strategic Leadership: Top Executives and Their Effects on Organizations*. Also recommended as overview of the leadership literature is Yukl's *Leadership in Organizations*. In the category of more academically oriented works, the special issue of *Organization Studies* entitled 'Interpreting Organizational Leadership', and edited by Susan Schneider gives a rich spectrum of ideas. The same is true for the special edition of the *Strategic Management Journal* entitled 'Strategic Leadership', and edited by Donald Hambrick.

For more specific readings taking an organizational leadership perspective, the classics with which to start are John Kotter's *The General Managers* and Gordon Donaldson and Jay Lorsch's *Decision Making at the Top: The Shaping of Strategic Direction*. Good follow-up readings are the book by Warren Bennis, *On Becoming a Leader*, and the book by Burt Nanus, *Visionary Leadership: Creating a Compelling Sense of Direction for Your Organization*. For leadership literature further away from the 'control pole', readers are advised to turn to Peter Senge's book *The Fifth Discipline: The Art and Practice of the Learning Organization* and Edward Schein's *Organizational Culture and Leadership*. The book by Henry Sims and Peter Lorenzi, *The New Leadership Paradigm: Social Learning and Cognition in Organizations*, is also a challenging book, but not easy to read.

For a critical reaction to the leadership literature, Manfred Kets de Vries has many excellent contributions. His article 'The Leadership Mystique' is very good, as are his books with Danny Miller, entitled *The Neurotic Organization* and *Unstable at the Top*. Miller also has many thought-provoking works to his name, of which *The Icarus Paradox: How Excellent Companies Can Bring About Their Own Downfall* is highly recommended. In the more academic literature, stimulating commentaries are given in the articles 'The Romance of Leadership' by James Meindl, S. Ehrlich and J. Dukerich, and in 'The Ambiguity of Leadership', by Jeffrey Pfeffer. The reading by Pfeffer and Robert Sutton in this chapter is based on their book, *The Knowing–Doing Gap*, which is quite accessible and very interesting.

For a good reading highlighting the importance of organizational dynamics for both strategy process and strategy content, Ralph Stacey's book *Strategic Management and Organizational Dynamics* is a good place to start. Gerry Johnson's *Strategic Change and the Management Process* also provides provocative ideas about the relationship between strategy and the organizational context. Richard Pascale's *Managing on the Edge: How Successful Companies Use Conflict to Stay Ahead* is also stimulating reading. Finally, for the academically more adventurous, Joel Baum and Jitendra Singh's volume, *Evolutionary Dynamics of Organizations*, gives plenty of food for thought, as does Howard Aldrich's recent *Organizations Evolving*.

REFERENCES

Ackoff, R.L. (1980) *Creating the Corporate Future*, Chichester: Wiley.

Aldrich, H. (1999) *Organizations Evolving*, London: Sage.

Allison, G. (1969) 'Conceptual Models and The Cuban Missile Crisis', *The American Political Science Review*, Vol. 63, No. 3, September, pp. 689–718.

Amabile, T.M. (1998) 'How to Kill Creativity', *Harvard Business Review*, Vol. 76, No. 5, September–October, pp. 76–87.

Argyris, C. (1990) *Overcoming Organizational Defenses: Facilitating Organizational Learning*, Needham, MA: Allyn & Bacon.

Arrow, K.J. (1963) *Social Choice and Individual Values*, New Haven, CT: Yale University Press.

Barney, J.B. (1991) 'Firm Resources and Sustained Competitive Advantage', *Journal of Management*, Vol. 17, No. 1, pp. 99–120.

Bass, B.M. (1990) *Bass and Stogdill's Handbook of Leadership*, Third Edition, New York: The Free Press.

Baum, J.A.C., and Singh, J.V (eds) (1994) *Evolutionary Dynamics of Organizations*, Oxford: Oxford University Press.

Bavelas, A. (1964) 'Leadership: Man and Function', in: H.H. Leavitt and L.R. Pondy (eds), *Readings in Managerial Psychology*, Chicago: University of Chicago Press.

Beinhocker, E.D. (1999) 'Strategy at the Edge of Chaos', *The McKinsey Quarterly*, No. 1, pp. 24–39.

Bennis, W. (1989) *On Becoming a Leader*, Reading, MA: Addison-Wesley.

Bennis, W., and Nanus, B. (1985) *Leaders: The Strategies for Taking Charge*, New York: Harper & Row.

Bennis, W., and Nanus, B. (1997) *Leaders: Strategies for Taking Charge*, New York: HarperBusiness.

Birnbaum, R. (1988) *How Colleges Work: The Cybernetics of Academic Organization and Leadership*, San Francisco: Jossey-Bass.

Bourgeois, L.J., and Brodwin, D.R. (1983) 'Putting Your Strategy into Action', *Strategic Management Planning*, March–May.

Bower, J.L. (ed.) (1991) *The Craft of General Management*, Boston: Harvard Business School Publications.

Brown, M.G. (1998) 'Using Measurement to Boost Your Unit's Performance, *Harvard Management Update*, Vol. 3, p. 1.

Calder, B. (1977) 'An Attribution Theory of Leadership', in: B. Staw and B. Salancik (eds), *New Directions in Organizational Behavior*, Chicago: St. Clair.

Cannella, A.A., and M.J., Monroe (1997) 'Contrasting Perspectives on Strategic Leaders: Toward a More Realistic View of Top Managers', *Journal of Management*, Vol. 23, No. 3, pp. 213–237.

Chandler, A.D. (1962) *Strategy and Structure: Chapters in the History of the American Industrial Enterprise*, Cambridge, MA: MIT Press.

Chandler, A.D. (1977) *The Visible Hand*, Cambridge, MA: Harvard University Press.

Chen, C.C., and Meindl, J.R. (1991) 'The Construction of Leadership Images in the Popular Press: The Case of Donald Burr and People Express', *Administrative Science Quarterly*, Vol. 36, No. 4, December, pp. 521–551.

Child, J. (1972) 'Organizational Structure, Environment, and Performance: The Role of Strategic Choice', *Sociology*, January, pp. 2–22.

Cohen, D. (1998) 'Toward a Knowledge Context: Report on the First Annual U.C. Berkeley Forum on Knowledge and the Firm', *California Management Review*, Vol. 40, No. 3, Spring, p. 23.

Cohen, H. (1998) 'The Performance Paradox', *Academy of Management Executive*, Vol. 12, p. 30.

Conger J.A. (1999) 'Charismatic and Transformational Leadership in Organizations', *The Leadership Quarterly*, Vol. 10, No. 2, Summer, pp. 145–179.

Cyert, R.M. (1990) 'Defining Leadership and Explicating the Process', *Non-Profit Management and Leadership*, Vol. 1, No. 1, Fall, pp. 29–38.

Cyert, R.M., and March, J.G. (1963) *A Behavioral Theory of the Firm*, Englewood Cliffs: Prentice Hall.

De Geus, A. (1988) 'Planning as Learning', *Harvard Business Review*, March-April, pp. 70–74.

Donaldson, G., and Lorsch, J.W. (1983) *Decision Making at the Top: The Shaping of Strategic Direction*, New York: Basic Books.

Drucker, P. (1973) *Management: Tasks, Responsibilities, Practices*, New York: Harper & Row.

Etzioni, A. (1961) *A Comparative Analysis of Complex Organizations*, New York: Free Press.

Finkelstein, S. (1992) 'Power in Top Management Teams: Dimensions, Measurement, and Validation', *Academy of Management Journal*, Vol. 35, No. 3, August, pp. 505–538.

Finkelstein, S., and Hambrick, D.C. (1996) *Strategic Leadership: Top Executives and Their Effects on Organizations*, West, St. Paul.

French, J., and Raven, B.H. (1959) 'The Bases of Social Power', in: D. Cartwright (ed.), *Studies of Social Power*, Ann Arbor: Institute for Social Research.

Glassman, R.M. (1986) 'Manufactured Charisma and Legitimacy', in: R.M. Glassman and W.H. Swatos, Jr. (eds), *Charisma, History, and Social Structure*, New York: Glenwood Press.

Goold, M., and Quinn, J.J. (1990) *Strategic Control: Milestones for Long-Term Performance*, London: Hutchinson.

Greenleaf, R.K. (1977) *Servant Leadership: A Journey into the Nature of Legitimate Power and Greatness*, New York: Paulist Press.

Greenwood, R., and Hinings, C.R. (1996) 'Understanding Radical Organizational Change: Bringing Together the Old and the New Institutionalism', *Academy of Management Review*, Vol. 21, No. 4, October, pp. 1022–1054.

Greiner, L.E. (1972) 'Evolution and Revolution as Organizations Grow', *Harvard Business Review*, July–August, pp. 37–46.

Hambrick, D.C. (1987) 'The Top Management Team: Key to Strategic Success', *California Management Review*, Vol. 30, No. 1, Fall, pp. 88–108.

Hambrick, D.C. (ed.) (1989) 'Guest Editor's Introduction: Putting Top Managers Back in the Strategy Picture', *Strategic Management Journal*, Vol. 10, Special Issue, Summer, pp. 5–15.

Hambrick, D.C., and Finkelstein, S. (1987) 'Managerial Discretion: A Bridge between Polar Views of Organizational Outcomes', in: B.M. Staw and L.L. Cummings (eds), *Research in Organizational Behavior* (Vol. 9), JAI Greenwich: CT, pp. 369–406.

Hambrick, D.C., and Mason, P.A. (1984) 'Upper Echelons: The Organization as a Reflection of Its Top Managers', *Academy of Management Review*, Vol. 9, No. 2, April, pp. 193–206.

Hampden-Turner, C., and Trompenaars, A. (1993) *The Seven Cultures of Capitalism: Value Systems for Creating Wealth in the United States, Japan, Germany, France, Britain, Sweden, and the Netherlands*, New York: Doubleday.

Hannan, M.T., and Freeman, J. (1977) 'The Population Ecology of Organizations', *American Journal of Sociology*, Vol. 82, No. 5, March, pp. 929–964.

Hargadon, A. (1998) 'Firms as Knowledge Brokers', *California Management Review*, Vol. 40, No. 3, Spring, pp. 209–227.

Harper, D. (1987) *Working Knowledge: Skill and Community in a Small Shop*, Chicago: University of Chicago Press.

Hayward, M.L.A., Rindova, V.P., and Pollock, T.G. (2004) 'Believing One's Own Press: The Causes and Consequences of CEO Celebrity', *Strategic Management Journal*, Vol. 25, No. 7, pp. 637–653.

Hedberg, B.L.T., Bystrom, P.C., and Starbuck, W.H. (1976) 'Camping on Seesaws: Prescriptions for a Self-Designing Organization', *Administrative Science Quarterly*, Vol. 21, No. 1, March, pp. 41–65.

Hofstede, G. (1993) 'Cultural Constraints in Management Theories', *Academy of Management Executive*, Vol. 7, No. 1, pp. 8–21.

House, R.J. (1971) 'A Path-Goal Theory of Leadership Effectiveness', *Administrative Science Quarterly*, Vol. 16, No. 3, September, pp. 321–339.

House, R.J., and Aditya, R.N. (1997) 'The Social Science Study of Leadership: Quo Vadis?', *Journal of Management*, Vol. 23, No. 3, May–June, pp. 409–474.

Ireland, R.D., and Hitt, M.A. (1999) 'Achieving and Maintaining Strategic Competitiveness in the 21st Century: The Role of Strategic Leadership', *Academy of Management Executive*, Vol. 13, No. 1, February, pp. 43–57.

Jensen, M.C., and Meckling, W.H. (1994) 'The Nature of Man', *Journal of Applied Corporate Finance*, Vol. 7, No. 2, Summer, pp. 4–19.

Johnson, G. (1987) *Strategic Change and the Management Process*, Oxford: Blackwell.

Johnson, G. (1988) 'Rethinking Incrementalism', *Strategic Management Journal*, Vol. 9, No. 1, January–February, pp. 75–91.

Kakabadse, A., Myers, A., McMahon, T, and Spony, G. (1995) 'Top Management Styles in Europe: Implications for Business and Cross-National Teams', *European Business Journal*, Vol. 7, No. 1, pp. 17–27.

Kelley, R.E. (1988) 'In Praise of Followers', *Harvard Business Review*, Vol. 66, No. 6, November–December, p. 142.

Kets de Vries, M.F.R. (1994) 'The Leadership Mystique', *Academy of Management Executive*, Vol. 8, No. 3, August, pp. 73–92.

Kets de Vries, M.F.R., and Miller, D. (1984) *The Neurotic Organization*, San Francisco: Jossey-Bass.

Kets de Vries, M.F.R., and Miller, D. (1988) *Unstable at the Top: Inside the Troubled Organization*, New York: New American Library.

Khandwalla, P.N. (1977) *The Design of Organizations*, New York: Harcourt, Brace, Jovanovich.

Klein, K.J., and House, R.J. (1998) 'Further Thoughts on Fire: Charismatic Leadership and Levels of Analysis', in: F. Dansereauand and F.J. Yammarino (eds), *Leadership: The Multi-Level Approaches*, Stamford, CT, JAI Press, Vol. 2, pp. 45–52.

Kohn, A. (1992) *No Contest: The Case Against Competition*, Boston, MA: Houghton Mifflin.

Kotter, J.P. (1982) *The General Managers*, New York: Free Press.

Kotter, J.P. (1990) 'What Leaders Really Do', *Harvard Business Review*, Vol. 68, No. 3, May–June, p. 103.

Lawrence, P.R., and Lorsch, J.W. (1967) 'Differentiation and Integration in Complex Organizations', *Administrative Science Quarterly*, March, pp. 1–47.

Leavy, B., and Wilson, D. (1994) *Strategy and Leadership*, London: Routledge.

Leonard-Barton, D. (1995) *Well-Springs of Knowledge: Building and Sustaining the Sources of Innovation*, Boston: Harvard Business School Press.

Lessem, R., and Neubauer, F.F. (1994) *European Management Systems*, London: McGraw-Hill.

Levy, D. (1994) 'Chaos Theory and Strategy: Theory, Application, and Managerial Implications', *Strategic Management Journal*, Vol. 15, pp. 167–178.

Lorange, P. (1974) 'A Framework for Management Control Systems', *Sloan Management Review*, Vol. 16, No. 1, Fall, pp. 41–56.

Lorange, P., Scott, M.F., and S. Ghoshal (1986) *Strategic Control*, St. Paul: West.

MacDuffie, J.P., and Helper, S. (1997) 'Creating Lean Suppliers: Diffusing Lean Production Through the Supply Chain', *California Management Review*, Vol. 39, No. 4, Summer, pp. 118–150.

Mann, L., Samson, D., and Dow, D. (1998) 'A Field Experiment on the Effects of Benchmarking and Goal Setting on Company Sales Performance', *Journal of Management*, Vol. 24, p. 82.

March, J.G., and Simon, H.A. (1958) *Organizations*, New York: Wiley.

Meindl, J.R., Ehrlich, S.B., and Dukerich, J.M. (1985) 'The Romance of Leadership', *Administrative Science Quarterly*, Vol. 30, No. 1, March, pp. 78–102.

Meyer, J.W., and Zucker, L.G. (1989) *Permanently Failing Organizations*, Newbury Park: Sage Publications.

Miles, R.E., and Snow, C.C. (1978) *Organizational Strategy: Structure and Process*, New York: McGraw-Hill.

Miller, D. (1990) *The Icarus Paradox: How Excellent Companies Can Bring About Their Own Downfall*, New York: Harper Business.

Miller, D., and Friesen, PH. (1980) 'Momentum and Revolution in Organizational Adaptation', *Academy of Management Journal*, Vol. 23, No. 4, December, pp. 591–614.

Miller, D., and Kets de Vries, M. (1987) *Unstable at the Top*, New York: New American Library.

Mintzberg, H. (1979) *The Structure of Organizations*, Englewood Cliffs, NJ: Prentice Hall.

Mintzberg, H. (1982) 'If You're Not Serving Bill and Barbara, Then You're Not Serving Leadership', in: J.G. Hunt, U. Sekaran, and C.A. Schreisheim (eds), *Leadership: Beyond Establishment Views*, Carbondale: Southern Illinois University.

Mintzberg, H. (1989) *Mintzberg on Management*, New York: Free Press.

Mintzberg, H. (1991) 'The Effective Organization: Forces and Forms', *Sloan Management Review*, Vol. 32, No. 2, Winter, pp. 54–67.

Misumi, J. (1985) *The Behavioral Science of Leadership*, Ann Arbor: University of Michigan Press.

Morgan, G. (1986) *Images of Organization*, London: Sage.

Nadler, D.A., and Tushman, M.L. (1990) 'Beyond the Charismatic Leader: Leadership and Organizational Change', *California Management Review*, Vol. 32, No. 2, Winter, pp. 77–97.

Nanus, B. (1992) *Visionary Leadership: Creating a Compelling Sense of Direction for Your Organization*, San Francisco: Jossey-Bass.

Nelson, R.R., and Winter, S.G. (1982) *An Evolutionary Theory of Economic Change*, Reading, MA: Harvard University Press.

Nonaka, I. (1988) 'Creating Organizational Order Out of Chaos: Self-Renewal in Japanese Firms', *California Management Review*, Vol. 30, No. 3, Spring, pp. 57–73.

Nonaka, I., and Konno, N. (1998) 'The Concept of "Ba": Building a Foundation for Knowledge Creation', *California Management Review*, Vol. 40, No. 3, Summer, pp. 40–41.

Pascale, R.T. (1990) *Managing on the Edge: How Successful Companies Use Conflict to Stay Ahead*, London: Viking Penguin.

Peters, T.J., and Waterman, R.H. (1982) *In Search of Excellence*, New York: Harper & Row.

Pettigrew, A. (1985) *The Awakening Giant*, Oxford: Blackwell.

Pfeffer, J. (1977) 'The Ambiguity of Leadership', *Academy of Management Review*, Vol. 2, No. 1, January, pp. 104–112.

Pfeffer, J. (1982) *Organizations and Organization Theory*, Boston: Pitman.

Pfeffer, J. (1992) *Managing With Power: Politics and Influence in Organizations*, Boston, MA: Harvard Business School Press.

Pfeffer, J. (1997a) *Human Resources at the AES Corporation: The Case of the Missing Department, Case SHR-3*, Stanford University, Stanford, CA: Graduate School of Business.

Pfeffer, J. (1997b) *The Men's Wearhouse: Success in a Declining Industry, Case HR-5*, Stanford, CA: Graduate School of Business, Stanford University.

Pfeffer, J., and Salancik, G. (1978) *The External Control of Organizations: A Resource Dependency Perspective*, New York: Harper & Row.

Pfeffer, J., and Sutton, R.I. (1999a) 'Knowing "What" to Do is Not Enough: Turning Knowledge Into Action', *California Management Review*, Vol. 42, No. 1, Fall, pp. 83–108.

Pfeffer, J., and Sutton, R.I. (1999b) *The Knowing–Doing Gap: How Smart Companies Turn Knowledge Into Action*, Boston, MA: Harvard Business School Press.

Pondy, L.R., Boland, J.R., and Thomas, H. (eds) (1988) *Managing Ambiguity and Change*, New York: Wiley.

Porter, M.E. (1990) *The Competitive Advantage of Nations*, London: Macmillan.

Quinn, J.B. (1980) 'Managing Strategic Change', *Sloan Management Review*, Summer, pp. 3–20.

Quinn, J.B. (1985) 'Managing Innovation: Controlled Chaos', *Harvard Business Review*, Vol. 63, No. 3, May–June, pp. 73–84.

Rowe, W.G. (2001) 'Creating Wealth in Organizations: The Role of Strategic Leadership', *Academy of Management Executive*, Vol. 15, No. 1, February, pp. 81–94.

Ruggles, R. (1998) 'The State of the Notion: Knowledge Management in Practice', *California Management Review*, Vol. 40, No. 3, p. 83.

Rumelt, R.P. (1995) 'Inertia and Transformation', in: C.A. Montgomery (ed.), *Resource-based and Evolutionary Theories of the Firm: Towards a Synthesis*, Boston: Kluwer Academic Publishers, pp. 101–132.

Schein, E.H. (1985) *Organizational Culture and Leadership*, San Francisco: Jossey-Bass.

Schein, E.H. (1993) 'On Dialogue, Culture, and Organizational Learning', *Organizational Dynamics*, Vol. 22, No. 2, pp. 40–51.

Schneider, S.S. (ed.) (1991) 'Interpreting Organizational Leadership', *Organization Studies*, Special Issue, Vol. 12.

Selznick, P. (1957) *Leadership in Administration: A Sociological Interpretation*, New York: Harper & Row.

Semler, R. (1994) 'Why My Employees Still Work for Me', *Harvard Business Review*, January–February, p. 64.

Semler, R. (1995) *Maverick*, London: Arrow Business.

Semler, R. (2003) *The Seven-day Weekend*, Century.

Senge, P. (1990a) *The Fifth Discipline: The Art and Practice of the Learning Organization*, New York: Doubleday.

Senge, P.M. (1990b) 'The Leader's New Work: Building Learning Organizations', *Sloan Management Review*, Vol. 32, No. 1, Fall, pp. 7–23.

Simons, R. (1991) 'Strategic Orientation and Top Management Attention to Control Systems', *Strategic Management Journal*, Vol. 12, No. 1, pp. 49–62.

Simons, R. (1994) 'How New Top Managers Use Control Systems as Levers of Strategic Renewal', *Strategic Management Journal*, Vol. 15, No. 3, March, pp. 169–189.

Simons, R. (1995) *Levers of Control: How Managers Use Innovative Control Systems to Drive Strategic Renewal*, Boston, MA: HBS Press.

Sims, H.P., and Lorenzi, P. (1992) *The New Leadership Paradigm: Social Learning and Cognition in Organizations*, London: Sage.

Smircich, L., and Stubbart, C. (1985) 'Strategic Management in an Enacted World', *Academy of Management Review*, Vol. 10, No. 4, pp. 724–736.

Stacey, R.D. (1992) *Managing Chaos: Dynamic Business Strategies in an Unpredictable World*, London: Kogan Page.

Stacey, R.D. (1993a) 'Strategy as Order Emerging from Chaos', *Long Range Planning*, Vol. 26, No. 1, pp. 10–17.

Stacey, R.D. (1993b) *Strategic Management and Organizational Dynamics*, London: Pitman.

Stalk, G., Evans, P., and Shulman, L.E. (1992) 'Competing on Capabilities: The New Rules of Corporate Strategy', *Harvard Business Review*, Vol. 70, No. 2, March–April, pp. 57–69.

Stewart, T.A. (1998) 'Knowledge, the Appreciating Commodity', *Fortune*, October 12, pp. 199.

Stopford, J.M., and Baden-Fuller, C. (1990) 'Corporate Rejuvenation', *Journal of Management Studies*, July, pp. 399–415.

Strebel, P. (1994) 'Choosing the Right Change Path', *California Management Review*, Vol. 36, No. 2, Winter, pp. 29–51.

Tannenbaum, R., and Schmidt, W.H. (1958) 'How to Choose a Leadership Pattern', *Harvard Business Review*, Vol. 36, No. 2, March–April, pp. 95–101.

Taylor, A. III (1997) 'How Toyota Defies Gravity', *Fortune*, December, p. 8.

The Conference Board (1997) *HR Executive Review*, Vol. 5, No. 3, p. 3.

Tichy, N., and Cohen, E. (1997) *The Leadership Engine: How Winning Companies Build Leaders at Every Level*, New York: Harper Collins.

Tichy, N., and Devanna, M. (1987) *The Transformational Leader*, New York: Wiley.

Tichy, N.M., and Ulrich, D.O. (1984) 'SMR Forum: The Leadership Challenge: A Call for the Transformational Leader', *Sloan Management Review*, Vol. 26, No. 1, Fall, pp. 59–68.

Tjosvold, D. (1986) *Working Together to Get Things Done*, D.C. Heath, MA: Lexington.

Trice, H.M., and Beyer, J.M. (1993) *The Cultures of Work Organizations*, Englewood Cliffs, NJ: Prentice Hall.

Tucker, R.C. (1968) 'The Theory of Charismatic Leadership', *Daedalus*, Vol. 97, No. 3, pp. 731–756.

Tushman, M.L., Newman, W.H. and Romanelli, E. (1986) 'Convergence and Upheaval: Managing the Unsteady Pace of Organizational Evolution', *California Management Review*, Vol. 29, No. 1, Fall, pp. 29–44.

Vroom, V.H., and Jago, A.G. (1988) *The New Leadership: Managing Participation in Organizations*, Englewood Cliffs, NJ: Prentice Hall.

Wack, P. (1985) 'Scenarios: Uncharted Waters Ahead', *Harvard Business Review*, Vol. 64, No. 5, September–October, pp. 73–89.

Waldman, D.A., and Yammarino, F.H. (1999) 'CEO Charismatic Leadership: Levels-of-Management and Levels-of-Analysis Effects', *Academy of Management Review*, Vol. 24, No. 2, pp. 266–285.

Weick, K.E. (1979) *The Social Psychology of Organizing*, New York: Random House.

Wheatly, M.J., and Kellner-Rogers, M. (1996) 'Self-Organization: The Irresistible Future of Organizing', *Strategy, and Leadership*, Vol. 24, No. 4, pp. 18–25.

Yoshino, M. (2002) *Nissan Motor Co. 2002*, Boston, MA: Harvard Business School Press.

Yukl, G. (1994) *Leadership in Organizations*, Third Edition, Englewood Cliffs, NJ: Prentice Hall.

Zalesnik, A. (1977) 'Managers and Leaders: Are They Different?', *Harvard Business Review*, Vol. 55, No. 3, May-June, pp. 67–78.

Zalesnik, A. (1989) *The Managerial Mystique: Restoring Leadership in Business*, New York: Harper & Row.

Zbaracki, M. (1998) 'The Rhetoric and Reality of Total Quality Management', *Administrative Science Quarterly*, Vol. 43, pp. 602–636.

THE INTERNATIONAL CONTEXT

There never were, since the creation of the world, two cases exactly parallel.

Philip Dormer Stanhope (1694–1773); English Secretary of State

INTRODUCTION

As firms move out of their domestic market on to the international stage, they are faced with differing business arenas. The nations they expand to can vary with regard to consumer behaviour, language, legal system, technological infrastructure, business culture, educational system, labour relations, political ideology, distribution structures and fiscal regime, to name just a few. At face value, the plurality of the international context can seem daunting. Yet, the question is how important the international differences are for firms operating across borders. Do firms need to adapt to the international diversity encountered, or can they find ways of overcoming the constraints imposed by distinct national systems, structures and behaviours? This matter of understanding and dealing with international variety is one of the key topics for managers operating across borders.

A second question with regard to the international context is that of international linkages – to what extent do events in one country have an impact on what happens in other countries? When a number of nations are tightly linked to one another in a particular area, this is referred to as a case of international integration. If, on the other hand, there are very weak links between developments in one country and developments elsewhere, this is referred to as a situation of international fragmentation. The question for managers is how tightly linked nations around the world actually are. Countries might be quite different, yet developments in one nation might significantly influence developments elsewhere. For instance, if interest rates rise in the United States, central bankers in most other countries cannot ignore this. If the price of oil goes down on the spot market in Rotterdam, this will have a 'spill over effect' towards most other nations. And if a breakthrough chip technology is developed in Taiwan, this will send a shockwave through the computer industry around the world. If nations are highly integrated, the manager must view all countries as part of the same system – as squares on a chessboard, not to be judged in isolation.

When looking at the subjects of international variety and linkages, it is also important to know in which direction they have been moving, and will develop further, over time. Where a development towards lower international variety and tighter international linkages on a worldwide scale can be witnessed, a process of globalization is at play. Where a movement towards more international variety and a loosening of international linkages is apparent, a process of localization is taking place.

For managers operating in more than one nation, it is vital to understand the nature of the international context. Have their businesses been globalizing or localizing, and what can be expected in future? Answers to these questions should guide strategizing managers in choosing which countries to be active in and how to manage their activities across borders. Taken together, these international context questions constitute the issue of international configuration, and will be the focus of the further discussion in this chapter.

THE ISSUE OF INTERNATIONAL CONFIGURATION

How a firm configures its activities across borders is largely dependent on how it deals with the fundamental tension between the opposite demands of globalization and localization. To understand these forces, pulling the organization in contrary directions, it is first necessary to further define them. Globalization and localization are terms used by many, but explained by few. This lack of uniform definition often leads to an unfocused debate, as different people employ the same terms, but actually refer to different phenomena. Therefore, this discussion will start with a clarification of the concepts of globalization and localization. Subsequently, attention will turn to the two central questions facing the international manager: which countries should the firm be active in and how should this array of international activities be managed? This first question, of deciding on which geographic areas the organization should be involved in, is the issue of international composition. The second question, of deciding on the organizational structure and systems needed to run the multi-country activities, is the issue of international management.

Dimensions of globalization

Clearly, globalization refers to the process of becoming more global. But what is global? Although there is no agreement on a single definition, most writers use the term to refer to one or more of the following elements (see Figure 10.1):

- Worldwide scope. 'Global' can simply be used as a geographic term. A firm with operations around the world can be labelled a global company, to distinguish it from firms that are local (not international) or regional in scope. In such a case, the term 'global' is primarily intended to describe the spatial dimension – the broadest possible international scope is to be global. When this definition of global is employed, globalization is the process of international expansion on a worldwide scale (e.g. Patel and Pavitt, 1991).

- Worldwide similarity. 'Global' can also refer to homogeneity around the world. For instance, if a company decides to sell the same product in all of its international markets, it is often referred to as a global product, as opposed to a locally tailored product. In such a case, the term 'global' is primarily intended to describe the variance dimension – the ultimate level of worldwide similarity is to be global. When this definition of global is employed, globalization is the process of declining international variety (e.g. Levitt, 1983, Reading 10.1 in this book).

- Worldwide integration. 'Global' can also refer to the world as one tightly linked system. For instance, a global market can be said to exist if events in one country are significantly impacted by events in other geographic markets. This contrasts to local markets, where price levels, competition, demand and fashions are hardly influenced by developments in other nations. In such a case, the term 'global' is primarily intended to describe the linkages dimension – the ultimate level of worldwide integration is to be global. When this definition of global is employed, globalization is the process of increasing international interconnectedness (e.g. Porter, 1986).

FIGURE 10.1   Internationalization and globalization of the firm

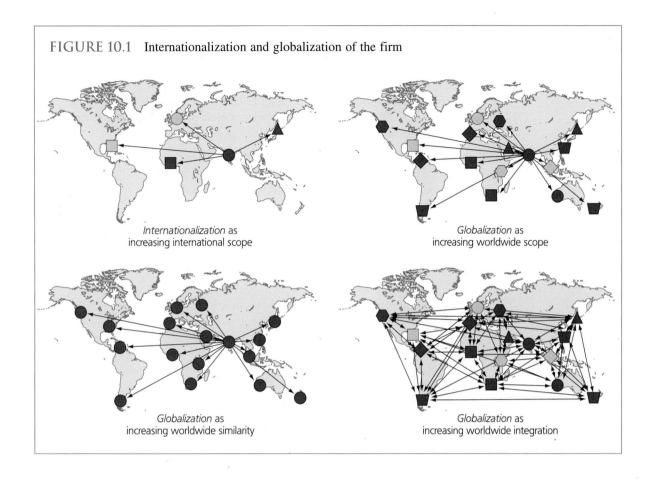

Internationalization as
increasing international scope

Globalization as
increasing worldwide scope

Globalization as
increasing worldwide similarity

Globalization as
increasing worldwide integration

So, is for example McDonald's a global company? That depends along which of the above three dimensions the company is measured. When judging the international scope of McDonald's, it can be seen that the company is globalizing, but far from global. The company operates in approximately half the countries in the world, but in many of these only in one or a few large cities. Of McDonald's worldwide revenues, more than half is still earned in the United States. This predominance of the home country is even stronger if the composition of the company's top management is looked at (Ruigrok and Van Tulder, 1995). However, when judging McDonald's along the dimension of international similarity, it is simple to observe that the company is relatively global, as it takes a highly standardized approach to most markets around the world. Although, it should be noted that on some aspects as menu and interior design there is leeway for local adaptation. Finally, when judging McDonald's along the dimension of international integration, the company is only slightly global, as it is not very tightly linked around the world. Some activities are centralized or coordinated, but in general there is relatively little need for concerted action.

As for localization – the opposite of the process of globalization – it is characterized by decreasing international scope, similarity and integration. From the angle of international strategy the most extreme form of localness is when firms operate in one country and there is no similarity or integration between countries (e.g. the hairdressing and driving school businesses). However, this equates local with national, while firms and businesses can be even more local, all the way down to the state/province/department/district and municipal playing fields.

Levels of globalization

The second factor complicating a clear understanding of the concept of globalization is that it is applied to a variety of subjects, while the differences are often not made explicit. Some people discuss globalization as a development in the economy at large, while others debate globalization as something happening to industries, markets, products, technologies, fashions, production, competition and organizations. In general, debates on globalization tend to concentrate on one of three levels of analysis:

- Globalization of companies. Some authors focus on the micro level, debating whether individual companies are becoming more global. Issues are the extent to which firms have a global strategy, structure, culture, workforce, management team and resource base. In more detail, the globalization of specific products and value-adding activities is often discussed. Here it is of particular importance to acknowledge that the globalization of one product or activity (e.g. marketing) does not necessarily entail the globalization of all others (e.g. Prahalad and Doz, 1987; Bartlett and Ghoshal, 1987, Reading 10.4).

- Globalization of businesses. Other authors are more concerned with the meso level, debating whether particular businesses are becoming more global. Here it is important to distinguish those who emphasize the globalization of markets, as opposed to those accentuating the globalization of industries (see Chapter 5 for this distinction). The issue of globalizing markets has to do with the growing similarity of worldwide customer demand and the growing ease of worldwide product flows (e.g. Levitt, 1983, Reading 10.1; Douglas and Wind, 1987, Reading 10.2). For example, the crude oil and foreign currency markets are truly global – the same commodities are traded at the same rates around the world. The markets for accountancy and garbage collection services, on the other hand, are very local – demand differs significantly, there is little cross-border trade and consequently prices vary sharply. The globalization of industries is quite a different issue, as it has to do with the emergence of a set of producers that compete with one another on a worldwide scale (e.g. Prahalad and Doz, 1987; Porter, 1990a, 1990b). So, for instance, the automobile and consumer electronics industries are quite global – the major players in most countries belong to the same set of companies that compete against each other all around the world. Even the accountancy industry is relatively global, even though the markets for accountancy services are very local. On the other hand, the hairdressing and retail banking industries are very local – the competitive scene in each country is relatively uninfluenced by competitive developments elsewhere.

- Globalization of economies. Yet other authors take a macro level of analysis, arguing whether or not the world's economies in general are experiencing a convergence trend. Many authors are interested in the macroeconomic dynamics of international integration and its consequences in terms of growth, employment, inflation, productivity, trade and foreign direct investment (e.g. Kay, 1989; Krugman, 1990). Others focus more on the political realities constraining and encouraging globalization (e.g. Klein, 2000; McGrew and Lewis, 1992). Yet others are interested in the underlying dynamics of technological, institutional and organizational convergence (e.g. Dunning, 1986; Kogut, 1993).

Ultimately, the question in this chapter is not only whether economies, businesses and companies are actually globalizing, but also whether these developments are a matter of choice. In other words, is global convergence or continued international diversity an uncontrollable evolutionary development to which firms (and governments) must comply, or can managers actively influence the globalization or localization of their environment?

International composition

An international firm operates in two or more countries. When a firm starts up value-adding activities in yet another country, this process is called internationalization. In Figure 10.2 an overview is presented of the most common forms of internationalization. One of the earliest international growth moves undertaken by firms is to sell their products to foreign buyers, either directly (internet or telephone sales), through a travelling salesperson, or via a local agent or distributor. Such types of export activities are generally less taxing for the organization than the establishment of a foreign sales subsidiary (or sales unit). Serving a foreign market by means of a sales subsidiary often requires a higher level of investment in terms of marketing expenditures, sales force development and after-sales service provision. A firm can also set up a foreign production subsidiary (or 'off-shore' production unit), whose activities are focused on manufacturing goods to be exported back to the firm's other markets. Alternatively, a firm can begin an integrated foreign subsidiary that is responsible for a full range of value-adding activities, including production and sales. In practice, there are many variations to these basic forms of internationalization, depending on the specific value-adding activities carried out in different countries. For example, some subsidiaries have R&D, assembly and marketing their portfolio of activities, while others do not (Birkenshaw and Hood, 1998).

When establishing a foreign subsidiary the internationalizing firm must decide whether to purchase an existing local company (entry by acquisition) or to start from scratch (greenfield entry). In both cases the firm can work independently or by means of a joint venture with a local player or foreign partner. It is also possible to dispense with the establishment of a subsidiary at all, by networking with local manufacturers, assemblers, sales agents and distributors (as discussed in Chapter 7).

The issue of international composition deals with the question of where the firm wants to have a certain level of involvement. The firm's strategists must decide where to allocate resources, build up activities and try to achieve results. The issue of international composition can be further subdivided into two parts:

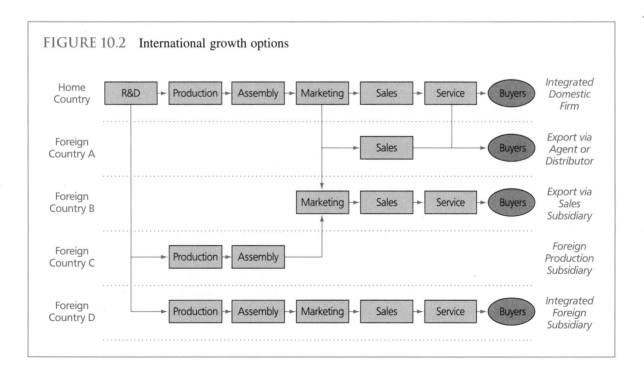

FIGURE 10.2   International growth options

■ International scope. The international composition of the firm depends first of all on the countries selected to do business in. The geographic spectrum covered by the firm is referred to as its international scope. The firm's strategists must decide how many countries they want to be active in, and which countries these should be.

■ International distribution. The international composition of the firm also depends on how it has distributed its value-adding activities across the countries selected. In some firms all national subsidiaries carry out similar activities and are of comparable size. However, in many firms activities are distributed less symmetrically, with, for example, production, R&D and marketing concentrated in only a few countries (Porter, 1986). Commonly some countries will also contribute much more revenue and profits than others, but these might not be the countries where new investments can best be made. It is the task of the firm's strategists to determine how activities can best be distributed and how resources can best be allocated across the various countries.

Just as a corporation's portfolio of businesses could be visualized by means of a portfolio grid, so too can a business's portfolio of foreign sales markets be displayed using such a matrix. In Figure 10.3 a fictitious example is given of a firm's international sales portfolio using the GE business screen as analysis tool. Instead of industry attractiveness along the vertical axis, country attractiveness is used, calculating items such as market growth, competitive intensity, buyer power, customer loyalty, government regulation and operating costs. Following a similar logic, firms can also evaluate their international portfolios of, for instance, production locations and R&D facilities.

Deciding which portfolio of countries to be active in, both in terms of international scope and distribution, will largely depend on the strategic motives that have stimulated the firm to enter the international arena in the first place. After all, there must be some good reasons why a firm is willing to disregard the growth opportunities in its home market and to enter into uncertain foreign adventures. There must be some advantages to being international that offset the disadvantages of foreignness and distance. These advantages of having activities in two or more countries – cross-border synergies – will be

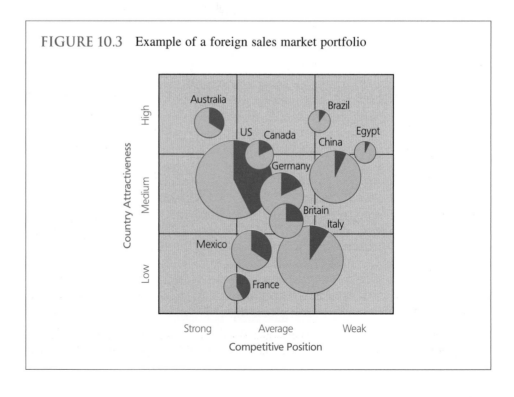

FIGURE 10.3   Example of a foreign sales market portfolio

discussed in more detail, after an account of the second international configuration question, the issue of international management.

International management

A firm operating in two or more countries needs to find some way of organizing itself to deal with its border-spanning nature. As managing across borders is difficult and costly, the simplest solution would be to organize all operations on a country-by-country basis, and to leave all country units as autonomous as possible. Yet, internationalization is only economically rational if 'the international whole is more than the sum of the country parts' (see Chapter 6). In other words, internationalization only makes sense if enough cross-border synergies can be reaped to offset the extra cost of foreignness and distance.

Therefore, the firm needs to have international integration mechanisms to facilitate the realization of cross-border synergies. The three most important integration mechanisms used in international management are:

- Standardization. An easy way to reap cross-border synergies is to do the same thing in each country, without any costly adaptation. Such standardization can be applied to all aspects of the business model (see Chapter 5) – the product offerings, value-adding activities and resources employed. Standardization is particularly important for achieving economies of scale (e.g. Hout, Porter and Rudden, 1982; Levitt, 1983), but can be equally valuable for serving border-crossing clients who want to encounter a predictable offering (e.g. Hamel and Prahalad, 1985; Yip, 1993).

- Coordination. Instead of standardizing products or activities, international firms can also align their varied activities in different countries by means of cross-border co-ordination. Getting the activities in the various countries aligned is often inspired by the need to serve border-crossing clients in a coordinated manner (e.g. global service level agreements), or to counter these clients' policy of playing off the firm's sub-sidiaries against one another (e.g. cross-border price shopping). International co-ordination can be valuable when responding to, or attacking, competitors as well. A coordinated assault on a few markets, financed by the profits from many markets (i.e. cross-subsidization), can sometimes lead to competitive success (Prahalad and Doz, 1987).

- Centralization. Of course, activities within the firm can also be integrated at one cen-tral location, either in the firm's home country or elsewhere. Such centralization is often motivated by the drive for economies of scale (e.g. Buckley and Casson, 1985; Dunning, 1981), but might be due to the competitive advantage of a particular country as well. For example, production costs might be much lower, or quality much higher, in a certain part of the world, making it a logical location for centralized production. Centralization of knowledge intensive activities is sometimes also needed, to guard quality or to ensure faster learning than could be attained with decentralized activities (e.g. Porter, 1990b; Dunning, 1993).

It is up to the firm's strategists to determine the most appropriate level of standardization, coordination and centralization needed to function efficiently and effectively in an in-ternational context. The level chosen for each of these three characteristics will largely determine the organizational model adopted by the international firm.

In their seminal research, Bartlett and Ghoshal (1989) distinguish four generic organizational models for international firms, each with its own mix of standardization, coordination and centralization (see Figure 10.4):

- Decentralized federation. In a decentralized federation, the firm is organized along geographic lines, with each full-scale country subsidiary largely self-sufficient and

FIGURE 10.4   Generic organizational models for international firms
(adapted from Bartlett and Ghoshal, 1995)

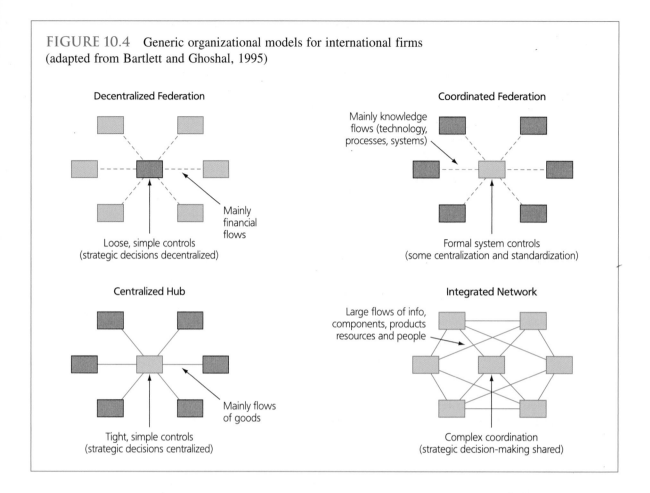

autonomous from international headquarters in the home country. Few activities are centralized and little is coordinated across borders. The level of standardization is also low, as the country unit is free to adapt itself to the specific circumstances in its national environment. Bartlett and Ghoshal refer to this organizational model as 'multinational'. Another common label is 'multi-domestic' (e.g. Prahalad and Doz, 1987; Stopford and Wells, 1972).

■ Coordinated federation. In a coordinated federation, the firm is also organized along geographic lines, but the country subsidiaries have a closer relationship with the international headquarters in the home country. Most of the core competences, technologies, processes and products are developed centrally, while other activities are carried out locally. As a consequence, there is some standardization and coordination, requiring some formalized control systems (i.e. planning, budgeting, administration). Another name employed by Bartlett and Ghoshal to refer to this organizational model is 'international'.

■ Centralized hub. In a centralized hub, national units are relatively unimportant, as all main activities are carried out in the home country. Generally a highly standardized approach is used towards all foreign markets. As centralization and standardization are high, foreign subsidiaries are limited to implementing headquarters' policies in the local markets. Coordination of activities across countries is made easy by the dominance of headquarters. Bartlett and Ghoshal use the term 'global' to describe this organizational model.

■ Integrated network. In an integrated network, the country subsidiaries have a close relationship with international headquarters, just as in the coordinated federation, but also have a close relationship with each other. Very little is centralized at the international headquarters in the home country, but each national unit can become the worldwide centre for a particular competence, technology, process or product. Thus subsidiaries need to coordinate the flow of components, products, knowledge and people between each other. Such a networked organization requires a certain level of standardization to function effectively. Another name used by Bartlett and Ghoshal for this organizational model is 'transnational'.

Which international organizational model is adopted depends strongly on what the corporate strategist wishes to achieve. The preferred international management structure will be largely determined by the type of cross-border synergies that the strategists envisage. This topic of multi-country synergies will be examined more closely in the following section.

THE PARADOX OF GLOBALIZATION AND LOCALIZATION

The axis of the earth sticks out visibly through the center of each and every town or city.

Oliver Wendell Holmes (1809–1894); American physician, poet and essayist

It requires almost no argumentation that internationally operating companies are faced with a tension between treating the world as one market and acknowledging national differences. During the last few decades, achieving a balance between international uniformity and meeting local demands has been the dominant theme in the literature on international management. All researchers have recognized the tension between international standardization and local adaptation. The key question has been whether international firms have the *liberty* to standardize or face the *pressure* to adapt.

However, since the mid-1980s, this standardization–adaptation discussion has progressed significantly as strategy researchers have moved beyond the organizational design question, seeking the underlying strategic motives for standardization and adaptation (e.g. Bartlett and Ghoshal, 1987; Porter, 1986; Prahalad and Doz, 1987). It has been acknowledged that international standardization is not a matter of organizational convenience that companies naturally revert to when the market does not demand local adaptation. Rather, international standardization is a means for achieving cross-border synergies. A firm can achieve cross-border synergies by leveraging resources, integrating activities and aligning product offerings across two or more countries. Creating additional value in this way is the very *raison d'être* of the international firm. If internationalizing companies would fully adapt to local conditions, without leveraging a homegrown quality, they would have no advantage over local firms, while they would be burdened by the extra costs of international business (e.g. overcoming distance and foreignness). Therefore, international companies need to realize at least enough cross-border synergies to compensate for the additional expenses of operating in multiple countries.

Much of the theoretical discourse has focused on the question which cross-border synergies can be achieved on the ultimate, global scale. Most researchers identify various potential opportunities for worldwide synergy, yet recognize the simultaneous demands to meet the specific conditions in each local market (e.g. Dicken, 1992; Yip, 1993). These possibilities for reaping global synergy will be examined first, followed by the countervailing pressures for local responsiveness.

The demand for global synergy

Striving for cross-border synergies on as large a scale as possible can be an opportunity for an international firm to enhance its competitive advantage. However, realizing global synergies is often less an opportunity than a competitive demand. If rival firms have already successfully implemented a global strategy, there can be a severe pressure to also reap the benefits of globalization through standardization, coordination or centralization.

There are many different types of cross-border synergies. In accordance with the business model framework described in Chapter 5, these synergies can be organized into three categories: aligning product offerings, integrating activities and leveraging resources (see Figure 10.5).

Synergy by aligning positions.   The first way to create cross-border synergies is to align market positions in the various countries in which the firm operates. Taking a coordinated approach to different national markets can be necessary under two circumstances – namely to provide a concerted cross-border product offering to customers and to stage a concerted cross-border attack on competitors:

- Dealing with cross-border customers. An international firm is ideally placed to offer border-crossing customers an internationally coordinated product or service offering. Whether it is for a tourist who wants to have the same hotel arrangements around the world, or for an advertiser who wants to stage a globally coordinated new product introduction, it can be important to have a standardized and coordinated offering across

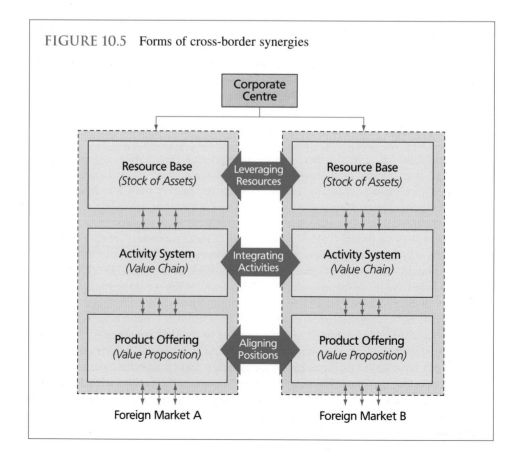

FIGURE 10.5   Forms of cross-border synergies

various nations. It might be equally necessary to counter the tactics of customers shopping around various national subsidiaries for the best deals, or to meet the customer's demand to aggregate all global buying via one central account.

■ Dealing with cross-border competition. An international firm is also in an ideal position to successfully attack locally oriented rivals, if it does not spread its resources too thinly around the world, but rather focuses on only a few countries at a time. By coordinating its competitive efforts and bringing its global power to bear on a few national markets, an international firm can push back or even defeat local rivals country-by-country. Of course, an international company must also have the capability of defending itself against such a globally coordinated attack by a rival international firm.

Synergy by integrating activities.   Cross-border synergies can also be achieved by linking the activity systems of the firm in its various national markets. Integrating the value-creation processes across borders can be useful to realize economies of scale and to make use of the specific competitive advantages of each nation:

■ Reaping scale advantages. Instead of organizing the international firm's activity system on a country-by-country basis, certain activities can be pooled to reap economies of scale. Commonly this means that activities must be centralized at one or a few locations, and that a certain level of product and/or process standardization must be accepted. Economies of scale can be realized for many activities, most notably production, logistics, procurement and R&D. However, scale advantages might be possible for all activities of the firm. Although scale advantages are often pursued by means of centralization, it is often possible to achieve economies by standardizing and coordinating activities across borders (e.g. joint procurement, joint marketing campaigns).

■ Reaping location advantages. For some activities certain locations are much more suited than others, making it attractive to centralize these activities in the countries that possess a particular competitive advantage. A national competitive advantage can consist of inexpensive or specialist local inputs, such as raw materials, energy, physical infrastructure or human resources, but can also be due to the presence of attractive buyers and related industries (Porter, 1990a, Reading 10.3).

Synergy by leveraging resources.   A third manner in which cross-border synergies can be realized is by sharing resources across national markets. Such resource leveraging can be achieved by physically reallocating resources to other countries where they can be used more productively, or by replicating them so they can be used in many national markets simultaneously:

■ Achieving resource reallocation. Instead of leaving resources in countries where they happen to be, international firms have the opportunity to transfer resources to other locations, where they can be used to more benefit. For example, money, machinery and people can be reallocated out of countries where the return on these resources is low, into countries where they can reap a higher return. Managers specializing in market development might be sent to new subsidiaries, while older machinery might be transferred to less advanced markets (Vernon, 1966; Buckley and Casson, 1976).

■ Achieving resource replication. While leveraging tangible resources requires physical reallocation or sharing (see reaping scale advantages), intangible resources can be leveraged by means of replication. Intangibles such as knowledge and capabilities can be copied across borders and reused in another country. This allows international companies to leverage their know-how with regard to such aspects as technology, production, marketing, logistics and sales (Kogut and Zander, 1993; Liebeskind, 1996).

For all of these cross-border synergies it holds that the wider the geographic scope, the greater the potential benefit. Where possible, realizing these synergies on a global scale would result in the highest level of value creation.

These opportunities for global synergy represent a strong demand on all companies, both international and domestic. If a company can reap these synergies more quickly and successfully than its competitors, this could result in a strong offensive advantage. If other companies have a head start in capturing these global synergies, the firm must move quickly to catch up. Either way, there is a pressure on companies to seek out opportunities for global synergy and to turn them to their advantage.

The demand for local responsiveness

Yet the pressure to pursue global synergies is only half the equation. Simultaneously, companies must remain attuned to the specific demands of each national market and retain the ability to respond to these particular characteristics in a timely and adequate manner. In other words, firms must have the capability to be responsive to local conditions. If they lose touch with the distinct competitive dynamics in each of their national markets, they might find themselves at a competitive disadvantage compared to more responsive rivals.

While business responsiveness is always important, it becomes all the more pressing when the differences between various national markets are large. The more dissimilar the national markets, the more pressure on the international firm to be attuned to these distinct characteristics. The most important differences between countries include:

- Differences in market structure. Countries can differ significantly with regard to their competitive landscape. For example, in some national markets there are strong local competitors, requiring the international firm to respond differently than in countries where it encounters its 'regular' international rivals. Another difference is that in some countries there are only a few market parties, while in other countries the market is highly fragmented among numerous competitors. There can also be large differences from country to country in the background of competitors – in some countries conglomerates dominate the business scene, while in other countries single business competitors are more frequent.

- Differences in customer needs. Customers in each national market can have needs that are significantly different than the needs exhibited in other countries. The nature of these customer differences can vary from divergent cultural expectations and use circumstances, to incompatible technical systems and languages employed.

- Differences in buying behaviour. Not only the customers' needs can differ across countries, but so can their buying behaviour. For example, customers can be different with regard to the way they structure buying decisions, the types of information they consider and the relationship they wish to have with their suppliers.

- Differences in substitutes. National markets can also differ with regard to the types of indirect competition that needs to be faced. In some countries, for instance, beer brewers have to deal with wine as an important rival product, while in other markets tea or soft drinks might be the most threatening substitutes.

- Differences in distribution channels. Countries can exhibit remarkable differences in the way their distribution channels work. For example, countries can vary with regard to the kinds of distribution channels available, the number of layers in the distribution structure, their level of sophistication, their degree of concentration and the negotiating power of each player.

- **Differences in media structure.** National markets can have very different media channels available for marketing communication purposes. In the area of television, for instance, countries vary widely with regard to the number of stations on the air (or on the cable), the types of regulation imposed, the amount of commercial time available, and its cost and effectiveness. In the same way, all other media channels may differ.

- **Differences in infrastructure.** Many products and services are heavily dependent on the type of infrastructure available in a country. For example, some products rely on a digital telephone system, high-speed motorways, 24-hour convenience stores, or a national healthcare system. Some services require an efficient postal service, poor public transport, electronic banking or cable television.

- **Differences in supply structure.** If a company has local operations, the differences between countries with regard to their supply structures can also force the company to be more locally responsive. Not only the availability, quality and price of raw materials and components can vary widely between countries, but the same is true for other inputs such as labour, management, capital, facilities, machinery, research, information and services.

- **Differences in government regulations.** As most government regulations are made on a country-by-country basis, they can differ significantly. Government regulations can affect almost every aspect of a company's operations, as they range from antitrust and product liability legislation, to labour laws and taxation rules.

Responsiveness to these local differences is not only a matter of adaptation. Simple adaptation can be reactive and slow. Being responsive means that the firm has to have the ability to be proactive and fast. As each market develops in a different way and at a different pace, the international firm needs to be able to respond quickly and adequately to remain in tune.

It is clear that international managers cannot afford to neglect being responsive to local conditions. Yet, at the same time, they need to realize cross-border synergies to create additional value. Unfortunately for managers, these two key demands placed on the international firm are, at least to some extent, in conflict with one another. Striving for cross-border synergies on a global scale will interfere with being locally responsive and vice versa. Therefore, the question is how these two conflicting demands can be reconciled – how can the international manager deal with the paradox of globalization and localization?

EXHIBIT 10.1 SHORT CASE

ING DIRECT: KEEPING THE FLEET TOGETHER?

Few start-ups grow from zero to ten thousand employees in only 12 years. Even among high-tech and internet companies such spectacular growth is rare. But it is even stranger when it happens in a mature and conventional industry like consumer banking. Yet, since starting its first country unit in Canada in 1997, ING Direct has grown at this phenomenal rate, to become the world's leading direct bank. After Canada, ING Direct entered Spain and Australia in 1999, followed by France and the US in 2000, Italy

and Germany in 2001, the UK in 2003 and Austria in 2004. In each case, its formula has been to open a consumer bank without branch offices, offering only a savings account with high interest rates, no fees and instantly accessible via a call centre or internet. Once established, each country unit has then expanded its services to other banking products, such as mortgages, brokerage and payment accounts, depending on the customer needs in each country. In this way, ING Direct has attracted more than 22 million clients in its nine countries of operation, with savings balances of over €200 billion and €116 billion worth of mortgages. In these countries ING

▶

Direct scores first or second in customer satisfaction, reaching a brand recognition averaging 87%.

While ING Direct started in Canada, it is actually headquartered in the Netherlands and part of the large financial services company, the ING Group. Its founding father is Hans Verkoren, who had a long career within the Dutch Postbank organization. As its name implies, the Postbank was initially part of the Dutch post office and provided a type of direct banking through the mail system. It was eventually merged into the ING Group (originally meaning International Netherlands Group) and Hans Verkoren was positioned to look for international growth opportunities for the bank. Instead of entering foreign markets by acquiring local rivals and working hard to add some value to them, Verkoren had the idea of taking the Postbank concept and applying it abroad through new start-ups. Verkoren got the ING board to accept this idea. Canada was suggested as a good place to start since it was accessible, not too big and far enough away from headquarters. Since this beginning, ING Direct has been a largely autonomous unit within the ING corporation, with the understanding that it shouldn't operate in the Netherlands or Belgium, to avoid cannibalizing ING's large retail banking business in these countries.

While at many other banks 'financial innovation' has meant that even bank managers don't know exactly how a product works, at ING Direct innovation has meant simplification. From the outset, it has been ING Direct's philosophy to offer a focused range of simple and transparent products, taking away the burden of banking for their customers. The company found that simpler products make it easier for customers to make decisions, while at the same time lowering the cost to ING Direct. Being transparent about conditions and fees helps people to overcome their distrust of banks and feel that the company has their best interest in mind. To this mix ING Direct adds very competitive rates and excellent customer service, which to most banking customers is an entirely new experience. All this is possible because ING Direct operates with one of the lowest cost structures in the industry, while working hard to make sure that 'lean' does not become 'mean'. Actually, while a low cost outfit, ING Direct invests a lot in its 'orange spirit', emphasizing values such as honesty, transparency, optimism, customer focus,

innovativeness, teamwork and having a 'can do' attitude. As a rule of thumb, new employees are hired first and foremost because of their 'orangeness', with technical skills coming in second. Unsurprisingly, there are very few employees that originally come from the banking industry.

In all markets that ING Direct has entered the local competition was caught off guard by this rule-breaker-out-of-nowhere. In most cases, ING Direct's business model was dismissed as inappropriate for the local market or, at best, interesting for a minor market niche. However, after the initial phases of denial and shock, many competitors have tried to copy ING Direct's low cost model, putting pressure on ING Direct to stay one step ahead in the innovation game. Yet, while it is relatively easy to set up a bare bones internet savings bank, most competitors have found it difficult to match ING Direct's consistently high customer service and positive brand image.

Since 2008, the vision of ING Direct, as espoused by its Global Management Team (GMT), has been to become the world's most preferred consumer bank. CEO Dick Harryvan: 'This means moving out of our savings niche and offering a full range of banking services.' In its first ten years, ING Direct aimed at being a customer's second bank, offering only selective services, while leaving 'bread and butter' banking products, such as payment accounts, to be provided by a customer's primary bank. But the ING Direct strategy is now aimed at taking the role of primary bank, which is a frontal assault on the big national players, which in most countries have not seen serious new rivals for decades.

What Harryvan and the other GMT members have not changed is their unwavering belief that consumer banking is a local business and that therefore the ING Direct country units need to have autonomy to be responsive to the local demands. According to Harryvan 'retail is detail', requiring a decentralized structure in which country managers can tailor their product range, marketing and operations to the specific national circumstances. Not only are consumers extremely different in each local market, Harryvan points out, but so are competitors, banking regulations and tax incentives.

Take the French market, for instance, where consumers can save €15 300 per person tax free via a product called Livret A, which, until 2009, was only available via three French banks, but closed to all others. For ING Direct this has meant that they need to focus on the market segment that has more than this amount to save. Getting French consumers to move away from their traditional banks has been hard work anyway, as they prefer to have a personal relationship with their bankers and internet penetration has been slow.

In the same way, the Italians and the Spanish are also not very internet-minded, while having the same preference for face-to-face contact. One of the solutions used in Italy is to approach potential new customers through booths in shopping malls and by organizing music events at beach resorts during the summer. Another innovation has been to open ING Direct Cafés in major cities, as a way to make the bank less virtual and allow clients to interact face-to-face with ING Direct staff. The first café evolved in Toronto, where customers wanted to visit the ING Direct offices to check whether the company really existed, and has since spread to the US, Spain and France, but each in their own way.

Another big difference is in people's saving habits. While the Spanish have high per capita savings, for years Americans have had a negative savings rate. The Germans like to keep their money fixed in one bank, while in the UK many consumers shop around for the best interest rates. Italians like to save in cash, while Australians like to accumulate capital by owning their own home. Actually, in Australia ING Direct has more mortgages than savings, while in most other countries it is the other way around. In France ING Direct doesn't even offer mortgages, as the margin on these products is extremely low.

In each country the competitive landscape is also very different. In the US and Germany, ING Direct faces a mix of a few big competitors, with many regionally oriented savings banks. In Canada, Australia, France, Austria and Spain, however, the market is dominated by a few large national banks, who tend to see ING Direct as a market spoiler. Particularly in Spain, competitors have reacted quite aggressively. In each case, ING Direct has had to find a sustainable competitive position, differentiating itself from the local alternatives. Therefore, each ING Direct country unit develops its own advertising, sometimes knocking the competition, such as in Italy and Spain, sometimes totally ignoring them, as in Germany and Austria. Each unit even uses different icons in their advertising; in the

US an orange ball, in Germany the famous basketball player Dirk Nowitzki, in Italy a pumpkin, in the UK and Australia a lifebuoy, in Canada the Dutch actor Fredrik de Groot, in Spain an orange bench and in France, for a long time, the beautiful model Dina. Even the name ING Direct is not standardized everywhere. In Germany and Austria the company is called ING DiBa, due to the initial acquisition of a direct bank by that name.

If you add the differences in national regulation to this picture, it is clear why from the outset ING Direct decided to work with highly empowered country units. Having strong local management has been key to nimbly adapting to the unfolding competitive game in each geographic market. Yet autonomy has not meant independence. A key pillar of ING Direct's strategy has been to keep the separate country units together in a 'fleet of companies'. In the view of Harryvan and his fellow GMT members, strong country units have a lot of ideas, innovations and experiences to share, as long as they see the mutual benefit. For instance, they can share new products, new marketing concepts, IT systems, best practices and key people.

To facilitate cross-border synergizing, ING Direct has Councils for each functional area, bringing together senior managers from each country unit. For more specific topics, Working Groups, Expert Groups and Circles have been formed to enable joint learning and the exchange of best practices. To encourage global networking the top 200 managers come together each year at a Global Conference and more than 700 have been sent to a Business Management Program focused on culture, strategy and sharing. ING Direct also has a competence-finder function on their intranet, so that each person can find their counterparts in each of the other units. But most importantly, the GMT has worked hard at keeping the common Orange Spirit alive, stressing key principles and values that underpin sharing and team work.

Yet, as local competitors have recovered from their initial shock and are now attempting to beat ING Direct at its own game, the company has no other option than to stay at least one step ahead. Some commentators have suggested that the best way forward is to allow each country unit even more leeway to evolve to fit the local environment, accepting that the fleet of companies will float apart and have less to share. Others have advocated the opposite, recommending that ING Direct move towards more globally standardized products and systems, allowing them to roll out innovations worldwide and reduce their costs even further. Merging the disparate fleet into a supertanker might make the company extremely efficient and virtually unstoppable.

Separate ships, a supertanker or keeping a fleet of companies? This is the challenging question for the ING Direct captains to answer as the company sets sail for the next leg of the race.

Co-author: Martijn Rademakers

Sources: *The Orange Spirit*, 2007; *ING Direct Company Brochure*, 2008; Kuhlmann and Philp, 2009; company interviews.

PERSPECTIVES ON THE INTERNATIONAL CONTEXT

Nothing is more dangerous than an idea, when you have only one idea.
Alain (Emile-Auguste Chartier) (1868–1951); French poet and philosopher

When doing business in an international context, it is generally accepted that the challenge for firms is to strive for cross-border synergies, while simultaneously being responsive to the local conditions. It is acknowledged that international managers need to weigh the specific characteristics of their business when reconciling the paradox of globalization and localization – some businesses are currently more suited for a global approach than others. Where opinions start to diverge is on the question of which businesses will become more global, or can be made more global, in the near future. To some managers it is evident that countries are rapidly becoming increasingly similar and more closely interrelated. To them globalization is already far advanced and will continue into the future, wiping out the importance of nations as it progresses. Therefore, they argue that it is wise to anticipate, and even encourage, a 'nationless' world, by focusing on global synergies over local responsiveness. Other managers, however, are more skeptical about the speed and impact of globalization. In their view, much so-called globalization is quite superficial, while at a deeper level important international differences are not quickly changing and cross-border integration is moving very slowly. They also note that there are significant counter-currents creating more international variety, with the potential of loosening international linkages. Therefore, wise managers should remain highly responsive to the complex variety and fragmentation that characterizes our world, while only carefully seeking out selected cross-border synergy opportunities.

These differing opinions among international strategists are reflected in differing views in the strategic management literature. While there is a wide spectrum of positions on the question of how the international context will develop, here the two opposite poles in the debate will be identified and discussed. On the one side of the spectrum, there are the managers who believe that globalization is bringing Lennon's dream of the 'world living as one' closer and closer. This point of view is called the 'global convergence perspective'. At the other end of the spectrum are the managers who believe that deep-rooted local differences will continue to force firms to 'do in Rome as the Romans do'. This point of view is referred to as the 'international diversity perspective'.

The global convergence perspective

 According to proponents of the global convergence perspective, the growing similarity and integration of the world can be argued by pointing to extensive economic statistics, showing significant rises in foreign direct investment and international trade. Yet, it is simpler to observe things directly around you. For instance, are you wearing clothing unique to your country, or could you mingle in an international crowd without standing out? Is the television you watch, the vehicle you drive, the telephone you use and the timepiece you wear specific to your nation, or based on the same technology and even produced by the same companies as those in other countries? Is the music you listen to made by local bands, unknown outside your country, or is this music equally popular abroad? Is the food you eat unique to your region, or is even this served in other countries? Now compare your answers with what your parents would have answered 30 years ago – the difference is due to global convergence.

Global convergence, it is argued, is largely driven by the ease, low cost and frequency of international communication, transport and travel. This has diminished the importance of distance. In the past world of large distances, interactions between countries were few and international differences could develop in relative isolation. But the victory of technology over distance has created a 'global village', in which goods, services and ideas are easily exchanged, new developments spread quickly and the 'best practices' of one nation are rapidly copied in others. Once individuals and organizations interact with one another as if no geographic distances exist, an unstoppable process towards cultural, political, technological and economic convergence is set in motion – countries will become more closely linked to one another and local differences will be superseded by new global norms.

Of course, in the short run there will still be international differences and nations will not be fully integrated into a 'world without borders'. Managers taking a global convergence perspective acknowledge that such fundamental and wide-ranging changes take time. There are numerous sources of inertia, e.g. vested interests, commitment to existing systems, emotional attachment to current habits and fear of change. The same type of change inhibitors could be witnessed during the industrial revolution, as well. Yet, these change inhibitors can only slow the pace of global convergence, not reverse its direction – the momentum caused by the shrinking of distance can only be braked, but not stopped. Therefore, firms thinking further than the short term, should not let themselves be guided too much by current international diversity, but rather by the emerging global reality (Ohmae, 1990).

For individual firms, global convergence is changing the rules of the competitive game. While in the past most countries had their own distinct characteristics, pressuring firms to be locally responsive, now growing similarity offers enormous opportunities for leveraging resources and sharing activities across borders, e.g. production can be standardized to save costs, new product development can be carried out on an international scale to reduce the total investments required, and marketing knowledge can easily be exchanged to avoid reinventing the wheel in each country. Simultaneously, international integration has made it much easier to centralize production in large-scale facilities at the most attractive locations and to supply world markets from there, unrestrained by international borders. In the same manner, all types of activities, such as R&D, marketing, sales and procurement, can be centralized to profit from worldwide economies of scale.

An equally important aspect of international integration is that suppliers, buyers and competitors can also increasingly operate as if there are no borders. The ability of buyers to shop around internationally makes the world one global market, in which global bargaining power is very important. The ability of suppliers and competitors to reap global economies of scale and sell everywhere around the world creates global industries, in which competition takes place on a worldwide stage, instead of in each nation separately. To deal with such global industries and global markets, the firm must be able to align its market activities across nations.

These demands of standardization, centralization and coordination require a global firm, with a strong centre responsible for the global strategy, instead of a federation of autonomous national subsidiaries focused on being responsive to their local circumstances. According to proponents of the global convergence perspective, such global organizations, or 'centralized hubs' (Bartlett and Ghoshal, 1995), will become increasingly predominant over time. And as more companies switch to a global strategy and a global organizational form, this will in turn speed up the general process of globalization. By operating in a global fashion, these firms will actually contribute to a further decrease of international variety and fragmentation. In other words, globalizing companies are both the consequence and a major driver of further global convergence.

EXHIBIT 10.2 THE GLOBAL CONVERGENCE PERSPECTIVE

IKEA: THE WORLD IS FLAT

Whether you are in Abu Dhabi, Adelaide, Amsterdam, Ancona, Antwerp, Arhus, Arlon, Athens, Atlanta, Augsburg or Austin, you have one. Together with about 300 other locations around the world, these cities have an IKEA. The bright yellow and blue stores can be found in 39 countries and counting – the pace of new store openings varies between 10 and 30 per year, depending on the state of the global economy. In 2008 IKEA was visited over 632 million times, leading to sales of approximately €22.5 billion, making them the world's largest home furnishing retailer by far.

Despite operating in countries as varied as Saudi Arabia, China, the US, Russia, Japan and the UK, IKEA's success formula has remained surprisingly constant over the years, ever since founder Ingvar Kamprad set up a warehouse showroom in a disused factory in Almhult, Sweden, in 1953. Kamprad set out 'to offer a wide range of home furnishing items of good design and function at prices so low, that the majority of people can afford to buy them'. So, instead of selling expensive hand-crafted items, he teamed up with open-minded suppliers to design basic furniture of good quality, that could be mass-produced using local inexpensive softwoods and new wood-based materials such as plywood and particle boards. An innovative breakthrough was to let the customers assemble the products themselves, selling them as flat packs, saving production and shipping costs, while making it easier for customers to transport their own purchases.

IKEA still has its entire range of 9500 products custom-designed and then manufactured by one of its 1380 suppliers in 54 countries. All these products are sold under the IKEA brand name and share a typical Scandinavian design – simple elegance achieved by clear lines and natural materials. This is probably one of the most interesting aspects of IKEA's international expansion, which started in 1973, when the company entered the Swiss market. IKEA has remained quintessentially Swedish. Most products are of Swedish design, all have Swedish names, the store restaurants serve Swedish food and the company culture strongly reflects such Swedish values as equality, honesty, openness, modesty, reliability and simplicity. IKEA's store formula also embodies many of these qualities. While the aircraft-hangar-sized stores benefit from scale efficiencies, IKEA has been able to create a quality atmosphere through human-scale dimensions in the store lay-out. Visiting an IKEA store is intended to be more like a day out for the entire family than a shopping trip.

In its expansion to other markets, IKEA has not been culturally insensitive, but rather guided by the philosophy to keep it simple, as this means lower cost. In practice this philosophy has lead to a 'standardize-unless' approach to each national market – first try it the global way and only when this doesn't work, look for an intelligent local solution. It is usually not difficult to find an expensive local alternative, but with a global mindset and some creativity, a simple international standard can often be found. The result has been an assortment that is 95% globally standardized, store formats that are largely identical and the supply chain that is globally leveraged.

On the merchandise side, IKEA has occasionally made some small local adjustments, such as in the US, where beds are sold in non-metric sizes and kitchens are bigger to allow for American appliances and pizza plates. When it comes to store layout, locations serving cities with a lot of small apartments like Hong Kong and Tokyo, have the freedom to devote more room to space saving furniture and accessories. In countries where fewer people own their own vehicles, such as China, stores have been built closer to the city centre and public transport, instead of IKEA's regular policy of locating outside cities on cheap land, with plenty of space for parking. In the UK, where local regulations have made it difficult to build big boxes outside of cities, IKEA has been experimenting with an alternative store layout spread over three floors instead of the standard two. Another exception in China is that the IKEA annual catalogue, which is distributed to 200 million people, has been replaced by smaller monthly brochures, although these are still made in Sweden, to keep the IKEA feel.

Within the international organization the functions of branding, product development, concept development, purchasing and training are strongly controlled by headquarters, to ensure standardization and leverage global scale. The functions of physical distribution and retailing are regionally divided. To lower exchange rate risks and transport costs, IKEA tries to produce the larger furniture items close to each region, which has lead to a growth in local production in the US and China. Yet, smaller items generally come from a global source, which is often IKEA itself – the company's Swedwood arm operates 49 factories and sawmills in 11 countries.

So, how far can IKEA go with its global approach? When IKEA first started in Germany, currently its largest market, many warned about their conservatism. When the first American store was opened in 1985, it was billed as IKEA's likely Waterloo. When entering China in 1998, many feared that finally IKEA would be humbled. And when IKEA built its first Japanese store in Tokyo in 2006, industry experts were sure that IKEA would fail, as all other retailers before it. Kamprad, in his 80s, supports the current CEO Anders Dahlvig's philosophy to keep expanding: 'The temples of design in places like Milan or God knows where overflow with beautiful, original furniture that costs extortionate amounts of money. The vast majority of people don't have six figure amounts in the bank and don't live in enormous apartments … it is for just such people that I created IKEA. For everybody who wants a comfortable house in which to live well. A need that crosses all countries, races and religions.'

Sources: www.ikea.com; *Wall Street Journal*, 3 March 2006; Burt, Johansson & Thelander, 2008.

The international diversity perspective

To managers taking an international diversity perspective, the 'brave new world' outlined in the previous sub-section is largely science fiction. People around the world might be sporting a Swatch or a Rolex, munching Big Macs and drinking Coke, while sitting in their Toyota or Nissan, but to conclude that these are symptoms of global convergence is a leap of faith. Of course, there are some brand names and products more or less standardized around the world, and their numbers might actually be increasing. The question is whether these manufacturers are globalizing to meet increasing worldwide similarity, or whether they are actually finally utilizing the similarities between countries that have always existed. The actual level of international variety may really be quite consistent.

It is particularly important to recognize in which respects countries remain different. For instance, the world might be drinking the same soft drinks, but they are probably doing it in different places, at different times, under different circumstances and for different reasons in each country. The product might be standardized worldwide, but the cultural norms and values that influence its purchase and use remain diverse across countries. According to proponents of the international diversity perspective, it is precisely these fundamental aspects of culture that turn out to be extremely stable over time – habits change slowly, but cultural norms and values are outright rigid. Producers might be lucky to find one product that fits in with such cultural diversity, but it would be foolish to interpret this as worldwide cultural convergence.

Other national differences are equally resilient against the tides of globalization. No countries have recently given up their national language in favour of Esperanto or English. On the contrary, there has been renewed emphasis on the local language in many countries (e.g. Ireland and the Baltic countries) and regions (e.g. Catalonia and Quebec). In the same way, political systems have remained internationally diverse, with plenty of examples of localization, even within nations. For instance, in Russia and the United States the shift of power to regional governments has increased policy diversity within the country. Similar arguments can be put forward for legal systems, fiscal regimes, educational systems and technological infrastructure – each is extremely difficult to change due to the lock-in effects, vested interests, psychological commitment and complex decision-making processes.

For each example of increasing similarity, a counter-example of local initiatives and growing diversity could be given. Some proponents of the international diversity perspective argue that it is exactly this interplay of divergence and convergence forces that creates a dynamic balance preserving diversity. While technologies, organizing principles, political trends and social habits disperse across borders, resulting in global convergence, new developments and novel systems in each nation arise causing international divergence (Dosi and Kogut, 1993). Convergence trends are usually easier to spot than divergence – international dispersion can be more simply witnessed than new localized developments. To the casual observer, this might suggest that convergence trends have the upper hand, but after more thorough analysis, this conclusion must be cast aside.

Now add to this enduring international diversity the reality of international economic relations. Since World War II attempts have been made to facilitate the integration of national economies. There have been some regional successes (e.g. the North American Free Trade Association and the European Union) and some advances have been made on a worldwide scale (e.g. the World Trade Organization). However, progress has been slow and important political barriers remain.

The continued existence of international diversity and political obstacles, it is argued, will limit the extent to which nations can become fully integrated into one borderless world. International differences and barriers to trade and investment will frustrate firms' attempts to standardize and centralize, and will place a premium on firms' abilities to adapt and decentralize. Of course, there will be some activities for which global economies of scale can be achieved and for which international coordination is needed, but this will not become true for all activities. Empowering national managers to be responsive to specific local conditions will remain an important ingredient for international success. Balancing globalization and localization of the firm's activities will continue to be a requirement in the future international context.

Ideally, the internationally operating company should neither deny nor regret the existence of international diversity, but regard it as an opportunity that can be exploited. Each country's unique circumstances will pose different challenges, requiring the development of different competences. Different national 'climates' will create opportunities for different innovations. If a company can tap into each country's opportunities and leverage the acquired competences and innovations to other countries, this could offer the company an important source of competitive advantage. Naturally, these locally leveraged competences and innovations would subsequently need to be adapted to the specific circumstances in other countries. This balancing act would require an organization that combined strong local responsiveness with the ability to exchange and coordinate internationally, even on a worldwide scale. International organizations blending these two elements are called 'transnational' (Bartlett and Ghoshal, 1995), or 'heterarchical' (Hedlund, 1986). However, in some businesses the international differences will remain so large that an even more locally responsive organizational form might be necessary, operating on a federative basis.

EXHIBIT 10.3 THE INTERNATIONAL DIVERSITY PERSPECTIVE

IMTECH: GLOBAL TECHNOLOGY MADE LOCAL

Shouldn't technology be driving globalization? Shouldn't 'best practice' technical solutions be rolled out in the same way everywhere around the world? Not according to René van der Bruggen, CEO of Europe's largest technical services provider, Imtech. In his view, technology might be global, but applying information and communication technology, as well as electrical and mechanical engineering knowhow to serve B2B clients requires local skills and local people. Since starting the company in 1993 as a division within the Internatio-Müller conglomerate, Van der Bruggen has believed in organizing Imtech on a country-by-country basis, to get the maximum of local responsiveness as possible. Over the years, Imtech has grown by acquiring strong ICT, mechanical and electrical companies in various European markets and then merging them into integrated technical service providers, but always with a clear focus on the national market and with strong local management. By 2009, Imtech had grown to a turnover of almost €4 billion, with major operations in Germany, the United Kingdom, the Nordics, Belgium, the Netherlands and Spain, while starting up in Ireland, Austria, Switzerland and a number of Eastern European countries.

Imtech's clients can be categorized into three distinct segments; buildings, industry and infrastructure. In the buildings segment, Imtech complements the general contractor by providing the entire technical installation in and around the building structure. Simply put, anything that has to do with pipes or wires is Imtech's responsibility, whether this is for offices, laboratories, airports, museums, stations, stadiums, hospitals or shopping centres. Not only does Imtech install all technical systems, but they can also design and maintain

them. In the industry segment, Imtech provides a similar service, designing, installing and maintaining the technical intestines of factories and refineries, including everything from security systems to logistics automation and clean room technology. In the infrastructure segment, the 'objects' on which Imtech works are tunnels, bridges, traffic management systems, railway systems, parking systems, high voltage transport lines and public lighting, whereby their customers are usually governments or semi-public organizations.

To be successful in all these areas requires a high level of technical competence, but according to Van der Bruggen this is not really what clients pay for. Clients have a problem and they are willing to pay for a solution – for a tailored solution. Finding the right solution requires 'customer intimacy'; a deep understanding of the client's situation, needs and organizational complexities, as well as the ability to adapt to unforeseen circumstances. As clients have a lot at stake, they need to trust their supplier and know that the supplier is not flying in with a standard global approach and flying out as soon as the going gets tough. Therefore, clients generally prefer to build up a long term relationship with local firms, who know the local circumstances, speak the local language, can circumvent the local political icebergs and who have a local reputation at stake. At the same time, for Imtech this local knowledge allows them to estimate the risk profile of each project, which is generally the big difference between making a profit and incurring a loss.

Working with country-based units has another great benefit that Van der Bruggen likes to highlight – entrepreneurship. Instead of trying to manage everything from headquarters in Gouda, just outside of Rotterdam, Van der Bruggen prefers to decentralize authority and initiative to the countries, where strong local managers can shape their own units, but also shoulder the responsibility for reaching the agreed results. This does not mean that Imtech ignores cross-border synergy potential, but only that intra-firm cooperation needs to be voluntary, not imposed from head office. Van der Bruggen prefers to bring senior people together in management development programs and task forces, so that they build horizontal networks in the company and exchange information, know-how and customer leads where relevant. The emphasis is on synergizing without centralizing.

Yet, being a pragmatist, Van der Bruggen does not impose the same approach on the entire firm, as there is a fourth client segment that is much less localized,

namely the marine and offshore business. Imtech, with its roots in the Rotterdam harbour, provides the technical installations in all sorts of floating objects, such as luxury yachts, cruise ships, naval vessels, dredging ships, transporters and oil rigs. As this business is very international, with many globally operating customers, Imtech strikes more of a balance between being global and local. But here too there is a deep understanding that the competitive advantage of really knowing your local customer is very hard to beat, even with the best of technologies.

Sources: www.imtech.eu; company interviews.

INTRODUCTION TO THE DEBATE AND READINGS

You may say I'm a dreamer,
but I'm not the only one;
I hope some day you'll join us,
and the world will live as one.
John Lennon (1940–1980); British
musician and songwriter

When I am in Milan,
I do as they do in Milan;
but when I go to Rome,
I do as Rome does.
St. Augustine (354–430); Roman
theologist and philosopher

So, is the international context moving towards increased similarity and integration, or will it remain as diverse and fragmented as at the moment? And what does this mean for the international configuration of firms? Should managers anticipate and encourage global convergence by emphasizing global standardization, centralization and coordination? They would choose to place more emphasis on realizing value creation by means of global synergies, accepting some value destruction due to a loss of local responsiveness. Or should managers acknowledge and exploit international diversity by emphasizing local adaptation, decentralization and autonomy? They would then focus on being locally responsive, accepting that this will frustrate the realization of cross-border synergies.

Again, the strategic management literature does not provide a uniform answer to the question of which international strategy firms can best pursue. On the contrary, the variety of opinions among strategy theorists is dauntingly large, with many incompatible prescriptions being given. At the core of the debate within the field of strategy is the paradox of globalization and localization. Many points of view have been expounded on how to reconcile these opposing demands, but no common perspective has yet emerged. Hence, it is up to individual managers to find their own approach in dealing with the challenge of the international context.

To help strategizing managers to come to grips with the variety of perspectives on this issue, four readings have been selected that each shed their own light on the debate. As in previous chapters, the first two readings will be representative of the two poles in this debate (see Table 10.1), while the second set of two readings will bring in extra arguments to add further flavour to the discussion.

TABLE 10.1   Global convergence versus international diversity perspective

	Global convergence perspective	*International diversity perspective*
Emphasis on	Globalization over localization	Localization over globalization
International variety	Growing similarity	Remaining diversity
International linkages	Growing integration	Remaining fragmentation
Major drivers	Technology and communication	Cultural and institutional identity
Diversity and fragmentation	Costly, convergence can be encouraged	Reality, can be exploited
Strategic focus	Global-scale synergies	Local responsiveness
Organizational preference	Standardize/centralize unless	Adapt/decentralize unless
Innovation process	Centre-for-global	Locally leveraged
Organizational structure	Global (centralized hub)	Transnational (integrated network)

Reading 10.1, representing the global convergence perspective, is 'The Globalization of Markets' by Theodore Levitt. This article, published in the early 1980s, has probably been the most influential at starting the debate about globalization in the business literature. Levitt's thesis is that the world is quickly moving towards a converging commonality.

He believes that 'the world's needs and desires have been irrevocably homogenized'. The force driving this process is technology, which has facilitated communication, transport and travel, while allowing for the development of superior products at low prices. His conclusion is that 'the commonality of preference leads inescapably to the standardization of products, manufacturing and the institutions of trade and commerce'. The old-fashioned multinational corporation, that adapted itself to local circumstances is 'obsolete and the global corporation absolute'. While a clear proponent of the global convergence perspective, it should be noted that Levitt's bold prediction of global convergence is focused on the globalization of markets. In particular, he is intent on pointing out that converging consumer demand in international markets facilitates – even necessitates – the reaping of economies of scale through the standardization of products, marketing and production. With this emphasis on the demand side, Levitt pays far less attention to the supply side – the globalization of industries and the competition within industries – that other global convergence proponents tend to accentuate (see Reading 10.3). And although he strongly advises companies to become 'global corporations', he does not further detail what a global company should look like (see Reading 10.4). Overall, Levitt views globalization more as growing international similarity, while paying less attention than some other authors to the possibility of growing international integration.

As a direct response to 'the sweeping and somewhat polemic character' of Levitt's argumentation, Susan Douglas and Yoram Wind's article, 'The Myth of Globalization', has been selected for Reading 10.2 as representative of the international diversity perspective. Douglas and Wind believe that many of the assumptions underlying Levitt's global standardization philosophy are contradicted by the facts. They argue that the convergence of customer needs is not a one-way street; divergence trends are noticeable as well. Furthermore, they believe that Levitt is mistaken in arguing that economies of scale in production and marketing are an irreversible force driving globalization. According to Douglas and Wind, many new technologies have actually lowered the minimum efficient scale of operation, while there are also plenty of industries where economies of scale are not an important issue. The authors conclude by outlining the specific circumstances under which a strategy of global standardization might be effective. Under all other circumstances, Douglas and Wind reiterate, the international strategist will have to deal with the existence of international diversity and search for the right balance between global standardization and local adaptation.

In Reading 10.3, 'The Competitive Advantage of Nations', Michael Porter introduces a different angle to the debate on globalization. Porter agrees with proponents of the global convergence perspective that the world is becoming highly integrated, although in some industries more than others (see Porter, 1986). However, Porter does not agree that the world is in all ways becoming more similar. In fact, Porter argues the opposite – growing international integration encourages international diversity. Global integration, according to Porter, does not make geographic location and nationality unimportant, as some authors seem to suggest (e.g. Ohmae, 1989), but in some ways more important. This is due to the process of local specialization, by which clusters of interconnected buyers, suppliers, competitors, and related and supporting industries evolve, that reinforce each other in innovating and becoming more competitive. Porter argues that such local clusters of firms operating in a particular sector will develop if there is a strong national diamond, that is, a challenging competitive environment with advantageous factor and demand conditions, and a strong infrastructure of related and supporting industries. And once a strong diamond has been established, it can have a self-perpetuating momentum, by winning in global competition and by attracting excellent companies and individuals from other countries. Porter therefore concludes that companies should recognize the specific characteristics of the national diamond in their home country and try to exploit and improve its unique strengths. He also advises companies to seek out and tap into strong local clusters abroad, to supplement their home-based advantages and to compensate for any home-based disadvantages. In short, international diversity is a reality, but can be exploited by the internationally operating company.

In the final reading, 'Transnational Management', Christopher Bartlett and Sumantra Ghoshal bring the issue of organization into the debate on globalization. Bartlett and Ghoshal do not take a direct stance on the issue of global convergence and international diversity. They are more concerned with clarifying the various pressures on international organizations and outlining the different organizational forms that can be adopted. The thrust of their argument is that globalization has forced the international company to manage across borders, as opposed to the old multinational corporation that was organized on a country-by-country basis. In the old multinational, emphasis was placed on strong geographic management to be responsive to the local circumstances. But to deal with, and benefit from, international integration and similarities, companies have to be able to do more. Global functional management is needed to learn and transfer competences worldwide, while global business management with global product responsibilities is needed to achieve worldwide efficiency. Bartlett and Ghoshal argue that optimizing learning, efficiency and responsiveness simultaneously is the challenge facing the new transnational organization. They believe that every organization must find its own dynamic balance between these forces; there is not one best organizational response to globalization, because the extent of globalization is never the same.

READING

10.1

The globalization of markets

By Theodore Levitt[1]

A powerful force drives the world toward a converging commonality, and that force is technology. It has proletarianized communication, transport, and travel. It has made isolated places and impoverished peoples eager for modernity's allurements. Almost everyone everywhere wants all the things they have heard about, seen, or experienced via the new technologies.

The result is a new commercial reality – the emergence of global markets for standardized consumer products on a previously unimagined scale of magnitude. Corporations geared to this new reality benefit from enormous economies of scale in production, distribution, marketing, and management. By translating these benefits into reduced world prices, they can decimate competitors that still live in the disabling grip of old assumptions about how the world works.

Gone are accustomed differences in national or regional preference. Gone are the days when a company could sell last year's models – or lesser versions of advanced products – in the less developed world. And gone are the days when prices, margins, and profits abroad were generally higher than at home.

The globalization of markets is at hand. With that, the multinational commercial world nears its end, and so does the multinational corporation.

The multinational and the global corporation are not the same thing. The multinational corporation operates in a number of countries, and adjusts its products and practices in each – at high relative costs. The global corporation operates with resolute constancy – at low relative cost – as if the entire world (or major regions of it) were a single entity; it sells the same things in the same way everywhere.

Which strategy is better is not a matter of opinion but of necessity. World-wide communications carry everywhere the constant drumbeat of modern possibilities to lighten and enhance work, raise living standards, divert, and entertain. The same countries that ask the world to recognize and respect the individuality of their cultures insist on the wholesale transfer to them of modern goods, services, and technologies. Modernity is not just a wish but also a widespread practice among those who cling, with unyielding passion or religious fervour, to ancient attitudes and heritages.

Who can forget the televised scenes during the 1979 Iranian uprisings of young men in fashionable French-cut trousers and silky body shirts thirsting with raised modern weapons for blood in the name of Islamic fundamentalism?

In Brazil, thousands swarm daily from preindustrial Bahian darkness into exploding coastal cities, there quickly to install television sets in crowded corrugated huts and, next to battered Volkswagens, make sacrificial offerings of fruit and fresh-killed chickens to Macumban spirits by candlelight.

A thousand suggestive ways attest to the ubiquity of the desire for the most advanced things that the world makes and sells – goods of the best quality and reliability at the lowest price. The world's needs and desires have been irrevocably homogenized. This makes the multinational corporation obsolete and the global corporation absolute.

Living in the Republic of Technology

Daniel J. Boorstin, author of the monumental trilogy *The Americans*, characterized our age as driven by 'the Republic of Technology (whose) supreme law … is convergence, the tendency for everything to become more like everything else'.

In business, this trend has pushed markets toward global commonality. Corporations sell standardized products in the same way everywhere – autos, steel, chemicals, petroleum, cement, agricultural commodities and equipment, industrial and commercial construction, banking and insurance services, computers, semiconductors, transport, electronic instruments, pharmaceuticals, and telecommunications, to mention some of the obvious.

Nor is the sweeping gale of globalization confined to these raw material or high-tech products, where the universal language of customers and users facilitates

[1]Source: Reprinted by permission of Harvard Business Review. From 'The Globalization of Markets' by T. Levitt, May–June 1983, Vol. 61. © 1983 by Harvard Business School Publishing Corporation, all rights reserved.

standardization. The transforming winds whipped up by the proletarianization of communication and travel enter every crevice of life.

Commercially, nothing confirms this as much as the success of McDonald's from the Champs Elysées to the Ginza, of Coca-Cola in Bahrain and Pepsi-Cola in Moscow, and of rock music, Greek salad, Hollywood movies, Revlon cosmetics, Sony televisions, and Levi jeans everywhere. 'High-touch' products are as ubiquitous as high-tech.

Starting from opposing sides, the high-tech and the high-touch ends of the commercial spectrum gradually consume the undistributed middle in their cosmopolitan orbit. No one is exempt and nothing can stop the process. Everywhere everything gets more and more like everything else as the world's preference structure is relentlessly homogenized.

Consider the cases of Coca-Cola and Pepsi-Cola, which are globally standardized products sold everywhere and welcomed by everyone. Both successfully cross multitudes of national, regional, and ethnic taste buds trained to a variety of deeply ingrained local preferences of taste, flavour, consistency, effervescence, and aftertaste. Everywhere both sell well. Cigarettes, too, especially American-made, make year-to-year global inroads in territories previously held in the firm grip of other, mostly local, blends.

These are not exceptional examples. (Indeed their global reach would be even greater were it not for artificial trade barriers.) They exemplify a general drift toward the homogenization of the world and how companies distribute, finance, and price products. Nothing is exempt. The products and methods of the industrialized world play a single tune for all the world, and all the world eagerly dances to it.

Ancient differences in national tastes or modes of doing business disappear. The commonality of preference leads inescapably to the standardization of products, manufacturing, and the institutions of trade and commerce. Small nation-based markets transmogrify and expand. Success in world competition turns on efficiency in production, distribution, marketing, and management, and inevitably becomes focused on price.

The most effective world competitors incorporate superior quality and reliability into their cost structures. They sell in all national markets the same kind of products sold at home or in their largest export market. They compete on the basis of appropriate value – the best combinations of price, quality, reliability, and delivery for products that are globally identical with respect to design, function, and even fashion.

That, and little else, explains the surging success of Japanese companies dealing world-wide in a vast variety of products – both tangible products like steel, cars, motorcycles, hi-fi equipment, farm machinery, robots, microprocessors, carbon fibres, and now even textiles, and intangibles like banking, shipping, general contracting, and soon computer software. Nor are high-quality and low-cost operations incompatible, as a host of consulting organizations and data engineers argue with vigorous vacuity. The reported data are incomplete, wrongly analysed, and contradictory. The truth is that low-cost operations are the hallmark of corporate cultures that require and produce quality in all that they do. High quality and low costs are not opposing postures. They are compatible, twin identities of superior practice.

To say that Japan's companies are not global because they export cars with left-side drives to the United States and the European continent, while those in Japan have right-side drives, or because they sell office machines through distributors in the United States but directly at home, or speak Portuguese in Brazil is to mistake a difference for a distinction. The same is true of Safeway and Southland retail chains operating effectively in the Middle East, and to not only native but also imported populations from Korea, the Philippines, Pakistan, India, Thailand, Britain, and the United States. National rules of the road differ, and so do distribution channels and languages. Japan's distinction is its unrelenting push for economy and value enhancement. That translates into a drive for standardization at high quality levels.

Vindication of the Model T

If a company forces costs and prices down and pushes quality and reliability up – while maintaining reasonable concern for suitability – customers will prefer its world-standardized products. The theory holds at this stage in the evolution of globalization, no matter what conventional market research and even common sense may suggest about different national and regional tastes, preferences, needs, and institutions. The Japanese have repeatedly vindicated this theory, as did Henry Ford with the Model T. Most important, so have their imitators, including companies from South Korea (television sets and heavy construction), Malaysia (personal calculators and microcomputers), Brazil (auto parts and tools), Colombia (apparel), Singapore (optical equipment), and yes, even from the United States (office copiers, computers, bicycles, castings),

Western Europe (automatic washing machines), Rumania (housewares), Hungary (apparel), Yugoslavia (furniture), and Israel (pagination equipment).

Of course, large companies operating in a single nation or even a single city don't standardize everything they make, sell, or do. They have product lines instead of a single product version, and multiple distribution channels. There are neighbourhood, local, regional, ethnic, and institutional differences, even within metropolitan areas. But although companies customize products for particular market segments, they know that success in a world with homogenized demand requires a search for sales opportunities in similar segments across the globe in order to achieve the economies of scale necessary to compete.

Such a search works because a market segment in one country is seldom unique; it has close cousins everywhere precisely because technology has homogenized the globe. Even small local segments have their global equivalents everywhere and become subject to global competition, especially on price.

The global competitor will seek constantly to standardize his offering everywhere. He will digress from this standardization only after exhausting all possibilities to retain it, and he will push for reinstatement of standardization whenever digression and divergence have occurred. He will never assume that the customer is a king who knows his own wishes.

Trouble increasingly stalks companies that lack clarified global focus and remain inattentive to the economics of simplicity and standardization. The most endangered companies in the rapidly evolving world tend to be those that dominate rather small domestic markets with high value-added products for which there are smaller markets elsewhere. With transportation costs proportionately low, distant competitors will enter the now-sheltered markets of those companies with goods produced more cheaply under scale-efficient conditions. Global competition spells the end of domestic territoriality, no matter how diminutive the territory may be.

When the global producer offers his lower costs internationally, his patronage expands exponentially. He not only reaches into distant markets, but also attracts customers who previously held to local preferences and now capitulate to the attractions of lesser prices. The strategy of standardization not only responds to world-wide homogenized markets but also expands those markets with aggressive low pricing.

The new technological juggernaut taps an ancient motivation – to make one's money go as far as possible. This is universal – not simply a motivation but actually a need.

The hedgehog knows

The difference between the hedgehog and the fox, wrote Sir Isaiah Berlin in distinguishing between Dostoevski and Tolstoy, is that the fox knows a lot about a great many things, but the hedgehog knows everything about one great thing. The multinational corporation knows a lot about a great many countries and congenially adapts to supposed differences. It willingly accepts vestigial national differences, not questioning the possibility of their transformation, not recognizing how the world is ready and eager for the benefit of modernity, especially when the price is right. The multinational corporation's accommodating mode to visible national differences is medieval.

By contrast, the global corporation knows everything about one great thing. It knows about the absolute need to be competitive on a world-wide basis as well as nationally and seeks constantly to drive down prices by standardizing what it sells and how it operates. It treats the world as composed of few standardized markets rather than many customized markets. It actively seeks and vigorously works toward global convergence. Its mission is modernity and its mode, price competition, even when it sells top-of-the-line, high-end products. It knows about the one great thing all nations and people have in common: scarcity.

Nobody takes scarcity lying down; everyone wants more. This in part explains division of labour and specialization of production. They enable people and nations to optimize their conditions through trade. The median is usually money.

Experience teaches that money has three special qualities: scarcity, difficulty of acquisition, and transience. People understandably treat it with respect. Everyone in the increasingly homogenized world market wants products and features that everybody else wants. If the price is low enough, they will take highly standardized world products, even if these aren't exactly what mother said was suitable, what immemorial custom decreed was right, or what market-research fabulists asserted was preferred.

The implacable truth of all modern production – whether of tangible or intangible goods – is that large-scale production of standardized items is generally cheaper within a wide range of volume than small-scale production. Some argue that CAD/CAM (computer aided design/computer aided manufacturing) will allow companies to manufacture customized products on a small scale – but cheaply. But the argument misses the point. If a company treats the world as one or two distinctive product markets, it can serve the world more economically than if it treats it as three, four, or five product markets.

Different cultural preferences, national tastes and standards, and business institutions are vestiges of the past. Some inheritances die gradually; others prosper and expand into mainstream global preferences. So-called ethnic markets are a good example. Chinese food, pitta bread, country and western music, pizza, and jazz are everywhere. They are market segments that exist in world-wide proportions. They don't deny or contradict global homogenization but confirm it.

Many of today's differences among nations as to products and their features actually reflect the respectful accommodation of multinational corporations to what they believe are fixed local preferences. They believe preferences are fixed, not because they are but because of rigid habits of thinking about what actually is. Most executives in multinational corporations are thoughtlessly accommodating. They falsely presume that marketing means giving the customer what he says he wants rather than trying to understand exactly what he'd like. So they persist with high-cost, customized multinational products and practices instead of pressing hard and pressing properly for global standardization.

I do not advocate the systematic disregard of local or national differences. But a company's sensitivity to such differences does not require that it ignore the possibilities of doing things differently or better.

With persistence and appropriate means, barriers against superior technologies and economics have always fallen. There is no recorded exception where reasonable effort has been made to overcome them. It is very much a matter of time and effort.

A failure in global imagination

Many companies have tried to standardize world practice by exporting domestic products and processes without accommodation or change – and have failed miserably. Their deficiencies have been seized on as evidence of bovine stupidity in the face of abject impossibility. Advocates of global standardization see them as examples of failures in execution.

In fact, poor execution is often an important cause. More important, however, is failure of nerve – failure of imagination.

Consider the case for the introduction of fully automatic home laundry equipment in Western Europe at a time when few homes had even semiautomatic machines.

The growing success of small, low-powered, low-speed, low-capacity, low-priced Italian machines, even against the preferred but highly priced and highly promoted brand in West Germany, was significant. It contained a powerful message that was lost on managers confidently wedded to a distorted version of the marketing concept according to which you give the customer what he says he wants. In fact the customers said they wanted certain features, but their behaviour demonstrated they'd take other features provided the price and the promotion were right.

In this case it was obvious that under prevailing conditions, people preferred a low-priced automatic over any kind of manual or semiautomatic machine and certainly over higher priced automatics, even though the low-priced automatics failed to fulfil all their expressed preferences. The supposedly meticulous and demanding German consumers violated all expectations by buying the simple, low-priced Italian machines.

This case illustrates how the perverse practice of the marketing concept and the absence of any kind of marketing imagination let multinational attitudes survive when customers actually want the benefits of global standardization. People were asked what features they wanted in a washing machine rather than what they wanted out of life. Selling a line of products individually tailored to each nation is thoughtless. Managers who took pride in practising the marketing concept to the fullest did not, in fact, practice it at all. Data do not yield information except with the intervention of the mind. Information does not yield meaning except with the intervention of imagination.

Cracking the code of Western markets

Since the theory of the marketing concept emerged a quarter of a century ago, the more managerially advanced corporations have been eager to offer what customers clearly want rather than what is merely convenient. They have created marketing departments supported by professional market researchers of awesome and often costly proportions. And they have proliferated extraordinary numbers of operations and product lines – highly tailored products and delivery systems for many different markets, market segments, and nations.

Significantly, Japanese companies operate almost entirely without marketing departments or market research of the kind so prevalent in the West. Yet, in the colourful words of General Electric's chairman John F. Welch Jr., the Japanese, coming from a small cluster of resource-poor islands, with an entirely alien culture and an almost impenetrably complex language, have cracked the code of Western markets. They have done it not by looking with mechanistic thoroughness at the way markets are different but rather by searching for meaning with a deeper wisdom. They have discovered the one great thing all markets have in common – an overwhelming desire for dependable, world-standard modernity in all things, at aggressively low prices. In response, they deliver irresistible value everywhere, attracting people with products that market-research technocrats described with superficial certainty as being unsuitable and uncompetitive.

The wider a company's global reach, the greater the number of regional and national preferences it will encounter for certain product features, distribution systems, or promotional media. There will always need to be some accommodation to differences.

In its highly successful introduction of Contac 600 (the timed-release decongestant) into Japan, Smith-Kline Corporation used 35 wholesalers instead of the 1000-plus that established practice required. Daily contacts with the wholesalers and key retailers, also in violation of established practice, supplemented the plan, and it worked.

Denied access to established distribution institutions in the United States, Komatsu, the Japanese manufacturer of lightweight farm machinery, entered the market through over-the-road construction equipment dealers in rural areas of the Sunbelt, where farms are smaller, the soil sandier and easier to work. Here inexperienced distributors were able to attract customers on the basis of Komatsu's product and price appropriateness.

In cases of successful challenge to prevailing institutions and practices, a combination of product reliability and quality, strong and sustained support systems, aggressively low prices, and sales-compensation packages, as well as audacity and implacability, circumvented, shattered, and transformed very different distribution systems. Instead of resentment, there was admiration.

The differences that persist throughout the world despite its globalization affirm an ancient dictum of economics – that things are driven by what happens at the margin, not at the core. Thus, in ordinary competitive analysis, what's important is not the average price but the marginal price, what happens not in the usual case but at the interface of newly erupting conditions. What counts in commercial affairs is what happens at the cutting edge. What is most striking today is the underlying similarities of what is happening now to national preferences at the margin. These similarities at the cutting edge cumulatively form an overwhelming, predominant commonality everywhere.

To refer to the persistence of economic nationalism (protective and subsidized trade practices, special tax aids, or restrictions for home market producers) as a barrier to the globalization of markets is to make a valid point. Economic nationalism does have a powerful persistence. But, as with the present almost totally smooth internationalization of investment capital, the past alone does not shape or predict the future.

Reality is not a fixed paradigm, dominated by immemorial customs and derived attitudes, heedless of powerful and abundant new forces. The world is becoming increasingly informed about the liberating and enhancing possibilities of modernity. The persistence of the inherited varieties of national preferences rests uneasily on increasing evidence of, and restlessness regarding, their inefficiency, costliness, and confinement. The historic past, and the national differences respecting commerce and industry it spawned and fostered everywhere, is now subject to relatively easy transformation.

Cosmopolitanism is no longer the monopoly of the intellectual and leisure classes; it is becoming the established property and defining characteristic of all sectors everywhere in the world. Gradually and irresistibly it breaks down the walls of economic insularity, nationalism, and chauvinism. What we see today as escalating commercial nationalism is simply the last violent death rattle of an obsolete institution.

The successful global corporation does not abjure customization or differentiation for the requirements of markets that differ in product preferences, spending patterns, shopping preferences, and institutional or legal arrangements. But the global corporation accepts and adjusts to these differences only reluctantly, only after relentlessly testing their immutability, after trying in various ways to circumvent and reshape them.

READING

10.2

The myth of globalization

By Susan Douglas and Yoram Wind[1]

I n recent years, globalization has become a key theme in every discussion of international strategy. Proponents of the philosophy of 'global' products and brands, such as Professor Theodore Levitt of Harvard, and the highly successful advertising agency, Saatchi & Saatchi, argue that in a world of growing internationalization, the key to success is the development of global products and brands, in other words, a focus on standardized products and brands world-wide. Others, however, point to the numerous barriers to standardization, and suggest that greater returns are to be obtained from adapting products and marketing strategies to the specific characteristics of individual markets.

The growing integration of international markets as well as the growth of competition on a world-wide scale implies that adoption of a global perspective has become increasingly imperative in planning strategy. However, to conclude that this mandates the adoption of a strategy of universal standardization appears naïve and oversimplistic. In particular, it ignores the inherent complexity of operations in international markets, and the formulation of an effective strategy to penetrate these markets. While global products and brands may be appropriate for certain markets and in targeting certain segments, adopting such an approach as a universal strategy in relation to all markets may not be desirable, and may lead to major strategic blunders. Furthermore, it implies a product orientation, and a product-driven strategy, rather than a strategy grounded in a systematic analysis of customer behaviour and response patterns and market characteristics.

The purpose of this article is thus to examine critically the notion that success in international markets necessitates adoption of a strategy of global products and brands. Given the restrictive characteristic of this philosophy, a somewhat broader perspective in developing global strategy is proposed which views standardization as merely one option in the range of possible strategies which may be effective in global markets.

The traditional perspective on international strategy

Traditionally, discussion of international business strategy has been polarized around the debate concerning the pursuit of a uniform strategy world-wide versus adaptation to specific local market conditions. On the one hand, it has been argued that adoption of a uniform strategy world-wide enables a company to take advantage of the potential synergies arising from multicountry operations, and constitutes the multinational company's key competitive advantage in international markets. Others however, have argued that adaptation of strategy to idiosyncratic national market characteristics is crucial to success in these markets.

Fayerweather, in his seminal work in international business strategy, described the central issue as one of conflict between forces toward unification and those resulting in fragmentation. He pointed out that within a multinational firm, internal forces created pressures toward the integration of strategy across national boundaries. On the other hand, differences in the sociocultural, political, and economic characteristics of countries as well as the need for effective relations with the host society, constitute fragmenting influences that favour adaptation to the local environment.

Recent discussion of global competitive strategy echoes the same theme of the dichotomy between the forces that have triggered the globalization of markets and those that constitute barriers to global competition. Factors such as economies of scale in production, purchasing, faster accumulation of learning from operating world-wide, decrease in transportation and distribution costs, reduced costs of product adaptation, and the emergence of global market segments have encouraged competition on a global scale. However, barriers such as governmental and institutional constraints, tariff barriers and duties, preferential treatment of local firms, transportation costs, differences in customer demand, and so on, call for nationalistic or 'protected niche' strategies.

Compromise solutions such as 'pattern standardization' have also been proposed. In this case, a global promotional theme or positioning is developed, but execution is adapted to the local market. Similarly, it has been pointed out that even where a standardized product is marketed in a number of countries, its positioning may be adapted in each market. Conversely, the positioning may be uniform across countries, but the product itself adapted or modified.

Although this debate first emerged in the 1960s, it has recently taken on a new vigour with the widely publicized pronouncements of proponents of 'global standardization' such as Professor Levitt and Saatchi & Saatchi.

The sweeping and somewhat polemic character of their argument has sparked a number of counterarguments as well as discussion of conditions under which such a strategy may be most appropriate. It has, for example, been pointed out that the potential for standardization may be greater for certain types of products such as industrial goods or luxury personal items targeted to upscale consumers, or products with similar penetration rates. Opportunities for standardization are also likely to occur more frequently among industrialized nations, and especially the Triad countries where customer interests as well as market conditions are likely to be more similar than among developing countries.

The role of corporate philosophy and organizational structure in influencing the practicality of implementing a strategy of global standardization has also been recognized. Here, it has been noted that few companies pursue the extreme position of complete standardization with regard to all elements of the marketing mix, and business functions such as R&D, manufacturing, and procurement in all countries throughout the world. Rather, some degree of adaptation is likely to occur relative to certain aspects of the firm's operations or in certain geographic areas. In addition, the feasibility of implementing a standardized strategy will depend on the autonomy accorded to local management. If local management has been accustomed to substantial autonomy, considerable opposition may be encountered in attempting to introduce globally standardized strategies.

An examination of such counterarguments suggests that there are a number of dangers in espousing a philosophy of global standardization for all products and services, and in relation to all markets world-wide. Furthermore, there are numerous difficulties and constraints to implementing such a strategy in many markets, stemming from external market conditions (such as government and trade regulation, competition, the marketing infrastructure, and so on), as well as from the current structure and organization of the firm's operations.

The global standardization philosophy: The underlying assumptions

An examination of the arguments in favour of a strategy of global products and brands reveals three key underlying assumptions:

- Customer needs and interests are becoming increasingly homogeneous world-wide.
- People around the world are willing to sacrifice preferences in product features, functions, design, and the like for lower prices at high quality.
- Substantial economies of scale in production and marketing can be achieved through supplying global markets.

There are, however, a number of pitfalls associated with each of these assumptions. These are discussed here in more detail.

Homogenization of the world's wants

A key premise of the philosophy of global products is that customers' needs and interests are becoming increasingly homogeneous world-wide. But while global segments with similar interests and response patterns may be identified in some product markets, it is by no means clear that this is a universal trend. Furthermore, there is substantial evidence to suggest an increasing diversity of behaviour within countries, and the emergence of idiosyncratic country-specific segments.

Lack of evidence of homogenization. In a number of product markets ranging from watches, perfume, and handbags to soft drinks and fast foods, companies have successfully identified global customer segments, and developed global products and brands targeted to these segments. These include such stars as Rolex, Omega and Le Baume & Mercier watches, Dior, Patou or Yves St. Laurent perfume. But while these brands are highly visible and widely publicized, they are often, with a few notable exceptions such as Classic Coke or McDonald's, targeted to a relatively restricted upscale international customer segment.

Numerous other companies, however, adapt lines to idiosyncratic country preferences, and develop local brands or product variants targeted to local market segments. The Findus frozen food division of Nestlé, for example, markets fish cakes and fish fingers in the United Kingdom, but beef bourguignon and coq au vin in France, and vitello con funghi and braviola in Italy. Similarly, Coca-Cola in Japan markets Georgia, cold coffee in a can, and Aquarius, a tonic drink, as well as Classic Coke and Hi-C.

Growth of intracountry segmentation price sensitivity.   Furthermore, there is a growing body of evidence that suggests substantial heterogeneity within countries. In the United States, for example, the VALS (Value of American Lifestyles) study has identified nine value segments, while other studies have identified major differences in behaviour between regions and subcultural segments. Many other countries are also characterized by substantial regional differences as well as different lifestyle and value segments.

Similarly, in industrial markets, while some global segments, often consisting of firms with international operations, can be identified, there also is considerable diversity within and between countries. Often local businesses constitute an important market segment and, especially in developing countries, may differ significantly in technological sophistication, business philosophy and strategy, emphasis on product quality, and service and price, from large multinationals.

The evidence thus suggests that the similarities in customer behaviour are restricted to a relatively limited number of target segments, or product markets, while for the most part, there are substantial differences between countries. Proponents of standardization counter that the international strategist should focus on similarities among countries rather than differences. This may, however, imply ignoring a major part of a local market, and the potential profits that may be obtained from tapping other market segments.

Universal preference for low price at acceptable quality

Another critical component of the argument for global standardization is that people around the world are willing to sacrifice preferences in product features, functions, design, and the like for lower prices, assuming equivalent quality. Aggressive low pricing for quality products that meet the common needs of customers in markets around the world is believed to further expand the global markets facing the firm.

Although an appealing argument, this has three major problems.

Lack of evidence of increased price sensitivity. Evidence to suggest that customers are universally willing to trade off specific product features for a lower price is largely lacking. While in many product markets there is invariably a price-sensitive segment, there is no indication that this is on the increase. On the contrary, in many product and service markets, ranging from watches, personal computers, and household appliances to banking and insurance, an interest in multiple product features, product quality, and service appears to be growing.

Low price positioning is a highly vulnerable strategy. Also, from a strategic point of view, emphasis on price positioning may be undesirable, especially in international markets, since it offers no long-term competitive advantage. A price-positioning strategy is always vulnerable to new technological developments that may lower costs, as well as to attack from competitors with lower overhead, and lower operating or labour costs. Government subsidies to local competitors may also undermine the effectiveness of a price-positioning strategy. In addition, price-sensitive customers typically are not brand or source loyal.

Standardized low price can be overpriced in some countries and underpriced in others. Finally, a strategy based on a combination of a standardized product at a low price, when implemented in countries that vary in their competitive structure as well as the level of economic development, is likely to result in products that are overdesigned and overpriced for some markets and underdesigned and underpriced for others. Cost advantages may also be negated by transportation and distribution costs as well as tariff barriers or price regulation.

Economies of scale of production and marketing

The third assumption underlying the philosophy of global standardization is that a key force driving strategy is product technology, and that substantial economies of scale can be achieved by supplying global markets. This does, however, neglect three critical and interrelated points:

1 Technological developments in flexible factory automation enable economies of scale to be achieved

at lower levels of output and do not require production of a single standardized product.

2 Cost of production is only one and often not the critical component in determining the total cost of the product.

3 Strategy should not be solely product driven but should take into account the other components of a marketing strategy, such as positioning, packaging, brand name, advertising, PR, consumer and trade promotion and distribution.

Developments in flexible factory automation. Recent developments in flexible factory automation methods have lowered the minimum efficient scale of operation and have thus enabled companies to supply smaller local markets efficiently, without requiring operations on a global scale. However, diseconomies may result from such operations due to increased transportation and distribution costs, as well as higher administrative overhead, and additional communication and coordination costs.

Furthermore, decentralization of production and establishment of local manufacturing operations enables diversification of risk arising from political events, fluctuations in foreign exchange rates, or economic instability. Recent swings in foreign exchange rates, coupled with the growth of offshore sourcing have underscored the vulnerability of centralizing production in a single location. Government regulations relating to local component or offset requirements create additional pressures for local manufacturing. Flexible automation not only implies that decentralization of manufacturing and production may be cost efficient but also makes minor modifications in products or models in the latter stages of production feasible, so that a variety of model versions can be produced without major retooling. Adaptations to product design can thus be made to meet differences in preferences from one country to another without loss of economies of scale.

Production costs are often a minor component of total cost. In many consumer and service industries, such as cosmetics, detergents, pharmaceuticals, or financial institutions, production costs are a small fraction of total cost. The key to success in these markets is an understanding of the tastes and purchase behaviour of target customers' distribution channels, and tailoring products and strategies to these rather than production efficiency. In the detergent industry, for example, mastery of mass-merchandising techniques

and an effective brand management system are typically considered the key elements in the success of the giants in this field, such as Procter & Gamble (P&G) or Colgate-Palmolive.

The standardization philosophy is primarily product driven. The focus on product- and brand-related aspects of strategy in discussions of global standardization is misleading since it ignores the other key strategy variables. Strategy in international markets should also take into consideration other aspects of the marketing mix, and the extent to which these are standardized across country markets rather than adapted to local idiosyncratic characteristics.

Requisite conditions for global standardization

The numerous pitfalls in the rationale underlying the global standardization philosophy suggests that such a strategy is far from universally appropriate for all products, brands, or companies. Only under certain conditions is it likely to prove a 'winning' strategy in international markets. These include:

- the existence of a global market segment;
- potential synergies from standardization;
- the availability of a communication and distribution infrastructure to deliver the firm's offering to target customers world-wide.

Existence of global market segments

As noted previously, global segments may be identified in a number of industrial and consumer markets. In consumer markets these segments are typically luxury- or premium-type products. Global segments are, however, not limited to such product markets, but also exist in other types of markets, such as motorcycle, record, stereo equipment, and computer, where a segment with similar needs and wants can be identified in many countries.

In industrial markets, companies with multinational operations are particularly likely to have similar needs and requirements world-wide. Where the operations are integrated or coordinated across national boundaries, as in the case of banks or other financial institutions, compatibility of operational systems and equipment may be essential. Consequently, they may seek vendors who can supply and service their operations world-wide, in some cases developing glo-bal contrasts for such purchases. Similarly, manu-facturing companies with world-wide operations may source globally in order to ensure uniformity in qual-ity, service and price of components, and other raw materials throughout their operations.

Marketing of global products and brands to such target segments and global customers enables develop-ment of a uniform global image throughout the world. In some markets such as perfume or fashions, association with a specific country of origin or a foreign image in general may carry a prestige connotation. In other cases, for example, Sony electronic equipment, McDonald's hamburgers, Hertz or Avis car rental, IBM computers, or Xerox office equipment, it may help to develop a world-wide reputation for quality and service. Just as multinational corporations may seek uniformity in supply world-wide, some consumers who travel ex-tensively may be interested in finding the same brand of cigarettes and soft drinks, or hotels, in foreign countries. This may be particularly relevant in product markets used extensively by international travellers.

While the existence of a potential global segment is a key motivating factor for developing a global pro-duct and brand strategy, it is important to note that the desirability of such a strategy depends on the size and economic viability of the segment in question, the strength of the segment's preference for the global brand, as well as the ability to reach the segment ef-fectively and profitably.

Synergies associated with global standardization

Global standardization may also have a number of synergistic effects. In addition to those associated with a global image noted above, opportunities may exist for the transfer of good ideas for products or promo-tional strategies from one country to another.

The standardization of strategy and operations across a number of countries may also enable the acquisition or exploitation of specific types of expertise that would not be feasible otherwise. Expertise in assessing country risk or foreign exchange risk, or in identifying and in-terpreting information relating to multiple country markets, for example, may be developed.

Such synergies are not, however, unique to a strategy of global standardization, but may also occur wherever operations and strategy are coordinated or integrated across country markets. In fact, only cer-tain scale economies associated with product and

advertising copy standardization, and the develop-ment of a global image as discussed earlier, are unique to global standardization.

Availability of an international communication and distribution infrastructure

The effectiveness of global standardization also de-pends to a large extent on the availability of an inter-national infrastructure of communications and dis-tribution. As many corporations have expanded overseas, service organizations have followed their customers abroad to supply their needs world-wide.

Advertising agencies such as Saatchi & Saatchi, McCann Erickson, and Young & Rubicam now have an international network of operations throughout the world, while many research agencies can also supply services in major markets world-wide. With the grow-ing integration of financial markets, banks, investment firms, insurance and other financial institutions are also becoming increasingly international in orientation and are expanding the scope of their operations in world markets. The physical distribution network of shippers, freight forwarding, export and import agents, customs clearing, invoicing and insurance agents is also becom-ing increasingly integrated to meet demand for interna-tional shipment of goods and services.

Improvements in telecommunications and in logistical systems have considerably increased capa-city to manage operations on a global scale and hence facilitate adoption of global standardization strategies. The spread of telex and fax systems, as well as satellite linkages and international computer linkages, all con-tribute to the shrinking of distances and facilitate glo-balization of operations. Similarly, improvements in transportation systems and physical logistics such as containerization and computerized inventory and handling systems have enabled significant cost savings as well as reducing time required to move goods across major distances.

Operational constraints to effective implementation of a standardization strategy

While adoption of a standardized strategy may be desirable under certain conditions, there are a number of constraints that severely restrict the firm's ability to develop and implement a standardized strategy.

External constraints to effective standardization

The numerous external constraints that impede global standardization are well recognized. Here, four major categories are highlighted, namely

1 government and trade restrictions;
2 differences in the marketing infrastructure, such as the availability and effectiveness of promotional media;
3 the character of resource markets, and differences in the availability and costs of resources;
4 differences in competition from one country to another.

Government and trade restrictions. Government and trade restrictions, such as tariff and other trade barriers, product, pricing or promotional regulation, frequently hamper standardization of the product line, pricing, or promotional strategy. Tariffs or quotas on the import of key materials, components, or other resources may, for example, affect production costs and thus hamper uniform pricing or alternatively result in the substitution of other components and modifications in product design. Local content requirements or compensatory export requirements, which specify that products contain a certain proportion of components manufactured locally or that a certain volume of production is exported to offset imports of components or other services, may have a similar impact.

The existence of cartels such as the European steel cartel, or the Swiss chocolate cartel, may also impede or exclude standardized strategies in countries covered by these agreements. In particular, they may affect adoption of a uniform pricing strategy as the cartel sets prices for the industry. Cartel members may also control established distribution channels, thus preventing use of a standardized distribution strategy. Extensive grey markets in countries such as India, Hong Kong, and South America may also affect administered pricing systems, and require adjustment of pricing strategies.

The nature of the marketing infrastructure. Differences in the marketing infrastructure from one country to another may hamper use of a standardized strategy. These may, for example, include differences in the availability and reach of various promotional media, in the availability of certain distribution channels or retail institutions, or in the existence and efficiency of the communication and transportation network. Such factors may, therefore, require considerable adaptation of strategy of local market conditions.

Interdependencies with resource markets. Yet another constraint to the development of standardized strategies is the nature of resource markets, and their operation in different countries throughout the world as well as the interdependency of these markets with marketing decisions. Availability and cost of raw materials, as well as labour and other resources in different locations, will affect not only decisions regarding sourcing of and hence the location of manufacturing activities but also marketing strategy decisions such as product design. For example, in the paper industry, availability of cheap local materials such as jute and sugar cane may result in their substitution for wood fibre.

Cost differentials relative to raw materials, labour, management, and other inputs may also influence the trade-off relative to alternative strategies. For example, high packaging cost relative to physical distribution may result in use of cheaper packaging with a shorter shelf life and more frequent shipments. Similarly, low labour costs relative to media may encourage a shift from mass media advertising to labour-intensive promotion such as personal selling and product demonstration.

Availability of capital, technology, and manufacturing capabilities in different locations will also affect decisions about licensing, contract manufacturing, joint ventures, and other 'make-buy' types of decisions for different markets, as well as decisions about countertrade, reciprocity, and other long-term relations.

The nature of the competitive structure. Differences in the nature of the competitive situation from one country to another may also suggest the desirability of adaptation strategy. Even in markets characterized by global competition, such as agricultural equipment and motorcycles, the existence of low-cost competition in certain countries may suggest the desirability of marketing stripped-down models or lowering prices to meet such competition. Even where competitors are predominantly other multinationals, preemption of established distribution networks may encourage adoption of innovative distribution methods or direct distribution to short-circuit an entrenched position. Thus, the existence of global competition does not necessarily imply a need for global standardization.

All such aspects thus impose major constraints on the feasibility and effectiveness of a standardized strategy, and suggest the desirability or need to adapt to specific market conditions.

Internal constraints to effective standardization

In addition to such external constraints on the feasibility of a global standardization strategy, there are also a number of internal constraints that may need to be considered. These include compatibility with the existing network of operations overseas, as well as opposition or lack of enthusiasm among local management toward a standardized strategy.

Existing international operations. Proponents of global standardization typically take the position of a novice company with no operations in international markets, and hence fail to take into consideration the fit of the proposed strategy with current international activities. In practice, however, many companies have a number of existing operations in various countries. In some cases, these are joint ventures, or licensing operations or involve some collaboration in purchasing, manufacturing or distribution with other companies. Even where foreign manufacturing and distribution operations are wholly owned, the establishment of a distribution network will typically entail relationships with other organizations, for example, exclusive distributor agreements.

Such commitments may be difficult if not impossible to change in the short run, and may constitute a major impediment to adoption of a standardized strategy. If, for example, a joint venture with a local company has been established to manufacture and market a product line in a specific country or region, resistance from the local partner (or government authorities) may be encountered if the parent company wishes to shift production or import components from another location. Similarly, a licensing contract will impede a firm from supplying the products covered by the agreement from an alternative location for the duration of the contract, even if it becomes more cost efficient to do so.

Conversely, the establishment of an effective dealer or distribution network in a country or region may constitute an important resource to a company. The addition of new products to the product line currently sold or distributed by this network may therefore provide a more efficient utilization of company resources than expanding to new countries or geographic regions with the existing line, as this would require substantial investment in the establishment of a new distribution network.

In addition, overseas subsidiaries may currently be marketing not only core products and brands from the company's domestic business, but may also have added or acquired local or regional products and brands in response to local market demand. In some cases, therefore, introduction of a global product or brand may be likely to cannibalize sales of local or regional brands.

Advocates of standardization thus need to take into consideration the evolutionary character of international involvement, which may render a universal strategy of global products and brands suboptimal. Somewhat ironically, the longer the history of a multinational corporation's involvement in foreign or international markets, and the more diversified and far-flung its operations, the more likely it is that standardization will not lead to optimal results.

Local management motivation and attitudes. Another internal constraint concerns the motivation and attitudes of local management with regard to standardization. Standardized strategies tend to facilitate or result in centralization in the planning and organization of international activities. Especially if input from local management is limited, this may result in a feeling that strategy is 'imposed' by corporate headquarters, and/or not adequately adapted or appropriate in view of specific local market characteristics and conditions. Local management is likely to take the view 'it won't work here – things are different', which will reduce their motivation to implement a standardized strategy effectively.

A framework for classifying global strategy options

The adoption of a global perspective should not be viewed as synonymous with a strategy of global products and brands. Rather, for most companies such a perspective implies consideration of a broad range of strategic options of which standardization is merely one.

In essence, a global perspective implies planning strategy relative to markets world-wide rather than on a country-by-country basis. This may result in the identification of opportunities for global products and brands or integrating and coordinating strategy across national boundaries to exploit potential synergies of operating on an international scale. Such opportunities should, however, be weighed against the benefits of adaptation to idiosyncratic customer characteristics.

The development of an effective global strategy thus requires a careful examination of all international options in terms of standardization versus adaptation open to the firm.

A firm's international operations are likely to be characterized by a mix of strategies, including not only global products and brands, but also some regional products and brands and some national products and brands. Similarly, some target segments may be global, others regional, and others national. Hybrid strategies of this nature thus enable a company to take advantage of the benefits of standardization and potential synergies from operating on an international scale, while at the same time not losing those afforded by adaptation to specific country characteristics and customer preferences.

READING 10.3

The competitive advantage of nations
By Michael Porter[1]

Companies, not nations, are on the front line of international competition. Yet, the characteristics of the home nation play a central role in a firm's international success. The home base shapes a company's capacity to innovate rapidly in technology and methods and to do so in the proper directions. It is the place from which competitive advantage ultimately emanates and from which it must be sustained. A global strategy supplements and solidifies the competitive advantage created at the home base; it is the icing, not the cake. However, on the one hand, while having a home base in the right nation helps a great deal, it does not ensure success. On the other hand, having a home base in the wrong nation raises fundamental strategic concerns.

The most important sources of national advantage must be actively sought and exploited, unlike low factor costs obtainable simply by operating in the nation. Internationally successful firms are not passive bystanders in the process of creating competitive advantage. Those we studied were caught up in a never-ending process of seeking out new advantages and struggling with rivals to protect them. They were positioned to benefit the most from their national environment. They took steps to make their home nation (and location within the nation) an even more favourable environment for competitive advantage. Finally, they amplified their home-based advantages and offset home-based disadvantages through global strategies that tapped selectively into advantages available in other nations.

Competitive advantage ultimately results from an effective combination of national circumstances and company strategy. Conditions in a nation may create an environment in which firms can attain international competitive advantage, but it is up to a company to seize the opportunity.

The context for competitive advantage

These imperatives of competitive advantage constitute a mind-set that is not present in many companies. Indeed, the actions required to create and sustain advantage are unnatural acts. Stability is valued in most companies, not change. Protecting old ideas and techniques becomes the preoccupation, not creating new ones.

The long-term challenge for any firm is to put itself in a position where it is most likely to perceive, and best able to address, the imperatives of competitive advantage. One challenge is to expose a company to new market and technological opportunities that may be hard to perceive. Another is preparing for change by upgrading and expanding the skills of employees and improving the firm's scientific and knowledge base. Ultimately, the most important challenge is overcoming complacency and inertia to act on the new opportunities and circumstances.

The challenge of action ultimately falls on the firm's leader. Much attention has rightly been placed on the importance of visionary leaders in achieving unusual organizational success. But where does a leader get the vision, and how is it transmitted in a way that produces organizational accomplishment? Great leaders are influenced by the environment in which they work. Innovation takes place because the home environment stimulates it. Innovation succeeds because the home environment supports and even forces it. The right environment not only shapes a leader's own perceptions and priorities but provides the catalyst that allows the leader to overcome inertia and produce organizational change.

Great leaders emerge in different industries in different nations, in part because national circumstances attract and encourage them. Visionaries in consumer electronics are concentrated in Japan, chemicals and pharmaceuticals in Germany and Switzerland, and computers in America. Leadership is important to any success story, but is not in and of itself sufficient to explain such successes. In many industries, the national environment provides one or two nations with a distinct advantage over their foreign competitors. Leadership often determines which particular firm or firms exploit this advantage.

More broadly, the ability of any firm to innovate has much to do with the environment to which it is exposed, the information sources it has available – and consults – and the types of challenges it chooses to face. Seeking safe havens and comfortable customer relationships only reinforces past behaviour. Maintaining suppliers who are captive degrades a source of stimulus, assistance, and insight. Lobbying against stringent product standards sends the wrong signal to an organization about norms and aspirations.

Innovation grows out of pressure and challenge. It also comes from finding the right challenges to meet. The main role of the firm's leader is to create the environment that meets these conditions. One essential part of the task is to take advantage of the national 'diamond' (see Figure 10.3.1 and Exhibit 10.3.1) that currently describes competition in the industry.

The new rules for innovation

A company should actively seek out pressure and challenge, not try to avoid them. Part of the task is to take advantage of the home nation in order to create the impetus for innovation. Some of the ways of doing so are:

- Sell to the most sophisticated and demanding buyers and channels. Some buyers (and channels) will stimulate the fastest improvement because they are knowledgeable and expect the best performance. They will set a standard for the organization and provide the most valuable feedback. However, sophisticated and demanding buyers and channels need not be the firm's only customers. Focusing on them exclusively may unnecessarily diminish long-term profitability. Nevertheless, serving a group of such buyers, chosen because their needs will challenge the firm's particular approach to competing, must be an explicit part of any strategy.

- Seek out the buyers with the most difficult needs. Buyers who face especially difficult operating

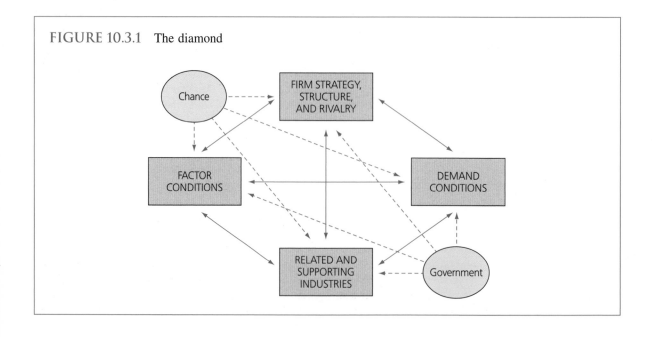

FIGURE 10.3.1 The diamond

EXHIBIT 10.3.1   ELEMENTS OF THE DIAMOND

COMPETITIVE ADVANTAGES AND DISADVANTAGES

The 'diamond' provides a framework for assessing important areas of competitive strength and weakness.

Factor conditions. International rivals will differ in the mix and cost of available factors and the rate of factor creation. Swedish automobile firms, for example, benefit from the solidarity wage system that makes the wages of Swedish auto workers closer to those of other Swedish industries, but relatively lower than the wages of auto workers in other advanced nations.

Demand conditions. Competitors from other nations will face differing segment structures of home demand, differing home buyer needs, and home buyers with various levels of sophistication. Demand conditions at their home base will help predict foreign competitors' directions of product change as well as their likely success in product development, among other things.

Related and supporting industries. Competitors based in other nations will differ in the availability of domestic suppliers, the quality of interaction with supplier industries, and the presence of related industries. Italian footwear firms and leather goods producers, for example, have early access to new tanned leather styles because of the world-leading Italian leather tanning industry.

Firm strategy, structure, and rivalry. The environment in their home nation will strongly influence the strategic choices of foreign rivals. Italian packaging equipment firms, for example, reflect their Italian context. They are mostly small and managed by strong, paternal leaders. Owners of firms have personal relationships with significant buyers. This makes them unusually responsive to market trends and provides the ability to custom-tailor machinery to buyer circumstances.

---

requirements (such as climate, maintenance requirements, or hours of use), who confront factor cost disadvantages in their own businesses that create unusual pressures for performance, who have particularly tough competition, or who compete with strategies that place especially heavy demands on the firm's product or service, are buyers that will provide the laboratory (and the pressure) to upgrade performance and extend features and services. Such buyers should be identified and cultivated. They become part of a firm's R&D programme.

■ Establish norms of exceeding the toughest regulatory hurdles or product standards. Some localities (or user industries) will lead in terms of the stringency of product standards, pollution limits, noise guidelines, and the like. Tough regulating standards are not a hindrance but an opportunity to move early to upgrade products and processes. Older or simplified models can be sold elsewhere.

■ Source from the most advanced and international home-based suppliers. Suppliers who themselves possess competitive advantage, as well as the insight that comes from international activities, will challenge the firm to improve and upgrade as well as provide insights and assistance in doing so.

■ Treat employees as permanent. When employees are viewed as permanent instead of as workers who can be hired and fired at will, pressures are created that work to upgrade and sustain competitive advantage. New employees are hired with care, and continuous efforts are made to improve productivity instead of adding workers. Employees are trained on an ongoing basis to support more sophisticated competitive advantages.

■ Establish outstanding competitors as motivators. Those competitors who most closely match a company's competitive advantages, or exceed them, must become the standard of comparison. Such competitors can be a source of learning as well as a powerful focal point to overcome parochial concerns and motivate change for the entire organization.

The true costs of stability

These prescriptions may seem counterintuitive. The ideal would seem to be the stability growing out of obedient customers, captive and dependent suppliers, and sleepy competitors. Such a search for a quiet life, an understandable instinct, has led many companies to buy direct competitors or form alliances with them. In a closed, static world, monopoly would indeed be the most comfortable and profitable solution.

In reality, however, competition is dynamic. Complacent firms will lose to other firms who come from a more dynamic environment. Good managers always run a little scared. They respect and study competitors. Seeking out and meeting challenges is part of their organizational norm. By contrast, an organization that values stability and lacks self-perceived competition breeds inertia and creates vulnerabilities.

In global competition, the pressure of demanding local buyers, capable suppliers, and aggressive domestic rivalry are even more valuable and necessary for long-term profitability. These drive the firm to a faster rate of progress and upgrading than international rivals, and lead to sustained competitive advantage and superior long-term profitability. A tough domestic industry structure creates advantage in the international industry. A comfortable, easy home base, in contrast, leaves a firm vulnerable to rivals who enjoy greater dynamism at home.

Perceiving industry change

Beyond pressure to innovate, one of the most important advantages an industry can have is early insight into important needs, environmental forces, and trends that others have not noticed. Japanese firms had an early and clear warning about the importance of energy efficiency. American firms have often gotten a jump in seeing demand for new services, giving them a head start in many service industries. Better insight and early warning signals lead to competitive advantages. Firms gain competitive position before rivals perceive an opportunity (or a threat) and are able to respond.

Perceiving possibilities for new strategies more clearly or earlier comes in part from simply being in the right nation at the right time. Yet it is possible for a firm to more actively position itself to see the signals of change and act on them. It must find the right focus or location within the nation, and work to overcome the filters that distort or limit the flow of information.

- Identify and serve buyers (and channels) with the most anticipatory needs. Some buyers will confront new problems or have new needs before others because of their demographics, location, industry, or strategy.

- Discover and highlight trends in factor costs. Increases in the costs of particular factors or other

inputs may signal future opportunities to leapfrog competitors by innovating to deploy inputs more effectively or to avoid the need for them altogether. A firm should know which markets or regions are likely to reflect such trends first.

- Maintain ongoing relationships with centres of research and sources of the most talented people. A firm must identify the places in the nation where the best new knowledge is being created that is now or might become relevant to its industry. Equally important is to identify the schools, institutions, and other companies where the best specialized human resources needed in the industry are being trained.

- Study all competitors, especially the new and unconventional ones. Rivals sometimes discover new ideas first. Innovators are often smaller, more focused competitors that are new to the industry. Alternatively, they may be firms led by managers with backgrounds in other industries not bound by conventional wisdom. Such 'outsiders,' with fewer blinders to cloud their perception of new opportunities and fewer perceived constraints in abandoning past practices, frequently become industry innovators.

- Bring some outsiders into the management team. The incorporation of new thinking in the management process is often speeded by the presence of one or more 'outsiders' – managers from other companies or industries or from the company's foreign subsidiaries.

Interchange within the national cluster

A firm gains important competitive advantages from the presence in its home nation of world-class buyers, suppliers, and related industries. They provide insight into future market needs and technological developments. They contribute to a climate for change and improvement, and become partners and allies in the innovation process. Having a strong cluster at home unblocks the flows of information and allows deeper and more open contact than is possible when dealing with foreign firms. Being part of a cluster localized in a small geographic area is even more valuable.

Buyers, channels, and suppliers

The first hurdle to be cleared in taking advantage of the domestic cluster is attitudinal. It means recognizing that home-based buyers and suppliers are allies in international competition and not just the other side of transactions. A firm must also pursue:

- regular senior management contact;
- formal and ongoing interchange between research organizations;
- reciprocity in serving as test sites for new products or services;
- cooperation in penetrating and serving international markets.

Working with buyers, suppliers, and channels involves helping them upgrade and extend their own competitive advantages. Their health and strength will only enhance their capacity to speed the firm's own rate of innovation. Open communications with local buyers or suppliers, and early access to new equipment, services, and ideas, are important for sustaining competitive advantage. Such communication will be freer, more timely, and more meaningful than is usually possible with foreign firms.

Encouraging and assisting domestic buyers and suppliers to compete globally is one part of the task of upgrading them. A company's local buyers and suppliers cannot ultimately sustain competitive advantage in many cases unless they compete globally. Buyers and suppliers need exposure to the pressures of world-wide competition in order to advance themselves. Trying to keep them 'captive' and prevent them from selling their products abroad is ultimately self-defeating.

An orientation toward closer vertical relationships is only just starting to take hold in many American companies, though it is quite typical in Japanese and Swedish companies. Interchange with buyers, channels, and suppliers always involves some tension, because there is inevitably the need to bargain with them over prices and service. In global industries, however, the competitive advantage to be gained from interchange more than compensates for some sacrifice in bargaining leverage. Interchange should not create dependence but interdependence. A firm should work with a group of suppliers and customers, not just one.

Related industries

Industries that are related or potentially related in terms of technology, channels, buyers, or the way buyers obtain or use products are potentially important to creating and sustaining competitive advantage. The presence in a nation of such industries deserves special attention. These industries are often essential sources of innovation. They can also become new suppliers, buyers, or even new competitors.

At a minimum, senior management should be visiting leading companies in related industries on a regular basis. The purpose is to exchange ideas about industry developments. Formal joint research projects, or other more structured ways to explore new ideas, are advisable where the related industry holds more immediate potential to affect competitive advantage.

Locating within the nation

A firm should locate activities and its headquarters at those locations in the nation where there are concentrations of sophisticated buyers, important suppliers, groups of competitors, or especially significant factor-creating mechanisms for its industry (such as universities with specialized programmes or laboratories with expertise in important technologies). Geographic proximity makes the relationships within a cluster closer and more fluid. It also makes domestic rivalry more valuable for competitive advantage.

Serving home base buyers who are international and multinational

To transform domestic competitive advantage into a global strategy, a firm should identify and serve buyers at home that can also serve abroad. Such buyers are domestic companies that have international operations, individuals who travel frequently to other nations, and local subsidiaries of foreign firms. Targeting such buyers has two benefits. First, they can provide a base of demand in foreign markets to help offset the costs of entry. More important, they will often be sophisticated buyers who can provide a window into international market needs.

Improving the national competitive environment

Sustaining competitive advantage is not only a function of making the most of the national environment. Firms must work actively to improve their home base by upgrading the national diamond (see Figure 10.3.1 and Exhibit 10.3.1). A company draws on its home nation to extend and upgrade its own competitive advantages. The firm has a stake in making its home base a better platform for international success.

Playing this role demands that a company understands how each part of the 'diamond' best contributes to competitive advantage. It also requires a long-term perspective, because the investments required to improve the home base often take years or even decades to bear fruit. What is more, short-term profits are elevated by foregoing such investments, and by shifting important activities abroad instead of upgrading the ability to perform them at home. Both actions will diminish the sustainability of a firm's competitive advantages in the long run.

Firms have a tendency to see the task of ensuring high-quality human resources, infrastructure, and scientific knowledge as someone else's responsibility. Another common misconception is that, because competition is global, the home base is unimportant. Too often, US and British companies in particular leave investments in the national diamond to others or to the government. The result is that companies are well managed but lack the human resources, technology, and access to capable suppliers and customers needed to succeed against foreign rivals.

Where and how to compete

A firm's home nation shapes where and how it is likely to succeed in global competition. Germany is a superb environment for competing in printing equipment, but does not offer one conducive to international success in heavily advertised consumer packaged goods. Italy represents a remarkable setting for innovation in fashion and furnishing, but a poor environment for success in industries that sell to government agencies or infrastructure providers.

Within an industry, a nation's circumstances also favour competing in particular industry segments and with certain competitive strategies. Given local housing conditions, for example, Japan is a good home base for competing globally in compact models of appliances and in appliances that are inherently compact (such as microwave ovens) but a poor home base for competing in full-size refrigerators. Within compact appliances, the Japanese environment is particularly conducive to differentiation strategies based on rapid new model introduction and high product quality.

The national diamond becomes central to choosing the industries to compete in as well as the appropriate strategy. The home base is an important determinant of a firm's strengths and weaknesses relative to foreign rivals.

Understanding the home base of foreign competitors is essential in analysing them. Their home nation yields them advantages and disadvantages. It also shapes their likely future strategies. The diamond serves as an important tool for competitor analysis in international industries.

Choosing industries and strategies

The likelihood that a firm can achieve breakthroughs or innovations of strategic importance in an industry is also influenced by its home nation. Innovation and entrepreneurial behaviour is partly a function of chance. But it also depends to a considerable degree on the environment in which the innovator or entrepreneur works. The diamond has a strong influence on which nation (and even on which region within that nation) will be the source of an innovation.

Important innovations in Denmark, for example, have occurred in enzymes for food processing, in natural vitamins, in measuring instruments related to food processing, and in drugs isolated from animal organs (insulin and the anticoagulant heparin). These are hardly random in a nation whose exports are dominated by a large cluster of food-and-beverage-related industries. A firm or individual has the best odds of succeeding in innovation, or in creating a new business, where the national diamond provides the best environment.

The national circumstances most significant for competitive advantage depend on a firm's industry and strategy. In a resource- or basic factor-driven industry, the most important national attribute is a supply of superior or low-cost factors. In a fashion-sensitive industry, the presence of advanced and cutting-edge customers is paramount. In an industry heavily based on scientific research, the quality of factor-creating mechanisms in human resources and technology, coupled with access to sophisticated buyers and suppliers, is decisive.

Cost-oriented strategies are more sensitive to factor costs, the size of home demand, and conditions that favour large-scale plant investments. Differentiation strategies tend to depend more on specialized human resources, sophisticated local buyers, and world-class local supplier industries. Focus strategies rest on the presence of unusual demand in particular segments or on factor conditions or supplier access that benefits competing in a particular product range.

As competition globalizes, and as developments such as European trade liberalization and free trade between the United States and Canada promise to eliminate artificial distortions that have insulated domestic firms from market forces, firms must increasingly compete in industries and segments where they have real strengths. This must increasingly be guided by the national diamond.

A firm can raise the odds of success if it is competing in industries, and with strategies, where the nation provides an unusually fertile environment for competitive advantage. The questions in Figure 10.3.2 are designed to expose such areas. Of major importance is a forward-looking view in answering these questions. The focus must be on the nature of evolving competition, not the past requirements for success.

Diversification

While diversification is part of company strategy in virtually every nation, its track record has been mixed at best. Widespread diversification into unrelated industries was rare among the international leaders we studied. They tended instead to compete in one or two core industries or industry sectors, and their commitment to these industries was absolute. For every widely diversified Hitachi or Siemens, there were several Boeings, Koenig & Bauers, FANUCs, Novo

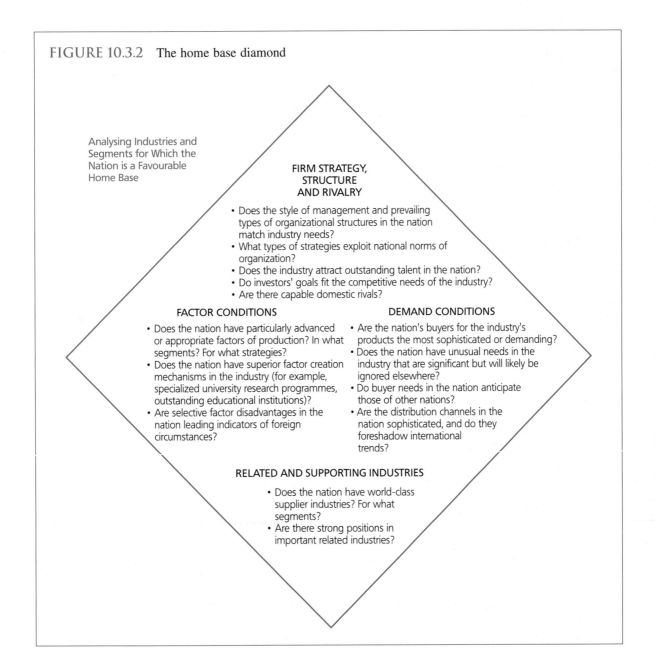

FIGURE 10.3.2   The home base diamond

Analysing Industries and Segments for Which the Nation is a Favourable Home Base

FIRM STRATEGY, STRUCTURE AND RIVALRY
- Does the style of management and prevailing types of organizational structures in the nation match industry needs?
- What types of strategies exploit national norms of organization?
- Does the industry attract outstanding talent in the nation?
- Do investors' goals fit the competitive needs of the industry?
- Are there capable domestic rivals?

FACTOR CONDITIONS
- Does the nation have particularly advanced or appropriate factors of production? In what segments? For what strategies?
- Does the nation have superior factor creation mechanisms in the industry (for example, specialized university research programmes, outstanding educational institutions)?
- Are selective factor disadvantages in the nation leading indicators of foreign circumstances?

DEMAND CONDITIONS
- Are the nation's buyers for the industry's products the most sophisticated or demanding?
- Does the nation have unusual needs in the industry that are significant but will likely be ignored elsewhere?
- Do buyer needs in the nation anticipate those of other nations?
- Are the distribution channels in the nation sophisticated, and do they foreshadow international trends?

RELATED AND SUPPORTING INDUSTRIES
- Does the nation have world-class supplier industries? For what segments?
- Are there strong positions in important related industries?

Industries, and SKFs, who are global competitors but heavily focused on their core industry.

Internal diversification, not acquisition, has to a striking degree been the motivation for achieving leading international market positions. Where acquisitions were involved in international success stories, the acquisitions were often modest or focused ones that served as an initial entry point or reinforced an internal entry. The reasons for this track record in diversification are not hard to understand when viewed in light of my theory.

Internal diversification facilitates a transfer of skills and resources that is quite difficult to accomplish when acquiring an independent company with its own history and way of operating. Internal entry tends to increase the overall rate of investment in factor creation. There is also an intense commitment to succeed in diversification into closely related fields because of the benefits that accrue to the base business and the effect on the overall corporate image. Unrelated diversification, particularly through acquisition, makes no contribution to innovation. The implications of my theory for diversification strategy are as follows:

- New industries for diversification should be selected where a favourable national diamond is present or can be created. Diversification proposals should be screened for the attractiveness of the home base.

- Diversification is most likely to succeed when it follows or extends clusters in which the firm already competes.

- Internal development of new businesses, supplemented by small acquisitions, is more likely to create and sustain competitive advantage than the acquisition of large, establishment companies.

- Diversification into businesses lacking common buyers, channels, suppliers, or close technological connections is not only likely to fail but will also undermine the prospects for sustaining advantage in the core businesses.

Locating regional headquarters

The principles I have described carry implications for the choice of where to locate the regional headquarters responsible for managing a firm's activities in a group of nations. Regional headquarters are best placed not for administrative convenience but in the nation with the most favourable national diamond. Of special importance is choosing a location that will expose the firm to significant needs and pressures lacking at home. The purpose is to learn as well as raise the odds that information passes credibly back to the home base.

Selective foreign acquisitions

Foreign acquisitions can serve two purposes. One is to gain access to a foreign market or to selective skills. Here the challenge of integrating the acquisition into the global strategy is significant but raises a few unusual issues. The other reason for a foreign acquisition is to gain access to a highly favourable national diamond. Sometimes the only feasible way to tap into the advantages of another nation is to acquire a local firm because an outsider is hard-pressed to penetrate such broad, systemic advantages. The challenge in this latter type of acquisition is to preserve the ability of the acquired firm to benefit from its national environment at the same time as it is integrated into the company's global strategy.

The role of alliances

Alliances, or coalitions, are final mechanisms by which a firm can seek to tap national advantages in other nations. Alliances are a tempting solution to the dilemma of a firm seeking the home-base advantages of another nation without giving up its own. Unfortunately, alliances are rarely a solution. They can achieve selective benefits, but they always involve significant costs in terms of coordination, reconciling goals with an independent entity, creating a competitor, and giving up profits. These costs make many alliances temporary and destined to fail. They are often transitional devices rather than stable arrangements. No firm can depend on another independent firm for skills and assets that are central to its competitive advantage. If it does, the firm runs a grave risk of losing its competitive advantage in the long run. Alliances tend to ensure mediocrity, not create world leadership. The most serious risk of alliances is that they deter the firm's own efforts at upgrading. This may occur because management is content to rely on the partner. It may also occur because the alliance has eliminated a threatening competitor.

READING

10.4

Transnational management

By *Christopher Bartlett and Sumantra Ghoshal*[1]

Changes in the international operating environment have forced MNCs to optimize global efficiency, national responsiveness, and world-wide learning simultaneously. For most companies, this new challenge implies not only a fundamental strategic reorientation, but also a major change in organizational capability.

Implementing such a complex three-pronged strategic objective would be difficult under any circumstances, but in a world-wide company the task is complicated even further. The very act of 'going international' multiplies a company's organizational complexity. Most companies find it difficult enough balancing product divisions that carry overall responsibility for achieving operating efficiency and strategic focus with corporate staffs whose functional expertise allows them to play an important counterbalance and control role. The thought of adding capable geographically oriented management and maintaining a three-way balance of organizational perspectives and capabilities among product, function, and area is intimidating. The difficulty is further increased because the resolution of tensions among the three different management groups must be accomplished in an organization whose operating units are often divided by distance and time and whose key members are separated by barriers of culture and language.

Beyond structural fit

Because the choice of a basic organizational structure has such a powerful influence on the management process in an MNC, much of the earlier attention of managers and researchers alike was focused on trying to find which formal structure provided the right 'fit' under various conditions. The most widely recognized study on this issue was Stopford and Wells's (1972) research on the 187 largest US-based MNCs in the late 1960s. Their work resulted in a 'stages model' of international organization structure that became the benchmark for most work that followed.

Stopford and Wells defined two variables to capture strategic and administrative complexity that faced most companies as they expanded abroad: the number of products sold internationally ('foreign product diversity', shown on the vertical axis in Figure 10.4.1) and the importance of international sales to the company ('foreign sales as a percentage of total sales', shown on the horizontal axis). Plotting the structural change in their sample of 187 companies, they found that worldwide corporations typically adopt different organizational structures at different stages of international expansion.

According to this model, world-wide companies typically manage their international operations through an international division at the early stage of foreign expansion, when both foreign sales and the diversity of products sold abroad are limited. Subsequently, those companies that expand their sales abroad without significantly increasing foreign product diversity typically adopt an area structure. Other companies that expand by increasing their foreign product diversity tend to adopt the world-wide product division structure. Finally, when both foreign sales and foreign product diversity are high, companies resort to the global matrix.

Although these ideas were presented as a descriptive model, consultants, academics, and managers alike soon began to apply them prescriptively. For many companies, it seemed that structure followed fashion more than strategy. And in the process, the debate was often reduced to generalized discussions of the comparative value of product versus geography-based structures and to simplistic choices between 'centralization' and 'decentralization'.

Confronted with the increasing complexity, diversity, and change in the 1980s, managers in many world-wide companies looked for ways to restructure. Conventional wisdom provided a ready solution: the global matrix. But for most companies, the result was disappointing. The promised land of the global matrix turned out to be an organizational quagmire from which they were forced to retreat.

---

[1]Source: Reprinted from Chapter 5 of *Transnational Management: Text, Cases, and Readings in Cross-Border Management*, second edition, R. D. Irwin Inc., 1995. Reproduced with permission from McGraw-Hill Companies Inc.

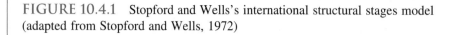

FIGURE 10.4.1   Stopford and Wells's international structural stages model (adapted from Stopford and Wells, 1972)

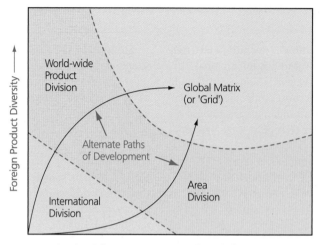

Failure of the matrix

In theory, the solution should have worked. Having front-line managers report simultaneously to different organizational groups (such as business managers reporting to both the area and the functional groups or area managers reporting along functional and business lines) should have enabled the companies to maintain the balance among centralized efficiency, local responsiveness, and world-wide knowledge transfer. The multiple channels of communication and control promised the ability to nurture diverse management perspectives, and the ability to shift the balance of power within the matrix theoretically gave it great flexibility. The reality turned out to be otherwise, however, and the history of companies that built formal global matrix structures was an unhappy one.

Dow Chemical, a pioneer of global matrix organization, eventually returned to a more conventional structure with clear lines of responsibility being given to geographic managers. Citibank, once a textbook example of the global matrix, similarly discarded this mode of dual reporting relationships after a few years of highly publicized experimentation. And so too did scores of other companies that experimented with this complex and rather bureaucratic structure.

Most encountered the same problems. The matrix amplified the differences in perspectives and interests by forcing all issues through the dual chains of command so that even a minor difference could become the subject of heated disagreement and debate. While this strategy had proven useful in highly concentrated domestic operations, the very design of the global matrix prevented the resolution of differences among managers with conflicting views and overlapping responsibilities. Dual reporting led to conflict and confusion; the proliferation of channels created informational logjams; and overlapping responsibilities resulted in turf battles and a loss of accountability. Separated by barriers of distance, time, language, and culture, managers found it virtually impossible to clarify the confusion and resolve the conflicts.

As a result, the management process was slow, acrimonious, and costly. Communications were routinely duplicated, approval processes were time-consuming, and constant travel and frequent meetings raised the company's administrative costs dramatically. In company after company, the initial appeal of the global matrix structure quickly faded into a recognition that a different solution was required.

Building organizational capability

The basic problem underlying a company's search for a structural fit was that it focused on only one organizational variable – formal structure – and this single tool proved to be unequal to the task of capturing the complexity of the strategic task facing most MNCs. First, as indicated earlier, this focus often forced managers to ignore the multidimensionality of the environmental forces as they made choices between product versus geographically based structures and debated the relative advantages of centralization versus decentralization. Furthermore, structure defined a static set of roles, responsibilities, and relationships in a dynamic and rapidly evolving task environment. And finally, restructuring efforts often proved harmful, as organizations were bludgeoned into a major realignment of roles, responsibilities, and relationships overnight.

In an increasing number of companies, managers now recognize that formal structure is a powerful but blunt instrument of strategic change. Moreover, given the complexity and volatility of environmental demands, structural fit is becoming both less relevant and harder to achieve. Success in coping with managers' multidimensional strategic task now depends rather more on building strategic and organizational flexibility.

To develop multidimensional and flexible strategic capabilities, a company must go beyond structure and expand its fundamental organizational capabilities. The key tasks become to reorient managers' thinking and reshape the core decision-making systems. In doing so, the company's entire management process – the administrative system, communication channels, and interpersonal relationships – become the tools for managing such change.

Administrative heritage

While industry analysis can reveal a company's strategic challenges and market opportunities, its ability to fulfil that promise will be greatly influenced – and often constrained – by existing asset configurations, its historical definition of management responsibilities, and the ingrained organizational norms. A company's organization is shaped not only by current external task demands but also by past internal management biases. In particular, each company is influenced by the path by which it developed – its organizational history – and the values, norms, and practices of its management – its management culture. Collectively, these factors constitute a company's administrative heritage. It can be, at the same time, one of the company's greatest assets – the underlying source of its key competencies – and also a significant liability, since it resists change and thereby prevents realignment or broadening of strategic capabilities. As

managers in many companies have learned, often at considerable cost, while strategic plans can be scrapped and redrawn overnight, there is no such thing as a zero-based organization. Companies are, to a significant extent, captives of their past, and any organizational transformation has to focus at least as much on where the company is coming from – its administrative heritage – as on where it wants to get to.

The importance of a company's administrative heritage can be illustrated by contrasting the development of a typical European MNC whose major international expansion occurred in the decades of the 1920s and 1930s, a typical American MNC that expanded abroad in the 1940s and 1950s, and a typical Japanese company that made its main overseas thrust in the 1960s and 1970s. Even if these companies were in the same industry, the combined effects of the different historical contexts in which they developed and the disparate internal cultural norms that influenced their management processes led to their adopting some very different strategic and organizational models.

Decentralized federation

Expanding abroad in a period of rising tariffs and discriminatory legislation, the typical European company found its budding export markets threatened by local competitors. To defend its various market positions, it was forced to build local production facilities. With their own plants, various national subsidiaries were able to modify products and marketing approaches to meet widely differing local market needs. The increasing independence of these fully integrated national units was reinforced by the transportation and communications barriers that existed in that era, limiting the headquarters' ability to intervene in the management of the company's spreading world-wide operations.

The emerging configuration of distributed assets and delegated responsibility fit well with the ingrained management norms and practices in many European companies. Because of the important role of owners and bankers in corporate-level decision making, European companies, particularly those from the United Kingdom, the Netherlands, and France, developed an internal culture that emphasized personal relationships rather than formal structures, and financial controls more than coordination of technical or operational detail. This management style, philosophy, and capability tended to reinforce companies' willingness to delegate more operating independence and strategic freedom to their foreign subsidiaries. Highly autonomous national companies were often managed more as a portfolio of offshore investments than as a single international business.

The resulting organization and management pattern was a loose federation of independent national subsidiaries, each focused primarily on its local market. As a result, many of these companies adopted what we have described as the multinational strategy and developed a decentralized federation organization model that is represented in Figure 10.4.2.

Coordinated federation

US companies, many of which enjoyed their fastest international expansion in the 1950s and 1960s, developed under very different circumstances. Their main strength lay in the new technologies and management processes they had developed as a consequence of being located in the world's largest, richest, and most technologically advanced market. After

the war, their foreign expansion focused primarily on leveraging this strength, particularly in response to demands generated by postwar reconstruction and the granting of independence to previously colonized nations.

Reinforcing this strategy was a professional managerial culture in most US-based companies that contrasted with the 'old boy network' that typified the European companies' processes. The management approach in most US-based companies was built on a willingness to delegate responsibility, while retaining overall control through sophisticated management systems and specialist corporate staffs. The systems provided channels for a regular flow of information, to be interpreted by the central staff. Holding the managerial reins, top management could control the free-running team of independent subsidiaries and guide the direction in which they were headed.

The main handicap such companies faced was that parent-company management often adopted a parochial and even superior attitude toward international operations, perhaps because of the assumption that

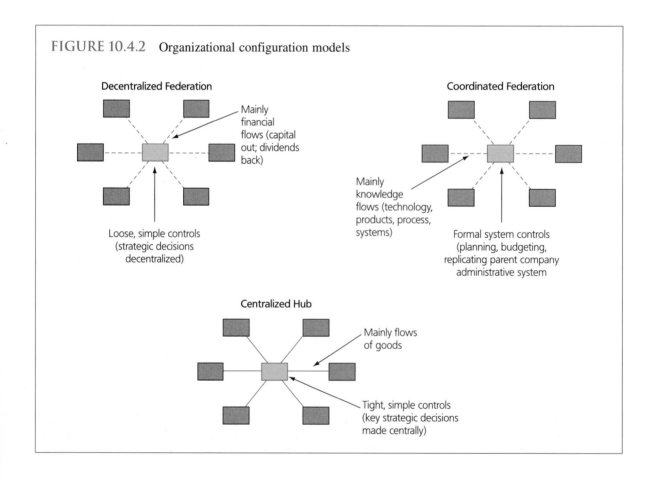

FIGURE 10.4.2   Organizational configuration models

new ideas and developments all came from the parent. Despite corporate management's increased understanding of its overseas markets, it often seemed to view foreign operations as appendages whose principal purpose was to leverage the capabilities and resources developed in the home market.

None the less, the approach was highly successful in the postwar decades, and many US-based companies adopted what we have described as the international strategy and a coordinated federation organizational model shown in Figure 10.4.2. Their foreign subsidiaries were often free to adapt products or strategies to reflect market differences, but their dependence on the parent company for new products, processes, and ideas dictated a great deal more coordination and control by headquarters than in the decentralized federation organization. This was facilitated by the existence of formal systems and controls in the headquarters–subsidiary link.

Centralized hub

In contrast, the typical Japanese company, making its main international thrust since the 1970s, faced a greatly altered external environment and operated with very different internal norms and values. With limited prior overseas exposure, it chose not to match the well-established local marketing capabilities and facilities that its European and US competitors had built up. (Indeed, well-established Japanese trading companies often provided it with an easier means of entering foreign markets.) However, it had new, efficient, scale-intensive plants, built to serve its rapidly expanding domestic market, and it was expanding into a global environment of declining trade barriers. Together, these factors gave it the incentive to develop a competitive advantage at the upstream end of the value-added chain. Its competitive strategy emphasized cost advantages and quality assurance and required tight central control of product development, procurement, and manufacturing. A centrally controlled, export-based internationalization strategy represented a perfect fit with the external environment and the company's competitive capabilities.

Such an approach also fitted the cultural background and organizational values in the emerging Japanese MNC. At the foundation of the internal processes were the strong national cultural norms that emphasized group behaviour and valued interpersonal harmony. These values had been enhanced by the paternalism of the zaibatsu and other enterprise groups.

They were also reflected in the group-oriented management practices of *nemawashi* and *ringi* that were at the core of Japanese organizational processes. By keeping primary decision making and control at the centre, the Japanese company could retain this culturally dependent management system that was so communications intensive and people dependent.

Cultural values were also reflected in one of the main motivations driving the international expansion of Japanese MNCs. As growth in their domestic market slowed and became increasingly competitive, these companies needed new sources of growth so they could continue to attract and promote employees. In a system of lifetime employment, growth was the engine that powered organizational vitality and self-renewal. It was this motivation that reinforced the bias toward an export-based strategy managed from the centre rather than the decentralized foreign investment approach of the Europeans. As a result, these companies adopted what we have described as a global strategy, and developed a centralized hub organizational model, shown in Figure 10.4.2, to support this strategic orientation.

The transnational challenge

We advanced the hypothesis that many world-wide industries have been transformed in the 1980s from traditional multinational, international, and global forms toward a transnational form. Instead of demanding efficiency, responsiveness, or learning as the key capability for success. These businesses now require participating firms to achieve the three capabilities simultaneously to remain competitive.

Table 10.4.1 summarizes the key characteristics of the decentralized federation, coordinated federation, and centralized hub organizations as the supporting forms for companies pursuing the multinational, international, and global strategies. A review of these characteristics immediately reveals the problems each of the three archetypal company models might face in responding to the transnational challenge.

With its resources and capabilities consolidated at the centre, the global company achieves efficiency primarily by exploiting potential scale economies in all its activities. In such an organization, however, the national subsidiaries' lack of resources and responsibilities may undermine their motivation and their ability to respond to local market needs. Similarly, while the centralization of knowledge and skills allows the global company to be highly efficient in developing and managing innovative new products and processes, the central groups

TABLE 10.4.1   Key organizational characteristics

	Decentralized Federation	Coordinated federation	Centralized hub
Strategic approach	Multinational	International	Global
Key strategic capability	National responsiveness	World-wide transfer of home country innovations	Global-scale efficiency
Configuration of assets and capabilities	Decentralized and nationally self-sufficient	Sources of core competencies centralized, others decentralized	Centralized and globally scaled
Role of overseas operations	Sensing and exploiting local opportunities	Adapting and leveraging parent-company competencies	Implementing parent-company
Development and diffusion of knowledge	Knowledge developed and retained within each unit	Knowledge developed at the centre and transferred to overseas units	Knowledge developed and retained at the centre

often lack adequate understanding of the market needs and production realities outside their home market. Limited resources and the narrow implementation role of its overseas units prevent the company from tapping into learning opportunities outside its home environment. These are problems that a global organization cannot overcome without jeopardizing its trump card of global efficiency.

The classic multinational company suffers from other limitations. While its dispersed resources and decentralized decision making allows national subsidiaries to respond to local needs, the fragmentation of activities also leads to inefficiency. Learning also suffers, because knowledge is not consolidated and does not flow among the various parts of the company. As a result, local innovations often represent little more than the efforts of subsidiary management to protect its turf and autonomy, or reinventions of the wheel caused by blocked communication or the not-invented-here (NIH) syndrome. In contrast, the international company is better able to leverage the knowledge and capabilities of the parent company. However, its resource configuration and operating systems make it less efficient than the global company, and less responsive than the multinational company.

The transnational organization

There are three important organizational characteristics that distinguish the transnational organization from its multinational, international, or global counterparts. It builds and legitimizes multiple diverse internal perspectives able to sense the complex environmental demands and opportunities; its physical assets and management capabilities are distributed internationally but are interdependent; and it has developed a robust and flexible internal integrative process. In the following paragraphs, we will describe and illustrate each of these characteristics.

Multidimensional perspectives

Managing in an environment in which strategic forces are both diverse and changeable, the transnational company must develop the ability to sense and analyse the numerous and often conflicting opportunities, pressures, and demands it faces world-wide. Having a limited or biased management perspective through which to view developments can constrain a company's ability to understand and respond to some potential problems or opportunities.

The transnational organization must have broad sensory capabilities able to reflect the diverse environmental opportunities and demands in the internal management process. Strong national subsidiary management is needed to sense and represent the changing needs of local consumers and the increasing pressures from host governments; capable global business management is required to track the strategy of global competitors and to provide the coordination necessary to respond appropriately; and influential functional management is needed to concentrate corporate knowledge, information, and expertise, and facilitate its transfer among organizational units.

Unfortunately, however, in many companies, power is concentrated with the particular management group that has historically represented the company's most critical strategic tasks – often at the cost of allowing other groups to represent different needs. For example, in multinational companies, key decisions were usually dominated by the country management group since they made the most critical contribution to achieving national responsiveness, which lay at the centre of the strategic approach of such companies. In global companies, by contrast, managers in world-wide product divisions were typically the most influential, since strong business management played the key role in the company's efforts to seek global efficiency. And in international companies, functional management groups often came to assume this position of dominance because of their roles in building, accumulating, and transferring the company's skills, knowledge, and capabilities.

In transnational companies, however, biases in the decision-making process are consciously reduced by building up the capability, credibility, and influence of the less powerful management groups while protecting the morale and capabilities of the dominant group. The objective is to build a multidimensional organization in which the influence of each of the three management groups is balanced.

Distributed, interdependent capabilities

Having sensed the diverse opportunities and demands it faces, the transnational organization must then be able to make choices among them and respond in a timely and effective manner to those that are deemed strategically important. When a company's decision-making process and organizational capabilities are concentrated at the centre – as they are in the global organization's centralized hub configuration – it is often difficult to respond appropriately to diverse world-wide demands. Being distant from the front-line opportunities and threats, the central group's ability to act in an effective and timely manner is constrained by its reliance on complex and intensive international communications. Furthermore, the volume and diversity of demands made on the central group often result in central capabilities being overloaded, particularly where scarce technological or managerial resources are involved.

On the other hand, multinational organizations with their response capabilities spread throughout the decentralized federation of independent operations suffer from duplication of effort (the reinventing-the-wheel syndrome), inefficiency of operations (the 'locally self-sufficing scale' problem), and barriers to international learning (the not-invented-here syndrome).

In transnational organizations, management breaks away from the restricted view that assumes the need to centralize activities for which global scale or specialized knowledge is important. They ensure that viable national units achieve global scale by giving them the responsibility of becoming the company's world source for a given product or expertise. And they tap into important technological advances and market developments wherever they are occurring around the globe. They do this by securing the cooperation and involvement of the relevant national units in upgrading the company's technology, developing its new products, and shaping its marketing strategy.

One major consequence of the distribution of assets and responsibilities is that the interdependence of world-wide units automatically increases. Simple structural configurations like the decentralized federation, the coordinated federation, and the centralized hub are inadequate for the task facing the transnational corporation. What is needed is a structure we term the *integrated network* (see Figure 10.4.3).

In the integrated network configuration, national units are no longer viewed only as the end of a delivery pipeline for company products, or as implementors of centrally defined strategies, or even as local adapters and modifiers of corporate approaches. Rather, the assumption behind this configuration is that management should consider each of the world-wide units as a source of ideas, skills, capabilities, and knowledge that can be harnessed for the benefit of the total organization. Efficient local plants may be converted into international production centres; innovative national or regional development labs may be designated the company's 'centre of excellence' for a particular product or process development; and creative subsidiary marketing groups may be given a lead role in developing world-wide marketing strategies for certain products or businesses. The company becomes a truly integrated network of distributed and interdependent resources and capabilities.

Flexible integrative process

Having established management groups representing multiple perspectives to reflect the variety of environmental demands and pressures and a configuration based on distributed and interdependent assets and organizational capabilities, the transnational organization requires a management process that can resolve the diversity of interests and perspectives and integrate the

FIGURE 10.4.3 Integrated network model

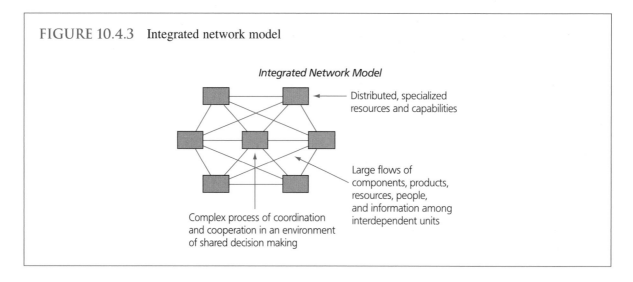

Integrated Network Model

Distributed, specialized resources and capabilities

Large flows of components, products, resources, people, and information among interdependent units

Complex process of coordination and cooperation in an environment of shared decision making

dispersed responsibilities. However, it cannot be bound by the symmetry of organizational process that follows when the task is seen in simplistic or static terms (e.g. 'Should responsibilities be centralized or decentralized?'). It is clear that the benefits to be gained from central control of world-wide research or manufacturing activities may be much more important than those related to the global coordination of the sales and service functions. We have also seen how the pattern of functional coordination varies by business and by geographic area (aircraft engine companies need central control of more decisions than multinational food packagers; operations in developing countries may need more central support than those in advanced countries). Furthermore, all coordination needs change over time due to changes in the international operating environment, the life cycles of products and technologies, or the company's stage of development.

Thus, management must be able to differentiate its operating relationships and change its decision-making roles by function, across businesses, among geographic units, and over time. The management process must be able to change from product to product, from country to country, and even from decision to decision.

This requires the development of rather sophisticated and subtle decision-making machinery based on three different but interdependent management processes. The first is a supportive but constrained escalation process that allows top management to intervene directly in the content of certain decisions – a subtle and carefully managed form of *centralization*. The second is a managed organizational process in which the key management task is to structure individual roles and supportive systems to influence specific key decisions through *formalization*. The third is a self-regulatory capability in which top management's role is to establish a broad culture and set of relationships that provide an appropriate organizational context for the delegated decisions – a sophisticated management process driven by *socialization*.

THE INTERNATIONAL CONTEXT IN INTERNATIONAL PERSPECTIVE

A truth on this side of the Pyrenees, a falsehood on the other.
Montaigne (1533–1592); French moralist and essayist

What a curious title, one might be inclined to think: 'The international context in international perspective'. Isn't this a case of the snake biting itself in its own tail? Of course, the answer is no. Similar to all previous chapters, an international angle can be used to view the debate between proponents of the global convergence perspective and those of the international diversity perspective. The question of interest is whether strategists in certain countries are more inclined towards a specific perspective. In other words, are there nations where the global convergence perspective is more prevalent, while in other nations the international diversity perspective is more widespread?

This is a tantalizing question, but as before, it must be concluded that little comparative research has been done on the issue. As a stimulus to the debate whether there are national differences in international context perspective, we would like to put forward a number of factors that might be of influence on how the paradox of globalization and localization is dealt with in different countries. It goes without saying that more international comparative research is required before a clear picture can be formed about the actual international differences.

Of course, if the proponents of the global convergence perspective are entirely right, the factors mentioned below will become less and less important as countries grow more similar. All of the international differences in strategic management preferences discussed in the concluding pages of each of the preceding chapters will also wither away. However, if international diversity remains a characteristic of our world, the way strategy paradoxes are dealt with differently in each country will continue to be an important issue to discuss.

Level of nationalism

The prospect of global convergence is a dream to some, but a nightmare to others. It is inspiring for those who would like to see a borderless world, in which like-minded people would see eye-to-eye. It is frightening for those who prefer to keep a diverse world, in which local autonomy and retaining of national culture are highly valued. Although global convergence enthusiasts and detractors can be found in each country, some nations seem more troubled by the prospect of further globalization than others. In some countries the belief is widespread that foreign values, norms, habits and behaviours are being imposed, that are undermining the national culture, and that the country's ability to decide its own fate is being compromised. This leads many to argue that global convergence should be, and will be, curtailed. In other countries such nationalism is far less pronounced, and the advantages of globalization are more widely accepted. In general, it can be expected that strategists from countries with a strong streak of nationalism will gravitate more toward the international diversity perspective, while strategists from less nationalist countries will be more inclined towards the global convergence perspective.

Size of country

In general, smaller countries are more exposed to the international context than larger countries. Smaller countries commonly export more of their gross domestic product than larger countries, and import more as well. Hence, their companies are more used to dealing with, and adapting to, a high number of foreign suppliers, customers and competitors. Moreover, companies from smaller countries, confronted with a limited home market, are forced to seek growth in foreign markets earlier than their counterparts in larger countries. During this early internationalization, these companies do not have the benefit of scale economies in the home market and therefore are usually more inclined to adapt themselves to the demands of foreign markets. Companies in larger markets normally grow to a significant size at home, thereby achieving certain economies of scale through national standardization, while also establishing a domestically oriented management style. When they do move abroad, as a more mature company, their international activities will tend to be modest compared to domestic operations and therefore they will be less inclined to be locally adaptive.

It stands to reason that this difference in exposure to the international context has an influence on how strategists from different countries perceive developments in the international context. Generally, strategists from smaller countries, to whom adaptation to international variety has become second nature, will favour the view that international diversity will remain. Strategists from larger countries will be more inclined to emphasize the growing similarities and to seek opportunities for international standardization.

Preference for central decision-making

This point is linked to the debate in the previous chapter, where the paradox of control and chaos was discussed. It was argued that in some countries there is a stronger emphasis on the role of top management in running the firm. In these countries there is usually a strong chain of command, with clear authority and responsibilities, and a well-developed control system. To remain manageable from the top, the organization must not become too complex to comprehend and steer. Usually this means that business units are structured along simple lines and that strategy is not too varied by product or geographic area. As soon as each product or geographic area requires its own specific strategy, the ability to run things centrally will diminish. Strategists with a strong preference for central decision-making will therefore be less inclined to acknowledge pressures for local responsiveness. Quite the opposite, they will be searching for opportunities to standardize their approach to different countries, which will allow for a more centralized decision-making structure. Strategists from countries with a tradition of more decentralized decision-making, are more likely to accept international diversity as a workable situation (e.g. Calori, Valla and De Woot, 1994; Turcq, 1994; Yoneyama, 1994).

FURTHER READING

There have been few writers as radical as Theodore Levitt, but quite a large number of stimulating works from the global convergence perspective. A good place for the interested reader to start would be Kenichi Ohmae's *The Borderless World: Power and Strategy in the Interlinked Economy* and George Yip's *Total Global Strategy*. For a stronger balancing of perspectives, the reader should turn to *The Multinational Mission*, by C.K. Prahalad and Yves Doz, and *Competition in Global Industries* by Michael Porter. For a critical review of the globalization literature, *The Logic of International Restructuring* by Winfried Ruigrok and Rob van Tulder makes for stimulating reading.

Most of this literature emphasizes strategy content issues, while largely neglecting strategy process aspects. A well-known exception is the article 'Strategic Planning for a Global Business' by Balaji Chakravarthy and Howard Perlmutter. With regard to the management of large international companies, *Managing Across Borders: The Transnational Solution*, *by Christopher Bartlett and Sumantra Ghoshal, is highly recommended.*

REFERENCES

Bartlett, C.A., and Ghoshal, S. (1987) 'Managing Across Borders: New Organizational Responses', *Sloan Management Review*, Vol. 29, No. 1, Fall, pp. 43–53

Bartlett, C.A., and Ghoshal, S. (1989) *Managing Across Borders: The Transnational Solution*, New York: Harvard Business School Press,.

Bartlett, C.A., and Ghoshal, S. (1995) *Transnational Management: Text, Cases, and Readings in Cross-Border Management*, Second Edition, New York: R.D. Irwin Inc.

Birkenshaw, J., and Hood, N. (1998) *Multinational Corporate Evolution and Subsidiary Development*, London: Macmillan.

Buckley, P.J., and Casson, M.C. (1976) *The Future of the Multinational Enterprise*, London: Macmillan,.

Buckley, P.J., and Casson, M.C. (1985) *The Economic Theory of the Multinational Enterprise*, London: Macmillan.

Calori, R., Valla, J.-P., and de Woot, P. (1994) 'Common Characteristics: The Ingredients of European Management', in: R. Calori and P. de Woot (eds), *A European Management Model*, London: Prentice Hall.

Chakravarthy, B.S., and Perlmutter, H.W. (1985) 'Strategic Planning for a Global Business', *Columbia Journal of World Business*, Vol. 20, Summer, pp. 3–10.

Dicken, P. (1992) *Global Shift: The Internationalisation of Economic Activity*, London: Chapman.

Dosi, G., and Kogut, B. (1993) 'National Specificities and the Context of Change: The Co-evolution of Organization and Technology', in: B. Kogut (ed.), *Country Competitiveness: Technology and the Organizing of Work*, Oxford: Oxford University Press.

Douglas, S.P., and Wind, Y. (1987) 'The Myth of Globalization', *Columbia Journal of World Business*, Vol. 22, Winter, pp. 19–29.

Dunning, J. (1986) *Japanese Participation in British Industry: Trojan Horse or Catalyst for Growth?*, Dover, NH: Croom Helm.

Dunning, J. (1993) *The Globalization of Business*, London: Routledge.

Dunning, J.H. (1981), *International Production and the Multinational Enterprise*, London: Allen and Unwin.

Ghoshal, S., and Nohria, N. (1993) 'Horses for Courses: Organizational Forms for Multinational Companies', *Sloan Management Review*, Winter, pp. 23–35.

Govindarajan, V., and Gupta, A.K. (1999) 'Taking Wal-Mart Global: Lessons from Retailing's Giant', *Strategy and Business*, No. 4.

Gupta, A.K., and Govindarajan, V. (2000) 'Managing Global Expansion: A Conceptual Framework', *Business Horizons*, Vol. 43, No. 2, March–April, pp. 45–54.

Hamel, G., and Prahalad, C.K. (1985) 'Do You Really Have a Global Strategy?', *Harvard Business Review*, Vol. 63, No. 4, July–August, pp. 139–148.

Hedlund, G. (1986) 'The Hypermodern MNC – A Heterarchy?', *Human Resource Management*, Vol. 25, pp. 9–35.

Hout, T.M., Porter, M.E., and Rudden, E. (1982) 'How Global Companies Win Out', *Harvard Business Review*, Vol. 60, No. 5, September–October, pp. 98–108.

Kay, J. (1989) 'Myths and Realities', in: Davis, E. (ed.), 1992: *Myths and Realities*, London: Centre for Business Strategy.

Klein, N. (2000) *No Logo, Taking Aim at the Brand Bullies*, London: Flamingo.

Kogut, B. (1985) 'Designing Global Strategies: Comparative and Competitive Value-Added Chains', *Sloan Management Review*, Summer, pp.15–28.

Kogut, B. (ed.) (1993) *Country Competitiveness: Technology and the Organizing of Work*, Oxford: Oxford University Press.

Kogut, B., and Zander, U. (1993) 'Knowledge of the firm and the Evolutionary Theory of the Mul', *Journal of International Business Studies*, Vol. 24, No. 4; pp. 625–645.

Krugman, P.R. (1990) *Rethinking International Trade*, Cambridge, MA: MIT Press.

Levitt, T. (1983) 'The Globalization of Markets', *Harvard Business Review*, Vol. 61, No. 3, May–June, pp. 92–102.

Liebeskind, J. (1996) 'Knowledge, Strategy and the Theory of the Firm', *Strategic Management Journal*, Vol. 17, Special Issue, Winter, pp. 93–107.

McGrew, A.G., and Lewis, P.G. (eds) (1992) *Global Politics: Globalisation and the Nation-State*, Cambridge: Polity Press.

Morrison, A.J., Ricks, D.A., and Roth, K. (1991) 'Globalization versus Regionalization: Which Way for the Multinational?', *Organizational Dynamics*, Winter, pp. 17–29.

Ohmae, K. (1989) 'Managing in a Borderless World', *Harvard Business Review*, Vol. 67, No. 3, May–June, pp. 152–161.

Ohmae, K. (1990) *The Borderless World: Power and Strategy in the Interlinked Economy*, London: Fontana.

Patel, P., and Pavitt, K. (1991) 'Large Firms in the Production of the World's Technology: An Important Case of "Non-Globalisation"', *Journal of International Business Studies*, Vol. 22, No. 1, pp. 1–21.

Pitt, M. (1996) 'IKEA of Sweden: The Global Retailer', in: C. Baden-Fuller and M. Pitt (eds), *Strategic Innovation*, London: Routledge.

Porter, M.E. (1986) *Competition in Global Industries*, New York: Free Press.

Porter, M.E. (1990a) *The Competitive Advantage of Nations*, London: Macmillan.

Porter, M.E. (1990b) 'New Global Strategies for Competitive Advantage', *Planning Review*, Vol. 18, No. 3, May–June, pp. 4–14.

Prahalad, C.K., and Doz, Y. (1987) *The Multinational Mission: Balancing Local Demands and Global Vision*, New York: Free Press.

Reich, R. (1991) *The Work of Nations: Preparing Ourselves for 21st Century Capitalism*, New York: Alfred Knopf.

Rodrik, D. (1997) 'Has Globalization Gone Too Far', *California Management Review*, Vol. 39, No. 3, Spring, pp. 29–53.

Ruigrok, W., and van Tulder, R. (1995) *The Logic of International Restructuring*, London: Routledge.

Stopford, J.M., and Wells L.T. (1972) *Strategy and Structure of Multinational Enterprise*, New York: Basic Books.

Teece, D.J. (1981) 'The Multinational Enterprise: Market Failure and Market Power Considerations', *Sloan Management Review*, Spring, pp. 4–17.

Turcq, D. (1994) 'Is There a US Company Management Style in Europe?', in: R. Calori and P. de Woot (eds), *A European Management Model*, London: Prentice Hall.

Vernon, R. (1966) 'International Investment and International Trade in the Product Life Cycle', *Quarterly Journal of Economics*, Vol. 80, No. 2, May, pp. 190–207.

Vernon, R., and Wells, L.T. (1986) *The Economic Environment of International Business*, Fourth Edition, Englewood Cliffs, NJ: Prentice Hall.

Wortzel, L.H. (1990) 'Global Strategies: Standardization Versus Flexibility', in: H. Vernon-Wortzel and L.H. Wortzel (eds), *Global Strategic Management*, New York: Wiley.

Yip, G.S. (1993) *Total Global Strategy: Managing for Worldwide Competitive Advantage*, London: Prentice Hall.

Yoneyama, E. (1994) 'Japanese Subsidiaries: Strengths and Weaknesses', in: R., Calori and P. de Woot (eds), *A European Management Model*, London: Prentice Hall.

PURPOSE

ORGANIZATIONAL PURPOSE

Corporation, n. An ingenious device for obtaining individual profit without individual responsibility.

The Devil's Dictionary, Ambrose Bierce (1842–1914); American columnist

INTRODUCTION

At the beginning of this book, strategy was defined as a course of action for achieving an organization's purpose. Subsequently, nine chapters were spent looking at strategy from many different angles, but scant attention was paid to the organizational purposes that firms want to achieve. How to set a course for the organizational vessel through turbulent waters was discussed, but the question of why the journey was being undertaken in the first place was hardly raised – the focus was on means, not on ends. This lack of attention to the subject of organizational purpose is a notable feature of the strategic management literature. This might be due to the widespread assumption that it is obvious why business organizations exist. Some writers might avoid the topic because it is highly value-laden and somehow outside the realm of strategic management.

Yet, in practice, managers must constantly make choices and seek solutions based on an understanding of what their organization is intended to achieve. It is hardly possible for strategizing managers to avoid taking a stance on what they judge to be the purpose of their organization. They are confronted with many different claimants who believe that the firm exists to serve their interests. Demands are placed on the firm by shareholders, employees, suppliers, customers, governments and communities, forcing managers to weigh whose interests should receive priority over others. Even when explicit demands are not voiced, managers must still determine who will be the main beneficiary of the value-creation activities of the firm.

Where managers have a clear understanding of their organization's purpose, this can provide strong guidance during processes of strategic thinking, strategy formation and strategic change. The organizational purpose can function as a fundamental principle, against which strategic options can be evaluated. Yet, while of central importance, organizations can be guided by more principles than organizational purpose alone. For example, they can be strongly influenced by certain business philosophies and values. The broader set of fundamental principles giving direction to strategic decision-making, of which organizational purpose is the central element, is referred to as the 'corporate mission'.

Determining the corporate mission is a challenging task, not least because there are so many different views on how it should be done. In this chapter, the issue of corporate mission will be explored in more detail, with the intention of uncovering the conflicting perspectives on the subject of organizational purpose that lie at the heart of the divergent opinions.

THE ISSUE OF CORPORATE MISSION

Corporate mission is a rather elusive concept, often used to refer to the woolly platitudes on the first few pages of annual reports. To many people, mission statements are lists of lofty principles that have potential public relations value, but have little bearing on actual business, let alone impact on the process of strategy formation. Yet, while frequently employed in this hollow manner, a corporate mission can be very concrete and play an important role in determining strategic actions.

A good way to explain the term's meaning is to go back to its etymological roots. 'Mission' comes from the Latin word *mittere*, which means 'to send' (Cummings and Davies, 1994). A mission is some task, duty or purpose that 'sends someone on their way' – a motive or driver propelling someone in a certain direction. Hence, 'corporate mission' can be understood as the basic drivers sending the corporation along its way. The corporate mission consists of the fundamental principles that mobilize and propel the firm in a particular direction.

The corporate mission contributes to 'sending the firm in a particular direction' by influencing the firm's strategy. To understand how a mission impacts strategy, two topics require closer attention. First, it is necessary to know what types of 'fundamental principles' actually make up a corporate mission. These elements of corporate mission will be described below. Secondly, it needs to be examined what types of roles are played by a corporate mission in the strategy formation process. These functions of corporate mission will also be described (see Figure 11.1).

Besides the 'what' of corporate mission, it is equally important to explore the 'who' – who should determine a corporate mission. In the previous chapters the implicit assumption has consistently been that managers are the primary 'strategic actors' responsible for setting the direction of the firm. But in fact, their actions are formally monitored and controlled by the board of directors. In this way, the direction of the firm must be understood as a result of the interaction between management ('the executives') and the board of directors. As the name would imply, directors have an important influence on direction.

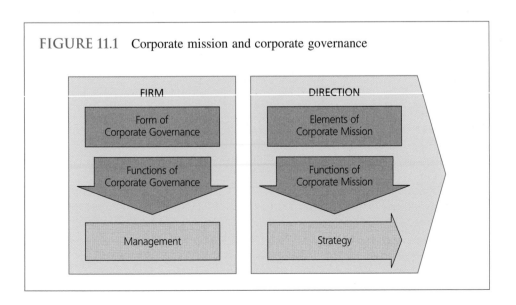

FIGURE 11.1   Corporate mission and corporate governance

The activities of the board of directors are referred to as 'corporate governance' – directors govern the strategic choices and actions of the management of a firm. And because they have such an important role in setting the corporate mission and strategy, their input will be examined here as well. First, an overall review will be presented of the various functions of corporate governance. Then it will be examined what the different forms of corporate governance are, as this can significantly influence the eventual mission and strategy that are followed (see Figure 11.1).

Elements of a corporate mission

Organizational purpose can be defined as the reason for which an organization exists. It can be expected that the perception that managers have of their organization's purpose will give direction to the strategy process and influence the strategy content (e.g. Bartlett and Ghoshal, 1994; Campbell and Tawadey, 1990). Sometimes strategizing managers consciously reflect on, or question, the organizational purpose as they make strategic choices. However, more often their view of the organization's purpose will be a part of a broader set of business principles that steers their strategic thinking. This enduring set of fundamental principles, that forms the base of a firm's identity and guides its strategic decision-making, is referred to as the corporate mission.

While the purpose of an organization is at the heart of the corporate mission, three other components can also be distinguished (see Figure 11.2):

- Organizational beliefs. All strategic choices ultimately include important assumptions about the nature of the environment and what the firm needs to do to be successful in its business. If people in a firm do not share the same fundamental strategic beliefs, joint decision-making will be very protracted and conflictual – opportunities and threats will be interpreted differently and preferred solutions will be very divergent (see Chapter 2). To work swiftly and in unison, a common understanding is needed. The stronger the set of shared beliefs subscribed to by all organizational

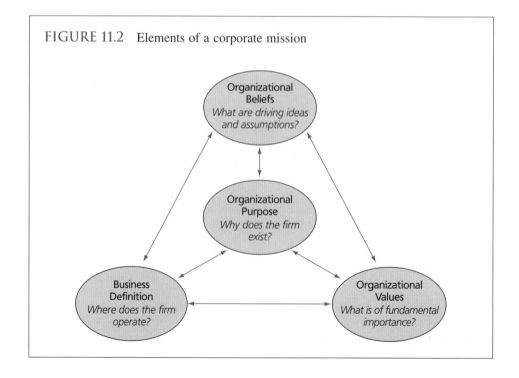

FIGURE 11.2   Elements of a corporate mission

members, the easier communication and decision-making will become, and the more confident and driven the group will be. Where researchers refer to the organizational ideology ('system of ideas') as their 'collective cognitive map' (Axelrod, 1976), 'dominant logic' (Prahalad and Bettis, 1986) or 'team mental model' (Klimoski and Mohammed, 1994), companies themselves usually simply speak of their beliefs or philosophy.

■ Organizational values. Each person in an organization can have their own set of values, shaping what they believe to be good and just. Yet, when an organization's members share a common set of values, determining what they see as worthwhile activities, ethical behaviour and moral responsibilities, this can have a strong impact on the strategic direction (e.g. Falsey, 1989; Hoffman, 1989). Such widely embraced organizational values also contribute to a clear sense of organizational identity, attracting some individuals, while repelling others. Although it can be useful to explicitly state the values guiding the organization, to be influential they must become embodied in the organization's culture (e.g. McCoy, 1985; Collins and Porras, 1996, Reading 11.3).

■ Business definitions. For some firms, any business is good business, as long as they can make a reasonable return on investment. Yet, if any business is fine, the firm will lack a sense of direction. In practice, most firms have a clearer identity, which they derive from being active in a particular line of business. For these firms, having a delimiting definition of the business they wish to be in strongly focuses the direction in which they develop. Their business definition functions as a guiding principle, helping to distinguish opportunities from diversions (e.g. Abell, 1980; Pearce, 1982). Of course, while a clear business definition can focus the organization's attention and efforts, it can lead to short-sightedness and the missing of new business developments (e.g. Ackoff, 1974; Levitt, 1960).

The strength of a corporate mission will depend on whether these four elements fit together and are mutually reinforcing (Campbell and Yeung, 1991). Where a consistent and compelling corporate mission is formed, this can infuse the organization with a sense of mission, creating an emotional bond between organizational members and energizing them to work according to the mission.

A concept that is often confused with mission is vision. Individuals or organizations have a vision if they picture a future state of affairs they wish to achieve (from the Latin *vide* – to see; Cummings and Davies, 1994). While the corporate mission outlines the fundamental principles guiding strategic choices, a strategic vision outlines the desired future at which the company hopes to arrive. In other words, vision provides a business aim, while mission provides business principles (see Figure 11.3).

Generally, a strategic vision is a type of aim that is less specific than a short-term target or longer-term objective. Vision is usually defined as a broad conception of a desirable future state, of which the details remain to be determined (e.g. Senge, 1990). As such, strategic vision can play a similar role as corporate mission, pointing the firm in a particular direction and motivating individuals to work together towards a shared end.

Functions of corporate mission

The corporate mission can be articulated by means of a mission statement, but in practice not everything that is called a mission statement meets the above criteria (e.g. David, 1989; Piercy and Morgan, 1994). However, firms can have a mission, even if it has not been explicitly written down, although this does increase the chance of divergent interpretations within the organization.

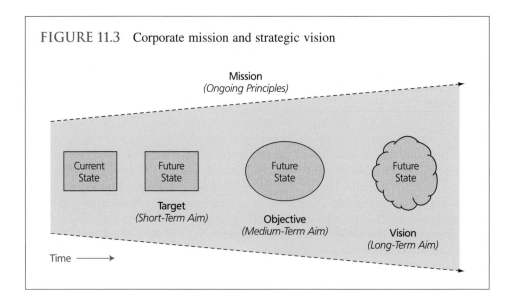

FIGURE 11.3   Corporate mission and strategic vision

In general, paying attention to the development of a consistent and compelling corporate mission can be valuable for three reasons. A corporate mission can provide:

- Direction. The corporate mission can point the organization in a certain direction, by defining the boundaries within which strategic choices and actions must take place. By specifying the fundamental principles on which strategies must be based, the corporate mission limits the scope of strategic options and sets the organization on a particular heading (e.g. Bourgeois and Brodwin, 1983; Hax, 1990).

- Legitimization. The corporate mission can convey to all stakeholders inside and outside the company that the organization is pursuing valuable activities in a proper way. By specifying the business philosophy that will guide the company, the chances can be increased that stakeholders will accept, support and trust the organization (e.g. Klemm, Sanderson and Luffman, 1991; Freeman and Gilbert, 1988).

- Motivation. The corporate mission can go a step further than legitimization, by actually inspiring individuals to work together in a particular way. By specifying the fundamental principles driving organizational actions, an *esprit de corps* can evolve, with the powerful capacity to motivate people over a prolonged period of time (e.g. Campbell and Yeung, 1991; Peters and Waterman, 1982).

Especially these last two functions of a corporate mission divide both management theorists and business practitioners. What is seen as a legitimate and motivating organizational purpose is strongly contested. What the main factors of disagreement are will be examined in a later section of this chapter.

Functions of corporate governance

The subject of corporate governance, as opposed to corporate management, deals with the issue of governing the strategic choices and actions of top management. Popularly stated, corporate governance is about managing top management – building in checks and balances to ensure that the senior executives pursue strategies that are in accordance with the corporate mission. Corporate governance encompasses all tasks and activities that are intended to supervise and steer the behaviour of top management.

In the common definition, corporate governance 'addresses the issues facing boards of directors' (Tricker, 1994: xi). In this view, corporate governance is the task of the directors and therefore attention must be paid to their roles and responsibilities (e.g. Cochran and Wartick, 1994; Keasey, Thompson and Wright, 1997). Others have argued that this definition is too narrow, and that in practice there are more forces that govern the activities of top management. In this broader view, boards of directors are only a part of the governance system. For instance, regulation by local and national authorities, as well as pressure from societal groups, can function as the checks and balances limiting top management's discretion (e.g. Mintzberg, 1984; Demb and Neubauer, 1992). Whether employing a narrow or broad definition, three important corporate governance functions can be distinguished (adapted from Tricker, 1994):

■ Forming function. The first function of corporate governance is to influence the forming of the corporate mission. The task of corporate governance is to shape, articulate and communicate the fundamental principles that will drive the organization's activities. Determining the purpose of the organization and setting priorities among claimants are part of the forming function. The board of directors can conduct this task by, for example, questioning the basis of strategic choices, influencing the business philosophy, and explicitly weighing the advantages and disadvantages of the firm's strategies for various constituents (e.g. Freeman and Reed, 1983, Reading 11.2; Yoshimori, 1995, Reading 11.4).

■ Performance function. The second function of corporate governance is to contribute to the strategy process with the intention of improving the future performance of the corporation. The task of corporate governance is to judge strategy initiatives brought forward by top management or to actively participate in strategy development. The board of directors can conduct this task by, for example, engaging in strategy discussions, acting as a sounding board for top management, and networking to secure the support of vital stakeholders (e.g. Baysinger and Hoskisson, 1990; Donaldson and Davis, 1995; Zahra and Pearce, 1989).

■ Conformance function. The third function of corporate governance is to ensure corporate conformance to the stated mission and strategy. The task of corporate governance is to monitor whether the organization is undertaking activities as promised and whether performance is satisfactory. Where management is found lacking, it is a function of corporate governance to press for changes. The board of directors can conduct this task by, for example, auditing the activities of the corporation, questioning and supervising top management, determining remuneration and incentive packages, and even appointing new managers (e.g. Parkinson, 1993; Spencer, 1983).

These functions give the board of directors considerable influence in determining and realizing the corporate mission. As such, they have the ultimate power to decide on the organizational purpose. Therefore, it is not surprising that the question to whom these functions should be given is extremely important.

Forms of corporate governance

There is considerable disagreement on how boards of directors should be organized and run. Currently, each country has its own system of corporate governance and the international differences are large. Yet even within many countries, significant disagreements are discernible. In designing a corporate governance regime, three characteristics of boards of directors are of particular importance (adapted from Tricker, 1994):

■ Board structure. Internationally, there are major differences between countries requiring a two-tier board structure (e.g. Germany, the Netherlands and Finland), countries with a one-tier board (e.g. United States, Britain and Japan), and countries in which companies are free to choose (e.g. France and Switzerland). In a two-tier system there is a formal division of power, with a management board made up of the top executives and a distinct supervisory board made up of non-executives with the task of monitoring and steering the management board. In a one-tier (or unitary) board system, executive and nonexecutive (outside) directors sit together on one board (see Figure 11.4).

■ Board membership. The composition of boards of directors can vary sharply from company to company and from country to country. Some differences are due to legal requirements that are not the same internationally. For instance, in Germany by law half of the membership of a supervisory board must represent labour, while the other half represents the shareholders. In French companies labour representatives are given observer status on the board. In other countries there are no legal imperatives, yet differences have emerged. In some cases outside (non-executive) directors from other companies are common, while in other nations fewer outsiders are involved. Even within countries, differences can be significant, especially with regard to the number, stature and independence of outside (non-executive) directors.

■ Board tasks. The tasks and authority of boards of directors also differ quite significantly between companies. In some cases boards meet infrequently and are merely asked to vote on proposals put in front of them. Such boards have little formal or informal power to contradict the will of the CEO. In other companies, boards meet regularly and play a more active role in corporate governance, by formulating proposals, proactively selecting new top managers, and determining objectives and incentives. Normally, the power of outside (non-executive) directors to monitor and steer a company only partly depends on their formally defined tasks and authority. To a large degree their impact is determined by how proactive they define their own role.

The question in the context of this chapter is how a board of directors should be run to ensure that the organization's purpose is best achieved. What should be the structure, membership and tasks of the board of directors, to realize the ends for which the organization exists?

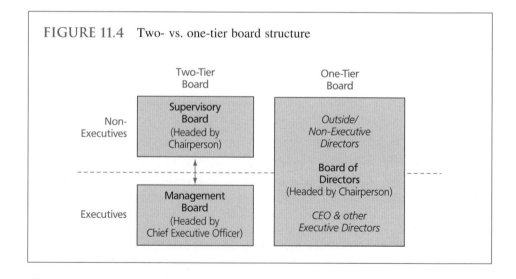

FIGURE 11.4   Two- vs. one-tier board structure

THE PARADOX OF PROFITABILITY AND RESPONSIBILITY

Property has its duties as well as its rights.

Thomas Drummond (1797–1840); English public administrator

Discussions on what firms should strive to achieve are not limited to the field of strategic management. Given the influential position of business organizations in society, the purpose they should serve is also discussed by theorists in the fields of economics, political science, sociology, ethics and philosophy. Since the industrial revolution, and the rise of the modern corporation, the role of business organizations within the 'political economic order' has been a central theme in many of the social sciences. It has been the topic that has filled libraries of books, inspired society-changing theories and stirred deep-rooted controversies.

The enormous impact of corporations on the functioning of society has also attracted political parties, labour unions, community representatives, environmentalists, the media and the general public to the debate. All take a certain position on the role that business organizations should play within society and the duties that they ought to shoulder. Here, too, the disagreements can be heated, often spilling over from the political arena and negotiating tables into the streets.

In countries with a market economy, it is generally agreed that companies should pursue strategies that ensure economic profitability, but that they have certain social responsibilities that must be fulfilled as well. But this is where the consensus ends. Opinions differ sharply with regard to the relative importance of profitability and responsibility. Some people subscribe to the view that profitability is the very purpose of economic organizations and that the only social responsibility of a firm is to pursue profitability within the boundaries of the law. However, other people argue that business corporations are not only economic entities, but also social institutions, embedded in a social environment, which brings along heavy social responsibilities. In this view, organizations are morally obliged to behave responsibly towards all parties with a stake in the activities of the firm, and profitability is only a means to fulfil this duty.

Most managers accept that both economic profitability and social responsibility are valuable goals to pursue. Yet, as organizational purpose, profitability and responsibility are at least partially contradictory. If managers strive towards profit maximization, shareholders might be enamoured, but this will bring managers into conflict with the optimization of benefits for other stakeholders. In other words, to a certain extent there is a tension between the profitability and responsibility (e.g. Cannon, 1992; Demb and Neubauer, 1992; Drucker, 1984; Yoshimori, 1995, Reading 11.4).

The demand for economic profitability

It is clear that business organizations must be profitable to survive. Yet simple profitability, that is having higher income than costs, is not sufficient. To be an attractive investment, a company must earn a higher return on the shareholders' equity than could be realized if the money were deposited in the bank. Put differently, investors must have a financial incentive to run a commercial risk; otherwise they could just as well bring their money to the bank or buy low risk government bonds.

Yet, offsetting the risk carried by investors is but a small part of the larger picture. Once a corporation has established a track record of profitability, this inspires trust among financiers. Such trust makes it much easier to raise new capital, either through borrowing (at more attractive rates) or by issuing new shares. And of course, new capital can be used to further the competitive objectives of the organization. Where companies have not been particularly profitable in the past, and cannot authoritatively project an attractive level of profitability in the future, they will find it difficult or virtually impossible to find new financing. This can significantly weaken the position of the firm and undermine its long-term competitiveness.

For publicly traded corporations strong profitability is usually reflected in higher share prices, which is not only beneficial to the shareholders at that moment, but also makes it easier to acquire other firms and to pay with shares. Moreover, a high share price is the best defence against a hostile takeover and the best negotiating chip for a friendly one. In both publicly and privately held companies, retained profits can also be an important source of funds for new investments.

In short, profitability is not only a *result*, but also a *source*, of competitive power. Profitability provides a company with the financial leeway to improve its competitive position and pursue its ambitions.

The demand for social responsibility

As economic entities engaging in formalized arrangements with employees, suppliers, buyers and government agencies, corporations have the legal responsibility to abide by the stipulations outlined in their contracts. Equally, they are bound to stay within the 'letter of the law' in each jurisdiction in which they operate. However, being good corporate citizens entails more than just staying out of court.

Companies are more than just 'economic machines' regulated by legal contracts. They are also networks of people, working together towards a common goal. And as members of a social group, people within a company need to develop a sense of 'community' if they are to function properly. One of the most basic needs is to build a level of trust among people – a feeling of security that each individual's interests will be taken into account. Trust evolves where people feel certain that others will behave in a socially responsible manner, instead of letting their own self-interest prevail without limitation. Once there is enough trust between people, they can engage in productive teamwork and invest in their mutual relationships.

Hence, social responsibility – that is, acting in the interest of others, even when there is no legal imperative – lies at the basis of trust. And where there is trust, people are generally willing to commit themselves to the organization, both emotionally and practically. Emotionally, they will become involved with, and can become strongly connected to, the organization, which can lead to a sense of pride and loyalty. Practically, they will be willing to invest years acquiring firm-specific knowledge and skills, and in building a career. Such commitments make people dependent on the organization, as they will be less able and inclined to job-hop. It is therefore vital that the organization rewards such commitment by acting responsibly, even where this hurts profitability; otherwise the bond of trust can be seriously damaged.

Acting in the interest of all employees is a limited form of social responsibility. Just as it is beneficial for trust to evolve within organizations, it is important for trust to develop between the organization and its broader environment of buyers, suppliers, governments, local communities and activist groups. Therefore, it is important that these organizations also come to trust that the organization is willing to act in a socially responsible way, even when this entails sacrificing profitability.

EXHIBIT 11.1   SHORT CASE

FONTERRA: CREAMING THE PROFITS IN DAIRY?

Fonterra is easily one of the world's top ten dairy companies – quite an achievement for a firm based in the small, isolated country of New Zealand. An important part of its business is supplying bulk ingredients such as milk powder, butter and cheese to international markets. In 2008 it was the world's largest international trader of milk products, claiming to be responsible for a third of international dairy trade. It also owns valuable international brands including Anchor, Anlene and Anmum. As global dairy consumption is forecast to continue rising at over 2.5% per year, Fonterra's strategic position looks highly attractive. On the other hand, size and prominence seldom come without controversy. Fonterra faces conflicting pressures on its strategy, from the farmers who own the business and from other influential stakeholders.

Fonterra was founded in its present form in 2001 by a merger of the two largest farmer-owned co-operatives and the Dairy Board, which at that time held a statutory export monopoly. Since then, the dairy industry in New Zealand has continued to expand, growing production volumes from 13 billion litres of milk to 15 billion litres in 2006/2007. This expansion has been possible because New Zealand's climate allows for a highly efficient model of milk production: the cattle graze almost exclusively on natural pasture, eliminating the expense and energy consumption of heated barns and food concentrate. As a result, milk production is not only cost efficient, but also generates lower carbon emissions than other production methods, even after accounting for shipping. The costs of producing a kilogram of milk solids in New Zealand are lower than in almost any other country, although rising prices for suitable land threaten this lowest-cost position.

In common with other dairy businesses around the world, Fonterra is a farmer-owned cooperative, with 10 500 owner-suppliers. The shares farmers own are in proportion to the quantity of milk they supply. Fonterra's shares are not traded on any stock exchange, as non-suppliers cannot buy them, and the New Zealand government has no direct involvement with the business. The shares represent a

significant financial commitment for the dairy farmers. Many of the farmers are actually highly indebted, due to the cost of land purchases and investment in irrigation, facilities and stock that many have made during the recent expansion.

Fonterra's governance structure reflects its constitution as a cooperative. Not only do the farmers directly elect nine of the 13 board members, but they also have further oversight of the board via the 35-member elected Shareholders' Council. The Shareholders' Council in turn appoints a Milk Commissioner to mediate in any disputes between Fonterra and individual shareholders. In practice, the farmers indeed have a strong influence on board behaviour. Given the trend towards fewer, larger dairy farms, this influence seems destined to increase.

Another important constraint on Fonterra's strategic freedom to manoeuvre is that profits normally have to be paid out as dividends to the farmers each year. Because the firm has little or no discretion to retain profits, it must fund growth and investment via extra farmer equity capital and by issuing debt. This works out when farmers increase the volumes of milk they supply to the cooperative, because equity capital flows in and the business can use this capital to fund capacity expansion. However, this dependency on gaining supply volumes biases Fonterra's management towards processing bulk commodity products and away from creating higher value-added. Fonterra's cooperative structure also means that if suppliers decide to exit – whether by leaving the industry or electing to supply an alternative processor – the cooperative has to buy back these suppliers' shares at their current fair value. This potentially exposes Fonterra to redemption risk if suppliers desert in sufficient numbers to undermine the balance sheet. The board has proposed to mitigate this risk by opening the business to ownership by shareholders who are not milk suppliers, but so far the current shareholders have rejected its proposals.

From the outset, a central strategic issue at Fonterra has been how, and to what extent, to build businesses that add value beyond the efficient processing and trading of commodity dairy products. Although New Zealand's efficient dairy industry means that farmers can profit from the sale of commodities, volatile commodity prices and exchange rates undermine the value of this strategy. So too do trade barriers and farm subsidies in major markets such as the European Union and the United States.

Many of Fonterra's options to develop new sources of value creation draw on its processing and logistics expertise to manage international operations. This often involves partnership agreements with overseas suppliers and customers. The co-operative already sources around 20% of its milk from outside New Zealand. From a shareholder's perspective, this can be problematic because it means that New Zealand farmers' capital helps finance ventures that, by some arguments, compete with their own milk production. The problem is compounded by the fact that many of the opportunities for Fonterra lie in fast-growing markets in developing countries. This in turn increases the risk involved in such ventures and requires more specialist skills at managing politically complex transnational relationships. Commentators have argued that the skills and preferences of Fonterra's farmer-dominated board are not closely aligned with managing multinational ventures. Furthermore, the higher levels of business risk sit uncomfortably with the financial position of many of Fonterra's owners and the cooperative's fund raising constraints.

One of Fonterra's international ventures was a joint venture agreement with the Sanlu dairy company in China. This arrangement came to an abrupt end in 2008 when Sanlu was struck by a milk contamination scandal that affected thousands of infants and led to the death of at least six. Because it held a 43% equity stake in the business, Fonterra became embroiled in the scandal. It became clear that Fonterra's oversight of this business was weak at both board and operational levels to the extent that it either did not know about, or was unable to curtail, the contamination scandal for many months after it first came to the attention of Sanlu's management. Subsequently, Sanlu went bankrupt and Fonterra had to write off over NZ$200 million of its investment in the venture. For some commentators, this set of events highlights the extent to which Fonterra's international strategy sits uncomfortably with its ownership and governance structure. This misalignment is likely another reason for the so far unsuccessful efforts by the board and management team to open up the international and branded product parts of Fonterra's business to outside equity capital.

As well as dealing with pressures from shareholders, Fonterra must manage its relationship with other influential stakeholders. In lobbying for support, it is not shy to point out that in 2008 it contributed 25% of New Zealand's export revenues. It also makes much of the economic spin-off effects of its activities, which extend beyond dairy farmers to communities, regions and cities. These spin-offs mean that the economic fortunes of the business have a major influence on those of New Zealand as a whole. However, power and importance at this level often does not engender popularity. Fonterra not only controls a very high proportion of the liquid milk supply to the domestic market, but also owns several of the major brands of cheese, butter and yoghurt. When the international commodity milk price is high, dairy prices rise for domestic consumers, and they tend to see this as profiteering at their expense.

Another important area of stakeholder interest in Fonterra comes from the environmental impact of its activities. Many of these impacts come from dairy farming itself, and hence Fonterra does not directly control them, but stakeholders still see them as inextricably linked to Fonterra. Intensive dairying is both a major consumer of water for irrigation and potentially a polluter of water via run-off of effluent and nitrogen fertilizer. The pollution threatens local ecosystems and threatens to undermine the unusually pure municipal water supply enjoyed by domestic consumers. The high water consumption threatens these same water supplies due to over-extraction of this historically lightly regulated resource. Fonterra has targets to improve the industry's performance in these areas, but critics say these are nowhere near enough. In March 2009, Fonterra acknowledged that 11% of its farmers were still in breach of the regulations for effluent run-off.

Perhaps the most crucial long-term stakeholder challenge for Fonterra and the dairy industry is its contribution to New Zealand's emissions of greenhouse gases. The problem arises principally from methane emissions, which are a by-product of cows' digestion. Because methane is a much more potent greenhouse gas than carbon dioxide, these represent New Zealand's largest contributor to greenhouse emissions, at over 30% of the total. Because New Zealand is a party to the Kyoto agreement, it must pay directly for above-quota emissions, triggering the government to consider how and to what extent farmers should contribute to this expense.

Despite this apparently daunting set of challenges, Fonterra remains a successful, growing firm that is a leader in its industry. The decision Fonterra's board and management faces if it is to sustain this performance is whether and to what degree to take into account the diverse set of stakeholder concerns about its activities. If it spends heavily to address these concerns, it risks compromising the immediate interests of its owners, and hence losing their support. If it does too little, it risks

undermining its operating environment (for example by stimulating unfavourable legislation), and hence compromising its owners' future interests. Within the business, the board and management must deal with the latent conflict between competing shareholder interests. They have a delicate path to tread in resolving the tension between respecting the fundamental values perceived by many owners and keeping pace with a dynamic global industry. Quite a few issues to chew over a few times.

Co-author: Paul Knott.

Source: www.fonterra.com; www.lic.co.nz; *Sunday Star Times*, 26 September 2008; *The New Zealand Farmers Weekly*, 16 March 2009; Ministry for the Environment (www.mfe.govt.nz), NZ's greenhouse gas inventory 1990–2007; Ministry of Foreign Affairs & Trade (www.mfat.govt.nz), Kyoto Protocol Part II.

PERSPECTIVES ON ORGANIZATIONAL PURPOSE

Perfection of means and confusion of goals . . . characterize our age.

Albert Einstein (1879–1955); German-American physicist

Firms require a certain measure of economic profitability if they want to compete and survive, and they need to exhibit a certain amount of social responsibility if they are to retain the trust and support of key stakeholders. In itself, this creates a tension, as the two demands can be at odds with one another. Often, socially responsible behaviour costs money, which can only be partially recouped by the increased 'social dividend' it brings. But if profitability and responsibility are both seen as the ultimate purpose of business firms, then the tension is even stronger, as optimizing the one will be in conflict with maximizing the other. Emphasizing profitability means subjecting all investments to an economic rationale – socially responsible behaviour should only be undertaken if the net present value of such an investment is attractive or there is no legal way of avoiding compliance. Emphasizing responsibility means subjecting all activities to a moral or political rationale – asking who has a legitimate and pressing claim to be included as a beneficiary of the activities being undertaken, which can severely depress profitability.

Hence, it is not surprising to find that the paradox of profitability and responsibility strongly divides people across many walks of life, not only business managers and management theorists. The main point of contention is whether firms should primarily be run for the financial benefit of the legal owners, or for the broader benefit of all parties with a significant interest in the joint endeavour. Should it be the purpose of firms to serve the interests of their shareholders or of their stakeholders? Should profitability be emphasized because economic organizations belong to the providers of risk capital, or should responsibility be emphasized because organizations are joint ventures bringing together various resource providers by means of a social contract?

While there are many points of view on the 'right' organizational purpose in the strategy literature, here the two diametrically opposed positions will be identified and discussed. At the one pole of the debate are those people who argue that corporations are established to serve the purposes of their owners. Generally, it is in the best interest of a corporation's shareholders to see the value of their stocks increase through the organization's pursuit of profitable business strategies. This point of view is commonly referred to as the 'shareholder value perspective'. At the other end of the spectrum are those people who argue that corporations should be seen as joint ventures between shareholders, employees, banks, customers, suppliers, governments and the community. All of these parties hold a stake in the organization and therefore can expect that the corporation will take as its responsibility to develop business strategies that are in accordance with their interests and values. This point of view will be referred to as the 'stakeholder values perspective'.

The shareholder value perspective

To proponents of the shareholder value perspective it is obvious that companies belong to their owners and therefore should act in accordance with the interests of the owners. Corporations are instruments whose purpose it is to create economic value on behalf of those who invest risk-taking capital in the enterprise. This clear purpose should drive companies, regardless of whether they are privately or publicly held. According to Rappaport (1986, p. xiii, Reading 11.1), 'the idea that business strategies should be judged by the economic value they create for shareholders is well accepted in the business community. After all, to suggest that companies be operated in the best interests of their owners is hardly controversial.'

There is some disagreement between advocates of this perspective with regard to the best way of advancing the interests of the shareholders, particularly in publicly held companies. Many people taking this point of view argue that the well being of the shareholders is served if the strategy of a company leads to higher share prices and/or higher dividends (e.g. Hart, 1995; Rappaport, 1986). Others are less certain of the stock markets' ability to correctly value long-term investments, such as R&D spending and capital expenditures. In their view, stock markets are excessively concerned with the short term and therefore share prices myopically overemphasize current results and heavily discount investments for the future. To avoid being pressured into short-termism, these people advocate that strategists must keep only one eye on share prices, while the other is focused on the long-term horizon (e.g. Charkham, 1994; Sykes, 1994).

According to supporters of the shareholder value perspective, one of the major challenges in large corporations is to actually get top management to pursue the shareholders' interests. Where ownership and managerial control over a company have become separated, it is often difficult to get the managers to work on behalf of the shareholders, instead of letting managers' self-interest prevail. This is known as the principal–agent problem (e. g. Jensen and Meckling, 1976; Eisenhardt, 1989) – the managers are agents, working to further the interests of their principals, the shareholders, but are tempted to serve their own interests, even when this is to the detriment of the principals. This has led to a widespread debate in the academic and business communities, especially in Britain and the United States, about the best form of corporate governance. The most important players in corporate governance are the outside, or non-executive, members on the board of directors. It is one of the tasks of these outsiders to check whether the executives are truly running the company in a way that maximizes the shareholders' wealth. For this reason, many proponents of the shareholder value perspective call for a majority of independent-minded outside directors on the board, preferably owning significant amounts of the company's stock themselves.

The emphasis placed on profitability as the fundamental purpose of firms does not mean that supporters of the shareholder value perspective are blind to the demands placed on firms by other stakeholders. On the contrary, most exponents of this view argue that it is in the interest of the shareholders to carry out a 'stakeholder analysis' and even to actively manage stakeholder relations. Knowing the force field of stakeholders constraining the freedom of the company is important information for the strategy process. It is never advisable to ignore important external claimants such as labour unions, environmental activists, bankers, governmental agencies and community groups. Few strategists would doubt that proactive engagement is preferable to 'corporate isolationism'. However, recognizing that it is expedient to pay attention to stakeholders does not mean that it is the corporation's purpose to serve them. If parties have a strong bargaining position, a firm might be forced into all types of concessions, sacrificing profitability, but this has little to do with any moral responsibility of the firm towards these other powers. The only duty of a company is to maximize shareholder value, within the boundaries of what is legally permissible.

The important conclusion is that in this perspective it might be in the interest of shareholders to treat stakeholders well, but that there is no moral obligation to do so. For instance, it might be a good move for a troubled company not to lay off workers if the resulting loyalty and morale improve the chances of recovery and profitability later on. In this case the decision not to fire workers is based on profit-motivated calculations, not on a sense of moral responsibility towards the employees. Generally, proponents of the shareholder value perspective argue that society is best served by this type of economic rationale. By pursuing enlightened self-interest and maintaining market-based relationships between the firm and all stakeholders, societal wealth will be maximized. Responsibility for employment, local communities, the environment, consumer welfare and social developments are not an organizational matter, but issues for individuals and governments (Friedman, 1970).

EXHIBIT 11.2   THE SHAREHOLDER VALUE PERSPECTIVE

GENERAL ELECTRIC: YOUR COMPANY

Few companies are as widely known and admired as General Electric. Between 1998 and 2007, it was elected 'The World's Most Respected Company' by a panel of 1000 CEOs from around the globe, although after taking a big hit during the economic crisis it slid to third place in 2008 and ninth place in 2009. This standing is all the more surprising given the fact that GE defies the conventional industry wisdom that conglomerates should have become extinct. With its US$183 billion in sales coming from such businesses as power plant turbines, airplane engines, television broadcasting, medical equipment, household appliances, locomotives, aircraft leasing and financial services, GE is a highly diversified company.

Much of the popularity of GE has been due to the man who was at the helm of the company from 1981 to 2001, Jack Welch. In a speech at New York's Pierre Hotel, soon after taking over as CEO, Welch outlined his approach to 'fast growth in a

low growth economy', which since then has been recognized as the start of the shareholder value movement. His strategy focused on restructuring and integrating businesses, to be able to realize a predictable stream of profits for shareholders, outstripping overall GDP growth. This quickly gave him the nickname, Neutron Jack, as his hard-nosed method of restructuring was said to have the same impact as a neutron bomb – the buildings were left standing, but all of the people were gone. During these early years of his tenure, he thoroughly shook up the company, introducing the rule that GE should exit any business in which it could not be number one or two, on the premise that only these two top spots hold the promise of superior profitability. Subsequently, he drove the company hard, with one clear focus: maximizing shareholder value. His style at the corporate centre was that of a very demanding and challenging sparring partner for the business units, constantly setting high financial targets for each to achieve.

Welch's impact has been enormous. GE is characterized by a results-oriented culture, in which financial performance is the name of the game. The clear sense of purpose within the company has made a mission statement redundant – it is engrained in the firm that success means giving the shareholders 10%-plus earnings growth per year and 20%-plus return on total capital per year. Executive compensation packages are strongly tied to financial performance, to encourage them to pursue what is best for the shareholders. And to further motivate employees to serve the interests of the owners, GE has stimulated widespread share ownership within the company, which currently totals approximately 10% of the company's stock.

Since taking over from Welch in 2001, Jeffrey Immelt has continued working in the same shareholder-value driven way. This has not meant that GE has disregarded its employees or other stakeholders, as they are crucial for long-term success. For instance, GE has recognized that investing in human resources is an important means for achieving the purpose of shareholder value creation. Similarly, GE has been at the forefront of the development of environment-friendly technologies, particularly in engines and wind turbines, but with the clear objective of making money by pleasing customers.

For many years the financial results have been above average, although not as high as the overly optimistic expectations at the end of Welch's tenure in 2000, when GE shares traded at around US$60. Unfortunately, as the economic crisis hit, GE also took a few knocks and its share price tumbled to around US $ 10, which didn't make its shareholders particularly happy. This was soon followed by a downgrading of its prized triple-A credit rating and the first cut in its annual dividend since 1940. However, as Immelt pointed out, 'in a tough environment in 2008, we set a record for revenue and had our third-highest earnings year ever. . . . Our earnings declined 19% versus a decline in S&P 500 earnings of 35%. That's not the kind of outperformance we like, but it was still better than the broad market.' In the 2008 annual shareholder letter he also stressed that what's ultimately important is 'that GE is positioned to lead in a reset world'.

Despite newspapers reporting that Welch had changed his mind and now thought that shareholder value 'was a dumb idea', the opposite is the case. Welch has restated that firm's should strive to achieve sustained shareholder value by balancing long term strategy with short-term results. The fact that some people have equated shareholder value with squeezing the business for short-term profitability was the dumb idea to which Welch was referring.

As Welch, Immelt too is still committed to creating sustained shareholder value, promising GE shareholders that 'your GE team' is dedicated to maximizing the value of 'your company'.

Source: www.ge.com; *GE Annual Report 2008*; *The Economist*, 4 May 2002; *Financial Times*, 12 March 2009; *Business Week*, 16 March 2009.

The stakeholder values perspective

 Advocates of the stakeholder values perspective do not see why the supplier of one ingredient in an economic value-creation process has a stronger moral claim on the organization than the providers of other inputs. They challenge the assumption that individuals with an equity stake in a corporation have the right to demand that the entire organization work on their behalf. In the stakeholder values perspective, a company should not be seen as the instrument of shareholders, but as a coalition between various resource suppliers, with the intention of increasing their common wealth. An organization should be regarded as a joint venture in which the suppliers of equity, loans, labour, management, expertise, parts and service all participate to achieve economic success. As all groups hold a stake in the joint venture and are mutually dependent, it is argued that the purpose of the organization is to serve the interests of all parties involved (e.g. Berle and Means, 1932; Freeman and Reed, 1983, Reading 11.2).

According to endorsers of the stakeholder values perspective, shareholders have a legitimate interest in the firm's profitability. However, the emphasis shareholders place on stock price appreciation and dividends must be balanced against the legitimate demands of the other partners. These demands are not only financial, as in the case of the shareholders, but also qualitative, reflecting different values held by different groups (e.g. Clarke, 1998; Freeman, 1984). For instance, employees might place a high value on job security, occupational safety, holidays and working conditions, while a supplier of parts might prefer secure demand, joint innovation, shared risk-taking and prompt payment. Of course, balancing these interests is a challenging task, requiring an on-going process of negotiation and compromise. The outcome will in part depend on the bargaining power of each stakeholder – how essential is its input to the economic success of the organization? However, the extent to which a stakeholder's interests are pursued will depend on the perceived legitimacy of their claim as well. For instance, employees usually have a strong moral claim because they are heavily dependent on the organization and have a relatively low mobility, while most shareholders have a spread portfolio and can 'exit the corporation with a phone call' (Stone, 1975).

In this view of organizational purpose, managers must recognize their responsibility towards all constituents (e.g. Clarkson, 1995; Alkhafaji, 1989). Maximizing shareholder value to the detriment of the other stakeholders would be unjust. Managers in the firm have a moral obligation to consider the interests and values of all joint venture partners. Managing stakeholder demands is not merely a pragmatic means of running a profitable business – serving stakeholders is an end in itself. These two interpretations of stakeholder management are often confused. Where it is primarily viewed as an approach or technique for dealing with the essential participants in the value-adding process, stakeholder management is *instrumental*. But if it is based on the fundamental notion that the organization's purpose is to serve the stakeholders, then stakeholder management is *normative* (e.g. Buono and Nichols, 1985; Donaldson and Preston, 1995).

Most proponents of the stakeholder values perspective argue that, ultimately, pursuing the joint interests of all stakeholders it is not only more just, but also more effective for organizations (e.g. Jones, 1995; Solomon, 1992). Few stakeholders are filled with a sense of mission to go out and maximize shareholder value, especially if shareholders bear no responsibility for the other stakeholders' interests (e.g. Campbell and Yeung, 1991; Collins and Porras, 1994). It is difficult to work as a motivated team if it is the purpose of the organization to serve only one group's interests. Furthermore, without a stakeholder values perspective, there will be a deep-rooted lack of trust between all of the parties involved in the enterprise. Each stakeholder will assume that the others are motivated solely by self-interest and are tentatively cooperating in a calculative manner. All parties will perceive a constant risk that the others will use their power to gain a bigger slice of the pie, or even rid themselves of their 'partners'. The consequence is that all stakeholders will vigorously guard their own interests and will interact with one another as adversaries. To advocates of the stakeholder values perspective, this 'every person for themselves' model of organizations is clearly inferior to the partnership model in which sharing, trust and symbiosis are emphasized. Cooperation between stakeholders is much more effective than competition (note the link with the embedded organization perspective in Chapter 7).

Some exponents of the stakeholder values perspective argue that the narrow economic definition of stakeholders given above is too constrictive. In their view, the circle of stakeholders with a legitimate claim on the organization should be drawn more widely. Not only should the organization be responsible to the direct participants in the economic value-creation process (the 'primary stakeholders'), but also to all parties affected by the organization's activities. For example, an organization's behaviour might have an impact on local communities, governments, the environment and society in general, and therefore these groups have a stake in what the organization does as well. Most supporters of the stakeholder values perspective acknowledge that organizations have a moral responsibility towards these 'secondary stakeholders' (e.g. Carroll, 1993; Langtry, 1994).

However, opinions differ whether it should actually be a part of business organizations' purpose to serve this broader body of constituents.

The implication of this view for corporate governance is that the board of directors should be able to judge whether the interests of all stakeholders are being justly balanced. This has led some advocates of the stakeholder values perspective to call for representatives of the most important stakeholder groups to be on the board (e.g. Guthrie and Turnbull, 1994). Others argue more narrowly for a stronger influence of employees on the choices made by organizations (e.g. Bucholz, 1986; Blair, 1995). Such co-determination of the corporation's strategy by management and workers can, for instance, be encouraged by establishing work councils (a type of organizational parliament or senate), as is mandatory for larger companies in most countries of the European Union. Yet others emphasize measures to strengthen corporate social responsibility in general. To improve corporate social performance, it is argued, companies should be encouraged to adopt internal policy processes that promote ethical behaviour and responsiveness to societal issues (e.g. Epstein, 1987; Wartick and Wood, 1998). Corporate responsibility should not be, to quote Ambrose Bierce's sarcastic definition, 'a detachable burden easily shifted to the shoulders of God, Fate, Fortune, Luck, or one's neighbour'.

EXHIBIT 11.3   THE STAKEHOLDER VALUES PERSPECTIVE

PATAGONIA: LET MY PEOPLE GO SURFING

'No longer can we assume the Earth's resources are limitless; that there are ranges of unclimbed peaks extending endlessly beyond the horizon. Mountains are finite, and despite their massive appearance, they are fragile.' This is not Al Gore speaking in the 2006 movie *An Inconvenient Truth*, but Yvon Chouinard in his climbing equipment catalogue in 1974. Having started as teenage rock climber and surfer in California in the 1950s, Chouinard stumbled into making gear for his fellow climbers, but soon realized how this hardware was defacing the cliffs he loved so much. This set him on the path to building a company that was responsible and sustainable, while making a living and having fun at the same time. As the company branched out of climbing equipment into outdoor sportswear, it was eventually renamed Patagonia, which like Timbuktu and Shangri-La evokes a sense of mystery and natural beauty. Since then, Patagonia has grown to be a leading global supplier to avid climbers, hikers, skiers and surfers, employing more than 1300 people in 2009 and achieving sales estimated to around US$300 million.

The person Chouinard embodies much of what Patagonia stands for. According to Holger Bismann, Director at Patagonia Europe since September 2008,

'sustainability is Chouinard's true business and inspires every choice he makes.' While being a retired millionaire, Chouinard still drives an old Subaru, doesn't own a television or a cell phone and lives in a house made of 100% recycled materials. True to the title of his memoirs, *Let my people go surfing*, he lets his employees go surfing, hiking or climbing for half a day per week and joins them whenever he can. Chouinard's philosophy has been to treat his employees as he himself would like to be treated, but to do so with people who share his values, passion and sense of responsibility. This has led to an informal and friendly company culture, where people dress as they like, have flexible working hours and collaborate closely. Decision-making is very open and participative, with high levels of employee empowerment. Being all committed to social and ecological integrity, there is a strong emphasis on finding ways to do no harm to the environment and contribute to the wellbeing of stakeholders wherever possible.

It starts with little things like the way waste is collected and electricity and food are consumed in their offices. Employees are also allowed to take two months of paid leave to go abroad and work on an environmental project they select themselves, based on the assumption that people will contribute most to society if they work on what they like best. Within each region of Patagonia, employees are also asked to join committees that are empowered to spend the 1% of sales that is reserved each year to fund preservation proposals. These committees work intensely to coordinate projects, such as pollution reduction plans, wildlife conservation and the founding of new national parks. Since 1985, when Patagonia joined the Conservation Alliance, made up of more than 1000 business that levy a 1% 'earth tax' on themselves, the company has donated over US$40 million to environmental causes.

Besides donating to others, Patagonia wants to work in a sustainable way itself. For example, in 1996 Patagonia shifted entirely to organically grown cotton, although it was more expensive. But knowing the enormous ecological damage done by industrial pesticides, and that one of its biggest users are cotton growers, Patagonia felt it had no choice. The upside has not only been a positive impact on the environment, but it turns out that organic cotton is of better quality and improves the feel of Patagonia's products. Another example has been Patagonia's unwillingness to use the well-known fabric Gore-Tex, which is widely employed by its competitors. Although the cheaper Gore-Tex would improve Patagonia's margins, it is a noxious

material that can't be recycled. Where Patagonia uses non-natural materials, such as polyester, it mostly uses recycled ingredients. It was the first company to produce fleece made from recycled soda bottles and to create infant clothing from adult clothing scraps, through the Common Threads Recycling Program, started in 2005. 'Up to now, 61% of our 2009 winter collection has been made out of recycled materials, 77% out of e-fibres, and 65% is recyclable', says Bismann.

To Patagonia, creating great products, making an honest living, having fun, respecting people and protecting the environment are all one package, labelled sustainability. Maximizing profit to the detriment of all other responsibilities makes no sense in their eyes. Or as the current CEO of Patagonia, Casey Sheahan, recently put it: 'There is no business done on a dead planet.'

Co-author: Mariapia Di Palma

Source: www.patagonia.com; www.freeonlineresearchpapers.com/patagonia-business-analysis; *Incentive Magazine*, 7 July 2008; *Climbing*, 16 July 2009.

INTRODUCTION TO THE DEBATE AND READINGS

The business of America is business.
Calvin Coolidge (1872–1933); American president

A business that makes nothing but money is a poor kind of business.
Henry Ford (1863–1947); American industrialist

So, what should be the purpose of a firm? Should managers strive to maximize shareholder value or stakeholder values? Should it be the purpose of business organizations to pursue profitability on behalf of their owners, or should firms serve the interests and promote the values of all of their stakeholders in a balanced way?

This debate has been going on for some time now, made all the more relevant by the mounting political pressure in many countries to reform their system of corporate governance. The proponents of the shareholder value perspective are lobbying for more receptiveness to the interests of the shareholders on the part of the board, to increase top management accountability and to curb perceived executive self-enrichment at the expense of shareholders. The advocates of the stakeholder values perspective are vying for a system that would bring more receptiveness to the interests of stakeholders, to ensure that firms do not become more myopically 'bottom line' oriented. While both sides do agree on one or two points (e.g. corporate governance is generally too weak), on the whole, little consensus can be found on how to deal with the paradox of profitability and responsibility. Therefore, again, managers cannot look to the strategy literature to glean the best practice and apply it to their own situation, but will need to determine their own point of view on what they believe should be the purpose of the organization.

To help managers make up their own mind, this section will present four readings. As before, the first set of two readings will represent the two poles in the debate (see Table 11.1), so that the reader can gain a sharper understanding of the breadth of opinions on this topic. The second set of two readings will add extra arguments to the debate, to further deepen the discussion. In all other chapters, the international perspective was only introduced at the end of the readings section, but here the international dimension is too predominant to keep out of the debate for so long.

Therefore, instead of a separate 'international perspective' paragraph, a special reading has been inserted as Reading 4.4 to pay more explicit attention to the international differences in view regarding organizational purpose.

Selecting the first reading to represent the shareholder value perspective was a simple task. Alfred Rappaport's highly influential book *Creating Shareholder Value* is the classic text in the field. Although the largest part of his book details how the shareholder value approach can be applied to planning and performance evaluation processes, the first chapter is a compelling exposition of his underlying views on the purpose of a business organization. This first chapter, entitled 'Shareholder Value and Corporate Purpose', has been reprinted as Reading 11.1. Rappaport's argument is straightforward – the primary purpose of corporations should be to maximize shareholder value. Therefore, 'business strategies should be judged by the economic returns they generate for shareholders, as measured by dividends plus the increase in the company's share price'. Unlike some other proponents of the shareholder value perspective, Rappaport does not explicitly claim that shareholders have the moral right to demand the primacy of profitability. His argument is more pragmatic – failing to meet the objective of maximizing shareholder value will be punished by more expensive financing. A company's financial power is ultimately determined by the stock markets. Hence, management's ability to meet the demands of the various corporate constituencies depends on the continuing support of its shareholders. Creating shareholder value, therefore, precedes the satisfaction of all other claims on the corporation. It should be noted, however, that Rappaport's arrows are not directed at the demands of employees, customers, suppliers or debtholders, but at top management.

He carefully states that senior executives may in some situations pursue objectives that are not to the benefit of shareholders. His preferred solution is not to change corporate

TABLE 11.1   Shareholder value versus stakeholder values

	Shareholder value perspective	*Stakeholder values perspective*
Emphasis on	Profitability over responsibility	Responsibility over profitability
Organizations seen as	Instruments	Joint ventures
Organizational purpose	To serve owner	To serve all parties involved
Measure of success	Share price and dividends (shareholder value)	Satisfaction among stakeholders
Major difficulty	Getting agent to pursue principal's interests	Balancing interests of various stakeholders
Corporate governance through	Independent outside directors with shares	Stakeholder representation
Stakeholder management	Means	End and means
Social responsibility	Individual, not organizational matter	Both individual and organizational
Society best served by	Pursuing self-interest (economic efficiency)	Pursuing joint-interests (economic symbiosis)

governance structures, but to more tightly align the interests of both groups, for example by giving top managers a relatively large ownership position and by tying their compensation to shareholder return performance (in later writings he does favour more structural reforms; e.g. Rappaport, 1990).

The opening reading on behalf of the stakeholder values perspective (Reading 11.2) is also a classic – 'Stockholders and Stakeholders: A New Perspective on Corporate Governance', by Edward Freeman and David Reed. This article in *California Management Review* and Freeman's subsequent book *Strategic Management: A Stakeholder Approach* were instrumental in popularizing the stakeholder concept. In their article, Freeman and Reed challenge 'the view that stockholders have a privileged place in the business enterprise'. They deplore the fact that 'it has long been gospel that corporations have obligations to stockholders . . . that are sacrosanct and inviolable'. They argue that there has been a long tradition of management thinkers who believe that corporations have a broader responsibility towards stakeholders other than just the suppliers of equity financing. It is their conviction that such a definition of the corporation, as a system serving the interests of multiple stakeholders, is superior to the shareholder perspective. Their strong preference for the stakeholder concept is largely based on the pragmatic argument that, in reality, stakeholders have the power to seriously affect the continuity of the corporation. Stakeholder analysis is needed to understand the actual claims placed by constituents on the firm and to evaluate each stakeholder's power position. Stakeholder management is a practical response to the fact that corporations cannot afford to ignore or downplay the interests of the claimants. Only here and there do Freeman and Reed hint that corporations have the moral responsibility to work on behalf of all stakeholders (which Freeman does more explicitly in some of his later works, e.g. Freeman and Gilbert, 1988; Freeman and Liedtka, 1991). In their opinion, the consequence of the stakeholder concept for corporate governance is that 'there are times when stakeholders must participate in the decision-making process'. However, they believe that if boards of directors adopt a stakeholder outlook and become more responsive to the demands placed on corporations, structural reforms to give stakeholders a stronger role in corporate governance will not be necessary.

In a chapter on organizational purpose, it is hard to avoid the most influential authors in this field, Jim Collins and Jerry Porras, whose two books on the topic, *Built to Last* (1997) and *Good to Great* (2001), have sold millions of copies. The reading reprinted here is the *Harvard Business Review* summary of *Built to Last*, titled 'Building Your Company's Vision'. In this article, Collins and Porras argue that successful companies are those capable of preserving a core ideology, while simultaneously adapting their products and processes to achieve a challenging long-term goal. These firms have a strong sense of identity, coming from an enduring set of core values and a core organizational purpose, while at the same time they are driven to change what they do by a vivid picture of what they could achieve in the long run. These two elements, core ideology and envisioned future – which in this book are called mission and vision – need to be combined to ensure that a firm is 'built to last', according to Collins and Porras. They carry on to explain in more detail how the organizational ideology/mission is based on core values and a core purpose, giving many inspiring examples. They also go on to argue that an envisioned future (vision) can actually be provoked by setting a 'Big, Hairy, Audacious Goal' – a highly ambitious long-term aim that helps to stretch the imagination, rally the troops and sets the overall direction. In the context of this chapter it is important to note that Collins and Porras haven't helped to clarify the terminology (calling the core ideology and envisioned future together the vision), but they have underlined the importance of mission and vision, while reemphasizing that the two need to go hand in hand. When it comes to the nature of the organizational purpose, Collins and Porras also have a clear view: 'maximizing shareholder wealth does not inspire people . . . [it] is the standard off-the-shelf purpose for those organizations that have not yet identified their true core purpose. It is a substitute – and a weak one at that.' Indirectly quoting Peter Drucker, they reiterate that the best and the most dedicated people are ultimately volunteers, who will only be inspired by 'meaning', not by 'money', however you answer the question, 'who does the organization belong to?'

Reading 11.4 actually picks up on this very question – 'who does the organization belong to?' In this article, 'Whose Company Is It? The Concept of the Corporation in Japan and the West', Masaru Yoshimori compares the Japanese view of organizational purpose with European and American conceptions. He points out that the ultimate issue dividing the shareholder value and stakeholder values perspectives is their view of organization ownership. Yoshimori has looked at this issue by asking middle managers in Britain, France, Germany, the United States, and Japan the simple question, 'In whose interest should the firm be managed?' He reports that the countries studied fit into three categories. In Britain and the United States, the shareholder value perspective, which he refers to as the 'monistic' concept of the corporation, is most prevalent. In Japan, on the other hand, the stakeholder values perspective is by far the predominant outlook. In the Japanese 'pluralistic' concept of the corporation, the employees' interests take precedence, closely followed by those of the main banks, major suppliers, subcontractors, and distributors. According to Yoshimori, most managers in Germany and France exhibit a 'dualistic' concept of the corporation, in which shareholder and employee interests are both taken into consideration. Yoshimori carries on to explain the most important differences between these five countries, and he weighs the costs and benefits of each. He concludes that in all countries corporate governance is poorly developed, and that nations have a lot to learn from one another. In his opinion, international cross-fertilization will lead to a partial convergence of corporate governance systems in the various countries. However, 'the concept of the corporation is firmly rooted in the historic, economic, political and even socio-cultural traditions of the nation', and therefore it is improbable 'that any one concept should drive out another at least in the foreseeable future'.

READING

11.1

Shareholder value and corporate purpose

By Alfred Rappaport[1]

Corporate mission statements proclaiming that the primary responsibility of management is to maximize shareholders' total return via dividends and increases in the market price of the company's shares abound. While the principle that the fundamental objective of the business corporation is to increase the value of its shareholders' investment is widely accepted, there is substantially less agreement about how this is accomplished.

On the cover of its 1984 annual report Coca-Cola states that 'to increase shareholder value over time is the objective driving this enterprise'. On the very next page the company goes on to say that to accomplish its objective 'growth in annual earnings per share and increased return on equity are still the names of the game'. In contrast, Hillenbrand Industries, a producer of caskets and hospital equipment, also declares its intention to provide a superior return to its shareholders, but to accomplish that objective management is focusing not on earnings but rather on creating 'shareholder value', which, it explains in the 1984 annual report, 'is created when a company generates free cash flow in excess of the shareholders' investment in the business'.

Both Coca-Cola and Hillenbrand Industries acknowledge their responsibility to maximize return to their respective shareholders. However, Coca-Cola emphasizes accounting indicators, earnings-per-share growth, and return on equity, while Hillenbrand Industries emphasizes the cash-flow based shareholder value approach to achieve shareholder returns. There are material differences between these two approaches to assessing a company's investment opportunities. Maximizing earnings-per-share growth or other accounting numbers may not necessarily lead to maximizing return for shareholders.

The growing interest

Numerous surveys indicate that a majority of the largest industrial companies have employed the shareholder value approach in capital budgeting for some time. Capital budgeting applications deal with investment projects such as capacity additions rather than total investment at the business level. Thus, we sometimes see a situation where capital projects regularly exceed the minimum acceptable rate of return, while the business unit itself is a 'problem' and creates little or no value for shareholders. This situation can arise because capital expenditures typically represent only a small percentage of total company outlays. For example, capital expenditures amount to about 10 per cent of total outlays at General Motors, a particularly capital intensive company.

During the past 10 years, the shareholder value approach has been frequently applied not only to internal investments such as capacity additions, but also to opportunities for external growth such as mergers and acquisitions. Recently a number of major companies such as American Hospital Supply, Combustion Engineering, Hillenbrand Industries, Libbey-Owens-Ford, Marriott, and Westinghouse have found that the shareholder value approach can be productively extended from individual projects to the entire strategic plan. A strategic business unit (SBU) is commonly defined as the smallest organizational unit for which integrated strategic planning, related to a distinct product that serves a well-defined market, is feasible. A strategy for an SBU may then be seen as a collection of product-market related investments and the company itself may be characterized as a portfolio of these investment-requiring strategies. By estimating the future cash flows associated with each strategy, a company can assess the economic value to shareholders of alternative strategies at the business unit and corporate levels.

The interest in shareholder value is gaining momentum as a result of several recent developments:

- The threat of corporate take-overs by those seeking undervalued, undermanaged assets.

- Impressive endorsements by corporate leaders who have adopted the approach.

- The growing recognition that traditional accounting measures such as EPS and ROI are not reliably

[1]Source: This article was adapted with the permission of The Free Press, a Division of Simon & Schuster Adult Publishing Group, from *Creating Shareholder Value: The New Standard for Business Performance* by Alfred Rappaport. © 1986 by Alfred Rappaport.

linked to increasing the value of the company's shares.

- Reporting of returns to shareholders along with other measures of performance in the business press such as *Fortune*'s annual ranking of the 500 leading industrial firms.

- A growing recognition that executives' long-term compensation needs to be more closely tied to returns to shareholders.

Endorsements of the shareholder value approach can be found in an increasing number of annual reports and other corporate publications. One of the more thoughtful statements appears in Libbey-Owens-Ford's 1983 annual report and is reproduced as Exhibit 11.1.1.

Combustion Engineering's vice president for finance states that 'a primary financial objective for Combustion Engineering is to create shareholder value by earning superior returns on capital invested in the business. This serves as a clear guide for management action and is the conceptual framework on which CE's financial objectives and goals are based.'

Whether or not executives agree with the well publicized tactics of raiders such as Carl Icahn and T. Boone Pickens, they recognize that the raiders characterize themselves as champions of the shareholders. The raiders attack on two fronts. First, they are constantly searching for poorly managed companies, where aggressive changes in strategic directions could dramatically improve the value of the stock. Second,

EXHIBIT 11.1.1   LIBBEY-OWENS-FORD STATEMENT

A GREATER EMPHASIS ON SHAREHOLDER VALUE

Libbey-Owens-Ford's mission statement specifies that its primary responsibility is to its shareholders, and that the company has a continuing requirement to increase the value of our shareholders' investment in LOF. This is not just a contemporary business phrase, but the basis for a long-term company strategy. It evaluates business strategies and plans in terms of value to our shareholders, not just on the incremental income that the results will contribute to the bottom line. It requires a greater emphasis on developing strategies and plans that will increase shareholder value as measured by the market appreciation of our stock and dividends.

Traditional accounting measures may not tell the entire story

Traditionally, the most popular way to determine whether a company is performing well is through such accounting measurements as earnings per share (EPS) and return on investment. These measures do, of course, give an indication of a company's performance, but they can be misleading in that often they do not measure the increase or decrease in shareholder value. Sustained growth as measured by EPS does not necessarily reflect an increase in stock value.

This occurs because earnings do not reflect changes in risk and inflation, nor do they take into vested in thebusiness to finance its growth. Yet these

are critical considerations when you are striving to increase the value of the shareholders' investment.

Cash flow analysis is emphasized

LOF stresses the importance of cash flow measurement and performance. Individual operating companies must analyse the cash flow effects of running their businesses. Where cash comes from and what cash is used for must be simply and clearly set forth. LOF's cash and short-term investments increased $46.3 million during 1983.

The shareholder value approach

The shareholder value approach taken by LOF emphasized economic cash flow analysis in evaluating individual projects and in determining the economic value of the overall strategy of each business unit and the corporation as a whole. Management looks at the business units and the corporation and determines the minimum operating return necessary to create value. It then reviews the possible contribution of alternative strategies and evaluates the financial feasibility of the strategic plan, based on the company's cost of capital, return on assets, the cash flow stream and other important measurements.

This disciplined process allows LOF to objectively evaluate all its corporate investments, including internal projects and acquisitions, in light of our primary goal to increase shareholder value.

Source: Libbey-Owens-Ford Company 1983 Annual Report.

they identify undervalued assets that can be redeployed to boost the stock price. As a result, many executives recognize a new and compelling reason to be concerned with the performance of their company's stock.

Executives have also become increasingly aware that many accrual-based accounting measures do not provide a dependable picture of the current and future performance of an organization. Numerous companies have sustained double-digit EPS growth while providing minimal or even *negative* returns to shareholders. Hillenbrand Industries, for example, points out in its 1984 annual report (p. 4) that 'public companies that focus on achieving short-term earnings to meet external expectations sometimes jeopardize their ability to create long-term value'.

Considerable attention has focused recently on the problems associated with rewarding executives on the basis of short-term accounting-based indicators. As a reflection of the increasing scrutiny under which executive compensation has come, business publications such as *Fortune* and *Business Week* have begun to publish compensation surveys that examine the correlation between the executives' pay and how well their companies have performed based on several measures – including returns to shareholders. For example, *Business Week's* executive compensation scoreboard now includes a 'pay–performance index' for 255 companies in 36 industries. The index shows how well the top two executives in each company were paid relative to how shareholders fared. The index is the ratio of the executive's three-year total pay as a percentage of the industry average to the shareholders' total three-year return as a percentage of the industry average. If an executive's pay and shareholders' return are both at the industry average, the index is 100. The lower the index, the better shareholders fared. The broad range in the pay–performance index, even within industries, has further fuelled the interest in achieving shareholder value. For the 1982–1984 period, for example, *Business Week* reported a pay–performance index of 59 for Roger Smith, CEO of General Motors, and an index of 160 for Phillip Caldwell, CEO of Ford Motor.

When the shareholder value approach first gained attention toward the end of the 1970s, even the executives who found the concept an intriguing notion tended to think that the approach would be very difficult to implement. The task of educating managers seemed substantial, and they were also not eager to develop a new planning system if it might involve upheaval in the corporate information system. Recent advances in technology have put impressive analytical potential at management's disposal. Managers' decisions are now greatly facilitated by microcomputer software. New approaches thus can more readily be incorporated without displacing existing information systems.

Management versus shareholder objectives

It is important to recognize that the objectives of management may in some situations differ from those of the company's shareholders. Managers, like other people, act in their self-interest. The theory of a market economy is, after all, based on individuals promoting their self-interests via market transactions to bring about an efficient allocation of resources. In a world in which principals (e.g. stockholders) have imperfect control over their agents (e.g. managers), these agents may not always engage in transactions solely in the best interests of the principals. Agents have their own objectives and it may sometimes pay them to sacrifice the principals' interests. The problem is exacerbated in large corporations where it is difficult to identify the interests of a diverse set of stockholders ranging from institutional investors to individuals with small holdings.

Critics of large corporations often allege that corporate managers have too much power and that they act in ways to benefit themselves at the expense of shareholders and other corporate constituencies. The argument is generally developed along the following lines. Responsibility for administering companies or 'control' is vested in the hands of professional managers and thereby has been separated from 'ownership.' Since the ownership of shares in large corporations tends to be diffused, individual shareholders are said to have neither influence on nor interest in corporate governance issues such as the election of board members. Therefore, boards are largely responsive to management which, in turn, can ignore shareholders and run companies as they see fit.

The foregoing 'separation of ownership and control' argument advanced by Berle and Means in 1932 has been a persistent theme of corporate critics during the intervening years. There are, however, a number of factors that induce management to act in the best interests of shareholders. These factors derive from the fundamental premise that the greater the expected unfavourable consequences to the manager who decreases the wealth of shareholders, the less likely it is that the manager will, in fact, act against the interests of shareholders.

Consistent with the above premise, at least four major factors will induce management to adopt a shareholder orientation: (1) a relatively large ownership position, (2) compensation tied to shareholder return performance, (3) threat of take-over by another organization, and (4) competitive labour markets for corporate executives.

Economic rationality dictates that stock ownership by management motivates executives to identify more closely with the shareholders' economic interests. Indeed, we would expect that the greater the proportion of personal wealth invested in company stock or tied to stock options, the greater would be management's shareholder orientation. While the top executives in many companies often have relatively large percentages of their wealth invested in company stock, this is much less often the case for divisional and business unit managers. And it is at the divisional and business unit levels that most resource allocation decisions are made in decentralized organizations.

Even when corporate executives own shares in their company, their viewpoint on the acceptance of risk may differ from that of shareholders. It is reasonable to expect that many corporate executives have a lower tolerance for risk. If the company invests in a risky project, stockholders can always balance this risk against other risks in their presumably diversified portfolios. The manager, however, can balance a project failure only against the other activities of the division or the company. Thus, managers are hurt by the failure more than shareholders.

The second factor likely to influence management to adopt a shareholder orientation is compensation tied to shareholder return performance. The most direct means of linking top management's interests with those of shareholders is to base compensation, and particularly the incentive portion, on market returns realized by shareholders. Exclusive reliance on shareholder returns, however, has its own limitations. First, movements in a company's stock price may well be greatly influenced by factors beyond management control such as the overall state of the economy and stock market. Second, shareholder returns may be materially influenced by what management believes to be unduly optimistic or pessimistic market expectations at the beginning or end of the performance measurement period. And third, divisional and business unit performance cannot be directly linked to stock price.

Rather than linking incentive compensation directly to the market returns earned by shareholders, most

Fortune 500 companies tie annual bonuses and long-term performance plans to internal financial goals such as earnings or accounting return on investment. These accounting criteria can often conflict with the way corporate shares are valued by the market. If incentives were largely based on earnings, for example, management might well be motivated to pursue economically unsound strategies when viewed from the perspective of shareholders. In such a situation what is economically irrational from the shareholder viewpoint may be a perfectly rational course of action for the decision-making executives.

The third factor affecting management behaviour is the threat of take-over by another company. Tender offers have become a commonly employed means of transferring corporate control. Moreover the size of the targets continues to become larger. During the 1979–1985 period, 77 acquisitions each in excess of $1 billion were completed. The threat of take-over is an essential means of constraining corporate managers who might choose to pursue personal goals at the expense of shareholders. Any significant exploitation of shareholders should be reflected in a lower stock price. This lower price, relative to what it might be with more efficient management, offers an attractive take-over opportunity for another company which in many cases will replace incumbent management. An active market for corporate control places limits on the divergence of interests between management and shareholders and thereby serves as an important counterargument to the 'separation of ownership and control' criticisms.

The fourth and final factor influencing management's shareholder orientation is the labour market for corporate executives. Managerial labour markets are an essential mechanism for motivating management to function in the best interests of shareholders. Managers compete for positions both within and outside of the firm. The increasing number of executive recruiting firms and the length of the 'Who's News' column in the *Wall Street Journal* are evidence that the managerial labour market is very active. What is less obvious is how managers are evaluated in this market. Within the firm, performance evaluation and incentive schemes are the basic mechanisms for monitoring managerial performance. As seen earlier, the question here is whether these measures are reliably linked to the market price of the company's shares.

How managers communicate their value to the labour market outside of their individual firms is less apparent. While the performance of top-level corporate officers can be gleaned from annual reports and other publicly available corporate communications, this is not generally the case for divisional managers. For corporate level executives, the question is whether performance for shareholders is the dominant criterion in assessing their value in the executive labour market. The question in the case of division managers is, first, how does the labour market monitor and gain insights about their performance and second, what is the basis for valuing their services.

'Excellence' and restructuring

Two of the most visible business phenomena of the first half of the 1980s have been the publication of Peters and Waterman's *In Search of Excellence* and the unprecedented surge in the restructuring of companies. The 'excellence phenomenon' certainly provided no obvious encouragement for management to link its decisions more closely with the objective of maximizing returns to shareholders. In contrast, the more recent restructuring movement is clearly a manifestation of top management's growing concern with its company's share price and shareholder returns.

As US corporations began the 1980s, saddled with a decade of inflation and lagging productivity, nothing could have come as better news than the idea that not all excellent companies are Japanese. It was in this climate that *In Search of Excellence*, published in 1982, became an absolute sensation. Its longevity on the top of the best-seller list along with its wide coverage in the business press provided an extraordinary platform for the authors' ideas.

The basic purpose of *In Search of Excellence* was to identify key attributes of corporate excellence that are common among successful American corporations. To choose the 'excellent' companies, Peters and Waterman began by assembling a list of 62 US companies that were considered 'successful' by business leaders, consultants, members of the business press, and business school professors. From that list they selected 36 'excellent' companies based on superior performance for such financial measures as return on total capital, return on equity, return on sales, and asset growth. Eight attributes of corporate excellence were identified – a bias for action; staying close to the customer; autonomy and entrepreneurship; productivity through people; hands-on, value-driven management; sticking to the knitting; simple organization form and lean staff; and simultaneous loose-tight properties.

Even though the 'excellent' firms exhibited superior financial (accounting) performance over the 1960–1980 period, they did not provide consistently superior returns to shareholders via dividends plus share price appreciation. The excellent companies did not perform significantly better than the market. Indeed, they did not consistently outperform their respective industry groups or closest competitors. These results once again raise questions about the use of accounting measures to gauge the economic performance of corporations. Since the eight attributes of corporate excellence are not associated with systematically superior returns to shareholders, efforts to emulate these attributes may be ill advised.

While *In Search of Excellence* became 'must reading' in many organizations during 1982 and 1983, a certain degree of disenchantment set in during the following two years as a number of 'excellent' companies experienced strategic setbacks. Atari, Avon Products, Caterpillar Tractor, Digital Equipment, Hewlett-Packard, Levi Strauss, and Texas Instruments serve as examples.

But if emulating excellent companies has lost some of its lustre, a new focal point of interest has captured the imagination of management during the past couple of years – restructuring. Hardly a day passes without some company announcing a major restructuring of its businesses or capital structure. Restructuring involves diverse activities such as divestiture of underperforming businesses or businesses that do not 'fit', spin-offs directly to shareholders, acquisitions paid for with 'excess cash', stock repurchases, debt swaps, and liquidation of overfunded pension funds. In many cases, these restructurings are motivated by a desire to foil a take-over bid by so-called 'raiders' who look for undermanaged companies where changes in strategic direction could dramatically increase the value of the stock, and for companies with high liquidation values relative to their current share price. There is, of course, no better means of avoiding a take-over than increasing the price of the stock. Thus, increasing share price has become the fundamental purpose of corporate restructuring.

In contrast to the earlier euphoria over emulating excellent companies, the current restructuring movement is solidly based on shareholder value creation principles. In 1985, the Standard & Poor's 500 appreciated 26 per cent in price. Goldman Sachs estimates that corporate restructuring accounted for about 30 per cent of that price change. However, the early stage of the restructuring movement, which I call 'Phase I restructuring', is largely based on one-time transactions such as those listed above rather than changes in day-to-day management of the business.

The necessary agenda for the second half of the 1980s seems clear. Companies need to move from Phase I restructuring to Phase II restructuring. In Phase II, the shareholder value approach is employed not only when buying and selling businesses or changing the company's capital structure, but also in the planning and performance monitoring of all business strategies on an ongoing basis. Frequently, the most difficult issue in this area is how to go about estimating the impact of strategies on shareholder value. Fortunately, relatively straightforward approaches do exist for estimating the shareholder value created by a business strategy, and an increasing number of major companies have begun to use them.

Most companies already use the same discounted cash-flow techniques used in the shareholder value approach to assess the attractiveness of capital investment projects and to value prospective acquisition targets. This approach can be extended to estimate the value creation potential of individual business units and the strategic plan for the entire company.

In Phase II restructuring it will also become increasingly important that executive compensation be tied closely to the shareholder value driven plans so that management will be strongly motivated to make decisions consistent with creating maximum returns to shareholders. A successful implementation of Phase II restructuring not only ensures that management has met its fiduciary responsibility to develop corporate performance evaluation systems consistent with the parameters investors use to value the company, but also minimizes the Phase I concern that a take-over of an undermanaged company is imminent.

Rationale for shareholder value approach

Business strategies should be judged by the economic returns they generate for shareholders, as measured by dividends plus the increase in the company's share price. As management considers alternative strategies, those expected to develop the greatest sustainable competitive advantage will be those that will also create the greatest value for shareholders. The 'shareholder value approach' estimates the economic value of an investment (e.g. the shares of a company, strategies, mergers and acquisitions, capital expenditures) by discounting forecasted cash flows by the cost of capital. These cash flows, in turn, serve as the foundation for shareholder returns from dividends and share-price appreciation.

The case for why management should pursue this objective is comparatively straightforward. Management is often characterized as balancing the interests of various corporate constituencies such as employees, customers, suppliers, debtholders, and stockholders. As Treynor (1981) points out, the company's continued existence depends upon a financial relationship with each of these parties. Employees want competitive wages. Customers want high quality at a competitive price. Suppliers and debtholders each have financial claims that must be satisfied with cash when they fall due. Stockholders as residual claimants of the firm look for cash dividends and the prospect of future dividends which is reflected in the market price of the stock.

If the company does not satisfy the financial claims of its constituents, it will cease to be a viable organization. Employees, customers, and suppliers will simply withdraw their support. Thus, a going concern must strive to enhance its cash-generating ability. The ability of a company to distribute cash to its various constituencies depends on its ability to generate cash from operating its businesses and on its ability to obtain any additional funds needed from external sources.

Debt and equity financing are the two basic external sources. The company's ability to borrow today is based on projections of how much cash will be generated in the future. Borrowing power and the market value of the shares both depend on a company's cash-generating ability. The market value of the shares directly impacts the second source of financing, that is, equity financing. For a given level of funds required, the higher the share price, the less dilution will be borne by current shareholders. Therefore, management's financial power to deal effectively with corporate claimants also comes from increasing the value of the shares. Treynor, a former editor of the *Financial Analysts Journal*, summarizes this line of thinking best:

> *Those who criticize the goal of share value maximization are forgetting that stockholders are not merely the beneficiaries of the corporation's financial success, but also the referees who determine management's financial power.*
>
> *Any management – no matter how powerful and independent – that flouts the financial objective of maximizing share value does so at its own peril.*

READING

11.2

Stockholders and stakeholders: A new perspective on corporate governance

By Edward Freeman and David Reed[1]

Management thought has changed dramatically in recent years. There have been, and are now underway, both conceptual and practical revolutions in the ways that management theorists and managers think about organizational life. The purpose of this article is to understand the implications of one of these shifts in world view; namely, the shift from 'stockholder' to 'stakeholder'.

The stakeholder concept

It has long been gospel that corporations have obligations to stockholders, holders of the firm's equity, that are sacrosanct and inviolable. Corporate action or inaction is to be driven by attention to the needs of its stockholders, usually thought to be measured by stock price, earnings per share, or some other financial measure. It has been argued that the proper relationship of management to its stockholders is similar to that of the fiduciary to the *cestui que trustent*, whereby the interests of the stockholders should be dutifully cared for by management. Thus, any action taken by management must ultimately be justified by whether or not it furthers the interests of the corporation and its stockholders.

There is also a long tradition of departure from the view that stockholders have a privileged place in the business enterprise. Berle and Means (1932) were worried about the 'degree of prominence entitling (the corporation) to be dealt with as a major social institution'. Chester Barnard argued that the purpose of the corporation was to serve society, and that the function of the executive was to instil this sense of moral purpose in the corporation's employees (Barnard, 1938). Public relations and corporate social action have a history too long to be catalogued here. However, a recent development calls for a more far-reaching change in the way that we look at corporate life, and that is the good currency of the idea of 'stakeholders'.

The stakeholder notion is indeed a deceptively simple one. It says that there are other groups to whom the corporation is responsible in addition to stockholders: those groups who have a stake in the actions of the corporation. The word *stakeholder*, coined in an internal memorandum at the Stanford Research Institute in 1963, refers to 'those groups without whose support the organization would cease to exist'. The list of stakeholders originally included shareowners, employees, customers, suppliers, lenders, and society. Stemming from the work of Igor Ansoff and Robert Stewart (in the planning department at Lockheed) and, later, Marion Doscher and Stewart (at SRI), stakeholder analysis served and continues to serve an important function in the SRI corporate planning process.

From the original work at SRI, the historical trail diverges in a number of directions. In his now classic *Corporate Strategy: An Analytic Approach to Business Policy for Growth and Expansion*, Igor Ansoff (1965) makes limited use of the theory:

> *While as we shall see later, 'responsibilities' and 'objectives' are not synonymous, they have been made one in a 'stakeholder theory' of objectives. This theory maintains that the objectives of the firm should be derived by balancing the conflicting claims of the various 'stakeholders' in the firm: managers, workers, stockholders, suppliers, vendors.*

Ansoff goes on to reject the stakeholder theory in favour of a view which separates objectives into 'economic' and 'social' with the latter being a 'secondary modifying and constraining influence' on the former.

In the mid-1970s, researchers in systems theory, led by Russell Ackoff (1974) 'rediscovered' stakeholder analysis, or at least took Ansoff's admonition more seriously. Propounding essentially an open systems view of organizations, Ackoff argues that many social problems can be solved by the redesign of fundamental institutions with the support and interaction of stakeholders in the system.

A second trail from Ansoff's original reference is the work of William Dill, who in concert with Ackoff, sought to move the stakeholder concept from the periphery of corporate planning to a central place. In 1975 Dill argued:

> *For a long time, we have assumed that the views and the initiative of stakeholders could be dealt with as externalities to the strategic planning and management process: as data to help management shape decisions, or as legal and social constraints to limit them. We have been reluctant, though, to admit the idea that some of these outside stakeholders might seek and earn active roles with management to make decisions. The move today is from stakeholder influence towards stakeholder participation.*

Dill went on to set out a role for strategic managers as communicators with stakeholders and considered the role of adversary groups such as Nader's Raiders in the strategic process. For the most part, until Dill's paper, stakeholders had been assumed to be nonadversarial, or adversarial only in the sense of labour-management relations. By broadening the notion of stakeholder to 'people outside . . . who have ideas about what the economic and social performance of the enterprise should include', Dill set the stage for the use of the stakeholder concept as an umbrella for strategic management.

A related development is primarily responsible for giving the stakeholder concept a boost; namely, the increase in concern with the social involvement of business. The corporate social responsibility movement is too diverse and has spawned too many ideas, concepts, and techniques to explain here. Suffice it to say that the social movements of the sixties and seventies – civil rights, the antiwar movement, consumerism, environmentalism, and women's rights – served as a catalyst for rethinking the role of the business enterprise in society. From Milton Friedman to John Kenneth Galbraith, there is a diversity of arguments. However, one aspect of the corporate social responsibility debate is particularly relevant to understanding the good currency of the stakeholder concept.

In the early 1970s the Harvard Business School undertook a project on corporate social responsibility. The output of the project was voluminous, and of particular importance was the development of a pragmatic model of social responsibility called 'the corporate social responsiveness model' (Ackerman and Bauer, 1976). It essentially addressed Dill's question with respect to social issues: 'How can the corporation respond proactively to the increased pressure for positive social

change?' By concentrating on responsiveness instead of responsibility, the Harvard researchers were able to link the analysis of social issues with the traditional areas of strategy and organization.

By the late 1970s the need for strategic management processes to take account of nontraditional business problems in terms of government, special interest groups, trade associations, foreign competitors, dissident shareholders, and complex issues such as employee rights, equal opportunity, environmental pollution, consumer rights, tariffs, government regulation, and reindustrialization had become obvious. To begin to develop these processes, The Wharton School began, in 1977 in its Applied Research Center, a 'stakeholder project'. The objectives of the project were to put together a number of strands of thought and to develop a theory of management which enabled executives to formulate and implement corporate strategy in turbulent environments. Thus, an action research model was used whereby stakeholder theory was generated by actual cases.

To date the project has explored the implications of the stakeholder concept on three levels: as a management theory; as a process for practitioners to use in strategic management; and as an analytical framework.

At the theoretical level the implications of substituting *stakeholder* for *stockholder* needs to be explicated. The first problem at this level is the actual definition of *stakeholder.* SRI's original definition is too general and too exclusive to serve as a means of identifying those external groups who are strategically important. The concentration on generic stakeholders, such as society and customers, rather than specific social interest groups and specific customer segments produces an analysis which can only be used as a background for the planning process. Strategically useful information about the actions, objectives, and motivations of specific groups, which is needed if management is to be responsive to stakeholder concerns, requires a more specific and inclusive definition.

We propose two definitions of *stakeholder:* a wide sense, which includes groups who are friendly or hostile, and a narrow sense, which captures the essence of the SRI definition, but is more specific.

■ The wide sense of stakeholder. Any identifiable group or individual who can affect the achievement of an organization's objectives or who is affected by the achievement of an organization's objectives. (Public interest groups, protest groups, government agencies, trade associations, competitors, unions, as well as employees, customer segments, share-owners, and others are stakeholders, in this sense.)

■ The narrow sense of stakeholder. Any identifiable group or individual on which the organization is dependent for its continued survival. (Employees, customer segments, certain suppliers, key government agencies, shareowners, certain financial institutions, as well as others are all stakeholders in the narrow sense of the term.)

While executives are willing to recognize that employees, suppliers, and customers have a stake in the corporation, many resist the inclusion of adversary groups. But from the standpoint of corporate strategy, *stakeholder* must be understood in the wide sense: strategies need to account for those groups who can affect the achievement of the firm's objectives. Some may feel happier with other words, such as *influencers*, *claimants*, *publics*, or *constituencies*. Semantics aside, if corporations are to formulate and implement strategies in turbulent environments, theories of strategy must have concepts, such as the wide sense of *stakeholder*, which allow the analysis of all external forces and pressures whether they are friendly or hostile. In what follows we will use *stakeholder* in the wide sense, as our primary objective is to elucidate the questions of corporate governance from the perspective of strategic management.

A second issue at the theoretical level is the generation of prescriptive propositions which explain actual cases and articulate regulative principles for future use. Thus, a *post hoc* analysis of the brewing industry and the problem of beverage container legislation, combined with a similar analysis of the regulatory environments of public utilities have led to some simple propositions which serve as a philosophical guideline for strategy formulation. For example:

■ Generalize the marketing approach: understand the needs of each stakeholder, in a similar fashion to understanding customer needs, and design products, services, and programmes to fulfil those needs.

■ Establish negotiation processes: understand the political nature of a number of stakeholders, and the applicability of concepts and techniques of political science, such as coalition analysis, conflict management, and the use and abuse of unilateral action.

■ Establish a decision philosophy that is oriented towards seizing the initiative rather than reacting to events as they occur.

■ Allocate organizational resources based on the degree of importance of the environmental turbulence (the stakeholders' claims).

Other prescriptive propositions can be put forth, especially with respect to issues of corporate governance. One proposition that has been discussed is to 'involve stakeholder groups in strategic decisions', or 'invite stakeholders to participate in governance decisions'. While propositions like this may have substantial merit, we have not examined enough cases nor marshalled enough evidence to support them in an unqualified manner. There are cases where participation is appropriate. Some public utilities have been quite successful in the use of stakeholder advisory groups in matters of rate setting. However, given the breadth of our concept of stakeholder we believe that co-optation through participation is not always the correct strategic decision.

The second level of analysis is the use of stakeholder concepts in strategy formulation processes. Two processes have been used so far: the *Stakeholder Strategy Process* and the *Stakeholder Audit Process*. The Stakeholder Strategy Process is a systematic method for analysing the relative importance of stakeholders and their cooperative potential (how they can help the corporation achieve its objectives) and their competitive threat (how they can prevent the corporation from achieving its objectives). The process is one which relies on a behavioural analysis (both actual and potential) for input, and an explanatory model of stakeholder objectives and resultant strategic shifts for output. The Stakeholder Audit Process is a systematic method for identifying stakeholders and assessing the effectiveness of current organizational strategies. By itself, each process has a use in the strategic management of an organization. Each analyses the stakeholder environment from the standpoint of organizational mission and objectives and seeks to formulate strategies for meeting stakeholder needs and concerns.

The use of the stakeholder concept at the analytical level means thinking in terms which are broader than current strategic and operational problems. It implies looking at public policy questions in stakeholder terms and trying to understand how the relationships between an organization and its stakeholders would change given the implementation of certain policies.

One analytical device depicts an organization's stakeholders on a two-dimensional grid map. The first dimension is one of 'interest' or 'stake' and ranges from an equity interest to an economic interest or marketplace stake to an interest or stake as a 'kibitzer' or influencer. Shareowners have an equity stake; customers and suppliers have an economic stake; and single-issue groups have an influencer stake. The second dimension of a stakeholder is its power, which ranges from the formalistic or voting power of stockholders to the economic power of customers to the political power of special interest groups. By *economic power* we mean 'the ability to influence due to marketplace decisions' and by *political power* we mean 'the ability to influence due to use of the political process'.

Figure 11.2.1 represents this stakeholder grid graphically. It is of course possible that a stakeholder has more than one kind of both stake and power, especially in light of the fact that there are stakeholders who have multiple roles. An employee may be at once shareholder, customer, employee, and even kibitzer. Figure 11.2.1 represents the prevailing world view. That is, shareholders and directors have formal or voting power; customers, suppliers, and employees have economic power; and government and special interest groups have political power. Moreover, management concepts and principles have evolved to treat this 'diagonal case.' Managers learn how to handle stockholders and boards via their ability to vote on certain key decisions, and conflicts are resolved by the procedures and processes written into the corporate charter or by methods which involve formal legal parameters. Strategic planners, marketers, financial analysts, and operations executives base their decisions on marketplace variables, and an entire tradition of management principles is based on the economic analysis of the marketplace. Finally, public relations and public affairs managers and lobbyists learn to deal in the political arena. As long as the real world approximately fits into the diagonal, management processes may be able to deal effectively with them.

A more thoughtful examination, however, reveals that Figure 11.2.1 is either a straw man or that shifts of position have occurred. In the auto industry, for instance, one part of government has acquired economic power in terms of the imposition of import quotas or the trigger price mechanism. The Securities and Exchange Commission might be looked at as a kibitzer with formal power in terms of disclosure and accounting rules. Outside directors do not necessarily have an equity stake, especially those women, minorities, and academics who are becoming more and more normal for the boards of large corporations. Some kibitzer groups are buying stock and acquiring an equity stake, and while they also acquire formal power, their main source of power is still political. Witness the marshalling of the political process by church groups in bringing up, at annual meetings, issues such as selling infant formula in the Third World or investing in South Africa. Unions are using their political power as well as their formal clout as managers of large portions of pension funds to influence the company. Customers are being organized by consumer advocates to exercise the voice option and to politicize the marketplace. In short, the real world looks more like Figure 11.2.2. (Of course, each organization will have its own individual grid.) Thus,

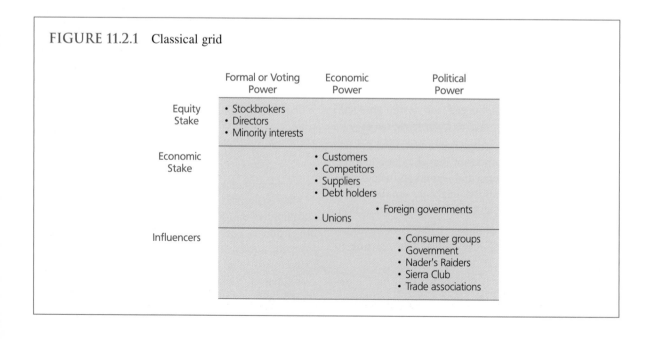

FIGURE 11.2.1   Classical grid

	Formal or Voting Power	Economic Power	Political Power
Equity Stake	• Stockbrokers • Directors • Minority interests		
Economic Stake		• Customers • Competitors • Suppliers • Debt holders • Unions	• Foreign governments
Influencers			• Consumer groups • Government • Nader's Raiders • Sierra Club • Trade associations

FIGURE 11.2.2   'Real world' stakeholder grid

	Formal or Voting Power	Economic Power	Political Power
Equity Stake	• Stockbrokers • Directors • Minority interests		• Dissident stockholders
Economic Stake		• Suppliers • Debt holders • Customers • Unions	• Local governments • Foreign governments • Consumer groups • Unions
Influencers	• Government • SEC • Outside directors	• EPA/OSHA	• Nader's Raiders • Government • Trade associations

search for alternative applications of traditional management processes must begin, and new concepts and techniques are needed to understand the shifts that have occurred and to manage in the new environment.

There is a need to develop new and innovative management processes to deal with the current and future complexities of management issues. At the theoretical level, stakeholder analysis has been developed to enrich the economic approach to corporate strategy by arguing that kibitzers with political power must be included in the strategy process. At the strategic level, stakeholder analysis takes a number of groups into account and analyzes their strategic impact on the corporation.

Stakeholder analysis and corporate democracy

The debate on corporate governance and, in particular, corporate democracy has recently intensified. Proposals have been put forth to make the corporation more democratic, to encourage shareholder participation and management responsiveness to shareholder needs, and to make corporations more responsive to other stakeholder needs and, hence, to encourage the participation of stakeholders in the governance process. Reforms from cumulative voting to audit committees have been suggested.

Corporate democracy has come to have at least three meanings over the years, which prescribe that corporations should be made more democratic: by

increasing the role of government, either as a watchdog or by having public officials on boards of directors; by allowing citizen or public participation in the managing of its affairs via public interest directors and the like; or by encouraging or mandating the active participation of all or many of its shareholders. The analysis of the preceding section has implications for each of these levels of democratization.

The propositions of stakeholder analysis advocate a thorough understanding of a firm's stakeholders (in the wide sense) and recognize that there are times when stakeholders must participate in the decision-making process. The strategic tools and techniques of stakeholder analysis yield a method for determining the timing and degree of such participation. At the absolute minimum this implies that boards of directors must be aware of the impact of their decisions on key stakeholder groups. As stakeholders have begun to exercise more political power and as marketplace decisions become politicized, the need for awareness to grow into responsiveness has become apparent. Thus, the analytical model can be used by boards to map carefully the power and stake of each group. While it is not the proper role of the board to be involved in the implementation of tactical programmes at the operational level of the corporation, it must set the tone for how the company deals with stakeholders, both traditional marketplace ones and those who have political power. The board must decide not only whether management is managing the affairs of the corporation, but indeed, what are to count as the affairs of the corporation. This involves assessing the stake and power of each stakeholder group.

Much has been written about the failure of senior management to think strategically, competitively, and globally. Some have argued that American businesspersons are 'managing [their] way to economic decline' (Hayes and Abernathy, 1980). Executives have countered the critics with complaints about the increase in the adversarial role of government and in the number of hostile external interest groups. Yet if the criteria for success for senior executives remain fixated on economic stakeholders with economic power and on short-term performance on Wall Street, the rise of such a turbulent political environment in a free and open society should come as no surprise. If the board sees itself as responsive only to the shareholder in the short term, senior management will continue to manage towards economic decline.[2] We have argued that the problem of governing the corporation in today's world must be viewed in terms of the entire grid of stakeholders and their power base. It is only by setting the direction for positive response and negotiation at the board level that the adversarial nature of the business-government relationship can be overcome.

If this task of stakeholder management is done properly, much of the air is let out of critics who argue that the corporation must be democratized in terms of increased direct citizen participation. Issues which involve both economic and political stakes and power bases must be addressed in an integrated fashion. No longer can public affairs, public relations, and corporate philanthropy serve as adequate management tools. The sophistication of interest groups who are beginning to use formal power mechanisms, such as proxy fights, annual meetings, the corporate charter, to focus the attention of management on the affairs of the corporation has increased. Responsive boards will seize these opportunities to learn more about those stakeholders who have chosen the option of voice over the Wall Street Rule. As boards direct management to respond to these concerns, to negotiate with critics, to trade off certain policies in return for positive support, the pressure for mandated citizen participation will subside.

[2]It is arguable whether responsiveness to nonmarket stakeholders is in the long-term interest of the corporation. We believe that there is no need to appeal to utilitarian notions of greatest social good or altruism or social responsibility. Rather the corporation fulfils its obligations to shareholders in the long term only through proper stakeholder management. In short we believe that enlightened self-interest gives both reasons why (personal motivation) and reasons for (social justification) taking stakeholder concerns into account. The development of this argument is, however, beyond our present scope.

Building your company's vision

By James C. Collins and Jerry I. Porras[1]

Companies that enjoy enduring success have core values and a core purpose that remain fixed while their business strategies and practices endlessly adapt to a changing world. The dynamic of preserving the core while stimulating progress is the reason that companies such as Hewlett-Packard, 3M, Johnson & Johnson, Procter & Gamble, Merck, Sony, Motorola, and Nordstrom became elite institutions able to renew themselves and achieve superior long-term performance. Hewlett-Packard employees have long known that radical change in operating practices, cultural norms, and business strategies does not mean losing the spirit of the HP Way – the company's core principles. Johnson & Johnson continually questions its structure and revamps its processes while preserving the ideals embodied in its credo. In 1996, 3M sold off several of its large mature businesses – a dramatic move that surprised the business press – to refocus on its enduring core purpose of solving unsolved problems innovatively. We studied companies such as these in our research for *Built to Last: Successful Habits of Visionary Companies* and found that they have outperformed the general stock market by a factor of 12 since 1925.

[1]Source: This article was adapted by permission of *Harvard Business Review*. From 'Building Your Company's Vision' by James C. Collins and Jerry I. Porras, September/October 1996. © 1996 by the Harvard Business School Publishing Corporation, all rights reserved.

Truly great companies understand the difference between what should never change and what should be open for change, between what is genuinely sacred and what is not. This rare ability to manage continuity and change – requiring a consciously practiced discipline – is closely linked to the ability to develop a vision. Vision provides guidance about what core to preserve and what future to stimulate progress toward. But *vision* has become one of the most overused and least understood words in the language, conjuring up different images for different people: of deeply held values, outstanding achievement, societal bonds, exhilarating goals, motivating forces, or *raisons d'être*. We recommend a conceptual framework to define vision, add clarity and rigor to the vague and fuzzy concepts swirling around that trendy term, and give practical guidance for articulating a coherent vision within an organization. It is a prescriptive framework rooted in six years of research and refined and tested by our ongoing work with executives from a great variety of organizations around the world.

A well-conceived vision consists of two major components: *core ideology* and *envisioned future* (see Figure 11.3.1). Core ideology, the yin in our scheme, defines what we stand for and why we exist. Yin is unchanging and complements yang, the envisioned future. The envisioned future is what we aspire to become, to achieve, to create – something that will require significant change and progress to attain.

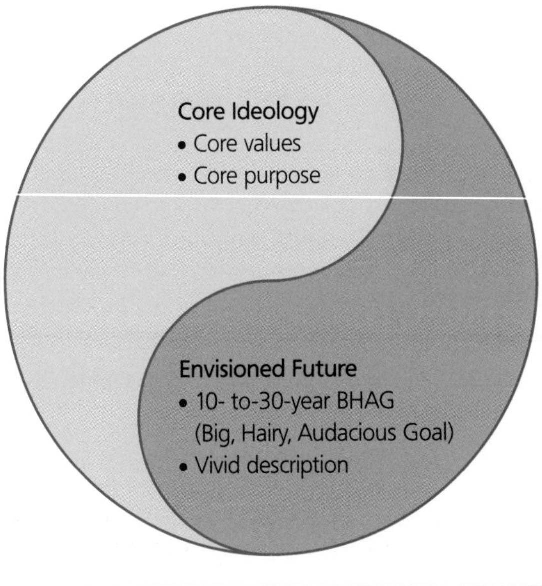

Core ideology

Core ideology defines the enduring character of an organization – a consistent identity that transcends product or market life cycles, technological breakthroughs, management fads, and individual leaders. In fact, the most lasting and significant contribution of those who build visionary companies is the core ideology. As Bill Hewlett said about his longtime friend and business partner David Packard upon Packard's death not long ago, 'As far as the company is concerned, the greatest thing he left behind him was a code of ethics known as the HP Way.' HP's core ideology, which has guided the company since its inception more than 50 years ago, includes a deep respect for the individual, a dedication to affordable quality and reliability, a commitment to community responsibility (Packard himself bequeathed his $4.3 billion of Hewlett-Packard stock to a charitable foundation), and a view that the company exists to make technical contributions for the advancement and welfare of humanity. Company builders such as David Packard, Masaru Ibuka of Sony, George Merck of Merck, William McKnight of 3M, and Paul Galvin of Motorola understood that it is more important to know who you are than where you are going, for where you are going will change as the world around you changes. Leaders die, products become obsolete, markets change, new technologies emerge, and management fads come and go, but core ideology in a great company endures as a source of guidance and inspiration.

Core ideology provides the glue that holds an organization together as it grows, decentralizes, diversifies, expands globally, and develops workplace diversity. Think of it as analogous to the principles of Judaism that held the Jewish people together for centuries without a homeland, even as they spread throughout the Diaspora. Or think of the truths held to be self-evident in the Declaration of Independence, or the enduring ideals and principles of the scientific community that bond scientists from every nationality together in the common purpose of advancing human knowledge. Any effective vision must embody the core ideology of the organization, which in turn consists of two distinct parts: core values, a system of guiding principles and tenets; and core purpose, the organization's most fundamental reason for existence.

FIGURE 11.3.1 Articulating a vision

Core Ideology
- Core values
- Core purpose

Envisioned Future
- 10- to-30-year BHAG (Big, Hairy, Audacious Goal)
- Vivid description

Core values

Core values are the essential and enduring tenets of an organization. A small set of timeless guiding principles, core values require no external justification; they have *intrinsic* value and importance to those inside the organization. The Walt Disney Company's core values of imagination and wholesomeness stem not from market requirements but from the founder's inner belief that imagination and wholesomeness should be nurtured for their own sake. William Procter and James Gamble didn't instil in P&G's culture a focus on product excellence merely as a strategy for success but as an almost religious tenet. And that value has been passed down for more than 15 decades by P&G people. Service to the customer – even to the point of subservience – is a way of life at Nordstrom that traces its roots back to 1901, eight decades before customer service programmes became stylish. For Bill Hewlett and David Packard, respect for the individual was first and foremost a deep personal value; they didn't get it from a book or hear it from a management guru. And Ralph S. Larsen, CEO of Johnson & Johnson, puts it this way: 'The core values embodied in our credo might be a competitive advantage, but that is not *why* we have them. We have them because they define for us what we stand for, and we would hold them even if they became a competitive *dis*advantage in certain situations.'

The point is that a great company decides for itself what values it holds to be core, largely independent of the current environment, competitive requirements, or management fads. Clearly, then, there is no universally right set of core values. A company need not have as its core value customer service (Sony doesn't) or respect for the individual (Disney doesn't) or quality (Wal-Mart Stores doesn't) or market focus (HP doesn't) or teamwork (Nordstrom doesn't). A company might have operating practices and business strategies around those qualities without having them at the essence of its being. Furthermore, great companies need not have likable or humanistic core values, although many do. The key is not *what* core values an organization has but that it has core values at all.

Companies tend to have only a few core values, usually between three and five. In fact, we found that none of the visionary companies we studied in our book had more than five: most had only three or four (see Exhibit 11.3.1) And, indeed, we should expect

---

EXHIBIT 11.3.1   CORE VALUES ARE A COMPANY'S ESSENTIAL TENETS

Merck

- Corporate social responsibility
- Unequivocal excellence in all aspects of the company
- Science-based innovation
- Honesty and integrity
- Profit, but profit from work that benefits humanity

Nordstrom

- Service to the customer above all else
- Hard work and individual productivity
- Never being satisfied
- Excellence in reputation; being part of something special

Philip Morris

- The right to freedom of choice
- Winning–beating others in a good fight
- Encouraging individual initiative
- Opportunity based on merit; no one is entitled to anything
- Hard work and continuous self-improvement

Sony

- Elevation of the Japanese culture and national status
- Being a pioneer–not following others; doing the impossible
- Encouraging individual ability and creativity

Walt Disney

- No cynicism
- Nurturing and promulgation of "wholesome American values"
- Creativity, dreams, and imagination
- Fanatical attention to consistency and detail
- Preservation and control of the Disney magic

that. Only a few values can be truly *core* – that is, so fundamental and deeply held that they will change seldom, if ever.

To identify the core values of your own organization, push with relentless honesty to define what values are truly central. If you articulate more than five or six, chances are that you are confusing core values (which do not change) with operating practices, business strategies, or cultural norms (which should be open to change). Remember, the values must stand the test of time. After you've drafted a preliminary list of the core values, ask about each one: If the circumstances changed and *penalized* us for holding this core value, would we still keep it? If you can't honestly answer yes, then the value is not core and should be dropped from consideration.

A high-technology company wondered whether it should put quality on its list of core values. The CEO asked, 'Suppose in ten years quality doesn't make a hoot of difference in our markets. Suppose the only thing that matters is sheer speed and horsepower but not quality. Would we still want to put quality on our list of core values?' The members of the management team looked around at one another and finally said no. Quality stayed in the *strategy* of the company, and quality-improvement programmes remained in place as a mechanism for stimulating progress; but quality did not make the list of core values.

The same group of executives then wrestled with leading-edge innovation as a core value. The CEO asked, 'Would we keep innovation on the list as a core value, no matter how the world around us changed?' This time, the management team gave a resounding yes. The managers' outlook might be summarized as, 'We always want to do leading-edge innovation. That's who we are. It's really important to us and always will be. No matter what. And if our current markets don't value it, we will find markets that do.' Leading-edge innovation went on the list and will stay there. A company should not change its core values in response to market changes; rather, it should change markets, if necessary, to remain true to its core values.

Who should be involved in articulating the core values varies with the size, age, and geographic dispersion of the company, but in many situations we have recommended what we call a *Mars Group*. It works like this: Imagine that you've been asked to re-create the very best attributes of your organization on another planet but you have seats on the rocket ship for only five to seven people. Whom should you send? Most likely, you'll choose the people who have a gut-level understanding of your core values, the highest level of credibility with their peers, and the highest levels of competence. We'll often ask people brought together to work on core values to nominate a Mars Group of five to seven individuals (not necessarily all from the assembled group). Invariably, they end up selecting highly credible representatives who do a super job of articulating the core values precisely because they are exemplars of those values – a representative slice of the company's genetic code.

Even global organizations composed of people from widely diverse cultures can identify a set of shared core values. The secret is to work from the individual to the organization. People involved in articulating the core values need to answer several questions: What core values do you personally bring to your work? (These should be so fundamental that you would hold them regardless of whether or not they were rewarded.) What would you tell your children are the core values that you hold at work and that you hope *they* will hold when they become working adults? If you awoke tomorrow morning with enough money to retire for the rest of your life, would you continue to live those core values? Can you envision them being as valid for you 100 years from now as they are today? Would you want to hold those core values, even if at some point one or more of them became a competitive *dis*advantage? If you were to start a new organization tomorrow in a different line of work, what core values would you build into the new organization regardless of its industry? The last three questions are particularly important because they make the crucial distinction between enduring core values that should not change and practices and strategies that should be changing all the time.

Core purpose

Purpose, the second part of core ideology, is the organization's reason for being. An effective purpose reflects people's idealistic motivations for doing the company's work. It doesn't just describe the organization's output or target customers; it captures the soul of the organization (see Exhibit 11.3.2). Purpose, as illustrated by a speech David Packard gave to HP employees in 1960, gets at the deeper reasons for an organization's existence beyond just making money. Packard said,

EXHIBIT 11.3.2 CORE PURPOSE IS A COMPANY'S REASON FOR BEING

3M: To solve unsolved problems innovatively

Cargill: To improve the standard of living around the world

Fannie Mae: To strengthen the social fabric by continually democratizing home ownership

Hewlett-Packard: To make technical contributions for the advancement and welfare of humanity

Lost Arrow Corporation: To be a role model and a tool for social change

Pacific Theatres: To provide a place for people to flourish and to enhance the community

Mary Kay Cosmetics: To give unlimited opportunity to women

McKinsey & Company: To help leading corporations and governments be more successful

Merck: To preserve and improve human life

Nike: To experience the emotion of competition, winning, and crushing competitiors

Sony: To experience the joy of advancing and applying technology for the benefit of the public

Telecare Corporation: To help people with mental impairments realize their full potential

Wal-Mart: To give ordinary folk the chance to buy the same things as rich people

Walt Disney: To make people happy

I want to discuss why a company exists in the first place. In other words, why are we here? I think many people assume, wrongly, that a company exists simply to make money. While this is an important result of a company's existence, we have to go deeper and find the real reasons for our being. As we investigate this, we inevitably come to the conclusion that a group of people get together and exist as an institution that we call a company so they are able to accomplish something collectively that they could not accomplish separately – they make a contribution to society, a phrase which sounds trite but is fundamental . . . You can look around [in the general business world and] see people who are interested in money and nothing else, but the underlying drives come largely from a desire to do something else: to make a product, to give a service – generally to do something which is of value.

Purpose (which should last at least 100 years) should not be confused with specific goals or business strategies (which should change many times in 100 years). Whereas you might achieve a goal or complete a strategy, you cannot fulfil a purpose; it is like a guiding star on the horizon – forever pursued but never reached. Yet although purpose itself does not change, it does inspire change. The very fact that purpose can never be fully realized means that an organization can never stop stimulating change and progress.

In identifying purpose, some companies make the mistake of simply describing their current product

lines or customer segments. We do not consider the following statement to reflect an effective purpose: 'We exist to fulfil our government charter and participate in the secondary mortgage market by packaging mortgages into investment securities.' The statement is merely descriptive. A far more effective statement of purpose would be that expressed by the executives of the Federal National Mortgage Association, Fannie Mae: 'To strengthen the social fabric by continually democratizing home ownership.' The secondary mortgage market as we know it might not even exist in 100 years, but strengthening the social fabric by continually democratizing home ownership can be an enduring purpose, no matter how much the world changes. Guided and inspired by this purpose, Fannie Mae launched in the early 1990s a series of bold initiatives, including a programme to develop new systems for reducing mortgage underwriting costs by 40 per cent in five years; programmes to eliminate discrimination in the lending process (backed by $5 billion in underwriting experiments); and an audacious goal to provide, by the year 2000, $1 trillion targeted at 10 million families that had traditionally been shut out of home ownership – minorities, immigrants, and low-income groups.

Similarly, 3M defines its purpose not in terms of adhesives and abrasives but as the perpetual quest to solve unsolved problems innovatively – a purpose that is always leading 3M into new fields. McKinsey & Company's purpose is not to do management consulting but to help corporations and governments be more successful: in 100 years, it might involve methods other than consulting. Hewlett-Packard doesn't exist to make electronic test and measurement equipment but to make technical contributions that improve people's lives – a purpose that has led the company far afield from its origins in electronic instruments. Imagine if Walt Disney had conceived of his company's purpose as to make cartoons, rather than to make people happy; we probably wouldn't have Mickey Mouse, Disneyland, EPCOT Center, or the Anaheim Mighty Ducks Hockey Team.

One powerful method for getting at purpose is the *five whys*. Start with the descriptive statement 'We make X products' or 'We deliver X services', and then ask, 'Why is that important?' five times. After a few whys, you'll find that you're getting down to the fundamental purpose of the organization.

We used this method to deepen and enrich a discussion about purpose when we worked with a certain market-research company. The executive team first met for several hours and generated the following statement of purpose for their organization: To provide the best market-research data available. We then asked the following question: Why is it important to provide the best market-research data available? After some discussion, the executives answered in a way that reflected a deeper sense of their organization's purpose: To provide the best market research data available so that our customers will understand their markets better than they could otherwise. A further discussion let team members realize that their sense of self-worth came not just from helping customers understand their markets better but also from making a *contribution* to their customers' success. This introspection eventually led the company to identify its purpose as: To contribute to our customers' success by helping them understand their markets. With this purpose in mind, the company now frames its product decisions not with the question 'Will it sell?' but with the question 'Will it make a contribution to our customers' success?'

The five whys can help companies in any industry frame their work in a more meaningful way. An asphalt and gravel company might begin by saying, 'We make gravel and asphalt products'. After a few whys, it could conclude that making asphalt and gravel is important because the quality of the infrastructure plays a vital role in people's safety and experience; because driving on a pitted road is annoying and dangerous; because 747s cannot land safely on runways built with poor workmanship or inferior concrete; because buildings with substandard materials weaken with time and crumble in earthquakes. From such introspection may emerge this purpose: To make people's lives

better by improving the quality of man-made structures. With a sense of purpose very much along those lines, Granite Rock Company of Watsonville, California, won the Malcolm Baldrige National Quality Award – not an easy feat for a small rock quarry and asphalt company. And Granite Rock has gone on to be one of the most progressive and exciting companies we've encountered in *any* industry.

Notice that none of the core purposes fall into the category 'maximize shareholder wealth'. A primary role of core purpose is to guide and inspire. Maximizing shareholder wealth does not inspire people at all levels of an organization, and it provides precious little guidance. Maximizing shareholder wealth is the standard off-the-shelf purpose for those organizations that have not yet identified their true core purpose. It is a substitute – and a weak one at that.

When people in great organizations talk about their achievements, they say very little about earnings per share. Motorola people talk about impressive quality improvements and the effect of the products they create on the world. Hewlett-Packard people talk about their technical contributions to the marketplace. Nordstrom people talk about heroic customer service and remarkable individual performance by star salespeople. When a Boeing engineer talks about launching an exciting and revolutionary new aircraft, she does not say, 'I put my heart and soul into this project because it would add 37 cents to our earnings per share.'

One way to get at the purpose that lies beyond merely maximizing shareholder wealth is to play the 'Random Corporate Serial Killer' game. It works like this: Suppose you could sell the company to someone who would pay a price that everyone inside and outside the company agrees is more than fair (even with a very generous set of assumptions about the expected future cash flows of the company). Suppose further that this buyer would guarantee stable employment for all employees at the same pay scale after the purchase but with no guarantee that those jobs would be in the same industry. Finally, suppose the buyer plans to kill the company after the purchase – its products or services would be discontinued, its operations would be shut down, its brand names would be shelved forever, and so on. The company would utterly and completely cease to exist. Would you accept the offer? Why or why not? What would be lost if the company ceased to exist? Why is it important that the company continue to exist? We've found this exercise to be very powerful for helping hard-nosed, financially focused executives reflect on their organization's deeper reasons for being.

Another approach is to ask each member of the Mars Group, How could we frame the purpose of this organization so that if you woke up tomorrow morning with enough money in the bank to retire, you would nevertheless keep working here? What deeper sense of purpose would motivate you to continue to dedicate your precious creative energies to this company's efforts?

As they move into the twenty-first century, companies will need to draw on the full creative energy and talent of their people. But why should people give full measure? As Peter Drucker has pointed out, the best and most dedicated people are ultimately volunteers, for they have the opportunity to do something else with their lives. Confronted with an increasingly mobile society, cynicism about corporate life, and an expanding entrepreneurial segment of the economy, companies more than ever need to have a clear understanding of their purpose in order to make work meaningful and thereby attract, motivate, and retain outstanding people.

Discovering core ideology

You do not create or set core ideology. You *discover* core ideology. You do not deduce it by looking at the external environment. You understand it by looking inside. Ideology has to be authentic. You cannot fake it. Discovering core ideology is not an intellectual exercise. Do not ask, 'What core values should we hold?' Ask instead, 'What core values do we truly and passionately hold?' You should not confuse values that you think the organization ought to have – but does not – with authentic core values. To do so would create cynicism throughout the organization. ('Who're they trying to kid? We all know that isn't a core value around here!') Aspirations are more appropriate as part of your envisioned future or as part of your strategy, not as part of the core ideology. However, authentic core values that have weakened over time can be considered a legitimate part of the core ideology – as long as you acknowledge to the organization that you must work hard to revive them.

Also be clear that the role of core ideology is to guide and inspire, not to differentiate. Two companies can have the same core values or purpose. Many companies could have the purpose to make technical contributions, but few live it as passionately as Hewlett-Packard. Many companies could have the purpose to preserve and improve human life, but few hold it as deeply as Merck. Many companies could

have the core value of heroic customer service, but few create as intense a culture around that value as Nordstrom. Many companies could have the core value of innovation, but few create the powerful alignment mechanisms that stimulate the innovation we see at 3M. The authenticity, the discipline, and the consistency with which the ideology is lived – not the content of the ideology – differentiate visionary companies from the rest of the pack.

Core ideology needs to be meaningful and inspirational only to people inside the organization; it need not be exciting to outsiders. Why not? Because it is the people inside the organization who need to commit to the organizational ideology over the long term. Core ideology can also play a role in determining who *is* inside and who is not. A clear and well-articulated ideology attracts to the company people whose personal values are compatible with the company's core values; conversely, it repels those whose personal values are incompatible. You cannot impose new core values or purpose on people. Nor are core values and purpose things people can buy into. Executives often ask, 'How do we get people to share our core ideology?' You don't. You can't. Instead, find people who are predisposed to share your core values and purpose; attract and retain those people; and let those who do not share your core values go elsewhere. Indeed, the very process of articulating core ideology may cause some people to leave when they realize that they are not personally compatible with the organization's core. Welcome that outcome. It is certainly desirable to retain within the core ideology a diversity of people and viewpoints. People who share the same core values and purpose do not necessarily all think or look the same.

Don't confuse core ideology itself with core-ideology statements. A company can have a very strong core ideology without a formal statement. For example, Nike has not (to our knowledge) formally articulated a statement of its core purpose. Yet, according to our observations, Nike has a powerful core purpose that permeates the entire organization: to experience the emotion of competition, winning, and crushing competitors. Nike has a campus that seems more like a shrine to the competitive spirit than a corporate office complex. Giant photos of Nike heroes cover the walls, bronze plaques of Nike athletes hang along the Nike Walk of Fame, statues of Nike athletes stand alongside the running track that rings the campus, and buildings honour champions such as Olympic marathoner Joan Benoit, basketball superstar Michael Jordan, and tennis pro John McEnroe. Nike people who do not feel stimulated by the competitive spirit and the urge to be ferocious simply do not last long in the culture. Even the company's name reflects a sense of competition: Nike is the Greek goddess of victory. Thus, although Nike has not formally articulated its purpose, it clearly has a strong one.

Identifying core values and purpose is therefore not an exercise in wordsmithery. Indeed, an organization will generate a variety of statements over time to describe the core ideology. In Hewlett-Packard's archives, we found more than half a dozen distinct versions of the HP Way, drafted by David Packard between 1956 and 1972. All versions stated the same principles, but the words used varied depending on the era and the circumstances. Similarly, Sony's core ideology has been stated many different ways over the company's history. At its founding, Masaru Ibuka described two key elements of Sony's ideology: 'We shall welcome technical difficulties and focus on highly sophisticated technical products that have great usefulness for society regardless of the quantity involved; we shall place our main emphasis on ability, performance, and personal character so that each individual can show the best in ability and skill.' Four decades later, this same concept appeared in a statement of core ideology called Sony Pioneer Spirit: 'Sony is a pioneer and never intends to follow others. Through progress, Sony wants to serve the whole world. It shall be always a seeker of the unknown. . . . Sony has a principle of respecting and encouraging one's ability . . . and always tries to bring out the best in a person. This is the vital force of Sony.' Same core values, different words.

You should therefore focus on getting the content right – on capturing the essence of the core values and purpose. The point is not to create a perfect statement but to gain a deep understanding of your organization's core values and purpose, which can then be expressed in a multitude of ways. In fact, we often suggest that once the core has been identified, managers should generate their own statements of the core values and purpose to share with their groups.

Finally, don't confuse core ideology with the concept of core competence. Core competence is a strategic concept that defines your organization's capabilities – what you are particularly good at – whereas core ideology captures what you stand for and why you exist. Core competencies should be well aligned with a company's core ideology and are often rooted in it; but they are not the same thing. For example, Sony has a core competence of miniaturization – a strength that can be strategically applied to a wide array of products and markets. But it does not have a core *ideology* of miniaturization. Sony might not even have miniaturization as part of its strategy in 100 years, but to remain a great company, it will still have the same core values described in the Sony Pioneer Spirit and the same fundamental reason for being – namely, to advance technology for the benefit of the general public. In a visionary company like Sony, core competencies change over the decades, whereas core ideology does not.

Once you are clear about the core ideology, you should feel free to change absolutely *anything* that is not part of it. From then on, whenever someone says something should not change because 'it's part of our culture' or 'we've always done it that way' or any such excuse, mention this simple rule: If it's not core, it's up for change. The strong version of the rule is, *If it's not core, change it!* Articulating core ideology is just a starting point, however. You also must determine what type of progress you want to stimulate.

Envisioned future

The second primary component of the vision framework is *envisioned future.* It consists of two parts: a 10–30-year audacious goal plus vivid descriptions of what it will be like to achieve the goal. We recognize that the phrase *envisioned future* is somewhat paradoxical. On the one hand, it conveys concreteness – something visible, vivid, and real. On the other hand, it involves a time yet unrealized – with its dreams, hopes, and aspirations.

Vision-level BHAG

We found in our research that visionary companies often use bold missions – or what we prefer to call *BHAGs* (pronounced BEE-hags and shorthand for Big, Hairy, Audacious Goals) – as a powerful way to stimulate progress. All companies have goals. But there is a difference between merely having a goal and becoming committed to a huge, daunting challenge – such as climbing Mount Everest. A true BHAG is clear and compelling, serves as a unifying focal point of effort, and acts as a catalyst for team spirit. It has a clear finish line, so the organization can know when it has achieved the goal; people like to shoot for finish lines. A BHAG engages people – it reaches out and grabs them. It is tangible, energizing, highly focused. People get it right away; it takes little or no explanation. For example, NASA's 1960s moon mission didn't need a committee of wordsmiths to spend endless hours turning the goal into a verbose, impossible-to-remember mission statement. The goal itself was so easy to grasp – so compelling in its own right – that it could be said 100 different ways yet be easily understood by everyone. Most corporate statements we've seen do little to spur forward movement because they do not contain the powerful mechanism of a BHAG.

Although organizations may have many BHAGs at different levels operating at the same time, vision requires a special type of BHAG – a vision-level BHAG that applies to the entire organization and requires 10 to 30 years of effort to complete. Setting the BHAG that far into the future requires thinking beyond the current capabilities of the organization and the current environment. Indeed, inventing such a goal forces an executive team to be visionary, rather than just strategic or tactical. A BHAG should not be a sure bet – it will have perhaps only a 50% to 70% probability of success – but the organization must believe that it can reach the goal anyway. A BHAG should require extraordinary effort and perhaps a little luck. We have helped companies create a vision-level BHAG by advising them to think in terms of four broad categories: target BHAGs, common-enemy BHAGs, role-model BHAGs, and internal-transformation BHAGs (see Exhibit 11.3.3)

Vivid description

In addition to vision-level BHAGs, an envisioned future needs what we call *vivid description* – that is, a vibrant, engaging, and specific description of what it will be like to achieve the BHAG. Think of it as translating the vision from words into pictures, of creating an image that people can carry around in their heads. It is a question of painting a picture with your words. Picture painting is essential for making the 10–30-year BHAG tangible in people's minds.

For example, Henry Ford brought to life the goal of democratizing the automobile with this vivid description: 'I will build a motor car for the great multitude. . . . It will be so low in price that no man making a good salary will be unable to own one and enjoy with his family the blessing of hours of pleasure in God's great open spaces. . . . When I'm through, everybody will be able to afford one, and everyone will have one. The horse will have disappeared from our highways, the automobile will be taken for granted. . . . [and we will] give a large number of men employment at good wages.'

The components-support division of a computer-products company had a general manager who was able to describe vividly the goal of becoming one of the most sought-after divisions in the company: 'We will be respected and admired by our peers. . . . Our solutions will be actively sought by the end-product divisions, who will achieve significant product "hits" in the marketplace largely because of our technical contribution. . . . We will have pride in ourselves. . . . The best up-and-coming people in the company will seek to work in our division. . . . People will give unsolicited feedback that they love what they are doing. . . . [Our own] people will walk on the balls of their feet. . . . [They] will willingly work hard because they want to. . . . Both employees and customers will feel that our division has contributed to their life in a positive way.'

In the 1930s, Merck had the BHAG to transform itself from a chemical manufacturer into one of the preeminent drug-making companies in the world, with a research capability to rival any major university. In describing this envisioned future, George Merck said at the opening of Merck's research facility in 1933, 'We believe that research work carried on with patience and persistence will bring to industry and commerce new life; and we have faith that in this new laboratory, with the tools we have supplied, science will be advanced, knowledge increased, and human life win ever a greater freedom from suffering and disease. . . . We pledge our every aid that this enterprise shall merit the faith we have in it. Let your light so shine – that those who seek the Truth, that those who toil that this world may be a better place to live in, that those who hold aloft that torch of science and knowledge through these social and economic dark ages, shall take new courage and feel their hands supported.'

Passion, emotion, and conviction are essential parts of the vivid description. Some managers are uncomfortable expressing emotion about their dreams, but that's what motivates others. Churchill understood that when he described the BHAG facing Great Britain in 1940. He did not just say, 'Beat Hitler.' He said, 'Hitler knows he will have to break us on this island or lose the war. If we can stand up to him, all Europe may be free, and the life of the world may move forward into broad, sunlit uplands. But if we fail, the whole world, including the United States, including all we have known and cared for, will sink into the abyss of a new Dark Age, made more sinister and perhaps more protracted by the lights of perverted science. Let us therefore brace ourselves to our duties and so bear ourselves that if the British Empire and its Commonwealth last for a thousand years, men will still say, "This was their finest hour."'

EXHIBIT 11.3.3   BIG, HAIRY, AUDACIOUS GOALS AID LONG-TERM VISION

Target BHAGs can be quantitative or qualitative

- Become a $125 billion company by the year 2000 (Wal-Mart, 1990)

- Democratize the automobile (Ford Motor Company, early 1900s)

- Become the company most known for changing the worldwide poor-quality image of Japanese products (Sony, early 1950s)

- Become the most powerful, the most serviceable, the most far-reaching world financial institution that has ever been (City Bank, predecessor to Citicorp, 1915)

- Become the dominant player in commercial aircraft and bring the world into the jet age (Boeing, 1950)

Common-enemy BHAGs involve David-versus-Goliath thinking

- Knock off RJR as the number one tobacco company in the world (Philip Morris, 1950s)

- Crush Adidas (Nike, 1960s)

- Yamaha *wo tsubusu!* We will destroy Yamaha! (Honda, 1970s)

Role-model BHAGs suit up-and-coming organizations

- Become the Nike of the cycling industry (Giro Sport Design, 1986)

- Become as respected in 20 years as Hewlett-Packard is today (Watkins-Johnson, 1996)

- Become the Harvard of the West (Stanford University, 1940s)

Internal-transformation BHAGs suit large, established organizations

- Become number one or number two in every market we serve and revolutionize this company to have the strengths of a big company combined with the leanness and agility of a small company (General Electric Company, 1980s)

- Transform this company from a defence contractor into the best diversified high-technology company in the world (Rockwell, 1995)

- Transform this division from a poorly respected internal products supplier to one of the most respected, exciting, and sought-after divisions in the company (Components Support Division of a computer products company, 1989)

A few key points

Don't confuse core ideology and envisioned future. In particular, don't confuse core purpose and BHAGs. Managers often exchange one for the other, mixing the two together or failing to articulate both as distinct items. Core purpose – not some specific goal – is the reason why the organization exists. A BHAG is a clearly articulated goal. Core purpose can never be completed, whereas the BHAG is reachable in 10 to 30 years. Think of the core purpose as the star on the horizon to be chased forever; the BHAG is the mountain to be climbed. Once you have reached its summit, you move on to other mountains.

Identifying core ideology is a discovery process, but setting the envisioned future is a creative process. We find that executives often have a great deal of difficulty coming up with an exciting BHAG. They want to analyse their way into the future. We have found, therefore, that some executives make more progress by starting first with the vivid description and backing from there into the BHAG. This approach involves starting with questions such as, 'We're sitting here in 20 years; what would we love to see?' 'What should this company look like?' 'What should it feel like to employees?' 'What should it have achieved?' 'If someone writes an article for a major business magazine about this company in 20 years, what will it say?' One biotechnology company we worked with had trouble envisioning its future. Said one member of the executive team, 'Every time we come up with something for the entire company, it is just too generic to be exciting – something banal like "advance biotechnology worldwide".' Asked to paint a picture of the company in 20 years, the executives mentioned such things as 'on the cover of *Business Week* as a model success story . . . the *Fortune* most admired top-ten list . . . the best science and business graduates want to work here . . . people on airplanes rave about one of our products to seatmates . . . 20 consecutive years of profitable growth . . . an entrepreneurial culture that has spawned half a dozen new divisions from within . . . management gurus use us as an example of excellent management and progressive thinking,' and so on. From this, they were able to set the goal of becoming as well respected as Merck or as Johnson & Johnson in biotechnology.

It makes no sense to analyse whether an envisioned future is the right one. With a creation – and the task is creation of a future, not prediction – there can be no right answer. Did Beethoven create the right Ninth Symphony? Did Shakespeare create the right *Hamlet*? We can't answer these questions; they're nonsense. The envisioned future involves such essential questions as 'Does it get our juices flowing?' 'Do we find it stimulating?' 'Does it spur forward momentum?' 'Does it get people going?' The envisioned future should be so exciting in its own right that it would continue to keep the organization motivated even if the leaders who set the goal disappeared. City Bank, the predecessor of Citicorp, had the BHAG 'to become the most powerful, the most serviceable, the most far-reaching world financial institution that has ever been' – a goal that generated excitement through multiple generations until

it was achieved. Similarly, the NASA moon mission continued to galvanize people even though President John F. Kennedy (the leader associated with setting the goal) died years before its completion.

To create an effective envisioned future requires a certain level of unreasonable confidence and commitment. Keep in mind that a BHAG is not just a goal; it is a Big, Hairy, Audacious Goal. It's not reasonable for a small regional bank to set the goal of becoming 'the most powerful, the most serviceable, the most far-reaching world financial institution that has ever been', as City Bank did in 1915. It's not a tepid claim that 'we will democratize the automobile', as Henry Ford said. It was almost laughable for Philip Morris – as the sixth-place player with 9% market share in the 1950s – to take on the goal of defeating Goliath RJ Reynolds Tobacco Company and becoming number one. It was hardly modest for Sony, as a small, cash-strapped venture, to proclaim the goal of changing the poor-quality image of Japanese products around the world (see Exhibit 11.3.4). Of course, it's not only the audacity of the goal but also the level of commitment to the goal that counts. Boeing didn't just envision a future dominated by its commercial jets; it bet the company on the 707 and, later, on the 747. Nike's people didn't just talk about the idea of crushing Adidas; they went on a crusade to fulfil the dream. Indeed, the envisioned future should produce a bit of the

---

EXHIBIT 11.3.4 PUTTING IT ALL TOGETHER

SONY IN THE 1950S

Core ideology

Core values

- Elevation of the Japanese culture and national status
- Being a pioneer – not following others; doing the impossible
- Encouraging individual ability and creativity

Purpose

To experience the sheer joy of innovation and the application of technology for the benefit and pleasure of the general public.

Envisioned Future

BHAG

Become the company most known for changing the worldwide poor-quality image of Japanese products.

Vivid description

We will create products that become pervasive around the world . . . We will be the first Japanese company to go into the U.S. market and distribute directly . . . We will succeed with innovations that U.S. companies have failed at – such as the transistor radio . . . Fifty years from now, our brand name will be as well known as any in the world . . . and will signify innovation and quality that rival the most innovative companies anywhere . . . 'Made in Japan' will mean something fine, not something shoddy.

'gulp factor': when it dawns on people what it will take to achieve the goal, there should be an almost audible gulp.

But what about failure to realize the envisioned future? In our research, we found that the visionary companies displayed a remarkable ability to achieve even their most audacious goals. Ford did democratize the automobile; Citicorp did become the most far-reaching bank in the world; Philip Morris did rise from sixth to first and beat RJ Reynolds worldwide; Boeing did become the dominant commercial aircraft company; and it looks like Wal-Mart will achieve its $125 billion goal, even without Sam Walton. In contrast, the comparison companies in our research frequently did not achieve their BHAGs, if they set them at all. The difference does not lie in setting easier goals: the visionary companies tended to have even more audacious ambitions. The difference does not lie in charismatic, visionary leadership: the visionary companies often achieved their BHAGs without such larger-than-life leaders at the helm. Nor does the difference lie in better strategy: the visionary companies often realized their goals more by an organic process of 'let's try a lot of stuff and keep what works' than by well-laid strategic plans. Rather, their success lies in building the strength of their organization as their primary way of creating the future.

Why did Merck become the preeminent drug-maker in the world? Because Merck's architects built the best pharmaceutical research and development organization in the world. Why did Boeing become the dominant commercial aircraft company in the world? Because of its superb engineering and marketing organization, which had the ability to make projects like the 747 a reality. When asked to name the most important decisions that have contributed to the growth and success of Hewlett-Packard, David Packard answered entirely in terms of decisions to build the strength of the organization and its people.

Finally, in thinking about the envisioned future, beware of the We've Arrived Syndrome – a complacent lethargy that arises once an organization has achieved one BHAG and fails to replace it with another. NASA suffered from that syndrome after the successful moon landings. After you've landed on the moon, what do you do for an encore? Ford suffered from the syndrome when, after it succeeded in democratizing the automobile, it failed to set a new goal of equal significance and gave General Motors the opportunity to jump ahead in the 1930s. Apple Computer suffered from the syndrome after achieving the goal of creating a computer that nontechies could use. Start-up companies frequently suffer from the We've Arrived Syndrome after going public or after reaching a stage in which survival no longer seems in question. An envisioned future helps an organization only as long as it hasn't yet been achieved. In our work with companies, we frequently hear executives say, 'It's just not as exciting around here as it used to be; we seem to have lost our momentum.' Usually, that kind of remark signals that the organization has climbed one mountain and not yet picked a new one to climb.

Many executives thrash about with mission statements and vision statements. Unfortunately, most of those statements turn out to be a muddled stew of values, goals, purposes, philosophies, beliefs, aspirations, norms, strategies, practices, and descriptions. They are usually a boring, confusing, structurally unsound stream of words that evoke the response 'True, but who cares?' Even more problematic, seldom do these statements have a direct link to the fundamental dynamic of visionary companies: preserve the core and stimulate progress. That dynamic, not vision or mission statements, is the primary engine of enduring companies. Vision simply provides the context for bringing this dynamic to life. Building a visionary company requires 1 per cent vision and 99 per cent alignment. When you have superb alignment, a visitor could drop in from outer space and infer your vision from the operations and activities of the company without ever reading it on paper or meeting a single senior executive.

Creating alignment may be your most important work. But the first step will always be to recast your vision or mission into an effective context for building a visionary company. If you do it right, you shouldn't have to do it again for at least a decade.

Whose company is it? The concept of the corporation in Japan and the West

By Masaru Yoshimori[1]

Available evidence seems to suggest that in terms of corporate governance countries may be divided into three groups: with monistic, dualistic and pluralistic concepts of the corporation. The monistic outlook is shareholder-oriented and looks at the firm as the private property of its owners. This concept is prevalent in the United States and the UK. The dualistic concept also puts a premium on the shareholder interest, but the interests of employees are taken into account as well. This is an adapted form of the monistic concept and is widely shared in Germany and to a lesser degree in France. The view that the firm is a social institution where people develop themselves freely ranked first among six alternative definitions, according to Albach's survey of leading German companies in 1975, though it slipped to the third rank in 1991 (Albach, 1994).

The pluralistic approach assumes that the firm belongs to all the stakeholders, with the employees' interests taking precedence. This is the concept specific to Japan which manifests itself in the form of long-term employment for employees and long-term trading relations among various other stakeholders (the main bank, major suppliers, subcontractors, distributors), loosely called *Keiretsu*.

This three-part categorization is supported by the results of a mail survey undertaken by the author with managers and executives in the five countries under review (see Figure 11.4.1). The shareholder-centred Anglo-American outlook starkly contrasts with the employee-centred Japanese perspective, with Germany and France in between but significantly more oriented towards 'shareholder value' than Japan. The findings on Japan are consistent with the results of other studies. For instance, a survey carried out in 1990 by *Nippon Keizai Shimbun* on 104 employees of large corporations showed a majority of 80 per cent replying that the company belongs to its employees; 70 per cent believed that the company exists for the benefit of society as a whole. The concept that the firm is the property of shareholders ranked third with 67 per cent.

Clearly Japan puts the interest of employees before that of shareholders. Her current unemployment rate of around 3 per cent even in a prolonged recession is a testimony to this. Though increasingly challenged, job security is still defended as the mainstream ideology, as two major spokesmen of the Japanese business community recently proclaimed: Fumio Sato, Chairman of Toshiba Corporation, said that to discharge employees is 'the most serious sin' a president can commit and Takeshi Moroi, Chairman of Chichibu Cement, said that job security is the 'responsibility of the corporation'.

Key implications of the different approaches

The central characteristic of the Japanese pluralistic concept is the alignment of the company's goals and interests with those of the stakeholders. This leads to a higher degree of cohesion between the firm's stakeholders, i.e. shareholders, management, employees, the main bank, major suppliers and distributors. They pull together toward a common purpose: the company's survival and prosperity. They share the implicit consensus that their respective interests are realized and promoted through their long-term commitment and cooperation with the firm. Maximization of general benefit, or the firm's 'wealth maximizing capacity', as Drucker (1991) puts it, and not self-interest, is the name of the game. Michael Porter characterizes such relationship as 'a greater community of interest' and categorizes it as 'quasi integration', that is an intermediate form between long-term contracts and full ownership. According to Porter (1980), this type of interdependent relationship among the stakeholders combines some of the benefits of vertical integration without incurring the corresponding costs. Suzuki and Wright (1985) argue that a Japanese company, though legally independent, should be regarded rather as a division of a big conglomerate. This 'network

[1]Source: This article was adapted from *Long Range Planning*, Vol. 28, No. 4, M. Yoshimori, 'Whose Company Is It? The Concept of the Corporation in Japan and the West', pp. 33–45, © 1995. With permission from Elsevier.

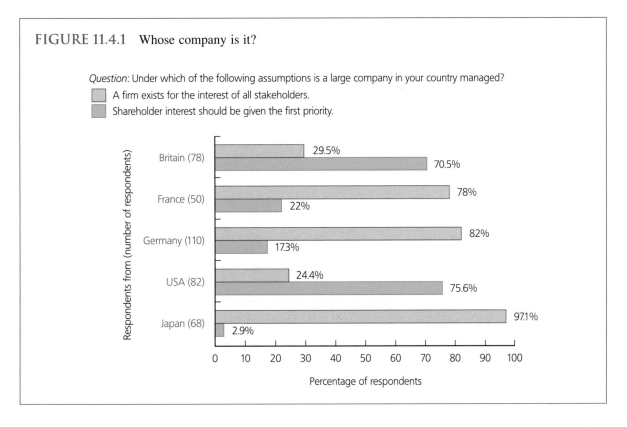

FIGURE 11.4.1   Whose company is it?

Question: Under which of the following assumptions is a large company in your country managed?

A firm exists for the interest of all stakeholders.

Shareholder interest should be given the first priority.

structure' provides a system of collective security in time of crisis, as will be illustrated later.

Within the Japanese concept of the corporation, the company president is the representative of both the employees and the other stakeholders. The source of legitimacy of the president is derived primarily from his role as the defender of job security for the employees. This is understandable given the fact that the employees constitute the most important power base for the president, as Figure 11.4.2 indicates. His secondary role is as the arbitrator for the divergent interests of the stakeholders so that a long-term balance of interests is achieved.

In contrast, under the Anglo-American 'monistic' concept where shareholders' interests are given primacy, the CEO represents the interests of the shareholders as their 'ally', according to Abegglen and Stalk, though their respective objectives may diverge at times. Understandably other stakeholders also seek to maximize their respective interests. In this 'zero-sum game', the firm ends up as a mere vehicle by which to satisfy the self-centred needs of the different

stakeholders. The company then becomes an organization 'external' to the interests of its stakeholders, as Abegglen and Stalk (1985) point out, with no one caring about the long-term destiny of the firm itself. This makes a turnaround process more difficult, once a firm is confronted with financial difficulties.

The relationship between the firm and its main bank

In the Japanese *Keiretsu* the main bank assumes a pivotal role owing to its monitoring and disciplinary function based on its financial and equity claims. The main bank is not to be confused with the Zaibatsu[2] institution, as any bank, whether *Zaibatsu* or non-*Zaibatsu* in origin, can assume this role. The firm's main bank relations are characterized as follows:

- The main bank is typically the largest or one of the largest providers of loans and makes available on a preferential basis long-term and comprehensive financial services covering deposits, discounting of

---

[2] *Zaibatsu* is a prewar conglomerate under family ownership and control. Mitsubishi, Mitsui, Sumitomo, and other *Zaibatsu* controlled a majority of Japan's large industrial, financial and service firms before World War II. They were broken up by the Occupation forces after the war. Today the firms of a former *Zaibatsu* form a loose federation based on their common tradition and business relationship.

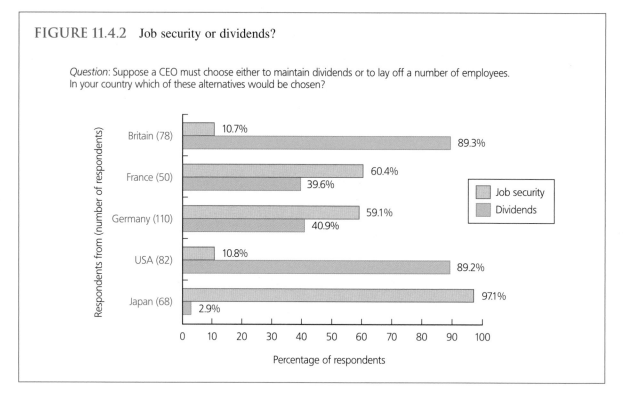

FIGURE 11.4.2   Job security or dividends?

Question: Suppose a CEO must choose either to maintain dividends or to lay off a number of employees. In your country which of these alternatives would be chosen?

notes, foreign exchange transactions, advice in financial planning, agents on other loans, etc.

■ Cross-shareholdings and interlocking directorships result in information sharing through official and personal contacts.

■ The rescue of a client firm is attempted when it is targeted in a hostile take-over bid. Thus none of the hostile take-over attempts by a well-known raider, Minebea, were successful. An attempt to acquire Janome, a sewing machine maker, was thwarted by its main bank, Saitama Bank, another raid on Sankyo Seiki was frustrated by its main bank, Mitsubishi Bank who later arranged for an equity participation by Nippon Steel.

■ Direct intervention in the turnaround process occurs in case the borrower company faces serious financial distress.

This main bank support is the most important motivation for Japanese firms to have a main bank. Typically the bailout measures range from the provision of emergency finance at an early stage in the crisis to, if the situation becomes more serious, the reduction of or exemption from interest payments, the engineering of a financial reorganization, the bank sending its own executives to supervise the reorganization, and finally the replacement of ineffectual management, the

reorganization of the assets and an arrangement for an alliance or merger with another firm. The intervention by the main bank may have effects similar to an external take-over.

A recent mail survey of 305 listed companies excluding financial corporations suggests that 70 per cent of them believe that their main bank would provide them with support in case of a crisis. The results of another poll of 354 corporations of Nikkeiren (The Japanese Federation of Employers' Associations) published in August 1994, indicated that 81.6 percent are in favour of maintaining the main bank system.

A Japan–US comparison of stakeholder relations

The relations among stakeholders in Japan, in particular the firm–main bank relations, may be better understood when a firm faces a crisis. The turnaround processes of Toyo Kogyo, manufacturer of Mazda passenger cars, and of Chrysler are contrasted.

Toyo Kogyo

In 1974, Toyo Kogyo was confronted with a financial crisis due to its large stockpile of unsold cars. Mazda

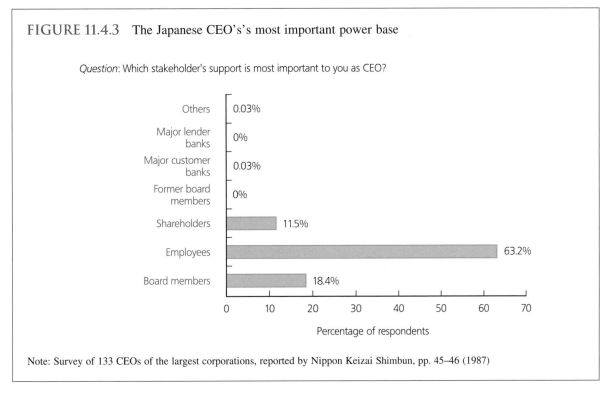

FIGURE 11.4.3   The Japanese CEO's's most important power base

Question: Which stakeholder's support is most important to you as CEO?

Note: Survey of 133 CEOs of the largest corporations, reported by Nippon Keizai Shimbun, pp. 45–46 (1987)

cars powered by Wankel rotary engines were less fuel-efficient, a serious disadvantage after the first oil crisis of 1973. Sumitomo Bank, the main bank, played a vital role in the bailout operations.

- Sumitomo Bank made a public assurance to stand by the distressed company, and a commitment to carry any new loans.
- Sumitomo Bank sent a team of seven directors to control and implement the reorganization process.
- Sumitomo Bank replaced the president with a new, more competent successor.
- Sumitomo Bank co-ordinated negotiations with the other lenders to establish a financial package.
- Sumitomo group companies switched their car purchases to Mazda and bought 8000 vehicles over six years.
- No lay-off of employees but factory operators joined the sales force.
- The suppliers and subcontractors agreed to extend payment terms from 189 to 210 days, resulting in estimated savings in interest payments of several billion yen.
- They also agreed to price reductions of 14 per cent over two and a half years. Joint cost reduction programmes were also implemented, with cost reductions of ¥123 billion over 4 years.

- The employees accepted rescheduling of bonus payments, contributing ¥4 billion in increased annual cash flow. They also agreed to restraints in wage and bonus increases.

Chrysler

In the turnaround process at Chrysler, the stakeholders – the banks, the union, and the dealers – distrusted each other, were afraid of being stuck with an unfair burden and shunned responsibility for saving the firm. Its lead bank, Manufacturers Hanover Trust, did not or could not make an assurance to bail Chrysler out, although the bank's chairman had been on the Chrysler board for years. The chairman declared that he would approve no more unguaranteed loans to Chrysler because of its fiduciary responsibility to its shareholders and depositors. Lack of solidarity of the lenders and other stakeholders made the turnaround process dependent on government guarantees. As Iacocca sarcastically wrote, 'it took longer to get $655 million in concessions from the four hundred lending institutions than it did to get the loan guarantees of $1.5 billion passed by the entire US Congress.' For him, 'the congressional hearings were as easy as changing a flat tyre on a spring day, compared to dealing with the banks'. Such financial concerns occupied top management for most of one year.

- Manufacturers Hanover Trust arranged for an agreement on a $455 million revolving credit with 80 American banks.
- Manufacturers Hanover Trust's chairman pleaded in Congress for a Federal loan guarantee for Chrysler.
- Manufacturers Hanover Trust urged its colleagues to accept Chrysler's packages of concessions.
- The labour union agreed to a wage restraint and curtailment of paid days off.
- Suppliers agreed to price reductions.

Legal restrictions on banks in the United States

Contrary to Japan and Germany, the United States traditionally put a premium on investor protection by insisting on complete and accurate disclosure of company information, portfolio diversification and on a sharp line of demarcation between investor and manager roles. Thus the Glass–Steagall Act, the Bank Holding Company Act of 1956, the Investment Company Act of 1940, the ERISA Act of 1974 and finally the rules against insider trading all combine to prohibit or inhibit investing funds of banks and pension plans in the stock of any single corporation, and participation in the management of the portfolio and borrower companies. This legal framework coupled with banks' preference for liquidity over investment has made the US financial market the most transparent, fair, efficient, liquid and low-cost in the world. The downside is fragmented equity holding, and arm's length or even antagonistic relations between shareholders and management.

The roles of the German 'Hausbank'

In Germany where the Hausbank has a similar role to the Japanese main bank, many firms regard it as a kind of 'insurance, bearing appropriate premiums in good times and offering corresponding protection when things go less well', according to Schneider-Linné, a member of the Management Board of Deutsche Bank. German main banks do take initiatives to reorganize their client firms in financial distress. Their part in rescuing companies, however, seems to be more limited in scope and commitment than that of Japanese main banks. The most significant difference is that the German main bank does not get directly involved in the management of the distressed firm and that the rescue concept itself is usually left to management consultancy firms. The German bank usually confines itself to rescheduling interest and principal payments or reducing interest charges and debts, giving advice to management and bringing in suitable new management.

The flaws in the Japanese concept of the corporation

Needless to say, Japan's close-knit, inward-looking concept of the corporation has its downsides. The most serious one is inefficient monitoring of top management. Indeed, there has been practically no control exercised over top management except through the product market. Through cross-shareholdings, cross-directorships and long-term business relations, Japanese managers have isolated themselves from take-over threats and shareholder pressures and thus have been able to pursue expansionist strategies throughout the post-war period, particularly during the high-growth period up until the mid-1970s. Certainly their growth-oriented strategies have been beneficial to companies, as many Japanese firms rose to dominant positions in the international market. In the process managers have not generally sought to maximize their personal income as in some other countries. The remuneration level of Japanese top executives is much lower than international levels.

But the potential risk of ineffective monitoring of top management was inherent in the Japanese governance system, as it is also in Germany. This flaw became apparent in the second half of the 1980s in horrendous wastes of capital through reckless and unrelated diversifications and investments, and illegal or unethical behaviour of many large firms. We now examine major dysfunctions of the Japanese monitoring system.

Ritualized general meeting of shareholders

The Japanese general meeting of shareholders is without doubt the least effective among the countries under review as a monitor over management. It has degenerated into a mere formality, as nearly everything is decided between the management and the major shareholders before the meeting takes place.

A mail survey carried out in June 1993 by the Japan Association of Statutory Auditors on 1106 public corporations revealed that nearly 80 per cent of their general meetings of shareholders ended in less than half an hour including recess time. Less than three per cent last for more than an hour. At the meeting not a single question was posed by shareholders in 87 per cent of the companies studied, not to speak of shareholder proposals which were not made at all in 98 per cent of the companies.

Limited monitoring power of the chairman of the board

Unlike in Anglo-American and French companies, board chairmanship and presidency of Japanese corporations are seldom assumed concurrently by the same person. At first sight, therefore, the supervisory function of the chairman and the executive function of the president seem to be clearly separated. Theoretically the chairman is expected to exercise control over the president. But this is not the case, because the Japanese board chairmanship is usually an honorary, symbolic or advisory position, the last step on the ladder before retirement from the company after having been president for several years. The chairman rarely interferes with the day-to-day managerial activities of the president, though his advice may be occasionally sought on major strategic decisions or on the appointment of key managerial positions. He spends most of his time representing the firm at external functions and activities, such as meetings of trade and economic associations, government commissions, etc. This 'half-retired' position of the chairman of the board is well illustrated by the fact that in 96 per cent of the firms the president, not the chairman, presides over the general meeting of shareholders.

Board members are appointed by the president

The fundamental cause of the board's dysfunction is that in most large firms nearly all of the board members are appointed by the president and naturally pledge their allegiance to him. In addition there are no or very few outside directors. If any, they are typically representatives from affiliated companies such as suppliers, subcontractors, etc. with little influence on the president. There is no distinction, therefore, between directors and officers. The board members are supposed to monitor the president who is their immediate superior, with obvious adverse consequences.

Boards are too large

The average board in Japanese companies is larger than in any of the other industrialized nations

examined here. Sakura Bank, second largest bank in revenue in 1993, is the champion with 62 board members. The average board size for the top three construction firms is about 52, for the top three trading companies close to 50, and for the three largest automobile and banking companies around 43.

This inflation of board sizes is due to the fact that board membership is often a reward for long and faithful service or major contributions to the company. The title of board member is useful to obtain business from major customers. In short, the Japanese board of directors has been transformed into a motivating and marketing tool. With such a large board with most directors engaged in day-to-day line activities, it is practically impossible to discuss any matter of importance in detail, let alone advise and sanction the president.

Ineffective statutory auditors

Large listed corporations are legally subject to two monitoring mechanisms: statutory auditors and independent certified public accountants. Neither is functioning properly. The primary auditing function of statutory auditors is to prevent any decisions by the directors to be taken or implemented which are judged to be in violation of laws or articles of incorporation, or otherwise detrimental to the company. Statutory auditors thus perform both accounting and operating audits to protect the interests of the company and the stakeholders by forestalling any adverse decisions and actions before it is too late. On paper they are given powerful authority, including the right to suspend illegal actions by a board member. But actual use of this power is unheard of. The root cause of the lack of monitoring by the statutory auditors is that they are selected by the president whom they are supposed to monitor.

A study conducted by Kobe University reveals that 57 per cent of statutory auditors are selected by the president and 33 per cent by directors or the executive committee and endorsed by the president. This shows that 90 per cent of the statutory auditors are indeed chosen by the president for perfunctory approval at the shareholders' meeting.

Flawed corporate governance in the West

Nor do the monitoring capabilities of Western boards function perfectly due firstly to the CEO assuming the board chairmanship (except in Germany where this is legally prohibited), secondly due to the psychological and even economic dependence of outside (non-executive) directors on the CEO/chairman, and lastly due to multiple directorships.

CEO/chairman duality – USA, UK, and France

These three countries share the same problem as expressed by the chairman of Delta Metal: 'The problem with British companies is that the chairman marks his own papers.' In the United States, 75 per cent of large manufacturing companies are run by the CEO-chairman, according to a survey by Rechner and Dalton (1989). CEO duality is also prevalent in the UK where in 60 per cent of large firms including financial corporations the chairman is also the CEO, according to a Korn Ferry International survey. In France firms can opt either for the conventional single board or the two-tier board system inspired by the German model. An overwhelming majority of large firms have the traditional single board where in most cases the chairman is also the CEO, as the title Président Directeur-Général indicates.

In Germany the separation between the supervisory board and the management board is legally assured as no member of the one board is allowed to be a member of the other at the same time. Theoretically, the German system precludes the power concentration on the CEO-chairman as seen in other countries, thus assuring independent monitoring by the chairman of the supervisory board over the management board. But the reality does not altogether reflect the intention of the legislation. According to an empirical study by Gerum (1991) on 62 large firms, this monitoring mechanism functions effectively only in firms whose supervisory board is dominated by one or more block-vote holders. The study shows that in a majority of 64 per cent of the sample firms the management board influences the supervisory board. Only in 13 per cent of firms does the supervisory board discharge its oversight functions over the management board. In the remaining 23 per cent of firms, the supervisory board is strongly involved in the decision making of the management board, a power concentration similar to the Anglo-American, French and Japanese situations. The researcher concludes that this represents 'pathological traits' in the light of the objectives sought by the law (Gerum, 1991).

Lack of neutrality of outside directors – USA and Europe

In the United States the board chairman (who is often also the CEO as mentioned already) recommends candidates for outside directors in 81 per cent of the 600 firms surveyed by Korn Ferry International. In the UK 80 per cent of the non-executive (outside) directors are selected from among the 'old-boy network', reducing their monitoring potential, as reported by Sir Adrian Cadbury. A similar situation is observed in France where new candidates for board membership are recommended by the CEO-chairman in 93.5 per cent of the firms controlled by owner-managers, and in 92 per cent of firms under managerial control, according to a study by Charreaux and Pitol-Belin (1990). In Germany, no hard data are available, but the preceding findings of Gerum on the dominance of the management board over the supervisory board lead us to infer that in a majority of large firms it is the managers on the management board that effectively determine who will be the members of the supervisory board.

Multiple directorships – USA and Europe

This is a phenomenon that does not exist in Japan. All the Western countries reviewed here share this convention. In the United States 72 per cent of the CEOs of the largest 50 corporations serve on the board of other firms and 50 per cent of them have more than six outside directorships, according to Bassiry and Denkmejian (1990). In Germany the maximum number of board memberships is set at 10 without counting directorships in subsidiary companies. Bleicher's study of directors (1987) shows that 36 per cent of his sample assume directorship in more than three corporations. Whenever there is spectacular corporate mismanagement, further reduction in the maximum number of directorships is urged, often to five. In the UK 58 per cent of directors assume non-executive directorship positions in other companies and 81 per cent of them hold two to four directorships (Nash, 1990). In France the legal limit is eight directorships plus five at subsidiary firms. Of 13 000 directors, 47 per cent have one to 13 outside director positions, two per cent have 14 to 50 positions, according to a survey by Bertolus and Morin (1987).

The question is to what extent they can be counted on to be an effective monitor and advisor. They surely have enough problems in managing their own company. They do not have in-depth knowledge or information on the business and internal problems of the other companies where they serve as outside directors.

Which system will win out?

The inevitable and tempting question which follows from this kind of international comparison is which system has superiority, if any at all, over the other in the long run in the light of two fundamental criteria: efficiency and equity.

As for efficiency we have limited evidence but one of the first empirical studies revealing a positive correlation between efficiency and the pluralistic concept of the corporation was offered by Kotter and Heskett (1992). They report that firms with cultures that emphasized the importance of all the stakeholders (customers, stockholders, and employees) outperformed by a huge margin firms that did not (see Table 11.4.1). If sufficient similar evidence is accumulated, we may conclude that the pluralistic concept does enhance a firm's efficiency.

The pluralistic concept seems to be more conducive to an equitable distribution of the firm's income, and fairer sharing of risk and power among the stakeholders. This will increase organizational cohesion and survivability, as we have seen in the comparative case studies. Under the monistic concept of the corporation, employees tend to incur a disproportionately higher risk, as their job security is jeopardized in favour of shareholder/manager interests. They are usually the first to bear the brunt of poor decision-making by top management, even if they are not responsible for it. This makes it difficult to expect a high commitment from them, under normal conditions or in crisis situations.

Applicability of the pluralistic concept

The pluralistic concept of the corporation may find wider applicability in countries outside Japan and may be a more viable and universal way for the modern corporation to promote efficiency and equity. It is not an ideology unique to Japan. An almost identical concept of the corporation was put forward in 1917 in Germany by Walther Rathenau and in the United States by Adolf Berle/Gardiner Means in 1932, and by Ralph Cordiner in the 1950s.

Walther Rathenau, who was to become Foreign Minister later, succeeded his father as the CEO of the electric engineering firm AEG. In an influential article in 1917 he asserted that 'a big business is not only a product of private interests but it is, individually and collectively, a part of the national economy and of the whole community' (Rathenau, 1923). This thesis is believed to have been instrumental in the later development of the concept of 'the firm itself' *(Unternehmen an sich)*, which is close to the pluralistic approach. It paved the way for a dilution of shareholder rights, the protection of management positions, the post-World War II co-determination, and the justification of 'hidden reserves' and shares with multiple votes.

Most probably influenced by Rathenau (quoted twice in their seminal work), Berle and Means (1932) conclude their book with exactly the same proposition. In the last chapter titled 'The New Concept of the Corporation', they suggest:

> *neither the claims of ownership nor those of control can stand against the paramount interests of the community. . . . The passive property right (i.e. diffused ownership) . . . must yield before the largest interests of the society. It is conceivable indeed it seems almost essential if the corporate system is to survive that the 'control' of the great corporation should develop into a purely neutral technocracy, balancing a variety of claims by various groups in the*

TABLE 11.4.1   The pluralistic concept may bring better performance – a US study

11-year growth	Firms emphasizing value to customers, shareholders & employees (%)	Other firms
Revenue	682	166
Workforces	282	36
Stock prices	901	74
Income	756	1

Study carried out between August 1987 and January 1991 with 202 US firms.
Based on: John P. Kotter and James L. Heskett, Corporate Culture and Performance, p. 11 (1992).

community and assigning to each a portion of the income stream on the basis of the public policy rather than private cupidity.

A similar ideology was espoused by Ralph Cordiner, CEO of General Electric in the 1950s who advocated that top management, as a trustee, was responsible for managing the company 'in the best interest of shareholder, customers, employees, suppliers, and plant community cities'. This concept of the corporation did not last, however, primarily because of the rise of the hostile take-over in the late 1970s, according to Peter Drucker.

Emerging convergence

The concept of the corporation is firmly rooted in the historic, economic, political and even socio-cultural traditions of the nation. Each approach has its own positive and adverse sides. It would be improbable nor would it be necessary, therefore, that any one concept should drive out another at least in the foreseeable future. Through the cross-fertilization process, nations will be correcting the flaws in their systems, while retaining the core norms. In the process different concepts of the corporation may slowly converge, but certainly not totally. Some signs of such partial convergence are already discernible.

Japan

Japan and Germany are edging towards the Anglo-American model for increased openness and transparency, emphasis of shareholder interest and shorttermism. In Japan the traditional emphasis on job security is being eroded and the process seems to be irreversible in the long run for various reasons: firms' tendency to place merit before seniority, perspectives of low growth economy, the changing industrial structure, competitive pressures from the rapidly developing Asian countries, the increasingly detached attitude of young employees to their company, and so on.

Yotaro Kobayashi, Chairman of Fuji Xerox, for instance, made an almost unprecedented declaration for a Japanese executive to the effect that Japanese management giving top priority to employees was no longer tenable. Several companies recently announced their target return on equity to show their emphasis on shareholder wealth. Mitsubishi Corporation has declared that it will raise ROE from currently 0.6 per cent to eight per cent by the year 2000. Other listed corporations such as Marubeni, Omron, Daikin, etc. are following suit.

The amended Commercial Code came into force in October 1993, albeit under the usual (salutary)

pressure from the United States. Every large company is now required to increase the minimum number of statutory auditors from two to three. The newly introduced stockholders' representative action makes it easier for shareholders to bring lawsuits against company directors as the court fee has been fixed at a flat rate of only ¥8200 per case, regardless of the size of the claim. The number of shareholders eligible for access to confidential financial documents has been expanded to those with at least three per cent ownership, down from the former 10 per cent. This revision may be a small step forward but it is still progress.

USA

In the United States, conversely, the traditional restrictions on concentration of funds in a single investment and of board representation at portfolio companies are breaking down. Anti-take-over regulations have been introduced in a number of States, so that the interests of the company, i.e. all stakeholders and particularly employees, are taken into account. Employees are regarded as a major stakeholder and are involved in small group activities and share ownership. Long-term business relations are being introduced notably in the automobile industry between subcontractors and assemblers.

Germany

In Germany legislation against insider trading is finally being passed. The US style audit committee is advocated by senior executives and by scholars as one of the effective remedies to ensure the proper monitoring of the supervisory board. Shareholder activism by Anglo-American institutional shareholders as well as domestic individual shareholders is increasing. In an unprecedented move the CEO and CFO of Metallgesellschaft were simply fired for their responsibility in the alleged mismanagement of oil futures business. Increased reliance on the New York capital markets and the future location of the EU's central bank in Frankfurt am Main will certainly accelerate the Anglo-Americanization process. Disclosure by Daimler-Benz of its hidden assets to conform to the SEC regulations for listing on the New York Stock Exchange is symbolic.

Conclusion

The business organization is one of the few social institutions where the deficit of democracy is pronounced, compared with the national governance system. Lack of consensus as to whose interest the company should be promoting, and insufficient checks and balances among various corporate governance mechanisms are some of the evidence. As Professor Rappaport (1990) of the Northwestern University stresses, corporate governance is 'the last frontier of reform' of the public corporation. This reform is a daunting challenge, but it will determine the economic fate of any industrialized nation in the next century.

FURTHER READING

Readers interested in delving deeper into the topic of organizational purpose have a richness of sources from which to choose. A good introductory work is the textbook *International Corporate Governance* by Robert Tricker, which also contains many classic readings and a large number of interesting cases. One of the excellent readings reprinted in Tricker's book is Henry Mintzberg's article 'Who Should Control the Corporation?', which provides a stimulating insight into the basic questions surrounding the topic of organizational purpose. Another good overview of the issues and literature in the area of corporate governance is presented in the book *Strategic Leadership: Top Executives and Their Effects on Organizations* by Sydney Finkelstein and Donald Hambrick.

Other worthwhile follow-up readings on the topic of corporate governance include the book by Ada Demb and Friedrich Neubauer, *The Corporate Board: Confronting the Paradoxes*, and an excellent comparison of five national governance systems given in the book *Keeping Good Company*, by Jonathan Charkham. Recent edited volumes well worth reading are *Capital Markets and Corporate Governance*, by Nicolas Dimsdale and Martha Prevezer, and *Corporate Governance: Economic, Management and Financial Issues*, by Kevin Keasey, Steve Thompson and Mike Wright.

For further reading on the topic of shareholder value, Alfred Rappaport's book *Creating Shareholder Value* is the obvious place to start. A good follow-up reading is Michael Jensen's article 'Corporate Control and the Politics of Finance'. For a very fundamental point of view, Milton Friedman's classic article 'The Social Responsibility of Business is to Increase Its Profits' is also highly recommended. For a stinging attack on the stakeholder concept, readers are directed to 'The Defects of Stakeholder Theory', by Elaine Sternberg.

For a more positive view of stakeholder theory, Edward Freeman's *Strategic Management: A Stakeholder Approach* is still the book at which to begin. Only recently has stakeholder theory really attracted significant academic attention. Excellent works in this new crop include 'Instrumental Stakeholder Theory: A Synthesis of Ethics and Economics', by Thomas Jones, and 'The Stakeholder Theory of the Corporation: Concepts, Evidence, and Implications', by Thomas Donaldson and Lee Preston.

On the topic of corporate social responsibility, there are a number of good books that can be consulted. Archie Carroll's, *Business and Society: Ethics and Stakeholder Management* can be recommended, while the book *International Business and Society*, by Steven Wartick and Donna Wood, has a stronger international perspective. Good articles include 'The Corporate Social Policy Process: Beyond Business Ethics, Corporate Social Responsibility and Corporate Social Responsiveness', by Edwin Epstein, and the more academic A Stakeholder Framework For Analyzing and Evaluating Corporate Social Performance', by Max Clarkson.

For an explicit link between strategy and ethics, the book *Corporate Strategy and the Search For Ethics*, by Edward Freeman and Daniel Gilbert, provides a good point of entry. The more recent article 'Strategic Planning As If Ethics Mattered', by LaRue

Hosmer, is also highly recommended. Many books on the general link between ethics and business, such as Thomas Donaldson's *Ethics in International Business*, deal with major strategy issues as well.

Finally, on the topic of corporate mission a very useful overview of the literature is given in the reader *Mission and Business Philosophy*, edited by Andrew Campbell and Kiran Tawadey. Good follow-up works not in this reader are Derek Abell's classic book *Defining the Business: The Starting Point of Strategic Planning*, and the article 'Mission Analysis: An Operational Approach', by Nigel Piercy and Neil Morgan. An interesting book emphasizing the importance of vision is *Built To Last: Successful Habits of Visionary Companies*, by James Collins and Jerry Porras.

REFERENCES

Abbeglen, J., and Stalk, G. (1985) *Kaisha, the Japanese Corporation*, New York: Basic Books.

Abell, D. (1980) *Defining the Business: The Starting Point of Strategic Planning*, Englewood Cliffs, NJ: Prentice Hall

Ackermann, R.W., and Bauer R.A. (1976) *Corporate Social Performance: The Modern Dilemma*, Reston, VA.: Reston

Ackoff, R.L. (1974) *Redesigning the Future*, New York: Wiley.

Albach, H. (1994) 'Wertewandel Deutscher Manager', in: H. Albach, (ed.), *Werte und Unternehmensziele im Wandel der Zeit*.

Alkhafaji, A.F. (1989) *A Stakeholder Approach to Corporate Governance: Managing a Dynamic Environment*, Westport, CT: Quorum Books.

Ansoff, I. (1965) *Corporate Strategy: An Analytic Approach to Business Policy for Growth and Expansion*, New York: McGraw-Hill.

Axelrod, R. (1976) *The Structure of Decision: The Cognitive Maps of Political Elites*, Princeton, NJ: Princeton University Press.

Barnard, C. (1938) *The Function of the Executive*, Cambridge, MA: Harvard University Press.

Bartlett, C.A., and Ghoshal, S. (1994) 'Changing the Role of Top Management: Beyond Strategy to Purpose', *Harvard Business Review*, November–December, pp. 79–88.

Bassiry, G.R., and Denkmejian, H. (1990) 'The American Corporate Elite: A Profile', *Business Horizons*, May–June.

Baysinger, B.D., and Hoskisson, R.E. (1990) 'The Composition of Boards of Directors and Strategic Control: Effects of Corporate Strategy', *Academy of Management Review*, Vol. 15, No. 1, January, pp. 72–81.

Berle, A.A., and Means, G.C. (1932) *The Modern Corporation and Private Property*, New York: Transaction Publishers, Mcmillan.

Bertolus, J., and Morin, F. (1987) 'Conseil d'Administration', *Science et Vie Économie*, Vol. 33, November.

Blair, M. (1995) *Ownership and Control: Rethinking Corporate Governance for the Twenty-First Century*, Washington: Brookings Institution.

Bleicher, K. (1987) *Der Aufsichtsrat im Wandel*, Guetersloh: Verlag Bertelsmann-Stiftung.

Bourgeois, L.J., and Brodwin, D.R. (1983) 'Putting Your Strategy into Action', *Strategic Management Planning*, March–May.

Bucholz, R.A. (1986) *Business Environment and Public Policy*, Englewood Cliffs, NJ: Prentice Hall.

Buono, A.F., and Nichols, L.T (1985) *Corporate Policy, Values and Social Responsibility*, New York: Praeger.

Cameron, K.S. (1986) 'Effectiveness as a Paradox: Consensus and Conflict in Conceptions of Organizational Effectiveness', *Management Science*, 549, May.

Campbell, A., and Tawadey, K. (1990) *Mission and Business Philosophy*, Oxford: Butterworth-Heinemann.

Campbell, A., and Yeung, S. (1991) 'Creating a Sense of Mission', *Long Range Planning*, Vol. 24, No. 4, August, pp. 10–20.

Cannon, T. (1992) *Corporate Responsibility*, London: Pitman.

Carroll, A.B. (1993) *Business and Society: Ethics and Stakeholder Management*, Second Edition. Cincinnati: South-Western Publishing.

Charkham, J. (1994) *Keeping Good Company: A Study of Corporate Governance in Five Countries*, Oxford: Oxford University Press.

Charreaux, G, and Pitol-Belin, J. (1990) *Le Conseil d Administration.*

Clarke, T. (1998) 'The Stakeholder Corporation: A Business Philosophy for the Information Age', *Long Range Planning*, Vol. 31, No. 2, April, pp. 182–194.

Clarkson, M.B.E. (1995) 'A Stakeholder Framework For Analyzing and Evaluating Corporate Social Performance', *Academy of Management Review*, Vol. 20, No. 1, January, pp. 92–117.

Cochran, P.L., and Wartick, S.L. (1994) 'Corporate Governance: A Review of the Literature', in: R.I. Tricker (ed.), *International Corporate Governance: Text, Readings and Cases*, Singapore: Prentice-Hall.

Collins, J.C., and Porras, J. (1994) *Built To Last: Successful Habits of Visionary Companies*, London: Random House.

Collins, J.C., and Porras, J. (1996) 'Building Your Company's Vision', *Harvard Business Review*, Vol. 75, No. 5, September–October, pp. 65–77.

Collins, J. (2001) *Good to Great*, New York: HarperCollins.

Cummings, S., and Davies, J. (1994) 'Mission, Vision, Fusion', *Long Range Planning*, Vol. 27, No. 6, December, pp. 147–150.

David, F.R. (1989) 'How Companies Define Their Mission', *Long Range Planning*, Vol. 22, No. 1, February, pp. 90–97.

Demb, A., and Neubauer, F.F. (1992) *The Corporate Board: Confronting the Paradoxes*, Oxford: Oxford University Press.

Dill, W.R. (1975) 'Public Participation in Corporate Planning: Strategic Management in a Kibitzer's World', *Long Range Planning*, pp. 57–63.

Dimsdale, N., and Prevezer, M. (eds) (1994) *Capital Markets and Corporate Governance*, Oxford: Oxford University Press.

Donaldson, L., and Davis, J.H. (1995) 'Boards and Company Performance: Research Challenges the Conventional Wisdom', *Corporate Governance*, Vol. 2, pp. 151–160.

Donaldson, T. (1989) *Ethics in International Business*, London: Oxford University Press.

Donaldson, T., and Preston, L.E. (1995) 'The Stakeholder Theory of the Corporation: Concepts, Evidence, and Implications', *Academy of Management Review*, Vol. 20, No. 1, January, pp. 65–91.

Drucker, P.F. (1984) 'The New Meaning of Corporate Social Responsibility', *California Management Review*, Vol. 26, No. 2, Winter, pp. 53–63.

Drucker, P.F. (1991) 'Reckoning with the Pension Fund Revolution', *Harvard Business Review*, March–April.

Eisenhardt, K.M. (1989) 'Agency Theory: An Assessment and Review', *Academy of Management Review*, Vol. 14, No. 1, January, pp. 57–74.

Emshoff, J.R., and Freeman, R.E. (1981) 'Stakeholder Management: A Case Study of the U.S. Brewers Association and the Container Issue', in: R. Schultz (ed.), *Applications of Management Science*, Greenwich: JAI Press.

Epstein, E.M. (1987) 'The Corporate Social Policy Process: Beyond Business Ethics, Corporate Social Responsibility, and Corporate Social Responsiveness', *California Management Review*, Vol. 29, No. 3, Spring, pp. 99–114.

Falsey, T.A. (1989) *Corporate Philosophies and Mission Statements*, New York: Quorum Books.

Finkelstein, S., and Hambrick D.C. (1996) *Strategic Leadership: Top Executives and Their Effects on Organizations*, St. Paul: West.

Forbes, D.P., and Milliken F.J. (1999) 'Cognition and Corporate Governance: Understanding Boards of Directors as Strategic Decision-Making Groups', *Academy of Management Review*, Vol. 24, No. 3, July, pp. 489–505.

Freeman, R.E. (1984) *Strategic Management: A Stakeholder Approach*, Boston: Pitman/Ballinger.

Freeman, R.E., and Gilbert Jr., D.R. (1988) *Corporate Strategy and the Search for Ethics*, Englewood Cliffs, NJ: Prentice Hall.

Freeman, R.E., and Liedtka, J. (1991) 'Corporate Social Responsibility: A Critical Approach', *Busines Horizons*, July–August.

Freeman, R.E., and Reed, D.L. (1983) 'Stockholders and Stakeholders: A New Perspective on Corporate Governance', *California Management Review*, Vol. 25, No. 3, Spring, pp. 88–106.

Friedman, M. (1970) 'The Social Responsibility of Business is to Increase Its Profits, *The New York Times Magazine*, September 13.

Gerum, E. (1991) 'Aufsichtratstypen: Ein Beitrag zur Theorie der Organisation der Unternehmungsführung', *Die Betriebswirtschaft*, No. 6.

Goodpaster, K.E. (1991) 'Business Ethics and Stakeholder Analysis', *Business Ethics Quarterly*, January.

Guthrie, J., and Turnbull, S. (1994) 'Audit Committees: Is There a Role for Corporate Senates and/or Stakeholder Councils?', *Corporate Governance*, Vol. 3, pp. 78–89.

Harrison, J.R. (1987) 'The Strategic Use of Corporate Board Committees', *California Management Review*, Vol. 30, pp. 109–125.

Hart, O.D. (1995) *Firms, Contracts and Financial Structure*, Clarendon Press, Oxford.

Hax, A.C. (1990) 'Redefining the Concept of Strategy and the Strategy Formation Process', *Planning Review*, May–June, pp. 34–40.

Hayes, R., and Abernathy, W (1980) 'Managing Our Way to Economic Decline', *Harvard Business Review*, Vol. 58, No. 4, pp. 66–77.

Hoffman, W.M. (1989) 'The Cost of a Corporate Conscience', *Business and Society Review*, Vol. 94, Spring, pp. 46–47.

Hosmer, L.T. (1994) 'Strategic Planning as if Ethics Mattered', *Strategic Management Journal*, Vol. 15, Summer, pp. 17–34.

Jensen, M.C. (1991) 'Corporate Control and the Politics of Finance', *Journal of Applied Corporate Finance*, Vol. 4, pp. 13–33.

Jensen, M.C., and Meckling, W.H. (1976) 'Theory of the Firm, Managerial Behavior, Agency Costs, and Ownership Structure', *Journal of Financial Economics*, Vol. 3, No. 4, October, pp. 305–360.

Jones, T.M. (1995) 'Instrumental Stakeholder Theory: A Synthesis of Ethics and Economics', *Academy of Management Review*, Vol. 20, No. 2, April, pp. 404–437.

Keasey, K., Thompson, S., and Wright, M. (eds) (1997) *Corporate Governance: Economic, Management, and Financial Issues*, Oxford: Oxford University Press.

Kiefer, C.F., and Senge, P.M. (1987) *Metanoic Organizations: Experiments in Organizational Innovation*, Framingham, MA: Innovation Associates.

Klemm, M., Sanderson, S., and Luffman, G. (1991) 'Mission Statements', *Long Range Planning*, Vol. 24, No. 3, June, pp. 73–78.

Klimoski, R., and Mohammed, S. (1994) 'Team Mental Model: Construct or Metaphor', *Journal of Management*, Vol. 20, pp. 403–437.

Kotter, J.P., and Heskett, J.L. (1992) *Corporate Culture and Performance*, New York: Free Press.

Langtry, B. (1994) 'Stakeholders and the Moral Responsibilities of Business', *Business Ethics Quarterly*, Vol. 4, pp. 431–443.

Levitt, T. (1960) 'Marketing Myopia', *Harvard Business Review*, Vol. 38, July–August, pp. 45–56.

McCoy, C.S. (1985) *Management of Values*, Cambridge, MA: Ballinger.

Mintzberg, H. (1984) 'Who Should Control the Corporation?', *California Management Review*, Vol. 27, No. 1, Fall, pp. 90–115.

Mitchell, R.K., Agle, B.R., and Wood, D.J. (1997) 'Toward a Theory of Stakeholder Identification and Salience: Defining the Principle of Who and What Really Counts', *Academy of Management Review*, Vol. 22, No. 4, October, pp. 853–886.

Mohn, R. (1989) *Success Through Partnership*, London: Bantam.

Mueller, R.K. (1989) *Board Compass*, Lexington, MA: Lexington Books.

Nash, T. (1990) 'Bit Parts and Board Games', *Director*, October.

Parkinson, J.E. (1993) *Corporate Power and Responsibility*, Oxford: Oxford University Press.

Pearce, J.A. (1982) 'The Company Mission as a Strategic Tool', *Sloan Management Review*, Spring, pp. 15–24.

Peters, T.J., and Waterman, R.H. (1982) *In Search of Excellence*, New York: Harper & Row.

Piercy, N.F., and Morgan, N.A. (1994) 'Mission Analysis: An Operational Approach', *Journal of General Management*, Vol. 19, No. 3, pp. 1–16.

Porter, M.E. (1980) *Competitive Strategy: Techniques for Analyzing Industries and Competitors*, New York: Free Press.

Prahalad, C.K., and Bettis, R.A. (1986) 'The Dominant Logic: A New Linkage Between Diversity and Performance', *Strategic Management Journal*, November–December, pp. 485–601.

Rappaport, A. (1986) *Creating Shareholder Value: The New Standard for Business Performance*, New York: Free Press.

Rappaport, A. (1990) 'The Staying Power of the Public Corporation', *Harvard Business Review*, January–February. Vol. 68, No. 1, p. 96.

Rathenau, W (1923) *Vom Aktienwesen, eine geschäftliche Betrachtung*, Fischer, Berlin.

Rechner, P.L., and Dalton, D.R. (1989) 'The Impact of CEO as Board Chairperson on Corporate Performance: Evidence vs. Rhetoric', *The Academy of Management Executive*, Vol. 3, No. 2, pp. 141–144.

Senge, P. (1990) *The Fifth Discipline: The Art and Practice of the Learning Organization*, New York: Doubleday.

Solomon, R.C. (1992) *Ethics and Excellence: Cooperation and Integrity in Business*, New York: Oxford University Press.

Spencer, A. (1983) *On the Edge of the Organization: The Role of the Outside Director*, New York: Wiley.

Sternberg, E. (1997) 'The Defects of Stakeholder Theory', *Corporate Governance: An Internationa Review*, Vol. 5, No. 1, January, pp. 3–10.

Stone, C.D. (1975) *Where the Law Ends*, New York: Harper & Row.

Suzuki, S., and Wright, R.W (1985) 'Financial Structure and Bankruptcy Risk in Japanese Companies', *Journal of International Business Studies*, Spring, pp. 97–110.

Sykes, A. (1994) 'Proposals for Internationally Competitive Corporate Governance in Britain and America', *Corporate Governance*, Vol. 2, No. 4, pp. 187–195.

Treynor, J.L. (1981) 'The Financial Objective in the Widely Held Corporation', *Financial Analyst Journal*, March–April, pp. 68–71.

Tricker, R.I. (ed.) (1994) *International Corporate Governance: Text, Readings and Cases*, Singapore: Prentice Hall.

Walsh, J.P., and Seward, J.K. (1990) 'On the Efficiency of Internal and External Corporate Control Mechanisms', *Academy of Management Review*, Vol. 15, pp. 421–458.

Wartick, S.L., and Wood, D.J. (1998) *International Business and Society*, Oxford: Blackwell.

Yoshimori, M. (1995) 'Whose Company Is It? The Concept of the Corporation in Japan and the West', *Long Range Planning*, Vol. 28, pp. 33–45.

Zahra, S.A., and Pearce, J.A. (1989) 'Boards of Directors and Corporate Financial Performance: A Review and Integrative Model', *Journal of Management*, Vol. 15, pp. 291–334.

CASES

Those who have read of everything are thought to understand everything too, but this is not always so; reading furnishes the mind only with the materials of knowledge, it is thinking that makes what is read ours. It is not enough to cram ourselves with a great load of collections; unless we chew them over and over again, they will not give us strength and nourishment.

John Locke (1632–1704); English philosopher

As Locke correctly observed, true understanding requires more than just reading. Ideas, concepts and perspectives must be chewed over before they can be absorbed in our minds. A good way of achieving this is by means of case discussions. Therefore, 22 long cases (and 11 short cases) have been included in this book, giving the reader ample opportunity to apply the theoretical concepts to practical situations.

In the table below an overview is presented of the fit between the cases and the chapters. Three stars indicates an excellent fit between a case and the strategic issues discussed in the chapter, while two stars points to a good match and one star means that there is only a partial (reasonable) fit. As this table shows, at least two cases have an excellent fit with each chapter.

TABLE VI.1   Link between cases and chapters

Case	Chapter 1	2	3	4	5	6	7	8	9	10	11
London Heathrow	***	**	*	**	*	*	*	*	*	*	*
Honda Motors	***	**	**	*	*	*	*	*	*	*	
Apple		***		**	**			*	**	*	*
Gucci	*	***	*	*	**			*	*	*	
UPS		*	***	**	*	***		**			
DSM		*	***	**	*	*		*			
Ferrari	*	**	**	***	**	*	**	*	*	*	
COSCO		**	***	**	**	**			**	***	*
Starbucks in US		*	**	***	*	*		**	*	***	
Pep Stores		*	**	***	***	**		*	**		**
Nestle		**	**	**	***	*		**		*	**
Aditya Birla Group		*	*	***	***	***		*	**	**	
Air-France - KLM			*	**	**	**	***	**		*	**
BT Group		**	**		**		***	**		*	
NCR and WiFi		*	**				**	***		*	
VION			**	**	*	**	**	***		*	*
HP		*	**	***		*		*	***		***
BP			**	**	*	**		*	***		**
Wal Mart			*		*	***	**	*	**	***	
Kentucky Fried Chicken					**	**	*			***	
Pharmac			*				*		**		***
Nike									**	**	***

Reconciling managerial dichotomies at Honda Motors

By Andrew Mair[1]

By following a corporate policy that stresses originality, innovation, and efficiency in every facet of its operations – from product development and manufacturing to marketing – Honda has striven to attain its goal of satisfying its customers.

(Honda Annual Report, 1997)

Honda Motor Co., the Japan-based manufacturer of cars, motorcycles and power products like lawnmowers and small boat engines, is one of the great success stories of the post-war Japanese economy (see Exhibit 1 and Tables 1 and 2). Established in 1948, since the 1970s Honda has been widely recognized as a pioneering Japanese manufacturer and as one of the world's leading motor industry companies. Honda was the first Japanese manufacturer to make its products in Europe, when its Belgian motorcycle factory opened in 1963. Honda became the first Japanese firm to manufacture automobiles in North America when it opened its Ohio assembly plant in 1982. Honda took the risk of entering into a long and complex relationship during the 1980s with a European company universally considered to be one of

EXHIBIT 1 SIGNIFICANT MILESTONES IN HONDA'S DEVELOPMENT

1946	Soichiro Honda sets up Honda Technical Research Institute in Hamamatsu, producing auxiliary engines for bicycles, and later, machine tools.
1948	Company renamed Honda Motor Co. Ltd. First production Honda vehicle, 90cc B-type motorcycle.
1952	Exports begin (to Philippines).
1954	Soichiro Honda visits European car manufacturers. First exports (of 200cc K-type 'Juno' scooter) to USA.
1955	Honda becomes largest Japanese motorcycle manufacturer.
1959	American Honda Motor Co. Inc. [sales subsidiary] established.
1961	European Honda GmbH (now Honda Deutschland GmbH) [sales subsidiary] established in Hamburg.
1962	NV Honda Motor SA (now Honda Belgium NV) established to assemble and sell mopeds in Europe (production begins 1963) [the first

	manufacturing facility opened by any Japanese company in the West].
1963	T360 lightweight truck and S360 sports car, first Honda 4-wheeled vehicles, go on sale.
1965	Honda UK Ltd. [sales subsidiary] established in London.
1968	First exports of N360 and N600 micro-cars. Cumulative motorcycle production passes 10 million.
1971	CVCC low emission automobile engine announced.
1972	First generation Civic automobile introduced.
1973	Soichiro Honda and Takeo Fujisawa retire to become Supreme Advisors.
1976	First generation Accord announced. Civic production reaches 1 million after 4 years.
1977	IAP Industriale SpA (now Honda Italia Industriale SpA) established in Italy [subsidiary to manufacture motorcycles].
1978	Honda of America Manufacturing, Inc. set up to make motorcycles in the USA (production begins 1979). Cumulative production of

[1]Source: This case was written by Andrew Mair, Birkbeck College, University of London. A previous version of this case study appeared as 'Honda Motors: a paradoxical approach to growth,' in C. Baden-Fuller and M. Pitt (eds), *Strategic Innovation: An International Casebook*, London: Routledge, 1996, pp. 435–461. The author acknowledges the helpful comments of Charles Baden-Fuller and Martyn Pitt. This version has been updated and revised. Copyright © 1997 by Andrew Mair, by permission of Cengage Learning.

	motorcycles exceeds 30 million. Cumulative car production exceeds 5 million.
1979	Company signs technical collaboration with British Leyland [now Rover Group], covering BL production of Triumph Acclaim car (production in the United Kingdom begins 1981) [first of several joint car developments between the firms lasting until late 1990s].
1982	European Head Office established in Belgium. Honda of America begins car production.
1984	Plans to double Honda of America car manufacturing capacity to 300,000 units/year. Honda Research of America (now Honda R&D North America) established.
1985	Plans announced to double car production in Canada from 40,000 to 80,000 cars/year.
1986	Honda of America begins engine manufacture.
1988	Plans announced for second US car assembly plant. VTEC variable valve timing system principle announced. Plans announced to build R&D centre in Europe.
1989	Soichiro Honda inducted into America's Automotive Hall of Fame [as first Japanese];

	Honda Accord becomes overall best selling automobile model in the United States.
1990	Agreement with Rover under which Honda acquires minority shareholding in Rover. Accord Aerodeck becomes the first American built car model to be exported both to Japan and to Europe.
1992	European production of Honda Accord begins at Swindon, United Kingdom.
1994	Honda unwinds formal relationship with Rover and BMW purchases Rover from its parent company; announcement of further investments in North America to take annual production capacity from 600,000 to 800,000 by 1999, with 150,000 of these vehicles exported.
1995/6	Successful entry into growing 'light truck' market niches in Japan and North America with Odyssey minivan and CR-V sports utility vehicle.
1997	Production of new 'Asian car' (City model) starts in Thailand as overseas production approaches half of total car production at Honda.

Source: Excerpted from *Honda European Information Handbook* (1991–1992) and Honda Annual Reports.

the least capable automobile manufacturers in the West, British Leyland (now Rover Group).

By the late 1980s, only 25 years after the firm entered the automobile industry, the 'industry of industries', Honda had become one of the world's top ten producers. Indeed, automobile production had come to dominate Honda's activities, responsible for nearly four-fifths of its turnover. By the mid 1990s Honda also stood head and shoulders above other leading automobile producers in international sales (with 77 per cent of its sales by volume outside its home market region), and had become the most international of all automobile companies in production, with 46 per cent of its manufacturing output by volume outside its home market region (see Table 3).

TABLE 1   Growth of Honda's world-wide automobile production, 1960–1995

Year	Automobiles/Light trucks (000 units)
1960	0
1965	52
1970	393
1975	957
1985	1,363
1990	1,928
1995	1,794

Source: Honda Annual Reports, Japan Automobile Manufacturers Association.

TABLE 2 Snapshot of Honda activities, 1997

Product range	Annual unit sales (000s)	Percentage of sales by value
Motorcycles	5,198	13.0
Automobiles	2,184	79.9
Power products	2,648	7.1
(engines, tillers, portable generators, outboard motors, lawnmowers, etc.)		

■ **Focus on internal combustion engines**
    Honda produced over 10 million internal combustion engines world-wide in 1996-7, about 40,000 per day.

■ **Regional sales breakdown by value**

Japan	34%
North America	42%
Europe	11%
others	13%

■ **Factories**
    Honda has a wide international production network, with 89 production facilities in 33 countries.

■ **Employees**
    Honda directly employs 101,100 people, approximately 1/3 of them in japan.

Source: Honda Annual Report 1996–7.

TABLE 3 World production and sales of new passenger cars in 1994

Producers	Production 1994 (Output in 1000s)	Geographic distribution of production (in %)				Geographic distribution of sales (in %)			
		North America	Europe	Japan	Others	North America	Europe	Japan	Others
Ford	3,959	54.6	37.1		8.3	53.3	35.8	0.2	10.7
Ford (& Mazda)	4,928	46.6	29.8	16.7	7.0	49.3	32.3	5.5	12.9
General Motors	5,486	59.7	30.1		10.2	61.4	28.4	0.4	9.8
GM (& Isuzu)	5,537	59.1	29.9	0.9	10.1	60.8	28.1	0.5	10.6
Honda	1,561	38.9	3.3	54.1	3.7	53.2	10.7	23.0	13.0
Nissan	2,081	22.0	9.8	64.5	3.7	31.7	18.3	36.5	13.5
Toyota	3,836	12.7	2.2	72.2	12.9	21.4	8.2	36.9	33.5
V.A.G	2,980	8.2		71.8	20.1	9.3	63.3	1.2	26.2
Fiat	2,137		62.7		37.3	0.1	60.2	0.2	39.6
Renault	1,613		86.5		13.5	0.0	81.0	0.1	18.9
PSA Peugo-Citroën	1,798		98.5		1.5	0.0	84.9	0.3	14.7
BMW-Rover	1,027	(*)	97.8		2.2	8.7	75.6	2.9	12.8
Mercedes	599	(*)	97.5		2.5	12.9	69.9	5.6	11.6

Source: Bélis-Bergouignan, Bordenave and Lung (1998).
(*) New plants have been opened in North America since 1994.

TABLE 4   Honda's recent financial performance

Fiscal year*	Nets sales (¥bn)	Net income of sales (%)	Research and development (¥bn)
1985	2,740	4.7	114
1986	3,009	4.9	135
1987	2,961	2.8	150
1988	3,229	3.1	164
1989	3,489	2.8	184
1990	3,853	2.1	186
1991	4,302	1.8	194
1992	4,391	1.4	192
1993	4,132	0.9	199
1994	3,863	0.6	189
1995	3,966	1.6	203
1996	4,252	1.7	221
1997	5,293	4.2	251

*Ends 28th February up to 1987, 31st March from 1988. Fiscal year therefore includes 9 or 10 months of previous calender year. Figures for 1988 are author's estimate for comparative purposes, based on 12/13 of previous 13 months.

All yen conversions are at then-current exchange rates. During the above period, the value of the US dollar declined from 251 yen in February 1985 to 89 yen in March 1995 and then rose to 124 yen in March 1997. During the same period, Honda's unit automobile sales in North America remained roughly constant, proportionately, at apporximately half of world-wide Honda sales.

Compared to its Japanese rivals, Honda has remained a relatively small player in its domestic market, with market share consistently under 10 per cent, on a par with Mazda and Mitsubishi, not far ahead of Daihatsu and Suzuki. But from a global perspective, Honda's early and rapid internationalization, first of sales during the 1970s, then of production during the 1980s, propelled the company spectacularly out of the ranks of mid-sized Japanese automobile producers to a status alongside Toyota and Nissan as one of the global Japanese 'Big Three' automobile producers. And Honda was now significantly more international than either Toyota or Nissan in both sales and production. Continued growth of sales and production during the first half of the 1990s was hindered – as in the early 1970s – by world recession. But the geographical spread of Honda's activities meant that, unlike some of its Japanese competitors, the firm was able to sustain profitability right through the post-'bubble economy' slump in the Japanese economy during the early 1990s (see Table 4).

In the global automobile industry, Honda's achievements on the technology front are well recognized, ranging from its cutting-edge low pollution and low fuel consumption engine technologies to its achievement in powering World Champion Formula 1 (F-1) racing cars for six years in a row during the 1980s. In 1989 the company's founder, Soichiro Honda, became the first Japanese to be accepted into Detroit's symbolic Automotive Industry Hall of Fame.

It is perhaps not surprising that examples of strategic management practice at Honda became widely quoted in the management literature during the 1980s. An undoubtedly successful firm was attracting the attention it deserved. But was that success a result of good management or was it due to a series of fortunate coincidences? One problem with the way Honda has been analyzed in the management literature is that its management innovations have been treated as a series of isolated stories frequently described in only a few sentences, and seemingly brought forth to justify or legitimize this or that new theory (Mair, 1998).

Is there anything more fundamental, more deep-seated, that underlies Honda's recognized proclivity for innovative and pioneering management strategies?

Reconciling dichotomies: A method for innovative strategic thinking?

Underlying Honda's innovative strategic management, there appears to lie a process that might be described as 'reconciling dichotomies'. To see how it seems to work consider the dozens of dichotomous categories that pervade management thinking and permeate all aspects and functions. There are dichotomies in buyer–supplier relations (e.g. vertical integration and market relationships), work organization (e.g. efficient and humane), product development processes (e.g. sequential and simultaneous development), and business strategy (e.g. cost and differentiation), to name but a few.

Why are these dichotomies important? Strangely, although we can come up with lists of them, few Western managers consider them to be of any significance. And yet if we were to consider them as paradoxes or poles that implicitly require to be solved, we would discover a novel method for developing new ideas about traditional management problems.

In the West, the traditional, ingrained and implicit approach to the puzzles that dichotomous concepts represent has been twofold:

1. Assume a trade-off between them: hence, to take the example of the group–individual dichotomy, to gain the advantages of individualism it is necessary to sacrifice some of the benefits of the group, and vice versa.

2. Conceive of change management in terms of switching from one dichotomized – and mutually exclusive – pole to the other. Any attempt to sit in the middle (trying to keep elements of both group- and individual-oriented organizational forms, for instance) has been thought of as 'muddling through', ending up with 'the worst of both worlds'.

If these ways of thinking seem self-evidently true to many in the West, to Honda they do not. The case study examines Honda's very different way of thinking.

An example: 'Right-first-time' or 'build in quality'

To illustrate the Honda approach, let us look at a very significant instance of the thought process that characterizes dichotomy reconciliation and observe how it works. This example is well understood in Japan (it

was not invented by Honda) and has also increasingly been accepted by many Western managers in recent years.

Western management thinking has traditionally assumed trade-offs between product quality, cost and delivery: high quality cost more and took longer; low cost meant low quality too; fast delivery cost more and risked low quality. But the Japanese-developed 'right-first-time' principle inherent in the 'just-in-time' production system has revealed that there are better ways to manage these dichotomies. By focusing on how to 'build in quality' to products rather than 'test in quality' afterwards, it is possible to reduce costs (less waste and downtime) and to rationalize production with minimal stocks, hence reducing delivery lead times too.

This example involves a strategic approach to manufacturing, and it has widespread ramifications for marketing, product positioning and competitive strategy. Yet significant as the example is, it has been taken up almost in isolation in the West. Few realize that it represents just one example of a wholly different way of strategic thinking rather than a solution to one particular management problem. There are many more dichotomies waiting to be discovered and reconciled, thereby providing innovative impetus to strategic thinking across the range of management functions.

Nobuhiko Kawamoto's reforms

Shortly after taking office as company president in 1991, Nobuhiko Kawamoto introduced significant reforms to the top management structure at Honda. Since the retirement in 1973 of the joint company founders, inventive engineer Soichiro Honda and financial mastermind Takeo Fujisawa, during their company's 25th anniversary year (see Exhibit 2), Honda had become well known in the business world for the collective decision-making process utilized by its top executives, a process in which few of them seemed to have clear individual responsibilities. The collective process was symbolized in the physical layout of the Honda headquarters 'board room', in which none of the executives had their own offices, but instead shared an open space where there were not only individual desks but also various areas for them to meet, sit and talk together.

There was no doubt that Kawamoto's new ideas were significant. He established a clear hierarchy at executive level, with two leading executives joining him to form an innermost leadership circle. He also announced that executives could have private offices if

EXHIBIT 2 HONDA'S LEADERS

- Soichiro Honda, founded company 1948; retired 1973.

- Takeo Fujisawa, joined company 1949, in effect business manager, leaving Soichiro Honda free to concentrate on engineering and product strategy; retired 1973.

- Kiyoshi Kawashima, joined company 1947, before it was officially formed; ran works motor racing teams in 1960s; company president, 1973–1983.

- Tadashi Kume, joined company 1953; ran works motor racing teams in 1960s; principal engineer in design and development of Life and Civic models; company president, 1983–1990.

- Nobuhiko Kawamoto, joined company 1963; consecutively chief engineer, director and president of Honda R&D, 1970–1991; company president and CEO, 1991–.

they so wished. Moreover, Honda's global management structure was reorganized with clear and direct lines of responsibility to the top management group.

Kawamoto's reforms made front page news in the Western business press. *The Wall Street Journal* ran the headline 'Just as US Firms Try Japanese Management, Honda is Centralizing: Kawamoto Finds "Teamwork" Is No Longer Enough To Boost Market Share: Coming Soon: Private Offices' (Chandler and Ingrassia, 1991). *Fortune* followed suit, with 'A US-Style Shakeup at Honda: CEO Kawamoto has abandoned consensus management for American-looking organization charts. Result: Communications and decision-making are getting faster' (Taylor, 1991). As far as strategic decision making was concerned, the clear impression given was that Honda's penchants for groupism and horizontal communication were on the way out, with individualism and vertical structure the order of the new day. Apparently a Japanese company with a particularly Japanese management style had now decided that a Western style was superior after all.

But was this interpretation valid? Was Honda a firm whose strategic management decision making switched from a collectivist mode to an individualist mode? In fact, the true picture is rather different, and the view presented in the Western business press is, arguably, uninformed.

The joint board room had actually been set up in the mid 1960s by Takeo Fujisawa, who saw it as an adjunct structure to Soichiro Honda's highly individualistic style, a means of encouraging executives to talk about problems and solutions with each other, and to prepare younger managers for the day the founders would retire. In other words, the organizational structure to promote collective decision making existed alongside the individualist Honda (who is said

once to have hit an engineer over the head with a spanner to drive home a point!).

Kawamoto's changes were only one of a series of periodic reorganizations at Honda. When Honda and Fujisawa retired in 1973, new president Kiyoshi Kawashima shifted Honda further towards a collective decision-making mode with the wide-ranging committee structure that he set up. When Tadashi Kume in turn succeeded Kawashima as president in 1983, he too instituted his own changes. Thus each new president has deliberately sent a shock wave of reorganization (of interrelationships as much as of people) through the firm. Indeed Kawamoto was by no means dispensing with collective decision making; what he was doing was injecting a strong dose of individual responsibility into the existing framework.

Kawamoto's changes are best interpreted less as a switch to a new type of structure, as the Western press had it, from one pole of a dichotomy to another, than as a change in emphasis. A useful way to visualize this process is to think of the organization as a sailing ship on a narrow tack against the wind, progressing in a zig-zag fashion, first towards individualism and vertical structure, then back towards collectivism and horizontal structure, then back again. All the while, the ship moves forward despite sailing against the wind, as each tack builds on the achievements of the last, despite the apparently dramatic changes of direction (see Figure 1).

Reconciling dichotomies at Honda

Honda's approach to the individual–group dichotomy in the strategic decision-making process is exemplary of Honda's approach to innovation in management. Honda appears to have implemented a systematic

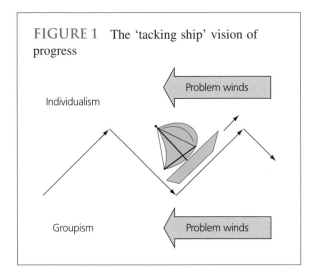

FIGURE 1   The 'tacking ship' vision of progress

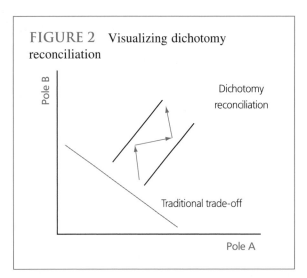

FIGURE 2   Visualizing dichotomy reconciliation

approach to resolving some of the great dilemmas of twentieth-century management.

Traditional dichotomous pairs of concepts are used in the West as an underlying framework to think about management. Thus in the case of Kawamoto's reforms, there is, first, the collective (or group) versus the individual, and second, vertical structure and horizontal structure. 'Reconciliation' in this context refers to an approach in which the two poles are somehow (and that is the challenge) made compatible with each other.

The way in which Kawamoto 'changed tacks' from a group-based to an individual-based trajectory (not structure) is a classic example of dichotomy reconciliation, Honda-style. Honda's strategic thinking rejects the typical Western simple trade-off and emphatically rejects the typical Western idea that failure to select clearly one or the other pole leads to indecision. Honda's solution to the group-individual dichotomy and the horizontal–vertical dichotomy is to progress flexibly with a 'tacking' motion along a well defined and fairly narrow path. In other words, the reconciliation sought is always one which incorporates 'the best of both worlds' (see Figure 2).

The refusal to accept static trade-offs, and the rejection of any obligation to choose one pole or the other, lie behind many of Honda's strategic innovations. The process can be seen at work across a wide range of activities at Honda, and constitutes the hallmark of its strategic innovation.

Organizational process: Competition and the individual

Let us take a closer look at how the individual–group dichotomy is played out at Honda. Honda has a remarkable penchant for praising the successes of individual employees and for encouraging a sense of competition among them. Company-wide quality circle (called NH Circles; for New, Now, Next Honda) competitions have focused on the achievements of individual people (albeit, characteristically, working in small groups). Within Honda R&D, the subsidiary company that develops Honda products, competitive and individual-based basic research activities deliberately foster individual inventiveness. The competitive nature of employee suggestion schemes at Honda's North American operations, with awards given to annual 'winners', also fosters individualism.

In similar vein, individual managers remain closely associated with the projects and products for which they have been responsible; Tadashi Kume was lauded as the principal engineer behind the Life and Civic automobiles. Kawamoto has been known as 'Mr NSX' after the aluminium-bodied super-sports car Honda developed in the late 1980s, and he was also associated with Honda's successes in the 1980s on the Grand Prix racing circuit.

What is most interesting, however, is that individualism and competition are not stressed over and above loyalty and cooperation; each 'pole' within the individual-group dichotomy is a tendency that 'has its place' in a way that maximizes the contribution each can make, while minimizing any negative impacts of overemphasis on either individual or group. Hence alongside the stress on individual achievement can be observed the promotion of group processes: collective decision making, in the corporate board room for instance; team working, the tight and disciplined cooperation of the various people involved in F-1 racing being communicated as a model of behaviour for all employees; and interdepartmental cooperation in the product development process, which is organized into highly cooperative 'SED' (Sales-Engineering-Development) teams that are explicitly differentiated from the individualist and competitive character of the basic research process.

Organizational structure

A classic dichotomy in organizational structures is between vertical and horizontal structures. Recently many consultants have been advising large companies to dispense with vertical, hierarchical structures in favour of process-oriented horizontal linkages. Indeed a driving force behind reform of organizational structure at Honda has been the avoidance of 'big business disease'. In the Honda view, when a company grows bigger and adopts overly rigid vertical structures of organizational control, it can lose the small-firm vitality and the horizontal linkages and communication that are so vital to innovation and dynamism.

At Honda there are regular drives to battle 'big business disease'. But significantly, these take place within, rather than replacing, a strongly hierarchical structural framework. Thus after he became Honda President in 1983, Tadashi Kume launched a series of initiatives to prevent bureaucratic structures from hardening. These included round-table meetings between executives and front-line supervisors to cut across layers of vertical hierarchy, regular round-table meetings between executives and middle-level managers, and the encouragement of 'diagonal' linkages whereby manufacturing managers, for instance, held discussions to share viewpoints with front-line sales staff.

In similar vein, strategic thinking about the career paths of individuals has been woven into organizational thinking to keep structure flexible and innovative. Honda's 'expert' system, developed during the 1950s and 1960s, allows technical experts to be promoted in a clearly vertical fashion without having to enter the ranks of management, on the grounds that the latter would be a sure-fire route to poor lower-level management since many technical experts desire promotion but do not actually want to manage other people. Moreover, managers can follow diagonal promotion paths (simultaneous vertical and horizontal moves). An example is the marketing manager who was put in charge of expanding one of Honda's North American factories in the late 1980s. One advantage Honda gained from this appointment was that manufacturing and engineering staff were obliged to be very

clear about what they were doing and began to question taken-for-granted procedures.

Honda has pursued web-like organizational forms mixing group and individual processes, vertical and horizontal structures, and formal and informal relationships and positions to the point that it is well nigh impossible for anyone entering the firm from outside to understand precisely what Honda's organizational structure is.

Is Honda a 'Japanese' firm?

One dichotomy pervasive in the Western management literature is the grand division between Western firms and management methods, on the one hand, and Japanese firms and methods on the other hand. Many management theorists and practitioners have held to the idea that Japanese firms are fundamentally different from Western firms: whether in organizational structures, company cultures, labour relations, inter-firm relationships, manufacturing systems, work organization, or marketing strategies. Analysts created a 'Japanese model' of management diametrically opposed, in classic dualist fashion, to the Western model. Their argument was that adherence to this Japanese model explained much of Japan's economic successes during the 1970s and 1980s (see Table 5).

It may therefore seem strange even to pose the question of whether Honda can be considered a 'Japanese' firm. But remember that only one third of Honda's turnover now derives from Japan, and the company runs over 80 manufacturing facilities throughout the world, nearly all of them outside Japan. The crux of the issue, however, is whether Honda is actually managed in a 'Japanese' way. Many assume that it must be, given its roots in a country with a particularly strong and unique culture. And yet Japanese analysts agree that Honda does not easily fit the 'Japanese model'. In Japan Honda has deliberately set out to counter what it views as negative traits of 'Japanese-ness'. It deliberately stresses decentralized management structures, praises the achievements of individuals, makes merit the key to promotion, and awards responsibility to younger employees: all this in a Japanese society founded on centralization, collective decision making and responsibility, status and seniority, and respect for elders. The point to grasp is that Honda has struggled to overcome the innovation-deadening impacts of these cultural forces. Soichiro Honda himself has been the model, portrayed as exemplary of an individualist who cared nothing for the position of his supposed 'betters', deliberately crossed

TABLE 5 The 'Japanese model' seen as diametrically opposed to the 'Western model'

'Western management model'	*'Japanese management model'*
Overall description	
▪ Mass	▪ Lean
▪ Standardized	▪ Flexible
▪ Fordist	▪ Post-Fordist
Work process	
▪ Taylorist	▪ Post-Taylorist
▪ Do Workers	▪ Think workers
▪ Unskilled	▪ Polyvalent
Production organization and logistics	
▪ Large-lot production	▪ Small-lot production
▪ Just-in-case	▪ Just-in-time
▪ Push system	▪ Pull system
Organization	
▪ Vertical	▪ Horizontal
▪ Fragmented duties	▪ Broad duties
▪ Individual as responsible	▪ Group as responsible
Labour relations	
▪ Job control focus	▪ Employment conditions focus
▪ Cross-company unions	▪ Enterprise unions
▪ Hire and fire	▪ Job-for-life
Industry organization	
▪ Separated firms	▪ *Keiretsu* families
▪ Distant inter-firm relations	▪ Close inter-firm relations

status barriers, and promoted younger individuals across seniority levels. The result is that in Japan Honda is commonly viewed as a peculiarly 'un-Japanese' firm.

Thus Honda has injected so-called Western attributes into the way it functions, which co-exist with the 'Japanese' features that employees bring with them – the results of their upbringing in Japan – as they enter the firm. Rather than pursuing a 'Japanese model' distinct from a 'Western model', the big picture reveals Honda's innovation to be its simultaneous incorporation of both models so as to work consciously and deliberately with elements of each: precisely what we saw earlier in Kawamoto's reforms.

Product strategy: Guiding the technology development process

A recognized source of competitive advantage for Honda has been its 'core competence' in the advanced internal combustion engines which power the whole range of its products. But Honda's product strength goes far deeper: a dichotomy-reconciling approach characterizes both the mental process of technology research and the philosophy behind the actual product designs. The technology and design features of Honda products are the embodiments of successful reconciliations of dichotomies which deliver direct and immediate competitive advantage.

The classic example of Honda's technology is the CVCC (compound vortex controlled combustion) engine, designed during the 1969–1971 period. Indeed the CVCC engine is used within the firm to represent and communicate Honda's approach to technology. The compromise tackled and overcome by the CVCC engine was widely accepted in the world's automobile industry, namely a trade-off among the various pollutants emitted from internal combustion engines. According to the traditional view, attempts to reduce emissions of one chemical inevitably led to increases in others. The only way out of the dilemma, it was

EXHIBIT 3   HOW THE CVCC ENGINE SIMULTANEOUSLY REDUCED POLLUTANTS IN A WAY PREVIOUSLY THOUGHT IMPOSSIBLE

Regular engine
- Supply of a denser mixture of air and fuel decreases NOx but increases CO and HC.
- Supply of a thinner mixture of air and fuel decreases CO and HC but increases NOx.
- As the mixture grows thinner, NOx and CO will decrease but the engine may die.

Sources of pollutants
- The higher the temperature of the gas in the cylinder, the greater the amount of NOx emitted.
- The more quickly the temperature of the gas in the cylinder falls in the process of expansion, the greater the amount of unignited fuel emitted as HC.

- The greater the amount of dense fuel supplied, the greater the amount of CO emitted due to lack of oxygen resulting from oxidation.

Merits of CVCC engine
- Decrease in NOx by lowering the maximum combustion temperature.
- Decrease in HC by prolonging the time the temperature of oxidation is maintained.
- Decrease in CO by supplying very thin mixed gas so as to make sufficient oxygen available.

Source: Mito (1990).

believed, was to add a process (e.g. catalytic conversion) to clean up the pollutants after combustion.

Honda engineers proceeded from the assumption that it would be more rational not to create pollutants in the first place than to have to clean them up. The CVCC engine design therefore denied the taken-for-granted compromises. The technical solution was to place two connected combustion chambers in each cylinder. A fuel-thin mixture of fuel and air was injected into a main combustion chamber. A fuel-rich mixture was injected into a smaller chamber where the spark plug was located. When the spark ignited the mixture, combustion spread from the smaller to the main chamber, with the result that the fuel and oxygen burned more completely, and with less fuel used, compared to a conventional engine. Each of these characteristics helped reduce a different pollutant, resulting in an engine in which the old trade-offs were overcome (see Exhibit 3).

The thinking embodied in the VTEC (variable valve timing and lift electronic control) family of engines that Honda first introduced in 1989 derives from a similar approach. The conventional dichotomy and associated trade-off tackled by the VTEC engines was fuel economy versus engine power; to improve fuel economy meant losing power. However, in the VTEC engine the innovative variable valves (the mechanisms which let fuel and air in and out of the combustion chamber), in conjunction with the electronically controlled fuel injection system, control the ratio of fuel to air according to driving conditions. In normal mode, a fuel-thin mixture provides fuel economy. But at high engine speeds with the driver's foot pressed hard on the accelerator a fuel-richer mixture provides significantly more power. Figure 3 illustrates both the performance economy trade-off of Honda's conventional engines, and the dichotomy-reconciling leap achieved by VTEC engines in Honda Accord automobiles.

While in product terms Honda is perhaps best known for its technologically innovative engines, refusal to accept taken-for-granted trade-offs characterizes all aspects of Honda's strategic approach to technological change. This is well illustrated in the revealing language used by a Honda engineer describing an apparently mundane technological advance made by Honda R&D at its North American operations (see Exhibit 4).

Designing automobiles

In addition to its technologically innovative products, Honda's product development process is respected within the automobile industry for its sheer speed. During the 1970s and 1980s Honda led the Japanese automobile industry's drive to reduce development lead times: today automobiles are being manufactured only two years after the launch of their development process. Until recently five to six years or longer was the norm in the West, and few manufacturers achieve better than three to four years. Honda's speed has been attained in two ways. The first is its organizational approach to the

FIGURE 3   The VTEC engine compared to the conventional fuel consumption–acceleration trade-off

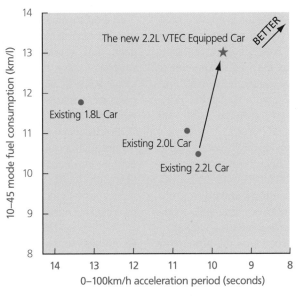

Source: Japan Autotech Report (1993).

product development process, based on the SED teams mentioned above. The SED teams work together on projects from start to finish, in contrast to the traditional sequential development process utilized in the West where each function makes its specialized input in turn (marketing, design, product engineering, production engineering and manufacturing).

The second is Honda's particular model replacement system. What is most significant about this system is the way it challenges an important dichotomy observed in the Western automobile industry. This is between the 'complete model change', in which the whole design process starts from scratch with every component redesigned for a totally new automobile, and the 'facelift', in which only a small number of components are redesigned to give an older model a more modern image. As adherents of this dichotomous approach, for decades Western automobile makers have made complete model changes perhaps every eight to ten years, and given facelifts to their models perhaps every two to four years. Most Honda models are changed every four years. Thus new Honda Accords were introduced in 1981, 1985, 1989, 1993 and 1997, and new Civics in 1979, 1983, 1987, 1991 and 1995. Western automobile makers, wedded to their traditional approach, claimed that Honda was not 'properly' replacing models in these short cycles, but simply giving its models a cosmetic facelift.

Yet Honda's strategic approach to model replacement means that it does not face the same dichotomous choices. The process at Honda can be described schematically as follows. Honda's model changes are neither complete changes nor mere facelifts. Instead, every four years, when a Honda model is 'officially' replaced, the components the driver can see or otherwise notice are replaced: the exterior body shape, the interior design, the lights. Then, also every four years with a two-year lag after the official model change, vital unseen components are changed, and new engines, gearboxes, braking systems, for instance, are introduced. The outcome is best described as a 'rolling' or 'iterative' model change programme with significant and regular changes to each model (and hence a regular boost to customer interest). The traditional distinction between complete change and facelift is dispensed with in favour of a smoother, more fluid and flexible approach. Manufacturing systems (for instance, sizes and shapes of machinery) and whole vehicle design configurations (for instance, sizes and shapes of components and the spaces they fit in) are preplanned as far as possible to allow for the expected evolution of models and components.

This iterative process of model evolution is put into practice in three 'dimensions'. The first is over time, as described above. Thus the 1993 replacement for the Today model, sold in Japan, shared 40 per cent of its

EXHIBIT 4   WE AREN'T INTERESTED IN TRADE-OFFS

When it comes to weight reduction, the auto industry's appetite is insatiable. Honda is no exception.

As part of a corporate goal to reduce weight in its automobiles, Honda of America Manufacturing Inc. in Marysville, Ohio, is the first automaker in the United States to use a lightweight underbody coating, or sound deadener, with expanded polymeric microspheres supplied by Pierce & Stevens Corp. of Buffalo, NY.

Besides lightweight, Honda sought several other attributes from any new underbody coating, including reduced volatile organic compound emissions and an improved durability standard.

Honda also wanted improved 'line-side workability' – the ease-of-use characteristics judged by those who work with the product on the production line.

In addition, the product could not require any modifications to the existing sound-deadener delivery and application systems.

It was a tall order, but according to Trish Peters, assistant manager of the Marysville plant's auto paint department, reformulations either meet all of Honda's standards or they aren't used at all.

'We aren't interested in trade-offs', she said. 'We won't accept lesser performance in any aspect of a product to get improvement in some other aspect. Our sound-deadener suppliers – there are several – know this. They accepted our goals and came back to us with formulations that included polymeric microspheres – what we call "plastic balloons".'

'We reduced the weight of the deadener by 30 to 40 per cent', said Lee Manville of the Marysville auto paint production staff. 'We got better adhesion of the product to the body surface and were able to reduce film build (the amount applied) while improving our durability standard.'

'We're satisfied with the performance of the reformulated sound deadener – for now', said Peters. 'Honda has trained us not to make or accept assumptions about the performance of anything we use. Our department's goals – to improve existing materials and find new materials – are like our corporate goals to improve quality and drive down costs. They never end.'

Source: Fleming (1993).

components with its predecessor. Second, it is practiced laterally, in the development of parallel, 'sister' models for different market segments. The third dimension is geographical, in which models developed for different world markets are frequently spin-offs from existing models (neither entirely different, nor mere cosmetic changes). Hence both the Accord and Civic models that Honda was manufacturing in Europe in the mid-1990s were spin-offs, with significant engineering changes, from automobiles first manufactured for the Japanese market.

Strategies for production and logistics: The assembly line

What philosophy guides how Honda actually makes its products? Honda has sought to combine the advantages inherent in what have normally been seen in the West as dichotomous and mutually exclusive production and logistics systems.

Honda first experimented with a 'free-flow' assembly line at its Kumamoto motorcycle plant on the Japanese island of Kyushu in the late 1970s. This system was an attempt to combine productive efficiency with human dignity. Efficiency and dignity have been treated as polar opposites in the traditional Western strategy for manufacturing design which regarded the mind-numbing and alienating continuous assembly line, with its fragmentation of tasks carefully orchestrated by time-and-motion staff, as the epitome of efficiency, and viewed the efforts of the Swedish automobile manufacturers Volvo and Saab to develop more personally satisfying forms of 'group work' in the 1970s and 1980s as necessarily sacrificing efficiency.

Honda's free-flow assembly line, the first of its type in the Japanese motor industry, was based on a series of separate carriers upon which partially completed vehicles were placed (or hung). The carriers followed each other from workstation to workstation but their speed of movement was not controlled centrally as with the traditional chain-driven line. Advantages were sought in terms of efficiency and dignity. On the one hand both manual and automated assembly tasks could be undertaken more accurately since the separate carriers could stop at each workstation. Moreover, work could be completed satisfactorily before the carrier was sent on its way. On the other hand production workers could be given a sense of control over the production process since they could make the decision that the task had been executed properly and that the carrier should now move to the next workstation. The free-flow principle was later adopted for the new third automobile assembly line built at the Suzuka factory in the late 1980s, where Honda has continued to experiment with it.

Production planning

Honda has also developed an innovative strategy for the planning of production, a strategy which exhibits characteristics of both the traditional dichotomous poles. One pole is 'large-lot mass production', in which manufacturing is organized so that thousands of identical or virtually identical products are made in a row, or series. This implies the use of dedicated machinery and, indeed, in the Western automobile industry each factory frequently can make only a single automobile model, which is changed every few years. To many, the automobile industry is the epitome of large-lot mass production. In this system the goal is to reduce costs, achieved at the expense of product variety (the trade-off within the Western mass production system).

At the other extreme is the 'one-piece-flow' production system said to characterize at least some firms in the Japanese automobile industry. In this system each assembly line can handle several different models with minimal if any changeover time, and the partly finished vehicles coming down the line are sequenced in 'lots of one', i.e. each vehicle is different from that preceding and following it (colours, options, engines, numbers of doors, models). The objective of this system is to permit far greater product variety (to the point of 'customized' products individually ordered). One drawback is the very complex logistics system needed to supply components to the assembly line in the correct order. In general terms, the Toyota-developed 'just-in-time' production and logistics system can be seen as a dichotomy reconciliation permitting both product variety and productive efficiency.

Honda's own innovative strategy for production planning has been to develop a 'small batch' production system based around the key number 60 and its factors (30, 15, 12, etc.). Automobiles are sent down the assembly lines in batches in which each vehicle is exactly the same (including colour). Workers therefore execute exactly the same tasks for each batch. Components are delivered to the assembly line in batches (lot sizes, colours, optional extras) which exactly match the vehicles they will be fitted into. The objective is to combine the advantages of large-lot production (simpler logistics and quality control, less likelihood of error, easier to programme production schedules) and of small-lot production (ability to offer a wider range of products to consumers and greater worker involvement and satisfaction).

Making production planning and product marketing coherent

This small batch production system is closely linked to Honda's strategy towards marketing and sales. Honda has tended not to offer its customers the spectacular breadth of choice developed by other Japanese automobile manufacturers during the Japanese 'bubble economy' of the late 1980s. Some firms expanded product variety so far that Japanese customers could choose among several dozen different steering wheels per model, a level of consumer choice which was soon recognized to have got out of hand. Honda's strategy emphasizes the high technology built into all its products and it was quick to offer features like advanced engines (though often available in only two sizes per model), anti-lock brakes, electric windows and sun-roofs as standard rather than optional extras, thus simplifying product variety within each model type.

In operations management, an important dichotomy distinguishes 'push'-based production planning and logistical systems from 'pull'-based systems. In the former, said to be typically Western, production schedules for particular models are set out months in advance, and alignment of output levels with customer demand tends to focus on sales strategy (e.g. discounting may be necessary). In the latter, said to be typically Japanese, automobiles are only made to customer order.

Honda's approach to production planning is to operate a combination push-pull system. When planning at the annual scale, production levels of particular models can be varied up or down as a function of demand, because flexible equipment means that production lines can be used for various models (in gross terms, a pull system). When undertaking monthly planning, an 'un-Japanese' push system fixes the total mix of products and appropriate schedules several months in advance, based on market forecasts. Simultaneously a small-scale inventory pull system is utilized for everyday production planning, where it helps deal with unforeseen difficulties: if, for instance, there is a problem with a certain colour of paint in the paint shops, components makers may be alerted in a matter of hours that the production schedule has been altered and they will need to respond accordingly. The outcome at Honda is the simultaneous operation of pull- and push-based production planning systems rather than dominance of one type over the other.

Relationships with components makers

In the analysis of inter-firm relationships, in particular buyer–supplier relations in the components supply chain, a distinction is traditionally made in the West between vertical integration and market relationships (reflected in the 'make or buy?' decision). Honda's approach to relationships with its components suppliers transcends this dichotomy and others associated with supply chain management. In Japan Honda has only a handful of components makers that might be considered to belong to its supplier 'family', and is the only firm in the Japanese automobile industry not to organize its own 'suppliers association' as a forum for suppliers to meet and solve common problems. Honda does build long-term relationships with its suppliers, but these are not buttressed by the institutional mechanisms (cross-shareholding, 'family' relationships, supplier associations) often said to govern long-term relationships in Japan.

In North America, where a substantial network of more than 80 Japanese 'transplant' component makers has developed to supply Honda with components, Honda invested its own capital in a number of the early arrivals as a means of reducing the risk for its smaller Japanese partners. Other than this, formal linkages in North America are non-existent. And yet in operational terms Honda intervenes directly in the 'internal' activities of its component makers when it believes this necessary. For a number of components Honda arranges the purchase of the raw materials, for example steel and aluminium, two or three tiers back along the supply chain, which will eventually find their way into Honda automobiles, gaining advantages in price and quality. Honda engineers also visit suppliers regularly, and may be stationed in their factories for a time if serious problems arise in components delivery and quality.

Thus relationships with component makers are based on complex combinations of close control and open, commercial relationships, creating a structure which defies the polar types in traditional views of buyer-supplier relations. The goal is clearly to reconcile the dichotomy to gain the advantages accruing from each polar type of organizing.

The same refusal to fit easily into traditional categories holds for the number of supplier firms from which Honda sources each component. The traditional dichotomous choice between 'dual/multiple' sourcing strategy versus 'single' sourcing strategy is bypassed by Honda, where sourcing strategy is based on elements of both. Thus Honda sources a certain type of seat (the basic version, say) for its Accord model from supplier A, in single-sourcing fashion, and simultaneously sources a different type of seat (perhaps a high-tech electronic version) from supplier B, also in single-sourcing fashion. The two suppliers are not in direct competition, yet Honda can subtly play them off (in dual-sourcing fashion) since each is aware of the other's existence and willingness to expand its market share when plans are made for the next Accord model change. Honda gains the advantage of both single sourcing (stable relationships with one supplier) and dual sourcing (an element of competition).

Honda's ability to find solutions even reaches into the geographical pattern of its relationships with component makers in North America. The traditional approach is to choose between purchasing from component makers located very long distances away, often to allow cheap labour sources in other regions and countries to be exploited (a feature of the 'Western model'), and the spatially concentrated production system at Toyota City in Japan, where hundreds of supplier companies and nearly all Toyota's production capacity are concentrated into a few square kilometres, which is particularly advantageous for just-in-time logistics.

In North America, where Honda has greatly influenced the general location choices made by its Japanese component makers, the geographical pattern reflects both spatial dispersal and spatial concentration. In Ohio, where Honda's main manufacturing base has been constructed, there are now more than 40 Japanese-owned firms making automobile components, nearly all of which supply Honda. Concentration within a two-hour travel-time permits just-in-time 'pull' logistics to be operated on a day-to-day basis. However, within Ohio the factories are dispersed to small town locations 10 to 20 miles apart; this way, their local labour markets are separated and the new investments and jobs they represent will not drive up local wages. Distant from Honda too, they can offer wages only half to two-thirds those paid at the automobile assembly plant. In other words, Honda's network of component makers is designed to combine the advantages of spatial concentration and spatial dispersal.

Honda's strategic challenges

How does Honda manage the key dichotomies of strategic management: planning vs. learning, market positioning vs. developing internal resources, and within the resource-based perspective, product-related core competencies vs. process-related core capabilities? The many Western observers of Honda from the academic and consultancy worlds in recent years have tended to lay the emphasis on one pole to the exclusion of the other, and have battled it out among themselves to claim that Honda is *either* a planner *or* a learner, *either* a market positioner *or* a resource builder, *either* a competency-based diversifier *or* a capabilities predator. Similarly, followers of trends in multinational enterprise organization have been quick to claim that Honda exemplifies a polar position as a 'post-national' or 'stateless' corporation operating in a 'borderless' world (Mair, 1997, 1998).

Judging by the evidence of Honda's strategic capability to reconcile dichotomies, these analysts may be missing the point. As the energies of debate have been channelled into ceaseless either/or argument, meanwhile Honda may have been focusing its strategic effort, and mobilizing its dichotomy-reconciling strategic capability, precisely on reconciling the apparently incompatible poles of strategic dichotomies in a way that consigns these debates to the irrelevant margins.

Have Honda's strategists therefore implemented detailed planned strategies with precision whilst simultaneously learning and adjusting strategy to business environment change? One clue may be found by reversing the normal assumption that the formulation and execution of detailed strategic plans is inevitably a long-term process such that learning from environmental change can only extend to marginal tweaks. What if learning were the long term and planning the short term? A strategically agile company might be able to make operational (treat as short-term variables) parameters previously considered strategic (necessarily fixed in the short term). The strategy process would then consist of a series of rapid formulation-implementation pulses over time. And indeed Honda's rapid and iterative new product development process and flexifactory manufacturing infrastructure appear to support just such an approach.

Can a market positioning and resource-based view of strategy content be reconciled in innovative ways?

Here Honda appears to have faced difficult challenges at a number of points in its history, without always succeeding, particularly in reconciling the company's core competencies in engine design as well as its engineers' pursuit of technological mastery to the evolution of market demand. Significantly, notwithstanding Honda's image as a designer of sporty and technically innovative cars, fully three quarters of the company's global sales comprise the relatively conservative and simple Civic and Accord models, which, broadly speaking, occupy the market position (once thought unattainable) which combines high quality with low cost based on core capabilities residing at the heart of Honda's product design and production process. What core-competency related product technology breakthroughs might provide the basis for novel and successful market positions in future? Not surprisingly, along with other industry companies, Honda has recently invested huge resources into developing new low-pollution power sources for its vehicles (electric, solar power, for example), in the drive to focus its competencies on potential breakthrough market positions.

Which matters most to the consumer, Honda's core competencies in mechanical technologies, or its core capabilities in managing the whole value chain from raw materials to dealer networks via product design and production processes? This dichotomy seems plainly false, at Honda at least. The company focuses on both resources because both matter to purchasers of its products: if to varying degrees. Purchasers of the top-of-the-range super sports NSX model are presumably attracted by the car's driving and handling characteristics, features intimately related to product technology, whereas purchasers of a small engine three-door Civic model may focus more on cost, quality, and reliability (hence in some countries, notably the United Kingdom, Honda has struggled to shake off a market image as a maker of cars for the over 60s), product features associated more with core design and production process capabilities.

The grand dichotomies of business and corporate strategy are clearly more complex, multilayered concepts and practices than those associated with operations, human resources and other functional-level strategies. Yet Honda seems destined to pitch the company's collective intellect full-force into the struggle to find ways of reconciling them for competitive advantage. Each time Honda succeeds in finding new solutions, the competitive map in its chosen industries will be redrawn, just as it has been at regular intervals over the past 50 years.

References

Bélis-Bergouignan, M.-C, Bordenave, G., and Lung, Y. (1998) Global strategies in the automobile industry, *Regional Studies* (forthcoming).

Chandler, C. and Ingrassia, P. (1991) Just as US Firms Try Japanese Management, Honda is Centralizing: Kawamoto Finds 'Teamwork' Is No Longer Enough To Boost Market Share: Coming Soon: Private Offices, *The Wall Street Journal*, 4th November, pp. 1 and A10.

Fleming, A. (1993) Honda switches to lighter underbody coating, *Automotive News*, 12th April, p. 20.

Japan Autotech Report (1993) Vol. 175, p. 23.

Mair, A. (1997) Strategic localization: the myth of the post-national enterprise, in Cox, K.R. (ed.), *Spaces of Globalization: Reasserting the Power of the Local*, New York: Guildford, pp. 64–88.

Mair, A. (1998) Learning from Honda, *Journal of Management Studies*.

Mito, S. (1990) *The Honda Book of Management: A Leadership Philosophy for High Industrial Success*, London: Kogan Page.

Taylor III, A. (1991) A US-Style Shakeup at Honda: CEO Kawamoto has abandoned consensus management for American-looking organization charts. Result: Communications and decision-making are getting faster, *Fortune*, 20 December.

London Heathrow: The airport's expansion dilemma

By Prabhu Sethuraman and Abdul Syed[1]

I am firmly opposed to this expansion of Heathrow Airport as it runs contrary to all the growing evidence we now have on the impact of aviation on climate change.

Ken Livingstone, London Mayor

If fears about climate change are allowed to frustrate the overwhelming economic case for extra runway capacity at the national hub, the country's entire economic direction would come into question.

Willie Walsh, British Airways Chief Executive

London-Heathrow (Heathrow), UK's only hub airport and one of Britain's most important economic assets, is full, operating at 99 per cent of permitted runway capacity and susceptible to foreign competition. The airport's operator and broader business lobbies believe that an additional runway and a terminal at Heathrow would meet the increased passenger capacity and help sustain UK's competitiveness as a global hub. However, environmentalists suggest that the airport's expansion would increase the greenhouse-gas emissions and question Britain's role in climate change. Various solutions were proposed to deal with Heathrow's current expansion dilemma. Proposals like the mixed mode operation of Heathrow's existing runways, building a Greenfield airport at Thames estuary, integrating air/rail services and expanding Gatwick have been suggested as alternatives to Heathrow's expansion. Gordon Brown, Britain's prime minister is yet to make a decision about Heathrow's future. Should he press ahead with Heathrow's expansion? What would the implications be?

London-Heathrow airport

London is a North Atlantic gateway to Europe, and acts as a hub between Europe and Latin America. It is however too far west to operate as a hub to Asia and the Far East, or as an intra-European hub. For historical reasons, Heathrow was developed as a major international hub airport[2] with BAA[3] as the hub operator. Since its privatization in 1987, BAA has owned and operated Heathrow. BAA also operates other airports like London Gatwick, London Stansted, Glasgow, Edinburgh, Aberdeen and Southampton in the UK. BAA was later acquired by a consortium led by the Spanish Grupo Ferrovial[4] for £9 billion, in June 2006.

Heathrow is the world's third busiest International hub airport carrying around 68 million passengers per annum (mppa) (Exhibit 1). It is a main gateway to the global economy supporting billions of pounds of British exports and thousands of UK jobs, and encourages hundreds of International businesses to locate in the UK. Local passengers – those travelling to and from the hub – provide the backbone of the airport system while transfer passengers provide the volume to double frequencies and significantly increase the number of destinations served.

One-third of Heathrow's passengers are transfer passengers, who are regarded as critical as they help maintain a global network of direct overseas air routes. In fact, it is because of them that around two-thirds of all UK long haul flights depart from Heathrow. For instance, there may not be sufficient local demand to support regular, frequent flights to the Middle-East, but because many transfer passengers use Heathrow, it creates enough demand for airlines to operate a long haul route. This is not just beneficial to the airport operator, but bigger the network of its direct air routes, the more attractive a city and a country become to businesses.

Heathrow, located 24 kilometres or 15 miles west of Central London, was built during the Second World War – to be less vulnerable to enemy bombers. It had

---

[1]Source: © 2009, IBS Research Center.

[2]The term 'hub airport' represents an airport whose facilities can handle large volumes of connecting passengers in a short span of time. The aim of a hub is to minimize the connect time between flights, while offering the maximum number of possible connections.

[3]Widely or albeit erroneously referred to as the 'British Airports Authority' by both media and the public, the company admits its name is strictly 'BAA Limited' and does not stand for anything.

[4]Ferrovial is one of the world's leading construction groups, specializing in four strategic lines of business – airports, construction, transport infrastructure and services throughout Spain, the UK, Portugal and rest of the world.

EXHIBIT 1   TOTAL TERMINAL PASSENGERS, 2007

Rank	Airport	Passengers (million)
1	Atlanta	89.3
2	Chicago O'Hare	76.2
3	Heathrow	67.9
4	Tokyo-Haneda	66.7
5	Los Angeles	61.9
6	Dallas Fort Worth	59.8
7	Paris-CDG	59.7
8	Frankfurt	53.9
9	Beijing	53.7
10	Madrid	52.1

Source: 'Top Ten World Airports – 2007', http://www.baa.com, 2007

up to nine runways of which only three survived, and just two, running east–west, proved suitable for regular use. In 1946, the airport changed hands from military to civil and construction of terminals and an air traffic control tower followed later.

Heathrow's first terminal (then called the Europa building and today's Terminal 2) was opened for short-haul flights in 1955. The Oceanic building (today's Terminal 3), mainly operating long-haul flights was opened in 1961, and Terminal 1, mainly handling UK domestic and European flights, in 1968. All three terminals formed a cluster at the centre of the airport's site causing perpetual traffic congestion (Exhibit 2).

Increased congestion in the central area led to the birth of a £200 million Terminal 4 on the airport's southern side in 1986. Though a modern facility, the terminal is an inconvenient 10–20 minute transfer from the heart of Heathrow. The government gave BAA the approval to build a fifth terminal in November 2001, following the longest public enquiry in British planning history – around 4 years. Terminal 5 (T5) – a £4.3 billion ($8.5 billion) glass–steel masterpiece situated within the airport's existing boundary – is exclusively for British Airways (BA).

T5, however, experienced teething problems in its first eight days, since its opening on March 27th 2008. Many flights were cancelled, hundreds of passengers stranded and around 20 000 bags went missing. Sir Peter Hall, president of the Town and Country Planning Association calls Heathrow's history 'as a series of minor planning disasters that together make up one of the country's truly great planning catastrophes'.

Nevertheless, Heathrow has brought economic benefits to London and other adjoining areas. According to Oxford Economic Forecasting (OEF), a consultancy, business passengers induce wider economic benefits than do leisure passengers. OEF also reveals that 32 per cent of all UK companies regard Heathrow as vitally important and 22 per cent as very important (Exhibit 3). In addition, Heathrow is most strongly valued by companies based in London or counties close to Heathrow. However, OEF acknowledges that business travel accounts for only a third of Heathrow's passengers.

Heathrow is over-utilized because it is cheaper for airlines, and due to rapid growth in transit and transfer passengers (Exhibit 4). According to the Civil Aviation Authority (CAA), the UK aviation regulatory body, these were only 9 per cent of the total in 1992, but they reached 35 per cnt by 2004. The airport currently serves around 68 mppa using buildings and systems designed for 45 mppa. With T5 in use, the airport's total passenger capacity is expected to reach 90 mppa.

Owing to capacity constraints, the number of destinations served by Heathrow has fallen from 227 in 1990 to 180 in 2007, a 20 per cent change, as airlines have used their scarce existing slots to concentrate on the most profitable routes. Consequently, Heathrow has slipped from second in 1990 to fourth in 2004 and is expected to slip further to seventh in 2010 in the European rankings for the most number of destinations served. At a time when Chinese airlines are seeking to expand routes to Europe, Heathrow's two runways operate at 99 per cent permitted runway capacity, whereas its rivals have 25 per cent spare capacity (Exhibit 5). Amsterdam has five full-size runways (with 47.8 million terminal passengers), Paris Charles de Gaulle (CDG) and Madrid have four each and Frankfurt expects to have its fourth by 2010. Elsewhere, Dubai has six runways and is in a rush to become a global hub linking Asia with the rest of the world. Heathrow's lack of capacity for growth is a potential threat to the continued pre-eminence of London as Europe's financial centre. Moreover, Heathrow is bursting at the seams. A plane takes off or lands at Heathrow every 45 seconds, and the tiniest mishap, such as a thunderstorm or high winds, can cause delays and cancelled flights.

As demand for air travel has risen, governments have attempted to relieve Heathrow by diverting

EXHIBIT 2 LONDON-HEATHROW AIRPORT

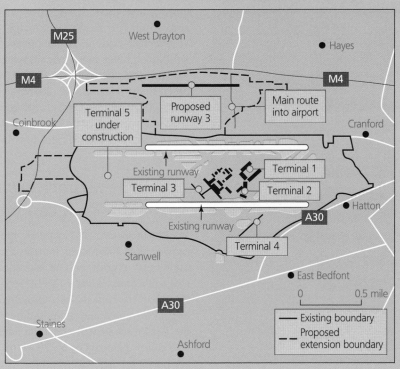

Source: http://www.telegraph.co.uk, November 24th 2007

EXHIBIT 3 IMPORTANCE OF AIRPORTS – ALL UK COMPANIES

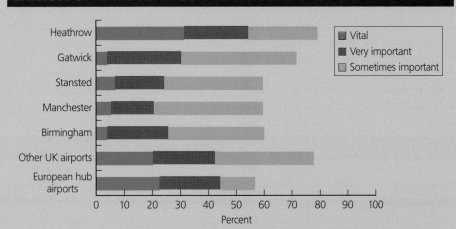

Sources: 'The Economic Contribution of the Aviation Industry in the UK', www.oef.com/Free/pdfs/Aviation2006Final.pdf, October 2006, page 56

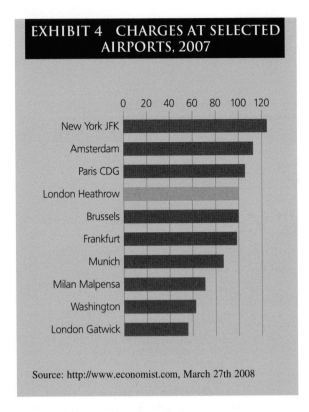

EXHIBIT 4 CHARGES AT SELECTED AIRPORTS, 2007

Source: http://www.economist.com, March 27th 2008

traffic to other airports close to London. Gatwick, that opened in the late 1950s and Stansted, in the 1970s are the two preferred airports for low-cost carriers, such as easyJet and Ryanair. However, they are nearly as full as Heathrow, and airlines have had little incentive to move their long haul routes and transfer traffic from Heathrow. According to Civil Aviation Authority's (CAA) estimates, the passenger-traffic to, from and within Britain, is not likely to fall below its long-term trend of 5 per cent putting Heathrow's image as UK's major hub airport in jeopardy.

Meanwhile, the Competition Commission, deluged with complaints from airlines and passengers about BAA's poor performance, is investigating whether its monopoly in the south-east has contributed to Heathrow's awfulness. BAA's parent Ferrovial, however, aims to change Heathrow's image with continued investment. Expansion is the demand of both BAA and BA, which holds more than 40 per cent of take-off and landing slots at the airport. Two new runways are proposed in the south-east by 2030: the first at Stansted by 2011–2012, followed as quickly as possible by a third short runway at Heathrow. It is also proposed to safeguard land for a second runway at Gatwick after 2019.

The airport expansion programme

BAA's proposals at Heathrow are two-fold: a new runway at 2,200 metres long to accommodate all but the largest aircraft, and an additional passenger terminal with direct access to rail services. Expansion at Heathrow is conceivable, provided BAA meets EU targets on noise and air pollution. OEF believes that the third runway will create an additional capacity of 31 million passengers by 2030, of which 9.7 million are business passengers and the rest leisure. OEF also estimates the third runway contribution to GDP to be £7.2 billion by 2030, at 2005 prices.

The Department of Transport (DfT) suggests that expansion will increase the number of annual flights from around 480 000 per year to 720 000 by 2020, and fully meet the air quality limits. BAA and the government think that because aircrafts are getting quieter and cleaner, the extra flights will be bearable. However, the Environment Agency – the government's principal environmental advisor – is disputing this conclusion. It claims a third runway would contribute to global warming. John Sauven, executive director of Greenpeace, believes, 'There is no need whatsoever

EXHIBIT 5 HEATHROW – VULNERABLE TO FOREIGN COMPETITION

Airport	2007 Passenger numbers (mppa)	Runways	Destinations Served	2007 ATMs (Arrivals & Departures)	2010 ATM Capacity	% full
Heathrow	67.5	2	180	477,000	480,000	99%
Frankfurt	52.8	3	265	490,000	660,000	74.2%
Paris CDG	56.8	4	223	541,000	710,000	76.2%
Amsterdam	46.1	5	260	440,000	600,000	73.3%

Source: http://www.heathrowairport.com

for a third runway. If everybody took trains to Manchester, Paris, Scotland and Brussels rather than flying, then a third runway would not need to be built.'

The airport expansion would also require additional land, with a loss of around 700 homes, including the community of Sipson. Residents are fighting to save their village and believe that Heathrow's current noise and air pollution already amount to an environmental disaster that expansion will only worsen. Moreover, since most arriving planes use a flight path across the capital, they claim that accident rates could go up. Their fears were reinforced by the January 2008 crash of BA Boeing 777 that landed short of the runway ripping off part of its undercarriage.

Hundreds of protestors – wearing 'Stop Airport Expansion' T-shirts – opposed Heathrow's expansion plans. A member protested, 'It's a stupid idea to sign an agreement in Bali saying we want to save the planet and then we read there was going to be a third runway. The area, skies and planet won't take it.' But another group, called 'Future Heathrow', is lobbying for the airport's expansion. Lord Soley, the group's director and the Labour peer, opines that Heathrow could lose business to European rivals if not expanded. He considers the airport 'critically important to the economic prosperity of west London and the Thames Valley'. Rival hubs, on the other hand, have more capacity now than Heathrow will ever have (Exhibit 6).

Meanwhile, Ruth Kelly, UK transport secretary, provoked the fury of environmental campaigners with her proposals to expand Heathrow. In a written statement to parliament she said, '. . . for too long it [Heathrow] has operated at nearly full capacity, with relatively minor problems causing severe delays to passengers. If nothing changes, Heathrow's status as a world-class airport will be gradually eroded – jobs will be lost and the economy will suffer.'

Passenger-traffic forecasts suggest that, shortly after the third runway opens, in 2020, Heathrow will burst at the seams. Construction of new airport capacity is feasible only when many complex issues are resolved. So, if these issues rule out airport expansion as the principal solution, how else can Brown address the problem of chronic under-capacity on the ground? Proposals like the mixed mode operation of Heathrow's existing runways, building a Greenfield airport at Thames estuary, adopting an intermodal strategy and expanding Gatwick have been suggested as alternatives to Heathrow's expansion.

One of the alternatives suggested is the mixed mode operation of existing runways. Currently, the two runways at Heathrow are used either for take-off or landing at any one time, known as 'segregated' mode. During the day, on westerly operations, one runway is used for landings from 07:00 till 15:00 GMT and the other from 15:00 GMT until after the last departure. This arrangement runs for a week and the order is reversed every week. At night, there is runway alternation on both the westerly and easterly operations after the last departure at 06:00 GMT.

As a measure to deal with under-capacity in the interim period, BAA has asked the government to support the simultaneous use of its runways, referred to as 'mixed mode', by 2015. OEF estimates the introduction of mixed mode operations would allow for an additional capacity of 12 million passengers by 2030, of which 4.3 million constitute business passengers and the rest leisure. BA opines that mixed mode operations would allow Heathrow to serve more

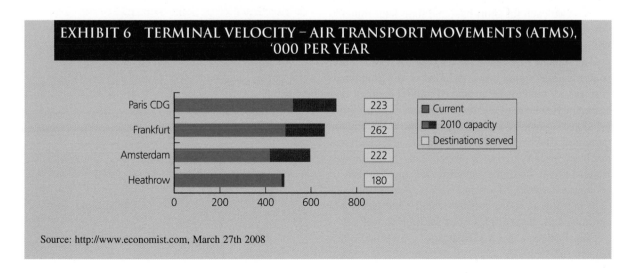

EXHIBIT 6   TERMINAL VELOCITY – AIR TRANSPORT MOVEMENTS (ATMS), '000 PER YEAR

Source: http://www.economist.com, March 27th 2008

destinations, including long haul services – currently not served from anywhere in the UK – that would otherwise go to continental hubs. These additional routes could have a mix of business and leisure use, while additional frequency on existing routes would be highly attractive to business passengers by adding flexibility in scheduling.

Willie Walsh, the BA chief executive, said the mixed mode operation could raise the annual total flights from the current limit to 520 000 – 550 000 a year, and reduce the emissions from the planes as they wait to land. He felt reducing such queuing would cut BA aircraft's emissions alone by 76 000 tonnes of CO_2 annually, an amount equivalent to the emissions from 150 round trips to New York. However, Mayor Ken Livingstone disagreed, and felt that 'the vast majority of Londoners living under the Heathrow flight path value the half a day's peace and quiet they get from runway alternation and want to see this retained.'

Another alternative is to move Heathrow away from densely populated neighbourhoods. Since the 1960s, major cities including Paris, Milan, and New York have moved their airports when faced with chronic under-capacity problem. 'In Hong Kong, the government spent 6 years and $20 billion building an airport on an artificial island and linking it by bullet train to the city.' A marine location is generally popular with residents' groups as it would keep away aircraft noise from inhabited areas, and could be used 24 hours a day. In Britain, however similar proposals have been blocked. In the 1970s, a scheme to build an airport on Maplin Sands in Essex was neglected because of lack of funds. The government also had the option to build a £33 billion hub on an artificial island in the Thames estuary in 2005. In fact, Bluebase, the architectural firm behind the plan, proposed four runways – two each for short haul and long haul routes – where planes could land and take-off round the clock without disrupting residents.

The scheme that would have called for regeneration of the Thames region however failed on the grounds of cost, risk of seabirds being sucked into jet engines, and before high-speed rail the 28-mile distance from central London was considered too great. Mark Willingale, partner of Bluebase, however believes that the DfT was not keen in carrying out a proper study, even though Bluebase had used the department's own model of economic benefits to obtain 'spectacular' results. In fact, the airport at the estuary would have easily accommodated all the flights from Gatwick as well.

The backlash against Heathrow's awfulness has resurrected demands to move the capital's main hub

airport to the Thames estuary. Boris Johnson, London Mayoral candidate is calling on the government to reexamine plans for a new airport in the estuary. He feels it is not impossible to move the capital's biggest airport as others have done it with much success. He further cautioned the government not to 'entrench a planning error of the 1960s by further expansion at Heathrow. We should look at whether there's a solution to the east, in the Thames estuary.' However, Lord Solely fears the new hub would put 72 000 Heathrow airport workers' lives in jeopardy, and deems the move to the estuary unrealistic.

The third alternative is to develop an intermodal strategy that focuses on limiting the rate of growth in air passenger numbers by encouraging travellers to use other forms of transport. By doing so, landing slots for short haul destinations – of less than 500 km – at airports can be withdrawn which in turn creates additional slots for long haul destinations. While this strategy is beneficial – as the time gains of flying over such short distances are often small, particularly when taking account of boarding times – short flights have a relatively large environmental impact per passenger kilometre because of high fuel usage during take-off and landing.

EXHIBIT 7   TIME-TAKEN FROM HEATHROW BY AIR AND TRAIN

Destination	Flights per day *	Time by plane (hrs)	Time by train (hrs)
Paris	60	3	3
Amsterdam	50	3.25	8
Edinburgh	40	2.5	4.75
Manchester	36	2.5	2.5
Brussels	30	3.25	2.75
Glasgow	28	2.75	5.75
Newcastle	12	2.75	3.15
Leeds/Bradford	10	2.5	2.5
Rotterdam	6	3.25	7
Durham/Tees Valley	6	2.5	3.25

*Figures are those of a typical day and could vary throughout the year Note: 1.5-hour check-in time added for domestic flights, 2 hour for European flights & the required half hour for Euro Star travellers. Journey times to/from the stations or airports not included.
Source: 'Short-Haul Flights: Clogging up Heathrow's Runways', www.hacan.org.uk, November 2006

HACAN – the organization representing residents under the Heathrow flight path – believes Heathrow could cut back around 100 000 flights annually, if there were no flights to and from the destinations where there exists a good rail alternative. Currently, Paris is the top destination from Heathrow with 60 flights a day between the two cities followed by Amsterdam (Exhibit 7). HACAN suggests that the government needs to restrict short haul landing slots,

impose higher taxes on short haul flights and offset the higher taxes on aviation with reductions in other taxes business pays.

Fast rail connections are happening all over Europe. Airports at Amsterdam, Paris and Frankfurt are well linked to high-speed rail networks. By networking air and rail traffic, Frankfurt airport has been a trendsetter of the intermodal hub strategy. The Frankfurt airport intermodal transportation hub is

EXHIBIT 8 FULL TEXT DR. CAROLINE LUCAS' LETTER

Dear Secretary of State,

I would like to take this opportunity to contribute to the Government's consultation regarding the proposed expansion of Heathrow Airport by means of a third runway. I am utterly opposed to the proposals and hope that you will give proper consideration to the views of the many thousands of my constituents whose lives will be further adversely affected should any expansion go ahead.

The government has said that the expansion will only go ahead if the area affected by 'aircraft noise' post- expansion would not be greater than the area affected in 2002. But this base line is deceptive. First, Concorde was still operating in 2002. Because of the way the Department for Transport (DfT) measures noise, Concorde's retirement in 2003 would allow BAA Ferrovial to bring in many more planes without extending the area affected . . .

Second, the area which should not be expanded is the so-called '57 decibel contour' – the area where noise levels average out at 57 decibels or higher over the course of a year. But the recent ANASE (Attitudes to Noise from Aviation Sources in England) study . . . found that in reality significant annoyance starts at around 50 decibels – a result that's consistent with the findings of the World Health Organisation (WHO). That means that many more people than previously admitted are affected by aircraft noise. At Heathrow, there are 258,000 residents inside the 57 decibel area, but over 2 million inside the 50 decibel contour . . . The DfT has commissioned a sequence of models of future 'air pollution' at Heathrow. The models make assumptions about emissions from aircraft, airport vehicles, cars at monitoring points near the airport; and then predict air pollution levels up to 2030. Yet just about every assumption going into these models is contentious, and adds to the

uncertainty of the predictions . . . That means that the total uncertainty arising from the model assumptions may well exceed the difference between the modelled levels of air pollution and the EU air quality limits. In those circumstances, it is almost impossible for the government to know whether it can meet air quality standards . . .

Aviation is the fastest-growing source of greenhouse gas emissions, with cumulative growth of 87 per cent between 1990 and 2004, a rate of over 4 per cent a year. At current rates of growth, the increased emissions from this sector will neutralise more than a quarter of the reductions required by the EU's Kyoto target by 2012 . . . Evidence from the World Development Movement suggests that the extra annual CO_2 from a third runway would be equivalent to all the CO_2 produced by Kenya in one year, yet international aviation is left out of the government's flagship climate change bill.

Some economists say that, as long as emissions are declining somewhere in the economy, it doesn't matter where the cuts are being made. However, the European Emissions Trading Scheme (ETS) takes no account of the other gases from aviation, which at altitude, are even more powerful greenhouse gases than CO_2 . . . I urge you to now start listening to the voices of local people and abide by the government's own stated commitment to reducing CO_2 emissions, by withdrawing the third runway expansion proposals for Heathrow immediately.

Yours sincerely,

Caroline Lucas – Green Party MEP for South East England.

Sources: Compiled by the authors from 'Heathrow expansion would be a "social and environmental disaster", says Green Principal Speaker in submission to consultation', www.greenparty.org.uk, February 26th 2008

connected to all transportation systems: Rail, road, and even waterways. With the future expansion of the high-speed rail network, Frankfurt airport will become one of Europe's key integrated transportation complexes. Heathrow's transport infrastructure, on the other hand, is far from the likes of Frankfurt and other European rivals.

The fourth alternative is to expand and use London-Gatwick Airport for both short- and long-haul services. Gatwick, located 43 kilometres or 27 miles south of central London, is the busiest single runway airport in the world. It is regarded as the only existing British airport with the potential to compete with Heathrow. It has good transport links and its main flight path is over the channel and farmland. The airport currently serves 79 airlines that operate from Gatwick's two terminals, serving 227 destinations. Gatwick's annual passenger traffic is around 35 million in 2007 and is expected to reach around 40 million by 2015. In 2007, Gatwick's passenger mix was 70 per cent UK leisure passengers, 10 per cent UK business passengers and 20 per cent foreign passengers.

Roy Griffins, chairman of London City Airport and a former head of civil aviation at the DfT, believes an expanded Gatwick might be able to lure a big airline alliance with lower prices and the promise of its own terminal. Another runway could support more traffic than Heathrow does now, but the 1979 legal agreement does not permit a new runway before 2019. Nevertheless, BAA's monopolistic hold over London's main airports has meant it has little incentive to consider expansion at Gatwick as a viable alternative.

Heathrow is clearly important to the economy, but the critical question is whether the expansion of Heathrow is essential to UK's economy? Steve Ridgway, chief executive of Virgin Atlantic, thinks, 'Limiting growth at Heathrow wouldn't prevent climate change because that growth would only go elsewhere. It would only serve to damage the UK's competitiveness, as well as limit the choice available to the huge number of people living in London who want to travel to visit friends and family.' On the other hand, Dr. Caroline Lucas, Green Party Principal Speaker and a Member of the European Parliament, in her letter to the Secretary of State, labelled the expansion plans as 'irresponsible, deceptive and environmentally disastrous' (Exhibit 8). It remains to be seen what Brown would do regarding Heathrow's future.

Strategic leadership and innovation at Apple Inc.

By Loizos Heracleous and Angeliki Papachroni[1]

Stop and look at Apple for a second, since it's an odd company. . . . While most high-tech firms focus on one or two sectors, Apple does all of them at once . . . Apple is essentially operating its own closed miniature techno-economy. . . . If you follow conventional wisdom, Apple is doing it all wrong. And yet . . . this is the company that gave us three of the signature technological innovations of the past 30 years: the Apple II, the Macintosh and the iPod.

(Grossman, 2005)

Voted as the most innovative company for three consecutive years during 2006–2008 and as America's number 1 most admired company, Apple seemed to have it all: innovative products that have redefined their markets (such as the iMac and the iPod), a consumer base as loyal as a fun club, and a business model characterized by vertical integration and synergies that no competitor could easily imitate. The Apple brand had transcended the barriers of the computer industry to traverse the consumer electronics, record, movie, and the video and music production industries (see Figure 1 for an outline of Apple's product and service portfolio). In 2008 the Apple brand was listed as the 24th most valuable global brand (up from 33rd place the previous year), valued at $13.7bn.

After a lacklustre period during 1989–1997 when Apple was nearly written off, its dynamic comeback was impressive. Between 2003 and 2008 Apple's sales tripled to $24 billion and profits increased to $3.5 billion, up from a mere $24 million (see Table 1 for an outline of Apple's financial performance during 2006-8). Apple topped Fortune 500 companies for total return to shareholders both over 2003-2008 (94 per cent return) as well as over 1998–2008 (51 per cent return), a remarkable achievement.

But things haven't always been that rosy for the company once known as the underdog of the computer industry. During the time when Steve Jobs was not part of the organization (1985–1997) Apple progressively degenerated to the point of struggling for survival. Apple charged premium prices and operated through a closed proprietary system, at a time when more economical, IBM-compatible PCs gained mass appeal. Its cost base was high compared with its major competitors. This combination of factors led to shrinking market share and lower profitability. Apple lost momentum in the PC industry, despite the effort of three different CEOs to reverse the downfall (see Table 2 for a timeline of Apple's CEO tenures).

John Sculley attempted to gain market share (at the time around 7 per cent) by introducing lower priced products that still had a technological edge, forged alliances with IBM to work on a joint operating system and multimedia applications, and outsourced much of manufacturing to subcontractors to cut costs. A joint alliance was also formed with Novell and Intel to reconfigure Apple's OS to run on Intel chips. By the end of Sculley's tenure in 1993, however, market share was at around 8 per cent, and Apple's gross profits reduced from around 50 per cent to 34 per cent.

During Spindler's tenure, the alliances with Intel and Novell, as well as with IBM, were exited, and a decision was taken to license Apple's OS to companies that would make Mac clones (a decision reversed by Jobs in 1997). There was focus on international growth, and more cost-cutting efforts. With performance remaining flat, Spindler was replaced by Gil Amelio. In 1996, under Amelio, Apple went through three successive restructurings and further cost cutting. At the same time, Amelio aimed to return Apple to its premium price, differentiation strategy. The biggest challenge at the time was the release of Apple's new generation operating system in response to the release of Microsoft's Windows 95, which had received great attention upon its release one year earlier. Apple's OS system named Copland, on the other hand, was so behind schedule that the company decided to turn to external help. Ironically, Apple turned to NeXT, a software company founded by Steve Jobs after his departure from Apple in 1985. Meanwhile, Apple's market share fell to 3 per cent and Amelio was forced out by the board of directors.

[1]Source: This case was prepared by Professor Loizos Heracleous and Angeliki Papachroni. Warwick Business School, January 2009. Reproduced with permission from the authors and www.ecch.com.

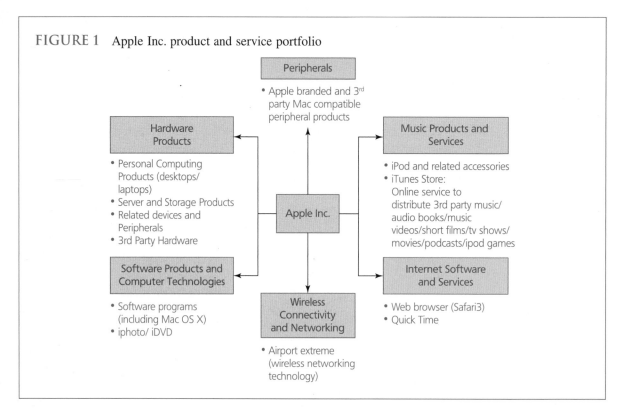

FIGURE 1   Apple Inc. product and service portfolio

After NeXT's help with the new version of Apple's operating system, Apple's executive board resolved to buy the company. A year later, in July 1997, Jobs was offered the title of Apple's CEO, after spending a few months as a consultant at Apple. This was a crucial time in the company's history. Apple's stock had sank to $3.30 and the company reported a net loss of $708 million in its second quarter that year, flirting with bankruptcy. At the same time competitors like Dell and Microsoft were thriving, following the tech boom of the late 1990s. Jobs took on the role of Interim CEO in 1997 and then became CEO during 2000.

The competitive landscape

By 2009, the computer technology industry had undergone some profound changes that shaped the competitive context within which Apple operated. IBM, the once undisputed leader in PC manufacturing, has moved away from its traditional territory of computer hardware and with a focus on computer technology, research and service consulting became a very different company from what it used to be in the 1990s. In 2009 IBM was the world's second largest software company after Microsoft, and its acquisition of PwC Consulting in 2002 marked IBM's serious entry to the business services sector. After selling its

PC and laptop business to Chinese company Lenovo in 2005 (a segment it had itself created) to allow more strategic focus on services, and higher end servers, IBM's strategy also moved to encompass open business approaches. IBM was a significant contributor to open source movements such as Linux by investing in the program's development, growth and distribution (Linux is supported on all modern IBM Systems) and in 2005 the company gave away approximately 500 software patents (valued over $10 million) so as to enhance global innovation and profit from newly created business opportunities. Through these actions, IBM aimed to enlarge the global market for IT products and services and to benefit by responding to this demand. IBM made over 50 acquisitions during 2002–2007, building a portfolio around 'networked, modularized and embedded technologies, including service-oriented architecture (SOA), information on demand, virtualization and open, modular systems for businesses of all sizes'. With IBM exiting the PC manufacturing industry the competitive environment in this front included HP, Dell, Acer and Lenovo, which together accounted for more than 50 per cent of worldwide PC shipments in 2007.

Following the launch of the IBM PC, Microsoft dominated the PC operating system market mostly because it offered an open standard that multiple PC

TABLE 1   Selected Apple financial data

	2008	Change	2007	Change	2006
Net sales by operating segment:					
Americas net sales	$ 14,573	26%	$ 11,596	23%	$ 9,415
Europe net sales	7,622	40%	5,460	33%	4,096
Japan net sales	1,509	39%	1,082	(11)%	1,211
Retail net sales	6,315	53%	4,115	27%	3,246
Other Segments net sales	2,460	40%	1,753	30%	1,347
Total net sales	$ 32,479	35%	$ 24,006	24%	$ 19,315
Unit sales by operating segment:					
Americas Mac unit sales	3,980	32%	3,019	24%	2,432
Europe Mac unit sales	2,519	39%	1,816	35%	1,346
Japan Mac unit sales	389	29%	302	(1)%	304
Retail Mac unit sales	2,034	47%	1,386	56%	886
Other segments Mac unit sales(a)	793	50%	528	58%	335
Total Mac unit sales	9,715	38%	7,051	33%	5,303
Net sales by product:					
Desktop	$ 5,603	39%	$ 4,020	21%	$ 3,319
Portables	8,673	38%	6,294	55%	4,056
Total Mac net sales	14,276	38%	10,314	40%	7,375
iPod	9,153	10%	8,305	8%	7,676
Other music related products and services	3,340	34%	2,496	32%	1,885
iPhone and related products and serives	1,844	NM	123	NM	–
Peripherals and other hardware	1,659	32%	1,260	15%	1,100
Software, service, and other sales	2,207	46%	1,508	18%	1,279
Total net sales	$ 32,479	35%	$ 24,006	24%	$ 19,315
Unit sales by product:					
Desktops	3,712	37%	2,714	12%	2,434
Portables	6,003	38%	4,337	51%	2,869
Total Mac unit sales	9,715	38%	7,051	33%	$ 1,391
Nets sales per Mac unit sold	$ 1,469	0%	$ 1,463	5%	$ 1,391
iPod unit sales	54,828	6%	51,630	31%	39,409
Net sales per iPod unit sold	$ 167	4%	$ 161	(17)%	$ 195
iPhone unit sales	11,627	NM	1,389	NM	–

NM = Not Meaningful

Source: Apple Inc. Annual Report, 2008

makers could incorporate into their products. Windows OS became the standard operating system in the industry with more than 85 per cent of all PCs in the world running on some Windows version. Microsoft's revenue reached $60.4 billion in fiscal year 2008, an increase of 18 per cent over the previous year. By 2009 Microsoft faced increased competition in the software front from Apple, HP, IBM and Sun Microsystems, as well as Linux OS derived from UNIX. Microsoft's portfolio also included the online search

TABLE 2   Timeline of Apple's Chief Executive
Officers

1977–1981	Michael Scott
1981–1985	Mike Markkula
1985–1993	John Sculley
1993–1996	Michael Spindlee
1996–1997	Gil Amelio
1997–2000	Steve Jobs (Interim CEO)
2000–2009	Steve Jobs

(Source: Authors)

and advertising business (MSN portals, Live Search
etc) in which the company sought to invest further.
This was indicated by Microsoft's interest in acquiring
Yahoo, a deal which by the end of 2008 had not
reached agreement. The failing of initial talks led to
calls for the resignation of Yahoo's CEO, who indicated that he would resign as soon as a successor
was found. In late 2008 Microsoft's interest in Yahoo
was rekindled, but only in its search business. Microsoft's position in the entertainment industry was
holding strong with the Xbox 360 console selling
more than 19 million units and Xbox Live having
more than 12 million members.

The computer vendors: Hewlett-Packard and Dell

After the acquisition of Compaq in 2002 that brought
significant scale in its desktop and laptop product
lines, HP became the world's largest PC vendor, surpassing rival Dell in 2007 with a 3.9 per cent market
share lead. In 2007 the company's reported revenue
was $104 billion, making it the first IT company
in history to exceed revenues of $100 billion, and
the world's largest technology company in terms of
sales after IBM. HP's portfolio included personal
computing, imaging and printing-related products and
services, and enterprise information technology infrastructure, including enterprise storage and servers,
technology support and maintenance, consulting and
integration and outsourcing services.

Dell Inc. offered a range of product categories including desktop personal computers, servers and networking products, storage, mobility products, software
and peripherals, and services. It was the first computer
company to sell customized PCs directly to consumers
without using intermediaries. Once the leading PC
vendor in terms of both profitability and market share,
Dell faced increased competition in the desktop and

notebook business that made it difficult to sustain its
earlier growth and profitability rates. Although Dell
had based its success in its distinctive business model
of direct sales and built to order manufacturing, in
2007 the company initiated a strategic change program
that included investment in the design and release of
consumer friendly products through retail distribution.

Gaining scale from significant acquisitions, Acer
became the third largest PC vendor in the world. Acer
focused on the consumer market and in particular in
the production of notebook PCs. Lastly China-based
Lenovo became the fourth biggest PC vendor after
acquiring IBM's PC business for $1.75 billion. Leno-
vo had a strong position in the Chinese market where
it held 35 per cent market share.

Microprocessors: Intel

In the microprocessors front Intel was the undisputed
leader accounting for more than 80 per cent share in
the market of PC Central Processing Units. AMD was
Intel's closest competitor in terms of market share.
Intel's portfolio additionally included wired and
wireless Internet connectivity products and communications infrastructure products. The company was
effective in guiding the co-evolution of its offerings
with those of its customers, and had relentlessly driven
the evolution of computing power down a predictable
trajectory of semiconductor density increase, cost
reduction and performance improvement. As a result
the 2007 fiscal year ended with an 8 per cent revenue
increase, at $38.3 billion, with net income of $7 billion,
up by 38 per cent over 2006. By 2007 Intel was investing in new product areas such as mobile internet
devices and ultra-mobile PCs that leveraged on its
micro-processor   architecture   and   manufacturing
technology.

Apple 1997–2009: Turnaround and re-building an innovative organization

The return of Steve Jobs to Apple in 1997 marked the
beginning of a new era for the company. Jobs worked
for a salary of $1 per year for 30 months, leading
Apple's successful turnaround. His priority was to revitalize Apple's innovation capability. 'Apple had
forgotten who Apple was,' as he noted in an interview,
stressing that it was time for Apple to return to its core
values and build on them. At the time, Michael Dell
was asked at an investor conference what Jobs should

do with Apple. He replied 'I'd shut it down and give the money back to the shareholders'.

According to a former Apple executive who participated in Jobs' first meeting with the top brass on his return to Apple, Jobs went in with shorts, sneakers, and a few days' of beard, sat on a swivel chair, spun slowly, and asked them what was wrong with Apple. Jobs then exclaimed that it was the products, and that there was no sex in them anymore. Upon taking charge, Jobs announced that Microsoft would invest $150 million in Apple, reaffirming its commitment to producing Microsoft Office and other products for the Mac, and soon scrapped the Mac OS licensing programme, that he believed was cannibalizing Mac sales. He axed 70 per cent of new products in development, kept 30 per cent that he believed were 'gems', and added some new projects that could offer breakthrough potential. He also revamped the marketing message to take advantage of the maverick, creative Apple brand, and repriced stock options to retain talent (and pushed for the resignation of board members who did not agree with the repricing).

In January 2000, when Apple became profitable with a healthy share price, Apple announced that it would buy Jobs a Gulfstream V jet, at a cost of $88 million, fulfilling Jobs' request for an aeroplane so he could take his family on vacation to Hawaii and fly to the East coast. Larry Ellison, Oracle CEO and a board member at Apple, said that the time, 'with what he's done, we ought to give him five airplanes!'.

Innovation at Apple

Long before it was voted as the world's most innovative company, Apple had placed its trademark on a long list of technological breakthroughs including the mouse, the graphical user interface, colour graphics, built-in sound, networking and wireless LAN, FireWire and many more. Apple's approach over the years had been to make use of a personal computer as easy and intuitive as possible through developing a highly responsive operating system, establishing standard specifications to which all applications software packages were expected to conform, strict control of outside developers, and delivering computers that did what they promised.

Apple's innovations enhanced the consistency across applications, which translated to ease of use, an attribute that helped to explain to some extent Apple's loyal consumer base. Another significant characteristic of Apple's approach to innovation was the diffusion of innovation across the value chain with both high end and low end products that appealed to a much wider audience ranging from amateurs to professionals (see Figure 2 for an outline of Apple's key product innovations). According to Jobs, 'Apple's DNA has always been to try to democratize technology. If you make something great then everybody will want to use it'.

Many of the disruptive innovations Apple has introduced are based on what employees call 'deep collaboration', 'cross pollination' or 'concurrent engineering'. This refers to products not developed in discrete stages but by 'all departments at once – design, hardware, software – in endless rounds of interdisciplinary design reviews'. In an interview about how innovation is fostered in the company, Jobs noted that the system for innovation is that there is no system:

The reason a lot of us are at Apple is to make the best computers in the world and make the best software in the world. We know that we've got some stuff that (is) the best right now. But it can be so much better. . . . That's what driving us. . . . And we'll sleep well when we do that.

Although Apple has been envied for its ability to catch the wave in new technology fronts earlier than competitors (such as in the case of iTunes and the iPhone) Jobs describes it as a rather slow process:

Things happen fairly slowly, you know. They do. These waves of technology, you can see them way before they happen, and you just have to choose wisely which ones you are going to surf. If you choose unwisely, then you can waste a lot of energy, but if you choose wisely, it actually unfolds fairly slowly.

Redefining the PC industry

Loyal to the value of user friendliness, Steve Jobs led the launch of the first iMac in 1998, his first project after his return to the company. The iMac, or 'the computer for the rest of us', its slogan when it was launched, revolutionized desktop computing by combining technological advancements and unique design. The combination of a CPU, a CD ROM drive and a modem all packed in a translucent case, that could support all 'plug and play' peripherals that were designed for Windows based machines, for the compelling price of $1299 marked Apple's dynamic comeback.

Even though the iMac was the fastest selling Macintosh model ever, Apple refused to rest on its laurels, continually updating its hardware and operating

FIGURE 2   Timeline of Apple's innovations

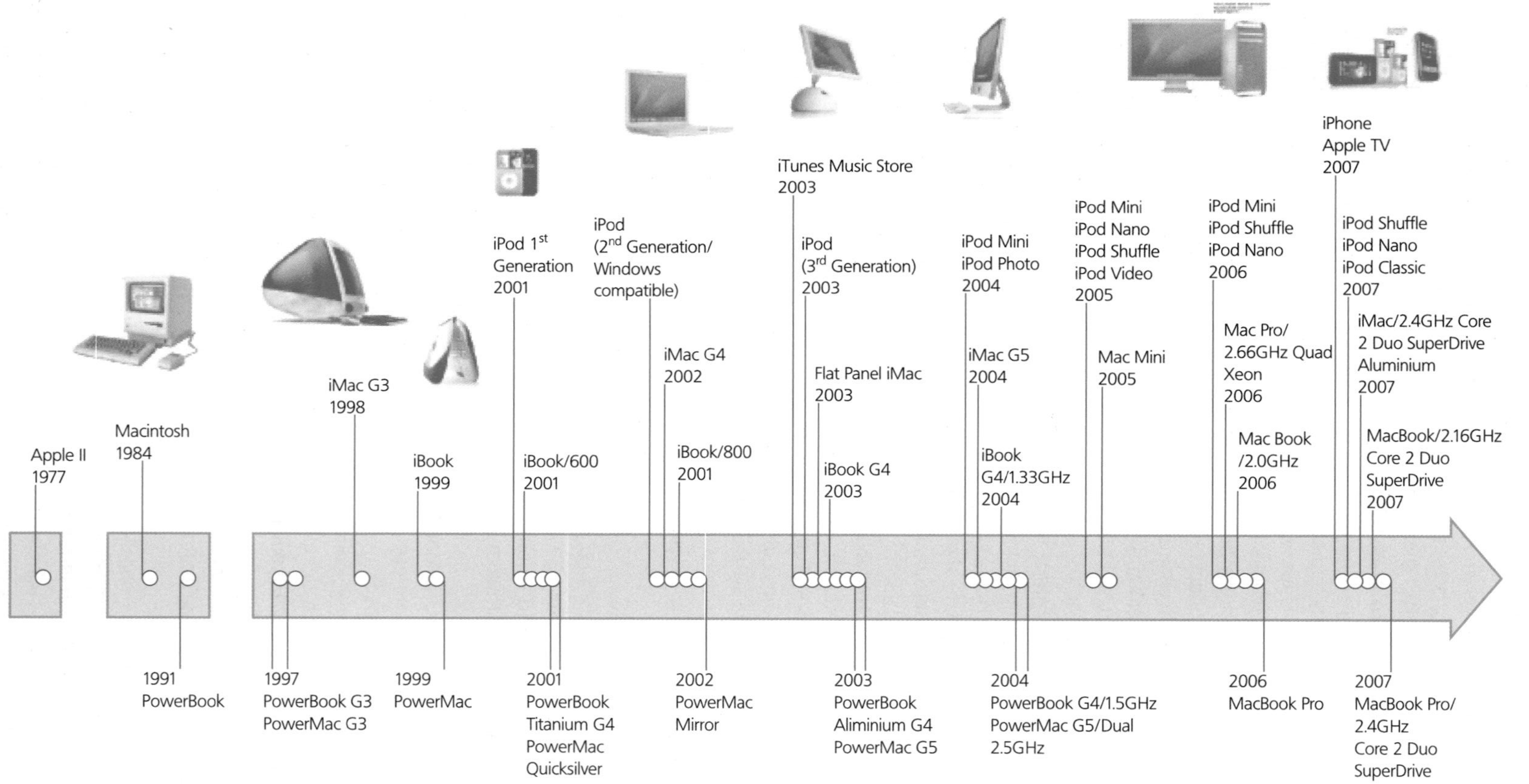

Note: Figure shows selected product offerings that are indicative of their categories. Consumer segment products are shown *above* the timeline, and professional segment products are shown *below* the timeline.

system, and launching updated models and software almost every 4 months. Most importantly the iMac was the first Apple product with wide consumer acceptance, since 70 per cent of sales where adding to the Macs already in use, helping Apple double its worldwide market share to 6 per cent by the end of 1998.

In parallel Steve Jobs proceeded to simplify Apple's product mix in terms of four lines of desktop and portable computers designed for both the professional and consumer markets. Following the iMac's success, the iBook was launched in 1999. This consumer portable computer featured an optional AirPort wireless networking hub that allowed up to ten Macs to share an Internet connection. Just six weeks after the iBook's unveiling, Apple had received more than 140 000 advance orders, making it a success equal to the iMac.

After the introduction of the iMac and the iBook, Apple's figures looked a lot healthier. In October 1999 Apple announced its eighth consecutive profitable quarter and closed that fiscal year with revenues of $6.1 billion and net earnings of $601 million. Whereas most of Apple's innovations led to an even more closed Apple archipelagos (software and hardware integration), at the same time Jobs decided to loosen control in other areas, for example the use of standard interfaces, such as the USB port. This change made the Mac a more open system since users of a Mac Mini for example could use a non-Mac keyboard. In the years to follow, a variety of innovative proprietary applications, developed in-house, supported the Macintosh product lines. These include programs such as those in the iLife package (iDVD, iMovie, iPhoto,) that offered editing and creative opportunities to users as well as Apple's own Web browser, Safari, developed in 2003.

Breakthrough innovation in consumer electronics and entertainment industries

In 2001 Apple introduced its first iPod, launching a new era for the company as it entered the consumer electronics industry. Capitalizing on the emerging trend of MP3 music, Apple introduced a breakthrough product that soon became synonymous with the MP3 music player category. With impeccable design and easy to use menu, the iPod could load 1000 songs in just 10 minutes and play music for 10 hours. The integration with the iTunes 2.0 software also made synchronizing music libraries a matter of few seconds. A year later, in 2002 Apple released more capacious iPods that could also work with Windows, a move that helped to skyrocket iPod sales. By the end of 2003 more than one million iPods were sold marking the first substantial stream of revenues apart from the Macintosh. Since then the iPod product range has been renewed every 3 to 5 months and the company announced in 2007 that it sold the 100 millionth iPod. These numbers made the iPod the fastest selling music player in history.

Arguably, one the most important innovations for Apple has been the launch of the iTunes Music store in 2003, a revolutionary service through which consumers could access and purchase online music for only $0.99 per song. The iTunes Music Store was compatible with all iPods (running both in Macs as well as Windows based computers) and served as Apple's Trojan horse to what Jobs has envisioned as the digital hub where digital content and Apple devices would be seamlessly interconnected. The downloaded songs had royalty protection and could only be played by iPods, bringing the interoperability between Apple's hardware, software and content to a new level and creating higher barriers to entry in this ecosystem.

Apple's next big innovation was the iPhone, a device combining a phone, a music player and a personal computer that was expected to redefine the mobile phone industry in the same way iPod and iTunes revolutionized the music industry. According to Jobs, 'It was a great challenge: Let's make a great phone that we fall in love with. Nobody had thought about putting operating systems as sophisticated as an OS X inside a phone, so that was a real question'. iPhone's success is attributed not only to its technological capacity but also to its design: 'We had a different enclosure design for this iPhone until way too close to the introduction to ever change it. And it came one Monday morning and I said: I just don't love it. And we pushed the reset button. That happens more than you think because it is not just engineering and science. There is art too.' According to Burrows and Grover (2006), 'Jobs' true secret weapon is his ability to meld technical vision with a gut feel of what regular consumers want and then market it in ways that make regular consumers want to be part of tech's cool club.'

Playing by different rules: Sticking with a proprietary ecosystem

Apple's innovations have redefined existing product categories such as music players, and helped the company successfully enter hotly contested new markets such as the entertainment industry. Key to these achievements have been the focus on design, the consumer experience, and the seamless integration of hardware and software (such as in the case of the iPod and iTunes).

The tight integration of its own operating system, hardware and applications, has been a strategy followed diligently by Apple. As Steve Jobs says: 'One of our biggest insights [years ago] was that we didn't want to get into any business we didn't own or control the primary technology, because you'll get your head handed to you. We realized that for almost all future consumer electronics, the primary technology was going to be software. And we were pretty good at software.'

Apple is nearly unique among contemporary technology companies in doing all of its own design in-house, at its Cupertino campus. Other companies have outsourced most or all of their product design function, relying on outsourced design manufacturers (ODMs) to develop the products that with minor adaptations will fit into their product lines. Apple however believes that having all the experts in one place – the mechanical, electrical, software, and industrial engineers, as well as the product designers, leads to a more holistic perspective on product development; and that a critical mass of talent makes existing products better and opens the door to entirely new products. According to Jobs, '. . . you can't do what you can do at Apple anywhere else. The engineering is long gone in the PC companies. In the consumer electronics companies they don't understand the software parts of it. There's no other company that could make a MacBook Air and the reason is that not only do we control the hardware, but we control the operating system. And it is the intimate interaction between the operating system and the hardware that allows us to do that. There is no intimate interaction between Windows and a Dell computer'.

The company's tightly knit proprietary system has been frequently seen as the reason for Apple's loss of initial momentum in the PC industry and increasing isolation until the mid 1990s. According to Kahney, 'When Jobs returned to Apple in 1997, he ignored everyone's advice and tied his company's proprietary software to its proprietary hardware'. He has persisted in following this strategy over the years even when all other Silicon Valley firms turned towards openness and interoperability. Tony Fadell, Vice President of engineering in the iPod division, notes that Apple aims to develop a self-reinforcing, synergistic system of products rather than a series of individual products: 'The product now is the iTunes Music Store and iTunes and the iPod and the software that goes on the iPod. A lot of companies don't really have control, or they can't really work in a collaborative way to truly make a system. We're really about a system'.

Over the years, there have been some notable exceptions to this proprietary approach. In order to reach a broader consumer base, in late 2003 Apple offered a Windows compatible version of iTunes allowing not only Windows users to use the iPod but more importantly to familiarize them with Apple products. Another milestone came with the company's switch from PowerPC processors made by IBM to Intel chips, a decision announced in mid-2005. This decision allowed Macs to run Windows software, implied lower switching costs for new Mac consumers and also allowed software developers to adapt more easily their programs for Apple. A previous alliance with Microsoft occurred in 1997 when Microsoft agreed to invest $150 million in Apple, reaffirming its commitment to develop core products such as Microsoft Office for the Mac.

Apple has developed a series of strategic alliances in the course of its efforts to become the centre of the digital hub, where digital content would be easily created and transferred to any Apple device. Development of the iPod, iTunes and iPhone have necessitated these alliances, since entry in the entertainment and consumer electronics markets would not have been possible without some key strategic partners (for example the big record labels for iTunes such as EMI, Sony BMG, Universal and Warner Brothers, or YouTube for the iPhone). In this process of building systems, Apple has been very selective about its partners. Rather than aiming for the most partners, Apple focuses on engaging with the best companies for a specific purpose (for example Apple has partnered with Google, in developing mapping and video applications for the iPhone).

At the same time Apple has proceeded with a number of acquisitions intended to strengthen its core competencies. For example, in 2002 Apple acquired the German specialist in music software, Emagic, as well as Prismo Graphics, Silicon Grail and Nothing Real, three small companies involved in professional level video creation and production. In April 2008 Apple also announced the acquisition of the boutique microprocessor company PA Semi, known for its highly sophisticated and low priced chips. With that acquisition Apple is said to be moving towards bringing its chip design in-house, building an ever more tightly knit ecosystem that helps to prevent copycat designs from rivals and to design chips for supporting specific new products or applications. According to COO Tim Cook: 'One traditional management philosophy that's taught in many business schools is diversification. Well, that's not us. We are the antibusiness school'.

In 2001, Apple created a retail division to enable it to sell its products directly to the public. By mid-2008 there were 215 retail stores, most of them in the US, accounting for almost 20 per cent of total revenues. In 2006 Apple entered into an alliance with Best Buy, and by the end of 2007 Apple products could be purchased in over 270 Best Buy stores.

Corporate culture and human capital

According to Apple's COO Tim Cook, Apple 'is not for the faint of heart'. Apple's culture is all about intense work and perfectionism but in a casual environment. Jobs stimulates thinking out of the box and encourages his employees to experiment and share with others 'the coolest new thing' they have thought of. It may not be accidental that Apple's emblem of corporate culture is a pirate flag with an Apple rainbow coloured eye patch, designed after a famous Jobs quote: 'It's better to be a pirate than join the navy.' This flag was hanging over the Macintosh building as Apple's team was working on the first iMac, to act as a reminder of their mission. 'Processes lead according to Jobs to efficiency, not innovation nor new ideas. These come from people meeting up in the hallways, calling each other in the middle of the night to share a new idea or the solution to a long thought as unsolved problem'.

Along with the rebel spirit that Jobs wants to maintain, Apple has a tradition of long working hours and relentless pursuit of perfection. Each manufacturing and software detail is worked and reworked until a product is considered perfect, thus providing a seamless integration of software and hardware. Apple's engineers spend so much time on each and every product that they are able to foresee and respond to any possible difficulties a consumer might encounter when using it. 'It's because when you buy our products, and three months later you get stuck on something, you quickly figure out [how to get past it]. And you think, "Wow, someone over there at Apple actually thought of this!" And then six months later it happens again. There's almost no product in the world

that you have that experience with, but you have it with a Mac. And you have it with an iPod'.

Apple's employees are not paid astronomically. They are not pampered, nor do they enjoy unique privileges beyond what most large companies offer. They are talented people with passion for excellence, proud to be part of the Apple community. Moreover they want to be part of a company that believes that the best way to predict the future is to invent it. This pride stems from a corporate culture that fosters innovation and a sense of Apple's superiority against competitors. Apple recruits talent of the highest calibre, and Jobs is known for approaching people who are known as the best in what they do and recruiting them to Apple. According to Gus Mueller, founder of a software development firm that develops software for Apple, 'Apple only hires top-notch folks. I know a number of people there, and they are all super smart and creative. I don't know a single person who shouldn't be there'. As Steve Jobs said: 'We may not be the richest guy in the graveyard at the end of the day, but we're the best at what we do. And Apple is doing the best work in its history.'

Steve Jobs' leadership

When Jobs returned to Apple in 1997 after an absence of 12 years, he arrived with much historical baggage. He was Apple's co-founder at the age of 21, and was worth $200 million by the age of 25. He was then forced to resign by the age of 30, in 1985, after a battle over control with CEO John Sculley which ended in Jobs losing all operational responsibilities. Jobs (who had been executive VP and General Manager of the Macintosh division) was considered a threat to the company, accused of trying to 'play manager' and control areas over which he had no jurisdiction. He was considered 'a temperamental micromanager whose insistence on total control and stylish innovation had doomed his company to irrelevance'.

Twenty-two years later however Jobs was voted as one of the greatest entrepreneurs of all time by *Business Week*. His personality left a mark on Apple in a way that only a few leaders had achieved, making his name synonymous with the company and its remarkable turnaround. Described by his colleagues as brilliant, powerful and charismatic, he could also be a demanding and impulsive perfectionist. As Jobs puts it: 'My job is not to be easy on people. My job is to take these great people we have and to push them and make them even better. How? Just by coming up with more aggressive visions of how it could be'.

Many believe that Jobs' achievement of being regarded as one of the greatest technology entrepreneurs is not based so much on his knowledge of technology (he is not an engineer or a programmer, neither does he have an MBA or college degree) but on his innate instinct for design, the ability to choose the most talented team and 'the willingness to be a pain in the neck for what matters for him most'. With regard to the iMac, for example, a product concept he and Jonathan Ive, Head of design had envisioned, the engineers were initially sceptical: 'Sure enough, when we took it to the engineers, they said, "Oh." And they came up with 38 reasons. And I said, "No, no, we're doing this." And they said, "Well, why?" And I said, "Because I'm the CEO, and I think it can be done." And so they kind of begrudgingly did it. But then it was a big hit.' Jobs has cited himself as 'co-inventor' on 103 separate Apple patents.

Jobs could be both inspirational but also experienced as scary. According to Guy Kawasaki, former head of developers, 'Working for Steve was a terrifying and addictive experience. He would tell you that your work, your ideas, and sometimes your existence were worthless right to your face, right in front of everyone. Watching him crucify someone scared you into working incredibly long hours. . . . Working for Steve was also ecstasy. Once in a while he would tell you that you were great and that made it all worth it'. Apart from displaying such behaviours as parking his car in handicapped places and publicly losing his temper, Jobs often made his employees burst into tears through direct and personal criticism. Robert Sutton, management professor at Stanford, discussed Steve Jobs in his book 'The no asshole rule' in the chapter on the virtues of assholes. Sutton then reflected further on his discussion of Steve Jobs in his blog, suggesting that Jobs may be mellowing as he gets older. Yet, according to Palo Alto venture capitalist Jean-Louis Gasse, a former Apple executive who once worked with Jobs, 'Democracies don't make great products. You need a competent tyrant'.

The high praise as well as high criticism made people try harder, jump higher and work later into the night. Jobs is credited with imposing discipline on Apple, a quality that the company had lacked for years. The company that used to be known as the 'ship that leaks from the top' due to its relaxed management style and corporate culture was soon transformed into a tightly controlled and integrated machine after Jobs' arrival. At Pixar, things were seen differently than at Apple however. Reportedly Jobs spent less than a day per week there, and was hands off, particularly on the creative front. According to a Pixar employee, 'Steve doesn't tell us what to do . . . Steve's our benevolent benefactor'.

Jobs' charisma is depicted in the way he briefed his team concerning a new product: 'Even though Steve didn't draw any of the lines, his ideas and inspiration made the design what it is. To be honest, we didn't know what it meant for a computer to be "friendly" until Jobs told us'. As author Scott Kelby put it: 'There is one thing I am certain of: Steve's the right man to lead Apple. There's never been anyone at Apple who has had the impact that Steve has since his return. He may be a tyrant, demanding, unforgiving and the worst boss ever. But he is also a visionary. A genius. A man who gets things done. And the man who kept Apple afloat when a host of other nice guys couldn't'.

Jobs brought his own brand of strategic thinking to Apple: 'The clearest example was when we were pressured for years to do a PDA, and I realized one day that 90 per cent of the people who use a PDA only take information out of it on the road. Pretty soon cell phones are going to do that so the PDA market's going to get reduced to a fraction of its current size. So we decided not to get into it. If we had gotten into it we wouldn't have the resources to do the iPod'. Jobs has often said 'I'm as proud of what we don't do as I am of what we do'.

Challenges on Steve Jobs' watch

In October 2003 Jobs was diagnosed with pancreatic cancer. Whereas this disease is fatal, his case was a rare but treatable form, if operated on. Jobs, a vegetarian and Buddhist, decided not to get operated but to follow a special diet and to seek alternative medical approaches that he believed would cure him. Apple's board of directors was aware of his condition, but a decision was made to not disclose it to investors. The board of Pixar, the other public company where Jobs was CEO, was not aware of his condition. In July 2004, after a scan revealed a growth in the tumour, Jobs finally had the surgery. The next day his employees and the media found out about his situation, through an email he sent his employees that was released to the press. On the day of the announcement Apple's shares dropped by 2.4 per cent, a relatively low figure, bearing in mind the severity of the situation. Assuring everyone that he was cured, Jobs returned to his duties a few months later.

Jobs' recent tenure has also been marred by other issues. In 2006, after a series of articles in the *Wall Street Journal* about options backdating, Apple set up a board committee to examine whether it had engaged in this practice, and the committee concluded that it had done so between 1997 and 2001 with regard to 6428 option grants (around a sixth of the total). There were no backdating issues before Jobs took over as CEO. Disney also investigated option grants at Pixar during Jobs' CEO tenure and found irregularities as well. However, Steve Jobs did not personally benefit from the options backdating, and Apple has been extremely co-operative with the SEC investigation on the issue. The SEC filed charges against Apple's former general counsel and CFO for organizing the backdated option grants and falsifying relevant documentation. In a public statement, the CFO said that he had made Jobs aware of the accounting implications of the backdated options.

When Jobs took over at Apple in 1997, he restructured the board of directors to create a new board with six members, two of which remained from the earlier board. The new members included Oracle CEO Larry Ellison, a close friend of Jobs, as well as Intuit CEO Bill Campbell, a former employee of Apple and Jobs' neighbour. Former SEC chairman Arthur Levitt was surprised to be first invited by Jobs to join the new board, and then 'dis-invited', after Jobs had read one of Levitt's speeches on corporate governance and concluded that the issues Levitt mentioned in that speech were not applicable to Apple.

This tight relationship between Jobs and Apple along with his health status that some perceive as fragile, have given room for speculation about his replacement, should that be necessary. *Fortune* magazine named Tim Cook, Apple's COO as the most probable candidate for the position. Cook's role in Apple's operations since 1998 has given him a prominent position next to Jobs, as he is the only person to have a vast area of responsibility apart from Jobs himself and the one who replaced him while he was recovering from his pancreatic operation. In any case Jobs' plans regarding his future successor remain veiled. Jobs' immense influence on Apple has given pause for scepticism regarding Apple's future without him. As Fortune's editor Elkind notes: 'In the 26 years that Fortune has been ranking America's Most Admired Companies never has the corporation at the head of the list so closely resembled a one-man show'.

Looking to the future

In January 2007, Apple Computer changed its name to Apple Inc., signifying a shift away from its computer vendor roots. Since 2006, revenues from desktop and portable computers were accounting for less than half of Apple's total revenues. By early 2009, Apple had come a long away: it had produced the world's fastest personal computer, introduced a series of attractive new Macintosh models with a reliable, competitive operating system known for its astonishing backward compatibility, created a cult following of iPod users, and begun its inroads into the mobile phone industry with the iPhone.

Despite Apple's impressive comeback, its share in the worldwide PC industry hovered below 3 per cent, and the growth prospects of the iPod and iPhone were far from guaranteed. The company was faced with the threat of commoditization as the iPod market in developed countries showed some signs of maturity and music over mobile phones was becoming increasingly popular. Apple's competitors were introducing alternative products and some were attempting to copy Apple's approach to doing business. Sony for example, hired one of Apple's former executives, Tim Schaaff, as the company's new senior vice president for software development, and set the goal of imitating Apple's interoperability amongst products. In September 2008 T-Mobile, a mobile operator owned by Germany's Deutsche Telekom, presented its new phone, the G1, made by HTC, a Taiwanese manufacturer. The device was the first to be based on the Android software (Google's open-source operating system), while Samsung, HTC, LG Electronics, and Motorola were among the companies that said they would also produce phones that ran on Android.

E-giant Amazon set up its own online music store in September 2007 to provide music compatible with both Windows Media Player, iTunes and any MP3 player device. Half of the tracks available through Amazon MP3 store were priced at $0.89 compared to Apple iTunes' price at the time of $1.29. Finally MySpace, the world's largest social network, announced in April 2008 its cooperation with Sony, Universal and Warner to form Myspace Music, a one stop shop where visitors could communicate, share and buy music.

Some analysts believed that Apple's closed system might once again hold the company back from its potential mass appeal (as in the 1980s with the Mac OS) and recommended that Apple's future should be more based on openness and partnerships.

In January 2009, Jobs announced that he was taking leave of absence from Apple until June, due to health issues relating to a 'hormone imbalance'. COO Tim Cook would handle day-to-day operations, and Jobs would stay involved in major strategic decisions.

Commentators disagreed on the degree of impact Jobs' absence would have. Some said that the new products Apple would introduce over the following 18 months had already been developed under Jobs' leadership, and that Cook would manage Apple effectively in Jobs' absence. Others, however, believed that Jobs' motivational role, negotiation skills and creative vision were crucial for Apple.

Meanwhile, a week later Apple announced that its performance for the last quarter of 2008 beat expectations, with a net profit of $1.61 billion. By that time, it also emerged that the Securities and Exchange Commission were carrying out an investigation to ensure that Jobs' health related disclosures did not mislead investors.

By early 2009, Apple was faced with some critical decisions regarding its strategy for the future. Was its competitive advantage becoming eroded through product imitation, and attempts by other companies to duplicate Apple's key competencies? Should Apple focus more on the consumer electronics or the computer markets? Was it time for Apple to re-think its closed proprietary ecosystem? What would happen to Apple if it lost Steve Jobs for good? Was Apple still on the rollercoaster that characterized its history, at risk of heading downwards, after its upward climb?

References

Burrows, P. and Grover, R. (2006) Steve Jobs' magic kingdom. *Business Week*, 6 February. http://www.businessweek.com/magazine/content/06_06/b3970001.htm, accessed on 23 December 2008.

Grossman, L., (2005) How Apple does it, *Time*, October 16, http://www.time.com/time/magazine/article/0,9171,1118384,00.html, accessed on 1 December 2008.

Kahney, L. (2008) How Apple got everything right by doing everything wrong, *Wired Magazine*, April, pp. 137–142

Envy me? The rise and fall of Gucci

By Sally Simmons and Manfred Kets de Vries[1]

In 1993, Maurizio Gucci signed away his 50% holding in Gucci, thereby ending his family's ownership of a company that for three generations had been a by-word for luxury and glamour. The Gucci name had become synonymous with having made it – the label proclaimed the wearer's standing and significance. It had assumed an iconic status all its own.

But despite its success, the company had been the scene of bitter family feuding for more than two decades, turning son against father, brother against brother. Greed, rivalry, intrigue and violence ultimately tore the family and the company apart. Indeed, they almost seemed intent on destroying the source of their wealth and success. But if the Gucci saga was more than the Florentine drama the media loved to bill it as, its denouement was nothing less than tragic.

Part 1: Guccio Gucci

The Savoy Hotel in London attracted the great and the not so good from the day it opened in 1898. It was here that Oscar Wilde brought Bosie and other boyfriends; that Dame Nellie Melba had a dessert and toast named after her; that Messrs Ritz and Escoffier kicked off their careers; that George Gershwin played Rhapsody in Blue to its first UK audience; that Laurence Olivier met Vivien Leigh, and that Noel Coward entertained guests during an air raid in World War II. Today, it still provides celebrity tabloid fodder when the likes of Michael Douglas and Catherine Zeta Jones take to the dance floor, or Elton John lets his bath overflow, flooding a £1400-a-night suite.

All that, of course, happens upstairs. Downstairs, as when it first opened, the hotel service community attracts a multinational staff. It was here that, in 1899, Guccio Gucci turned up at the age of 17 and talked his way into a job as a humble kitchen assistant.

Italian emigration had been increasing steadily since the mid-19th century, mainly from rural areas in the north of the country where industrialization had failed to alleviate the poverty resulting from years of war and unrest Emigrants moved primarily to Austria, France and Germany, but some went to the UK, settling mainly in Scotland and London. In the 1850s there were an estimated 4000 Italians in the country, mostly artisans but also confectioners, shopkeepers, restaurateurs and retailers. By the 1890s there were more than 4000 of them established in Scotland alone, with the second-largest community in Wales, working mainly in the services supporting the shipping industry and the mines.

It is not clear what Guccio was escaping from back home but it must have been something significant to convince him that washing up below stairs in smoggy London was better than working in his family's straw hat business in the Tuscan sun. Very little is known of his early circumstances. The facts have been obscured by the more glamorous version of his dynastic history that he favoured later in life. His father, Gabriello, was not a successful businessman and the straw hats eventually failed. But neither were they peasants – his daughter remembered her grandparents as 'just simple folk with a little interest coming in from capital saved'.

Guccio worked his passage to London as a stoker on a steamer. He apparently had great charm and good looks as a young man, and he was ambitious. At The Savoy he gained promotion, becoming a waiter in its prestigious restaurant, and in less than three years he had accumulated enough money in appreciative tips to return to Italy and marry his sweetheart, Aida Calvelli, the mother of an illegitimate son who (it has been speculated) may have been one reason for Guccio's decision to leave his home town in the first place.

Guccio took back with him memories of the gilded stratum of society he had served. The clientele of The Savoy ranged from royalty (a bell was rung in the hotel when they approached) to the nouveaux riches who liked to advertise their wealth as they travelled: luggage, leather, labels – the trappings that indicated someone had arrived (in every sense of the word), might not stay long, but could afford to live in luxury in the most expensive hotels in the most exciting cities in the world.

[1]Source: This case was written by Sally Simmons of the Cambridge Editorial Partnership, under the supervision of Manfred Kets de Vries, Raoul de Vitry d'Avaucourt Chaired Professor of Leadership Development at INSEAD. Copyright © 2007 INSEAD.

While in London he had developed a remarkable insight for a poor man: far from meaning nothing, cost was immensely significant to the fabulously rich. The higher the price of luxury goods, the more desirable they became. They were the insignia – of class, rank, success, fortune – that their exclusive peer group recognized. Guccio Gucci understood these people and saw that beneath their superficiality there was an expectation of superior quality – enviable goods had to be worth envying – which he thought he knew how to satisfy.

All this was in the future, however. Guccio and Aida married shortly before the birth of their first child and only daughter, Grimalda, in 1903. They went on to have three sons, Aldo (1905), Vasco (1906) and Rodolfo (1912). A fourth boy died in childhood. Aida's illegitimate son, Ugo, was raised as their own. Before the first world war, Guccio worked in a variety of businesses and was the manager of a Florentine leather goods shop when he was called up to join the army in his mid-thirties. After the war he joined Franzi, manufacturers of quality leather goods, learning the trade from the bottom up: from the selection and treatment of hides in the tannery to the running of the retail business. Aida and the family remained in Florence while he worked in Rome, joining his family at weekends.

Quality

The war brought European travel to a halt, but by 1922, when Guccio decided to go into business, peace was established and tourists had begun to return to the streets and galleries of Italy's major cities. When shop premises became available in the Via della Vigna Nuova in Florence, a short walk from the Duomo and Piazza della Repubblica, Guccio judged it was time to build on his experience in London and his skills and knowledge of the luxury goods market. He left Franzi and went into partnership with an acquaintance, a Signor Calzolani, who provided the initial capital to back Guccio's business plans. However, their relationship was never easy and as soon as the business was stable Guccio bought Calzolani out of the partnership.

The new House of Gucci stocked quality leather goods that Guccio bought in from struggling German wholesalers, and was soon making a profit. But its local reputation centred on the high quality and superior workmanship of its repairs. After a while he expanded the small workshop to allow freelance craftsmen to create new lines for the shop. He selected workers carefully, employing only the best, and they turned out an eclectic range of items, from large pieces of heavy luggage and handbags to small gift pieces like belts, wallets, key fobs and jewellery cases. The high turnover of these accessories sustained the company's sales in difficult times. When leather supplies were scarce, particularly in the pre-war era, designs were adapted to include materials like canvas and wicker, but quality was never compromised.

Guccio is famously quoted as having said, 'Quality is remembered long after the price is forgotten' – so frequently that it has been described as the company motto. In fact, his motto was something quite different – 'Stay small to remain great' – a policy that, unlike Guccio's take on quality, was bitterly contested throughout the company's history.

By the mid-1930s Gucci's reputation had spread worldwide, more or less by word of mouth among moneyed travellers. Customers came from the UK, France, Germany and the US, countries that would again be at war before the end of the decade.

Guccio's eldest son Aldo, like his other children, had grown up in the business but was the only one to take an active role in the company before the second world war. Fearless, energetic and imaginative, Aldo was frustrated by his father's 'stay small' strategy and the slow growth of the business, which essentially waited for customers to come to it rather than reaching out to them. It was Aldo who devised the timeless GG symbol that appeared on all Gucci products and became an internationally recognized stamp of wealth and privilege. And it was he who petitioned for a second store in Rome, persuading his father that the tourists there would spend in a day what those in Florence spent in a week. The shop, which set new standards of opulence and cost a fortune to fit out, opened just months before Hitler invaded Poland. In such circumstances it should have been a disaster. In the event, it saved the company.

World War II and after

The Guccis were relatively lucky during the war. Aldo remained at the store in Rome, an 'open' city spared the Allied bombings. Vasco ran the factory in Florence. Rodolfo, a budding film star, joined the troops' entertainment service. Ugo, always a problem, joined Mussolini's Fascist forces and survived, but became a threat and an embarrassment to the family. After the war, Guccio bought out his interest in the business and further contact was effectively ended. The war's implications for the Gucci customer base were paralleled within the family. Aldo's wife was English; Rodolfo's German. Aldo's three young children, who had divided their time between Italy and England throughout the 1930s, now saw the two sides of their family potentially pitched against one another. While their father escaped military service, their mother was active in the Roman resistance, helping Allied prisoners to freedom at great risk to her safety, an undertaking for which she was later decorated.

Rome, in 1945, was full of American soldiers with time on their hands and money to spend. Within a surprisingly short time tourists began to return to those European cities that had escaped the bombing. Aldo's astute purchase meant that Gucci was better placed than its competitors in the early years of post-war recovery. The new store was stocked with lower- priced gift items (all now bearing the GG design) that made easily transported, unique presents and were snapped up in impressive quantities. More than a trademark was being established. 'A status symbol is not born,' said Aldo Gucci, some years later. 'It becomes one when it is accepted by a certain elite, and everyone then becomes eager to buy it.'

Myths and symbols

It is unclear where Gucci's equestrian motif, with its overtones of old European class, came from. Guccio liked the linked-stirrups effect that the GG initials produced and it seems to have been a small step from that to the proliferation of the hunting and racing symbols in Gucci lines and colours, which recalled racing silks. The symbolism spawned its own myth: the straw hat-making ancestors were transmuted into makers of high-class saddles for the Italian aristocracy, and the Gucci ancestors were almost ennobled. Guccio bought into his own fable to the extent of convincing himself and others that he had been The Savoy's maitre d', rather than a junior waiter and dish washer, a myth that persisted long after his death.

Whatever their origins, the Gucci style and legend were in tune with the times. Aldo found an outlet for his frustrated ambitions in establishing Gucci as the last word in style and taste. Stock and shop fittings attained the highest levels of quality and perfection, and orders rolled in from customers who were among the richest, most glamorous and prominent people in the world. By the early 1950s, film stars and royalty (even film stars who became royalty, like Grace Kelly, a lifelong customer) – the sort of people Guccio had served at The Savoy – were coming to his shop to buy goods bearing his initials for their exclusive cachet.

Part II: Sons and brothers

By the early 1950s, Gucci was in a position to expand internationally – to take its products to its customers in their own markets. But Guccio's 'stay small' policy was inflexible and it was made clear that, while he lived, the company would remain in Italy and in the family, notwithstanding the ambitions and vision of its younger members.

Ironically, at a time when the company was on the brink of becoming a spectacular success, relationships were becoming increasingly strained. The family saga, hidden for many years, was marked by envy, suspicion, antagonism and rivalry almost from the company's inception. Much of the Gucci phenomenon can be explained by its Italian context, but to understand what happened to the company we have to understand what happened in the family.

'Siamo Gucci'

Inconsistency seems to have been a defining feature of Guccio's existence. Uneducated but clever, he considered the family to be the centre of his life yet remained emotionally distant from his children, insisting they address him formally and encouraging competition between his sons: 'He liked to provoke arguments between them, setting one against the other.' The family's apparent closeness belied a growing fragmentation. Guccio's marriage endured despite his womanizing, although Aida reacted to his infidelities with violence. In some cases it was too close to home, extending to female members of the shop staff, a habit his sons and grandsons acquired in their turn. Guccio combined an aggressive temperament with a need for control: it was a brave son who contradicted him or challenged his business decisions. While he insisted that all his sons, including the useless Ugo, should have shares of equal value in the company, his daughter Grimalda, allegedly his favourite child, was blatantly excluded: the company was to be run only by Gucci men. Even when he seemingly allowed his sons a longer rein, he never relinquished control. Refusing to fund their ventures with company money, he would refer them to the bank and, behind their backs, instruct the bank to issue a loan. His sons thought they were acting independently but Guccio was pulling the strings. Although he traded in luxury goods, his parsimony was legendary and his sons were retained on far lower salaries than those that managers in similar businesses commanded.

Guccio's apparent even-handedness ignored the fact that his sons did not put an equal amount of work and commitment into the company. Aldo and Vasco were involved in the business throughout their adult lives but their attitudes were very different. Vasco, who ran the Florence factory, was easy-going to the point of laziness. Although he had inherited his fair share of Gucci creativity, he was happiest in the country indulging his passion for hunting. Aldo was his father's right-hand man, although their relationship was strained as Guccio consistently blocked his son's attempts to move the company in new directions. Aldo's son Paolo, who was later to play a major role in the company, believed that his grandfather was suspicious of Aldo's motives: 'He was afraid he'd take over.'

Rodolfo was the only son to have chosen a different course. His good looks had brought him moderate success in the cinema, but his career collapsed after the war and he was only too glad to be welcomed as a late entry into the family business, where his father put him on an equal basis with Aldo, opening a store in Milan which Rodolfo was asked to run. An egotistical man who had inherited his father's controlling personality, Rodolfo made himself the subject of a lifetime's study, spending years and a fortune on the preparation of a lengthy autobiographical film.

In retrospect, it seems inevitable that the perceived – and real – unfairness should fuel competitiveness and jealousy between the Gucci sons, particularly Aldo and Rodolfo. And the family dynamics – rivalry, volatility, suspicion – were mirrored in the business, resulting in disorganization, secrecy and caution. Although in principle it was all in the family, there was no sense of everyone pulling together in the same direction. Guccio's sons' ambitions were blocked while their egos were indulged. The fragmentation in the family was reflected in retail chaos: everyone felt entitled to have their say, resulting in a multiplicity of styles and lines with no management of design or product development.

Occasionally the spontaneity and rush to market paid off. When Princess Grace visited the store in Florence in search of a floral silk scarf, Guccio immediately put one into production. (The same print was later retrieved from the archive and used as the basis of Gucci's wildly successful haute-couture collection in the summer of 2004). However, this sort of happy opportunism was rare and the proliferation of products became unmanageable and uneconomic. Paolo Gucci remarked: 'Nothing was checked in advance or test marketed. We just went ahead and shoved the new line in the windows. At one time we had hundreds of handbags, all different.'

Some are more equal than others

In 1952 Aldo made his move. Perhaps he had a sense of power sifting down through the generations and reinforcing his position, as by now all three of his sons – Roberto, Paolo and Giorgio – had joined the company. In association with a US lawyer, Frank Dugan, and behind his father's back, Aldo established Gucci Shops Incorporated in the United States. Guccio remained in the dark about this treacherous move until Vasco and Rodolfo travelled to New York for the opening of the first store on Fifth Avenue. Guccio was predictably enraged, a feeling exacerbated by his sense of insecurity over company money being invested in a country of which he knew little and understood less.

But his sons didn't have to ride out their father's wrath for long. Guccio died suddenly in the summer of 1953, of heart failure. He was 72. Although he did not live to see the glory days of the company in the 1960s and 1970s, in retrospect his family were relieved that he was spared the internecine battles that accompanied them.

His death unleashed his sons' ambitions and removed the major obstacle to their plans for expansion. Vasco was the only one to echo his father's caution, but his temperament made him no match for Aldo and Rodolfo, who briefly united to oppose him. The initial period following Guccio's death was one of uneasy strategic alliances: Rodolfo and Aldo against Vasco, and all three against their sister Grimalda, whose petition to gain an equal share in her father's estate was ruthlessly quashed by her brothers in court.

The relationship between Aldo and Rodolfo settled into one of increasing antagonism. Their deep-seated rivalry seeped into every area of their lives. Alexandra Murkowska, who worked for both brothers during her 12 years with the company, recounted how they competed for women, came to blows over the slightest pretext, and even raced one another on the autostrada. Both were determined to be top dog: Aldo considered he wore the Gucci crown but Rodolfo wanted a piece of it. Murkowska's role was to establish some consistency and structure within the company and to a certain extent she succeeded, although constantly torn by their turf wars: 'They switched their minds all the time, but you had to ride it.' She felt that she understood their motivation: 'The Guccis are all about power.'

'We are no worse than any other family, I suppose.'

Both Aldo and Rodolfo cultivated their individual power bases and protected their interests by grooming their sons for careers in the company. Roberto and Giorgio initially worked for their father in New York, before Aldo's overbearing personality and their own family concerns brought them back to Italy, where Paolo, who was becoming the strongest creative voice in Gucci, worked in the Florence headquarters with Vasco. Meanwhile Rodolfo focused all his plans and ambitions on his only child, Maurizio, who became the focus of his life after the early death of his wife. Some years younger than his cousins, Maurizio's childhood in his father's Swiss mansion should have been idyllic. In reality, his father's possessiveness and fears for his safety, with the controlling temperament he had inherited from Guccio, meant that he had little personal freedom and an isolated adolescence. Supervised on his rare outings by his father or the family chauffeur, he spent his weekends and holidays working in the Milan store.

By 1967 Aldo had opened Gucci stores across the United States, from California to the east coast, in addition to offices in Japan. He had plans for Canada, South Africa and Australia as well. With the opening of a custom-built factory supervised by Paolo in Scandicci, on the outskirts of Florence, production increased, but Paolo was struggling with the institutionalized chaos of Gucci management. His father and uncles still commissioned new product lines without consulting anyone, and held impromptu meetings with no agenda whenever they felt the need to assert themselves. Uncle Rodolfo was his particular *bête noire:* 'I'd suddenly be confronted with an idea he'd thought up for a handbag, already in full-scale production. . . . There'd been no pre-planning, consideration of size, price or quantity. Just an impetuous rush into production, the way the firm had been doing things for the past 50 years.'

The climate of suspicion and intrigue filtered down to succeeding generations. Just as Aldo had gone behind his father's back to set up the first operation in New York, Giorgio secretly set up a Gucci boutique in Rome, selling affordable gift items and accessories that attracted younger customers. It was a huge success but Rodolfo had difficulty seeing it as anything other than disloyal, until a greater betrayal shook his world.

After taking a degree in economics in Milan, Maurizio Gucci had worked for seven years with his uncle Aldo in New York, where the physical and emotional distance from home gave him a chance to make a realistic assessment of his family and the company: 'The difference between my father and my uncle was that my uncle was a marketing man, a developer. He was the one who handled the expansion side . . . the one, in fact, who was building up everything in the company. . . . What fascinated me most was how different he was from my father, who was an actor in everything he did. My uncle wasn't playing a part; it was the real thing with him.' This aversion to acting, an inevitable part of his rebellion against his overbearing father, also informed Maurizio's attitude towards the family myths, which he refused to perpetuate: 'We must do away with all this kind of noblesse about our ancestry. . . . In my own family I insist that we do not carry on as if we came from some sort of kingdom. . . . Nor must we give the impression that we have some special right to be on top of the world.'

When Maurizio eventually broke away, he did so in the way best calculated to hurt his father. In 1972, at the age of 24, he married Patrizia Reggiani, the daughter of a truck driver. Rodolfo disapproved of Patrizia, whom he suspected of being a fortune hunter, and was determined to prevent the match. When direct appeals to the Reggiani family and displays of rage and grief failed, Rodolfo and Maurizio were estranged for some time. Although they were reconciled after the wedding, the resentment never abated. Paolo Gucci said later, 'His father didn't trust him. . . . He knew his son was tremendously ambitious, despite his immaturity. I think in a way . . . he was a little afraid of Maurizio.'

Rodolfo subsequently moved to prevent his son owning an independent share in Gucci. His bitterness meant that Maurizio was not included in the major venture that began the year of the wedding – the launch of Gucci Parfums. At the time it seemed little more than an attractive sideline to keep Aldo's sons happy. Aldo, Roberto, Paolo, Giorgio and Rodolfo each took a 20 per cent share in the new company. No one could foresee that Gucci Parfums would grow to become more valuable than the original company. And everyone except Paolo failed to take seriously the power imbalance that was being established in the third generation. 'We are all in the family and these are only family squabbles.'

It was the death of Vasco in 1975 that effected the biggest change in Gucci since the death of Guccio 22 years earlier. Uniting to retain their brother's share in the company by buying out Vasco's widow (they had no children), Aldo and Rodolfo became joint owners of Gucci, Rodolfo retaining 50 per cent of the shares, while Aldo kept 40 per cent and divided the other 10 per cent between his three sons.

As the third generation moved into increasingly responsible positions, and despite the fact that Gucci was doing better than ever, the gulf between cousins, uncles and brothers widened. Family relationships were more fractured than ever, with Paolo and Giorgio both at odds with their father, and Rodolfo and Maurizio nursing their mutual hurt over the fall-out from the latter's marriage. The divisions were even more dramatically marked within the share structure of the company (see Exhibit 1). Roberto, Paolo and Giorgio together owned 60 per cent of Gucci Parfums and 10 per cent of Guccio Gucci while Maurizio had nothing and any future influence would depend entirely on the goodwill of his father. 'He expected me to be his creature,' he remarked later. 'Well, a young man does not always accept such direction indefinitely.'

Part III: Mutually assured destruction

By the late 1970s Gucci was everywhere. Yet the brand's ubiquity was not matched by its profitability. In 1978, the year Gucci announced a record turnover of $48 million, the company registered zero profits. There should have been far more money around than there was. Furthermore, the fratricidal and patricidal dynamics within the family were becoming increasingly overt. Aldo vs. Rodolfo was an old story, but now a new confrontation began to threaten the company's future: Paolo vs. Aldo.

When Paolo had tackled his Uncle Rodolfo head on over his interference with the management of Guccio Gucci in Florence, Rodolfo had sacked him and Aldo had promptly employed his son in New York, making him head of Gucci Shops Inc. However, when Paolo announced his intention to market a series of lines under his own name, Aldo was outraged, fired his son, and started legal proceedings to block the Paolo Gucci brand. Paolo was out of work and effectively out of the company, although he still retained his shares.

His revenge was devastating. For some time he had been monitoring the company accounts and he knew where the money was going: Aldo was involved in a huge tax evasion scheme. Faced with the prospect of his father's intransigent litigation, he played his trump card: he would present the US revenue service with evidence of the fraud.

Although Paolo knew the implications of his threat, he did not hesitate to act: 'If they wanted my extinction, why should I not have theirs? They were the ones who had chucked me out, forbidding me even to use my own name to make a living. Why should I spare any of them?' Although the ensuing loss of share value would wipe out his own fortune, he handed the evidence he held to the authorities, and waited.

Into the maelstrom of accusation and counter-accusation came Maurizio, but he took care to remain on the sidelines. He, too, was playing a waiting game. His father Rodolpho, who was seriously ill with cancer, owned 50 per cent of Gucci. Maurizio was his sole heir and had ambitions for Gucci. He wanted to secure the future of the company and to rekindle the reputation for exclusivity and quality that was beginning to suffer from the proliferation of lower-priced accessories and branded goods entering the market. Products at the lower end of the market were easily imitated and stores and street markets around the world were flooded with fake Gucci lines. Fighting brand theft was costly, time-consuming and a losing battle. The only way forward was to reposition the company: Maurizio wanted to go multinational and license the production of Gucci goods.

Rodolfo died in 1983. In 1985, at the age of 81, Aldo was imprisoned for tax fraud, convicted largely on the testimony of his son. Between those dates, Maurizio, taking over his father's half-share of the company, manoeuvred both Aldo and Paolo off the board and out of Gucci, but not before they had agreed to the setting up of Gucci Licensing Services. The new company was valued at $800 million. The rest of the family soon followed them. For the first time since his grandfather had opened his store on the Via della Vigna Nuova, one man was back in charge of the company, and he was the only Gucci still in it.

Un uomo solo

Paradoxically, as the Gucci family disintegrated, the company itself grew stronger. The damaging aftershock of Aldo's conviction and the media frenzy over the family meltdown subsided and it became clear that the company was in good health, if under-active. It had two major problems: imitation had reduced its image to one of a 'tacky airport brand' and it had no vision.

Maurizio recognized that he couldn't go it alone and made two major appointments. Dawn Mello, a specialist in retailing turnaround, was brought in as

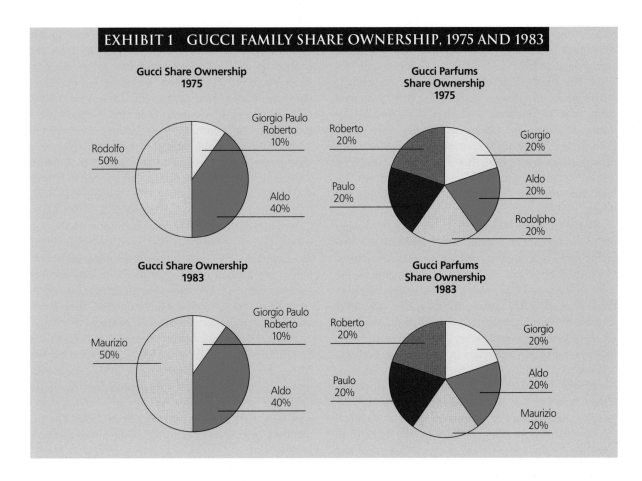

EXHIBIT 1   GUCCI FAMILY SHARE OWNERSHIP, 1975 AND 1983

Gucci Share Ownership 1975 — Rodolfo 50%, Giorgio Paulo Roberto 10%, Aldo 40%

Gucci Parfums Share Ownership 1975 — Roberto 20%, Giorgio 20%, Aldo 20%, Rodolpho 20%, Paulo 20%

Gucci Share Ownership 1983 — Maurizio 50%, Giorgio Paulo Roberto 10%, Aldo 40%

Gucci Parfums Share Ownership 1983 — Roberto 20%, Giorgio 20%, Aldo 20%, Maurizio 20%, Paulo 20%

creative director, and Domenico De Sole, the lawyer who had helped Maurizio gain control of the group and had overseen the purchase of the balance of the family's shares by Investcorp, became CEO of Gucci America.

De Sole streamlined the company's operations and arranged the start of repayments and fines to the IRS. By 1989 Gucci America was turning an annual profit of around $20 million. Between them, Mello and De Sole had the vision and the ability to reposition Gucci in the market.

They were hampered, however, by the man who had appointed them. Maurizio had his own ideas for dealing with the quality crisis. Against De Sole's advice, he announced the immediate closing down of the Gucci Accessories Collection, the wholesale business that supplied Gucci outlets in major department stores and duty-free concessions. The cuts meant a loss of $110 million in revenue, but Maurizio was adamant: Gucci must not only move up market but once again define what the market should be. 'The bitterness of poor quality is remembered long after the sweetness of low price has faded from memory,' Aldo had once

said, echoing his own father's motto. Maurizio wanted to erase that bitterness for good.

Nobody doubted his commitment to the company but his business judgement was highly questionable. His actions brought Gucci to the verge of bankruptcy, despite the success of Mello's ready-to-wear and couture ranges, which repositioned Gucci among the world's leading fashion houses. In 1993, after four years in charge, Maurizio was voted off the board and sold his shares in the company to Investcorp, the other leading shareholder. Forty years after the death of its founder, the last member of the Gucci family to be working in the company signed it away.

The beautiful men move in

From 1993 to 2003 the Gucci story was one of riches to riches. In 1990, Mello made the appointment that definitively redefined the company's image when she asked Tom Ford to design for the company. Ford's charisma and personal attractiveness had always brought him as much attention and publicity as his designs. Now, with De Sole's backing, he set about moving the company in an entirely new direction, devising a series of collections that wiped out the stirrups-and-saddles and Princess Grace image for good. His flamboyant, overtly sexy clothes, and the provocative advertising campaigns that promoted them, shot the company to the top of the fashion industry. Madonna and Gwynneth Paltrow wore Gucci Ford designs to award ceremonies and fashion commentators fawned on him. 'It was hot! It was sex! You just knew that wearing those clothes would make you look like you were living on the edge – doing it and having it all!'

By the time the 'Gucci sex factor' began to wear off at the end of the decade, and Tom Ford and Domenico De Sole had moved on to other ventures, Gucci had been named European Company of the Year (1998), and had seen off two major takeover bids, leveraging the power of its major ally PPR (Pinault-Printemps-Redoute), now the majority shareholder in the Gucci Group, which owned or part-owned a range of companies in the fashion, perfume and jewellery industry, including Yves Saint Laurent, Alexander McQueen, Stella McCartney, Roger & Gallet, Van Cleef & Arpels and Fendi. Gucci was the group's top performer. Although profits slumped catastrophically in 2003, blamed on the fall-off in spending by the super-rich after the SARS scare and Iraq War, Gucci sales climbed by 19 per cent in 2005 following Frida Giannini's 'flora' collection, for which she resurrected the print Guccio Gucci had designed for Princess Grace. Giannini's challenge was to maintain Gucci's position in the market while exorcizing 'the glamorous, media-savvy ghost of Tom Ford', the man who put it there. She looked set to succeed and take the company to heights that Guccio, his sons and grandsons could never have foreseen.

Part IV: 'I want to see him dead'

But what of Maurizio? His ill-fated tenure at Gucci was not the only upheaval in his life at that time. When the death of Rodolfo released the final bond in their difficult relationship, his response had been disproportionate. The teenager whose enormously wealthy father had bought him only a modest car while his friends drove Porsches, allowing him out on his bike only if the chauffeur went with him, bought himself a private plane, several luxury properties and ocean-going yachts, and filled his garages with fast cars and motorbikes.

The indulgence in forbidden treats was understandable, but it seemed that his freedom from the controlling relationship prompted him to lay waste to every perceived constriction, including his marriage. His wife recalled him saying, 'First I had my father, now I have you. I have never been free in all my life. I didn't enjoy my youth, and now I want to be free.' On 22 May 1985, he told Patrizia that he was going on a short business trip, packed a case and left their Milan apartment. The following day he sent a friend to tell her that he would not be returning. The marriage was over.

Maurizio was generous, if implacable. After a protracted divorce, in 1991 Patrizia was awarded $500 000 annual alimony. Maurizio continued to support their two daughters. However, he could maintain neither his family nor himself in the style to which they had become accustomed. With his personal debts mounting to more than $40 million as Gucci faltered, they could only be defrayed when he sold out of Gucci in 1993.

Patrizia's response to the divorce – 'I want to see him dead' – was taken no more seriously by her friends than the recriminations that follow the break-up of any marriage. One explanation for her erratic behaviour seemed to have been identified when she was diagnosed with a brain tumour in 1992. The tumour was successfully removed without any apparent ill effects.

Remaining in Milan to be near his children, Maurizio gradually began to rebuild his life, starting a new business venture and settling down with a new partner, Paola Franchi. On 23 September 1995, he was shot dead on the steps outside his office as he arrived at the start of the day's business. Eighteen months later, Patrizia was arrested and charged with his murder. At her subsequent trial she was found guilty of having hired a hit man to kill her ex-husband, and sentenced to life imprisonment. Her appeal to have her conviction overturned, on the grounds that brain surgery had affected her personality, was dismissed in a ruling by the European Court of Human Rights in June 2005. On 25 January 2006, Italy's highest court of appeal rejected a motion to release her on medical grounds and confirmed that she would complete her 26-year jail sentence.

Epilogue

Envy eats nothing but its own heart.

German proverb

Guccio Gucci understood envy. He must have known it himself, working below stairs at The Savoy Hotel.

It was clearly a strong motivating force within his own family and the destructive rivalry that developed between his sons was handed down in turn to the third generation, ultimately tearing the family apart. It was the principle on which he founded the company, building on people's envy of the super-rich, glamorous and successful.

Gucci products are still promoted on that basis. In 2004, without the slightest hint of irony, the company announced the launch of a new fragrance: 'Envy Me'.

Strategic planning at United Parcel Service

By David A. Garvin and Lynne C. Levesque[1]

We fully recognize that it is not possible to develop a true strategic plan more than a few years out and that business plans should have an even shorter horizon. But we are convinced that it is possible and wise, indeed necessary, to develop a set of very long-range scenarios that can form the foundation for our future strategic plans.

Michael (Mike) J. Eskew, Chairman and Chief Executive Officer, United Parcel Service

As Mike Eskew walked through the long, open atrium of UPS's corporate headquarters late in March 2005, he thought about his upcoming lunch meeting with Vice President of Corporate Strategy Vern Higberg. Higberg was preparing a presentation for the senior management strategy committee, the Strategy Advisory Group, on improvements to the strategic-planning process. While the company had made major progress in planning for the future over the past 10 years, Eskew had charged Higberg and his colleagues with developing recommendations for moving forward, citing one of his predecessors, who had said, 'The future of our company will be no better or worse than the quality of planning we do to prepare for it.'

Company background

In 1907, 19-year-old Jim Casey borrowed $100 from friends to start the small company that eventually became UPS. From its humble origins delivering messages for the city of Seattle, Washington, UPS had grown into a $37 billion corporation (see Exhibit 1). Over the 98 years since its founding, it had transformed itself several times, first into a package-delivery company, then into an international air transportation company, and finally, in the late 1990s, into a logistics company. In November 1999, after 92 years as a private company, UPS went public in the largest corporate initial public offering (IPO) to date.

By 2005, UPS was the world's largest package-delivery company, as well as a leading global provider of specialized transportation and logistics services. It served more than 200 countries and territories worldwide. UPS Airlines, as of 2005, was one of the 10 largest airlines in the United States. The acquisition of Mail Boxes Etc. had provided the company with over 3500 retail locations in the United States. With a workforce of 384 000, only Wal-Mart and McDonald's had more employees.

Organization

In 2002, when Mike Eskew, an industrial engineer and 30-year veteran at UPS, became the company's ninth CEO, he found a highly centralized, hierarchical organization with a traditional structure at the top. A Management Committee met weekly, with a full-day meeting once a month, to provide the day-to-day management of the company. Various other committees and staff groups assisted the CEO and Management Committee, including a Strategy Advisory Group – a subgroup of the Management Committee – that met monthly to address more strategic issues (see Exhibit 2).

Within this structure, the responsibilities of corporate staff and field operations in the regions were clearly delineated. Senior management and staff, working in a collegial, consensus-building culture at corporate headquarters, set direction, determined priorities and budgets, and defined initiatives and rollout plans. The more hierarchically run field was responsible for execution and meeting revenue and cost goals. The Corporate Strategy Group's (CSG's) strategic-planning manager, Ed Rogers, explained: 'All strategic decisions are made by the corporate office. UPS does tactical, rather than strategic, planning at the regional level. There is a clear line between strategy and execution, since the regions focus on delivering on the next quarter's business. They also have rollout responsibility' Said one observer, 'One side of me says it would be nice to have more autonomy in the regions, but we're in a network business, and what's best for one region could easily foul things up for other regions or the overall network.'

[1]Source: Copyright © 2005 President and Fellows of Harvard College.

EXHIBIT 1   FINANCIAL PERFORMANCE

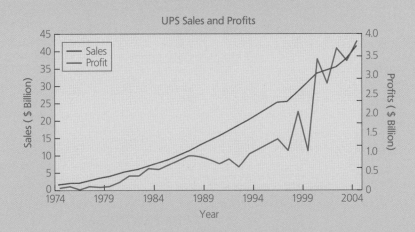

($ million)	1974	1984	1994	2000	2004
Total Revenue	**1,303**	**6,833**	**19,576**	**29,771**	**36,582**
Operating expenses	1,226	6,104	18,020	25,249	31,593
Operating profit	77	729	1,556	4,522	4,989
Other expenses and taxes	32	252	613	1,588	1,656
Net Income	**45**	**477**	**943**	**2,934**	**3,333**
Year-end stock price	a	a	a	59	85
Employees (year-end)	67,900	141,000	285,000	359,000	384,000

Source: Standard & Poors, Compustat accessed April 25, 2005; company web page, accessed April 25, 2005.
aUPS went public in 1999.

Culture

Over the years, the company had acquired a reputation for being relentlessly focused on efficiency and execution. Founder Casey instilled a desire to run the company 'like a military operation, ordering recruits to be polite at all times and to place speed above all other virtues.' Carefully researched work methods, developed by industrial engineers and rooted in time and motion studies, coupled with time-tested policies and procedures, led to UPS's reputation for low-cost and highly predictable customer service. UPS reportedly tracked its drivers so closely that it even knew how many times they shifted gears in the course of a day.

Along with efficiency and discipline, Casey had left a legacy of continuous improvement, which he called 'constructive dissatisfaction,' and a set of strong values that included service excellence, employee ownership, and a commitment to stability for the company's employees, shareholders, and customers. The result was a loyal workforce, with extremely low turnover. It was not uncommon for employees to spend their entire working career at UPS. Internal promotion was standard practice. All of the company's CEOs were long-term employees who had risen through the ranks along with their peers. Most senior managers had business or engineering degrees yet had started their careers at UPS as part-time package-handling employees or package-delivery drivers.

Evolution of strategic planning at UPS

Through its growth years from 1907 to 1997, UPS had shifted from message delivery to package delivery as opportunities arose (see Exhibit 3). Until the early 1990s, there was no formal strategic-planning process.

EXHIBIT 2   ORGANIZATION CHART

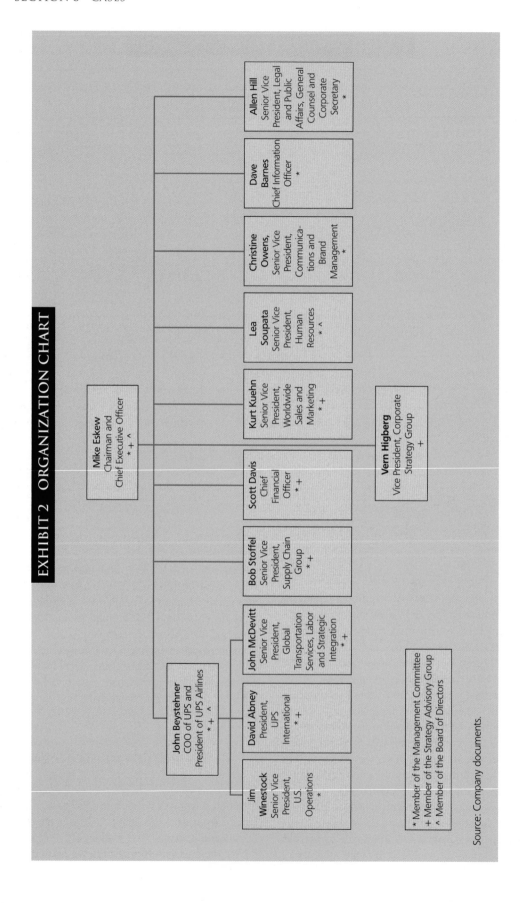

Mike Eskew
Chairman and
Chief Executive Officer
* + ^

John Beystehner
COO of UPS and
President of UPS Airlines
* + ^

Jim Winestock
Senior Vice President,
US Operations
*

David Abney
President,
UPS International
* +

John McDevitt
Senior Vice President,
Global Transportation Services, Labor and Strategic Integration
* +

Bob Stoffel
Senior Vice President,
Supply Chain Group
* +

Scott Davis
Chief
Financial
Officer
* +

Kurt Kuehn
Senior Vice President,
Worldwide Sales and Marketing
* +

Lea Soupata
Senior Vice President,
Human Resources
* ^

Christine Owens,
Senior Vice President,
Communications and Brand Management
*

Dave Barnes
Chief Information Officer
*

Allen Hill
Senior Vice President, Legal and Public Affairs, General Counsel and Corporate Secretary
*

Vern Higberg
Vice President, Corporate Strategy Group
+

* Member of the Management Committee
+ Member of the Strategy Advisory Group
^ Member of the Board of Directors

Source: Company documents.

Instead, strategy was the responsibility of a small group of senior managers and involved little more than a series of discrete, *ad hoc* projects. In the mid-1970s, one task force had recommended that UPS expand globally; its members had then been charged with opening up Canada and Germany. Roughly 10 years later, a second task force, soon named the Strategic Technology Group, was formed to identify major gaps in technology. It then became responsible for overseeing an $11 billion investment in technology and was later reintegrated into the technology and engineering groups. In 1991, then CEO Oz Nelson and his senior managers introduced a corporate mission and strategy statement that codified the values of the founder and refocused the company on the four constituencies it intended to serve: customers, UPS people, shareowners, and communities.

The decade of the 1990s

In the early 1990s, competition from both private companies (e.g., Federal Express) and large government-supported agencies (e.g., Deutsche Post) started to threaten UPS's position. Senior leaders became concerned that the company's execution mentality was hindering management's ability to see significant changes in the environment.

EXHIBIT 3 UPS TIMELINE OF SELECTED KEY DATES IN THE STRATEGIC PLANNING PROCESS

Year	Event
1907	United Parcel Service (UPS) founded in Seattle, Washington (as American Messenger Company)
1991	Corporate Mission and Strategy Statement introduced
1996	Strategy Advisory Group and Corporate Strategy Group formed
1997	First scenario-planning session
1999	UPS Charter completed and broadly communicated
2002	■ Management Committee off-site, resulting in Centennial Plan ■ Strategy Road Map developed
2004	Second scenario-planning session
2005	Management Committee review and update of Strategy Road Map

Source: Company documents.

In 1996, Jim Kelly, the soon-to-be CEO, began to address these challenges. He set up the Strategy Advisory Group, a small subset of his direct reports, to meet monthly for half a day to consider and debate strategic issues. Kelly also established the CSG, a staff organization of 20 people, most of them tenured UPS managers with significant line and staff experience. He expected the CSG to develop the strategic processes for planning for the future, to research and frame key strategic issues, and to assist the Management Committee and the Strategy Advisory Group in strategy development.

After surveying consultant offerings, the CSG decided to design its own strategic process. The process that ensued was actually a series of discrete activities, some linked more closely than others, involving a relatively small group of managers at headquarters. Activities included scenario planning, strategic planning, and support for strategic decision-making and strategy implementation. Higberg described the process as 'not the most nimble, since it uses multiple tools and methodologies. But so long as we have the backing at the top, we can use any approach it takes to make it work.' The CEO played a central role. In fact, Higberg observed, 'At UPS, strategy is owned by our chairman. We exist to support him and work at his direction. He is our chief strategist.'

The implementation of the new strategic process involved several steps that unfolded over a period of years. An important first step was a scenario-planning session held in 1997. Two years later, in 1999, senior management completed a crucial second step when they drafted the UPS Charter, redefining UPS's mission and purpose and providing a detailed statement of the company's values and strategies. The new mission and purpose moved UPS from 'leadership in package distribution' to 'enabler of global commerce' (see Exhibit 4).

Into the new century

In January 2002, shortly after Eskew became CEO, he convened a Management Committee executive retreat whose purpose was 'to focus the group on the kind of company we were going to be in 2007 – on our 100th anniversary'. The outcomes from that meeting formed the 'Centennial Plan', the third step in the strategic process. As UPS's version of a five-year strategic plan, the Centennial Plan was designed to guide the company to its centennial anniversary by providing themes and broad, overarching direction. Shortly thereafter, the fourth step in the strategic process, a 'Strategy Road Map', was developed to take the Centennial Plan to an

---

EXHIBIT 4 UPS CHARTER

Our Values – *Our enduring beliefs*

- We believe that integrity and excellence are the core of all we do.
- We believe that attention to our customers' changing needs is central to the success of UPS.
- We believe that people do their best when they feel pride in their contributions, when they are treated with dignity, and when their talents are encouraged to flourish in an environment that embraces diversity.
- We believe that innovation fortifies our organization through the discovery of new opportunities to serve our people and our customers.

Our Purpose – *Why we're in business*

We enable global commerce.

Our Mission – *What we seek to achieve*

We fulfill our promise to our constituents throughout the world in the following ways:

- We serve the evolving distribution, logistics, and commerce needs of our customers worldwide, offering excellence and value in all we do.
- We sustain a financially strong company, with broad employee ownership, that provides a long-term competitive return to our shareowners.
- We strive to be a responsible and well-regarded employer by providing our people with an impartial, rewarding, and cooperative environment with the opportunity for advancement.

- We build on our legacy as a caring and responsible corporate citizen through the conduct of our people and company in the communities we serve.

Our Strategy – *The UPS plan of action*
Create the future though One Company.
One Vision. One Brand

- We will continue to expand our distribution and supply chain solutions to synchronize the world of commerce – the flow of goods, information, and funds.
- We will expand our position as a trusted broker between buyers and sellers worldwide.
- We will harness the appropriate technology to create new services and to strengthen our operations and networks.
- We will attract and develop the most talented people whose initiative, good judgment, and loyalty will help realize our company's mission.
- We will continually study customers' behavior, anticipate their needs, and design our products and services to exceed their expectations.
- We will create a practice of innovation that leads to sustainable growth.
- We maintain an environment that enables us to treat every customer as if they are our only one.
- We will leverage the UPS brand to maximize brand loyalty among all constituencies.

Source: Company website, accessed on August 15, 2005.

---

executable level of detail. Since the Centennial Plan was segmented by years, an annual plan could be separated out and translated into regional business plans that were handed down to the regions to execute.

With these steps completed, Eskew, in early 2004, decided that it was time for another scenario-planning session. He was concerned that UPS was getting closer to 2007 – the end of the first scenario-planning session horizon – and believed that management needed to be thinking further out. As he put it, 'I felt comfortable that we understood the strategy and had initiatives to carry us through the next five years, but I didn't

know what came after that.' Shortly after the scenario-planning exercise was completed, the Management Committee met in early 2005 to revisit and update the Strategy Road Map.

1997 Scenario planning

To address the distinctive UPS challenge, described by one manager as 'less a struggle with execution and getting things done than with coming up with creative ideas about what to do,' senior management in 1997 reviewed alternative long-range planning approaches. They ultimately chose to bring in consultants from Global Business Network to facilitate a set of scenario-planning workshops. These workshops were preceded by a series of interviews inside and outside UPS that led to the definition of the key focal issue facing UPS: 'The future of UPS's global business in an ever-changing competitive environment.' Working through the various stages of the process, the participants created four different scenarios that could impact UPS's future.

Axes of uncertainty

Participants, primarily UPS managers representing different functions and generally reporting to a Management Committee member, went through several hours of discussion over driving forces and critical uncertainties. They eventually defined two axes of uncertainty. The horizontal axis was the 'Market Environment', or the flow of goods and funds across borders, a continuum that ranged from regional and national markets with trade barriers to a more global market with a free flow of goods. The vertical axis was 'Demand Characteristics', or the nature of consumers and the type of goods and delivery mechanisms they required. This continuum went from traditional consumers, requesting more traditional goods and services, to proactive, sophisticated consumers (which UPS called 'prosumers'), demanding high value-added services and active engagement in supply-chain activities.

Scenarios

In combination, these two axes produced four scenarios (see Exhibit 5). The first scenario, 'Tangled Paths', depicted a future with a highly competitive business marketplace, constrained by strong regional and nationalistic government regulations, where consumers desired more variation in products. The second scenario, representing the 'Regressive World', described a future similarly constrained by regional and nationalistic government regulations but with a more traditional supply chain, competitive landscape, and set of consumers. The third scenario, 'Global Scale Prevails', portrayed a global marketplace with slower adoption of new technology because of stable demand, more traditional consumers, and industry consolidation. Finally, the last scenario, named 'Brave New World', described a future with a deregulated, globalized marketplace, providing mass customization of goods and services to

proactive consumers and populated with new forms of competition and virtual organizations, such as alliances and business webs.

The teams went on to outline specific characteristics of each of the scenarios, to position UPS and its competitors within the scenarios, and to identify implications and possible strategies for the company's logistics business, technology and government affairs efforts, brand, workforce, and culture (see Exhibit 6). No early warning signals were defined in 1997. Instead of creating narratives to describe the scenarios, the teams decided to use an outside media company to prepare dramatic presentations with sets constructed to illustrate each scenario so that senior management could 'experience' the scenarios. Actors were hired to improvise events in the future scenarios, and videotapes were produced to describe the alternative futures.

Outcomes

The sessions produced several outcomes – both tangible and intangible. They included the eventual definition of the Corporate Charter and change in the company's mission statement, identification of key themes and insights, the creation of a platform for management discussions, and a mind-set shift for at least some managers.

Corporate charter The insights from these sessions and the discussions they sparked resulted in the eventual definition, in 1999, of the UPS Charter, which guided the company until 2002. The Charter incorporated the change in the company's purpose from 'serving the package-delivery needs of our customers' to 'enabling global commerce', a move that reflected both the more global nature of the business as well as its intended focus on end-to-end supply-chain solutions. It also included detailed strategy statements. According to Eskew, 'The Charter served as a springboard for a series of events, starting with the decision to go public in November 1999, and then for the company's five-year strategic plan.'

Themes and strategic conversations The scenario-planning sessions also led senior management to define several 'themes' for UPS's future. These themes included (1) a proactive shift directly to the end consumer, eliminating usage barriers; (2) leveraging this end-consumer positioning to win additional business-to-business customers within the demand chain; (3) a focus on customer solutions that integrated goods movement and financial and information services; (4) identification of opportunities to be selectively captured across entire

EXHIBIT 5   1997 SCENARIO CHARACTERISTICS

Focal Issue: "The future of UPS's global business in an ever-changing competitive environment"

Pro-sumers

Tangled Paths

- Strong local and regional government regulations
- Restrictions on flow of goods
- Technology available and governments struggle to regulate
- Consumers demand more variations in products
- Highly competitive market, with non-traditional niche players

Brave New World

- Deregulation and globalization
- Scope economies vs. scale
- Technology with open standards and fluid systems
- Customization of goods and services
- Virtual organizations, non-traditional competitors

Regional/National ← Market Environment → *Global*

Demand Characteristics

Regressive World

- Strong local and regional government regulations
- Restrictions on flow of goods
- Technology a mix of proprietary systems
- Traditional supply chain and product offering
- More traditional competition from domestic and regional players

Global Scale Prevails

- Deregulation and globalization
- Scope economies vs. scale
- Technology adopted at a slower pace, proprietary systems prevalent
- Traditional consumption and consumers
- Industry consolidation of competitors

Traditional Consumers

Source: Company documents.

demand chains, with integrated solutions between companies; and (5) the maintenance of a global growth perspective.

The themes and the scenarios themselves provided a common vocabulary for discussions at Strategy Advisory Group meetings, as well as a guide for investigating growth opportunities and competitive strategies. Senior managers would pepper their discussions of acquisitions and other growth alternatives with phrases such as, 'That seems like a "Regressive World" option', or 'That would move us more toward "Global Scale" or "Brave New World".' They also developed a shorthand for referring to the scenarios. 'Global Scale Prevails' was 'asset heavy', whereas 'Brave New World' was 'asset light'. Looking back on the process, Eskew commented on the influence of the scenario sessions on their thinking:

> We came out of the first scenario-planning session understanding that it would be difficult to say which way the world would go. We all liked the top-right quadrant, the 'Brave New World' scenario, and didn't like the top-left

> quadrant, or 'Tangled Paths' scenario. Left to our own devices, we would probably have ended up in 'Global Scale Prevails', focusing totally on physical assets and missing more virtual opportunities. We thought that we should try to move to 'Brave New World', but we had no control over how the world was going to turn out. What impact would the Seattle protests at the World Trade Organization meeting have on the scenarios, for example? A few years later, we wondered about the impact of the terrorist attacks in New York.

Mind-set shift   A more subtle impact was the change in mind-sets. As Rogers put it, 'The session got us thinking far beyond the business-planning horizon.' Higberg believed the sessions had a more subtle impact as well:

> As much as anything else, the scenarios are a mind-set, a place where you're going to live, a context. If the world shifts, we're at least ready for some of the options ahead. If the competition

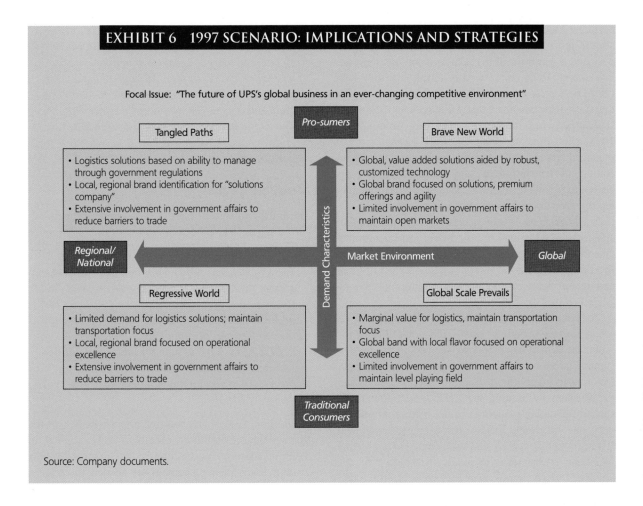

EXHIBIT 6   1997 SCENARIO: IMPLICATIONS AND STRATEGIES

Focal Issue: "The future of UPS's global business in an ever-changing competitive environment"

Source: Company documents.

does things differently, how do we respond? If there's a major disruption in the economy, what do we do? Out of the scenario-planning exercise, we got much richer outcomes than if we had only done competitive analyses, based on trend lines and a view of the world as all about just slugging it out for market share. Without scenario planning, you don't see the big changes until they are history.

However, other participants in the 1997 session were less positive. Some felt that the exercise lacked realism. One of them observed: 'I don't think that way. I'm a marketing guy, not a process guy. I could see the four alternative quadrants, but for some of them, I just couldn't believe that they could happen.'

Use of the scenarios

The scenarios provided, in Higberg's view, the backdrop for strategic decisions at UPS; there was no formal or mechanical link. The acquisition of Mail Boxes Etc. provided an example of the subtle interplay of the scenarios with strategic choices. Coming out of the 1997 scenario-planning session, senior managers realized the importance of establishing a retail presence to serve more proactive consumers and had begun to pilot a company-owned and operated retail store concept. After considerable analysis of the business and financial aspects of the deal and as the wisdom of moving toward virtual assets in the 'Brave New World' scenario became even more evident, UPS instead decided in 2001 to acquire Mail Boxes Etc., a franchised network of retail stores providing shipping and business services.

The evolution of the decision to build a service-parts logistics business also illustrated how strategic choices were made at UPS against the backdrop of the scenarios. After the first scenario-planning session and the change in purpose to 'enabling global commerce', Eskew had asked the CSG to explore new opportunities.

Strategy Advisory Group members could not agree on several proposals. Although they fit with the new purpose and at least two of the scenarios and met return on investment (ROI) and other key thresholds, they were felt to be too far from UPS's core capabilities. Finally, the CSG recommended that UPS scale up the small service-parts logistics business that had come with the 1995 acquisition of SonicAir. This business, which managed returns processing, spare-parts fulfilment, equipment refurbishment, and warranty repairs, appeared to fit with the expected support needs of the then rapidly growing technology business sector in the asset-light 'Brave New World' scenario. After the dot-com crash, the CSG reanalysed the market and determined that there continued to be significant unmet customer need for a single point of contact for fixing fulfilment and repair problems in the more traditional 'Global Scale Prevails' scenario as well.

As these examples demonstrate, UPS's use of the scenarios in evaluating options did not follow a formula. At times, the scenarios seemed to be used to support almost any investment, using a particular quadrant to justify the decision. Managers rationalized the decision by arguing that UPS was following the scenario-planning guidelines of not betting on one and only one quadrant. Eskew, for example, explained: 'Even though Brave New World would say go virtual, we made investments in assets that didn't fit that quadrant.' Higberg was clear they recognized the dangers of betting on one quadrant or one official future:

> The key is not to fall in love with one quadrant. The acquisitions that worked best were the 'no-brainers', or those that were able to work in all four worlds. If we've made mistakes, it's because we bet on the upper-right quadrant, totally. For example, in the 1997 session we assumed the dot-com world would materialize into an enormous fulfilment market for UPS. The strategies that were just focused on that upper-right quadrant, such as e-logistics, did not work out because of timing and the dot-com crash. We learned we should go for options that can pay off in multiple worlds, such as brokerage activities, air-freight forwarding, and service-parts logistics.

At the same time, despite acknowledgement of this warning, at least one observer indicated, 'There seems to be a gravitational pull toward one of the futures.' Senior Vice President of Worldwide Sales and Marketing Kurt Kuehn explained some of the inconsistency among the different views:

> It's a chicken and egg kind of thing. UPS is big enough to influence the direction of the world, so perhaps there is a value on betting on a particular future. In fact, we have to make bets because the world doesn't move perfectly to one quadrant. Or maybe we accept the fact that all four of the quadrants will coexist simultaneously, and we have to figure out how to prosper in each one.

Strategic plans

The third major step in the UPS strategic process occurred when Eskew became CEO at the beginning of 2002. He recalled:

> The Charter had seen us through the 1999 IPO and up to 2002, but it needed to be refined. Jim Casey's company was going to be 100 years old in 2007. Our job in 2002 was to start planning then to position the company to be where we need to be in 2007, to plan for future capabilities and accomplishments, and to identify missing pieces. After all, nothing happens overnight in a company like this.

In addition, Eskew was worried about whether all the Management Committee members were aligned in their expectations for the future, since many were new to their assignments: 'I knew we needed to create a future together and felt that if we didn't focus on these longer-term issues in an off-site, we would keep talking only about the day-to-day responsibilities and numbers.' One CSG manager described another reason for the planning session: 'Prior to the off-site, there was no framework that aligned the various corporate initiatives and projects with the strategy. We had no control over the 300 or so functional projects; they were being run on their own. We needed a separate effort to pull them together, since that was not the purpose of the scenario-planning exercise.'

Eskew focused the session on qualitative, not quantitative, expectations. He observed:

> Strategy development is not necessarily about numbers. Yet it is very hard for operationally minded execs to get beyond the numbers. In fact, there was almost a rebellion at the off-site. They wanted me to tell them the numbers. I did my best at that meeting to stay away from numbers. Instead, I described the future verbally. I wanted to talk about capabilities and what we needed to build for the future. I didn't want to frame the discussion with an ambitious growth-rate

number. Now, of course, we have quickly added numbers to the plan because we can't operate without them. It just isn't our nature.

Centennial plan

To prepare for the off-site, managers were given an assignment: come to the meeting with 40 to 50 predictions about UPS's future. According to one observer, 'The diversity of opinions was astounding.' There were different assumptions about the future size of the company, its profitability, the percentage of business that would continue to come from US domestic small-package delivery, and whether UPS would be a truly global company or a US company with international operations.

The group distilled the predictions to a manageable set. They then reached consensus on what became known as the Centennial Plan. The Plan included three components. The first was a qualitative set of 'Goals and Characteristics for the year 2007' that addressed issues such as the UPS brand, competition, growth and profitability, people, customers, operational efficiency, cost control, and quality. Second, the group developed an overarching sense of corporate direction, with the goal of creating a global, unified company with 'one vision and one brand.' This objective underscored the need for continued integration of the dispersed logistics units into one cohesive group.

Finally, senior management worked backwards from the proposed UPS of 2007 to identify a set of four Strategic Imperatives:

- **Winning Team:** Attracting and developing a highly skilled, diverse, and aligned global workforce
- **Value-Added Solutions:** Providing customers with value-added services combining movement of goods, information, and funds
- **Customer Focus:** Building customer loyalty and expanding UPS's services worldwide
- **Enterprise Excellence:** Creating an environment of high-quality service and value.

Strategy road map

To ensure implementation of the four Strategic Imperatives, which were considered 'skeletal', individual Management Committee members were assigned responsibility for each of them. Imperative teams were formed the next month with team members from the various functional staff areas.

The teams added detailed measures and goals to each of the imperatives and broke them down into 24 more discrete projects, or 'critical initiatives'; these initiatives, in turn, were supported by more than 100 specific projects. Under the 'Winning Team' imperative, for example, there were initiatives to improve employee and labour relations indices and employee turnover ratios. Together, the entire set of critical initiatives became known as the Strategy Road Map.

According to one senior executive, 'We believed that everything the company did from that time on should tie into those imperatives. If not, we needed to question the value of the new project.' At the same time, the Strategy Road Map had no direct connection to the scenario-planning sessions. Rogers observed: 'The Strategy Road Map was constructed *in consideration* of the scenario-planning process. You'll find consistency of thought between the two but not a direct linkage. Why? They are different types of exercises. You need different types of people involved in each one. There are some of us who have had a foot in both, but not many.'

Strategic implementation

The Management Committee established a process to oversee and manage the Strategy Road Map and implement the Centennial Plan. A Project and Program Oversight Committee was responsible for providing project management support and rigor to the initiatives, applying standards, monitoring progress, resolving resource conflicts, and aligning the functions with the critical initiatives. This support was considered necessary because, in one CSG manager's view, 'If these projects were easy and compartmentalizable, we would have already done them.' Project priorities were set by the CEO, since, as another CSG manager commented, 'not all initiatives are created equal.'

McDevitt's role

Within the next few months, progress on some of these initiatives seemed to stall. Therefore, in March 2003, Eskew asked John McDevitt to join the Management Committee from his post of vice president of Air Operations to be in charge of 'strategic integration'. Perspectives on what this role meant varied. To some managers, McDevitt was 'the coordinator of strategic initiatives'; to others, he was 'the champion of strategy execution'. Still others saw him as a neutral 'tie-breaker on the Management Committee'. According to one senior manager, 'McDevitt was brought in to help resolve deadlocks. Before that time, Eskew was the only one who could do that at the Management Committee level, and he needed help.' McDevitt's role, according to Eskew, was 'to oversee these efforts and put in the discipline we needed to accomplish the 2007 plan. He made sure that the four strategic imperatives were actually aligned and executed and that development activities were moving forward at the right speed, with the right support, and with the right sense of urgency'.

McDevitt confessed that he had a real challenge defining the job when he took it on: 'In the beginning, I jokingly told people, "Don't ask me what I do. At this point, I don't know. But when I do, you'll be the second to know!"' He elaborated:

The job involved a lot of change, since various parts of the organization were working on different projects and often using competing metrics. Roles were not always consistently defined. There were also different opinions about what we were trying to accomplish and how to get these imperatives operationalized. My responsibility was to make sure that all the teams delivered what they said they were going to deliver. I also made sure ideas went from being a gleam in the eye to reality.

An example: Trade Direct

McDevitt's role in the Trade Direct project, a critical initiative under the Value-Added Solutions Imperative, illustrated his contribution. Trade Direct was a new service offering that would take goods manufactured abroad and link them into the US delivery system, seamlessly addressing customs, regulatory, logistics, and information-processing needs. The project involved two groups: the Supply Chain Solutions logistics group, which would handle the movement of the goods from China, for example, to the US, and US Operations, which would move the goods into the UPS physical-delivery system, bypassing warehousing and obtaining large savings for customers. The project had been in the planning stages since 2000, and despite agreement on the opportunity, different parts of the organization were at odds over conflicting priorities and goals.

To get the project moving, McDevitt took over direct ownership, since in his view, 'We clearly needed a Management Committee member to come in and drive it.' He took several steps to get the project back on track: 'We set up meetings with all participants and uncovered the problems. For example, we needed an approach for coming up with the funds to cover IT costs. The issues were elevated and made visible to the Management Committee, and we made sure accountability was assigned.' McDevitt believed he was able to do this because 'I had access to all of the players because I reported directly to the CEO.' He attributed his success with Trade Direct and other initiatives to 'accountability through visibility': 'I worked through the staff that already existed. I went to imperative team meetings and met separately with team leaders below the Management Committee members. Then, every month, there were report outs on the Strategic Imperatives at the Management Committee meeting. Nobody wanted to be behind. That's just in the DNA of UPS.'

Scenario planning: Horizon 2017

After considerable strategic progress, Eskew announced at the 2004 Management Conference that UPS needed to embark on another scenario-planning exercise to look further into the future. Kuehn described the reasoning: 'We found ourselves in a situation where the timing of some of our plans was beginning to go beyond 2007. We needed to revisit the scenarios and recalibrate our compasses, since the magnetic poles had moved a bit around globalization and trade flows, for example. We had to be sure that we were not chasing a straw man.' Eskew added:

It was critical for us to look as far down the road as we could at all the factors and forces affecting our future to think about the kind of capabilities that were needed and the roles that UPS might play to meet the needs of current and future customers. There was too much ambiguity. The old scenarios were becoming dated and hard to recognize. We needed to paint some new pictures so that we could refine our strategy for the next decade.

At the same time, there was concern, voiced by Higberg and others, that 'we certainly didn't want to just repeat the 2007 exercise'. There was speculation that the scenarios would not change drastically, although the implications might be different. Most, however, believed that 'we would be more sophisticated the second time around'.

Process

The Horizon 2017 session, as it came to be called, was similar to the 1997 session in format and process, with three important variations. First, Eskew and the CSG decided to take the scenarios and implications deeper, to regional levels as opposed to a single global picture. Second, to prepare for the Horizon 2017 session, the preparatory interviews were even more extensive and added the perspectives of academics, consultants, politicians, and key customers, selected from a list of those who pushed UPS the hardest and had a clear idea of what they wanted from UPS in its supply-chain efforts (see Exhibit 7). The interviews resulted in the definition of the key issue for Horizon 2017: 'The future(s) of UPS's world market and major regional markets in 2017'.

A third variation involved participants. As before, participants from operations were excluded. Rogers explained the reasoning: 'We weren't going to pull operations folks from the field to do this touchy-feely stuff. It's very hard for them to suddenly break out of their day-to-day tactical responsibilities. And besides, most staff personnel have had operations experience during some part of their career.' Because they were concerned that familiarity with the 1997 scenarios might bias the thinking and development process, management deliberately limited the number of participants and facilitators who had been part of the 1997 sessions. Finally, participants in this session were

more globally diverse and were from lower levels in the organization. As Higberg put it, 'We wanted a balance of seasoned veterans at UPS with people young enough to be here in 2017.'

Eskew kicked off the session and made it very clear that this was not a strategic plan for 2017. He noted: 'Plans for the next one, three, and five years would be more robust and more detailed than scenarios. Scenario planning is more about helping UPS see forks in the road and figuring out which one to take.' Over the course of three workshops spaced over four months, the participants developed drivers, the scenario framework, and scenario characteristics.

Axes of uncertainty While the axes of uncertainty chosen by the participants addressed demand and marketplace characteristics and were thus similar to the axes from the 1997 session, the Horizon 2017 axes incorporated more complex facets of each. This time, the horizontal axis was the range of possible business models and demand characteristics, moving from traditional, proprietary business models and focused, incremental demand to a more proactive, open, and collaborative world of commerce. The vertical axis addressed the global and regional business environments, which ranged from bordered, chaotic,

---

EXHIBIT 7 SAMPLE QUESTIONS, EXCERPTED FROM INTERVIEW QUESTIONS FOR 2004 SESSION

External non-customer interview questions

- What external factors will affect the transportation and logistics industry over the next decade?

- What will deliver success (for transportation and logistics companies) 10–12 years out, and how will that differ from today?

- Paint me a picture of how transportation and logistics may look in 2017. Which current competitors will be strong players, and what kinds of new entrants do you see emerging?

External customer interview questions

- What will make a company successful in your industry in the next decade? (What's going to be different?)

- If we could answer one question about the future to help your company succeed, what would that question be?

- What is going to stop being true in your industry over the next decade?

UPS management internal interview questions

- How would you describe success for UPS over the next 10–12 years? What would it look like for us? What would be the results?

- How would you like UPS to be viewed within the industry? Within the financial community? Among customers? Among employees?

- If I could answer any question for you, what would you want to know? What would you like to know that would give UPS a jump on the competition?

Source: Company documents.

EXHIBIT 8   HORIZON 2017 SCENARIO CHARACTERISTICS

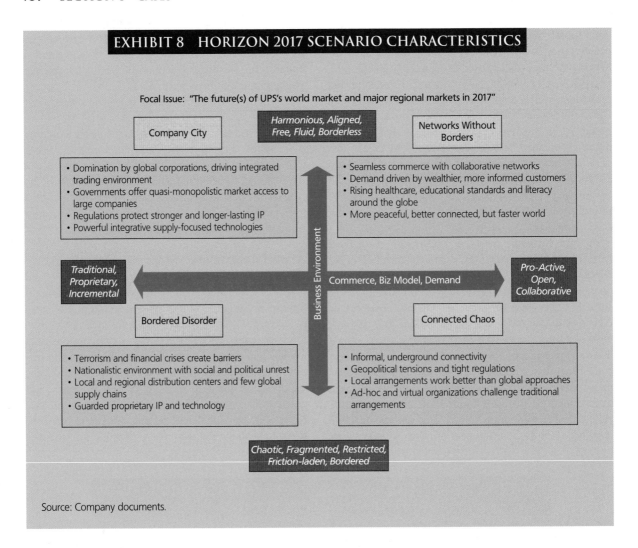

Focal Issue: "The future(s) of UPS's world market and major regional markets in 2017"

Company City
- Domination by global corporations, driving integrated trading environment
- Governments offer quasi-monopolistic market access to large companies
- Regulations protect stronger and longer-lasting IP
- Powerful integrative supply-focused technologies

Harmonious, Aligned, Free, Fluid, Borderless

Networks Without Borders
- Seamless commerce with collaborative networks
- Demand driven by wealthier, more informed customers
- Rising healthcare, educational standards and literacy around the globe
- More peaceful, better connected, but faster world

Traditional, Proprietary, Incremental ← Commerce, Biz Model, Demand → *Pro-Active, Open, Collaborative*

Business Environment

Bordered Disorder
- Terrorism and financial crises create barriers
- Nationalistic environment with social and political unrest
- Local and regional distribution centers and few global supply chains
- Guarded proprietary IP and technology

Connected Chaos
- Informal, underground connectivity
- Geopolitical tensions and tight regulations
- Local arrangements work better than global approaches
- Ad-hoc and virtual organizations challenge traditional arrangements

Chaotic, Fragmented, Restricted, Friction-laden, Bordered

Source: Company documents.

restricted, and fragmented to borderless, harmonious, free, and holistic.

Scenarios   These axes formed the framework for four scenarios (see Exhibit 8). In the upper-left quadrant was the 'Company City' future dominated by large corporations, with a growing middle class and the proliferation of powerful, integrated supply-focused technologies. The lower-left quadrant described a 'Bordered Disorder' world, with a highly regulated, protectionist environment with slow growth in developing nations, guarded intellectual property and technology, and an increase in security threats and environmental and financial shocks. In the lower-right quadrant, 'Connected Chaos' defined a future full of global unrest, 'amoral' commerce, and informal connectivity that was difficult for governments to control. Finally, the upper-right quadrant, called 'Networks without Borders', defined a highly connected, stable

world with low barriers to market entry and fast-moving technologies aimed at consumers.

The participants then drafted story lines and provided more detail for each of the four scenarios. Subsequently, consultants turned this work into cohesive, internally consistent scenario stories at the UPS global level and provided broad descriptions of the four scenarios at the regional level. These documents were then distributed to participants for review prior to the third session. Finally, the participants met in regional teams to define implications for technology and infrastructure initiatives, growth strategies and options, and workforce development at both the global and regional levels (see Exhibit 9). Unlike in the 1997 session, the participants also identified early warning signals to indicate movement toward one scenario or another. However, the system to monitor the signals was, according to one CSG manager, 'loose' (see Exhibit 10).

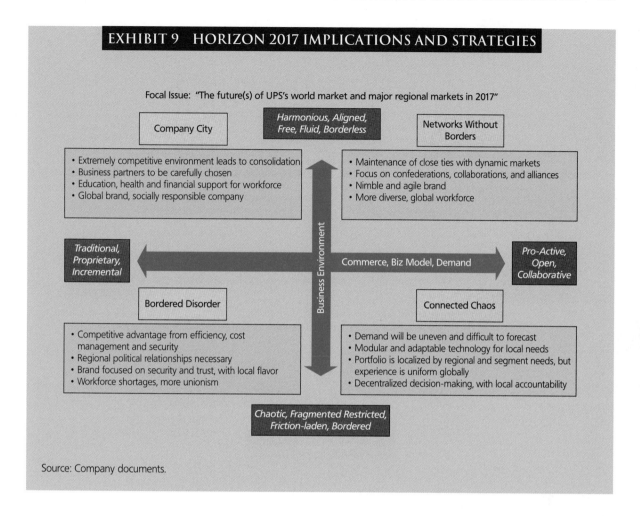

EXHIBIT 9   HORIZON 2017 IMPLICATIONS AND STRATEGIES

Focal Issue: "The future(s) of UPS's world market and major regional markets in 2017"

Company City

Harmonious, Aligned, Free, Fluid, Borderless

Networks Without Borders

- Extremely competitive environment leads to consolidation
- Business partners to be carefully chosen
- Education, health and financial support for workforce
- Global brand, socially responsible company

- Maintenance of close ties with dynamic markets
- Focus on confederations, collaborations, and alliances
- Nimble and agile brand
- More diverse, global workforce

Business Environment

Traditional, Proprietary, Incremental

Commerce, Biz Model, Demand

Pro-Active, Open, Collaborative

Bordered Disorder

Connected Chaos

- Competitive advantage from efficiency, cost management and security
- Regional political relationships necessary
- Brand focused on security and trust, with local flavor
- Workforce shortages, more unionism

- Demand will be uneven and difficult to forecast
- Modular and adaptable technology for local needs
- Portfolio is localized by regional and segment needs, but experience is uniform globally
- Decentralized decision-making, with local accountability

Chaotic, Fragmented Restricted, Friction-laden, Bordered

Source: Company documents.

As it had in the first scenario-planning exercise, the Strategy Advisory Group served as both an incubator and a skeptic for the process. It reviewed the results as the teams progressed through critical points and had many discussions around the scenarios, their implications, and possible strategies.

Results

The 2004 session produced scenarios that had more similarities than differences when compared with the 1997 scenarios. For Higberg, this was not a concern. 'I was more worried that it would be a 90-degree turn rather than a 10- to 20-degree change. Roughly 60% of the characteristics of the scenarios were the same as in 1997. The other 40% were what's interesting.' Some of the hypotheses developed in 1997, such as industry consolidation and continued growth of the Internet, had become reality. In addition, some of the huge open technological issues had been clarified. However,

there were some surprises; they included the rise of safety and terrorist threats and the fall of the dot-coms. Despite the lack of major changes in direction, Higberg was convinced the session was valuable: 'It validated and reaffirmed our direction. It also provided a much richer understanding of regional nuances.'

In March 2005, senior management was still digesting the scenarios that had been produced. Since most of the company was focused on executing the Centennial Plan and Strategy Road Map, discussions about implications were limited to the Strategy Advisory Group members and staff in CSG, Marketing, Public Affairs, and Investor Relations.

Senior management reactions

Senior managers differed in their views on the value and applicability of the process. Kuehn believed the sessions had value, since 'they helped get our eyes above the horizon a little bit and be more sensitive to

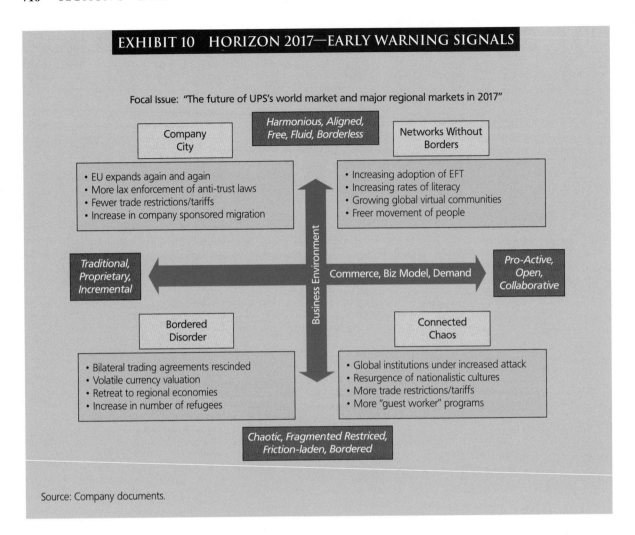

EXHIBIT 10   HORIZON 2017—EARLY WARNING SIGNALS

Focal Issue: "The future of UPS's world market and major regional markets in 2017"

Company City

Harmonious, Aligned, Free, Fluid, Borderless

Networks Without Borders

- EU expands again and again
- More lax enforcement of anti-trust laws
- Fewer trade restrictions/tariffs
- Increase in company sponsored migration

- Increasing adoption of EFT
- Increasing rates of literacy
- Growing global virtual communities
- Freer movement of people

Business Environment

Traditional, Proprietary, Incremental

Commerce, Biz Model, Demand

Pro-Active, Open, Collaborative

Bordered Disorder

Connected Chaos

- Bilateral trading agreements rescinded
- Volatile currency valuation
- Retreat to regional economies
- Increase in number of refugees

- Global institutions under increased attack
- Resurgence of nationalistic cultures
- More trade restrictions/tariffs
- More "guest worker" programs

Chaotic, Fragmented Restriced, Friction-laden, Bordered

Source: Company documents.

the major forces shaping the world.' Other managers saw value in using the scenarios to fine tune their tracking of the competition and to define appropriate lobbying initiatives. McDevitt also found the scenarios helpful: 'We don't want to just plod along. The scenarios helped us see where the opportunities are. Also, once we have them, we can look back and see where we were accurate in our work, and we can see what did and did not materialize.'

Eskew continued to believe in the merit of the sessions:

Our goal is not to predict the future but to start thinking about the ramifications of the various scenarios, so that we can align our planning behind them. The exercise allows us to more effectively build in midcourse corrections and backup strategies as we create the next three- to five-year strategic plan for the organization. It is a significant undertaking and a big time commitment. But, in our business we can't afford to be caught flat-footed by trends – trends that we could have anticipated – but that sneak in under our radar screen.

More tactical, operationally minded members of the Management Committee questioned the worth of the exercise. They found the exercise too abstract and difficult to apply. These managers, one executive observed, tended to see the exercise as 'pipe dreams, daydreaming, and happy talk. They had a hard time suspending disbelief long enough to free up their thinking.'

These differing opinions were not surprising, for they reflected a fundamental tension in the company. One observer commented: 'The mixed perceptions on the immediate value of the exercise reflect the tactical and strategic dichotomy that lies at the heart of the UPS character. UPS at its best is a mix of execution and vision.' Or as Kuehn put it, 'If only 10% of the managers get it, maybe that's okay.'

Participant reactions

Participants in the sessions also had a variety of reactions to the exercise. Some participants struggled with the process. According to one: 'At first, everybody had trouble seeing the possible, since most managers in the company are so focused on the short term. It was also difficult to keep the perspective in mind that this was not about UPS but rather about how the world affected UPS. It was irrelevant that UPS existed.' In addition, despite the desire to limit the transfer of knowledge from the 1997 session, it was difficult to keep the two exercises separate and distinct. One participant commented: 'The two axes caused problems. They were very similar to the previous versions, and the names of the 1997 scenarios were well ingrained in our minds.'

There were several other concerns with the sessions. Most revolved around value, purpose, and goals. Some participants were skeptical about the value of the sessions. According to one: 'Scenario planning looks pretty, but does it have any impact on what people do?' Another admitted the session had no impact on his work. A third participant observed, 'It was hard to understand what scenario planning was all about. It was very clear that sessions were not to be used to develop strategy. And we didn't really feel we were in a strategy process in the first meeting. Instead it felt like we were in Saturday Night Live. It was wacky. It felt fun, but frivolous.' However, he went on to acknowledge that the impact of the session was more subtle and affected his own thinking process: 'I used to lay out a series of steps and say, "Here's where we need to go, here's the plan." What I had never done is say, "If this happens, is the plan still right?" Now, I'll say, "Let's look at what might happen if our competitors do x. How would things change? Are we prepared?"'

Strategy road map status

In January 2005, shortly after the conclusion of the 2004 scenario-planning sessions, the Management Committee members spent a day reviewing the status of the Strategy Road Map. Since roughly 50% of the members who had been at the original meetings in 2002 had retired, the session also served to give the new members a chance to hear the plans directly from the CEO.

Prior to the meeting, McDevitt and Eskew had handed out homework assignments. They asked each of the members to review the Road Map and their assignments, the original 2002 direction, and the current status of the initiatives. Members were expected to report on the status of the projects, the importance of the effort, and what needed to be added or dropped. In preparation for the meeting, McDevitt went to the teams and asked them the same questions. Books were prepared for the meeting that included a report on each critical initiative, comparing the two perspectives of the Management Committee members and the teams to highlight whether they were in agreement. Management Committee members, who had not seen the book beforehand, spent the day – after receiving a brief summary of the strategic process, including a short overview of the November 2004 scenario planning – going through each initiative, item by item. The Strategy Road Map was then refined, as needed.

McDevitt commented on the outcome of the session, 'After reviewing the book, we found that we weren't that far off course. I felt comfortable that we could move forward appropriately. This was the team that would personally take responsibility for the initiatives, since they will for the most part be here in 2007.' When asked if his work was done, however, McDevitt replied, 'While the exercise was very beneficial, I can't say it's complete. You never know when the next Trade Direct will come up. Even though we are much more attuned to these cross-functional issues and have achieved a certain degree of strategic integration, there is a strong tendency to go back to your area and focus there.'

In fact, the need for someone with McDevitt's responsibilities was currently under review. With the retirement of UPS's global transportation chief in mid-February 2005, Eskew had asked McDevitt to take on that role. But he had not resolved the future of McDevitt's strategic-integration responsibility. McDevitt had argued that he should keep the old responsibilities in addition to his new ones as transportation chief, since he believed that the needs of the old job had changed. But Eskew was not convinced of the wisdom of that recommendation.

UPS: Beyond the centennial

Before resolving the question of McDevitt's role, Eskew wanted to place the decision in the larger context of strategic planning at UPS. He had two primary concerns. First, he was worried that the strategic-planning process might need changes to keep UPS on the leading edge. The company had managed to transform itself several times over the past almost 100 years. But could it continue to do so with the current processes? Did there need to be a clearer, more direct link between the different components of the strategic process, for example?

The second concern specifically involved the scenario-planning exercise. Eskew knew that the exercise had helped him see the future differently, but he was not sure of its organizational impact. He was not convinced that the scenarios were really forming the foundation for future strategic plans. Were managers thinking broadly and creatively enough? How could they incorporate the possibility of wild-card events that they had not even considered in the last session? Were they doing enough to monitor early warning signals? Should participation be broadened to include field management? Or, was scenario planning an exercise that only really benefited senior managers and strategists of the company?

Strategy and performance management at DSM

By Marjolein Bloemhof and Philippe Haspeslagh[1]

It was April 2003, and Hans Dijkman, Business Group Director of DSM Melamine, had just attended a Business Strategy Dialogue (BSD) meeting. DSM Melamine was the global leader in the manufacturing and marketing of melamine, a chemical compound used to make highly resistant surfaces, supplying almost one third of world demand. However, Dijkman and his team faced significant challenges in terms of cost competitiveness, aggressive competition, market maturity in Europe and the US, and emerging growth, particularly in China.

Business Strategy Dialogues had been introduced at DSM in the mid-90s to help structure the firm's strategy development process. The BSD process consisted of five distinct phases resulting in a thorough review of the industry, market trends, customer needs, competition and the position of the relevant business group. In 2001, as part of its new Value Based Business Steering (VBBS) system, DSM had also started to align its strategic planning and financial management processes by introducing Strategic Value Contracts. These contracts contained both performance indicators to monitor the implementation of strategy, and value drivers to measure economic value-creation.

BSDs were initiated whenever either the business or corporate felt the need, on average every three years. DSM Melamine was currently performing its fourth BSD at the request of Dijkman who felt that the current 'actively maintain' strategy would soon fail to achieve the financial performance targeted in his Strategic Value Contract.

Management of DSM Melamine had been discussing the possibility of pursuing a 'grow and build' strategy. They felt that they had reached the limits of cost reduction and that the only way to grow for DSM Melamine was by investing in new melamine plants. Dijkman, however, doubted whether corporate management would agree with this change. Would they emphasize the corporate strategy of becoming a specialties company and thus be reluctant to invest heavily in a commodity such as melamine, or would

they let VBBS principles prevail and let themselves be swayed by Melamine's financial track record?

From state mines to specialty company

DSM origins go back to 1902 when the Dutch government founded Dutch State Mines (DSM) as a state-owned coal-mining company. In the 100 years of its existence DSM reinvented itself several times from what was originally a coal mining company, first, as a petrochemicals business, then a commodity chemicals business, and more recently a specialties company.

DSM became a public company in 1989. In 1993, Simon de Bree was appointed CEO and under his leadership DSM continued working on a portfolio shift towards advanced chemical and biotechnical products for the life sciences industry and performance materials. These activities were characterized by good earnings, quality, and strong growth. When de Bree stepped down in July 1999 he was hailed for having reduced the company's exposure to cyclicality and improved its structure by shifting towards a larger share of value-added products. He left the company in good shape both financially and portfolio-wise. Peter Elverding, the board member in charge of integrating Gist Brocades at that time, succeeded de Bree as CEO. Under his guidance, DSM was able to complete its strategic transformation into a specialty chemical company.

By 2003, the company had more than 20 000 employees spread across 200 offices and production sites in 40 countries. It was the leading producer of life science products, performance materials and industrial chemicals, and had a turnover of €6 billion in 2002 (Exhibit 1). Its headquarters were located in Heerlen, in the south of the Netherlands, close to the site of the former coalmines. In 2002, on the 100th anniversary of its foundation, DSM was given royal status and renamed Royal DSM.

[1]Source: Reprinted with permission of INSEAD, Fontainebleau, France.

Vision 2005: 'Focus and value strategy'

One year after his appointment, Elverding announced the outcome of the Corporate Strategy Dialogue conducted in 2000 and labelled 'Vision 2005: Focus and Value'. With the implementation of Vision 2005, DSM would complete its strategic transformation into a specialty chemicals company. Elverding announced that DSM was planning to spin off its petrochemical business. This decision was not without emotion as the petrochemicals business was regarded by many as the 'roots' of the chemical company.

EXHIBIT 1 KEY FIGURES ON DSM

Balance Sheet (€ million)	2002	2001
Fixed assets	3,639	4,442
Current assets	5, 357	4,133
Total assets	8,996	8,575
Capital employed	4,570	5,763
Group equity	5,186	4,298
Provisions	682	809
Net debt	−1,038	867
Total group equity and liabilities	8,996	8,575
Income Statement (€ million)		
Ongoing Activities		
Net sales Life Science Products	2,168	2,237
Net sales Performance Materials	1,767	1,855
Net sales Polymers & Industrial Chemicals	1,268	1,302
Net sales Other Activities	433	357
Total, ongoing activities	5,636	5,751
Operating profit plus depreciation and amortization (EBITDA)	767	741
Operating profit (EBIT)	383	336
Capital expenditure (including acquisitions)	496	561
Discontinued activities		
Net sales	1,029	2,219
Operating profit plus depreciation and amortization (EBITDA)	125	301
Operating profit (EBIT)	67	185
Total		
Net sales	6,665	7,790
Operating profit plus depreciation and amortization (EBITDA)	892	1,042
Operating profit (EBIT)	450	521
Capital expenditure (including acquisitions)	536	652
Profit on ordinary activities after taxation	349	369
Net profit	1,188	1,415
Dividend	199	199
Depreciation and amortization	442	521
Cash flow	1,630	1,936
Workforce at 31 December	18,375	21,504

In addition, Elverding announced ambitious targets of increasing annual sales by approximately 60 per cent to € 10 billion by 2005, despite the planned withdrawal from the petrochemicals business, which provided one-third of the company's turnover in 2000. At least 80 per cent of sales would have to be generated by specialty products; the rest would come from industrial chemicals, such as melamine and caprolactam, where DSM was already the global leader. Acquisitions would account for half of the sales increase and the remainder would be achieved through organic growth, roughly 6 per cent per year.

Besides focusing on a global leadership position in the specialties business, Vision 2005 also addressed DSM's desire to increase its market capitalization as management felt that the company's stock was undervalued. There were several reasons for this underperformance, including concerns about DSM's portfolio breadth relative to the size of the company, but management believed that the main reason was the market's perception that DSM still was a cyclical stock with predominantly a commodity profile. Management hoped that the implementation of Vision 2005 would turn DSM into a real specialties company, leading to a re-rating and appreciation of its market capitalization. A major part of the Vision 2005 strategy was accomplished when DSM successfully sold its petrochemicals business to Saudi Arabian Basic Industry Corp (SABIC) in June 2002. With a total net consideration of €2.25 billion, this transaction was the largest single deal in DSM's history. In a separate transaction, DSM sold its entitlement to an annual portion of the net profits of EBN[2] to the Dutch government in December 2001. These transactions created a solid cash cushion of over €3 billion to fund the expansion of the specialty portfolio targeted in Vision 2005. To protect its cash trove from unwanted parties, and to keep the funds and transformation process transparent, DSM took the unusual step of placing the revenues from the disposals of EBN and the petrochemicals business into a new subsidiary, DSM Vision 2005 BV. The use of these resources required approval by the governing board of the foundation, which consisted of three members of DSM's managing board and three members of the supervisory board. After the divestment of petrochemicals, DSM had become a substantially smaller company, but with a portfolio that matched the desired profile. Specialties now represented well over two-thirds of total sales, justifying a reclassification from 'bulk commodity player' to 'specialty player'.

In February 2003, Elverding was able to announce the next step in implementing Vision 2005 as DSM signed a contract to acquire Hoffman-La Roche's vitamins, carotenoids and fine chemicals business for €1.75 billion, the largest acquisition it had ever made.[3] The acquisition would help restore its total sales, which had been reduced to less than € 6 billion as a result of the divestment of petrochemicals, to over €8 billion. More importantly, it would boost the specialty part of DSM's portfolio and help achieve the goal of 80 per cent of sales in specialties two years ahead of the scheduled date (2005). Various analysts were skeptical about the acquisition, however, because of the price pressure and the low growth prospects of the business.

The DSM organization

DSM had a decentralized organizational structure built around 15 business groups (consisting of various business units) that were empowered to execute all business functions. The business groups were grouped into three strategic clusters, mainly for reporting purposes (Exhibit 2). DSM believed that this structure ensured a flexible, efficient and fast response to market changes. The business group directors reported directly to the managing board of directors. Staff departments at corporate level supported the managing board and the business groups. The business groups contracted the services of a number of shared service departments, DSM Research, and intergroup product supplies at market prices.

The managing board of directors was a collegial board with five members. It was responsible for making decisions about the company's strategy, its portfolio policy, and the deployment of resources. Most board members were 'board delegates' for various business groups. The top management team consisted of the 15 business group directors and the corporate vice- presidents reporting to the board. The third layer of management consisted of 300 senior executives. The top 300 were considered 'corporate property'; they were on one central payroll and

[2]EBN: Energie Beheer Nederland, the entity controlling the state participations in the exploration, production and marketing of natural gas in the Netherlands, the management of which was entrusted by the State to DSM.

[3]The deal was closed in September 2003, after the final approval of the anti-trust authorities was obtained. Roche's Vitamins & Fine Chemicals business was renamed DSM Nutritional Products (DNP).

EXHIBIT 2 ORGANIZATIONAL STRUCTURE, AS OF MARCH 2003

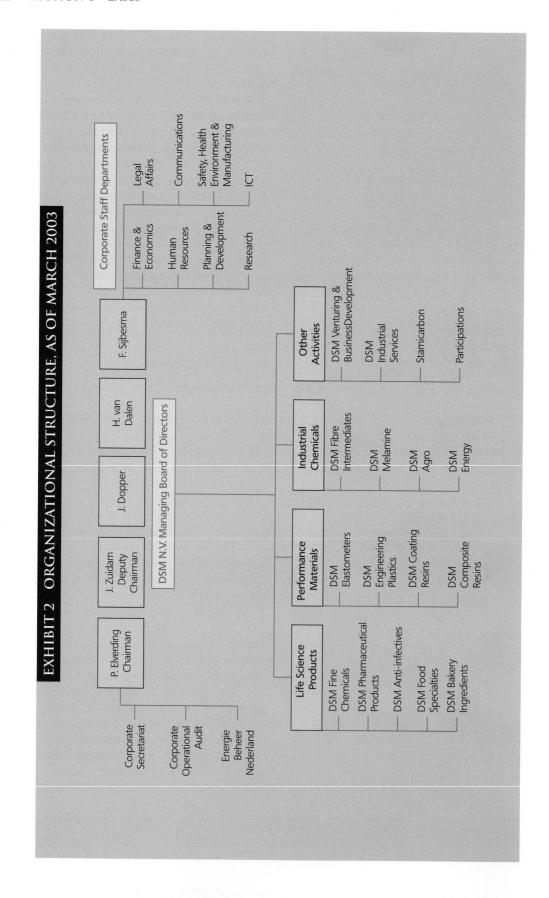

Corporate had the authority to relocate these executives within DSM if they felt the need to do so.

DSM's corporate culture was traditionally informal and consensus-oriented, as is the case in many Dutch companies. Long-standing careers at DSM were encouraged. However, because DSM had been a cyclical company where 90 per cent of the business results were the outcome of external circumstances that could not be influenced, DSM historically did not have a strong accountability culture.

The strategic planning process at DSM

Until the early 1990s, DSM had operated a traditional strategic planning process with planning and budget cycles taking place throughout the year However, DSM management was no longer satisfied with this process. They felt that Corporate Planning owned the strategic planning process and that it served too many different purposes (corporate, divisional, business and functional strategy, internal and external). The process had become routine over time and had degenerated into a 'numbers exercise'. The link between strategy and performance was not clear, but more importantly, top management felt that the quality of strategy development was poor. Most of the strategies focused mainly on cost reduction. The primary beneficiary of such strategies was not the company but its customers, since most of the cost savings were typically passed on to them through price reductions. To enhance the quality of the strategy development process, a new approach called the Business Strategy Dialogue (BSD) was introduced in 1992. These BSDs led to Corporate Strategy Dialogues (CSDs) which were intended to improve the corporate strategy development process.

Corporate strategy dialogue

DSM's strategy development process started with an extensive study of the current situation and the outlook for the company for the next few years. The Corporate Strategy Dialogue was held every three years with a team of 40–50 company-wide executives. It was aimed at developing a long-term corporate strategy, with evaluations and choices being made about portfolio composition, investment priorities and geographical spread. The whole process took six to nine months and was wide-ranging, involving intensive discussions in DSM Corporate top meetings, with the supervisory board and the Central Works Council. The end product was a shortlist of corporate top priorities.

The first CSD was performed in 1994, followed by another in 1997 and a third in 2000. Besides new themes that were defined in each CSD, a number of common themes had consistently been part of the CSD, such as profitable growth, leadership position, coherent portfolio, reduction of cyclicality, growth markets, reduction of dollar-sensitivity, geographical spread, and being an attractive employer.

Once the priorities were set, the corporate strategic plan was to be implemented over the next two to three years. Focusing all energy on realizing its corporate priorities had allowed DSM to achieve most of them before their target dates.

Business strategy dialogue

The businesses were responsible for developing and implementing their (approved) Business Strategy Dialogues (BSDs). The purpose of a BSD was to provide a consistent method and terminology to help structure the strategy development process and improve its quality. BSDs were mostly initiated by the business groups themselves, but were sometimes requested by corporate. They occurred at regular intervals of three years on average.

The BSD process consisted of five phases with several steps within each phase. The five phases were: Characterizing the Business Situation; Analyzing the Business System at Macro Level; Analyzing the Business System at Micro Level; Options and Strategic Choice and Action Planning and Performance Measurement (see Exhibit 3). But before a BSD could be started, some preparatory work had to be done.

Starting up. One of the first things to be done was to identify a facilitator and a challenger. To facilitate the implementation of the BSDs, Corporate had trained around 30 'facilitators' to support the business teams in its creative thinking process. They were selected from the top 350 executives and asked by the Chairman of DSM to become a facilitator. The task of a facilitator was to prepare the strategy development process with the business group director by defining the scope of the exercise, discussing the composition of the core team, examining the time schedule, drafting a list of important strategic issues, and appointing a project manager who was responsible for the operational part of the strategy development process. The most important role of the facilitator, however,

EXHIBIT 3 THE STRATEGY DEVELOPMENT PROCESS

Phase	I Business Situation	II Macro Business System	III Micro Business System	IV Options/ Strategic Choice	V Actions & Performance Measurement
Tools	Strategic data checklist	Facilitators	Facilitators	Facilitators	Management reporting format
Duration	2-4 months	2 days	2 days	1-2 days	Continuous
Objective	Gather basic information for BSD	Analyze business dynamics, drivers and strategic groups	Understand own capabilities, analyze options, strength/ weaknesses	Understand options, select performance indicators and targets	Continuously measure progress
Tasks	■ Environmental and market analysis ■ Competitor assessment ■ Analysis of manufacturing, R&D, technology, HRM, finance, processes	■ Discuss business chain ■ Analyze dynamics ■ Determine industry drivers ■ Characterize strategic groups	■ Formulation and evaluation of options ■ Detailed KSF analysis ■ Qualifiers ■ Differentiators ■ Formulation of indicators ■ Targets from competitive benchmarking		■ Progress control ■ Action plan ■ Target setting ■ Continuous improvement program
Output	■ Document with required information ■ Strategy support database	■ Strategic groups ■ Industry drivers	■ Capabilities ■ Organizational/ HR assessment	■ Strategic plan outline ■ Strategic mission ■ KSFs ■ Indicators ■ Targets	■ Strategic contract versus targets

was to make sure that the BSD led to real strategic options and a real choice, as expressed by Marthijn Jansen, facilitator: 'The role of the facilitator is to make sure that the BSD focuses on the right issues, that in the "options phase" the conversation diverges, and that in the defining of the KPIs phase, everything converges to a clear path and a clear view of the implications of the choices made.'

In addition to a facilitator, a 'challenger' was selected. The challenger had an important role as he/she had to question the BSD team about the assumptions, analyses and conclusions it made. Challengers were chosen from the top 100 managers within DSM. In addition to the internal challenger, a business group could also ask 'outsiders' to challenge them on specific issues. These outsiders – often (technology) specialists – also shared their knowledge.

The core team in the BSD typically consisted of the complete business management team supported by specialists from further down the organization. They were advised not to have more than 10 to 12 people as management felt that larger groups did not allow for effective discussion and hampered the creativity of the process. In large or complicated businesses sub-groups were formed to address specific questions. The BSD process consisted of workshops and discussion sessions led by the facilitator. Input and participation by all concerned was considered very important.

Characterizing the business situation. The objective of this phase was to collect and structure the necessary information to be used as input to the BSD. The Group provided the businesses with a strategic data checklist of the information that might be useful for the BSD such as environmental and market analysis, competitor assessments and analysis of manufacturing, R&D, HRM, finance and processes. Data were supplied by functional discipline. In addition to data gathering, the checklist offered a useful format for summarizing and presenting the information. The data set was structured in accordance with questions such as:

- What business are you competing in?
- Which other businesses and products are you competing with?
- How attractive is the industry in terms of growth and profitability?
- What is your competitive position (benchmarks)?
- What are the dynamics? What trends can be expected in your business system?

Practice showed that this phase could take two to four months. Corporate management emphasized that the businesses should not view this information-gathering phase as a checklist exercise but rather approach it from an 'issue-driven' angle.

Analyzing the business system at macro level. In this phase, which took approximately two days, the industry in which the business unit competed was analysed from the outside in, based on Porter's Five Forces model. The discussion focused on the examination of the value added in the business chain, the customers, the competitors, the business dynamics and the drivers of the industry. An important step was the analysis of the different generic strategies followed by key competitors. Understanding generic strategies forced the businesses to categorize the different ways in which a business could compete in the industry. A strategic group was defined as a cluster of companies following the same generic strategy. The outcome of this phase included a basic understanding of the 'rules of the game', i.e. the strategic groups in which the business might compete and a preliminary view of the key success factors (KSFs) that must be met in order to compete successfully within a certain strategic group.

Analyzing the business system at micro level. In this phase the organization was analysed from the inside out, by looking at the internal process. Important tools for the analysis of the internal value chain were market segmentation, activity-based costing, internal or (preferably) external benchmarking of functions, and assessment of the technological position. The conclusions of the micro-discussion included an analysis of the business unit's capabilities – both strengths and weaknesses – to compete in its strategic group. This phase took on average two days.

Options and strategic choice. After having assessed the competitive environment and the business unit's capabilities to compete successfully in its environment, the outcome of both steps were compared, i.e. internal capabilities were compared with the list of KSFs (see Exhibit 4). This allowed the business to make a choice as to the strategic group in which it wanted to compete. Furthermore, it allowed the business to verify whether it really could serve the selected market segments and determine what steps were necessary to achieve or sustain leadership within the strategic group.

Action planning and performance measurement. Once the strategic choice had been made, the strategy had to be translated into an action plan and linked to performance measurement. Based on the strategic mission and objectives of the business unit a limited number of performance indicators that were important to the corresponding KSFs were selected. Performance indicators monitored the implementation of the strategy and were the measurable part of the KSFs, allowing comparisons with competitors and performance monitoring over time. Examples of performance indicators included market share, pipeline of products, quality, customer satisfaction, and cost per unit. The objective of performance measurement was to provide periodic information on the progress made toward the defined targets for each performance indicator. Furthermore, it helped management set objectives and target levels for the next period.

Annual Strategic Review (ASR). The Annual Strategic Review (ASR) was performed by each business group, and comprised a progress report on the implementation of the BSD, an update or reassessment of major business risks, an updated sensitivity analysis and updated financial projections. The ASRs of the business groups constituted the building blocks of the corporate ASR whose purpose was to monitor the execution of the Corporate Strategy Dialogue. An

EXHIBIT 4 DSM MELAMINE: STRATEGIC GROUPS, BSD 1999

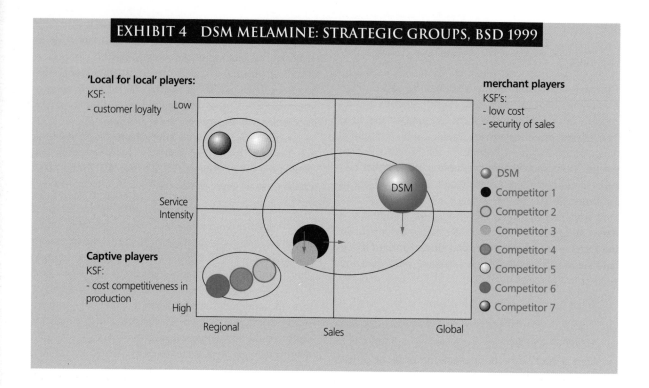

important element in the review was the confirmation that the chosen strategy in the BSD was still valid and that the implementation was on track. Therefore, the validity of the main assumptions on which the strategy was based had to be checked and the consequences of changes in the business environment for the strategy evaluated.

Benefits and challenges of the BSD system

Benefits. In 2000, six years after its implementation, the BSD had become an accepted system for developing business strategy. DSM management was pleased with the improved quality of strategy formulation and the team-building aspects. One business group director coming from outside DSM commented: 'The strategic planning process is very good at DSM. It is a robust and effective process. And it is a living system, contrary to many other companies where people just "feed" the system.'

Many people valued the 'challenger' part of the BSD, where someone from outside the business group challenged the assumptions and outcomes of the BSD. One business group director recalled: 'Corporate said to us: "The BSD is nice but not rigorous enough.

Come back when you have really looked at the intrinsic value of each market segment. Not at macro level, but at market segment level." This was very good because it forced us to get a real grounding in segments.'

People agreed that the BSD process greatly enhanced the insights and understanding of the business. In addition, it forced alignment, both across functions in the business unit and with respect to the strategy. Furthermore, people felt that the BSD gave legitimacy to initiate changes later on when the business got to the implementation phase. Another big advantage of the process was that strategy development became a three-yearly process with just an annual update. One top executive of corporate planning commented: 'Performing a BSD is a lot of work. But once you are done, you are done for two to three years.'

Challenges. The final phase of the BSD – translating strategy into performance measurement – remained a challenge. Hein Schreuder, Corporate Vice President Strategy & Development, expressed his concern: 'DSM invests heavily in a good strategic diagnosis, but the ultimate focus should be on delivery.'

Although DSM had improved the quality of strategic thinking in the planning process, the question remained indeed how to link it with execution.

Value based business steering

In 2000, Henk van Dalen, Director of the DSM Polyethylenes business group, was appointed to the managing board. He believed that the necessary step to implement Vision 2005 and its promise for performance was a more intense focus on value-creation in the businesses. According to the newly introduced Value-Based-Business Steering (VBBS) concept, the overall target for DSM was to create value for all of its stakeholders, i.e. shareholders, employees, customers, and society.

DSM approached VBBS from three different angles. The first was accountability as the basis for financial control. The second was alignment of DSM's strategic business planning processes to materialize its promise for performance. The third was the introduction of new financial operating metrics that translated Vision 2005 and BSDs into economic value terms. DSM decided to start with the third angle because it had the biggest impact on the organization and was a first step in aligning strategy with performance measurement. As a result, VBBS was strongly driven by the finance department – at least initially.

New financial business steering metrics

A new set of performance metrics was developed for internally measuring and managing financial performance in terms of value-creation. Cash Flow Return on Investment (CFROI) became DSM's new yardstick for measuring the performance of its businesses. Contrary to other value-based management companies, DSM decided to use CFROI only for internal reporting and financial performance measurement, while ROI remained the performance measure for external reporting. A reason for this decision was that DSM felt that the complex CFROI calculations were difficult to explain to investors. Furthermore, DSM first wanted to see if the new metrics would work.

Total Shareholder Return was an important external performance indicator related to value-creation for DSM as a whole, but could not be directly linked to the performance of individual business groups. DSM chose to introduce Cash Value Added (CVA) to translate value-creation from a capital market point of view into an objective internal DSM measure. CVA represented the cash surplus generated ('value realized') by a business once all capital providers had been compensated. To determine the 'value created' by a business, DSM measured the increase in value

(delta CVA) from year to year. Because DSM was a decentralized company, the group did not impose delta CVA targets; instead, target setting was done in a bottom-up fashion. To achieve a positive delta CVA and thus create value, a business could work on two key value drivers: by improving CFROI or by investing in profitable projects.

Investments were evaluated against the Internal Rate of Return (IRR) hurdle, i.e. the before-tax weighted average cost of capital (WACC). If an investment met the WACC hurdle, it created value. However, DSM imposed an additional performance standard by plotting the current business position and the historical performance of a business group on a so-called 'C-curve' (see Exhibit 5).

The C-curve provided a clear indication of the preferred route to value-creation for a business depending on its current return. Three basic scenarios could be distinguished. For businesses that generated returns below the WACC, restructuring and improving the return was priority number one. Businesses that had returns around the WACC needed to improve their performance and were encouraged to explore methods to increase CFROI. Finally, businesses that had returns well above the WACC found themselves in a position that was profitable; the way to create value for this kind of businesses was to grow while improving or maintaining CFROI.

Operationalizing VBBS. Value-creation for DSM as a whole was translated into the internal value-creation measure delta CVA. This measure could be applied at the business group level, but also at lower levels such as business units or product/market combinations. The next step in the VBBS process was to translate the abstract concept of value-creation into operational actions using the concept of value drivers. DSM defined a value driver as an 'operational variable which can be influenced by acts of management and which has a direct link with value-creation'. Examples of value drivers included: working capital as a percentage of sales, raw material costs per ton, production costs per ton, and sales price per ton.

At this stage, the difference between value drivers and performance indicators became clear. Performance indicators were developed during the BSD and monitored the implementation of the strategy. Value drivers were developed during the VBBS analyses and monitored how the implemented strategy resulted in economic value-creation. Performance indicators applied to the strategic and tactical level and provided early warning signs ('leading indicators'). In contrast,

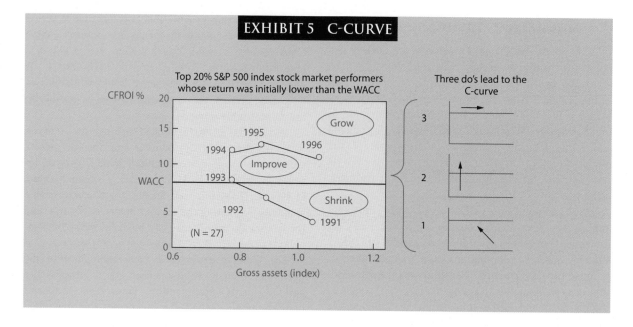

EXHIBIT 5   C-CURVE

Top 20% S&P 500 index stock market performers whose return was initially lower than the WACC

Three do's lead to the C-curve

value drivers applied to the operational level of the organization and were financial and often results-based and therefore 'lagging indicators'.

Value drivers and performance indicators did not necessarily have a one-to-one relationship. One performance indicator (e.g. market share) could influence multiple value drivers (e.g., volume, margin, cost), and vice versa, one value driver could be affected by several performance indicators. For the commodity businesses, value drivers and performance indicators often covered the same variables. For example, a value driver could be cost per ton, while the corresponding performance indicator would be a relative measure – costs compared to competitors. However, the link was much less clear for the specialty activities where factors such as the management of the innovation pipeline would be decisive for success. There could be a significant time lag between the filling of the pipeline with new products and the value-creation caused by higher sales volume resulting from these new products.

Once the metrics were defined and the concept of VBBS was clear, DSM started with the strategic assessment of its various businesses. These assessments yielded valuable new insights into the positioning of specific businesses. For example, some businesses that accounting wise (i.e., based on ROI) looked like diamonds in the portfolio, turned out to be value-destroying businesses from a CFROI perspective. Loek Radix, Director of Corporate Finance, explained: 'I was almost physically attacked when I delivered that message. But the strategic assessments were a huge eye-opener about how we should manage a

certain type of business. Before, there was an atmosphere of complacency in successful businesses. There was no mindset at all about delta value. However, it is not important what today's value is; it is important what the evolution in value is.'

Although people got excited about the results from the VBBS assessments, implementing the new metrics and coming up with value drivers turned out to be a technically difficult and time consuming process. Although the consultants were able to explain the concept of CFROI and CVA, translating this into specific measures was extremely complex. According to Radix: 'The sweaty part starts when you really have to develop the metrics in detail. Questions like: "What do I do with foreign investment?" or "What is the percentage of economic depreciation?" were difficult to answer. We had to re-define items during the process. That was not really helping us in the introduction of VBBS and we got pushback from the operating managers.'

In early 2002, the general knowledge of the VBBS system in the DSM organization was still limited. Although top management understood the big picture, a survey testing more detailed knowledge showed that even at the executive level a lot still had to be learned. One corporate manager estimated that it would take three to five years for people to really understand and work with the new system. However, at corporate level, VBBS thinking had already significantly changed the strategic approach vis-à-vis the businesses. Whereas previously corporate finance used to strive for consensus, the department was now more able to challenge the businesses, helped by the C-curve. According to Radix:

> Before we had a culture of managing conflict in our department. Now we are able to say, 'No, we don't agree, we oppose this investment.' We now challenge businesses whose CFROI is above the WACC to grow, and we refuse to give additional investment money to businesses whose CFROI is below WACC. We now say 'If you don't have 8 per cent CFROI, then your first task is to get that CFROI before you get money for investments.' As a business unit manager you can no longer say: 'I will grow out of the misery.' VBBS and the C-curve really helped to challenge in a different way.

More than new metrics: Creating strategic alignment through strategic value contracts

Although VBBS within DSM was still very much metrics oriented, right from the early days DSM was aware that it was much more than just adopting new metrics: DSM management felt that it gave them the tools and insights to align the business strategies to performance measurement. The connection between strategy and performance measurement was made by elaborating the BSD into Strategic Value Contracts (SVCs).

From 2001 on, each new BSD had to result in a SVC. A SVC was a summary of the main conclusions of a BSD translated into measurable targets for the next three years. It contained two main sections which had to be explicitly approved by the managing board: (1) bottom line results focusing on CFROI and CVA and the breakdown thereof in controllable value drivers, and (2) strategic goals laid down in the strategic mission and the implementation specified in terms of key success factors, performance indicators and strategic milestones. Thus, both performance indicators for monitoring strategy implementation, and value-based measures for monitoring value-creation were incorporated into the contract. Future performance of the business would be monitored against the agreed-upon SVC.

DSM felt that the SVC was a strong communication tool and helped the implementation of strategy and VBBS at the business group levels. It explained the steps of how businesses were planning to execute their strategy. This led to more transparency and helped the management board ask the right questions and challenge the business groups. One management

board member explained: 'What always had frustrated me about the BSD was that a strategy was developed, but monitoring the implementation of this strategy was difficult. I am very pleased with the Strategic Value Contract because people are now forced to implement the strategy. Now, people really have to finish the BSD. That is much clearer.'

The SVC was signed by the business group director and the business group referee in the managing board, who signed on behalf of the entire managing board. A successor taking over responsibility for someone's business also had to take over the existing SVC. Proposals for substantial modifications to the contract could only result from major changes in the business environment and had to be approved by the managing board. In early 2002, two business groups had their SVC and five other contracts were in progress. By 2003, nearly all business groups had their SVC.

Compensation

In the past, not meeting targets was widely tolerated at DSM, largely as a result of the fact that DSM had been a cyclical company where 90 per cent of the businesses results were beyond the firm's control. DSM management felt that it had to change this 'culture of excuse' and high level of 'cyclicality tolerance' as DSM transformed into a specialties company. The implementation of SVCs supported this change in culture.

DSM felt that the next step in the implementation of VBBS was to link it with the managers' performance evaluation system. In 2002, it rolled out a new performance appraisal system for its executives which evaluated managers based on their ability to develop sustainable strategies and get them approved (BSD), the achievement of targets set in the SVC, and a number of enabling factors, such as having the right processes and workforce in place. The management board evaluated the top 30 executives, who in turn appraised the managers below them. This appraisal was used to determine managers' salary evolution.

The second element of the compensation system was a short-term incentive programme which ranged from 20 per cent to 30 per cent on top of the base salary. This incentive scheme was linked to VBBS by replacing ROI with delta CVA and calculating bonuses based on the current year's delta CVA. Thus, executive compensation was linked both to personal targets and to financial performance measures, such as CFROI, delta CVA and CVA. Lower management was held responsible for the relevant value drivers. Finally, DSM introduced a personnel share option scheme alongside the existing management option scheme in 2001.

When SVCs and the new performance appraisal system were first introduced, managers felt uncomfortable as the pressure on them gradually mounted. On the other hand, the contracts made it clear what was expected of them and improved communication both between the business groups and Corporate and within the business group itself. SVCs also led to a demand from the business group directors with respect to key individuals in their organization. Previously, corporate HR had the authority to move people around and managers typically changed jobs every 18 months to two years. Under the new system, however, some business group directors claimed that they were unable to achieve their SVC targets if they could not keep their key managers. DSM management therefore decided that employees would not move around for a period of three years, but also stated that business group directors had 'corporate' responsibilities in terms of training and follow up of people.

In 2002, DSM was unable to meet its ambitious profitability targets due to unfavorable economic developments. However, a number of corporate improvement targets relating to safety, health and the environment, and a number of targets linked to the Group's strategy were realized. The overall realization was 20 per cent. Moreover, the Supervisory Board had used its discretionary powers to grant an additional bonus to the members of the Managing Board amounting to 10 per cent of their fixed annual salary, in recognition of their extraordinary efforts in strategically repositioning the company.

The BSD and VBBS process at work at DSM Melamine

The DSM Melamine business group was part of the 'Industrial Chemicals' cluster. It was the global leader in the manufacturing and marketing of melamine, supplying almost one third of global demand. Melamine is a heat- and scratch-resistant plastic mainly used in impregnating resins and adhesive resins for laminated flooring and panels in the wood-processing industry. It is also used in car paints, durable plastic tableware, euro bank notes, and flame-retardants. The gas-phase production technology that DSM Melamine used to produce melamine was a proprietary technology developed in 1967 and was a highly sophisticated process technology. The raw materials

for the production of melamine were natural gas, ammonia, carbon dioxide, and urea. Since ammonia and carbondioxide were by-products of melamine production, melamine plants had to be built close to a urea plant.

In 2001, world consumption of melamine was nearly 700 000 metric tons, valued at approximately $700 million. DSM Melamine was well established with advanced production plants on three continents and a sophisticated technical support system in place for its customers. In 2002, DSM Melamine's image was one of a global reliable supplier of 'hassle-free' product in Europe, Americas, and Asia Pacific. It earned more than half of its sales from long-term contracts with large customers who considered melamine a strategic purchase item and valued security of supply.

The melamine market was subject to high volatility. Demand for most downstream markets for melamine was greatly influenced by general economic conditions. Consequently, demand followed the fortunes of the leading world economies. Furthermore, demand and capacity had not always been in balance, leading to significant price fluctuations. In 1998, for example, the melamine market was characterized by supply shortages caused by technical problems at several melamine producers worldwide. High imports from overseas by melamine consumers via traders raised spot prices to levels of €3500 /ton. In 1999, however, prices collapsed to €800–900/ton. One of the major challenges for melamine producers was therefore to balance supply and demand.

Forecasting demand was not sufficient, however. An accurate estimate of global melamine supply was also needed to avoid major under- or over-supply. This was hard to predict because of the many unplanned maintenance shutdowns at several melamine producers worldwide. The management of DSM Melamine had worked hard to improve its estimates of capacity utilization vis-à-vis global nameplate capacity.

The early BSDs

DSM Melamine started in 1992 with its first BSD, followed by others in 1995 and 1999. The BSD process proved to be very helpful in addressing the problems and challenges the business group was facing and dramatically changed its performance (see Exhibit 6).

BSD 1992. The main outcome of the 1992 BSD was the final approval of a US$80 million project to dismantle a relatively new melamine plant at Geleen in the Netherlands, and reconstruct it in Indonesia. DSM Melamine had made the decision to build the plant in Geleen in 1989 when it predicted a 5 per cent annual growth in melamine in Europe. However, since then melamine sales and prices in Western Europe had declined as demand in key markets in the former Soviet Union stagnated and exports to Eastern Europe slumped. The management team of DSM Melamine had to decide whether to close, sell, or relocate the plant that had been built only in 1992. Management decided to rebuild it in Indonesia where its Jakarta-based business Joint Venture, DSM Kaltim Melamine, in which it had a 60 per cent stake, would own and operate the plant. DSM had wanted to build a Southeast Asian melamine plant for some time as the Asia/Pacific region was a fairly new market that was developing at a fast pace, especially in countries with major wood-processing industries. The Geleen plant was dismantled in 1994 and rebuilt in Indonesia in 1997, thereby reducing the company's worldwide melamine capacity for three to four years. The plant was the largest melamine plant in the Far East and the first to be built in Southeast Asia.

BSD 1995. In 1995, the second BSD led to a major strategic breakthrough in the eyes of management. The strategy was to 'actively maintain' its global leadership position in terms of market share, technology, cost and customer image. Competition was based on 'price over volume' and DSM Melamine wanted to grow at the prevailing market rate. A breakthrough in the BSD process occurred when DSM Melamine woke up to the fact that it did not have the right technology to grow with the market. Instead of continuing to build large plants with gas-phase production technology – which would cover the growth of the market for the next four to five years – management decided to acquire Shortened Liquid Phase (SLP) technology in 1997. This technology, which required fewer production steps to produce high-quality melamine, would enable DSM Melamine to build smaller plants while still being cost competitive with the traditional gas-phase plants. However, to achieve the same quality level as the melamine obtained in DSM's gas-phase process, the SLP technology had to be upgraded.

BSD 1999. In 1999, a third BSD was performed. The project motivated by the new review was to build a fourth Melamine plant in Geleen based on the new liquid (phase technology, which required an investment of) € 90 million. A portion of that investment would be used to expand urea production at the site. The melamine plant was expected to come on-stream by end 2003.

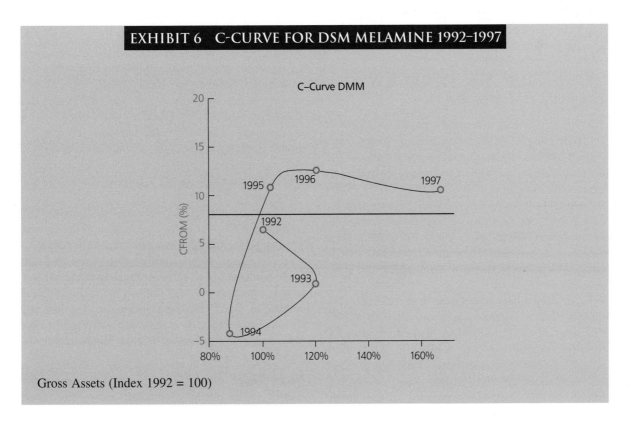

EXHIBIT 6   C-CURVE FOR DSM MELAMINE 1992–1997

C–Curve DMM

Gross Assets (Index 1992 = 100)

The strategy that followed the 1999 BSD was to continue the 'actively maintain' strategy. Management of DSM Melamine expected worldwide consumption of melamine to grow by 5-6 per cent per annum. This growth was concentrated in Europe and to a lesser extent Asia (China) and the Americas. Accordingly, DSM Melamine planned to expand its global capacity by 30kt every two to three years in addition to de-bottlenecking the existing plants.

Key success factors for the actively maintain strategy were 'lowest cost delivered' by de-bottlenecking existing gas-phase plants and new low cost technology, and 'security of sales'. The latter could be achieved by negotiating long-term contracts with global key customers, meeting the requirements for strategic customer alliances, and differentiating service levels.

The Strategic Value Contract

In 2001, the first SVC was drafted for DSM Melamine. Since it was DSM's first experience with these contracts, it was primarily viewed as a learning experience. The subsequent 2003 contract, signed in September 2002, was considered the first 'real' contract. It was based on the 1999 BSD and would be revised at the end of 2003, once the 2003 BSD was finished. (Exhibit 7 shows an extract of the SVC for the period 1999–2003.)

The 2003 BSD process

The 2003 BSD was initiated by the management of DSM Melamine (DMM), as the Annual Strategic Review of 2002 had shown that its current strategy would not enable the business group to achieve the ambitious targets set forth in the SVC. Projections by DMM showed that the group would have a zero or negative delta CVA from 2004 onwards and reach a major negative delta CVA in 2007. These calculations were based on assumptions from the corporate planning group which had predicted a major economic slowdown for 2007.

In addition, the environment had changed considerably. After experiencing strong demand in 1998 and most of 2000, melamine markets declined or remained stagnant in most regions in 2001. High natural gas costs, lower margins, depressed demand, and significant capacity additions during 1998–2001 forced many melamine producers to curtail production in 2001. Producers such as Melamine Chemicals and Namhae Chemical exited the market. However, industry experts expected the demand for melamine in the US and Western Europe to recover and grow at nearly 3 per cent per year from 2001 to 2006. Demand in Southeast Asia, particularly in China, was expected to experience much higher growth rates because of increasing production of laminates for both domestic use and exports. In the 1999 BSD, DMM had not actively looked into China, as the main investment opportunities were seen to be in Europe (see Exhibit 8). However, because of the impressive annual growth rate (15 per cent) of the Chinese melamine market, the management of DMM wanted to investigate the impact of China on its current strategy.

Kick-off. The BSD 2003 of DMM started with a kick-off meeting in September 2002 with the BSD global management team, including the management team from Sittard, the general manager of America, the general manager of Indonesia, and the facilitator. Although the facilitator typically came from outside the business group, DMM decided to ask its own Director of Planning and Projects, Martijn Jansen, to act as facilitator. In his former function at corporate planning, Mr. Jansen had been facilitator for various business groups and was therefore perceived as very experienced in this role. He was expected to spend half of his time on the BSD process for a period of six months. The challenger, Jos Goessens, Business Group Director of Plastic and Engineering, was asked to join the BSD team in January 2003.

One of the criticisms of previous BSDs was that people felt that they were used to 'sell' a project to top management. The BSD team wanted to prevent this from happening again in 2003 and therefore stressed the importance of challenging each other during the whole process and making a serious effort at identifying alternatives.

As DMM wanted to perform an 'issue-driven' BSD, the BSD team started with identifying the subjects on which they thought decisions were needed. A total of 35 issues were identified ranging from subjects such as marketing & sales, operations, R&D, personnel & organization, and finance, to regional issues related to DMM Indonesia, America, Europe, and China. The next step was to decide which information was needed on these issues to make decisions and who should provide it.

Value teams. The BSD team decided to create so-called 'value teams' for each issue, who were

EXHIBIT 7 EXTRACT OF THE STRATEGIC VALUE CONTRACT FOR DSM MELAMINE 1999–2003

Strategic mission

Actively maintain global leadership in market share, technology, cost, and customer image.

1. **Financial performance measures:**
   - EBITDA (m€)
   - CFROI (%)
   - CVA (m€)
   - Delta CVA (m€)

2. **Key Success Factors and Performance Indicators**
   Security of sales
   - Long-term contract with global key customers
   - Meet the requirements for strategic customer alliances
   - Differentiate service levels
   - Volume sold under contract
   - Share of Integrated Panel Producers
   - Share global customers

   Lower cost
   - De-bottlenecking existing gas-phase plants
   - New low cost technology
   - Capability to Produce (CTP)
   - Controllable fixed out of pocket cost/m ton

3. **Value drivers:**
   - Unit production cost DSM Kaltim Melamine
   - Unit production cost DSM Melamine Americas
   - Unit production cost DSM Melamine Europe
   - Production volume
   - Average sales price
   - Sales volume existing plants

4. **Strategic actions and milestones**
   - Defined per project

5. **Required resources**
   - Pre-approval for the next 3 years

6. **Sensitivity items**
   - Global utilization rate
   - USD/EUR currency rate

EXHIBIT 8   BSD 1999 REGIONAL GROWTH RATES: FORECASTS VERSUS REALIZATION

	1999 Forecast	1998–2002 Realization
Europe	4.0%	4.5%
American	5.4%	0.0%
Asia Pacific (APAC)	5.9%	2.9%
China	7.7%	33%

responsible for gathering information (i.e. phase I of the BSD – characterizing the business situation) and performing phase II (i.e., analysing the business system at macro level). By implementing value teams DMM wanted to involve as many people as possible in the BSD process, thereby creating a large platform for the BSD. The value teams presented the results of phase I and II to the BSD team in December 2002. The micro analysis was finalized in February 2003. The next phase was options and strategic choice (phase IV).

Options and strategic choice.   A main point of discussion in the BSD 2003 was DSM Melamine's position in the US, Indonesia and China. Its 50–50 joint venture with Cytec was the largest player in the US with the highest prices. However, the business was not profitable because of high raw material costs. DSM Melamine had the best plant in the world located in Indonesia, but profits there were unsatisfactory due to unstable raw material supply and the negative impact on demand of the Asian crisis. Consequently, it was unable to realize the low cost production necessary. Furthermore, DSM Melamine did not yet have a position in China, which the marketing managers viewed as the fastest growing market.

Management felt that the existing 'actively maintain' strategy may no longer be the best, especially since VBBS required businesses to deliver a positive delta CVA every year. According to one of the managers at DMM:

VBBS has its limits. It is nice for a start-up business but for a mature business it is very difficult to produce a positive delta CVA year after year. It is not easy to create value within a three-year contract in a business like melamine where it takes two to four years for a plant to be operational. So VBBS can lead to short-termism. You have the choice to either increase

CFROI on the existing asset base by cutting costs or raising prices, or you can increase the asset base. However, the latter takes more time and involves greater risk.

If DSM did not have VBBS, we would probably continue with our current 'actively maintain' strategy.

In February, after the macro and micro session, management felt that it should present Corporate with the basic choice to either grow the business – as Dijkman and his team felt that they had reached the limits of cost reduction – or otherwise divest.

Growing the business

In the ASR 2002, it was concluded that DSM Melamine could grow faster than was currently the case but that it lacked the capacity to do so. Management wondered if it should be more aggressive and investigated growth opportunities in, for example, Trinidad, a Caribbean island with natural gas production, the Middle East, Europe, and China (see Exhibit 9 for the choice on growth ambitions, ranging from 'give up market share' to 'aggressive growth'). In Europe, DMM's main competitors, such as Agrolinz, were following 'grow/build' scenarios in response to growing worldwide demand. Leon Halders, Vice-President Marketing & Sales DSM Melamine, noted:

Our two main competitors in Europe are growing heavily, one is tripling and the other is doubling. They are not part of a large company like DSM, but part of a company where melamine is the most attractive business. Melamine is profitable, but because we are part of DSM with a certain strategic mission, we are not the spearhead of DSM strategy.

Although DMM had looked into several growth options, China still seemed the most natural and promising market because of its high growth rates. However, questions remained. First of all there was the question of how DMM, which positioned itself as a main supplier, should enter the Chinese market which was currently a spot market. Another issue was the fact that DMM's existing customers had no significant production base yet in China, which meant that it would have to build a customer base. Finally, a wave of capacity expansion in 2004–2006 was expected to result in oversupply. According to industry analysts, approximately 210 thousand metric tons of melamine was added between 1998 and 2001, with China

EXHIBIT 9   DSM MELAMINE CHOICE ON GROWTH AMBITIONS

Market share target

20%	25%	25%	30%
Give up market share	**Organic growth**	**Active growth**	**Aggressive growth**
■ Price over volume	■ Organic growth with existing customer base	■ Gain market share	■ "Volume over price" policy for plant load
■ "Europe only"		■ Access to new Integrated Panel Producers customers	■ Secure lowest cost position worldwide
■ Lose market leadership	■ China as opportunity market only	■ Significant market share in China	■ Acquisition may bring growth without price erosion
■ Max short term cash	■ No new production capacity	■ Build lowest cost plant, leave high cost plant	
■ Irreversible:	■ Accept gradual loss of market share	■ Signal commitment to leadership	
– give up China			
– lose scale economies			
– technology standstill			
– competitors build			

accounting for nearly half of new capacity. If all announced capacity expansions were completed, global capacity utilization was expected to fall to approximately 80 per cent in 2006 from 86 per cent in 1998. Some anticipated melamine projects were likely to be postponed or cancelled as a result. But, despite the above challenges, the BSD team still believed in major growth opportunities in China.

As DSM Melamine's financial performance exceeded the WACC, requests for investment to build new melamine plants were justifiable from a VBBS point of view. Dijkman, however, wondered if corporate management would agree with this new strategy, as it was not in line with DSM's corporate strategy of becoming a specialties company. Furthermore, investments in melamine plants always involved large amounts of money (between 50 and 100 million euro), which in the first few years would significantly lower DMM's CFROI.

The corporate perspective on DSM Melamine

At corporate level, DSM management faced a dilemma. From a financial perspective and in line with VBBS principles, investments in DSM Melamine would make perfect sense. On the other hand, following the corporate strategy of becoming a specialty company, one could question how much more to invest in the remaining commodities business such as

melamine. It was also important to think through how investors and analysts would react if DSM were to invest further in its melamine business. Earlier in 2003, the management board had already committed to a €50 million proposal of Caprolactam, its other remaining commodity business.

Another issue confronting the management board was the permanent challenge of balancing short-term requirements and long-term value. Big investments would significantly lower DMM's CFROI and only increase CVA in the long-term.

While debating the dilemma on the growth opportunities for DSM Melamine, however, Corporate was also challenging the business on the cost side. It agreed that DSM Melamine had a good low cost position, but as one corporate executive explained: 'We push DSM Melamine. The business has excellent low costs but we are not interested in costs per ton. We would like DSM Melamine to benchmark itself against competitors in its BSD 2003 so that they can see their relative cost position.'

The broader issues. In addition to the strategic issues facing DSM Melamine, Corporate also had to tackle the remaining challenges of the BSD and VBBS processes. First, VBBS implementation was heavily centralized in the sense that the corporate centre, as opposed to the business groups, was driving the change. Although the corporate centre had trained facilitators and provided tools to support the implementation, the process was complex and somewhat slow, with significant differences in progress on implementation between the various business groups. The question was how DSM could speed up the process. Top management hoped that the new appraisal system would help the implementation move forward.

Another concern related to how BSDs and SVCs could be effectively translated into specific actions and program management. Thus far, it had been entirely up to the business groups whether and how to operationalize the chosen strategy in terms of value drivers, or how to integrate the SVC with the performance measurement system such as the balanced scorecard. Business groups chose their own way to resolve these issues, with the outcome often being dependent on the consultant that had been hired.

The real test for the future was 'consequence management'. What should DSM do if a business group did not meet its contract, given DSM's historical culture of tolerance for mediocre performance?

Finally, there were some more fundamental questions. Implementing the new financial metrics had led to greater emphasis on short-term performance. DSM felt that this short-term focus could be hazardous for a specialty company that heavily depended on innovation and R&D. For example, in 2000 one of DSM's most successful and profitable products was Stanyl, a product which had been 10 years in development, with negative EPs throughout all those years. How would these kinds of investment projects be handled under the new approach?

Transforming the prancing horse: Ferrari 1950–2004

By Mark Jenkins[1]

I n 2004 Ferrari won their sixth successive world championship constructors title, the first time this had ever happened since the award began in 1958. Furthermore driver Michael Schumacher won his fifth successive drivers' world championship, the first time a driver had ever achieved such a concentrated dominance, his previous world championships for the Benetton team in 1994 and 1995 also meant that he had now achieved a total of seven drivers' world championships making him the most successful driver since F1 began in 1950. However, this success had not come without controversy. At the Austrian Grand Prix of 2002 Ferrari were accused of unsporting behaviour when their second driver, Rubens Barrichello, who had dominated the race, moved over to allow Michael Schumacher to win, thereby maximizing Schumacher's world championship points. Whilst there was a furore in the press, the Ferrari management remained stoical about their approach. After all, this success had been a long time coming, their 1999 constructors' title had been their first for 16 years, during which the honours had been dominated by the British based Williams, McLaren and Benetton teams. Moreover Ferrari's focus had always been to secure the drivers' championship and Schumacher's title in 2000 had been Ferrari's first since Jody Scheckter in 1979, a gap of 21 years. The roots of Ferrari's 2000 victory can be traced back to the appointment of a new chairman, Luca di Montezemolo in 1991, the fact that it took Ferrari ten years to reinvent itself into a world championship winner, meant that those involved in this journey felt justified in savouring the fruits of victory for as long as possible.

The Prancing Horse

Born in 1898, Enzo Ferrari achieved his boyhood ambition of becoming a racing driver. Legend has it that on his first victory at the 1923 Circuito del Savio he was presented the prize by Countess Paolina Baracca, the mother of first world war fighter pilot Francesco Baracca who had used an image of a prancing horse on the side of his plane. The countess offered Ferrari the horse logo so that he could use it for his racing cars, an offer he gratefully accepted. However Ferrari's career as a driver was soon behind him and in November 1929 he created Scuderia Ferrari (SF) based in Modena, between Parma and Bologna in northern Italy. SF focused on the preparation and competition of racecars for enthusiasts, thereby creating one of the first specialist motorsport companies. They exclusively raced Alfa Romeo cars and in 1932 Alfa Romeo outsourced all its motorsport activity to be run by SF. 1932 was also the year that Ferrari used the prancing horse logo, a black horse on a yellow background – the historic colour of Modena, to symbolize Scuderia Ferrari. The partnership with Alfa Romeo proved to be very successful, winning 144 out of 225 races in the period up to 1937. However during the late thirties the German Mercedes and Auto Unions began to dominate racing and following the second world-war Alfa Romeo split with SF and Enzo Ferrari went on to build his first car.

The Ferrari 125 made its debut in May 1947 having been designed and developed over the previous two years. Most of the design and development had focused on the creation of the Ferrari supercharged 12-cylinder engine, the first in a long line of Ferrari *dodici cilindri* engines. The Ferrari 125 entered the new F1 championship when it began in 1950, but it was not until 1951 that a Ferrari won a Grand Prix and in 1952 driver Alberto Ascari won the driver's world championship. The early fifties were of unparalleled success for Ferrari and the other Italian teams of Alfa Romeo and Maserati who were all based in northern Italy. Italy were now the world leaders in motorsport engineering with designs which focused on supercharged 4.5 litre engines positioned in front of the driver, their blood red cars a reflection of the earlier days of grand prix racing when cars were colour coded by country of origin with British racing green for the Vanwalls and BRMs, and the silver Mercedes and Auto-Unions from Germany.

---

[1]Source: © 2005, M. Jenkins, Cranfield School of Management.

The 1950s were also a tragic time for Ferrari, overall safety standards were poor and many drivers died in Ferrari cars. As a consequence Ferrari often had to endure a great deal of criticism from the press, Ferrari had lost his son Dino in 1956, and for many this loss hardened his attitude to life and to the loss of drivers. The role of the driver was simply to do a job – bring victory to the red cars of Ferrari and if they did not there was always another to take their place. He was also very frugal about driver's wages as former world champion Phil Hill remarked: 'The Old Man's line was very much that you drove for Ferrari for the honour of it. And he wasn't kidding.' Similarly it was also claimed that Enzo liked to manage the situation so no particular driver was able to gain the credit for success, as the following observation by former driver Stirling Moss illustrates: 'I never drove for him, but I've no doubts that in my day he would allow different drivers to win by giving them better cars sometimes, thereby giving the impression that the driver didn't count for anything – that it was the *car* which had won.'

Ferrari himself had a rather enigmatic approach to running the company. After the death of his son Dino he very rarely left the Modena area, and hardly ever attended races, preferring to spend his time either in the factory or at the Ferrari test facilities. He relied on the Italian media – who had always shown a keen interest in Ferrari – and his closest advisors for information which often created a highly political atmosphere in the team.

However, the Italian supremacy was challenged towards the end of the fifties with the British constructor Cooper developing small 2.0 litre cars which positioned the engine behind the driver and whose designs focused on maximizing mechanical grip as opposed to the emphasis on engine power preferred by the Italians. Cooper dominated the world championships of 1959 and 1960 using the 'bought in' Coventry Climax engine which had been originally designed to power water pumps for fire engines. They were followed by Lotus who, like Cooper, produced lightweight agile cars with high levels of mechanical grip.

Ferrari initially resisted the trend being pioneered by the British constructors whom he referred to as 'assemblatori' or 'garagistes'. He defended the engine layout of the Ferrari with the analogy that the 'horse' had always pulled, not pushed, the cart. Although not an engineer himself, the designers who Ferrari employed (Alberto Massimino, Gioachino Colombo, Carlo Chiti and Mauro Forghieri) had learnt their trade as engine designers and so the design of a new car would always start with the engine. Ferrari himself

often referred to 'the song of the twelve' underlining the distinctive high pitched note of the Ferrari engine. However by 1960 the dominance of the British cars was clear, and Ferrari had to build a lighter rear-engined car, which they did using a highly effective V6 engine. The Dino 156 (1.5 litre, V6) or 'shark nose' dominated 1961 and gave Ferrari a further world title. However, the advances made in chassis construction by other teams had meant that they were increasingly uncompetitive and in 1964 the Ferrari 158 was launched with a similar monocoque type chassis to the Lotus 25 of 1962. In 1964 Ferrari tried out the 'Flat 12' engine developed by Mauro Forghieri, it was this 12 cylinder unit that was seen to be the future for Ferrari.

Ferrari renaissance:
The mid-seventies

In the late sixties Ferrari merged with Italian automotive manufacturer Fiat. This was, in effect, a benign acquisition, with Fiat acquiring 40% of the equity in Ferrari, thereby providing a huge injection of cash to support R&D activities. This allowed the construction of a private Grand Prix circuit at Fiorano close to the SF factory at Maranello. The technical team used this facility to engage in a period of intensive development focusing on the 'flat 12' engine.

The new ownership and influence from Fiat meant increased resources, but also increased pressure for results. In the early seventies F1 was dominated by the Ford DFV engine. Built by Cosworth Engineering near Northampton and funded by the Ford Motor Company, the DFV was F1's first purpose built engine it was light, powerful and relatively inexpensive. In 1968 the engines were available for 7500 each and were fully capable of winning a Grand Prix. This enabled the British constructors, who specialized in chassis design, to become increasingly competitive. In 1971 and 1973 every Grand Prix was won by a car using a DFV engine. The impact of the DFV engine was that it made the cars both very light and very powerful, at a time when tyre technology was relatively primitive, this left the designers searching for other ways to increase grip. The answer came from aerodynamics with aircraft type 'wings' being used to create downforce or aerodynamic grip allowing the cars to both enter and exit corners at vastly increased speeds.

During this time Enzo himself had been suffering from ill health, now in his seventies he made the decision to appoint a team manager to run the day-to-day activities of the F1 team. Luca di Montezemolo was a

25-year-old lawyer who was also connected to Fiat's Agnelli dynasty. In addition Mauro Forghieri had been recalled to Ferrari in 1973 as technical director. In 1975 the fruits of Forghieri's creative ideas and the intensive testing at Fiorano were exemplified in the new 312T which featured a wide low body with a powerful flat 12, 12-cylinder engine and a revolutionary transverse (sideways mounted) gearbox which improved the balance of the car making it handle extremely well. The engine was originally designed by Forghieri in 1964, and when asked why he didn't take the opportunity to copy the V8 DFV his response was unequivocal: 'I used the 12 cylinder because it is the story of the factory (at Maranello). We make 6 and 8 cylinder engines for our cars, but the 12 is the best. Every engineer that comes to Ferrari, first wants to work on engines and second the 12 cylinder engines. There are economic reasons as we already have many of the parts and components, but most importantly it is the history of Ferrari.'

Although the new car was not ready until the season had already started, driver Niki Lauda, with the support of team-mate Clay Regazzoni, was able to easily secure both the drivers and constructors world championships. The Ferraris dominated the 1975 season. With their elegant handling and the power advantage of the engine, they were in a class of their own. This unprecedented run of Ferrari success continued through to 1978 and in 1979 when they won both the drivers and constructors championships, but perhaps their greatest moment was in 1979 when Ferrari's finished first and second at the Italian grand prix at Monza. Sending the fanatical Italian fans or tifosi, and the Italian press into a complete frenzy.

Ferrari, the end of an era: 1980–1990

However in 1980 312T5 car was outclassed by the competition. New innovations in aerodynamics brought the 'ground effect' revolution, pioneered by Lotus and quickly adopted by Williams and Brabham. Here the underside of the car featured two 'venturi, or channels either side of the driver. These were aerodynamically designed to create a low pressure area under the car which sucked the car to the track allowing faster cornering. Sliding strips of material or 'skirts' were used to create a seal for the air flowing under the car. Whilst the Ferrari's engine was one of the most powerful it was a 'flat 12' meaning that the cylinders were horizontal to the ground creating a low

and wide barrier which gave little opportunity to create the ground effect achieved with the slimmer V8 DFV engines. In 1978 Alfa Romeo had launched a V12 engine to replace their flat 12 for this very reason. No such initiative had been taken at Ferrari who were concentrating on a longer term project to develop a V6 turbocharged engine. Autosport correspondent Nigel Roebuck commented on this change of fortune: 'Maranello's flat-12, still a magnificent racing engine, is incompatible with modern chassis. Villeneuve and Scheckter were competing in yesterdays cars.' The lowest point came in the Canadian Grand Prix when the reigning world champion, Jody Scheckter, failed to qualify his Ferrari for the race, a bit like Italy failing to qualify for the soccer World Cup. Once again the full wrath of the Italian press descended on the team.

In the mid-eighties more and more investment was poured into the Italian facilities but with no dramatic effect on performance. A key problem was that new developments in aerodynamics and the use of composite materials had emerged from the UK's motorsport valley. Rather than a valley this was an area to the west, north and south of London where the major British F1 teams were located. These teams bought in their engines from specialist suppliers such as Cosworth, Renault, Honda and Porsche. They therefore focused their expertise on the design and development of the chassis which featured advance materials such as the carbon composite monocoque (a term for the one piece chassis) which had been pioneered by McLaren's John Barnard in the early 1980s. These teams also used sophisticated 'moving ground' wind tunnels which were available at local universities in Cranfield, Southampton and Imperial College London to perfect their aerodynamic performance.

In 1984, British designer Harvey Postlethwaite became the first non-Italian Technical Director of Ferrari. In 1986 British designer John Barnard was recruited to the top technical role. However Barnard was not prepared to move to Italy as he felt that his technical team and network of contacts in the UK would be essential to the success of his position. Surprisingly Enzo Ferrari allowed him to establish a design and manufacturing facility near Guildford in Surrey that became known as the Ferrari 'GTO' or Guildford Technical Office. The fact that Barnard was defining the technical direction of Ferrari meant that he became increasingly involved in activities at both sites. However the geographical separation between the car and engine departments led to development of various 'factions' within Ferrari, making Barnard's job increasingly difficult. In 1987 on arrival at

Maranello he ordered a ban on the consumption of wine at the midday canteen, there was uproar with the workforce seeing this as an insult to their professionalism.

Enzo Ferrari's death in 1988 created a vacuum which was filled by a series of executives from the Fiat organization for a number of years. It was written into the contract that on Enzo's death Fiat's original stake would be increased to 90%, this greater investment led to attempts to run Ferrari as a formal subsidiary of the Fiat group. Barnard became frustrated with the interference and politics of the situation and left to join Benetton in 1989. Ferrari had recruited world champion Alain Prost to drive for them in 1990, but whilst the GTO designed 1990 car was highly competitive (an example of this Ferrari 641 now resides in New York's Museum of Modern Art), the organization was falling apart and in 1991 Prost was fired by the Ferrari management for criticising the car and therefore the sacred name of Ferrari. Former driver Patrick Tambay commented on the situation as follows: 'No one's in charge anymore. When the Old Man was alive the buck stopped with him. Maybe he took some curious decisions – but at least he took them. I'm not saying that Ferrari will never win again, but the fabric of what the name meant has gone. There are so many layers of management, so many bosses reporting to bosses, until ultimately it gets to Gianni Agnelli (Chairman of Fiat).'

Transforming the Prancing Horse: 1990–2004

However at the end of 1991, Fiat's chairman Gianni Agnelli appointed Luca di Montezemolo as CEO with a mandate to do whatever was needed to take Ferrari back to the top. Montezemolo had been team manager for Ferrari during the successful period in the mid-seventies, subsequently he had taken on a range of high-profile management roles including running Italy's hosting of the Soccer World Cup in 1990. di Montezemolo accepted the role on the basis that Ferrari and in particular, the racing operation, was independent of Fiat. 'I have not been in the Fiat management stream for ten years. Maranello is another world and has to be treated as such.'

In an article in *Autosport* he described the situation as follows:

After I arrived last December (1991) I spent five months working to understand the situation. To understand the manpower, to understand the

potential of the car. Once I had absorbed all this I decided to approach the whole situation in a completely different manner. Ferrari had become an inflexible monolith of a company which was no good for racing. As a result I decided to divide it into three small departments: future developments and special projects in the UK under John Barnard; the engine department in Maranello under Paolo Massai and finally the Scuderia Ferrari under Harvey Postlethwaite which is the place where we build the cars and manage the team.

I also wanted to build up a a strong relationship between our UK facility and Italy in order to take full advantage of the F1 'silicon valley' in England for chassis development and specialist sub-contractors while still harnessing the huge potential of Maranello.

When asked why he was repeating the 'GTO' initiative which Enzo Ferrari had set up with Barnard and which had ultimately ended with Barnard leaving and taking the facility with him, Montezemolo had a very clear response:

I think that the GTO concept of Enzo Ferrari was a super idea. Unfortunately, at the time Ferrari was very old and the situation was managed in a bad way. But the fundamental idea was very good. For me the approach is slightly different. First of all, I am in charge of the company with full powers, so I can take a decision without anyone else taking a parallel initiative. I take my responsibilities and I want the people in the company to follow my ideas. If they follow, I am very happy. If they don't then there are many other doors, many possibilities available to them outside Ferrari. My objective is to create a smaller racing department which contains less bureaucracy, of course, there will be a lot of discussion between the engine and chassis departments. In Maranello we have a huge organization geared to building cars, but I want to take advantage of the UK facilities, and for a world-wide company like Ferrari it is certainly not a scandal to have an affiliate in the UK. If you want to make pasta, then you have to be in Parma, I want to make a sophisticated F1 project so I want to be involved in England. Then it is up to me to put everything together.

In August 1992 John Barnard signed a five-year contract with Ferrari to design and develop their new cars.

In an effort to avoid a 'them and us' situation between the UK and Italy a number of Italian technical people were recruited to work for Barnard in the UK, and a number of English technicians were redeployed to Maranello.

At the launch of the 1992 car, Luca di Montezemolo broke with tradition, and introduced a new numbering system based on the year a car would be racing, an approach which has been followed from 1992 up to the championship winning F2003-GA (in recognition of Fiat's Gianni Agnelli who passed away in January 2003). Prior to this the numbering of many Ferrari cars had been based on the characteristics of the engine – the 312 of 1971 representing 3.0 litre 12 cylinders, the 126C4 of 1984 representing a 12° 'V' angle with 6 cylinders, and C standing for 'Compression' or turbo-charging.

> At Ferrari we have always devoted and will continue to devote, great attention to racing, racing is part of the history, the culture and the traditions of this company. We live in a country which, especially in recent times, people have yelled and complained a bit too much. We hope that the only noise around here will be our engine as it sets new lap records at Fiorano. We are looking for a revival here, and with an eye to the future we have tried to put together a group which combines young engineers, many of them with the highest qualifications, and people whose enthusiasm and abilities will make a notable contribution. We have a lot of work to do, we have a lot of ground to make up on the opposition. We have code-named the new car F92A to demonstrate that we are turning a new page in our history.

When asked about drivers in 1992 he also gave some indication of his thinking: 'the main priority is the new organization. We are lucky because it is a big challenge to offer a driver the chance to help re-establish Ferrari to a competitive level. I want a driver who is motivated and prepared to work with us. Motivation is everything in a driver, as Niki Lauda reminds us!'

In addition to the structural changes, di Montezemolo had also brought in some familiar faces from Ferrari's successful period in the mid seventies, driver Niki Lauda acted as a consultant to the team and Sante Ghedini took on the role of team manager. With an Englishman heading up design he followed this up with the appointment of a Frenchman, Jean Todt, to handle the overall management of the team. Todt had no experience in F1 but had been in motorsport

management for many years and had recently led a successful rally and sportscar programme at Peugeot. Driver Gerhard Bergher commented on Todt's team building skills 'I was able to bring some links in the chain to Ferrari, but it took Todt to join them together. Ferrari is now working as a team for the first time. He has made a huge difference.' Chief Mechanic Nigel Stepney joined Ferrari in 1993, but his first impressions were not positive.

'When I joined Ferrari at the beginning of 1993, it was like being thrown into the lion's den. I was in a non-position, regarded as John Barnard's spy and not allowed to take any responsibility.' However he recalled the arrival of Jean Todt as a turning point in the team. 'It was like Julius Caesar every day. People getting sacked and leaving every five minutes. You never knew who was boss – not until Jean Todt arrived, took control of the situation and instilled organization, stability and loyalty into the team.'

However the physical separation between design and development in Guildford and the racing operation in Maranello led to increased problems and eventually Barnard and Ferrari parted company for the second time in 1996. This opened the way for Ferrari to recruit, not only driver Michael Schumacher, but also a number of the key individuals in the Benetton technical team which had helped him to his world titles in 1994 and 1995. The arrival of Schumacher provided new impetus for the team, as Nigel Stepney recounted: 'Once Schumacher arrived, everyone started putting us under incredible pressure. We weren't quite ready as we still needed key people, but at some point you just have to go for it and get the best driver around. He was the icing on the cake and it sent out signals that we were serious again.' Todt and di Montezemolo also chose not to make a direct replacement for the role of technical supremo who would both lead the design of the car and the management of the technical activity. They split the role between a chief designer, Rory Byrne, who had overall responsibility for designing the car, and Ross Brawn who managed the entire technical operation, these were roles which both had undertaken in working with Schumacher at Benetton. However the contractual arrangement with John Barnard had been one where the GTO designers were paid through his private company. When he left they all went with him and Byrne and Brawn faced the task of building up from scratch a new design department – around 50 people, based in Italy. The engine department continued to develop Ferrari's engines, but in line with new technologies and developments these were now lighter V10s to compete with the Renault and Mercedes engines, rather than the beloved, but now dated Ferrari *dodici cilindri*. As part of their recruitment of Michael Schumacher in 1996 Ferrari entered into a commercial partnership with tobacco giant Phillip Morris to use their Marlboro brand on the Ferrari cars. In a novel arrangement Phillip Morris, rather than Ferrari, paid Schumacher's salary, and also made a significant contribution to Ferrari's annual operating budget. However there was one price to pay which was too high for many long-term Ferrari aficionados: the blood red Ferrari of old was now replaced by a bright orange red which was more closely matched to the Marlboro colour scheme, but most importantly was more effective on television than the original Ferrari red.

In addition to Marlboro, Ferrari also entered into a long-term partnership with Shell to provide both financial and technical support to the team (for example Shell were able to develop fuels for Ferrari which were lighter and delivered more power on combustion thereby improving both the weight distribution and performance of the car). This was a departure for Ferrari who had previously always worked with Italian petroleum giant Agip. In these kinds of arrangements Ferrari led a trend away from selling space on cars to long-term commercial arrangements, with coordinated marketing strategies for commercial partners to maximize the benefits of their investments. Ferrari also had a particular style of doing business with their partners as described by Raul Pinnel of Shell: 'They took me straight to a restaurant and offered me some wine. Normally I don't drink wine at lunch, but I realized it would be rude if I did not oblige. They asked me about my family, my friends, my history, and my life in general. I kept thinking when are they going to get to business? I kept checking my watch and worrying about my plane departure time. Finally, I told them of my concern, they said, "Don't worry; we've got a car ready for you. And now we know you and like you. You are part of the family." They gave me a big bear hug, we talked and after we agreed certain things in principle, they poured me into a Ferrari for the drive to catch my plane.'

To many the team now revolved around Schumacher, rather than, as in the past, the drivers who were honoured to work for Ferrari. Jean Alesi, a former Ferrari driver observed that 'Schumacher does whatever he wants, and they do whatever he says.' This was in marked contrast to Enzo Ferrari who had famously rejected a number of top class drivers because they wanted too much money, such as Jackie

Stewart in 1970 and Ayrton Senna in 1986 whose wage demands Enzo described as 'imaginativo!'

Another key part of this revised organization was the relationship between engine design and the other critical areas of aerodynamics and chassis development, as summarized by Ross Brawn: 'I really felt that if we could get into a situation where the engine was completely integrated into the car, then that must be the best situation. So one of the things that was important to myself and Rory was to have someone who understood that and luckily Paolo (Martinelli, Engine Director) very quickly appreciated our ideas and was completely receptive to the idea of a fully integrated engine as part of the car package.' Paolo Martinelli had worked on engines in Ferrari for many years, and was one in a long line of brilliant Italian engine designers, but he recognized that there was a need for change which was supported at the top of the organization and that real progress could be made by working closely with the other areas of the car: 'I think it was very important that there was trust and direction from the top management.' This approach is best summarized by Brawn: 'Our efforts have always been not to make everything as good as it can be, but to work together as a complete package.'

This rejuvenated team provided the basis for Michael Schumacher's dominance of F1. In 1997 they raced the Barnard developed Ferrari and finished second in the constructors championship. Although as this was Ferrari's 50th anniversary there was high anticipation that this was to be their year, as Nigel Stepney recounts: '1997 was a great disappointment for the team as we so nearly won the championship, we felt we had the right way of working; we just had to keep at it and not panic.' Their competitiveness continued to improve and in 1999 they won the constructors championship – although the driver's championship went to Mika Hakkinen in a McLaren-Mercedes, Stepney again recalls: 'It was a very stressful year, we lost Michael Schumacher after he broke his leg at Silverstone. Then we made mistakes such as the pit-stop at the Nurburgring. But although we paid the price in one respect, we gained from the experiences. We realized that as a team, we had to pace ourselves, to switch off and recharge our batteries sometime.'

There was clear momentum in the company now to secure the world championships and what followed was a complete domination by Ferrari in the period 2000–2004. For Montezemolo this was the culmination of a process which had started from the moment of his appointment in 1991: 'At the beginning of the '90s, we reorganized the team and invested a lot in new technology. Now we're getting the benefit of what we did three, four years ago, in Formula 1, you can't change everything in 12 months. We had a strong mechanical knowledge, and it was important to keep that, but we had to find out about things we didn't know such as aerodynamics, electronics and perhaps most importantly, team work. It's because of all that change that we have a very strong team today.'

APPENDIX A: SUMMARY OF WORLD CHAMPIONS

Year	Driver	Car/Engine	Constructor's Cup
1950	Giuseppe Farina	Alfa Romeo	
1951	Juan Manuel Fangio	Alfa Romeo	
1952	Alberto Ascari	Ferrari	
1953	Alberto Ascari	Ferrari	
1954	Juan Manuel Fangio	Maserati	
1955	Juan Manuel Fangio	Mercedes-Benz	
1956	Juan Manuel Fangio	Lancia-Ferrari	
1957	Juan Manuel Fangio	Maserati	
1958	Mike Hawthorn	Ferrari	Vanwall
1959	Jack Brabham	Cooper/Climax	Cooper/Climax
1960	Jack Brabham	Cooper/Climax	Cooper/Climax
1961	Phil Hill	Ferrari	Ferrari
1962	Graham Hill	BRM	BRM
1963	Jim Clark	Lotus/Climax	Lotus/Climax
1964	John Surtees	Ferrari	Ferrari
1965	Jim Clark	Lotus/Climax	Lotus/Climax
1966	Jack Brabham	Brabham/Repco	Brabham/Repco
1967	Denny Hulme	Brabham/Repco	Brabham/Repco
1968	Graham Hill	Lotus/Ford	Lotus/Ford
1969	Jackie Stewart	Matra/Ford	Matra/Ford
1970	Jochen Rindt	Lotus/Ford	Lotus/Ford
1971	Jackie Stewart	Tyrrell/Ford	Tyrrell/Ford
1972	Emerson Fittipaldi	Lotus/Ford	Lotus/Ford
1973	Jackie Stewart	Tyrrell/Ford	Lotus/Ford
1974	Emerson Fittipaldi	McLaren/Ford	McLaren/Ford
1975	Niki Lauda	Ferrari	Ferrari
1976	James Hunt	McLaren/Ford	Ferrari
1977	Niki Lauda	Ferrari	Ferrari
1978	Mario Andretti	Lotus/Ford	Lotus/Ford
1979	Jody Scheckter	Ferrari	Ferrari
1980	Alan Jones	Williams/Ford	Williams/Ford
1981	Nelson Piquet	Brabham/Ford	Williams/Ford
1982	Keke Rosberg	Williams/Ford	Ferrari
1983	Nelson Piquet	Brabham/BMW	Ferrari
1984	Niki Lauda	McLaren/Porsche	McLaren/Porsche

Year	Driver	Car/Engine	Constructor's Cup
1985	Alain Prost	McLaren/Porsche	McLaren/Porsche
1986	Alain Prost	McLaren/Porsche	Williams/Honda
1987	Nelson Piquet	Williams/Honda	Williams/Honda
1988	Ayrton Senna	McLaren/Honda	McLaren/Honda
1989	Alain Prost	McLaren/Honda	McLaren/Honda
1990	Ayrton Senna	McLaren/Honda	McLaren/Honda
1991	Ayrton Senna	McLaren/Honda	McLaren/Honda
1992	Nigel Mansell	Williams/Renault	Williams/Renault
1993	Alain Prost	Williams/Renault	Williams/Renault
1994	Michael Schumacher	Benetton/Ford	Williams/Renault
1995	Michael Schumacher	Benetton/Renault	Benetton/Renault
1996	Damon Hill	Williams/Renault	Williams/Renault
1997	Jacques Villeneuve	Williams/Renault	Williams/Renault
1998	Mika Hakkinen	McLaren/Mercedes	McLaren/Mercedes
1999	Mika Hakkinen	McLaren/Mercedes	Ferrari
2000	Michael Schumacher	Ferrari	Ferrari
2001	Michael Schumacher	Ferrari	Ferrari
2002	Michael Schumacher	Ferrari	Ferrari
2003	Michael Schumacher	Ferrari	Ferrari
2004	Michael Schumacher	Ferrari	Ferrari

Notes: Constructors championship is based on the cumulative points gained by a team during the season. Currently each team is limited to entering two cars and drivers per race.

COSCO

By Lily Zhang, Gary Liu and Peter Lorange[1]

B y 2007, China Ocean Shipping (Group) Company (COSCO) owned and operated a varied merchant fleet of some 800 vessels. It included about 140 container ships, with a carrying capacity of over 430 000 twenty-foot equivalent units (TEUs), and about 500 dry bulk vessels with a carrying capacity of up to 38 million deadweight tonnes (DWT). COSCO was the second largest shipping company in the world, with total carrying capacity of more than 50 million DWT; it was also the No.1 dry bulk shipping company.

Back in 1998, the shipping industry was experiencing tough times in its business cycle because of the Asian financial crisis. Wei Jiafu, the recently appointed president and CEO of COSCO, was reconsidering the corporate strategy. Was it possible to build a business model that would help COSCO pull through hard times, given that the industry was typically cyclical?

Background

Founded in 1961, COSCO was the first international shipping carrier in China. In May 1967 one of COSCO's liners embarked on a maiden voyage to Western Europe, marking the beginning of the first international liner service in China. In 1978 COSCO's regular container liner business came into operation as the first of its kind in China.

In the 1980s, as developed western economies began to pay more attention to services and high-tech products and to transfer manufacturing eastward. Some developing eastern countries took up the challenge and evolved to become manufacturing bases. All of this changed the shipping industry, with eastern countries emerging as the drivers of the industry. In 1982 COSCO established COSCO America in California; it then established COSCO North America Limited in partnership with Norton Lilly. In 1988 COSCO restructured a joint venture it had in UK by purchasing the shares held by its business partner, thus giving it a wholly owned subsidiary in London. The establishment of a new COSCO UK marked the beginning of COSCO's transnational business operations in the international arena.

In the 1990s China's economy and foreign trade started to grow fast. This 'China factor' became increasingly influential in the world economy and the global shipping industry. Besides all the external factors, COSCO's growth could also be attributed to its skills in leveraging the capital markets. In 1993 COSCO acquired a company listed on the Singapore Stock Exchange and changed its name to COSCO Investment (Singapore), which was later renamed COSCO Corporation. In 1994 COSCO Pacific began trading on the Hong Kong Stock Exchange.

Wei Jiafu was born in 1950 and obtained a master's degree in shipping management engineering and a doctorate in shipping and ocean structure design. Before becoming COSCO's CEO in 1998 – the 36th year in his shipping career – Wei was a senior executive in many COSCO subsidiaries, both at home and abroad. During his tenure as the president of COSCO (Singapore) Ltd, he had managed to turn it into a listed company in 1993 – a double first. It marked the first entry of COSCO and of a state-owned enterprise (SOE) into the international capital market.

'Two transformation' strategy

In 1998 Wei Jiafu decided to initiate a 'two transformation' strategy at COSCO: Transformation from a global shipping carrier to a global logistics operator based on the shipping business, and from a cross-border business player to a multinational conglomerate. To carry out the transformation from a carrier to a logistics operator, COSCO planned to extend the industry value chain and move into logistics, terminal operations, ship repair and shipbuilding businesses.

Logistics

COSCO Logistics was set up in 2002. The company had eight regional subsidiaries across the nation, covering a wide range of areas from Dalian, Qingdao, Shanghai and Ningbo in northern and eastern China to Wuhan, Xiamen and Guangzhou in central and

[1]Source: Copyright © 2008 by IMD – International Institute for Management Development, Lausanne, Switzerland.

southern China. In 2007 COSCO Logistics (Hong Kong), COSCO Logistics (Western Asia) and COSCO Logistics (America) began operations. COSCO Logistics owned or operated about 250 000 square meters of warehouses, some 2.65 million square meters of stockyards, over 1200 vehicles and 231 feeder barges totaling 187 480 DWT. The company also launched nine double-stacked train (DST) services linking hub ports with major inland markets.

COSCO Logistics explored a number of market segments, including home appliances, automobiles, power plants, chemicals, exhibitions and retail. It held a leading position in China in fields like home appliance logistics, automobile logistics and nuclear logistics, ranking No.1 for three years in a row in China's top 100 Logistics Enterprises.

Besides COSCO Logistics, COSCO also had a number of logistics arms covering a wide range of territories, including North America, Europe, Japan, South Korea, Singapore, Australia, South Africa and West Asia.

Terminal operations

In 2003 COSCO entered into joint venture agreements with two major ports in northern China – Tianjin Port and Dalian Port. COSCO held a 14 per cent and a 30 per cent equity interest, respectively. In 2007 COSCO signed individual strategic cooperation agreements with Xiamen City (southern China) and Jiangsu Province (eastern China) to develop Haicang Port and Lianyungang Port. COSCO also invested in overseas terminals, including the Antwerp Gateway in Belgium, the Suez Canal Container Terminal in Egypt and terminals in Singapore, Hong Kong and Long Beach in the US.

By 2007 COSCO had invested in 20 more terminals around the world and owned more than 100 berths. Its total annual throughput amounted to 30 million standard containers, being the fifth largest in the world.

Ship repair and building

COSCO set up Nantong COSCO KHI Ship Engineering Ltd (NACKS) with Kawasaki Heavy Industries in 1999. NACKS was mainly engaged in building bulk carrier, oil tanker and post-Panamax container vessels. NACKS constructed a series of 5400 TEU container ships in 2001 and a 300 000 DWT very large crude carrier (VLCC) in 2002. It had ascertained the leading position in Chinese shipbuilding industry.

In 2001 COSCO Shipyard Group was founded. It became a leading company in China for ship repair, ship conversion, shipbuilding and marine engineering construction. It owned five major subsidiaries strategically located in the most important sites along China's coastline: Nantong, Dalian, Zhoushan, Guangzhou and Shanghai. By 2007 the docks of COSCO Shipyard had a total capacity of 1.85 million tons, with two docks able to handle 300 000 tons of capacity, four docks with a capacity of 150 000 to 200 000 tons and six docks of 40 000 to 80 000 tons, 31 berths, two shipbuilding berths, and four water slides as well as two supporting water splits. The company annually repaired over 600 various vessels for more than 140 world-renowned shipping companies in over 50 countries. As of 2006, COSCO had gained orders for ocean engineering and shipbuilding valued at RMB 20 billion.

According to a ranking by the China Ship Engineering Association, COSCO Shipyard Group's three branch companies in Nantong, Dalian and Guangzhou are No. 1, No. 3 and No. 7, respectively, in terms of competitiveness among China's ship engineering companies.

Entering international capital markets

At the same time, to realize the transformation from a cross-border business player to a multinational company, COSCO needed to enter the international capital markets. This would allow it to benchmark against leading multinational companies and improve management and corporate governance.

In 2002 the COSCO Shipping subsidiary launched an initial public offering (IPO) on the Shanghai Stock Exchange. Three years later, China COSCO Holdings Company Limited (China COSCO) made its IPO on the main board of the Hong Kong Stock Exchange, formally launching COSCO's core shipping business on the global capital markets. China COSCO raised US $ 1.2 billion through the IPO – the largest sum in the history of the global shipping industry. China COSCO began trading on the Shanghai Stock Exchange in June 2007 (Exhibit 1).

Continuous innovation

COSCO was well known in China for its innovation and reform. Being an SOE, the company was courageous in its reforms. In the late 1990s, the salary system in its subsidiaries was changed to give staff more incentives. Meanwhile, COSCO expatriates enjoyed

EXHIBIT 1 COSCO'S LISTED SUBSIDIARIES

Subsidiary	Trading Code	Listing Venue
China COSCO	1919.HK	Hong Kong
China COSCO	601919.SS	Shanghai
COSCO Pacific	1199.HK	Hong Kong
COSCO International	0517.HK	Hong Kong
COSCO Corporation	COSC.SI	Singapore
COSCO Shipping	600428.SS	Shanghai
Sino-Ocean Land	3377.HK	Hong Kong
China International Marine Containers	000039.SS	Shenzhen

similar benefits to those of local people in other countries. In 2004 COSCO Bulk Carrier adopted so-called virtual stocks as a new incentive plan. The return on these virtual stocks was related to factors such as total profit, return on assets and operational efficiency.

Because of the size of the organization, COSCO was continuously upgrading its management systems. In 1997 it implemented the COSCO Global Cash Management System, in which all the revenues of all overseas subsidiaries were entered to give a unified COSCO account. In addition, an SAP system was implemented to oversee all the subsidiaries' financial activities. In 2003 COSCO invested RMB 1 billion in introducing an Integrated Regional Information System (IRIS-2), a set of container management information systems developed by Orient Overseas Container Line.

From owning to leveraging

COSCO's latest management innovation was the concept of transitioning 'from owning to leveraging'. COSCO defined the change in three levels. The first was the operating level, where 'from owning to leveraging' referred to changing from owning ships to chartering ships for its shipping business. By February 2007, COSCO only owned half of the ships it used and chartered the rest. By the end of the year, chartered ships accounted for 60% of COSCO's profits. For COSCO Logistics, the number of warehouses owned was less than 10% of the total warehouses used by COSCO.

The second level was about financial assets. COSCO's target capital structure for expansion would be 5:4:1, that is, 50 per cent from the capital market, 40 per cent from bank loans and 10 per cent from company's profits. At this level, 'from owning to leveraging' meant COSCO would not only list its own assets, use commercial notes, securitization and other capital market instruments for financing, but it would also invest in the financial sector. To date, COSCO had invested several billion RMB in banking, security and investment funds and was the No. 2 shareholder of China Merchant Bank, one of most famous banks in China. COSCO hoped that finance would also become its supportive business.

The third level was related to resources. COSCO established strategic cooperation partnerships with regional governments and other large companies to leverage various resources. These companies included China National Offshore Oil Corporation (CNOOC), China Petrochemical Corporation (Sinopec), Shenhua Group, China Nonferrous Metal Mining Group, Baosteel Group and Guangzhou Baiyun Airport, among others. For example, in 1997 COSCO and three other shipping carriers formed CKYH, the world's largest liner service alliance. COSCO signed strategic cooperation agreements with Jiangsu Province and Hebei Province for cooperation in shipping, terminal building, ship repair and building, logistics, infrastructure development and exploitation of energy resources.

Challenges ahead

By 2007 COSCO had grown into a $ 17 billion corporation, providing services in international shipping, logistics and terminal operation, ship repair and building, financing, IT and the like. Ships and containers bearing the COSCO logo shuttled between 1500 ports in more than 160 countries and regions around the globe. The number of COSCO staff had increased to 80 000, of which 5000 were non-Chinese.

At the end of 2007, COSCO faced many opportunities, with some external and internal challenges ahead:

■ Cross-border operation and involvement in several parts of the industry chain means greater exposure to risk – political, country, economic, event-related. For example, the subprime debt crisis threatened to lead the US into recession and to slow the growth of the world economy, which in turn would hit demand for the import and export of raw materials and manufactured goods. This would have a negative impact on bulk, tanker and container shipping, which would result in slower growth of the terminal, shipbuilding and logistics businesses. How to cope with and manage the risks posed a great challenge to COSCO.

- How to turn from cyclical development to sustainable development? Shipping carriers like COSCO used to conduct so-called reverse operations, for example, buying ships at market lows. COSCO's efforts to build a sustainable model included forming strategic cooperation partnerships and entering the international capital market when the market was booming. This would lay a solid foundation for COSCO to pull through hard times. Shipping is typically a cyclical industry, but with dramatic changes. Is the sustainable development model viable? Can it really smooth the ups and downs of the industry cycle?

- Expanding beyond organic growth. Integrating outside resources via acquisition would be a faster way to achieve expansion than to rely on organic growth. But it required more organization capabilities in order to consolidate the acquired assets. How to turn COSCO into a 'system integrator'?

- Balance between business sectors. Was the present emphasis on each business sector the best way to realize optimal resource utilization of the group as a whole? Could greater synergy be achieved if some adjustments were made to the weight of each sector?

CASE 9

Starbucks in US: Too much coffee spilling all over?

By Shanul Jain[1]

Over the past 10 years, in order to achieve the growth, development and scale necessary to go from less than 1,000 stores to 13,000 stores and beyond, we have had to make a series of decisions that, in retrospect, have lead to the watering down of the Starbucks experience.

Howard Schultz, Chairman and CEO, Starbucks

In 2008, Starbucks, with over 15 000 stores in 43 countries and serving 50 million customers a week, was the world's leading retailer, roaster and brand of specialty coffee. During the 1990s and after, the company expanded rapidly – especially in the US, reaching a count of over 10 000 locations by 2007 – becoming not just the largest but also the most ubiquitous coffee shop that commanded premium prices.

However, trouble started brewing at Starbucks in 2006 and come 2008, it threatened to spill over. With sales of $9.4 billion and its growth targets and expansion into Asia being on track, it would seem that all was well. In fact, Starbucks was facing its first serious crisis in many years – its share price had fallen by more than 40 per cent for the first time since it listed and some store sales had declined in the US – its biggest market. Starbucks' reinstated founder CEO, Howard Schultz acknowledged that the chain had lost its soul and no longer resembled the neighbourhood store but rather a chain of cookie-cutter stores. The year 2008 therefore, was one of reckoning, at least for US operations.

To restore the exclusivity of the brand – US store expansion would be slowed down and the company would focus on global operations. Schultz announced that Starbucks would close 600 underperforming stores in the US – this from a retailer that prided itself on having shuttered just a few stores due to misjudged locations in its entire history. Had the purveyor of premium coffee grown too fast and commoditized its brand? Was it time for the company to rethink its US growth strategy? Had Starbucks run out of steam after Schultz's departure and did his return hint at the gravity of problems at one of the iconic brands? What

are Schultz's priorities and how should he go about addressing them?

Starbucks: Brewing premium coffee

In 1971, three academicians and coffee enthusiasts – Jerry Baldwin, Gordon Bowker and Zev Siegel – started a specialty coffee store, Starbucks Coffee, Tea and Spice, in Seattle's Pike Place Market. The firm did not sell coffee by the cup but samples were sometimes available for tasting.

In 1982 the company hired Schultz (Exhibit 1) as director of retail operations and marketing. In 1983, on a buying trip to Italy, Schultz came across the Italian coffee bars and reminiscences, 'I discovered the ritual and romance of the coffee bars in Italy. I saw how popular they were and how vibrant. Each one had its own unique character, but there was one common thread: the camaraderie between the customers, who knew each other well, and the barista (counter-worker), who was performing with flair.' Italy, with a population of about 56.6 million in 1983, had about 200 000 coffee bars with 1500 alone in Milan, a city the size of Philadelphia. Schultz remarked, 'It seemed they were on every street corner and all were packed.' It was here that he heard a customer order a café latte and trying it concluded that it was 'the perfect drink' and one which he had to introduce the Americans to.

On returning to Seattle, Schultz shared his idea of serving fresh-brewed coffee in Starbucks stores with the founders. Starbucks' differentiating factor would be recreating the coffee-bar culture in the US, where every visit would be an experience, a special treat; and the stores, a place to meet friends and visit. The founders however were unwilling to modify Starbucks' format. In 1985, Schultz left the company to start his own Italian-style espresso bars. However, raising money for the venture was not easy. Schultz got rejected by 217 of the 242 people he spoke to. Sceptics said, 'Americans are never going to spend a

[1]Source: Copyright IBSCDC, 2009.

EXHIBIT 1 HOWARD SCHULTZ: PROFILE

Howard Schultz was born in 1953 in Brooklyn and grew up in Bayview Project, a government-subsidized housing unit. His family had little money, but Schultz was determined to escape poverty. He became the first member in his family to get a college education and got a degree in business and marketing. After college, he joined Xerox Corporation.

Later he worked for Hammarplast, a Swedish maker of stylish kitchen equipment and house wares and rose to be the vice president and general manager of US operations. While there, he got curious about a company in Seattle that was ordering an extraordinary number of specially shaped coffee filters. He visited Seattle and there was taken in by the enthusiasm of the Starbucks' founders and talked them into hiring him. Schultz joined Starbucks Coffee Company as director of operations and marketing in 1982, when the Company had only four stores.

In August 1987, Schultz purchased Starbucks Coffee Company. Widely known as the architect of Starbucks brand image, he served as chief executive officer of the Company from 1987 to 2000. During that period, the Company went public in 1992 becoming the first specialty coffee company to become a public company. Under his leadership the company achieved exceptional US and international growth. From 2000 onward, in his role as chairman, Schultz focused on the Company's global strategies and expansion.

He returned as chairman and chief executive officer in 2008 when the company started facing trouble. He has to now focus on giving the correct strategic direction to the company.

Under Schultz's leadership, Starbucks was one of the first companies in North America to offer two unique benefits to its eligible full- and part-time partners: healthcare benefits, and grants in the form of stock options, called Bean Stock. Starbucks is now the leading retailer, roaster and brand of specialty coffee in the world.

dollar and a half for coffee.' Investors saw coffee as a commodity business and thought that the espresso-bar concept lacked any basis for sustainable competitive advantage and argued that there was no scope for building a brand around a commodity product.

However, Schultz persisted and his first espresso bar, *Il Giornale* (meaning 'daily' in Italian) opened in Seattle in April 1986 in a building that later became the highest skyscraper in Seattle. The store tried to replicate the Italian-style coffee bar – Italian opera played in the background, the baristas wore white shirts and bow ties and all service was stand-up. However, when parts of the concept did not appeal to the American tastes, the company was quick to make changes. Chairs were added when customers demanded a place to sit, music was varied when they complained about the incessant opera and even non-fat milk was provided for their drinks. Throughout, however, care was taken 'not to make so many compromises that we would sacrifice our style and elegance'. Within 6 months, *Il Giornale* was serving about 1000 customers a day. The second store opened 6 months later in the Seattle Trust Tower at Second and Madison, another downtown high-rise.

In 1987, Schultz got an opportunity to buy Starbucks that was bigger with six stores compared to *Il Giornale*'s three. He believed that Starbucks and *Il Giornale*

complemented each other and that he 'understood and valued what Starbucks stood for'. With the backing of investors, Schultz acquired Starbucks for $3.8 million in August 1987. The new entity was named Starbucks Corporation and it was a hybrid retail coffee-bean store and an espresso bar/café. The name Starbucks was chosen as it was more established and 'connoted a product that was unique and mystical, yet purely American'. The goal of the merged entity was to open 125 stores in 5 years and the vision Schultz had was, 'Customers would respect our brand so much that they would talk of "a cup of Starbucks coffee". Perhaps we could change the way Americans drank coffee.'

Starbucks: Sizing up a brand

Starbucks was positioned as a 'third' place between work and home where one could come, listen to music, relax and have great coffee. The barista's were expected to be friendly and to know customers' names and their favourite drink on their next visit. The need to be pleasant and friendly with customers was emphasized and baristas were trained to 'just say yes' to customer requests. Schultz believed that if Starbucks could always manage this then, 'the Starbucks brand will stand for a meaningful, personal experience no matter how ubiquitous we become.'

The store design and ambience were given particular attention. Details like the style of chairs, the edges of countertops and the texture of slate floors were all thoroughly looked into. Colourful banners and posters were used for better visual impact. To keep the aroma of coffee pure, the company did not sell chemically flavoured beans, soup or cooked food and prepared foods were kept covered. Smoking in the stores was banned and employees were asked to not wear perfume or cologne. Schultz maintains that it is due to this that the brand value was built. For Schultz, '(Starbucks) brand is based on the experience we control in our stores. When a company can create a relevant, emotional and intimate experience, it builds trust with the customer. We have benefited by the fact that our stores are reliable, safe and consistent, where people can take a break.'

A key factor in Starbucks' growth was the strong employee culture. The employees' ideas and connection to the customers was an essential element in the 'Starbucks Experience'. Schultz believed that a generous benefits package was a key competitive advantage. Two-thirds of the work force comprised part-timers. Starbucks became the first private and later the first public company to offer healthcare benefits to both full-time and part-time employees working at least 20 hours a week. All employees were eligible for stock option grants through Bean Stock, the company-wide stock option plan. It also referred to all its employees as 'partners'. Schultz said, 'We built our brand first with our people, not consumers – the opposite approach from that of the crackers-and-cereal companies.'

Starbucks' approach towards employees benefited the company with a turnover rate lower than the retail industry average. The turnover rate for Starbucks' baristas was about 60–65 per cent, much lower than the 150–400 per cent a year for other national retailers. One store manager remarked, 'Morale is very high in my store among staff. I have worked for a lot of companies, but I have never seen this level of respect. It is a company that is very true to its workers and it shows. Our customers always comment that we are happy and having fun. In fact a lot of people ask if they can work here.'

The high employee morale in Starbucks stores resulted in some of the company's best-selling products being master-minded by its 'partners'. At the company stores in California, the baristas received constant demand for blended drinks which the company did not have on the menu. The partners' request for such a drink was declined because the company thought that

it was something a true coffee connoisseur would not appreciate. However, the 'partners' began experimenting without official permission. After trials and improvements an icy blend of dark-roasted coffee and milk was developed and was named Frappuccino. The drink was a runaway hit with $52 million in sales in the first full year on the national market. Schultz remarked that Frappuccino was, 'The best mistake I didn't make.'

Schultz's objective was to make Starbucks a national company with a presence in every major city. Early on in 1987 Starbucks opened a store in Chicago, but that failed due to misjudged location. Schultz knew that Starbucks had to succeed in Chicago to attract venture capitalists and prove that the idea was transportable throughout North America. To tackle the problem, experienced managers were hired and the prices charged were raised to compensate for the high rent and labour costs. The stores in Chicago began to turn profitable and acquired a critical mass of customers. However, the root of the problem was believed to be that 'there just weren't enough of them (stores)'. The need was for more Starbucks stores and greater presence.

Starbucks accelerated its store openings and opened 15 new stores in 1988 reaching a total of 35 stores. Schultz was eager to expand to ensure that Starbucks would be way ahead even if some local coffee roasters and retailers decided to go national at a later date. Schultz believed that Starbucks needed to invest ahead of the growth curve. Growth and earnings however were not possible simultaneously and the company lost $330 000, $764 000 and $1.2 million in 1987, 1988 and 1989 respectively.

Starbucks: Growth strategy

In 1990, Starbucks turned a profit, had 84 stores and was opening more stores than laid out in the original plan. The company went public in 1992 and the IPO raised $29 million. With the additional capital, Starbucks sped up its expansion. The rapid expansion was helped by a sophisticated store-development process based on a 6-month opening schedule. There was an in-house team of architects and designers to ensure that each store would convey the right image and character. As a result, the company was able to open a store every business day.

Starbucks tried to be first in each market and gain a foothold there before moving to another city. It opened stores in highly visible, high-traffic downtowns and residential neighbourhoods. In each region the company worked without side brokers to scout for the best locations. An error in judgement would mean that the company would lose at least $500 000 in costs (including inventory, equipment and write-down for lease-hold improvement) along with the cost of getting out of the lease. A 'flagship' store would cost even more. Location was important and Schultz believed, 'In the building of a retail brand you have to create awareness and attract people's favour-able attention. You have to become in vogue. You need opinion leaders who naturally endorse your pro-duct.' The first store in Chicago was in a prime loca-tion, one block away from Sears Tower. In New York, the stores opened in Fairfield and Westchester coun-ties where many opinion-makers who worked in Manhattan stayed. In California the company opened its first store in LA. The idea was to make Starbucks the preferred brand of Hollywood to give it mileage.

Starbucks also identified prospective cities through its mail-order business. The business had started in the mid 1970s and since mail-order buyers made an extra effort to obtain Starbucks products, they hap-pened to be the most loyal customers. The company targeted those cities and neighbourhoods where its mail-order customers were clustered. The strategy worked – of the first 1000 stores Starbucks opened, only two had to be shuttered because of misjudge-ment in site.

Starbucks spent very little on traditional advertising and 'the stores reputation grew mostly by word of mouth.' In a customer survey in California people re-marked, 'Starbucks is so social. We go to Starbucks store because of a social feeling.' The company mostly advertised through the print medium as the target market comprised relatively educated people who did more reading than the average person.

The company opened thousands of stores and in-itially a typical store was between 200 and 4000 sq. ft. The stores opened later ranged from 1000 to 1700 sq. ft. There were some stores directly across the street from each other to make it easier for customers to get their cup of coffee and increase awareness of the brand. Although some cannibalization was inevitable, the company believed that opening multiple stores in the same area helped build the brand and also enhanced convenience for its customers.

On Starbucks' strategy *Fortune* wrote:

The strategy is simple: Blanket an area completely, even if the stores cannibalize one another's business. A new store will often capture about 30 per cent of the sales of a nearby Starbucks, but the company considers that a good thing: The Starbucks-everywhere approach cuts down on delivery and management costs, shortens customer lines at individual stores, and increases foot traffic for all the stores in an area. A typical customer stops by 18 times a month; no American retailer has a higher frequency of customer visits. Even in a down economy, when other retailers have taken a beating, Starbucks store traffic has risen between 6 per cent and 8 per cent a year.

To expand outside North America, Starbucks Coffee International was formed in 1995. The first stores opened in Tokyo, Japan in the high-fashion Ginza district in 1996, in a joint venture with SAZABY Inc., amid doubts whether the Japanese known to dislike carrying to-go food or beverages on the street would warm to the concept. Also, in Tokyo, there was a coffee shop on almost every corner. However, on the opening day, there were long lines with people stand-ing patiently for their drink. The success of Starbucks in a country where green tea was the national drink showed that the brand had the same power outside as it had in North America.

Most Starbucks stores were company-owned and even though the area was leased, the company bore the entire cost of design and construction. The licensee model was avoided to keep the company in full control of the quality of its products and the character and location of its stores. Licensing was done if there was no other way for the company to serve a particular market. Starbucks stuck to this model even when other retailers expanded in a big way by franchizing na-tionwide. Since Starbucks owned its stores, it did not have to answer to unhappy franchisees about cannibalization.

Apart from increasing the number of stores, the company also formed a number of partnerships to serve a broader customer base. It set up the North American Coffee Partnership with Pepsi to manu-facture and distribute coffee drinks. The partnership was initially viewed as strange because, 'Starbucks appeals to sophisticated consumers with discriminat-ing tastes, while Pepsi aims to appeal to the broadest consumer base possible.' The partnership's first product, Mazagran – a cold, carbonated coffee bev-erage – was a failure. However, the next product – bottled Frappuccino – was an instant hit and heralded Starbucks' entry into the supermarket and the ready-to-drink beverage business. Starbucks also formed al-liances with Dreyer's Grand Ice Cream to introduce super premium ice cream and acquired Tazo LLC, a premium tea company.

Initially, Starbucks' consumers could buy coffee at Starbucks store only. Schultz was as opposed to wholesaling as he was to franchizing. However, the opportunity to attract new customers was too appealing and to reach customers in different locations Starbucks partnered with bookstore chains Barnes and Nobles and Chapters Inc., food and beverage company Kraft Foods, hotel chains Host Marriott International and Hyatt International and also got the accounts of United Airlines and Horizon Air. It experimented with drive-through windows – the technique mirrored those by fast-food chains that are more grab-and-go – in locations where speed and convenience were important to customers and with kiosks in supermarkets, building lobbies and other public places. All the time while expanding Schultz wondered, 'How far can you extend a brand before you dilute it.'

Because of the diverse and distant locations where Starbucks was opening its stores, the company started using FlavorLock bags to retain the freshness of the coffee and according to Schultz, 'The reintroduction of FlavorLock bags was a key decision that made our expansion strategy feasible. It allowed us to sell and serve coffee with the highest freshness standards even in stores thousands of miles form our roasting plant.' Also, to keep up with the rapid pace of expansion, Starbucks switched from hand-operated La Marzocco espresso machines to automatic Verisimo ones. These machines helped to standardize and speed up the coffee-making process.

Starbucks came to be known for its dark roast specialty coffee and also leveraged the brand to build complementary products and services. The company produced a successful line of music CDs (a suggestion made by a partner) as a result of an extremely popular in-house music programme. The company also acquired its own music label, Hear Music and launched Hear Music Coffeehouses which housed an extensive digital and physical music inventory. A partnership with Apple allowed customers at participating Starbucks outlets to download music from the iTunes Wi-Fi Music Store. Apart from music, other entertainment initiatives encompassed book, film and technology-based initiatives to appeal to new and existing Starbucks customers.

Starbucks usually opened to near-capacity crowds in every new location. However, with success also came the brickbats. The company was often accused of wiping out the small local retailers. It was also targeted by the anti-globalization activists who accused the company of exploiting farmers in the third-world countries from where coffee was sourced. Starbucks was a purveyor of specialty coffee – differentiated by origin and type. It was distinguished from commodity coffee which tended to be sold in large quantities at a low price. The quality of coffee that Starbucks purchased was usually sourced directly from the growers on a negotiated basis and at a bit higher prices. Long-term fixed-price contracts were worked out to ensure an adequate supply even in case of contingencies. Starbucks was very exacting in its standards and the company's chief coffee procurer would trail mountains in Kenya, Guatemala, Indonesia and elsewhere to look for the perfect beans. While maintaining a strict quality check, Starbucks also worked to be more socially responsible and started a preferred supplier programme, sourcing beans from those growers who were committed to socially and environmentally responsible farming. Suppliers who fitted Starbucks' criteria were paid a premium for their produce.

In other initiatives, the company worked with CARE and Conservation International to promote environmentally responsible methods of growing coffee. The company also committed to purchase Fair Trade Certified coffee. The entire process of buying the coffee to making it available to customers was tightly controlled by the company, making it vertically integrated – an approach quite different from other brand-name consumer-products companies.

In the 1990s, Starbucks expanded rapidly and Schultz to oversee the company's international expansion handed the post of CEO to Orin Smith, a Starbucks veteran, and himself assumed the role of chairman and chief global strategist in 2000. By 2004, Starbucks was opening on an average three stores per day in the US. In Manhattan alone, the company had almost 200 stores. On these numbers Schultz remarked, 'We're not even approaching anything close to saturation. We think the market is very, very large. These are the early days of the growth of the company.' By the end of fiscal 2006, stores numbered 12 440 and Starbucks offered coffee in a variety of choice and flavours – almost 55 000 by the company's count.

Starbucks: Brand dilemmas

Starbucks brought coffee drinking into the mainstream. It was largely credited with changing the way Americans viewed and drank their coffee. On an average, Starbucks drew on a population base of around 80 000 and in some states like California below 20 000. In Times Square in New York there was one Starbucks for every 0.04 square miles and for every 1442 people. Soon, with the company opening on average six to seven stores per day, some markets were saturated.

Business Week wrote: 'The coffee quality has been declining, especially as stores went from brewing coffee to pushing buttons on machines. The atmosphere of the stores has become all-too familiar. And with people so short of time, most stores are places to stop and go, rather than hang out.'

With the increase in focus on profitability, comfy couches were out and promotional music stands and racks of coffee-related knick-knacks took their place. In the first sign of trouble, same store sales declined in the US from 9 per cent in 2005 to 7 per cent in 2006.

With the growth in coffee sales declining, Starbucks introduced warm breakfast sandwiches to boost sales. It was serving breakfast sandwiches across 700 locations and they were expected to add $700 000 to each store's annual sales. Since Starbucks' cafés were not equipped for in-store cooking, the sandwiches were cooked and assembled in a central location and shipped to individual destinations daily. Here they were re-heated and served to customers. Soon however, there were complaints that the smell of baked sandwiches overpowered the aroma of coffee. Also, baristas were instructed to ask customers whether they wanted sandwiches with their coffee, a technique that seemed unnatural to most as the idea at Starbucks was for baristas to remember the names and preferences of customers. A barista remarked, 'The more and more business they get in the store, the more it seems like another fast-food job.'

Starbucks was also seeing the entry of more players in the specialty coffee market. The market for specialty coffee in the US had grown from $11.05 billion in 2005 to $12.27 billion in 2006. For customers, the coffee quality and a convenient location were the most important coffeehouses characteristics and price was the least. Coffee bars and espresso carts sprouted all across the US. Espressos were also being sold at gas-stations and convenience stores. There were about 25 000 coffeehouses in the US in 2007 as compared to 585 in 1987. A number of independent coffee roasters and cafés, targeting a particular area were thriving and re-focusing their attention on the art and craft of coffee selection, roasting, brewing and presentation. The growing market attracted a number of fast-food retailers as well (Exhibit 2). McDonald's – the world's largest fast-food chain – and Dunkin' Donuts added specialty coffee to their offerings. McDonald's

EXHIBIT 2 MAIN US SPECIALITY COFFEE COMPETITORS

Company	Revenues ($) of Stores	Number Stores	Franchised	Type
Starbucks	9.41 billion	10,684	3,891	Specialty coffee roaster and retailer.
McDonald's	22.7 billion	13,862	11,272	Quick-service restaurant chain.
Dunkin' Donuts	5.3 billion	7,988	5,769	Coffee and baked goods chain.
Tim Hortons (Canada based)	1.9 billion	398	356	Quick-service restaurant chain.
Pan era Bread	1.07 billion	1,167	666	Chain of bakery-cafe restaurants.
Krispy Kreme	429 million	245	145	Chain of doughnut stores.
Peet's Coffee & Tea	249 million	166	N/A	Specialty coffee roaster and marketer.
Caribou Coffee	257 million	484	12	Gourmet coffeehouse operator.
Tully's Coffee	60 million	128	N/A	Specialty coffee retailer, roaster and wholesaler.
Diedrich Coffee	37 million	146	139	Specialty coffee roaster, wholesaler and retailer.
Coffee Bean & Tea Leaf	N/A	183	N/A	Specialty coffee and tea retailer.

launched McCafe selling lattes and cappuccinos, with plans to serve coffee in its nearly 14 000 US restaurants in 2008. Dunkin' Donuts was also aggressively moving to grab the market of affluent women and professionals – two strong bases for Starbucks.

In February 2007, Schultz wrote an internal memo to company executives where he warned about the commoditization of the Starbucks brand. Schultz stated that while the decision of moving to automatic espresso machines, using flavour locked packaging, streamlining store design were necessary to gain efficiencies of scale and were right at the time, they had eroded the 'romance and theatre' associated with the coffee making process. The height of the new espresso machines blocked the visual sight line the customer previously had to watch the drink being made and for the intimate experience with the barista. For the stores he said they 'no longer have the soul of the past and reflect a chain of stores vs. the warm feeling of a neighbourhood store. People even call our stores sterile, cookie cutter, no longer reflecting the passion our partners feel about our coffee.'

While the same store sales at Starbucks declined, prices for food commodities reached an all-time high in the US. If earlier consumers were not price conscious, they now cut back on spending amid declining home values and higher fuel prices. People were unwilling to spend on a cup of premium coffee at Starbucks while cheaper options were available. In February 2007, *Consumer Reports*, a trade magazine, rated McDonald's filter coffee as better not just in flavour but also price than the same sort of beverage served up at Starbucks. Starbucks coffee was rated as, 'strong, but burnt and bitter enough to make your eyes water instead of open.' The price at McDonald's was $1.35 in March 2007, 20 lower than Starbucks' $1.55. At Starbucks, depending on the size, a cup of coffee could cost as much as $5. Joe Buckley, restaurant analyst for Bear Stearns remarked, 'The Starbucks customer 5 years ago shrugged everything off, because (the company) had such an affluent base. Starbucks has been very successful broadening their customer base, but one result of doing that is their customers are not quite as indifferent to what is going on around them.'

Starbucks also fell behind Dunkin' Donuts and McDonald's in the 2008 Customer Loyalty Engagement Index of Brand Keys, a brand consulting firm in New York, after holding the top spot for the past 4 years. Robert Passikoff, chief executive Brand Keys, said, 'They took their eye off the brand to become more efficient, walking away from what gave them their differentiation.'

Starbucks' share, which had been on a constant upswing ever since the company went public, also slumped. The share price plummeted by 42 per cent – making it one of the worst performers on the NASDAQ stock exchange. Walter Todd, a principal at Greenwood Capital Associates LLC, an investment advisory firm remarked, 'The perception is that Starbucks is oversaturated in the US and that the quality of the experience has deteriorated as they have grown.'

Even though the share price and same store sales declined, the Starbucks brand continued to be among the most valuable brands in the world. The brand value constantly increased and in 2008 Interbrand ranked Starbucks as the 85th most valuable brand with a brand value of $3.9 billion (Exhibit 3).

Along with an increase in brand value, there was an increase in sales as well. In 2007, Starbucks had $9.4 billion in revenue as compared to $7.8 billion in 2006. The company's financial performance was highly dependent on its US operating segment, which comprised 78 per cent of total net revenues (Exhibit 4). Starbucks had over 10 000 locations in the US (Exhibit 5). About two-thirds of outlets were wholly owned by the company and the remaining operated by licensees who paid fees for use of the Starbucks brand name. However, the same store sales that started declining in 2006 further fell in 2007 (Exhibit 6). Even though same store sales were within the company's stated target range, it was accomplished through two fairly quick price increases. Starbucks had raised prices 7 times since 1997, but there had been little effect on demand. Now, however, its customer base was eroding with many people shifting to cheaper premium coffee from competitors. Starbucks' share further slumped by 12 per cent in early 2008 – such a dismal stock performance was a first in the company's history.

Analysts believed that the company had grown far too fast. *The Economist* wrote, 'While Starbucks has expanded so have its rivals. The firm's home market seems to have reached saturation point. To restore the company's shine Mr Schultz will need to make Starbucks special again.'

In January 2008, Schultz returned as CEO. He argued that rising dairy prices, increasing competition and a faltering economy were not the company's main problems. The company had spent the last several years 'trying to invest ahead of the growth curve – in people, process, infrastructure, roasting plants, coffee

EXHIBIT 3   STARBUCKS' INTERBRAND / *BUSINESS WEEK* BRAND RANKING

Year	Rank	Value ($ million)	Change	Business Week's *Comment*
2008	85	3,879	7%	There are not many places left in this world where absolutely everyone is invited. Starbucks says, "come in, sit where you want, bring what you want, wear what you want, and enjoy yourself." Starbucks built a comfy couch for the planet, and brought community and hospitality back into a culture that had lost it.
2007	88	3,631	17%	Starbucks has mastered the challenges of ensuring a consistent sense of 'Starbucks' permeates consumers' worlds. From its retail environments and non-traditional advertising policy, to its fair trade coffee, the experience is unmistakably Starbucks. One brand transcends it all.
2006	91	3,099	20%	Starbucks brings in customers with lifestyle marketing, pushing music, books and lunch food to get them to stick around.
2005	99	2,576	7%	Profits and share price remain high, now Starbucks is pushing to become a force in music distribution.
2004	98	2,400	17%	Global expansion, new products, and yet more variations on the humble cup of Java boost the coffee huts appeal.
2003	93	2,136	9%	This fast-growing brand continued to corner the US market, although it hit some speed bumps overseas.
2002	93	1,960	12%	Starbucks hasn't stumbled yet. There are still gaps to fill in the US as it gears up for expansion in Asia and Europe.
2001	88	1,760	32%	Shows the biggest jump in brand value as it keeps expanding its coffee empire into every nook and cranny
2000	88	1,330	—	Fastest growing brand

buying, and that had taken focus away from the customers' store experience'. He added 'This is a problem that I think we've created, and as a result of that, that we can fix.' He stated he would bring a 'laser-like' focus to improving the customer experience and in making sure that the 'Starbucks experience' was markedly different from rivals.

He outlined a major restructuring initiative to slow the company's pace of US store openings. Initially, the company announced that it would be closing 100 under-performing locations in the US. The number was upped to 600 stores in July 2008. Schultz believed that the

company had not produced enough 'exciting' products, only variations of products and no blockbuster new products. Other initiatives would be to introduce new products and store designs, re-train baristas and improve offerings for its customers. The company would try to boost sales at existing stores while opening fewer locations. The focus would be on improving the 'customer experience' at US stores and streamlining management.

Industry analysts also had their take on what Starbucks should do. Dean Crutchfield, a senior vice-president of marketing at Wolff Olins, a branding firm, said, 'Starbucks really needs to refocus on the

EXHIBIT 4   STARBUCKS' FINANCIALS ($ MILLION)

Item	2007		2006		2005		2004		2003	
	Total	US	Total	US	Total	US	Total	US	Total	US
Net revenues	9,411.49	7,348.99	7,786.94	6,178.55	6,369.3	5,334.46	5,294.25	4,490.85	4,075.52	3,472.45
Cost of sales including occupancy costs	3,999.12	2,956.23	3,178.79	2,374.48	2,605.21	2,086.70	2,191.44	1,782.58	1,681.43	1,358.83
Store operating expenses	3,215.88	2,684.19	2,687.81	2,280.04	2,165.91	1,848.83	1,790.16	1,546.87	1,379.57	1,199.02
Other operating expenses	294.13	204.67	253.72	190.62	197.02	162.79	171.64	144.85	141.34	119.96
Depreciation and amortisation expenses	467.16	348.19	387.21	284.62	340.17	250.41	289.18	210.44	244.67	173.74
General and administrative expenses	489.24	85.94	479.38	93.75	357.11	85.36	304.29	80.22	244.55	45.00
Income from equity investees	108.00	0.76	93.93	0.15	76.74	45.57	59.07	37.45	36.90	28.48
Operating income	1,053.94	1,070.51	893.95	955.17	780.61	945.92	606.58	763.32	420.85	604.36
Net Interest income (expense)	2.41		12.29		15.83		14.14		11.62	
Income before	1,056.36		906.24		796.44		620.72		432.47	
Net earnings	672.63		564.25		494.46		388.97		265.35	

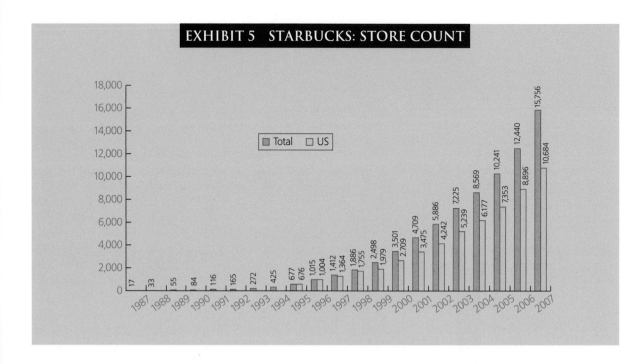

EXHIBIT 5   STARBUCKS: STORE COUNT

Total / US store counts:

Year	Total	US
1987	17	
1988	33	
1989	55	
1990	84	
1991	116	
1992	165	
1993	272	
1994	425	
1995	677	676
1996	1,015	1,004
1997	1,412	1,364
1998	1,886	1,755
1999	2,498	1,979
2000	3,501	2,709
2001	4,709	3,475
2002	5,886	4,242
2003	7,225	5,239
2004	8,569	6,177
2005	10,241	7,353
2006	12,440	8,896
2007	15,756	10,684

EXHIBIT 6   STARBUCKS COMPARABLE STORE SALES

Region	2007	2006	2005	2004	2003	2002	2001	2000
US	4	7	9	11	9	7	5	9
International	7	8	6	6	7	1	3	12
Consolidated	5	7	8	10	8	6	5	9

Compiled by the author

luxury coffee experience; the smells, the sounds and they could mix up the retail presence to be less cookie-cutter, perhaps using a modular system of bars and furniture. A different store design could give different locales their own sense of richness.'

The solution, as Schultz put in his memo was, 'to get back to the core. Push for innovation and do the things necessary to once again differentiate Starbucks from all others.' Starbucks had to rise to the challenge of staying small while growing big.

Pep Stores: Retailing to low-income consumers

By Catherine McPherson, Steven Michael Burgess and Mlenga Jere[1]

Pep Stores is an Every Day Low Prices (EDLP) discount retailer catering to low income consumers in the various markets in which it operates. In addition to its core products of clothing, footwear, and textiles, the stores stock a range of 'everyday home essentials'. The chain consists of over 1400 stores in South Africa and other African countries including Angola, Zambia, Zimbabwe, Mozambique, and Malawi and is the largest same brand retailer in South Africa. In existence for over 40 years, the Pep chain has been listed and delisted from the Johannesburg Stock Exchange, enjoyed periods of profitability as well as times of financial disappointment, and witnessed a changing consumer profile as South Africa transited to democracy.

> *Pep currently has the country's third highest Return on Operating Assets in the clothing industry, it is also the number three brand of clothing, it has the best retail distribution system, the biggest store network and, most importantly, Pep believes it has developed the best band of people working in retail in South Africa.*
>
> www.pepstores.co.za

Pep is privately owned by Pepkor, a South African-based investment holding company, which has interests in various value retail chains in Africa, Poland and Australia (See Exhibit 1 and 2 for Pepkor milestones and current organizational structure). In 2005, the chain sold over 400 million units at an average price of R14 per unit, and enjoyed a turnover of R5.9 billion and operating profit of R607 million.

Discovering a recipe for retail success

Renier van Rooyen formulated a recipe for retail success while running successful general dealership and clothing outlets in South Africa's Northern Cape province. He realized that poor people had little disposable income but their collective buying power was immense. His idea was to provide clothing cheaply – but not cheap clothing – to South Africa's low and middle income groups and capitalize on large volumes with low profit margins.

Pep Stores (Pty) Limited was founded in Upington, Northern Cape, on 17 August 1965, a time when people defined as 'non-white' by Apartheid legislation were marginalized and treated like second-class citizens in South Africa. Many people of colour, especially blacks, lived a large part of their lives in rural 'homelands', which were set out by the Apartheid government to enforce the segregated living of the different races and tribes. Although a bloated, inefficient bureaucracy offered some employment opportunities, life in the homelands was bleak and many people relied on meagre remittances from family members 'lucky enough' to transit 'influx control' and get permission to work in the city.

Notwithstanding Apartheid-era legislation, van Rooyen held liberal political views and refused to treat people differently because of racial classification. He believed that new clothing helped restore the dignity of poor people by enabling them to look and feel good. Driven by this vision, he adopted self-service retailing, so customers could explore the merchandise without a service counter separating them from the goods for sale, and allowed everyone to use the same in-store dressing rooms, ignoring the racial controversy it generated initially.

Growth and early years of Pep

There were three Pep stores in 1966. By 1968, there were 18. This growth and expansion was taking place mainly in the rural areas, close to Pep's target market. By this time, Pep had built a head office and storage facilities in Kuils River, Cape Town. Pep identified the 'Coloured'[2] population as its main customer base,

---

[1] Source: ©2009, University of Cape Town Graduate School of Business.

[2] Under Apartheid legislation, people of mixed race ancestry were classified as Coloured, and included many Afrikaans-speaking descendants of the first Dutch settlers and Khoisan inhabitants of the Cape and indentured servants brought to South Africa from Malaysia, who often speak English in the home.

EXHIBIT 1   PEPKOR MILESTONES

1965:	Pep Stores is started in Upington in the Northern Cape of South Africa
1972:	Pep Stores is listed on the JSE Securities Exchange.
1979:	The company enters food retailing with the take?over of Shoprite, which in turn acquires Grand Bazaars.
1982:	The name of the holding company is changed from Pep Stores to Pepkor Limited.
1986:	The discount clothing chain Ackermans is acquired. The group lists its clothing interests on the JSE Securities Exchange as Pep Limited and its food interests as Shoprite Holdings Limited.
1991:	Pepkor acquires control of the retail chains Smart Group Holdings, Cashbuild, Checkers and Stuttafords. Checkers is brought in under the Shoprite name. The group extends its interests to the United Kingdom with the opening of the first Your More Store outlet in Scotland.
1992:	Pep's interest in Botswana is listed on the Botswana Stock Exchange.
1993:	Pepkor acquires the controlling interest in the British company Brown & Jackson plc with its wholly?owned subsidiary, the retail chain Poundstretcher. Pep's interest in Namibia is listed on the Namibian Stock Exchange.
1997:	Pepkor consolidates its UK retail interests in Brown & Jackson.
1998:	The group extends its interests to Australia by acquiring the clothing chain Best & Less with its 84 stores.
1999:	Pep Limited is delisted from the JSE Securities Exchange South Africa
2000:	Cashbuild and Stuttafords are disposed of. The group undergoes dramatic restructuring. Pepkor unbundles its interest in Shoprite and Brown & Jackson to shareholders. Pepkor's pyramid structure falls away, resulting in the delisting and disappearance of Pepgro, Pepkor's ultimate holding company. The businesses remaining in the group are the value clothing retailers Pep, Ackermans and Best & Less.
2003:	Pepkor acquires the assets of Fashion Africa (Fashaf) and with that the Dunns chain.
2004:	Delisted from the JSE Securities Exchange South Africa. At the end of that year it acquires the stores in Poland from Tradehold.
2005	Shoe City is taken over.

and bought and sold clothing to suit their tastes. Positioning itself as a low cost retailer, the merchandise mix focused on basic items rather than more expensive fashion clothing. Van Rooyen stressed the importance of a positive-thinking work force that had a shareholding in the business and relied on pamphlet distribution to promote his stores' merchandise (some say this was because many of his customers could not read and therefore did not buy newspapers).

Buoyed by continued rapid growth and expansion, Pep began manufacturing in 1971 to guarantee appropriate clothing in the quantities needed and cut distribution costs. A year later, Pep was listed on the Johannesburg Stock Exchange in order to fund additional expansion. That year, Pep comprised 163 stores and 2 manufacturing units, with a turnover of R22 million. By 1981, Pep had grown to 464 stores and 10 factories, with a turnover of R202 million.

Pep stores had developed a characteristic sensitivity to the needs of its target market and a willingness to accommodate and adapt to those needs.

www.pepstores.co.za

The listed Pep Stores Limited had been acquiring other chains. A new holding company Pepkor Limited was listed in 1982, with four operating divisions: non-food retail, food retail, manufacturing, and property. In 1986, Pepkor listed its clothing business separately as Pep Stores Limited, comprising Pep Stores and Ackermans, a budget clothing operation that had been acquired. The store location strategy was to secure relatively small sites of about 400 square metres on main commuter roads. Noting that although 70 per cent of Pep's outlets in 1986 were located in rural areas, substantially less of its revenues were generated

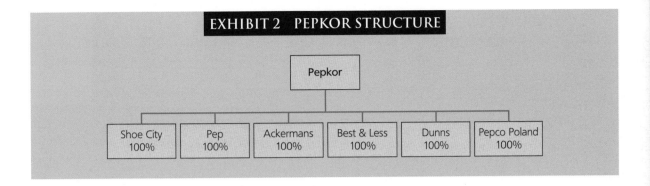

EXHIBIT 2 PEPKOR STRUCTURE

from those stores, Pep announced that its future expansion would focus on urban areas. By 1990, Pep's 25th birthday year, the chain consisted of 660 stores and 5697 employees.

Pep in the 1990s: As South Africa changes, the chain loses focus

The early 1990s was a time of great social and political uncertainty in South Africa. Nelson Mandela had been released from prison in 1990 but it was not certain that the country could successfully transit to post-Apartheid rule. The effects of international anti-Apartheid sanctions and uncertainty combined to produce one of South Africa's worst-ever recessions, resulting in unemployment, social violence, and reduced consumer spending. Pep annual reports of this period referred to adverse trading conditions and acknowledged the hard times it was experiencing. Even the country's first democratic elections in 1994, in which many of Pep's customers were eligible to vote for the very first time in their lives, did not have a marked improvement on Pep's fortunes.

Other factors impacted on sales. Competitors were making credit available for the first time to many lower middle-income consumers, who shopped at Pep for school clothing and many other goods. A bad drought affected many rural areas, Pep's heartland. Apartheid legislation that limited movement was abolished. So was the bloated homeland administration. The resulting mass migration to the urban areas included many traditional Pep customers and impacted negatively on Pep's rural operations. Pep responded by re-evaluating its operations in an effort to improve profitability. Market research was conducted to examine the changing needs of its customers. A new marketing strategy focused on three key areas: geographical expansion into Africa; upgrading and re-evaluating the

position of existing branches; and development of sophisticated information systems.

In 1992, Pep Managing Director Basil Weyers indicated that future expansion would be in urban areas. Not ruling out opportunities in rural areas, he nonetheless indicated that busier locations in major metropolitan areas would be the primary focus in the future. Pep also refocused on maximizing the development of its staff and provided ongoing training. While 1997 saw turnover and operating profit increasing again, Pep's operating profit for 1998 literally nosedived – by 47 per cent for the year (from R192 million in 1997 to R102 million in 1998) (Figure 1).

The South African economy had faced a series of knocks including a weakening of the Rand and high interest rates, which in turn lead to job losses and resulting cutbacks in consumer spending due to decreased disposable income. Reflecting on the state of the economy and job creation Christo Wiese, Pepkor's Chairman, noted in his review contained in the group's 1998 annual report that the average absorption capacity of the formal economy had declined from 82.7 per cent in 1980 to 53.9 per cent in 1994, and that these effects were being felt most keenly among the majority of Pep's customers. He also noted that the growth in real private consumption expenditure had declined from 3.9 per cent in 1996 to 2 per cent in 1997. The spending of the growing middle class, he noted, was being curtailed by heavier tax burdens and reduced government spending that played out as less benefits per tax rand.

In the market sector in which Pepkor's subsidiaries mainly operate, high interest rates only have an indirect effect. Much more important to the group is unemployment, social disintegration and violence. Weather conditions, in the form of a very mild winter, adversely affected clothing sales in particular. As

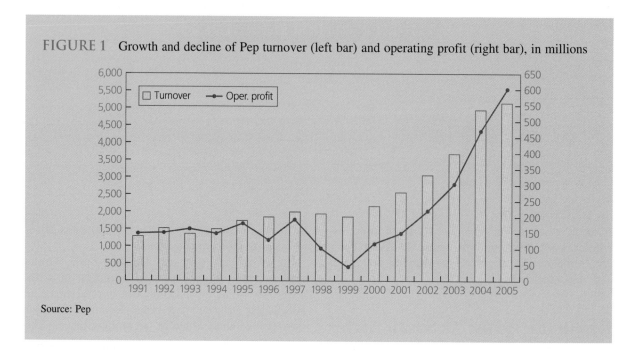

FIGURE 1 Growth and decline of Pep turnover (left bar) and operating profit (right bar), in millions

Source: Pep

disposable income dropped, competition for it intensified, which invariably had had a negative effect on profit margins.

JF Le Roux, Pepkor Chief Executive Officer, 1998 Annual Report

But Pep's performance could not be blamed on external factors alone. The firm also had to look inwards to examine what had lead to such a disappointing performance. In 1998, the Pep chain was composed of 941 stores in South Africa and a further 300 branches in the rest of Africa. Manufacturing operations had been cut back and had supplied just 11 per cent of the chain's stock for the year under review. Wiese acknowledged that Pep as a business had lost focus, and as a result had moved away from its original premise of being the lowest price discounter to being more of a value retailer, which had driven customers elsewhere. Further, the chain had extended its range of merchandise, which had pushed up operating expenses, created cluttered shopping environments, and eroded the departmentalization of the stores. Steps to remedy the situation included the appointing of new management, lead by a new Managing Director, Andre Labuschaigne, in February of 1998. The new management team was tasked with refocusing the business and returning it to the original price proposition and lowering of costs. A year later, in 1999, with a slight decrease in turnover from R1945 billion to R1875 billion, and a dismal R51 million profit for the year, compared to the previous year's R89 million profit, Wiese had to accept that the turnaround of Pep would take longer than expected.

The business climate during the year under review showed scant if any improvement on the previous year. A virtually static GDP was accompanied by rocketing interest rates ... the stifling effect of these rates on general spending impacted disastrously on consumers in the lower income groups.

Christo Wiese, Pepkor Chairman, 1999 Annual Report

Wiese reaffirmed his confidence in Labuschaigne and his management team and determined that the most effective manner in which to tackle Pep's problems was to 'reorganize all aspects of the business in depth in order to position Pep in a new league.' Pep stock was then delisted from the stock exchange.

Breathing new life into Pep

Labuschaigne had been tasked with building a management team that could reposition Pep as a lowest price retailer. His ambition was to recreate the uniqueness of the original Pep in a manner that could fit with the new South Africa, a country vastly different from the one into which Pep was born. Labuschaigne was a 'people person' and a charismatic leader whose primary strength was addressing people issues.

He immediately set out to formulate a new vision, mission and value statement for Pep and improve staff morale. All staff were consulted and invited to contribute to the process. The new vision, mission, and values were captured in the following statements:

- Our vision: Delighted customers: our focus and pleasure.
- Our mission: We strive to be the friendliest and most exciting retailer offering up-to-date and durable products at the best prices
- Our values: Honesty. Passion. Resourcefulness.

Labuschaigne then formally put processes in place to breathe new life into Pep's organizational culture. His lasting legacy at Pep is the corporate culture, Sikhula KunYe, which was his brainchild. Formalized under the name 'Sikhula KunYe' (we are growing together), and depicted using a mature oak tree, the revitalized culture emphasized personal empowerment, accountability through performance measurement and management, and reward for good performance through bonuses and public recognition. Staff were referred to as 'Dynamos' and greeted one another with a new 'high five' gesture.

Under Sikhula Kunye, Pep committed itself to becoming a learning organization:

EXHIBIT 3   SELECTED PEP-PERMINTS

- A candle loses nothing by lighting another candle. The race for quality has no finishing line.
- It's a funny thing about life – if you refuse to accept anything but the very best you will often get it.
- Attitude is a little thing that makes a big difference. Heart is what separates the good from the great.
- Show your customers how much you care about them, and they will show you how much they care about you / us.
- Doing the best at this moment puts you into the best place for the next moment. Our brightest blazes are commonly kindled by unexpected sparks.

(Pep: 40 years of honesty, passion and resourcefulness)

... constantly revitalizing itself – a goal that could be achieved through continuous feedback, higher levels of learning and stretch goals.

www.pepstores.co.za

Labuschaigne broke down levels of hierarchy within Pep by introducing a less formal dress code. He encouraged more decentralized decision-making and personal initiative. He fostered communication across all levels of staff by sharing company performance, new initiatives and more. He personally set about motivating staff through his PEP-permints (i.e., 'words of wisdom') that he shared with staff via email. And he instilled a culture of learning and performance by establishing retail courses and training programs in conjunction with a local university.

Responding to change

Market research was conducted to identify why Pep had lost customers, and as a result, revenue and profit. The results showed that Pep customers 'had become more sophisticated'. Broadly speaking, the change was the result of the socio- economic impact of the long-overdue arrival of democracy in South Africa. Denied dignity and respect for so long, the elections filled ordinary South Africans with hope, new aspirations, and the desire to 'be somebody'. Even if home and motorcar ownership remained dreams for many people, 'anyone could gain status by dressing smartly'.

The research further pointed out that Pep was considered cheap, and so was the merchandise. Pep responded by upgrading its product range without increasing prices; putting pressure on suppliers to improve quality; implementing stock distribution programs that could track customer preferences at each store; enhancing store layouts and appearance by introducing aesthetic standards, and printed price cards and point of sale material. The corporate identity (logo), while retaining its original character, was modernized. New products and services were also introduced by Pep based on changing consumer needs and spending patterns.

The arrival of cellular phones in South Africa meant that consumers were spending a portion of their disposable income on something other than clothing. In response, Pep began selling airtime, and was the first company in South Africa to sell it electronically, as well as to introduce mobile electronic airtime tills during peak times when the store tills were busy. This innovation arose as a result of Frank Bavenboer, Pep Operations Finance Manager, who was sent to the Babson Retail College in America as part of Pep's executive management training programmed. While in New York, Bavenboer noticed that the bus companies were selling tickets from portable tills, and implemented the concept in Pep stores. Pep Bank also was introduced, leveraging Pep's brand name and relationship with the target market and its distribution network, with the running of the bank left to an established South African banking institution.

While Pep had started to follow its shoppers into the urban areas almost a decade before, changing consumer habits meant that more of Pep's market were now not just shopping in metropolitan areas, but in the shopping malls. As a result, 167 unprofitable stores were closed within a few years and Pep moved where its customers were going, opening 11 stores in shopping malls in 2000 alone. By 2000, the efforts were bearing fruit: Pep enjoyed a 180 per cent increase in operating profit to R118 million in that year, and in 2002 posted an operating profit of R220 million. Other favourable outcomes included a market share increase of 20 per cent between 2000 and 2002, improving staff morale, and stronger supplier relations.

But not everything went smoothly. When management challenged staff to reduce shrinkage (i.e., stock losses), one outlet responded inappropriately in August 2000. The white manager of the Louis Trichardt (Northern Cape) Pep store and one of the shop assistants stripped a young black shopper partially naked and painted her with PVC paint, after allegedly catching her shoplifting underwear worth R2.99. The national press got wind of the story and it threatened to be a public relations disaster in a country where the humanistic philosophy of ubuntu (*viz.*, 'a person is a person through other people') is a cherished cultural norm. Pep responded by publishing full-page advertisements in many newspapers apologizing for the incident. The staff involved were immediately suspended and dismissed after due process.

Aiming high: The R1BOP challenge

Having weathered the storms of the 1990s, and encouraged by improved performance in the early years of the new decade, it was time for a change. Operations Director and board member George Steyn was appointed as Managing Director of Pep in 2005, after serving approximately 20 years with the firm. He

began his Pep career as an assistant store manager and worked his way through various divisions of the business including logistics, planning and buying. Under Steyn's leadership, the organization immediately set itself a new goal: to achieve R1 billion operating profit by the year 2009. The goal was communicated to all staff, and internally the project was given a name: R1BOP (R1 Billion Operating Profit). A R1BOP strategy was agreed, with new revenue and expense targets that challenged the business to be more efficient. 'Every department has a challenge to save costs,' says Marcus Banga, Marketing Director of Pep. 'This is a no frills business, but it's a nice business, a *lekker* business', he adds.

In November, 2006, Steyn made the retailer's goal public in a press release. Having delisted from public trading in previous years, Pep was not obliged to divulge any financial information, yet Pep publicized its ambitions and revealed that annual turnover to June 2006 was over R5 billion. It offered the media and public a glimpse of just how profitable the Pep business was. By the time of the announcement, turnover growth at Pep in the year to date was up 20 per cent, even though core products had not performed as well as expected for the previous four months. In the public announcement of Pep's R1BOP target, Steyn reiterated the chain's commitment to continually offer low prices in order to grow market share and anticipated turnover growth of between 15 per cent and 20 per cent per year for the coming five years. Low prices would be maintained by dropping the margins on clothing and leveraging the efficiencies generated by economies of scale. At the time of the announcement, Pep viewed its strategic response to market demands as two distinct parts: 'what the customers don't see' and 'what the customers see', essentially the internal workings of the organization that facilitated market orientation and the market oriented Pep that customers interacted with.

What the customers don't see

The Sikhula KunYe corporate culture was instilled and going strong by 2006. Pep emphasized performance among its staff through various awards and sales targets and awarded prizes based on performance (stores were categorized by tiers in terms of turnovers; e.g. R5 million stores, R10 million stores etc.) as well as an annual 13th paycheck for all staff. The most prestigious of these are the national and regional Sikhula KunYe Awards, which are awarded annually in Cape Town to 'Dynamos' who best live the Pep culture according to the votes of fellow employees. The prize includes cash, a floating trophy, and most considerable esteem in the firm.

Pep is probably one of the few companies in the world where people so actively share and live the corporate culture.

Marcus Banga, Pep Marketing Director

Canteens and social events were fostering much greater connectedness among staff. Regular information sessions were facilitating the sharing of customer knowledge as well as corporate strategies and performance milestones among the whole organization. *KwaPep,* Pep's internal magazine, regularly listed all members of staff who had recently celebrated long service awards. In February 2007, 126 staff had observed anniversaries for service exceeding 20 years, 53 for 25 years, and 25 for 30 years. More than 180 others observed more than 10 years of service.

Pep formalized most roles and responsibilities within the organization. This included formalizing expectations for teamwork, so that knowledge and problem solving were shared. The marketing team worked closely with sales and operations to deliver better products to customers and work more efficiently. Pep felt it centralized decision-making more than at other companies – to the degree that some decisions that were previously delegated to the regions, had been brought back under the authority of central office. Pep's point of view was that with 1400 stores, effective delegation of decision-making was a big challenge. Centralization was a calculated choice based on the Pep business model, because, according to Marcus Banga, centralization simplified processes, helped to save costs, and contributed to the company's national competence.

Pep realized early on the importance of investing in and establishing business processes and information technologies to facilitate operational efficiencies and keep costs down. By the time of the R1BOP challenge, many of the systems that had been in planning for many years were now being implemented. However, even in the investment of systems that would help Pep to improve efficiencies and cut costs, the firm maintained its cost savings approach to business.

What we have is what is necessary to help us run our business – it's the stuff that will make us better than we are now. This is because it's not technology that drives growth but the use and application of it. We want to arrive at the point where we are comfortable with what we have.

Technology is expensive and it changes regularly. We are a business that needs to manage costs – if not we will be expensive to the customer.

Marcus Banga, Pep Marketing Director

Steyn was well aware that cost cutting only went so far in achieving the R1BOP operating profit objective, Pep had to strengthen its marketing efforts. Pep's management reaffirmed its commitment to marketing by allocating generous marketing budgets and appointing Marcus Banga as Marketing Director in early 2006.

Under Labuschaigne's direction, most advertising functions were outsourced to an advertising agency. Banga established Pep's marketing function and brought advertising back in-house to be part of the marketing function. This move was intended to avoid the duplication of effort that often occurs between a client's marketing department and the agency's advertising executives. It also facilitated quicker turnaround of creative work. A more streamlined briefing process was created, which entailed a standard brief format. This included a list of standard questions to make sure 'everyone at Pep and the agency was on the same page':

1. Do we have enough merchandise to run the promotion?
2. Are we getting good mileage from our spend?
3. Have we got Point of Sale to support the promotion?
4. Does it reach our customers (in the case of pamphlets)?
5. Is it relevant to the customer?
6. What are the key messages?
7. What are the creative parameters?
8. Is this a call to action, or a normal advert?

The new brief paid immediate dividends. Banga proudly related the success of the previous three promotions Pep had run, describing it as 'unprecedented'. Consumer off-take of promotion items over three days had exceeded expectations considerably. One example of the success of recent campaigns was the Birthday Promotion Cellular Deal: The two-week plan was to sell 50 000 units, but 40 000 units were sold during the first week alone. In July 2007, Pep flighted its first brand advertisement on *Generations* on SABC1 (South African Broadcasting Corporation Channel 1) as part of its brand repositioning.

Banga felt that success depended on Pep sourcing the lowest cost merchandise of the highest quality from around the world, but predominantly China. Some products were imported from Africa, including Zimbabwe, Lesotho, and Zambia. Local suppliers were also used, although a big challenge was to find local suppliers who could produce the quantities required by Pep in the time frame provided. The emphasis on low-cost made it critical for the buyers to locate good quality products at reasonable prices. Since the beginning, Pep's focus had been on providing basic items of good quality and low price. Fashion items had been avoided due to the higher cost and perceived inconsistency with the Every Day Low Prices strategy. Pep does not hold sales and only occasionally marks items down. Unsold seasonal basic items were put back into storerooms until the following season, whereas fashion items would not have been saleable a year later. However, to instil a sense of excitement in the merchandise offering, and to complement the range of basic items that the stores sold, Pep often uses opportunistic buying to provide high fashion items and international brands at very low prices to its customers.

Pep also owns its own factory, which it ran as a cost rather than a profit centre, with the objective being to break even and pass the cost savings on to the customer. The factory manufactures Pep's school wear (Pep's share of the school wear market is above 50 per cent) and other items. The factory employed 2200 people, and consistent with its caring culture, which one Pep employee described as paternalistic, the factory only operated a day shift from 8am to 5pm.

What the customers see

Pep viewed its offering to its customers as a pentagon, the five corners representing:

- Place – size, location, layout and design of stores
- Sales force – service, knowledge, climate
- Communications – positional and promotional
- Product – Style and fashion, intensity, assortment
- Value – price and quality.

In 2006, Pep continued with store refurbishments, an ongoing programme that began three years earlier. This programme saw existing stores being upgraded and new stores boasting a cleaner, more departmentalized look. These new-look stores – there were 250 of them, out of a total of 1300 stores, by 2006 – were described within Pep as 'Blue Sky' stores. Blue Sky concept stores were designed to address public perceptions of Pep outlets, which shoppers sometimes described as 'clumped' and 'filthy'.

Pep stores were designed to 'scream', with loud colours and big price points, and lots of clothes piled onto shelves and clothing racks, creating a 'bargain-store' feel but also the feel of a leading chain. When the Blue Sky layout was implemented, stores retained their customary bazaar-like character, but featured increased departmentalization to capitalize on shopper problem solving. The bazaar-like feel ensured that Pep was a 'fun place to shop' and reaffirmed the positioning as a discount retailer. The upgrading of the interiors communicated the desire to treat Pep customers to a satisfying shopping experience. Banga commented that the result was a retail outlet that felt like the clothing it sold: low cost but not cheap. Shopping centre managers approved of the new Blue Sky stores. This was important for Pep because traditional customers were doing more shopping in regional malls in addition to traditional store locations near commuter hubs and on busy streets.

Customer service starts with staff

Staff morale and its implications for improved customer service also motivated the Blue Sky store initiative. Customer service had always been a priority at Pep. A book was commissioned to celebrate the retailer's 40th birthday in 2005. Called *Pep Stories: 40 Years of Honesty, Passion and Resourcefulness,* the book contained over 100 stories submitted by Pep staff. Many proudly related anecdotes of satisfied customers, and employees going the extra mile. One of the stories was about an elderly lady who collapsed in a chemist, but made her way across the road to the local Pep store because, her husband said, she knew she would be looked after by Pep staff. 'The focus on the customer is huge,' says Banga.

Pep's approach to customer service started with a focus on Pep staff, who were encouraged to love and respect themselves and then translate what they felt for themselves to what they felt for the customer and coworkers. This was an extension of the Sikhula KunYe culture, which encompassed personal growth, growth of colleagues and growth of customers. Simply put, staff were expected to be 'ladies and gentlemen serving ladies and gentlemen'. Pep's mandate to all staff was that all customers should be treated with dignity and respect, friendliness and personal service. Especially in the rural areas and small towns, where Pep still had the majority of their stores and dominated

Somewhere in South Africa lives a man called Pepsy, so named because a Pep store manager in the town where he was born opened his store on a freezing cold night to help the newborn's father choose clothes for him because his birth had come sooner than expected. Elsewhere there are three triplets called Patience, Esther and Purity. Their unemployed mother named them for the three letters P.E.P. after a Pep store manager arranged for a donation of clothes for the three newborns, whose overwhelmed and poverty-stricken mother had only expected to give birth to one child. These are just two of many stories contained in *Pep Stories: 40 Years of Honesty, Passion and Resourcefulness* that illustrate how Pep staff go out of their way for their customers, and how much that effort is appreciated.

the clothing market, 'everyone knew everyone' and store managers developed close personal relationships with all their customers.

Changing customers and merchandising

Over the years, the traditional focus on clothing, footwear, and textiles for the whole family changed. Stores sold an FMCG[3] range of brand name washing powders, dishwashing liquid, toiletries, household cleaners, baby products, and other goods. Priced at or below major supermarket prices, Pep stocked these items as an added value service. This was especially true in the rural towns where small 'spaza' shops charged a premium for FMCGs, due to higher distribution costs and lack of competition on FMCG brands. Pep's logistics network delivered quality brands to customers where they wouldn't otherwise receive them and appreciated it, according to Banga.

Other successful new product line additions since 2005 included a health and wellness range, homeware merchandise in certain stores, and white goods and household appliances. The health and wellness range consisted of natural (non-pharmaceutical) products, including a male libido booster, a herbal mixture containing African potato extract, an elixir recommended to boost energy levels and help with arthritis and rheumatism, and a nutritionally enriched dry cereal that could be mixed with milk or warm water. According to Banga, the wellness range was enormously popular during the test phases, and the products were 'flying off the shelf'. He felt that this range was another value added product for low-income consumers, who were very often not able to access adequate health services, especially in the rural areas.

The new homeware departments in some Blue Sky stores were so successful that Pep decided to introduce stand-alone Pep Home-ware stores. Home-ware merchandise included bedding, towels, bathroom accessories, cooking utensils, glassware, and other items. The rationale behind the introduction of such goods was based on the changing demographics and psychographics of its traditional customer base. Increased government spending, low interest rates, relatively strong economic growth, and increasing consumer credit benefited the growing emerging middle class. Home ownership increased as people moved into better accommodation. The desire to beautify the home was universal and affordable decorative items helped customers to feel good about their homes and themselves – an extension of Pep's core mission.

Pep also introduced white and electronic goods, such as fridges, microwaves, flat screen televisions, and DVD players. These goods were not held in stock at the stores, but rather advertised and showcased in catalogues prominently displayed in-store. Goods ordered in-store were collectable by customer's home within seven days. These white goods were described internally by Pep as 'good quality'. Recognized low-end brands, such as Hi-Sense and Telefunken, were backed by after-sales service, manufacturer guarantees, and Pep's guarantee that applied to all merchandise. While the product line had not been heavily promoted by Pep, with only pamphlets being used to communicate price and availability, the catalogue concept and product range was proving to be exceptionally lucrative for the stores as it achieved double digit growth rates each year. Banga's belief was that catalogue selling had much more potential and that the concept could be used to sell a whole host of other goods.

Pep had always made heavy use of pamphlet distribution as their primary means of advertising, and this was still the case in 2007. Pep also used television (mainly SABC 1, the TV channel most watched by its target market) to advertise its promotions and merchandise. More work also was being done to build the Pep brand, but not by using the traditional above-the-

---

[3]Fast moving consumer goods, also called consumer packaged goods in some countries.

line brand-building commercials, about which Banga said, 'No one believes those "airy-fairy" ads.'

Activities planned to build the Pep brand and counter the 'cheap and nasty' image people had of Pep included partnering with *Generations* (the popular TV drama) so that Pep was written into the story line; sponsoring the *Wini-Khaya* programme (a TV show where people sent an SMS costing R7.50 and stood a chance to win a home), and *The Pep Challenge,* a 3-minute TV insert in which Pep clothing was compared to similar merchandise from other stores. Some inserts featured 'quality experts' who appraised the two products and concluded which offered better quality. Pep also placed fashion spreads in the popular magazines *You, Huisgenoot* and *Drum,* which showed readers how to mix and match Pep items for maximum fashion effect. Radio also was employed to advertise great deals at Pep.

Even with the trend towards consumer credit, Pep had remained steadfast in its refusal to issue store credit. According to Banga, South Africa had an 80–90 per cent rejection rate for store credit applications, and for Pep customers, a store credit rejection would be a personal rejection. 'Customers tend to believe that brands believe in them,' said Banga, 'and a credit rejection destroys this notion.' Pep also felt strongly that customers didn't need credit to shop at Pep. It was with a sense of paternalism that Pep decided not to give credit to customers. Instead, all stores offered a lay-by service whereby customers could pay a small deposit to have their chosen items set aside and the rest of the purchase price paid in instalments.

While Pep acknowledged that they had lost some customers to competitors offering credit, Banga believed that customers would return to Pep after buying expensive items and reaching maximum credit limits on store credit cards. He also noted that rising interest rates were making credit purchases more expensive and driving customers back to Pep. In late 2006, it was reported that Pep's main competition, Jet Stores (which offered credit), had experienced less than expected performance, with sales growth of 12 per cent. The financial press suggested Jet's performance was due to the effects of rising interest rates on credit retailers.

Marketing's role in the R1BOP challenge

The R1BOP challenge was based on a simple premise: to be profitable and remain faithful to its EDLP strategy, Pep had to run on an EDLC (Every Day Low Cost) basis. Eliminating bottlenecks caused by slow moving or non-selling merchandise in stores made an important contribution by opening shelf space for exciting new products and increasing inventory turnover. Banga felt that good marketing could contribute to achieving the R1 billion target by successfully repositioning Pep, attracting new customers, and improving perceptions of the product range. This would not only increase the number of shoppers but also their average purchase and off-take. The way to achieve these objectives, according to Banga, was to ensure that Pep stocked every basic item a customer would need in their home.

In order to keep customers and attract new ones, Pep also needed to differentiate itself from its competition in the market including discount retailers like Jet stores. Banga felt that Pep's quality was superior. He acknowledged that not providing credit had lost Pep some customers, but felt that Pep was winning them back with better quality and service. Pep's approach was to focus on what Pep did and strive to do it better rather than focus on what the competition was doing.

Banga distinguished between Pep customers who aspired to shop elsewhere and those that actually shopped there, acknowledging that many Pep customers would like to shop at top fashion stores.

Pep is not an aspirational brand, but it is an inspirational brand. Every time people start to accept Pep they feel inspired; they feel like something massive is happening in their lives.... Nobody aspires to be a Pep person, but we are giving them the inspiration to be the best they can be with what they have.

Marcus Banga, Pep Marketing Director

In 2006, more than 60 per cent of Pep's stores were located in the rural areas where Pep had originally established itself and remained virtually unchallenged. Its continued success derived from its low-cost and world-class logistics system and the low concentration of shoppers in rural areas. It was thought to be unlikely that the pricing advantages provided by these rural distribution and store network capabilities would be eroded easily by new or potential competition.

Shifting customer demographics presented an important challenge to Pep. Pep's traditional customers typically were classified as LSM 1–5[4], especially LSM 1–3. Living standards in the post-Apartheid-era were increasing

[4]LSMs (living standard measures) are a popular measure of objective well-being in emerging markets, see the South African Advertising Research Foundation website for more information (www.saarf.co.za).

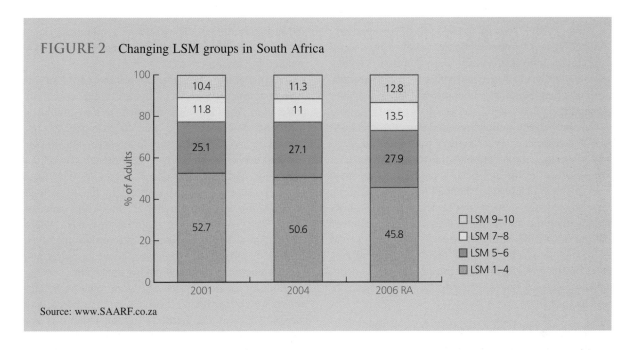

FIGURE 2 Changing LSM groups in South Africa

Source: www.SAARF.co.za

most rapidly in low LSMs (see Figure 2). Pep knew that customers were primarily from LSM 2 to LSM 6 and included all races. However, it was not clear how living standards or sociodemographics affected retail preferences or perceptions of Pep in the changing environment.

Repositioning the Pep brand

To understand the changing environment of retailing, Pep appointed a strategic marketing consultancy to segment the market and evaluate its brand positioning. The qualitative and quantitative research was conducted with a random sample of 1000 LSM2 to LSM7 consumers. It examined sociodemographic, behavioural, and life context dimensions, dreams for the future, spontaneous category associations, attitudes towards credit, and purchase behaviour. The result was a psychographic and sociodemographic profile for each segment that helped marketing and salespeople understand how segments answered questions such as 'Who am I?', 'What makes me different?', 'Where does clothing fit into my life?' and 'Why am I important to you (Pep)?' The results informed thinking about Pep's brand, guided buying, assisted with individual store strategies, and provided insight and understanding.

Gender, age, ethnicity, household income, life stage, geographical location and culture, and the quality of an existing relationship with Pep were identified as important influences. As an example, women placed considerable importance on the excitement of the shopping experience. They judged value by weighing complex attributes, such as quality, lowest price, and clothing style and fashion. They generally shopped with children or someone else, for themselves and others, and used their own and household funds for purchases. They often browsed but also shopped specific items. Although conscious of fashion brands, store brands and where one shopped had low importance. They preferred store credit to lay-by[5] and were frustrated by not being able to get credit at Pep. They spent a greater portion of their money on linen and health and beauty products.

In comparison, men said they never shop at Pep. They shopped mainly for themselves, when they did shop, and did not need store credit. They tended to shop for specific items and clothing style and fashion were important. Appearance was more important than practicality of clothing. They spent more of their budget on shoes, and regularly took their wife with them when they shopped. Ethnicity was related to shopping differences, although it was not clear how much of the difference was due to living standards and how much to culture. Black consumers often travelled by taxi to shop for predetermined items and paid for purchases with cash. Coloured shoppers used a motor car to visit a nearby mall to browse with children and bought mainly

---

[5]When something is sold on lay-by (also called layaway), the retailer holds the good from sale while the customer makes payments. The goods are released only when the price is paid in full.

on store credit. Neither group said they regularly shopped at Pep. However, Banga believed that social desirability influenced many Pep shoppers to deny shopping at the chain. He noted that focus group participants often admitted shopping at Pep only after prompting.

The probability sample included Pep customers and non-Pep customers. Pep shoppers were more likely to buy clothing, cellular products, airtime, and shoes at Pep, but not health and beauty products. They paid cash, planned in advance, shopped for a specific item, and wanted the lowest price. Unconcerned about brands, they did not socialize heavily. They preferred buying in cash or on lay-by because they were afraid of getting into debt. Most of their shopping money went on linen and financial services.

The shopping process of Pep customers typically was as follows:

- Someone in the household needed something
- They were informed of a special
- They compared prices
- They paid with cash
- They did not shop for special occasions or buy gifts.

People, who did not shop at Pep, typically spent money on cellular products and health and beauty products, bought on credit at a variety of stores, browsed for items, and sought the best quality. They spent more on cellular telephony, clothing, and appliances. When shopping, they typically:

- Were less likely to be prompted by practical considerations, such as a child outgrowing clothing.
- Browsed and tried clothing on that caught their attention
- Used a store credit card, not cash
- Did not shop alone
- Shopped for clothes for a special occasion.

Unaided awareness of Pep was higher among women and they were more likely to say they shopped there. Shoppers in metropolitan areas with more than 100 000 people spontaneously mentioned Pep less often than others. Shoppers in towns with populations below 100 000 mentioned Pep more frequently. They shopped mostly for clothing and shoes but not health and beauty aids. People in large towns went to a specific store for something new and generally paid in cash. People in towns with less than 8000 people planned purchases for specific items at specific stores and monitored prices. They were not influenced much by TV commercials, but read pamphlets. They avoided buying on credit.

In terms of age, spontaneous awareness for Pep was highest among people over 35 years of age, especially those over 50. Over 50s shopped at Pep regularly, spent more on linen, and paid in cash for specific items they had planned to buy in advance. The 35–44-year-old cohort spent more of their money on cellular telephony, did not consider brands important, and generally shopped when someone in the household needed something and sought out areas with a range of shops. The 16–24 cohort reported that they would never shop at Pep because they did not like the style. Further, they liked to try on items, loved shopping, and considered store and brand names important.

Clothing quality, price, fashion, and value for money were identified as the most important drivers of shopping choices and therefore suitable to be used as a basis for segmentation. Five consumer segments were identified (proportion of the total population):

1. Price: Consumers who buy primarily based on low price (24 per cent)
2. Price Plus: Consumers who buy based on a combination of price and quality (17 per cent)
3. Value: Consumers whose decision was based on 'value for money' (14 per cent)
4. Quality: Consumers who based their decisions on perceived best quality of goods (18 per cent)
5. Fashion: Consumers whose decision was based on fashion and style of merchandise (27 per cent)

The first two segments shopped at Pep more often than others. *Price* buyers also shopped at Ackermans. *Price Plus* buyers also shopped at Jet, Mr Price, and Ackermans. These low-income consumers shared common characteristics across segments. They placed more importance on 'the collective' than high-income consumers, who were more self-directed. People were more trusting than high-income consumers but were concerned generally about having enough money.

Using the results, Pep identified its core target market as parents with children and young single couples of all races between the ages of 25 and 40, in the LSM 2 to LSM 4 groups. Grandparents in LSM 2 to LSM 6 were also identified as a core target group. Parents with children and young singles between the ages of 25 and 40 within the LSM 5–6 group were identified as Pep's secondary market. The study resonated with management, confirming Pep's belief that their customers did not have enough money. They believed that their philosophy of helping everyone look and feel good remained relevant and that the product mix strategy based on 'everyday home essentials' was appropriate for the broader market. New findings offered Pep insight into the different needs and wants of different market segments, as well as how significant these differences were.

Banga felt that the varied aspirations of the segments were a key finding. Youth displayed high levels of personal aspiration. Parents and older consumers had much greater aspiration for their loved ones than themselves. They were the caretakers and care givers who were concerned for others and more hopeful for the future of others than for themselves. One of Pep's lessons from the segmentation was that the LSM 5–6 group was less of a key market than they had originally thought.

Even though the youth had no desire to shop at Pep according to the research, Banga believe they had potential to grow into Pep customers when they had children and faced the realities of constrained finances and expanding needs. In order to entrench the Pep

brand in their minds in the present, Pep was exploring introducing selected brand name clothing. However, these brands would need to appeal to the youth while still fitting into Pep's price range. 'We'll never be the Nike store, or even Edgars,' said Banga. 'We're cool being Pep.' Based on the research and findings, Pep's strategy going forward was to focus on the LSM2–4 group, whose typical household income ranged from R1200 to R3900 per month. This is where Pep 'dominated' and they would continue to focus their energies there. However, they realized that it was important to secure a foothold in the LSM 5 and 6 groups, as this market, while characterized as being more aspirational than a typical Pep customer, also liked a bargain. As one respondent said, even 'rich people' occasionally shopped for bargains at Pep for goods of a purely functional nature.

Conclusion

The new millennium had seen a dramatic turnaround in Pep's financial performance. The organization had

APPENDIX A: THE PEP RECIPE

We want to be:
- The best Clothing, Footwear, Textiles, Home ware and Cellular retailer by making it possible for everyone to look and feel good

Because we offer:
- The lowest prices for everyone
- A variety of up-to-date, durable products and an exciting shopping experience the biggest store network in the best possible locations
- The friendliest service

We manage to do this because we:
- Understand our customers
- Only employ honest and the most passionate and resourceful Dynamos
- Nurture a Sikhula KunYe culture that encourages growth, dignity, respect and fun are striving to the world-class by doing everything better every day
- Are supported by tailor-made and simple systems and processes
- Run the most effective distribution network
- Build strong, collaborative relationships with our suppliers operate at the lowest cost in everything we do
- Sell on a cash basis only

So that:
- We delight our customers
- Our Dynamos receive fair reward and recognition we create wealth for all stakeholders

been structured to meet the market's demands and gained new insights into its customers. New ambitions had been formulated and the whole organization was working towards the 2009 goal. But in order to satisfy customers and win new ones, Pep was investing heavily in advertising, store upgrading and broadening its product range, essentially evolving into a purveyor of everyday home essentials from its original positioning as a clothing, footwear, and textiles retailer. And these costs would have to come from somewhere.

Pep's R1BOP challenge was putting pressure on the organization to not only increase sales but also reduce costs, and the firm had acknowledged that increases in sales would have to be accompanied by decreasing costs. But if costs kept rising, and operating profit continued to increase, it would mean that the customer would have to pay for these investments at the till. And that would mean that Pep had, inadvertently, slipped back into being a value retailer rather than a lowest cost store.

Nestlé in 2008

By David E. Bell and Mary Shelman[1]

Choose the right direction, start walking and you have a good chance of getting there.

Old Chinese saying

Paul Bulcke looked out his office window onto the placid waters of Lake Geneva in April 2008 and thought about his new role as head of the world's largest food and beverage company. 'Our overall business vision of becoming the world's recognized leader in nutrition, health, and wellness remains unchanged,' the 29-year Nestlé veteran remarked. 'This is a very strong vision and the basic pieces are in place. Now it's up to us to make it work. My challenge is to deliver the organic growth and improved margins necessary to meet our targets. That will happen through swift execution.'

Nestlé's historic success was built on deep agricultural supply chains, strong local market teams, and strategic acquisitions. Sales in 2007 had for the first time exceeded CHF 100 billion[2] – a figure previous CEO and now Chairman Peter Brabeck referred to in Nestlé's 2007 annual report as an 'almost mystical barrier'. Looking to the future Bulcke commented, 'The biggest danger we face is that we become complacent.' In a company with an extensive portfolio of billion-dollar brands, years of rock-solid financial performance, and where the average tenure of managers was measured in decades, how was Bulcke to keep Nestlé moving forward with a sense of urgency when there were no big threats looming on the horizon?

Nestlé history

In 1867 pharmacist Henri Nestlé of the small lake town of Vevey, Switzerland, developed a nutritious infant formula from cow's milk, wheat flour, and a little sugar, to which he applied a unique drying process that retained most of the mixture's nutrients.

Created for mothers and babies unable to breastfeed, the formula proved effective in curbing infant mortality due to malnutrition. Nestlé marketed the formula as Farine Lactée Nestlé (Nestlé's Milk Cereal) and used the symbol of a bird feeding babies in a nest (the name Nestlé meant 'little nest' in German) as a trademark to give the company a clean, healthy, nurturing, and caring image. Sales soon expanded into other European countries, thereby giving the company an international orientation very early.

In 1905 Nestlé merged with its chief rival, the Anglo-Swiss Condensed Milk Company, ending years of fierce competition. The combined firm grew rapidly through mergers, geographical expansion, and entry into new product categories including chocolate. By the early 1900s, Nestlé operated milk and infant food processing plants in the United States (US), Britain, Germany, and Spain. The firm began manufacturing in Australia in 1907 and soon established warehouses in Singapore, Hong Kong, and Bombay to supply the rapidly growing Asian markets. In 1920 Nestlé opened a factory in Brazil, the first in a series of Latin American processing facilities.

As Nestlé entered into new markets it worked to establish local supply chains, which often meant organizing basic agricultural capabilities all the way back to the farm level.[3] The company's 'milk district model,' first introduced in Switzerland in the 1870s as a way to ensure adequate milk supplies, had been replicated and adapted for use in Latin America, the Caribbean, Asia, Africa, and most recently Inner Mongolia.

Throughout the years Nestlé constantly developed new products and improved and adapted existing ones to suit changing consumer tastes. In 1937, after eight years of development, Nestlé's R&D laboratories invented the '*Nescafé*' process to manufacture premium-quality soluble (instant) coffee. Initially created to help solve the Brazilian coffee industry's large coffee surplus, *Nescafé* revolutionized coffee drinking around the world. The same drying process was used

---

[1] Source: Copyright © 2008, 2009 President and Fellows of Harvard College.

[2] All amounts in the case are in Swiss francs (CHF) unless otherwise noted. On December 31, 2007, CHF 1.00 = $1.126.

[3] Although Nestlé worked back to the farm level, the company did not own any agricultural land or operate commercial farms.

to make *Nestea* (an instant tea) in the early 1940s. The chocolate powder *Nesquik* was introduced in 1948.

After World War II Nestlé merged with Maggi, a large European producer of food enhancers and prepared foods such as soups. Numerous acquisitions followed in canned and frozen foods, bottled water, ice cream, and pet foods. Nestlé encouraged managers of the acquired companies to stay, with new operations typically remaining intact and reporting to the Nestlé country managers in each market. Nestlé also expanded beyond food with the 1974 purchase of a 25 per cent interest in French cosmetics firm L'Oréal and the 1977 acquisition of Alcon Laboratories, a U.S. firm specializing in eye care products. (See Exhibit 1 for Nestlé timeline and key acquisitions.)

The Maucher years, 1980–1997

Seasoned Nestlé manager Helmut Maucher became CEO in 1980 at a critical time. After years of after-tax profits in excess of 4 per cent, profits had declined between 1978 and 1981. Maucher undertook a radical programme of change within the once highly bureaucratic company. He shed several underperforming brands, slashed inefficiencies, revived cash flows, reorganized top management, reinvigorated Nestlé's culture of quality, emphasized the value of the Nestlé brand umbrella, and refocused the firm's energies on remaining the world's leading branded food company.

Maucher extended the reach of the company beyond its core of coffee, milk, and chocolate-related products,

EXHIBIT 1   NESTLÉ TIMELINE AND SELECTED MAJOR ACQUISITIONS, 1866–2007

1866	Anglo-Swiss Condensed Milk Co.
1867	Henri Nestlé's infant cereal
1905	Nestlé & Anglo-Swiss Condensed Milk Co. (New name after merger)
1929	Peter, Cailler, Kohler, Chocolats Suisses S.A.
1938	*Nescafé* launch
1947	Nestlé Alimentana S.A. (New name after merger with Maggi)
1960	Cross & Blackwell (canned goods)
1969	Vittel (water), Deer Park (water)
1971	Ursina-Franck (Swiss food company)
1973	Stouffer (frozen foods)
1974	L'Oréal (cosmetics; minority interest)
1977	Nestlé S.A. (new name); Alcon (ophthalmology pharmaceutical company)
1985	Carnation (dairy, pet food and catering), Friskies (pet food)
1986	Herta (meat products)
1988	Buitoni-Perugina (Italian foods), Rountree (*KitKat, Smarties, After Eight*)
1992	Perrier (water)
1993	Finitalgel (ice cream)
1994	Alpo (pet food)
1998	San Pellegrino (water), Spillers Petfoods
2000	PowerBar (energy bar)
2001	Ralston Purina (pet food)
2002	Scholler (ice cream), Chef America (*Hot Pockets*)
2002	Alcon spin off and IPO
2003	Mövenpick (ice cream), Dreyer's Grand Ice Cream, Powwow (water)
2004	Valio (ice cream)
2005	Wagner, Proteika, Musashi (nutrition business)
2006	Jenny Craig (diet centers), Uncle Tobys (Australian breakfast foods)
2007	Novartis Medical Nutrition, Gerber (baby food), Henniez (water)

Sources: Company documents.

to new corners of the globe and into new product categories. Two primary objectives were to improve Nestlé's market share in the US and to make Nestlé the world leader in certain high growth market segments (e.g., mineral waters and chocolate/confectionery). The company's $3 billion takeover of the American food giant Carnation in 1985 was, at that time, one of the largest in the history of the food industry.

The Brabeck era, 1997–March 2008

Brabeck, another Nestlé veteran, became CEO in June 1997 upon Maucher's retirement. As articulated in his inaugural speech, Brabeck's goal was to achieve worldwide sustainable competitiveness through four 'strategic pillars': (1) low cost, highly efficient operations; (2) renovation and innovation of the Nestlé product line; (3) universal availability; and (4) improved communication with consumers through better branding. Together, these pillars would enable achievement of the 'Nestlé Model,' a term used to describe the company's long-term objectives of organic growth between 5 per cent and 6 per cent each year; continued year-after-year improvement in earnings before interest and tax (EBIT) margin; and improved capital management.

Brabeck made a number of moves to improve the performance and market orientation of the CHF60 billion company. The research and development (R&D) programme was restructured to be more responsive to consumers and to better deliver the 'renovation and innovation' necessary for organic growth. Previously composed of small decentralized units spread all over the world, R&D efforts were shifted to a few large, resource-intensive centers organized by product groups. Emphasis was put on looking for ways to reinvigorate old brands, such as finding multiple uses for them. An established brand such as *Nesquik*, for example, which was traditionally sold as a powder used in milk, was developed into syrup form and also into ready-to-drink varieties. Brabeck also launched a '60/40' preference rating system for products that required Nestlé offerings to be preferred by 60 per cent of participants in blind tests against direct competitors including other national brands and private labels. Products that failed to achieve the 60 per cent level were reformulated, discontinued, or sold.

In mid-2000 Brabeck initiated GLOBE (Global Business Excellence), a comprehensive information system that ultimately would tie all of Nestlé's businesses together under a common technology infrastructure. First introduced in 2002, GLOBE was designed to capture data (one of the first steps was the standardization of data based on the same definitions and units), manage information, and create knowledge which could be shared among the company's many SBUs and geographies. GLOBE's online real-time reports brought important insights into both the production and the selling sides of Nestlé's businesses. For the first time, managers could easily calculate total worldwide purchases of raw materials and the distribution of spending amongst suppliers. In addition, the firm could measure total worldwide sales to individual accounts, allowing for better customer management. GLOBE also allowed synchronization of data between manufacturing and retailers, leading to improved order fulfilment. And once tied into the GLOBE system, retailers could add new products to their store inventories with one 'click' of the mouse.

Over time, the company had in some instances moved away from its basic agricultural and processing roots. For example, several cocoa and dairy processing plants were sold and ingredients were bought from outside suppliers. 'We sold businesses where we could not add value,' explained CFO James Singh. 'In those cases buying the ingredient [instead of processing it yourself] may not cost you more and at the same time may relieve you of the need to invest in facilities and to devote attention to those businesses. For example, we got out of cocoa roasting but we did not get out of chocolate.'

Several major acquisitions during Brabeck's tenure solidified Nestlé's position in key categories such as bottled water, coffee, ice cream, and infant formula. A Nestlé manager explained that Brabeck 'acquired brands of great potential'. For example, the $10.3 billion purchase of Ralston-Purina in 2001 created a global platform for pet foods.

Brabeck was known for his vocal dismissal of two management paradigms popular in the 1990s: that all firms needed to undergo radical change to keep up and that firms should 'focus' in order to achieve operating efficiency. Instead, he championed a model of year-on-year growth even in the face of adverse external events, agile local businesses, and a strong company culture as 'the social glue that keeps everything together'.

During Brabeck's 12-year tenure as CEO, sales grew 78 per cent from CHF60.5 billion to CHF107.6 billion in 2007 while EBIT grew 142 per cent (from CHF6.2 billion to CHF15 billion). Nestlé's share price increased 323 per cent from CHF122.90 to CHF520.00 and shareholder returns during that period were 408 per cent. (See Exhibits 2, 3, 4, and 5 for financial information, Exhibit 6 for results of the Nestlé Model, and Exhibit 7 for results compared to selected competitors.)

Nestlé's new vision: Beyond food to nutrition, health, and wellness

Along with operational changes, Brabeck was instrumental in moving Nestlé from a technology- and processing-driven food and beverage company towards a broader vision of nutrition, health, and wellness. 'It all started with a fundamental strategic decision,' recalled Singh. 'The CEO, the Executive Board, and the board of directors all agreed that Nestlé should try to create a new industry. We recognized that consumers were increasingly aware of the link between food, health, and personal well being. Our ultimate goal was to be recognized by consumers as 'the' nutrition, health, and wellness company and to deliver a competitive return to our shareholders at the same time.'

Brabeck created a new Division of Nutrition that reported directly to the CEO. Three major acquisitions were made in the specialty nutrition area to establish a platform for growth: Jenny Craig (2006), a US chain of weight loss centres which allowed Nestlé to enter into the area of weight management; Novartis Medical Nutrition (2007), which reinforced Nestlé's position in healthcare nutrition; and Novartis's Gerber baby foods business (2007), which extended the company's leadership across key areas of infant nutrition. Singh explained how Nestlé targeted strategic acquisitions, using the Novartis examples: 'We identified these as

EXHIBIT 2   CONSOLIDATED INCOME STATEMENT 2007

In millions of CHF	2007	2006
Sales	107 552	98 458
Cost of goods sold	(45 037)	(40 713)
Distribution expenses	(9 104)	(8 244)
Marketing and administration expenses	(36 512)	(34 465)
Research and development costs	(1 875)	(1 734)
EBIT Earnings Before Interest, Taxes, restructuring and impairments	15 024	13 302
Net other income/(expenses)	(590)	(516)
Profit before interest and taxes	**14 434**	**12 786**
Net financing cost		
Financial income	576	537
Financial expense	(1 492)	(1 218)
	(916)	(681)
Profit before taxes and associates	**13 518**	**12 105**
Taxes	(3 416)	(3 293)
Share of results of associates	1 280	963
Profit from continuing operations	**11 382**	**9 775**
Net profit/(loss) on discontinued operations	–	74
Profit for the period	**11 382**	**9 849**
of which attributable to minority interests	733	652
of which attributable to shareholders of the parent (Net profit)	10 649	9 197
As percentage of sales		
EBIT Earnings Before Interest, Taxes, restructuring and impairments	14.0%	13.5%
Profit for the period attributable to shareholders of the parent (Net profit)	9.9%	9.3%
Earnings per share from continuing operations (in CHF)		
Basic earnings per share	27.81	23.71
Fully diluted earnings per share	27.61	23.56

Source: Company documents.

EXHIBIT 3   CONSOLIDATED BALANCE SHEET 2007

In millions of CHF	2007		2006	
Assets				
Current assets				
Liquid assets				
Cash and cash equivalents	6 594		5 278	
Short-term investments	2 902		6 197	
		9 496		11 475
Trade and other receivables		15 421		14 577
Assets held for sale		22		74
Inventories		9 272		8 029
Derivative assets		754		556
Prepayments and accrued income		805		594
Total current assets		**35 770**		**35 305**
Noncurrent assets				
Properly, plant, and equipment		22 065		20 230
Gross value	49 474		47 077	
Accumulated depreciation and impairment	(27 409)		(26 847)	
Investments in associates		8 936		8 430
Deferred tax assets		2 224		2 433
Financial assets		4 213		2 778
Employee benefits assets		811		343
Goodwill		33 423		28 513
Intangible assets		7 217		3 773
Total noncurrent assets		**78 889**		**66 500**
Total assets		**114 659**		**101 805**
Liabilities and equity				
Current liabilities				
Trade and other payables		14 179		12 572
Liabilities directly associated with assets held for sale		7		–
Financial liabilities		24 541		15 494
Tax liabilities		856		884
Derivative liabilities		477		470
Accruals and deferred income		3 266		3 059
Total current liabilities		**43 326**		**32 479**
Noncurrent liabilities				
Financial liabilities		6 129		6 592
Employee benefits liabilities		5 165		5 415
Deferred tax liabilities		1 398		706
Other payables		1 081		366
Provisions		3 316		3 039

In millions of CHF		2007		2006
Total noncurrent liabilities		**17 099**		**48 957**
Total liabilities		**60 425**		**48 957**
Equity				
Share capital		393		401
Share premium and reserves				
Share premium	5 883		5 926	
Reserve for treasury shares	7 839		4 550	
Translation reserve	(6 302)		(5 205)	
Retained earnings	52 285		49 963	
		59 705		55 234
Treasury shares		(8 013)		(4 644)
Total equity attributable to shareholders of the parent		**52 085**		**50 991**
Minority interests		2 149		1 857
Total equity		**54 234**		**52 848**
Total liabilities and equity		**114 659**		**101 805**

Source: Company documents.

EXHIBIT 4   CONSOLIDATED CASH FLOW STATEMENT 2007

In millions of CHF	2007	2006
Operating activities		
Profit from continuing operations	11 382	9 775
Less share of results of associates	(1 280)	(963)
Depreciation of property, plant, and equipment	2 620	2 581
Impairment of property, plant, and equipment	225	96
Impairment of goodwill	251	38
Depreciation of intangible assets	591	580
Impairment of intangible assets	6	–
Increase/(decrease) in provisions and deferred taxes	162	(338)
Decrease/(increase) in working capital	82	348
Other operating cash flows	(600)	(341)
Operating cash flow	**13 439**	**11 676**
Investing activities	**(4 971)**	**(4 200)**
Capital expenditure	(619)	(689)
Expenditure on intangible assets	323	98
Sale of property, plant, and equipment	(11 232)	(6 469)
Acquisition of businesses	456	447

In millions of CHF	2007	2006
Disposal of businesses	264	323
Cash flows with associates	26	(30)
Other investing cash flows	(15 753)	(10 520)
Investing cash flows		

	2007	2006
Financing activities		
Dividend paid to shareholders of the parent	(4 004)	(3 471)
Purchase of treasury shares	(5 455)	(2 788)
Sale of treasury shares	980	906
Cash flows with minority interests	(205)	(191)
Bonds issued	2 023	1 625
Bonds repaid	(2 780)	(2 331)
Increase in other noncurrent financial liabilities	348	134
Decrease in other noncurrent financial liabilities	(99)	(289)
Increase/(decrease) in current financial liabilities	9 851	6 393
Decrease/(increase) in short-term investments	3 238	6 393
Other financial cash flows	–	(4)
Financing cash flow	**3 897**	**(30)**
Translation differences on flows	(64)	(360)
Increase/(decrease) in cash and cash equivalents	**1 519**	**766**
Cash and cash equivalent at beginning of year	5 278	4 658
Effects of exchange rate changes on opening balance	(203)	(146)
Cash and cash equivalents retranslated at beginning of year	**5 075**	**4 512**
Cash and cash equivalents at end of period	**6 594**	**5 278**
Cash at bank and in hand	2 610	2 380
Time deposits	3 039	2 579
Commercial paper	945	319

Source: Company documents.

two objectives we wanted to accomplish. We believed they could be truly transformational to our business. We developed mutual value-added relationships with key executives at Novartis and waited for the appropriate time to execute.'

Yet the nutrition, health, and wellness vision was not limited to a single division; indeed, the new strategy would be implemented in all Nestlé categories from infant formula to candy to pet food. Committees of executives from different businesses and departments were assembled to informally discuss ways to promote well being through new product development

and also through improving the nutritional foundation of existing products.

The 60/40 benchmarking standard was enhanced to require a nutritional advantage, leading to '60/40+.' 'One of our opportunities is to update our current products to be relevant,' explained Singh. 'It's about taking out things – salt, sugar, fat – to give them a healthier profile and then putting in other things – whole grains, more calcium, Omega-3s, antioxidants – to make them more nutritious. Every year one-third of our product portfolio is 60/40+ tested.' Between 2003 and 2006, Nestlé adjusted recipes to remove 34 000 metric tons of

EXHIBIT 5   FINANCIAL INFORMATION – FIVE-YEAR REVIEW

In millions of CHF	2007	2006	2005	2004	2003
Results					
Sales	107 552	98 458	91 115	84 690	87 979
EBIT Earnings Before Interest, Taxes, restructuring and impairments	15 024	13 302	11 876	10 760	11 006
as % of sales	14.0%	13.5%	13.0%	12.7%	12.5%
Taxes	3 416	3 293	2 647	2 404	2 307
Net profit	10 649	9 197	8 081	6 621	6 213
as % of sales	9.9%	9.3%	8.9%	7.8%	7.1%
as % of average equity attributable to shareholders of the parent	20.7%	18.7%	18.6%	17.4%	17.3%
Total amount of dividend	4 691	4 004	3 471	3 114	2 800
Depreciation of property, plant, and equipment	2 620	2 581	2 382	2 454	2 408
as % of sales	2.4%	2.6%	2.6%	2.9%	2.7%
Balance sheet and cash flow statement					
Current assets	35 770	35 305	41 765	35 285	36 233
of which liquid assets	9 496	11 475	17 393	15 282	15 128
Noncurrent assets	78 889	66 500	60 953	51 832	53 328
Total assets	114 659	101 805	102 718	87 117	89 561
Current liabilities	43 326	32 479	35 854	29 075	30 365
Noncurrent liabilities	17 099	16 478	17 796	17 743	21 373
Equity attributable to shareholders	52 085	50 991	47 498	39 236	36 880
Minority interests	2 149	1 857	1 570	1 063	943
Net financial debt	21 174	10 971	9 725	10 171	14 355
Operating cash flow	13 439	11 676	10 205	10 412	10 125
as % of net financial debt	63.5%	106.4%	104.9%	102.4%	70.5%
Free cash flow	8 231	7 018	6 557	6 640	6 361
Capital expenditure	4 971	4 200	3 375	3 260	3 337
as % of sales	4.6%	4.3%	3.7%	3.8%	3.8%
Data per share					
Weighted average number of shares	382 880 947	384 801 089	388 812 564	388 449 957	387 018 429
Basic earnings from continuing operations	27.81	23.71	20.82	16.97	16.05
Basic earnings from discontinued operations	–	0.19	(0.04)	0.07	–
Equity attributable to shareholders	136.03	132.51	122.16	101.01	95.29
Dividend	12.20	10.40	9.00	8.00	7.20
Pay-out ratio based on total basic earnings per share	43.9%	43.5%	43.3%	46.9%	44.8%
Stock prices (high)	553.50	448.30	404.30	346.00	314.50
Stock prices (low)	426.50	355.00	298.30	276.00	233.30
Yield	2.2/2.9	2.3/2.9	2.2/3.0	2.3/2.9	2.3/3.1
Market capitalization	**195 661**	**166 152**	**152 576**	**115 237**	**119 876**
Number of personnel (in thousands)	**276**	**265**	**250**	**244**	**253**

Sources: Company documents.

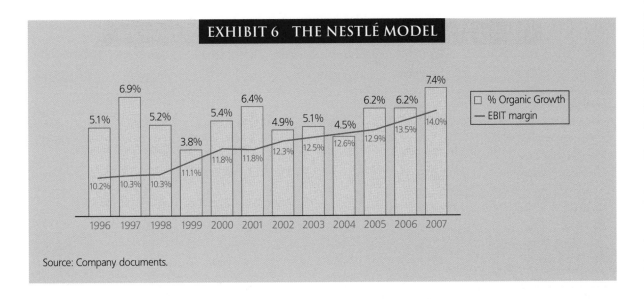

EXHIBIT 6 THE NESTLÉ MODEL

Source: Company documents.

trans fatty acids, 5000 metric tons of salt, and 204 000 metric tons of sugar from products. Nutritional improvements were also introduced in indulgence categories such as ice cream (e.g., Nestlé's *Dreyer's Slow Churned* brand used low temperature freezing technology that produced ice creams with 50 per cent less fat and 30 per cent less calories yet tasted as rich and creamy as their full-fat equivalents), confectionary (e.g., chocolate snacks made with healthy ingredients such as fibre or yogurt fillings), and chocolate (e.g., Nestlé supported Australia's 'switch to dark' campaign). For pet foods, Nestlé introduced offerings with natural ingredients and developed special formulations for different ages, sizes, and breeds.

Other target areas for nutrition, health, and wellness included:

Functional benefits. The firm looked to add new functional benefits – labelled by Nestlé as 'branded active benefits' or 'BABs' – to the main product platforms. For example, *Nido* powdered milk for children was expanded by adding probiotics and proprietary BABs which strengthened the child's defence against harmful germs, leading to unique products targeted at the 1+, 3+ and 6+ age segments. By 2008, 13 individual BABs had been developed and incorporated into hundreds of products to improve digestive health, immune defences, weight management, physical and mental development, and healthy aging.

Specialty nutrition products. Another opportunity was the development of scientifically proven products for people with special needs, such as infants and children, athletes, or those suffering from specific health conditions such as obesity or cancer or recovering from surgery or chemotherapy. For example, *Nutren Balance* bars were formulated to provide better glucose control for people with diabetes and *Clinutren* was a range of easy-to-digest oral nutritional supplements with high protein content to build muscle and promote recovery after surgery. Nutrition products could also assist with general malnutrition, a condition often found among the elderly even in wealthy countries.

Services. As nutrition became more tailored to individual situations and conditions, Nestlé leaders believed that services increasingly could complement a science-based product portfolio. For example, in the weight loss area Nestlé's Jenny Craig Centers provided members (who paid an annual fee) with weekly personal nutrition counselling sessions and an individualized food plan. The centres stocked and sold a broad line of frozen and shelf-stable foods carrying the Jenny Craig brand. Members unable to come to a center could receive nutritional and lifestyle advice on the Jenny Direct website and by phone, and order meals that were delivered directly to their homes. Another possibility under review was home delivery of special foods for those who were ill or lacked mobility. Nestlé HomeCare provided a broader offering by providing patients with a full service at home that included training by a dietician, product delivery, and access to a 24-hour hot-line.

One Nestlé manager characterized the company as being much better at thinking about what it wanted to be in 10 years' time compared to its competitors: 'Every food company talks about wellness, but Nestlé's product portfolio is better positioned to deliver wellness products. Dairy products, cereals, and water

EXHIBIT 7 SELECTED FOOD COMPANY RESULTS, 2003–2007

	2003	2004	2005	2006	2007
Nestlé					
Revenue ($ bil.)	65.6	70.0	73.8	78.3	89.8
Operating margin %	10.7	10.8	12.9	13.5	14.0
Profit margin %	9.4	9.2	11.2	13.3	12.6
Asset turnover	0.99	0.98	0.96	0.96	0.99
Return on assets %	7.02	7.60	8.94	9.60	10.52
Kraft					
Revenue ($ bil.)	31.0	32.2	34.1	34.4	37.2
Operating margin %	19.8	14.8	13.9	13.2	11.6
Profit margin %	11.1	8.3	7.7	8.9	10.0
Asset turnover	0.52	0.54	0.59	0.61	0.60
Return on assets %	5.97	4.47	4.56	5.50	4.19
General Mills					
Revenue ($ bil.)	10.5	11.1	11.2	11.6	12.4
Operating margin %	18.2	20.2	20.1	16.9	16.5
Profit margin %	8.9	9.5	11.0	9.411.0	13.1
Asset turnover	0.60	0.62	0.62	0.64	0.68
Return on assets %	5.75	9.79	6.86	5.99	6.29
Unilever					
Revenue ($ bil.)	53.9	54.6	48.6	52.3	58.8
Operating margin %	13.0	8.6	13.4	13.6	13.1
Profit margin %	10.6	7.1	12.0	12.2	12.9
Asset turnover	1.14	1.16	1.01	1.10	1.14
Return on assets %	7.36	5.43	10.14	13.87	11.69
Groupe Danone					
Revenue ($ bil.)	14.9	17.1	16.3	17.6	17.5
Operating margin %	12.2	12.4	13.1	13.3	12.1
Profit margin %	11.2	11.1	12.3	12.8	10.7
Asset turnover	0.88	1.00	0.87	0.84	0.58
Return on assets %	5.63	2.31	9.78	9.29	18.82

Source: Compiled from Hoover's, Morningstar, Reuters Financial, Nestlé Annual Reports (2002–2004), General Mills Annual Report (2004), and Groupe Danone Annual Report (2005).

just make more sense to consumers looking for a nutritional boost than colas and cookies. We have positioned ourselves to be ready.'

What should we eat?

The new nutrition, health, and wellness vision was enabled by basic scientific research and state-of-the-art tools such as nutrigenomics – the study of the relationships between diet, genes, function, and health – to produce revolutionary new product ideas. This called for a changed role for R&D, which historically had focused on improvements in raw materials or processing technologies.

'"What should we eat?" is the big question,' explained Werner Bauer, executive vice president of innovation, technology, research and development. 'The answer seems to change every day. The problem is in the translation of basic science into specific diet and nutrition recommendations. Over the last 10 years we have developed more specific understandings of the link between nutrition and health through nutrigenomics to replace the generalized knowledge we had before.'

Basic research was conducted at the Nestlé Research Center (NRC) in Switzerland, the biggest private facility for fundamental research on food, nutrition, and the link to health in the world. Overall, Nestlé Research comprised the NRC and 23 Product Technology and R&D centres worldwide that were focused on particular products or geographies. Nestlé also initiated a new model of 'open innovation' that encompassed more than 300 external research collaborations spanning a global network of more than 5000 scientists and technologists in top universities, research establishments, and private firms. Internal and external R&D efforts were augmented with investments in companies working on novel technologies and product ideas. In 2007, Nestlé committed to invest over CHF1.5 billion over the next 10 years in start-up and growth-phase companies in the areas of food, nutrition, health, and wellness.

According to Bauer, the focus on science-based nutrition and the internal goal of fewer and bigger breakthrough innovations was causing R&D efforts to move towards a pharmaceutical model, based on patents to protect core technologies, clinical trials, claims development, and regulatory approvals. The ultimate goal of research was to create an innovation pipeline with projects in different phases at any given time with some in development or conceptualization, some in clinical or consumer trials, and others in their launch phase.

Since many of the new products coming out of R&D had global applications, an 'innovation acceleration team' was created to support rapid product introductions. Composed of R&D and supply chain experts, the team's job was to act as a catalyst and execution specialist to coordinate product launches in multiple top priority markets. Prior to these teams, new products were introduced in markets only after the local country manager decided to add them to their portfolios.

Nestlé in 2008

Nestlé's food and beverage sales were CHF100.3 billion out of total group sales of CHF107.6 billion in

2007. Organic growth in food and beverages was 7.1 per cent, including 4 per cent real internal growth and 3.1 per cent due to price increases. EBIT of CHF15 billion rose by CHF1.7 billion over the previous year, even in the face of substantial increases in agricultural raw materials and distribution costs.

Product and brand portfolio

Nestlé's product portfolio ranged from baby food to coffee and ice cream to pet foods. About 70 per cent of sales came from 29 'billionaire' brands (see Exhibit 8); the umbrella Nestlé brand covered 40 per cent of group sales. While many brands were global, Nestlé believed that there was no standard worldwide taste: product formulations could vary widely from country to country, or even within a country. The firm organized its more than 8,000 products into five main business categories and two global divisions (see Exhibit 9). Nestlé main product categories included:

Powdered and liquid beverages. Nestlé beverage products included roast, ground, and instant coffee, teas, water (run as a globally managed business, see section below), and other products such as chocolate- and malt-based drinks. Billionaire brands in this group included *Nescafé* (the world's largest coffee brand, accounting for 23 per cent of global coffee consumption), *Milo*, *Nesquick*, *Nestea*, and *Nespresso* – a proprietary pod-based, individual-cup coffee brewing system that had become Nestlé's fastest growing product.

Milk products and ice cream. The category included dairy products such as powdered and condensed milks, ice cream, and yogurts. It also included Cereal Partners Worldwide, Nestlé's joint venture with General Mills for breakfast cereals outside North America. Billionaire brands in shelf-stable dairy included *Nestlé*, *Nido* (the world's leading brand of powdered milk for one-to-six year olds), *Coffee-mate*, and *Carnation*. Billionaire ice cream brands of *Nestlé*, *Dreyer's*, and *Edy's* were augmented by premium brands such as *Mövenpick* and *Häagen-Dazs*.[4]

Prepared foods and cooking aids. This division contained a wide variety of product lines, from frozen foods (e.g., *Stouffer's*, *Lean Cuisine*, *Hot Pockets*), to soups, bouillon, and sauces (*Maggi*, *Cross & Blackwell*), to pasta and sauces (*Buitoni*), to delicatessen products and cold meats (*Herta*).

---

[4]Nestlé licensed the Häagen-Dazs brand from General Mills.

EXHIBIT 8 PORTFOLIO OF BILLIONAIRE BRANDS

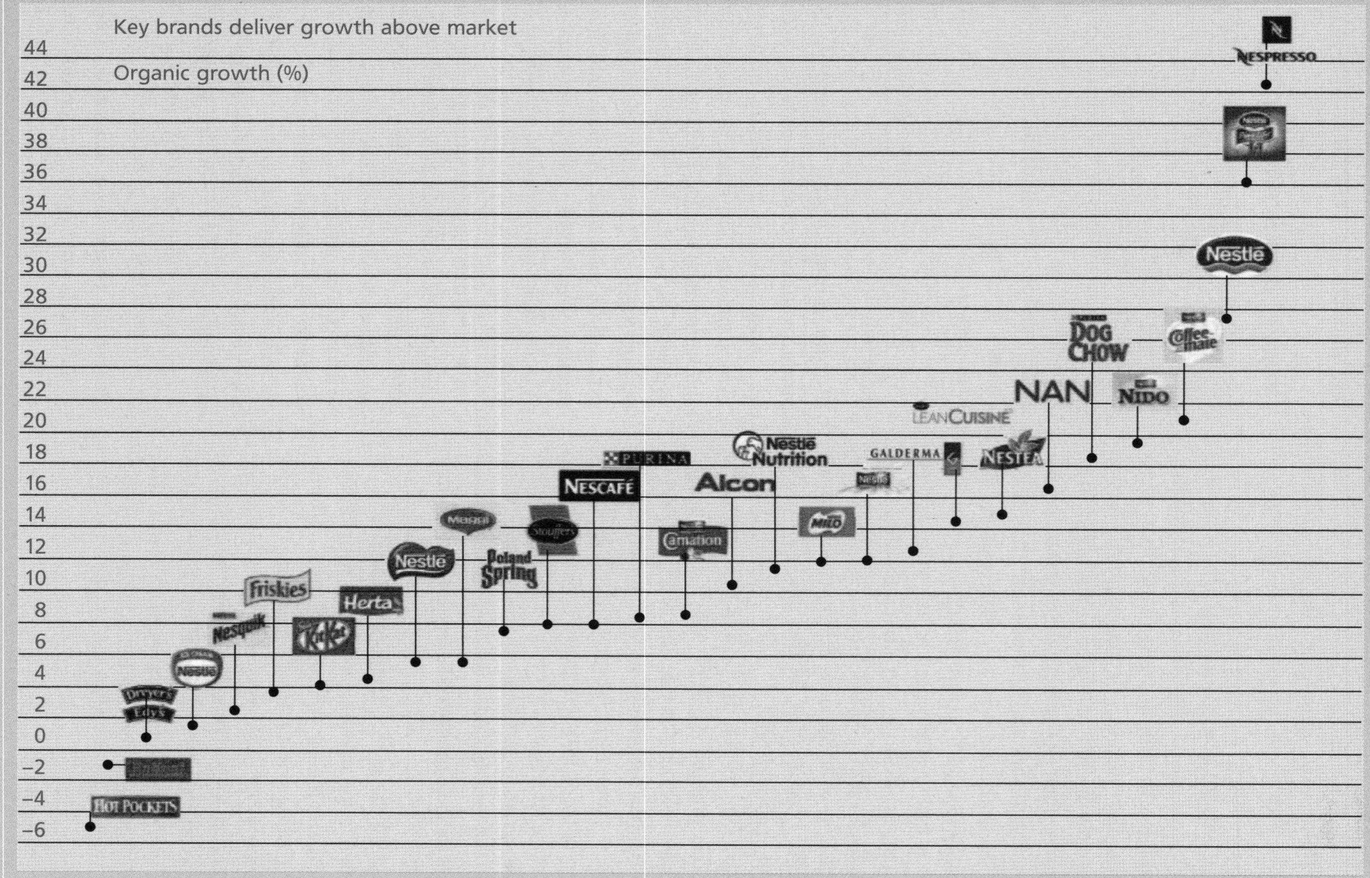

Key brands deliver growth above market

Organic growth (%)

Sources: Company documents.

EXHIBIT 9   RESULTS BY PRODUCT GROUP, 2005–2007

In millions of CHF	2005	2006	2007		RIG (%)	OG (%)
Beverages						
Soluble coffee	8 783	9 477	10 371	**36.7%**		
Nestlé Waters	8 787	9 636	10 404	**36.8%**		
Other	6 272	7 679	7 470	**26.5%**		
Total sales	23 842	25 882	28 245	**100.0%**	6.6	8.9
EBIT	4 131	4 475	4 854	**17.2%**		
Capital expenditure	752	1 105	1 409			
Milk products, Nutrition and Ice cream						
Milk products	9 881	10 820	11 742	**40.3%**		
Nestlé Nutrition	5 270	5 864	8 343	**29.0%**		
Ice cream	7 023	7 424	7 521	**25.8%**		
Other	1 101	1 227	1 409	**4.9%**		
Total sales	23 275	25 435	29 106	**100.0%**	2.8	8.3
EBIT	2 598	3 003	3 744	**12.9%**		
Capital expenditure	689	702	933			
Prepared dishes and cooking aids						
Frozen and chilled	9 656	10 307	10 705	**57.9%**		
Culinary and other	7 017	7 328	7 799	**42.1%**		
Total sales	16 673	17 635	18 504	**100.0%**	3.2	4.0
EBIT	2 176	2 323	2 414	**13.0%**		
Capital expenditure	261	272	305			
Confectionery						
Chocolate	8 640	9 103	9 754	**79.6%**		
Sugar confectionery	1 207	1 204	1 207	**9.9%**		
Biscuits	947	1,092	1,287	**10.5%**		
Total sales	10 794	11 399	12 248	**100.0%**	2.3	5.3
EBIT	1 257	1 309	1 426	**11.6%**		
Capital expenditure	194	258	316			
PetCare						
Total sales	10 569	11 420	12 130	**100.0%**	3.8	7.0
EBIT	1 532	1 730	1 876	**15.5%**		
Capital expenditure	274	345	402			
Nestlé FoodServices (Out-of-Home)						
Total sales	6 132	6 913	7 237	**100.0%**	2.5	5.5
Alcon						
Sales	5 452	6 123	6 679	**100.0%**	10.6	10.7
EBIT	1 751	2 038	2 326	**34.8%**		
Capital expenditures	195	267	264			
Health and beauty joint ventures						
Nestlé's share of sales	510	564	640			
Associated companies						
Nestlé's share of results	896	963	1 280			

Notes: RIG = Real Internal Growth; OG = Organic Growth.

Confectionary. Nestlé was the world's leading chocolate and confectionery company with approximately 8.1 per cent global market share including Geroto in Brazil. Leading global brands such as *Nestlé, Crunch,* and *KitKat* (except in the US where it was sold by Hershey) were complemented by strong local brands such as *Cailler, Milky Bar, Baby Ruth,* and *Butterfinger.*

PetCare. With its 2001 acquisition of Ralston Purina, Nestlé became the second largest pet food company in the world with a 24.8 per cent share by 2007. Billionaire pet food brands included *Purina, Dog Chow,* and *Friskies.* Nestlé estimated the global dog and cat food market at $46 billion in 2007. The 60/40+ test was also applied to pet care products and Purina scientists carried out over 20 000 taste tests each year.

Pharmaceutical. Nestlé's non-food interests included majority ownership of Alcon and minority ownership of L'Oréal, the world's largest cosmetics company. Nestlé also had two joint ventures with L'Oréal: dermatology-focused Galderma and Laboratoires innéov, focused on beauty-related nutritional supplements sold in pharmacies.

In addition to product categories, there were two globally managed businesses in early 2008:

Nestlé Waters. By 2007, Nestlé Waters included 72 brands of bottled water sold worldwide. Billionaire brands included Nestlé *Pure Life,* which was sold around the world, and *Poland Spring.* Water was produced at 100 factories in 38 countries. Almost 50 per cent of water sales were in North America, 44 per cent in Europe, and 7 per cent in other regions. *Pure Life* (a purified, mineralized, bottled water) was a good example of Nestlé's innovative research, explained Bauer:

> *Obviously water itself is not an invention but what you do with it is. Our objective was to make a good quality water that we could sell around the world at an affordable price, which is especially important in areas where the local water is not safe to drink. We were tired of relying on local sources [of water], which varied tremendously due to mineral content and purity. So the CEO asked if we could make clean and nutritional water in a factory. Our research team designed a process where first we take everything out of the local water, then remineralize it to meet the local country tastes. Pure Life varies by country, but what is similar is the engineering – the technology behind it.*

Nestlé Nutrition. This stand-alone, globally led business unit was comprised of four businesses: infant nutrition; healthcare nutrition; performance nutrition; and weight loss. Nestlé was the world leader in infant nutrition (over 70 per cent of Nestlé Nutrition sales in 2007); the world number two in healthcare nutrition; the world leader in science-based performance nutrition; and the North American leader in customized weight management. Billionaire nutrition brands included *Nestlé, NAN* (infant formula), and *Gerber* (which was a multi-billionaire brand).

Organization

Although Nestlé employed over 275 000 people and sold products in 130 countries, the Nestlé organization was decentralized and relatively flat. The CEO and 12 top managers formed the Executive Committee, which reported to the board of directors (see Exhibit 10). Forty-three regional organizations reported to three zones (Zone Europe, Zone Americas, and Zone Asia, Oceania and Africa), each run by a zone manager who was located at Nestlé headquarters. They managed their zones by region, working with each regional and country manager to set revenue and profit goals. (See Exhibit 11 for sales by zone.)

Country managers – called market heads – were given a large degree of autonomy in matters dealing directly with consumers. The company felt local management understood the cultural traits, tastes, and motivations of consumers, and could best translate that knowledge into products tailored to meet their needs, which in turn would lead to long-term consumer-product relationships. Nestlé was considered a local company in many countries, remarked Corporate Communications Director Rudolph Ramsauer: 'The Nestlé market head is very well respected. In smaller countries, they almost have official status – like an ambassador would.'

Nestlé's policy was to develop local management as soon as possible; however, Francisco Castañer, executive vice president in charge of human resources, explained that this took time:

> *People begin down in the ranks and then move up over time. We invest a lot in training and in giving cross experiences. As managers move to different assignments around the world, they get to know others at their level and this forms a strong bond. For example, in China, India, and Russia today our top managers are primarily expats. In comparison, we have nationals running Brazil and Mexico where we started several decades ago.*

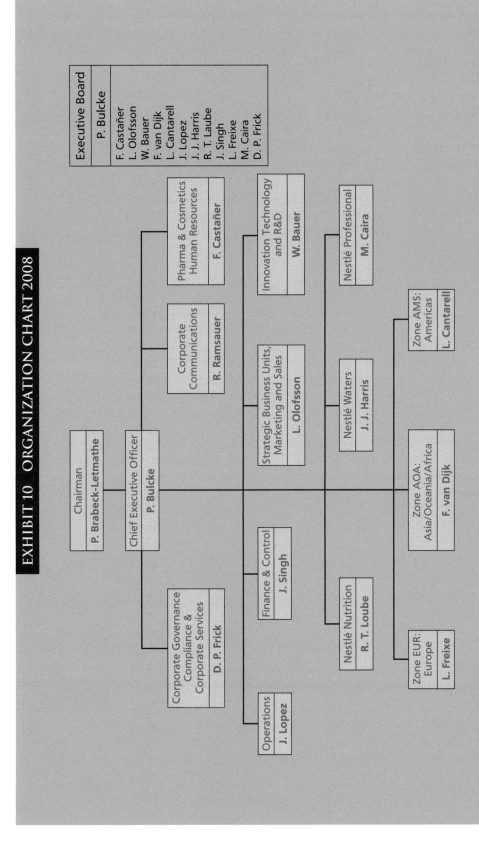

EXHIBIT 10 ORGANIZATION CHART 2008

Executive Board

P. Bulcke

F. Castañer
L. Olofsson
W. Bauer
F. van Dijk
L. Cantarell
J. Lopez
J. J. Harris
R. T. Laube
J. Singh
L. Freixe
M. Caira
D. P. Frick

Chairman
P. Brabeck-Letmathe

Chief Executive Officer
P. Bulcke

Corporate Governance Compliance & Corporate Services
D. P. Frick

Finance & Control
J. Singh

Operations
J. Lopez

Corporate Communications
R. Ramsauer

Pharma & Cosmetics Human Resources
F. Castañer

Strategic Business Units, Marketing and Sales
L. Olofsson

Innovation Technology and R&D
W. Bauer

Nestlé Nutrition
R. T. Loube

Nestlé Waters
J. J. Harris

Nestlé Professional
M. Caira

Zone EUR: Europe
L. Freixe

Zone AOA: Asia/Oceania/Africa
F. van Dijk

Zone AMS: Americas
L. Cantarell

Sources: Company documents.

EXHIBIT 11 RESULTS BY GEOGRAPHIC AREA, 2005–2007

In millions of CHF	2005	2006	2007		RIG (%)	OG (%)
Zone Europe						
Western	22,726	23,241	24,476	86.0%		
Eastern and Central	2,873	3,411	3,988	14.0%		
Beverages	5,286	5,598	6,168	21.7%		
Milk products and Ice cream	3,295	3,436	3,556	12.5%		
Prepared dishes and cooking aids	8,631	8,858	9,254	32.5%		
Confectionery	5,025	5,174	5,593	19.6%		
PetCare	3,362	3,586	3,893	13.7%		
Total sales	25,599	26,652	28,464	100.0%	2.0	3.0
EBIT	3,082	3,109	3,412	12.0%		
Capital expenditure	797	812	932	3.3%		
Zone Americas						
USA and Canada	19,412	20,603	20,824	63.3%		
Latin America and Caribbean	9,544	10,684	12,093	36.7%		
Beverages	3,505	3,770	4,007	12.2%		
Milk products and ice cream	8,787	9,470	10,159	30.9%		
Prepared dishes and cooking aids	5,916	6,395	6,543	19.8%		
Confectionery	4,117	4,420	4,678	14.2%		
PetCare	6,631	7,232	7,539	22.9%		
Total sales	28,956	31,287	32,917	100.0%	3.3	8.1
EBIT	4,364	4,946	5,359	16.3%		
Capital expenditure	908	1,125	1,371	4.2%		
Zone Asia, Oceania and Africa						
Oceania and Japan	4,676	4,624	4,571	27.6%		
Other Asian markets	5,626	6,466	6,983	42.2%		
Africa and Middle East	3,994	4,414	5,002	30.2%		
Beverages	5,168	5,436	5,685	34.3%		
Milk products and Ice cream	4,854	5,365	5,572	34.4%		
Prepared dishes and cooking aids	2,112	2,370	1,886	16.4%		
Confectionery	1,586	1,731	1,886	11.4%		
PetCare	576	602	699	4.2%		
Total sales	14,296	15,504	16,556	100.0%	4.4	8.8
EBIT	2,334	2,571	2,697	16.3%		
Capital expenditure	546	588	675	4.1%		
Nestlé Waters						
Europe	3,959	4,179	4,551	43.7%		
USA and Canada	4,222	4,805	5,118	49.2%		
Other regions	606	652	735	7.1%		
Total sales	8,787	9,636	10,404	100.0%	5.0	6.6
EBIT	709	834	851	8.2%		
Capital expenditure	601	923	1,043	10.0%		

In millions of CHF	2005	2006	2007		RIG (%)	OG (%)
Nestlé Nutrition						
Europe	2,063	2,314	2,807	**33.3%**		
Americas	1,800	2,236	3,897	**46.2%**		
Asia, Oceania and Africa	1,407	1,414	1,730	**20.5%**		
Total sales	5,270	5,964	8,434	**100.0%**	6.5	9.7
EBIT	932	1,009	1,447	**17.2%**		
Capital expenditure	134	194	271	**3.2%**		

Notes: RIG = Real Internal Growth; OG = Organic Growth.

Nestlé's leadership believed that, as a Swiss firm with a very small home market (less than 2 per cent of sales were in Switzerland), the company was better positioned than competitors to understand the trends of the world. 'We have to think about the world food supply and international issues such as the WTO and bilateral trade agreements,' explained a Nestlé manager. 'We sit here on our little lake in Switzerland and have to think beyond our boundaries. The distance means we [at headquarters] are not involved in the day-to-day details, and that gives us time to think about the right things. The oxygen is here to do that.'

'The job of headquarters is to be the platform for shaping, defining, thinking,' added Bulcke. 'There are no contract negotiations here at Vevey. That is all handled in the markets. Our job is to make sure that all of that energy is aligned and to provide guidance to where the journey is heading. Our people must walk in the same direction with the right tools and strategies.'

Castañer explained the role of Nestlé's unique culture in making that happen:

Nestlé is a company of unwritten culture – a strong personal culture. We rely more on this than on management 'systems.' Most of our top managers have been here over 25 years. With that amount of time, they are really aligned with the principles and objectives of the company. It's therefore a problem when we recruit someone from another company. They are rarely successful here. It's often a difference in priorities. They are often more focused on short-term results than we are. The safest way to join at a high level is through an acquisition. We have a very good track record in developing people from acquired companies.

R&D

Nestlé's R&D spending had more than doubled since 1998, reaching CHF1.88 billion (approx. 1.75 per cent of revenues) in 2007 with about 60 per cent invested to support food, nutrition, health and wellness and 40 per cent in pharmaceutical businesses. Nestlé's Research Center in Switzerland had a permanent staff of 700, including over 300 scientists. In addition, each of the 23 Product Technology Centers (PTCs) located around the world was responsible for category-specific innovation aligned with one or more of the Nestlé SBUs and global businesses. To encourage information sharing, Nestlé organized 20 to 25 R&D strategy conferences each year. The firm had also created a network of 'experts' – thousands of people around the world who volunteered to answer questions.

R&D had a critical role to play in delivering the Nestlé's model, explained Bauer. 'Given our internal growth targets, CHF3 billion of new sales has to come from renovation or innovation each year,' he said. 'Therefore we must understand the global business strategy to see where R&D should be working. The goal is to identify the sweet spot of three elements: what is needed by the consumer, what is technically and scientifically feasible, and what is commercially viable.' Prioritization was crucial given the numerous opportunities. Ten research projects that had the ability to be 'transformational' were selected each year and monitored at the corporate level.

Singh commented on R&D's role in the company's growth:

Nestlé was founded on invention and, 140 years later, this spirit is still here. We have a spirit of discovery, especially today since what we become in the future will be driven by our ability to innovate today. Nespresso is a great example of a true invention that created a new industry. Nestlé built the unique business model, technology, machine, capsules – the entire experience. It took 15 years to get to the first billion [dollars] of revenues, but only three years to get to the second. Nespresso is now growing 40 per cent a year – the fastest of all Nestlé brands.

Operations and raw material sourcing

In 2007 Nestlé operated 480 factories in 86 countries. About half of the factories were in developing countries and most of these produced for the local market. 'We don't open a factory in a cheap place to produce products to sell to an expensive place,' explained Jose Lopez, executive vice president of operations. 'Our goal for food has always been local, affordable, and fresh. That's good for the world.' For example, over 90 per cent of Nestlé products made in China were sold in China.

To support its global operations, Nestlé spent about CHF13 billion a year on agricultural materials including dairy (51 per cent), coffee (15 per cent), sugar (9 per cent), and cocoa (8 per cent). Over 60 per cent of purchases were from emerging economies. Lopez remarked how Nestlé operated differently from other large food companies:

In developing countries, we buy agricultural commodities from local markets and often directly from farmers – over 600 000 of them – rather than on the world market. We want to establish ourselves as partners of choice for the farmer. We form a direct link with them, offering them technical advice and a reliable market for their product. We need them to have a long-term, sustainable business.

Lopez credited the company's philosophy of creating 'shared value' (see Exhibit 12) with partially shielding the firm from the recent run-up in agricultural commodity prices, which he felt was no surprise:

Farm prices have been falling in real terms since 1970. They needed to go up so farmers could stay in business. We can manage the price increases. But what is different today is the volatility. Farmers used to be predictable, planting basically the same things year in and year out. Decisions were often driven by subsidies, which were slow to change. Now you see farmers with their PCs, watching the prices

to see what to plant. They've moved from a seasonal clock to a Wall Street clock. Farmers are now vibrating with the rest of the world. It's a new world with more volatility. And the ability to plan has become more demanding.

Lopez also explained how globalization was impacting Nestlé's supply chain on both the sourcing and demand sides:

Ten years ago we used to talk explicitly about globalization. Now no one talks about it. It's become a reality. But the impact of globalization has been different than we thought it would be. For those of us in the West, globalization meant developing countries opening their markets for us to sell to. Yet that's not how it turned out. When a country like China is the tenth largest buyer of a commodity, they are a taker. But when they become the third largest buyer they set the rules on what we eat. So instead of being globalized, we are learning to react to globalized markets. If everyone in China decides to have one more cup of coffee every day, then the cost of coffee beans will increase and we must build many more factories.

Bulcke takes over

In April 2008 Bulcke replaced Brabeck as CEO, part of a carefully planned succession almost two years in the making. Like his predecessor, Bulcke was a Nestlé veteran who had advanced through a series of increasingly challenging country assignments before moving to headquarters in Vevey. His postings included Peru, Ecuador, Chile, and several locations in Europe. Immediately prior to being appointed CEO, Bulcke was head of Nestlé's largest business unit, Zone Americas.

The new CEO shared his predecessor's philosophies of leadership and the importance of the Nestlé culture in obtaining long-term performance:

The Nestlé model is one of steady growth and margin improvement. It is not management by surprise. This model is so inherent in our structure and culture that we don't have major restructurings. We try to anticipate and be proactive so we don't have to react, because then you end up overreacting. We don't need short-term gimmicks that might jeopardize the long-term results.

EXHIBIT 12   CREATING SHARED VALUE

Shared value minimizes adverse business impacts along the value chain and maximizes positive contributions to Nestlé, our shareholders, and society.

Agriculture and Sourcing

- Agricultural and local supplier development
- Purchasing practices (e.g., direct sourcing)
- Sustainable agriculture/supply chain approach
- Industry initiatives

Value to Nestlé: traceability; quality assurance; reliable supply; committed growers; improved cost management and sustainable returns on investment.

Value to society: scalable standards of economic, social, and environmental sustainability.

Environment and Manufacturing

- Environmental practices
- Labour health and safety
- Workforce development

- Food safety standards

Value to Nestlé: increased production; reduced costs; reduced consumption of resources and generation of waste.

Value to society: fewer resources used; reduced environmental impact; employment opportunities.

Products and Consumers

- New/reformulated products for nutrition, health, and wellness
- Increased knowledge of nutrition/health
- Public-private partnerships

Value to Nestlé: entry into new/growing markets; wider brand recognition; consumer trust; product and brand differentiation.

Value to society: access to range of affordable, nutritional products; increased awareness of health/nutrition issues.

Bulcke did see a different path for the company over the coming years:

Our future growth will come from internal growth, which is different from the past where we have had a number of important acquisitions. We have built an incredible foundation. Our top strength is our product and brand portfolio. People use our products every day of their lives, every minute of the day. In addition, R&D is now a fantastic platform and it is up to us to leverage it better. It must be aligned with our consumer platforms, to make sure we are a consumer-driven company. Our third strength is our global presence. We have time-tested expertise in every corner of the world. We know where to be, how to work in that country. Finally, we have our people and our Nestlé culture, which is strong in every part of the world. My challenge is to drive growth from this asset base while being as efficient and as productive as possible.

Bulcke saw GLOBE as an important vehicle for continuous improvement. GLOBE would allow best practices to be identified and shared across plants and business units. This was crucial in enabling Nestlé to shift from organization by country to organization by business. 'Before GLOBE, every market was like a

small kingdom,' explained Bulcke. 'Our world wasn't global. Products were adapted to every market. Today, our science-based platform requires us to generate demand differently. We are rolling out more products worldwide. Certain products need to be globally managed. For example, we don't do marketing for medical nutrition. Instead of communicating with the final customer, we must inform doctors, pharmacies, and health professionals who recommend the product to patients. All of the professional communication is done centrally.'

Growth platforms

Four complementary platforms had been identified that could double the company's sales over the next 10 years (see Exhibit 13): (1) health, nutrition, and wellness; (2) emerging markets; (3) out-of-home consumption; and (4) 'premiumization' of existing products.

Health, nutrition, and wellness. The nutrition, health, and wellness strategy continued to be implemented in all categories and regions (see Exhibit 14). 'This must be first,' remarked Bulcke. 'It will be the mainstream of our business.' Nestlé Nutrition had grown to CHF11 billion in 2007 with high margins and high growth potential. Nutrition was a focal point for the firm's R&D efforts, which were then useful in other businesses. For

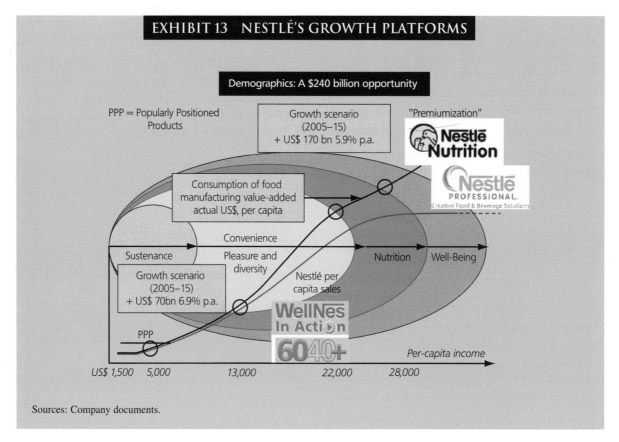

EXHIBIT 13   NESTLÉ'S GROWTH PLATFORMS

Sources: Company documents.

example, Nestlé's pet food division provided an early ability to introduce and test products, such as a planned Alzheimer's product for dogs. 'Our advantage is that we are the only company with both a big nutrition business and a big food business, so we can support the scientific research and quickly get the product to consumers in multiple forms while advising them of the benefits,' commented a Nestle manager.

Bauer acknowledged the challenge of developing global products given differences in nutritional requirements across geographic areas and incomes:

There will be more bifurcation in the future. For countries in the basic stage of development, we must look at what that country is lacking. For example, the population might be deficient in iron and zinc due to eating crops grown on poor soils. The effect of many deficiencies is often worst on physical development, including brain development, much of which happens during the last months of pregnancy. However, it is often difficult to find these relationships, because with humans we can't do intervention studies. Animal studies are very important because they can act as a proxy.

Emerging markets. Nearly 90 per cent of the world population was projected to live in developing and emerging countries by 2010 (see Exhibit 15). While over a third of Nestlé's 2007 sales came from the developing world, Bulcke believed this figure could reach 40 per cent to 50 per cent over the next 10 years. Nestlé planned to reach 1 billion new consumers through a portfolio of 'popularly positioned products' (PPPs) designed to provide good nutrition at an affordable price on a daily basis to people at the base of the pyramid. In 2007, PPPs were present across Africa, Asia, and Latin America and accounted for 6 per cent of Nestlé revenues. Nestlé managers estimated that this consumer segment offered a 10-year $70 billion opportunity for profitable growth.

The challenge was to leverage Nestlé's rural presence and develop new business models and distribution structures that reduced system costs. Products should be made more affordable by producing locally, using less packaging, or adapting the unit size to local needs. For example, Nestlé's PPP products included smaller, less-expensive pack sizes such single serving sachets of instant milk powder or 'two-stick' *KitKat* bars instead of the normal four-stick package. PPP products should also address specific nutritional

EXHIBIT 14 NUTRITION ACROSS THE PORTFOLIO

Transforming product portfolio towards healthier nutrition is also driving growth

Sales CAGR 2004–2007

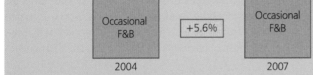

	2004	2007
BAB		BAB
+23.7%		
Nutrition enhanced F&B		Nutrition enhanced F&B
+7.8%		
Everyday F&B		Everyday F&B
+6.2%		
Occasional F&B		Occasional F&B
+5.6%		

Optimizing Nutrition:

- **Adding/enhancing**
  - 2005–2007: Whole Grains: 700 million additional servings in Europe
  - Health benefits: BABs
  - Micronutrients: vitamins, minerals, trace elements...

- **Reducing**
  - 2003–2006: TFAs: 34,000 metric tons removed
  - 2005–2006: Salt: 5,000 metric tons removed
  - 2003–2006: Sugar: 240,000 metric tons removed

Sources: Company documents.

EXHIBIT 15 MORE OPPORTUNITY FOR PPPS

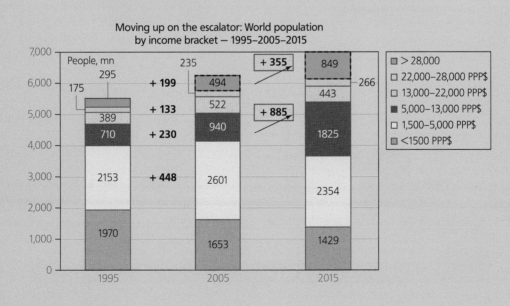

Moving up on the escalator: World population by income bracket — 1995–2005–2015

Sources: Company documents.

needs, such as iron or Vitamins B or D, along with local needs, such as replacing milk ingredients in areas with high incidence of lactose intolerance. And new distribution options, such as direct delivery in Brazil or street carts for ice cream, could supplement traditional venues such as supermarkets or kiosks.

Out-of-home consumption. Given the growing need for convenience and rising economic standards, consumers throughout the world were eating more meals in restaurants and other non-home settings. In mature economies, between 30 per cent and 50 per cent of consumer spending on food and beverages was for food prepared outside of the home. Nestlé estimated the size of the out-of-home market at $400 billion. 'It's a large but complicated market,' commented Bulcke. 'There are many more actors that have relationships with consumers. Today we are the largest player in the sector with $7 billion in revenues. But that is from just being there, not from any concentrated actions. We need to crack the code.' Nestlé Professional was being separated as a globally

managed business beginning in 2008. The unit was initially concentrating on two areas: branded beverage solutions such as coffee and teas (where Nestlé also provided the machines) and customized culinary solutions which had a nutritional focus.

Premiumization. Nestlé managers recognized a growing super-premium sector and saw the opportunity to develop exclusive, high-quality versions of its existing products that would appeal to higher income consumers. 'We see demand for premium products even in the developing world,' said Bulcke. 'Two years from now there will be more potential premium and luxury goods consumers in China than in the whole of Western Europe. Our goal with these products is not to be everywhere. We don't need to be in every supermarket with the lowest price. This is about value, not volume.' Along with the highest quality ingredients, premium and luxury products might include unique components (e.g., the machine used to produce *Nespresso*), personalized services (e.g., a telephone or internet help line), or distribution channels (e.g., '*Nespresso* Corners' in

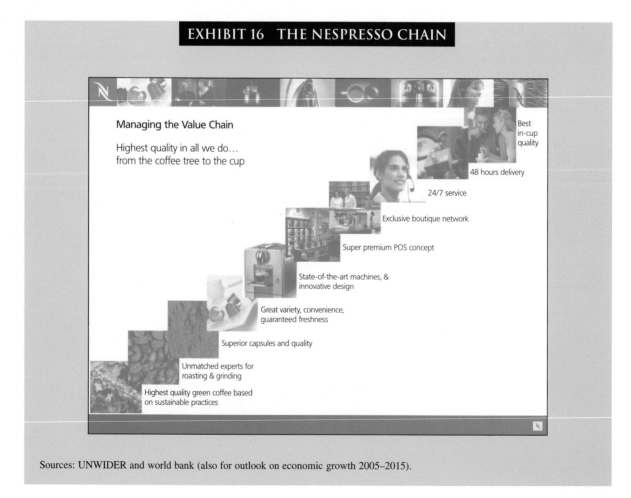

EXHIBIT 16   THE NESPRESSO CHAIN

Managing the Value Chain

Highest quality in all we do…
from the coffee tree to the cup

Best in-cup quality

48 hours delivery

24/7 service

Exclusive boutique network

Super premium POS concept

State-of-the-art machines, & innovative design

Great variety, convenience, guaranteed freshness

Superior capsules and quality

Unmatched experts for roasting & grinding

Highest quality green coffee based on sustainable practices

Sources: UNWIDER and world bank (also for outlook on economic growth 2005–2015).

department stores, stand-alone *Nespresso* Boutiques in major cities, or home delivery). Examples of Nestlé premium and luxury brands included *Mövenpick* and *Häagen-Dazs* in ice cream, *Nespresso* and *Dolce Gusto* in coffee (see Exhibit 16), *Perrier* in water, *Nestlé Noir* and *Perugina* in chocolates, and *Purina Pro Plan* and *Purina ONE* in pet foods.

Looking ahead

Bulcke knew there were many changes on the horizon that would affect Nestlé's business. Global retailers such as Wal-Mart and Carrefour continued to grow larger and more powerful. Consumers around the world had access to more sources of information than ever before and were increasingly requiring products that met environmental, ethical, and social production standards. At the same time, the price of basic agricultural commodities was increasing, hurting all consumers but especially those in the lowest economic tier. How did a company like Nestlé remain relevant, dynamic, and at the same time provide essential industry leadership in areas such as nutrition and sustainable sourcing while keeping products affordable? How should Bulcke balance local autonomy with global coordination as more science-based products with multi-market roll-out potential were developed?

While keeping the primary focus on organic growth, should Bulcke continue to look for acquisitions to bring into the Nestlé fold? The firm was well positioned to act should opportunities arise: just three days before Bulcke's first day as CEO, the company sold 25 per cent of its shareholding in Alcon to Novartis for $10.6 billion, with Novartis also acquiring a call option on Nestlé's remaining shares that could amount to an additional $24.8 billion or more in either 2010 or 2011. And after April 2009 Nestle would be able to sell its 30 per cent stake in L'Oréal, which could generate estimated capital gains of at least $22 billion.

Bulcke was confident that Nestlé was on course with the right vision, organization, and culture. 'It's like the old Chinese saying,' he said. 'If you choose the right direction and start walking and you don't stop, then there is a good chance you will get where you intend to go.'

Aditya Birla Group: The Indian multinational

By Ashok Som[1]

Kumar Mangalam Birla was on his way to his office at the Aditya Birla House. He had received an email request from ESSEC Business School to showcase Aditya Birla Group to a group of executives from the third largest bank in France. Usually requests came from professors and students of foreign business schools, not from executives from a foreign bank. As he entered his fifth floor corner office, he wondered what would be the best way to showcase the group. Would he speak about the growth of the group? Or about the redesign he had undertaken since he inherited the business in 1995, when he was 25 years old and fresh out of London Business School? Or would he suggest a presentation usually presented to analysts? As he looked at the portrait of his father, the legendary Aditya Vikram Birla, then shifted his focus to the Raza and Hussain paintings, he thought why not showcase the group's evolution from the point in time he accepted the challenge of running the group 10 years before.

In 1995, he Birla inherited the $1.5 billion[2] conglomerate with interests in textiles, cement, tea, sponge iron, aluminium, fertilizers, shipping, carbon black, palm oil refining, chemicals and a clutch of small businesses. About 25 per cent of the revenues came from textiles, a sector that was highly regulated and fragmented with margins as low as in the range of 8–10 per cent. In cement, there were two separately listed companies where lack of synergies was adding to the costs. The group had no competencies in refining and had made a half-hearted foray into it. Birla could not grow the fertilizer business as it was highly regulated, which obstructed plans of expansion. The high cross-holdings within the group and the unplanned diversification that came from the opportunistic responses of the 'license raj' made capital allocation highly complex. Within 10 years, he steered the group to a $8.3 billion conglomerate by focusing on market leadership and size in its chosen sectors. It institutionalized the rule of three – to be within the top three players in the world or at least the region – in each of its businesses. It considerably reduced its dependence on its fibre business. Today, the group is a dominant player in all of the sectors in which it operates, which include viscose staple fibre, non-ferrous metals, cement, viscose filament yarn, branded apparel, carbon black, chemicals, fertilizers, sponge iron, insulators and financial services. Under Birla's leadership, the group became a world leader in viscose staple fibre, grew to become Asia's largest integrated aluminium producers and the fastest-growing copper company in Asia. It is the 11th largest cement producer in the world and the seventh largest in Asia, where it is also the fourth largest producer of carbon black. The company is the world's largest single-location palm oil refinery and the world's No. 1 in insulators, with its joint venture with NGK of Japan. In India, it is a premier branded garments player; the most energy efficient private sector fertilizer plants; it is the second-largest producer of viscose filament yarn, the number two private sector insurance company and the fourth-largest asset management company. It has a market cap of $12 billion, employs 72 000 from 20 different nationalities and 30 per cent of its revenue comes from operations in Thailand, Indonesia, Malaysia, Philippines, Egypt, Canada, Australia and China.

But how did it all happen? It was not an easy task...

Growth of the group

The Aditya Birla Group's roots can be traced back to the 19th century, when Seth Shivnarain Birla began trading in cotton in the picturesque town of Pilani, set

---

[1]Source: Associate Professor of the Management Department at ESSEC Business School, Paris. The case was written with permission from Mr. Kumar Mangalam Birla, co-ordinated by Dr. Pragnya Ram, Group Executive President, Communications. The case draws upon archival data, interviews and insights from the top-management team at Aditya Birla Management Corporation Ltd. It is intended to be used as a basis for class discussion rather than to illustrate either effective or ineffective handling of a business situation.

[2]For simplicity the whole text assumes that US$1 = 50 Indian Rupees

amidst the Rajasthan desert. It was here that Seth Shiv Narayan Birla started trading in cotton, laying the foundation for the House of Birlas.

Through India's arduous times of the 1850s, the Birla business expanded rapidly. In the early part of the 20th century, the group's founding father, Ghanshyamdas (G.D) Birla, set up industries in critical sectors such as textiles and fibre, aluminium, cement and chemicals. As a close confidante of Mahatma Gandhi, he played an active role in the Indian freedom struggle. It was at Birla House in Delhi that the luminaries of the Indian freedom struggle often met to plot the downfall of the British Raj. G.D Birla found no contradiction in pursuing his business goals with the dedication of a saint, emerging as one of the foremost industrialists of pre-independence India. The principles by which he lived were soaked up by his grandson, Aditya Vikram Birla, the group's legendary leader (see Exhibit 1 for the family tree).

A formidable force in Indian industry, Mr. Aditya Birla dreamt of setting up a global business empire at the age of 24. He was the first to put Indian business on the world map as far back as 1969. In the then vibrant and free market South East Asian countries, he ventured to create world-class production bases, setting up 19 companies outside India, in Thailand, Malaysia, Indonesia, the Philippines and Egypt. Interestingly, for Mr. Aditya Birla, globalization meant more than just geographic reach. He believed that a business could be global even while being based in India. Therefore, back in his home-territory, he single-mindedly put together the building blocks to make its Indian business a global force. Under his stewardship, his companies rose to be the world's largest producer of viscose staple fibre, the largest refiner of palm oil, the third largest producer of insulators and the sixth largest producer of carbon black. In India, the company attained the status of the largest single producer of viscose filament yarn, apart from being a producer of cement, grey cement and rayon grade pulp. The group was also the largest producer of aluminium in the private sector, the lowest first cost producer in the world and the only producer of linen in India's textile industry. At the time of his untimely death due to prostate cancer in 1995 at the age of 52, the group's revenues topped $1.5 billion globally, assets, comprising 55 plants, were $1.3 billion, employees numbered 75000 and there were 600 000 shareholders. Most importantly, his companies had earned the respect and admiration of the people as one of India's finest business houses. Through this outstanding record of enterprise, he helped create enormous wealth for the nation, and respect for Indian entrepreneurship in South East Asia. In his time, his success was unmatched by any other industrialist in India.

After Aditya Vikram Birla's death, Kumar Mangalam Birla started shaping and reshaping his companies relentlessly (see Exhibit 2 for the group's mission statement). From its diverse portfolio, Mr. Birla decided to focus on cement, aluminium, viscose staple fibre, carbon black which he regarded as value businesses, along with knowledge sector industries such as telecom, software, insurance and branded apparel. The group grew and consolidated its portfolio through a spate of acquisitions and greenfield projects.

Diversified conglomerate: Portfolio of businesses

The Aditya Birla Group has more than 40 national and international companies that operate under two flagship companies – Grasim and Hindalco. The other major companies are Aditya Birla Nuvo (Indian Rayon, Indo Gulf, etc.) and Idea Cellular. Grasim includes cement and VSF, Hindalco comprises metals, and Nuvo is a conglomerate with a balanced portfolio of businesses in the manufacturing, brands and services sectors. In the words of Mr. Birla:

> Our clear focus is to attain the leadership position in every business we are into. It is to be achieved through value added products, services, capacity expansion through organic and inorganic growth, sweating assets and cost reduction. Every business has been categorized according to the geographical leadership roles they can play and the focus is very much on profitability and growth rather than size or footprint.

In the cement business (see Exhibit 3), with the acquisition of the L&T Cement business at $440 million, the group is the largest producer of cement in the country, with a capacity of 31 million tons per annum. During 2004–2005, the L&T brand name was phased out and re-branded UltraTech Cement. The change was achieved without any loss of market share and both brands – Grasim and UltraTech – prospered. Synergies were gained through integration in procurement and logistics due to cross-manufacturing. In India, Grasim and Ultratech were both domestic and exports market leader with an overall 21 per cent market share.

In the non-ferrous metals business, the group, in an attempt to become a global player, embarked on a $2.5

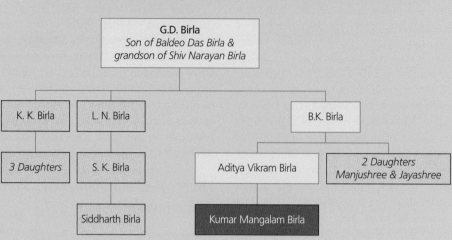

EXHIBIT 1 EARLY FAMILY HISTORY AND FAMILY TREE

The Birla's hail from the Marwar province of Rajasthan, located in North-West of India. The traders and merchants of Rajasthan founded their business empires in West Bengal, specially in Kolkata, where they were called '*Marwaris*' which literally meant inhabitants from Marwar. Marwaris are known for their entrepreneurship and sound business acumen.

Seth Shiv Narayan Birla, a Maheswari Marawari from Pilani, Rajasthan way back in 1857 wanted to diversify from the traditional money lending business with items as security. He left for Mumbai and set up his business as a cotton dealer. His business was very successful and he returned to Pilani with a lot of wealth and built a huge mansion that is today known as Birla Haveli. Seth Shiv Narayan Birla's son, Baldeo Das Birla amassed a lot of wealth by starting business houses in Kolkata and Mumbai. Initially their income was from trading in opium and silver that was often forced by the British raj. They diversified to jute, sugar, tea and other commodities as opportunity arose and slowly emerged as one of the richest families of India.

G.D. Birla, son of Baldeo Das Birla, was an inborn entrepreneur and wanted to focus and diversify his father's business into jute. His business fared well in Kolkata, the then jute capital of India, amidst competition from British and Scottish merchants. He founded many educational institutes and amongst them the most successful and well-known seat of higher education was in his village, the Birla Institute of Technology and Science (BITS), Pilani. G.D. Birla became interested in politics and was influenced by Pandit Malaviya and Lala Lajpat Rai and later on became a follower of Mahatma Gandhi, the Father of the Indian Nation and a financier of the Congress Party. Birla Houses in Kolkata, Delhi and Mumbai were given over to Mahatma when he visited these cities and later on his assassination, these houses were donated to the nation.

Birlas were, and are, a very close-knit family and do not marry outside sub-caste. They are strict vegetarians and teetotalers. They create enormous wealth and show life-long courtesy towards people they employ. They have a passion for building temples, educational institutions and hospitals. The Aditya Birla Group today spends more than US$150mn running 16 hospitals and 45 schools.

billion investment plan to grow the aluminium business. In aluminium, Hindalco (see Exhibits 4 and 5) through capacity expansions and two large Greenfield projects, planned to be among the top ten global producers of aluminium by 2010. The capacity expansions were in

Muri in Jharkhand, where production increased from 110 000 metric tons per annum (tpa) to 500 000 metric tpa by 2006, and an increase from 65 000 metric tpa to 146 000 metric tpa of aluminium at Hirakud in Orissa by 2007. The two greenfield projects were in Aditya

EXHIBIT 2   VISION, MISSION, VALUE

Vision:

To be a premium global conglomerate with a clear focus on each business.

Mission:

To deliver superior value to our customers, shareholders, employees and society at large.

Values:

Integrity – We define integrity as honesty in every action. We shall act and take decisions in a manner that these are fair, honest and follow the highest standards of professionalism. Integrity shall be the cornerstone for all our dealings, be it with our customers, our employees, suppliers, our partners, shareholders, the communities we serve or the government.

Commitment – On the foundation of integrity, we see commitment as doing whatever it takes to deliver as promised. Each one of us shall take ownership for our own work, teams and the part of the organisation we are responsible for. Through this value, we shall build an even sharper results-oriented culture that is high on reliability and accountability. Our commitment is likely to make us a formidable leader and competitor in every market that we are in.

Passion – We define passion as a missionary zeal arising out of an emotional engagement with work which inspires each one to give his or her best. All of us are expected to be enthusiastic in the pursuit of our goals and objectives. We shall recruit and actively encourage employees with a 'fire in the belly'. With this value, we hope to build a culture of innovation and breakthrough thinking, leading to superior customer satisfaction and value creation.

Seamlessness – We understand seamlessness as thinking and working together across functional silos, hierarchy levels, across business lines and geographies. Each one of us shall demonstrate high level of teamwork through sharing and collaborative efforts and garner the synergy benefits from working together. Before we can truly benefit from a borderless world, we need to build a borderless organization. We visualize free flow of knowledge and information across the group. I am reminded of the words of my father, the late Aditya Vikram Birla:

'Our search for knowledge is not limited to within the group.

We seek knowledge from every nook and corner, from our competitors, suppliers, customers et al.

Even the worst run units in India would have something to teach us. It is with this humility that we seek knowledge.'

Speed – One step ahead always. We look upon speed as responding to internal and external customers with a sense of urgency. We shall continuously seek to crash timelines and ensure expeditious completion of our tasks. Through this value, we hope to build an agile and proactive organisation that is prompt to respond to the present and future needs of our customers.

Aluminium with a capacity of 100 0000 metric tpa of aluminium and 260 000 metric tpa of aluminium in Orissa, and Utkal Aluminium, a joint venture with Alcan for setting up a 150 0000 metric tpa plant with a 325 000 metric tpa aluminium smelter in Jharkhand. The copper business was in the process of commissioning its new line of 250 000 tons per annum at a cost of $240 million, taking its total capacity to 500 000 tpa, which would make it the world's largest smelter at a single location. The group acquired Nifty Copper Mines, Australia in 2003 for a total investment of $235 million and commissioned it in December 2005. This project supplied more than 160 000 tpa of copper concentrate to the Dahej smelter in Gujarat, India.

Internationally, ten copper mines were earmarked for acquisition by Hindalco Industries in Brazil, Chile, Peru in 2006. Referring to Hindalco and speaking about the mining business, Ravi Kastia, MD, Essel Mining reflected:

In this business, resources determine the profit. TISCO/HINDALCO have the lowest cost because of the quality, low cost of raw materials and energy. If one takes the difference, 70–80 per cent of the profit is in the access to raw materials. The production process itself does not bring in a substantial difference in the profit margin. For example, POSCO of Korea can run

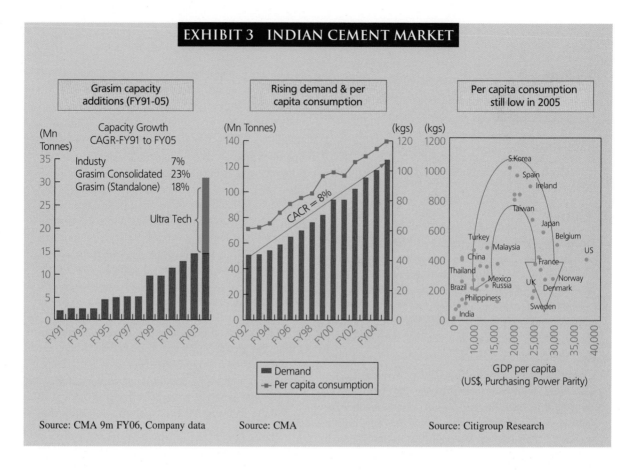

EXHIBIT 3   INDIAN CEMENT MARKET

| Grasim capacity additions (FY91-05) | Rising demand & per capita consumption | Per capita consumption still low in 2005 |

Source: CMA 9m FY06, Company data   Source: CMA   Source: Citigroup Research

a steel plant similar to that of TISCO with 17000 people, while TISCO after 5 years of restructuring reduced its workforce from 100000 to 40 000.

In the viscose staple fibre (VSF) (see Exhibit 6) business, the group acquired the AV Nackawic Pulp Plant in New Brunswick in Canada in a JV with Tembec. This captive source of high quality pulp is used for fibre units in India, Thailand and Indonesia. With a capacity of 180000 tpa, this acquisition significantly enhanced the company's competitiveness in the fibre business.

Indo-Bharat Rayon, in Indonesia, at a cost of $39 million, is setting up its new plant of 37000 tpa for manufacturing speciality fibres that will take its total capacity to 150000 tpa. Today, the group is the largest VSF producer in the world with more than 21 per cent global market share. According to Mr. Birla:

The acquisition of Saint Anne Nackawic Pulp Mill move is consistent with our strategy of reinforcing our competitive edge in the cellulose man-made fibre sector through setting up fully integrated operations. My father, Aditya Birla, first looked beyond India 30 years ago. As

globalization picked up, 30 per cent of our turnover started coming from overseas. We plan to increase it to 40 per cent by the end of the decade. The underlying logic in many of our businesses is simple: If you want leadership position, you have to be global in it. While we have made significant strides in globalization, our group still has a long way to go.

In the carbon black (see Exhibit 7) business, the group was among the top four global producers, with operations at various locations. In India, it is known as Hi-Tec Carbon. Alexandria Carbon Black (ACB) commissioned its fourth line of 50 000 tpa, taking its total capacity to 190 000 tpa in 2005 and making it the largest single location manufacturing capacity of carbon black in the world. ACB, with an investment of $30 million, would further increase its capacity of 60500 tpa, at a cost of $30 million. Thai Carbon Black commissioned its 5th line of 44 000 tpa at a cost of $20 million, on par with ACB. Also in 1995, the carbon black business commissioned a new plant in Liaoning, China, with a capacity of 36 000 tpa, at a cost of $17 million, marking the commissioning of the group's

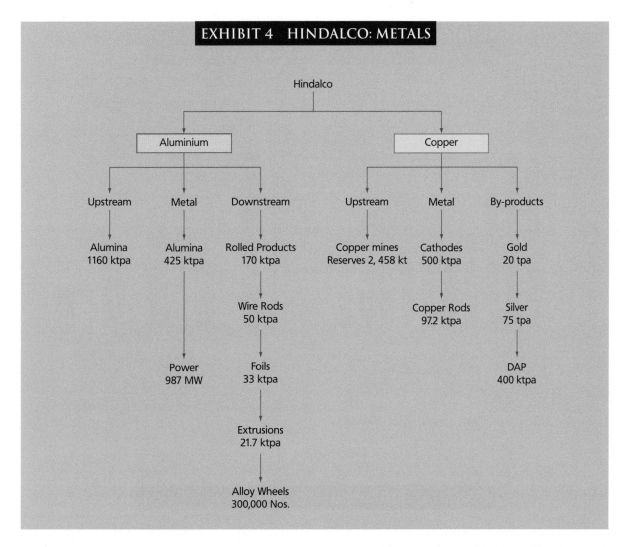

EXHIBIT 4   HINDALCO: METALS

first investment in China. Later plans including growing the business through Brownfield and Greenfield ventures, as well as targeting new locations. With these expansions, the group's carbon black capacity stood at 650 000 tpa, making it the fourth largest in the world. Most importantly, it had clout due to the size and operational effectiveness due to partnerships with three global tire companies, Michelin, Goodyear and Bridgestone.

In the new age (high growth) business, the group's interest in garments rose with its acquisition of Madura Garments, in financial services, with life insurance and asset management, joint ventures, in telecom with full control of Idea Cellular in 2006 and in IT services and BPO. The Aditya Birla Nuvo (see Exhibits 8 and 9) was created by a three-way merger of Indian Rayon, Indo Gulf and Birla Global to create a resource pool that could fund growth plans in these high growth businesses. Aditya Birla Nuvo aimed to expand its high growth businesses quickly. For example, Madura Garments intended to transform itself into a lifestyle brand, tie up strategically with global brands, and to double its retail space in three years. Transworks, the BPO division, planned to build scale and diversify. Aditya Birla Nuvo intended to enter pension funds and banks, if allowed to do so.

With these steps, the group had initiated measures to untangle the cross-holdings which were the legacy of the *licence raj*, redesign and redefine the group's companies which stemmed from the environment, culture and heritage of family business houses in India.

Redesigning and redefining the group

The Aditya Birla Group decided to sustain and grow its business where it had clear strength, a dominant

EXHIBIT 5 GLOBAL ALUMINIUM COMPETITORS AND DOMESTIC MARKET SHARE

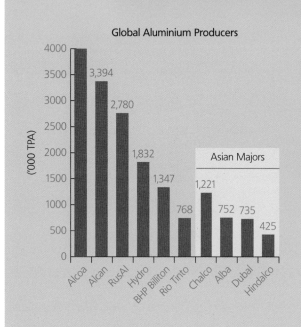

Global Aluminium Producers

Asian Majors

Source: CRU – Oct. 2005

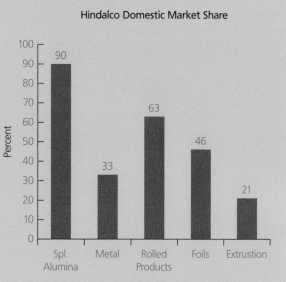

Hindalco Domestic Market Share

Source: Company data, Aluminium Association of India

EXHIBIT 6 BUILDING GLOBAL PRESENCE IN VSF

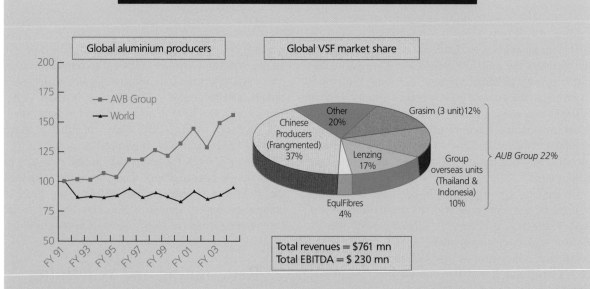

Global aluminium producers

- AVB Group
- World

Global VSF market share

Chinese Producers (Frangmented) 37%

Other 20%

Grasim (3 unit) 12%

Lenzing 17%

AUB Group 22%

Group overseas units (Thailand & Indonesia) 10%

EquiFibres 4%

Total revenues = $761 mn
Total EBITDA = $ 230 mn

Source: Company Data. Fiber Organon

EXHIBIT 7   BUILDING GLOBAL PRESENCE IN CARBON BLACK: 4TH IN THE WORLD AND FASTEST GROWING

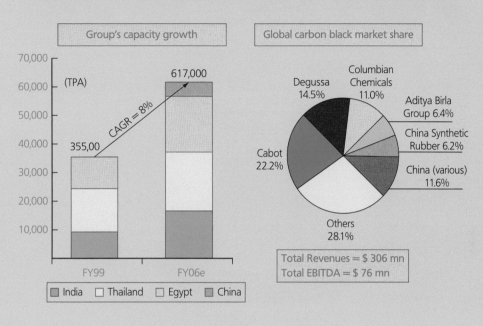

Source: Company Data. Freedonia Carbon Black Report 2005

EXHIBIT 8   ADITYA BIRLA NUVO: RESTRUCTURING FOR A BALANCED PORTFOLIO

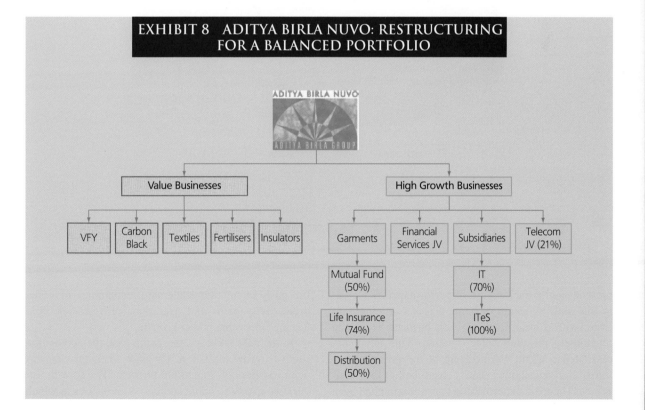

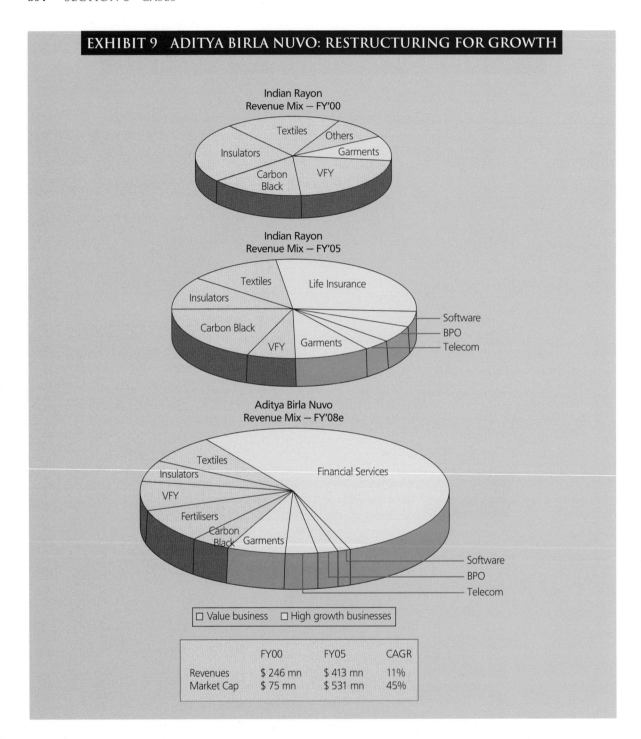

EXHIBIT 9   ADITYA BIRLA NUVO: RESTRUCTURING FOR GROWTH

Indian Rayon
Revenue Mix — FY'00

Indian Rayon
Revenue Mix — FY'05

Aditya Birla Nuvo
Revenue Mix — FY'08e

☐ Value business   ☐ High growth businesses

	FY00	FY05	CAGR
Revenues	$ 246 mn	$ 413 mn	11%
Market Cap	$ 75 mn	$ 531 mn	45%

presence and a track record of performance. This was in line with its vision of being a premium conglomerate, with a clear focus at each business level and relentlessly pursuing value creation. This intent necessitated constant restructuring of the group's portfolio, and redesigning and consolidating the businesses. The logic underpinning consolidation had been the push for market leadership, economies of scale, productivity gains and operational efficiencies, coalescing into value added growth.

In the past 10 years, the group took the acquisition route to grow, unlike in the past when growth was achieved through greenfield projects. The growth imperative had been value addition in industries in which the group operated rather than on asset growth as before. When Mr. Kumar Mangalam Birla joined the group, he dropped some mega-projects such as paper, sugar and steel that the group had embarked upon. Earlier, the overall portfolio was predominantly fibre-based businesses which were being replaced by non-ferrous metals and cement. The share of textiles had since dropped from a quarter of the group's turnover to below 5 per cent, while the share of metals and cement had increased to 62 per cent. The group had branched out into consumer products, services and telecom, while the family fortune was founded on commodities. The group was consolidating each of its businesses (see Exhibit 10 for the time line of restructuring). In the words of Mr. Birla,

We still have a very strong presence in the commodities sector and I am very comfortable with that. But I see our group as a conglomerate. I am quite happy being involved in a variety of businesses, provided I am sure that we can attain a dominant position in those businesses. So you'll find us now in mutual funds, insurance and branded garments. In fact, we're the market leaders in the branded garment business. The focus has been on placing larger bets on fewer businesses. It's a portfolio issue and it's a much tighter portfolio today. We have taken hard decisions on exiting businesses, but I am glad we did. We are on a

cleaner wicket now. We have legitimate reason to believe that as a group we can soon enter the Fortune 500 list.

On redesigning the group's portfolio, Mr. Birla commented,

We had the cement businesses in Indian Rayon and Grasim. We brought that under the Grasim umbrella. We completed the change by moving copper from Indo Gulf to Hindalco. We acquired Indal to consolidate our non-ferrous metal business. Next, we consolidated the cement business under Grasim by acquiring L&T cement and re-christened it as Ultratech. There isn't any other overlap as such across companies. Further re-defining the group, we undertook a three-way merger of group companies Indian Rayon, Birla Global Finance and Indo Gulf Fertilisers. The new entity, Aditya Birla Nuvo, will be a strong conglomerate. This landmark restructuring, valued at over US$100mn, is one of the major consolidations of its kind in India. The restructuring is a major step in shareholder value creation. It creates a company that captures opportunities in the evolving Indian economy through focussed value businesses, such as carbon black, VFY, textiles and fertilisers, and driving high growth businesses namely garments, IT/ITES, financial services (life insurance, mutual funds) and

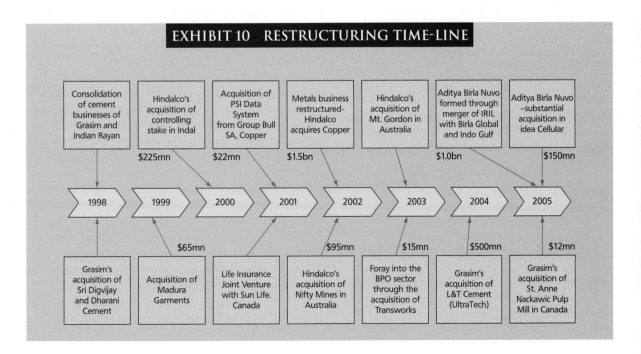

EXHIBIT 10   RESTRUCTURING TIME-LINE

Consolidation of cement businesses of Grasim and Indian Rayan	Hindalco's acquisition of controlling stake in Indal	Acquisition of PSI Data System from Group Bull SA, Copper	Metals business restructured- Hindalco acquires Copper	Hindalco's acquisition of Mt. Gordon in Australia	Aditya Birla Nuvo formed through merger of IRIL with Birla Global and Indo Gulf	Aditya Birla Nuvo –substantial acquisition in idea Cellular
	$225mn	$22mn	$1.5bn		$1.0bn	$150mn
1998	**1999**	**2000**	**2001**	**2002**	**2003**	**2004**	**2005**
	$65mn		$95mn	$15mn	$500mn	$12mn
Grasim's acquisition of Sri Digvijay and Dharani Cement	Acquisition of Madura Garments	Life Insurance Joint Venture with Sun Life. Canada	Hindalco's acquisition of Nifty Mines in Australia	Foray into the BPO sector through the acquisition of Transworks	Grasim's acquisition of L&T Cement (UltraTech)	Grasim's acquisition of St. Anne Nackawic Pulp Mill in Canada

telecom. We don't need to do that across companies that do not add value.

The Aditya Birla Group had chosen to have all major investments in India. This might seem ironic, especially since, frustrated by the regulatory environment, Kumar Mangalam Birla's father, Aditya Vikram Birla, was among the first Indian industrialists to establish global outposts back in 1973. The underlying assumption of this investment had been value creation in its businesses which were essentially rooted in India. The first step was the acquisition of a 74.6 per cent equity stake in Indal from Alcan, at an investment of a little more than $200 million.

Moving on to copper, it achieved leadership status commanding a market share of more than 45 per cent within a short span of three years from its first commissioning. Here the expansion had more to do with being cost competitive rather than growing the business in size. When the Birlas first ventured into copper in the mid-1990s, they started the business more as a domestic play. The differential between the import duty for the metal and its raw material was high (nearly 30 per cent). This allowed local companies to earn a good margin in just being converters. There was also a robust demand for copper in telecom cables.

The next redesigning occurred with the decision to consolidate Indo-Gulf's copper business with Hindalco. Simultaneously, Hindalco made a second open offer for the shares of Indal. All these moves took the group toward unifying its non-ferrous metals businesses and transforming Hindalco into a globally competitive non-ferrous metals powerhouse. Bringing Indal into the group's fold helped the group position itself along every link in the value chain of the business, from metal to downstream products, where the Hindalco-Indal combined accounted for 70 per cent of the market share in India. According to Debu Bhattacharya, Managing Director of Hindalco:

I inherited Hindalco, which had been very successful from its very inception. Though it is small and somewhat boutique in nature, its efficiency, operational parameters, and cost structures are of very high standard. It was not easy to expand the capacity in pre-liberalization era. To make Hindalco a global company, we had to focus on operational performance, scale and scope efficiency. High-grade bauxite availability in India and opening up of coal-blocks for the private industry, gave us a global

competitive advantage. After 1999, when copper production commenced at Dahej, there had been continuous growth in copper production, which corresponded to a growth rate of more than 30 per cent YoY (Year-On-Year) and at the current capacity of 0.5 million tonne of copper/year, it is one of the largest single-location Copper Smelter in the world. We have identified expansion plans worth US$5.0 billion in our Aluminium business. We have continuously evaluated both green-field and brown-field options. Inorganic growth, through acquisition, is also on our radar system and our investment is justified primarily on the basis of commercial and economic attractiveness. Geographical location has relatively low weightage in making a final choice.

Post-redesigning, Indo-Gulf restricted its activities to fertilizers, with a brand that commanded a huge equity, strong cash flows and a leadership position in the fertilizer industry. It was well positioned to take advantage of any opportunities that might arise from the disinvestment programme of the Indian government.

The next step was to de-merge the Insulator Division – one of the group's best performing businesses – and transfer it to a separate 50:50 joint venture with NGK of Japan, the leading global player in the business. The partnership with NGK helped strengthen the leading position that the Insulator business already enjoyed in the domestic market. With the JV, the Insulator Division acquired the latest in product and manufacturing technology with opportunities for accessing the global marketing network.

A slew of initiatives was taken to consolidate the operations of Grasim. The pulp and fibre plants at Mavoor were closed down and the loss-making fabric operations at Gwalior was sold. In three years, Grasim became much leaner and stronger – the debt/equity ratio improved from 0.93 to 0.58, interest charges fell by 42 per cent, operating profit increased 68 per cent and workforce rationalization strengthened from 24400 to 16600. Along with this, the cement business was restructured by consolidating it under Grasim in 1998, a move that triggered the consolidation process in the Indian cement industry. These, coupled with smaller acquisitions, helped the group emerge as the third largest producer in India. Consolidating and building in size and scale, the group acquired L&T Cement to become the largest producer in India and the 11th largest in the world, with gross margins of

28.2 per cent. Grasim was expected to be among the most profitable cement companies in the world.

The group divested its stake in Mangalore Refineries and Petrochemicals Ltd (MRPL) to Oil and Natural Gas Company (ONGC), the state owned giant. The sell off of MRPL indicated the group's resolve to rationalize its portfolio of businesses with a view on the future.

Indian Rayon had been a beneficiary of the restructuring efforts and witnessed significant activity. Subsequent to the restructuring of the cement business, the group focused on strengthening the competitiveness in the existing businesses of Viscose Filament Yarn, carbon black and insulators through a combination of low cost Brownfield expansions, quality and brand orientation and by setting up joint ventures with major global players. Exiting from value destructive businesses was integral to this strategy. While these helped the group strengthen its cash flows from traditional businesses, they offered limited growth prospects. Given this constraint and the need to invest in growth businesses of the future, new opportunities were pursued, including the acquisition of Madura Garments, an entry into the newly opened insurance sector and a foray into the software and BPO sectors. While propelling growth, these strategic moves helped achieve a balanced portfolio and transformed Indian Rayon into a leader in promising growth sectors of the future.

Indo Gulf had a strong brand name in its Shaktiman branded urea. Functioning in an over-regulated industry structure and a controlled pricing regime, Indo Gulf couldn't achieve growth quickly. With the demerger of the copper business from Indo Gulf in 2001, the idea was to make it a major player in the fertilizer market. With no changes in the fertilizer sector on the horizon, the merger with Indian Rayon was expected to help Indo Gulf shareholders migrate to a high growth business. Mr. Birla reflected:

Even though the fertilizer business has seen steady profits, regulatory uncertainties constrain growth avenues, making accelerated value creation difficult. Becoming a part of the Indian Rayon shareholder fraternity should provide Indo Gulf shareholders a broader canvas to participate in enhanced value creation. For Birla Global shareholders, they extend their participation in financial services beyond mutual funds into life insurance as the financial services business of the group gets consolidated under Indian Rayon. This transaction will strengthen the financials of Indian Rayon, open new opportunities and should result in enhanced investor interest. The company has a demonstrable record of managing a diverse portfolio with razor sharp focus in each business.

In September 2005, a three-way merger created the Aditya Birla Nuvo which had a swap ratio of Indian Rayon: Indo Gulf, 1:3 and Indo Rayon: Birla Global Finance, 1:3. This swap ratio translated into a reasonable premium to both Indo Gulf and Birla Global Finance shareholders based on the current Indian Rayon share price. Besides the approvals of shareholders of the three companies, the merger needed the consent of the high courts of Maharashtra, Uttar Pradesh and Gujarat. The new shareholding pattern included promoters' shareholding at 38 per cent, financial institutions at 15 per cent and banks at 22 per cent. The remaining 25 per cent was held by the public. Prior to the reorganization, the promoters held 28.6 per cent in Indian Rayon, 58 per cent in Indo Gulf and 75 per cent in Birla Global. The idea was to make Aditya Birla Nuvo a diversified, high-growth company.

'They provide us with robust cash flow but they do not have very large cash requirement to carry them forward. We will use the cash flow to invest in high-growth areas that we are trying to promote. The intent is to grow into businesses like financial services, telecom, IT and IT-enabled businesses,' reflected Sanjeev Aga, the MD of the new conglomerate.

In the telecom business, in March 2006, the Aditya Birla Group acquired 48 per cent of Tata Group's stake in Idea Cellular for $969 million, raising its share equity in the country's fifth-largest mobile provider to 98 per cent. After much speculation, the group decided to stay in the telecom sector. The deal presented substantial growth opportunity in the mobile telecom sector despite Idea Cellular's subscriber base of just over 7 million and the fact that it lagged behind other competitors such as Hutch, Bharati, BSNL and Reliance. It had a debt of about $1 billion and needed fresh investments not only to reduce its debt-equity ratio, but also to expand and grow in an intensely competitive marketplace.

Summing up, Mr. Birla restated:

From all of this, a clear trend emerges. Our strategy dictates that we get out of businesses where we are bit players and strengthen the businesses where we have clear competencies, so that we get to the top of the league or consolidate our position there, as the case may be. This leads to a sharper and tighter business portfolio with our firepower being better targeted.

Financing the growth

According to Mr. Birla:

Funding is the least of our worries – our cash flow is healthy and our liquidity position comfortable. In the past, both our organic and inorganic growths have been funded through our own cash flows and I see no exception to this in the future. We have an under-leveraged balance-sheet which we can leverage tellingly – very few corporates are in the same comfortable position as Hindalco in this respect. Our debt-equity ratio presently is 0.32 per cent. Moreover, the group companies have been imminently successful in raising finance for major investment decisions. We have raised funds at very competitive rates. For example, Hindalco has been able to raise over US$1400 at only 65 bps above the 5 year government securities for its recent expansion programme. Even for our other major ventures like the acquisition of UltraTech stake by Grasim was enabled largely through internal accruals and using minimal debt. The recent acquisition of Cingular stake in Idea Cellular too did not entail large borrowings. We have made substantial investments to meet with the expectations of our multiple stakeholders which include besides investors, our employers, our customers, Government and society at large. All our Group companies are highly credible in terms of delivering value to its stakeholders. All the companies are AAA rated companies by various rating agencies. Even the equity/loan offering programmes of the company in the domestic markets as well as the overseas markets have been met with huge investor responses.

To cite an example of cash flow, in the aluminium business in the past few years, the leading aluminium companies in the world, like Alcan (capacity 3.5 million tonnes) and Alcoa (capacity 4.1 million tonnes), have consolidated, buying out smaller players across Europe and the US. The 10 top players controlled more than 50 per cent of the market. In the process, greater scale helped bring down the cost of production. Now, price movements in the aluminium

business are dictated by the London Metals Exchange (LME), which acts as the benchmark. So far, Hindalco has been able to keep its costs down and make hefty profits. Last year it released nearly $300 million of free cash flow. Elaborating on scale and scope, Debu Bhattacharya, MD of Hindalco comments:

Staying in the business with the same capacity is like running on the treadmill. You just stay where you are. We can reduce costs only to an extent. Beyond that, there is a crying need to increase scale.

The goal for the future was summed-up as:

Our goal is to achieve 30 per cent CAGR in 5 years for the strategic businesses. We plan to double these businesses every 3 years, 4 times in 6 years. In order to do so, our resource requirements could be substantial. For this we intend using our internal resources (we are still under-leveraged), private equity and other innovative financial products.

Dev Bhattacharya and Bharat K. Singh, Business Strategy Cell.

Managing the diversified conglomerate

The restructuring process started in 1996, a year after the death of Mr. Aditya Birla, under the leadership of Mr. Kumar Mangalam Birla. The group launched for the first time a corporate identity that would serve as its logo. The group chose 'Aditya' which meant the Rising Sun'. Dr. Pragnya Ram, Group Executive President, Corporate Communications, in her article quoting Mr. Birla had summarized:

The new logo overshot the agenda in an amazing way. The impact of a symbol could be so enormous, is something that took us by surprise. At that time when the organization was going through a turmoil, the symbol of the Rising Sun brought different parts of the group together, helped us as an organization to re-energize ourselves, cross the bridge, and to get started on the path of change. The corporate identity served the need to relate, to belong to a club, to an association, and make an emotional connect with the name 'Aditya Birla' that weaved the group into an integrated whole. The Rising Sun, in a strange way brought a new optimism and served as a rallying point for the organization.

That really, in a strategic way, was the first positive step for us in our process of change.

Notwithstanding the group logo, The Aditya Birla Group, as an entity, was unknown, although the name Aditya Birla was a much vaunted one. There was no brand recognition, so it was a challenge to attract the brightest and the best of talent to work with the group. It was at that point, Aditya Birla Management Corporation Limited (ABMCL) was created. Dr. Pragnya Ram, Group Executive President, Corporate Communications, reflected,

The Corporate Cell at ABMCL is the group's apex decision making body and it provides strategic direction to the group Companies. Mr. Birla is the non-executive Chairman with eight Directors representing the major businesses and the HR. function.

In the words of Mr. K.K. Maheswari, Business Head, Chemicals:

ABMCL assist Mr. Birla in taking decisions. The group Logo and the ABMCL were ways so that employees could have ownership with the Brand rather than the family, and that in turn would make the group move from a paternalistic culture to a professional culture. The management model under Mr. Aditya Birla was of a very decentralized structure wherein there was very little synergistic contact between the different Units of the group. To overcome this and establish an institutionalized sharing of best practices, he started the concept of Birla Management Centre way back in 1989. It was through such forums and through the interventions of Chairman's office that the group was able to obtain the benefits of its collective strength. Under Mr. Kumar Managalam Birla, the group has developed a powerful corporate centre that does not command and control but leverages the group's strength and resources and facilitates innovation. It has clearly defined the group values and the corporate policies and practices be it on HR, communication, world class manufacturing etc. which need to be followed by all the Units of the group. In this corporate cell mode, best practices have been studied and implemented by HR within the group. The model is to help everyone grow and develop within the group. The Senior Management go through a Leadership Development program. Mr. Kumar Mangalam Birla takes a lot

of interest in development of leaders and the talent in the group. He leads the group by role modelling. For example, the entire senior management team was participating in the leadership development workshop. We got our report card with our leadership profile. Mr. Birla opened his report and started discussing the implications of the observations in the report and how it could be used for further development. It is this commitment to processes, to reflect and develop from within, intervene where necessary and be a part of the process is what makes his leadership different.

Dr. Santrupt Misra, Director HR, further explained:

A great admirer of Jack Welch, Mr. Birla modelled the ABMCL along the lines of GE Capital. The ABMCL is the central nervous system of the group which allows for individual businesses to function to their optimum under their respective managements, while leveraging the expertise of the corporate cell. About 20 business leaders and those with group-wide responsibilities are housed at the headquarters they report directly to the Chairman. Not even his secretary is allowed to get between him and them. He gives them complete freedom to run their businesses, but also holds them accountable for their performance. Mr. Birla starts from a position of trust and continues to do so unless proven otherwise, but it is in no way abdication. He has his own antennae and picks rare moments to assess people. If you pass muster at those points, then you have his trust forever.

Dr. Bharat K. Singh, Director, Corporate Strategy & Business Development Cell pointed out:

ABMCL hosts Active Centres of Excellence. The job of ABMCL is to 'think like a company, and not as a Group'. Its role is to integrate and co-ordinate the group's activities as if it was managed as a Company – integration of people, systems, fungibility, create an integrated entity. Within this framework, there are Business Review Councils to review the strategy as well as the operating performance of businesses. Each of the group companies has a Board of high quality independent directors who have a reputation and the expertise in related areas that fit in with the group's businesses. The board is accountable to the Company and the shareholders. The Board provides strategic guidance and ensures performance through effective monitoring. It is also committed to the protection of minority shareholder interests, equitable treatment of all shareholders as well as transparency and timely disclosures.

With the group identity and his team at ABMCL in place, Mr. Birla started deconstructing and re-constructing businesses:

During the time of Aditya Birla, most of the businesses were small units and if not they were spilt into small units as licenses (during the License Raj) were difficult to come by. Growth was stunted in every way possible and competition within India was self-inflicted. The first priority for any licence was employment generation and to manage more employment. In 1991, with liberalization, markets opened up, business paradigms were re-defined, there were pressures from shareholders and the main question was 'how does the group operate as a group and not as an amalgamation of loosely knit companies?' Transition is never easy for any company. The initial phase of transition was more externally driven (because of market forces, customers and shareholders) as they wanted certain amount of clarity and understand-ability. In the early 1990s, the group started transitioning to a professional organization for the sake of stakeholder's interest (manly employees). It was painful, compelling and entailed a learning process. At the beginning, financial markets did not view the restructuring process very kindly but we continued to restructure with a focussed business strategy – in our key business areas. In some ways the AB Group was a pioneer/leader to change the mindset of a large diversified family owned business group to a focussed professionally managed conglomerate.

Bharat K. Singh, Director, Business Strategy and Dev Bhattacharya, Strategy.
Exhibits 11 and 12 depict the organizational structure of the group in 1999 and 2006, respectively. Sanjeev Aga, Managing Director, Aditya Birla Nuvo explained,

Our structure is entirely divisional, unit based that gives it high clarity. But it creates confusion and contradiction at the top level as we have 20–25 businesses to understand. We have

distributed the Governance role with corporate functions at the conglomerate level. The Chairman is responsible for the corporate functions. It was required to synergise values, brands, HR policies, technologies, and finance across the whole group. This interplay between support/corporate function and business line has to be improved. It works well (common office) on the whole. I would tend to favour bringing in little more accountability, responsibility at the business head level as this inter-linkage of corporate function and business units sometimes tend to favour non-performance. People sometimes feel proprietorial but not necessarily entrepreneurial. We have room to function as a matrix organization and be supportive and safe. But they are not necessarily the trait of great companies. If it does not pay to work in a humane manner we have to change and it won't be devoid of cost.

K.K. Maheswari, Business Head, Chemicals commented, 'The organization structure now is evolving but is more logical now. It is divisional – with each business responsible for one product.'

Cultural heritage of Marwari family businesses

In traditional Marwari business families, scions aren't expected to have a mind of their own. Typically, they are expected to continue family traditions and customs, and play the benefactor 'babu.'[3] It is very hierarchical, usually with no woman in the top-echelons with a prevalent control-and-command management style. In order to do away with the 'babu culture' that was so prevalent at Birla companies, Mr. Birla launched a 360-degree feedback programme that allowed managers to question even his leadership style. It's not just ancient financial practices or power centres within the group that he has thrown out of the window. Complacency at AV Birla today is just not tolerated. No one today doubts Birla's ability to expand his empire even though concerns remain about uncertainty related to line of reporting and accountability. At the top sits Kumar Manglam Birla, and despite the delegation of authority, people still prefer to wait for 'Babu's' orders directly.

---

[3] 'Babu' culture symbolized looking up to the head of the company always for direction and decisions.

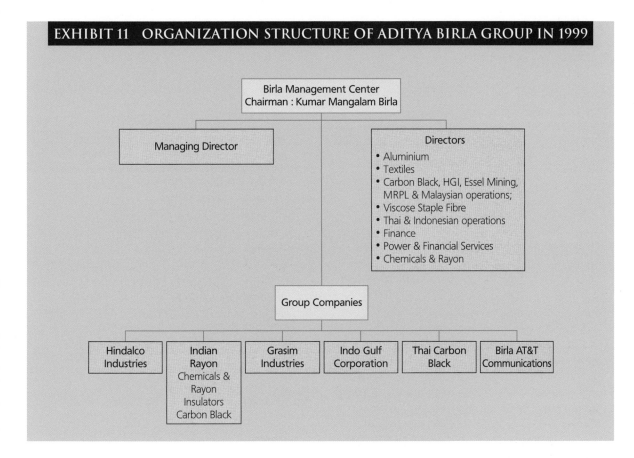

EXHIBIT 11 ORGANIZATION STRUCTURE OF ADITYA BIRLA GROUP IN 1999

Changing this mindset is clearly Birla's biggest challenge now. Kumar Mangalam's answer to the unprecedented challenges has been simple: He has assembled an impressive group of professionals and he listens to them, empowers and delegates, while he himself scans the environment to anticipate changes.

according to notes of one industry spokesman. In the words of Mr. Birla:

As the concept of core competency assumed primacy, given our diversified corporations, we had to face a major reassessment from stakeholders. Foreign investors, particularly, began questioning the very logic of diversification. To me core competency is a snapshot of an organization's key skills at a given point in time. There is nothing that neither stops a company from acquiring core competency nor in losing its core competency if they do not focus on holding a particular skill.

What is more important is the willingness to learn and the capacity to absorb from others and nurturing the excitement that it evokes.

I wanted the conglomerate that I inherited, to move with deregulation, liberalization and globalization. I took time to study, review, analyse, and filter what our stakeholders had to say, I worked out a roadmap along with my team to respond to the turbulent and challenging times that lay ahead.

Turning a patriarchal group into a meritocracy was not easy by any means. According to his grandfather, B.K. Birla:

Kumar Mangalam Birla had to let go of 350 Vice Presidents above the age of 60 in one day which was unheard of in those days at the Birla empire – most of these people were old loyalists who had worked for Aditya Birla for years, ending the 'womb-to-tomb'[4] policy once and for all. So retiring them couldn't have been easy for Kumar Mangalam too, but he did it because, well, he

---

[4] 'Womb-to-tomb' policy meant that there was no fixed retirement age and loyalists of the family stayed on with the company as many years they could work and be of help to the company (similar to the age old Japanese system). When they could not work anymore they would request the 'babu' to guarantee their children a job in the company.

EXHIBIT 12   ORGANIZATION STRUCTURE OF ADITYA BIRLA GROUP IN 2006

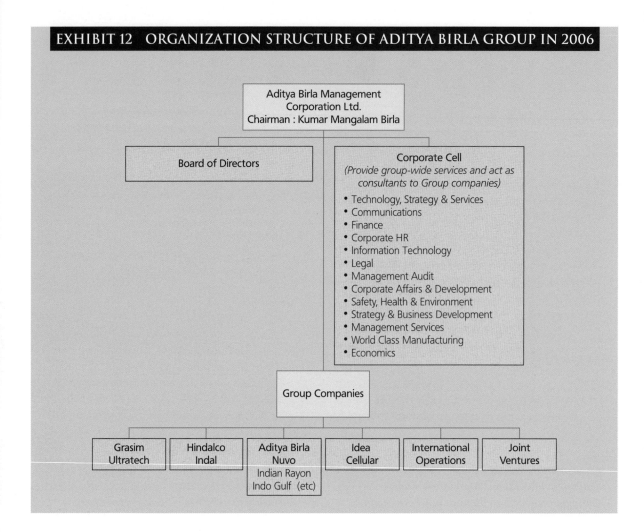

had to – the needs of the organization demanded that he did so. Along with Santrupt Misra, Director HR (hired from Levers in 1996) Birla introduced a path-breaking retirement policy that saw 325 senior executives step down after years of service. The executives were between the ages of 62 to 65. Together with this he built a team by hiring senior people from outside, a marked departure from the past. They recruited Bharat Singh (1996), Debu Bhattacharya (1998), Pragnya Ram (1998), Sanjeev Aga (1998) and Sumant Sinha (2002). This removed at one shot the impression that those who were not sure of finding a suitable job outside join Birla companies. They have been replaced with 190 young executives. It was the passing away of the AV Birla era.

Kumar Mangalam Birla replied:

When I took over as Chairman, people in the group were about twice my age. I had great respect for them personally (a strong 100000 workforce with an average age of 58), but I also felt the need for change. The company was in mourning. At meetings seniors, who had worked with my father, would frequently break down and cry at the mention of his name. For me this was traumatic. I felt that if people never retired, then there was no place for younger people to rise. So it was important to institute a retirement policy. I also felt that the company should instil meritocracy rather than compliance, the so called Kith-and-Kin policy[5]. So I instituted a policy that vetted all applications from family members of existing employees. None of this made me very popular but I thought it needed to

---

[5]'Kith-and-Kin' policy meant guaranteed jobs for family members in the group. It happened that if one son was very bright, he went to work for a multinational. The other son, if he wasn't good enough for anywhere else, was sent off to work for the group.

be done and now, I think people are much more accepting of the policy.

One of the senior manager noted:

> Both G.D. Birla and A.V. Birla were more focused on relatively short-term goals. K.M. Birla takes a long-term view while he is far more demanding. Initially, Mr. Birla was trying to understand; now he is in complete command. Earlier he would seek answers, now he gives us the direction. In the initial days, Mr. K.M. Birla replaced the 'Pratha system',[6] which was the group's main benchmark with value addition principles that took into account the cost of capital. The Cash Value Added (CVA)[7] principle calculated the value added out of the capital investment that led the group to focus on profitability, asset productivity and growth. This was a change in mindset as it shifted the focus from day-to-day operational focus to the concept of added value vis-à-vis cost of capital and risk associated with the business.

According to Mr. K.K. Maheswari, Business Head, Chemicals, who had worked closely with Mr. Aditya Birla before working with Mr. Kumar Mangalam Birla:

> Mr. Aditya Birla built a substantial part of the group, especially the overseas operation's from scratch. He was involved in many of these businesses from the stage of conception, formulating the strategy for the same, implementing the projects and running them on a day to day basis. Mr. Aditya Birla's management style was very much hands on managerially and operationally. He himself motivated his workforce by actively interacting with them and would review and oversee the operations personally. He was personally involved. He took decisions with personal initiative. With his sharp intellect and vision, he was able to lead different businesses in their global perspectives and guide them towards aiming for and achieving superior results and growth. His management style had certain overall common traits of aiming for the highest

operation excellence, execution of projects speedily and at the lowest cost and the reporting systems. Despite his active involvement, he ran the business in a decentralized style with the Business Heads having full responsibility and authority of running the business in their own preferred style. This resulted in different businesses having different styles of management – the preferred style of the Business Heads. The organization structure earlier was of different Unit Heads reporting to certain Business Heads based on historical reasons of the growth emanating in a particular corporate entity or region. For example, cement business of Rajashree Cement reported to the Director, who was responsible for the VFY business and was instrumental in setting up the cement business in Indian Rayon (now Aditya Birla Nuvo Ltd). At the same time, the cement business of Grasim reported to the Director, who was earlier looking after its Chemical Business and was instrumental in setting up the cement business for Grasim Chemicals. The overseas operations were looked after by the Directors, who had conceptualized and implemented those projects. Thai Rayon reported to the Director of Thailand operation while the similar operations in India which were part of Grasim reporting to the Director in charge of Grasim's VSF business. The group practiced life-time employment policy. People rarely moved from one business to another. The Directors took decisions directly consulting Mr. Aditya Birla. To that effect uniformity across businesses was never possible as micro-cultures existed within the group. Level of delegation varied widely depending on the personal relationship with Mr. Birla. Though the overall Group objectives had certain common themes but it was managed in a decentralized fashion. Mr. Birla was the leader, motivator, and had responsibility for success. Training was imparted when required.

Continuing on the changes, Mr. Maheswari commented:

> With Mr. Kumar Mangalam Birla the size of businesses increased considerably. The business

---

[6]'Pratha system' was a manual system suited for relatively small production systems for determining input costs such as plant capacity utilization, energy consumption vis-à-vis and daily cash profits as compared to budgeted profits. GD Birla had developed the system of accountability based on partha, in which each company in the group had to draw up a series of informed estimates of how much it would cost to manufacture a particular volume of production, sell it and meet a profit target based on this estimate. The amount of capital it takes to support the manufacturing was also taken into account.

[7]CVA = (Gross cash flow) − [(Cost of Capital) − (Gross Cash investment)]

environment has changed. He has adopted his own managerial style reflecting the changed business environment and the challenges of managing a group which would be much bigger in size compared to the group he inherited. He has therefore delegated the day to day operations to the Business Heads. He personally gets involved only in strategy formulation, decisions impacting the long term growth of a business large capital expenditure and HR related matters. He has institutionalized the HR processes wherein the senior level appointments and movements in the group are done in joint consultation of businesses and HR. Common policies on HR pertaining to recruitment, inter unit movements, job bands, compensation, welfare etc., have been put in place to bring about uniformity in the group's working and culture. The businesses have been consolidated on the basis of product structure and report to one common Business Head rather than the earlier structure wherein similar businesses reported to different Business Heads. The concept of Country Head has been done away with and even the overseas operations are now structured on the basis of businesses. He personally handpicks the Heads of various businesses and the next level of direct reports. The Presidents of various Units have full freedom to run their operations under the overall supervision of the Business Heads. Mr. Birla gets involved only in quarterly reviews or monthly reviews in the case of larger Units and provides total freedom to take decisions on operational matters. Certain other processes like world class manufacturing have also been institutionalized so that the entire Group focuses on preparing itself for external competition and benchmarking itself with the best in the world. To motivate people for healthy competition and to share their best practices, systems like annual awards have been instituted, where the Units showcase their achievements and are publicly recognized for their excellence.

Commenting on the transformation of culture Ravi Kastia, MD, Essel Mining said:

I think cultural baptism is required. The company had a G.D. Birla culture before – which was entrepreneurial and full responsibility was with the Business unit head (individualized) to manage and run the business unit. Now, it is more professionalized with streamlined systems and processes that add value from the centre and run from the corporate centre. Processes and systems are subservient to objectives, KRAs etc. The key question is how one can contribute without having silo visions and learn from the overall process.

While Sanjeev Aga, M.D, Aditya Birla Nuvo commented:

The Aditya Birla Group combines the qualities of a good international organization with an Indian Ethic, where everything is not contractual or confrontational, but unwritten bonds and expectations also play a part. There is no bias of gender, caste, or creed. There was originally a preponderance of managers from certain backgrounds, but all that has vanished, almost unnoticed.

Summarizing, Mr. Birla reflected:

As I look back on our group's journey over nearly a decade, I do believe that we have changed in some very fundamental ways. In fact the genetic coding of our group stands altered substantially. We have become a transnational, multi-cultural entity. Ten years ago women executives were few and far between. Today women constitute more than 6 per cent of our employees and the number is on the rise. As we venture into new countries the world over, our group's geographic spread has changed phenomenally and as a result the organization is faced with the challenge of having to integrate with a culture that is foreign to it and, practices it has been unexposed to. For example, in our group, an Indian manager who moves to Thailand on expatriation takes time to adjust to the fact that the night shift has only women workers, something that is illegal in India. Similarly, an Indian Manager who is posted to our Australian mines can find the task of ferrying workers to the mine site by an aircraft, to and fro each day, a rather unusual experience. I have to say that our long-standing presence overseas and the exposure it brought with it, has made the task of adapting to different cultures a lot easier. However, much as we have changed, we continue to constantly reinvent ourselves.

Concluding, Mr. Birla categorically pointed out:

We are not a family run business. My mother and I are the only members of the family in the business. I have no other family member in the business.

Decision making

As the group redesigned itself from a paternalistic, centralized decision making system to a decentralized, consensus based process; it worked on discussing decisions in Business Review Councils to have a seamless integration between and within businesses. Sanjeev Aga, Managing Director, Aditya Birla Nuvo, explained:

Our group is run as a conglomerate, with leaders of individual businesses interfacing with corporate functions which serve across different businesses, whereas our competitors are generally single focus companies. Decision-making in conglomerates can tend to be slower. But we expect that our organizational design will preempt any such impediment, and empowerment and speed of decision making will rival our competition.

Speed

On the speed of decision making, Ravi Kastia, Managing Director, Mining, believed:

We have about 70 physical plants and about 72000 people. Business Units had ownership mentality; they were largely governed by the systems and procedures of the head of the BU. As we grow the important question is how much control is required and with what speed we can take decisions – there are inherent tradeoffs. Here the key question and the debate rest on: What is the role of the corporate centre? I would say that among the three largest business groups in India, the first generation business houses are the fastest. The older business houses are the slowest and we are in the middle, getting to come close to first generation houses.

Summarizing, Mr. Kumar Manglam believed:

Today, every company puts a premium on speed. We loathe anything that is not fast enough, for obvious reasons. In a process of transformation however, one learning that stands out for us is that it is only infinite and indefinite patience that brings immediate results. We have, I find when I look back, in some instances, tended to fall a prey to what one might call the 'last mile exhaustion'. It is that period in the journey of change where the novelty of the new ideas had faded, when sufficient ground had been covered, where the goal was near, but yet not quite so. It is sustaining the organization's will-power and stamina through that last mile that very often makes or breaks the process of change.

Style of management: Intellectual curiosity at the top

According to Bharat K. Singh, Director, Business Strategy:

We as a group have transitioned to a new management style. Mr. Birla believes in democracy, empowerment, stretch vision and wants this to have a cascading effect within the company. In our company 'anyone can say anything and Mr. Birla will listen. The implementer of the idea and the executor of the plan have to agree and take ownership. Only then will Mr. Birla give his assent'. Employees take responsibilities which creates ownership. The Business Units should decide the next steps.

Kumar Mangalam's grandfather, B.K. Birla agreed:

My style of management was no different from my father's (G.D.) and Aditya's was about 20–25 per cent different from mine, but Kumar Mangalam's is completely different. At the core of Kumar Mangalam's management style are the twin virtues of patience and persuasion. He employs that not only with his own people, but also with associates outside. A classic example of that is the group's acquisition of L&T's cement division. Negotiations for the deal stretched over two years – long enough for a less-dogged CEO to walk away from it. But Kumar Mangalam kept at it relentlessly.

L&T's never-say-die Chairman and Managing Director, A.M. Naik commented, 'His style, very simply put, is to win over the person across the table with a lot of patience. He just won't give up. He is very charming and friendly even in the thick of negotiations. He gets exactly what he wants by actually winning you over.'

Adds Debu Bhattacharya, MD, Hindalco, 'What excited me was his ability to delegate and yet be supportive when you need it.'

According to Ravi Kastia, MD, Mining:

> On one hand centralization of the processes brings about a uniform culture within the group while it kills independence and local initiative that was the strength of the group before. Again 'the role of corporate in a diversified group such as ours has to be debated and clarified'. One way to achieve professionalized culture is churning of people, transfer of BU heads every 5 years, and localize management.

Summarizing, Kumar Mangalam Birla reflected:

> I think my father was more hands on. My style is much more to give people freedom to do their own thing. As long as they deliver, I don't like to get involved. They should have the freedom to do what they think necessary. I am available if they need me and I will hold them accountable but I will not interfere needlessly. People used to say that when my father phoned somebody, then that person would stand up while answering the phone. He was great at bilateral motivation and contact. My style is more group-oriented. I like motivating groups of people. I find that in business, it is more important to empower a whole group than to depend on a single individual. So in that sense, my approach is less bound by the baggage of tradition.

Building human capital

In the words of Dr. Santrupt Misra, Director HR and IT:

> My main task was getting people to understand that we need change. Next was getting them to change the 'mindset'. There was a clear disconnect between the people in the organization and the external environment. We had to make our employees believe that we mean business and we will change. The third step was to continue to prepare for the change. Two examples that were drastic in this respect were to set up a retirement and a training policy. People never believed that in the group this policy will ever hold. Everyone was asking 'Can there be a special way for me? We aren't yet ready to retire.' During succession planning, we had questions like 'What if my boss does not

> retire?' One of the comments that I received on training was 'Are you going to teach old dogs new tricks'. We had to reinforce that to be a professionalized managed organization we have to build systems and be consistent in applying them. The past was nice and necessary but today the cost-value equation has changed completely. We pay too many people; we pay them too little and also expect little from them. This does not hold today anymore.

Mr. Kumar Mangalm Birla believed that their most important asset was its people. Over the last few years, the focus on employees was building competencies and meritocracy. The growth (see Exhibit 13) required the next push to be on the people front. The group in 2002 created a management talent pool that identified more than 200 managers as performers and put them on a fast track. With the goal to provide for systematic and structured processes for career growth, the HR Department trained more than 100 managers as job analysts and another 100 as job evaluators. With this evaluation, 5000 jobs were evaluated, resulting in the formation of 11 distinct job bands. Together with this, the HR Department continued to enhance the quality and the pace of the institutionalization of the systems and processes that embraced the entire life cycle of the employees' engagement with the organization. Several new initiatives were taken toward the well-being of the employees, particularly in the area of health-care, education of their children and other critical aspects that would have a significant bearing on his or her performance. For this, setting bigger challenges and giving incentives to achieve them was the key in preparing the organization for growth. Consistently, the group contemporized a talent pool through lateral inductions across all levels. The HR Department established a group Management Trainee Scheme that helped recruit entry level managers from reputed business schools and academic institutions. To track employee satisfaction, the group institutionalized the process of Organisational Health Survey, which is a well regarded tool globally. The process links rewards to performance and encourages excellence has been institutionalized both at the individual and at the team level.

Dr. Misra continued:

> We had to invest in capability development. Some of us thought it was a waste. But we had to prepare the group for globalization and to gain benefits from India's economic liberalization. In some ways we changed everything little by little. Later we changed few things completely, but

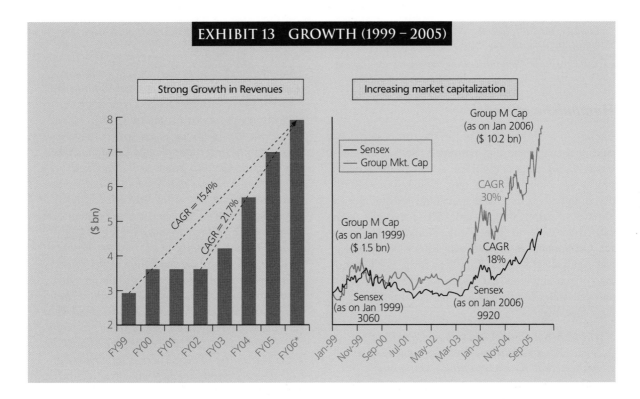

EXHIBIT 13   GROWTH (1999 – 2005)

Strong Growth in Revenues

Increasing market capitalization

never thought of changing the core of the company, its values, the respect for individuals that the company fosters, empowering people, bringing in innovation and the emotional connect that the employees have with Aditya Birla. To implement and institutionalize this change process we did lots of communication, intense face-to-face, travelled to almost every factory in the first 2 years, lots of training programmes with 300 Senior Managers at MDI Gurgaon for Strategic Leadership programme, undertook lots of small policy and system initiatives for e.g., trying to change the dogma of 'Kith and Kin' organization, bringing in the concept of Meritocracy, preserving the emotional equity with Aditya Birla, the quest for excellence, and making our organization world-class that started with the Logo (in 1996), cultural renewal, transformation, benchmarking, building the Leadership Development Centre called 'Ganyodaya'. It symbolized that we as a group were committed to people investment. Our resources are world-class and in some sense we had to destroy some of the old cultural mindset of a family organization. We brought in internal competition to re-kindle outside competition. This was achieved by internal job postings. It enabled

people to believe in the system and process that we put in place and employees could see that they can apply, without asking permission from their boss or without personal requests. It was open and transparent. It created turmoil on one hand, but signalled that changes were going to happen. We promoted teamwork, moving away from islands of power-centres, participated extensively in business school campus activities and recruitment. It signalled end of Kith and Kin company culture. HR was a Strategic Partner in this change process from the very beginning. HR is involved in all strategic decisions, in every function and is represented in the Board, in Management Committees etc.

Communication

Dr. Pragnya Ram, Executive President, Corporate Communications commented:

The process of transformation is about communication, communication and more communication. Proactive, clear, honest and simple open two-way communication across the organization is the key to diffusing seamlessness in our operations and processes. Some of the channels we use are interface with the Chairman, enhancing the corporate image and *identity, media relations, internet, investor relations support, servicing business sectors with business communication managers etc.*

Humanistic attitude

The group inherently believed in the trusteeship concept of management and portrayed itself as a value-based, caring corporate citizen. A part of the group's profits are ploughed back into meaningful welfare-driven initiatives that make a qualitative difference to the lives of marginalized people. These activities were carried out under the aegis of the Aditya Birla Centre for Community Initiatives and Rural Development andspearheaded by Mrs. Rajashree Birla. For Corporate Citizen activities, the group received prestigious national and international awards. According to Ms. Rajashree Birla:

For us in the Aditya Birla Group, Corporate Social Responsibility (CSR) is very much a part of the overall business portfolio. Our entire group's community work is carried out under the banner of The Aditya Birla Centre for Community Initiatives and Rural Development, which I am privileged to lead. It is anchored by our corporate communications team and we have 150 people working exclusively for our social projects. We work in around 3700 villages and reach out to approximately five million people every year. Of these, more than 60 per cent live below the poverty line. It is anchored by Dr. Pragnya Ram from our Corporate Communications and we have a strong team of 250 people who works to raise literacy levels, take health-care to the hut-step of the villagers, and train them to eke out a sustainable livelihood, empower women, provide basic amenities and espouse social reform. Our second project is on a partnership with Habitat for Humanity International – an international NGO working in the areas of housing for the marginalized section of society. We have committed to construct 500 houses in the next 3 years, of which 100 have been constructed in Uttar Pradesh and reconstruction of houses is being undertaken in Cuddalore for the Tsunami affected. The third community work is promoting widow-remarriages and dowryless marriages. In 2005, more than 500 widows have been remarried. Together with this we run 45 schools and 16 hospitals. We annually spend about US$18millon.

On being asked what kind of values does Mr. K.M Birla portray, he replied:

Simple things. The Birlas are very conscious about punctuality. We are not ostentatious. We have a great sense of family. I remember that during my vacations I would always go off to Calcutta to be with my grandparents. We are taught to respect older people. Good manners and regard for other people are considered very important. I believe that no child in India must have to skip school for the sake of pursuing a livelihood. And no student ought to be denied an opportunity for higher education for lack of funds. It started out as an internal touch-point. I wanted to capture certain values that I wanted this Group to embody: youth, dynamism, trust, tradition, modernity, growth and quality. These are the values that I strive for and I wanted some way of embodying them. My calling is to build an organization that can create value; anything else is a subset of that. There is an element of legacy here, but I don't see myself as a catalyst of change as such, only change as a subset of organization building.

Mr. Debu Bhattacharya, MD, Hindalco summarized:

In the context of MNC, let me speak about Hindalco, which, by itself, is shaping to be an MNC As a group, we already operate in 19 countries and it is our ambition to feature in the Fortune 500 Company list. We not only focus on size, we also aspire to be the best in Asia and, indeed, in the world in whatever business segment we operate in. India is going through a metamorphosis and we would like to take part in that journey. However, this transformation would need a change in the mindset from 'being the best in India' to aim to become 'the best in the world', and in this journey our non-Executive Chairman plays a key role.

Weaving the future: The emerging challenges

Over the last 10 years, the strategy of redesigning the organization worked considerably well. During that time, the group pulled off a string of acquisitions at home and abroad. The group was reasonably professionalized with systems and processes and a strong brand identity, gaining over the long placed paradigm of loyalty over competence. It had geared itself to compete in a global marketplace.

In 2005, Kumar Mangalam Birla and his grand-father B.K. Birla acquired a majority stake (57 per cent) in Pilani Investment & Industries Corporation, the holding company of the Birla clan. It marked the watershed in the history of the Birla family and brought the curtain down on what had been a contentious chapter in relations between the various Birla families. It kicked off a shift to a more transparent corporate structure. Industry sources familiar with the development pegged the acquisition cost close to $70 million. Apart from a 37 per cent stake in Century Textiles, Pilani Investments held shares in most Birla group of companies like Indian Rayon, Hindalco, Grasim, Bihar Caustic, Birla VXL, Cimmco Birla, Jayshree Tea, Kesoram Industries, Mysore Cements, Mangalam Cement, Sutlej Industries, Zuari and Tanfac. Century Textiles and Industries (valued at $500 milion), along with Century Enka, the flagship company of B.K. Birla group companies. As per B.K. Birla's succession plan, Mr. Kumar Mangalam Birla, his grandson, inherited Century Textiles, of which he had been nominated to the Board in 2006. The change in stakeholding sig-nalled the dominance of the 38-year-old Kumar Man-galam, the youngest Birla and the most successful of them all (see Exhibit 14 for the financial statement).

With these events, the group seemed well positioned to selectively acquire businesses and technologies from Europe and the US where companies were struggling to cope with rising costs of manpower, environmental clean-up and overhead. According to Mr. Birla:

We can see a discernible shift in supply chains to Asia which present enormous opportunities for us to consolidate our hold on some of these industries, globally. We are now in the phase of re-scaling, re-scoping and re-designing the supply chain integration to gain access and

growth in these markets. Being a conglomerate we seek global growth in multiple businesses simultaneously and this leads to several management challenges. The complexities facing us today are multifold: global competitive pressures, changes in technology, changing customer requirements, demanding investors, and businesses competing for resources.

Collectively the group faced some challenges. The *first* challenge was developing a global corporate mindset within a family owned business that had a history strongly rooted in India. It was important to ask whether the company wanted to be a true MNC or just an Indian company operating internationally. Being a true-blue MNC was only partly about geo-graphic spread (see Exhibit 15 for details on growth and internationalization recently achieved). It was more a mindset of leveraging resources seamlessly; eager to build unique capabilities to transcend the barriers of language and cultures to create value. It was about being global in attitude, without letting go of the company's roots. The *second* challenge was to be responsive to local cultures on one hand, while commanding brand equity abroad. Without recogni-tion it was difficult to access talent – the key resource to making the company global. The *third* challenge was the respect of the values that the group epito-mized. These values were a moral contract between the employees and the organization and went beyond business and economic transactions. The *fourth* chal-lenge was the ability of the group to morph commod-ity businesses into customer-centric businesses, such as from cement to ready-mix concrete, from alumi-nium to foil. This might be the only way to insulate commodities from business cycles by going down-stream closer to the consumer.

Speaking about future challenges, K.K. Maheswari, Business Head, Chemicals commented:

Before, capital was scarce. Today resources are readily available. We as a large group had advantage and could command effective borrowing rates. We were cost-effective in that sense. Today, the rules of the game have changed. Competition is intense. There is free flow of goods and services. The socio-economic environment is also changing. Today we not only compete with India companies but slowly we are seeing the trend that we have begin to compete with global players who have focused businesses. Now we cannot have only an Indian strategy but any strategy we built for ourselves should include

EXHIBIT 14 FINANCIAL STATEMENT OF THE GROUP

(In Million US$)	2003	2004	2005
Sales	4627	5565	7245
PBIT	842	908	1234
PBT	709	803	1115
PAT	528	532	695
Shareholders funds		5044	5441
Total borrowings		1823	2224
No. of People			72000

EXHIBIT 15   GROWTH AND INTERNATIONALIZATION RECENTLY ACHIEVED

- Overseas operations contribute over 30% of Group revenues

- Successful operations in 18 countries across 4 continents
  - *Manufacturing across 9 countries*

- Successful recent ventures
  - *Acquired St. Anne Nackawic Pulp Mill in* **Canada**
  - *VSF expansion in* **Indonesia** *making it the world single largest VSF plant*
  - *Expansions in Carbon Black across units in* **Egypt, Thailand and China**
  - *Acrylic fibre in* **Egypt**
  - *Copper mines in* **Australia**

the global players in each segment. For example, in the chemicals business, we thought our Indian competitors was Gujrat Alkali, DCM Shriram, Kanoria etc but now we find that we are competing against Dow Chemicals, Dupont, Honeywell (in the Fluorine business), Degusa, Solvay (in Peroxide business), Resolution Chemical (in Epoxy business). To understand the scale, Dow Chemicals is a $40 billion company. The entire Indian chemicals business is about $30 billion and we as a total group are $7 billion. India produces only about 2 million tons of caustic soda whereas the global consumption is of 50 million tons and the major player has a capacity which is almost 10 million tons. This calls for a different level of strategizing and competencies to compete against these global majors with much larger size.

Speaking about future challenges, Debu Bhattacharya, MD, Hindalco commented:

For Aditya Birla Group to be a Fortune 500 company, I see four major challenges. They are (1) Growth itself (both green and brown) (2) Ability to adopt new cutting-edge technologies along with developing appropriate band width to carry out large number of projects in remote locations (3) Funding; and most importantly (4) People. Funding, per se, should be manageable,

as Hindalco has demonstrated through its recent Rights Issue and tying up of significantly large debt funding. However, the situation is very different in the area of people. As India is experiencing a growth phase with 8–9 per cent GDP growth, the main challenge for any corporate in India is going to be to attract, nurture and retain the right professionals, and more importantly to keep them motivated for the right challenges. At the end of the day, we have to have bodies and minds, who not only are capable of delivering results, but are excited to work in a challenging atmosphere to run these businesses. In effect, we should be able to generate exciting discomfort across the teams, which will help them achieve seemingly impossible tasks. Indians have run businesses very successfully both in India as well as in developed economies. With easy adaptability that Indians have demonstrated over the years, it will not be difficult for Indian companies to turn global. Indeed, our group's experiences as well as the recent acquisitions abroad by Indian companies, justify this confidence.

On being a true MNC, Ravi Kastia, MD, Mining, explained:

Leadership development is a challenge for us. Leadership can only be nurtured if we can strive to build trust (as before) with higher respect of verbal communication and tolerance for genuine mistakes. Respect comes when 70–80 per cent business decisions are right. If there are no mistakes, it means there was no decision taken. If everything is run by set systems and processes, technically, it will dampen entrepreneurship, risk taking ability and speed in decision making, which were our strength before. Our group can become a true MNC if we can nurture 20 per cent leaders and 80 per cent followers. We had decision takers those who can stick their neck out rather than report superlative results.

Reflecting on the challenges, Mr. Birla responded:

While these challenges will have to be dealt with at each individual business level, it has to be in the context of the overall Group vision. We have a portfolio of businesses that we are in, and consequently there are an array of sunrise businesses in India like mobile telephony, insurance, BPO etc. which present significant growth opportunities for the next 10 years. All this, while not compromising on the performance or growth of our existing businesses. This can sometimes present conflicting objectives, which needs to be managed in the best interests of the stakeholders. We do not shy away from creative destruction of businesses, which do not have a potential for rapid growth. This allows us to free up the capital deployed in under performing assets and the management time for more rewarding high growth businesses.

On being asked how to reach the Fortune 500 threshold (see Exhibit 16 for details), several top managers replied:

We have to change orbits – become top-notch and do things differently. Strategy, structure, systems – these hygiene factors will take us thus far but will also restrict us after a point. In the businesses and times in which we operate, systems and processes can not substitute people capabilities. We want processes to be institutionalized, but not fossilized. For example, introducing incentives for junior and middle managers is good, but not path-breaking. We have to facilitate and filter to attract and retain talent. The stability and the value systems of the group have been helpful. We are striving to be a class act, but are not yet there. The senior

leadership team will be confronted with this challenge. We can extrapolate and grow, but to be world-class, we have to change orbits, not necessarily disruptively, but it will certainly be a very conscious effort coming from the heart. Thought leadership and doggedness will be essential constituents to pitchfork us into the Fortune 500 League.

To be in the league of a Fortune 500 company, we need more cost-effective expansions. We have to see Asia as a market, if not the world as a market. Resource allocation has to be done in sectors which will give us the maximum returns. In a diversified group as ours there are always conflicting priorities and there is sometimes difficulty in convincing the Chairman where we should be and where we should allocate more funds for the future. I could manage reasonable capital allocation for the Chemicals business after the house was set in order. Once the Chemical Business could show sustained profitability, we have been allocated over USD 100 million for our growth initiatives. The Chemical Business is different from other businesses as it involves a basket of large number of products and for every product segment there are different raw material requirements, different processes, different competitors and different set of customers with different requirements. In India, companies had earlier not paid much attention to developing R&D and new technology. Recognising the importance of this, the group has created its own technology cell that would help in development of technology and developing value added products. And above all hiring and grooming talent to manage and lead the business growth initiatives will also be a challenge.

To be successful, there is a saying – if you want to catch fish, you have to get wet. As Indians we have confidence in our abilities, we are clear what we want to do and we are committed in our endeavour to make this Group a world-class company be it a MNC or a Fortune 500 company.

Summarizing, Mr. Kumar Mangalam Birla reflected:

We need to work towards attaining a leadership position in our key businesses. This means taking a quantum leap and doubling our growth. We may need to grow at an average 15 per cent

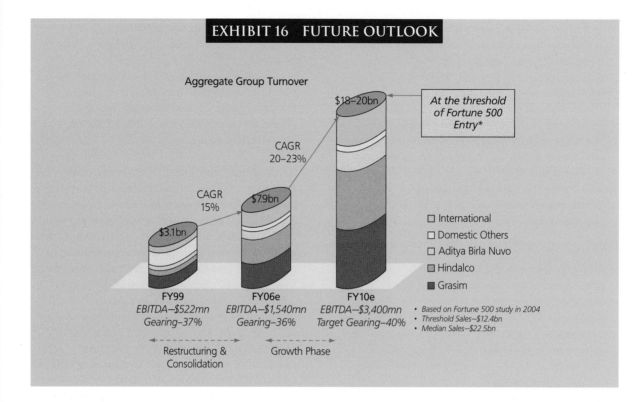

p.a. in dollar terms over the next 7 years. This may translate to a higher growth expectation from some businesses to account for lower growth in others. In rayon fibre we aim to be the number one player in the world with a market share in excess of 30 per cent. In non-ferrous metals, we plan to be the largest integrated aluminium player in Asia with significant presence in down-stream customer facing businesses. In cement, we target to remain the largest player in India and look selectively at other attractive markets to diversify our global reach. In carbon black, our target is to be one of the top three global players with a commanding presence in all significant markets in the world. My own goal for our business is to build a world-class MNC. My calling is to build an organization that can create value for its multiple stakeholder, anything else is a subset of that. We are working towards having an unbeatable employment brand which by 2010 will be well recognized even beyond the shores of India. I am a proud Indian and an important part of my mission is that of taking India to the world through extending our footprint across continents and building on 'Brand India'. We have set our sight on entering the League of the Fortune 500 by the turn of the decade.

CASE

13

Air France-KLM: Changing the rules of the game

By Ashok Som[1]

Jean-Cyril Spinetta, CEO of Air France since 1997 and CEO of Air France KLM since the merger, could be proud of the company's achievements since 2003, the year of the merger announcement. In the early days after the announcement, many analysts considered it 'nonsense', asserting there was no need for a merger because of the geographical proximity (400 km) and the small foreseeable synergies the two companies would realize. Despite great opposition from industry experts, Air France and KLM completed the merger on May 5, 2004.

After the deal was publicly accepted, industry skeptics considered the merger an adventure and a challenge. The two companies each had a strong corporate identity and culture, and both were among the oldest in Europe and the respective national champion. They had been competing in the same field for decades.

Alliances were the traditional way of cooperating in the airline industry. 'Star alliance' was the first global alliance in 1997 and its success led others to follow a similar strategy. The idea of a merger between two companies so close to each other did not seem realistic in the airline market as it might in others. Industry analysts predicted that the downsides of the merger would outweigh the upsides. The stock prices dropped 7.4 per cent at €13.12 in the week the merger was announced (see Exhibit 1 for Air France-KLM stock prices). Jean-Cyril Spinetta and Leo M. van Wijk – CEO of KLM until the merger – worked day and night to convince analysts, public authorities and stockholders of the merger's advantages, asserting that: 'A consolidation was necessary to create a global player in a global market. A single income statement for two companies is better than one for the two of them.'

What led to the merger? What was the logic behind this deal? Why a merger instead of another alliance? How did they lead the merger? What were the implications of the merger? These were some of the questions that those close to the industry were asking.

The airline industry

To know who actually was the first to make something heavier than the air fly is nearly impossible since many claim to have made this breakthrough. The French Clement Ader or the Wright brothers are the most famous engineers who worked in the field. WWI provided a tremendous platform to what actually began as a defence industry. Because of that historical heritage, the aircraft industry was geographically clustered and so was the airline industry, which appeared between WWI and WWII.

In every country, governments and authorities wanted to form a strong national defence, stronger than their enemy's. For example, during the 1920s and 1930s in France, government officials actively promoted the development of a domestic commercial aviation industry. They were convinced that aviation would be an important part of the country's economic growth. They also believed that a strong aerial presence would extend France's political and diplomatic influence in an unstable world. Pierre-Etienne Flandin, Assistant Secretary of State for Aeronautics from January 1920 to February 1921 had vigorously pushed for the consolidation within the industry. A decade later, Air France became a legal entity in August 1933 as the result of a merger between five private sector airlines: Air Union, Société Générale de Transport Aérien (S.G.T.A.), Compagnie Internationale de Navigation Aérienne (C.I.D.N.A.), Air Orient and the then bankrupt Aéropostale.

This national structure was emphasized in each country by the names of the companies: British Airways, Alitalia, Air France, Iberia, Swiss Air, and so on. To protect these companies, authorities used to limit access to their sky and supported their position with geopolitical reasons. Spinetta sums it up quite clearly:

Before 1990, air transport in Europe was governed by a complex web of bilateral service agreements between the different European

[1]Source: © 2009 Ashok Som. All Rights Reserved.

EXHIBIT 1   AIR FRANCE – KLM STOCK PERFORMANCE

states. Once the traffic rights were obtained, the two States concerned allocated them to one or more of their airlines. ... The development of traffic rights is still based on bilateral treaties between countries.

In the US market, regulations and needs were different and several big companies were able to develop earlier, although there were no public companies initially. Globally, 249 airline companies were registered at the IATA (International Air Transport Association) in 2007.

A fragile industry

Airliners have three main revenue sources: passengers, freight and maintenance services. Originally focused on diplomats and top businessmen, airlines soon widened their market targeting tourists, families, students and even commuters. Hence, the passenger market exploded to 2.1 billion in 2006 (see Exhibit 2–4 for an outlook of the market evolution for passengers, emerging countries and cargo traffics). According to the different needs of these passengers, airlines adapted their offerings by proposing minimum services for low-cost companies to high-level premium food in first-class cabins. Big airlines addressed

both targets, whereas others chose to focus on one of the two.

Freight was not an original activity for airlines but it progressively became a profitable area. Airlines took seriously this area of business as it allowed an optimization of every flight with goods carried along with passengers. Some companies began to use their installations (hubs, warehouses) to develop an exclusive and autonomous freight activity. For example, in 2006, Air France-KLM operated in their hubs at Charles de Gaulle and Schiphol, 21 aircraft of which 14 were Boeing 747 and seven were Boeing 777 that were dedicated to cargo activity.

Finally, enjoying the exclusive control of the national hubs, some airlines provided competitors with maintenance programs for their fleet. For example, with 5000 employees and operating revenue of €4950 million, KLM Engineering & Maintenance was the largest technical maintenance business in the Netherlands in 2006.

Both passenger and freight demand need steady economic growth. Air travel was and still is extremely sensitive to changes in the economy. Discretionary travel has always been one of the first expenses cut by companies and individuals during a recession. For example, the first Gulf War and the economic crises that

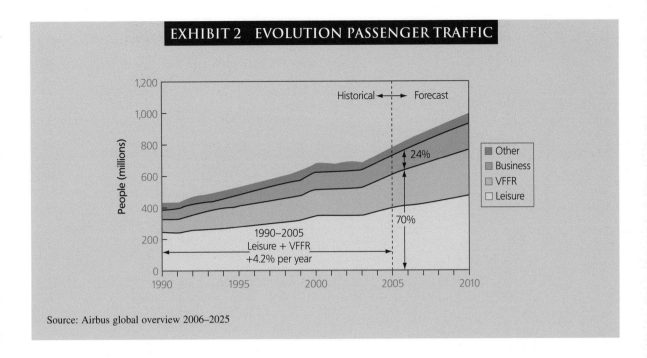

EXHIBIT 2   EVOLUTION PASSENGER TRAFFIC

Source: Airbus global overview 2006–2025

followed in the early 1990s led to a series of concentration moves within the airline industry because of decreasing demand. The same cause, emphasized by the terrorist attacks in 2001, led to the restructuring in this case. Such declines in business hit airlines especially hard because they have high fixed costs, such as fuel and labor costs, that cannot be quickly or easily reduced.

Another important cost item for an airline is fuel. Fuel prices can rise sharply during international crises, particularly military tensions in the Middle East. Fuel is a fixed cost because it must be consumed in the quantity amounts whether the airline is at a 75 per cent or a 100 per cent occupancy rate.

In addition to the decline in demand for air travel resulting from economic difficulties, other non-market factors can create a significant public disinclination toward air travel, such as the SARS epidemic in Asia and the threat of terrorism, which impacted the market between 2001 and 2003. During that time, the market grew not at all, whereas the average growth between 1993 and 2006 was 4.5 per cent per year. At the beginning of 2006, although the market grew by 5.5 per cent, the overall performance of airline companies was a negative margin of $5 billion.

Yet, many challenges remained for airlines which aimed to generate consistent profits. Technological innovation and flexibility were considered to be the key for profitability. The IATA director stressed that:

'Growth and profitability are two elements that are completely different.'

Aircraft providers

Supplying a booming demand on the domestic market, US aircraft providers such as Boeing, Lockheed, McDonnell Douglas grew quickly. In the mid-1970s, Airbus emerged propelled by European subsidies. Underestimated by the American giants, Airbus soon became a competitive force to reckon with in the field of aircraft manufacturing. In 1997, after Boeing merged with McDonnell Douglas, Airbus was the only competitor, relying on a focused strategy to overtake Boeing or to at least become a co-leader in the industry, thus ushering in an era of a duopolistic market.

The airline business model was greatly impacted by technological innovations of engineers. In the early 1950s, first jet aircrafts like the Boeing 707 were the key to allowing non-stop flights from Europe to the eastern coast of the United States; New York was then 8 hours from Paris. The tourism demand then became a major driver and with low fuel prices until 1973, long range flights developed exponentially. In 1969, Boeing launched the B747-100, which was able to carry 380 passengers worldwide. It was also in 1969 that Airbus launched its first aircraft, the A300, a wide body plane, adding to the competition. After several oil crises, aircraft providers focused on economical

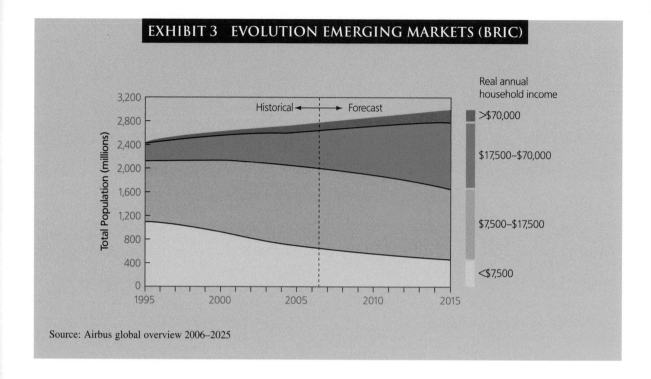

EXHIBIT 3 EVOLUTION EMERGING MARKETS (BRIC)

Source: Airbus global overview 2006–2025

aircrafts like the Boeing Dreamliner 787, allegedly 20 per cent more fuel efficient than any other wide bodied aircraft. The Airbus A350 should be its direct competitor in 2012.

Airlines enjoyed these breakthroughs which widened their offering from 100 to 550 passengers and across more than 20 800 km with the Boeing 777-300 ER which allowed a great flexibility to airliners.

Regarding the relationships between airlines and aircraft providers, the equation could be summed up in the following way: When airlines have to renew their fleet (and aircraft manufacturers know that happens once a decade), the bargaining power of the airline manufacturers relied on the contract. The bigger the fleet, the cheaper was the price for renewing the fleet. This became more and more evident with the 'family or series' concept. Another trend was to renew the fleet more often, following the path of technological evolutions, although this trend was a financial challenge.

Yet, the influence of the airlines was crucial when Airbus or Boeing launched a new model. The two manufacturers needed a contract before the aircraft even flew because stakes were high. For example, Airbus had to improve its new offering to satisfy clients who were more attracted by the Boeing 787. They designed an entirely new aircraft with the A350 XWB which included higher standards with upgraded

technology, was more fuel efficient and could have any customized cabin. Aircraft providers understood that big airlines would pick either one of the two providers, not both.

Cost management

SG&A and fuel have always been the two main expenses for airliners. They were also the two main areas of improvement for airlines which aimed at realizing economies of scales very early. There were different ways of realizing those economies.

With fuel consumption, a simple calculation could show the average fuel consumption (AFC) for a regular commercial flight. To reduce total fuel needs, companies had to rely on technological progress. In this case a young fleet is a strong asset, which was supported by projects of Boeing 787 (which used to be the 7E7, with the E standing for economical) and the Airbus A350 launched during the oil crisis of 2004–2006. The other driver was the number of passengers. Airlines decided to work on optimizing occupancy rates. Pricing methods or yield management were key activities to sell seats on aircrafts. Customer fidelity programmes and code sharing were two other popular practices in 2005. The global occupancy rate in 2006 was 77 per cent, the highest since the late 1940s. During the late 1940s, the bottleneck was the available number of aircrafts.

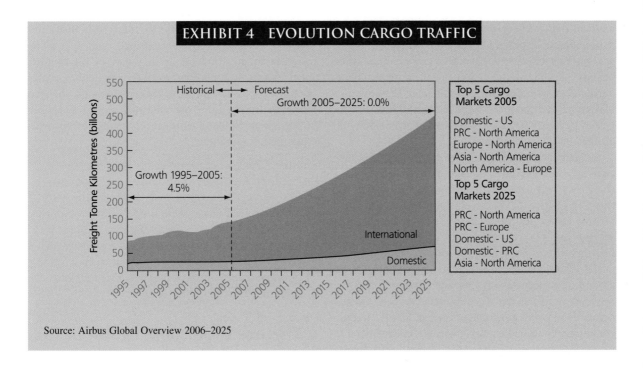

EXHIBIT 4 EVOLUTION CARGO TRAFFIC

Source: Airbus Global Overview 2006–2025

Another solution was to secure the cost of fuel. Companies contracted expensive insurances or bought financial instrument derivatives on oil to secure this price but it was only fruitful in high volatile environments. For example, Air France-KLM paid for 84 per cent of its oil at $38 in 2005–2006 and the rest at $44, whereas the average prices where skyrocketing to $80.

The proportion of fixed costs which threatened the financial structures of airlines at every downturn was the first obstacle airliners tried to adjust to. Yet, layoffs and other labour cost cutting measures were difficult to implement due to a highly unionized workforce. Equipment costs were fixed and expensive (a typical wide-body aircraft cost about $200 million) and although leasing is heavily used for aircraft, lease payments continue regardless of whether the aircraft is in service or not. The success of the family concept and the economies of scale allowed on training programs was a result of the cost policy led by airlines and aircraft providers.

Deregulation, consolidation and 'Open Sky'

Many of the airlines operating today in the US trace their beginnings to delivering mail for the Post Office under government contracts; their dependence on these contracts was also the initial basis for government control over the industry. Although the US never had a state-owned airline, between 1938 and 1978 the Civil Aeronautics Board (CAB) regulated the prices charged by scheduled airlines operating between federal states. It also regulated the number of carriers and until 1977, the CAB permitted no new entrants on routes that were already supplied by two or more carriers.

Deregulation of the airline industry was pioneered in the United States with the passage of the 1978 Deregulation Act by Congress. With a single stroke the government eliminated state control over fares and routes, and for the first time gave airlines the opportunity to operate as a true business. Dozens of new airlines were created in 1971, among which Southwest Airlines. In later years as consolidation became the rule of the game many were absorbed into the larger airlines.

Since the early 1950s, every attempt to create an 'all-Europe' air carrier failed. For example, at the beginning of what would become the European Union, the major airlines of France, West Germany, Belgium and Italy worked on plans to create Air Union. This was to be a full-fledged European airline that could, by integrating resources and services, meet the competition presented by American carriers. However, unable to work together, the project failed by 1964 and each country reverted back to promoting its own national flag-carrying champion. It was inconceivable to liquidate a national carrier even when the airline was losing money, so the national carriers were often heavily subsidized by their respective governments during economic downturns. In the end, the countries of Europe had produced more than 100 airline companies by the 1980s, compared with approximately 30 airlines in the United States.

A landmark development in the history of European aviation was the privatization of British Airways (BA). BA had been the quintessential European national flag carrier. It was regal, steeped in tradition and boasted the world's most extensive international route service. But it was also highly inefficient with bloated management, a strike-prone workforce and large financial losses for the government. The financial turnaround of British Airways became a prime objective for Margaret Thatcher's government. As was already being done with government-owned assets in telecommunications and energy, plans were formalized to privatize the carrier, and BA's shares were finally floated on the London Stock Exchange in 1987.

Over the past two decades airline privatization has become a worldwide trend. With a few exceptions, the majority of airlines outside North America were fully owned by their governments in 1980. Now that number has been significantly reduced, with a growing number of governments selling part or all of their airlines (see Exhibit 5 to see the deregulation evolution). Moreover, the decreasing regulations changed the way traffic rights are allocated among European competitors. Spinetta stressed this impact of this evolution on the market:

> *Any European carrier benefits from total freedom to acquire traffic rights and establish itself in another European country. Contrary to preconceived ideas, there are no more protectionist barriers inside Europe. ... Ever since the 1st of January 1993, all European carriers have known that the days when European air transport was organized around national champions are over.*

The need for cooperation in the airline industry

Although the first attempts did not lead to a transnational company, for want of synergy, airlines never gave up. Cooperation developed in the form of

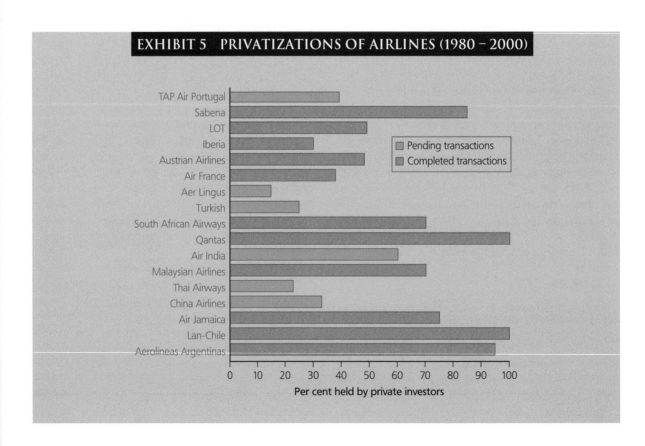

EXHIBIT 5   PRIVATIZATIONS OF AIRLINES (1980 – 2000)

alliances. In 1998, the Chairman of KLM summed up the process, asserting that:

> *Europe established a unified market, which is now an economic reality, [trading] rules changed significantly, but the airline industry remained static, based on a 'national champion' in each country. This is nonsense, this is obsolete.*

Star Alliance and its mates

Deregulation led to more intense competition in the major airfields, yet a national airline facing more intense competition could always keep a competitive advantage thanks to its national facilities. How could Air France compete with American giant companies that controlled every hub on American soil? How could Lufthansa obtain a significant market share in France? Before Star Alliance, Northwest Airlines and KLM were operating together as the forerunners of the modern airline alliance system (see Exhibit 6 for details of the major alliances and the partner airlines) since 1993, although there had been earlier pairings and groupings of airlines for decades on a less formal level.

In 1997, Star Alliance was formed, considered a milestone in the industry because of the number of

EXHIBIT 6   ALLIANCE COMPOSITIONS 2006

	Star Alliance	OneWorld	Sky Team
Passengers/year	425 millions	242.6 millions	372.9 millions
Market share	23.6%	13.5%	20.7%
Members	Adria Airways Air Canada Air New Zealand ANA Asiana Airlines Austrian Airlines Blue1 bmi Croatia Airlines LOT Polish Airlines Lufthansa SAS Singapore Airlines South African Airways Spanair Swiss International Air Lines TAP Portugal Thai Airways International United US Airways	Aer Lingus American Airlines British Airways Cathay Pacific Finnair Iberia LAN Qantas	Aeroflot Aeroméxico Air France-KLM Alitalia Continental Czech Airlines Delta Korean Air Northwest
Network Strengths	North America (AC, UA, US) Central America (AC, UA, US) Caribbean (AC, US) Europe (BD, LH, TP, JK, LO, LX, OS, SK, KF, LO, JP, OU) Middle East (LH, OS) Africa (LH, SA) Asia (SQ, TG, NH, OZ, UA) Australia & NZ(NZ, UA) Pacific Islands (NZ)	US & Canada (AA) Mexico & Central America (AA) Caribbean (AA, LA) South America (LA, IB) Western Europe (BA, EI, AY, IB) Asia (CX) Australia & New Zealand (QF) Pacific Islands (QF, LA) Middle East (RJ)	US & Canada (DL, CO, NW) Mexico & Central America (AM, CO, DL) Caribbean (DL, CO) Western Europe (AF, KL, AZ, SU) Central & Eastern Europe (OK, AZ) Middle East (AF, AZ) Africa (AF) Asia (KE, NW) Pacific Islands (CO)
Network Weaknesses	South America	Africa	South America (Copa) Australia & NZ

agents involved and because it speeded up the creation of other alliances. In 2006, Star Alliance ran 16 930 daily flights to 842 airports in 152 countries.

In 1998, OneWorld was launched when American Airlines, British Airways, Canadian Airlines, Cathay Pacific and Qantas announced their intention to form a new alliance. A year later, OneWorld became operational. In 2006, the alliance was the third largest, reaching more than 600 destinations in 135 countries around the world, operating more than 8000 daily flights. It was the only alliance with a full network in Australia and the only alliance with a member based in South America.

On June 22, 1999, Air France and Delta (the second biggest airline carrier after American Airlines at the time) announced the creation of a global alliance, the fourth after Star Alliance, OneWorld and Wings. It was a pure commercial alliance with the aggregation of programs for customers' fidelity, the harmonization of services and the handling of passengers as well as coordination of the trans-Atlantic flights. The alliance was complementary for both companies: Delta Airlines was focused on the American continent, whereas Air France focused on the European, African and Asian continents. A year later, four major airlines, Aero México, Air France, Delta Air Lines and Korean Air launched, a global alliance focused on the passenger. They also operated a cargo alliance called Cargo with all current members except Continental Cargo.

Alliances were meant to broaden and standardized the offer of every member by (a) cooperation in scheduling; (b) a unique office for ticketing; (c) code sharing to optimize occupancy rates; (d) easier flight transfer operations; (e) frequent flyer programmes; and (f) shared airport lounges. For airlines, the point was to reduce fixed costs and to share best practices.

Are there other real synergies?

OneWorld was the first airline alliance to establish a central management system. Based in Vancouver, Canada, it had a managing director who reported to an alliance board that was made up of the chief executives of each of the member airlines. The role of chairman of the board was held on a rotating basis. Function heads for commercial, IT, public relations, airports and customer service, and a global project director reported to the managing partner.

Member airlines also developed common specifications as widely as possible across their engineering and maintenance activities, aligning their policies and procedures and working together to develop and support solutions that could be applied throughout the airline industry. Costs were also reduced through bulk buying and by sharing parts between one another.

The reciprocal use of the hubs was at the heart of the alliance strategy: forming an alliance with Air France, Delta got access to the hub of Roissy Charles de Gaulle and thus to the European market; accordingly Air France got access to Delta's hub in Atlanta and thus to the American market (refer Exhibit 7 for the hub model). When asked about the prospects of alliances, Spinetta said: 'Alliances are a reasoned response to the antiquated regulatory system and facilitators for providing indirect access into restricted markets.'

In his mind, global alliances were still far from reaching their limits in terms of efficiency and development of the airline cooperation. Moreover, the discrepancies between international regulations kept it

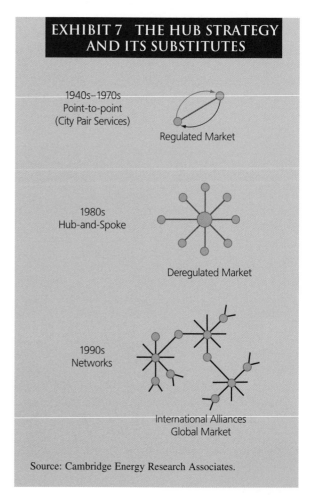

EXHIBIT 7   THE HUB STRATEGY AND ITS SUBSTITUTES

1940s–1970s
Point-to-point
(City Pair Services)

Regulated Market

1980s
Hub-and-Spoke

Deregulated Market

1990s
Networks

International Alliances
Global Market

Source: Cambridge Energy Research Associates.

difficult for a national airline to take over a competitor. Spinetta gave this example:

If, for example, BA was to take over Iberia, a non-European country could say – we'll withdraw the traffic rights we gave to Spain, because they will now be exploited by a British and not a Spanish carrier. This major contradiction between European and international law, which still exists, continues to hamper mergers and groupings.

The Air France-KLM deal

Air France

The history of France's air-carrier industry began in 1909 with the advent of *Compagnie Générale Trans-aérienne*. This company mainly operated dirigibles and seaplanes and operated in the airmail business. The first passenger airlines appeared at the end of World War I. At that time, passenger transportation was developing fast, but only 6786 passengers were carried in 1922; five times more would be carried ten years later. Driven by the financial crisis in the early 1930s, an airline was created and named Air France in August 1933. On June 26, 1945, the French civil aviation industry was nationalized and the former private company Air France became state-owned.

After the war, new technology aircrafts enabled French air transport to take off again and to continue its former expansion. On July 1, 1946, the first Paris–New York flight was made and the airline regained its position among the world's leading airlines. It operated a fleet of 130 aircraft and got off to a flying start over the next few years.

From 1965 to 1970, Air France was increasingly subjected to international competition. Air traffic increased at that time at an average yearly rate of 7.5 per cent. In 1972, Air France set up a cargo division and developed this activity, which grew considerably. Being a pioneer, Air France became a leader in cargo transportation. On January 21, 1976, Air France introduced the supersonic Concorde. Two years later the economy faced a downturn due to the increasing oilprices.

In the 1980s the airline industry faced increasing competition with the early deregulation acts. Price wars, the haphazard development of charter airlines and chronic overcapacity characterized this period. Air France coped with the situations by expanding its consumer base. It became one of the top airlines in the world in terms of mass air travel. Yet top management commitment and their intent remained a critical issue. Numerous people politically appointed came and went but did not show consistent leadership and strategy for the company (refer to Exhibit 8 for the list of CEOs of Air France).

Because of the crisis in the early 1990s, Air France, UTA and Air Inter merged to form one of the world's largest air transport groups, the Air France Group, on January 12, 1990. During the 1990s, Air France experienced difficult financial problems and was forced to restructure, which ushered in radical changes. Air France was seeking rationalization and cost reduction possibilities. Plans for annual savings were set up and subsequently abandoned due to lack of efficiency.

On September 18, 1997, Jean-Cyril Spinetta, became the new CEO of Air France. The Initial Public Offering on the February 22, 1999 marked an important stage in the company's history. The IPO was highly successful since the shares were priced at the upper end of the book-building range and were oversubscribed ten times.

In June 1999, Air France signed a long-term partnership agreement with Delta Air Lines which laid the foundation for a global alliance in which Air France invested much of its energy. Through the development of the alliance, Air France managed to stress its global dimension, becoming the second largest airline in the alliance behind Delta.

In 2003, some days before the merger, Air France was struggling with the SARS epidemic consequences, the Iraq war and weak European growth, which impacted results; core businesses generated $12.3 billion in revenue including passenger transport (83 per cent), freight (11.6 per cent), maintenance services (4.3 per cent) and others (1.1 per cent). Yet this turnover represented a 3 per cent decline compared with 2002–2003 and that stressed the need for consolidation.

Koninklijke Luchtvaart Maatschappij (KLM)

Koninklijke Luchtvaart Maatschappij (KLM), the Royal Dutch Airlines, was founded on October 7, 1919, which made it the world's oldest international airline. With its primary hub (still) located in Amsterdam (Schiphol) the carrier started its first scheduled flight on May 17, 1920, connecting Amsterdam and London. KLM became the pioneer in intercontinental flights with its flight to Indonesia. Subsequently, regularly scheduled flights to the Far

EXHIBIT 8   PROFILE OF CHAIRMEN OF AIR FRANCE

Air France has a long history of Chairmen who have been appointed by government. These appointments were mostly a return favour or based upon lifelong friendships. The accumulated profits/losses per chairman for the last 20 years:

Marceau Long (1984–1987). Profits: €134 mn
Appointed by François Mitterrand, as remuneration for his efforts for the French State. He was head of Air France awaiting another job: becoming Vice-president of the 'Conseil d'Etat'. Not knowing anything about business, and not having ever heard of Boeing and overbooking, and not eager to learn, he left the management of Air France totally to the techno-structure in place.

Jacques Friedmann (1987–1988). Profits: €360 mn
His childhood friend Jacques Chirac appointed him, to fulfil the ungrateful task of replacing the industry leaders appointed by the socialist government. Starting his job part-time, he realized after a few months that managing Air France was a full time job. Faced with an outdated fleet he launched an investment programme, without taking care of the finances.

Bernard Attali (1988–1993). Loss: €1, 77 bn
Appointed because his brother, Jacques Attali was a close friend of Jacques Chirac, the French prime minister until 1988. Did not know anything about air transport, but that didn't stop him from acquiring Air Inter and UTA at insupportable debt rates. He left the company in a state of near bankruptcy, deep in the biggest crisis Air France ever experienced.

Christian Blanc (1993–1997). Loss: €1,26 bn
Known for his qualities as a tough negotiator and tempered character. He was appointed by the French prime minister Edouard Balladur in the middle of the big crisis in 1993. He dealt briskly with major personnel strikes and was responsible for obtaining the government subsidy of 20 bn Francs. This subsidy allowed Air France to survive and it directed Air France towards privatization. He was also responsible for the beginnings of the hub strategy.

Jean-Cyril Spinetta (1997–present).
Christian Blanc was replaced by Jean-Cyril Spinetta in 1997. Blanc successfully brought Air France back in the black and wanted the French government to completely privatize Air France. Lionel Jospin, the French prime minister at the time refused so Blanc left the company. Spinetta was appointed, having had previous experience in the business, at the helm of Air Inter. Spinetta's main accomplishments are the further expansion of the CdG hub and the formation of a successful alliance.

East began in 1929. In May 1946, KLM became the first continental European airline to open transatlantic services to the United States. KLM had three core activities: passenger transport, cargo transport and engineering and maintenance businesses.

With 4.4 million passengers carried to 142 destinations in more than 70 countries in 2003, KLM was ranked 14th in worldwide international passengers carried and 7th worldwide in terms of international passengers' kilometres flown

KLM started to operate its transatlantic routes between the Netherlands and the United States under a far-reaching alliance with Northwest Airlines, which offered its customers seamless travel options between North America and Europe, Africa, the Middle East and India. The long-standing cooperation and trust between these two partner airlines had shown that such an alliance could deliver substantial benefits despite stiff competition and a flagging economy.

In October 2001, KLM and Continental Airlines joined in a temporary commercial alliance and also concluded a fully reciprocal frequent flyer agreement. In May 2002, a code sharing agreement between the two was reviewed covering selected connecting flights between Newark and Houston (the two hubs controlled by Continental Airlines) and other domestic destinations in the United States with selected connecting flights across Europe, Africa and the Middle East. By June 2003, this contract was expanded to make a co-terminus with the KL/NWA Enhanced Alliance Implementation Agreement.

In 2003, KLM was at a crossroad. Its declining position in business and individual air travel had adversely impacted its financial situation. Also, with the saturation of air travel providers in Europe, KLM was close to filing Chapter 11 bankruptcy. In this context, there was a need for consolidation in light of the challenges facing the industry

The merger

On September 30, 2003, the merger between Air France and KLM Royal Dutch Airlines was announced. The new group, which would be named Air France-KLM, would become operative in the first quarter of 2004 after being approved by the U.S Securities and Exchange Commission (SEC). Spinetta commented on the merger: 'this is the creation of the first European airline group and a consolidation of the airline industry.'

The merger was a tender offer based on a stock swap: 11 AF shares + 10 stock options for 10 shares of KLM stock. It represented a premium of 40 per cent for KLM shareholders and the strategic aspect of the move was clearly valuable. The strategic rationale for this merger was clear in the minds of Spinetta and Van Wijk. They were (a) structural changes and a consolidation of the European airline landscape were required to create more profitability (b) further reinforced cooperation was required (c) both companies were complementary: two widespread brands, two modern hubs (Paris CDG and Schiphol Amsterdam), complementary networks on medium-haul flights, as well as long-haul flights and the creation of one of the biggest suppliers for maintenance activities.

The foreseeable advantages

The new group would serve 226 destinations with a fleet of 540 planes and 106 000 employees. Air France-KLM would continue to develop its three principle activities: passenger (77 per cent of turnover), cargo (14 per cent) and maintenance (4 per cent). In the meantime, the group could be reinforced by a possible integration of Alitalia.

One of the main consequences of the merger was the dilution of the equity and the transformation of Air France, a state owned company to a publicly owned company (see Exhibit 9 for the equity breakdown evolution).

The expected synergies of Air France-KLM were meant to increase consolidated operating revenues. The merger was a 'market extension M&A'. The new company could optimize its management, benefit from a larger network and extend its maintenance activities. In addition, due to its dominant position, cost savings could be realized from increased bargaining power (purchasing power when buying new planes) and commercial distribution. The expected cost savings was €500 million a year, which would be reached through economies of scale and scope.

The merger of Air France and KLM had direct consequences on, with Air France-KLM the new powerful member. As a result of the growing attractiveness of, other airline carriers were integrated in the alliance like Aeroflot, the Russian carrier which opened up the promising market of the former Soviet Union. Thanks to KLM's long standing partnerships with Northwest and Continental and, from there, their probable integration into the alliance, new dimensions could be brought to its transatlantic strategy. That was possibly a reason the Franco-Dutch merger was ratified by U.S. and European regulatory authorities with some difficulties: lobbyists were not satisfied that the new alliance would be able to control a fourth of the world's air traffic.

Moreover, the merger of Air France and KLM pushed Air France into a new dimension: it surpassed British Airways as Europe's leading airline and its position within was aligned to Delta's. Spinetta said:

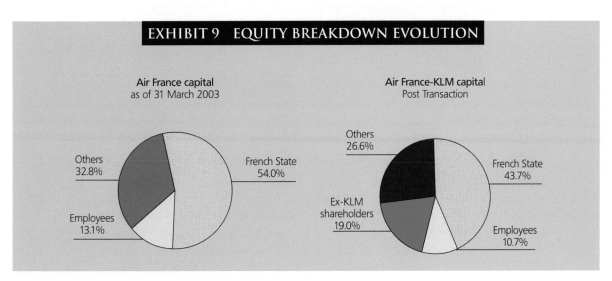

EXHIBIT 9 EQUITY BREAKDOWN EVOLUTION

Air France capital
as of 31 March 2003

Others 32.8%
French State 54.0%
Employees 13.1%

Air France-KLM capital
Post Transaction

Others 26.6%
French State 43.7%
Ex-KLM shareholders 19.0%
Employees 10.7%

'We were at risk because we were middleweight champions in a heavyweight contest.'

Also the deal forced Air France's European competitors, like the German Star Alliance member Lufthansa, to fortify its efforts searching for a new member in the U.S. Furthermore, some analysts expected that the Franco-Dutch merger would have a snowball effect with Alitalia, Swiss and Iberia quickly becoming the next takeover candidates. Air France and Alitalia had been regularly in contact; the two companies had been sharing codes and collaborating since 2002. It must be underlined that Spinetta was on Alitalia's board of directors until January 17, 2007 and Giancarlo Cimoli, Alitalia's CEO, was on Air France's board until January 18, 2007. As Robert Czerwensky, an equities analyst at Vereins and Westbank commented: 'An important market effect would be that every country would no longer have its own airlines for the sake of prestige.'

Following this pattern, the airline industry was reconstructed around the three existing global alliances. An aviation consultant commented: 'This is the destiny of the industry, but I regret to see that no more than three global alliances are in place, that a fourth failed.'

The side effects

Nevertheless, many issues had to be addressed. For example, different corporate cultures (French and Dutch) needed to be reconciled and the two-hub, long-haul route system had to be established and managed. Also, the French and Dutch airlines shared many identical destinations that had to be rationalized immediately. In order to not cannibalize each other and to stay ahead of rivals, they decreased prices and initiated competition on the European market. The merger's impact on could be critical, as a transportation consultant pointed out:

> It could either slow it [the development] down, which the French carrier putting more emphasis on the materialization of its KLM partnership, or boost it with the Air France-KLM merger acting as a catalyst for faster integration and deeper cooperation with other members.

Also, the diversity of alliance members was striking. Air France and Alitalia were state-controlled units, whereas CSA Czech was dominantly owned by a national property fund and Delta and Korean Airlines were publicly owned. This might be a concern since coordination among the partners had to still consider non-business interests such as political interferences which were not in line with 's new dominant position. Another problem to keep in mind was the possible integration of Continental and Northwest. According to some experts, bringing Delta, Continental and Northwest into the same alliance was a challenge due to their high rivalry in the North American market.

But leaders were afraid of other difficulties that could attack profitability plans and growth. As Spinetta warned: 'The Europeans do not create sufficient runway capacity to cope with growth, a weakness that will further concentrate traffic growth in a small number of existing hubs.'

EXHIBIT 10 KEY DATES IN THE AF-KLM MERGER

- 30 September 2003: Air France and KLM officially announce their merger through Air France's friendly public exchange offer for KLM.

- 11 February 2004: Approval received from the European and US anti-trust authorities.

- 29 March 2004: Go-ahead received from the *Commission des Participations et des Transferts* for equity interests and transfers.

- 5 April 2004: Exchange offering launched on KLM securities.

- 5 May 2004: Launch of the new company on the Paris, Amsterdam and New York stock exchanges.

- 15 September 2004: Holding company set up.

- 22 February 2005: AIR FRANCE KLM named Airline of the Year by Air Transport World Magazine

- 23 March 2005: AIR FRANCE KLM launches its joint frequent flyer program, Flying Blue, replacing Air France's Fréquence Plus and KLM's Flying Dutchman programms.

EXHIBIT 11   KEY FIGURES: AIR FRANCE-KLM PERFORMANCE IN 2006

- World's leading airline group in terms of turnover: €21.04 bn in revenues (+10%)
- Europe's leading airline group in terms of market share
- World's leading airline group for freight transported (revenue tonne-kilometres)
- 102,000 employees
- 70 million passengers
- 565 aircrafts in operation
- 225 destinations including 110 long-haul and 125 medium-haul

Activity breakdown (sales revenue)-2006

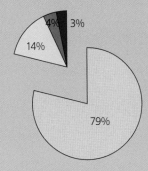

□ Passengers   □ Cargo - Fret   ■ Maintenance   ■ other activities

Unrestricted competition was not yet a reality in the airline industry and the political interferences were still too high.

The birth of a global leader

The synergies gained from that merger could create a social threat in Europe where layoffs and restructuring are traditionally unpopular. It was all the more true since Air France had been state owned until the merger and KLM was a national pride. Mergers had already been tried in the field but had failed and Spinetta explained why: 'In the past, many mergers have failed because they have concentrated too much on cost-cutting and downsizing and not enough on growing market share and revenues. Right from the beginning, we decided on an offensive rather than defensive strategy.'

Therefore, the two companies backed themselves up with social negotiations and guarantees given to every stakeholder for an eight year period: (a) Air France and KLM would retain their respective home bases, their operating licenses and all their air traffic rights; (b) the multi-hub system around Paris CDG and Schiphol would be developed homogeneously; (c) the national identities, logos and brands of the two companies would be safeguarded; (d) the two maintenance services would be protected; and (e) no discrimination in promotion decisions would be guaranteed.

Regarding commercial synergies, the two companies enjoyed a broader network with several new destinations available. They also worked on the optimization of unprofitable routes and began offering reduced fares to attract new customers, combined with an ambitious goal of a 10 per cent cost cut per year, which would come from a reduction of the number of services and the number of crew attendants in medium haul flights. Anticipating a negative reaction from customers and a publicity campaign pointing out the decreasing quality of services, Air France decided to stress the modernization of its fleet and began in 2005 a marketing campaign to target business travellers. Air France launched the common frequent flyer programme, a merger of the Air France and KLM programmes. It strengthened the Air France KLM brand and allowed cost savings by reducing the number of offices across the world.

The main synergy was gained in IT systems. Air France and KLM had to align the way they packaged

EXHIBIT 12 INCOME STATEMENT (2004–2005)

In €m	2005–06	2004–05 pro forma	change
Turnover	21,448	19,467	+10,2%
Operating income	936	553	+69.3%
Operating margin	4.4%	2.8%	+1.6
Income from operating activities	1,455	1,931	ns
Net income, Group share	913	1,704[1]	ns
Net income before restatements relating to the recognition of pension fund surpluses	913	706	+29.3%
Net income per share (in €)	3.47	6.59[1]	
Dividend per share (in €)	0.30	0.15	
Operating cash flow	2,656	2,054	+29.3%
Operating cash flow margin	12.4%	10.6%	+1.8
Net debt (in €bn)	4,380	5,640	
Equity (in €bn)	7,853	6,020	
Gearing	0.56	0.94	

(1) After write-back of total negative goodwill arising on KLM acquisition of 1.35 billion

and sold their services to customers. They could, in this way, improve the quality of service and gain both on the cost and the revenue sides. Spinetta illustrated that:

If we have to cancel an AF flight between Paris and Shanghai, we must be able to rapidly offer our customer from Barcelona or elsewhere a good alternative, in other words a KLM flight to Shanghai through Amsterdam. Aligning your IT systems makes this kind of thing possible.

For the fiscal year 2004–2005, Air France and KLM released their financial results jointly. The turnover was up by 7.3 per cent at €19.02 billion, the EBIT was up 33.4 per cent, whereas oil costs went up 33.3 per cent.

For the fiscal year 2005–2006, the company announced a 10 per cent boom of it turnover to €21.4 billion, a €936 million net income and a €1 billion free cash flow. Air France was then the largest airline and the most profitable; able to overcome skyrocketing oil prices (refer to Exhibit 7 for oil price evolution). The synergies which were meant to represent $400 million to $500 million over 5 years were revised to $600 million at the end of 2006.

The future

Overcoming analysts' pessimism and every external pitfall (oil prices, social constraints, political pressure),

Spinetta and Van Wijk made Air France and KLM a global leader in the airline industry. While American companies were filing bankruptcy under Chapter 11, Air France increased its market share, industrial efficiency and profitability. In 2006, the new group was the world leader in terms of the number of passengers (70 million), turnover (€21.4 billion) and freight volume (1 330 000 tons). The market also had changed its mind and the stock traded at more than €35 in the first months of 2007 and analysts stressed: 'While its competitors are struggling, Air France KLM look well placed to gain market shares in a sector increasingly clustered between high-end companies and discounters.'

Spinetta won his place next to Carlos Ghosn as the French businessman of the year in 2005. The streak continued with a very promising 2006–2007 and Spinetta asserted:

Thanks to the merger, Air France KLM is the world leader and benefits from a unique competitive position which is contributing to the continued improvement of our results. ... Over the medium term, we are targeting capacity growth of 5 per cent in line with the market demand and including significantly more flights to India and China.

CASE 14

BT Group: Bringing external innovation inside

By Felipe Monteiro and Donald N. Sull

As he prepared to board British Airways flight 284, from San Francisco to London, Jean-Marc Frangos, BT's Senior Vice President, Technology and Innovation, nostalgically remembered his flight from San Francisco to first present the activities of his team in Silicon Valley to BT executives. Almost six years earlier, in June 2000, Frangos, a London Business School alumnus, had been assigned to head BT's Technology Scouting unit in Palo Alto, at that time a brand new unit designed to spot emerging business models and technologies developed in the United States. After six years in that function, Frangos had analysed hundreds of technologies and crossed the Atlantic almost every two months trying to connect what he was seeing in Silicon Valley with the needs of BT's lines of business in the UK.

In May 2006, most BT executives believed that BT's ability to source and commercialize external innovation was paramount for BT's survival. Although BT, one of Europe's largest telecommunications providers, with revenues exceeding £19.5 billion in fiscal year 2006, was still the dominant telecommunications player in the UK (at the end of 2005, it had 59 per cent of the residential and 41 per cent of the business voice market in the UK), the revenues from its traditional businesses were declining significantly (see Exhibits 1–3 for BT's financial indicators; and Exhibit 4 for BT's share performance). A combination of market deregulation and the convergence of formerly distinct industries presented BT with an intensity of competition that many executives believed was unprecedented in the industry. In addition, analysts predicted the imminent entry of big media players, such as BskyB, into the telecommunications market. Media players planned, for example, to use BT's copper local loops to connect directly to the end customers, offering them broadband and other services. BT's senior management team believed the group would either need to generate innovative services and products or fail in the market. BT's Group Chief Technology Officer (GCTO), Matt Bross, shared this assessment. Bross, who joined BT in 2002 was brought in by Chief Executive Officer, Ben Verwaayen. Bross frequently emphasised the mantra that 'we have to innovate the way we innovate'. (See Exhibit 5 for a summary of BT's new approach to innovation). He was also the driving force behind BT's 21st Century Network, a transformational project aimed at re-inventing BT's network and systems in order to enable them to deliver the innovation in the markets it served.

Against this competitive backdrop, Frangos' unit gained visibility within the Group, and the scope of the unit was expanding. By 2006, Frangos oversaw not only the Silicon Valley unit but also scouting teams in China and Japan, as well as the UK-based Innovation Central and Applied Technology Centre, charged with the task of articulating and testing emerging technologies identified outside the Group. Unlike some technology scouting units of other companies, Frangos' unit was measured against aggressive 'innovation dividend' targets, i.e., concrete financial benefits to BT either in terms of cost benefits or revenue generation rather than the number of reports written or companies visited. In 2005, for instance, Frangos's area was tasked to deliver £500 million in innovation dividends to the BT Group.

As he boarded the plane, Frangos contemplated three alternatives to increase the innovation dividend his unit could deliver: first, he could try to hire more managers to work in the existing scouting units. This would certainly increase the volume of external technologies being accessed by BT, but Frangos was not entirely convinced this increase in staff size would translate into higher innovation dividends. A second alternative would be to establish scouting units in other parts of the world. Israel and India, for instance, were considered strategic for the telecommunication industry. If, on the one hand, Frangos acknowledged that it was necessary to have scouts in areas, other than Silicon Valley, China and Japan, he feared he would get less and less mileage as the geographic scope of his scouting team expanded. Finally, Frangos wondered whether he needed to have more of his own people in the UK. All these options seemed promising

EXHIBIT 1   BRITISH TELECOM GROUP BALANCE SHEET

Year to March (£rnn)	2005	2006	2007e	2008e	2009e
Goodwll and other intangible assets	1,259	1,641	1,390	1,139	886
Property plant and equipment, gross	38,108	38,108	41,180	44,144	47,039
Accumulated depreciation	−22,722	−22,619	−25,272	−27,936	−30,604
Property plant and equipment, net	15,386	15,489	15,908	16,208	16,435
Other non current assets	133	84	99	115	131
Deferred tax assets	1,434	764	638	506	367
Non current assets	**18,212**	**17,978**	**18,036**	**17,968**	**17,819**
Inventories	106	124	124	124	124
Trade and other receivables	4,269	4,199	4,339	4,312	4,272
Other financial assets	3,634	434	434	434	434
Cash and cash equivalents	1,312	1,965	2,976	2,790	2,018
Current assets	**9,321**	**6,722**	**7,872**	**7,661**	**6,848**
Total assets	**27,533**	**24,700**	**25,908**	**25,628**	**24,667**
Loans and other borrowings	4,261	1,940	1,940	1,940	1,940
Trade and other payables	6,772	6,540	6,756	6,700	6,618
Other current liabilities	1,020	1,000	1,000	1,000	1,000
Current liabilities	**12,053**	**9,480**	**9,696**	**9,640**	**9,658**
Loans and other borrowings	7,744	7,995	8,913	8,673	7,660
Deferred tax liabilities	1,715	1,605	1,605	1,605	1,505
Retirement benetrt obligations	4,781	2,547	2,139	1,696	1,231
Other non current labilities	1,145	1,566	1,566	1,566	1,566
Non current liabilities	**15,385**	**13,613**	**14,123**	**13,440**	**11,852**
Called up share capital	432	432	132	o118	o118
Reserves	−387	1,123	1,905	2,615	3,324
Total equity shareholders' fords	45	1,555	2,037	2,497	3,206
Minority interest	50	62	52	52	52
Total equity	**95**	**1,607**	**2,089**	**2,549**	**3,258**
Total liabilities	**27,533**	**24,700**	**25,908**	**25,628**	**24,667**

Source: BT, Morgan Stanley Research (BT Group plc Report. July 6, 2006)

growth avenues. Frangos, however, had clearly in mind that the goal of his area was to continue delivering a substantial level of innovation dividends for BT, not just bringing more external ideas that would have no impact inside the company.

As the captain announced that the plane was ready to take-off, Frangos decided to take advantage of the 10-hour flight to London to finalize the plan he would present to Matt Bross, BT's Group Chief Technology Officer, the following morning.

Background

British Telecommunications plc (the predecessor name for BT Group) emerged out of the 1984 Telecommunication Act, which created two telecommunication service providers (BT and Mercury) and also established the Office of Telecommunications (OFTEL), as the independent regulatory body charged with overseeing the telecommunications industry. Initially, the British government held 49 per cent of BT's

EXHIBIT 2   BRITISH TELECOM GROUP CASH FLOW STATEMENT

Year End March(£m)	2005	2006	2007e	2008e	2009e
Operating profit (pre G/W)	2,693	2,633	2,647	2,729	2,816
Exceptionals	−59	18	0	0	0
Depreciation	2,844	2,884	2,966	2,983	2,970
Working capital	253	120	0	0	0
Movement in provisions	175	277	−112	−112	−112
Net cash from operating activities	**5,906**	**5,932**	**5,502**	**5,600**	**5,673**
Capital expenditure	−2,945	−2,874	−3,055	−3,055	−3,007
Acquisitions/disposals of financial investments	537	−1	0	0	0
Taxation	−332	−390	−494	−541	−592
Dividends from associates/JVs	2	1	1	1	1
Free cash flow	**3,168**	**2,668**	**1,954**	**2,005**	**2,076**
Interest	−886	−901	−595	−595	−595
Equity free cash flow	**2,282**	**1,767**	**1,359**	**1,410**	**1,481**
Dividends	−784	−907	−1,095	−1,197	−1,265
Acquistions	119	−167	0	0	0
Disposals	−537	0	0	0	0
Shares Issued/bought back	−193	−339	0	0	0
Net cash/debt Impact from cash flows	**887**	**354**	**264**	**213**	**216**
Acquired debt	−159	0	0	0	0
Currency/other non-cash movements	−91	160	0	0	0
Net cash (debt) movement	**637**	**514**	**264**	**213**	**216**
Loans repayments	−1,292	−2,946	0	0	0
Management of liquid resources	712	3,221	0	0	0
Currency/other non-cash movements	247	−160	0	0	0
Cash movement	**305**	**629**	**264**	**213**	**216**
Net debt B/F	−8,530	−7,893	−7,379	−7,115	−6,902
Net debt C/F	−7,893	−7,379	−7,116	−6,902	−6,686
EFCF/share (p)	26.8	21.0	16.3	16.9	17.7
FCF/share (p)	37.2	31.7	23.4	24.0	24.8
FCF yield on EV (%)	11.7	9.8	7.2	7.4	7.6
FCF yield on equity (%)	11.8	9.1	7.0	7.3	7.6

Source: BT Group, West LB Research Estimates (BT Group Equity Research Report, 1 August 2006)

shares but sold its share to investors over the following decade.

During the 1990s, BT aspired to become a global player in the telecommunications industry and expanded into the US market. In June 1994, BT acquired a 20 per cent stake in MCI Communication Corporation, the second largest carrier of long distance telecommunications in the US, and established a US$1 billion joint-venture called Concert Communications Services. By the end of 1996, the joint venture between BT and MCI had emerged as a leading supplier of global telecommunication services to 3000 multinationals companies with more than US$1.5 billion in revenue under contract. BT executives initiated a merger with MCI, but WorldCom disrupted the deal with a share offer for MCI. BT executives declined to match WorldCom's offer, and the BT/MCI merger never occurred. In 1997, BT sold its stake in MCI to

EXHIBIT 3 BRITISH TELECOM GROUP PROFIT & LOSS ACCOUNT

Year End March(£m)	2005	2006	2007e	2008e	2009e
Turnover	**18,429.0**	**19,514.0**	**19,923.5**	**20,205.6**	**20,306.1**
BT Global Services	7,488.0	8,772.0	9,122.9	9,396.6	9,584.5
BT Retail	8,698.0	8,507.0	8,228.6	7,915.7	7,647.2
BT Wholesale	9,095.0	7,343.0	7,453.1	7,564.9	7,640.6
Openreach		5,142.0	5,126.2	5,151.9	5,177.6
EBITDA	**5,537.0**	**5,517.0**	**5,613.9**	**5,712.2**	**5,785.3**
BT Global Services	961.0	926.0	977.5	1,080.6	1,150.1
BT Retail	754.0	716.0	748.8	712.4	688.3
BT Wholesale	3,864.0	1,861.0	1,929.8	1,942.1	1,950.5
Openreach		1,983.0	1,926.7	1,946.0	1,965.5
EBITDA margin (%)	**30.0**	**28.3**	**28.2**	**28.3**	**28.5**
BT Global Services	12.8	10.6	10.7	11.5	12.0
BT Retail	8.7	8.4	9.1	9.0	9.0
BT Wholesale	42.5	25.3	25.9	25.7	25.5
Openreach		38.6	37.6	37.8	38.0
Depreciation	**−28440.0**	**−2,884.0**	**−2,966.4**	**−2,982.8**	**−2,970.4**
BT Global Services	−550.0	−638.0	−657.0	−657.0	−657.0
BT Retail	−147.0	−147.0	−158.0	−158.0	−158.0
BT Wholesale	−1,914.0	−1,102.0	−1,150.0	−1,150.0	−1,150.0
Openreach		−800.0	−795.1	−803.1	−811.1
BT Global Services	411.0	288.0	320.5	423.6	493.1
BT Retail	607.0	569.0	590.8	554.4	530.3
BT Wholesale	1,950.0	759.0	779.8	792.1	800.5
Openreach		1,183.0	1,131.6	1,142.9	1,154.3
JVs/associates (inc.Concert)	−14.0	−16.0	−18.0	−20.0	−22.0
Exceptional operating costs	274.0	−137.0	0.0	0.0	0.0
Share of JV exceptionals	−25.0	0.0	0.0	0.0	0.0
Interest	−599.0	−472.0	−295.0	−295.0	−295.0
Pre tax profit (pre goodwill etc.)	**2,080.0**	**2,177.0**	**2,370.4**	**2,454.4**	**2,541.9**
Pre tax profit	2,329.0	2,040.0	2,370.4	2,454.4	2,541.0
Taxation	−541.0	−533.0	−580.8	−601.3	−622.8
Exceptionals	16.0	41.0	25.0	0.0	0.0
Minorities	1.0	−1.0	0.0	0.0	0.0
Net income to equity (pre GW/excpt)	**1,540.0**	**1,643.0**	**1,789.7**	**1,853.1**	**1,919.1**
Net income	1,805.0	1,547.0	1,814.7	1,853.1	1,919.1
EPS (p)(pre GW/excpt)	**18.1**	**19.5**	**21.4**	**22.2**	**23.0**
EPS (p)(post)	21.2	18.4	21.7	22.2	23.0
EPS(p) diluted(post)	21.0	18.1	21.6	22.0	22.8
DPS(p)	10.4	11.9	13.7	14.6	15.4

Source: BT Group, West LB Research Estimates (BT Group Equity Research Report, 1 August 2006)

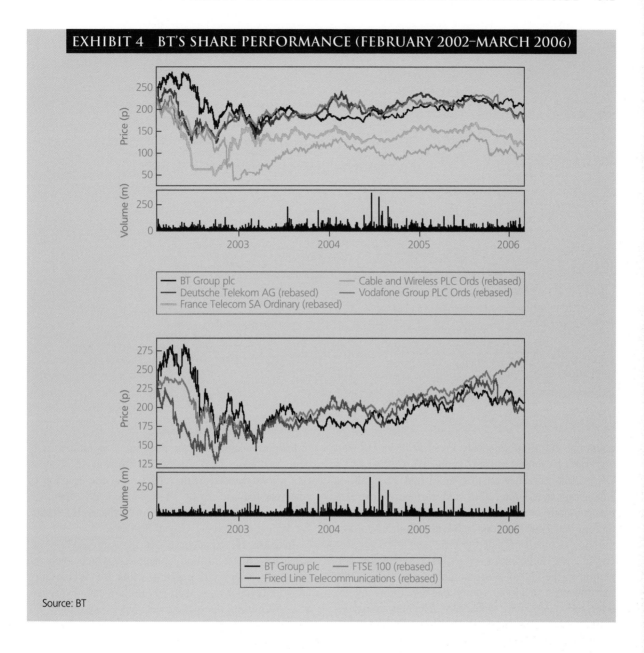

EXHIBIT 4 BT'S SHARE PERFORMANCE (FEBRUARY 2002–MARCH 2006)

Source: BT

WorldCom, booking a profit of over US$2 billion on the original investment.

BT executives maintained their ambition to become the world's first truly integrated global telecommunications service firm, offering a range of technologically advanced communications services to global enterprises. In July 1998, BT announced its intentions to form a global venture with AT&T. The venture, owned equally by BT and AT&T, combined the trans-border assets and operations of both companies, including international networks, international call traffic, and international services for business customers. The joint venture (also called Concert) launched in January 2000 as 'the leading global telecommunications company serving multinational business customers, international carriers and internet service providers worldwide'. Concert had a direct sales force serving approximately 270 multinational customers. Through its network of global distributors, Concert served an additional 29 000 customers worldwide. In addition to using BT's and AT&T's extensive networks in the UK and the US, Concert built a new state-of-the-art high speed Internet Protocol (IP) backbone network spanning 21 cities in 17

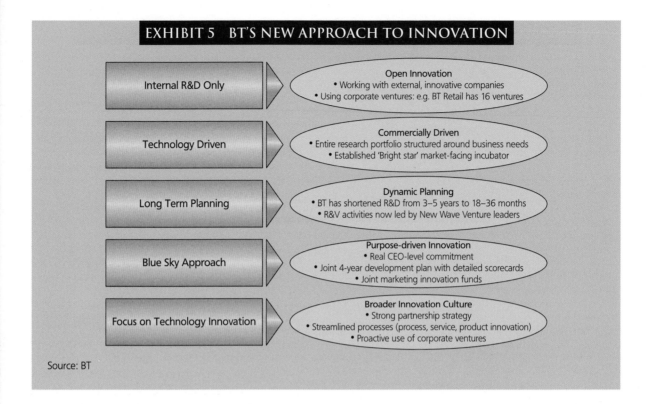

EXHIBIT 5   BT'S NEW APPROACH TO INNOVATION

Internal R&D Only →
Open Innovation
- Working with external, innovative companies
- Using corporate ventures: e.g. BT Retail has 16 ventures

Technology Driven →
Commercially Driven
- Entire research portfolio structured around business needs
- Established 'Bright star' market-facing incubator

Long Term Planning →
Dynamic Planning
- BT has shortened R&D from 3–5 years to 18–36 months
- R&V activities now led by New Wave Venture leaders

Blue Sky Approach →
Purpose-driven Innovation
- Real CEO-level commitment
- Joint 4-year development plan with detailed scorecards
- Joint marketing innovation funds

Focus on Technology Innovation →
Broader Innovation Culture
- Strong partnership strategy
- Streamlined processes (process, service, product innovation)
- Proactive use of corporate ventures

Source: BT

countries. BT simultaneously invested in its UK network and its mobile infrastructure. BT Cellnet (BT's UK mobile operation at that time) had 11.2 million customers by March 2001 and through European-based mobile companies – such as Telfort, Viag Interkom and Esat Digifone – BT also had 5.7 million mobile customers outside the UK.

The new millennium witnessed a significant correction in the global telecommunications sector. With the downturn in global equity markets following the dot.com crash, the wholesale telecommunications market experienced an abrupt slowdown. In 2000/2001, several of BT's UK wholesale customers went bankrupt, reducing BT's external sales by £200 million. In addition, BT took a £3 billion charge against goodwill in its Viag Interkom involvement. Earnings were also reduced by higher interest charges, following the acquisition of businesses and 3G licences (in the UK, BT Cellnet acquired a 3G licence for over £4 billion) and a downturn in demand for the services offered by many of BT's international operations. In the 2002 financial year, the new Chairman – Sir Christopher Bland – and new CEO – Ben Verwaayen – initiated a comprehensive financial and organizational restructuring, which included the UK's largest-ever rights issue (raising £5.9 billion), the spin off BT's wholly-owned mobile assets

in Europe renamed O₂, the disposal of significant non-core businesses and assets, the unwind of Concert (BT's joint venture with AT&T) and the creation of customer-focused lines of business. BT then re-organized into three main lines of business: BT Retail, BT Wholesale and BT Global Services.

In 2006, BT Retail provided network services and solutions to 18 million consumers which included practically every UK business while BT Wholesale's network handles more than 300 million calls every day and 350 million internet connections every month. BT Global Services, on the other hand, had an international scope and addressed the networked IT services needs of multi-site organizations including multinational enterprises with far-flung global operations. It provided a range of specialist network-centric propositions and practices spanning high performance networking, applications management, outsourcing and managed services, and business transformation. BT's 21st century global internet protocol (IP) infrastructure, used in 71 countries, should extend to 160 countries by the end of 2007 and already connected more than 160 000 customer sites in 2005 (see Exhibits 6–8 for more information about BT's lines of business).

In the 2006 financial year, 87 per cent of BT's revenues were derived from operations within the UK.

EXHIBIT 6 BT LINES OF BUSINESS		
	2006	*2005**
BT Retail		
Revenue	8,452	8,698
Gross margin	2,354	2,354
SG&A before leaver costs	1,541	1,576
EBITDA before leaver costs	813	778
Leaver costs	22	24
EBITDA	791	754
Depreciation and amortisation	147	147
Operating profit	644	607
Capital expenditure	153	170
BT Wholesale		
External revenue	4,226	3,820
Internal revenue	5,006	5,275
Revenue	9,232	9,095
Variable cost of sales	2,201	2,162
Gross variable profit	7,031	6,933
Network and SG&A before leaver costs	3,103	3,007
EBITDA before leaver costs	3,928	3,926
Leaver costs	34	62
EBITDA	3,894	3,864
Depreciation and amortisation	1,902	1,914
Operating profit	1,992	1,950
Capital expenditure	2,013	1,981
BT Global Services		
Revenue	8,632	7,488
EBITDA before leaver costs	1,050	1,020
Leaver costs	49	59
EBITDA	1,001	961
Depreciation and amortisation	638	550
Operating profit	363	411
Capital expenditure	702	605

BT and the UK telecom industry in 2005: Regulation, convergence and competition

The UK telecommunications market was one of Europe's largest, with aggregate revenues from all service providers estimated at £44.6 billion in 2004, of which wholesale activity accounted for around 19 per cent (£8.6 billion) and retail revenues for 81 per cent (£36 billion). In the 12 months to 30 September 2005, fixed-line revenues fell to £10.3 billion – down by 9 per cent compared with the previous 12 months – while revenues from mobile communications grew by 16 per cent to £13.6 billion. In September 2005, Ofcom's data showed that 57 per cent of the country's 15.5 million internet connections were over broadband and it was estimated that by December 2005 there were almost 9.8 million broadband connections across the UK. Ofcom's research also showed that there were 62.5 million mobile subscriptions – a figure that was higher than the total UK population, suggesting that a significant number of people had two or more mobile subscriptions. In 2006, three inter-related forces shaping the UK telecommunications industry were particularly affecting BT: A regulatory review; a renewed trend towards convergence and intense competition.

The Office of Communications' (Ofcom) Strategic Review of Telecommunications

In 2003, the Communications Act created a new regulatory body called Ofcom, charged with regulating the UK communications industries, including television, radio, telecommunications and wireless communications services. Ofcom took on the functions and duties of five previously separate regulators: Oftel (telecoms), Radiocommunications Agency (spectrum), ITC (television), the Radio Authority (radio) and the Broadcasting Standards Commission (standards, fairness and privacy in relation to all broadcasters including the BBC).

Since its inception Ofcom aimed to increase competition, innovation and investment certainty in the UK telecommunications sector. According to Ofcom's published reports, the core problem in the UK telecommunications industry was in the fixed line market. Ofcom estimated that in the 20 years since BT's privatization, regulators had failed to stimulate the competition required for long-term consumer benefit and

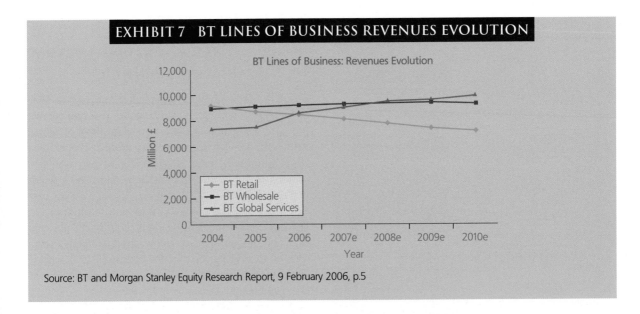

EXHIBIT 7   BT LINES OF BUSINESS REVENUES EVOLUTION

Source: BT and Morgan Stanley Equity Research Report, 9 February 2006, p.5

EXHIBIT 8   BT LINES OF BUSINESS

	BT Retail	*BT Wholesale*	*BT Global Services*
Main services	Voice services, broadband, mobility, ICT solutions	Network services and solutions within the UK	IT services, consulting/ system integration, global carrier,
Target market	Consumers and small and medium enterprises (SMEs)	Fixed and mobile communication companies, internet service providers and other service providers.	Large multi-site organizations.
Number of employees	18,000		30,000
Number of customers	18 million	700 +	10,000
Examples of key customers	Atomized customer base	BT Retail, Vodafone, Cable&Wireless, AOL, Wanadoo	Ministry of Defense, NHS, Inbev, Bristol-Myers Squibb, Barclays, Lloyds, Honeywell, EDS
Competitors	Ntl/Telewest, Cable&Wireless, Easynet, AOL, Wanadoo, Skype, Google		Accenture, EDS, IBM, Atos Origin

spur investment in next generation core and access networks. Ed Richards, Ofcom's COO explained:

Anyone wanting to offer anything close to a national service faces this bottleneck: no-one other than BT can viably supply the line between the customer and the exchange, and in many cases from the exchange further back to the

network, too ... Anyone wanting to compete with BT in the parts of the network that are competitive needs access to this bottleneck. Yet BT is a vertically integrated company. Its wholesale customers, to whom it sells access to this bottleneck, are also its retail competitors. So the combination of vertical integration and market power in this bottleneck part of the network gives BT an incentive to discriminate against its wholesale customers.

In 2004, Ofcom launched the proposal of a Strategic Review of Telecommunications. After considering other options, Ofcom reached an agreement with BT to secure 'real equality of access', i.e., BT committed to behavioural and organizational changes to ensure that its competitors benefited from access to products and processes equivalent to those offered to BT's own retail businesses. This 'real of equality access' policy had two dimensions: First the policy required that BT's own downstream operations use the same products, processes and prices as those used by their rivals – 'equivalence of input' in the jargon. The second established an operational separation within BT to ensure that those responsible for overseeing BT's bottleneck assets had the same incentives to serve other operators in practice and on the ground with the same zeal, efficiency and enthusiasm as they served the BT's own retail business.

This organizational change in BT set up a new, division called Openreach, which controlled the bottleneck asset: the national access network – the metaphorical 'first mile' where millions of calls, web searches and business deals originated each day. Openreach had its own brand, significant discretion over capital expenditure, and linked bonuses to Openreach's performance, not BT's. Openreach was expected to have approximately 30 000 people, of these, 25 000 engineers. These people came almost equally from BT Wholesale and BT Retail.

Convergence

The term convergence in the telecom sector usually described the power of digital media to combine voice, video, data, and text, in new applications, devices and networks. In this regard, convergence arose from the transition from analogue to digital where different forms of content – including voice, pictures, text, audio or visual – now represented undifferentiated bits of data. Convergence could take place at any stage in the value chain (see Exhibit 9 for the telecommunications industry value chain).

Convergence in network platforms, for example, could offer traditional analogue applications, such as voice phone calls, to be offered on digital platform, with voice over internet protocol (VoIP) the main example. Wireless and fixed line networks were also converging and industry analysts expected that the boundaries between fixed and mobile networks would blur as additional spectrum, such as WiFi and WiMAX, roaming across both. TV services delivered over broadband connections (IPTV) represented an example of convergence of services. Convergence was also happening at the device level where telephones could operate on both fixed and mobile network, mobile phones provided mobile TV services and PCs provided internet as well as voice services.

Traditionally focused firms were increasingly merging with other players to capture the opportunities emerging from convergence. A number of big deals had taken place since the beginning of 2005 ITV purchased Friends Reunited for £120 million; Emap bought WGSN for £140 million, EasyNet was acquired by BskyB for £211 million, not to mention Ebay's acquisition of Skype for US$2.6 billion. Sean Williams, Ofcom's Board Director, commented:

In a period of less than 6 months [up to February 2006] we have had the merger of the cable companies ntl and Telewest, and their further bid for Virgin Mobile; the acquisition of Energis by Cable & Wireless, on top of its previous acquisition of Bulldog; the acquisition of Easynet by BskyB; the acquisition of Your Communications by Thus; the acquisition of O2 by Telefonica, the acquisition of One.Tel [UK] and Tele2 [UK] by Carphone Warehouse. . . . Has there been a 6-month period with so many large transactions? Not for a long time.

Competition

BT executives believed that the group faced the most intense competition in its history because the agreement with Ofcom that opened access to the 'first mile' of its network coincided with heightened convergence in the industry. Competition came not only from traditional rivals, but from a wide variety of companies, ranging from large players in the wireless (e.g. Vodafone, T-Mobile, O2) and cable (e.g. ntl/Telewest) segments to hundreds of niche service providers, as well as media operators (e.g. BskyB) entering the fray. (See Exhibit 10 for a table with UK telecom market players).

BT remained the single largest player in the UK telecoms sector. In 2004 its overall share of the UK telecoms revenue was just over 41 per cent. And at the end of 2005, BT had 59 per cent of the residential and 41 per cent of the business voice market in the UK. Analysts, however, believed that BT faced several risks including competition driven by fixed to mobile substitution, voice over IP and unbundling strategies

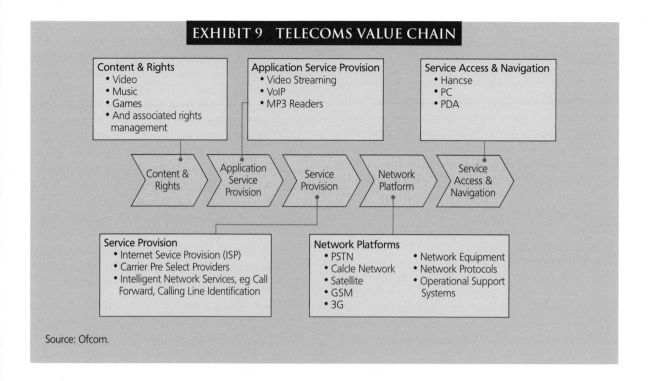

EXHIBIT 9   TELECOMS VALUE CHAIN

Content & Rights
- Video
- Music
- Games
- And associated rights management

Application Service Provision
- Video Streaming
- VoIP
- MP3 Readers

Service Access & Navigation
- Hancse
- PC
- PDA

Content & Rights → Application Service Provision → Service Provision → Network Platform → Service Access & Navigation

Service Provision
- Internet Sevice Provision (ISP)
- Carrier Pre Select Providers
- Intelligent Network Services, eg Call Forward, Calling Line Identification

Network Platforms
- PSTN
- Calcle Network
- Satellite
- GSM
- 3G
- Network Equipment
- Network Protocols
- Operational Support Systems

Source: Ofcom.

EXHIBIT 10   UK TELECOM MARKET PLAYERS

Type	Examples	Number of Players
BT		1
Cable	ntl, Telewest	2
Corporate alt-nets	Cable & Wireless, Energis	c.20
Other alt-nets	Easynet	c.20
Mobile networks	Vodafone, O2, Orange, T-Mobile, 3	5
Major service providers	Centrica, Virgin, AOL, Wanadoo	c.20
Niche service providers		Several hundreds

Source: Ofcom, The Communications Market 2005, p. 109.

that have been announced at the end of 2005 by several operators. In addition, BT faced competition from players using BT's infrastructure to sell directly to end customers, such as the Carrier Pre-Select (CPS) and Wholesale Line Rental (WLR) markets (see Appendix for a glossary of telecom terms and abbreviations). In November 2005, the base of CPS in the UK totalled 5.55 million and major players in this market were One.tel, Homecall, Tele2 and Carphone Warehouse. At the end of 2005, the WLR base in the UK totalled 1.88 million.

Many analysts believed that the major threat facing BT was the acceleration in local loop unbundling (LLU). Local loop unbundling enabled operators other than BT to connect directly to the end consumer via BT's copper local loops and then add their own equipment to offer broadband and other services. In fact, the number of LLU lines grew from fewer than 50 000 in the first quarter of 2005 to over 200 000 by the end of the year, and according to the Office of the Telecommunications Adjudicator this total had increased to 250 000 by February 2006. In February

2006, Ofcom asked BT to prepare for 2–3 million LLU by the end of 2006. One of the most worrying concerns from a BT perspective was the long-term threat posed by a potential combination of media companies and alternative operators. Industry analysts had long speculated about the emergence of 'infotainment' companies that integrate media content with telecommunication services delivered directly to the home. Deutsche Bank, for instance, estimated that 'under a quite realistic scenario for BT, the company would effectively lose 2 per cent of its group revenue and 6 per cent of its group EBITDA from an aggressive and successful media operators entrance into telecoms unbundling'. (See Exhibit 11 for key financials of major European telcos).

BT had already suffered a significant revenue decline in its traditional market (primarily retail voice calls and access). By 2005, this revenue decline had apparently stabilized and market analysts acknowledged that the stickiness of BT's consumer base was still quite high. Analysts also praised BT's 'willingness to grab the VoIP bull by the horns and adopt a proactive strategy'. There seemed to be however a consensus in the industry that the revenue decline in the traditional market was likely to accelerate in the future. Some analysts forecast that BT Retail minute calls would fall from 113.10 billion in 2005 to 22.46 billion by 2011. Ben Verwaayen, BT Group's CEO, explained: 'Fixed-voice telephone calls may no longer be the only way to measure the success of a communication company, but they remain fundamental to our business'. At the end of 2005, BT was managing to offset this revenue decline by developing 'New Wave' revenues (e.g. ICT, Broadband and Mobility), which accounted for approximately 30 per cent of BT's revenues. New Wave was dominated by the Global Services business (19 per cent of revenues) and Broadband (7 per cent) which together comprised 26 per cent of New Wave's total 30 per cent group revenue.

Management stated that defending BT's traditional market would not ensure future survival. Rather, BT was determined to introduce a series of innovative services that could offset the revenue declines from increased competition in the 'last mile', fixed to mobile substitution and voice over IP. Verwaayen noted:

Today, BT is a very different company from the one that I joined three years ago. As our customers' needs have changed and continue to change, so we have found and continue to find

new ways of meeting those needs, investing in innovative products and services which add value to our customers and to BT.

Innovating innovation

Against this context, BT executives believed that that introducing innovative services and products was critical to the Group's survival at the beginning of 2006. And industry analysts argued that incumbent telcos like BT could only achieve the required innovation by fundamentally restructuring the way they approached innovation:

There are three reasons why telcos need to rethink their innovation strategies: 1. The telco cash cows are in decline and risky new bets take years to deliver; 2. Telcos struggle with lack of focus, old structures, stiff cultures, convoluted processes, and fragmented networks in the face of new, integrated service delivery requirements and; 3. Telcos' business-as-usual approach to innovation won't help.

BT had a long history of technological innovations with a total worldwide portfolio of 7700 current patents and applications, 141 of which had been filed for in the 2006 fiscal year. The BT Group invested £727 million in research and development (R&D) in the 2005/06 financial year. This investment comprised capitalized software development costs of £401 million and R&D operating costs of £326 million. This compares with £522 million in the 2005 financial year, which comprised £265 million of capitalized software development and £257 million of R&D operating costs. BT R&D was headquartered in Adastral Park, a 99-acre site near Ipswich, UK, where a number of scientists from blue-chip companies (e.g. Alcatel, Xerox, Siemens) and academic institutions (University of College London, CMI-Cambridge/MIT) interacted with BT researchers. (See Exhibit 12 for BT's innovation track record).

Although BT had a long tradition of technological innovations, Bross believed that the company's innovation efforts should be more commercially – rather than technologically driven, with the entire research portfolio structured around business needs. In particular, he had radically transformed BT Research into this open hybrid model, re-aligned it with BT's business and commercial priorities through a Research Investment Board governance body with representation from all operational divisions. Bross had set the

EXHIBIT 11   EUROPEAN TELCOS COMPARATIVE SHEET

Companies	Net Revenue 2004/5 [CAGR 2005-2008E]	Group EBITDA 2004/5 [CAGR 2005-2008E]	Group Capex 2004/5 [CAGR 2005-2008E]	Normalised Equity Free Cashflow 2004/5 [CAGR 2005-2008E]	Dividends per Share 2004/5 [CAGR 2005-2008E]	Group EBITDA margin 2004/5 [CAGR 2005-2008E]
Belgacom	5,506 [−1.6%]	2,369 [−3.6%]	556 [−6.2%]	1,227 [−1.4%]	1.93 [5.2%]	43.0 % [38.7%]
British Telecom	27,418 [−1.3%]	8,152 [−3.5%]	4,433 [−3.3%]	2,058 [−8.3%]	0.15 [−0.3%]	29.7 % [−2.3%]
Cable & Wireless	4,340 [2.3%]	627 [17.5%]	496 [−6.3%]	32 [−197.4%]	0.06 [10.0%]	14.4 % [15.0%]
Deutsche Telecom	57,360 [2.8%]	19,617 [0.1%]	5,366 [7.7%]	10,311 [−4.1%]	0.62 [0.0%]	34.2 % [−2.7%]
France Telecom	46,158 [3.3%]	17,923 [2.8%]	5,215 [5.9%]	6,424 [7.9%]	0.48 [7.9%]	38.8 % [−0.5%]
KPN	11,820 [1.3%]	4,835 [1.7%]	1,665 [5.9%]	1,984 [0.2%]	0.35 [11.8%]	40.9 % [0.4%]
Portugal Telecom	5,960 [0.3%]	2,319 [2.1%]	761 [−4.3%]	1126 [12.6%]	0.35 [10.0%]	38.9 % [1.8%]
Swisscom	6,451 [−0.3%]	2,815 [−1.7%]	729 [4.9%]	1,536 [−11.1%]	8.98 [6.3%]	43.6 % [−1.5%]
Telekom Austria	4,058 [2.7%]	1,569 [4.6%]	548 [−1.6%]	760 [6.3%]	0.24 [24.5%]	38.7 % [1.8%]
Telefonica	30,821 [4.4%]	12,222 [6.9%]	3,771 [4.2%]	6,840 [6.0%]	0.5 [5.0%]	39.7 % [2.4%]
Telecom Italia	28,292 [3.0%]	12,864 [3.6%]	5,003 [−5.8%]	4,576 [8.1%]	0.11 [5.0%]	45.5 % [0.6%]
TeliaSonera	9,056 [−0.3%]	3,187 [2.7%]	1,098 [−4.1%]	1,578 [4.0%]	0.13 [11.6%]	36.7 % [3.1%]
Telenor	7,613 [4.8%]	2,680 [6.0%]	1,598 [−4.1%]	784 [31.0%]	0.19 [11.0%]	35.2 % [1.1%]
Vodafone	41,611 [5.8%]	14,669 [1.9%]	6,204 [1.6%]	5,833 [−16.5%]	0.03 [14.8%]	35.3 % [−3.7%]

EBITDA= debt servicing-tax-changes in working capital; CAPEX= other FCF items. Normalized for tax assets.

Source: Adapted from Credit Suisse, European First Factsheet, 28 February 2006.

EXHIBIT 12   BT INNOVATION TRACK RECORD

1970s	1980s	1990s	2000s	2010s
Optics	Wireless	Broadband	Web services	Pervasive intelligence

	2005 Innovation Results
○ 1977–Optical fibre launch	• Created the world's first fully converged fixed–mobile service 'Fusion'
○ 1979–First digital network demonstration (Project X)	
○ 1985–First transoceanic optical fibre cable (TAT 8)	• First European Telco to create partnership with Yahoo for value–added services 'BT communicator'
○ 1985–Cellular radio (Cellnet)	
○ 1990–World's largest fibre to home trial	
○ 1991–UK ISDN coverage	• Early recognition of VoIP reflected in new 21 CN architecture
○ 1994–First major ADSL trial Colchester	
○ 1995–Optical packet routing demo	
○ 1997–WDM trials	• 32% growth of New Wave turnover with UK £4.5 billion compared to 30% growth in 2004
○ 1999–Colossus IP network	
○ 2000–World's first GPRS network	
○ 2000–World's first telephony IP network	
○ 2000–IN platform	
○ 2001–First VDSL trial	
○ 2005 Fusion	

Source: BT

direction for the Technology community, insisting that projects had to fit one of three magnet objectives: Improving BT consumers' personal lifestyle, improving BT customers' professional lifestyle, or improving the future state of Business. Bross had also moved BT from a theoretical to an experimental approach to Innovation, and both the new shape of BT Research and Frangos' Innovation team were designed to serve this new approach (please refer back to Exhibit 5).

Lars Godell, from Forrester Research, commented:

Traditionally, the dominant telco culture has focused on internal needs, not those of customers. Telcos reward R&D employees for participation in international standardization bodies and for publishing papers. More recently, they have rewarded employees for filing patents. Between 1996 and 2001, European telecom patent filings grew 167 per cent. But on average less than 10 per cent of patents have commercial relevance, and less than 1 per cent have critical importance.

BT's top management team was convinced that being technologically innovative was no longer enough. Rather, BT had to introduce new services that could offset the revenue decline in its traditional business. If BT were to survive the increasing level of competition, deregulation and consolidation in the telecommunications sector, it had to increase the speed

and impact of new services to boost the company's 'New Wave' revenues.

Open innovation

Open innovation was not a new expression for BT. In fact, the company had actively managed its patent portfolio (e.g. licensing, spinning out new businesses) for years. Bross, however, believed that BT could do more by moving towards a model where BT leveraged the power and speed of external partners to accelerate the creation of new services. Bross summarized:

In my view, nobody has a crystal ball on what customers really want and oftentimes, I don't think they know what they want, but what's absolutely for sure is that they'll know good when they see it. So we needed to build a team of people out there scouting the globe for those innovative services that customers in other parts of the world are already buying and that we can do on our platforms here very quickly. . . .

External innovation models had attracted growing interest as a way for companies to import new ideas and expertise through R&D collaboration with outside parties. According to Hank Chesbrough, Professor at the University of California, Berkeley and author of the influential book *Open Innovation* companies should open their R&D to outside sources of innovation. Contrary to the established model of innovation pioneered by large multinationals in the 20th century, Chesbrough, argued that companies should adopt an open innovation model where 'valuable ideas can come from inside or outside the company as well. [Open Innovation] places external ideas and external paths to market on the same level of importance as that reserved for internal ideas and paths to market during the Closed Innovation era.' At the end of 2005, many in the telecommunications industry saw a trend towards growing standardization on the Internet Protocol and an increasing focus on commercializing new technologies rather than inventing them internally. KPN, the Dutch telecom, took open innovation to the extreme by giving away its R&D lab (KPN Valley) to the Dutch Organization for Applied Scientific Research (TNO) in January 2003.

Bross believed open innovation would require BT to reorganize its R&D function to enhance its ability to identify, understand, select from, and connect to the wealth of available external knowledge. He established that two of R&D's key objectives would be to identify global sources of innovation (product, service, process, social), seed into the lines of business and lead hot house innovation processes at BT and second to build external innovation-based strategic partners globally.

Débuting at Silicon Valley

BT's commitment to access external technologies dated back to the late 1990s when BT and AT&T established the second Concert joint-venture. At that time, non-compete clauses in the joint venture contract precluded BT from establishing businesses in the US, which competed with AT&T's operations. BT executives remained interested in gaining access to new technologies emerging in the US market and therefore a new venture fund with AT&T to make mutually agreed investments in start up companies. At that time, BT executives viewed the venture fund as a means of getting early insight into new emerging technologies. In the end, however, the venture fund never materialized. A senior manager at BT involved in that process explained:

One of the main reasons [for the failure] was whilst we wanted early insight into new technologies, what AT&T wanted out of the venture fund was to see a lot of business development work that they were already doing.... And when we got to the nitty gritty, everything that we wanted to do they didn't want to do, and vice versa.

BT subsequently established a stand-alone venture fund in Silicon Valley designed to gain early insight into emerging business models and technologies. In 2000, Frangos and Rob Hull, Vice President, Business Development, went to Palo Alto, California to set up the fund. Both had spent about 10 years within BT, in a variety of roles including sales, commercial, and strategy, before moving to Silicon Valley. Both had technical backgrounds and degrees in electronics. Hull noted:

We are more technical than most people and we both have the ability to go deep quickly if we need to. Now we're not technical experts, but I guess we just have the ability to use a fair amount of logic and sound questioning and analytical skills to explore areas that are new to us, by drawing on previous knowledge.

In the early days in Silicon Valley, Frangos and his team relied on venture capitalists (VCs), such as Sequoia and Granite Ventures, to arrange the majority of their meetings with startups. Frangos recalled:

At the beginning we invested in a couple of funds that gave us a foot in the door in this venture capital start-up market.... It is a very tight-knit network of people who know each other in Silicon Valley and you have to have friends there.... That's the way we bought our way into this, by participating in those funds; they were well known in the Valley and very well connected and they helped us open the doors to a number of other people....

Having funds to invest with VCs not only opened doors in Silicon Valley but also created some internal stability for Frangos's team. Hull described:

Having these investments also gave BT the reason for sticking people out here ... You can never gauge whether that was actually the final reason ... Looking in retrospect, we could have been quite easily pulled back in the first six to nine months because nothing much was happening on the investment and BT wasn't really ready to digest that innovation...

When the venture capital bubble burst, BT's appetite for investing softened, but did not stop entirely, unlike many other telcos. BT's interest in external innovation sources remained high. The decision not to make any further investment in new funds, but to focus on individual companies, in fact allowed Frangos and Hull to focus on partnerships and technologies BT was really interested in. At the same time that they were trying to understand what was going on in the Valley and building up new relationships with local firms, they were also cultivating a few internal champions. Frangos noted:

> Our first [internal] customers used to pay us money, essentially an internal transfer, and for that, we would give them newsflashes, a weekly report, we would host them out here and show them new ideas.... They got good value from us and at the same time these initial experiences made us think about how we funnel ideas and work through a process to sell those ideas internally.... By April 2002 we had contracts and relationships with about five or six different business units in BT.

Technology scouts in California...

By 2002, the team at Silicon Valley served primarily as technology scouts on behalf of BT, although BT kept open the possibility to do some minor corporate venture investing. Frangos' unit focused their activity on identifying and screening innovative new technologies and business models, qualifying them, and communicating them back to various units within BT.

Identifying new technologies and business models

BT's Palo Alto team employed a number of means to access external technologies. Their target was to identify any company that had a significantly new technology that BT could potentially use, but they did not restrict their search to start ups. A major source of new insights were the portfolio review sessions with a list of 20 to 25 leading venture capitalists in Silicon Valley. During these sessions, VCs presented their portfolio firms, and how they envisioned the market evolving in the future. In exchange, BT shared with the VCs the technologies and business models it would like to see those start-ups develop, so these interactions with VCs were perceived by both parties as a mutually beneficial exchange of information. Frangos frequently participated in industry conferences and searched for mid-sized companies beyond the start-up stage, but not yet 'at the top of the page' when it came to technology suppliers to BT.

On top of that, BT established, in partnership with other telecommunication companies (e.g. Telecom Italia, Bell Canada, SK Telecom, Swisscom, Deutsche Telekom), the 'Service Provider's Investment Forum' a monthly meeting of representatives from wireless and wireline carriers's venture capital and R&D divisions in Silicon Valley. Usually, three start-ups presented at each of those meetings. Frangos explains:

> It is a bit like a club and there are our competitors although not so much our competitors.... I mean if you look at France Telecom, they have activities in the UK so therefore they are our competitors but mostly the innovation goes into their domestic market and it is always very interesting for us to have a technology adopted by more than just us. In fact, if another major telco, for instance Deutsche Telekom, adopts a technology that was presented during these meetings, it is likely to be easier for us to convince BT to adopt it as well.

BT's Silicon Valley team 'saw' (i.e. had some touch point, not necessarily a physical meeting) between 800 and 1200 companies each year, including companies that sent a business plan, or that BT representatives met at a conference, through a VC, etc. Out of those companies, BT managers in Palo Alto made approximately 200–250 sit down visits per year (see Exhibit 13). Hull explains how this first cut was usually done:

> We examine their website, we look at anything they would have sent to anybody in the company (slides, white paper, email) and typically that first cut filters out most companies ... But if we have doubts, or we think that they might have something interesting, then we follow up with a call. In that case we have a quick chat with the guys, on the phone, before we meet....

Having decided to meet the company, they usually spent one hour and a half with the target company, normally on the company's premises, and met with their management team to understand what they were doing, what their financing plans were about, 'getting under the skin of the company' in Hull's words.

Initial assessment

After this meeting with the company, the team conducted an initial evaluation of the technologies they identified See Exhibit 14 for a list of Key Qualification Criteria used by BT Technology Scouting Unit to assess external technologies. Given their multi-disciplined background, Frangos and his team were

EXHIBIT 13   SUMMARY BT TECHNOLOGY SCOUTING ACTIVITIES

	2001	2002	2003	2004	2005
Total companies analysed	300	600	800	1000	1200
Total face-to-face meetings	200	250	300	300	400
Total companies downstreamed	50	50	60	60	60
Total companies BT UK engaged in initial conversations	10	20	30	40	40
Total companies BT UK eventually did some business with	1	2	2	3	4

EXHIBIT 14   KEY QUALIFICATION CRITERIA USED BY BT TECHNOLOGY SCOUTING UNIT TO ASSESS EXTERNAL TECHNOLOGIES

- **Technology** – Is it significantly different to the status quo? – Is it believable? – Does it fit with BT's strategic direction and legacy systems? – Who are the company's partners? – Does the solution port to the UK/Europe from a technical perspective?

- **Market** – Is there a credible market? – Is this a target market for BT? – What are the barriers to entry? – Is it tactical or strategic? – Does it unnecessarily cannibalise existing services?

- **Company** – Where is the company in development cycle (pre-product, early trials, late

trials, general release)? – Does it have enough financial backing? – Could it support BT in the UK/ Europe/Worldwide for service, sale support etc? – Is it credible? – Who are its customers?

- **Deal** – Is deal framework (e.g. license, white label, sell....) compatible with BT lines of business? – What does it need off BT to make it work? – What would BT need to launch service?

Source: BT

generally able to do a first cut qualification without recourse back to the experts at BT's headquarters. If BT's team at Silicon Valley was really interested in the company they visited and if their initial assessment was positive, they would frequently refer to the scientists from BT's research labs in the UK who could help identify any major flaws in the technology. To assess the commercial viability of the new technology, Frangos and his team generally contacted a BT line manager or a local VC. Frangos explained:

> *We can call someone in BT Retail, Wholesale or BT Global, with whom we have a good relationship and who knows really well BT's needs in that area to assess whether there is a good fit.... Sometimes we pick up the phone and call any of our VC partners and they will normally know at least one company in their portfolio that does the same thing. We then call the company suggested by the VCs and they*

> *usually know their competitors. This generates a list of five or six companies working in the same technological space.*

'BT'izing' the technologies

For those technologies that were considered promising, the Silicon Valley team performed another task: to translate them and their business implications into a language that people within BT in the UK could relate to, or, in other words 'BT'ize' the technologies. Hull explained:

> *Most start up companies have a 'shotgun proposition'.... They have a deck of slides designed to get them funding, in which they say they can do too many things.... That's absolutely no use, if that deck is presented to BT. We've got to really help them [the entrepreneurs] focus down to the sharp end of the needle, the*

one area of their proposition that is very clearly aligned with the BT problem set. We actually find that in order to get BT interested in the technology of a new company, the last thing you do is simply send the company's technology description to BT. Instead, we need to do the articulation of the idea to our people in the UK whereby we absolutely focus it on, and put it in the language the BT people will understand.

...'Doctors' and 'Salesmen' in the UK

Technology scouting in Silicon Valley was only one half of the story. The other half consisted of two tasks: understanding on an ongoing basis the real needs of the lines of business in the UK and 'selling' the external technologies within BT. Frangos used a medical metaphor to illustrate the first task:

It is hard to know what the 'patient' [lines of business] really suffers from.... Is the problem really that they need new stuff, is it a channel problem, is it a product problem, is it a process problem, is it a people problem? Usually they can't tell where it hurts.... I need to go to the operating divisions and say: 'tell me where you have real problems, which technology could solve' but extracting that 'book of pain points' takes a long time; multiple interviews with the lines of business and drilling through questions like that.... Those pain points have never been written down anywhere.

In Frangos' view, he and his team required a deep understanding of 'what are BT's real strategic priorities and that is more difficult than what it looks like' before scouting for new technologies in Silicon Valley. Understanding BT's pain points was an ongoing activity requiring significant time. Frangos spent approximately one week every two months in BT's headquarters in London when he typically met with between 10–20 line managers. He estimated that half of those meetings were 'letting people know what he has seen' – and the other half entailed collecting the information about emerging threats and opportunities. Frangos usually met heads of division, CEOs of division, product managers, and research staff:

The most important thing is to have your radar in such a way so the technologies you identify at Silicon Valley are really useful as opposed to 'a

nice to have'.... I have been in the company 15 years now and I know people at corporate, divisional and research levels.... It takes that kind of multi faceted approach to know the priorities in the company.... Being able to identify the mapping of what you see with the various interests is the challenge here.... You won't find the cure for your patient if you don't really understand what he suffers from.

Salesmanship

With time BT's Silicon Valley mission changed from simply 'alerting' BT's headquarters about what was happening in Silicon Valley, to finding lines of business interested in adopting the external technologies they identified. As a consequence, their main output changed from newsflashes and quarterly trend reports, to one-page summaries about the companies they were seeing. Those one-pagers, called 'heads-up', which included the target company's, location, date of visit, confidentiality status, funding (how much money that company had, if they were raising money, who were the investors) were sent to managers in the lines of business. Those transfer memos were very succinct. Unlike the traditional R&D scientists that usually wrote thirty-page reports about new technologies, and took several weeks to do so, Frangos's team opted for speed rather than depth. 'Quite often, the senior managers would rather have something very quick that says, red, amber, green, rather than a twenty page report that usually gives you more questions than answers', explained Hull. On top of that, Frangos believed it was critical to flag not only the external technology per se but more importantly its local context, i.e., how the local community in Silicon Valley reacted to it:

We have many ideas internally but the interesting thing about external ideas is that other people are putting money on it. And that is proof that there is a group of intelligent people somewhere ready to put their money where their mouth is and fund the company. In many instances we may have already had something similar but not in a position where it was credible enough to launch. That same idea developed externally with a whole ecosystem around it, all the large technology companies adopting or funding the idea, a number of early customers taking that idea and doing something with it is a completely different story.... Now compare this with a research guy in a lab coming up with the same idea and trying to have a meeting with his boss, let alone with the head of the division, to show his idea. . . . It is much more difficult for him to get his boss' attention because there is limited market proof around it. So the external factor brings with it a level of market credibility that helps us sell the idea internally.

If Frangos and his team failed to find anyone within BT interested in a new technology, all their earlier activities (e.g. scouting the environment in Silicon Valley, meeting companies, evaluating and translating an external technology) added little value. Hull explained how he and his colleagues followed-up within BT:

All of these people [BT line managers] have got fifteen hours of work to do in their business day, and you've just given them the sixteenth hour. So you need to chase to make sure that, they understand that yours is not being done. . . . Chasing is important but it's an unpleasant part of the job . . . You know, the number of times that I reply to my own sent mail, and say, have you had a chance to look at this, can we have a call to discuss this please?

Frangos added:

You can't push people to the extreme; you need to let them digest the information. . . . You could shout it until you're blue in the face and still not get an action and that doesn't serve my cause because I want an answer. And I want the answer to be good, I want the answer to be that's a good idea, we ought to do that. So, like a persistent salesman, we have to try one, two, three, four, five, six times. . . . It may not work in the first time and we have to be constantly alert to see when a window has opened.

External innovation in 2006

BT senior management was pleased with the track record of Frangos' team in terms of bringing external innovation inside BT. In less than six years, BT's unit in Silicon Valley assessed a couple of thousand external technologies which generated hundreds of leads to the lines of business in the UK. More importantly, they brought external technologies in areas that were crucial for BT's future (see Exhibit 15 for the key technological areas scouted by the Silicon Valley

team). Mark Bagley, VP Technology, in Silicon Valley, explained:

The notoriously hard to target Small to Medium Enterprise Business segment [2–100 employees], for instance, has been a target for BT for some years. But with the application of a new method of delivery, born of Silicon Valley, called Software as a Service (SaaS) this segment is now within reach. We are also identifying a number of collaborative tools and social applications in the Internet that enable BT Retail to offer a whole new range of services to the younger demographic. . . . Those social applications have a great potential in terms of generating 'New Wave' revenues and these are technologies and business models that BT finds hard to develop internally at the scale and rate seen in Silicon Valley.

Frangos' team was recognized within BT by their big hits every year, i.e., external technologies that enabled BT to launch highly successful and innovative services, and by the £500mn per annum on average they generated to BT in innovation dividends (see Exhibit 16). By the beginning of 2006, Frangos' responsibilities had expanded considerably. Although the structure of the Silicon Valley team remained practically the same since the unit was established in 2000, Frangos also managed technology scouting teams in China and Japan. 'On the back of the successes of the Palo Alto team, I was told we should actually make sure that we were covering other technology hotspots in the world.' Frangos also assumed responsibility for a group of sixteen people working in the UK called 'Innovation Central' and also for the Applied Technology Centre (ATC) charged with rapid prototyping of promising technologies and services (see Exhibit 17 for BT's External Innovation area organizational chart and structure:

It became clear things could be more effective if I had people down on the floor [in the UK]. . . . Now when we reach a point where we have an initial contact between the external company and someone in BT who is in charge of something, and if we feel at that point there is some degree of attraction, then we start getting the rest of my team involved, i.e., the Innovation Central guys and the ATC guys. . . . In other words, if there's real interest, we start looking at how we can help that guy who has seen the external company sell it internally. Although this

EXHIBIT 15   KEY TECHNOLOGY AREAS SCOUTED BY THE SILICON VALLEY TEAM

Broadband
Consumer Application Platform
Personal Content Management
Home Monitoring
WellBeing
Global IP Interconnect

Mobility
Consumer VOIP
Converged Messaging
In-car services
E-Directories
Mobile TV

Information Technology
Hosted Applications Services
Business Comms Dashboard
Network APIs for Applications
Managed Security Outsourcing
Data Center Virtualization
XML switching

NG Customer Experience
Digital Home Support
Service Agent Technology
Voice Command and Authentication
Knowledge Management

Process Innovation
Network Management Security
Massive Logs Exploitation
Field Force Optimization
Data Integrity Validation
Provision Improvements

Network Technologies (21CN)
Deep Packet Inspection
Mobility Session Management
Wimax and WiBro
Ethernet
Home Gateways

Source: BT

EXHIBIT 16   SUMMARY INNOVATION SUCCESSES FROM THE TECHNOLOGY SCOUTING TEAM

Year	Product/ Service/ Solution description	Estimated innovation dividends/strategic impact
2005/6	Network attached computing for lower cost highly scalable virtual application server platform	High
2005/6	Enterprise Wiki platform for internal collaboration tools	Low
2005/6	Web 2.0 content / directory remote access, sharing & back-up service concept	Medium
2005/6	Wideband voice for consumer broadband customers	Low
2004/5	UMA GSM / Bluetooth / WiFi roaming mobile solution	High
2004/5	Automated text service agent for customer self support	Medium
2004/5	Wireless VoIP platform	Low
2003/4	ATA based VoIP consumer proposition	High
2003/4	Broadband IP traffic monitoring and filtering	Low

Source: BT Group

EXHIBIT 17 BT EXTERNAL INNOVATION ORGANIZATIONAL CHART

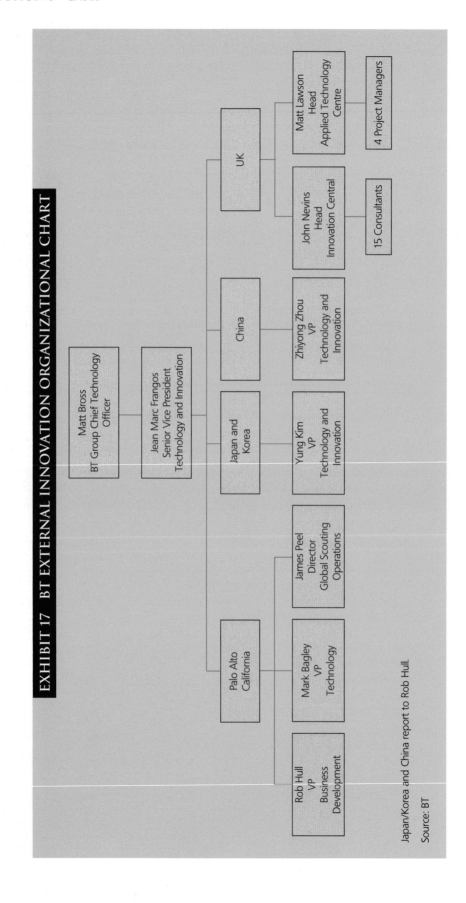

Japan/Korea and China report to Rob Hull.

Source: BT

external technology might be something that is really helpful to him for next year he still needs to achieve his objective of this year . . . . We help him put together the case, we help him with the presentation, and we help him to make more introductions to his peers and to his senior management.

Paired with the expansion of the area under his responsibility, however, also came aggressive targets in terms of innovation dividends that external innovation should generate for BT. Frangos's target was £500m for 2005 and another £500m for 2006. 'So far, in any given year if we manage to get four or five of these technology companies to actually do something with BT then that's a successful year'. Frangos wondered how he could increase the number of external technologies that would eventually become innovations that BT's customers would vote with their wallets. Frangos believed that there was no problem with the supply of interesting external technologies and he knew that BT needed to introduce innovative services. Growing the innovation dividends brought by his area should then be a feasible target.

As he considered how to grow the innovation dividend, Frangos considered a few options. First he could grow the existing scouting units. He had three managers in Palo Alto but only one covering China and another one covering both Japan and Korea. Yung Kim who was responsible for the scouting activities in Japan and Korea, for instance, believed those markets were three or four years ahead of the UK and offered huge potential for BT to develop new technologies with local start-ups. Kim found it challenging to cover two countries at the same time. 'The problem with more people in the same geography is that having more volume does not necessarily mean we will have better ideas. This is not a question of volume but a question of quality. And I don't want to have hundreds of new technologies coming in without being really relevant to BT. On top of that, these people in the countries are not junior people, they are expatriates and therefore the costs of increasing staff outside the UK is quite significant', pondered Frangos.

A second possibility was to expand the scouting teams to other important technological clusters in the world, such as Israel and India. Frangos was already

EXHIBIT 18   ORGANIZATIONAL STRUCTURE OF BT'S EXTERNAL INNOVATION AREA

Innovation is also learning from others		**Innovation Scouting Team**
8 people Tech/Bus. Mgt profiles		• Identify Innovation from all external sources • Help calibrate Research • Ensure LoBs consider opportunities • An independent view for Senior Management • Measured on Innovation Dividend
Articulating is as important as inventing		**Innovation Central**
15 people Consultant profiles		• Articulation Engine—Creates sales pitch for ideas • Cross organization structured brainstorms • Consultant methodology • Presentations, Draft business cases and MRDs • Measured on Innovation Dividend
A demo is worth a thousand slides		**Applied Technology Center**
5 people Project Mgt profiles		• Creates concept demonstrations and prototypes • Helps to clarify concepts • Delivers a clearer set of specs for development (OneIT) • Measured on Innovation Dividend

Source: BT.

exploring the possibility of having someone cover Israel out of the UK:

> *I started employing consultants in Israel and we did a year and a half of consultants and it wasn't too good. . . . I have now decided to send Mike Hodgson who works for the ATC in the UK on a quarterly basis to Israel. . . . Mike has worked with me before in Palo Alto, so he knows what companies to look for, so that's much more efficient than trying to brief consultants. . . . We were spending hours and hours on the phone trying to brief them about what we were looking for, and they couldn't understand that we didn't have a precise list of things, a shopping list for them.*

Likewise, BT had also hired, on a part-time basis, a manager to start the scouting activities in India. But if hiring people with the adequate technological and business experience to work in the scouting unit Silicon Valley was not trivial (see Exhibit 19 for the job description of VP, Technology, Silicon Valley) finding the right managers for the other offices around the world might prove even more difficult. 'Scaling a team liked this is very difficult. Everyone in my team has been hand-picked,' explained Frangos. With the exception of Zhiyong Zhou in China, all other managers in Silicon Valley and Japan had a long experience within BT. Nevertheless, these jobs were quite challenging even for a seasoned BT manager. Kim, from the Japan office, for example, had worked in many different areas within BT for more than 20 years. He still found it difficult, however, to get people in the UK to act on the technologies and new businesses he spotted: 'Sometimes I feel I am a hunting dog in the forest but there is no one with a gun to shoot the prey. … I wish I had someone in the UK working for me that could help me get some action from the lines of business.'

Frangos was aware of the risk of increasing the number of people scouting for technologies in different parts of the globe and not having enough action from headquarters. Therefore, his third alternative would be to have some managers in the UK whose job would be to 'sell' the technologies identified by the scouting units around the world to BT's lines of business in the UK. 'This is certainly a very interesting option but I have to be sure that people I am hiring can be good sales people. They have to be credible on their own, their personal credibility is what matters. And again it is not easy to scale a team like this'. Finally, Frangos had recently seconded two of his managers in

the UK to the lines of business and he wondered whether this could be a promising way of increasing the innovation dividends generated by his area. Frangos explains:

> *There are two managers from Innovation Central who are now part of BT Retail. The idea was to get our guys embedded in the lines of business. I believe this way we can disseminate the interest in external innovation through those 'disciples' that are seconded to the lines of business. We have implanted transmission belts directly in the operational divisions. The downside for my area, however, is that I have less people in my team. And although theoretically they have to come back to my team whether they really will is an open question.*

After a couple of hours working on his laptop Frangos realized that it was running out of battery and that he had not brought the inflight power adaptor. '*Ce n'est pas grave*', he thought in French, 'I have enough to start this discussion with Matt tomorrow'. He saved his work, turned off the laptop, sipped a glass of wine and decided to take advantage of the remaining 7 hours of his flight to sleep. Next morning, he would have to deal with an 8-hour time difference and go straight to BT's Centre at Newgate Street in the City of London. Just the start of a long week of meetings, relentlessly driving innovation and change throughout BT.

Appendix: Glossary of telecom terms and abbreviations

3G (or 3-G) is short for third-generation technology. It is usually used in the context of cell phones. The services associated with 3G provide the ability to transfer both voice data (a telephone call) and non-voice data (such as downloading information, exchanging email, and instant messaging). In marketing 3G services, video telephony has often been used as the flag-ship killer application for 3G. A certain euphoria was created, which led to huge spectrum-licensing fees in many countries, especially in Europe, where spectrum auctions generated many billions of euros for the respective countries. Since these spectrum licensing fees were collected many years before any income could be expected from 3G business, and since enormous investments are necessary to build the 3G networks, many telecommunication operators got into great financial difficulties, which greatly delayed 3G roll-out in all countries except Japan and South Korea, where such

EXHIBIT 19   JOB DESCRIPTION FOR THE POSITION OF VP, TECHNOLOGY, SILICON VALLEY (ABRIDGED)

The Technology & Innovation team includes a team based in Silicon Valley, California and reports directly to the BT Group CTO. The U.S. based team provides an Innovation Scouting service to BT Group and directly to senior executives across the BT Lines of Business. This is based on an active monitoring of the US start-up community and the established US Communications Service Providers. The process includes a first pass technical and commercial qualification of specific technologies/companies and services of relevance to BT. This Innovation Scouting is delivered via a number of means including service innovation propositions and reports, conference reports, technology trend analysis, as well as ad-hoc discussions & presentations to BT domain experts. The VP, Technology provides the core technical expertise to the US Venturing team but shares the objectives and responsibilities of the team with regards to Innovation Scouting, Relationship Management, and Technology Investments. Success is measured in terms of the number and quality of innovations introduced and adopted by BT and/or investments generating a substantial advantage to BT.

Innovation Scouting – Provide Innovation services to customers across the BT Group, including:

1. Providing first level technical judgment on new technologies in terms of their differentiation and value to the BT Group. Further validating technologies with BT domain experts (e.g. in the context of proper diligence projects or simple email/phone interactions)

2. Analyzing/synthesizing various technical information in concise communications (including formal deliverables as mentioned above)

3. Organizing & hosting visits and selecting appropriate agenda items for senior executive visits to Silicon Valley

4. Organizing hand-over to Innovation Central and/or Applied Technology Centre teams for further articulation/evangelization.

A significant & broad technical background is necessary to fulfill this role. The candidate must be a recognized expert in their current & previous technical domains, although the ability to assimilate and come up to speed on a wide range of technologies is also essential.

Technical experience should include at least one, but preferably a number of the following: a) Infrastructure technologies relevant to BT's 21C (Core, Metro, Access, CPE); b) Service delivery/intelligence infrastructures and Capabilities; c) NetworkIT (Data Centre, Security, Integration, CRM, Managed Desktop, Managed LAN, Integrated Comms, etc.). Systems & software, for example OSS/BSS and customer support systems along with their applicability to BT's strategic thrusts around Broadband, Mobility and NetworkIT.

The candidate must have direct experience, or at least knowledge of, current engineering and operational practise (appropriate to their given domain of expertise), although their recent background may be engineering or research. In addition the candidate must: 1. demonstrate an intuitive feel for LoBs innovation priorities, their future and present requirements, and be able to communicate at senior level with LoBs; 2. have a clear ability to assimilate the wide range of technology propositions relevant to BT and demonstrate sound technical judgment regarding the viability and potential of new technologies; 3.demonstrate a strategic technical mind

Good personal connections (within BTexact and/or BT Procurement and/or LoB Innovation, Product&Portfolio Strategy and Operational teams) are necessary to successfully fulfill the role, especially in creating linkage between start-ups and the appropriate areas of BT. More general attributes include being:

1. A self starter;

2. An articulate communicator able to present and convince;

3. At ease with senior executives within BT as well as external companies;

4. at ease in customer facing situations

The candidate should have a basic understanding of the mechanics of private equity for start-up companies, be proficient with PC and IT (autonomous, no need for support) and able to move to the US for at least 2 years.

spectrum licensing fees were avoided since priority was set on national IT infrastructure development. The first country which introduced 3G on a large commercial scale was Japan. In 2005 about 40 per cent of subscribers use 3G networks only, and 2G is on the way out in Japan. It is expected that during 2006 the transition from 2G to 3G will be largely completed in Japan.

ADSL Asymmetric Digital Subscriber Line (ADSL) is a form of DSL, a data communications technology that enables faster data transmission over copper telephone lines than a conventional modem can provide. The distinguishing characteristic of ADSL over xDSL is that the volume of data flow is greater in one direction than the other, i.e. it is asymmetric. Providers usually market ADSL as a service for people to connect to the Internet in a relatively passive mode: able to use the higher speed direction for the 'download' from the Internet but not needing to run servers that would require bandwidth in the other direction.

ASP An application service provider (ASP) is a business that provides computer-based services to customers over a network. The most limited sense of this business is that of providing access to a particular application program (such as medical billing) using a standard protocol such as HTTP.

CPS Carrier Pre-Selection. Consumers choose to preselect an alternative operator for calls but still pay the wireline incumbent (e.g. BT) for access.

DSL Digital Subscriber Line, or DSL, is a family of technologies that provide digital data transmission over the wires of a local telephone network. DSL is the principal competition of cable modems for providing high speed Internet access to home consumers in Europe and North America

IP The Internet Protocol (IP) is a data-oriented protocol used for communicating data across a packet-switched internetwork. IP is a network layer protocol in the internet protocol suite and is encapsulated in a data link layer protocol (e.g., ethernet). As a lower layer protocol, IP provides the service of communicable unique global addressing amongst computers.

GSM The Global System for Mobile Communications (GSM) is the most popular standard for mobile phones in the world. GSM service is used by over 1,5 billion people across more than 210 countries and territories. The ubiquity of the GSM standard makes international roaming very common between mobile phone operators, enabling subscribers to use their phones in many parts of the world.

Local loop unbundling (LLU) is the process of allowing telecommunications operators to use the twisted-pair telephone connections from the telephone exchange's central office to the customer premises. This local loop is owned by the incumbent local exchange carrier (ILEC). It is considered an application of the 'essential facilities' doctrine found in U.S. and, arguably, EC antitrust law. LLU is generally opposed by the ILECs, which in most cases used to be state monopoly enterprises before the telecommunications sector was liberalised. New entrants argue that, since they cannot economically duplicate the incumbent's local loop, they cannot actually provide certain services, such as ADSL, without LLU, thus allowing the incumbent to monopolise the respective market and stifle innovation. They point out that alternative access technologies, such as Wireless local loop (WLL) have proven uncompetitive and/or impractical, and that under current pricing models, the incumbent is guaranteed a fair price for the use of his facilities, including an appropriate return on investment.

MVNO Mobile virtual network operators which offer retail mobile services by leasing network capacity from operators

PSTN The public switched telephone network (PSTN) is the concentration of the world's public circuit-switched telephone networks, in much the same way that the Internet is the concentration of the world's public IP-based packet-switched networks. Originally a network of fixed-line analog telephone systems, the PSTN is now almost entirely digital, and now includes mobile as well as fixed telephones.

VoIP Voice over Internet Protocol (also called VoIP, IP Telephony, Internet telephony, and Broadband Phone) is the routing of voice conversations over the Internet or through any other IP-based network. The voice data flows over a general-purpose packet-switched network, instead of traditional dedicated, circuit-switched telephony transmission lines.

Wi-Fi (also WiFi, Wi-fi, Wifi, or wifi) is a brand originally licensed by the Wi-Fi Alliance to describe the underlying technology of wireless local area networks (WLAN) based on the IEEE 802,11 specifications. Wi-Fi was intended to be used for mobile computing devices, such as laptops, in LANs, but is now often used for increasingly more applications, including Internet access, gaming, and basic connectivity of consumer electronics such as televisions and DVD players. A person with a Wi-Fi device, such as a computer, telephone, or personal digital assistant

(PDA) can connect to the Internet when in proximity of an access point. The region covered by one or several access points is called a hotspot.

WiMAX is an acronym that stands for Worldwide Interoperability for Microwave Access, a certification mark for products that pass conformity and interoperability tests for the IEEE 802,16 and ETSI HiperMAN standards. WiMAX is a standards-based wireless technology that provides high-throughput broadband connections over long distances. WiMAX can be used for a number of applications, including 'last mile' broadband connections, hotspots and cellular backhaul, and high-speed enterprise connectivity for business

WLR. Wholesale line rental. By renting voice lines from the wireline incumbent, alternative carriers charge for access as well as voice calls.

VION Food Group: Riding the waves of change in the European meat industry

By Martijn Rademakers, Marcel van Gils and Hester Duursema[1]

S even men in the eye of a hurricane – that is how to picture the spring 2008 strategy meeting when the executive board[2] of the VION Food Group, head-quartered in Son en Breugel, the Netherlands, sat down to exchange thoughts and views on future strategies for the company. With annual sales exceeding €7.1 billion, a solid financial position (Exhibit 1) and more than 16 000 employees, VION is one of the largest meat processors in Europe, leading in fresh beef and holding second position in fresh pork[3].

The tranquillity of their meeting in the boardroom was in great contrast to the howling wind produced by a hefty storm outside. It did not go unnoticed that the storm formed a perfect metaphor for the dynamics of the international meat industry which they, originating as a rendering operation, entered as a newcomer less than 5 years previously. Enjoying the tailwind from a series of well-timed acquisitions, VION has grown to be a leading meat processor in Europe. The industry dynamics, however, are generating ever stronger headwinds, particularly in the form of mounting competition from global players.

The battle for Europe's meat markets began during 2005, not long after the rise of VION as a leading firm in the industry. The competitive battling continued and seems to be accelerating in 2008. In search of growth markets, large global firms, including Smith-field Foods based in the USA or Brazil's JBS Swift and Perdigão, are penetrating and expanding into European territory. Neither are incumbent competitors such as Danish Crown in Denmark and Tönnies in Germany sitting still. So with VION still digesting part of the takeovers constituting the VION Fresh Meat division as a leading meat producer in Europe, the seven men in the boardroom are engaged in the on-going quest for a robust, competitive strategy in an ever changing industry environment. The VION executive board members are keen not just to defend the company's position but also to move forward and grow in attractive market segments.

What should VION do to be different and, in the eyes of the consumer, outperform the competition? In tune with this, how can they foresee which rules of the game are developing fastest in the industry and have to be followed, and which ones can be pro-actively changed to help them secure a sustainable competitive position in the European meat industry?

Ownership, governance and *raison d'être*

VION is a private firm owned by a single shareholder, the Dutch farmers union ZLTO (The Dutch Organization for Agriculture and Horticulture, Southern Region). By 2008, ZLTO had more than 18 000 members, of which 30–40% are livestock farmers. For more than a century the organization has been fur-thering the interests of its members (farmers and hor-ticulturists) particularly in the levels of income and business continuity (Exhibit 2).

The VION governance structure is designed to se-cure a high degree of management discretion on the owner side. Apart from the demand that company activities be consonant with the ZLTO mission, i.e. furthering the long-term interests of its members and securing a steady stream of dividends, it is VION's Executive Board running the company and setting the strategy.

To keep a clear division line between the company and the farmers union, a multi-layered governance structure was put in place, including a trust office

---

[1]Source: M. Rademakers, M. van Gils & Hester Duursema, 2008.

[2]The Executive Board includes Daan van Doorn (Chief Executive Officer), Ton Lammers (Chief Finance Officer), Peter Beckers (Chief Strategy Officer), and four Chief Operational Officers: Dirk Kloosterboer (Ingredients Division), Uwe Tillmann and Geert Janssen (Fresh Meat Division), and Ton Christiaanse (Convenience).

[3]On June 14, 2008, VION signed an agreement to acquire Grampian, one of the UK's largest food companies (sales €2.5 billion, 17.500 employees). The acquisition, which yet needs to be approved by the European competition authorities, would strengthen the position of VION in the UK markets for fresh pork, bacon, and sausages.

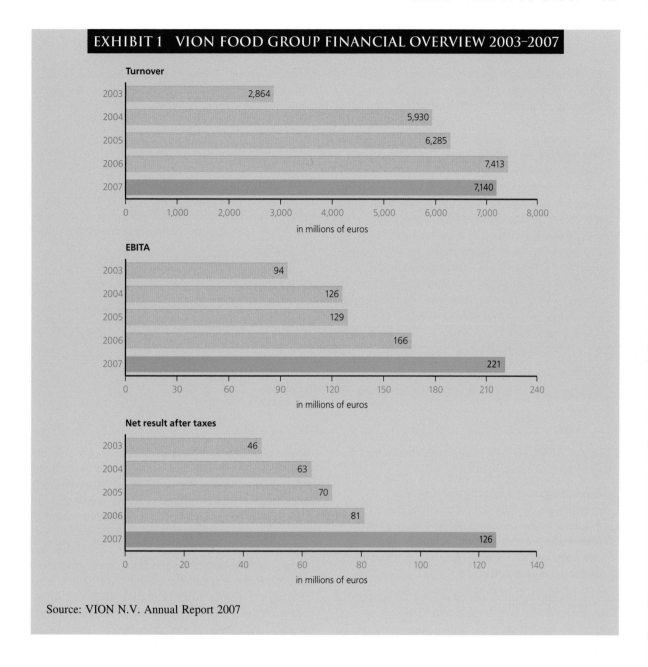

EXHIBIT 1   VION FOOD GROUP FINANCIAL OVERVIEW 2003–2007

Turnover

Year	Value
2003	2,864
2004	5,930
2005	6,285
2006	7,413
2007	7,140

in millions of euros

EBITA

Year	Value
2003	94
2004	126
2005	129
2006	166
2007	221

in millions of euros

Net result after taxes

Year	Value
2003	46
2004	63
2005	70
2006	81
2007	126

in millions of euros

Source: VION N.V. Annual Report 2007

between ZLTO and VION. The VION supervisory board includes four members from the outside and four who represent ZLTO, a composition that balances strategic influence between this single shareholder and the VION executive board even further.

The lines of separation laid down in VION's governance structure enable ZLTO to act as a strategic shareholder with influence on long-term developments only, while the executive board runs the company shielded from short-term political dynamics within and around the farmers union. The structure also protects against potential conflicts deriving from the supplier relations between VION on one hand and livestock farmers with ZLTO membership on the other.

The VION *raison d'être*, i.e., the ultimate intended impact of the company's strategic actions, is to secure long-term market demand for goods produced by farmers in the Dutch agricultural complex. At the time of VION's strategic transformation in 2005, the

EXHIBIT 2 ZLTO

ZLTO is a union of farmers and horticulturalists in the Dutch provinces Noord-Brabant, Zeeland, and the southern part of Gelderland. By 2008, the union listed approximately 18,000 members. The union furthers the interests of individual members, groups of members and entrepreneurs, and the collective interests of its members.

ZLTO is comprised of 65 departments divided over 4 regions, each with its own management team. Every member of the management team of a department has a portfolio with one or more policy issues in it. All portfolios, in turn, are represented in an administrative platform advising ZLTO's management team.

The organization has three separate divisions including ZLTO Interest Protection, ZLTO Projects, and ZLTO Advice, plus several related staff services.

ZLTO Interest Protection

ZLTO Interest Protection promotes the interests of members who desire to be both market-driven and society-oriented. Through its extended network, ZLTO Interest Protection is able to influence the future and innovation capacity of the agricultural and horticultural industries.

ZLTO Projects

ZLTO Projects stimulates structural teamwork within groups of agricultural entrepreneurs, initiatives for innovation in the agricultural sector, and practical execution of policies monitored by these groups of entrepreneurs.

ZLTO Advice

The advisers and specialists of ZLTO Advice offer tailor-made solutions for individual agricultural entrepreneurs. They are the experts to talk to regarding important choices for the future, such as succession and members' investments to grow their businesses.

chairman of ZLTO and supervisory board member Anton Vermeer expressed that vision:

A healthy meat processing industry is a prerequisite for long-term survival of the livestock farmers. It is an indispensable layer linking the primary production system on the one hand and the industry for food distribution and retail on the other.

The leadership position of VION in the market for fresh meat in the Netherlands and Germany, placed against the backdrop of the above statement, can be seen as a way to secure a sustainable market for cattle farmers in the Netherlands. The key defence mechanism against attacks on their market by foreign players is a set of seemingly unchangeable rules of the game in the fresh meat industry[4]. First, high-quality fresh meat is highly perishable and therefore cannot be transported over long distances in an economically viable way. New entrants would have to buy market share by taking over meat production plants in VION's own backyard. The alternative, namely to set up new fresh meat production plants in a highly

mature industry, is not considered to be a viable option. Second, supermarkets and food service clients demand just-in-time delivery, which also hampers long-distance transportation of fresh meat and increases both the complexity and long-term nature of buyer–supplier relations.

In addition to the above, it can be argued that furthering the development of the Dutch meat processing industry alone will not be enough. The Dutch agricultural sector at large is facing the challenge of securing demand for their goods in a globalizing food industry with ever fewer and larger international players on the processing and retail side who are driving cross-border competition.

Company history

VION originated as an animal by-products processor in the 1930s, expanded the business via takeovers in the 1980s, branched out in value-added products based mainly on gelatin in the 1990s, and made a massive move into the meat industry in the period 2004–2005. On July 1, 2006, the company gave itself

---

[4]It should be stressed here that these rules of the game are true for fresh meat only. For frozen meat and meat products, the situation differs, as these products are less perishable and better transportable over long distances – in the case of frozen meat, even from continent to continent.

a new name, switching from SOVION to VION Food Group. This marked the completion of the strategic transformation from an animal by-products processor, gelatin and drug delivery company with €760 million sales in 2002 towards a leading, €7.1 billion company in the European meat industry. That was not an easy journey. The commonly accepted view at the time was that the ailing meat industry in the Netherlands was just about to collapse, along with parts of the German meat industry. As illustrated by CEO Daan van Doorn:

> Five years ago banks were not willing to invest in the meat industry, which made it difficult to find the required capital to pursue our strategy.

By contrast, newspapers have devoted whole pages to VION since the turnaround and the company has received nominations which include Best European Entrepreneur of the Year, and Growth Strategy of the Year. In 2008 major activities of the VION corporation revolve around the markets for beef, lamb and pork (approximately 86 per cent of annual turnover) in Western Europe, driven by a business that encompasses slaughtering and meat processing. At the same time, the company is expanding into the convenience food business, while remaining active as a leading and growing European firm in animal by-products processing, and as a worldwide leading player in the gelatin business (Exhibit 3).

VION corporation: Three divisions and a business unit[5]

VION consists of three divisions (Fresh Meat, Ingredients, Convenience) and one separate business unit (Banner). The principle at corporate headquarters is to provide the divisions and their business units with a high level of autonomy under strict financial control. The basic idea is to enable the units to respond optimally to market and industry developments and keep corporate overheads as low as possible.

VION fresh meat

Active in processing, producing and obtaining economic value from meat products (pork, beef and lamb), VION Fresh Meat employed 6447 persons in 44 operating plants and 14 country offices in 2007, realizing a turnover of €5.4 billion. The Fresh Meat division operates worldwide, with meat processing plants concentrated in the Netherlands and Germany, and with sales offices all across Europe plus one in Australia. Key customers served by the division include *retailers* (such as Ahold, Wal-Mart, Aldi, Metro Group, Carrefour and Tesco), *food service companies* (such as Burger King and McDonald's), and the branded *food industry* (including Unilever and Nestlé). The VION Fresh Meat strategy is largely focused on margin-driven growth in the Dutch, German and UK markets, and increased export to Italy, France, Spain, Greece, Eastern European countries, the USA and countries in Asia. In line with the corporate philosophy of high business unit autonomy and market responsiveness, VION Fresh Meat and the constituting business units are linked with the other VION divisions and businesses on a pragmatic and transactional basis.

VION Ingredients: With 62 operating plants around the world, five international offices and 4512 employees, the Ingredients division achieved a turnover of €0.7 billion in 2007. The VION Ingredients division is the European market leader in blood products and animal proteins. Business units of the division include Sobel, Rousselot, and Sobel 5Q. The Sobel business unit, operating in the animal by-products industry, includes Rendac (collecting and processing fallen stock and other risk-involved animal by-products), Sonac (producing and selling ingredients from animal-based raw materials), and Ecoson (producing biofuels from slaughter by-products). Rousselot is the second largest gelatin producer in the world with a market share of 19% behind the number one Gelita which had a 24% market share in 2007. Rousselot gelatin is used by clients in the food and pharmaceutical industries, and the adhesives and photo paper industries among others. Sobel 5Q is a business unit which coordinates the sale of slaughter by-products originating from all VION operations. The VION Ingredients strategy is aimed at consolidation of its leading positions in the market for fat in Europe and blood products in China, strengthening of the Sonac position in natural casings, and expansion of Rousselot (gelatin) in South America.

---

[5]VION plans to integrate Grampian into a new division, VION UK. This division will be managed from the UK and led by Ton Christiaanse who will be appointed CEO VION UK. Peter Barr, formerly chairman of the Meat and Livestock Commission in the UK, will be appointed as non-executive Chairman of the Board of VION UK. In the UK, VION currently has four business operations. Key Country Foods is a major UK retail bacon processor. VION also holds a majority share in J&J Tranfield (acquisition of majority of shares in beginning of 2008), a leading supplier and manufacturer of pizza and sausages. VION Food UK Ltd is responsible for the sales of bacon, fresh pork, beef and convenience products to the UK market. VION company Oerlemans Foods offers fresh frozen vegetables, potato products and fruit through its UK sales office.

EXHIBIT 3 ACQUISITIONS AND JOINT VENTURES BY VION IN 2007 AND 2008

VION UK (Grampian will be integrated into the new VION division, VION UK)

2008: Acquisition of Grampian Country Food Group Ltd, one of the UK's leading food companies, supplying the major multiples with chicken, pork, beef and lamb. The company currently employs 17,500 staff (of which 4,500 in Thailand), with an annual turnover of £1.7 billion (€2.5 billion) and has production locations in the UK and Thailand. The head office is located in Livingston, Scotland.

VION Fresh Meat

2007: 50% acquisition of Südfleisch in Germany

2008: Joint venture with the Russian RAMFOOD. RAMFOOD is specialized in the production of fresh and pre-packed meat and sausages. The company supplies the Russian retail and food service market in the Moscow area. RAMFOOD Group of Companies consists of a slaughter plant, a meat processing plant, a transport company, warehousing facility, distribution center and own retail outlets. The company has an annual turnover of rubles 3,2 billion (more than €86 million) and employs well over 1,300 employees.

VION Ingredients

2008: Joint venture with the Brazilian company Rebière, one of the leading companies in the Brazilian gelatin market, and one of the top 10 gelatin companies in the world. Rebière has about 400 employees.

2007: Joint venture with the Chinese company Wuhan NPC. The company is the largest producer of plasma powder and hemoglobin powder destined for animal feed in China.

2007: Acquisition of Gebr. Smilde, a producer and processor of animal fats for human consumption, with activities in the Netherlands, Germany and Austria. The company achieved a turnover of €285 million in 2006 and has about 200 employees.

2007: Joint venture with Combinatie Teijsen van den Hengel (CTH), a Netherlands-based company processing and selling natural sausage casings, based on slaughter by-products. CTH has production locations in Belgium, Germany, the Netherlands, Poland, Portugal, Spain and China, and employs about 500 persons.

VION Convenience

2008: Acquisition of a majority of the shares of J&J Tranfield. Tranfield is specialized in the production of sausages and pizza for the UK retail and food service market. Tranfield has an approximate turnover of €175 million and 1400 employees.

2007: Acquisition of the Dutch-based Oerlemans Foods. Oerlemans Foods is a Dutch company specializing in fresh frozen vegetables, potato products and fruit for the food service, retail and industrial markets. The company achieves 50 percent of its turnover in the Netherlands, Germany and the United Kingdom. Oerlemans is a €120 million turnover company and has about 750 employees.

2007: Acquisition of shares in Christian Salvesen, a transporter of frozen foods.

VION convenience

This division concentrates on the development, production, and marketing of meat-based convenience foods and also non-meat foods including fish, vegetables and vegetarian products. In 2007 the division achieved a turnover of €1.2 billion with 3884 employees, 30 plants and 14 international offices (shared with the Fresh Meat division). The seven business units of the division include Frozen Retail, Frozen Vegetables, Processed Meat & Chilled Food, VION Retail NL (serving retailers with customized food products and services), Pre-packed Fresh, Food Service and

Tranfield. The strategy of this division revolves around innovation, consolidation and optimization of the brand portfolio, and further development of market research and intelligence. VION Convenience aims to further internationalize its product portfolio via sales offices, and the division is expected to double its sales to about €2.5 billion within the next five years.

Banner

Banner is a separate business unit, prominent in the development and production of gelatin and non-gelatin based oral dosage forms for the pharmaceutical, food supplement and cosmetics industries. The business unit is mentioned separately since it no longer fits in with VION's aim to be market leader (top 3) in selected market segments. The money that can be made by selling Banner can be used for further acquisitions.

European meat industry wisdoms

The meat industry receives serious attention from observers and analysts working for governments, EU offices, universities, journals, consultancies, and also the leading meat companies, who try to understand what is going on in the business and where it is heading. From the vast stream of information, thoughts and opinions, five major industry wisdoms can be distilled which seem to drive strategic thinking in the contemporary European meat business.

1. Food retail is leading and consolidating, food suppliers need to follow. The retail consolidations are outpacing those of food processors and producers. The retailer bargaining power increases due to these consolidations plus the strength of their private labels or store labels, so they have alternative resources for purchasing, and they are able to negotiate favourable prices due to large volumes.

2. Bigger is better in meat production. The meat industry is largely a commodity business where economies of scale and high volumes drive costs down, particularly in slaughtering.

3. The pressure on margins remains high. Competition in the meat industry is intense and is intensifying further, among other reasons due to the increasing export power of Brazilian meat companies, the aggressive price policies of producers operating from relatively low-cost countries within the European Union, and the rising strength of the euro over the dollar and other currencies. Further pressure on margins is caused by rising costs to secure food safety, preventing and fighting cattle diseases, as well as societal pressures for natural environment protection measures and animal welfare. On the other hand, margins can be improved or sustained through processing slaughter by-products into value-added products.

4. Future growth of demand is in value-added food propositions. Differentiation is believed to be an escape route from the current commoditization trap, but most meat companies in Europe have problems distinguishing themselves from their competitors. They use similar production methods, of course leading to products with almost identical quality and taste. In this light, it is relevant to note that fresh meat is a 'must-have' item for supermarkets, and on-time delivery and freshness is at least as crucial as a good price.

5. Access to a stable pool of farmers able to supply both good quality and quantity at a competitive price is the bedrock of the processor's value-adding processes. Farmers, however, tend to be suspicious of the attempts by meat firms to work on a partnership basis with them instead of trading for cattle and pigs on a spot-market driven, transactional basis with a focus on price. This hampers the attempts of meat processors to enhance the performance of farmers.

Considering that a majority of the meat companies in Europe have these five wisdoms on their radar screen, an important question is, which competitors will be able to take advantage of those forces by acting upon them, and how? Which competitors will be best in playing by the rules of the game in this industry? Which competitors will be able to bend the rules in their favour, or set new ones?

The competitive landscape of the European meat industry

A glance at the meat industry in Europe shows a crowd of global, national and local companies. Some are consolidating their positions, some are struggling, and others have a foothold for further expansion.

European meat firms generally focus on slaughtering and processing, whereas most companies from other continents also incorporate downstream activities such as farming and sometimes even genetics. The worldwide operating meat firms (Exhibit 4) differ in terms of species they process. Most companies, however, have pork and beef in their portfolio. The competitors also differ in the levels of integration of their value chains, ranging from genetics and cattle breeding to convenience food manufacturing (Exhibit 5). A third key difference is the ownership structure, including cooperatives (e.g., Danish Crown), publicly listed firms (e.g., Smithfield), and privately held companies (e.g., VION). All global meat competitors with operations in Europe show a solid home base, while increasingly seeking market opportunities overseas.

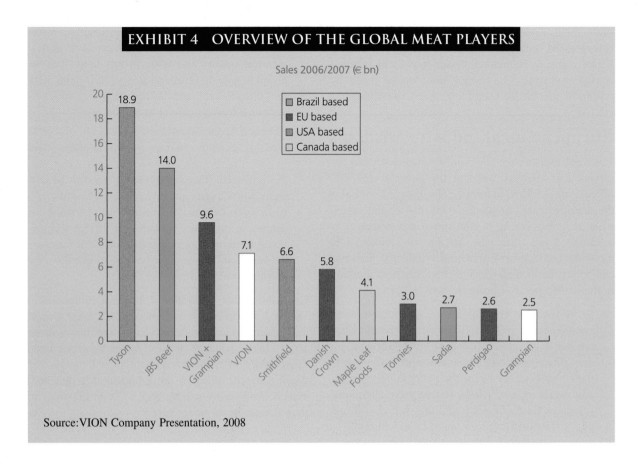

EXHIBIT 4 OVERVIEW OF THE GLOBAL MEAT PLAYERS

Sales 2006/2007 (€ bn)

Source: VION Company Presentation, 2008

Pork

Regarded from a global perspective, seven out of the top 20 pork producers are European companies operating from their domestic regions, while eight of the largest producers are US-American, four are Brazilian, and one is of Chinese origin (Exhibit 6). Looking at seven large European pork producers and with non-European competitors moving in, the European pork business is becoming quite crowded, and that is driving increasingly strong competitive pressures. Seen in this light, consolidation is likely to progress on a Europe-wide scale. The world's top three pork producers, Smithfield Foods (USA), Danish Crown (Denmark) and VION are competing both for access to European customers and to the suppliers. Danish Crown is the largest fresh pork processor in Europe with a 10.7 per cent market share in 2007, with VION following in a close second position (8.9 per cent), and the German Tönnies placing third (4 per cent). Smithfield Foods, considered the world's number 1 pork producer, entered the European market in 2005, starting up and acquiring operations in Romania and Poland. Meanwhile, they have built positions through acquisitions and joint ventures in Spain and France, with some smaller operations in the UK and the Netherlands.

Beef

VION became the European market leader in fresh beef, with a 7.4 per cent market share after acquiring a 50 per cent stake in the Germany-based Südfleish in 2007. Second largest in Europe is the Irish Food Group, operating 23 processing plants and realizing a turnover of around €1 billion in 2007. Cremonini, a leading beef processor in Italy, is the third largest player in the European beef scene. In 2007, Cremonini's beef processing company INALCA was acquired by the Brazil-based JBS Swift, the world's largest beef producer entirely focused on beef activities. By contrast, the USA-based Smithfield Foods has divested all beef activities, selling their beef unit to JBS Swift for US$565 million in cash in March 2008.

EXHIBIT 5 BUSINESS SCOPE OF MAJOR GLOBAL MEAT COMPANIES

Global Meat Competitors	Species					Value chain stages				Geographics							
	Beef	Pork	Poultry	Lamb	Dairy	Genetics	Farming	Slaughter	Processing	W-EU	E-EU	US	SA	Canada	Asia	Aus.	Russia
JBS Friboi S.A/Swift	✓	✓	✓	✓			✓	✓	✓	✓		✓	✓	✓	✓	✓	✓
Perdigao S.A.	✓	✓	✓		✓		✓	✓	✓			✓	✓	✓	✓		✓
Sadia S.A.	✓	✓	✓			✓	✓	✓	✓		✓	✓	✓		✓		✓
Smithfield	✓	✓	✓			✓	✓	✓	✓	✓	✓	✓	✓		✓		✓
Tyson	✓	✓	✓			✓	✓	✓	✓	✓		✓	✓	✓	✓		✓
Cargill Meat solutions	✓	✓	✓				✓	✓	✓	✓		✓	✓	✓	✓	✓	
Danish Crown	✓	✓						✓	✓	✓	✓	✓			✓		
VION	✓	✓		✓				✓	✓	✓	✓				✓	✓	
Tönnies	✓	✓						✓	✓	✓	✓						
Grampian	✓	✓		✓			✓	✓	✓	✓	✓						
Maple Leaf Foods		✓	✓			✓	✓	✓	✓	✓		✓		✓	✓		

Legend:
☐ Brazil based
■ USA based
☐ EU based
☐ Canada based

Source: Adapted from VION Food Group documnets, 2007

EXHIBIT 6 THE 20 LARGEST PIG PROCESSORS IN THE WORLD

Company and country	Pigs slaughtered/ year
1: Smithfield Foods (PSF-Animex) *USA/Poland*	30 million
2: Danish Crown (Flagship-Sokolow) *Denmark/UK/Poland*	22 million
3: Vion *Netherlands/Germany*	19 million
4: Tyson Foods (IBP) *USA*	17 million
5: Cargill (Excel-Seara) *USA/Brazil*	10.4 million
6: Fribol (Swift) *USA/Brazil*	10 million
7: Tönnels *Germany*	10 million
8: Olymel *Canada*	8 million
9: Maple Leaf *Canada*	7 million
10: Hormel Foods *USA*	6 million
11: Westfleisch/Barfuss *Germany*	5.4 million
12: Sadia *Brazil*	4.1 million
13: Seaboard *USA*	4 million
14: Coorperl *France*	3.7 million
15: Perdigao *Brazil*	3.5 million
16: Indiana Packers *USA*	3.3 million
17: Socopa Country Foods *UK*	3.1 million
18: Grampain Country Foods *UK*	3 million
19: Ng Fung Hong/Shanghai Food Group *China*	3 million
20: Aurora *Brazil*	2.7 million

Source: DLG/Agriculture, 2007

Lamb

In the less crowded and much smaller market for lamb meat, JBS Swift is VION's main competitors. The key players in this market are well established in geographical territories which have high entry barriers that, in turn, are rooted in the land-bound nature of lamb production.

VION's meat strategy

The VION Fresh Meat division has the bulk of its activities geographically focused in the Netherlands, and Germany. The driving philosophy is to be market leader (in pork, beef and lamb) through margin driven growth and increased exports to the UK, Italy, France, Spain, Greece, Eastern European countries, the USA, and Asia. To achieve this, VION stays close to its strengths: building and maintaining durable relations with farmers and customers, exploiting the core capability of growing through acquisitions and turning the acquired processing companies around. Moreover, expanding and developing capabilities to thrive in differentiation-driven business, as opposed to low-cost activities, is high on the managerial agenda. In tune with this, the VION Convenience division assists VION Fresh Meat in the ongoing search for new products. Innovation, receiving top management attention since 2005, can be considered to be another spearhead. As VION's Chief Strategy Officer Peter Beckers puts it: 'In generics innovation is possible as well.'

Apart from defending the relatively stable meat business activities in Europe through cost cutting, and seeking growth through ongoing innovation of processes, technologies and propositions to customers, it has been no secret that an important part of VION's future growth will be realized through acquisitions and joint ventures in the meat industry. According to CFO Ton Lammers, VION has a war chest of 150 to 200 million euros for future acquisitions. More capital will become available with the projected divestment of Banner. Adding value to slaughter by-products can also deliver financial advantages for VION and reduce the pressure on fresh meat margins. On top of that, VION acquisition power can be boosted even further, as Lammers explained in a 2007 interview: 'On Earnings Before Tax Depreciation and Amortization (EBITDA) of almost 300 million, one can borrow over 1 billion euro.'

The question remains, where should VION seek value-adding takeovers and what is the right timing, given the competitive situation? In case opportunities in beef and pork processing run out in Northwest Europe, VION would not be short of options. New opportunities lie ahead both in Southern and Eastern Europe, and in meat business based on other species.

Looking ahead

With the European meat market under siege of leading global protein companies, and stiff competition from within, VION executive board members tend to take the emerging industry dynamics as a source of new opportunities for VION. However, there are concerns as well. The diversity of distinctive and hard-to-copy strengths which VION faces in major competitors confronts the company with much food for thought.

For instance, Smithfield Foods is well-geared for competing on costs when it comes to pork processing, as the company is known to run a highly efficient, low-cost business model, driven by high levels of supply chain integration (including farming), large scale, and focus. Their business model based on full vertical integration has been honed over the past decades. Yet they are successfully branching into convenience food. Also growing turkey in their domestic USA market, and with robust bridgeheads vested in Eastern and Southern Europe, they may begin competing in the northwestern regions of Europe at some point in time. Being a publicly listed firm, Smithfield enjoys access to relatively cheap capital for takeovers.

Brazil-based companies are also eagerly seeking chances to increase their stake in Europe. Sadia, the biggest poultry producer in the world, has shown interest in the UK-based Grampian Country Foods, together with another Brazil-based food company called Perdigão. Moreover, the JBS-Inalca joint venture established in Italy in 2007 has provided another Brazilian giant with a firm foothold in the European Union. The Brazilian competition has the advantage of very low-cost domestic production, a huge unexploited potential for exports, and economies of scale – both in terms of production, sales power, and capital for takeovers. As an illustration of the Brazilian cost advantages over their European counterparts: in 2007, the production costs of one kilogram of pig meat were on average 1.50 euros in the Netherlands versus 1.08 euros in Brazil (2004 cost prices corrected for feed price increases). If and when the European Union allows the import of Brazilian meat, this could have serious consequences for VION.

Closer to home, Danish Crown cooperative, enjoys substantial advantages from stable and high-quality supplies on the basis of mutually attractive purchasing arrangements with livestock farmers who are members of the cooperative. As a consequence, the company is likely to be well-geared for competing both on differentiation and cost through smart inputs into its processing activities. Danish Crown, however, is also known to operate with low solvency levels, driven by limited market conformity when it comes to the price they have to pay for members' supplies.

Considering VION amidst its competitors, some industry observers take the distinctive VION ownership structure as an advantage. Having ZLTO as a single shareholder allows for a long-term strategy, rather than a focus on quarterly profits. The farmers, though, are not de facto supplying VION. Tönnies, a privately owned German company, competes with VION for supplies. As a consequence, VION cherishes both the capabilities and the attitude required to live up to the daily challenges of a free market setting on the supply side.

Being part of a multi-business corporation, though loosely integrated, provides the VION Fresh Meat division with potentially distinctive strengths through cross-business synergies. VION, however, has yet to develop the synergies that could make a difference in terms of outperforming the competition. For example, VION is likely to enjoy benefits from a closer touch and better grasp of consumer market needs through the Convenience business relations.

But none of these advantages are strong enough, distinctive enough, or difficult for competition to copy. None of these will secure a long-term sustainable position in the European meat industry by default.

So the storm outside the office building was not their greatest concern as the executive board talked strategy in the VION boardroom that day. More than enough questions were on the table. Could they rely on the charts? Were the mainstays strong enough to ride the waves of a competitive race on the pan-European and even global scale? Which of their strengths should they practice to perfection? When is it time to sail across the wind? Where could they draw sufficient unique market power to maintain the lead and put more distance between themselves and their competition in the European meat industry?

NCR and Wi-Fi

By Wolter Lemstra[1]

The train is scheduled to leave Platform 5 in 10 minutes from London Kings Cross to Darlington. It is the first day of a new phase in the career of Bruce Tuch. Yesterday, he formally completed his last day as Chief Technology Officer for Mergers and Acquisition and as Head of European Venture Capital at Motorola. In that role, he had been working for many years with a lot of high-tech start-up companies. It was time for a new challenge and he was looking forward to meet again the same level of enthusiasm and entrepreneurial spirit he had enjoyed earlier in his career at NCR, AT&T, Lucent Technologies, Agere Systems and more recently at Motorola. With an e-ticket and coffee in his hand he jumps on the train wagon. The aroma of the fresh roasted coffee is pleasant in the anticipation of settling down.

This would be a long train ride, about 3 hours to the northern part of England, but it was the easiest way; considering he had just finished an early morning London meeting and was set up to talk in the evening with the owner of a company working on specialized components for wireless broadband communications systems, who had called for his 'expert advice'.

He always had liked trains and imagined a nice trip on the 'Orient Express', something he would have to arrange one day. Hey, what was that sign posted on the front cabin door? 'Free Wi-Fi'! Now that is going to make this trip just great! He logged-in and started to pull down his email list. The rolling landscape passing by started him to think about when all this had started. He never imagined, back in 1986 as a radio engineer, when starting the 'feasibility study' for the 'Wireless Local Area Network Project' at NCR (Utrecht, The Netherlands) into what the seed money received from Headquarters in Dayton, Ohio, would grow. Looking around, he saw five other 'wireless users' in his train wagon, one seemed to be working on some presentation, two others were using their browser to look at some schedules; he quickly glanced away since he really did not want to be nosey. The one Apple Mac user seems to be looking at pictures on some social

site. Apple, with a reputation as innovative firm, had played a key role in the success story of Wi-Fi.

But what can the history of Wi-Fi tell us about the future of broadband wireless communication? What advice should he give to this start-up company in Darlington? He could establish his credentials based on his hands-on involvement in the innovation journey of Wi-Fi, for more than 25 years. He knows how to work in start-up mode and how to deal with large corporations. He also learned, how stubborn the market can be, that it takes a lot of time and effort to move from selling to the early adopters to entering the mass market. The market positioning of the product of this start-up company would be crucial. Wi-Fi had been extremely successful in linking computers to the internet, but lots of money, billions of dollars have been invested in 3G mobile networks by powerful companies, such as Vodafone, Deutsche Telecom and AT&T. How will that affect Wi-Fi and the product positioning of the start-up company? What will be the new battleground? What will it take to win? Should they play by the rules of the game? Or should they try to change them? To convince them, he may have to tell them first about the innovation journey of Wi-Fi and the road to its global success.

Wi-Fi today

Wi-Fi has changed our way of life. Wi-Fi has given us freedom. Rather than being bound by wires, we use radio waves to connect our computer to the internet – at home, in the office, in hotels, at airports, at the university campus.

Increasingly, Wi-Fi provides access to the internet for remote communities in developing countries, bridging large distances, e.g., in the Himalayan mountains and in the Andes. Even in rural areas of developed countries, for instance, in Denmark a community based Wi-Fi initiative emerged to provide broadband wireless internet access, as the incumbent operator – TeleDenmark – failed to extend the infrastructure to less profitable areas in a timely manner. In

[1]Source: Wolter Lemstra, 2009.

a further development, municipal governments, in for instance the USA and Europe, have taken the initiative to role-out Wi-Fi networks to improve the economic and social infrastructure of their cities.

A new multi-billion dollar industry has been created. In 2008, the shipments of Wi-Fi chipsets grew to 380 million, representing a little short of US$5 billion in revenues, see Figure 1, based on InStat data. In the same year, more than 1200 new products were certified by the Wi-Fi Alliance for compliance with the Wi-Fi standards, known under the name of the organization that facilitated the creation of the family of Wireless Local Area Networking standards – the Institute of Electrical and Electronic Engineers – and the serial number of the Working Group involved: IEEE 802.11.

Recognizing that the Wireless-LAN market in 1998, only ten years earlier, was estimated at less than US$10 million, what has been the origin of this new industry, and which firms, or even individuals should be considered responsible for its creation? Moreover, is it the result of a 'grand strategic plan' by one of the leading firms in the ICT industry, or rather the result of a series of 'emerging opportunities' exploited by a number of companies over time? Is there a role model for success implied, that might be followed?

The involvement of NCR Corporation

The origin of Wi-Fi and the related industry is linked to a story of technological innovation aimed at solving a customer problem that goes back to the NCR Corporation in the early 1980s.

NCR was founded a century earlier, in 1879, as the National Manufacturing Company of Dayton, Ohio, to manufacture and sell mechanical cash registers, invented in 1879 by James Ritty. In 1884, the company and its patents were bought by John Henry Patterson and his brother Frank Jefferson and the company was renamed National Cash Register Company. NCR was formed into one of the first modern American companies, introducing new, aggressive sales methods and business techniques. The first sales training school was established in 1894. Nonetheless, the company also introduced a comprehensive social welfare programme for its factory workers.

Note that Thomas J. Watson Sr. worked his way up to general sales manager to become General Manager of Computing Tabulating Recording (CTR) Corporation in 1914 and President in 1915. In 1924, the CTR Corporation changed its name to International Business Machines Corporation, or simply IBM. Watson would play a central role in establishing what would become the IBM organization and culture.

In 1926, NCR went public with an issue of US$55 million in stock. In 1952, NCR acquired Computer Research Corporation and created a specialized electronics division. In 1957, the company introduced its first transistor-based computer, the NCR 304. In 1962 followed the introduction of the NCR-315 Electronic Data Processing System. In 1974, NCR commercialized the first bar code scanners. And in 1982, the company became

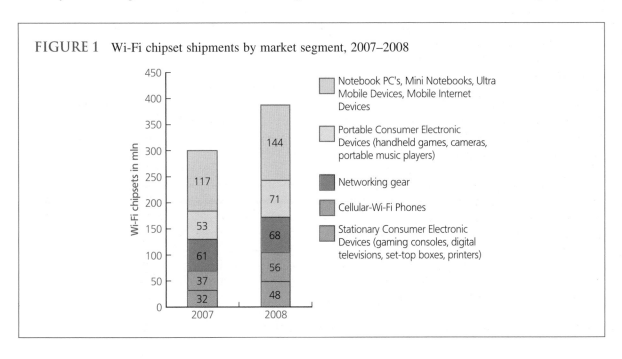

FIGURE 1 Wi-Fi chipset shipments by market segment, 2007–2008

involved in 'open systems architecture', with the introduction of the UNIX-based TOWER 16/32 computer. See Exhibit 1 for a historical timeline (NCR, 2009).

In the late 1970s and early 1980s a nagging issue for the NCR sales force had become the lack of mobility in the cash register product portfolio. Retail department stores, one of the main client groups of NCR, reconfigured the sales floor on a regular basis and the cost of rewiring the transaction terminals was a significant expense. To address this issue NCR had conducted a study into the use of infrared light technology, but according to Don Johnson at the NCR Corporate R&D organization in Dayton, Ohio, radio technology would be a much better option: 'if it was permitted, if we could make it work, and if we could turn it into affordable products'.

Obtaining permission to use radio waves for data communication is not a trivial affair. The use of the

EXHIBIT 1 NCR HISTORY TIMELINE

1884	John. H. Patterson founded the National Cash Register Company, maker of the first mechanical cash registers.
1894	NCR opened one of the first sales training schools.
1906	Charles P. Kettering designed the first cash register powered by an electric motor.
1914	NCR developed one of the first automated credit systems.
1926	NCR became publicly owned.
1952	NCR acquired Computer Research Corporation (CRC), of Hawthorne, California, which produced a line of digital computers with applications in aviation.
1953	NCR established the Electronic Division to continue to pursue electronic applications for business machines.
1957	NCR announced first fully transistorized business computers, the NCR 304.
1968	NCR's John L. Janning invented liquid crystal displays (LCD)
1974	Company changed its name to NCR corporation.
1974	NCR commercialized first bar code scanners.
1982	The first NCR Tower super-microcomputeer system was launched, establishing NCR as a pioneer in bringing industry standards and open systems architecture to the computer market.
1991	NCR acquired by AT&T.
1991	NCR purchased Teradata Corporation, acquiring its advanced and unique commercial parallel processing technology. NCR Teradata becomes the world's most proven and powerful database for data warehousing.

1994	NCR name changed to AT&T Global Information Solutions (GIS).
1995	AT&T announced spin-off of AT&T GIS by the end of 1996.
1996	AT&T GIS changed its name back to NCR Corporation in anticipation of being spun-off to AT&T shareholders by January 1997, as an independent, publicly-traded company.
1997	Signalling its evolution from a hardware-only company to a full solutions provider. NCR purchased Comprios Technologies, Inc., a leading provider of store automation and management software for the food-service industry, and Dataworks, a company that develops check-processing software.
1998	NCR finalized the transfer and sale of their computer hardware manufacturing assets to Solectron, confirming NCR's commitment to concentrate on the market-differentiated software and services components of the solutions portfolios.
2000	NCR acquired CRM provider Cares Integrated Solutions and services company 4 Front technologies, deepening NCR's solutions offerings in key markets.
2003	NCR granted patent for signature capture.
2005	Following the 2004 acquisition of travel self-service leader Kinetics, NCR further strengths its self-service portfolio by acquiring Galvanon, a leading provider of solutions for the health-care industry.
2007	NCR separated in two companies through the spin-off of the Teradata Data Warehousing business.
2009	NCR establishes its new corporate headquarters in Duluth, Georgia.

radio frequency waves is highly regulated and subject to licensing by government agencies. Only the use of short range devices, such as garage door openers, is licence-exempt, provided the equipment complies to strict regulations, which the manufacturer has to certify to the satisfaction of the National Regulatory Agency (NRA). In the Unites States this is the Federal Communications Commission (FCC).

The role of the US Federal Communications Commission

As a lucky coincidence, the radio regulations had become subject of reform under the Carter Administration (1977–1981). Carter's programme was one of deregulation, which had already affected the airline, trucking and railroad industries. The White-House facilitated a dialogue with regulators on basic concepts and an interagency committee occasionally organized workshops for agencies to exchange ideas on deregulation. FCC Chairman Charles Ferris (Oct, 1977 – Feb, 1981) intended to extend the deregulation spirit to apply to the radio frequency spectrum. He would like to end the practice whereby numerous requests for spectrum would be brought forward, based on special cases of technology application. The adagio was 'let us unrestrict the restricted technologies'. To that effect he hired in 1979 Dr. Stephen Lukasik as Chief Scientist at the FCC, a physicist famous for having been Director of ARPA from 1969, during the pioneering years of ARPAnet, which was the precursor of today's internet. Dr. Michael Marcus relays the story:

At that time I was working for the Institute for Defence Analyses, which I had joined in 1975. I was assigned to study options for Electronic Counter-Counter Measures, which was triggered by the 1973 Middle-East war showing an unexpected amount of communications warfare. In 1979 during a closed meeting on Electronic Warfare held in Chicago, the delegates were seated in alphabetical order, and as it happened I was seated next to Stephen Lukasik. I found out that Stephen was about to leave Xerox to become Chief Scientist of the FCC. He had been asked by FCC Chairman Charles Ferris to identify new communications technologies that were being blocked by anachronistic rules. I suggested that spread spectrum was such a technology and as a consequence I was invited by Stephen to join the FCC to follow up on the idea

EXHIBIT 2 INVENTION OF SPREAD SPECTRUM

The invention of the spread spectrum concept, in the form of frequency hopping, dates back to 1942 when a patent was granted to actress Hedy Lamarr and composer George Antheil: U.S. Patent # 2,292,387, issued on August 11, under the title: '*Secret Communications System*'. Hedy Lamarr, born as Hedwig Eva Maria Kiesler in 1913 in Vienna), had become notorious through her appearance in Gustav Machaty's film *Ecstasy,* a Czechoslovak film, in which she played a love-hungry young wife of an indifferent old husband.

In 1933 she married to Friedrich Mandl, an Austrian arms manufacturer, which exposed her to discussions on the jamming of radio-guided torpedoes launched from submarines. In 1937 Kiesler left Austria for America, under a contract with MGM. Here, she met with the composer George Antheil. Their combined insights in technology and music generated the idea to change the carrier frequency on a regular basis, akin to changing the frequency when striking another key on the piano. They presented their idea to the National Inventors Council and subsequently donated their patent to the US military, as a contribution to the war effort.

However, the first practical application was after the war, in the mid 1950s, in sonobuoys used to secretly locate submarines. The first serial production of systems based on the 'direct sequence' version of spread spectrum were most probably the Magnavox AN/ARC-50 and ARC-90 airborne systems. There are most probably other early systems that have remained classified.

In December 1979 the MITRE Corporation was requested by the FCC to investigate the potential civil usage of spread spectrum. Their report of 1980 resulted in a public consultation conducted by the FCC on the use of spread spectrum technology. The consultation process would lead to the landmark decision of 198. On May 9, the FCC decided to open up three radio frequency (RF) bands that were already designated for Industrial, Scientific and Medical (ISM) applications for the use by radio communication systems. There were two important conditions attached to the use: spread spectrum technology should be applied and the transmission power was to be limited to 1 Watt (FCC, 1985).

The prescription of spread spectrum technology was special as this technique had remained officially classified as military technology until 1981.

Involvement of the Dutch NCR Engineering centre

The 1985 decision by the FCC resolved the first item on Don Johnson's list of issues in realizing a Wireless LAN. The next step was 'to make it work'.

For that purpose seed money was made available by Headquarters for the execution of a feasibility study to be executed by the NCR Systems Engineering centre located in Utrecht, The Netherlands.

The Utrecht Systems Engineering centre was established to adapt the NCR products to the specific European requirements. The centre included a significant software development team working on integration of financial systems into the IBM-world, and another group of experts working on adapting the telephone modem technologies to the European standards. The Utrecht Centre had become a skill centre in modem communication designs. One of the designs was a wired Local Area Network (MIRLAN), which NCR deployed to wire-up their Cash Machines in stores before Ethernet became a standard. The choice of the Utrecht Engineering Centre for the execution of the technology investigation was based on this LAN experience, their signal processing expertise, hardware design experience, and the recently acquired radio technology knowledge from Philips Electronics, in Eindhoven, The Netherlands.

Bruce Tuch would become the leader of the research effort. A 'Brooklyn boy', who moved four years earlier straight out of university to the Radio Division of Philips Electronics in Eindhoven, following his wife's opportunity to study Veterinary Medicine in Utrecht, to be recruited by the NCR Engineering Centre in 1985.

The challenge facing the NCR engineers was that copper wires, coax and (shielded) twisted pair, differ from radio frequency spectrum in their transmission properties and in the way the medium can be accessed. Hence, new designs were required at the physical layer (PHY) and at the medium access layer (MAC) of the OSI protocol stack. See also Figure 2. Any possible further impact on the higher layers of the stack (network through application) would also have to be assessed as part of the feasibility study. The fewer layers would be affected the easier the Wireless LAN functionality could be integrated in existing products.

The first part of the feasibility project was to determine under what 'spread spectrum' conditions such products could be certified by the FCC. The logic here is that the more the signal is 'spread' over the radio frequency spectrum, the more the signal looks like 'noise' to others – the more systems can operate simultaneously in the same band. Moreover, there is also a trade off between the data rates to be achieved and the complexity of the total system and thus the costs. Interactions with the FCC on the issue of 'spreading' suggested that a Wireless Local Area Network could be realized operating at 1 Mbit/s or even higher. Based on this information and the results of indoor propagation studies the team set to work. The feasibility study resulted in a Wireless-LAN Demo unit and a set of related product specifications.

These results were to the satisfaction of HQ and Don Johnson moved to start the product development process, with the objective 'to turn it into affordable products'.

The development team in Utrecht was able to convince the Retail Systems Division that product development was also best carried out by the same team. In the summer of 1987, the team set out to create a Wireless Network Interface Card (Wireless-NIC) with a data rate of 2 Mbit/s, targeted at the retail markets that NCR was serving. The NIC would have to operate in the 900 MHz band, This lower band was selected to provide the maximum possible range and to reduce the cost of the electronics.

The creation of a new Medium Access Control protocol became the focus of the product development effort. To limit costs and to reduce the development time the team intended to leverage as much as possible existing MAC designs and to make use of existing protocol standards where possible. And, if an 'open' MAC standard could be found, the cost of the Intellectual Property (IP) involved would be minimal, as 'open standards' are based on an agreement that IP will be made available by participating firms on a 'fair, reasonable and non-discriminatory basis'.

The role of standards within NCR Corporation

Within NCR *de-facto* standards had been a curse rather than a blessing, as they were of a proprietary nature. Although the company was a leading provider of point-of-sale terminals, most of the time these terminals had to be connected to a back office computing system, mostly supplied by the leading mainframe provider IBM. Having a dominant position in this market, IBM used proprietary protocols to connect terminal equipment to its mainframes and mini-computers. As a

FIGURE 2 IEEE 802.11 standards mapped to the OSI reference model

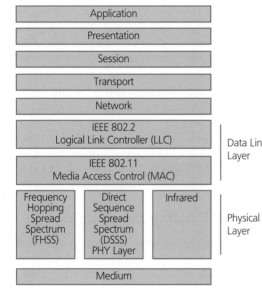

IEEE 802.11 related standards stack

- Application
- Presentation
- Session
- Transport
- Network
- IEEE 802.2 Logical Link Controller (LLC)
- IEEE 802.11 Media Access Control (MAC)
- Frequency Hopping Spread Spectrum (FHSS) | Direct Sequence Spread Spectrum (DSSS) PHY Layer | Infrared
- Medium

Examples of related protocols used in the context of the internet

HTTP, HTTPS, SMTP, POP3, IMAP, FTP, UUCP, NNTP, SSL, SSH, IRC, SNMP, SIP, RTP, Telnet, DNS

TCP, UDP, SCTP, DCCP

IPv4, IPv6, ICMP, ARP, IGMP

Data Link Layer — Ethernet, Wi-Fi, Token Ring, FDDI, PPP, ATM

Physical Layer — RS-232, EIA-422, RS-449, EIA-485, 10BaseT, 100BaseT, IEEE 802.11a, IEEE 802.11b, IEEE 802.11g, DSL, ADSL

Twisted pair copper, coax, fiber, radio, infra-red

Source: Reprinted from 'Network modernization in the telecom sector: The case of Wi-Fi' in The Governance of Network Industries (2009) edited by Künneke, Groenewegen and Auger, with permission from Edward Elgar.

result, much of the protocol expertise of the Utrecht development team originated from the analysis and subsequent emulation of IBM protocols. Bruce Tuch provides the rationale and the decision to go for a standards based approach:

Any proprietary system outside the scope of the NCR core business were considered to dilute the R&D efforts and it also could open up new 'choke points'. Therefore the business units which attended to standards that were seen to be in the interest of NCR received funding through the Corporate R&D organization. Although our Wireless LAN product was aimed at the vertical retail markets and according to corporate rules would not require a standards-based interface, it was understood that if we worked towards a standard the total market in the future would be greater than the relatively small vertical retail niche. At that time we had no idea how much bigger this would really become!

First product development task: Finding an existing MAC protocol

Finding a related MAC was in essence a search for a MAC protocol already being implemented using a wireless medium, or to find a MAC implemented for another medium that could be adapted to wireless use. Bruce Tuch relays the story about this search and how the link with IEEE as a relevant standards developing organization came about:

I knew already of ALOHA, which was one of the first Wireless Radio protocols, of which derivates had morphed into Ethernet and later the IEEE 802.3 standard for wired-LANs. Ethernet was a Carrier Sense Access with Collision Detection based mechanism; which relied on the wired medium to be able to detect collisions.[2] Unfortunately, in a wireless

---

[2] If two or more stations try to send information at the same time over the same medium a 'collision' of the signals will occur and the receiving station will not be able to detect and reconstruct the original signal properly. Hence, collisions should be avoided and/or a recovery procedure should be implemented.

environment we could not use this same mechanism. At the same time, another possible choice emerged: the Medium Access Control used in the Token Bus standard, another wired-LAN standard, which was very recently approved as IEEE 802.4. Being 'just a simple engineer', when I dove into the materials of the different standards organizations, it seemed more like the United Nations documents of engagement, and my eyes would roll. Luckily NCR supported standards making activities in various bodies. Vic Hayes was one of the experts that could guide one through this maze. It became clear that the standards body we needed to focus on was IEEE and in particular the '802' committee, given the market acceptance of this body for the standardisation of wired-LANs.

The development team recognized that having an already established group within IEEE 802 to sponsor a wireless protocol was a much faster process than trying to start a new standard from scratch. In IEEE 802.4 a Task Group was already working on a wireless variant of Token Bus driven by General Motors, but it seemed it was 'losing steam'. The Chair of the Task Group did not attend anymore, but the Executive Secretary was willing to convene a meeting on request of NCR in July 1988. In the following meeting in November, Vic Hayes of NCR was elected to take over the chair of this Task Group.

However, as Tuch observed: 'Making the 802.4 protocol fit with the wireless medium was like trying to use a boat to get across a swamp, instead of a hovercraft'.

Having concluded that the Token Bus protocol was not suitable for the purpose, the MAC used as part of the IEEE 802.3 Ethernet standard still might be adapted. One of the key issues here again was how to get it implemented using a wireless medium. A solution for the 'collision detection' problem was developed by representatives of NCR and Inland Steel and was presented to the IEEE 802.3 Ethernet standards group, to solicit interest to start a new wireless working group. They were apparently too busy on the evolution of the Ethernet standard towards higher data rates to support this initiative. With a negative vote for the proposal the political stage was set to 'start from scratch' with a new Wireless MAC standard. Under the leadership of Bruce Tuch of NCR, the companies interested in establishing a wireless local area network standard quickly generated the necessary paperwork

for the establishment of a new standardization project within the IEEE. At the July Plenary meeting, the IEEE 802 Executive Committee approved the request. With the subsequent approval by the Standards Board the new '802.11' Working Group was born, and Vic Hayes of NCR was appointed as the interim chairperson.

The decision to 'offer' the chair person to lead the Working Group is of strategic importance. The position provides full visibility of the activities of all participating firms and can be crucial to direct the standards making process in the desired direction. The challenge for the person involved is to combine the interest of the firm with the need to lead the Working Group in a manner acceptable to all parties involved.

For the Utrecht Engineering Team, the funding of the standards making effort by HQ in Dayton, Ohio made this decision much easier to take.

NCR taking the lead in IEEE 802.11

September of 1990, at the first meeting of the 802.11 Working Group Vic Hayes was elected as the Chair. At the November 1991 meeting of the Work Group two Sub Groups were established, the MAC group and the PHY group. On a case by case basis the sub groups made their own rules for what materials the proponents had to submit for the '802.11' membership to make a well informed decision. Once the proposals would be available, the two groups had the daunting task of selecting the appropriate technology for the project. In most of the cases the Task groups used a process of selection, whereby in each round of voting the proposal with the lowest number of supporting votes would be removed from the list, until a proposal would reach majority support.

Different perceptions – competing proposals

While companies cooperate in standards bodies, the work environment is highly competitive. Active contributors to the standards making process are jockeying for favourable positions, to optimally exploit their interests. Different firms may recognize different market opportunities and hence pursue different functionalities to be standardized. Moreover, their R&D development and Intellectual Property Right (IPR) positions may differ, leading to a different standardization strategy.

In the Wireless LAN standardization process a wide range of issues had to be resolved as contending proposals were being submitted. Some of these issues resulted in fierce battles with in the end both winners and losers.

Different perceptions on architecture: IBM vs NCR c.s.

The first point of contention was about the principle to be used in assigning capacity to a terminal based on the shared use of the radio frequency spectrum. A similar issue in the Wired-LAN arena had split the industry and led to three different incompatible standards having been approved by the IEEE.

For Wireless-LANs IBM proposed a centralized approach, while NCR together with Symbol Technologies and Xircom submitted a proposal that supported a decentralized mechanism. The merits of the two proposals were intensely debated and subjected to the voting process.[3] In the end the NCR-led proposal for a decentralized approach won the vote; one of the reasons being that this protocol would support 'ad hoc' networking, whereby a terminal would be able to independently coordinate communications with another terminal. IBM lost this battle.

The options left open by the FCC – Frequency Hopping and Direct Sequence.

The second area of contention was related to the PHY. In its 1985 Rule & Order the FCC had specified two different spread spectrum modulation techniques that could be used: Frequency Hopping (FH) and Direct Sequence (DS). When put to a vote in the PHY Task Group neither of the two modulation techniques obtained the required 75% level of support. Proponents of Frequency Hopping claimed it was easier to implement, while Direct Sequence had the promise of a more robust system with a higher data rate. The individuals in the Frequency Hopping camp feared that the required investment in silicon would be significant, while the Direct Sequence camp tried to refute the argument based on their experience in the implementation of pilot versions. As neither of the two groups could get the required level of support, the only way out was to include both modulation techniques in the standard.

Alternative European standard for WLAN – HIPERLAN.

Following the decision making by the FCC in the USA, an ad-hoc group on wireless-LANs within the CEPT, the body responsible for the harmonization of radio spectrum use in Europe, recommended that the 2.4 GHz band be opened for the licence-exempt use of wireless-LAN devices. Note that in Europe the 900 MHz band is used for mobile telephony – GSM, and thus could not be made available for wireless-LANs. The CEPT decision paved the way towards a global assignment of radio spectrum for Wireless-LANs.

The CEPT also identified the 5 GHz band as suitable for wireless-LANs. As often happens in Europe, this allocation of the spectrum would be tied to devices adhering to a specific standard, in this case the standard tagged HIPERLAN for High Performance Local Area Networks, yet to be developed. HIPERLAN was aimed at providing high-speed communications (24 Mbit/s typical data rate) and to be compatible with Ethernet and Token Ring standards. HIPERLAN was aimed to cover a range of 50 meters and to support asynchronous (data) and synchronous (voice, video) applications.

Vic Hayes had been invited to participate as an industry representative in the ad-hoc committee of CEPT, and in the related Technical Committee of ETSI[4]. This provided the Utrecht Team with a rather unique position to leverage its activities in IEEE and ETSI, and to align as far as (politically) possible the activities in the two standard setting bodies. Again the company volunteered to provide the chair person; Jan Kruys became the second chair of the ETSI-RES 3 committee.

The Committee published its first technical specification HIPERLAN/1 in 1997. A second version HIPERLAN/2 was developed to provide much higher data rates (up to 54 Mbit/s) and to support multi-media applications. A HIPERLAN2 Global Forum was established to support its deployment, supported by, e.g., Bosch, Dell, Ericsson, Nokia, Telia and TI.

Neither the HIPERLAN/1 standard nor HIPERLAN/2 standard, completed in 2004, have become a success. Alvarion, Motorola and SICE Communications were involved in early product introductions, but in the end game HIPERLAN had to compete with a much more matured IEEE 802.11 standard for which devices had been developed that had already reached a price point too low to compete with effectively.

NCR the *de-facto* leader in the Wireless LAN standard making process

From the account it may have become clear that the NCR Engineering Team had become the *de-facto*

---

[3]To reach agreement within the IEEE Working Groups and Task Groups individuals opposing a proposal in a vote have to explain the reasons for their opposition. By making these reasons explicit the group as a collective is invited to find ways to resolve the issue, and if successful, it has broadened the support for the resulting proposal.

[4]ETSI: European Telecommunication Standards Institute.

leader in the standards making process in IEEE 802.11 Working Group. This is further illustrated in Figure 3 showing the number of contributions from each company having submitted 10 or more documents from the start of IEEE 802.11 in 1990 till the end of 1999. Recall that in 1991 NCR was acquired by AT&T. In 1996 AT&T divests NCR and creates Lucent Technologies. In the process the wireless-LAN activities move to Lucent Technologies.

This count includes the documents provided for administrative purposes, such as meeting minutes, agendas, ballot results and planning presentations. With 531 contributions, representing 23% of the total and almost four times as many as the next company in the sequence, the leadership role that NCR, and subsequently AT&T and Lucent Technologies, has assumed in the development of the IEEE 802.11 standard is becoming obvious.

Introducing the Wireless LAN products in the market

The decision by NCR Corporation to exploit the new business opportunity through the development of an open standard in cooperation with others was an important step in realizing its Wireless LAN vision. However, while manufacturing partners can be aligned through the standardization process, real products are required to convince potential customers of the benefits that Wireless LANs can provide. Market research initiated by NCR to establish the right product positioning strategy indicated that LAN (re-)wiring was cumbersome and expensive, estimated at US$200–1500 per 'drop'. Also the lack of expertise was mentioned as an issue. The connection of PC adaptors to the coax cable and localizing faults in the early Ethernet systems was know to be cumbersome. Lower overall cost was identified as the key feature of Wireless-LANs.

Well ahead of a formal standard being approved, NCR launched its first WaveLAN product for the US market at Networld in Dallas, in September of 1990. The product operated at 915 MHz, providing a data rate of 2 Mbit/s. It was a desktop PC plug-in board, requiring an external antenna. The general product release was in May 1991, after radio certification and manufacturing start-up issues had been resolved. Prospective customers appeared to be fascinated by the technology, but the benefits were perceived as marginal and the price as too high. At the product launch the price was set at US$1395 per card, which included the Novell Netware driver. This compared favourably with the

competing Wireless LAN product of Motorola, Altair. For the NCR development team the Altair had been the development benchmark. However, Motorola had opted to implement a product in the 18 GHz band, involving a different technology, that was inherently more expensive, and made it virtually impossible to reach a cost base lower than US$1000. Moreover, it would be very difficult, if not impossible, to scale down the product to make it portable.

However, in comparison a wired-LAN ARCNet card was sold at US$300, an Ethernet card at $495, and a Token Ring card at $645. Giving the difference in implementation only a Total Cost of Ownership calculation would provide for a fair comparison. Although this improved the business case significantly, within short NCR would lower the price to $995.

In the course of 1991, it became clear that the product was incomplete in the view of prospective customers. Multiple Access Points (AP) would be needed to cover larger buildings, to be connected to the wired-LAN infrastructure; plus the capability of roaming (also called hand-off) between the APs. The concept was easily described and readily adopted, given its similarity with cellular communication. The implementation looked relatively easy as the client stations, PC/laptop, could keep track of the signal strength of each AP within reach and switch the connection to the AP with the best transmission performance. However, the R&D efforts increased significantly when the system had to be 'scaled-up', and became comparable to the efforts involved in the development of the NIC.

Security concerns

As it is much easier to eavesdrop on a wireless system than on a wired system the level of security provided by WLANs raised doubts in the minds of prospective customers, which in turn frustrated its adoption. From the outset WaveLAN included as an option a Data Encryption Security (DES) chip. This chip was used until the IEEE standard was implemented, which included the so-called Wired Equivalent Privacy (WEP) algorithm, providing a basic authentication and encryption method. WEP was designed in the 1990s and was purposely weak, to remain within the confines of existing US export regulations.

Global versus local products

The differences between the early successes in the 915 MHz US market and the 'international' market adopting

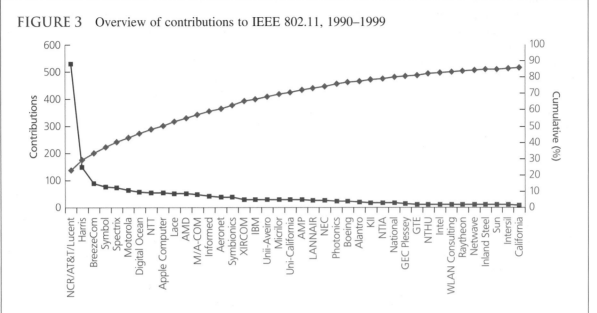

FIGURE 3   Overview of contributions to IEEE 802.11, 1990–1999

Source: 'The Shaping of the IEEE 802.11 Standard: The role of the Innovating Firm in the Case of Wi-Fi' in *Information Communication Technology Standardization for E-business Sectors* edited by Kai Jakobs. Copyright 2009, IGI Global, www.igi-global.com. Reprinted by permission of the publisher.

2.4 GHz raised the strategic question whether a global product or localized products should be pursued. The 2.4 GHz band was also available in the USA. The 915 MHz lower frequency range had the advantage of a larger reach, as attenuation of radio waves increases with frequency. However, in the 2.4 GHz band more spectrum had been assigned and hence more channels could be accommodated and used simultaneously, increasing the system performance. While on the one hand a global product would be more cost effective, product costs at 2.4 GHz would be higher than at 915 MHz. Moreover, as the products would provide the same functionality, it would be difficult to differentiate in pricing.

The decision was essentially determined by market forces. Competitors who were only marketing products in the 2.4 GHz band pushed the advantage of more channels, which gave the customers the impression that the 2.4 GHz product was providing a higher data rate. With the illusion of higher speed the issue of a shorter range became a mute point. As Cees Links, Product Line Manager of Wireless LANs at NCR, observed:

This shift in the market implied a further set back for the Wireless LAN business case. The shift to a 2.4 GHz product would further erode the margins, which were already very tight, at or below 10 per cent, while 30 per cent was desirable. The cost of a 2.4 GHz radio was estimated to be US$350 or more. To combine a competitive market price with a reasonable margin the costs should come down to $250 or less. Aggressive cost reduction efforts would have to be started immediately, and hence, the integration of functionality into a smaller chipset. There was one advantage, we would not have to spend a lot of marketing dollars in moving the early adopters from the 'old' 915 MHz product to the 'new' 2.4 GHz product.

First large scale application

In 1993, AT&T was successful in closing the first contract for large scale deployment of WaveLAN at the Carnegie Mellon University (CMU) in Pittsburgh, Pennsylvania. The project involved the deployment of Access Points to serve 10 000 students, faculty and staff moving about the university campus. The acquisition of CMU as a client would provide a perfect test bed for a large scale deployment of WLANs.

Ten years into the product development effort

Summarizing the situation in early 1997 Cees Links, Product Line Manager, concludes:

While the early product development period 1987–1991 had been cumbersome, the period 1991–1994, involving the general availability of the WaveLAN product and a major marketing and sales effort, had not been much better. We had essentially 'doubled our bets' with adding a 2.4 GHz product, but there were no real profits in sight. After the first period we had a Wireless LAN card, after the second period we had a Wireless LAN system. Hence, we could bridge into a wired environment, and we could roam through buildings while staying connected. After the first period we had a US-only product, after the second we had a worldwide product. This was all encouraging in terms of progress. However, the cost was still too high and the speed of 2 Mbit/s was to low compared with Wired LANs. Moreover, the market acceptance of Wireless LANs was still very low. There were serious concerns raised about the lack of a standard. All companies, the major ones Proxim, Aironet, and now AT&T, and the many smaller ones including Breezecom, WaveAccess, Xircom, all had different products. All of them were telling the prospects why they were the best and what was wrong with the technology of the competitor. The consequence of this all was that prospective customers did not trust anybody – 'data was precious, and radio waves were weird' – so the prevailing attitude was 'wait and see'. It was clear what we needed was standards, higher speeds, and lower costs.

In the period 1995–1997 the Wireless LAN industry was struggling to keep afloat. The companies were only marginally profitable, and overpowered by the hype around cellular. And according to Cees Links:

The cellular phone industry did not understand LANs and were about to make the same mistake as their wired predecessors had made with ISDN, assuming that data was just a variation of voice.

Having become part of the big AT&T through the acquisition of NCR in 1991, the Wireless LAN activities had become part of Lucent Technologies in 1996, and thereby a marginal activity in the scheme of the multi-billion dollar public telecommunications equipment business.

Note that to solve the channel conflict between AT&T the operator and AT&T the equipment vendor, the company decided to split into three independent companies: AT&T – the operator of long-distance and international communication services, Lucent Technologies – the equipment division, which included Bell Labs, and NCR, the computing business – to become an independent entity again. In this move the WaveLAN activities moved from AT&T Global Information Systems to Lucent Technologies.

The telecom industry represented by e.g. Alcatel, Ericsson, Lucent Technologies, Nokia, Nortel, Motorola and Siemens were riding the cellular wave and were already looking for the 'next big thing'. Although many executives were expecting that wireless data was going to be important, these public networking companies were not used to work with unlicensed spectrum, in fact they were not used to the Ethernet protocol either. These companies were network centric and not PC centric. Optical fibre attracted most of their investments, and 3G (UMTS in Europe) was to be the next 'promise'.

By 1997 the investments in establishing a standard for Wireless LANs culminated in the approval of IEEE 802.11, which covered 1 and 2 Mbit/s, Frequency Hopping and Direct Sequence Spread Spectrum operating at 2.4 GHz. April 1998, Lucent Technologies announced its IEEE 802.11 compliant WaveLAN product – a PC-card with an integrated antenna – to be introduced at the Networld+InterOP show in Las Vegas.

In 1997 a few important developments occurred in parallel, having major impact on the strategy that was being followed by the Lucent Technologies Wireless-LAN team: (1) the HomeRF consortium is formed; and (2) the IEEE 802.11 community starts the development of a standard for higher data rates.

Targeting a different market segment – the HomeRF consortium

In 1997, an industry consortium was initiated and led by Proxim, targeting Wireless LANs for application in the home. They concluded that voice communication (telephony) had to be supported by the new Wireless LAN standard. Companies that were involved in the HomeRF development included: Butterfly Communications, Compaq, HP, IBM, Intel, iReady, Microsoft, Motorola, Proxim, OTC Telecom, RF Monolithics, Samsung and Symbionics (Lansford, 1999). The consortium adopted the Frequency Hopping method as the basis for their standard proposal, supporting a data rate of 1.6 Mbit/s.

The choice for Frequency Hopping by the consortium, implied that NCR became one of the few companies pursuing only the Direct Sequence variant of spread spectrum technology. Knowing that the consortium was backed by some important firms, such as Intel and Motorola, put significant pressure on the Utrecht development team.

When the IEEE 802.11b project adopted an 11 Mbit/s data rate (see below) the consortium announced a second release of the specification for speeds of 6 Mbit/s up to 10 Mbit/s. This required the consortium to file a letter requesting an interpretation or waiver at the FCC, permitting Frequency Hopping devices to widen the channels from 1 MHz to 3 and 5 MHz on November 11, 1998. The FCC agreed and released a Notice of Proposed Rulemaking on June 24, 1999. This request revealed the maximum possible data rate as a (major) weakness of the HomeRF proposal, which subsequently could be exploited by the Lucent Technologies Team in pursuing the Direct Sequence version.

The HomeRF battle in the 802.11 Working Group was fierce. Vic Hayes provides as an illustration some anecdotal evidence:

> The battle went so far that an officer of the IEEE EMC committee (also happening to be an employee of a firm with high stakes in the HomeRF work) called me after the September 1999 meeting of IEEE 802.11 coercing me to stop submitting IEEE 802.11 Reply Comments to the FCC pending approval by that committee, based on the IEEE rules according to that person. I knew the rules of the IEEE very well to state that each group within the IEEE had the freedom to submit papers to the US government, provided the IEEE_USA had approved it. The person was not able to direct me to any evidence that we had to receive approval from the EMC Committee. Waiting for the approval of that committee would have been killing for the filing of our comments, as the deadline would have passed.

HomeRF was positioned as a low cost solution combining existing DECT[5] technology with the proposed IEEE standard. In April 2000 Intel announced its Anypoint wireless home networking and in November Proxim unveiled its Symphony HRF. Despite the support of major payers in the industry the HomeRF initiative failed. According to Lansford the reasons for the failure were twofold[6]:

1. Because none of the consortium members except Proxim were developing PHY silicon, they were forced to switch to the OpenAir PHY developed by Proxim. Many companies in the HomeRF Industry Consortium felt this made the standard a proprietary system, and

2. The adoption of IEEE 802.11b standard in 1999 and its support by several silicon vendors (including Harris and Lucent Technologies) drove down prices relatively quickly compared to the single silicon source for HomeRF. The HomeRF consortium had assumed that FH products would always be cheaper than DS products, but market competition invalidated that assumption.

Bruce Tuch concluded that in comparison with IEEE 802.11 the HomeRF initiative was 'too little, too late':

> The proposed HomeRF standard only supported 1.6 Mbit/s, with the goal to be able to go to 10 Mbit/s higher speeds in the future, when the FCC would approve the new rule making proposals. The fact that HomeRF also supported voice services was not a 'market need', voice was not driving the usage model. Getting the IEEE 802.11b standard at 11 Mbit/s accepted in 1999 was the key nail on the HomeRF coffin.

Increasing the data rate – the turbo version

With the implementations of the various manufacturers being based on the same open standard this allows for very little product differentiation. Hence, what often can be observed is that manufacturers try to enhance the functionality of the standard product to create differentiation. In communication systems this is often done by increasing the data rate by providing a 'turbo option'. This was also the strategy pursued by the Lucent Technologies team, as the IEEE 802.11 Working Group was focusing on standards improvements in the area of security and quality of service. For that purpose, Bruce Tuch engaged the support of Bell Labs scientist and mathematician Israel bar-David, who would spend his sabbatical year in Utrecht to support the design of a 10 Mbit/s version. The 'theorist' Israel worked closely with system engineer Rajeev Krishnamoorthy, on the practical aspects of the

---

[5]DECT: Digital Enhanced Cordless Telecommunications. Originally Digital European Cordless Telecommunications.
[6]Lansford has been Co-Chair of the Technical Committee for the HomeRF Industry Working Group and wireless system architect with Intel Corporation.

algorithms. This gave birth to a 8 Mbit/s Pulse Position Modulation (PPM) technique. The product development for this differentiated Turbo product (chip set and NIC cards) were completed and ready for market introduction.

However, the momentum in the IEEE standards arena was very strong and did not end with the completion of the 2Mbit/s version of the standard in 1997. Following the approval in the IEEE of the 100 Mbit/s Ethernet standard in 1993, high speed wired-LAN products had been introduced in the market and during the final editing of the IEEE 802.11-1997 version of the Wireless LAN standard it was becoming clear to everybody in the '802.11' community that also higher data rate Wireless-LANs would be required. The goal being set was to extend the performance and the range of applications in the 2.4 GHz band, and specify a higher data rate wireless access technology suitable for data, voice and image information services in the lower 5 GHz band.

This result forced Lucent Technologies to quickly change its strategy from pursuing a proprietary 'turbo' solution to support a standards-based high data rate version of IEEE 802.11. The good news was that Vic Hayes had remained the chair of Working Group 802.11 and the team could quickly resume its full contribution to the standards effort by proposing PPM for 802.11b in the 2.4 GHz band, enabling to influence the outcome, as well as submitting a proposal together with NTT of Japan for the 802.11a standard in the 5 GHz band.

Increasing the data rate – Lucent Technologies vs. Harris vs. Micrilor

The least contentious was the 802.11a variant with a data rate up to 54 Mbit/s in the 5 GHz band. There were two main proposals, one from Breezecom on a single carrier modulation method and one from Lucent Technologies together with NTT of Japan, based on a new modulation technique OFDM[7]. The voting was won by the Lucent Technologies and NTT combination.

The voting for the IEEE 802.11b standard in the 2.4 GHz band was much more contentious, and almost a war on the brink of tearing the 802.11 Working Group apart. The main contenders were Harris and Lucent Technologies, and a proposal from an outsider Micrilor, a start-up company with a proposal having some

significant technical advantages. Cees Links recalls the course of events:

When these three remaining proposals were left and subjected to the next round of voting, the Lucent Technologies proposal was voted out. What happened then is hard to describe, and challenged the democratic rules in IEEE. In the voting Micrilor came out with 52 votes and Harris with 51 votes, and one abstention. According to one set of rules, Micrilor had won the vote, but this was immediately contested, as Micrilor did not have a majority of the votes: 52 out of 104 votes is not 'more than 50 per cent'. A violent discussion started to unfold on the interpretation of the outcome of the vote with many real and emotional arguments floating around. Then Jeff Abramowitz, the 3Com Product Manager for Wireless-LANs, stood up and moved a motion in which he contested the whole voting procedure. According to the rules of IEEE, an IEEE member engineer should vote for the best technical proposal, and in his assessment, despite the voting having been 'closed', the reality of the voting was that the individual members had voted along party lines, that is, along the line of the company for which they worked. This was true to a high extent, but he phrased his motion in such a way, that the Harris proposal should be declared the winner, as the voting in favour of Micrilor had become an anti-Harris vote. It became clear that 3Com was a Harris supporter. The chaos this motion created was incredible, and the whole meeting went down in flames.

There was a degree of truth in the 3Com statement that most of the Lucent Technologies supporters had decided to side with Micrilor in the voting to avoid that Harris and their supporters would have an unfair advantage in the market, as they already had progressed substantially in their development efforts. In the same week the IEEE meeting took place, representatives of Lucent Technologies and Harris sat together and acknowledged a compromise was needed. Subsequently Harris and Lucent Technologies worked out a new radio transmission scheme, different from anything that had been proposed before, called Complementary Code Keying (CCK). The two parties could agree on this alternative proposal, as this would

---

[7]Orthogonal Frequency Division Multiplexing.

provide improved performance compared to the original Harris proposal and reduced complexity compared to the original Lucent Technologies proposal. Because this proposal gave no advantage/disadvantage to any other party the joint proposal was accepted in the next meeting of the Working Group six weeks later, resulting in the IEEE 802.11b standard for 11 Mbit/s.

An unexpected call from Steve Jobs

In the course of 1998 the Lucent Technology senior management started questioning the results of the Wireless-LAN project. This was after only two years of involvement and with limited visibility of what had been spent in the preceding decade. Slowly but surely resources were moved to other more promising radio projects, such as Wireless Local Loop. Nonetheless, the sales team kept pushing WaveLAN. The fortune of WaveLAN and for that matter Wireless-LANs would take a turn for the better following an unexpected call from Apple Headquarters, simply stating: 'Steve Jobs wants to have a meeting with Rich McGinn about wireless LANs.'

This request was received with some scepticism. In earlier sales calls it had become apparent that Apple was working with Motorola and had a clear preference for Frequency Hopping, while WaveLAN was based on Direct Sequence. Apple had also pursued other wireless solutions involving other companies, e.g. Plessey from the UK, Digital Ocean, and with a Bay-area start-up company Photonics they had explored an infra-red based solution. As Cees Links observed: 'I think Apple's quality was to "be there" when the technology and the standardization had reached the level that economic viability was around the corner. They reminded us that "timing is everything".'

Apparently Steve Jobs, who had returned to Apple as 'interim CEO' to reinvigorate the company, had decided that Wireless-LAN had to be the key differentiating feature for the iBook which was scheduled to be launched in 1999.[8] The meeting in the Apple Boardroom was an interesting one. Lucent brought some of the most Senior Managers to the meeting, including John Dickson, the Head of the Semiconductor Division, as had Apple. Cees Links recalls:

> Cordialities were exchanged, business cards handed out, etc. The meeting started at 2:00 PM, the companies at either side of the table, Lucent representatives with suits and ties, the Apple delegation was showing up Californian style. But, no Steve Jobs, the atmosphere became somewhat awkward: Steve had been delayed. Then Steve walks in, Californian style too, walks over to the Lucent side and shakes hands with everyone, needing no introduction. Steve starts talking, Wireless LANs are the greatest thing on earth, and this is what Apple wants, for about ten minutes straight. Rich McGinn tried a few comments, no traction. Then Steve asks: 'Are there any questions?' I tried to show a few slides: key wins, market positioning, product offering, value creation, etc. Presenting slides with Steve Jobs is actually quite easy: you put up the slide, and he will do the talking, not necessarily related to the slide. Then he asks for the next slide. Rich McGinn is chiming in a few words, he thinks 1999 will be the big year for DSL[9]: 'Will Apple be ready? ' That is: 'Will Apple PCs have DSL?' Steve Jobs: 'Probably not next year, maybe the year after, depends on whether there is a one standard worldwide...' Turning the conversation back to wireless-LANs: 'We need the radio card for $50, and I want to sell at $99.' Then Steve apologizes, he has to leave – stands up, says 'Hi!' and goes. The room falls silent.

For Steve Jobs the job was done, for Lucent Technologies the work started. The target was audacious, because early 1998 the cost level of the cards was still above US$100. The chipsets for the next round of cost reductions had been designed, but it was not clear whether the target set by Apple could be met by Spring of 1999. In the following months several rounds of negotiations took place to obtain agreement on the product definition. Apple wanted a special interface, moreover, they wanted three versions of the Access Point. Also the price was subject of some

---

[8] Apple had considered wireless connectivity as essential to the success of its laptops and PDA business. In early 1990 Apple petitioned the FCC to allocate 40 MHz of spectrum in the 1850-1990 MHz band earmarked for new technologies, in particular PCS, for a new radio service called Data-PCS. In the fall of 1993 this request was accommodated, however, the band was used by microwave users. Although relocation with compensation was agreed upon, there was no effective model for managing the relocation. Apple also filed a petition for rule making in 1995 for an allocation of 300 MHz in the 5GHz band, linked to the National Information Infrastructure initiative in the Clinton-Gore period. In 1997 the FCC created the Unlicensed-NII band within the existing 5 GHz ISM-band.

[9] DSL: Digital Subscriber Line.

tough negotiations. A complicating matter was that the initial agreement had been based on the existing 2 Mbit/s product, meanwhile, the standards making process had advanced substantially and the 11 Mbit/s version was expected to become available in 1999. Apple wanted to go directly to the 11 Mbit/s version, but did not want to accept a higher price for the increased data rate. It became an all or nothing negotiation.

The product was launched in New York at Macworld as the Apple Airport in July 1999, with the PC card priced at $99 and the Access Point at $299. At this price level the 11 Mbit/s Wireless LANs could compete effectively with the 10 Mbit/s wired Ethernet. The industry was shocked. Cees Links recalls:

> We were accused of 'buying' the market and that we were losing money on every card sold. But we were not. The mechanism we used was to 'forward' price the product. With the volume going up quickly the costs would also come down quickly, and the market share gained would bring in the margin. That is the theory – well, it worked in practice, and it worked very well as would turn out in the following years.

Dell was the first PC vendor to follow the trend set by Apple. Cees Links:

> I received an email that happened to have in its tail an original discussion with Michael Dell, who was furious about the fact that he had been beaten by Apple. Although, he had been offered the opportunity – going through my notes I can confirm I had called Michael Dell personally in 1992 to propose cooperation. In fact in 1993 Dell had tested our WaveLAN product, as well as products from the competition, but as they stated they were not convinced that a market existed for this type of technology.

However, the cooperation with Dell had an additional complicating factor: they used the Microsoft Operating System. As a consequence Lucent was faced with another hurdle to overcome. As Microsoft had become overloaded with requests to resolve interface issues, they had installed a new certification procedure called Wireless Hardware Quality Labs. Unfortunately some requirements in the certification program were incompatible with the operation of Wireless-LANs. This

required Lucent to work closely with Microsoft to resolve these issues. Initially some compromises were made and waivers obtained to expedite market deployment. Eventually the cooperation involved creating new software to support Wireless-LANs proper, to be included in the upcoming release of XP in 2001.[10]

With this effort done, the two world leading PC operating systems had in-built features to support Wireless-LANs, and hence another dimension of the 'whole product' concept had been resolved. Within a year all other PC vendors had followed the example set by Apple. Agere Systems[11] had almost a clean sweep of the Wireless-LAN market for PCs. This success is replacing the business user as the main target of Wireless LAN applications by the home user.

This new period posed new challenges. Ramping up volume in manufacturing became the key issue, which implied lead time reduction, improving inventory management, optimizing test capabilities. In the early days the radio part of the card had about 15 test points and involved manual calibration. Now, the cards are fully tested through software. The early cards had about 300 components, which had come down to 30 and would go down further to 10. All the result of moving from a production level of 100 cards per week in 1991 to 100 000 cards per week in 2001.

The Wi-Fi Alliance

With the approval of the IEEE 802.11 standard a number of implementation variants were allowed, in part a result of the FCC Report & Order which included the two spread spectrum options, frequency hopping and direct sequence. This could in practice lead to two companies claiming to be compliant, while the products would be incompatible. This situation forced the leading Wireless-LAN companies to collaborate. The Wireless Ethernet Compatibility Alliance (WECA) started operation in 1999, as a non-profit organization driving the adoption of a single Direct Sequence based world-wide standard for high-speed wireless local area networking, focussing on IEEE 802.11b compliance. Governed by a small Board, WECA quickly established an interoperability testing procedure and a seal of compliance, the Wi-Fi (Wireless Fidelity) logo. In 2002 it changed its name to the Wi-Fi Alliance, to acknowledge the power of

---

[10]In the cooperation with Microsoft the strategic importance of IEEE 802.11 being restricted to the PHY and MAC layers, showed in the relative ease of implementation of WLAN functionality within an existing PC Operating System environment (Tuch, 2009).

[11]In 2000 Agere Systems was established as a subsidiary of Lucent Technologies, the WLAN activities moved to this entity.

the Wi-Fi brand. As of July 2007, the organization had certified the interoperability of over 3500 products.

The penultimate success

By early 2001, Agere had reached the summit as supplier of Wi-Fi products with an approximately 50% market share, inclusive of the OEM[12] channel. By that time the market had grown to an US$1 billion annual level. Meanwhile, the business had reached break-even, see Figure 4. The objective formulated by Don Johnson at HQ back in 1986 had become a reality: 'we could turn it into affordable products.'

However, by the end of 2001 it became clear that the industry was moving into another phase. With the broad acceptance of Wi-Fi it was clear that the Wireless-LAN functionality would be progressively integrated into the various computer and networking products.

The competition would shift from the plug-ins toward the chipsets, as was confirmed by the moves of e.g. Intersil, Broadcom, Infineon, and AMD. As a consequence the ORiNOCO brand (as successor to WaveLAN) and the related infrastructure products, Access Points, Residential gateways and Outdoor Routers, were separated organizationally from the chip activities. In 2002, Agere sold the ORiNOCO business unit to Proxim in a friendly take-over valued at US$65 million. Agere Systems continued to develop the Wireless LAN technology and turned it into new chipsets. They also sold the technology to other chipset providers to allow the integration with other Input/Output technologies.

Meanwhile Intel had expanded its Wireless LAN expertise by acquiring Xircom in 1999. In 2003, Intel launched the Centrino chipset with built-in Wi-Fi functionality for mobile computers. This launch was supported with a US$300 million marketing campaign, essentially moving the success of the 'Intel inside' campaign to a 'Wi-Fi inside' campaign. This marks the ultimate success of Wi-Fi, having moved from PC adaptors, through plug-ins and integrated chipsets, to functionality that has become part of the hardware core of laptop computers. This also moved the industry into another era and ends the period of the specialty suppliers. As a result Agere Systems

discontinued its Wireless LAN activities in 2004.[13] The remaining WLAN expertise transitioned 'in person' to other firms, in particular to Motorola, a company active in the field of WiMAX, another member of the Wi-Family.

From a product to a service offering

While the initial application of WLANs had been targeted by its manufacturers to be in the corporate domain, and attempts by the HomeRF consortium had failed, Apple had effectively opened up the home networking market. The massive adoption by the users shaped the emerging market. This triggered another set of entrepreneurs, including telecom operators, to use Wi-Fi to provide (semi-)public access to the internet at 'hotspots'.

Hotspots

'Travel at blazing speeds on the internet – all from the comfort of your favourite cozy chair'. It has been the Starbucks initiative to provide wireless access to the internet in their coffee shops that has set off Wi-Fi as the preferred means of accessing the internet in public areas in general. For Starbucks it was the prospect of attracting more customers and keeping them longer in the coffeehouse, in particular after the rush hour, that made investments in the new service an interesting proposition. In January 2001, Starbucks, MobileStar and Microsoft announced their strategic relationship to create a high-speed, connected environment in Starbucks locations across North America. The service would be provided by MobileStar, a wireless ISP[14] established in 1996 with a focus on providing high-speed internet access for business travellers in 'hotspots' such as airports, hotels, convention centers, restaurants and other public places in the US. MobileStar would install Access Points in the Starbucks locations and connect these locations to the Internet using T1-lines.[15] Microsoft was to provide the portal facilitating an easy log-on procedure. MobileStar set out using a proprietary Frequency Hopping spread spectrum product supplied by Proxim, and subsequently moved to an IEEE 802.11 compliant Direct Sequence based product. By the end

---

[12]Original Equipment Manufacturer.

[13]While Intel would take a leading position in providing Wi-Fi functionality in laptops, Broadcom would become the leading provider of Wi-Fi chips to be included in access points, gateways and routers.

[14]ISP: Internet Service Provider.

[15]T1-lines are digital links at a data rate of 1.5 Mbit/s.

of the year MobileStar had equipped some 500 Star-bucks locations, but also had ran into financial diffi-culties. In the aftermath of the telecom market crash the private equity market had become very constrained, and the events of September 11th had severely limited business travel. The company seized operation in Oc-tober 2001 and subsequently the assets were acquired by VoiceStream, a cellular communications company, to be acquired by T-Mobile, a subsidiary of incumbent Deutsche Telekom, in 2001. By February 2002 the service at Starbucks was operating under the T-Mobile Hotspot brand. This acquisition made T-Mobile the largest hotspot provider in the USA.

Swisscom Eurospot, another European incumbent operator, is specifically targeting the hospitality in-dustry. Meanwhile, most of the 'hotspot' start-ups have been acquired by incumbent operators in an at-tempt to enter the market and quickly obtain a sig-nificant 'foot print'.

Community initiatives – Wi-Fi based networks

Wireless Internet Service Providers typically exploit Wi-Fi technology to provide internet access services for-a-profit, or in the case where the location owner exploits the 'hotspot', the objective may be to stimu-late the revenues of the core business. Next to these commercially oriented organizations, groups of vo-lunteers have emerged that are providing internet ac-cess for free or at very low cost. The shared internet Access and often also direct communications among community members is provided based on Wi-Fi Ac-cess Points being interconnected forming a wireless Neighbourhood Area Network (WNAN). These com-munities of volunteers are typically motivated by their enthusiasm to explore the possibilities of new technologies and their wish to demonstrate their technological savvy to others. These groups of Wi-Fi volunteers are in many ways similar to the early members of the 'Homebrew Computer Club' that emerged in Silicon Valley when the first do-it-yourself computer kits came on the market in the mid 1970s. Members would come together to trade computer parts, exchange schematics and programming tips.

A typical example of a Wi-Fi community in the Netherlands is 'Wireless Leiden', a group of volunteers that started in the year 2001 and has built a Neigh-bourhood Area Network that includes 60 nodes and is covering most of the Leiden city and is being linked to neighbouring towns to cover an area of about 500 km². Through the organization of volunteers the 'Wireless

Leiden' network is strongly embedded in the economic and social structure of the Leiden city. Companies that like to link their offices across the city or to their home, sponsor the network by providing the equipment for a network node at their premises, that will subsequently operate under their name. Other firms provide com-munication equipment in kind, or provide facilities for the group of volunteers to meet on a regular basis. The municipality supports the group by providing locations to place nodes and antennas. For a local church the 'Wireless Leiden' network provides live broadcast of the church service, and in return is allowed to place an antenna on the church tower. The network also provides inexpensive communication among schools in the city and provides access to the internet at the library and at the library busses that serve the city neighbourhood.

There is ample evidence that these Wi-Fi based NANs are important from an economic and social perspective in particular in (1) areas where incumbent telecom operators fail to provide broadband internet access in developed countries, a typical example is the peninsula of Djürsland in Denmark, and (2) in devel-oping areas where often the investment capital is lacking to provide the inhabitants with the very basic communication services such as telephony; typical examples are the rural areas in developing countries such as India, Latin America, and Africa. The moti-vation of these communities is in providing commun-ication services hitherto not being available. The Case of 'Wireless Leiden' is of interest because of its early start and its significant size, but also for the software development that was done to make Wi-Fi networking possible and for the entrepreneurial activities that it generated.

Municipal networks

Wireless municipal broadband access has become a major item in the USA with highly visible initiatives in, e.g., Philadelphia, San Francisco (involving Google) and Silicon Valley. The provisioning of city-wide Wi-Fi based connectivity is seen as a way for local governments to improve the availability and af-fordability of broadband access. Municipalities have thereby the opportunity to leverage their role as cus-tomer, when considering to become a supplier of broadband access. Reasons being stated for their in-volvement include: (1) the opportunity to fill the gap in available and affordable (wired) broadband access, where private firms fail to provide service or offer services at a price considered to be too high; (2) to create a 'third pipe' next to DSL and cable to improve

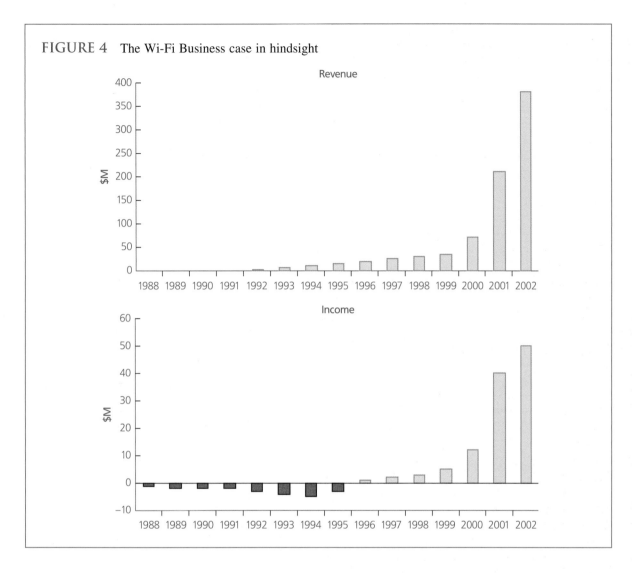

FIGURE 4   The Wi-Fi Business case in hindsight

competition; (3) making the city more competitive in attracting business; (4) improving intra- and inter-governmental communications, improving quality of work life for employees; (5) the availability of wireless technology at low cost, without the need for a licence; (6) the opportunity to offer services at lower costs of deployment, e.g., through ownership of rights-of-way, the use of municipal premises and leveraging internal use of the network. The role of local government in providing wireless broadband access is subject to intense debates, whether public funds may be used and whether these public initiatives infringe on private interests of the incumbent telecom and cable operators. This interest of municipalities in Wi-Fi deployment has resulted in additional law making at US State level, to regulate if and how municipalities can enter the wireless service provider sphere.

In a comparative study including European initiatives Van den Audenhove et al. conclude that local government motives to engage in wireless network deployment include policies related to the 'digital divide', city renewal, stimulating innovation, stimulating tourism, and improving the 'economic fabric' of the city.

In conclusion

With reference to Figure 5, Wi-Fi has evolved from its intended use in wireless corporate networking, with a market breakthrough in wireless home networking, to a wide variety of private entities and public-private partnerships exploiting its potential. Following a long gestation period, Wi-Fi is now reaching out to places and users that other networks cannot reach.

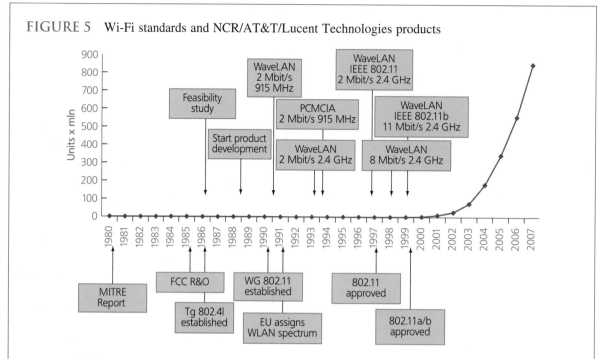

FIGURE 5   Wi-Fi standards and NCR/AT&T/Lucent Technologies products

Source: This figure appears in 'The Shaping of the IEEE 802.11 Standard: The role of the Innovating Firm in the Case of Wi-Fi' in *Information Communication Technology Standardization for E-business Sectors* edited by Kai Jakobs. Copyright 2009, IGI Global, www.igi-global.com. Reprinted by permission of the publisher.

As the train approached Darlington railway station, Bruce Tuch realized that in hindsight success can be explained relatively easily. As he had learned the hard way, predicting the road to global success is much more difficult. Tonight they will have to discuss the future of this start-up company. During the train ride he checked the information on their website and learned a lot about the company, but he will have to know more about their product, and they will need to spend ample time on exploring the forces that shape the converging wireless market place, as input to devise a strategy that may bring success. At the same time, he will have to make them aware that the road to success is long and winding, and strategies need to be flexible, to be adapted to changing circumstances, but always keeping the ultimate goal in mind.

As he steps onto the platform, he sees a sign towards the Stockton & Darlington Railway Museum and he recalls that the first passenger train was running from Stockton-on-Tees to 'Port Darlington' in 1825, giving birth to the public railway infrastructure. He hopes he will recognize some of the same entrepreneurial spirit in this start-up company, involved in the development of today's electronic communications infrastructure.

HP under Carly Fiorina and Mark Hurd

By Smitha Moganty[1]

I think the company's success will by my legacy. The company's failure will be my failure, with all the predictable consequences of that.

Carleton S. Fiorina, former CEO of HP, in 2002

HP is one of the world's great companies, with a proud history of innovation, outstanding talent and enviable positions in many of its product lines and services. It's a great honor to join its leadership team and have the opportunity to build on its success.

Mark V. Hurd, HP's CEO, in March 2005

She (Fiorina) was a 'celebrity CEO' known for her sales and marketing flair, Hurd is a low-profile, no-nonsense operations whiz. While many at HP felt Fiorina didn't mix enough with the troops, Hurd is known to walk the halls chatting with employees as he goes to get coffee.

BusinessWeek, in 2005

Introduction

In May 2006, Hewlett Packard Co. (HP) announced its second quarter results for the fiscal year 2005–2006. The company posted revenues of $22.6 billion – a five per cent increase over the revenues in the comparable quarter of the previous fiscal. Its earnings per share (EPS) for the quarter also shot up to $0.54 (later revised to $0.69, to include a favourable settlement in a prior period tax audit), from $0.37 in the second quarter of 2004–2005.

The second quarter of 2006 results were received well by investors and industry observers, because HP's financial performance had been unsatisfactory right from fiscal year 2002. (Refer to Exhibits 1 and 2 for a snapshot of HP's quarterly and annual financial results). As a result, the performance of HP's shares on the stock exchange had also remained lacklustre (Refer to Exhibit 3 for HP's share price from 1997 to 2006).

HP's poor earnings since 2002 were attributed largely to the effects of its much hyped merger with Compaq Computer Corporation in May 2002. The merger had been led by the company's then CEO, Carleton S. Fiorina, and was the largest merger in the computer industry at that time. Analysts said that the merger had not yielded the desired results because Fiorina had not been able to manage the operations of the combined company effectively. In February 2005, Fiorina was asked to resign by the HP board.

After Fiorina left, the board appointed Mark V. Hurd as its new CEO in March 2005. Under Hurd's management, HP's earnings started showing signs of improvement. The company's share price too was beginning to show an upward trend. In May 2006, HP was ranked #11 on the *Fortune* 500 list of the top 500 companies in the United States (as measured by gross revenue).

Background

William Hewlett (Hewlett) and David Packard (Packard), two electrical engineers from Stanford University, founded HP in 1938, in a garage behind Packard's home in Palo Alto, California. HP initially sold electronic instruments. The company's first product was a resistance-capacity audio oscillator, an electronic instrument used to test sound equipment. One of the big customers for the product was the Walt Disney Company, which used the product in the making of the movie *Fantasia.*

In 1940, Hewlett and Packard set up their own factory in Palo Alto, under the name Hewlett Packard. HP continued to grow as an electronic equipment company throughout the 1940s. The company was incorporated in 1947, after which Packard became the president and Hewlett the vice president. By the end of the 1940s, HP's revenues had crossed two million dollars and the company employed 166 people.

During the 1950s, HP gained prominence as a producer of innovative measuring and testing equipment of

[1]Source: Written under the direction of Shirisha Regani, and S.S George, ICFAI Center for Management Research (ICMR). It was compiled from published sources, and is intended to be used as a basis for class discussion rather than to illustrate either effective or ineffective handling of a management situation.

EXHIBIT 1   QUARTERLY FINANCIAL RESULTS OF HP FROM 2004 TO 2006

	Jan 2004	Apr 2004	July 2004	Nov 2004	Jan 2005	Apr 2005	July 2005	Nov 2005	Jan 2006	Apr 2006
Revenues (*in billions of $*)	19.5	20.1	18.9	21.3	21.4	21.5	20.8	22.9	22.7	22.6
Earnings per share	0.35	0.34	0.24	0.41	0.37	0.37	0.36	0.51	0.48	0.54

EXHIBIT 2   HP'S REVENUES FROM 1998 TO 2005

Year (*ending October 31st*)	1998	1999	2000	2001	2002	2003	2004	2005
Revenues (*in billions of $*)	39.4	42.3	48.8	45.2	56.6	73.0	79.9	86.7
Net (loss) earnings (*in billions of $*)	2.9	3.4	3.7	0.40	(0.90)	2.5	3.5	2.4

EXHIBIT 3   HP'S SHARE PRICE MOVEMENT FROM 1997 TO 2006

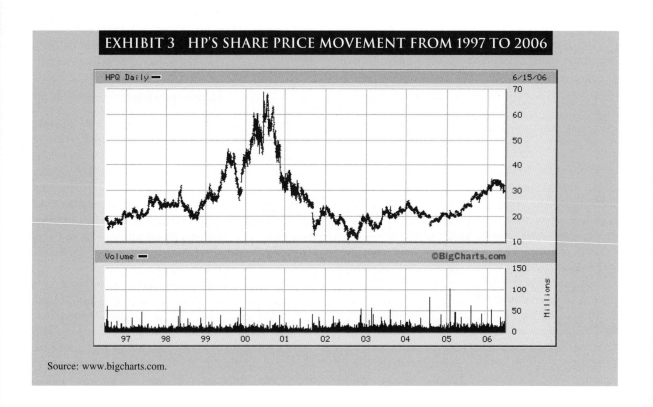

Source: www.bigcharts.com.

superior quality. The company went public in 1957. In 1958, HP made its first acquisition when it bought F.L. Moseley Company, a company that produced high-quality graphic recorders. HP began entering overseas markets towards the end of the 1950s. In 1959, it opened a marketing office in Switzerland and a manufacturing plant in Germany.

It was also during the 1950s that Hewlett and Packard formulated the HP corporate objectives. These objectives laid out HP's values relating to profit, customers, fields of interest, growth, people, management and citizenship. These corporate objectives also formed the basis for the 'The HP Way', which referred to the management style at the company (see Exhibit 4 for The HP Way). Over the years, Hewlett and Packard had transformed HP into a 'democratic' organization where all the employees were treated equally. Even in the 1950s, employees at all levels of the hierarchy addressed each other, and their bosses, by their first names.

During the 1960s, HP increased its presence in the international market. In 1963, the company entered the Asian market by forming a joint venture, Yokogawa Hewlett-Packard, with Yokogawa Electric Works of Japan. HP also made some acquisitions during the 1960s. The company entered the medical field with the purchase of Sanborn Company, a company that produced medical equipment. HP also purchased F&M Scientific Corporation, a maker of analytical instruments, in 1965.

In 1968, HP introduced the HP 9100A, a desktop scientific calculator that stored programs on magnetic cards and was capable of performing complex calculations. The HP 9100A was a breakthrough product at that time, as the calculators produced until then were mechanical machines that were noisy and operated on gears. On the other hand, the HP 9100A was an electronic device, and HP even used the term 'personal computer' while advertising the product – one of the first documented uses of the term, according to the company.

HP launched several other innovative computing devices during the 1970s. It introduced the first handheld scientific calculator (1972), the first handheld programmable calculator (1974) and the first alphanumeric, programmable, expandable calculator (1979), among others.

By the 1970s, the company had gained a reputation as a maker of superior quality computing devices and testing and measuring equipment. HP was also recognized for its strong technological capabilities and ability to introduce innovative products.

During the 1970s, Hewlett and Packard started leaving the day-to-day management of the company to John Young. Young became the CEO of HP in 1978. Under Young's management, HP entered the printer business. In the 1980s, the company launched inkjet and laser printers, and other printing products – products that would eventually help become the market leader in this segment. According to experts, the quality of the printers offered by HP was far superior to that of the printers offered by other company at that time. (Even in the early 2000s HP's printer business was the most profitable of all its businesses.)

By the end of the 1980s, HP's product portfolio included a wide array of products like minicomputers, desktop machines, portable computers, microcomputers, and medical and analytical products. In 1989, HP acquired Apollo Computer, which was then a leading manufacturer of workstations, to strengthen its position in that segment.

EXHIBIT 4 THE HP WAY

The HP Way was the management style followed by William Hewlett and David Packard. They believed that respecting employees as individuals fostered teamwork and innovation. Hewlett and Packard believed that when employees were given a certain amount of freedom in their work, it encouraged them to try out new ideas and perform better. They also practised 'management by walking around' and 'management by objectives'. They believed in a bottom-up approach to management. Said Carl Cottrell, former head of HP's European division, 'Everybody respected everybody else. Management was part of the team.'[1]

Hewlett and Packard gave as much importance to employees as to profits. In fact, HP was known as a company that cared for its employees. HP was a pioneer in introducing employee stock options. The company also introduced flexi-time that allowed employees to work according to their convenience. Hewlett and Packard were also against lay-offs. Ex-employees said that the management would rather reassign employees to new jobs than dismissing them. In the event that the management could not reassign an employee, he/she was allowed 'quit' so that their record remained clean.

It was said that the HP Way made the employees more loyal and committed to the organization. Further, analysts believed that the HP Way was largely responsible for HP becoming an innovative company in later years.

[1]Jocelyn Dong, 'The rise and fall of the HP Way,' www.paloaltoonline.com, April 10, 2002.

By 1990, HP had 92,000 employees and earned revenues of $13.2 billion. The company, even though it had grown in size, continued to follow the HP Way. HP's structure in the 1990s was such that each division was run like an independent unit. Each division had its own research and development wing and manufactured its own products. When a division grew too big, it was further split into smaller divisions. This resulted in HP becoming highly decentralized. This decentralized management structure caused delays in decision making. Some analysts predicted that, if HP continued to grow without changing its structure, it would have to face serious problems in the future.

During the 1990s, HP expanded its product line in the personal computer market to include products for individual consumers. Until then, HP's target consumers were universities, research centres and business consumers. HP bought the computer manufacturing unit of Texas Instruments (which manufactured UNIX-based PCs) in 1992. In 1995, HP launched HP Pavilion, a new personal computer. This product went on to become a huge success paving the way for the company to establish itself in the personal computer market. Further, the boom in the computer industry during the early 1990s helped HP achieve quick success. By the second half of the 1990s, HP had become the second-largest PC manufacturer in the US. Over the years, HP also expanded its market to several countries in the world.

However, by the end of the 1990s, the PC industry in the US was moving into a recession and this had an impact on HP. What's more, unlike companies like IBM and Sun Microsystems, HP had not taken advantage of the internet revolution in the mid-1990s, and this led to stagnation in the company's growth by the end of the 1990s.

It was also clear by then that the organizational structure and culture at HP were not appropriate for a company of its size and complexity, operating in a rapidly evolving market. HP's various divisions manufactured and sold more than 130 products. These divisions had little coordination between themselves, which led to duplication of efforts and resources. It was said that sometimes, as many as 50 HP salesmen approached the same customer at different times to sell their individual unit's products.

Over the years, HP had also begun to lag behind in innovation. After the inkjet printer in 1984, HP had not introduced any other breakthrough product. HP, once known for its innovations, seemed unable to cope with the changing conditions in the industry. Some analysts felt HP had turned into a staid company with an old-fashioned culture and an inability to innovate and make the most of the e-business revolution.

There was increasing dissatisfaction among employees too, with the way the company was managed. In late 1997, HP conducted a poll among 300 top-level executives. This poll revealed that the employees felt that HP lacked clear direction and that it had become too product-oriented. They also felt that HP needed an infusion of new thought and greater customer focus.

In order to bring more focus to its business, HP decided to concentrate on its computer business. Accordingly, it spun off its measurement, testing and medical equipment division into a new company called Agilent Technologies Inc. in early 1999. After the spin-off, HP was left with four main divisions – personal computers, inkjet printers, laser printers and servers.

Although the company took other measures like cutting costs and drafting a new internet strategy, it was still widely believed that what HP actually needed was a change in leadership.

Carly Fiorina

Carleton Fiorina was born in September 1954, in Austin, Texas. Her father was a professor of law and changed jobs very often. Consequently, Fiorina attended five different schools in England, Ghana and the US. Fiorina completed her BA in medieval history and philosophy from Stanford University in 1976. After that, she joined the law school at the University of California, Los Angeles. However, after a semester she discontinued her legal education. Later on, she received her postgraduate degree in business administration from Maryland University in 1980 and another postgraduate degree in Management from the Massachusetts Institute of Technology in 1988.

Fiorina joined AT&T as a sales representative in 1980. With her strong sales and marketing abilities, she began to climb the career ladder at the company at a brisk pace. Fiorina's main achievement at AT&T was in leading the successful spin-off of AT&T's telecommunication and networking equipment business into Lucent Technologies Inc. After this, she became the president of Lucent's consumer products business. At Lucent, Fiorina was credited with creating a new image for the company and for successfully conducting the company's IPO. Lucent went on to become a leader in the networking systems market during the early 1990s. Fiorina later rose to be president of Lucent's Global Services Provider business in 1998. Fiorina was ranked first in *Fortune*'s list of the '50 Most Powerful Women Executives in the US' in 1998.

Fiorina was appointed as the CEO of HP in July 1999. She was the first 'outsider' to become the CEO at HP.

HP under Fiorina

Soon after becoming the CEO, Fiorina announced that HP 'owed its customers and partners a clear vision and direction for the future' and that there was a need to speed up operations at the company. Fiorina also undertook a major marketing program to burnish the company's image in the market. New advertisements brought out by the company depicted HP's employees as a 'collection of fearless inventors' (Fiorina herself featured in many of these ads). In addition to new advertisements, the company launched a rebranding exercise and introduced a new company logo with the tagline 'Invent'. Reportedly, HP spent $200 million on the marketing and rebranding initiative.

In November 1999, Fiorina addressed Wall Street analysts and said that the sales growth targets for the company had been raised from seven per cent in 1999 to 15 per cent in 2000. Further, she announced that HP would cut costs, introduce new products and services to take advantage of the internet, and enter into alliances that would benefit the company over the next few years. She identified internet services and imaging as HP's key strategic growth areas. She said that HP had failed to realize the opportunities in the 'first chapter' of the internet. However, Fiorina said the company would now concentrate on taking advantage of the advances in internet technology. 'There is a great opportunity to leverage our assets and create a leadership position for ourselves in the internet's second chapter', she told the audience.

When Fiorina took over, HP was a highly decentralized organization with 83 different units, each having its own product groups, and research, manufacturing, sales and marketing departments. This complicated organizational structure was a source of great confusion among consumers. Business customers like Ford Motor Co. complained that several sales teams from HP approached them at different times, each trying to sell a narrow line of HP products instead of marketing a complete solution.

To streamline operations and marketing, Fiorina reorganized HP into a 'front-end, back-end organizational structure'. Under the new structure, Fiorina set up four organizations – two customer-facing organizations (one

for business customers and another for individual customers) and two focused on product generation (one for computing systems, and another for imaging and printing systems). The two 'customer-facing organizations' were the 'front-end' of the organizational structure. These two organizations were in fact 'two large sales and marketing groups' that dedicated themselves to managing customer relationships. The two 'product generation organizations' were the back-end of the company which were dedicated to the research and manufacturing of all HP products. The IT services segment was a component of the business customers' organization.

The new organizational structure was expected to enhance collaboration among the sales and marketing executives and also provide them a direct communication channel with the engineers. Fiorina believed that this would enable the engineers to better understand customer needs and problems and to develop new products accordingly. However, HP was still a vast company with numerous product lines. Therefore, it needed to have a great focus as well as excellent co-ordination among various product divisions in order to sustain the new structure.

As of October 2000, HP's main businesses included imaging and printing systems, computing systems and IT services. By 2000–2001, HP's revenues were falling and this was attributed mainly to decreasing revenues from its PC and server business. (Refer to Exhibit 5 for the HP's revenues from various business segments.) During this time, HP was facing tough competition from Dell. Dell, which was a direct seller, was able to eliminate intermediary margins to sell its products at low prices, and this helped it become the market leader in the PC and server segment.

In September 2001, Fiorina announced that HP would merge with Compaq Computer Corp.[2] in a $24 billion stock deal. Fiorina believed that the merger with Compaq would enable HP to strengthen its position in the PC and servers market. She also believed that the combined company could gain economies of scale in the PC and server business, cut costs and better equip itself to fight the mounting competition from Dell and IBM.

This merger was controversial from the start. The merger plans received a setback in November 2001, when Walter Hewlett (Walter), the eldest son of HP's co-founder William Hewlett, decided to use his 5.2 per

[2]In 2000, Compaq's main businesses included the consumer PC group, the commercial PC group and enterprise computing group. It employed close to 38,000 employees and sold its products and services in over 200 countries worldwide. The company had revenues of US$ 42.38 billion in 2000.

EXHIBIT 5   HP'S REVENUES FROM VARIOUS BUSINESS SEGMENTS (IN BILLIONS OF $)

Years (ending October 31st)	1999	2000	2001	2002	2003	2004	2005
Imaging and printing systems	18.5	20.4	19.4	20.4	22.6	24.1	25.1
Computing systems	17.3	20.6	17.7				
IT services	6.3	7.1	6.3				
Other	1.2	1.5	1.0				
Personal systems group				21.8	21.2	24.6	26.7
Enterprise systems group				16.1	15.3	15.0	16.7
HP services				12.3	12.3	13.8	15.5
Software						1.1	0.9

cent holding in the company to oppose the merger. Following this, David Woodley Packard, a relative of HP's co-founder Packard, and the Packard and Lucile Packard Foundation[3] also decided to use their stakes in the company to oppose the merger. Said Walter, 'After careful deliberation, consultation with my financial adviser, and consideration of developments since the announcement of the merger, I have decided to vote against the transaction. I believe that Hewlett-Packard can create greater value for stockholders as a stand-alone company than as a company combined with Compaq.'

Many industry observers too felt that the HP–Compaq merger did not make sense as it did not provide many real synergies to either company. This view was shared by HP's competitors as well, who foresaw with glee that the merger might instead create better opportunities for themselves. Ed Zander, president, Sun Microsystems, said, 'When two sick companies combine, I'm not sure what you get. This is a great opportunity for us, IBM and others to go after sales.' There were rumours that the HP–Compaq merger would never materialize. However, Fiorina was quick to brush aside these speculations. She said, 'We remain convinced it is in the best interests of share-owners. We remain convinced that this merger will occur....'

On March 19, 2002, after a proxy vote, HP announced that the majority of its shareholders were in favour of the proposed merger. Walter subsequently filed a suit against HP claiming that the company improperly gained votes from Deutsche Asset Management, one of the company's largest share-holders. This suit was resolved in May 2002, when the court ruled in favour of HP. In May 2002, HP paid $19 billion in stock for Compaq.

After the merger, HP had four main businesses – imaging and printing, personal systems, enterprise systems and HP services.

The HP–Compaq merger brought about many changes in HP, especially in the company's culture. Fiorina had earlier framed the 'Rules of the Garage' which, according to her, 'tried to capture the true spirit of HP' and 'ensured continued innovation' in the company. These rules emphasized performance, and although they did not seem to be in conflict with the HP Way, it was believed that Fiorina was trying to change the culture that was immortalized by the company's founders. (Refer to Exhibit 5 for the Rules of the Garage.)

The new rules did not find favour with many HP employees, who still believed in the HP Way and did not take easily to any change in the company's culture. One of the most radical steps that Fiorina took after the merger was to lay off more than 17 000 HP employees. This was a major shock to the employees, as under the HP Way employees were never laid off. Fiorina's popularity at the company had reached a low by this time, as she was believed to be putting profits ahead of people.

Commenting on Fiorina's management style, Shane Robison, executive vice president and chief strategy and technology officer at HP said, 'She's not in our offices every day beating on us, but she expects

---

[3]Created in 1964 by Packard and his wife Lucile Packard, the Packard and Lucile Packard Foundation is a philanthropic organization. It is the largest shareholder of HP.

us to be on top of what we're doing. She believes our culture should be based on performance, self-motivation and high achievement.' Fiorina made a drastic organizational change by bringing in a top-down approach in the company. Analysts observed that Fiorina tried to bring in the hierarchical system of management followed at AT&T and Lucent, to HP – a company that prided itself on its egalitarian work culture.

Critics also pointed out that Fiorina had started behaving like a celebrity during her tenure as HP's CEO, and this did not go down well with HP employees. Fiorina always travelled in a limousine, while all the previous CEOs of the company had used regular rented cars to visit employees at various locations. It was also said that Fiorina did not interact much with the employees personally. She communicated with them mostly through e-mails, webcasts, etc. This went against the HP Way where managers and other top executives interacted freely with employees and practised management by walking around. Against this background, Fiorina's 'movie star antics' only served to make her more unpopular at the company.

In 2003, Fiorina attempted another reorganization at HP. The company's product line now included a wide range of products ranging from digital cameras to printers and from personal computers to IT infrastructure. The company was reorganized into four main business divisions – customer solutions group, imaging and printing group, personal systems group and technology solutions group. HP offered products like personal computers, digital cameras, notebooks, etc. to individual consumers. At the same time, it provided IT infrastructure and services to businesses.

Some observers were doubtful as to whether HP would succeed in its strategy of offering a wide range of products to disparate customers. HP still faced stiff competition from Dell in the PC market and IBM in the services market, and this would make it difficult for the company to gain a lead in either of these markets.

Fiorina, however, believed that HP had a competitive advantage in that it offered high-technology innovative products at relatively low prices, thereby providing the 'best customer experience'. She believed that although Dell offered low-cost products, it was low on technology and its products did not match the quality of HP's products. On the other hand, though IBM's products and services were of superior quality, their prices were high and mainly targeted business customers. Hence HP was in a better position than its two main competitors, in Fiorina's view.

However, analysts remained skeptical. Cal Braunstein, chairman and CEO, Robert Frances Group Inc. commented, 'I think they've got the capability to be broad and deep. Whether they can execute is the real issue.'

Others doubted the competitive advantages that HP claimed in relation to Dell and IBM. It was believed that HP was too diversified and that its position in the market squeezed it between the two companies. Frank Gillett, principal analyst, Forrester Research said, 'The market challenges that are in place right now for HP are trying to compete with Dell in the commodity market while also filling out the mix to compete in the full-service high-end (market) with IBM.'

By 2004, Fiorina's critics had become even more vocal. HP had been posting disappointing earnings ever since its merger with Compaq. This took a toll on the company's stock price which was on a downward trajectory between 2002 and 2004. Moreover, even after its merger with Compaq, HP continued to post disappointing results from the PC and the storage and servers businesses. It was believed that HP was surviving on the revenues from the imaging and printing business alone.

EXHIBIT 6   THE RULES OF THE GARAGE

- Believe you can change the world.

- Work quickly, keep the tools unlocked, work whenever.

- Know when to work alone and when to work together.

- Share tools, ideas. Trust your colleagues.

- No politics. No bureaucracy. (These are ridiculous in a garage)

- The customer defines a job well done.

- Radical ideas are not bad ideas.

- Invent different ways of working.

- Make a contribution everyday. If it doesn't contribute, it doesn't leave the garage.

- Believe that together we can do anything.

Source: Lance Knobel, 'Rules of garage ensured innovation', http://www.digitalnpq.org, May 15, 2001.

Some industry observers said that Fiorina had failed to execute the diversification strategy properly. She kept all authority with herself and refused to delegate. In the third quarter of fiscal year 2003–2004, HP reported earnings of $586 million, with earnings per share of 24 cents – seven cents less than what had been forecast. After the announcement of the results, HP's share price dropped by 13 per cent. Following this, Fiorina fired three top HP executives whom she held responsible for the disappointing financial performance of the company.

By 2005, HP's share price still languished around the $20 level, a far cry from its peaks in 2000. Fiorina was blamed for not managing the company well. Investors held her responsible for the condition of the company. Analysts opined that Fiorina concentrated more on 'marketing' her vision (some even went so far as to say that Fiorina was more interested in marketing 'herself' during her presentations, as she was believed to be nurturing political ambitions) rather than focusing on aspects such as the company's structure and strategy to realize that vision. According to reports, Fiorina also opposed the HP board's decision to appoint a chief operating officer to manage the operations of the company. It was said that she was trying to do everything herself.

Criticisms were also beginning to be heard about Fiorina's vision of transforming HP from a computer manufacturing company to a 'consulting and computing powerhouse'. Fiorina was accused of having continuously over-promised and under-delivered as the CEO of HP. The merger between HP and Compaq was also being labelled as a big mistake as it had failed to show concrete results.

Some people were of the view that HP should spin off its lucrative imaging and printers business and focus on improving its computing devices and services business. Instead, Fiorina merged HP's personal systems group and the imaging and printing group in January 2005. This too drew criticism from industry observers. They felt that merging two product groups would only make the company's operations more complex and difficult.

HP's board too was believed to be unhappy with Fiorina's unwillingness or inability to delegate. As a result, her relationship with the HP board became more and more strained over time.

Finally, in February 2005, the board forced Fiorina to step down, citing differences over the execution of HP's strategy. Said Fiorina, 'While I regret the board and I have differences about how to execute HP's strategy, I respect their decision. HP is a great company and I wish all the people of HP much success in the future.'

Commenting on Fiorina's exit, Patricia Dunn (Dunn), non-executive chairman of HP said, 'Carly (Fiorina) was brought in to catalyze a transformation of HP. She did that in a remarkable fashion, and she executed the merger with her management team in a superior fashion. Looking forward, we think the job is very reliant on hands-on execution, and we thought a new set of capabilities was called for.'

After Fiorina left, HP's board appointed chief financial officer, Robert Wayman (Wayman) as the company's interim CEO. He was later replaced by Mark Hurd in March 2005.

Mark Hurd

Mark Hurd was born in New York City in 1957. He was a good tennis player and won a tennis scholarship to Baylor University, from where he received a bachelors degree in business administration in 1979. Hurd had also spent some time playing professional tennis.

Hurd joined NCR Corp. in 1980 as a fresh graduate. At NCR, Hurd became known for his excellent operational skills. In 1999, Hurd was promoted as the chief operating officer of Teradata, the data warehousing division of NCR. Hurd was credited with having increased the revenues of this division by almost 36 per cent during his tenure. In 2001, Hurd became the president and chief operating officer of NCR. He was later promoted as the company's CEO in 2003. Hurd turned NCR around by scrapping its unprofitable business units and implementing cost control measures.

Although NCR was a smaller organization than HP, both companies had some similarities in their businesses. The *Wall Street Journal* wrote that Hurd had in fact been running a 'mini HP' at NCR.

On March 29, 2005, HP named Hurd as its new CEO. 'Mark came to our attention because of his strong execution skills, his proven ability to lead top performing teams and his track record in driving shareholder value. He demonstrated these skills by turning around NCR, which, while smaller than HP, is a complex organization with multiple business segments', said Dunn, commenting on the choice of Hurd as CEO.

Industry observers opined that HP's choice might have been guided by the fact that Hurd was almost the polar opposite of Fiorina. While Fiorina was known for her marketing and sales abilities, Hurd was known for his execution skills. He was even called an 'operations whiz' by the media. Fiorina was a high-profile celebrity CEO. Whereas Hurd was known to maintain a very low profile and had a down-to-earth approach to his work.

Steve Milunovich, an analyst at Merrill Lynch, called Hurd a 'blue-collar CEO' who would concentrate on fixing the problems at HP rather than 'marketing' the company and its vision. He was perceived to be so different from Fiorina that the media nicknamed him 'anti-Carly'.

HP under Hurd

As a new CEO, Hurd said nothing about his vision for HP, and in fact, said that he did not even have a strategy. At an analysts' meeting held in July 2005, Hurd said that he did not intend to change the current HP strategy but would focus his efforts on attaining 'operational excellence' at the company. Hurd also said that he did not intend to spin off the profitable imaging and printing business, in spite of repeated suggestions from various quarters.

In late 2005, Hurd announced that he would lay off 14 500 workers – almost 10 per cent of HP's workforce – over the next 18 months. Most of the lay-offs were in the IT, finance and human resource departments. This was to be the biggest lay-off in the history of HP after the lay-off of 17 000 workers by Fiorina after the merger with Compaq. Apart from this, Hurd also announced that he would do away with some employee benefits like the worker-pension plan and the medical programmes among others. Hurd also scrapped the 'e-inclusion' programme as part of his cost cutting measures. Fiorina had started this programme in 2000 to promote the use of computers in developing countries.

Critics pointed out that though Hurd was different from Fiorina in his style of management, he too was going against HP's traditional values by cutting benefits and laying off employees. However, Hurd said that these were necessary cost-cutting measures and that he intended to save $1.9 billion a year through them. In response to a concern about whether he was trying to end the HP Way, Hurd said 'When things weren't right in the past, they were fixed. If things aren't right now, we've got to fix them. If that's countercultural to the past few years, so be it. We're just trying to run the fundamentals of a sound business.'

Hurd's next big move was restructuring HP. Hurd 'reversed' Fiorina's decision to combine imaging and printing businesses into one division by de-merging them. He reorganized HP into three main business divisions – the personal systems group, the technology solutions group and the imaging and printing group.

Hurd also took some bold decisions like hiring 'outsiders' for key posts in a company that had traditionally promoted from within to fill senior positions. For the post of chief information officer, Hurd brought in Randy Mott, the former CIO of Dell. He made Todd Bradley (Bradley), former CEO of PalmOne, head of HP's personal systems group. However, Hurd also posted HP veterans in important positions. For example, Ann Livermore and Vyomesh Joshi, two long-time HP executives, were named the heads of the enterprise solutions and imaging and printing businesses, respectively.

During her tenure, Fiorina had integrated the company's sales force in order to focus more on customer needs and preferences. In effect, there were two teams of sales people – one concentrating on marketing HP products to its business customers and the other marketing to its individual customers. Later in 2003, Fiorina had once again reorganized HP and created a new business division called 'customer solutions group'. This group was responsible for selling the entire portfolio of HP's products and services to business and government customers.

After the reorganization, HP's sales force was responsible for selling a wide range of products to different sets of customers. Further, the sales teams were required to report to different product heads. According to Hurd, this led to a 'matrixed' organizational structure. He observed that the heads of the main business divisions were not held responsible for sales revenues as they were not in charge of the sales forces for the products from their divisions. As Hurd saw it, the organizational structure was such that too many people were held accountable for a single task. Therefore, it was difficult to hold a single employee accountable for a particular task.

Hurd believed that HP had failed to execute its strategy well under Fiorina because employees were not assigned clear responsibilities for their work. He believed that the 'matrixed' organizational structure was to a large extent responsible for this. He said that he would make some changes in the HP structure so that there was more transparency with regard to reporting between executives and their subordinates.

Hurd decided to decentralize the company's workforce and make it more 'product-specific'. He divided the sales force between the three business divisions. Further, the heads of these divisions, Livermore,

Bradley and Joshi, were also given charge of their own sales forces. In addition, Hurd appointed Cathy Lyons, an HP veteran, as the company's vice-president and chief marketing officer. Lyons' task was to co-ordinate the activities of the sales forces of the three business divisions. According to Hurd, 'More than anything about the new model (it) is bringing clarity, accountability and responsibility across the company.'

Commenting on the reorganization, he said, 'The more accountable I can make you, the easier it is for you to show you're a great performer. The more that I make it a matrix, the more I give you the opportunity to blame others for something, or for you not to shine if you disagree with them.' Hurd believed that the way to make an individual more accountable for his/her work was to link his/her performance to results. Hurd, in fact, made this clear soon as he took over as HP's CEO. After his appointment, he was quoted as saying, 'I believe in an execution-oriented culture. My management style reflects a fundamental belief in cost discipline and focused investment in strategic growth initiatives.'

As part of his restructuring programme, Hurd had earlier dissolved the customer solutions group, created by Fiorina in early 2005. According to him, this group was not adding any value to the sales of the company. After this, Hurd integrated almost 100 of the largest enterprise partners of HP (in the Americas) into the direct sales force of the technology solutions group in order to improve the company's relation with value-added resellers. An in-house sales team was made responsible for overseeing the activities of the enterprise partners.

HP's direct sales force and the enterprise partners collaborated on such aspects as account mapping, which included planning and quota development among other things. Hurd expected that this kind of collaboration would lead to 'more streamlined decision-making, fewer conflicts and more profitable sales.' 'It allows these value partners to be uniquely aligned with the end-user selling organization within HP and drive the decision-making authority closer to the street', said John Thompson, vice president and general manager, solution partners organization for the Americas region.

According to Bradley, the reorganization of HP's sales force would remove some organizational layers and enable quicker decision-making. Analysts noted that the reorganization made HP more 'pragmatic and result-oriented than before'. It was said that the new sales force concentrated on selling a complete suite of HP products to customers, rather than the fragmented

approach they used earlier. Further, it also allowed the company to identify the most profitable combination of products to sell.

Under Fiorina's management, HP was known for its engineering prowess and marketing abilities. However, her strategies failed to emphasize sales growth sufficiently. In contrast, Hurd laid more emphasis on sales and the reorganization too was meant to bring in a 'sales culture' in HP. In this, Hurd apparently was strongly influenced by his tenure at NCR which had a strong sales culture and was the birthplace of concepts like sales training, dedicated territories and quota-based commissions.

In early 2006, Hurd announced his decision to close around 80 HP data centres (the company's information storehouses) spread across the world to achieve cost savings of $1 billion. Further, he announced that six existing data centres in the US would be made into larger offices to manage all the company's information including business transaction records, e-mails, etc. The closure of the data centres was expected to be completed over a period of three or four years.

Together with Mott, HP's chief information officer, Hurd also revamped the company's internal technology to bring about cost savings and achieve efficiencies. For example, Mott planned to bring in more automation in the six data centres in the US so that the number of workers needed would be less.

As of mid 2006, analysts were divided in their opinion on Hurd's stint as CEO. While Hurd had already proved that he was different from Fiorina in his approach to leadership, some questioned whether merely being different was enough for HP at that point.

Analysts were particularly skeptical about Hurd's decision to not make any strategic changes at HP. They felt that HP's strategy, which was to offer high-technology and low-cost products to a wide range of customers, had already proven to be unreliable. Hurd was also criticized for repeatedly saying that he did not have a vision or a long-term strategy for the company. Said, Michael Beer, professor, Harvard Business School, 'What he's doing appears to be absolutely right in this stage of development. But truly great companies have to do more than just focus on operations and performance.' According to him, to bring back HP's past glory as an innovative company, Hurd would have to create the right vision as well as execute it properly. Hurd was also criticized for not concentrating enough on ways to create new sources of revenue for the company.

There were also concerns whether an 'operational CEO', who was more concerned about the company's sales, would be able to revive HP as an innovative company. They pointed out that in his efforts to cut costs, Hurd had also reduced investment in R&D. According to analysts, the computing industry was highly competitive and companies needed to constantly innovate in order to survive in this market.

Even though Hurd had managed to improve the financial performance of HP within a year of his appointment, opinion was still divided on whether he would be able to help HP regain its past glory.

BP: The transformation of a corporate mind-set

By Manfred F.R. Kets de Vries & Elizabeth Florent-Treacy[1]

New Yorkers couldn't miss the huge billboards looming out at them in Manhattan's Times Square, trumpeting that BP believes in alternative energy: 'Like solar and Cappuccino'. Created by Ogilvy & Mather Worldwide, this multi-million dollar communication campaign stands as one of the clues to understanding John Browne himself as well as the famous CEO's strategy: BP has not only experienced a bold name change – it now stands for 'Beyond Petroleum' – but also a drastic revolution that propelled the oil company from an imperial past to one of the world's most respected companies.

The Anglo-Persian Oil Company was established in 1908. By World War II, the company was called Anglo-Iranian, which reflected its complete dependence on oil-rich fields in the Middle East. The oil company was renamed British Petroleum in 1954 before being booted out of Libya, Iran and Nigeria – all OPEC member countries. After the 1973 oil industry upheaval, BP had to re-invent itself. It chose to adopt a US/UK culture and concentrated on fields in North America and Europe, around Prudhoe Bay in Alaska and in the North Sea. But that was only the first step in a series of transformations that shook up the whole industry. By 2006, BP's turnover was about $262 billion. The company employed 96 000 people around the world and was active in exploration in 26 countries.

Transformational leadership: Three leaders, three personalities

Robert Horton, 'abrasive' leadership, 1989–1992

Robert Horton was BP's CEO from September 1989 to his ousting in June 1992. His fall from grace was precipitous, surprising even senior management. One of Horton's first actions as CEO was to announce that BP had to go through 'the corporate equivalent of perestroika and glasnost'. He initiated Project 1990 to transform the prevailing 'civil service' mentality and to create a new culture; the objectives of the transformation were both 'hard' and 'soft'. BP's hierarchical, bureaucratic structure would be replaced with a flatter organization leading to reductions of head office staff. Horton also realized that the corporate culture would have to change to make the new structure work. He wanted to get rid of the stuffiness, power hoarding and the atmosphere of distrust. David Simon, who would succeed Robert Horton as CEO, discussing those years later, remarked:

> Every time we change the management system in BP, it is usually the signal for a change in style and approach. We were a very bureaucratic, stylized, functional model. We had to get out of that bureaucratic model. The question was how to do it? We spent two years from 1990 to 1992, more or less obsessed … with cultural change, behavioural change, how to treat one another differently, and what things we needed to do to respond to the change of the outside environment. The whole issue was to take a behavioural process into a performance process.

But as senior managers met around conference tables to debate and implement Project 1990's radical proposals over the next year, it was felt that Horton was imposing change rather than fostering it. To make things worse, in 1992 BP's financial situation went from satisfactory to dismal: profits were down by 85 per cent from the previous year, and the company's debt-to-equity ratio rose to 81 per cent by March 1992.

Horton began a round of cost-cutting, which in turn exacerbated the severe morale problem at BP. Project 1990 soon became a euphemism for downsizing, and thereby lost its effectiveness in transforming corporate culture. In fact, BP, like other oil majors, had been slow to react to the more competitive, unstable business environment and volatile market of the 1980s,

[1]Source: Written by Manfred F. R. Kets de Vries, Raoul de Vitry d'Avaucourt Clinical Professor of Leadership Development and Director, INSEAD Global Leadership Centre, and Elizabeth Florent-Treacy, INSEAD Research Project Manager.

trying to maintain profitability through diversification rather than transformation.

Horton was correct in realizing that change was overdue, but he erred in insisting that it be done his way. At the heart of the problem was Horton's abrasive management style. Consensus had it that although Horton's 'straight-talking style and unconcealed ambition' may have worked in America – where Horton had headed Standard Oil Co. in Cleveland – he produced little more than resentment at BP's more conservative British headquarters. In an interview that appeared in Forbes in February 1992, Horton said: 'Because I am blessed with my good brain, I tend to get to the right answer rather quicker and more often than most people. That will sound frightfully arrogant, but it's true. So I have to rein in my impatience.'

Many felt that it was Horton's management style that brought him down. His style was too American and as a result, he never fully gained the trust and respect of his colleagues and subordinates. With the compliance of the executive directors, the board informed Horton that BP needed a change at the top. On June 25, 1992, Horton resigned from his position of Chairman and CEO of BP and was replaced by Lord Ashburton as Chairman and David Simon as CEO.

David Simon: 1992–1995

David Simon, Horton's successor, was well suited to be the leader of an Anglo-Saxon organization with an eye on expansion in continental Europe, South America and Asia. He spoke five languages, among them excellent French and German. In many ways, he was more European than typically British, particularly in his chatty, affable manner.

David Simon was originally hired as a university intern, working for BP during every long vacation, while studying for his degree at Cambridge. He later spent a year at INSEAD, in Fontainebleau, France, where he obtained an MBA in 1966, before spending the next ten years working for BP on the Continent. He visited filling stations throughout Europe, gaining grassroots experience and ideas that he would later draw on as CEO. In 1982, he became Chief Executive of BP Oil International; in 1986, a managing director of the BP Group; and in 1990, Chief Operating Officer of the BP Group. Finally, in 1992, he replaced Horton in the top spot.

The situation facing David Simon when he took over BP on June 25, 1992, was bleak. The organization needed to drastically revise its business strategy to reverse losses, and it had to repay billions of dollars in debt. Simon moved fast. He implemented a three-year plan with a simple name: '1-2-5'. The goals of that plan were to cut debt by $1 billion per year, build annual replacement-cost profits to $2 billion per year and keep capital spending below $5 billion per year. Over the following two years, he cut costs by selling off more than $6 billion worth of peripheral businesses, including the nutrition group, and by downsizing the workforce by almost 50 per cent, with a large reduction in middle management. He narrowed BP's core interest to petroleum only – 'finding it, extracting it, shipping it, refining it, converting it and selling it,' as he put it – through three main divisions: exploration, oil and chemicals. Oil production costs were slashed thanks to improved technology.

Simon's focus paid off. In August 1994, he declared that BP's recovery programme was nearly complete. The goals of the 1-2-5 strategy had been achieved a year ahead of schedule, which sent stockholder confidence soaring. By early 1996, BP's share price had more than doubled over the 1992 price, and the organization had better results than its arch-rival, Shell, in terms of return on capital. For David Simon, setting simple goals was an important part of developing a culture of continual performance improvement.

From there onwards, Simon made it clear to BP employees that they should be cost- and profit-conscious. He had a golden rule for attaining goals: 'Targeting is fundamental to achieving. If you do not target, you do not measure and you do not achieve.'

Equally important, Simon addressed the morale problem that had permeated the organization. Employees described him as a good communicator who, unlike his predecessor, inspired trust. Influenced by his background in marketing, Simon put great emphasis on 'people skills'.

Simon was careful to point out that, despite the uproar over Horton's management style, continuity of control and direction had been one of his own goals when he became CEO in 1992. At that time, he said: 'This is about the style of running the company at the top. It is not about changes in strategy.'

He had been an early and vocal proponent of Horton's Project 1990, and although Horton took much of the blame for the painful restructuring, Simon continued with it, and the transformation ultimately proved successful.

One top executive described Simon's accomplishments during his first three years as CEO as follows: 'What he has done so well is pull the company together in a very calming way, setting clear targets and telling people how they could achieve them.' An outside analyst commented: 'I think you have to put an awful lot of BP's recovery down to him. A complete cultural change has been put into place.'

Another executive said:

> It has been a big change in terms of the style and role of the leader. Simon's style is to encourage people to fill the space that he leaves around him. He has a very sophisticated and quite unique talent for guiding people without their really knowing he is doing it.

Simon once said that he keeps in mind a friend's advice: 'Listen first, think next and act after.' He later described his management style himself: 'I like talking through problems; I don't jump to conclusions. I love teamwork.' Simon's definition of bad management comes as no surprise: '[Bad managers are] managers who don't listen. Telling is not enough.' Thanks to his ability to communicate, Simon was said to be extremely efficient at 'changing the mind-set' within the organization:

> You spend a lot of time talking. And a lot of time listening. The process of direction and planning and agreeing on targets and agreeing on allocation of resources in this business is a continuous dialogue. I think it's important to have a very clear numerate focus – what is it we want to achieve? What are the targets related to change and the process of change? The whole organization can indulge in the dialogue on a continuous basis but it is resolved, it is clear, it isn't just a messy discussion. At some point in time, people will be able to say, 'This is what we are going to do.' Then people know why things are changing, and they can take pride in having achieved benchmarks along the way.

John Browne: 1995 to 2007

In July 1995, Simon became Chairman of BP, leaving his place as CEO to John Browne, and accepted, the same year, an invitation from the President of the European Commission to become a member of the newly formed Competitiveness Advisory Group. Browne, former head of BP's exploration division, who earned an honours degree in physics at the University of Cambridge, was trained as an engineer. Son of a BP man and an Auschwitz survivor, he spent his childhood abroad. Oil workers he met as a boy in Iran fascinated him. 'They were interesting and worldly people,' he remembers. He began his career with BP just out of university, working in the oilfields of Alaska. As a dyed-in-the-wool oilman, he was widely admired in the business community, and known for having turned BP's oil exploration division around in the early 1990s.

When John Browne became CEO, he took the reins of an organization that was in excellent financial shape. 'We have clawed our way back,' he said at the time. He described BP's new goal as being the best in each of its eleven criteria for business success, from oil exploration to business investment. According to Browne:

> What's important to us is that whatever business we're in, we focus on getting a position which is as close to dominating as possible. But we're going to do it in such a way that we don't imperil the financial structure of the company again.

Browne's aim was to create a 'distinctive' organization, with elements that competitors would have difficulty copying. He wanted to create a unique set of assets, including markets and provide unusual financial returns to investors. In BP's 1995 annual report, he wrote:

> To achieve distinctive performance from a portfolio of first-class assets requires continuous development of our organization and management processes. We are further decentralizing the organization in order to encourage personal initiative and creativity. Simultaneously, we are strengthening the sharing of experience and best practice so that BP's total competitive strength is greater than the sum of its parts.

By distinctive assets, Browne meant assets that a company has a disproportionate share of. He saw giant oilfields and market share as distinctive assets for BP in this sense. Technology also provided distinctiveness, as did BP's relationships with the rest of the world – customers, suppliers, governments, non-governmental organizations, communities, and so on – which BP thought of as long-term and based on mutual advantage. Browne also mentioned organization. By organization, he did not mean the design of the company but the process by which the company motivates its people and fosters creativity, learning, and the sharing of know-how. At a certain stage, Simon explained the respective roles of the CEO and the Chairman of the group when he discussed the dyad that he formed with Browne:

> The complementarity at the first level is that a lot of my responsibilities involve looking outside

and a lot of John's primary responsibility involves looking inside at the running and implementation. We complement each other in that way.

Knighted by the Queen in 1998 and made a life peer in 2001, Lord Browne of Madingley worked from an office that was appointed simply, apart from a David Hockney print and a table full of awards from US business magazines. An only child who never married, Browne seemed to have made BP the focus of his life. Browne admitted: 'When you don't have a real family, you build a surrogate one.'

A smoker of H. Upmann cigars (the Cuban brand favoured by Winston Churchill), John Browne spent half his time on the road. An art collector, photographer, and Trustee of the British Museum, he had a specific interest in crystal goblets and liked to spend time at his home in Venice. More surprisingly, and unlike his Texan counterparts, he preferred salmon to steak. Said John Stuzinski, a top investment banker at HSBC, and one of Browne's closest friends: 'He didn't come out of an oil well in Houston, and he is not a good old boy. He is a cosmopolitan, worldly business leader who wants BP to be at the top of the game.'

John Browne was known for his grasp of details, with colleagues claiming that he could spot the smallest error in a presentation. Executives had to be ready for him to drop in to their office at any time.

There are those who compared him to Jack Welsh, Steve Jobs or Bill Gates, while his detractors sometimes referred to him as 'The Sun King' saying that his control over the company was such that employees were sometimes afraid of giving him bad news.

For Craig Marsh, a consultant who worked with him at the time Browne was heading the exploration division:

People would not necessarily like John Browne, but would have immense respect for him. He is not as charismatic as other big names, but his power lies in his intellect and the certainty he has about what should be done. And he is almost always right. He is very good at driving people onto the picture of where the company should go. He can be brutal, but all of them are when they reach such a level of responsibility.

For the *Financial Times,* he was simply 'one of Europe's most influential businessmen for his feat of repeatedly changing the game for the world's oil industry'.

When John Browne became CEO, his objective was for BP to 'change in continuity'. Simon confirmed at the time that BP's first goal was 'strengthening the balance sheet, developing competitiveness in Europe and the Far East and achieving profitable, disciplined growth', to emerge with a streamlined, consolidated portfolio that offered improved financial returns and higher value growth. And that's precisely what Browne managed to achieve in his own way.

'This guy is a visionary,' said an Oppenheimer analyst, 'whether the issue is global warming, consolidation, or opportunities in Russia'. Browne always seemed to come before the competition and capitalize on what the business world calls 'the first mover's advantage'.

Changing the image

In 1997, John Browne broke away from the industry on the subject of the environment as he warned that there was evidence that CO_2 emissions might be changing the world's climate. Sounding more like an environmentalist than an oil baron, in a speech at Stanford University, Browne said:

Climate change is an issue which raises fundamental questions about the relationship between companies and societies as a whole and between one generation and the next. [Corporations] composed of highly skilled and trained people can't live in denial of mounting evidence gathered by hundreds of the most reputable scientists in the world.

His next step was to make sure that BP curbed pollution from its operation. BP increased investments in alternative energy and introduced its own emission trading system – imposing on the company Kyoto-style targets to reduce greenhouse gas emissions. The firm set a goal of reducing CO_2 emissions by 10 per cent by 2010, and met that target nine years ahead of schedule.

Under Browne's auspices, BP went through not only a striking identity shift but also a corporate rebranding exercise. It had shortened its name from British Petroleum to BP, coining it to the slogan 'Beyond Petroleum'. The BP logo was redesigned to an eco-friendly green, yellow and white sunburst. John Browne was alert to the dangers of 'heading a company in a world that – because of climate change, murmurings of war-for-oil and a host of other global crises – may hate oil companies, no matter how profitable they are.' So the whole idea was to change the image of BP to focusing on energy rather than just a petroleum company.

Initially mocked for the slogan, 'Beyond Petroleum', John Browne explained a few months later, at the Royal Festival Hall in London, what the much-hyped slogan meant for him:

> *It was a way of saying: look, there is a way of doing business which was the way petroleum companies used to be. We want to signal that we want to do it differently. I think we have to be careful to point out that it is not a literal statement. We are not getting out of the petroleum industry. We are one of the handful of the most successful companies in that business. And we intend to remain in that handful.*

For Paula Banks, who was at the time Senior Vice President for social strategy and policy at BP, the mission was far from simple. Daughter of a labourer and a former schoolteacher, she joined the company because she trusted John Browne's words: 'I heard his message and I saw the result. I believe BP means what it means', she told the *Guardian*. But she admits that rebranding the company has created confusion inside and outside the group.

Of course Browne's 'green' vision was not an act of pure altruism. Some of his detractors even argued that 'BP' now stood for 'Bigger Profits'. Lord Browne himself claimed that the company's efforts to control greenhouse gas emissions added 650 million dollars of market value to the company in three years, for an investment of just 20 million dollars.

So, behind a silk-smooth PR, was the image of the eco-friendly future of solar and renewable energy sincere? Although Browne's concerns over climate change won him some praise from environmentalists, controversial issues remained. Among those was Lord Browne's ambiguous position on sensitive questions like drilling oil in the Arctic National Wildlife Refuge, or BP's stake in Petrochina – the Chinese state-owned firm – that was building a contentious pipeline across Tibet.

When faced with that kind of antagonism, Browne counterattacked by citing pilot projects like those involving hydrogen fuel cells developed in service stations in Singapore, or even a multi-million dollar experiment to pump carbon dioxide back into the ground in Algeria. And when he was recently criticized about BP's role in building a pipeline from the Caspian Sea to Turkey, that might threaten environmentally sensitive areas in the Caucasus, he responded that the million-barrel-a-day pipeline would dramatically reduce tanker traffic in the Black Sea and the Bosphorus, making oil spills less likely.

In its pursuit of non-traditional energy sources and technologies, the multinational corporation announced in November 2005 the creation of a new low-carbon power business. The new company, called BP Alternative Energy, managed an investment program in solar, wind, hydrogen and combined-cycle-gas-turbine power generation, which could be worth $ 8 billion over the next decade.

Overall, BP's stand on environmental issues has also had an indirect impact on the whole industry, as even skeptical companies like Exxon were forced to adjust their public stance and policies on the issue of climate change.

Browne set out to 'create and sustain an image of himself as a different kind of oil executive leading a different kind of company.' In an attempt to measure the impact of that image and be able to capitalize on it, Browne had a 'reputation team' conduct extensive research, with stakeholders external to the corporation, about what BP meant and how petroleum companies should behave. The reputation building strategy centred on the close integration of retail marketing, advertising and communication.

BP's senior executive in the US was responsible for implementing the plan, and the reputation team was augmented by personnel from corporate headquarters in London and external consultants with expertise in advertising, public affairs, polling and government relations. Behind this worldwide operation lay the idea that brand reputation isn't just about connections with customers. It mainly determines whether governments award the company huge contracts or whether other businesses take on partnerships. BP's goal was to shape its corporate reputation with particular attention to the standing of the company and strengthening of its legitimacy in the United States where the bulk of BP's assets, stockholders and employees resided. A strong personal image of John Browne was 'assumed to help sustain the American asset value of the company in the same vein as other celebrity CEOs such as Jack Welch of GE, Steve Jobs of Apple, and Bill Gates of Microsoft'.

In another bold and much publicized move, John Browne took the decision to stop the US operations from making political contributions, a striking challenge for an oil supermajor in the country that sets the world's energy policy. By the same token, BP endorsed an anti-corruption policy and banned employees from making the 'facilitation' payments that ensured contracts were won in developing countries.

To complete his image as an icon of a modern senior executive, Browne offered equal benefits within BP for partners in same-sex relationships.

Changing the mind-set

John Browne is also the father of 'mega-mergers' in the oil industry. He had 'the strategic vision to transform BP in the late 1990s through a series of acquisitions', noted Philip Coggan in the *Financial Times*. BP was definitely transformed by the acquisition of Amoco, Arco and Burmah Castrol. The takeover of Amoco, the world's largest industrial merger ever, gave BP a huge position in the US. Amoco also brought with it big shares of Atlantic LNG, the rapidly expanding Trinidad liquefied natural gas project and one of the cornerstones of BP's growth in upstream markets. The second US takeover, Atlantic Richfield, gave it the missing piece in the US downstream jigsaw puzzle. But BP's bold acquisition spree was followed by a wave of sales of assets.

When many oil companies had portfolios featuring a large proportion of mature fields – which required higher operational costs to deliver the same amount of oil and natural gas out of the ground – BP sold some of its mature fields. 'We do actually divest as we invest – we are selling things that don't fit our strategy', explained John Browne. This was a way to boost efficiencies and profits, even if it made overall production harder to maintain. The ultimate goal was to sell oil and gas fields with relatively high production costs, from where BP had been pumping oil and gas for decades, requiring expensive maintenance and investment in new technology to keep production levels up. BP rather focused on properties with lower costs and higher profit margins, including those in Angola, Azerbaijan and the deep waters of the Gulf of Mexico.

In 2003, one of Browne's blockbusters was the $7 billion purchase of half of Russia's TNK, the first time a Western company had acquired a significant piece of a major Russian energy company. Browne was well aware of the risks of investing in Russia, but he justified his move in an interview with the Wall Street Journal: 'To ignore Russia if you are in the oil and gas business is to ignore the largest player.'

Although BP had been present in China for over a quarter of a century, it was gearing up for the race to acquire a bigger share of the fastest growing oil market in the world. In China, BP was building two new liquefied-natural-gas plants to help meet the country's demand for power. It was also exploring ways of shipping natural gas to China and South Korea from TNK-based facilities in eastern Siberia, a possible, multi-billion dollar project.

On a visit to Beijing in 2004, John Browne lobbied the Chinese government to strengthen cooperation with the British oil giant in petrochemicals, clean energy and new energy.

Beyond Chinese opportunities, BP kept a sharp eye on the Asian market as a whole. Twenty- five years ago, only one barrel of oil in seven was consumed in Asia, now it's one in three, and by 2020 it could be one in two.

Transforming the corporate culture

One of the great challenges that John Browne had to face following the complete reshuffling of BP's cards was to infuse a post acquisition corporate culture within the group. The new BP was a diverse organization, comprising employees of different nationalities and cultures. Although BP was one entity, legacy companies within BP still conducted business in their own way. More than 35 training programmes were taking place around the world, producing varying results.

A task force was then set up to try to unify such a disparate working population by creating an entirely new leadership development programme. It focused on the largest and most diverse population of leaders who became known as the 'first-level leaders' (FLL). Totalling more than 10 000 people, more than two-thirds of BP's total leadership, these employees worked in every business segment, including retail operations, chemical plants, refineries, and drilling platforms. Despite their differences, they had one key factor in common: their decisions had an enormous effect on BP's turnover, cost, quality, innovation, safety and environmental performance.

By the end of 2002, all targets set for the FLL development programme had been surpassed and the sessions were hailed a success. More than 4500 FLLs attended training sessions, and course attendees reported an 84 per cent satisfaction. Course demand was so high that more than a 120 courses were offered. Furthermore, the organization experienced no resistance to engaging the most senior-level group leaders, despite their hectic agendas.

The results of worldwide surveys not only proved that performance ratings of the FLLs who had attended the training sessions were much better than the ratings of the others. The results also showed that the training programme was having an effect on specific behaviours as well as an indirect impact on bottom-line performances.

Andy Inglis, Executive Vice-President and Deputy Chief Executive for Exploration & Production at BP, who was involved in shaping the new leadership of BP following a number of mergers and acquisitions at that time, recalls:

> *Following a series of major mergers and acquisitions, creating a corporate culture meant creating a fresh future for the new entity. Most of our people understood the strategic logic of mergers, but to create a vision for the new company, it was critical to establish common values for the leadership and therefore the organization. We achieved this by taking middle-level leaders in groups of fifty for 2 to 3 days and talking with them about the business, the strategy, planning the future, but mostly about values. In this way, our leadership had time to build relationships and share their experiences – there was a lot of personal time. During these sessions, what struck me most was the importance of the past – you have to respect it, even if we were talking at times about the primacy of one company. Since then, I believe it has been the rich combination of all of the best elements of these companies, their values and the synthesis of their strengths and brands that have made the new BP successful.*

In going through this process, Inglis was pleasantly surprised by the depth and breadth of the leadership talent that BP uncovered from within. With this raw material, BP's next task was how to genuinely blend the leadership to harness the best of the heritage companies and their incumbent skills. To make this happen, BP made sure that the number one and number two of each business unit around the world came from a different parent entity, for example one from BP and one from Amoco.

Inglis also explained how one of the keys to BP's distributed leadership model is 'space and boundaries'.

> *You have to be extremely clear about setting direction, defining boundaries and then allowing people space to get on with it. BP believes in a distributed leadership model. This is to facilitate decisions being taken at the level that has the right skills. As a senior leader, your role then becomes one of support – ensuring people have what they need to do the job they do best.*

John Browne always stressed the importance of Human Resources. Craig Marsh, who was consulting for BP when Browne was still heading the exploration division, details how new HR practices were introduced under his leadership (skill-based compensation, 360-degree appraisal, advanced management programmes …):

> *He identified about 30 managers who became drivers of performance, and stressed the importance of accountability and responsibility. He also installed a process of quarterly reviews and set up performance contracts. These included concrete targets in terms of explorations programs, safety, profits, revenue, as well as people skills.*

He also remembers the Andrew oilfield case. Located in the North Sea, it was discovered in the 1970s and sat on BP's shelf for 15 years. Numerous attempts had been made to develop the field but each plan had floundered.

> *One day, John Browne made it clear that he would not leave this under-performing asset sitting around. He brought a small team of engineers and contractors together and asked them to come up with a way to exploit it – or sell it. The idea was based on shared incentives and shared risks and, after weeks of work, the team actually did come back with a viable proposal.*

A few years later, asked how BP had gone from a functional, hierarchical company to a much more networking kind of organization, Browne answered:

> *The very embryonic ideas on process, the multitude of experimentation, the understanding of behaviour began to shape the organization that has developed.... Now we have an organization which is really distinctively flat. Very flat indeed. That wasn't the purpose. But it was the outcome. BP is now divided into business units, linked by process, deeply committed to motivation and working on getting more creativity in the organization.... But you have to have a balance; you have to be very human about it. If you have too much insecurity, you have a subsistence existence where people cannot be creative. They won't take risks.*

New management, new risks

Although Lord Browne's leadership proved successful – BP posted 29 per cent growth in the first quarter of 2005 – his frontier-type strategy was not without risks. For all its promise, Russia could end up becoming a major worry for BP. Although the TNK deal was more successful than many observers expected, BP is also increasingly dependent on Russia for the kind of financial returns Wall Street anticipates. As the international oil company gears up to acquire a bigger share of China's growing market, the same goes for BP investments in China.

On the other hand, and from a financial standpoint, John Browne had the reputation of being pretty cautious. 'It's just a detail, but at the time he was reviewing the profitability of oilfields, he would not base his estimates on a barrel higher than $14, whereas all other companies were basing their accounts on a barrel at $24', remembered one analyst.

Some detractors also say that BP's financial health came at a cost, and blame the oil giant for the 'lapses of security' that provoked the 2005 blast that killed 15 people and injured more than 170 at the Texas City Plant. In its final investigation report, BP acknowledged the fact that lapses in management at the refinery, along with the operation of substandard equipment, were among the root causes of the accident. Along the same lines, the US chemical Safety and Hazard Investigation Board accused BP of 'systematic lapses' in safety. From another standpoint, the recent and partial shutdown of the Prudhoe Bay oilfield, following the discovery of unexpectedly severe corrosion and a spill from an oil transit line, was perceived as yet another warning sign.

Asked if he worried that he cannot possibly know what is going on at BP's operations in Angola, Russia or China, the softly spoken cerebral man answered: 'Of course I know, when I wake up in the morning and shave, that things are going wrong. But equally I know that more things are going right than are going wrong, and I believe I have great people who will identify what is going wrong and who will do something about it.'

For years, a few commentators insisted that Lord Browne was 'losing his magic', stressing the financial-return induced risks of his strategy. But no one denies that Browne's image as a progressive industry thinker, who earned a reputation for being 'ahead of the pack'

in the cut-throat oil industry, paid dividends for BP stockholders. Employees as well as investors were aware of the 'Browne bonus effect': the willingness of the market to accept certain risky deals based, in part, on trust in Browne's management skills.

Lord Browne leaves the stage

As they focused on Browne's leadership, none of the observers – whether inside or outside the company – failed to notice that John Browne's succession was a major concern. He was expected to retire as he turned 60 in February 2008. It was said that Browne took the idea of his succession very seriously, handpicking long ago roughly a dozen potential candidates, who became known as 'the twelve apostles' inside the company.

Among potential successors were Tony Hayward, who ran BP Exploration; John Manzoni who headed BP's global refining and marketing units; and Iain Conn, who ran BP's global marketing and technology units. All three are British and BP lifers, and Browne and the board had kept these men in their sights.

Then, January 12, 2007, BP announced that John Browne would be stepping down 17 months early. Tony Hayward would take Browne's place the following July as chief executive officer. BP insiders said that the timing of Browne's departure was unrelated to criticism of BP's recent safety and management record, but the *Wall Street Journal* speculated that Hayward may have influenced an internal turning of opinion that precipitated Browne's departure.

John Browne had presided over an era (1995–2007) in which BP's market cap increased fivefold and earning per share more than 600 per cent. But now this legacy would be analysed, criticized, praised. Second guessing and hindsight-inspired analysis would come first; only time would tell if John Browne's vision and accomplishments would stand.

During his tenure as CEO, Simon had the habit of closing meetings with a quote from Dickens. Shortly after taking on the top job, Browne broke with tradition and ended a meeting with a quote from Shakespeare's *As you like it:* 'I will tell you the beginning; and if it pleases [you] may see the end for the best is yet to do.'

Although John Browne had bowed out, the play was far from over. Tony Hayward took the stage, and the world waited to see how events would unfold.

Wal-Mart in India

By Ayan Ghosh and Siddhartha Paul

Retailing is like a game of three dimensional chess where we operate as a local, regional and global player, so depending on the needs of the market we shall change our format and adapt.

John B.Menzer, Vice Chairman, Chief Administrative
Officer – Wal-Mart Stores, Inc.

On the 27th November 2006, Wal-Mart, the world's No. 1 retailer, announced a joint venture with Bharti Enterprise, (Bharti) a leading cell phone operator in India. Through the JV, the company would open hundreds of Wal-Mart branded superstores across India over the next five years. The retail shops were slated to be rolled out from August 15, 2007. This deal was a large-scale entry by a foreign multibrand retailer into the booming Indian market. Under the terms of the Bharti–Wal-Mart agreement, Bharti would own and operate the physical stores, while the supply chain would be managed jointly by Bharti and Wal-Mart. Although Wal-Mart had been considered as the number one retailer globally, the company had recently failed in some of its overseas markets. The major reason for its failure was its inability to judge local tastes. Due to this reason, Wal-Mart had to pull out from South Korea and Germany. On the other hand, Bharti had a vast retail distribution network and knowledge of the buying habits of the middle class Indians, but lacked necessary experience in discount and grocery stores. Due to such reasons, the analysts were skeptical about Wal-Mart's success in India.

Wal-Mart – The retail giant

In the year 1962, Sam Walton founded Wal-Mart Stores in Rogers, Arkansas. During the next five years of its operation, the company established 25 stores across the US. By 1967, the company had posted revenues of $12.6 million.

Wal-Mart had discount stores as well as super-centres. Its discount stores were department stores, which sold general merchandise, food items, drugs in a pharmacy centre, etc. Wal-Mart supercentres sold everything that a discount store sells. In addition, it also sold meat and poultry, baked goods, dairy products, frozen foods and garden produce.

On October 31, 1969, Wal-Mart Stores, Inc. was incorporated and it opened its first distribution centre in Bentonville, Arkansas in 1970. The basic philosophy of Wal-Mart was providing Every Day Low Prices (EDLP). According to this concept, the customers of Wal-Mart could procure high quality, branded and unbranded products at the lowest possible price and get value for their money. Compared to the pricing of its competitors, the products of Wal-Mart were priced much lower. This pricing strategy of Wal-Mart was instrumental in increasing loyalty from price conscious rural customers and thus increasing profit due to larger volumes. Wal-Mart was able to provide low prices by maintaining low costs. It procured its goods directly from the manufacturers avoiding any form of intermediaries. Being a large customer to most of its vendors, Wal-Mart used its bargaining power to bring down prices. In case the retailer failed to negotiate for lower prices, it switched vendors. Many vendors, in order to supply goods to Wal-Mart at lower prices shifted their manufacturing base to China and other third world nations, where the cost of labour was less expensive. Due to its massive size, Wal-Mart had the power to drive down costs in the retail and manufacturing sectors. Because of its efficient supply chain management, Wal-Mart had been able to attain the leader's position in the retail industry. Wal-Mart also used sophisticated barcode technology and hand-held computer systems, which made it easier to manage merchandise. The company's transportation system was fast and responsive, which made it possible for the goods to be shipped from the distribution centres to the stores within a very short span of time. Wal-Mart also invested heavily on IT and communications systems to track sales and inventories in stores across the US. During the 1980s, Wal-Mart continued to grow rapidly and by the year 1987, there were 1198 stores with sales of $15.9 billion. In 1998, Wal-Mart entered the grocery business and introduced the 'Neighborhood Market' concept with three stores in Arkansas. By 2005, the company controlled about 20% of the retail grocery and consumables business in the U.S. Wal-Mart's annual revenue increased from

$226 479 million in 2003 to $344 992 million in 2007. (Exhibit 1). On September 12, 2007, Wal-Mart introduced a new slogan in its advertisements, 'Save Money Live Better', replacing the 'Always Low Prices, Always' slogan, which it had used earlier.

As the US market was saturated, Wal-Mart planned to expand overseas. The United States made up only 4% of the world's total population. As a result, Wal-Mart was missing out on the potential customers of other nations. Moreover, as the disposable income of emerging markets was comparatively lower than that of the US, it provided a good opportunity for discount retailing. In order to survive, the company needed to grow and significant growth was possible only in the international arena. Additionally, to satisfy its shareholders, Wal-Mart had to show an increase in both sales and profits and so the company was left with no other option than to expand overseas.

Wal-Mart's global presence

Internationally, Wal-Mart was present in Puerto Rico, Canada, China, Mexico, Brazil, Germany, Britain, Argentina and South Korea. By July 1999, there were more than 130 000 employees working outside the United States out of a total worldwide workforce of more than 950 000. In 1993, the percentage of all Wal-Mart stores located outside the United States was 1 per cent that grew to 18 per cent by 1998 (Exhibit 2).

Between 1995 and 1998, Wal-Mart witnessed 5 per cent of its growth in sales and 4 per cent of the growth in profits from international operations (Exhibit 3). To successfully expand overseas, Wal-Mart exploited its buying power with domestic suppliers and procured goods at less cost. It also utilized domestically developed competencies in areas like efficient store management, logistics and merchandising skills and in the efficient use of technology.

Between 1991 and 1995, Wal-Mart concentrated on Mexico, Brazil, Argentina and Canada to establish its presence. In 1999, Wal-Mart entered Europe. Wal-Mart entered Canada through an acquisition, while in Mexico; it formed a 50:50 joint venture with Cifra, Mexico's largest retailer. Wal-Mart entered Brazil through a joint venture and due to the experience that it had gained in Latin America; Wal-Mart could enter Argentina through a wholly owned subsidiary. In 1996, Wal-Mart targeted Asia by focusing on China, which had a population of more than 1.2 billion.

Wal-Mart's entry in India

On the 27th November 2006, Wal-Mart announced a 50:50 joint venture with Bharti. The joint venture was named Bharti Wal-Mart Pvt. Ltd. Rising income and increased consumerism of the Indian urban population along with an upswing in rural consumption attracted Wal-Mart in India. The joint venture will roll out its retail stores from August 2007.

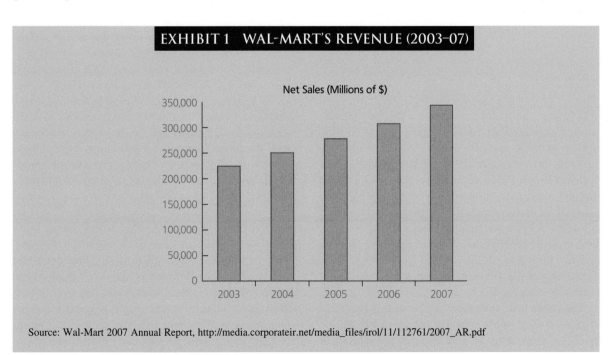

EXHIBIT 1   WAL-MART'S REVENUE (2003–07)

Net Sales (Millions of $)

Source: Wal-Mart 2007 Annual Report, http://media.corporateir.net/media_files/irol/11/112761/2007_AR.pdf

EXHIBIT 2   WAL-MART'S INTERNATIONAL STORES FROM 1993 TO 1998

Year ending 31/1	1993	1994	1995	1996	1997	1998
Wal-Mart stores	1848	1950	1985	1995	1960	1921
Supercenters	34	72	147	239	344	441
Sam's clubs	256	417	426	433	436	443
Domestic total	2138	2439	2558	2667	2740	2805
International	10	24	226	276	314	601
Total stores	2148	2463	2784	2943	3054	3406
International as % of total stores	1%	1%	8%	9%	10%	18%

EXHIBIT 3   FINANCIAL PROFILE OF WAL-MART'S INTERNATIONAL OPERATIONS

Year Ending 31/1		1995	1996	1997	1998
Sales ($ millions)	Wal-Mart discount Stores	51,967	55,243	55,815	57,915
	Sam's Clubs	18,908	19,068	19,785	20,668
	Supercenters	5,952	11,027	19,025	25,905
	Domestic total	76,827	85,338	94,625	104,488
	International	1,511	3,712	5,002	7,517
	International as % of total sales	2%	4%	5%	7%
Profit before tax ($ millions)	Wal-Mart discount stores	4,396	4,402	4,445	4,865
	Sam's Clubs	728	800	864	950
	Supercenters	310	618	1,103	1,554
	Domestic total	5,434	5,820	6,412	7,369
	International	−17	−16	24	262
	International as % of total profit	−0.3%	−0.3%	0.4%	3.4%

Wal-Mart's proposed investment in the venture would be around $100 million initially, rising to $450 million in a few years from 2007. Bharti would own and run the stores, while Wal-Mart would supply backend supply chain technology. Statistics showed that the retail industry accounted for 10 per cent of the GDP of India, which was projected to grow at 8 per cent. In India, the Indian retail industry was valued at about $300 billion and was expected to grow to $427 billion by 2010 and $637 billion by 2015. However, only 3 per cent of the retail industry in India was organized.

The organized retail sector in India was predicted to grow at 20 per cent annually and touch $23 billion by 2010. According to Tata Strategic Management Group, the top five organized retail categories by 2015 would be food, grocery and general merchandise, apparel, durables, food service and home improvement (Exhibit 4). This was prompting the leading brands like Reliance, Tatas and Birlas to invest in India. In 2006, Reliance Industries Ltd. was planning to invest more than $2 billion into its retail business division called Reliance Retail Ltd. The Aditya Birla Group was also to shell out over $1.3 billion by the year 2010. In the year 2006, Director of Tata Sons had announced that the company would debut in consumer durables product retailing through its arm Infiniti Retail and would be a part in the ongoing retail revolution, investing about $80 million and setting up about 100 stores dealing with electronic products.

EXHIBIT 4   ORGANIZED RETAIL MARKET IN INDIA

Category	2004	2015
Food, Grocery & General Merchandise	10%	42%
Clothes, Textile & Fashion Accessories	39%	16%
Durables & Mobiles	12%	12%
Food Service	7%	10%
Home Improvement	8%	7%
Jewellery & Watches	7%	3%
Footwear	9%	3%
Books, Music, Toys & Gifts	3%	1%
Others	5%	6%
Total	100%	100%

Source: 'Retail Revolution,' http://www.tata.com

Moreover, according to A.T. Kearney's Global Retail Development Index in 2004, India ranked as the second most emerging market based on the four key variables, country risk, market attractiveness, market saturation and time pressure (Exhibit 5).

A number of big retailers had ambitious plans in retailing in India. Metro, the number one retailer in Germany, had already opened wholesale stores in India. Tesco of the UK and Carrefour of France had been actively negotiating with several Indian companies for partnership. South Africa's Shoprite had already entered India.

India also had many hypermarkets. In 1997, the Kishore Biyani-led Future Group had entered its retail business with Pantaloon Retail outlet in Kolkata in 1997 and by 2007, it had grown into a retail giant with 140 stores across 32 cities in the country and ran the hypermarket chain Big Bazaar, supermarket chain Food Bazaar and malls called Central. Other big and medium retail players like Trent, Titan, Wills Lifestyle, Raymond, Café Coffee Day, Provogue, Trinethra, etc. were also in the retail business – be it in consumer products or in fashion apparels. Most of the globally famous brands like Nike, Levis, McDonald's, Domino, Benetton, Swarovski, Tommy Hilfiger, Revlon, Marks & Spencer, etc. had been operating through the franchisee model. The analysts believed that the scarcity of quality retail space and rising rentals could prove to be a hurdle for the organized retailers. This would mean that even the established players like Wal-Mart would have to struggle to find a retail space.

The road ahead

The announcement of Wal-Mart's tie-up with Bharti sent shockwaves amongst the existing and emerging retailers in India. This was so because Wal-Mart had a history of driving the 'mom and pop stores' and other big time retailers in the US out of business, every time they had opened a store. Wal-Mart retail stores might have a negative impact on small businesses in India and might force many small shops and traders to close. Experts believed that the retail industry in India was already very crowded and Wal-Mart's entry into India could devastate the small traders and their employees.

Wal-Mart was the largest private employer in the United States with 1.3 million employees and was a significant contributor to other countries like Mexico, Canada, and Brazil. However, the workers and unions, small businesses, environmental organizations, investors and political and religious leaders in the US and around the world had condemned the way Wal-Mart treated its workers. These institutions protested against Wal-Mart as it destroyed the local production and small businesses by importing most of its products from China.

Moreover, Wal-Mart might upset the import balance of India by importing massively from China rather than using local production. The analysts felt that after Wal-Mart's entry to the Indian retail sector, the market would be flooded with cheap Chinese-made goods. In 1995, Wal-Mart had imported about 6 per cent of its merchandise sold in the United States

EXHIBIT 5 GLOBAL RETAIL DEVELOPMENT INDEX (TOP 10 EMERGING MARKETS AS OF 2004)

			Country Risk (economic and political)	Market Attractive- ness	Market Saturation	Time Pressure	Total Score
1.	Russia	Eastern Europe	56	56	77	100	100
2.	India	Asia	62	34	92	72	88
3.	China	Asia	71	42	62	90	86
4.	Slovenia	Eastern Europe	83	60	43	76	84
5.	Croatia	Eastern Europe	61	53	55	93	83
6.	Latvia	Eastern Europe	64	55	54	89	82
7.	Vietnam	Asia	52	29	90	66	76
8.	Turkey	Mediterranean	50	58	67	65	75
9.	Slovakia	Eastern Europe	69	48	35	100	74
10.	Thailand	Asia	68	38	60	76	73

Legend:

0 – High Risk	0 – Low Attractiveness	0 – Saturated	0 – No time pressure
100 – Low Risk	100 – High Attractiveness	100 – Not Saturated	100 – Urgency to go

Source: 'Emerging Market Priorities for Global Retailers, The 2004 Global Retail Development Index, ATKEARNEY', http://www.atkearney.com

EXHIBIT 6 KEY SUCCESS FACTORS OF INTERNATIONAL RETAILERS ENTERING A NEW MARKET

Source: 'Emerging Market Priorities for Global Retailers', http://www.atkearney.com

from other countries including China. In the year 2004, 60% of its total merchandise was imported from more than 6000 suppliers in 63 countries, with Wal-Mart sourcing the majority of its goods from China. Wal-Mart purchased about $1.2 billion worth of goods from India, which was less than one-fifteenth of the amount that Wal-Mart sourced from China in the year 2004.

However, few were optimistic about Wal-Mart's entry into India. According to the analysts, Wal-Mart's efficient logistics services could be its biggest strong point when it enters the Indian market.

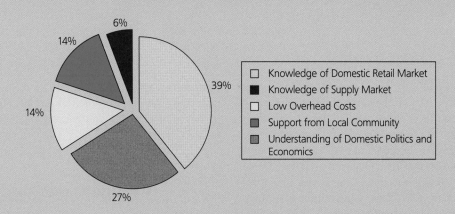

EXHIBIT 7   KEY SUCCESS FACTORS OF DOMESTIC COMPANIES WHEN COMPETING AGAINST INTERNATIONAL PLAYERS

- Knowledge of Domestic Retail Market
- Knowledge of Supply Market
- Low Overhead Costs
- Support from Local Community
- Understanding of Domestic Politics and Economics

Source: 'Emerging Market Priorities for Global Retailers', http://www.atkearney.com, 2004.

Purchasing power and new formats were the advantages that an international retailer had while entering a new market (Exhibit 6). Similarly, the main advantages that domestic companies had while competing against international retail giants were knowledge of the domestic retail market and knowledge of the supply market (Exhibit 7).

Moreover, the analysts were in favour of the deal as it would give the Indian consumers wider choice at a lower costs. However, it remained to be seen what consequences the deal would ultimately lead to. 'India is a very different place from the US or Canada. Wal-Mart's corporate myopia may not recognize that initially.'

Kentucky Fried Chicken and the global fast-food industry

By Jeffrey A. Krug[1]

Kentucky Fried Chicken Corporation (KFC) was the world's largest chicken restaurant chain and third largest fast-food chain. It held close to one-half of the US market in terms of sales and operated close to 14 000 restaurants in more than 100 countries. KFC was one of the first fast-food chains to go international in the late 1950s and was one of the world's most recognizable brands. KFC's early international strategy was to grow its company and franchise restaurant base throughout the world. It based its success on the number of countries in which it operated. By early 2007, however, KFC had refocused its international strategy on several high growth markets where the KFC concept was most popular and KFC had the greatest opportunities for market leadership. Its largest markets were China, Japan, Canada, Great Britain, Australia, South Africa, Malaysia, Mexico, Indonesia, South Korea, and the Philippines. With the notable exception of Mexico, KFC based most of its growth in these markets on franchises and joint ventures, which were operated by local businesspeople who understood the local market better than KFC. Franchises also allowed KFC to more rapidly expand into smaller countries that could only support a small number of restaurants. In the future, however, KFC hoped to make greater use of company owned restaurants, which gave it greater control over product quality, service, and restaurant cleanliness. This was particularly important in Europe, where the fast-food concept was less popular. In addition to Asia and Europe, Latin America was an appealing area for investment because of the size of its markets and geographical proximity to the United States. Mexico was of particular interest because of the North American Free Trade Agreement (NAFTA), a free trade zone between Canada, the United States, and Mexico that went into effect in 1994. McDonald's, Burger King, and Wendy's, however, were expanding into other countries in Latin America such as Argentina, Chile, Brazil, and Venezuela rapidly. KFC's task was to develop an effective strategy for penetrating the Latin American market more quickly and gaining quicker acceptance of its concept.

Company history

Fast-food franchising was still in its infancy in 1952 when Harland Sanders began his travels across the United States to speak with prospective franchisees about his 'Colonel Sanders Recipe Kentucky Fried Chicken'. By 1960, 'Colonel' Sanders had granted KFC franchises to more than 200 take-home retail outlets and restaurants across the United States. He had also established a number of franchises in Canada. By 1963, the number of KFC franchises had risen to more than 300 and revenues topped $500 million. The Colonel celebrated his 74th birthday the following year and was eager to lessen the load of running the day-to-day operations of his business. He sold his business to two Louisville businessmen – Jack Massey and John Young Brown Jr. – for $2 million. The Colonel stayed on as a public relations man and goodwill ambassador for the company. During the next five years, Massey and Brown concentrated on growing KFC's franchise system across the United States. In 1966, they took KFC public and the company was listed on the New York Stock Exchange. By the late 1960s, a strong foothold had been established in the United States. Massey and Brown then turned their attention to international markets. In 1969, a joint venture was signed with Mitsuoishi Shoji Kaisha, Ltd. in Japan and the rights to operate franchises in England were acquired. Subsidiaries were later established in Hong Kong, South Africa, Australia, New Zealand, and Mexico. By 1971, KFC had established 2450 franchises and 600 company-owned restaurants in 48 countries.

Heublein, Inc.

In 1971, KFC entered into negotiations with Heublein, Inc. to discuss a possible merger. The decision to pursue a merger was partially driven by Brown's desire to pursue other interests that included a political career (Brown was elected Governor of Kentucky in 1977). Several months later, Heublein acquired KFC. Heublein was in the business of producing vodka, mixed cocktails, dry gin, cordials, beer, and other alcoholic beverages. It had little experience, however, in the restaurant business. Conflicts quickly erupted between Colonel Sanders and Heublein management. In particular, Colonel Sanders was distraught over poor quality control and restaurant cleanliness. By 1977, new restaurant openings had slowed to only twenty a year. Few restaurants were being remodelled and service quality had declined. To combat these problems, Heublein sent in a new management team to redirect KFC's strategy. A 'back-to-the-basics' strategy was implemented and new restaurant construction was halted until existing restaurants could be upgraded and operating problems eliminated. A programme for remodelling existing restaurants was implemented, an emphasis was placed on cleanliness and service, marginal products were eliminated, and product consistency was reestablished. This strategy enabled KFC to gain better control of its operations and it was soon again aggressively building new restaurants.

R.J. Reynolds Industries, Inc.

In 1982, R.J. Reynolds Industries, Inc. (RJR) acquired Heublein and merged it into a wholly owned subsidiary. The acquisition of Heublein was part of RJR's corporate strategy of diversifying into unrelated businesses such as energy, transportation, food, and restaurants to reduce its dependence on the tobacco industry. Tobacco had driven RJR's sales since its founding in North Carolina in 1875. Sales of cigarettes and tobacco products, however, were declining as consumption continued to fall in the United States. Reduced consumption was largely the result of increased awareness among Americans of the negative health consequences of smoking.

RJR, however, had little more experience in the restaurant business than did Heublein when it acquired KFC 11 years earlier. In contrast to Heublein, which tried to actively manage KFC using its own managers, RJR allowed KFC to operate autonomously. RJR believed that KFC's executives were better qualified to operate the business than its own managers; therefore, KFC's top management team was left largely intact. In doing so, RJR avoided many of the operating problems that plagued Heublein during its ownership of KFC. In 1985, RJR acquired Nabisco Corporation for $4.9 billion. The acquisition of Nabisco was an attempt to redefine RJR as a world leader in the consumer foods industry. Nabisco sold a variety of well-known food products such as Oreo cookies, Ritz crackers, Planters peanuts, Lifesavers, and Milk-Bone dog biscuits. RJR subsequently divested many of its non-consumer food businesses. It sold KFC to Pepsi-Co, Inc. one year later.

PepsiCo, Inc.

PepsiCo, Inc. was formed in 1965 with the merger of the Pepsi-Cola Company and Frito-Lay, Inc. The merger created one of the largest consumer products companies in the United States. Pepsi-Cola's traditional business was the sale of soft drink concentrates to licensed independent and company-owned bottlers that manufactured, sold, and distributed Pepsi-Cola soft drinks. Pepsi-Cola's best known trademarks were Pepsi-Cola, Diet Pepsi, and Mountain Dew. Frito-Lay manufactured and sold a variety of leading snack foods such as Lay's Potato Chips, Doritos Tortilla Chips, Tostitos Tortilla Chips, and Ruffles Potato Chips.

PepsiCo believed the restaurant business complemented its consumer product orientation. The marketing of fast-food followed many of the same patterns as soft drinks and snack foods. Pepsi-Cola and Lay's Potato Chips, for example, could be marketed in the same television and radio segments, which provided higher returns for each advertising dollar. Restaurant chains also provided an additional outlet for the sale of Pepsi soft drinks. PepsiCo believed it could take advantage of numerous synergies by operating the three businesses under the same corporate umbrella. PepsiCo also believed that its management skills could be transferred among the three businesses. This practice was compatible with PepsiCo's policy of frequently moving managers among its business units as a means of developing future executives. PepsiCo's acquisition of KFC in 1986 followed earlier acquisitions of Pizza Hut and Taco Bell. The three restaurant chains were the market leaders in the chicken, pizza, and Mexican categories.

Following the acquisition of KFC, PepsiCo initiated sweeping changes. It announced that the franchise contract would be changed to give PepsiCo greater control over KFC franchisees and to make it easier to close poorly performing restaurants. Staff at KFC was reduced to cut costs and many KFC managers were replaced with PepsiCo managers. Soon after the acquisition, KFC's new personnel manager, who had just relocated from PepsiCo's New York headquarters, was overheard in the KFC cafeteria saying 'There will be no more home grown tomatoes in this organization.' Rumours spread quickly among KFC employees about their opportunities for advancement within KFC and PepsiCo. Harsh comments by PepsiCo managers about KFC, its people, and its traditions, several restructurings that led to layoffs throughout KFC, the replacement of KFC managers with PepsiCo managers, and conflicts between KFC and PepsiCo's corporate cultures created a morale problem within KFC. KFC's culture was built largely on Colonel Sander's laid-back approach to management. Employees enjoyed good job security and stability. A strong loyalty had been created over the years as a result of the Colonel's efforts to provide for his employees' benefits, pension, and other non-income needs. In addition, the Southern environment in Louisville resulted in a friendly, relaxed atmosphere at KFC's corporate offices.

PepsiCo's culture, in contrast, was characterized by a strong emphasis on performance. Top performers expected to move up through the ranks quickly. PepsiCo used its KFC, Pizza Hut, Taco Bell, Frito Lay, and Pepsi-Cola divisions as training grounds for its executives, rotating its best managers through the five divisions on average every two years. This practice created pressure on managers to demonstrate their management skills within short periods to maximize their potential for promotion. This practice reinforced feelings among KFC managers that they had few opportunities for advancement within the new company. One PepsiCo manager commented that 'You may have performed well last year, but if you don't perform well this year, you're gone, and there are 100 ambitious guys with Ivy League MBAs at PepsiCo's headquarters in New York who would love to have your job'. An unwanted effect of this performance driven culture was that employee loyalty was lost and turnover was higher than in other companies.

Kyle Craig, president of KFC's U.S. operations, commented on PepsiCo's relationship with KFC:

The KFC culture is an interesting one because it was dominated by a lot of KFC folks, many who have been around since the days of the Colonel. Many of those people were very intimidated by the PepsiCo culture, which is a very high performance, high accountability, highly driven culture. People were concerned about whether they would succeed in the new culture. Like many companies, we have had a couple of downsizings which further made people nervous. Today, there are fewer old KFC people around and I think to some degree people have seen that the PepsiCo culture can drive some pretty positive results. I also think the PepsiCo people who have worked with KFC have modified their cultural values somewhat and they can see that there were a lot of benefits in the old KFC culture.

PepsiCo pushes its companies to perform strongly, but whenever there is a slip in performance, it increases the culture gap between PepsiCo and KFC. I have been involved in two downsizings over which I have been the chief architect. They have been probably the two most gut-wrenching experiences of my career. Because you know you're dealing with peoples' lives and their families, these changes can be emotional if you care about the people in your organization. However, I do fundamentally believe that your first obligation is to the entire organization.

A second problem for PepsiCo was its poor relationship with KFC franchisees. A month after becoming president and chief executive officer in 1989, John Cranor addressed KFC's franchisees in Louisville to explain the details of the new franchise contract. This was the first contract change in 13 years. It gave PepsiCo greater power to take over weak franchises, relocate restaurants, and make changes in existing restaurants. In addition, restaurants would no longer be protected from competition from new KFC units and PepsiCo would have the right to raise royalty fees on existing restaurants as contracts came up for renewal. After Cranor finished his address, there was an uproar among the attending franchisees, who jumped to their feet to protest the changes. KFC's franchise association later sued PepsiCo over the new contract. The contract remained unresolved until 1996, when the most objectionable parts of the contract were removed by KFC's new president and CEO, David Novak. A new contract was ratified by KFC's franchisees in 1997.

PepsiCo's divestiture of KFC, Pizza Hut, and Taco Bell

PepsiCo's strategy of diversifying into three distinct but related markets – soft drinks, snack foods, and fast-food restaurants – created one of the world's largest food companies and a portfolio of some of the world's most recognizable brands. Between 1990 and 1996, PepsiCo's sales grew at an annual rate of more than 10 per cent, surpassing $31 billion in 1996. PepsiCo's growth, however, masked troubles in its fast-food businesses. Operating margins (profit after tax as a per centage of sales) at Pepsi-Cola and Frito Lay averaged 12 and 17 per cent, respectively. During the same period, margins at KFC, Pizza Hut, and Taco Bell fell from an average of more than eight per cent in 1990 to a little more than four per cent in 1996. Declining margins in the fast-food chains reflected increasing maturity in the US fast-food industry, intense competition, and the ageing of KFC and Pizza Hut's restaurant bases. As a result, PepsiCo's restaurant chains absorbed nearly one-half of PepsiCo's annual capital spending during the 1990s but generated less than one-third of PepsiCo's cash flows. This meant that cash had to be diverted from PepsiCo's soft drink and snack food businesses to its restaurant businesses. This reduced PepsiCo's corporate return on assets, made it more difficult to compete effectively with Coca-Cola, and hurt its stock price. In 1997, PepsiCo decided to spin off its restaurant businesses into a new company called Tricon Global Restaurants, Inc. The new company was based in KFC's headquarters in Louisville, Kentucky.

PepsiCo's objective was to reposition itself as a beverage and snack food company, strengthen its balance sheet, and create more consistent earning growth. PepsiCo received a one-time distribution from Tricon of $4.7 billion, $3.7 billion of which was used to pay off short-term debt. The balance was earmarked for stock repurchases. In 1998, PepsiCo acquired Tropicana Products, which controlled more than 40 per cent of the US chilled orange juice market. Because of the divestiture of KFC, Pizza Hut, and Taco Bell, PepsiCo sales fell by $11.3 billion and assets fell by $7.0 billion. Profitability, however, soared. Operating margins rose from 11 per cent in 1997 to 14 per cent in 1999 and ROA rose from 11 per cent in 1997 to 16 per cent in 1999. By focusing on high cash flow market leaders, PepsiCo raised profitability while decreasing its asset base. In 2001, PepsiCo acquired The Quaker Oats Company, which included Gatorade. Gatorade and Tropicana were moved into a separate division to increase efficiencies. By 2005, PepsiCo's sales exceeded $29 billion annually.

Yum! Brands, Inc.

The spin-off created a new, independent, publicly held company called Tricon Global Restaurants, Inc. The new company managed the KFC, Pizza Hut, and Taco Bell franchise systems. David Novak became Tricon's new CEO and moved quickly to create a new culture within the company. One of his primary objectives was to reverse the long-standing friction between management and franchisees that was created under PepsiCo ownership. Novak announced that PepsiCo's top-down management system would be replaced by a new management emphasis on providing support to the firm's franchise base. Franchises would have greater independence, resources, and technical support. Novak symbolically changed the name on the corporate headquarters' building in Louisville to 'KFC Support Center' to drive home his new philosophy.

In 2002, Tricon announced the acquisition of Long John Silver's and A&W All-American Food Restaurants. The acquisition increased Tricon's worldwide system to 32 500 restaurants. The acquisition signalled Tricon's decision to aggressively promote a multi-branding strategy that combined two brands in one restaurant and attracted a larger consumer base by offering them a broader menu selection in one location. One week after it announced the acquisition, shareholders approved a corporate name change to Yum! Brands, Inc. The new name reflected the company's expanding portfolio of fast-food brands (see Exhibit 1). In 2003, Novak announced the acquisition of Pasta Bravo, a made-to-order pasta and salad concept based in California. The acquisition followed several months of test marketing of the multibranding of Pasta Bravo and Pizza Hut.

Novak also initiated a plan to reduce the company-owned restaurant base by either closing poorly performing restaurants or selling company restaurants to individual franchisees. In 1997, 38 per cent of the restaurant base (KFC, Pizza Hut, and Taco Bell) was company-owned. By early 2005, company-owned restaurants had declined to 25 per cent of the total. The long-term goal was to reduce the company base to 20 per cent. The firm's new emphasis on supporting individual franchisees had an immediate effect on morale. In 1997, the year of the divestiture, the company recorded a loss of $111 million in net income. In 2004, net income was $740 million on sales of $9.0 billion, a return on sales of 8.2 per cent.

Fast-food industry

The National Restaurant Association (NRA) estimated that US food service sales increased by 5.5 per cent to $454 billion in 2004. More than 858,000 restaurants made up the U.S. restaurant industry and employed

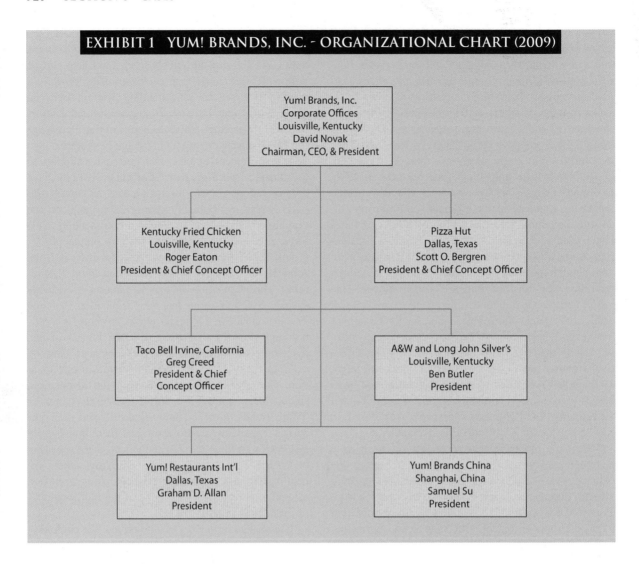

EXHIBIT 1   YUM! BRANDS, INC. - ORGANIZATIONAL CHART (2009)

Yum! Brands, Inc.
Corporate Offices
Louisville, Kentucky
David Novak
Chairman, CEO, & President

Kentucky Fried Chicken
Louisville, Kentucky
Roger Eaton
President & Chief Concept Officer

Pizza Hut
Dallas, Texas
Scott O. Bergren
President & Chief Concept Officer

Taco Bell Irvine, California
Greg Creed
President & Chief
Concept Officer

A&W and Long John Silver's
Louisville, Kentucky
Ben Butler
President

Yum! Restaurants Int'l
Dallas, Texas
Graham D. Allan
President

Yum! Brands China
Shanghai, China
Samuel Su
President

12 million people. Sales were highest in the full-service, sit-down sector, which grew 5.4 per cent to $157 billion. Fast-food sales grew by 5.9 per cent to $128 billion. Together, the full-service and fast-food segments made up about 63 per cent of all US food service sales.

Major fast-food segments

Eight major segments made up the fast-food segment of the restaurant industry: sandwich chains, pizza chains, family restaurants, grill buffet chains, dinner houses, chicken chains, non-dinner concepts, and other chains. Sales data for the leading chains in each segment are shown in Exhibit 2. Most striking is the dominance of McDonald's, which had sales of more 2than $24 billion in 2004. Sandwich chains made up the largest segment of the fast-food market.

McDonald's controlled 35 per cent of the sandwich segment, while Burger King ran a distant second with an 11 per cent market share. Sandwich chains, however, were struggling because of continued price discounting that lowered profits. The threat of obesity lawsuits and increased customer demand for more healthy food items and better service lowered demand for the traditional hamburger, fries, and soft drink combinations. Many chains attempted to attract new customers through price discounting. Instead of drawing in new customers, however, discounting merely lowered profit margins.

By 2005, most chains had abandoned price discounting and began to focus on improved service and product quality. McDonald's, Taco Bell, and Hardee's were particularly successful. They slowed new restaurant development, improved drive-thru service, and introduced a variety of new menu items. To meet

EXHIBIT 2 TOP U.S. FAST-FOOD RESTAURANTS (RANKED BY 2004 SALES, $000s)

Sandwich Chains	Sales	Change
McDonald's	24,391	10.3%
Burger King	7,920	3.1
Wendy's	7,870	5.6
Subway	6,270	10.2
Taco Bell	5,700	6.6
Arby's	2,830	4.4
Sonic Drive-In	2,666	13.0
Jack in the Box	2,570	8.9
Dairy Queen	2,360	9.0
Hardee's	1,702	2.4
Other Chains	5,530	19.8
Total Segment	69,809	8.8%

Pizza Chains	Sales	Change
Pizza Hut	5,200	3.3%
Domino's	3,173	5.7
Papa John's	1,727	0.5
Little Caesars	1,235	2.9
Chuck E. Cheese's	521	9.4
CiCi's Pizza	435	14.2
Total Segment	12,291	4.1 %

Family Restaurants	Sales	Change
Denny's	2,191	2.8%
IHOP	1,867	11.4
Cracker Barrel	1,574	6.3
Bob Evans	997	4.5
Waffle House	825	4.6
Perkins	787	0.0
Other Chains	1,842	4.0
Total Segment	10,083	5.2%

Grill Buffet Chains	Sales	Change
Golden Corral	1,340	7.5 %
Ryan's	765	-6.0
Ponderosa	516	-4.0
Total Segment	2,621	0.9%

Grill Buffet Chains	Sales	Change
Dinner Houses	Sales	Change
Applebee's	3,888	10.5 %
Chili's	2,875	14.8
Outback Steakhouse	2,539	6.3
Red Lobster	2,456	3.0
Olive Garden	2,283	5.5
T.G.I. Friday's	1,862	4.0
Ruby Tuesday	1,560	7.6
Cheesecake Factory	865	25.5
Romano's	740	5.9
Hooter's	731	9.1
Other Chains	9,566	16.8
Total Segment	26,365	10.4%

Chicken Chains	Sales	Change
KFC	5,000	1.3%
Chick-fil-A	1,746	13.8
Popeyes	1,338	5.0
Church's	691	-1.3
Boston Market	675	4.5
El Pollo Loco	427	7.9
Bojangles'	422	13.5
Total Segment	10,299	4.5%

Other Dinner Chains	Sales	Change
Panera Bread	1,163	28.1 %
Long John Silver's	800	3.0
Disney Theme Parks	756	7.0
Captain D's Seafood	525	3.8
Old Country Buffet	434	-2.7
Total Segment	3,678	10.0 %

Non-Dinner Concepts	Sales	Change
Starbuck's	4,060	30.9%
Dunkin' Donuts	3,380	13.6
7-Eleven	1,505	6.7
Krispy Kreme	975	1.9
Baskin-Robbins	535	4.9
Total Segment	10,455	16.8%

Source: Nation's Restaurant News.

health trends, McDonald's introduced premium salads and fruit salads while Burger King introduced a new line of low-fat, grilled chicken sandwiches. In contrast, Hardee's introduced a new 'Thickburger' menu that included -, half-pound and pound 'lean' Angus beef burgers in an attempt to distinguish itself from other hamburger chains. The shift from price discounting to new product introductions increased average ticket sales and helped sandwich chains improve profitability in 2004.

Dinner houses made up the second largest and fastest growing fast-food segment. Sales in the dinner house segment increased by ten per cent in 2004. Much of the growth in dinner houses came from new unit construction in suburban areas and small towns. Applebee's, Chili's, Outback Steakhouse, Red Lobster, and Olive Garden dominated the segment. Each chain generated sales of more than $2 billion in 2004. The fastest growing dinner houses, however, were newer chains generating less than $700 million in sales, such as Buffalo Wild Wings Grill & Bar, Texas Roadhouse, P. F. Chang's China Bistro, The Cheesecake Factory, and Red Robin Burgers & Spirits Emporium. Each chain was increasing sales at a 25 per cent annual rate. Dinner houses continued to benefit from rising household incomes in the United States. As incomes rose, families were able to move up from quick-service restaurants to more upscale, higher priced dinner houses. In addition, higher incomes enabled many professionals to purchase higher priced homes in new suburban developments, thereby providing additional opportunities for dinner houses to build new restaurants in unsaturated areas.

Increased growth among dinner houses came at the expense of sandwich chains, pizza and chicken chains, grilled buffet chains, and family restaurants. 'Too many restaurants chasing the same customers' was responsible for much of the slower growth in these other fast-food categories. Sales growth within each segment, however, differed from one chain to another. In the family segment, for example, Denny's (the segment leader), Perkins, and Shoney's shut down poorly performing restaurants while Waffle House, IHOP, Bob Evans, and Cracker Barrel expanded their bases. In the pizza segment, Pizza Hut and Papa John's closed underperforming restaurants while Little Caesars, Chuck E. Cheese's, and CiCi's constructed new restaurants. The hardest hit segment was grilled buffet chains. Declining sales caused both Sizzlin' and Western Sizzlin' to drop out of the list of Top 100 chains, leaving only three chains in the Top 100 (Golden Coral, Ryan's, and Ponderosa). Dinner

houses, because of their more upscale atmosphere and higher ticket items, were better positioned to take advantage of the aging and wealthier U.S. population. Even dinner houses, however, faced the prospect of market saturation and increased competition in the near future.

Chicken segment

KFC continued to dominate the chicken segment with sales of $5.0 billion in 2004, about half of chicken segment sales (see Exhibit 3). Its nearest competitor, Chick-fil-A, ran a distant second with sales of $1.7 billion. KFC's leadership in the U.S. market was so extensive that it had fewer opportunities to expand its US restaurant base, which was only growing at about one per cent per year. Despite its dominance, KFC was slowly losing market share as other chicken chains increased sales at a faster rate. KFC's share of chicken segment sales fell from 64 per cent in 1993 to less than 49 per cent in 2004, an 11-year drop of 15 per cent (see Exhibit 4). During the same period, Chick-fil-A and Boston Market increased their combined market share by 14 per cent. In the 1990s, many industry analysts predicted that Boston Market would challenge KFC for market leadership. Boston Market was a new chain that emphasized roasted rather than fried chicken. It successfully created the image of an upscale deli offering healthy, 'home-style' alternatives to fried chicken. To distinguish itself from more traditional fast-food, it refused to construct drive-thrus and established most of its units outside of shopping malls rather than at major city intersections.

On the surface, it appeared that Boston Market and Chick-fil-A's market share gains were achieved by taking customers away from KFC. Another look at the data, however, reveals that KFC's sales have grown at a stable rate during the last ten years. Boston Market, rather than drawing customers away from KFC, appealed to new consumers who did not regularly frequent KFC and wanted non-fried chicken alternatives. Boston Market was able to expand the chicken segment beyond its traditional emphasis on fried chicken by offering non-fried chicken products that appealed to this new consumer group. After aggressively growing its restaurant base through 1997, however, Boston Market fell on hard times as it was unable to handle mounting debt problems. It soon entered bankruptcy proceedings. McDonald's acquired Boston Market in 2000. The acquisition followed earlier acquisitions of Donatos Pizza in 1999 and Chipotle Mexican Grill in 1998. McDonald's hoped the

EXHIBIT 3 TOP CHICKEN CHAINS

	1998	1999	2000	2001	2002	2003	2004
Sales ($ millions)							
KFC	4,200	4,300	4,400	4,700	4,800	4,936	5,000
Chick-fil-A	764	943	1,082	1,242	1,373	1,534	1,746
Popeyes	843	986	1,077	1,179	1,215	1,274	1,338
Church's	620	705	699	721	720	700	691
Boston Market	929	855	685	640	641	646	675
El Pollo Loco	245	275	305	339	364	396	427
Bojangles'	250	270	298	333	347	375	422
Total	7,851	8,334	8,546	9,154	9,460	9,861	10,299
Sales per unit ($ 000s)							
KFC	823	822	820	871	877	898	905
Chick-fil-A	941	1,051	1,130	1,225	1,278	1,394	1,507
Popeyes	790	847	863	889	880	897	917
Church's	561	598	574	581	584	564	563
Boston Market	1,045	997	962	974	982	1,009	1,071
El Pollo Loco	939	1,019	1,094	1,157	1,190	1,277	1,343
Bojangles'	980	1,020	1,072	1,189	1,188	1,215	1,284
Total	827	845	850	896	909	1,038	1,084

acquisitions would help it expand its US restaurant base as there were few opportunities to expand the McDonald's concept. Chick-fil-A's early strategy was to establish sit-down restaurants in shopping malls. As more malls added food courts, however, malls became less enthusiastic about allocating separate store space to restaurants. As a result, Chick-fil-A began to open smaller units in shopping mall food courts and to build free-standing restaurants that competed head-to-head with existing chicken chains. Despite market share gains by Boston Market and Chick-fil-A, however, KFC's customer base has remained loyal to the KFC brand because of its unique taste.

The maturation of the US fast-food industry increased the intensity of competition within the chicken segment. With the exception of Chick-fil-A, most chains were no longer aggressively opening new restaurants. Restaurant profits were also threatened by rising input costs. Chicken prices, which represented about one-half of total food costs, increased dramatically in 2004. Boneless chicken breast, for example, cost $1.20 per pound in early 2001. By 2004, the price had risen to $2.50 per pound, an increase of more than 100 per cent. Chicken chains attempted to differentiate themselves based on unique product and customer

characteristics. KFC used animated images of the 'Colonel' to drive home its home-style image. It added new menu boards and introduced new products such as Oven Roasted Strips, Roasted Twister Sandwich Wraps, Popcorn Chicken, Honey BBQ Chicken, and Spicy BBQ Wings. Boston Market experimented with home delivery and began to sell through supermarkets. Popeyes continued to re-image its restaurants with its 'Heritage' design that included a balcony over the drive-thru, Cajun-style murals, and new signage. It recently introduced a Chicken Strip Po' Boy sandwich to expand its New Orleans-style menu of spicy chicken, jambalaya, etouffée, and gumbo. Bojangles' also promoted a Cajun décor but focused more heavily on core chicken products such as its Cajun Fried Chicken, Cajun Filet Sandwich, and Buffalo Bites. El Pollo Loco served marinated, flame-broiled chicken and other Mexican food entrees such as chicken burritos, tostada salads, and chicken nachos. Church's focused on adding drive-thru service while it also emphasized its 'made-from-scratch', Southern-style fried chicken and side dishes such as corn-on-the-cob, fried okra, and macaroni and cheese. Chick-fil-A continued to build free-standing restaurants to expand beyond shopping malls.

EXHIBIT 4   TOP CHICKEN CHAINS - MARKET SHARE

	KFC	Chick-fil-A	Popeyes	Church's	Boston Market	Pollo Loco	Bojangles'
Total							
1994	60.7	7.8	10.6	8.0	6.6	3.1	3.2
1995	56.6	7.7	10.1	7.7	11.6	3.0	3.3
1996	54.2	7.9	9.3	7.3	15.3	3.0	3.0
1997	52.5	8.5	9.5	7.6	15.8	3.1	3.0
1998	53.4	9.7	10.7	7.9	11.8	3.1	3.2
1999	51.6	11.3	11.8	8.5	10.3	3.3	3.2
2000	51.4	12.7	12.6	8.2	8.0	3.6	3.5
2001	51.3	13.6	12.9	7.9	7.0	3.7	3.6
2002	50.8	14.5	12.8	7.6	6.8	3.8	3.7
2003	50.1	15.6	12.9	7.1	6.6	4.0	3.8
2004	48.5	17.0	13.0	6.7	6.6	4.1	4.1

Trends in the restaurant industry

A number of demographic and societal trends influenced the demand for food eaten outside of the home. During the last two decades, rising incomes, greater affluence among a greater percentage of American households, higher divorce rates, and the fact that people married later in life contributed to the rising number of single households and the demand for fast-food. More than 50 per cent of women worked outside of the home, a dramatic increase since 1970. This number was expected to rise to 65 per cent by 2010. Double-income households contributed to rising household incomes and increased the number of times families ate out. Less time to prepare meals inside the home added to this trend. Countering these trends, however, was a slower growth rate of the US population and an overpopulation of fast-food chains that increased consumer alternatives and intensified competition.

Baby Boomers 35 to 50 years of age constituted the largest consumer group for fast-food restaurants. Generation X'ers (ages 25 to 34) and the 'Mature' category (ages 51 to 64) made up the second and third largest groups. As consumers aged, they became less enamoured with fast-food and were more likely to trade up to more expensive restaurants such as dinner houses and full-service restaurants. Sales of many Mexican restaurants, which were extremely popular during the 1980s, began to slow as Japanese, Indian, and Vietnamese restaurants became more fashionable. Ethnic foods were rising in popularity as US immigrants, who constituted 12 per cent of the US population in 2005, looked for establishments that sold their native foods.

Labour was the top operational challenge of US restaurant chains. Restaurants relied heavily on teenagers and college age workers. Twenty per cent of all employed teenagers worked in food service, compared to only four per cent of all employed men over the age of 18 and six per cent of all employed women. As the US population aged, fewer young workers were available to fill food service jobs. The short supply of high school and college students also meant they had greater opportunities outside of food service. Turnover rates were notoriously high. The National Restaurant Association estimated that about 96 per cent of all fast-food workers quit within a year, compared to about 84 per cent of employees in full-service restaurants.

Labour costs made up about 30 per cent of the fast-food chain's total costs, second only to food and beverage costs. To deal with the decreased supply of employees in the 16 to 24 age category, many restaurants were forced to hire lower quality workers, which affected service and restaurant cleanliness. To improve quality and service, restaurants increasingly hired elderly employees who were interested in returning to the work force. To attract more workers, especially the elderly, restaurants offered health insurance, non-contributory pension plans, and profit-sharing benefits that were generally not given only ten years before. To combat high turnover rates, restaurants also turned to better training programmes and mentoring systems that paired new employees with more experienced ones. Mentoring systems were particularly helpful in increasing the learning curve of new workers and providing better camaraderie among employees.

Intense competition in the mature restaurant industry made it difficult for restaurants to increase prices sufficiently to cover the increased cost of labour. Consumers made decisions about where to eat partially based on price. As a result, profit margins were squeezed. To reduce costs, restaurants eliminated low-margin food items, increased portion sizes, and improved product value to offset price increases. Restaurants also attempted to increase consumer traffic through discounting, by accepting coupons from competitors, by offering two-for-one specials, and by making limited-time offerings.

Technology was increasingly used to lower costs and improve efficiencies. According to the National Restaurant Association, restaurant operators viewed computers as their number one tool for improving efficiency. Computers were used to improve labour scheduling, accounting, payroll, sales analysis, and inventory control. Most restaurant chains also used point-of-sale systems that recorded the selected menu items and gave the cashier a breakdown of food items and the ticket price. These systems reduced serving times and cashier accuracy. Other chains like McDonald's and Carl's Jr. converted to new food preparation systems that allowed them to prepare food more accurately and a variety of sandwiches using the same process.

Higher costs and poor availability of prime real estate was another trend that negatively affected profitability. A plot of land suitable for a freestanding restaurant cost between $1.5 and $2.5 million. Leasing was a less costly alternative to buying. Nevertheless, market saturation decreased per store sales as newer units cannibalized sales from existing units. As a result, most food chains began to expand their US restaurant bases into alternative distribution channels in hospitals, airports, colleges, highway rest areas, gas stations, shopping mall food courts, and large retail stores or by dual branding with other fast-food concepts.

The global fast-food industry

Exhibit 5 lists the world's thirty-five largest restaurant chains. As the US market matured, more restaurants turned to international markets to expand sales. Foreign markets were attractive because of their large customer bases and comparatively little competition. McDonald's, for example, operated 48 restaurants for every one million US residents. Outside of the United States, it operated only one restaurant for every five million residents. McDonald's, KFC, Burger King, and Pizza Hut were the earliest and most aggressive chains to expand abroad beginning in the 1960s. By early 2005, at least 35 chains had expanded into a least one foreign country. McDonald's operated more than 13 000 US units and 17 000 foreign units in the 119 countries. With the acquisition of A&W and Long John Silver's, however, Yum! Brands became the world's largest restaurant chain in 2003. It operated more than 21 000 US and close to 33 000 non-US KFC, Pizza Hut, Taco Bell, A&W, and Long John Silver's restaurants in 88 countries. Because of their early expansion abroad, McDonald's, KFC, Burger King, and Pizza Hut had all developed strong brand names and managerial expertise operating in international markets. This made them formidable competitors for fast-food chains investing abroad for the first time. Subway, TCBY, and Domino's were more recent global competitors but were expanding more aggressively than McDonald's or KFC. By 2004, each was operating in more than 65 countries.

The global fast-food industry had a distinctly American flavour. Twenty-eight chains (80 per cent of the total) were headquartered in the United States. US chains had the advantage of a large domestic market and ready acceptance by the American consumer. European firms had less success developing the fast-food concept because Europeans were more inclined to frequent mid-scale restaurants, where they spent several hours enjoying multi-course meals in a formal setting. KFC had trouble breaking into the German market during the 1970s and 1980s because Germans were not accustomed to buying take-out or ordering food over the counter. McDonald's had greater success penetrating the German market because it made a number of changes to its menu and operating procedures to appeal to German tastes. German beer, for example, was served in all of McDonald's restaurants in Germany. In France, McDonald's used a different sauce on its Big Mac sandwich that appealed to the French palate. KFC had more success in Asia and Latin America, where chicken was a traditional dish.

Aside from cultural factors, international business carried risks not present in the domestic market. Long distances between headquarters and foreign franchises made it more difficult to control the quality of individual restaurants. Large distances also caused servicing and support problems. Transportation and other resource costs were higher than in the domestic

EXHIBIT 5 THE WORLD'S 35 LARGEST FAST-FOOD CHAINS IN 2004

	Franchise	Corporate Headquarters	Home Country	Countries
1.	McDonald's	Oakbrook, Illinois	U.S.A.	121
2.	KFC	Louisville, Kentucky	U.S.A.	99
3.	Pizza Hut	Dallas, Texas	U.S.A.	92
4.	Subway Sandwiches	Milford, Connecticut	U.S.A.	74
5.	TCBY	Little Rock, Arkansas	U.S.A.	67
6.	Domino's Pizza	Ann Arbor, Michigan	U.S.A.	65
7.	Burger King	Miami, Florida	U.S.A.	58
8.	T.G.I. Friday's	Dallas, Texas	U.S.A.	53
9.	Baskin Robbins	Glendale, California	U.S.A.	52
10.	Dunkin' Donuts	Randolph, Massachusetts	U.S.A.	40
11.	Wendy's	Dublin, Ohio	U.S.A.	34
12.	Chili's Grill & Bar	Dallas, Texas	U.S.A.	22
13.	Dairy Queen	Edina, Michigan	U.S.A.	22
14.	Little Caesar's Pizza	Detroit, Michigan	U.S.A.	22
15.	Popeyes	Atlanta, Georgia	U.S.A.	22
16.	Outback Steakhouse	Tampa, Florida	U.S.A.	20
17.	A&W Restaurants	Lexington, Kentucky	U.S.A.	17
18.	PizzaExpress	London, England	U.K.	16
19.	Carl's Jr.	Anaheim, California	U.S.A.	14
20.	Church's Chicken	Atlanta, Georgia	U.S.A.	12
21.	Taco Bell	Irvine, California	U.S.A.	12
22.	Hardee's	Rocky Mt., North Carolina	U.S.A.	11
23.	Applebee's	Overland Park, Kansas	U.S.A.	9
24.	Sizzler	Los Angeles, California	U.S.A.	9
25.	Arby's	Fr. Lauderdale, Florida	U.S.A.	7
26.	Denny's	Spartanburg, South Carolina	U.S.A.	7
27.	Skylark	Tokyo	Japan	7
28.	Lotteria	Seoul	Korea	5
29.	Taco Time	Eugene, Oregon	U.S.A.	5
30.	Mos Burger	Tokyo	Japan	4
31.	Orange Julius	Edina, Minnesota	U.S.A.	4
32.	Yoshinoya	Tokyo	Japan	4
33.	IHOP	Glendale, California	U.S.A.	3
34.	Quick Restaurants	Brussels	Belgium	3
35.	Red Lobster	Orlando, Florida	U.S.A.	3

market. In addition, time, cultural, and language differences increased communication and operational problems. As a result, most restaurant chains limited expansion to their domestic market as long as they were able to meet profit and growth objectives. As companies gained greater expertise abroad, they turned to profitable international markets as a means of expanding restaurant bases and increasing sales, profits, and market share. Worldwide demand for fast-food was expected to grow rapidly during the next two decades as rising per capita incomes eating out more affordable for greater numbers of consumers. In addition, the development of the internet was quickly breaking down communication and language barriers. Greater numbers of children were growing up with computers in their homes and schools. As a result, teenagers in Germany, Brazil, Japan, and the United States were equally likely to be able to converse about the internet. The internet also exposed more teenagers to the same companies and products, which enabled firms to quickly develop global brands and a worldwide consumer base.

Kentucky Fried Chicken corporation

Many of KFC's problems during the 1980s and 1990s surrounded its limited menu and inability to quickly bring new products to market. The popularity of its Original Recipe Chicken allowed KFC to expand through the 1980s without significant competition from other chicken chains. As a result, new product introductions were not a critical part of KFC's business strategy. KFC suffered one of its most serious setbacks in 1989 as it prepared to introduce a chicken sandwich to its menu. KFC was still experimenting with the chicken sandwich concept when McDonald's rolled out its McChicken sandwich. By beating KFC to the market, McDonald's developed strong consumer awareness for its sandwich. This significantly increased KFC's cost of developing awareness for its own sandwich, which KFC introduced several months later. KFC eventually withdrew the sandwich because of low sales. Today, about 95 per cent of chicken sandwiches are sold through traditional hamburger chains.

KFC's focus on fried chicken ('chicken-on-the-bone') became a serious problem by the 1990s as the US fast-food industry matured. In order to expand sales, restaurant chains began to diversify their menus to include non-core products, thereby cutting into the business of other fast-food segments. For example, hamburger and pizza chains, family restaurants, and dinner houses all introduced a variety of chicken items such as chicken sandwiches and chicken wings to expand their consumer bases. This made it difficult for KFC to increase per unit sales. By 2003, McDonald's boasted a menu that included hamburgers, chicken sandwiches, fish sandwiches, burritos, a full line of breakfast items, ice cream, and milkshakes. By diversifying its menu, McDonald's was able to raise annual sales to $1.5 million per restaurant. This compared with KFC's average restaurant sales of $883 000. In 2003, Yum! Brands conducted market research showing that customers preferred multiple menu offerings over single-concept menus like chicken or pizza by a 6-to-1 margin.

KFC's short-term strategy was to diversify its menu. It rolled out a buffet that included over 30 dinner, salad, and dessert items. The buffet was most successful in rural locations and suburbs but less successful in urban areas where restaurant space was limited. It then introduced Colonel's Crispy Strips and a line of chicken sandwiches that complemented its core fried chicken products. More recent product innovations include Popcorn Chicken, Chunky Chicken Pot Pie, and Twisters (a flour tortilla filled with chunks of chicken). To increase brand awareness for these new products, KFC introduced a new television campaign featuring a cartoon caricature of Colonel Sanders stating 'I'm a Chicken Genius!' It also featured Jason Alexander from the television sitcom 'Seinfeld' promoting Popcorn Chicken using the slogan 'There's fast food, then there's KFC.' Sandwiches and other non-core items, however, cannibalized sales of KFC's core chicken products. Most importantly, it did little to address the consumer's desire for greater menu variety beyond chicken.

Multibrand strategy

By 2000, the company began to open '2-in-1' units that sold both KFC and Taco Bell or KFC and Pizza Hut in the same location. Most of KFC's sales (64 per cent) and Pizza Hut's sales (61 per cent) were driven by dinner, while most of Taco Bell's sales (50 per cent) were driven by lunch (50 per cent). The combination of KFC and Taco Bell was a natural success because it increased per unit sales simply by filling up counter space left empty by KFC at lunch or Taco Bell at dinner. It became increasingly apparent, however, that the real value of combining restaurant concepts was in attracting greater numbers of consumers who wanted more menu variety. The acquisition of A&W and Long John Silver's in 2002 provided additional opportunities to create a variety of combinations of five highly differentiated fast-food category leaders. By 2005, Yum! Brands operated nearly 3000 multibrand restaurants worldwide that included KFC/Taco Bell, KFC/A&W, Taco Bell/Pizza Hut, and A&W/Long John Silver's. The company believed there was potential for opening 13 000 multibrand restaurants in the United States alone. The increase in per unit sales that resulted from multibranding meant that new restaurants could be opened in more expensive locations and lower population areas than were profitable with stand-alone restaurants.

International operations

KFC's early experience operating abroad put it in a strong position to take advantage of the growing trend toward global expansion. By early 2005, more than 58 per cent of KFC's restaurants were located outside of the United States. KFC was the most global of the five brands managed by Yum! Brands, Inc. The other brands had a significantly smaller percentage of their restaurant base outside of the United States – Pizza Hut (37 per cent), Taco Bell (four per cent), Long John Silver's (two per cent), and A&W (22 per cent). Historically, franchises made up a large portion of KFC's international restaurant base because franchises were owned and operated by local entrepreneurs who had a deeper understanding of local language, culture, customs, law, financial markets, and marketing characteristics. Franchising was also a good strategy for establishing a presence in smaller countries like Grenada, Bermuda, and Suriname, whose small populations could only support a single restaurant. The costs of operating company-owned restaurants were prohibitively high in these smaller markets. Of the 7000 KFC restaurants located outside of the United States, 77 per cent were franchisees, licensed restaurants, or joint ventures. In larger markets such as Mexico, China, Canada, Australia, Puerto Rico, Korea, Thailand, and the United Kingdom, there was a stronger emphasis on building company-owned restaurants. By coordinating purchasing, recruiting, training, financing, and advertising in these larger markets, fixed costs could be spread over a larger restaurant base. KFC could also maintain tighter control over product quality and customer service.

Latin American strategy

KFC operated 717 restaurants in Latin America in 2005 (Exhibit 6). Its primary presence was in Mexico, Puerto Rico, and the Caribbean. KFC established subsidiaries in Mexico and Puerto Rico in the late 1960s and expanded through company-owned restaurants. Franchises were used to penetrate countries in the Caribbean whose market size prevented KFC from profitably operating company-owned restaurants. Subsidiaries were later established in the Virgin Islands, Venezuela, and Brazil. KFC had planned to expand into these regions using company-owned restaurants. The Venezuelan subsidiary, however, was later closed because of the high costs of operating the small subsidiary. KFC had opened eight restaurants in Brazil but closed them by 2000 because it lacked the cash flow needed to support an expansion programme

in that market. Franchises were opened in other markets that had good growth potential such as Chile, Ecuador, and Peru. In 2003, KFC signed a joint venture agreement with a Brazilian partner that had a deeper understanding of the Brazilian market. KFC hoped the joint venture would help it reestablish a presence in Brazil.

KFC's early entry into Latin America gave it a leadership position over McDonald's in Mexico and the Caribbean. It also had an edge in Ecuador and Peru. KFC's Latin America strategy represented a classic internationalization strategy. It first expanded into Mexico and Puerto Rico because of their geographical proximity as well as political and economic ties to the United States. KFC then expanded its franchise system throughout the Caribbean, gradually moving away from its US base as its experience in Latin America grew. Only after it had established a leadership position in Mexico and the Caribbean did it venture into South America. McDonald's pursued a different strategy. It was late to expand into the region. Despite a rapid restaurant construction program in Mexico during the 1990s, McDonald's still lagged behind KFC. Therefore, McDonald's initiated a first mover strategy in Brazil and Argentina, large markets where KFC had no presence. By 2003, 55 per cent of McDonald's restaurants in Latin America were located in the two countries. Wendy's pursued a different strategy. It first expanded into Puerto Rico, the Caribbean, and Central America because of their geographical proximity to the United States. Wendy's late entry into Latin America, however, made it difficult to penetrate Mexico, where KFC, McDonald's, and Burger King had already established strong positions. Wendy's announced plans to build 100 Wendy's restaurants in Mexico by 2010; however, its primary objective was to establish strong positions in Venezuela and Argentina, where most U.S. fast-food chains had not yet been established.

Country risk assessment in Latin America

Latin America comprised some 50 countries, island nations, and principalities that were settled primarily by the Spanish, Portuguese, French, Dutch, and British during the 1500s and 1600s. Spanish was spoken in most countries, the most notable exception being Brazil where the official language is Portuguese. Catholicism was the major religion, though Methodist missionaries successfully exported Protestantism into many regions of Latin America in the 1800s, most

EXHIBIT 6 LATIN AMERICA RESTAURANT COUNT				
	McDonald's	*Burger King*	*Wendy's*	*KFC*
Mexico	261	154	16	274
Puerto Rico	112	163	46	97
Caribbean Islands	29	55	20	134
Central America	99	104	38	32
Subtotal	501	476	120	537
% Total	31%	82%	68%	83%
Colombia	25	0	3	9
Ecuador	10	13	0	39
Peru	10	12	0	25
Venezuela	129	20	33	5
Other Andean	45	6	0	5
Andean Region	219	51	36	83
% Total	14%	9%	25%	13%
Argentina	203	25	21	0
Brazil	584	0	0	0
Chile	70	23	0	30
Paraguay + Uruguay	28	6	0	0
Southern Cone	885	54	21	30
% Total	55%	9%	15%	5%
Latin America	1,605	581	143	650

notably on the coast of Brazil. Despite commonalities in language, religion, and history, however, political and economic policies differed significantly from one country to another. Frequent changes in governments and economic instability increased the uncertainty of doing business in the region.

Most US and Canadian companies realized that they could not overlook the region. Geographical proximity made communications and travel easier and the North American Trade Agreement (NAFTA) eliminated tariffs on goods shipped between Canada, Mexico, and the United States. A customs union agreement signed in 1991 (Mercosur) between Argentina, Paraguay, Uruguay, and Brazil eliminated tariffs on trade among those four countries. Other countries such as Chile had also established free trade policies that were stimulating strong growth. The primary task for companies investing in the region was to accurately assess the different risks of doing business in Latin America and to select the proper countries for investment. Miller developed a framework for analysing country risk that was a useful tool for

evaluating different countries for future investment. He argued that firms must examine country, industry, and firm factors to fully assess country risk.

Country factors addressed the risks associated with changes in the country's political and economic environment that potentially affected the firm's ability to conduct business. They included:

1. Political risk (e.g., war, revolution, changes in government, price controls, tariffs and other trade restrictions, appropriation of assets, government regulations, and restrictions on the repatriation of profits),

2. Economic risk (e.g., inflation, high interest rates, foreign exchange rate volatility, balance of trade movements, social unrest, riots, and terrorism), and

3. Natural risk (e.g., rainfall, hurricanes, earthquakes, and volcanic activity).

Industry factors addressed changes in industry structure that inhibited the firm's ability to successfully compete in its industry. They included:

1. Supplier risk (e.g., changes in quality, shifts in supply, and changes in supplier power),

2. Product market risk (e.g., consumer tastes and availability of substitute products), and

3. Competitive risk (e.g., rivalry among competitors, new market entrants, and new product innovations).

Firm factors examined the firm's ability to control its internal operations. They included:

1. Labour risk (e.g., labour unrest, absenteeism, employee turnover, and labour strikes),

2. Supplier risk (e.g. raw material shortages and unpredictable price changes),

3. Trade secret risk (e.g., protection of trade secrets and intangible assets),

4. Credit risk (e.g., problems collecting receivables), and

5. Behavioural risk (e.g., control over franchise operations, product quality and consistency, service quality, and restaurant cleanliness).

Many US companies considered Mexico to be one of the most attractive investment locations in Latin America. Mexico's population of 105 million exceeded one-third of that of the United States. It was three times larger than Canada's 32 million. Prior to 1994, Mexico levied high tariffs on many goods imported from the United States. Other goods were regulated by quotas and licensing requirements that made Mexican goods more expensive. As a result, many US consumers purchased less expensive products from Asia or Europe. In 1994, the long-awaited North American Free Trade Agreement (NAFTA) between Canada, the United States, and Mexico went into effect. NAFTA eliminated tariffs on goods traded among the three countries and created a trading bloc with a larger population and gross domestic product than the European Union. The elimination of tariffs led to an immediate increase in trade between Mexico and the United States. In 1995, only one year after NAFTA was signed, Mexico posted its first balance of trade surplus in six years. A large part of that surplus was attributed to greater exports to the United States. By 2003, almost 85 per cent of Mexico's exports were purchased by US consumers. In turn, about 68 per cent of Mexico's total imports came from the United States.

US investment in Mexico also increased significantly after NAFTA was signed, largely in the Maquiladoras located along the US–Mexican border. With the elimination of import tariffs, US firms could produce or assemble goods and transport them back into the United States more quickly and at significantly less cost than they could transport goods from Asia or Europe. Mexico's largest exports to the United States were automobiles, automobile parts, crude oil, petroleum products, and natural gas. A large portion of Mexico's automobile and auto part production was produced in US-owned plants. The cost of transporting automobiles back into the United States was more than offset by the lower cost of labour in Mexico. Today, 2600 US firms operate in Mexico and account for 60 per cent of all foreign direct investment in that country.

Despite the benefits, many Mexican farmers and unskilled workers strongly opposed NAFTA and US investment. The day after NAFTA went into effect, rebels rioted in the southern Mexican province of Chiapas on the Guatemalan border. After four days of fighting, Mexican troops drove the rebels out of several towns the rebels had earlier seized. Around 150 people were killed. The Mexican government negotiated a cease-fire with the rebels; however, armed clashes between rebel groups protesting poverty and lack of land rights continued to be a problem. Another protest followed the signing of NAFTA when 30 to 40 masked men attacked a McDonald's restaurant in the tourist section of Mexico City. The men threw cash registers to the floor, smashed windows, overturned tables, and spray-painted 'No to Fascism' and 'Yankee Go Home' on the walls.

Most Mexicans (70 per cent) lived in urban areas such as Mexico City, Guadalajara, and Monterrey. Mexico City's population of 18 million made it one of the most populated areas in Latin America. Many U.S. firms had operations in or around Mexico City. The fast-food industry was well developed in Mexico's cities. The leading US fast-food chains already had significant restaurant bases in Mexico, most importantly KFC (274 restaurants), McDonald's (261), Pizza Hut (174), Burger King (154), and Subway (71). Mexican consumers readily accepted the fast-food concept. Chicken was also a staple product in Mexico and helped explain KFC's wide popularity. Mexico's large population and ready acceptance of fast-food represented a significant opportunity for fast-food chains. Competition, however, was intense.

Despite Mexico's relative economic stability during the late 1990s and early 2000s, Mexico had a history of high inflation, foreign exchange controls, and government regulations. These often affected foreign firms' ability to make a profit. In 1989, President Salinas attempted to reduce high inflation by controlling the peso–dollar exchange rate, allowing the peso to depreciate by only one peso per day against the dollar. He also instituted price and wage controls. Firms like KFC were unable to raise prices and were closely monitored by Mexican authorities. However, smaller firms that supplied KFC and other US firms with raw materials continued to charge higher prices to compensate for inflation. KFC was soon operating at a loss, setting off heated debate in PepsiCo's headquarters. PepsiCo's finance group wanted to halt further restaurant construction in Mexico until economic stability improved. PepsiCo's marketing group wanted to continue expansion despite losses to protect its leading market share in Mexico. PepsiCo's marketing group eventually won the debate and KFC continued to build new restaurants in Mexico during the period.

When Ernesto Zedillo became Mexico's president in December 1994, one of his objectives was to continue the stability of prices, wages, and exchange rates achieved by ex-president Carlos Salinas. This stability, however, was achieved primarily on the basis of price, wage, and foreign exchange controls. While giving the appearance of stability, an over-valued peso continued to encourage imports that exacerbated Mexico's balance of trade deficit. At the same time, Mexican exports became less competitive on world markets. Anticipating a devaluation of the peso, investors began to move capital into US dollar investments. On December 19, 1994, Zedillo announced that the peso would be allowed to depreciate by an additional 15 per cent per year against the dollar. Within two days, continued pressure on the peso forced Zedillo to allow the peso to float freely against the dollar.

By mid-January 1995, the peso had lost 35 per cent of its value against the dollar and the Mexican stock market had plunged 20 per cent. By the end of the year, the peso had depreciated from 3.1 pesos per dollar to 7.6 pesos per dollar. In order to thwart a possible default by Mexico, the U.S. government, International Monetary Fund, and World Bank pledged $25 billion in emergency loans. Shortly thereafter, Zedillo announced an emergency economic package called the 'pacto' that included lower government spending, the sale of government-run businesses, and a wage freeze. By 2000, there were signs that Mexico's economy had stabilized. Interest rates and inflation, however, remained higher than in the United States, putting continuous pressure on the peso. This led to higher import prices and exacerbated inflation. In sum, optimism about future prospects for trade and investment in Mexico was tempered by concern about continued economic stability.

Brazil

Mexico's geographical proximity and membership in NAFTA partially explained why many US firms with little experience in Latin America expanded to Mexico first. Mexico's close proximity to the United States minimized travel and communication problems and NAFTA reduced the complexity of establishing production in Mexico and importing goods back into the United States. Many firms overlooked the potential of Brazil. Brazil, with a population of 182 million, was the largest country in Latin America and fifth largest country in the world. Its land base was as large as the United States and bordered ten countries. It was the world's largest coffee producer and largest exporter of sugar and tobacco. In addition to its abundant natural resources and strong export position in agriculture, Brazil was a strong industrial power. Its major exports were airplanes, automobiles, and chemicals. Its gross domestic product of $1.3 trillion was larger than Mexico's and the largest in Latin America (see Exhibit 7). Some firms did view Brazil as one of the most important emerging markets, along with China and India.

In 1990, US President George Bush initiated negotiations on a Free Trade Area of the Americas (FTAA) that would eliminate tariffs on trade within North, Central, and South America. The FTAA would create the world's largest free trade area with a combined gross domestic product of $13 trillion and 800 million consumers. In 1994, the presidents of 33 countries met with President Bush to negotiate details of the free trade agreement to go into effect by 2005. Many Brazilians opposed the FTAA because they feared Brazilian companies could not compete with more efficient US firms. Brazil imposed high tariffs of between 10 and 35 per cent on a variety of goods imported from the United States such as automobiles, automobile parts, computers, computer parts, engines, and soybeans. Other Brazilian firms, however, stood to gain substantially. To protect US producers from lower cost Brazilian goods, the United States imposed tariffs of between 10 and 350 per cent on imported Brazilian sugar cane, tobacco, orange juice concentrate, soybean oil, and women's leather footwear. FTAA would eliminate these tariffs. This would give US consumers the opportunity to buy Brazilian products at significantly lower prices.

Brazil played a leading role in negotiating trade and investment arrangements with other countries in Latin America. In 1991, Brazil, Argentina, Uruguay, and Paraguay signed an agreement to form a common market (Mercosur) that eliminated internal tariffs on goods traded among member countries and established a common external tariff. By 1995, 90 per cent of trade among member countries was free from trade restrictions. Member countries were allowed to impose tariffs on a limited number of products considered to be a threat to sensitive domestic industries. The hope was to expand Mercosur to include other countries in the region. Chile and Bolivia, for example, were offered associate memberships. Chile, however, later withdrew because it wanted to negotiate future membership in NAFTA. Like NAFTA, the signing of Mercosur had a dramatic effect on trade among its members. Argentina quickly became Brazil's second-largest trading partner after the United States, while Brazil became Argentina's largest trading partner. Brazilian officials made it clear that making Mercosur successful was their highest priority and that the Free Trade Area of the Americas might have to wait. Many believed Brazil was the major stumbling block to establishing FTAA by 2005.

Historically, the Brazilian government used a variety of tariffs and other restrictions on imports to encourage foreign investment in Brazil. The most highly visible example was automobiles that were taxed at rates up to 100 per cent during the 1980s and 1990s. By 2003, almost all global automobile companies, including General Motors, Mercedes-Benz, Toyota, Volkswagen, Honda, Fiat, and Peugeot were producing cars in Brazil for the Brazilian market. During the 1980s, the Brazilian government attempted to stimulate domestic production in a number of technology industries like computers through an outright prohibition on imports. An example was Texas Instruments (TI), a major computer manufacturer with semiconductor operations in São Paulo. TI was prohibited from using its own computers in its Brazilian production facilities. Instead, it was forced to use slower, less efficient Brazilian computers. The Brazilian government later eliminated such restrictions after it became clear that Brazilian computer firms were unable to compete head-to-head with global computer firms. Strong government regulations and the tendency of the Brazilian government to change regulations from year to year eventually caused TI to withdraw from Brazil, even though its plant was profitable.

During the 1980s and early 1990s, Brazil battled sustained cycles of high inflation and currency instability. Between 1980 and 1993, inflation averaged more than 400 per cent per year. Brazil's government attempted to reduce inflation through a variety of new currency programmes, price and wage controls, and the policy of indexation, which adjusted wages and contracts based on the inflation rate. In 1994, President Cardoso introduced the Real Plan, which restructured Brazil's currency system. The cruzeiro was eliminated and replaced with a new currency called the real. The real was pegged to the US dollar in an attempt to break the practice of indexation. By 1997, inflation had dropped to under seven per cent. Brazil's ability to successfully peg the real against the dollar was made possible in large part by the large foreign investment flows into Brazil during this period. The inflow of dollars boosted Brazil's dollar reserves, which could be used to buy the real on currency markets, thereby stabilizing the value of the real against the dollar.

By 1998, however, investors began to pull investments out of Brazil. Many investors were increasingly concerned about Brazil's growing budget deficit and pension system crisis. Pension benefits represented almost ten per cent of Brazil's gross domestic product. Almost half of Brazil's retirement payments went to retired civil servants who made up only five per cent of all retired Brazilians. The heavy demand on public funds for pension benefits diminished Brazil's ability to use fiscal and monetary policy to support economic development and promote stability. The Brazilian Central Bank attempted to reduce the outflow of investment capital by raising interest rates; however, dwindling dollar reserves finally reached a crisis in 1999, when Brazil abandoned its policy of pegging the real. The real was subsequently allowed to float against the dollar. The real depreciated by almost 50 per cent against the dollar in 1999.

The fast-food industry in Brazil was less developed than in Mexico or the Caribbean. This was partly the result of the structure of the fast-food industry that was dominated by US restaurant chains. US chains expanded further away from their home base as they gained experience operating in Latin America. As firms gained a foothold in Mexico and Central America, it was a natural progression to move into South America. McDonald's understood the importance of the Brazilian market and was early to expand there. By 2003, it was operating 584 restaurants. Many restaurant chains such as Burger King, Pizza Hut, and KFC built restaurants in Brazil in the early to mid-1990s but eventually closed them because of poor sales. In one example, Pizza Hut opened a restaurant in a popular restaurant section of Goiânia, a city of more than one million people about a two-hour drive from Brasìlia, Brazil's capital. When the restaurant opened, long lines of Brazilian customers wrapped around the block waiting to try Pizza Hut for the first time. Within a few

EXHIBIT 7 LATIN AMERICAN - ECONOMIC AND DEMOGRAPHIC DATA

	U.S.A.	Canada	Mexico	Colombia	Venezuela	Peru	Brazil	Argentina	Chile
Population (millions)	290.3	32.2	104.9	41.7	24.7	28.4	182.0	38.7	15.7
Growth Rate (%)	0.9	0.9	1.4	1.6	1.5	1.6	1.5	1.1	1.1
Origin (%)									
European	65.1	43.0	9.0	20.0	21.0	15.0	55.0	97.0	95.0
African	12.9			4.0	10.0		6.0		
Mixed African & European				14.0		37.0	38.0		
Latin American (Hispanic)	12.0								
Asian	4.2	6.0							
Amerindian or Alaskan native	1.5	2.0	30.0	1.0	2.0	45.0			3.0
Mixed Amerindian & Spanish			60.0	58.0	67.0				
Mixed African & Amerindian				3.0					
Other	4.3	26.0	1.0			3.0	1.0	3.0	2.0
GDP ($ billion)	10,400	923	900	268	133	132	1,340	391	151
Per Capital Income ($U.S.)	37,600	29,400	9,000	6,500	5,500	4,800	7.600	10,200	10,000
GDP Growth (%)	2.5	3.4	1.0	2.0	-8.9	4.8	1.0	-14.7	1.8
Inflation Rate (%)	1.6	2.2	6.4	6.2	31.2	0.2	8.3	41.0	2.5
Unemployment Rate (%)	5.8	7.6	3.0	17.4	17.0	9.4	6.4	21.5	9.2
Literacy Rate (%)	97.0	97.0	92.2	92.5	93.4	90.9	86.4	97.0	96.2

Source: U.S. Central Intelligence Agency, *The World Factbook,* 2003.

weeks, the lines were gone. Pizza Hut had opened a freestanding restaurant identical to those it operated in the United States. U.S. consumers were accustomed to waiting until a table was opened, sitting down and eating their meal, and leaving. Brazilian consumers did not mind waiting. However, they were accustomed to sitting outside with friends, socializing with a drink and hors d'oeuvres until a table was ready. Pizza Hut restaurants didn't accommodate this facet of Brazilian culture. Rather than change the structure of its operations, Pizza Hut sold the restaurant to Habib's, a popular Brazilian restaurant chain that sold Arab food.

Another problem was eating customs. Brazilians normally ate their big meal in the early afternoon. This could last two hours. It normally included salad, meat, rice and beans, dessert, fruit, and coffee. In the evening, it was customary to have a light meal such as a soup or small plate of pasta. Brazilians rarely ate food with their hands, preferring to eat with a knife and fork. This included food like pizza, which Americans typically ate with their hands. They also were not accustomed to eating sandwiches. If they did eat sandwiches, they wrapped the sandwich in a napkin. US fast-food chains catered to a different kind of customer, one who wanted more than soup but less than a full sit-down meal. US fast-food chains such as McDonald's were more popular in larger cities such as São Paulo and Rio de Janeiro, where business people were in a hurry. In smaller cities, however, traditional customs of eating were still popular. Food courts were well developed in Brazil's shopping malls. They included a variety of sit-down restaurants, fast-food restaurants, and kiosks. In the United States, in contrast, food courts consisted primarily of fast-food restaurants. US restaurant chains were, therefore, faced with a daunting task of changing Brazilians' eating habits – or convincing Brazilians of the attractiveness of fast-food, American style. The risk of not penetrating the Brazilian market, however, was significant given the size of Brazil's economy and McDonald's already significant presence.

Risks and opportunities

KFC faced difficult decisions surrounding the design and implementation of an effective Latin American strategy over the next twenty years. It wanted to sustain its leadership position in Mexico and the Caribbean but also looked to strengthen its position in other regions in South America, particularly in Brazil. Limited resources and cash flow limited KFC's ability to aggressively expand in all countries simultaneously. KFC also faced the task of adapting its entry strategy to overcome barriers to entry in countries where it had little presence such as Argentina, Paraguay, Uruguay, and Venezuela. In Brazil, KFC hoped a joint venture partner would help overcome cultural barriers that forced it to withdraw in 2000. How should KFC expand its restaurant base in Latin America given differences in consumer acceptance of the fast-food concept, intensity of competition, and culture? Should KFC open company-owned restaurants or rely on franchises to grow its restaurant base? In which markets should KFC approach joint venture partners as a means of more effectively developing the KFC concept? Could KFC approach markets like Brazil and Argentina cautiously in light of McDonald's and Wendy's aggressive first mover advantages in those countries, or should KFC proceed more aggressively? Last, in which countries should KFC establish subsidiaries that actively managed multiple restaurants in order to exploit synergies in purchasing, operations, and advertising? A country subsidiary that was supported by resources from KFC headquarters in Louisville could only be justified if KFC had a large restaurant base in the targeted country. KFC's Latin American strategy required considerable analysis and thought about how to most efficiently use its resources. It also required an in-depth analysis of country risk and selection of the right country portfolio.

CASE 21

PHARMAC: Keeping abreast of stakeholder interests

By Elizabeth Coster, Ljiljana Erakovic and Peter Smith[1]

It is the greatest good to the greatest number of people which is the measure of right and wrong...

Jeremy Bentham

As the PHARMAC board met on the ninth floor of their Wellington building in August 2008, their minds were not on the expansive harbour views below. The sparse boardroom was a sharp contrast to the intertwined web of divergent interests that had characterized the issue at hand. After almost three years of public debate, vested interests, fierce lobbying, legal challenges and questionable corporate behaviour, the board members were gathering to make the final decision that they hoped would draw the curtains on the highly publicized Herceptin affair. Radio and television journalists were poised to hear the outcome, as were breast cancer sufferers all over the country, none more so than the eight women who had summoned the board to the High Court. As the directors took their seats, each felt the burden of responsibility and reflected upon the journey that had brought them there ...

PHARMAC's role in the New Zealand health system

New Zealand's Pharmaceutical Management Agency (PHARMAC) was the body assigned by government to select and purchase the medicines required to treat the country's population. PHARMAC's principal duty was to secure the best health outcomes from pharmaceutical treatment for the population of New Zealand, within its allocated budget. In deciding which medicines to fund and on what terms they should be made available, PHARMAC made a social choice on behalf of the New Zealand public. That choice involved evaluating the benefits and costs of medicines against each other.

Established as a joint venture company in 1993, PHARMAC began its business in early 1994. Its shareholders were the four Regional Health Authorities (RHAs) responsible for the delivery of public care in New Zealand. A Labour-Alliance coalition Government, elected in November 1999, reformed the health sector. The RHAs were replaced with 21 Crown-owned, not-for-profit District Health Boards (DHBs). The move to DHBs signalled a significant shift in terms of governance, purchasing and accountability. The changes brought an emphasis on consultation with communities and meeting the needs of local populations. Amidst these changes PHARMAC became a Crown Entity.

As a Crown Entity, PHARMAC was accountable to the Minster of Health while acting on behalf of DHBs. Its role included economic assessment and price negotiation with drug companies, ensuring pharmaceutical purchasing remained within budget, and compiling the Pharmaceutical Schedule which detailed the medicines that were publicly subsidized for patients. PHARMAC played a significant role in the medicines system in overseeing pharmaceutical expenditure (see Exhibit 1), and contributed to promoting equity, improved health outcomes and cost-effectiveness.

For each purchasing decision, the PHARMAC board had a number of considerations, including government health funding priorities, the efficacy of existing medicines, and the clinical risks, benefits and value for money of new medicines. PHARMAC staff conducted financial and clinical assessment of new medicines, with counsel from clinical committees, to establish whether new drugs should be funded (the board's process for considering medicines for funding is outlined in Exhibit 2).

In its management of pharmaceutical expenditure, the board was required to consult with any sections of the public that it deemed to be affected by decisions. This occurred with every new pharmaceutical listing, and involved PHARMAC emailing information to all pharmaceutical suppliers, industry representatives, health professionals, and health professional organisations, as well as opening the PHARMAC website for consultation.

PHARMAC operated with what it labelled a 'very robust and comprehensive process' for making these social choices, based on a 'strong core of independent

[1]Source: The University of Auckland Business School, Auckland, New Zealand.

EXHIBIT 1   BODIES RELEVANT TO PHARMAC'S WORK

PHARMAC's Board

The PHARMAC board was appointed by and accountable to the Minister of Health. In 2008 the chairman of the board was Richard Waddel, an experienced professional director with an accounting background and health experience as a previous chair of the Auckland DHB and a member of the Otago DHB. The deputy chairman, Gregor Coster, was a university professor with a general practice background and significant governance experience in the public health sector as a Chair of several DHBs and on the board of the Health Funding Authority. They were joined by David Moore, a former CEO of PHARMAC; Adrienne von Tunzelmann had a public policy background and was involved in local body consultancy; David Kerr, a general practitioner, former Chair of Canterbury DHB and chairman of a top ten publicly listed company; and Kura Dunness, a chartered accountant of Maori descent who had health governance experience as a member of the Taranaki DHB.

PHARMAC's Management

Chief Executive, Matthew Brougham, managed PHARMAC's daily function. Supporting Brougham were six managers responsible for core areas of PHARMAC's operations: Medical, Funding & Procurement, Schedule and Contract Management, Access and Optimal Use, Analysis & Assessment, and Corporate. PHARMAC's fifty-four staff possessed a wide range of skills and experience in public health, economics analysis, business analysis, finance and law.

PHARMAC's Advisory Committees

- The **Consumer Advisory Committee (CAC)** was a group set up to voice the health consumer or patient perspective within the PHARMAC framework. The Committee's nine members represented diverse constituencies, including mental health, consumer rights, and the health of Maori, Pacific Island peoples, older people, women, families, and rural communities. The Committee provided input from a patient/health consumer perspective on a broad range of PHARMAC's activities, including around medicines funding issues. It was not, however, involved in the assessment of pharmaceutical funding applications. Reported directly to PHARMAC board.

- The **Pharmacology and Therapeutics Advisory Committee (PTAC)** was PHARMAC's primary clinical advisory committee. The group's role was to provide objective clinical advice to the PHARMAC board on applications to fund new pharmaceuticals. The committee comprised of 10 senior health practitioners from a range of specialties, who could ask for advice from 15 sub-committees, including over 70 health professionals feeding into PHARMAC's decision-making framework. (See Exhibit 2). Reported directly to PHARMAC board.

- The **Cancer Treatments Sub-Committee (CaTSoP)** was one such sub-committee that reported to PTAC. Comprised of oncologists (cancer specialists) the committee advised PTAC on any issues related to cancer treatment

clinical advice and sophisticated methods of assessing pharmaceutical cost-effectiveness'. But social choices could not be made on the basis of a technical assessment alone; they always involved explicit and implicit value judgments. The PHARMAC board had nine decision criteria that it considered (see Exhibit 3).

The pharmaceutical funding environment

Over the months and years in which the Herceptin drama played out, the pharmaceutical funding environment was challenging and complex. Rapid sharing of information meant that patients could access information about new medicines before PHARMAC could act on it. Direct to consumer marketing of pharmaceuticals often bypassed or pre-empted the recommendations of health professionals, which created increased public pressure for new pharmaceuticals to be subsidised.

PHARMAC faced an inherent tension between the motives of certain stakeholders and PHARMAC's role. For example, the commercial incentives of drug companies led them to seek premium prices, whereas PHARMAC acting on behalf of the New Zealand population had an interest in obtaining the lowest options which would then feedback to the PHARMAC board.

New Zealand Medicines and Medical Devices Safety Authority (Medsafe)

Medsafe was the business unit of the Ministry of Health which was responsible for the regulation of therapeutic products in New Zealand. In administering the Medicines Act 1981 and Regulations 1984, Medsafe was required to ensure that:

- medicines met acceptable standards of safety, quality and efficacy;
- personnel, premises and practices used to manufacture, store and distribute medicines complied

with requirements designed to ensure that products met acceptable standards right up until they were delivered to the end-user; and

- information about the selection and safe use of medicines was provided to health professionals and consumers.

Pre-marketing approval was mandatory for new and changed medicines. New medicines could not be marketed in New Zealand without the consent of the Minister of Health. Medsafe and PHARMAC worked independently and Medsafe was not involved in funding issues. Medsafe was a regualtory body responsible for registering drugs prior to PHARMAC considering them for funding.

prices. In the case of consumer and lobby groups, their motivation differed from PHARMAC's in that they focused on one specific health area, as opposed to PHARMAC's consideration of overall health outcomes. While there was sometimes vocal support for funding one particular treatment, the impact on the New Zealand public as a whole had to be considered.

Additionally, there was a constant balance to be struck between funding new medicines and maintaining subsidies for already funded treatments in the event that drug companies raised their prices. This balancing act was highlighted during 2007 when pharmaceutical companies AstraZeneca and GlaxoSmithKline raised prices of the heart medicine Metoprolol, and the thyroid treatment Levothyroxine. This move induced the PHARMAC board to raise its subsidies of the drugs accordingly, increasing spending by NZD 5 million per year. While raising subsidies to match the higher price served patients, effectively it meant spending more on the same products for no net health gain, limiting PHARMAC's ability to make new investments. While the pharmaceutical industry understandably wanted more money spent on medicines, drug companies' pricing decisions were a key factor in how many drugs PHARMAC could fund each year.

The challenge that faced pharmaceutical firms was the requirement for massive investment in research and development (R&D) in order to be successful in the industry. These expenses coupled with the failure of much R&D activity to yield marketable product created high risk, as revenue could only be gained

from the final selling of products. It had been estimated that the average cost to develop a drug ranged from USD 500 million to USD 2 billion, depending on the disease targeted, with an average 73 months invested in R&D. Significantly, it was estimated that only 20% of potential drugs made it to market. The drug company argument was that suitable pricing was essential to protect firms from the uncertainty of product development as well as to generate a profit comparable with the associated risk. Dropping prices may have required limiting R&D to those projects with the greatest chance of delivering return, thereby reducing the likelihood of innovation and denying society of the benefits of the goods that might have been.

Herceptin drama

It was in this challenging environment that PHARMAC received an application from the drug company Roche in December 2005 to fund the breast cancer drug Herceptin. At this time, Herceptin had not yet been approved by Medsafe, the body charged with the regulation of medicines and medical devices in New Zealand (see Exhibit 3). Significantly, Roche recommended the drug be funded for a period 12 months of sequential treatment for each patient. This time period was set out by the drug company, which was required to provide evidence for the benefits of this length of treatment. Herceptin (also known as Trastuzumab) was a drug used to treat HER 2 positive breast cancer. A pale yellow powder, it was dissolved into a

EXHIBIT 2   PHARMAC DECISION MAKING PROCESS

Decision making process

The process set out in this diagram is intended to be indicative of the process that may follow where a supplier or other applicant wishes a pharmaceutical to be funded on the Pharmaceutical Schedule. PHARMAC may, at its discretion, adopt a different process or variations of the process (for example, decisions on whether or not it is appropriate to undertake consultation are made on a case-by-case basis).

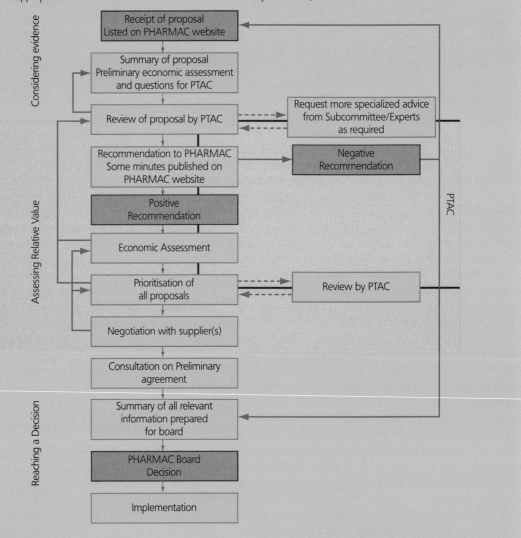

Source: Pharmaceutical Management Agency (2008) Information Sheet: Making funding decisions. Retrieved on May 11, 2009, from http://www.pharmac.govt.nz.

liquid and delivered intravenously. It could be used as a standalone treatment or in conjunction with additional chemotherapy. Treatment of early breast cancer aimed to both extend life and cure the disease. About 25% of all breast cancers were HER 2 positive and these cancers tended to occur in younger women, develop quickly, spread rapidly, and had a higher rate of recurrence.

EXHIBIT 3   DECISION CRITERIA

1. The health needs of all eligible people within New Zealand;

2. The particular health needs of Maori and Pacific peoples;

3. The availability and suitability of existing medicines, therapeutic medical devices and related products and related things;

4. The clinical benefits and risks of pharmaceuticals;

5. The cost-effectiveness of meeting health needs by funding pharmaceuticals rather than using other publicly funded health and disability support services;

6. The budgetary impact (in terms of the pharmaceutical budget and the government's overall health budget) of any changes to the Pharmaceutical Schedule;

7. The direct cost to health service users;

8. The government's priorities for health funding, as set out in any objectives notifies by the crown to PHARMAC, or in PHARMAC's Funding Agreement, or elsewhere; and

9. Such other criteria as PHARMAC thinks fit.

Source: Pharmaceutical Management Agency (Jan 2006). Operating Policies & Procedures, 3rd Edition. Retrieved on May 11, 2009, from http:/www.pharmac.govt.nz/procedures.

The Pharmacology and Therapeutics Advisory Committee (PTAC) considered the Roche's application in February 2006. While Roche had recommended a 12-month treatment of Herceptin, the drug company did not provide any evidence that this length of treatment was superior to a shorter option. The data supplied by Roche was incomplete. Internationally, trials had raised uncertainty as to the optimum length and sequencing of Herceptin treatment. Although Roche had not told the PHARMAC board, trials examining nine-week and 12-month treatments had produced comparable outcomes. PTAC concluded that further clinical research was required and recommended more information be sought from Roche and for Herceptin to be discussed by the cancer treatments sub-committee (CaTSoP) upon Medsafe approval.

In March 2006, Medsafe granted provisional consent for Herceptin in treatment for HER 2 positive early breast cancer. Concerns that the use of Herceptin might be linked to heart damage meant that the provisional consent was limited to those women who had a normal heart function prior to treatment, and required those receiving the drug to have their heart function monitored every three months during. Over the next few months, a cost-utility analysis of 12 months' Herceptin treatment was prepared by PHARMAC.

Two months later, in May 2006, the Cancer Treatments Sub-committee (CaTSoP) provided its recommendation to PTAC which concluded that there was insufficient evidence to warrant a funding recommendation for 12 months' treatment. The

Committee noted that the evidence provided in Roche's submission for Herceptin did not meet its requirements, and that an international trial called The FinHer Study examining a nine week treatment cast great doubt over the optimal length and timing of Herceptin treatment. The Committee believed that this uncertainty represented a large risk that should be resolved before any decision was made.

Following the Committee's recommendation, DHBs and PHARMAC decided not to fund Herceptin in the interim, and committed to an ongoing review of the drug. PHARMAC's Deputy Medical Director, Dr Dilky Rasiah confirmed:

We are continuing to examine the evidence that is emerging.... At the moment the data is not strong enough to support a positive funding decision, although we are open to funding Herceptin if better quality evidence becomes available.

District Health Boards' CEO David Meates supported the decision:

DHBs have to be mindful of Herceptin's cost, and the impact funding would have on associated services. ... Herceptin is a high cost drug, and in considering a [NZD] 20--25 million investment [about NZD 70 000 per patient per year] such as this, we need to be sure that Herceptin offers sufficient benefit.... We don't have that confidence at the moment.

By comparison, DHBs were budgeting a total of about NZD 35–40 million for all cancer drugs in 2006. In fact, 42 cancer drugs then cost a total of NZD 36 million per annum and this one drug alone would potentially add NZD 22 million per annum. Additionally, the adoption of Herceptin would have had associated costs such as echocardiograms (to monitor heart function), and hospital administration services owing to an increased risk of heart failure.

In August 2006, PTAC considered further data provided by Roche New Zealand. The data presented was a PowerPoint presentation, which unlike evidence normally submitted, had not been subjected to external peer review. The Committee found the presentation inadequate for making important clinical recommendations. PTAC concluded that the international FinHer trial cast doubt over the optimal length and timing of Herceptin treatment. Consequently PTAC requested that the Cancer Treatments Sub-Committee (CaTSoP) consider the clinical appropriateness of PHARMAC funding a nine week treatment of Herceptin for New Zealanders (as per the FinHer protocol).

By the end of 2006, PHARMAC announced its financial backing for an international trial to further investigate whether nine weeks or 12 months was the superior Herceptin treatment option. Dr Rasiah commented that the incentives of drug companies did not always align with the public interest. This related to concerns with company positions on pricing, treatment duration, sequencing and research decisions. Dr Rasiah reasoned that PHARMAC, in representing the public interest, needed to ask the 'hard questions' about these issues coupled with the ongoing assessment of evidence. Dr Rasiah said that while support for the trial had been committed, New Zealand's contribution was depended on assistance from New Zealand oncologists to recruit patients.

PHARMAC undertook a cost utility analysis of the proposed nine-week treatment and re-examined all the available evidence on Herceptin (see Exhibit 4). In a February meeting of PTAC the committee noted that data raised substantial doubts about the efficacy of sequential 12 months Herceptin. PTAC had requested that Roche provide full data from the N9831 trial, but this had not been provided. PHARMAC staff members were suspicious of the absence of these crucial trial results and later wrote that 'these missing data may confirm that sequential 12-month treatment is much less efficacious than [the nine week option] and than previously thought ... and either way the data are important and need to be published.'

In early March 2007, following consultation with DHBs, public consultation occurred on a draft proposal for the nine week treatment. PHARMAC's Dr Rasiah said: 'The nine-week regimen appears to be no less effective than 12 months but is less disruptive for patients, is less resource-intensive for hospitals, may also be safer for patients and is a quarter of the cost of 12 month treatment options.' From the DHBs' perspective, the CEO Meates held that the NZD 6 million per year cost to the DHBs was justifiable. The total cost included the drug itself and administration costs. 'One of our key concerns in considering 12 months Herceptin treatment was that investing up to NZD 25 million per year ... would curb our ability to fund other drugs and deliver existing hospital services to other patients', Meates concluded.

One month later, the PHARMAC board approved funding for concurrent 9 week Herceptin treatment from 1 July 2007. When Dr Rasiah announced this decision in May, he noted that 350 women each year would benefit:

> We have made this decision to fund nine weeks Herceptin because it can be justified under PHARMAC's decision criteria. These criteria include consideration of cost effectiveness, total cost, impact on DHB resources and Government priorities for health funding.

'This is great news for women with HER2 positive breast cancer. PHARMAC and DHBs have put in a tremendous amount of work to reach a solution that will improve outcomes for women ... while being affordable and pragmatic,' claimed Meates.

Public reactions

The decision was met with strong criticism from the public. The Herceptin Heroes, a group of breast cancer sufferers, said they were 'astounded' by what they labelled PHARMAC's 'misrepresentation of the efficacy' of the nine-week treatment. 'It seems they are being very careful to cover their backs rather than care for women with an aggressive disease.' Breast Cancer Aotearoa Coalition chairwoman Libby Burgess said PHARMAC's funding package was based 'purely on cost, not evidence. This radical decision is way out of step with the rest of the world. PHARMAC has ignored the recommendations of our oncologists and is forcing them to use an unproven treatment regimen'. Breast Cancer Action Trust spokesman Tim Short was astonished: 'I can't help but wonder whether there were other issues at play that have influenced their decision and whether it is really more of a political decision ... whether it was the cost that was considered rather than the medical advantages', he said. 'What price [do you put on] life?'

EXHIBIT 4   COST–UTILITY ANALYSIS OF HERCEPTIN

Cost effectiveness was determined by a cost-utility analysis (CUA). CUA was a technique widely used internationally, designed to provide information on the relative value for money of a pharmaceutical, that is, whether the health gains associated with a treatment were greater than the health gains from alternative options that could have been funded with that money. PHARMAC assessed the health gains obtained through its investments, and measured outcomes in Quality-Adjusted Life Years (QALYs). A QALY represented a year of life saved and evaluated both quantity and the quality of life enabled by healthcare intervention. Cost-utility analysis allowed PHARMAC to compare the cost per QALY of one drug against the cost per QALY of another drug.

This indicative cost-utility analysis examined the cost-effectiveness of adjuvant treatment with trastazumab (Herceptin) compared with standard treatment for early HER2-positive breast cancer. Key inputs in the model included reductions in the breast cancer disease events derived from the publishe one-year results of the HERA trial; 4-year persistence of effect; an 8% discount rate; quality of life scores based on HERA trial; and savings due to delays in hospital and other costs with treating fewer recurrences of breast cancer, balanced against the costs of extre cardiac monitoring side effects from trastazumab. The model was developed with clinical advice from PTAC and expert econmic review.

Under the analysis' base case scenario (the assumption of circumstances such as dosage, price, length of benefit etc. consderred to be most likely), the cost per QALY was estimated to be between $70 000 and $80 000 (12.5 to 14.3 QALYs gained per $1 million invested). The resutls of the CUA were very sensitive to the cost of trastazumab, duration of treatment, the assumed length of benefit (i.e. reduction in risk for recurring breast cancer), and the discount rate used.

There is clinical uncertainty with both duration of effect and optimal duration of treatment, and still a number of questions that need to be addressed regarding the use of trastazumab use in early HER2-positive breast cancer. Hence, based on the availbale information it is not possible to determine with sufficient certainty whether or not trastazumab is a cost-effective investment (relative to the other pharmaceutical investment options) at this time. In order for trastazumab to be considered as a cost effective investment, either:

- The overall cost would have to reduce significantly through a reduction in treatment duration (with the same clinical benefit) or through a significant price reduction; or
- The clinical benefit continues to increase following discontinuation of treatment (I.e. the disease free survival curves continue to diverge). It will however be several years before this information is clearly available.

Source: Pharmaceutical Management Agency (3 May 2007).

Maryanne Tipping, whose 32-year-old daughter Karen stayed in the United Kingdom to access Herceptin, said the decision was 'absolutely ridiculous'. Mrs Tipping said her daughter would remain overseas until she had finished her treatment. 'Why would she come home to a country where she wouldn't get it?' she said.

The government's response: Like bees to a honey pot...

In the Beehive (the popular name for the executive building of the New Zealand Government) many were keen to politicize the debate. The leader of the political party New Zealand First called the decision unethical and based on unsound research around a 'mythical nine-week treatment dreamt up by PHARMAC'. National Party representatives claimed PHARMAC's cancer experts were bullied into approving the nine-week programme. They argued that the Government had been claiming specialists had made the decision willingly when that was not the case and that the National Party would continue to lobby PHARMAC, astonished that the drug was given a low to medium priority when the rest of the world was moving to fund it.

Following the government's announcement, managing director of Roche New Zealand, Svend Petersen, sought an urgent meeting with Minister of Health in an effort to get the decision over-turned. 'This has the potential to be this Labour government's unfortunate experiment', he claimed and continued:

Internationally, there is no uncertainty about the optimum length of treatment with Herceptin. 23 OECD countries fund Herceptin for 52 weeks – New Zealand is the only country considering funding for nine weeks, and this is based purely on financial reasons.... This announcement makes a mockery of PHARMAC's mandate to make decisions based on the strongest possible clinical evidence, and flies in the face of international opinion and best practice.

He noted that decades of investment in biotechnology were finally producing significant advances across a range of diseases. 'While financial cost always accompanied innovation', Petersen said, 'breakthroughs such as Herceptin offered real value in return for the investment made.'

Scientific community: Hear our voices...

The scientific community was very critical of various clinical trials conducted by pharmaceutical companies. In 2008, the *Journal of the American Medical Association* (JAMA) published a study which reviewed 300 news articles about drug trials (all funded by pharmaceutical companies) and found that 42% failed to articulate the funding source. As a result readers were unaware of the publication biases as benefits of treatments were emphasized, while side effects were not mentioned and negative results remained unpublished. Furthermore, the *Journal of the Royal Society of Medicine* analysed media coverage of Herceptin (Trastuzumab) in Australia and in the United Kingdom. The paper concluded: 'Newspaper coverage of Trastuzumab has been characterized by uncritical reporting. Journalists (and consumers) should be more questioning when confronted with information about new drugs and of the motives of those who seek to set the news agenda.'

PHARMAC staff themselves started investigation against a backdrop of international drug company misconduct. They co-authored an article, published in the *Lancet*, a highly respected leading international medical journal, in May 2008. The article argued that Herceptin, as administered throughout much of the world (a 12-month sequential treatment) was much less effective

than widely believed because clinical trial data from nearly 1000 patients was effectively missing.

A lack of transparency was again highlighted when the use of lobby groups to promote the causes of drug companies became apparent in 2007/2008. Britain's *Guardian* newspaper reported on Cancer United, a body established by a worldwide public relations company, which was wholly funded by Roche. European MP's subsequently withdrew from their positions on Cancer United's board, amid concerns over the lack of transparency.

International claims: Across troubled waters

New Zealand was not the only country gripped with tension over drug funding. The majority of other countries, including Australia and the United Kingdom, did not have the limited budget or prioritization process of the New Zealand model. PHARMAC's equivalent body in the United Kingdom, the National Institute for Health and Clinical Excellence (NICE), made recommendations independent of budgetary considerations.

In a related saga, NICE was entangled in a controversy with Roche over cancer drug Avastin, as the drug company refused to provide data regarding its cost-effectiveness. NICE's Chair, Professor Sir Michael Rawlins concluded, '[Roche is] saying they felt they could not substantiate the high prices they expected to command in relation to the benefits of the product.' Avastin cost around USD 10 000 per month in Britain. He added: 'We have a finite amount of money for healthcare, and if you spend money one way, you can't use it in another.' Rawlins accused the industry of overpricing new medicines to boost profits and warned of 'perverse incentives' to hike drug prices, such as linking executives' pay to their company's share price:

We are being told we are being mean all the time, but what nobody mentions is why the drugs are so expensive.... Pharmaceutical companies have enjoyed double-digit growth year on year and they are out to sustain that, not least because their senior management's earnings are related to the share price. It's not in their interests to take less profit, personally as well as from the point of view of the business.... Traditionally the pharmaceutical industry will admit that they actually charged what they think the market will bear. The wiser ones are recognising that that model is no longer available.

Rawlins said cancer drugs, which NICE had been criticized for not endorsing, could be produced for about a tenth of their current cost. Dr Roy Vagelos, former Chief Executive of drug company Merck noted, '[t]here is a shocking disparity between value and price and it's not sustainable.' However, William Burns, the Chief Executive of Roche's pharmaceutical division and a member of the Board of Genentech (Herceptin's developer) defended its approach claiming:

As we look at Avastin and Herceptin pricing, right now the health economics hold up, and therefore I don't see any reason to be touching them. . . . The pressure of society to use strong and good products is there.

Back in New Zealand

This pressure was evidenced in June 2007 when eight women filed proceedings in the New Zealand High Court seeking judicial review of PHARMAC's funding decisions.

In August of 2007 the High Court heard the application for interim orders on the proceedings and found in favour of PHARMAC. This was to be followed in February 2008 by the High Court hearing on judicial review application.

Eight plaintiffs challenged PHARMAC decisions relating to the funding of Herceptin in the High Court. Twenty seven of the 28 grounds of appeal were not upheld. On 3 April 2008 the Court found:

- All allegations that the decisions were biased, unreasonable, pre-determined or irrational were without basis.

- The individual applications for Cancer Exceptional Circumstances funding were properly and robustly considered, and the applicants were 'afforded every opportunity' to put forward their cases.

- PTAC, PHARMAC's clinical advisory committee, was entitled to consider both the costs and benefits of medicines.

The court found that PHARMAC's decision to fund a nine-week treatment was robust. The Judge of the High Court labelled consultation as 'comprehensive':

The public was told, in clear terms, what PHARMAC's proposal was. All who wanted to express a view were heard. No procedural unfairness occurred. The decision to fund the nine week regime was not unreasonable or irrational in a legal sense. There was ample

EXHIBIT 5 THE TOP 15 DRUG EXPENDITURE GROUPS

Drug type	Main use	2007	2006	2005
Antiulcerants	Heartburn, stomach ulcers	75.5	73.8	68.6
Lipid Modifying Agents	Raised cholesterol (cardiovascular risk)	68.8	68.2	60.8
Antipsychotics	Mental health (psychoses)	56.9	53.4	48.6
Antidepressants	Mental health (depression)	30.6	29.7	27.3
Agents Affecting the Renin-Angiotensin System	Raised blood pressure (cardiovascular risk)	29.1	26.1	29.1
Immunosuppressants	Organ transplants, arthritis	27.9	28.3	27.8
Antiepilepsy Drugs	Epilepsy	27.8	24.8	21.4
Diabetes	Diabetes	26.3	22.5	20.6
Beta Adrenoceptor Blockers	Heart disease	24.5	21.3	17.6
Inhaled Long-acting Beta-adrenoceptor Agonists	Asthma	19.3	21.7	18.6
Analgesics Pain Relief	Pain relief	17.2	15.7	14.5
Diabetes Management	Blood glucose monitoring	17.1	16.3	19.5
Chemotherapeutic Agents	Cancers	16.6	13.7	11.3
Antibacterials	Bacterial infections	14.8	13.9	13.1
Calcium Channel Blockers	Heart disease	14.5	13.7	13.0

EXHIBIT 6   THE TRUTH ABOUT HERCEPTIN AND THE FINHER STUDY

Out of a total of 13,609 patients who have been involved in 8 clinical trials regarding the anti-cancer drug Trastuzumab (Herceptin), 8,724 were treated with Herceptin.

Sequential Herceptin studies

There are two large studies on the effectiveness of twelve months treatment with Herceptin after chemotherapy. One study of 1694 patients showed some benefit, the other study involving 985 patients did not. A third study involving 1694 patients has yet to be reported, and another study (N9831 arm A) is missing. Roche has said it is unable to supply the full data for the missing arm of N9831. This is a significant and worrying issue given the amount of money involved and the need for full disclosure by drug companies of all the results of drug trials.

FinHer study

The data on 116 patients in the FinHer study is for 3 years of follow-up and reveals that short duration concurrent treatment with Herceptin is effective at preventing recurrence of disease. In Finland both the 52-week course of concurrent treatment with Herceptin and the 9-week course are available to women. However, Finnish doctors prefer the 9-week course because there is less likelihood of cardiac damage and because the doctors were involved in the FinHer trial and saw for themselves the benefits to their patients of their 9-week course.

Sledge study

The data on 227 patients in the Sledge study is for 5 years of follow-up and it showed no difference in survival rates between those who received 10 weeks of concurrent treatment with Herceptin and those who received it concurrently for 52 weeks.

The results of these studies revealed that concurrent treatment with Herceptin results in significantly better efficacy than sequential treatment with the drug, all of which casts grave doubts on the superiority of the sequential treatment regime being promoted by Roche.

The pharmaceutical industry is an extremely powerful lobby group that has vested interest in the outcome of drugs they produce and market. As a recent article in *The Sunday Star Times* revealed, the reason other countries have not opted for the 9-week course of Herceptin is because in places like Britain it is the drug manufacturer who decides what treatment period they will request for their new drug, and of course in the case of Herceptin, Roche put forward the more expensive 52-week course of treatment.

Roche of course is not interested in funding further 9-week trials of Herceptin. The interest and position of drug companies around issues such as research choices, length of treatment, and treatment sequencing, not to mention pricing, do not always align with the public interest or even patient safety.

Source: Auckland Women's Health Council (March 2007). Newsletter.

---

evidence to support it being reasonable, though many may have disagreed.

The Court found that PHARMAC ought to have consulted on its 2006 decision not to fund Herceptin at that time. The court set that decision aside, ordering that PHARMAC consult on the funding of 12 months' Herceptin.

By the end of 2007, PHARMAC began the public consultation on the proposal to decline 12 months' Herceptin funding. In December 2007 the first PHARMAC forum had been held, bringing together a wide group of stakeholders to discuss PHARMAC's role and how PHARMAC could further improve. Subsequently

Chairman Richard Waddel lamented, 'It was clear that stakeholders had strongly divergent views on some key issues, underscoring that the interests of particular groups are not always aligned to the public interest that PHARMAC must serve.' PHARMAC proceeded cognizant of this challenge. PHARMAC Chief Executive Matthew Brougham said:

We acknowledge that a number of people have hopes of a 12- month treatment being funded. Our view in July 2006 was that funding 12 months's' Herceptin could not be justified under our decision criteria. Since then some new information has become available. This and any other new

The decision

information, along with consultation responses, will be taken into account before any decision is made.... We are expecting a high level of interest in the proposal, but consultation is not about counting votes. Consultation is about ensuring the decision maker has all relevant information before it when making a decision.... We want to assure people that PHARMAC has an open mind and is treating this as an opportunity to review all available materials, hear from all interested parties, and to ultimately make a robust decision having followed a fair and open process.

The consultation period closed on 10 June 2008 with over 300 submissions received. Brougham conceded that:

seeking to understand people's issues better and explaining our decisions does not miraculously make the decisions easier, nor lead to PHARMAC making decisions just to be liked. Better engagement does, however, enable the debate to shift to asking the right questions – is PHARMAC using good quality processes to make well-analysed and robust decisions ... ?'

Over the subsequent month CaTSoP and PTAC considered new information on Herceptin with a view to the PHARMAC board announcing a decision in August of 2008.

PHARMAC's public consultation culminated in a further decision not to fund a 12-month treatment, announced in August 2008. The Board argued that there was no new evidence which would support extension of the treatment beyond the current nine week regime. Brougham said PHARMAC's Board believed it was 'the most responsible decision that a reasonable and fair public agent could make'. He also added that money was not behind the PHARMAC's decision to decline the longer programme.

However, the Herceptin saga was not over. A general election was due in November 2008 and in the lead-up to the election, the opposition National (conservative) Party made a promise that a full 12-month programme of Herceptin would be made available to breast cancer patients should the party win the election. On December 10 2008 Prime Minister John Key made an announcement honouring this commitment, claiming this to be 'his proudest achievement in his government's first 100 days on office'. The Government negotiated the deal directly with Roche, providing initial funding of NZD 22 million independent of PHARMAC's budget to make the drug available. In PHARMAC's 15-year existence this was only the second occasion upon which the government had bypassed the agency's decision-making process.

Nike's dispute with the University of Oregon

By Rebecca J. Morris and Anne T. Lawrence

On April 24, 2000, Philip H. Knight, CEO of athletic shoe and apparel maker Nike Inc., publicly announced that he would no longer donate money to the University of Oregon (UO). It was a dramatic and unexpected move for the high-profile executive. A former UO track and field star, Knight had founded Nike's predecessor in 1963 with his former coach and mentor, Bill Bowerman. Over the years, Knight had maintained close ties with his alma mater, giving more than $ 50 million of his personal fortune to the school over a quarter century. In 2000, he was in active discussion with school officials about his biggest donation yet – millions for renovating the football stadium. But, suddenly, it was all called off. Said Knight in his statement: '[F]or me personally, there will be no further donations of any kind to the University of Oregon. At this time, this is not a situation that can be resolved. The bonds of trust, which allowed me to give at a high level, have been shredded.'

At issue was the University of Oregon's intention, announced April 14, 2000, to join the Worker Rights Consortium (WRC). Like many universities, UO was engaged in an internal debate over the ethical responsibilities associated with its role as a purchaser of goods manufactured overseas. Over a period of several months, UO administrators, faculty, and students had been discussing what steps they could take to ensure that products sold in the campus store, especially university-logo apparel, were not manufactured under sweatshop conditions. The University had considered joining two organizations, both of which purported to certify goods as 'no sweat'. The first, the Fair Labor Association (FLA), had grown out of President

Clinton's Apparel Industry Partnership (AIP) initiative and was vigorously backed by Nike, as well as several other leading apparel makers. The second, the Workers Rights Consortium, was supported by student activists and several US-based labour unions that had broken from the AIP after charging it did not go far enough to protect workers. Knight clearly felt that his alma mater had made the wrong choice. '[The] University [has] inserted itself into the new global economy where I make my living,' he charged. 'And inserted itself on the wrong side, fumbling a teachable moment.'

The dispute between Phil Knight and the University of Oregon captured much of the furore swirling about the issue of the role of multinational corporations in the global economy and the effects of the far-flung operations on their many thousands of workers, communities, and other stakeholders. In part because of its high-profile brand name, Nike had become a lightening rod for activists concerned about worker rights abroad. Like many US-based shoe and apparel makers, Nike had located its manufacturing operations overseas, mainly in Southeast Asia, in search of low wages. Almost all production was carried out by subcontractors, rather than by Nike directly. Nike's employees in the United States, by contrast, directed their efforts to the high-end work of research and development, marketing, and retailing. In the context of this global division of labour, what responsibility, if any, did Nike have to ensure adequate working conditions and living standards for the hundreds of thousands of workers, mostly young Asian women, who made its shoes and apparel? If this was not Nike's

[1]Source: Reprinted by permission from the *Case Research Journal*, Volume 21, Issue 3. 2001 by Anne T. Lawrence and Rebecca Morris and the North American Case Research Association. All rights reserved. Sources include articles appearing in the *New York Times, The Oregonian, Washington Post*, and other daily newspapers and material provided by Nike at its Web site www.nikebiz.com. Book sources include J. B. Strasser and L. Becklund, *Swoosh: The Unauthorized Story of Nike and the Men Who Played There* (New York: HarperCollins, 1993); D. R. Katz, *Just Do It: The Nike Spirit in the Corporate World* (Holbrook, Mass.: Adams Media Corporation, 1995); T. Vanderbilt, *The Sneaker Book* (New York: The New Press, 1998). Web sites for the Fair Labor Association and the Worker Rights Consortium may be found, respectively, at: www.fairlabor.org and www.workersrights.org. Ernst & Young's audit of Nike's subcontractor factories in Vietnam is available at: www.corpwatch.org/trac/nike/ernst. Coverage of Nike and the WRC decision in the University of Oregon student newspaper is available at: www.dailyemerald.com. A U.S. Department of Labor study of wages and benefits in the footwear industry in selected countries is available at: www.dol.gov/dol/ilab/public/media/reports/oiea/wagestudy. A full set of footnotes is available in the *Case Research Journal* version.

responsibility, then whose was it? Did organizations like the University of Oregon have any business pressuring companies through their purchasing practices? If so, how should they best do so? In short, what were the lessons of this 'teachable moment?'

Nike, Inc.

In 2000, Nike, Inc., was the leading designer and marketer of athletic footwear, apparel, and equipment in the world. Based in Beaverton, Oregon, the company's 'swoosh' logo, its 'Just Do It!' slogan and its spokespersons Michael Jordan, Mia Hamm, and Tiger Woods were universally recognized. Nike employed around 20 000 people directly, and *half a million* indirectly in 565 contract factories in 46 countries around the world. Wholly owned subsidiaries included Bauer Nike Hockey Inc. (hockey equipment), Cole Haan (dress and casual shoes), and Nike Team Sports (licensed team products). Revenues for the 12 months ending November 1999 were almost $ 9 billion, and the company enjoyed a 45 per cent global market share. Knight owned 34 per cent of the company's stock and was believed to be the sixth-richest individual in the United States.

Knight had launched this far-flung global empire shortly after completing his MBA degree at Stanford University in the early 1960s. Drawing on his firsthand knowledge of track and field, he decided to import low-priced track shoes from Japan in partnership with his former college coach. Bowerman would provide design ideas, test the shoes in competition, and endorse the shoes with other coaches; Knight would handle all financial and day-to-day operations of the business. Neither man had much money to offer, so for $ 500 a piece and a handshake, the company (then called Blue Ribbon Sports) was officially founded in 1963. The company took the name Nike in 1978; two years later, with revenues topping $ 269 million and 2700 employees, Nike became a publicly traded company.

From the beginning, marketing had been a critical part of Knight's vision. The founder defined Nike as a 'marketing-oriented company'. During the 1980s and early 1990s, Nike aggressively sought out endorsements by celebrity athletes to increase brand awareness and foster consumer loyalty. Early Nike endorsers included Olympic gold medallist Carl Lewis, Wimbledon champion Andre Agassi, and six members of the 1992 Olympic basketball 'Dream Team'. Later endorsers included tennis aces Pete Sampras and Monica Seles, basketball great Michael Jordan, and golf superstar Tiger Woods.

An important element in Nike's success was its ability to develop cutting-edge products that met the needs of serious athletes, as well as set fashion trends. Research specialists in Nike's Sports Research Labs conducted extensive research and testing to develop new technologies to improve the performance of Nike shoes in a variety of sports. For example, research specialists studied the causes of ankle injuries in basketball players to develop shoes that would physically prevent injuries, as well as signal information to the user to help him or her resist turning the ankle while in the air. Other specialists developed polymer materials that would make the shoes lighter, more aerodynamic, or more resistant to the abrasions incurred during normal athletic use. Findings from the Sports Research Labs were then passed on to design teams that developed the look and styling of the shoes.

Although it was the leading athletic footwear company in the world, Nike never manufactured shoes in any significant number. Rather, from its inception, the company had outsourced production to subcontractors in Asia, with the company shifting production locations within the region when prevailing wage rates became too high. In the early years, it had imported shoes form Japan. It later shifted production to South Korea and Taiwan, then to Indonesia and Thailand, and later yet to Vietnam and China.

The reasons for locating shoe production mainly in Southeast Asia were several, but the most important was the cost of labour. Modern athletic shoes were composed of mesh, leather, and nylon uppers that were hand-assembled, sewn and glued to composite soles. Mechanization had not been considered effective for shoe manufacturing due to the fragile materials used and the short life spans of styles of athletic shoes. Therefore, shoe production was highly labour-intensive. Developing countries, primarily in Southeast Asia, offered the distinct advantage of considerably lower wage rates. For example, in the early 1990s, when Nike shifted much of its shoe production to Indonesia, daily wages there hovered around $ 1 a day (compared to wages in the US shoe industry at that time of around $ 8 an hour).

Nike's subcontractor factories

Along with lower labour costs, Asia provided the additional advantage of access to raw material suppliers. Very few rubber firms in the United States, for example, produced the sophisticated composite soles demanded in modern athletic shoe designs. Satellite industries necessary for modern shoe production, plentiful in Asia, included tanneries, textiles, and plastic and ironwork mouldings. A final factor in determining where to locate production was differential tariff rates. In general, canvas sneakers were assessed higher tariffs than leather moulded footwear, such as basketball or running shoes. As a result, shoe companies had an incentive to outsource high-tech athletic shoes overseas, because tariffs on them were relatively low.

Many of Nike's factories in Asia were operated by a small number of Taiwanese and South Korean firms that specialized in shoe manufacturing, many owned by some of the wealthiest families in the region. When Nike moved from one location to another, often these companies followed, bringing their managerial expertise with them.

In 2000, Nike contracted with over 500 different footwear and apparel factories around the world to produce its shoes and apparel. Although there was no such thing as a typical Nike plant, a factory operated by the South Korean subcontractor Tae Kwang Vina (TKV) in the Bien Hoa City industrial zone near Ho Chi Minh City in Vietnam provided a glimpse into the setting in which many Nike shoes were made.

TKV employed approximately 10 000 workers in Bien Hoa City factory. The workforce consisted of 200 clerical workers, 355 supervisors, and 9465 production workers, all making athletic shoes for Nike. Ninety percent of the workers were women between the ages of 18 to 24. Production workers were employed in one of three major areas within the factory: the chemical, stitching, and assembly sections. Production levels at the Bien Hoa City factory reached 400 000 pairs of shoes per month; Nike shoes made at this and other factories made up fully 5 per cent of Vietnam's total exports.

Workers in the chemical division were responsible for producing the high-technology outsoles. Production steps involved stretching and flattening huge blobs of raw rubber on heavy duty rollers and baking chemical compounds in steel moulds to form the innovative three-dimensional outsoles. The chemical composition of the soles changed constantly in response to the cutting-edge formulations developed by the US design teams, requiring frequent changes in the production process. The smell of complex polymers, the hot ovens, and the clanging of the steel moulds resulted in a work environment that was loud and hot and had high concentrations of chemical fumes. Chemicals used in the section were known to cause eye, skin, and throat irritations; damage to liver and kidneys; nausea; anorexia; and reproductive health

hazards through inhalation or in some cases through absorption through the skin. Workers in the chemical section were thought to have high rates of respiratory illnesses, although records kept at the TKV operations did not permit the tracking of illnesses by factory section. Workers in the chemical section were issued gloves and surgical-style masks. However, they often discarded the protective gear, complaining that it was too hot and humid to wear them in the plant.

In the stitching section, row after row of sewing machines operated by young women hummed and clattered in a space the size of three football fields. One thousand stitchers worked on a single floor of the TKV factory, sewing together nylon, leather, and other fabrics to make the uppers. Other floors of the factory were filled with thousands of additional sewing machines producing different shoe models. The stitching job required precision and speed. Workers who did not meet the aggressive production goals did not receive a bonus. Failing to meet production goals three times resulted in the worker's dismissal. Workers were sometimes permitted to work additional hours without pay to meet production quotas. Supervisors were strict, chastising workers for excessive talking or spending too much time in the restrooms. Korean supervisors, often hampered by language and cultural barriers, sometimes resorted to hard-nose management tactics, hitting or slapping slower workers. Other workers in need of discipline were forced to stand outside the factory for long periods in the tropical sun. The Vietnamese term for this practice was *phoi nang,* or sun-drying.

In the assembly section, women worked side by side along a moving line to join the uppers to the outsoles through the rapid manipulation of sharp knives, skivers, routers, and glue-coated brushes. Women were thought to be better suited for the assembly jobs because their hands were smaller and more capable of the manual dexterity needed to fit the shoe components together precisely. During the assembly process, some 120 pairs of hands touched a single shoe. A strong, sweet solvent smell was prominent in the assembly area. Ceiling-mounted ventilation fans were ineffective since the heavy fumes settled to the floor. Assembly workers wore cotton surgical masks to protect themselves from the fumes; however, many workers pulled the masks below their noses, saying they were more comfortable that way. Rows and rows of shoes passed along a conveyor before the sharp eyes of the quality control inspectors. The inspectors examined each of the thousands of shoes produced daily for poor stitching or crooked connections between soles. Defective shoes were discarded. Approved shoes continued on the conveyor to stations where they were laced by assembly workers and finally put into Nike shoeboxes for shipment to the United States.

Despite the dirty, dangerous, and difficult nature of the work inside the Bien Hoa factory, there was no shortage of applicants for positions. Although entry level wages averaged only $ 1.50 per day (the lowest of all countries where Nike manufactured), many other workers viewed factory jobs as better than their other options, such as working in the rice paddies or pedalling a pedicab along the streets of Ho Chi Minh City (formerly Saigon). With overtime pay at one and a half times the regular rate, workers could double their salaries – generating enough income to purchase a motorscooter or to send money home to impoverished rural relatives. These wages were well above national norms. An independent study by researchers from Dartmouth University showed that the average annual income for workers at two Nike subcontract factories in Vietnam was between $ 545 and $5 66, compared to the national average of between $ 250 and $ 300. Additionally, workers were provided free room and board and access to on-site health care facilities. Many Vietnamese workers viewed positions in the shoe factory as transitional jobs – a way to earn money for a dowry or to experience living in a larger city. Many returned to their homes after working for Nike for two or three years to marry and begin the next phase of their lives.

The campaigns against Nike

In the early 1990s, criticism of Nike's global labour practices began to gather steam. *Harper's Magazine,* for example, published the pay stub of an Indonesian worker, showing that the Nike subcontractor had paid the woman just under 14 cents per hour, and contrasted this with the high retail price of the shoes and high salaries paid to the company's celebrity endorsers. The Made in the USA Foundation, a group backed by American unions, used a million dollar ad budget to urge consumers to send their 'old, dirty, smelly, worn-out Nikes' to Phil Knight in protest of Nike's Asian manufacturing practices. Human rights groups and Christian organizations joined the labour unions in targeting the labour practices of the athletic shoes firm. Many felt that Nike's anti-authority corporate image ('Just Do It!') and message of social betterment through fitness were incompatible with press photos of slight Asian women hunched over

sewing machines 70 hours a week, earning just pennies an hour.

By mid-1993, Nike was being regularly pilloried in the press as an imperialist profiteer. A CBS news segment airing on July 2, 1993, opened with images of Michael Jordan and Andre Agassi, two athletes who had multi-million-dollar promotion contracts with Nike. Viewers were told to contrast the athletes' pay checks with those of the Chinese and Indonesian workers who made 'pennies' so that Nike could 'Just Do It.'

In 1995, the *Washington Post* reported that a pair of Nike Air Pegasus shoes that retailed for $ 70 cost Nike only $ 2.75 in labour costs, or 4 per cent of the price paid by consumers. Nike's operating profit on the same pair of shoes was $ 6.25, while the retailer pocketed $ 9.00 in operating profits. Also that year, shareholder activists organized by the Interfaith Center on Corporate Responsibility submitted a shareholder proposal at Nike's annual meeting, calling on the company to review labour practices by its subcontractors; the proposal gathered 3 per cent of the shareholder vote.

A story in *Life* magazine documented the use of child labour in Pakistan to produce soccer balls for Nike, Adidas, and other companies. The publicity fallout was intense. The public could not ignore the photographs of small children sitting in the dirt, carefully stitching together the panels of a soccer ball that would become the plaything of some American child the same age. Nike moved quickly to work with its Pakistani subcontractor to eliminate the use of child labour, but damage to Nike's image had been done.

In October 1996, CBS News *48 Hours* broadcast a scathing report on Nike's factories in Vietnam. CBS reporter Roberta Baskin focused on low wage rates, extensive overtime, and physical abuse of workers. Several young workers told Baskin how a Korean supervisor had beaten them with a part of a shoe because of problems with production. A journalist in Vietnam told the reporter that the phrase 'to Nike someone' was part of the Vietnamese vernacular. It meant to 'take out one's frustration on a fellow worker'. Vietnamese plant managers refused to be interviewed, covering their faces as they ran inside the factory. CBS news anchor Dan Rather concluded the damaging report by saying, 'Nike now says it plans to hire outside observers to talk to employees and examine working conditions in its Vietnam factories, but the company just won't say when that might happen.'

The negative publicity was having an effect. In 1996, a marketing research study authorized by Nike reported the perceptions of young people aged 13 to

25 of Nike as a company. The top three perceptions, in the order of their response frequency, were athletics, cool, and bad labour practices. Although Nike maintained that its sales were never affected, company executives were clearly concerned about the effect of criticism of its global labour practices on the reputation of the brand they had worked so hard to build.

The evolution of Nike's global labour practices

In its early years, Nike had maintained that the labour practices of its foreign subcontractors, like TKV, were simply not its responsibility. 'When we started Nike,' Knight later commented, '… it never occurred to us that we should dictate what their factories] should look like.' The subcontractors, not Nike, were responsible for wages and working conditions. Dave Taylor, Nike's vice president of production, explained the company's position: 'We don't pay anybody at the factories and we don't set policy within the factories; it is their business to run.' When negative articles first began appearing in the early 1990s, however, Nike managers realized that they needed to take some action to avoid further bad publicity. In 1992, the company drafted its first Code of Conduct, which required every subcontractor and supplier in the Nike network to honour all applicable local government labour and environmental regulations, or Nike would terminate the relationship. The subcontractors were also required to allow plant inspectors and complete all necessary paperwork. Despite the compliance reports the factories filed every six months, Nike insiders acknowledged that the code of conduct system might not catch all violations. Tony Nava, Nike's country coordinator for Indonesia, told a *Chicago Tribune* reporter, 'We can't know if they're actually complying with what they put down on paper.'

In 1994, Nike tried to address this problem by hiring Ernst & Young, the accounting firm, to independently monitor worker abuse allegations in Nike's Indonesian factories. Later, Ernst & Young also audited Nike's factories in Thailand and Vietnam. A copy of the Vietnam audit leaked to the press showed that workers were often unaware of the toxicity of the compounds they were using and ignorant of the need for safety precautions. In 1998, Nike implemented important changes in its Vietnamese plants to reduce exposure to toxics, substituting less harmful chemicals, installing ventilation systems, and training personnel in occupational health and safety issues.

In 1996, Nike established a new Labor Practices Department, headed by Dusty Kidd, formerly a public relations executive for the company. Later that year, Nike hired GoodWorks International, headed by former US ambassador to the United Nations Andrew Young, to investigate conditions in its overseas factories. In January 1997, GoodWorks issued a glossy report, stating that 'Nike is doing a good job in the application of its Code of Conduct. But Nike can and should do better'. The report was criticized by activists for its failure to look at the issue of wages. Young demurred, saying he did not have expertise in conducting wage surveys. Said one critic, 'This was a public relations problem, and the world's largest sneaker company did what it does best: it purchased a celebrity endorsement.'

Over the next few years, Nike continued to work to improve labour practices in its overseas subcontractor factories, as well as the public perception of them. In January 1998, Nike formed a Corporate Responsibility Division under the leadership of former Microsoft executive Maria S. Eitel. Nike subsequently doubled the staff of this division. In May of that year, Knight gave a speech at the National Press Club, at which he announced several new initiatives. At that time, he committed Nike to raise the minimum age for employment in its shoe factories to 18 and in its apparel factories to 16. He also promised to achieve OSHA standards for indoor air quality in all its factories by the end of the year, mainly by eliminating the use of the solvent toluene; to expand educational programs for workers and in its micro-enterprise loan programme; and to fund university research on responsible business practices. Nike also continued its use of external monitors, hiring Pricewaterhouse Coopers to join Ernst & Young in a comprehensive programme of factory audits, checking them against Nike's code.

Apparel Industry Partnership

One of Nike's most ambitious social responsibility initiatives was its participation in the Apparel Industry Partnership. It was this involvement that would lead, eventually, to Knight's break with the University of Oregon.

In August 1996, President Clinton launched the White House Apparel Industry Partnership on Workplace Standards (AIP). The initial group was comprised of 18 organizations. Participants included several leading manufacturers, such as Nike, Reebok, and Liz Claiborne. Also in the group were several labour unions, including the Union of Needletrades, Industrial, and Textile Employees (UNITE) and the Retail, Wholesale and Department Store Union; and several human rights, consumer, and shareholder organizations, including Business for Social Responsibility, the Interfaith Center on Corporate Responsibility, and the National Consumer League. The goal of the AIP was to develop a set of standards to ensure that apparel and footwear were not made under sweatshop conditions. For companies, it held out the promise of certifying to their customers that their products were 'no sweat.' For labour and human rights groups, it held out the promise of improving working conditions in overseas factories.

In April 1997, after months of often-fractious meetings, the AIP announced that it had agreed on a Workplace Code of Conduct that sought to define decent and humane working conditions. Companies agreeing to the Code would have to pledge not to use forced labour, that is, prisoners or bonded or indentured workers. They could not required more than 60 hours of work a week, including overtime. They could not employ children younger than 15 years old or the age for completing compulsory schooling, whichever was older – except they could hire 14-year-olds if local law allowed. The code also called on signatory companies to treat all workers with respect and dignity; to refrain from discrimination on the basis of gender, race, religion, age, disability, sexual orientation, nationality, political opinion, or social or ethnic origin; and to provide a safe and healthy workplace. Employees' rights to organize and bargain collectively would be respected. In a key provision, the Code also required companies to pay at least the local legal minimum wage or the prevailing industry wage, whichever was higher. All standards would apply not only to a company's own facilities but also to their subcontractors or suppliers.

Knight, who prominently joined President Clinton and others at a White House ceremony announcing the code, issued the following statement:

> Nike agreed to participate in this Partnership because it was the first credible attempt, by a diverse group of interests, to address the important issue of improving factories worldwide. It was worth the effort and hard work. The agreement will prove important for several reasons. Not only is our industry stepping up to the plate and taking a giant swing at improving factory conditions, but equally important, we are finally providing consumers

some guidance to counter all of the misinformation that has surrounded this issue for far too long.

The Fair Labor Association

But this was not the end of the AIP's work; it also had to agree on a process for monitoring compliance with the Code. Although the group hoped to complete its work in six months, over a year later it was still deeply divided on several key matters. Internal documents leaked to the *New York Times* in July 1998 showed that industry representatives had opposed proposals, circulated by labour and human rights members, calling for the monitoring of 30 per cent of plants annually by independent auditors. The companies also opposed proposals that would require them to support workers' rights to organize independent unions and to bargain collectively, even in countries like China where workers did not have such rights by law. Said one nonindustry member, 'We're teetering on the edge of collapse.'

Finally, a subgroup of nine centrist participants, including Nike, began meeting separately in an attempt to move forward. In November 1998, this subgroup announced that it had come to agreement on a monitoring system for overseas factories of US-based companies. The AIP would establish a new organization, the Fair Labor Association (FLA), to oversee compliance with its Workplace Code of Conduct. Companies would be required to monitor their own factories, and those of their subcontractors, for compliance; all would have to be checked within the first two years. In addition, the FLA would select and certify independent external monitors, who would inspect 10 per cent of each firm's factories each year. Most of these monitors were expected to be accounting firms, which had expertise in conducting audits. The monitors' reports would be kept private. If a company were found to be out of compliance, it would be given a chance to correct the problem. Eventually, if it did not, the company would be dropped from the FLA and its termination announced to the public. Companies would pay for most of their own monitoring. The Clinton administration quickly endorsed the plan.

Both manufacturers and institutional buyers stood to benefit from participation in the Fair Labor Association. Companies, once certified for three years, could place an FLA service mark on their brands, signalling both to individual consumers and institutional buyers that their products were 'sweatshop-free'. It was expected that the FLA would also serve the needs of institutional buyers, particularly universities. By joining the FLA and agreeing to contract only with certified companies, universities could warrant to their student and others that their logo apparel and athletic gear were manufactured under conditions conforming with an established code of fair labour standards. Both parties would pay for these benefits. The FLA was to be funded by dues from participating companies (\$ 5000 to \$ 100 000 annually, depending on revenue) and by payments from affiliated colleges and universities (based on 1 per cent of their licensing income from logo products, up to a \$50 000 annual cap).

Although many welcomed the agreement – and some new companies signed on with the FLA soon after it was announced – others did not. Warnaco, a leading apparel maker that had participated in the Partnership, quit, saying that the monitoring process would require it to turn over competitive information to outsiders. The American Apparel Manufacturing Association (AAMA), an industry group representing 350 companies, scoffed at the whole idea of monitoring. 'Who is going to do the monitoring?' asked a spokesperson for the AAMA, apparently sarcastically. 'Accountants or Jesuit priests?' Others argued that companies simply could not be relied upon to monitor themselves objectively. Said Jay Mazur, president of UNITE, 'The fox cannot watch the chickens … if they want the monitoring to be independent, it can't be controlled by the companies.' A visit from an external monitor once every 10 years would not prevent abuses. And in any case, as a practical matter, most monitors would be drawn from the major accounting firms that did business with the companies they were monitoring and were therefore unlikely to seek out lapses. Companies would not be required to publish a list of their factories, and any problems uncovered by the monitoring process would be kept from the public under the rules governing nondisclosure of proprietary information.

One of the issues most troubling to critics was the code's position on wages. The code called on companies to pay the minimum wage or prevailing wage, whichever was higher. But in many of the countries of Southeast Asia, these wages fell well below the minimum considered necessary for a decent standard of living for an individual or family. For example, the *Economist* reported that Indonesia's average minimum wage, paid by Nike subcontractors, was only two-thirds of what a person needed for basic subsistence. An alternative view was that a code of conduct should require that companies pay a *living wage,* that is, compensation for a normal workweek adequate to provide for the basic needs of an average family, adjusted for the average number of adult wage earners per family. One problem with this approach, however, was that many countries did not systematically study the cost of living, relative to wages, so defining a living wage was difficult. The Partnership asked the US Department of Labor to conduct a preliminary study of these issues; the results were published in 2000.

The code also called on companies to respect workers' rights to organize and bargain collectively. Yet a number of FLA companies outsourced production to nondemocractic countries, such as China and Vietnam, where workers had no such rights. Finally, some criticized the agreement on the grounds it provided companies, as one put it, 'a piece of paper to use as a fig leaf.' Commented a representative of the needle trades unions, 'The problem with the partnership plan is that it tinkers at the margins of the sweatshop system but creates the impression that it is doing much more. This is potentially helpful to companies stung by public condemnation of their labour practices, but it hurts millions of workers and undermines the growing anti-sweatshop movement.'

The Worker Rights Consortium

Some activists in the antisweatshop movement decided to chart their own course, independent of the FLA. On October 20, 1999, students from more than 100 colleges held a press conference to announce formation of the Workers Rights Consortium (WRC) and called on their schools to withdraw from or not to join the FLA. The organization would be formally launched at a founding convention in April 2000.

The Worker Rights Consortium differed radically in its approach to eliminating sweatshops. First, the WRC did not permit corporations to join; it was comprised exclusively of universities and colleges, with unions and human rights organizations playing an advisory role. In joining the WRC, universities would agree to 'require decent working conditions in factories producing their licensed products'. Unlike the FLA, the WRC did not endorse a single, comprehensive set of fair labour standards. Rather, it called on its affiliated universities to develop their own codes. However, it did establish minimum standards that such codes should meet – ones that were, in some respects, stricter than the FLA's. Perhaps most significantly, companies would have to pay a living wage.

Companies were also required to publish the names and addresses of all of their manufacturing facilities, in contrast to FLA rules. Universities could refuse to license goods made in countries where compliance with fair labour standards was 'deemed impossible,' whatever efforts companies had made to enforce their own codes in factories there.

By contrast with the FLA, monitoring would be carried out by 'a network of local organizations in regions where licensed goods are produced', generally non-governmental organizations, independent human rights groups, and unions. These organizations would conduct unannounced 'spot investigations', usually in response to worker complaints; WRC organizers called this the 'fire alarm' method of uncovering code violations. Systematic monitoring would not be attempted. The consortium's governance structure reflected its mission of being an organization by and for colleges and universities; its 12-person board was composed of students, university administrators and human rights experts, with no seats for industry representatives. The group would be financed by 1 per cent of licensing revenue from participating universities, as well as foundation grants.

Over the course of the spring semester 2000, student protests were held on a number of campuses, including the University of Oregon, to demand that their schools join the WRC. By April, around 45 schools had done so. At UO, the administration encouraged an open debate on the issue so that all sides could be heard on how to ensure that UO products were made under humane conditions. Over a period of several months, the Academic Senate, the student body, and a committee of faculty, students, administrators, and alumni appointed by the president all voted to join the Consortium. Finally, after concluding that all constituents had had an opportunity to be heard, on April 12, 2000, University of Oregon President David Frohnmayer announced that UO would join the WRC for one year. Its membership would be conditional, he said, on the consortium's agreement to give companies a voice in its operations and universities more power in governance. Shortly after the University's decision was announced in the press, Phil Knight withdrew his philanthropic contribution. In his public announcement, he stated this main disagreements with the Workers Rights Consortium:

> Frankly, we are frustrated that factory monitoring is badly misconstructed. For us one of the great hurdles and real handicaps in the dialogue has been the complexity of the issue. For real progress to be made, all key participants have to be at the table. That's why the FLA has taken so long to get going. The WRC is supported by the AFL-CIO and its affiliated apparel workers' union, UNITE. Their main aim, logically and understandably, however misguided, is to bring apparel jobs back to the US. Among WRC rules, no company can participate in setting standards, or monitoring. It has an unrealistic living wage provision. And its 'gotcha' approach to monitoring doesn't do what monitoring should – measure conditions and make improvements.

INDEX